Lecture Notes in Computer Science 10736

Commenced Publication in 1973
Founding and Former Series Editors:
Gerhard Goos, Juris Hartmanis, and Jan van Leeuwen

More information about this series at http://www.springer.com/series/7409

Bing Zeng · Qingming Huang
Abdulmotaleb El Saddik · Hongliang Li
Shuqiang Jiang · Xiaopeng Fan (Eds.)

Advances in Multimedia Information Processing – PCM 2017

18th Pacific-Rim Conference on Multimedia
Harbin, China, September 28–29, 2017
Revised Selected Papers, Part II

 Springer

Editors
Bing Zeng
University of Electronic Science
  and Technology of China
Chengdu
China

Qingming Huang (iD)
University of Chinese Academy of Sciences
Beijing
China

Abdulmotaleb El Saddik
University of Ottawa
Ottawa, ON
Canada

Hongliang Li
University of Electronic Science
  and Technology of China
Chengdu
China

Shuqiang Jiang
Chinese Academy of Sciences
Beijing
China

Xiaopeng Fan
Harbin Institute of Technology
Harbin
China

ISSN 0302-9743   ISSN 1611-3349 (electronic)
Lecture Notes in Computer Science
ISBN 978-3-319-77382-7   ISBN 978-3-319-77383-4 (eBook)
https://doi.org/10.1007/978-3-319-77383-4

Library of Congress Control Number: 2018935899

LNCS Sublibrary: SL3 – Information Systems and Applications, incl. Internet/Web, and HCI

Printed on acid-free paper

This Springer imprint is published by the registered company Springer International Publishing AG
part of Springer Nature
The registered company address is: Gewerbestrasse 11, 6330 Cham, Switzerland

Preface

On behalf of the Organizing Committee, it is our great pleasure to welcome you to the proceedings of the 2017 Pacific-Rim Conference on Multimedia (PCM 2017). PCM serves as an international forum to bring together researchers and practitioners from academia and industry to discuss research on state-of-the-art Internet multimedia processing, multimedia service, analysis, and applications. PCM 2017 was the 18th in the series that has been held annually since 2000. In 2017, PCM was held in Harbin, China.

Consistent with previous editions of PCM, we prepared a very attractive technical program with two keynote talks, one best paper candidate session, nine oral presentation sessions, two poster sessions, and six oral special sessions. Moreover, thanks to the co-organization with IEEE CAS Beijing chapter, this year's program featured a panel session titled "Advanced Multimedia Technology." Social and intellectual interactions were enjoyed among students, young researchers, and leading scholars.

We received 264 submissions for regular papers this year. These submissions cover the areas of multimedia content analysis, multimedia signal processing and systems, multimedia applications and services, etc. We thank our 104 Technical Program Committee members for their efforts in reviewing papers and providing valuable feedback to the authors. From the total of 264 submissions and based on at least two reviews per submission, the Program Chairs decided to accept 48 oral papers (18.2%) and 96 poster papers, i.e, the overall acceptance ratio for regular paper is 54.9%. Among the 48 oral papers, two papers received the Best Paper and the Best Student Paper award. Moreover, we accepted six special sessions with 35 papers.

The technical program is an important aspect but only delivers its full impact if surrounded by challenging keynotes. We are extremely pleased and grateful to have two exceptional keynote speakers, Wenwu Zhu and Josep Lladós, accept our invitation and present interesting ideas and insights at PCM 2017. We would also like to express our sincere gratitude to all the other Organizing Committee members, the general chairs, Bing Zeng, Qingming Huang, and Abdulmotaleb El Saddik, the program chair, Hongliang Li, Shuqiang Jiang, and Xiaopeng Fan, the panel chairs, Zhu Li and Debin Zhao, the organizing chairs, Shaohui Liu, Liang Li, and Yan Chen, the publication chairs, Shuhui Wang and Wen-Huang Cheng, the sponsorship chairs, Wangmeng Zuo, Luhong Liang, and Ke Lv, the registration and finance chairs, Guorong Li and Weiqing Min, among others. Their outstanding effort contributed to this extremely rich and complex main program that characterizes PCM 2017. Last but not the least, we thank all the authors, session chairs, student volunteers, and supporters. Their contributions are much appreciated.

We sincerely hope that you will enjoy reading the proceedings of PCM 2017.

September 2017

Bing Zeng
Qingming Huang
Abdulmotaleb El Saddik
Hongliang Li
Shuqiang Jiang
Xiaopeng Fan

Organization

Organizing Committee

General Chairs

Bing Zeng — University of Electronic Science and Technology of China

Qingming Huang — University of Chinese Academy of Sciences, China

Abdulmotaleb El Saddik — University of Ottawa, Canada

Program Chairs

Hongliang Li — University of Electronic Science and Technology of China

Shuqiang Jiang — ICT, Chinese Academy of Sciences, China

Xiaopeng Fan — Harbin Institute of Technology, China

Organizing Chairs

Shaohui Liu — Harbin Institute of Technology, China

Liang Li — University of Chinese Academy Sciences, China

Yan Chen — University of Electronic Science and Technology of China

Panel Chairs

Zhu Li — University of Missouri-Kansas City, USA

Debin Zhao — Harbin Institute of Technology, China

Technical Committee

Publication Chairs

Shuhui Wang — ICT, Chinese Academy of Sciences, China

Wen-Huang Cheng — Taiwan Academia Sinica, Taiwan

Tongwei Ren — Nanjing University, China

Lu Fang — Hong Kong University of Science and Technology, SAR China

Special Session Chairs

Yan Liu — The Hong Kong Polytechnic University, SAR China

Yu-Gang Jiang — Fudan University, China

Wen Ji — ICT, Chinese Academy of Sciences, China

Jinqiao Shi — Chinese Academy Sciences, China

Feng Jiang — Harbin Institute of Technology, China

Tutorial Chairs

Zheng-jun Zha   Hefei Institute of Intelligent Machines,
                                  Chinese Academy of Sciences, China
Siwei Ma   Peking University, China
Chong-Wah Ngo   City University of Hong Kong, SAR China
Ruiqin Xiong   Peking University, China

Publicity Chairs

Liang Lin   Sun Yat-sen University, China
Luis Herranz   Computer Vision Center, Spain
Cees Snoek   University of Amsterdam and Qualcomm Research,
                                  The Netherlands
Shin'ichi Satoh   National Institute of Informatics, Japan
Zi Huang   The University of Queensland, Australia

Sponsorship Chairs

Wangmeng Zuo   Harbin Institute of Technology, China
Luhong Liang   ASTRI, Hong Kong, SAR China
Ke Lv   University of Chinese Academy of Sciences, China

Registration Chairs

Guorong Li   University of Chinese Academy of Sciences, China
Shuyuan Zhu   University of Electronic Science and Technology
                                  of China
Wenbin Yin   Harbin Institute of Technology, China

Finance Chairs

Weiqing Min   ICT, Chinese Academy of Sciences, China
Wenbin Che   Harbin Institute of Technology, China

Contents – Part II

Coding, Compression, Transmission, and Processing

Contents – Part I

Image Super-Resolution, Debluring, and Dehazing

Person Identity and Emotion

Multimedia Signal Reconstruction and Recovery

Text and Line Detection/Recognition

Social Media

3D and Panoramic Vision

Deep Learning for Signal Processing and Understanding

Content Analysis

A Competitive Combat Strategy and Tactics in RTS Games AI and StarCraft

Adil Khan[1](✉), Kai Yang[2], Yunsheng Fu[3], Fang Lou[3], Worku Jifara[1],
Feng Jiang[1], and Liu Shaohui[1]

[1] School of Computer Science and Technology, Harbin Institute of Technology,
Harbin 150001, People's Republic of China
adil.adil25@yahoo.com, worku.jifara@gmail.com,
{fjiang,shliu}@hit.edu.cn
[2] Chinese People's Liberation Army Aviation School, Beijing, People's Republic of China
yangkai4545@163.com
[3] Institute of Computer Applications, China Academy of Engineering Physics, Mianyang,
People's Republic of China
Fyun@yahoo.com, Lfang@163.com

Abstract. This paper presents a competitive combat strategy and tactics in RTS Games AI. To put it simply, if a player is building up base, he is losing out on creating an army and If he is building up his army, he is losing out on having a strong base. The key to winning, in StarCraft or any other RTS game is to balance strategy, tactics, macro and micro. To improve the game, one has to be able to keep track of everything that's going on over the entire map. And one must be able to give orders quickly and efficiently so in this paper we propose a competitive battle strategy with the help of a plot and decision tree. We simulate the strategy in MicroRTS developed in java EE by conducting a game-play between human player and MicroRTS AI (Game AI), though our proposed strategy outperforms the Game AI rarely as we did not account game playing-speed that makes a huge difference in victory but at least we succeeded in introducing a strategy that could well compete the Game AI and may defeat it but rarely.

Keywords: Combat strategy · Game AI · MicroRTS · Macro management
Real time strategy games · StarCraft

1 Introduction

Real time Strategy games are combat games in which a player try to dominate or destroy the opponent as quick as possible by managing and controlling resources, tactics and strategies [1]. Real time strategy is a sub-genre of strategy video games where the games do not progress or play incrementally [2]. The term 'Real Time Strategy' was first introduced in a magazine called BYTE in 1982 and the first game of this genre was Dune II developed by Westwood Studio and released by Virgin Interactive in 1992 followed by their seminal command & Conquer in 1995 [3]. On March 31, 1998 StarCraft was released for windows which was the first game in the StarCraft series based on science fiction real time strategy game and since then it grew in popularity among public in the

© Springer International Publishing AG, part of Springer Nature 2018
B. Zeng et al. (Eds.): PCM 2017, LNCS 10736, pp. 3–12, 2018.
https://doi.org/10.1007/978-3-319-77383-4_1

market [4]. Now this game is being played every day by millions of players or users and dominating and surpassing all other RTS games of this genre [5]. A 'strategy game' is a game in which the players intimidate and most often make independent strategic and tactical decisions that have a high importance in determining the outcome of the game. Almost all strategy games oblige internal decision tree style thinking, and typically very high situational consciousness or awareness [6].

Multiplayer online battle arena (MOBA) is a sub-genre of real time strategy video games in which the objective is to dominate and destroy the enemy's main structure like Bases, units, buildings and other resources [7]. Players typically have several abilities and benefits that improve over the progression of a game and that contribute in destroying the opponent team's overall strategy. Defense of the Ancients or "DotA" is one of the MOBA game. Players use commanding units known as heroes, and are supported by allied heroes and AI-controlled combatants called 'creeps'. Some of the best real time strategy games are StarCraft II: Wings of Liberty, StarCraft II: Legacy of the Void, Rome: Total War, Company of Heroes, Warcraft III: Reign of Chaos, Rise of Nations etc. We studied other related papers in the field that were either found outdated and specific to Some traditional strategic concepts or found with complicated and hybrid tactical and strategic techniques only, that is why we thought to write a paper with a unique and simple strategy or tactics pursuing updated information and literature, so this paper aims to introduce a simple but an efficient and competitive strategy for RTS games in the perspective of the current and recent past research and state of the arts in RTS games and StarCraft. It is organized as follows. Section 2 explains related work on RTS Games-AI and StarCraft. Section 3 presents a simple RTS game strategy with its decision tree. Section 4 includes experiments and implementation of the introduced strategy and Sect. 5 concludes the paper.

2   Related Work

Real time strategy games are fast paced combat games that were first introduced in 1990's and since then grew in a great popularity. RTS games face many challenges in AI research such as RTS games are played on large maps on which large numbers of units move around under player control collecting resources, constructing buildings, scouting, and attacking opponents with the goal of destroying all enemy buildings but this renders traditional full width search infeasible [8]. Combat strategy or map exploration is a common discovery oriented activity that players perform in modern video games. Exploration is a game mechanism that players need to master in order to collect resources and advance in the game [9]. In every RTS game, time is the most valuable resource before thinking about other resources. A player needs to keep himself aware of the time that he loses. It suggests that time is an important factor in composing a combat strategy always because if the opponent is faster so then it does not matter how clever the player is or how carefully the player base defenses and army compositions are [10], this also does not mean that speed trumps intelligence in RTS games but the speed is the foundation and backbone of an effective strategy. Along with speed, an effective combat strategy must need to be well composed of balanced, smart planning and responsive tactics [11]. According to the research community in RTS games, speed is more worthwhile than accuracy because in RTS games a player too often cannot afford to spend enough time in deciding where to place or manage a building, base or any other resource [12]. Developing computer controlled clusters to engage in fight, manage the usage of restricted resources, and form units and buildings in real time strategy games is a unique presentation in game-AI. But, tightly controlled online commercial game carry challenges to researchers interested in observing player's behavior and activities, constructing player's strategy models, and developing practical AI technology in them [13]. In place of setting up new programming settings or building a huge extent of agent's decision instructions by player's experience for directing real time AI research, the authors used reruns or replays of the commercial RTS game StarCraft to assess human player activities and to develop an intelligent system to learn humanoid decisions and performances. A case based reasoning approach was applied for the objective of training the system to learn and guess player strategies [14]. The researcher's analysis demonstrated that the suggested system is capable of learning and expecting individual player strategies, and that players provide signs of their private features through their building production orders.

3 Proposed Strategy and Decision Tree

In this section we present a competitive combat game strategy followed by its Decision tree with details as follows.

3.1 A Combat Strategy

Though it is not easy to program a game while planning any strategy for the first time without those who know playing RTS games like StarCraft. We thought over different strategies starting from rushes to complex micromanagement strategies. After all a simple Macro strategy was decided which is to out resource the enemy (opponent) by collecting the resources quickly than them that may result in victory in a long run. During the design, obviously we had a focus on worker units because of their certain role in success. During designing the units are required to act according to the strategy in finding and taking the remote resources to the base, if there is not any base near then it would start building one. Attacking units normally find the target and attack but sometimes workers will defend if they needed to, besides the bases and barrack will also keep producing attackers and workers to combat. We thought of a strong defense supporting the rush strategy by introducing the defense team that will guard the bases and will wait targeting until someone comes close. A percentage of defenders are assigned to attacking units called 'Assaults' to attack enemy when they are required or when they exceed a specific size or number. During units' production the ratio of defenders and assault is always kept balance. Also with the passage of time new units are assigned to assault team as the force grows larger. At least one of the three attack units i.e. Light, heavy and ranged would be opted to build at a specific time. For the proposed strategy we decided to work with a decision Tree, being one of the simplest, easiest to implement, but most importantly quickly adaptable. With a decision Tree, we would have no problem adding new nodes, and thus decisions and actions, our AI could take advantage off. We present the process of mapping out actions in the form of a tree or prototype developed in Visio 2016, to record the prototype. It let us easily set up, move around nodes. Upon beginning work on the base code for our AI, we needed two things. A base line tree code to build nodes, and some sort of knowledge base to keep all of the information our AI knew about the game, along with all other game settings. Our AI thus updates the knowledge base every frame before going through the decision tree to get unit actions (Fig. 1).

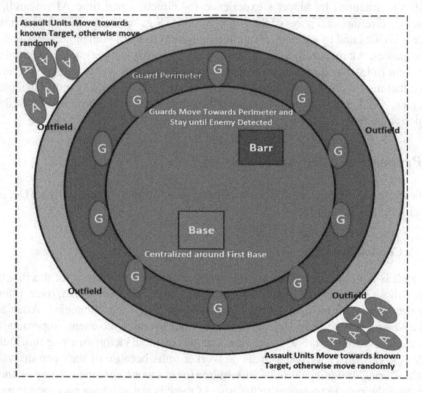

Fig. 1. An RTS combat game AI strategy

3.2 An RTS Combat Game Strategy Decision Tree

The tree consists of roughly 4 mini trees: Barracks, Base, Attack Units, and Workers. Each of these trees controls the specific type of unit. The 'Base' and 'Barracks' trees are roughly equivalent. The 'Base' simply checks if a worker cap has reached and to decide whether workers are to be build. The 'Barrack' is a little different, in so that the 'Barrack' first checks to see if the system will let build a particular unit, and if so, uses a random selection using weights. Each unit type has a weight associated with it in the 'Knowledge Base', and if the randomizer selects the range for that weight it will build that unit. For the attacking unit tree, it checks to see what team the unit is on, 'Assault' or 'Guard'. If it is an 'Assault Unit', it sees if it can attack an enemy, and if it can't it tries to move toward one if it has a target. If it has no target, it randomly moves. If it is a guard unit, it looks to see if there is a target and if there is, it moves and attack. If a guard unit does not have a target, they move towards the guard perimeter, and randomly move inside the perimeter. The 'Worker' has the most complex tree. It first checks to see if it needs to defend the base; if so, then it defends. Otherwise it checks if it's on the build or gather team. If the unit is on the build team, it checks to see if there aren't enough barracks, and if not, find space to build one (using a BFS) and builds one. Once the barracks cap has been reached it is reassigned to the gather team. The gather team first checks to see if the unit is holding a resource. If it is holding a resource, then it checks if a base is close enough to deposit it, and if it is, it will, otherwise it builds a new base next to resources. If it isn't holding resources, it tries to find the closest resources (using a BFS) and move towards them. Unfortunately, the breadth first search on this resource finding does not provide an optimal macro level solution. It does not factor in the amount of the resource (Fig. 2).

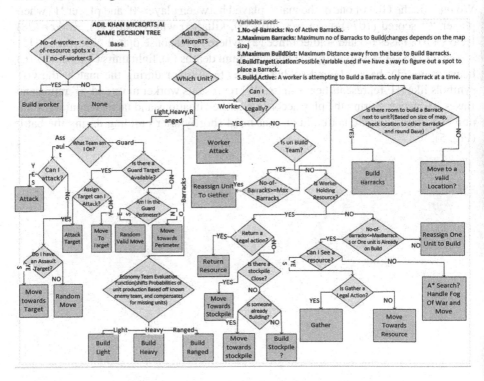

Fig. 2. An RTS combat game decision tree

4   Implementation/Experiment

We implemented our strategy in MicroRTS which is a simple RTS game designed for testing 'AI' procedures that provides the necessary features of an RTS game. MicroRTS supports six units and three building types each represent one tile. MicroRTS support configurable map sizes ranging from 8×8 to 32×32 in published publications. The game GUI and definitions of the unit types or resources types are notable in Fig. 3. Besides the unit and building types mentioned in Fig. 3, there are some other units with different specialties and buildings that we used in the MicroRTS like birds, 'sky archers', (air units), soldier offices and airports. We checked the performance of our introduced strategy against the built-in MicroRTS Game-AI by conducting a match between a human player (authors) and system AI where our proposed strategy shown a competitive performance against the Built-in Game-AI and even our strategy appeared successful in defeating the Game-AI but rarely because sometimes the system (Game AI) used to control and manage the resources, micro, macro and time efficiently as shown in the Fig. 4. Player '0' is the GAME-AI player and Player '1' is the human player (authors). We include the GUI of one of the match played between player '0' and player '1' where player '0' scored (1074), resources (40,235), kills (3) with Deaths (1), worker (28), Heavy (10), bases (4) and soldier office (2), where in response player '1' scored (415), resources (85, 111), kills only (1) with maximum deaths (3), light units (1), workers (6), heavy units (1), bases (1) and soldier office (1). Further during the match, the GUI symbols like 'H' represents heavy units, 'W' represents worker units and 'B' represents Bases. However, during the play according to the situations and tactics required, some units and buildings are not build or consumed shortly after building during the battle (Fig. 5).

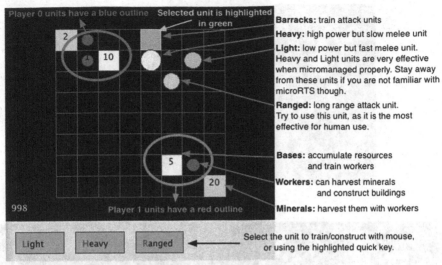

Player 0 units have a blue outline   Selected unit is highlighted in green

Barracks: train attack units

Heavy: high power but slow melee unit

Light: low power but fast melee unit. Heavy and Light units are very effective when micromanaged properly. Stay away from these units if you are not familiar with microRTS though.

Ranged: long range attack unit. Try to use this unit, as it is the most effective for human use.

Bases: accumulate resources and train workers

Workers: can harvest minerals and construct buildings

Minerals: harvest them with workers

Player 1 units have a red outline

Select the unit to train/construct with mouse, or using the highlighted quick key.

- **Select** units by left-clicking on them
- **Move** units by right-clicking on a destination
- **Attack** enemies by right-clicking on them
- **Harvest** minerals by right-clicking on them
- **Train** units by selecting them at the bottom of the screen
- **Construct** buildings by selecting the type of building at the bottom, and then right-clicking on the destination

Fig. 3. A MicroRTS GUI explaining numerous units or resource types [15].

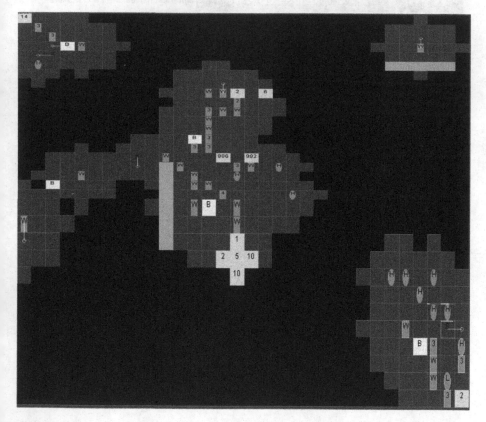

Fig. 4. Match played between human player and game AI (clear and visible GUI but in parts)

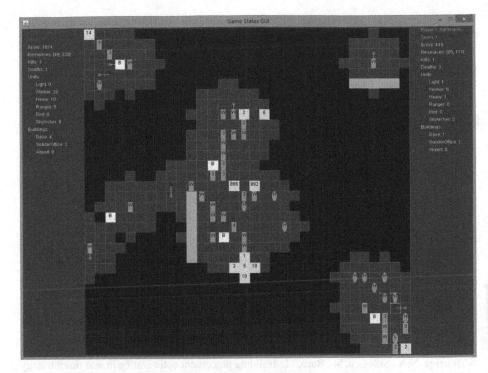

Fig. 5. Match played between human player and game AI (original GUI but adjusted)

5   Conclusion and Future Work

In this paper we introduced a competitive combat strategy for real time strategy games and StarCraft by implementing it in MicroRTS and played between human player and computer AI (Game-AI) that showed to be an efficient and a competitive strategy as far as real time performance is concerned during Game-play and observations but regardless of game-playing speed. In future, we are thinking to implement this strategy using a full-fledged game like Wargus or StarCraft using BWAPI, as MicroRTS is a small implementation of an RTS game, designed to perform AI research that initially helps to quickly test theoretical ideas, before moving on to full-fledged RTS games.

Author profile.   Adil Khan received C.T. from AIOU Islamabad Pakistan, MCSE from Microsoft, CCNA from Cisco, B.Ed from the University of Peshawar, BS Honors in Computer Science from Edwards college Peshawar, M.S in Computer Science from City University of Science and Information Technology Peshawar, and PhD from HIT, Harbin, China. In 2014-2016, he was a senior Lecturer in Higher Education Department KPK, Pakistan. He has published many publications in top-tier academic journals and conferences including IEEE and Springer. Currently, he is working as a Research Scientist in Game AI at the School of Computer Science and Technology, Harbin Institute of Technology, Harbin 150001 PR China. He is interested in Artificial Intelligence, Game

AI, Neural networks, RTS Games, FPS Games, Machine Learning. He can be reached at personal E-mails: adil.adil25@yahoo.com, Dradil@hit.edu.cn

Acknowledgement. Thanks for the support provided by CSC and Department of Computer Science, HIT Harbin, China.

References

1. Robertson, G., Watson, I.: A review of real-time strategy game AI. AI Mag. **35**(4), 75–104 (2014)
2. Si, C., Pisan, Y., Tan, C.T.: A scouting strategy for real-time strategy games, pp. 1–8 (2014)
3. Ontanón, S., et al.: A survey of real-time strategy game AI research and competition in StarCraft. IEEE Trans. Comput. Intell. AI Games **5**(4), 293–311 (2013)
4. Preuss, M., et al.: Reactive strategy choice in StarCraft by means of fuzzy control. In: 2013 IEEE Conference on Computational Intelligence in Games (CIG). IEEE (2013)
5. Farooq, S.S., et al.: StarCraft AI competition: a step toward human-level AI for real-time strategy games. AI Mag. **37**(2), 102–107 (2016)
6. Stanescu, M., et al.: Predicting army combat outcomes in StarCraft. In: AIIDE. Citeseer (2013)
7. Waltham, M., Moodley, D.: An analysis of artificial intelligence techniques in multiplayer online battle arena game environments. In: Proceedings of the Annual Conference of the South African Institute of Computer Scientists and Information Technologists. ACM (2016)
8. Barriga, N.A., Stanescu, M., Buro, M.: Building placement optimization in real-time strategy games. In: Tenth Artificial Intelligence and Interactive Digital Entertainment Conference (2014)
9. Si, C., Pisan, Y., Tan, C.T.: Understanding players' map exploration styles. In: Proceedings of the Australasian Computer Science Week Multiconference. ACM (2016)
10. Barriga, N.A., Stanescu, M., Buro, M.: Game tree search based on non-deterministic action scripts in real-time strategy games. IEEE Trans. Comput. Intell. AI Games, **PP**(99), 1 (2017). 10.1109/TCIAIG.2017.2717902
11. Stanescu, M., et al.: Evaluating real-time strategy game states using convolutional neural networks, September 2016
12. Chen, W., et al.: GameLifeVis: visual analysis of behavior evolutions in multiplayer online games. J. Vis. **20**, 651–665 (2017)
13. Lara-Cabrera, R., Cotta, C., Fernandez-Leiva, A.J.: A review of computational intelligence in RTS games. In: 2013 IEEE Symposium on Foundations of Computational Intelligence (FOCI), pp. 114–121 (2013)
14. Sourmelis, T., Ioannou, A., Zaphiris, P.: Massively multiplayer online role playing games (MMORPGs) and the 21st century skills: a comprehensive research review from 2010 to 2016. Comput. Hum. Behav. **67**, 41–48 (2017)
15. Ontanón, S.: The combinatorial multi-armed bandit problem and its application to real-time strategy games. In: Proceedings of the Ninth AAAI Conference on Artificial Intelligence and Interactive Digital Entertainment. AAAI Press (2013)

Indoor Scene Classification by Incorporating Predicted Depth Descriptor

Yingbin Zheng[1], Jian Pu[2], Hong Wang[1], and Hao Ye[1(✉)]

[1] Shanghai Advanced Research Institute, Chinese Academy of Sciences,
Beijing, China
{zhengyb,wang_hong,yeh}@sari.ac.cn
[2] Shanghai Key Lab for Trustworthy Computing,
School of Computer Science and Software Engineering,
East China Normal University, Shanghai, China
jianpu@sei.ecnu.edu.cn

Abstract. Depth cue is crucial for perception of spatial layout and understanding the cluttered indoor scenes. However, there is little study of leveraging depth information within the image scene classification systems, mainly because the lack of depth labeling in existing monocular image datasets. In this paper, we introduce a framework to overcome this limitation by incorporating the predicted depth descriptor of the monocular images for indoor scene classification. The depth prediction model is firstly learned from existing RGB-D dataset using the multiscale convolutional network. Given a monocular RGB image, a representation encoding the predicted depth cue is generated. This predicted depth descriptors can be further fused with features from color channels. Experiments are performed on two indoor scene classification benchmarks and the quantitative comparisons demonstrate the effectiveness of proposed scheme.

Keywords: Indoor scene classification · Predicted depth descriptor

1 Introduction

Scene understanding is a challenge problem in computer vision and multimedia research. As an important step for scene understanding, scene classification considers the semantic concepts and assigns images into their associated scene categories. With the development of internet and storage technologies in last decade, a few scene-centric datasets, such as Fifteen Natural Scene [1], MIT Indoor Scene [2] and SUN Database [3], have been proposed and a significant amount of progress has gone into recognizing scene via various image descriptors such as low-level features, mid-level features, and learning-based representations.

Most of previous scene classification frameworks are based on the color channels of the images. Recently, with the progress of the camera sensor technology, people can get affordable RGB-D cameras such as Microsoft Kinect and

© Springer International Publishing AG, part of Springer Nature 2018
B. Zeng et al. (Eds.): PCM 2017, LNCS 10736, pp. 13–23, 2018.
https://doi.org/10.1007/978-3-319-77383-4_2

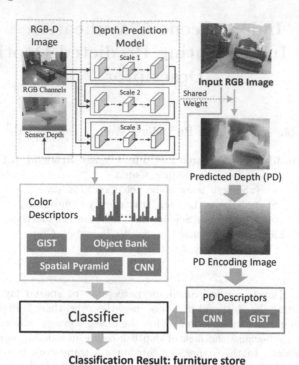

Classification Result: furniture store

Fig. 1. Overview of our frameworks. Depth prediction model is trained and employed to generate the predicted depth for an input RGB images. The features are extracted with predicted depth and color cues, and then applied to scene classifier.

Intel RealSense in the consumer market and take images with reliable depth information. These sensors have significantly boosted several research problems' revolution, e.g., pose recognition [4] and image segmentation [5]. There are also many works to assign semantic labels to an RGB-D images (e.g., [5–9]), and depth information are proved to be a very important cue for perception of spatial layout and understanding the cluttered indoor scenes. However, all of these approaches are trained using RGB-D datasets and then also tested in RGB-D images. Since the amount of RGB-D cameras and RGB-D images are order-of-magnitude smaller compared with that of traditional monocular RGB cameras, in real world application most of the images required to get the scene category are color images without depth channel. On the other hand, previous scene classification works seldom consider the depth perception within their feature designs. We believe that incorporating depth cue has the potential to further improve current color based scene classification approaches.

In this paper, we propose a framework by incorporating the predicted depth cue into descriptors of the monocular images for indoor scene classification. An overview of the framework is illustrated in Fig. 1. Our work is inspired by the progress on the depth estimation of monocular images. Starting with existing

RGB-D image dataset, a prediction model is trained and employed to generate the predicted depth. Then the depth encoding strategies are employed to map the raw predicted depth information into another intermediate channels. These intermediate channels form the regular RGB images and can be encoded into the image descriptors by employing different types of feature extractors. Finally, a multi-class classifier is applied on predicted depth features as well as the color features. The idea of constructing depth based representations for scene classification has been taken in [8–13]. Our novelty lies in the framework that combines depth prediction and descriptor generation upon the prediction. A framework that does pixel-wise prediction is not new, nor is the descriptor based on intermediate channels. But to the best of our knowledge, such a combination has not been proposed before for scene classification. Compared with these approaches using depth maps captured directly from the RGB-D sensors (namely, sensor depth), the predicted depth descriptors are extracted explicitly from RGB channels and can be applied to regular monocular images. The utilization of predicted depth makes our representation not limited by the RGB-D application and more widely available than the existing works. Although there are some loss on the depth metric, we show that the predicted depth features based on depth prediction model are with similar discriminant ability as the depth features obtained directly from depth sensors. Quantitative study shows predicted depth descriptors are consistently complementary with the color features.

The remainder of this paper is organized as follows. Section 2 reviews the related works on scene categorization and RGB-D applications. Section 3 describes our proposed approach. In Sect. 4, we demonstrate the quantitative study on scene categorization datasets. And finally, we conclude our work in Sect. 5.

2 Related Works

Scene Classification. A number of attempts to improve the scene classification task exist in the literature. As stated above, we can roughly summarize the descriptors for scene categorization into three groups: low-level features, mid-level features and learning-based representations. The low-level features try to acquire the global information (e.g., [14]) or appearance of local patches (e.g., [1]). Mid-level features focus on the meaning of image regions, for instance, [15] aim to describe objects in scene images, while [16,17] try to extract discriminative part representations. Recently, deep learning based approaches are proposed (e.g., [18–20]). Their models are trained from large scale image datasets [19,21] and achieve state-of-the-art performance. Our approach is different from the above approaches since we get a representation to describe images' depth information explicitly.

RGB-D. There are many previous works to assign semantic label to an RGB-D images. For example, [5,6] perform semantic segmentation on pixel level; [7] performs object detection on region level. Probably most similar to our approach is the works of [8,9] on using depth maps for scene categorization. Importantly, our framework is not limited to the RGB-D application but can be applied to regular color images.

3 Framework

We now elaborate the construction of our framework. We start by introducing the predicted depth image generation, followed by extracting the representation after the depth processing. Then predicted depth descriptors as well as the features directly extracted from color channels are employed for scenes classification.

3.1 From Input Image to Predicted Depth

Single image depth estimation is a long-standing problem and there exists a large body of literature [22–28]. Recently, several works have used the deep neural networks and led to major advances. As the focus of this paper is to exploit the adaptability of predicted depth cue for scene classification but not to design the depth prediction system, we use the state-of-the-art depth prediction model by multiscale convolutional network [24]. Here we briefly describe the prediction strategy.

First, all the images are resized to the resolution of 320 × 240 pixels and set as the input of a three scales network. Scale 1 contains 5 convolutional layers and 2 fully connected layers, which predicts a spatially varying set of features representing full-image view. Scale 2 is to predict at a mid-level resolution, by applying 5 convolutional layers and setting both input image and output features of the first scale as input. Scale 3 of the model employs a 4-convolutional-layer structure to refines the predictions. The multi-scale approach contains both coarse prediction from the entire image and fine prediction locally. The training procedure can be separated into two phases, which are the joint training of Scale 1 and 2, and further training of Scale 3 with frozen of previous scales. Both phases use stochastic gradient descent to learn the parameters. Given an image, the depth prediction model can output a 147 × 109 depth map and we bilinearly up-sample it back to the original image resolution.

3.2 From Predicted Depth to Descriptor

With the predicted depth, we are now able to build depth models for images with only color channels. A central issue in building a successful model is the design of the representation. There are a few approaches to make use of depth image based on past experiences on scene analysis and intuitions on what may be useful. One encoding method is to treat the predicted depth as a gray-level image by linearly scaling the depth values to the 0 to 255 range and then put the information into all of the RGB color channels to form an RGB image. Another approach is to map the predicted depth values with three properties of geocentric pose, i.e., horizontal disparity, height above ground, and angle

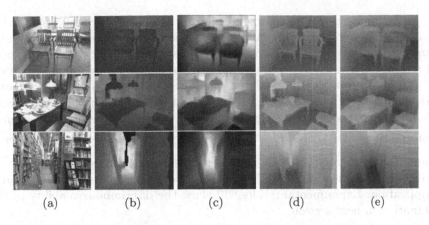

(a)   (b)   (c)   (d)   (e)

Fig. 2. Examples of RGB images (a), depth images (b), predicted depth images (c), HHA images based on sensor depth (d) and predicted depth (e).

of the pixel's local surface normal [7]. After scaling all three channels to 0 to 255 range, the depth information can be transformed into a color image, which has shown the efficiency in object detection task [7]. We refer the intermediate images as RGB and HHA, respectively. A few examples with the (predicted) depth images and their HHA encoding are illustrated in Fig. 2. We can observe the HHA encoding images from sensor depth and predicted depth are visually similar, although there are some loss for depth prediction. The experiments on SUN RGB-D will examine the effectiveness of this encoding for predicted depth.

Next we build the predicted depth descriptor upon the intermediate channels. Two types of feature are chosen for their performance and representative in scene classification, i.e., GIST and Convolution Neural Network (CNN) based features. GIST [14] is a global visual feature, capturing mainly the global texture distribution in depth images. CNN based features are usually learned from a large-scale image dataset, and proved to be more discriminative and accurate than hand-crafted features. Specifically, we use the structure of Alexnet [29] and VGG19 [30]. The Alexnet is with 5 convolutional layers and 3 fully connected (FC) layers, and VGG19 contains 16 convolutional layers and 3 FC layers. We employ the pretrained models learned from ImageNet [21] and then fine-tune the network using training set of the scene datasets. It has been shown that activations from the fully connected layers are with semantically meaningful embedding for recognition [18]. Thus, for each input image representing predicted depth, the 4096-dimensional deep features from the last FC layer are used as CNN representation.

3.3   From Descriptor to Scene Prediction

The Multi-class linear SVM classifier is adopted for the depth features. As displayed in Fig. 2, images representing the depth cue will lose details of the visual appearance. In order to benefit from the complementarity of regular features in color channels, we use the feature fusion to combine their respective classifier scores. Linear SVM is also applied on the color features. The late fusion strategy is employed as its efficiency in previous scene classification frameworks such as [31,32]. During the test phase, an input image receives a set of scores $S^d = (s_1^d, ..., s_n^d)$ from depth descriptor's classifier (n is the number of scene categories), and $S^{rgb} = (s_1^{rgb}, ..., s_n^{rgb})$ from color feature's classifier. The confidences of classifier that the image belongs to category i are computed by the softmax transformation of the scores: $c_i^d = \frac{\exp(s_i^d)}{\sum_{k=1}^n \exp(s_k^d)}, c_i^{rgb} = \frac{\exp(s_i^{rgb})}{\sum_{k=1}^n \exp(s_k^{rgb})}$. The overall confidence for category i is done by fusion of these confidences: $c_i = c_i^d \times c_i^{rgb}$. Finally, the image is assigned to the category with the highest confidence after multiplication. Experimental results will show the discriminative ability of the combination in next section.

4   Experiments

We evaluate the proposed framework on two indoor scene classification benchmarks: SUN RGB-D scene categorization [9] and the MIT Indoor Scene [2]. SUN RGB-D contains 10,335 images captured by RGB-D sensors (e.g., Kinect and Intel RealSense). Some of images are collected from NYU depth v2 [5], Berkeley B3DO [33], and SUN3D [34]. There are 19 scene categories with more than 80 images and we follow the standard train, validate and test split in the scene categorization benchmark. The MIT Indoor Scene contains 15,620 images labeled over 67 classes. We adopt the official train/test split to use 80 images per class for training and 20 for testing. The performance is evaluated by calculating the average accuracy on each category of both datasets. Throughout the experiments, we use the highly efficient multi-class linear LIBSVM for scene classification.

4.1   SUN RGB-D

Encoding strategy. We first examine the effectiveness of the HHA encoding for predicted depth. Both HHA and RGB encoding approaches are tested with Alexnet structure. The accuracy of RGB encoding is 19.4%, which is much lower than that of HHA (30.3%). We attribute this to the geocentric pose properties of HHA that avoid negative effects on the inaccuracy predicted on metric depth.

Predicted depth descriptors. As illustrated in Table 1, there is a gap between GIST and deep learning based features with more than 10% improvement on both the predicted depth and the fusion. The VGG19 network performs better than Alexnet, which indicates that a deeper network for extracting features might improve the discrimination of the depth feature.

Predicted depth vs. sensor depth. Overall, the predicted depth features achieve very impressive performance comparing with sensor depth. For example,

Table 1. Comparison for SUN RGB-D using sensor depth images and predicted depth images. Both approaches are with HHA encoding.

(a) Depth descriptor only.

Depth descriptor	Sensor depth	Predicted depth
GIST	20.1%	18.5%
Alexnet	35.7%	30.3%
VGG19	40.7%	35.2%

(b) Fusion of depth descriptor with color.

Depth descriptor	Sensor depth+color	Predicted depth+color
GIST	23.0%	22.8%
Alexnet	41.8%	39.2%
VGG19	44.5%	42.9%

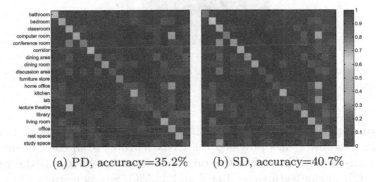

(a) PD, accuracy=35.2%   (b) SD, accuracy=40.7%

Fig. 3. Confusion matrices for classification result based on predicted depth (PD) and sensor depth (SD) VGG19 feature in SUN RGB-D.

the GIST feature with predicted depth produces an accuracy of 18.5%, with only a slight loss from the same feature representing sensor depth cue (20.1%). The confusion matrices of predicted depth and sensor depth VGG19 features are illustrated in Fig. 3. We see that although the average accuracy decreases from 40.7% to 35.2%, the confusion matrices between each two categories are with similar distribution. Another observation is the predicted depth VGG19 feature (35.2%) is on par with the feature using sensor depth (35.7%), which verifies that a stronger representation can fill in the gap between predicted depth and sensor depth.

Table 2. Comparisons of state-of-the-arts with only RGB images as inputs.

Method	This paper	Song et al. [13]	Wang et al. [12]	Zhu et al. [11]	Liao et al. [10]
Result	**42.9%**	42.7%	40.4%	37.0%	36.1%

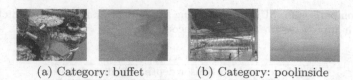

(a) Category: buffet   (b) Category: poolinside

Fig. 4. Challenging examples from two categories in MIT indoor dataset that have low prediction accuracies using our method. (Left: original image; Right: HHA image).

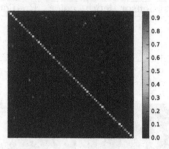

Fig. 5. Confusion matrix of MIT indoor using VGG19 feature on both RGB and predicted depth.

Fusion of depth and color. Since our focus is the depth information and the SUN RGB-D website[1] has provided the CNN features from color channels, we use these off-the-shelf color features on the feature combination (the result of GIST and CNN color features are 19.6% and 38.5%). Fusing features always leads to substantial performance gains, i.e., 18.5% to 22.8% for GIST and 35.2% to 42.9% for VGG19, which clearly show the value of joint modeling the predicted depth and color features for scene classification. The gap between sensor and predicted depth are also narrowed after cue fusion (−1.6% to −0.2% for GIST, and −5.5% to −1.6% for VGG19).

Comparison with state-of-the-arts. We compare to related methods on SUN RGB-D in Table 2. With only RGB images as inputs, our predicted depth descriptors outperforms previous approaches, which confirm the effectiveness of using predicted depth as an element for image feature construction. Our results are also better than some approaches considering both RGB and sensor depth channels as inputs, such as [11] (41.5%) and [10] (41.3%). A few works on multi-modal fusion obtain higher accuracy (e.g. [12,13]) and we believe that predicted depth descriptors is also complementary to the multi-modal fusion since they focus on different levels of information, which will be explored in the future.

---

[1] http://rgbd.cs.princeton.edu/.

Table 3. Classification accuracy for MIT Indoor dataset with color descriptor only and fusion of color and predicted depth descriptors.

	Color	Color+predicted depth
GIST [14]	28.66%	33.98%
Spatial Pyramid [1]	34.42%	42.41%
Object Bank [15]	37.60%	45.10%
VGG19 [30]	69.33%	70.57%

4.2 MIT Indoor

We also conduct experiments on the MIT Indoor dataset. Note that all the images from MIT Indoor are RGB channels only and without sensor depth information. Applying the predicted depth VGG19 features used in SUN RGB-D obtains the classification accuracy of 26.04%. As the MIT indoor dataset contains richer visual elements and the inter-category variance of depth layout between different classes is very little for the HHA images, only employing the predicted depth information may be not enough. Figure 4 shows two challenge examples. Thus, we fuse the predicted depth features with the visual features directly from color channels. Four popular RGB descriptors are selected, i.e., GIST [14], Spatial Pyramid [1], Object Bank [15], and VGG19 [30], which are corresponding to low-level feature (globally and locally), mid-level feature and learning-based feature. Table 3 gives the fusion results. Incorporating predicted depth feature boosts the performance with consistently improvement, which indicates the complementarity with predicted depth features and color features. Figure 5 illustrates the pre-category results for fusion of predicted depth and RGB VGG19 features with average accuracy of 70.57%.

5 Conclusion

In this paper, we have introduced a framework to incorporate predicted depth information into image descriptors for scene classification. After setting up the prediction model learned from RGB-D dataset, given an image, an encoding approach is used to transform the predicted depth map to the HHA image. The predicted depth representation is generated by using the GIST or CNN feature on HHA image. The scene classification result is computed by applying linear SVM on predicted depth features and features from color channels. Experimental comparisons with sensor depth features on SUN RGB-D benchmark show the effectiveness of predicted depth representation, and preliminary evaluations on MIT indoor dataset have confirmed the complementarity with the color features.

Acknowledgments. This work was supported in part by grants from NSFC (No. 61602459) and STCSM's program (No. 17511101902 and No. 17YF1427100).

References

1. Lazebnik, S., Schmid, C., Ponce, J.: Beyond bags of features: spatial pyramid matching for recognizing natural scene categories. In: CVPR, pp. 2169–2178 (2006)
2. Quattoni, A., Torralba, A.: Recognizing indoor scenes. In: CVPR (2009)
3. Xiao, J., Hays, J., Ehinger, K.A., Oliva, A., Torralba, A.: Sun database: large-scale scene recognition from abbey to zoo. In: CVPR, pp. 3485–3492 (2010)
4. Shotton, J., Sharp, T., Kipman, A., Fitzgibbon, A., Finocchio, M., Blake, A., Cook, M., Moore, R.: Real-time human pose recognition in parts from single depth images. Commun. ACM **56**(1), 116–124 (2013)
5. Silberman, N., Hoiem, D., Kohli, P., Fergus, R.: Indoor segmentation and support inference from RGBD images. In: Fitzgibbon, A., Lazebnik, S., Perona, P., Sato, Y., Schmid, C. (eds.) ECCV 2012, Part V. LNCS, vol. 7576, pp. 746–760. Springer, Heidelberg (2012). https://doi.org/10.1007/978-3-642-33715-4_54
6. Ren, X., Bo, L., Fox, D.: RGB-(D) scene labeling: features and algorithms. In: CVPR, pp. 2759–2766 (2012)
7. Gupta, S., Girshick, R., Arbeláez, P., Malik, J.: Learning rich features from RGB-D images for object detection and segmentation. In: Fleet, D., Pajdla, T., Schiele, B., Tuytelaars, T. (eds.) ECCV 2014, Part VII. LNCS, vol. 8695, pp. 345–360. Springer, Cham (2014). https://doi.org/10.1007/978-3-319-10584-0_23
8. Gupta, S., Arbelaez, P., Malik, J.: Perceptual organization and recognition of indoor scenes from RGB-D images. In: CVPR, pp. 564–571 (2013)
9. Song, S., Lichtenberg, S.P., Xiao, J.: Sun RGB-D: a RGB-D scene understanding benchmark suite. In: CVPR (2015)
10. Liao, Y., Kodagoda, S., Wang, Y., Shi, L., Liu, Y.: Understand scene categories by objects: a semantic regularized scene classifier using convolutional neural networks. In: ICRA (2016)
11. Zhu, H., Weibel, J.B., Lu, S.: Discriminative multi-modal feature fusion for RGBD indoor scene recognition. In: CVPR (2016)
12. Wang, A., Cai, J., Lu, J., Cham, T.J.: Modality and component aware feature fusion for RGB-D scene classification. In: CVPR (2016)
13. Song, X., Herranz, L., Jiang, S.: Depth CNNs for RGB-D scene recognition: learning from scratch better than transferring from RGB-CNNs. In: AAAI (2017)
14. Oliva, A., Torralba, A.: Modeling the shape of the scene: a holistic representation of the spatial envelope. IJCV **42**(3), 145–175 (2001)
15. Li, L.J., Su, H., Xing, E.P., Fei-Fei, L.: Object bank: a high-level image representation for scene classification semantic feature sparsification. In: NIPS (2010)
16. Juneja, M., Vedaldi, A., Jawahar, C.V., Zisserman, A.: Blocks that shout: distinctive parts for scene classification. In: CVPR, pp. 923–930 (2013)
17. Doersch, C., Gupta, A., Efros, A.A.: Mid-level visual element discovery as discriminative mode seeking. In: NIPS, pp. 494–502 (2013)
18. Razavian, A., Azizpour, H., Sullivan, J., Carlsson, S.: CNN features off-the-shelf: an astounding baseline for recognition. In: CVPR Workshops, pp. 806–813 (2014)
19. Zhou, B., Lapedriza, A., Xiao, J., Torralba, A., Oliva, A.: Learning deep features for scene recognition using places database. In: NIPS, pp. 487–495 (2014)
20. Gong, Y., Wang, L., Guo, R., Lazebnik, S.: Multi-scale orderless pooling of deep convolutional activation features. In: Fleet, D., Pajdla, T., Schiele, B., Tuytelaars, T. (eds.) ECCV 2014, Part VII. LNCS, vol. 8695, pp. 392–407. Springer, Cham (2014). https://doi.org/10.1007/978-3-319-10584-0_26

21. Deng, J., Dong, W., Socher, R., Li, L., Li, K., Fei-Fei, L.: ImageNet: a large-scale hierarchical image database. In: CVPR (2009)
22. Saxena, A., Sun, M., Ng, A.Y.: Make3d: learning 3d scene structure from a single still image. IEEE Trans. PAMI **31**(5), 824–840 (2009)
23. Liu, B., Gould, S., Koller, D.: Single image depth estimation from predicted semantic labels. In: CVPR (2010)
24. Eigen, D., Fergus, R.: Predicting depth, surface normals and semantic labels with a common multi-scale convolutional architecture. In: ICCV, pp. 2650–2658 (2015)
25. Liu, F., Shen, C., Lin, G.: Deep convolutional neural fields for depth estimation from a single image. In: CVPR (2015)
26. Zoran, D., Isola, P., Krishnan, D., Freeman, W.T.: Learning ordinal relationships for mid-level vision. In: ICCV (2015)
27. Wang, P., Shen, X., Lin, Z., Cohen, S., Price, B., Yuille, A.: Towards unified depth and semantic prediction from a single image. In: CVPR, pp. 2800–2809 (2015)
28. Chen, W., Fu, Z., Yang, D., Deng, J.: Single-image depth perception in the wild. In: NIPS (2016)
29. Krizhevsky, A., Sutskever, I., Hinton, G.E.: ImageNet classification with deep convolutional neural networks. In: NIPS (2012)
30. Simonyan, K., Zisserman, A.: Very deep convolutional networks for large-scale image recognition. In: ICLR (2015)
31. Pandey, M., Lazebnik, S.: Scene recognition and weakly supervised object localization with deformable part-based models. In: ICCV (2011)
32. Zheng, Y., Jiang, Y.-G., Xue, X.: Learning hybrid part filters for scene recognition. In: Fitzgibbon, A., Lazebnik, S., Perona, P., Sato, Y., Schmid, C. (eds.) ECCV 2012, Part V. LNCS, vol. 7576, pp. 172–185. Springer, Heidelberg (2012). https://doi.org/10.1007/978-3-642-33715-4_13
33. Janoch, A., Karayev, S., Jia, Y., Barron, J.T., Fritz, M., Saenko, K., Darrell, T.: A category-level 3d object dataset: putting the kinect to work. In: Consumer Depth Cameras for Computer Vision, pp. 141–165 (2013)
34. Xiao, J., Owens, A., Torralba, A.: Sun3d: a database of big spaces reconstructed using SFM and object labels. In: ICCV, pp. 1625–1632 (2013)

Multiple Thermal Face Detection in Unconstrained Environments Using Fully Convolutional Networks

Yezhao Fan[1](✉), Guangtao Zhai[1], Jia Wang[1], Menghan Hu[1], and Jing Liu[2]

[1] Institute of Image Communication and Network Engineering,
Shanghai Jiao Tong University, Shanghai, China
{yezhaofan,zhaiguangtao,jiaang,menghanHu}@sjtu.edu.cn,
humenghan89@163.com
[2] School of Electrical and Information Engineering,
Tianjin University, Tianjin, China
jliu_tju@tju.edu.cn

Abstract. Multiple thermal face detection in unconstrained environments has received increasing attention due to its potential in liveness detection and night-time surveillance. This paper presents an effective method based on fully convolutional network (FCN), density-based spatial clustering of applications with noise (DBSCAN) and non-maximum suppression (NMS) algorithm. Our proposed approach captures the thermal face features automatically using FCN. Then, an improved DBSCAN is used to detect all the faces in the thermal images. Finally, we use NMS to remove all of the bounding-boxes with an IOU (intersection over union). Experiments on RGB-D-T database show that the proposed method exceeds the state-of-the-art algorithms for single face detection on thermal images. We also build a new database with 10K multiple thermal face images in unconstrained environments. The results also show a high precision for multi-face detection tasks.

Keywords: Multiple thermal face detection
Fully convolutional network
Density-based spatial clustering of applications with noise
Nonmaximum suppression · Intersection over union

1 Introduction

With the advent of digital information age, millions of photos spread everywhere through the social net works such as Snapchat, Facebook and Twitter. Retrieving

This work was supported by the National Science Foundation of China (61422112, 61371146, 61521062, 61527804), National High-tech R&D Program of China (2015AA015905), and Science and Technology Commission of Shanghai Municipality (15DZ0500200).

relevant information especially for face recognition [1] and saliency detection [3] from the images makes it convenient for network users. And for face recognition, the prerequisite problem is to locate faces accurately. Hence, face detection is an active research area and has been researched for decades. Compared to the traditional face detection from RGB sources, thermal face detection may be more useful because the faces can be detected under the completely dark environment by thermal camera. Thermal face detection has a wide range of application including night-time surveillance [4] or rescuing after disaster.

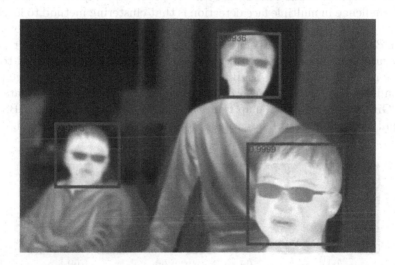

Fig. 1. An example of our database that contains multi-face thermal images in unconstrained environments, the bounding-boxes and corresponding scores show the result of the proposed approach.

For the past few years, thermal face detection has become one of the hottest research topics. In the past, most approaches extracted the features manually. For example, Majumder et al. [5] used fast independent component analysis (Fast ICA) and Gabor wavelet transform, which reduced dimension to accelerate face detection and recognition. Wu et al. [6] proposed a cascade detector to detect multi-face. And moment invariant is used to extract features for face detection in [7]. However, traditional thermal face detection approaches have some shortcomings, such as inefficient recognition rate, complicated feature extraction. These reasons impede development on the application.

Recently, convolutional neural network (CNN) has been exploited in computer vision tasks such as face recognition [8,10], object detection [11], and object classification [12]. Unlike the traditional algorithms, CNN captures the features by unsupervised learning [2] and enjoys the powerful ability to extract and select useful features automatically [13]. These results demonstrated outstanding performance in many kinds of computer vision tasks. In particular, the AlexNet showed that CNN has better results than other methods.

Different from CNN, FCN is composed of convolutional layers instead of fully-connected layers at the end of the network architecture. This makes it possible to run the network on the thermal images with any size and the output will be a probability map from the original image. Hence, FCN can be efficiently used for pixel-level tasks such as semantic segmentation [14] and object detection [15]. Besides, at the test time, because of no connected layers, there is no need to resize the input images, so that arbitrary-sized images can be input into the FCN, the output will be a correspondingly-sized probability map [16]. And compared to the region-based methods such as R-CNN [11], FCN is computation efficient.

The challenge in multiple face detection is that clustering method to locate all the faces in the images. And density-based spatial clustering of applications with noise (DBSCAN) is a classical clustering algorithm. It groups together points which contain many nearby neighbors. Points whose nearest neighbors too far away are marked as outliers. A DBSCAN-based method clustering image pixels based on DBSCAN [17] performs well in both image segmentation and data clustering. Given the probability map from the test images, the superior DBSCAN algorithm can well-cluster different faces to achieve multi-face detection.

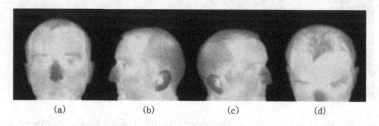

(a)   (b)   (c)   (d)

Fig. 2. The output of the thermal face images from dataset based on the ground truth.

In this paper, we present a FCN-based face detection algorithm. No additional preprocess (e.g.,segmentation [11]) is required. Compared to existing CNN architectures for thermal face detection [18], our network accept thermal images of arbitrary size. To detect all the faces, we propose an improved DBSCAN algorithm to cluster all the candidate points from the faces. Our approach produces both bounding-boxes and corresponding scores (see Fig. 1). A database composed of multi-face thermal images in unconstrained environments is established for further evaluating our algorithm.

We will start by discussing the details of the proposed approach in Sect. 2. Section 3 will present detailed experiments and results. And Sect. 4 will make a conclusion.

2 Proposed Method

In this section, we will detail the process of our training, clustering and localizing the thermal face. The key ideas are shown as follows:

Algorithm The proposed algorithm for thermal face detection
Process:
1: Training model by RGB-D-T database through FCN.
2: Clustering the thermal face regions for multi-face detection task by an improved DBSCAN algorithm.
3: Locate the faces by non-maximal suppression (NMS).

2.1 Fully Convolutional Networks

At the train time, FCN is a classification network. We input the images with the size of 227 × 227 by resizing the images and the output of the network is the corresponding score with 1 for positive samples (face images) and 0 for negative samples (non-face images).

We extract training examples from the RGB-D-T to train our model. To realize a classification net for distinguishing thermal face from background, we cut the images based on the ground truth provided by the RGB-D-T database. Figure 2 shows the examples of the output from the RGB-D-T database. It varies in head rotation, expression and illumination. This database contains about 15K positive samples. We get the negative samples about 15K by random selecting from thermal images against background.

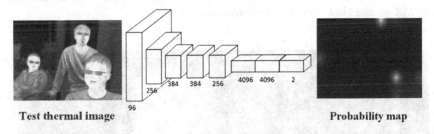

Test thermal image   **Probability map**

Fig. 3. The architecture of the proposed model is in the middle of the picture. At the test time, we input the thermal image to the model, the output will be a corresponding probability map.

AlexNet [12] is a classical network that consists of 8 layers, of which the first 5 are convolutional layers and the last 3 are fully-connected layers. We obtain the FCN by transforming the fully connected layers to convolutional layers. Similar to [14], the proposed thermal face classifier network changes the last 3 layers into convolutional layers. The architecture of our network is shown in the middle of Fig. 3.

We first train our network with images labeled by face and non-face. The trained network can predict scores for every input patch with the size of 227 × 227. The right of Fig. 3 shows the output of an image through the architecture of FCN. Every point of the probability map shows the FCN output, corresponding to the size of training input. It stands for the probability of having a face. Because of the convolutional filters, there is no need to resize. Kernels cover the entire of the input images with the stride of 32×32, so that arbitrary-sized images can be input to the network. The output would be a probability map (see Fig. 3), whose size is dependent on the input test image.

To detect all the different sized thermal faces in the images, we enlarge and shrink all the images and obtain the corresponding probability maps to consist a image pyramid. Unlike R-CNN, which uses SVM to get the final scores, we find that our network can output enough information for thermal face detection.

2.2   Clustering the Output Points and Locate the Bounding Box

The fully convolutional network above gives high response to all the regions highly related to the thermal faces. One single face would corresponds to multiple bounding boxes. Figure 4 shows a few possible potential bounding boxes. Therefore, it is essential to cluster the bounding boxes from the same thermal faces. Kmeans is designed to find k clusters on the dataset based on the distance to the cluster center. However, the hyper-parameter K, which represents the number of faces in the scene, is not available in unconstrained environments.

To overcome the drawback of K-means, DBSCAN is adopted in the proposed algorithm. It does not require any prerequisite knowledge of the face numbers. It is a density-based algorithm. The density is related to two parameters (ϵ and MinPts). ϵ is the radius of the neighborhood and the MinPts is the minimum number of points that core points contains.

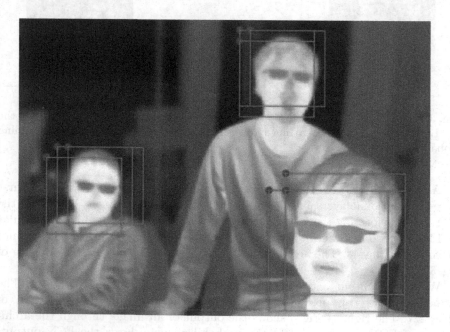

Fig. 4. The red points in the thermal image belong to different faces needed to cluster. (Color figure online)

Different from the original DBSCAN algorithm [19], which sets fixed parameters in advance, our proposed method adaptively update the value of ϵ. The method we presented can renew the value of ϵ. Therefore, all the faces can be accurately detected no matter how far away they are located. The ϵ is adaptively determined as follows:

$$\epsilon = 4\sqrt{\frac{(x1_{max} - x1_{min}) \times (x2_{max} - x2_{min}) \times K}{m \times \pi}}. \tag{1}$$

where x1 is the abscissa from all the possible points, x2 is the ordinate, m is the number of points, K is the MinPts and we set $K = 2$ in our algorithm.

From Fig. 5 we can see that our method can cluster the data of the bounding boxes very well. Data in Fig. 5(a) is relatively closer, especially for the blue points and the green points. And data in Fig. 5(b) is much farther, we can also classify images very well.

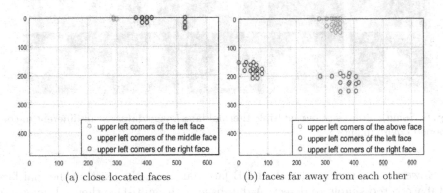

(a) close located faces   (b) faces far away from each other

Fig. 5. Two images of different relative position of faces. The relative position in (a) is closer than (b). Our improved DBSCAN can cluster the points regardless of the position of faces. (Color figure online)

After clustering all the points, we use NMS to locate the faces accurately. In each cluster, we remove all the bounding boxes with the scores under 90% of the maximum score. And then, we calculated the average of the locations from all the remained windows. And we use the maximum value as the score of our bounding box (see Fig. 1). Figure 7 shows the thermal face detection results with images that vary in rotations and occlusions from our database. Our proposed method can detect very well.

3 Experimental Results

In this section, we first use our model to detect single face on the thermal images from RGB-D-T database and compare with the state-of-the-art methods. To further validate our algorithm, we establish a multi-face thermal database in unconstrained environments. And finally, we report the evaluation results based on experimental results to assess our model in the following subsections.

3.1   Database description

A part of RGB-D-T database [20] is used to train our FCN model. RGB-D-T was collected from thermal camera. It contains 51 people with the resolution of 384 × 288. Three factors including head rotation, expression and illumination influence the thermal face detection. To train our model, we use the thermal faces from a part of RGB-D-T database to establish the train set. It contains about 12K thermal face images. We also extract the non-face regions randomly except the facial regions to train our model about 12K images. And 3K thermal images from the database to be our test set. We compare the face detection rate influenced by the different factors.

Fig. 6. Some examples of our multiple thermal face image database in different uncon-strained environments.

However, comparing with the RGB face database, the existing thermal face database is too simple to detect. A database with multi-face thermal images in unconstrained environments need to be established. To the best of our knowl-edge, this is the first database containing thermal images with multiple faces. It varies in the number of the people (one to three), head rotation (left, right, up and down), expression (neutral, smiling and laughing) and illumination (daylight and darkness). There are 10K thermal images taken in 10 different environment and the resolution of the images is 640 × 480. We also take the corresponding RGB images for the further research. Figure 6 is some of examples taken in five different environments. The first column of Fig. 6 is taken in the night-time con-tains only one person with neutral expression, and the second column contains three people with different head rotations and expressions in daylight. The per-son in third column stands against the window in the night-time varies in head rotation. The fourth column varies in the distance between them, and the last column has different expressions.

3.2   Parameter Setting

Based on the experiments of [8], we upscale the images by

$$factor = min(5, 4000/max(m, n)) \tag{2}$$

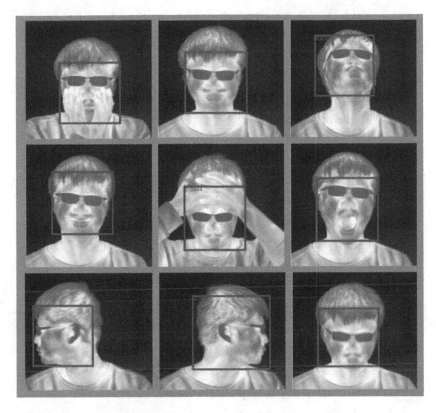

Fig. 7. Faces with different rotations and occlusions in our database.

where m is the number of row of the images, n is the number of column. And then, we down-scale the images by the scale of $\sqrt[3]{5} = 0.7937$. This makes it possible to detect all the faces even smaller than 45 pixels in large thermal images. We set the threshold equals to 0.95 to classify the regions for detection.

3.3   Results

According to the experiments on the RGB-D-T database, we compare with other methods considering three factors (head rotation, expression and illumination). As we can see in Table 1, our method has the best performance and improve the detection rate no matter what conditions. There is no doubt that we have no problem on detecting single thermal face against black background. Figure 8(a) shows the face detection rates from different methods.

Experimental results on our database is shown in Fig. 8(b). We can see that thermal images contained two people behave the worst. It is partly because the faces is closer to each other than images contained three people. When test the images contained only one person, our method can detect the thermal face no matter what influenced factor including head rotation, occlusion or expression. Based on the results, the proposed algorithm behaves well in our database.

Table 1. Face detection rate considering three factors

	Head rotation	Expression	Illumination
LBP	79.33	96.27	98.35
MI	59.37	91.76	94.51
HOG	90.27	98.79	99.18
Method [18]	90.27	98.79	99.18
Our method	98.13	100.00	100.00

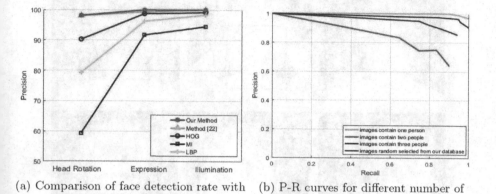

(a) Comparison of face detection rate with different algorithms

(b) P-R curves for different number of people in the images.

Fig. 8. Experiment results.

4   Conclusion

In this paper, we propose a FCN model to detect thermal face. The results on RGB-D-T show that our model has the best performance for thermal face detection. We establish a database consisted of multi-face thermal images in unconstrained environments. To validate the efficiency of the proposed algorithm, we test our model on the database. It performs better when faces are far away from each other than the faces is close. In general, our algorithm still work well.

References

1. Chen, Y., Chen, Y., Wang, X., et al.: Deep learning face representation by joint identification-verification. In: International Conference on Neural Information Processing Systems, pp. 1988–1996. MIT Press (2014)
2. Kstinger, M., Wohlhart, P., Roth, P.M., et al.: Annotated facial landmarks in the wild: a large-scale, real-world database for facial landmark localization. In: IEEE International Conference on Computer Vision Workshops, pp. 2144–2151. IEEE (2012)
3. Ke, G., Lin, W., Zhai, G., et al.: No-reference quality metric of contrast-distorted images based on information maximization. IEEE Trans. Cybern. **47**(12), 4559–4565 (2017)

4. Sarfraz, M.S., Stiefelhagen, R.: Deep perceptual mapping for thermal to visible face recognition (2015)
5. Majumder, G., Bhowmik, M.K.: Gabor-fast ICA feature extraction for thermal face recognition using linear kernel support vector machine. In: International Conference on Computational Intelligence and Networks, pp. 21–25. IEEE (2015)
6. Wu, B., Ai, H., Huang, C., et al.: Fast rotation invariant multi-view face detection based on real Adaboost. In: IEEE International Conference on Automatic Face and Gesture Recognition, pp. 79–84. IEEE Computer Society (2004)
7. Zaeri, N.: Moments invariant for expression invariant thermal human recognition. In: International Conference on Artificial Intelligence, Modelling and Simulation, pp. 92–96. IEEE (2015)
8. Farfade, S.S., Saberian, M.J., Li, L.J.: Multi-view face detection using deep convolutional neural networks, pp. 224–229 (2015)
9. Liu, Z., Luo, P., Wang, X., et al.: Deep learning face attributes in the wild, pp. 3730–3738 (2014)
10. Sun, Y., Wang, X., Tang, X.: Hybrid deep learning for face verification. In: IEEE International Conference on Computer Vision, pp. 1489–1496. IEEE Computer Society (2013)
11. Girshick, R., Donahue, J., Darrell, T., et al.: Rich feature hierarchies for accurate object detection and semantic segmentation. In: Proceedings of the IEEE Conference on Computer Vision and Pattern Recognition, pp. 580–587 (2014)
12. Krizhevsky, A., Sutskever, I., Hinton, G.E.: ImageNet classification with deep convolutional neural networks. In: International Conference on Neural Information Processing Systems, pp. 1097–1105. Curran Associates Inc. (2012)
13. Lecun, Y., Bengio, Y., Hinton, G.: Deep learning. Nature 521(7553), 436 (2015)
14. Shelhamer, E., Long, J., Darrell, T.: Fully convolutional networks for semantic segmentation. IEEE Trans. Pattern Anal. Mach. Intell. 39(4), 640 (2014)
15. Chen, L.C., Papandreou, G., Kokkinos, I., et al.: Semantic image segmentation with deep convolutional nets and fully connected CRFs. Comput. Sci. 4, 357–361 (2014)
16. Ben-Cohen, A., Diamant, I., Klang, E., Amitai, M., Greenspan, H.: Fully convolutional network for liver segmentation and lesions detection. In: Carneiro, G., et al. (eds.) LABELS/DLMIA -2016. LNCS, vol. 10008, pp. 77–85. Springer, Cham (2016). https://doi.org/10.1007/978-3-319-46976-8_9
17. Hou, J., Gao, H., Li, X.: DSets-DBSCAN: a parameter-free clustering algorithm. IEEE Trans. Image Process. 25(7), 3182–3193 (2016)
18. Wu, Z., Peng, M., Chen, T.: Thermal face recognition using convolutional neural network. In: International Conference on Optoelectronics and Image Processing, pp. 6–9. IEEE (2016)
19. Ester, M., Kriegel, H.P., Sander, J., et al.: A density-based algorithm for discovering clusters in large spatial databases with noise. In: KDD 1996, vol. 96, no. 34, pp. 226–231 (1996)
20. Simn, M.O., Corneanu, C., Nasrollahi, K., et al.: Improved RGB-DT based face recognition. IET Biometrics 5(4), 297–303 (2016)

Object Proposal via Depth Connectivity Constrained Grouping

Yuantian Wang[1], Lei Huang[1], Tongwei Ren[1(✉)], Sheng-Hua Zhong[2], Yan Liu[3],
and Gangshan Wu[1]

[1] State Key Laboratory for Novel Software Technology, Nanjing University,
Nanjing, China
wangyt@smail.nju.edu.cn, {leihuang,rentw,gswu}@nju.edu.cn
[2] College of Computer Science and Software Engineering, Shenzhen University,
Shenzhen, China
csshzhong@szu.edu.cn
[3] Computing Department, The Hong Kong Polytechnic University,
Hong Kong, China
csyliu@comp.polyu.edu.hk

Abstract. Object proposal aims to detect category-independent object candidates with a limited number of bounding boxes. In this paper, we propose a novel object proposal method on RGB-D images with the constraint of depth connectivity, which can improve the key techniques in grouping based object proposal effectively, including segment generation, hypothesis expansion and candidate ranking. Given an RGB-D image, we first generate segments using depth aware hierarchical segmentation. Next, we combine the segments into hypotheses hierarchically on each level, and further expand these hypotheses to object candidates using depth connectivity constrained region growing. Finally, we score the object candidates based on their color and depth features, and select the ones with the highest scores as the object proposal result. We validated the proposed method on the largest RGB-D image data set for object proposal, and our method is superior to the state-of-the-art methods.

Keywords: Object proposal · RGB-D image · Depth connectivity
Constrained grouping

1 Introduction

Object proposal aims to indicate the positions of category-independent object candidates in a given image with bounding boxes [1]. It can be used as a fundamental of numerous multimedia applications, such as object recognition [11], segmentation [14], tracking [18], image annotation [19], saliency analysis [16] and information retrieval [24]. Two paradigms are mainly used in current object proposal methods, named window scoring and grouping [26]. The former samples bounding boxes in a given image, measures the probability of each candidate box

© Springer International Publishing AG, part of Springer Nature 2018
B. Zeng et al. (Eds.): PCM 2017, LNCS 10736, pp. 34–44, 2018.
https://doi.org/10.1007/978-3-319-77383-4_4

in containing an object, *i.e.*, "*objectness*", and selects the boxes with the highest objectness scores as object candidates; the latter over-segments a given image into amounts of segments, and groups these segments into object candidates, which probably enclose objects.

(a)   (b)

Fig. 1. An example of the difference between color appearance and depth appearance in objectness representation. The monster truck is easier to distinguish in depth appearance (b) than in color appearance (a).

A key challenge in object proposal is the diversity and complexity of object appearance in color representation. Figure 1 shows an example. The monster truck in Fig. 1(a) has complicate color appearance, which is difficult to distinguish from the complex scene. In contrast, it can be easily identified from depth appearance in Fig. 1(b), because its surface is connected in depth while its boundary is disconnected from background. We can see that depth provides a powerful cue in detecting object candidates in RGB-D images [23]. However, RGB-D images usually suffer from low quality problem on depth appearance, which is caused by the limitation of capture devices and estimation algorithms, including inaccurate boundary and serious noise. It hampers the performance of object proposal methods, especially for the ones using pixel-level features, such as edges [12]. Compared to window scoring used in most existing object proposal methods on RGB-D images, grouping strategy has its natural advantage in combining depth cue into object proposal, because they work on region level necessarily. It helps to improve the robustness in handling low quality depth.

In this paper, we propose a novel object proposal method on RGB-D images with the constraint of *depth connectivity*. It can improve the key techniques in grouping based object proposal effectively, namely segment generation, hypothesis expansion and candidate ranking. Figure 2 shows an overview of the proposed method. We first generate segments using depth aware hierarchical segmentation on ultra-metric contour map. Next, we combine the segments into hypotheses hierarchically, and further expand these hypotheses to object candidates with depth connectivity constrained region growing. Finally, we score the object candidates based on their color and depth features, and select the ones with the highest scores as the object proposal result. We validate the proposed method on the largest public RGB-D image data set for object proposal, named *NJU1800*. Our method is superior the state-of-the-art methods.

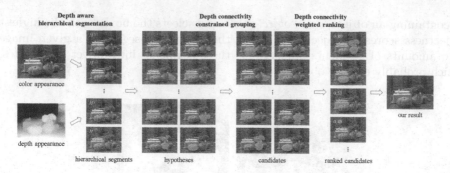

Fig. 2. An overview of our proposed method. To a given RGB-D image, we first over-segment it into segments. Next, we combine the segments into hypotheses and further expand the hypotheses to object candidates. Finally, we score the object candidates and select the ones with the highest scores as our result.

Our contributions mainly include:

- We define the depth connectivity between two segments, and utilize it to measure inner depth connectivity and boundary depth connectivity of an object candidate.
- We propose an object proposal method on RGB-D images with the constraint of depth connectivity, which improves hierarchical segmentation, hypothesis expansion and candidate ranking in grouping.
- We validate our method on the largest RGB-D image data set for object proposal, and our method outperforms the state-of-the-art methods.

2   Related Work

2.1   Object Proposal on RGB Images

Two paradigms are mainly used in the existing object proposal methods, named window scoring and grouping.

Window scoring based methods focus on the objectness measurement of the sampled bounding boxes. Some hand-crafted features were proposed to measure objectness, including object location and geometry properties [1], structured edge [26] and binarized normed gradient [7]. The boxes were ranked based on the extracted features, and the ones with the highest scores are selected as object candidates. Window scoring based methods are usually efficient, but they are hard to generate accurate candidates due to the limitation of discrete sampling.

In comparison, grouping based methods focus on segment generation and grouping. Carreira et al. [4] utilized constrained parametric mincuts and merged them based on object features, which was improved by applying edge detectors and multiple gragh cut segmentations [9]. Uijlings et al. [20] proposed selective search algorithm to merge similar super-pixels greedily, which could benefit from the combination with multiple features [17], multi-branch hierarchical segmentation [21], and region merging in high-complexity scenarios [22]. Manen et al. [15] merged randomized super-pixel connectivity graph with learned features. Arbeláez et al. [3] utilized multiscale hierarchical segmentation and combinatorial grouping with Pareto front model. Krähenbühl et al. [10] set object-like seeds and used classifiers in geodesic transform as object proposal results. Grouping based methods can provide more accurate candidates, but they usually suffer from low efficiency problem caused by iterative grouping.

A proposal refinement strategy was proposed in [6], which refined object candidates generated by different object proposal methods. The integration of window scoring based methods and the refinement strategy can obtain a good trade-off between proposal accuracy and efficiency [13].

2.2 Object Proposal on RGB-D Images

Object proposal methods on RGB-D images mainly focus on exploiting the effect of depth cue and integrating it into object proposal methods on RGB images. Xu et al. [23] first brought depth into objectness measurement by adaptively integrating color gradient and depth gradient. Liu et al. [12] detected multi-layered structured edges by decomposing the sparse edge map according to the corrected depth map, and ranked the bounding boxes with its maximum scores on all the depth layers. Liu et al. [13] generated bounding boxes by edge boxes method [26] and refined them through repartioning the super-pixels on their boundaries. Zhang et al. [25] provided a proposal refinement strategy with multiple trained high-level features, including CNN feature, depth geometric feature and semantic context feature.

The exiting object proposal methods on RGB-D images concentrate on extending windows grouping based methods and refinement strategies, but ignore the improvement of grouping based methods, which may impede them from generating object candidates with high accuracy.

3 Our Method

3.1 Depth Connectivity Measurement

Depth connectivity is the basic concept in our method, which is utilized to improve the performance of the key procedures. In this subsection, we introduce the measurement of depth connectivity.

In grouping based object proposal methods, a given image is first over-segmented into many segments. Assume s_i and s_j are two segments in the given image, and the average depths of all the pixels within them are d_i and d_j, respectively. Here, depth is normalized to the value range of $[0, 1]$, and larger depth value means image content is nearer. If s_i and s_j are adjacent, their depth connectivity $\phi_{i,j}$ is defined as:

$$\phi_{i,j} = 1 - |d_i - d_j|. \tag{1}$$

If s_i and s_j are not adjacent, but they belong to a segment combination, their depth connectivity is defined as:

$$\phi_{i,j} = \max_{p_k \in P_{i,j}} \varphi_k, \tag{2}$$

where $P_{i,j}$ is the set of all the connected paths between s_i and s_j within the segment combination; φ_k is the depth connectivity of p_k. Let $p_k : s_i \to s_{k_1} \to \cdots \to s_{k_{N_k}} \to s_j$, where N_k is the number of segments in p_k except s_i and s_j, φ_k is calculated as:

$$\varphi_k = \min\{\phi_{i,k_1}, \cdots, \phi_{k_{N_k},j}\}. \tag{3}$$

From Eqs. (1)–(3), we can see that depth connectivity between two segments is in the value range of $[0, 1]$. Larger depth connectivity value means two segments are more connected in depth.

Based on depth connectivity between two segments, we further define inner depth connectivity and boundary depth connectivity of an object candidate. To an object candidate c, its inner depth connectivity is measured as follows:

$$\psi^{in} = \min_{s_i, s_j \in S_c} \phi_{i,j}, \tag{4}$$

where S_c is the set of all the segments within c. The boundary depth connectivity of c is measured as follows:

$$\psi^{bd} = \frac{1}{|B_c|} \sum_{s_i \in B_c} \min_{s_j \in \Omega_i \setminus S_c} \phi_{i,j}, \tag{5}$$

where B_c is the set of all the segments in the boundary of c; Ω_i is the set of all the segments surrounding s_i; $|.|$ denotes the cardinality of a set.

3.2 Depth Aware Hierarchical Segmentation

We first generate the ultra-metric contour map using [2], which contains the contours weighted by brightness, color and texture gradients. The regions surrounded by the contours are treated as the segments.

Since all the segments are separated by the contours, there is one and only contour between every two segments. To two segments s_i and s_j, we denote the contour part between them as $e_{i,j}$, and measure its strength as follows:

$$\omega_{i,j} = \lambda \omega_{i,j}^U + (1 - \lambda)(1 - \phi_{i,j}), \tag{6}$$

where $\omega_{i,j}^U$ is the weight of $e_{i,j}$ in the ultra-metric contour map referring to [3]; $\phi_{i,j}$ is the depth connectivity between s_i and s_j; λ is a parameter for linear combination, which equals 0.7 in our experiments. For the value ranges of both $\omega_{i,j}^U$ and $\phi_{i,j}$ are $[0, 1]$, the value range of $\omega_{i,j}$ is $[0, 1]$.

Based on edge strength, we further merge the segments into different hierarchies $\{\mathcal{H}^*, \mathcal{H}^1, \mathcal{H}^2, ..., \mathcal{H}^L\}$ with Platt's method [5]. Here, $\mathcal{H}^*$ is the original segments before merging and $\mathcal{H}^L$ is the whole image. Based on the depth connectivity between two segments, i.e., the item $1 - \phi_{i,j}$ in Eq. (6), we can merge the adjacent segments with similar depth values, and prevent the merging of two segments which are not connected in depth but similar in color appearance.

3.3   Depth Connectivity Constrained Grouping

Based on $\{\mathcal{H}^*, \mathcal{H}^1, \mathcal{H}^2, ..., \mathcal{H}^L\}$ generated in hierarchical segmentation, we further generate hypotheses by combining the segments into singletons, pairs, triplets, and four-tuples on $\mathcal{H}^1, \mathcal{H}^2, ..., \mathcal{H}^{L-1}$, respectively. Inspired by [3], the adjacent segments without intersection on different hierarchies are preferred in hypothesis generation, and only the top fixed-number of hypotheses are retained.

Because the hypotheses are usually incomplete as compared to objects, we expand the hypotheses to generate object candidates. Considering the surface of an object is usually connected in depth, we use a greedy region growing strategy constrained by depth connectivity in hypothesis expansion. Assume Δ_h is the set of all the segments adjacent to a hypothesis h, we expand h iteratively till no segment can be grouped:

$$h^* \leftarrow h \cup \{s_i | s_i \in \Delta_h, \phi_{i,j} \geq \tau\}, \tag{7}$$

where s_j is a segment within h and it is adjacent to s_i; τ is a threshold, which equals 0.95 to avoid over-expansion in our experiments. We expand all the hypotheses and remove the repeated ones. The retained hypotheses after expansion are treated as object candidates.

3.4   Depth Connectivity Weighted Ranking

We score object candidates according to their color and depth features, and select the ones with the highest scores for object proposal.

In object candidate scoring based on color feature, we use a trained maximum marginal relevance model provided by [3], which uses the low level features including size, location, shape and boundary contour strength.

In object candidate scoring based on depth feature, we use both inner depth connectivity in Eq. (4) and boundary depth connectivity in Eq. (5). A candidate probably containing an object usually has high inner depth connectivity, because the surface of an object is connected in depth, and low boundary depth connectivity, because an object is usually disconnected from background in depth. However, the overemphasis of inner depth connectivity or boundary depth connectivity may degrade the performance of object proposal. Specifically, the overemphasis of inner depth connectivity may cause the preference of partial objects with similar depth, while the overemphasis of boundary depth connectivity may increase the rankings of the combinations of multiple objects with obvious boundaries. Hence, we balance the influences of inner depth connectivity and boundary depth connectivity in scoring object candidates based on depth features:

$$S^d = (\psi^{in})^\gamma - (\kappa(\psi^{bd}, \delta))^\gamma, \tag{8}$$

where γ is a parameter to nonlinearly emphasize high depth connectivity, which equals 4 in our experiments; κ is a function to punish high boundary depth connectivity with a parameter δ, which returns ψ^{bd} when it is smaller than δ, and 1 otherwise; δ equals 0.5 in our experiments. S^d is normalized to the value range of $[0, 1]$.

We combine the scores based on color and depth features linearly to obtain the final score of each object candidate:

$$S = \alpha S^c + (1 - \alpha)S^d, \tag{9}$$

where S^c is the score based on color feature; α is a parameter for combination, which equals 0.5 in our experiments.

Finally, we select the object candidates with the highest scores and generate their bounding boxes as the object proposal result.

4   Experiments

4.1   Data Set and Experiment Settings

We validated our method on the largest public RGB-D data set for object proposal *NJU1800*, which contains 1,800 RGB-D images with manually labelled ground truth [13].

All the experiments were conducted on a computer with Intel i5 2.8 GHz CPU and 8 GB memory. For all the other methods in comparison, we used their default settings suggested by the authors.

4.2   Experimental Results

We first compare our method with eight object proposal methods on RGB images, namely binarized normed gradients (BING) [7], edge boxes (EB) [26], objectness (OBJ) [1], geodesic object proposal (GOP) [10], multiscale combinatorial grouping (MCG) [3], selective search (SS) [20], multi-thresholding straddling expansion of edge boxes (M-EB) and multiscale combinatorial grouping (M-MCG) [6]. Figure 3 shows the comparison results on recall *vs.* candidate number under IoU = 0.8, average recall *vs.* candidate number [8] and recall *vs.* IoU on the top 1,000 candidates. It shows that our method outperforms all the methods on RGB images. It illustrates that our exploitation of depth in object proposal is effective, because inappropriate usage of depth will not improve object proposal performance [12].

We further compare our method with three object proposal methods on RGB-D images, namely adaptive integration of depth and color (AIDC) [23], depth-aware layered edge (DLE) [12] and elastic edge boxes (EEB) [13]. They can be treated as the extensions of BING, EB and M-EB by integrating depth, respectively. To provide more comprehensive evaluation, we adopt two baselines extended from other two open-source object proposal methods on RGB images, namely OBJ and M-MCG, by referring to [13], and denote them with OBJ* and M*-MCG. Figure 4 shows the comparison results under the same criteria to those in Fig. 3. It shows that our method is superior to other methods on RGB-D images. Figure 5 shows

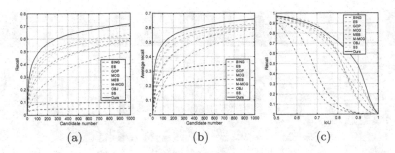

(a)   (b)   (c)

Fig. 3. Comparison with the state-of-the-art methods on RGB images. (a) Curve of recall *vs.* candidate number (IoU = 0.8). (b) Curve of average recall *vs.* candidate number. (c) Curve of recall *vs.* IoU on the top 1,000 candidates.

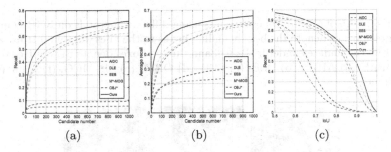

(a)   (b)   (c)

Fig. 4. Comparison with the state-of-the-art methods on RGB-D images. (a) Curve of recall *vs.* candidate number (IoU = 0.8). (b) Curve of average recall *vs.* candidate number. (c) Curve of recall *vs.* IoU on the top 1,000 candidates.

some examples of object proposal results generated by different methods on RGB-D images. The best bounding boxes as compared to the ones in ground truth within the top 1,000 candidates under IoU = 0.8 of each image are denoted with green boxes, and the omitted ones in ground truth are denoted with red boxes. we can see that our method can propose all the objects on various images, but other methods fail in some cases.

We also validate the efficiency of our method. Table 1 shows the running time of our method and other methods on RGB-D images. We can see that the running time of our method is similar to other grouping based methods with comparable performance, such as M*-MCG.

4.3   Discussion

In our experiments, we find some limitations of our method. For instance, our method may omit some objects in an image containing multiple objects with complex scene, such as the cups and two children in the top example in Fig. 6. Moreover, as shown in the bottom example in Fig. 6, our method fail in providing the accurate bounding boxes when the depth of two aircrafts are partially inaccurate.

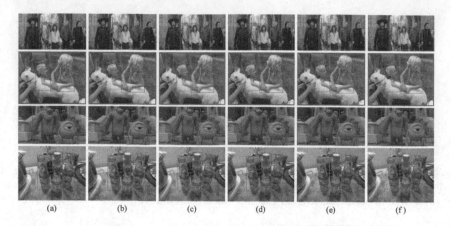

(a)   (b)   (c)   (d)   (e)   (f)

Fig. 5. Examples of object proposal results using different methods on RGB-D images. All the green boxes denote the best bounding boxes to the ones in ground truth within the top 1,000 candidates under IoU = 0.8, and the red boxes denote the omitted ones in ground truth. (a) AIDC. (b) DLE. (c) EEB. (d) OBJ*. (e) M*-MCG. (f) Ours. (Color figure online)

(a)   (b)   (c)

Fig. 6. Examples of our failure results. (a) Color appearance. (b) Depth appearance. (c) Our results (the green boxes and the red boxes have the same denotation to Fig. 5). (Color figure online)

Table 1. Efficiency evaluation of different methods on RGB-D images.

Method	Type	Language	Time per image (s)
AIDC	Window	C++	0.08
DLE	Window	C++ & Matlab	4.51
EEB	Integration	C++ & Matlab	22.34
OBJ*	Window	C++ & Matlab	4.19
M*-MCG	Grouping	C++ & Matlab	60.41
Ours	Grouping	C++ & Matlab	67.53

5   Conclusion

In this paper, we proposed an object proposal method on RGB-D images with the constraint of depth connectivity. Specifically, depth connectivity is used to improve the key techniques in grouping based object proposal, including segment generation, hypothesis expansion and candidate ranking. The proposed method was validated on the largest RGB-D image data set for object proposal *NJU1800*, and the experimental results showed that it outperforms the state-of-the-art methods on both RGB images and RGB-D images.

Acknowledgements. This work is supported by National Science Foundation of China (61321491, 61202320), and Collaborative Innovation Center of Novel Software Technology and Industrialization.

References

1. Alexe, B., Deselaers, T., Ferrari, V.: Measuring the objectness of image windows. TPAMI **34**, 2189–2202 (2012)
2. Arbeláez, P.: Boundary extraction in natural images using ultrametric contour maps. In: CVPR Workshop, p. 182 (2006)
3. Arbeláez, P., Pont-Tuset, J., Barron, J.T., Marques, F., Malik, J.: Multiscale combinatorial grouping. In: CVPR, pp. 328–335 (2014)
4. Carreira, J., Sminchisescu, C.: Constrained parametric min-cuts for automatic object segmentation. In: CVPR, pp. 3241–3248 (2010)
5. Chapelle, O., Vapnik, V., Bousquet, O., Mukherjee, S.: Choosing multiple parameters for support vector machines. Mach. Learn. **46**(1), 131–159 (2002)
6. Chen, X., Ma, H., Wang, X., Zhao, Z.: Improving object proposals with multi thresholding straddling expansion. In: CVPR, pp. 2587–2595 (2015)
7. Cheng, M.M., Zhang, Z., Lin, W.Y., Torr, P.H.S.: BING: binarized normed gradients for objectness estimation at 300fps. In: CVPR, pp. 3286–3293 (2014)
8. Hosang, J., Benenson, R., Dollár, P., Schiele, B.: What makes for effective detection proposals? TPAMI **38**(4), 814–830 (2016)
9. Humayun, A., Li, F., Rehg, J.M.: RIGOR: reusing inference in graph cuts for generating object regions. In: CVPR, pp. 336–343 (2014)
10. Krähenbühl, P., Koltun, V.: Geodesic object proposals. In: Fleet, D., Pajdla, T., Schiele, B., Tuytelaars, T. (eds.) ECCV 2014. LNCS, vol. 8693, pp. 725–739. Springer, Cham (2014). https://doi.org/10.1007/978-3-319-10602-1_47
11. Li, X., Jiang, S., Lv, X., Chen, C.: Learning to recognize hand-held objects from scratch. In: Chen, E., Gong, Y., Tie, Y. (eds.) PCM 2016. LNCS, vol. 9917, pp. 527–539. Springer, Cham (2016). https://doi.org/10.1007/978-3-319-48896-7_52
12. Liu, J., Ren, T., Bao, B.K., Bei, J.: Depth-aware layered edge for object proposal. In: ICME, pp. 1–6 (2016)
13. Liu, J., Ren, T., Wang, Y., Zhong, S.H., Bei, J., Chen, S.: Object proposal on RGB-D images via elastic edge boxes. NEUCOM **236**, 134–146 (2017)
14. Luo, B., Li, H., Meng, F., Wu, Q., Huang, C.: Video object segmentation via global consistency aware query strategy. TMM **PP**(99), 1 (2017)
15. Manen, S., Guillaumin, M., Gool, L.J.V.: Prime object proposals with randomized prim's algorithm. In: ICCV, pp. 2536–2543 (2013)

16. Qi, F., Zhao, D., Liu, S., Fan, X.: 3D visual saliency detection model with generated disparity map. Multimedia Tools Appl. **76**(2), 3087–3103 (2017)
17. Rantalankila, P., Kannala, J., Rahtu, E.: Generating object segmentation proposals using global and local search. In: CVPR, pp. 2417–2424 (2014)
18. Ren, T., Qiu, Z., Liu, Y., Yu, T., Bei, J.: Soft-assigned bag of features for object tracking. MMSJ **21**(2), 189–205 (2015)
19. Sang, J., Xu, C., Liu, J.: User-aware image tag refinement via ternary semantic analysis. IEEE Trans. Multimedia **14**(3), 883–895 (2012)
20. Uijlings, J.R.R., van de Sande, K.E.A., Gevers, T., Smeulders, A.W.M.: Selective search for object recognition. IJCV **104**(2), 154–171 (2013)
21. Wang, C., Zhao, L., Liang, S., Zhang, L.: Object proposal by multi-branch hierarchical segmentation. In: CVPR, pp. 3873–3881 (2015)
22. Xiao, Y., Lu, C., Tsougenis, E., Lu, Y., Tang, C.K.: Complexity-adaptive distance metric for object proposals generation. In: CVPR, pp. 778–786 (2015)
23. Xu, X., Ge, L., Ren, T., Wu, G.: Adaptive integration of depth and color for objectnes estimation. In: ICME, pp. 1–6 (2015)
24. Zhang, H., Zha, Z.J., Yang, Y., Yan, S., Gao, Y., Chua, T.S.: Attribute-augmented semantic hierarchy: towards a unified framework for content-based image retrieval. TOMM **11**(1s), 21 (2014)
25. Zhang, H., He, X., Porikli, F., Kneip, L.: Semantic context and depth-aware object proposal generation. In: ICIP (2016)
26. Zitnick, C.L., Dollár, P.: Edge boxes: locating object proposals from edges. In: Fleet, D., Pajdla, T., Schiele, B., Tuytelaars, T. (eds.) ECCV 2014. LNCS, vol. 8693, pp. 391–405. Springer, Cham (2014). https://doi.org/10.1007/978-3-319-10602-1_26

Edge-Aware Saliency Detection via Novel Graph Model

Hanpei Yang and Weihai Li[(⊠)]

Key Labotary of Electromagnetic Space Information,
Chinese Academy of Science University of Science and Technology of China,
Hefei, China
yanghanp@mail.ustc.edu.cn, whli@ustc.edu.cn

Abstract. Edge information takes an important role in distinguishing salient objects from background. In this paper, the screened edge information is utilized to roughly locate the salient object, which is combined with the color and texture to construct the feature space. Based on the feature space and fast background connection, a novel graph is put forward to effectively obtain the local and global cues and ease the blurry surrounds of the saliency maps while dealing with the intrinsic discontinuity and non-homogeneity within the salient object. Visual qualitative comparisons and comprehensive quantitatively evaluations on three benchmark datasets demonstrate that our method outperforms other state-of-the-art unsupervised methods and even some powerful supervised methods.

Keywords: Saliency detection · Edge information
Fast background connection · Blurry surrounds · Non-homogeneity

1 Introduction

The purpose of the salient object detection is to find the location of the eye-catching object, which is quite different from the traditional model that predict human fixations. The saliency detection technique is widely used in compression, recognition, image classification, attention retargeting and so on. Recent years have witnessed significant progress in saliency detection, which can be classified into biologically-inspired and computationally-oriented approaches. The first type utilizes the low-level features, such as color, movement, location, orientation to compute the saliency map. Work by Itti et al. [1] is a classical example, but it mostly generates blurry maps that are less useful for applications. Hou and Zhang [2] use spectral residual of the Fourier transform of an image to compute the saliency map, which tends to highlight the boundaries but not the entire salient object and is one of the examples of second type.

In recent years, a growing trend is toward graph-based propagation methods due to its simplicity and efficiency. Yang et al. [3] divide the image into superpixels, which are ranked based on their similarity to the boundaries and foreground seeds. Li et al. [4] propose the regularized random walks ranking to

© Springer International Publishing AG, part of Springer Nature 2018
B. Zeng et al. (Eds.): PCM 2017, LNCS 10736, pp. 45–55, 2018.
https://doi.org/10.1007/978-3-319-77383-4_5

formulate pixel-wise saliency maps from the superpixel-based background and foreground saliency estimations.

As shown in Fig. 1, the surrounds of salient objects in propagation-based saliency maps, such as BSCA [5] and GMR [3], are usually blurry. These methods simply use CIELab color space and location information to measure the similarity of two superpixels, which is not enough for complex images and the background superpixels around the salient objects are also assigned certain saliency value. Another phenomenon can be spotted that the detected saliency maps of images with intrinsic material discontinuity and non-homogenous color distribution within the salient objects are not highlighted uniformly, which is quite common in the sign post images. Numbers and texts in the sign posts are usually detected as background and assigned small saliency values.

Concerning two above-mentioned notorious and universal issues, we propose to use the edge information to roughly locate the salient objects and give more evidence to distinguish it from the background. A novel graph model takes fully advantage of the space location prior of the nodes, boundary prior, edge information, texture and color contrast to determine how different the superpixel is and how likely it belong to the part of salient objects. The main contributions of this work are listed as followed: (1) Edge based foreground probability is used as a superpixel feature to guide the graph construction. (2) A novel graph with novel feature space and fast background connection is proposed to explore the local as well as the global contrast between superpixels. (3) The proposed method improves the blurry surround of the saliency maps by propagation methods and the discontinuity of salient objects.

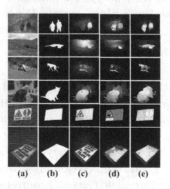

(a)   (b)   (c)   (d)   (e)

Fig. 1. Comparisons between saliency maps of propagation methods, from left to right: (a) Input image, (b) Ground truth, (c) BSCA15, (d) GMR13, (e) OURS.

2   Proposed Algorithm

In this section, we present the details of the proposed method. The image is first partitioned into N superpixels using SLIC algorithm [6]. Then, a novel graph model is constructed based on color prior, texture, edge information based foreground probability and space location information. Last, iteration evolution algorithm is used to propagate the saliency within a coarse saliency map gradually by exploring the impact of the neighboring superpixels and the current state of itself. The pipeline of the proposed algorithm is shown in Fig. 2.

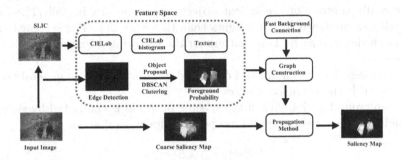

Fig. 2. Pipeline of the proposed algorithm.

2.1 Novel Graph Construction

Generally, in former research, a graph is constructed by taking the direct neighbors and the superpixels sharing the common boundaries as the final neighbors and their edge weights are computed by color and spatial distance in CIELab color space and Euclidean space. But these coarse settings are not sufficient for the complex images, so we put forward a strong feature space to give a more accurate description of superpixels and the similarity measurement. We also provide a novel neighbors selection method using boundary prior in the graph construction to better distinguish the salient object from the background.

Feature Extraction. A good feature descriptor can tell the small difference between two superpixels. In this section, we present three kinds of regional saliency features, including color $(3 + 256)$, texture (256), and edge based foreground probability (1), which results in 516 dimensional features to describe a superpixel. For color features, CIELab, denoted as c^{lab} is widely used in computer vision tasks for its propinquity to human vision. CIELab color histogram, denoted as his^{lab} is said to be effective in [7]. Consequently, we adopt these two color features to be part of the superpixel descriptor. For texture, we adopt the LBP features [8], denoted as his^{tex}. As can be observed, propagation based methods usually get the detected saliency maps with a blurry surround and the discontinuity inside the salient object. We try to improve these issues by introducing the edge based foreground probability as well as more accurate color and texture features. Edge information is of great importance in locating the foreground objects and give certain confidence to separate it from the background. The process meets two difficulties: the first is how to propagate the edge information to the whole salient object. The second one is how to propagate the values from pixel-level to superpixel-level to fit in our superpixel based feature extraction of following graph construction and keep the whole salient object highlighted at the same time. The details of the edge based foreground probability are listed as follows:

Step 1: canny detector is applied to the input image for the coarse edge map.
Step 2: the obtained edges are further processed by identifying whether they are the really contour of the salient objects, more details in [20]. The object boundaries are assigned higher weights than those are not. The screened canny edge map is denoted as E. This matters for the following foreground probability inference.
Step 3: the selective search method described in [9] is applied to generate object proposals. W is the proposal windows set.
Step 4: foreground probability of the specific proposal is computed by summing the weighted edges covered by the proposal window, as done in (1).

$$O(w) = \sum_{x \in w} E(x). \tag{1}$$

where $O(w)$ is the foreground probability of the proposal window w; $E(x)$ is the weight of pixel x in edge map. In order to propagate the foreground probability from the boundary to every pixel of salient object, we compute the summation foreground probability of all proposal windows covering the pixel, showed in (2). $O_p(x)$ is the foreground probability of pixel x.

$$O_p(x) = \sum_{w \in W \& x \in w} O(w). \tag{2}$$

Step 5: considering that we deal with the graph construction on the superpixel level, to propagate the foreground probability to the superpixels and to further strenthen the consistency of similar neighbor superpixels, we apply DBSCAN [21] to cluster the superpixels and assign the mean probability value of all pixels included in the cluster to the foreground probability of the cluster. The superpixels in the cluster share the same foreground probability. This measure is to make sure that the whole salient object is assigned the same value, avoiding that only the boundary superpixels around the salient object get highlighted. $O_r(S_i)$ is the foreground probability of the superpixel S_i and is computed as the average probability of the pixels included in the cluster. Figure 3 gives a more intuitionistic illustration of the process of how to generate the superpixel-wise foreground probability. Shown in Fig. 2, we successfully propagate the foreground probabality from the contour to the whole salient object.

$$O_r(S_i) = \frac{1}{\sum_{x \in clus_t} |x|} \sum_{S_i \in clus_t} \sum_{x \in S_i} O_p(x). \tag{3}$$

After step 1 to 5, we transform the edge information into the foreground probability of the superpixels. And then, it is used as a part of the superpixel feature descriptor to facilitate a more accurate graph construction.

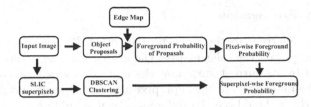

Fig. 3. The framework of edge based foreground probability.

Graph Construction. Graph model prevails in saliency detection research for its simplicity, explicitness and effectiveness. Traditionally, the graph is constructed in CIELab color space and Euclidean space, simply taking the locational neighbors. In this paper, we try to break this stereotype and give a more accurate and effective novel graph, which does good to the propagation methods and solving some notorious issues described in the introduction section. The process is detailed as below:

Step 1: for each superpixel (node of the graph), the initial neighbors of it are set as the locational direct neighbors and the superpixels that share the common boundaries with it.

Step 2: as certificated in former research, the boundary prior is effective, which means that the boundary superpixels are more likely to belong to the background. To make advantage of this characteristic, we connect each superpixel with a randomly chosen boundary superpixel. This give a more easier and faster way for the superpixels to connect to the background, which conforms the small-world network [10] and give a more direct way to measure how likely the superpixel resides in the background.

Step 3: the edge weight of the graph is computed as the similarity of connected superpixels. The weight plays an important role in distinguish the superpixels. A more robust similarity is especially required in complex scene, which can tell the small difference between superpixels. In this paper, we introduce the color, texture and edge based foreground probability to compose a strong feature descriptor.

$$sim(S_i, S_j) = \lambda_1 \left\| C_i^{\text{lab}} - C_j^{\text{lab}} \right\| + \lambda_2 \chi^2(his_i^{\text{lab}}, his_j^{\text{lab}}) + \\ \lambda_3 \chi^2(his_i^{\text{tex}}, his_j^{\text{tex}}) + \lambda_4 \left\| O_r(S_i) - O_r(S_j) \right\|. \tag{4}$$

where S_i, C_i^{lab}, his_i^{tex}, $O_r(S_i)$ are superpixel i, the CIELAB color of i, the CIELAB color histogram of i, the edge based foreground probability of i, respectively. $\lambda_1 - \lambda_4$ are the weighting parameters and set to 1, $\chi^2(h_1, h_2) = \sum_{i=1}^{K} \frac{2(h_1(i) - h_2(i))}{h_1(i) + h_2(i)}$ is the chi-squared distance between histograms h_1 and h_2 with k being the number of bins. It should be noticed that the edge weight of the connected superpixels are computed as done in (5), but when there is no connection between them, the edge weight is set to 0. σ is a constant and set to 0.1 as done in [3].

$$EW_{ij} = exp\{-sim(S_i, S_j)/\sigma\}. \tag{5}$$

2.2 Saliency Propagation

In this section, referring to the work by Qin et al. [5], we use the evolution
algorithm to propagate the saliency over the graph. The next state of the node
are determined by its current state and the state of nodes that connect to it.
To highlight the uniqueness of the superpixels, if the superpixel differs from its
neighbors greatly, it should keep its differences or it should be assimilated by its
neighbors. The update rule is shown in (6).

$$S^{t+1} = C \times S^t + (I - C) \times EW \times S^t. \tag{6}$$

$$c_i = -max(EW_{ij}). \tag{7}$$

$$C = \text{norm}(diag\{c_1, c_2, ..., c_N\}). \tag{8}$$

$EW = [EW_{ij}]_{N \times N}$ is the weight matrix of the edge in graph and also the
similarity of superpixel i and j. C is used to measure how likely the superpixel
should keep its saliency. Norm is the normalization operation. S^0 refers to the
coarse original saliency map and barrier distance [22] is applied to calculate it.
The saliency of the pixel is calculated by finding the minimum cost of all paths
starting from the pixel to the boundary pixels.

$$F(\pi) = \max_{i=0}^{k} I(\pi(i)) - \min_{i=0}^{k} I(\pi(i)). \tag{9}$$

$$D(t) = \min_{\pi \in \Pi_{B,t}} F(\pi). \tag{10}$$

where π is the path, from the specific pixel to boundary set B; $F(\pi)$ is the
cost function of the path; $D(t)$ is the salient value of the pixel t. The barrier
distance map is robust to the fluctuation of pixels, so we can roughly locate the
foreground object. Ours method can boost the coarse saliency map by a large
margin and the generation of the coarse map can be replaced by other methods,
which will be detailed in the experiment section.

3 Experiments

Datasets and Baselines. We evaluate our method on three datasets: ECSSD
[11], THUS10000 [12], and PASCAL-S [13], comparing to 10 state-of-the-art
methods: SR07 [2], FT09 [15], SF12 [16], HS13 [11], GMR13 [3], wCtr14 [17],
BSCA15 [5], RTMST16 [18], HDCT14 [19], DRFI14 [7]. The first eight algorithms are unsupervised and the last two are powerful supervised methods.
ECSSD [11] has 1000 semantically meaningful but structurally complex images.
THUS10000 is introduced by Liu et al. [12], containing 10000 images and pixel-
wise ground truths and is a descendant of the MSRA dataset. It is very challenging and also suitable for more comprehensive model evaluation. PASCAL-S
[13] contains annotations of the most salient objects over complex scenes taken
from PASCAL VOC dataset and is designed to avoid the dataset design bias.

Evaluation Metrics. Precision-recall curve, AUC, F-measure, MAE are common metrics in saliency detection. PR curve is calculated by binarizing the saliency map using thresholds ranging from 0 to 255. AUC is the area under the ROC curve that concerns two parameters, false positive rate and true positive rate, which can be obtained from the calculation process of PR curve. F-measure, $F_\beta = \frac{(1+\beta^2)Precision \times Recall}{\beta^2 Precison+Recall}$ (β^2=0.3 as done in other refernece), is utilized to get a harmonic mean of the precision and recall for a more comprehensive evaluation of quality of a saliency map. To measure the weighted, continuous saliency maps, the mean absolute error (MAE) between the saliency maps and the ground truths is evaluated as $MAE = \frac{1}{W \times H} \sum_{x=1}^{W} \sum_{y=1}^{H} |S(x,y) - G(x,y)|$.

Visual Comparisons. In Fig. 4, the visual comparison of saliency maps generated by different state-of-the-art methods are provided. Ours saliency maps highlight the salient objects uniformly. For instance, in the first row, the leopard has the similar color with the background, our algorithm can distinguish it from the background as a whole while other methods have a rather fuzzy detection or not uniformly highlight the whole object. Figure 1 aslo shows that our method sovle the discontinuity problem inside the salient object.

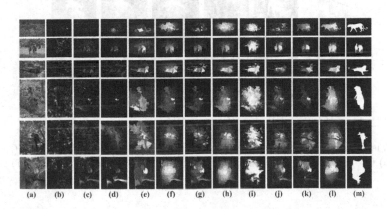

Fig. 4. Visual comparisons between ours and other ten state-of-the-art methods, from left to right: (a) Input image (b) SR07 (c) FT09 (d) SF12 (e) HS13 (f) GMR13 (g) wCtr14 (h) BSCA15 (i) RTMST16 (j) HDCT14 (k) DRFI14 (l) OURS (m) Ground truth.

Features. In this part, the features are exploited to show their effectiveness. In Fig. 5, **OURS** means the saliency map with all features mentioned before; **noob** is with all features except foreground probability; **nolab** is with all features except CIELab histogram and foreground probability. Comparing the adjacent two can get the effectiveness of CIELab and foreground probability. In Fig. 6, some saliency maps are provided to illustrate the effectiveness of different features. CIELab histogram and foreground probability can help distinguish the foreground from the background and give a clearer boundary of foreground.

Coarse Saliency Map can be calculated by other methods. SR07, FT09, SF12, GMR13 are used to illustrate the effectiveness of the proposed framework. In Fig. 7, the performance improvement of each coarse saliency map is quite obvious.

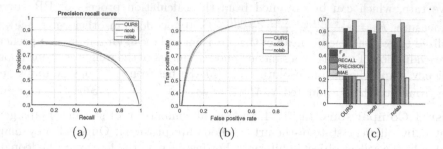

(a) (b) (c)

Fig. 5. Saliency performance with different features, from left to right: (a) PR curve, (b) ROC curve, (c) Precision, Recall, F_β & MAE on PASCAL-S dataset.

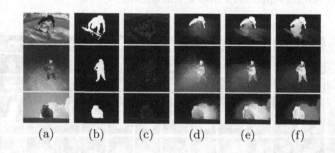

(a) (b) (c) (d) (e) (f)

Fig. 6. Visual saliency performance with different features, from left to right: (a) Input image (b) Ground truth (c) Screened edge detection map (d) nolab (e) noob (f) OURS.

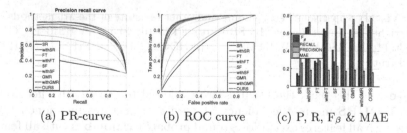

(a) PR-curve   (b) ROC curve   (c) P, R, F_β & MAE

Fig. 7. The proposed framework with different coarse maps on ECSSD.

As for the PR curve, our method slightly surpasses the powerful supervised method DRFI and these two methods exceed other state-of-the-art methods by a large margin, including the supervised HDCT method. The same situation can be observed in the ROC curves, except that our method has the comparable performance with the DRFI method. As for Fig. 8, our method has better precision, recall, F-measure, and MAE synthetically. For the first three parameters, the higher the better. For MAE, the lower the better. What's more, we don't have access to the source code of Grab method [14], but we can observe from the comparison with DRFI on ECSSD and THUS10000 datesets that our method outperforms the Grab method.

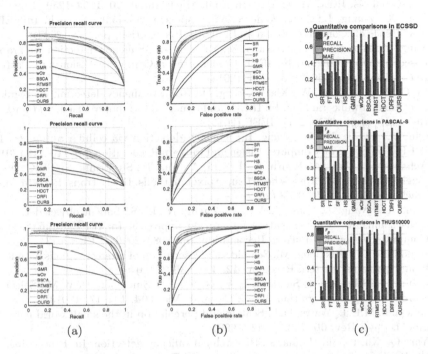

Fig. 8. Saliency performance of different methods, from left to right: (a) PR curve (b) ROC curve (c) Precision, Recall, F_β & MAE; from top to down: on ECSSD, on PASCAL-S, on THUS10000.

4 Conclusions

We present an edge-aware saliency detection method via graph based propagation model. Edge information can help distinguish the boundary of the salient object, and hence lessen the blurry surrounds of the objects. We propagate the edge information to the superpixel foreground probability to highlight the whole salient object uniformly. A novel graph model with boundary prior is proposed to better present the image, capture the local and global cues and give a fast connection between the superpixel and the background. Propagation method can help balance the impact of the node itself and its neighbors. Each node can evolve to a more accurate and robust state. Experiments on three public datasets demonstrate that our method can highlight the salient object and suppress the background effectively. Our method is also proved to be effective in solving intrinsic object discontinuity and non-homogenous color distribution within the salient objects.

References

1. Itti, L., Koch, C., Niebur, E.: A model of saliency-based visual attention for rapid scene analysis. IEEE Trans. Pattern Anal. Mach. Intell. **20**, 1254–1259 (1998)
2. Hou, X., Zhang, L.: Saliency detection: a spectral residual approach. In: IEEE Conference on Computer Vision and Pattern Recognition, pp. 1–8 (2007)
3. Yang, C., Zhang, L., Lu, H., Ruan, X., Yang, M.-H.: Saliency detection via graph-based manifold ranking. In: IEEE Conference on Computer Vision and Pattern Recognition, pp. 3166–3173. IEEE (2013)
4. Li, C., Yuan, Y., Cai, W., Xia, Y., Feng, D.: Robust saliency detection via regularized random walks ranking. In: IEEE Conference on Computer Vision and Pattern Recognition, pp. 2710–2717. IEEE (2015)
5. Qin, Y., Lu, H., Xu, Y., Wang, H.: Saliency detection via cellular automata. In: IEEE Conference on Computer Vision and Pattern Recognition, pp. 110–119 (2015)
6. Achanta, R., Shaji, A., Smith, K., Lucchi, A., Fua, P., Süsstrunk, S.: SLIC superpixels compared to state-of-the-art superpixel methods. IEEE Trans. Pattern Anal. Mach. Intell. **34**, 2274–2282 (2012)
7. Jiang, H., Wang, J., Yuan, Z., Wu, Y., Zheng, N., Li, S.: Salient object detection: a discriminative regional feature integration approach. In: IEEE Conference on Computer Vision and Pattern Recognition, pp. 2083–2090. IEEE (2013)
8. Heikkilä, M., Pietikäinen, M., Schmid, C.: Description of interest regions with local binary patterns. Pattern Recognit. **42**, 425–436 (2009)
9. Uijlings, J.R.R., van de Sande, K.E.A., Gevers, T., Smeulders, A.W.M.: Selective search for object recognition. Int. J. Comput. Vis. **104**, 154–171 (2013)
10. Newman, M.E.J., Watts, D.J.: Scaling and percolation in the small-world network model. Phys. Rev. **60**, 7332–7342 (1999)
11. Yan, Q., Xu, L., Shi, J., Jia, J.: Hierarchical saliency detection. In: Proceedings of the IEEE Conference on Computer Vision and Pattern Recognition, pp. 1155–1162 (2013)
12. Liu, T., Yuan, Z., Sun, J., Wang, J., Zheng, N., Tang, X., Shum, H.: Learning to detect a salient object. IEEE Trans. Pattern Anal. Mach. Intell. **33**, 353–367 (2011)
13. Li, Y., Hou, X., Koch, C., Rehg, J.M., Yuille, A.L.: The secrets of salient object segmentation. In: IEEE Conference on Computer Vision and Pattern Recognition, pp. 4321–4328 (2014)
14. Wang, Q., Zheng, W., Piramuthu, R.: GraB : visual saliency via novel graph model and background priors. In: IEEE Conference on Computer Vision and Pattern Recognition, pp. 535–543 (2016)
15. Achantay, R., Hemamiz, S., Estraday, F., Süsstrunky, S.: Frequency-tuned salient region detection. In: IEEE Conference on Computer Vision and Pattern Recognition Workshops, pp. 1597–1604 (2009)
16. Perazzi, F., Krahenbuhl, P., Pritch, Y., Hornung, A.: Saliency filters: contrast based filtering for salient region detection. In: Proceedings of the IEEE Conference on Computer Vision and Pattern Recognition, pp. 733–740 (2012)

17. Zhu, W., Liang, S., Wei, Y., Sun, J.: Saliency optimization from robust background detection. In: IEEE Conference on Computer Vision and Pattern Recognition, pp. 2814–2821 (2014)
18. Tu, W., He, S., Yang, Q., Chien, S.: Real-time salient object detection with a minimum spanning tree. In: IEEE Conference on Computer Vision and Pattern Recognition, pp. 2334–2342 (2016)
19. Kim, J., Han, D., Tai, Y., Kim, J.: Salient region detection via high-dimensional color transform. In: IEEE Conference on Computer Vision and Pattern Recognition, pp. 883–890. IEEE (2014)
20. Arbeláez, P., Maire, M., Fowlkes, C., Malik, J.: Contour detection and hierarchical image segmentation. IEEE Trans. Pattern Anal. Mach. Intell. **33**, 898–916 (2011)
21. Ester, M., Kriegel, H.P., Sander, J., Xu, X.: A density-based algorithm for discovering clusters in large spatial databases with noise. In: Proceedings of the 2nd International Conference on Knowledge Discovery and Data Mining, pp. 226–231 (1996)
22. Zhang, J., Sclaroff, S., Lin, Z., Shen, X., Price, B., Mech, R.: Minimum barrier salient object detection at 80 fps. In: IEEE International Conference on Computer Vision, pp. 1404–1412 (2015)

Multiple Kernel Learning Based on Weak Learner for Automatic Image Annotation

Hua Zhong, Xu Yuan, Zhikui Chen[(✉)], Fangming Zhong, and Yonglin Leng

School of Software Technology, Dalian University of Technology,
Dalian 116620, China
zkchen@dlut.edu.cn

Abstract. Image annotation is a challenging problem, which has attracted intensive attention recently due to the semantic gap between images and corresponding tags. However, most existing works neglect the imbalance distribution of different classes and the internal correlations across modalities. To address these issues, we propose a multiple kernel learning method based on weak learner for image annotation, which can acquire the semantic correlations to predict tags of a given image. More specifically, we first employ the convolutional neural network to extract the semantic features of images, and take advantage of the oversampling technique to generate new samples of minority classes which can solve the imbalance problem. Further, our proposed multiple kernel learning method is applied to obtain the internal correlations between images and tags. In order to further improve the prediction performance, we combine the boosting procedure with the multiple kernel learning to enhance the performance of classifier. We evaluate the proposed method on two benchmark datasets. The experimental results demonstrate that our method is superior to several state-of-the-art methods.

Keywords: Image annotation · Multiple kernel learning
Weak learner · Imbalance learning

1 Introduction

With the popularity of smart phones and the rapid development of social networks, the explosive growth image data have emerged over the Internet in the past few years, such as Facebook and Twitter. Some relevant keywords are assigned to images for organizing and managing the massive image data, which can effectively improve the performance of the web image search engines. However, it is almost impossible to manually annotate massive images due to the expensive cost. This makes automatic image annotation become a challenging problem and attract considerable attention.

The task of automatic image annotation is to predict several relevant keywords for a given image which accurately reflect its visual content. The essence of this task is to bridge the semantic gap between images and textual keywords.

In recent years, several researches [6–10,12–14] have been devoted to address the problem of semantic gap. In these researches, some works [9,10] treat annotation task as a problem of the joint likelihood distribution over the co-occurrence of images and tags, which directly learn the probability distribution over images for each tag. However, these works have no access to the internal correlations between images and tags. Inspired by this, a new baseline was introduced in [6] for the problem of image annotation, which attempted to convert this problem to a retrieval problem. In this work, K-nearest neighbors are employed to assign the tags for a given image. Following this line, a weighted nearest neighbor model was constructed to predict tags in [7]. Due to the wonderful annotation performance of nearest neighbor based methods, these methods [6–8] have attracted much attention.

In addition to the above methods, the discriminative model based methods [12–14] have also been widely investigated for addressing the annotation problem. For example, the support vector machine (SVM) was first introduced [12] by Cusano et al. for automatically annotating digital photographs. In this method, the unseen image is divided into image subdivisions which is classified by SVM, and then each pixel is assigned to one of the classes. Besides, a scheme of confidence based dynamic ensemble [13] was presented to overcome the lack of capability to assess the prediction quality. To improve the tolerance ability of misclassification, an SVM with variable tolerance is proposed in [14], which utilizes the kernel trick to further improve the performance of tag prediction.

Even though previous works have obtained impressive results, there are still three obvious shortcomings for them. First, some works apply the kernel learning model to obtain the correlations between images and tags. The success of these works is heavily dependent on the proper selection of single kernel functions. However, the kernel selection is time consuming and has weakly interpretability. Besides, many previous studies almost pay no attention to the imbalance distribution of image keywords. This problem can cause that the learning model produces poor performance over the minority classes, which can limit the overall performance over the entire dataset. Moreover, the low-level artificial visual features are employed to describe images in these researches, which are not rich enough to express the semantic information of images.

To overcome these shortcomings, we propose a multiple kernel learning model based on weak learner (WLMKL) to bridge the semantic gap between images and tags. Our model employs multiple kernel model to learn the correlations rather than single kernel model due to the stronger interpretability and flexibility. Specifically, in order to improve the expression ability of image features, convolutional neural network (CNN) features are extracted for describing high-level semantic information of images. Afterwards, we utilize a synthetic minority oversampling technique (SMOTE) to deal with the imbalance distribution of image keywords, which can avoid the issue that the overall performance of model is limited by the minority classes. In addition, the boosting procedure is incorporated into our model for further improving the prediction performance. This combination is then used to acquire a classifier for a given keyword, and the classifier

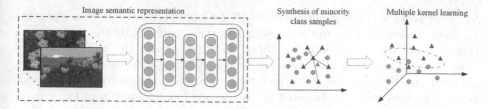

Fig. 1. The framework of our proposed model. The high-level semantic features of image are extracted by CNN, and the SMOTE method is employed to address the imbalance problem of data distribution. Furthermore, our model combines multiple kernel learning and weak learner to acquire the correlations between images and tags, which are used to predict tags for images.

discriminates whether an unseen image is annotated with the given keyword. The entire framework of WKMKL is depicted in Fig. 1. The performance of the proposed method is evaluated on two benchmark datasets, and the experimental results demenstrate that WLMKL outperforms several previous works.

The contributions of this work can be summarized as follows:

- We propose a novel multiple kernel learning model based on weak learner, which can effectively obtain the internal correlations between images and tags. It is worth noting that the selection of kernel function can be directly avoided.
- the imbalance learning method is employed to solve the problem of the imbalance distribution of image keywords, thus the minority classes will not limit the overall performance of our model.
- The boosting procedure is exploited to optimize the classifier on different combinations of the training sets, which can generate better classifier to obtain higher classification accuracy.

The rest of this paper is organized as follows. The details of our proposed model are described in Sect. 2. In Sect. 3 we present the data sets, experimental settings and experimental results in our experiment. Conclusions and future work are presented in Sect. 4.

2   Approach

In this section, we introduce our proposed model that utilizes the synthetic minority oversampling technique (SMOTE), the multiple kernel learning method and weak learner for automatic image annotation in detail. For modality representation, the details how to extract the features of images and represent the tags are provided. Sequentially, we employ SMOTE to enhance the minority classes, and the multiple kernel model is used for capturing the correlations between images and the annotation tags in high-dimensional space. Furthermore, the boosting algorithm is exploited for improving the accuracy of prediction.

2.1 Feature Representation

Inspired by previous works [22] on the image representation, we use convolutional neural networks (CNN) to extract image features. The results of related works [5,22,23] proved its outstanding capability for image representation. We take the outputs of full-connection layer as image feature. Furthermore, we apply PCA to improve the generalization ability. For each image, the image feature is denoted by I_i. We use $T_{i,j} \in \{0, 1\}$ to denote the tags of image. $T_{i,j} = 0$ if the j-th tag is absent for image i, and $T_{i,j} = 1$ otherwise. The distribution of tags conforms to the Bernoulli distribution. In final, we can obtain the vector T_i that consists of the absence/presence of all keywords for each image, and each image is annotated with suitable tags from all keywords. The details of feature representation can be further detailed in Sect. 3.

2.2 Imbalance Learning

Imbalance distribution of the datasets hinders the improvement of classification accuracy. The classes of skewed distribution are treated equally in traditional learning methods, which causes low accuracy over the minority classes. For addressing this problem, SMOTE [2] is utilized for generating synthetic samples of minority classes in this paper. The synthetic samples are generated by the samples and their k nearest neighbors in the minority classes. In order to synthesize a set of new samples $S_{synthetic}$ based on $S_{original}$, the original sample $S_{original}$ in a minority class and its $n(n < k)$ neighbors randomly selected from k nearest neighbors are used as stated in Eq. (1):

$$S_{synthetic}[i] = S_{original} + random(0, 1) * (L[i] - S_{original}) \tag{1}$$

where $i = 1, \cdots, n$, and L is set of n neighbors randomly selected from the k nearest neighbors of $S_{original}$. We can observe that the size of synthetic samples is n times to the original size.

Through this approach, we try to construct a set of synthetic samples for minority class, and broaden the decision region of minority class. In addition, the decision region can become more general by using this over-sampling technique.

2.3 Multiple Kernel Learning

The performance of conventional single kernel method depends heavily on the selection of kernel. While the selection of kernel function is difficult due to the different characteristics and application scenarios of various kernel functions. Especially on the high-dimensional data, the single kernel method is not applicable. Since the distribution of data in high-dimensional feature space is non-flat. Motivated by [1], our approach employs multiple kernel learning method to learn the correlations between images and the annotated tags. The interpretability of decision can be effectively enhanced by replacing single kernel with multiple kernel. The recent researches [3] have validated that the multiple kernel learning model can achieve better performance than the single kernel model.

In multiple kernel learning model, an equivalent kernel is a convex combination of multiple basic kernels, which replaces the conventional kernel for data mapping. Different data features can be exploited by different basic kernels. Thus, multiple kernel learning can become a more flexible approach on the high-dimensional heterogeneous data. Formally, the combined kernel function can be written as:

$$K = \sum_{n=1}^{N} \alpha_n K_n \quad s.t. \quad \alpha_n \geq 0, \sum_{n=1}^{N} \alpha_n = 1 \tag{2}$$

where N is the number of the basic kernels. K_n represents n-th basic kernel function, and α_n is its weight. The weights can be obtained by optimizing the multiple kernel learning model, which can be formulated as follows:

$$\min \frac{1}{2} \left(\sum_{i=1}^{m} \|g_i\| \right)^2 + c \sum_{i=1}^{n} \xi_i$$

$$s.t. \quad T_i \left(g\left(I_i \right) + b \right) \geq 1 - \xi_i \quad \text{and} \quad \xi_i \geq 0 \quad \forall i \tag{3}$$

$$w.r.t \quad g_i \in \mathbb{R}^{K_1} \times \mathbb{R}^{K_2} \times \cdots \times \mathbb{R}^{K_m}, \xi_i \in \mathbb{R}^n, b \in \mathbb{R}$$

where c and ξ_i represent the regularization parameter and the slack variable respectively.

Many methods are proposed to optimize the multiple kernel learning stated as Eq. (3) by transforming it to the dual problem [1,3,20]. In our proposed model, the SimpleMKL [3] is adopted as the solution for solving the SVM optimization problem, which wraps a SVM solver of the single kernel that is attained by the linear convex combination of multiple basic kernel. Furthermore, the weights of the convex combination can be optimized automatically. In SimpleMKL, the formulation of the dual problem can be represented as:

$$\max Q\left(\alpha, \beta\right) = \sum_{i=1}^{m} \beta_i - \frac{1}{2} \sum_{i=1}^{m} \sum_{j=1}^{m} \beta_i \beta_j T_i T_j \sum_{n=1}^{N} \alpha_n K_n$$

$$s.t. \begin{cases} \sum_{i=1}^{m} \beta_i T_i = 0 \\ \beta_i, \beta_j \in [0, c], \forall i \\ \alpha_n \geq 0, \sum_{n=1}^{N} \alpha_n = 1 \end{cases} \tag{4}$$

where β is the Lagrange multiplier, and the combination kernel $K = \sum_{n=1}^{N} \alpha_n K_n$ is used for the dual formulation. Supposing that β^* maximizes Eq. (4) and the kernel matrix K_n is positive definite, the optimal value of the dual problem is represented as

$$Q\left(\alpha\right) = \sum_{i=1}^{m} \beta_i^* - \frac{1}{2} \sum_{i=1}^{m} \sum_{j=1}^{m} \beta_i^* \beta_j^* T_i T_j \sum_{n=1}^{N} \alpha_n K_n \tag{5}$$

The dual problem has strict concavity property due to the positive definite K_i [1], which ensures the uniqueness of β^*. Assuming that the uniqueness of β^*

does not rely on α, then the objective function $Q(\alpha)$ is differentiable. Therefore, the differentiation of $Q(\alpha)$ with respect to α_n can be computed by

$$\frac{\partial Q}{\partial \alpha_n} = -\frac{1}{2} \sum_{i=1}^{m} \sum_{j=1}^{m} \beta_i^* \beta_j^* T_i T_j K_n \quad \forall n \tag{6}$$

The iterative procedure of the SimpleMKL algorithm is terminated if the stopping criterion can be met. There are many criterions for stopping the iteration, such as the duality gap, the KKT conditions and the variation of α. In the implementation of SimpleMKL, the duality gap is adopted as the stopping criterion, which can be further converted to another formulation

$$\max \sum_{i=1}^{m} \sum_{j=1}^{m} \beta_i^* \beta_j^* T_i T_j K_n - \sum_{i=1}^{m} \sum_{j=1}^{m} \beta_i^* \beta_j^* T_i T_j \sum_{n=1}^{N} \alpha_n^* K_n \leq \varepsilon \tag{7}$$

where α^* represents optimal primal variable. The proper weights of kernel functions can be obtained, and the primal multiple kernel learning problem can be effectively solved. Since the convergence rate of the SimpleMKL algorithm is faster than other multiple kernel learning methods, the proposed model is more efficient.

2.4   Weak Learning

In order to further improve the prediction accuracy over entire dataset, we employ the boosting algorithm in our model. Generally, each misclassified sample is given the equal weight whether it is a majority class or a minority class. The classification results will be skewed to the majority class if the skewed data distribution is not balanced. This problem can be avoided by using SMOTE in the beginning of our model. The synthetic samples can balance the skewed distribution, which make the boosting procedure perform efficiently. The AdaBoost.M2 [4] is used in our work, which is given more expressive power.

In each round p, the weak learner computes a weak hypothesis h_p on a distribution D_p. Some rules need to be followed for obtaining the weak hypothesis h_p. If $h_p(I_i, T_i) = 1$ and $h_p(I_i, T) = 0$, the prediction of h_p shows that the tag of I_i is T_i, rather than other tags T. Otherwise, If $h_p(I_i, T_i) = 0$ and $h_p(I_i, T) = 1$, the results of prediction is opposite. One prediction of h_p is chosen from both if $h_p(I_i, T_i) = h_p(I_i, T)$. Therefore, the pseudo-loss of hypothesis h_p on distribution D_p can be written as

$$\varepsilon_p = \frac{1}{2} \sum D_p(1 - h_p(I_i, T_i) + h_p(I_i, T)) \tag{8}$$

The goal of boosting procedure is to obtain a weak hypothesis h_p with low pseudo-loss. For this goal, the normalization constant Z_p is introduced, then the distribution D_p can be updated as follows:

$$D_{p+1} = \frac{D_p}{Z_p} \cdot \gamma_p^{\chi_p/2} \tag{9}$$

where γ can be calculated by $\gamma_p = \varepsilon_p/(1 - \varepsilon_p)$, and χ_p can be expressed as $\chi_p = 2 - (1 - h_p(I_i, T_i) + h_p(I_i, T))$. In the end, we can obtain the final hypothesis h_f by combining different hypotheses, which can be described as follows:

$$h_f = \arg\max_P \sum_{p=1}^{P} \left(\log \frac{1}{\gamma_p} \right) h_p(I, T) \tag{10}$$

The boosting algorithm can generate a powerful integration classifier based on the simple classifier, which transforms the weak learner to strong learner.

2.5   Multiple Kernel Learning Based on Weak Learner

The procedure of our proposed model is described in Algorithm 1. In order to represent the visual content of images, we utilize the CNN to extract the image features. Meanwhile, we take into account the problem of imbalance data. For addressing this problem, the SMOTE is employed to generate new samples of minority classes. Further, the multiple kernel learning model is used to train the classifier, and then the boosting procedure is exploited for improving the prediction accuracy over entire dataset. The iterative procedure is terminated until the number of maximal iterations is reached.

Algorithm 1. Multiple Kernel Learning model based on Weak Learner

---

Input: Training set of image and tag features I_{train} and T_{train}, Test set I_{test}, The number of boosting iterations P
Output: The prediction tags T_{pred}
 1: Generate the synthetic samples of minority classes using SMOTE Eq.(1)
 2: **Initialize** distribution D
 3: **Initialize** N basic kernel parameters and kernel types
 4: **for** $i = 0 \to P$ **do**
 5:     Train weak learner using SimpleMKL
 6:     Calculate the weak hypothesis h_p
 7:     Obtain the pseudo-loss with Eq.(8)
 8:     Set the value of γ_p and χ_p
 9:     Update D_{p+1} with Eq.(9)
10: **end for**
11: Obtain the final hypothesis h_f with Eq.(10)
12: **return** the result of prediction T_{pred}

---

3   Experiments

In this section, we first introduce two benchmark datasets for the evaluation of our method. Then, the feature extraction and the evaluation metric are described in detail. Subsequently, the experimental results are shown.

3.1 Data Sets

Two benchmark datasets are used for evaluating our proposed method. The brief description of these datasets are listed below.

Corel 5 K contains 4999 images and the manual image annotations, which is widely used for image annotation and image retrieval task [16]. Each image is annotated by an average of 3.5 tags, and all images cover 260 keywords. 4500 images are chosen as the training set, and the remained images are used for testing.

IAPR TC-12 consists of 19627 images of natural scenes. Each image is described with several language. This data set was initially published for cross-lingual retrieval [17]. There are 17665 images for training and 1962 images for testing. The dictionary contains 291 keywords with an average of 5.7 keywords per image.

3.2 Experimental Settings

Feature extraction is an essential part of our framework. Here, VGG [5] is applied to extract image features, which is a popular method for image features extracting. The extracted features by VGG have stronger expression capability than that extracted by conventional methods, such as SIFT and GIST. In our experiments, each image is represented by a 4096-dimensional vector. For reducing the feature dimension and enhancing the generalization ability, PCA is employed in our experiment. A 128-dimensional vector is obtained to represent image features in final.

In order to evaluate our method and compare with the previous works, we employ the standard evaluation metrics similar to [15]. The precision P, recall R and $F1$ score of different methods are computed in the testing set. Additionally, we compute the number of tags with non-zero recall value which is represented as $N+$.

As part of our experiment, we need to set multiple basic kernel. Several appropriate basic kernels are taken into account in our experiment, we exploit the Gaussian kernel and the Polynomial kernel as our basic kernel. Furthermore, these basic kernels are initialized to the same weight value. The weight values can be optimized in the step of multiple kernel learning.

3.3 Results

We evaluate the performance of WLMKL and compare it with several state-of-the-art works on the Corel-5K and IAPR TC-12 datasets. Table 1 reports the experimental results of our method and several previous works for automatic image annotation. The experimental results on two datasets are analyzed respectively as follows.

Note that our method achieves the highest R value, $F1$ value and $N+$ value on the Corel-5K dataset. The recall score is 30% higher than the state-of-the-art works. This may be because we consider the problem of imbalance distribution of data, and our method can generate the synthetic samples of minority classes. For the precision score, our method is comparable to other methods. In summary, our method outperforms state-of-the-art works on the Corel-5K dataset.

Table 1. The performance of our proposed method in terms of R (Recall), P (Precious), $F1$ and $N+$ (The number of tags with non-zero recall value) compared with several previous works on Corel-5K and IAPR TC-12 datasets.

Method	Corel-5K				IAPR TC-12			
	R	P	$F1$	$N+$	R	P	$F1$	$N+$
CRM [10]	19	16	17	107	-	-	-	-
MBRM [9]	25	24	24	122	23	24	23	223
JEC [6]	32	27	29	139	29	28	23	250
GS [18]	33	30	32	146	29	32	32	252
2PKNN [8]	40	**39**	39	177	32	**49**	39	274
Tagprop σML [7]	42	33	37	160	35	46	**40**	266
FastTag [21]	43	32	37	166	26	47	33	280
GLKNN [11]	47	36	41	184	36	41	38	282
KSVM-VT [15]	42	32	37	179	29	47	36	268
CCD [19]	41	36	38	159	29	44	35	251
LDMKL [24]	44	29	35	179	-	-	-	-
WLMKL	**56**	32	**41**	**210**	**47**	34	39	**286**

Specifically, we observe that our method outperforms the generative models [9,10] over all evaluation metrics. This may be explained by that the generative models pay more attention to a joint probability distribution over images and tags rather than the internal correlations between images and tags. Our methods is comparable with the nearest neighbor based methods [6–8,11]. Although these methods obtain higher precision, our method is superior to these methods in terms of the recall, $F1$ and $N+$ value. We also compare our method with KSVM-VT [15] which is the kernelized version of SVM with variable tolerance. The result shows that our method achieves better performance than KSVM-VT on Corel-5K dataset, which indicates our multiple kernel learning based model is more effective than the single kernel based method for image annotation. Besides, we compare our method with two multiple kernel models (CCD [19] and LDMKL [24]). As the results shown in Table 1, our method is superior to CCD and LDMKL in terms of the recall, $F1$ and $N+$ value, while is slightly worse than CCD at the precision score. Our method achieves a better overall performance than CCD and LDMKL, which proves the effectiveness of our multiple kernel learning method.

The comparison results on the IAPR TC-12 dataset are also displayed in Table 1. Compared to several previous works, our proposed method obtains better performance at the recall and $N+$ value, and the $F1$ score is slightly worse than the best one [7]. It is comparable to other methods at the precision of annotation. More specifically, we can observe that our method is superior to generative models at the overall performance, such as MBRM [9] and GS [18]. Our method acquires the higher recall and $N+$ values than the nearest neighbor based methods

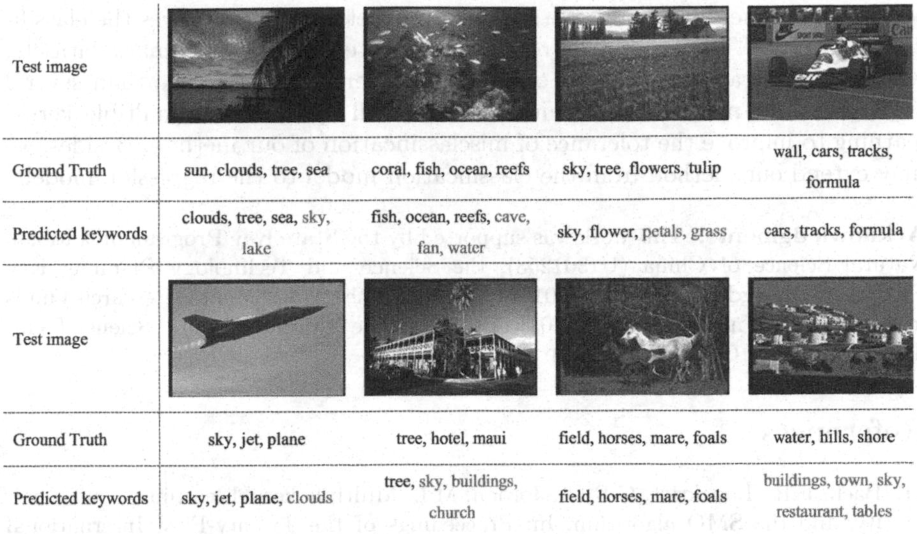

Fig. 2. The examples of image annotation by using WLMKL on Corel-5K dataset. This figure displays the given test images, the human annotations and the automatic annotations, respectively.

[6–8,11] and KSVM-VT [15], while being comparable at the precision value and aligns with the best one in term of $F1$ value. This may be because our method lacks a stronger tolerance for misclassification. Compared to CCD, the value of recall, $F1$ and $N+$ are higher, while it is comparable to CCD in term of precision. The comparison results reveal that our method still obtains the comparable performance to other method, which proves that our proposed method is effective on IAPR TC-12 dataset.

Figure 2 shows several examples of automatic image annotation on the Corel-5K dataset by using WLMKL. Different from the conventional methods, our method can find different number of keywords for image annotation, rather than a constant. The ground truth annotation and the prediction keywords of images are illustrated respectively. The prediction results can indicate the effectiveness of our method for image annotation.

4 Conclusion

We presented a multiple kernel learning method based on weak learner to bridge the semantic gap between images and tags for automatically image annotation. In this work, we employ convolutional neural network to extract the semantic content of image. In addition, an oversampling technique is applied to generate new samples of minority classes for addressing the imbalance problem of image keywords. We combine the multiple kernel learning with the weak learner for learning the internal correlations between images and tags, which avoids the selection of kernel function in the single kernel method and improves the classification accuracy. The experiment results are reported on two benchmark datasets, which demonstrate our method obtains the superior performance than several state-of-the-art methods. In future work, we will optimize the multiple kernel learning to improve the tolerance of misclassification of our method. Besides, we may extend our method from the classification model to the regression model.

Acknowledgments. This work was supported by the State Key Program of National Natural Science of China (U1301253), the Science and Technology Planning Key Project of Guangdong Province (2015B010110006), the Fundamental Research Funds for the Central Universities (DUT2017TB02), and the National Natural Science Foundation project of China (61672123).

References

1. Bach, F.R., Lanckriet, G.R.G., Jordan, M.I.: Multiple kernel learning, conic duality, and the SMO algorithm. In: Proceedings of the Twenty-First International Conference on Machine Learning, pp. 6–13. ACM, New York (2004)
2. Chawla, N.V., Bowyer, K.W., Hall, L.O., Kegelmeyer, W.P.: SMOTE: synthetic minority over-sampling technique. J. Artif. Intell. Res. **16**, 321–357 (2002)
3. Rakotomamonjy, A., Bach, F., Canu, S., Grandvalet, Y.: SimpleMKL. J. Mach. Learn. Res. **9**, 2491–2521 (2008)
4. Freund, Y., Schapire, R.R.E.: Experiments with a new boosting algorithm. In: International Conference on Machine Learning, pp. 148–156 (1996)
5. Simonyan, K., Zisserman, A.: Very Deep Convolutional Networks for Large-Scale Image Recognition. arXiv:1409.1556 [cs] (2014)
6. Makadia, A., Pavlovic, V., Kumar, S.: A new baseline for image annotation. In: Forsyth, D., Torr, P., Zisserman, A. (eds.) ECCV 2008. LNCS, vol. 5304, pp. 316–329. Springer, Heidelberg (2008). https://doi.org/10.1007/978-3-540-88690-7_24
7. Guillaumin, M., Mensink, T., Verbeek, J., Schmid, C.: TagProp: discriminative metric learning in nearest neighbor models for image auto-annotation. In: 2009 IEEE 12th International Conference on Computer Vision, pp. 309–316 (2009)
8. Verma, Y., Jawahar, C.V.: Image annotation using metric learning in semantic neighbourhoods. In: Fitzgibbon, A., Lazebnik, S., Perona, P., Sato, Y., Schmid, C. (eds.) ECCV 2012. LNCS, vol. 7574, pp. 836–849. Springer, Heidelberg (2012). https://doi.org/10.1007/978-3-642-33712-3_60
9. Lavrenko, V., Feng, S.L., Manmatha, R.: Multiple Bernoulli relevance models for image and video annotation. In: 2013 IEEE Conference on Computer Vision and Pattern Recognition, pp. 1002–1009. IEEE Computer Society, Los Alamitos (2004)
10. Lavrenko, V., Manmatha, R., Jeon, J.: A model for learning the semantics of pictures. In: Advances in Neural Information Processing Systems, pp. 553–560 (2003)
11. Su, F., Xue, L.: Graph learning on K nearest neighbours for automatic image annotation. In: Proceedings of the 5th ACM on International Conference on Multimedia Retrieval, pp. 403–410. ACM, New York (2015)
12. Cusano, C., Bicocca, M., Bicocca, V.: Image annotation using SVM. In: Proceedings of SPIE, pp. 330–338 (2003)
13. Goh, K.S., Chang, E.Y., Li, B.: Using one-class and two-class SVMs for multiclass image annotation. IEEE Trans. Knowl. Data Eng. **17**, 1333–1346 (2005)

14. Grangier, D., Bengio, S.: A discriminative kernel-based approach to rank images from text queries. IEEE Trans. Pattern Anal. Mach. Intell. **30**, 1371–1384 (2008)
15. Verma, Y., Jawahar, C.V.: Exploring SVM for image annotation in presence of confusing labels. In: ResearchGate, pp. 25.1–25.11 (2013)
16. Duygulu, P., Barnard, K., de Freitas, J.F.G., Forsyth, D.A.: Object recognition as machine translation: learning a lexicon for a fixed image vocabulary. In: Heyden, A., Sparr, G., Nielsen, M., Johansen, P. (eds.) ECCV 2002. LNCS, vol. 2353, pp. 97–112. Springer, Heidelberg (2002). https://doi.org/10.1007/3-540-47979-1_7
17. Grubinger, M.: Analysis and evaluation of visual information systems performance, Ph.D thesis. Victoria University, Melbourne (2007)
18. Zhang, S., Huang, J., Huang, Y., Yu, Y., Li, H., Metaxas, D.N.: Automatic image annotation using group sparsity. In: 2010 IEEE Computer Society Conference on Computer Vision and Pattern Recognition, pp. 3312–3319 (2010)
19. Nakayama, H.: Linear distance metric learning for large-scale generic image recognition, Ph.D thesis. The University of Tokyo, Japan (2011)
20. Zhang, Q., Chen, Z., Yang, L.T.: A nodes scheduling model based on Markov chain prediction for big streaming data analysis. Int. J. Commun. Syst. **28**, 1610–1619 (2015)
21. Chen, M., Zheng, A., Weinberger, K.: Fast image tagging. In: Proceedings of the 30th International Conference on Machine Learning (ICML-2013), vol. 28, pp. 1274–1282 (2013)
22. Murthy, V.N., Maji, S., Manmatha, R.: Automatic image annotation using deep learning representations. In: Proceedings of the 5th ACM on International Conference on Multimedia Retrieval, pp. 603–606. ACM, New York (2015)
23. Zhang, Q., Zhao, C., Yang, L.T., Chen, Z., Zhao, L., Li, P.: An incremental CFS algorithm for clustering large data in industrial internet of things. IEEE Trans. Industr. Inf. (2017). https://doi.org/10.1109/TII.2017.2684807
24. Jiu, M., Sahbi, H.: Nonlinear deep kernel learning for image annotation. IEEE Trans. Image Process. **26**, 1820–1832 (2017)

An Efficient Feature Selection for SAR Target Classification

Moussa Amrani[1(✉)], Kai Yang[2], Dongyang Zhao[3], Xiaopeng Fan[1], and Feng Jiang[1]

[1] School of Computer Science and Technology, Harbin Institute of Technology, Harbin 150001, People's Republic of China
amrani.lmcice@hotmail.com
[2] Chinese People's Liberation Army Aviation School, Jilin, China
[3] Beijing Institute of Computer Application, Beijing, China

Abstract. Selecting appropriate features is a prerequisite to attain the accuracy and the efficiency of SAR target classification. Inspired by the great success of BoVW, we address this issue by proposing an efficient feature selection method for SAR target classification. First, Graphic Histogram of oriented Gradients (HOG) based features is adopted to extract features from the training SAR images. Second, a discriminative codebook is generated using K-means clustering algorithm. Third, after feature encoding by computing the closest Euclidian distance, only two bags of features are considered. Fourth, for best result and lower time complexity, the Discriminant Correlation Analysis (DCA) is used to combine relevant information forming new discriminant features. Finally, for target classification, SVM is used as a baseline classifier. Experiments on MSTAR public release dataset are conducted, and the results demonstrate that the proposed method outperforms the state-of-the-art methods.

Keywords: Synthetic aperture radar · Target classification · HOG
DCA · BoVW

1 Introduction

Airborne and space borne synthetic aperture radar (SAR) has been a great success in targeting systems that it can work in all-weather day-and-night conditions and provides microwave images of extremely high-resolution. A SAR system sends electromagnetic pulses with high power from radar mounted on a moving platform to a fixed particular area of interest on the target and receives the echoes of the backscattered signal in a sequential way. SAR collects data from multiple viewing angles and combines them coherently to illuminate and attain a very high-resolution description of the target. SAR has been primarily utilized for many applications on a target [1] such as surveillance, reconnaissance, recognition and classification etc. However, the understanding of SAR images is hard to manually manipulate compared to optical images which describe a better appearance of a target. This leads to develop more creative automatic target recognition (ATR) algorithms for SAR images. Defining a good way to represent and recognize the targets in synthetic aperture radar automatic target recognition

© Springer International Publishing AG, part of Springer Nature 2018
B. Zeng et al. (Eds.): PCM 2017, LNCS 10736, pp. 68–78, 2018.
https://doi.org/10.1007/978-3-319-77383-4_7

(SAR-ATR) systems has become a challenging task. In this regard, developing a well-designed feature selection method is very important issue. Recently, many methods have been proposed to understand the target from SAR images; include geometric descriptors, such as peak locations, edges, corners, shapes [2], and transform-domain coefficients such as wavelet coefficients [3]. Although the above-mentioned methods may have some advantages, but most of these methods failed to achieve the promising classification performance (i.e., accuracy and time). In this paper, we address these problems using the Bag-of-Visual-Words (BoVW) paradigm [4], which can solve the multi-target SAR images classification effectively. The distributions of the proposal method mainly include four aspects. First, the ability of Graphic Histogram of oriented Gradients (HOG) is introduced. HOG based features [5] achieved a fast realization of feature extraction and a high precision performance than some other methods. Second, K-means clustering algorithm is adopted to generate a discriminative codebook, and also reduce the overall computational complexity. Meanwhile, the closest Euclidian distance between the extracted features and the visual dictionary is computed, and the two bags of features with high performance are considered. Third, for better classification accuracy and lower time complexity, the Discriminant Correlation Analysis (DCA) [6] is used to combine relevant information by concatenation forming new discriminant features. Finally, for simplicity, the linear support vector machine (SVM) is used as a baseline classier throughout the study. The simplicity comes from the fact that SVM applies a simple linear method to the data but in a high-dimensional feature space nonlinearly related to the input space. Moreover, even though we can think of SVM as a linear algorithm in a high-dimensional space, in practice, it does not involve any computations in that high dimensional space. Besides, the fusion between SVM classifier and the discriminant features is studied, which brings higher classifier precision than the common and the traditional method. The proposed method is evaluated on the real SAR images from Moving and Stationary Target Acquisition and Recognition (MSTAR) public release and the experimental results validate the effectiveness of the proposed method.

The rest of this paper is organized as follows: Sect. 2 describes the framework of the proposed method as well as introduces precisely: the feature extraction method using HOG, BoVW feature representation, and the feature fusion by concatenation using DCA. The experimental results are presented in Sect. 3. Finally, Sect. 4 gives the concluding remarks of the paper.

2 The Proposed Method

The proposed framework consists of the following four main steps as shown in Fig. 1: (1) HOG feature extraction; (2) using the BoVW paradigm to compute the bag of features based on k-means; (3) bag of features fusion based on DCA; and (4) using SVM as a baseline classifier for SAR target classification. The overall SAR target classification framework is given in Algorithm 1.

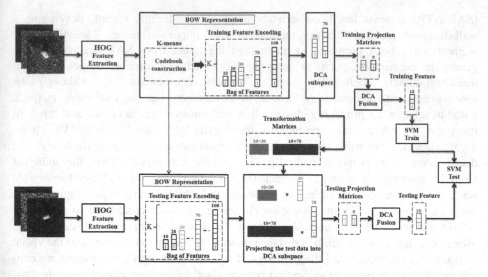

Fig. 1. Overall architecture of the proposed method.

Algorithm I : Feature selection and classification.

1: **Input:** $C_{train} = \{C_{tr1} \dots C_{trN}\}$ train category set, $C_{test} = \{C_{ts1} \dots C_{tsN}\}$ test category set, visual dictionary D.

2: **for** $i = 1$ to N **do**

3: Extract features from C_{train} and C_{test} using HOG-based feature.
$$X_{htrain} = \{x_{htrain_1}, x_{htrain_2}, \dots, x_{htrain_n}\} \quad X_{htest} = \{x_{htest_1}, x_{htest_2}, \dots, x_{htest_m}\}$$

4: Codebook generation using K-means clustering algorithm.

5: Select V_{train1} and V_{test1} using the Euclidian distance $d(X_{htrain}, D=30)$.

6: Select V_{train2} and V_{test2} using the Euclidian distance $d(X_{htrain}, D=70)$.

7: Compute the transformation matrix W_x and W_Y.

8: Project V_{train1}, V_{train2} into the DCA subspace. $V_{train1} = W_x * V_{train1}, V_{train2} = W_y * V_{train2}$

9: Project V_{test1}, V_{test2} into the DCA subspace. $V_{test1} = W_x * V_{test1}, V_{test2} = W_y * V_{test2}$

10: Fuse V_{train1}, V_{train2} and V_{test1}, V_{test2} by concatenation.

11: **end for**

12: Perform SVM classification

13: **Output:** Overall Accuracy

In the following subsections, we describe the main three steps of the proposed method (i.e., the feature extraction, feature representation, and feature fusion steps) with more details.

2.1 HOG Feature Extraction

In this paper, HOG features are adopted to enhance the target classification performance of the proposed method. The HOG feature extraction technique counts occurrences of gradient orientation in regions of interest (ROI) of SAR sample images as illustrated in Fig. 2.

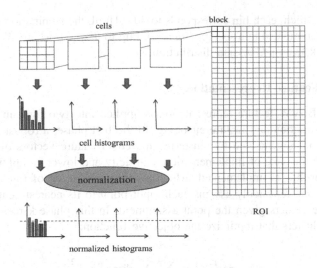

Fig. 2. HOG feature extraction framework.

For each pixel (x, y), the gradient computation is done by applying two discrete derivative kernels $G_h = [-1, 0, 1]$ and $G_v = [-1, 0, 1]^T$ to respectively obtain the horizontal difference $\partial_x(x_i, y_i)$, and the vertical difference $\partial_y(x_i, y_i)$. The gradient magnitude $m(x_i, y_i)$ and the orientation $\theta(x_i, y_i)$ are determined as follows:

$$m(x_i, y_i) = \sqrt{\partial_x(x_i, y_i)^2 + \partial_y(x_i, y_i)^2} \tag{1}$$

$$\theta(x_i, y_i) = \tan^{-1}\left(\frac{\partial_y(x_i, y_i)}{\partial_x(x_i, y_i)}\right) \tag{2}$$

First, a Histogram is generated [5, 7]. Second, as clarified in Fig. 3, each cell in the feature block is represented by 9-D orientation histograms. In order to reduce the effect of changes in contrast between the sample images of the same target class, the normalized histograms are divided into 16 * 16 pixel blocks, each cell size of 8 * 8 pixels. Finally, for preventing complexity, we quantify the orientation range from 0 to 360°

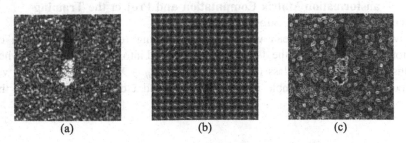

| (a) | (b) | (c) |

Fig. 3. HOG feature extraction of sample SAR image: (a) sample SAR image, (b) HOG features with a cell size of 8, (c) gradient magnitude of the SAR image.

into 9 bins, in which, each bin corresponds to 40°. Third, the summation of $m(x_i, y_i) * w_G(x_i, y_i)$ is accumulated in a specific bin according to $\theta(x_i, y_i)$, where $W_G(x_i, y_i)$ is the weighting mask from a Gaussian distribution.

2.2 BoVW Feature Representation

In this paper, BoVW feature representation is applied into two fundamental phases: codebook construction and feature encoding. In the first phase, a robust and discriminative codebook is generated by clustering the HOG feature vectors of the training feature set. For the sake of implementation simplicity and lower complexity k-means clustering algorithm is implemented; which starting with a set of randomly chosen initial centers, one repeatedly assigns each input point to its nearest center, and then recomputed the centers given the point assignment. In this phase k-means algorithm seeks to find clusters that minimize the objective function:

$$D\left(\{\pi_c\}_{c-1}^k\right) = \sum_{c=1}^{k} \sum_{a_i \in \pi_c} \|a_i - m_c\|^2 \tag{3}$$

$$m_c = \frac{\sum_{a_i \in \pi_c} a_i}{|\pi_c|} \tag{4}$$

where the centroid of the cluster π_c is denoted by m_c, and the number of visual words (i.e., the k values) is dependent on the used training dataset. In the second phase, the closest Euclidian distance between HOG feature vectors of the training and testing feature sets, and the constructed vocabulary are computed forming new robust bag of features that represent all the SAR targets.

2.3 Feature Fusion and Classification

The fusion of the two feature sets is done into two principal phases: in the first phase we calculated the transformation matrices Wx and Wy as well as projected the training feature sets into the DCA subspace, and then fused the two transformed training feature sets by concatenation. In the second phase, we projected the testing feature sets into the DCA subspace and fused the two transformed testing feature sets by concatenation.

2.3.1 Transformation Matrix Computation and Project the Training Feature Sets into the DCA Subspace

First, we computed the mean vectors of the training feature sets for each class. Therefore, the n columns of the data matrix are divided into c separate classes, where n_i columns belong to the ith class ($n = \sum_{i=1}^{c} n_i$). Let $x_{ij} \in X$ denote the feature vector corresponding to the jth sample in the ith class $\bar{x}_i$ and $\bar{x}$ denote the means of the x_{ij}

vectors in the ith class and the whole feature set, respectively. That is, $\overline{x_i} = \frac{1}{n}\sum_{j=1}^{n_i} x_{ij}$, and $\overline{x} = \frac{1}{n}\sum_{i=1}^{c}\sum_{j=1}^{n_i} x_{ij} = \frac{1}{n}\sum_{i=1}^{c} n_i \overline{x_i}$. Second, we diagonalized the between-class scatter matrix (S_b) for the two training feature sets, where:

$$S_{bx(p\times p)} = \sum_{i=1}^{c} n_i(\overline{x_i} - \overline{x})(\overline{x_i} - \overline{x})^T = \Phi_{bx}\Phi_{bx}^T \tag{5}$$

$$\Phi_{bx(p\times c)} = [\sqrt{n_1}(\overline{x_1} - \overline{x}), \sqrt{n_1}(\overline{x_1} - \overline{x}), \ldots \sqrt{n_1}(\overline{x_1} - \overline{x})] \tag{6}$$

Third, we projected the training feature sets in the between-class scatter matrices space to reduce the dimensionality of X from p to r as:

$$W_{bx}^T S_{bx} W_{bx} = I, \tag{7}$$

$$X'_{(r\times n)} = W_{bx(r\times p)}^T X_{(p\times n)} \tag{8}$$

where I is the between class scatter matrix, and X' is the projection of X in the space of I. Similar to the above step, the between-class scatter matrix for the second modality S_{by} is used to compute the transformation matrix W_{by}, which reduce the dimensionality of the training feature set Y from q to r as:

$$W_{by}^T S_{by} W_{by} = I \tag{9}$$

$$Y'_{(r\times n)} = W_{by(r\times p)}^T Y_{(q\times n)} \tag{10}$$

Fourth, after using the between-class scatter matrices to transform X and Y to X' and Y', respectively, the singular value decomposition (SVD) is utilized to diagonalize the between-set covariance matrix of the transformed feature sets $S'_{xy} = X'Y'^T$ as:

$$S'_{xy(r\times r)} = U\sum V^T \Rightarrow U^T S'_{xy} V = \sum \tag{11}$$

where $\sum$ is a non-zero diagonal matrix. Then, the between-set covariance matrix S'_{xy} is used to transform the training feature sets matrices as follows:

$$\overset{*}{X} = W_{cx}^T X' = W_{cx}^T W_{bx}^T X = W_x X \tag{12}$$

$$\overset{*}{Y} = W_{cy}^T X' = W_{cy}^T W_{by}^T X = W_y X \tag{13}$$

where $W_x = W_{cx}^T W_{bx}^T$ and $W_y = W_{cy}^T W_{by}^T$ are the final transformation matrices for X and Y respectively. Finally, the transformed training feature sets $\overset{*}{X}$ and $\overset{*}{Y}$ are fused by concatenation.

2.3.2   Project the Testing Feature Sets into the DCA Subspace

In this phase, the final transformation matrices and are used to transform the testing feature sets and as follows:

$$\overset{*}{X}_{test} = W_x X_{test} \tag{14}$$

$$\overset{*}{Y}_{test} = W_y X_{test} \tag{15}$$

Then, the projected testing feature sets $\overset{*}{X}_{test}$ and $\overset{*}{Y}_{test}$ are fused by concatenation. Finally, the linear SVM is trained to be able to classify unknown targets, into one of the learned class labels in the training set. More precisely, the classifier calculates the similarity of all trained classes and assigns the unlabeled targets to the class with the highest similarity measure.

3   Experimental Results

3.1   Dataset

In this section, the MSTAR public mixed target dataset is used for the evaluation of the system, which is downloadable [8]. This dataset Consists of SAR images of ground vehicle targets form different categories. All SAR images are with 1-foot resolution collected by Sandia National Laboratory (SNL). They are collected using the STAR-LOS X-band SAR sensor in a spotlight mode with a circular flight path from diverse depression angles.

3.2   Experimental Results

The effectiveness of the proposed method is evaluated on ten different vehicle targets from the dataset, which are: armored personnel carrier: BMP-2, BRDM-2, BTR-60, and BTR-70; tank: T-62, T-72; rocket launcher: 2S1; air defense unit: ZSU-234; truck: ZIL-131; bulldozer: D7. For the test, we used 3211 sample images with 15° of depression angle, and for the training, we used 3681 sample images with 17° of depression angle as illustrated in Table 1.

First, a Histogram is generated and normalized, and then the normalized histograms are divided into 16 * 16 pixel blocks, each cell size of 8 * 8 pixels. For lower complexity the orientation range is quantified into 9 bins, in which, each bin corresponds to 40°. Thus, the HOG features of SAR image are concatenated into a 7936-D feature. Second, we obtained the codebook of the features extracted from the training SAR images by applying the BOVW approach. Furthermore, the codebook constructed is used to compute the bag of features for both training and testing sets. Third, DCA is utilized to fuse the selected bag of features by concatenation. Finally, the classification of the targets with respect to its training set is done by comparing the bag of features of

Table 1. Number of training and testing samples used in the experiments for MSTAR dataset.

Target	Train		Test	
	Depression	No. Images	Depression	No. Images
BMP-2	17°	699	15°	587
BTR-70	17°	233	15°	196
T-72	17°	699	15°	588
BTR-60	17°	256	15°	196
2S1	17°	299	15°	274
BRDM-2	17°	299	15°	274
D7	17°	299	15°	274
T-62	17°	299	15°	274
ZIL-131	17°	299	15°	274
ZSU-234	17°	299	15°	274

the testing set to those of training set, this process is repeated five times. During our experimental analysis, the sensitivity of both cell and dictionary sizes are noticed through the variation of the cell and the dictionary sizes, respectively. The cell sizes are changed from 4 to 16, and the cell size of 8 produced the highest accuracy for the data set. In the same way, the classification accuracies with dictionary sizes from 10 to 100 are compared and the experiments showed that the features vectors of size 30 and 70 achieved the best results as shown in Fig. 4. To achieve the highest accuracy and lower time complexity, the feature vectors of size 30 and 70 are fused together forming new discriminant feature vector of size 18.

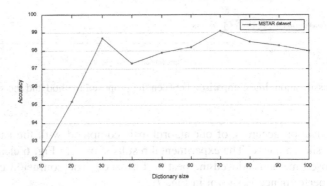

Fig. 4. Effect of the dictionary size on the classification accuracy.

The proposed method has a low-complexity time due to the small size of the used feature vectors (i.e., 18). Figure 5 shows the classification time of the proposed method compared with different approaches such as: A-Convnets [9], CNN [10], DWT + Real-Adaboost [11], BCS + Scattering centers [12], SVM + Scattering centers [12],

Object Matching + SIFT [13]. The test machine has an Intel(R) Core i5 processing unit @ 2.67 GHz, 4 GB internal memory and Microsoft Windows 10 Pro 64-bit. All methods have been implemented using MATLAB R2016a. All the classification time results are measured in millisecond (ms).

As shown in Fig. 5, the proposed method has lower classification time than other methods. BCS + Scattering centers [12] and SVM + Scattering centers [12] have the longest classification time due to the high dimension of the feature vectors size (i.e., 1024) that is used for classification. However, SVM + Scattering centers [12] has a lower classification time since SVM has a lower complexity than BCS. Both DWT + Real-Adaboost [11] and Object Matching + SIFT [13] used feature vectors of size 75 and 128, respectively. Therefore, their classification time is longer than the proposed method. CNN [10] and A-Convnets [9] classification needs GPU support and takes a lot of time, the reason being that CNN [10] used sparse auto encoder and a Convolutional neural network (CNN) for the feature extraction as well as a softmax layer, and A-Convnets [9] used a deep convolutional network with five trainable layers. Thus, the proposed method attained the lowest time complexity.

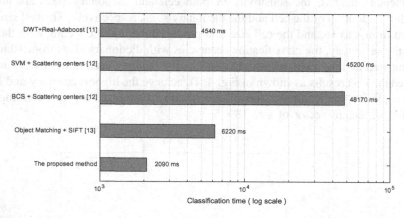

Fig. 5. The classification time comparison between the proposed method and the state-of-the-art methods.

The classification accuracy of our algorithm is compared with the same different approaches as shown above. The experimental results shown in Fig. 6 clearly interpret that our proposed method induced the best performance. The confusion matrix of the classification performance is shown in Fig. 7.

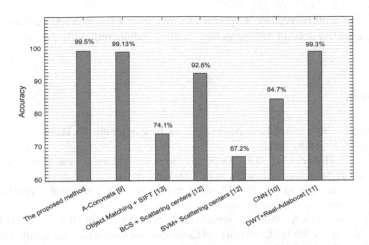

Fig. 6. The performance comparison between the proposed method and the state-of-the-art methods.

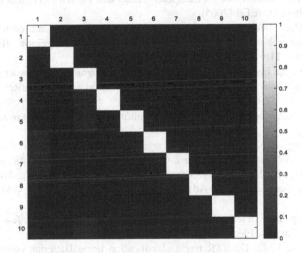

Fig. 7. Confusion matrix of the classification performance on MSTAR dataset: the rows and columns of the matrix indicate the actual and predicted classes, respectively.

4 Conclusion

Feature extraction plays a key role in the classification performance of SAR-ATR. It is very crucial to choose appropriate features to train a classifier, which is prerequisite. This paper proposed an efficient feature selection method, which takes advantages of BoVW to precisely represent the targets features, and then combine the relevant features together obtaining discriminative features. In contrast to previous SAR target classification studies which produced high complexity classification, the proposed method achieved high accuracy and low-complexity due to the small size of the discriminative feature vectors. Experimental results on the MSTAR dataset demonstrate the effectiveness of the proposed method compared with the state-of-the-art methods.

References

1. Ozdemir, C.: Inverse Synthetic Aperture Radar Imaging with MATLAB Algorithms, vol. 210. Wiley, Hoboken (2012)
2. Olson, C.F., Huttenlocher, D.P.: Automatic target recognition by matching oriented edge pixels. IEEE Trans. Image Process. **6**(1), 103–113 (1997)
3. Sandirasegaram, N.: Spot SAR ATR using wavelet features and neural network classifier, DTIC Document, Technical report (2005)
4. Sivic, J., Zisserman, A.: Video google: a text retrieval approach to object matching in videos. In: Proceedings of 9th IEEE International Conference on Computer Vision, vol. 2, pp. 1470–147, 13–16 October 2003
5. Dalal, N., Triggs, B.: Histograms of oriented gradients for human detection. In: 2005 IEEE Computer Society Conference on Computer Vision and Pattern Recognition (CVPR 2005), vol. 1, pp. 886–893. IEEE (2005)
6. Haghighat, M., Abdel-Mottaleb, M., Alhalabi, W.: Discriminant correlation analysis: Real-time feature level fusion for multimodal biometric recognition. IEEE Trans. Inf. Forensics Secur. **11**(9), 1984–1996 (2016)
7. Porikli, F.: Integral histogram: a fast way to extract histograms in cartesian spaces. In: 2005 IEEE Computer Society Conference on Computer Vision and Pattern Recognition (CVPR 2005), vol. 1, pp. 829–836. IEEE (2005)
8. SDMS: Mstar data. https://www.sdms.afrl.af.mil/index.php?collection=mstar. Accessed 23 Nov 2016
9. Chen, S., Wang, H., Xu, F., Jin, Y.Q.: Target classification using the deep convolutional networks for SAR images. IEEE Trans. Geosci. Remote Sens. **54**(8), 4806–4817 (2016)
10. Chen, S., Wang, H.: SAR target recognition based on deep learning. In: 2014 International Conference on Data Science and Advanced Analytics (DSAA), pp. 541–547. IEEE, October 2014
11. Zhao, X., Jiang, Y.: Extracting high discrimination and shift invariance features in synthetic aperture radar images. Electron. Lett. **52**(11), 958–960 (2016)
12. Zhang, X., Qin, J., Li, G.: SAR target classification using Bayesian compressive sensing with scattering centers features. Prog. Electromagnet. Res. **136**, 385–407 (2013)
13. Agrawal, A., Mangalraj, P., Bisherwal, M.A.: Target detection in SAR images using SIFT. In: 2015 IEEE International Symposium on Signal Processing and Information Technology (ISSPIT), pp. 90–94. IEEE, December 2015

Fine-Art Painting Classification
via Two-Channel Deep Residual Network

Xingsheng Huang, Sheng-hua Zhong$^{(\boxtimes)}$, and Zhijiao Xiao

College of Computer Science and Software Engineering, Shenzhen University,
Shenzhen 518000, People's Republic of China
huangxingsheng2016@email.szu.edu.cn,
{csshzhong, cindyxzj}@szu.edu.cn

Abstract. Automatic fine-art painting classification is an important task to assist the analysis of fine-art paintings. In this paper, we propose a novel two-channel deep residual network to classify fine-art painting images. In detail, we take the advantage of the ImageNet to pre-train the deep residual network. Our two channels include the RGB channel and the brush stroke information channel. The gray-level co-occurrence matrix is used to detect the brush stroke information, which has never been considered in the task of fine-art painting classification. Experiments demonstrate that the proposed model achieves better classification performance than other models. Moreover, each stage of our model is effective for the image classification.

Keywords: Image classification · Fine-art painting classification
Gray-level co-occurrence · Deep residual network

1 Introduction

In the history of world civilization, fine-art painting plays a very important role. Fine-art painting fully expresses the state of mind and social culture of mankind in different times. Nowadays, smart mobile devices have penetrated into every detail of people's daily life, which leads to the rapid development of digital collection of fine-art paintings. Hence, vast digital collections have been made available across the Internet and museums. With a large number of digital works collection, it is very important to automatically process and analyze the fine-art paintings. Moreover, automatic fine-art painting classification is an important task to assist the analysis of fine-art paintings, such as forging detection [1], object retrieval [2, 3], archiving and retrieval of works of fine-art [4, 5] and so on.

Since Krizhevsky and Hinton successfully applied the CNN model for image classification, there has been a significant shift away from shallow image descriptors towards deep features [6]. In the classification of natural images task, Ren et al. has achieved great success [7]. However, for the classification of fine-art paintings, CNN's performance is somewhat unsatisfactory. One of the main reasons is that the number of samples for fine-art painting classification is limited. For example, Painting-91, which is the largest number of fine-art painting dataset [8], only has 4266 images. Therefore,

© Springer International Publishing AG, part of Springer Nature 2018
B. Zeng et al. (Eds.): PCM 2017, LNCS 10736, pp. 79–88, 2018.
https://doi.org/10.1007/978-3-319-77383-4_8

considering the very limited training data, CNN is difficult to effectively extract features and achieve good performance.

Evidences from previous work show that CNN's success is, in the field of computer vision, relied on the availability of large-scale datasets with labels [9–14]. For example, for the classification of ImageNet, Krizhevsky proposed CNN model to effectively solve the problem of over-fitting [6]. One important reason is that the consistency of the up to 144 million parameters of the CNN model and the millions samples of ImageNet dataset. In view of the limited number of fine-art painting samples, Hentschel et al. proposed a fine-tuning method to solve this problem [15]. That is, a CNN model is firstly pre-trained on a large-scale dataset such as ImageNet, and then it is fine-tuned with the target dataset. Thus, the fine-tuning can, in the case of the limited sample of fine-art painting datasets, help us to construct an effective learning model based on the pre-trained CNN. Thus, in this paper, our proposed model also uses ImageNet dataset to pre-train our model.

With the stage of fine-tuning, CNN can solve the problem of insufficient data in the classification task of fine-art paintings. As we known, driven by the increases of depth, the notorious problem of vanishing/exploding gradients could hamper convergence of the deep networks. He et al. partially solved this problem by introducing a deep residual learning framework. Hence, our proposed model is based on deep residual neural networks [16–18].

In the task of fine-art painting classification, although some researchers tried to use some existing deep learning model or construct some new deep learning models, but all these models did not take into account the essential characteristics of fine-art paintings. Brush stroke is an important and powerful tool to understand the fine-art painting [19]. Unfortunately, this important character has never been considered in the classification of fine-art painting. Thus, in our work, we try to use the gray-level co-occurrence matrix (GLCM) to represent this information and it is set as the input of brush stroke information channel. In this paper, we propose a novel two-channel deep residual network for the classification task of fine-art paintings. This model is consisted of two channels, RGB channel and brush stroke information channel. This model firstly pre-trains on ImageNet dataset, and then it is fine-tuned with the fine-art painting dataset.

The rest of this paper is organized as followings. The second part briefly introduces the related work for fine-art painting classification. The third part introduces the architecture of our proposed model. The fourth part introduces the experimental setting and provides the experimental results. Finally, the conclusions are drawn in section five.

2   Related Work

Recently, CNN is widely used in the classification of fine-art painting images. Some researchers have suggested that CNN can be used as a feature extractor. Elgammal et al. investigated the effects of different features coupled with different types of metrics to perform the fine-art painting classification task. Although the CNN was employed, it was simply used as a feature extractor only [20]. As we described before, the number of samples in the fine-art painting datasets is very limited. Thus, some researchers try to combine the pre-training and fine-tuning stages to extract the effective image features from fine-art painting images. Tan et al. show that combine the pre-training and the fine-tuning stages can improve the performance of the deep learning model for the classification task of fine-art paintings [21]. Hentschel et al. pre-trained the deep representations on the ImageNet dataset and used fine-tuning for fine-art painting image datasets to evaluate the learned models [15].

More researchers have proposed novel models by reconstructing the structure of CNN to improve the performance of the classification task with fine-art painting images. Peng proposed cross-layer CNN is formed by cascading a number of modified CNN [22, 23]. Each modified CNN in the cross-layer is as same as Krizhevsky's CNN except that the convolution layer is removed. Tan replaced the last layer of CNN with a SVM classifier instead of a softmax layer [21].

3 Fine-Art Painting via Two-Channel Deep Residual Network

3.1 Two-Channel Deep Residual Network Architecture

In this part, we will introduce the details about the proposed model: fine-art painting via two-channel deep residual network (FPTD). The structure of the proposed FPTD is shown in Fig. 1. In RGB channel, the original RGB image of each fine-art painting image is input into the deep residual network (ResNet). In brush stroke information channel, the GLCM image is used to extract the brush stroke information and is input into the ResNet. The output of each channel is a 2048-dimensional vector, and 2048 is the number of kernel of the last convolution layer. Then, they are combined as a 4096-dimensional feature. This feature is input to the SVM classifier. We use LIBSVM Toolbox to implement SVM classifier and use the gaussian kernel and the grid

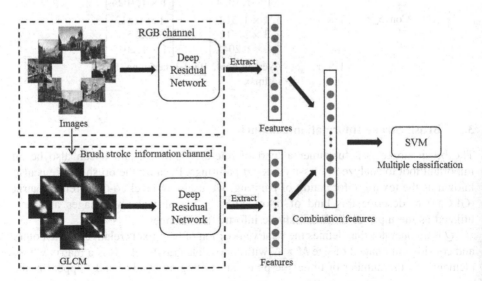

Fig. 1. Two-channel framework for fine-art paintings classification

optimization to find the optimal value of C in the parameter space [2−10: 1000] with a step of one [20]. To overcome the limitation of the number of samples, our model firstly pre-trains on ImageNet dataset, and then it is fine-tuned with the fine-art painting dataset.

3.2 RGB Channel

The RGB channel uses the original fine-art painting image as the input to learn the model. The output is a 2048-dimensional vector, and 2048 is the number of kernel of the last convolution layer. In this paper, we use two versions of ResNet, including 14 layers and 50 layers, The ResNet structure of each channel is shown in Table 1. To the setting of building blocks, the number of blocks stacked, and the down-sampling stages, we follow the previous work of He et al. [16].

Table 1. The architecture of ResNet in our proposed model

Layer name	Output size	14-layer ResNet	50-layer ResNet
Conv1	112×112	7×7, 64, stride 2	
Conv2_x	56×56	3×3 max pool, stride 2	
		$\begin{bmatrix} 1 \times 1, 64 \\ 3 \times 3, 64 \\ 1 \times 1, 256 \end{bmatrix} \times 1$	$\begin{bmatrix} 1 \times 1, 64 \\ 3 \times 3, 64 \\ 1 \times 1, 256 \end{bmatrix} \times 3$
Conv3_x	28×28	$\begin{bmatrix} 1 \times 1, 128 \\ 3 \times 3, 128 \\ 1 \times 1, 512 \end{bmatrix} \times 1$	$\begin{bmatrix} 1 \times 1, 128 \\ 3 \times 3, 128 \\ 1 \times 1, 512 \end{bmatrix} \times 4$
Conv4_x	14×14	$\begin{bmatrix} 1 \times 1, 256 \\ 3 \times 3, 256 \\ 1 \times 1, 1024 \end{bmatrix} \times 1$	$\begin{bmatrix} 1 \times 1, 256 \\ 3 \times 3, 256 \\ 1 \times 1, 1024 \end{bmatrix} \times 6$
Conv5_x	7×7	$\begin{bmatrix} 1 \times 1, 512 \\ 3 \times 3, 512 \\ 1 \times 1, 2048 \end{bmatrix} \times 1$	$\begin{bmatrix} 1 \times 1, 512 \\ 3 \times 3, 512 \\ 1 \times 1, 2048 \end{bmatrix} \times 3$
	1×1	Average pool, 1000-dimensional fc, softmax	

3.3 Brush Stroke Information Channel

The brush stroke is a fundamental part of fine-art paintings, and it can also be an important tool to analyze or classify fine-art paintings. Because the brush stroke is also known as the texture information of painting, we use gray-level co-occurrence matrix (GLCM) to describe this kind of information in fine-art painting images and it is utilized as the input of the brush stroke information channel.

Q is an operator that defines the relative position of two pixels relative to each other and consider an image I of size $M \times N$ with L possible gray levels. **G** is a matrix whose element g is the number of times the pixel pair with gray levels i and j appear at the position specified by Q in I, where $1 \leq i, j \leq L$. In this paper, Q is defined as one pixel immediately to the right. Hence, **G** could be defined as Eq. 1.

$$\mathbf{G} = (g_{ij})_{L \times L} \tag{1}$$

$$g_{ij} = |\{(x,y)|\mathbf{I}(x,y) = i, \mathbf{I}(x,y+1) = j, 8 \cdot m \leq x \leq 8 \cdot m+7, 8 \cdot n \leq y \leq 8 \cdot n+7\}| \tag{2}$$

$$m = 0, 1, 2, \cdots, \left\lfloor \frac{M}{8} \right\rfloor + 1 \tag{3}$$

$$m = 0, 1, 2, \cdots, \left\lfloor \frac{N}{8} \right\rfloor + 1 \tag{4}$$

In our work, we obtain the gray-level co-occurrence matrix **G** for each color channel (R, G, and B). And then we combine them as a 3D matrix, which is referred as GLCM image.

Figure 2 shows four sample images with different styles and their corresponding gray-level co-occurrence matrix images. Figures 2(a) and (c) are sample images of "neoclassicism". Figures 2(e) and (g) are sample images of "northern renaissance". Figures 2(b) and (d) are the corresponding GLCM image of Figs. 2(a) and (c), respectively. Figures 2(f) and (h) are the corresponding GLCM image of Figs. 2(e) and (g), respectively. We can find these two styles are not similar in style and in vision, and their GLCM image are different.

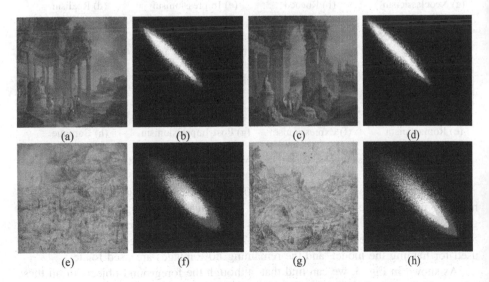

Fig. 2. (a) and (c) are sample images, which style is "neoclassicism". (b) and (d) are the extracted GLCM image of (a) and (c), respectively. (e) and (g) are sample images, which style is "northern renaissance". (f) and (h) are the extracted GLCM image of (e) and (g), respectively.

This GLCM image is used as the input of brush stroke information channel. The output of the brush stroke information channel is also a 2048-dimensional vector, and 2048 is the number of kernel of the last convolution layer. The structure of ResNet in brush stroke information channel and RGB channel is exactly the same, as shown in Table 1.

4   Experiment

In this section, we first introduce the experimental setting in Sect. 4.1. In Sect. 4.2, we evaluate the proposed method for the classification of fine-art painting on *style*, *genre* and *artist* datasets.

4.1   Experimental Setting

We conduct the experiments on three datasets to validate the performance of our method. The style dataset, the genre dataset and the artist dataset are downloaded from the WikiArt.org – Encyclopedia of fine-art painting website. The paintings in the website as well as the annotations are contributed by a community of experts [15].

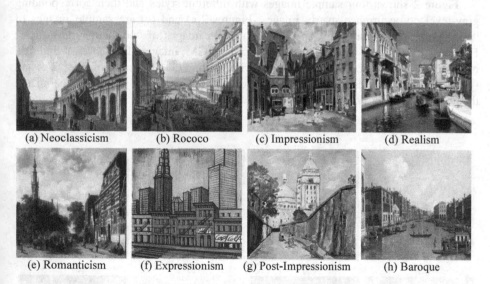

(a) Neoclassicism   (b) Rococo   (c) Impressionism   (d) Realism

(e) Romanticism   (f) Expressionism   (g) Post-Impressionism   (h) Baroque

Fig. 3. The sample images in the *style* dataset with different style labels

The *style* dataset is collected of a total 30825 images, including 25 styles, each style has 1233 pictures. The *genre* dataset has 28,760 images containing 10 genres and 2876 graphs for each genre. The *artist* dataset has 9766 images, including 19 artists, each has 514 images. We resize all images to 256 × 256, and 60% of images in each dataset are used for training the model, and the remaining 40% images are used for test.

As shown in Fig. 3, we can find that, although the foreground objects of all these images are "buildings", they actually belong to different style categories. It brings a lot of difficulty for the fine-art painting classification.

In our experiments, AlexNet and ResNet were trained using the stochastic gradient descent (SGD) with a batch size of 256 images. By following the setting of the AlexNet [6], their learning rate ε for the training epoch p with respect to the current epoch i is set to be

$$\varepsilon_i = 10^{-1-4\times\frac{i-1}{p-1}} \tag{5}$$

where p is a positive integer to ensure that the model is convergent. In our experiments, p is set to be 180. At that time, all the learning models are already converged.

4.2 Experimental Result

4.2.1 Fine-Tuning Is Useful to Improve Classification Accuracy

In Table 2, we provide the classification accuracies on three datasets. We compare AlexNet and ResNet with pre-training and without pre-training for the classification task of fine-art painting. We provide two versions of ResNet, 14 layers and 50 layers. Moreover, all the deep learning models here only include RGB channel.

Table 2. The comparisons of the classification performance on *style*, *genre* and *artist* datasets using different network structures with or without pre-training

Dataset	Network	Without pre-training		With pre-training	
		Top-1 error rates (%)	Top-5 error rates (%)	Top-1 error rates (%)	Top-5 error rates (%)
Style	AlexNet	69.23	31.76	56.71	19.12
	50-layer ResNet	67.16	27.08	**49.91**	**11.96**
	14-layer ResNet	**62.28**	**21.88**	51.5	13.22
Genre	AlexNet	51.18	10.38	34.95	4.15
	50-layer ResNet	51.61	9.69	**31.04**	**3.04**
	14-layer ResNet	**48.65**	**7.78**	32.91	3.43
Artist	AlexNet	53.74	19.28	27.34	5.6
	50-layer ResNet	57.82	19.33	**18.13**	**2.75**
	14-layer ResNet	**44.29**	**11.42**	19.61	2.93

From Table 2, we can find the performance of ResNet is better than AlexNet. This is because ResNet has the advantage that solves the problem of vanishing/exploding gradients. To each case, the models with pre-training achieve better performance than the models without it. It evidences that the pre-training is helpful to learn an effective model. Here, we can also find if we do not use ImageNet to pre-train the model, 14-layer ResNet could obtain smaller error rate. But this case does not happen in the case of the models with pre-training. That is because 50-layer ResNet gains better learning effect than 14-layer ResNet in the stage of pre-training [16].

4.2.2 Brush Stroke Information Is More Helpful to Improve the Classification Accuracy

In the previous section, we have verified that the pre-training stage could improve the performance for different classification tasks. In this section, we try to validate the effectiveness of the brush stroke information. We compare the proposed method FPTD with the model which has only one channel (RGB channel). Here, we provide the results of two versions of ResNet, 14 layers and 50 layers.

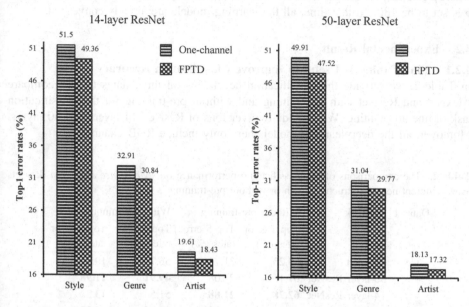

Fig. 4. The classification error rates comparisons of FPTD and one-channel model.

From Fig. 4, we can find the top-1 error rates of the proposed two-channel model FPTD are obviously less than the model with only one channel in each datatset. Moreover, the accuracy of the 50-layer ResNet is also better than the 14-layer ResNet. All the previous results demonstrate the importance of the brush stroke for the classification of fine-art paintings. Moreover, each stage of our model is effective for the fine-art painting classification.

5 Conclusion

Brush stroke is an important and powerful tool to understand the fine-art painting. Unfortunately, this important character has never been considered in the classification of fine-art painting. In this paper, we propose a novel model for fine-art painting classification via two-channel deep residual network, including RBG channel and brush stroke information channel. In detail, we take the advantage of the ImageNet to pre-train the deep residual network. The gray-level co-occurrence matrix is used to detect the brush stroke information, as the input of the brush stroke information channel. In order to validate the performance of our model, we run two experiments. In the first experiment, we find the pre-training is helpful to learn an effective model. We also find that the performance of ResNet is better than AlexNet, and the accuracy of 50-layer ResNet is better than 14-layer ResNet. In the second experiment, we find that the classification accuracy of our proposed two-channel model is obviously better than the model with only one channel. In future, we will try to integrate more characters of fine-art painting images into our model to improve the classification performance.

Acknowledgment. This work was supported by the National Natural Science Foundation of China (No. 61502311), the Natural Science Foundation of Guangdong Province (No. 2016A03 0310053), the Science and Technology Innovation Commission of Shenzhen under Grant (No. JCYJ20150324141711640, JCYJ20160422151736824), the Special Program for Applied Research on Super Computation of the NSFC-Guangdong Joint Fund (the second phase), the Shenzhen high-level overseas talents program, and the Tencent "Rhinoceros Birds" - Scientific Research Foundation for Young Teachers of Shenzhen University (2015, 2016).

References

1. Polatkan, G., Jafarpour, S., Brasoveanu, A., Hughes, S., Daubechies, I.: Detection of forgery in paintings using supervised learning. In: IEEE International Conference on Image Processing (ICIP), pp. 2921–2924 (2009)
2. Crowley, E.J., Zisserman, A.: In search of art. In: Agapito, L., Bronstein, M.M., Rother, C. (eds.) ECCV 2014. LNCS, vol. 8925, pp. 54–70. Springer, Cham (2015). https://doi.org/10.1007/978-3-319-16178-5_4
3. Crowley, E., Zisserman, A.: The state of the art: object retrieval in paintings using discriminative regions. In: British Machine Vision Conference (BMVC) (2014)
4. Mensink, T., Van Gemert, J.: The rijksmuseum challenge: museum centered visual recognition. In: Proceedings of International Conference on Multimedia Retrieval (ICMR), p. 451 (2014)
5. Gatys, L.A., Ecker A.S., Bethge, M.: A neural algorithm of artistic style. arXiv preprint arXiv:1508.06576 (2015)
6. Krizhevsky, A., Hinton, G.: Imagenet classification with deep convolutional neural networks. In: Advances in Neural Information Processing Systems (NIPS), pp. 1097–1105 (2012)
7. Ren, S., He, K., Girshick, R., Sun, J.: Faster R-CNN: towards real-time object detection with region proposal networks. In: Advances in Neural Information Processing Systems (NIPS), pp. 91–99 (2015)
8. Khan, F.S., Beigpour, S., Van-De-Weijer, J., Felsberg, M.: Painting-91: a large scale database for computational painting categorization. Mach. Vis. Appl. **25**(6), 1385–1397 (2014)
9. Zhong, S., Liu, Y., Hua, K.: Field effect deep networks for image recognition with incomplete data. ACM Trans. Multimedia Comput. Commun. Appl. (TOMM) **12**(4), 52 (2016)
10. Zhong, S., Liu, Y., Li, B., Long, J.: Query-oriented unsupervised multi-document summarization via deep learning. Expert Syst. Appl. (ESWA) **42**(21), 8146–8155 (2015)

11. Zhong, S., Liu, Y., Liu, Y.: Bilinear deep learning for image classification. In: Proceedings of 19th ACM International Conference on Multimedia (ACMMM) (2011)
12. Oquab, M., Bottou, L., Laptev, I., Sivic, J.: Learning and transferring mid-level image representations using convolutional neural networks. In: 2014 IEEE Conference on Computer Vision and Pattern Recognition (CVPR) (2014)
13. Lee, S.H., Chan, C.S., Wilkin, P., Remagnino, P.: Deep-plant: plant identification with convolutional neural networks. In: IEEE International Conference on Image Processing (ICIP), pp. 452–456 (2015)
14. He, K., Zhang, X., Ren, S., Sun, J.: Spatial pyramid pooling in deep convolutional networks for visual recognition. In: Fleet, D., Pajdla, T., Schiele, B., Tuytelaars, T. (eds.) ECCV 2014. LNCS, vol. 8691, pp. 346–361. Springer, Cham (2014). https://doi.org/10.1007/978-3-319-10578-9_23
15. Hentschel, C., Wiradarma, T.P., Sack, H.: Fine tuning CNNs with scarce training data-adapting ImageNet to art epoch classification. In: IEEE International Conference on Image Processing (ICIP) (2016)
16. He, K., Zhang, X., Ren, S., Sun, J.: Deep residual learning for image recognition. In: 2016 IEEE Conference on Computer Vision and Pattern Recognition (CVPR) (2016)
17. Zheng, M., Zhong, S., Wu, S., Jiang, J.: Steganographer detection via deep residual network. In: Proceedings of the IEEE International Conference on Multimedia and Expo (ICME) (2017)
18. Wu, S., Zhong, S., Liu, Y.: Deep residual learning for image steganalysis. In: Multimedia Tools and Applications (MTAP) (2017)
19. Li, L.: The relationship between the brush strokes and the image, the color, the emotion. J. Yangtze Univ. (Social Sciences), 34(9), 181–182 (2011)
20. Saleh, B., Elgammal, A.: Large-scale classification of fine-art paintings: learning the right metric on the right feature. arXiv preprint arXiv:1505.00855 (2015)
21. Tan, W.R., Chan, C.S., Aguirre, H.E., Tanaka, K.: Ceci n'est pas une pipe: a deep convolutional network for fine-art paintings classification. In: IEEE International Conference on Image Processing (ICIP) (2016)
22. Peng, K.C., Chen, T.: Cross-layer features in convolutional neural networks for generic classification tasks. In: IEEE International Conference on Image Processing (ICIP) (2015)
23. Peng, K.C., Chen, T.: A framework of extracting multi-scale features using multiple convolutional neural networks. In: International Conference on Multimedia and Expo (ICME) (2015)

Automatic Foreground Seeds Discovery for Robust Video Saliency Detection

Lin Zhang[✉], Yao Lu[✉], and Tianfei Zhou[✉]

Beijing Laboratory of Intelligent Information Technology, School of Computer
Science, Beijing Institute of Technology, Beijing, China
{zhanglin,vis_yl,tfzhou}@bit.edu.cn

Abstract. In this paper, we propose a novel algorithm for saliency
object detection in unconstrained videos. Even though various methods
have been proposed to solve this task, video saliency detection is still
challenging due to the complication in object discovery as well as the
utilization of motion cues. Most of existing methods adopt background
prior to detect salient objects. However, they are prone to fail in the case
that foreground objects are similar with the background. In this work, we
aim to discover robust foreground priors as a complement to background
priors so that we can improve the performance. Given an input video,
we consider motion and appearance cues separately to generate initial
foreground/background seeds. Then, we learn a global object appearance
model using the initial seeds and remove unreliable seeds according to
foreground likelihood. Finally, the seeds work as queries to rank all the
superpixels in images to generate saliency maps. Experimental results on
challenging public dataset demonstrate the advantage of our algorithm
over state-of-the-art algorithms.

Keywords: Video saliency · Foreground seeds discovery
Appearance model · Graph ranking

1 Introduction

Salient object detection currently has become an active research area of computer vision. Different from traditional research [11] that aims to predict human
fixations, salient object detection involves separating visually distinctive objects
from the background. It can help find the interesting objects or regions that
efficiently represent a scene and thus harness higher-level vision problems such
as object segmentation [12], image retargeting [5], object detection and recognition [22], etc.

In the past decades, hundreds of computational models have been proposed
for detecting salient or interesting objects in still images. They simulate the
selective perception characteristics of the human vision system using various
low-level features, *e.g.* color, shape, intensity. See [3] for the review. Benefit from
brilliant success in deep learning [13,15], we use deeply-learned feature as static

© Springer International Publishing AG, part of Springer Nature 2018
B. Zeng et al. (Eds.): PCM 2017, LNCS 10736, pp. 89–97, 2018.
https://doi.org/10.1007/978-3-319-77383-4_9

feature in our approach. More recently, following the recent advances in motion perception [4], many researchers attempt to compute spatio-temporal saliency for videos. They solve this problem by either extending previous image saliency detection models with additional temporal cues [18,20] or computing spatial and temporal saliency maps separately and then combining them [17,19]. Most of these methods use optical flow as motion cues to estimate saliency. However, these methods cannot detect those objects that initially stationary but move later on because they only evaluate per-frame motion contrast to find the regions that move saliently at each frame. To address this, we use long term trajectory as temporal cue, which can capture long-term dynamic objects.

Many existing methods adopt prior knowledge, *i.e.* background prior to help the estimation of saliency. They are difficult to deal with the cases that foreground objects are visually similar with the background. Inspired by supervised image editing methods, we note that foreground priors are also important for saliency estimation. Therefore, in this work, we aim to discover both foreground and background seeds. By considering long-term motion cues as well as objectness, we can discover relatively accurate foreground/background seeds. The initial seeds are then refined using non-local object appearance which are learnt by regularized least regression over initial foreground/background seeds. Finally, the saliency maps are obtained by ranking all the superpixels based on these seeds.

In summary, the main contributions of this paper are: (1) We devise novel techniques to discover foreground seeds using motion and static cues. (2) We develop a global appearance model to remove unreliable seeds. (3) Our approach has significant performance improvement over state-of-the-art methods on a challenging dataset, *i.e.* DAVIS.

2 Our Approach

Figure 1 shows an overview of the proposed algorithm for video saliency detection. Given an input video, we firstly decompose each frame into superpixels [1] (a), which enables our approach to avoid dealing with unnecessary details and reduce the computational cost. Next, we discover motion (b) and static (c) foreground/background seeds using long-term point trajectories and object appearance. To remove unreliable seeds and add new reliable seeds, we build an appearance model and compute the likelihood of each superpixel belonging to foreground (d). Finally, we rank all image superpixels to obtain saliency maps.

2.1 Seeds Discovery

Motion-Based Seeds. Given a video sequence, we link optical flow fields to generate dense point trajectories [16]. Among all trajectories, we remove those trajectories shorter than 5 frames. Then we compute motion saliency value for each trajectory, which is measured by the median distance between trajectory and all the other trajectories. Specifically, denote $\tau = \{tr^i\}_i$ as the set of trajectories in the video. The motion saliency of tr^i at time t is computed by:

$$s_t^i = median\{d_t(tr^i, tr^j), tr^j \in \mathcal{T}_t, j \neq i\} \tag{1}$$

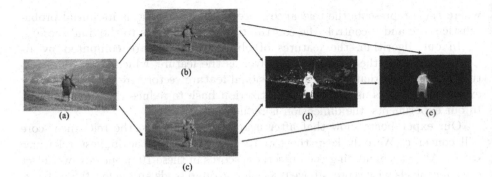

Fig. 1. (Best viewed in color) The framework of our algorithm. (a) an input frame (b) static-based foreground seeds (c) motion-based foreground seeds (d) foreground likelihood generated by appearance regression over the seeds (e) the final saliency map

where d_t indicates the distance between two trajectories tr^i and tr^j:

$$d_t(tr^i, tr^j) = \frac{1}{T}\{(u_t^i - u_t^j)^2 + (v_t^i - v_t^j)^2\} \tag{2}$$

We then follow [10] to fit a 1D Gaussian Mixture Model (GMM) to find a proper threshold so that we can separate the foreground trajectories from the background ones.

Besides, to deal with camera motion, we further estimate a camera model using background trajectories and associate each trajectory with a weight, which measures the motion difference between the trajectory and the camera motion. Then we consider those trajectories whose weights are larger than a threshold (0.85 in our experiments) as foreground trajectories, and those equal to 0 as background trajectories. We then choose the corresponding superpixels as foreground or background seeds.

Appearance-Based Seeds. Given an input video, we use MCG [2] to generate a set of object proposals and each proposal is associated with an objectness score. Note that MCG can generate many foreground object regions as well as a small number of background regions. Thus, we exploit this property and propose to remove those background regions using random walk.

In each frame, we build a graph in which each node is an object proposal and each edge denotes the feature distance between each two nodes. Denote the feature of nodes i and j as $\phi(i)$ and $\phi(j)$. The transition probability between i and j is:

$$p(i,j) = \frac{e^{-\gamma\|\phi(i)-\phi(j)\|_2}}{\sum_{m=1}^{k} e^{-\gamma\|\phi(i)-\phi(m)\|_2}} \tag{3}$$

Then we define the random walk over the graph as:

$$r_k(k) = \beta \sum_i r_{k-1}(i)p_{ij} + (1-\beta)v_j \tag{4}$$

where $r_k(j)$ represents the relevance score of the node j, v_j is its initial probabilistic score and β controls the contribution of both terms to the final score.

In our algorithm, the features of object proposals are computed by R-CNN [8]. We use the output of fc-7 layer as the feature, which is a 4096-d feature vector. Note that the high dimensional feature vectors are computationally expensive, we thus use iterative quantization hash to reduce the dimension [9]. In our experiments, the dimension is reduced to 256-d.

Our experiments show that after nearly 100 iterations, the relevance score will converge. We only keep the top 10 proposals with the highest relevance scores. After accumulating the objectness scores of these 10 proposals, we select the superpixels with scores above 0.8 as foreground seeds and below 0.2 as background seeds.

2.2   Foreground Appearance Estimation

In the previous section, we have discovered many foreground and background seeds. However, these seeds may be unreliable in that many background superpixels are considered as foreground seeds. Besides, some frames may have no foreground seeds. To solve this, we propose to learn a global appearance model using the initial seeds in all frames to refine the seed set. The non-local appearance model is demonstrated very robust in most scenarios.

We use bag-of-words over RGB color features since color is prove more robust than motion or texture features [24]. Given all the features of all seeds, we construct a few codewords which are defined as centers of learnt clusters. Let $X = [X_1, X_2, \ldots X_n]$ denote a $n \times d$ feature matrix where each X_i denote the feature vector of a superpixel and $Y = [Y_1, Y_2, \ldots Y_n]$ be a binary indicator vector to indicate foreground or background superpixels (*i.e.* $Y_i = 1$ means that X_i is a foreground superpixel and vice versa).

Given a k-word codebook $C = \{C_1, C_2, \ldots C_k\}$, we construct a codebook histogram Z with each element $Z_{ij} = \exp(-\frac{\|X_i - C_j\|}{\tau})$ where $\tau = 20$ is a constant. Then, the regression weight matrix W is computed by:

$$\min_W \|ZW - Y\|_F^2 + \lambda \|W\|_F^2 \tag{5}$$

For a superpixel with feature X_i, its codebook histogram $Z_i = [Z_{i1}, Z_{i2}, \ldots Z_{in}]$ will be computed first and its probability of being foreground is calculated by $Z_i W$.

Note that for complex videos, the initial set of seeds may be very noisy in some frames. However, using non-local appearance information, our appearance model are very robust to these noisy seeds. Besides, we can also discover additional reliable foreground seeds based on the appearance likelihood. See Fig. 2 the different stages of our algorithm in discovering foreground seeds.

2.3   Graph-Based Saliency Estimation

Given foreground and background seeds, we follow [23] to exploit global relationship among image data. The algorithm can rank the data concerning the intrinsic manifold structure accurately represented by the samples.

(a)   (b)   (c)   (d)

Fig. 2. (Best viewed in color) (a) foreground seeds detected using static cues (b) foreground seeds detected using motion cues (c) foreground object likelihood (d) refined foreground seeds. We only show foreground seeds here.

Represented by RGB color, superpixels in an image are denoted as $x = \{x_1, x_2, \ldots x_n\}$. A ranking function $f : x \rightarrow R^n$ allocates a score f_i to each superpixel x_i. Labeled superpixels work as queries. In our approach, foreground and background seeds work separately. Take foreground seeds as example. All foreground seeds have a indicator 1, the others have 0. So we get an indication vector $y = \{y_1, y_2, \ldots y_n\}$. Then we build a graph $G = (V, E)$ in the image. The graph nodes are image superpixels. Edges are defined by function of their Euclidean distance, for superpixel x_i and x_j, $w_{i,j} = e^{-\frac{\|x_i - x_j\|}{\sigma^2}}$. An affinity matrix is defined as $A = \{A_{ik}\}_{n \times n}$. Given G, the degree matrix is $D = diag\{d_{11}, \ldots d_{nn}\}$, with $d_{ii} = \sum_j a_{ij}$. Then the ranking scores are defined by:

$$f^* = arg \min_f \frac{1}{2}(\sum_{i,j=1}^n a_{ij}\|\frac{f_i}{\sqrt{d_{ii}}} - \frac{f_j}{\sqrt{d_{jj}}}\|^2 + \mu \sum_{i=1}^n \|f_i - y_i\|^2) \qquad (6)$$

The ranking function can be written as:

$$f^* = (I - \alpha S)^{-1}y \qquad (7)$$

In the equation, I denotes the identity matrix, $\alpha = \frac{1}{(1+\mu)}$, $S = D^{-\frac{1}{2}}AD^{-\frac{1}{2}}$.

We use foreground seeds work as query seeds to get a saliency map map_f. Similarly, background seeds help to get another saliency map map_b. Then, the final saliency map is calculated by the combination of the two maps

$$map = map_f * (1 - map_b) \qquad (8)$$

3   Experiments

We use DAVIS [14] to evaluate the performance of our proposed algorithm. It provides 50 high quality, full HD video sequences. These video sequences consist of multiple occurrences of common video object segmentation challenges such as occlusions, motion-blur and appearance changes. Each frame in all videos are attached with pixel-level labeling.

Metrics. We evaluate the performance of our algorithm using two metrics, *i.e.* Precision-Recall Curve (PR-Curve) and Mean Absolute Error (MAE). Precision is defined by the proportion of salient pixels correctly allocated in the

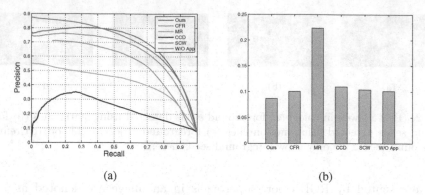

(a)   (b)

Fig. 3. (Best viewed in color) (a) PR_Curve results and (b) MAE of our algorithm in comparison with [6,7,18,21] and w/o app.

obtained saliency maps, while recall is the proportion of detected salient pixels in groundtruth numbers. The PR-Curve is computed by binarizing the obtained saliency map ranging [0, 255]. MAE is the average of absolute error between obtained saliency map and the groundtruth.

Performance of the proposed algorithm. We compare our algorithm with four state-of-the-art algorithms, MR [21], SCW [6], CFR [18] and CCD [7]. In these algorithms, MR [21] and CCD [7] are image saliency detection methods, while SCW [6] and CFR [18] are video saliency methods. Besides, to evaluate the importance of our global appearance model, we construct a baseline, *i.e.* w/o app, in which we do not refine the initial seeds.

The resulting PR-Curve is illustrated in Fig. 3(a). As can be seen in the figure, our algorithm ranks the highest for the most range. Especially when the recall is greater than 0.4, our algorithm performs the best of all algorithms. We also see that w/o app performs worse than our algorithm and SCW, thereby demonstrating the importance of our global appearance model for the refinement of the initial seed set. Figure 3(b) illustrates the MAE results of these methods. Our algorithm shows large performance improvement in comparison with others.

For further analysis, MR [21] uses only image boundary as background priors. Thus, it cannot deal with the cases that foreground and background are visually similar. As for the co-saliency method CCD [7], it cannot handle severe object appearance variations across frames. For SCW [6] and CFR [18], they use optical flow as temporal cues. Although they produce better results than other two methods, they may be easily fail due to the unstability of optical flow. On the contrary, our algorithm is superior in that (1) we consider not only background seeds but also robust foreground seeds to estimate the object saliency; (2) we use more stable long-term motion cues instead of short-term optical flow; (3) we introduce a global appearance model to refine initial seeds, thereby making our method more robust in complicated scenarios.

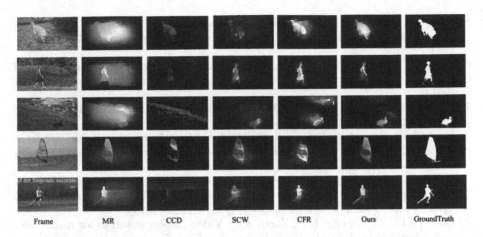

Fig. 4. Saliency maps of 5 frames by different methods. From left to right: the input frame, results by MR [21], CCD [7], SCW [6], CFR [18], Ours and groundtruth.

Qualitative analysis. Figure 4 illustrates some saliency maps generated by baseline methods and our approach. As can be seen, MR and CCD fail to locate the object when object resembles with background or object moves quickly. SCW cannot distinguish the foreground and background clearly, and CFR cannot deal with fast moving objects. By contrast, our approach performs well on all these situations.

4   Conclusions

In this work, we have presented a novel robust video saliency detection algorithm. Different from existing prior knowledge based saliency methods, we develop novel techniques to estimate robust foreground seeds based on motion and static information. Besides, the global appearance model is demonstrated effective to remove unreliable seeds. Experimental results on DAVIS dataset have shown that our algorithm can generate high-quality salient maps.

References

1. Achanta, R., Shaji, A., Smith, K., Lucchi, A., Fua, P., Süsstrunk, S.: Slic superpixels compared to state-of-the-art superpixel methods. IEEE Trans. Pattern Anal. Mach. Intell. **34**(11), 2274–2282 (2012)
2. Arbeláez, P., Pont-Tuset, J., Barron, J., Marques, F., Malik, J.: Multiscale combinatorial grouping. In: Computer Vision and Pattern Recognition (2014)
3. Borji, A., Cheng, M.M., Jiang, H., Li, J.: Salient object detection: a survey (2014). arXiv preprint: arXiv:1411.5878
4. Born, R., Groh, J., Zhao, R., Lukasewycz, S.: Segregation of object and background motion in visual area MT: effects of microstimulation on eye movements. Neuron **26**(3), 725–734 (2000)

5. Fang, Y., Chen, Z., Lin, W., Lin, C.W.: Saliency detection in the compressed domain for adaptive image retargeting. IEEE Trans. Image Process. **21**(9), 3888–3901 (2012)
6. Fang, Y., Wang, Z., Lin, W., Fang, Z.: Video saliency incorporating spatiotemporal cues and uncertainty weighting. IEEE Trans. Image Process. **23**(9), 3910–3921 (2014)
7. Fu, H., Cao, X., Tu, Z.: Cluster-based co-saliency detection. IEEE Trans. Image Process. **22**(10), 3766–3778 (2013)
8. Girshick, R., Donahue, J., Darrell, T., Malik, J.: Rich feature hierarchies for accurate object detection and semantic segmentation. In: Computer Vision and Pattern Recognition (2014)
9. Gong, Y., Lazebnik, S., Gordo, A., Perronnin, F.: Iterative quantization: a procrustean approach to learning binary codes for large-scale image retrieval. IEEE Trans. Pattern Anal. Mach. Intell. **35**(12), 2916–2929 (2013)
10. Guo, J., Li, Z., Cheong, L.F., Zhou, S.Z.: Video co-segmentation for meaningful action extraction. In: 2013 IEEE International Conference on Computer Vision (ICCV), pp. 2232–2239 (2013)
11. Itti, L., Koch, C., Niebur, E.: A model of saliency-based visual attention for rapid scene analysis. IEEE Trans. Pattern Anal. Mach. Intell. **20**(11), 1254–1259 (1998)
12. Ko, B.C., Nam, J.Y.: Object-of-interest image segmentation based on human attention and semantic region clustering. JOSA A **23**(10), 2462–2470 (2006)
13. Li, G., Yu, Y.: Deep contrast learning for salient object detection. In: Proceedings of the IEEE Conference on Computer Vision and Pattern Recognition, pp. 478–487 (2016)
14. Perazzi, F., Pont-Tuset, J., McWilliams, B., Van Gool, L., Gross, M., Sorkine-Hornung, A.: A benchmark dataset and evaluation methodology for video object segmentation. In: Proceedings of the IEEE Conference on Computer Vision and Pattern Recognition, pp. 724–732 (2016)
15. Simonyan, K., Zisserman, A.: Very deep convolutional networks for large-scale image recognition. CoRR abs/1409.1556 (2014)
16. Sundaram, N., Brox, T., Keutzer, K.: Dense point trajectories by GPU-accelerated large displacement optical flow. In: Daniilidis, K., Maragos, P., Paragios, N. (eds.) ECCV 2010, Part I. LNCS, vol. 6311, pp. 438–451. Springer, Heidelberg (2010). https://doi.org/10.1007/978-3-642-15549-9_32
17. Wang, W., Shen, J., Porikli, F.: Saliency-aware geodesic video object segmentation. In: Proceedings of the IEEE Conference on Computer Vision and Pattern Recognition, pp. 3395–3402 (2015)
18. Wang, W., Shen, J., Shao, L.: Consistent video saliency using local gradient flow optimization and global refinement. IEEE Trans. Image Process. **24**(11), 4185–4196 (2015)
19. Xi, T., Zhao, W., Wang, H., Lin, W.: Salient object detection with spatiotemporal background priors for video. IEEE Trans. Image Process. **26**, 3425–3436 (2017)
20. Xue, Y., Guo, X., Cao, X.: Motion saliency detection using low-rank and sparse decomposition. In: 2012 IEEE International Conference on Acoustics, Speech and Signal Processing (ICASSP), pp. 1485–1488. IEEE (2012)
21. Yang, C., Zhang, L., Lu, H., Ruan, X., Yang, M.H.: Saliency detection via graph-based manifold ranking. In: The IEEE Conference on Computer Vision and Pattern Recognition (CVPR), June 2013
22. Yu, H., Li, J., Tian, Y., Huang, T.: Automatic interesting object extraction from images using complementary saliency maps. In: Proceedings of the 18th ACM International Conference on Multimedia, pp. 891–894. ACM (2010)

23. Zhou, D., Weston, J., Gretton, A., Bousquet, O., Schölkopf, B.: Ranking on data manifolds. In: NIPS, vol. 3 (2003)
24. Zhou, T., Lu, Y., Di, H., Zhang, J.: Video object segmentation aggregation. In: 2016 IEEE International Conference on Multimedia and Expo (ICME), pp. 1–6. IEEE (2016)

Semantic R-CNN for Natural Language Object Detection

Shuxiong Ye, Zheng Qin[(✉)], Kaiping Xu, Kai Huang,
and Guolong Wang

School of Software, Tsinghua University, Beijing, China
{ysx15,xkp13,huang-k15,
wanggl16}@mails.tsinghua.edu.cn,
qingzh@tsinghua.edu.cn

Abstract. In this paper, we present a simple and effective framework for natural language object detection, to localize a target within an image based on description of the target. The method, called semantic R-CNN, extends RPN (Region Proposal Network) [1] by adding LSTM [20] module for processing natural language query text. LSTM [20] module take encoded query text and image descriptors as input and output the probability of the query text conditioned on visual features of candidate box and whole image. Those candidate boxes are generated by RPN and their local features are extracted by ROI pooling. RPN can be initialized from pre-trained Faster R-CNN model [1], transfers object visual knowledge from traditional object detection domain to our task. Experimental results demonstrate that our method significantly outperform previous baseline SCRC (Spatial Context Recurrent ConvNet) [7] model on Referit dataset [8], moreover, our model is simple to train similar to Faster R-CNN.

Keywords: Object detection · Natural language · RPN

1 Introduction

With the help of Convolutional Neural Networks (CNN), significant progress has been made in object detection [1–3, 10]. Faster R-CNN [1] can achieve very high precision when detecting some objects like cars on Pascal VOC dataset. However, traditional object detection models regard the number of object categories as fixed in training and inference. Moreover, one would prefer to detect objects with natural language query instead of fixed object categories since a natural language query can express more information than a simple category label. Such as "lady very back with white shirts next to man in hat" rather than a label of "lady" which includes information about object category, spatial configurations and interactions between objects.

Natural language object detection, where the goal is to localize the target by natural language query, is more challenging than traditional object detection, where the goal is to localize and classify different objects because it not only requires understanding of image content but also detail information of object included in query descriptions. Natural language object detection has a wide range of applications, for example, one would ask robot to pick up "red hat on the left". The detection framework is shown in Fig. 1.

© Springer International Publishing AG, part of Springer Nature 2018
B. Zeng et al. (Eds.): PCM 2017, LNCS 10736, pp. 98–107, 2018.
https://doi.org/10.1007/978-3-319-77383-4_10

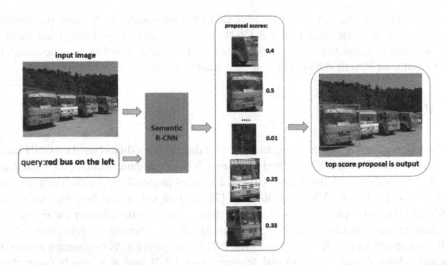

Fig. 1. Overview of natural language object detection. Our model, called Semantic R-CNN, takes an image and a natural language query as input and calculates score for each proposals generated by RPN module. Finally, the proposal with highest score is output as detecting result. (Color figure online)

In this paper, we divide the task into two sub-problems as SCRC method [7], one is the generation of candidate boxes and the other is retrieval target based on query text from candidate boxes. Our method, called Semantic R-CNN, extends RPN (Region Proposal Network) by adding a branch for calculating score for each Region of Interest (ROI) and picking the ROI with highest score, which solves these two sub-problems within a simple framework. Inspired by other image captioning models that use an LSTM to generate the text [4, 5], our model use LSTM branch to calculate scores for ROI. The LSTM network takes embedded query text, CNN representation of the ROI, their spatial configuration and global context as input and output score for each ROI. Visual representation of ROI and global context can be extracted by ROIpool [1, 2] based on feature map calculated by CNN, which is shared with RPN. The whole model can be easily trained end-to-end by SGD and error back propagation, moreover, we train RPN with multi-task loss used in Fast R-CNN [2] while training LSTM branch which allows two sub-problems to be adapted to each other.

Compared with previous visual-linguistic models such as Spatial Context Recurrent ConvNet (SCRC) [7], one of the advantages of using RPN to generating proposals is that it yields a much faster detection system than EdgeBox [6] because of shared convolutional computations. In addition, RPN can also produce ROI with higher accuracy than EdgeBox through training and benefit final precision of object detection. Our experiments results show that it significantly outperforms SCRC model. Not like SCRC using two CNN to extract image local and global descriptors, our model extracts them from same feature map generated by one CNN through ROI pool [1, 2], which makes the whole network more simpler and easier to be trained. The lack of large scale datasets with annotated object bounding boxes has been an unsolved problem until now, another advantage of using RPN is that it is easy to make use of large scale object detection datasets like ImageNet or MSCOCO by initializing RPN from pre-trained object detection model like Faster R-CNN, which transfers knowledge from former task to latter one and improves the performance. Our method achieves some competitive results on ReferIt dataset [8] with fast train and test speed.

2   Related Work

Object Detection: In recent years, many object detection methods based on CNN have been proposed. The R-CNN method [1] uses CNN to compute features for each proposal generated by Selective Search [9] and classifies proposal into object categories or background by linear SVM. Fast R-CNN [2] adds classifier and box regressor into CNN and computes proposal features from shared convolutional features which speed up training and reasoning. However, the time spent on generating region proposals is still a bottleneck in Fast R-CNN. Faster R-CNN [3] proposes RPN to generate region of interest which shared convolutional features with CNN and it is much faster than Selective Search and EdgeBoxes. Until now, many state-of-the-art object detection systems are still based on Faster R-CNN and our method is also inspired by it.

Image Captioning: An image given, image captioning system need to generate a natural language text to describe it. Most image captioning models are based on CNN and RNN which use CNN to extract high level image feature and use RNN to generate captions [12–14]. In [5], the image feature map extracted by GoogleNet is fed to LSTM model at -1 time step to generate captions. LRCN [4] uses two-layer LSTM with words embedding and visual features as input to predict captions. The method

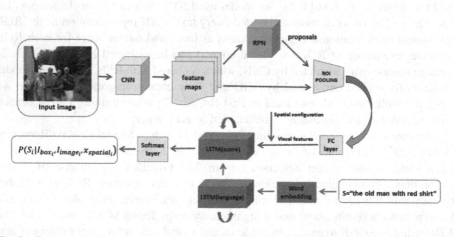

Fig. 2. Our model mainly consists of two modules, RPN module is used for generating region of interest (RoI) and LSTM module is used for calculating score for each RoI. Feature maps of input image is computed by CNN and local features of RoIs are extracted from global feature maps by RoI Pooling. LSTM module contains two LSTM units which are used for computing conditional probability of natural language query based on local and global visual features.

proposed in [13] also uses CNN to encode image feature, different from [5, 13] introduces the attention mechanism over image.

Referring Expression Comprehension: The most relevant work to our task is [7], which proposed SCRC model to solve similar task named natural language object retrieval, their method introduced two CNNs to extract image features of target and global context. They use three LSTMs to take visual features, 8-dimensional spatial configuration and embedded words as input to compute score for each bounding box. Mao [15] introduced a deep learning model includes CNN and LSTM to generate descriptions for unambiguous object, Additionally, they solved the inverse problem of localizing the referred target in the image with the same model which takes an image and natural language query as input (Fig. 2).

3 Our Method

3.1 Semantic R-CNN

Our method, called Semantic R-CNN, is composed of two modules. RPN [3] module is a fully convolutional network which is used to generate Region of Interest (ROI) and LSTM module consists of two LSTM units takes visual features of ROI, global context of image and spatial configuration as image context to compute a score for each candidate box. Inspired by Faster R-CNN [3], CNN in RPN is shared computation with CNN used to extract visual features and the two modules can be joint learned by different loss with backpropagation.

Feature map of whole image is computed by VGG16 [16] model which has 13 convolutional layers and it is input to fully convolutional layer in RPN to output a set of proposals as candidate boxes. The local descriptor I_{box} can be extracted from image feature map by ROI pooling [2, 10], which localizes feature map of the target using its location box. ROI pooling layer is followed by a full connection layer to get 1024-dimensional representation of local regions. The output of fc layers following feature map of whole image is regarded as global contextual feature I_{im}, which is also a 1024-dimensional vector. Combining I_{im} and I_{box} gives us a 2048-dimensional visual feature vector for the proposal and image. For each candidate box, we use 5-dimensional vector $[\frac{x1}{W}, \frac{y1}{H}, \frac{x2}{W}, \frac{y2}{H}, \frac{S_{box}}{S_{image}}]$ to encode the spatial configuration of the box as in [15], where (x1,y1) and (x2,y2) are the coordinates of the top left and bottom right corners of candidate box, S_{box} and S_{image} are the size of candidate box and image, H and W are the height and width of the image.

Concatenating spatial configuration with I_{im} and I_{box}, we can obtain a 2053-dimensional vector $[I_{box}, I_{im}, x_{spatial}]$ which encodes visual and location features. On the other hand, we use word embedding matrix to transform one-hot vectors of query into word embedding. $LSTM_{language}$ take words embedding as input and its hidden state at each time step t is regarded as the encoding of the natural language query. For input query, we expand it with two special tokens <bos> and <eos> which stand for the beginning and end of query sentence.

At each time step t, $LSTM_{score}$ take vector $[I_{box}, I_{im}, x_{spatial}]$ and hidden state of $LSTM_{language}$ as input and predict the conditional probability distribution $P(S_t|R, I)$.

Finally, we pick the region with highest score as detecting result and the score $P(S|R, I)$ is computed as:

$$P(S|R, I) = \prod\nolimits_{s_t \in S} P(s_t|s_{t-1}, \ldots, s_1, R, I) = \prod\nolimits_t softmax(Wh_{score}^t) \qquad (1)$$

Where $softmax(Wh_{score}^t)$ is a softmax function which outputs a probability distribution and we only use the probability value of word s_t. The dimension of hidden state for $LSTM_{language}$ and $LSTM_{score}$ is set to 1000 and the dimension of Wh_{score}^t is the same as the length of word dictionary.

3.2   Training RPN Module and LSTM Module

Our train data is a collection of triples (I, R, S), where I is an image, R represents a target within I and S is a natural language description of the target. There may be many target regions within an image, for a target, there may be many different descriptions. For example, "the white dog on the left" and "the white dog behind the woman" can describe the same object "dog" in an image. Inspired by approximate joint training in Faster R-CNN [3], we train RPN module and LSTM module with different loss, backward propagated signals from RPN loss and LSTM loss are combined for shared layers. For LSTM module, we use maximum likelihood training and the loss function is the negative log probability of the query sentence given visual features of image:

$$L(\theta) = -\sum\nolimits_{i=1}^{N} \log P(S_i|I_{box_i}, I_{image_i}, x_{spatial_i}; \theta) \qquad (2)$$

where N is the total number of training samples and $P(S_i|I_{box_i}, I_{image_i}, x_{spatial_i}; \theta)$ is computed by Eq. (1). For training RPN module, a binary class label is assigned to each RoI, RoI is assigned positive label when it's intersection-over-Union (IoU) overlap is higher than 0.7 with any ground-truth box or with highest IoU overlap with a ground-truth box, negative label is assigned to RoI which has IoU ratio lower than 0.3 for all ground-truth boxes. The multi-task loss in Faster R-CNN [3] is used for training RPN module which is defined as:

$$L(p_i, t_i) = \frac{1}{N_{cls}} \sum\nolimits_i L_{cls}(p_i, p_i^*) + \alpha \frac{1}{N_{reg}} \sum\nolimits_i p_i^* L_{reg}(t_i, t_i^*) \qquad (3)$$

where $L_{cls}(p_i, p_i^*)$ is classification loss over two classes (whether each region is an object or not) and $L_{reg}(t_i, t_i^*)$ is regression loss such as smooth L_1 which is activated only when p_i^* is equal to 1 (i.e. positive RoIs). N_{cls} and N_{reg} are used for normalization. By combining different loss for training RPN and LSTM, our model is learned to address region generation and score calculation simultaneously.

Non-maximum suppression (NMS) is used to reduce redundancy of proposals, the number of proposals is reduced from 6000 to 2000 for training. In testing, we select top-100 proposals as candidate boxes and calculate score for each box. Finally, detecting system returns box with highest score as final result. The parameters of CNN and RPN are initialized from Faster R-CNN model [3] which is pre-trained on MSCOCO dataset [17], that transfers knowledge from object detection to our task. The network architecture of CNN is the same as VGG16 [16]. The weights in LSTM module including words embedding matrix are initialized from Gaussian distribution. The learning rate is set to 0.001 at the beginning and is reduced to half for every 50000 iterations. We use a momentum of 0.9 and do not use weight decay. We set higher weight to LSTM loss than RPN loss and train whole model by SGD. Our model is implemented by using Caffe [18].

4 Experiments

4.1 Datasets and Analysis

Our method is evaluated on RefCLEF dataset [8] which is collected on top of IAPRTC-12 dataset [19] in a two-player game [8]. In ReferitGame [8], the first player is shown an image and a segmented object within the image, the player is asked to write a natural language expression to describe the target and the second player is asked to pick out the target which is described by the first player. Their descriptions will be included in Referit dataset only when they receive points.

There are 20000 images on this dataset, 99296 bounding boxes are used to show the locations of targets. For each bounding box, there may be more than one referring expressions collected to describe the target. There are total about 130000 referring expressions included on RefCLEF dataset, which means there are about 130000 triples (I, R, S) which can be used as training and testing samples. RefCLEF dataset contains both object regions and stuff regions. Object means entities with closed boundary and well-defined shape, such as "horse" and "dog", while stuff usually refers to entities

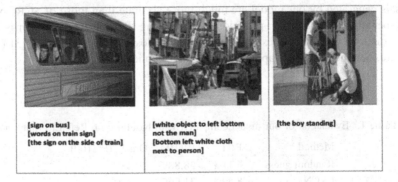

Fig. 3. Some example images on RefCLEF dataset, each image may contain multiple targets and each target is annotated by a bounding box and N referring expressions (there may be more than one description for each target).

without a well-defined shape, such as "sky" and "road". Figure 3 shows some examples on RefCLEF dataset.

4.2 Results and Discussion

We evaluate our model on RefCLEF dataset [8] and compare our results with LRCN model [4] and SCRC model [7]. We split the dataset into two subsets of 10000 training images and 10000 testing images as SCRC method [7], there are about 60000 training samples and 60000 testing samples, each sample is a tuple (I, R, S), where I is an image, R is a target region within the image annotated by bounding box and S is a description sentence describing the target.

We test the model in a scene which is very close to real applications, an image and a query text are fed into the system and the model retrieves a region from many generated proposals as detecting result. In testing, a detecting result is considered correct if the IoU of the output region and ground-truth box is at least 50%. We use top-1 precision P@1 as the measure of detection accuracy, which is the percentage of the highest scoring box being correct. We also calculate P@10 (percentage of at least one of the top-10 scoring region is correct) and P@100 (percentage of at least one of the top-100 scoring box or equivalently all candidate boxes is correct) as a comparison. we set the number of RoIs generated by RPN to be 100 because SCRC model uses 100 EdgeBox proposal as candidate box set in the experiment.

Table 1 shows the evaluation result on RefCLEF dataset, where P@1, P@10, P@100 and random guess precision (random guess is used to select the target from 100 candidate boxes which are generated by RPN) are reported. Both SCRC model and our model in Table 1 are a full model which includes spatial configuration and global context. Our method significantly outperforms SCRC model and LRCN model. Compared with our method, SCRC model uses EdgeBox method to generate proposals and it's not an efficient model which allows proposal generation module and LSTM module to be trained jointly. Instead, our method Semantic R-CNN uses RPN as proposal generation module and combines it with CNN module which allows the whole net to be learned jointly and the cost of proposal generation is almost zero because of shared convolutional computations. P@100 and P@10 of random guess shows that proposals generated by our model are much more accurate than those of SCRC which greatly benefits final detection precision. The running time of entire system is about 230 ms on K40 GPU when testing which is very close to Faster R-CNN [3] (5fps), Therefore, our model can be applied to real-time applications.

Table 1. Evaluation of our model compared with baselines on RefCLEF dataset

Method	P@1	P@10	Oracle (P@100)
Random guess	6.11%	38.88%	79.43%
LRCN	8.59%	31.86%	59.38%
SCRC	17.93%	45.27%	59.38%
Semantic R-CNN	**40.58%**	**71.49%**	**79.43%**

Fig. 4. Some testing examples on RefCLEF dataset which are localized correctly (i.e. IoU ≥ 0.5). The blue box is retrieved box and green box is the ground truth. (Color figure online)

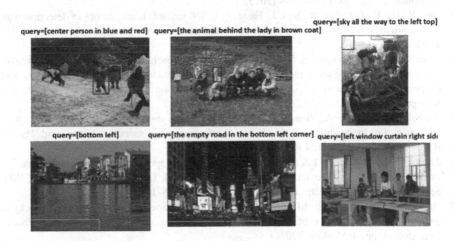

Fig. 5. Some failure cases on RefCLEF dataset (i.e. IoU < 0.5). The red box is incorrect localized target and the green box is the ground truth. (Color figure online)

Figure 4 shows some examples which are localized correctly (the localized region has at least 50% IoU with ground truth). As shown in Fig. 4, objects are distinguished by their attributes and positional relationships and our model can capture information contained in the query text and find the target. In addition, some stuff regions, such as "sky", are also localized correctly by our model.

Figure 5 shows some failure cases. Some failures cases are caused by multiple similar objects appearing in the image and it's hard to distinguish them by ambiguous query. There are also some meaningless annotations and queries on testing dataset, such as "bottom left" which causes failure in detection.

5   Conclusion

In this paper, we have proposed Semantic R-CNN to address natural language object detection. By using RPN for proposal generation, our model combines proposal generation module and object retrieval module into a network which can be learned jointly by different loss. Experiment result shows that our model significantly outperforms baseline models and the speed of testing is almost real-time.

References

1. Girshick, R., Donahue, J., Darrell, T., Malik, J.: Rich feature hierarchies for accurate object detection and semantic segmentation. In: Proceedings of the IEEE Conference on Computer Vision and Pattern Recognition, pp. 580–587 (2014)
2. Girshick, R.: Fast R-CNN. In: Proceedings of the IEEE International Conference on Computer Vision, pp. 1440–1448 (2015)
3. Ren, S., He, K., Girshick, R., Sun, J.: Faster R-CNN: towards real-time object detection with region proposal networks. In: Advances in Neural Information Processing Systems, pp. 91–99 (2015)
4. Donahue, J., Anne Hendricks, L., Guadarrama, S., Rohrbach, M., Venugopalan, S., Saenko, K., Darrell, T.: Long-term recurrent convolutional networks for visual recognition and description. In: Proceedings of the IEEE Conference on Computer Vision and Pattern Recognition, pp. 2625–2634 (2015)
5. Vinyals, O., Toshev, A., Bengio, S., Erhan, D.: Show and tell: a neural image caption generator. In: Proceedings of the IEEE Conference on Computer Vision and Pattern Recognition, pp. 3156–3164 (2015)
6. Zitnick, C.L., Dollár, P.: Edge boxes: locating object proposals from edges. In: Fleet, D., Pajdla, T., Schiele, B., Tuytelaars, T. (eds.) ECCV 2014. LNCS, vol. 8693, pp. 391–405. Springer, Cham (2014). https://doi.org/10.1007/978-3-319-10602-1_26
7. Hu, R., Xu, H., Rohrbach, M., Feng, J., Saenko, K., Darrell, T.: Natural language object retrieval. In: Proceedings of the IEEE Conference on Computer Vision and Pattern Recognition, pp. 4555–4564 (2016)
8. Kazemzadeh, S., Ordonez, V., Matten, M., Berg, T.L.: Referitgame: referring to objects in photographs of natural scenes. In: EMNLP, pp. 787–798 (2014)
9. Uijlings, J.R., Van De Sande, K.E., Gevers, T., Smeulders, A.W.: Selective search for object recognition. Int. J. Comput. Vis. **104**(2), 154–171 (2013)
10. He, K., Zhang, X., Ren, S., Sun, J.: Spatial pyramid pooling in deep convolutional networks for visual recognition. In: Fleet, D., Pajdla, T., Schiele, B., Tuytelaars, T. (eds.) ECCV 2014. LNCS, vol. 8691, pp. 346–361. Springer, Cham (2014). https://doi.org/10.1007/978-3-319-10578-9_23
11. Yang, Z., He, X., Gao, J., Deng, L., Smola, A.: Stacked attention networks for image question answering. In: Proceedings of the IEEE Conference on Computer Vision and Pattern Recognition, pp. 21–29 (2016)

12. Guadarrama, S., Rodner, E., Saenko, K., Zhang, N., Farrell, R., Donahue, J., Darrell, T.: Open-vocabulary object retrieval. In: Robotics: Science and Systems, vol. 2, p. 6. Citeseer (2014)
13. Xu, K., Ba, J., Kiros, R., Cho, K., Courville, A., Salakhudinov, R., Zemel, R., Bengio, Y.: Show, attend and tell: neural image caption generation with visual attention. In: International Conference on Machine Learning, pp. 2048–2057 (2015)
14. Levi, K., Weiss, Y.: Learning object detection from a small number of examples: the importance of good features. In: Proceedings of the 2004 IEEE Computer Society Conference on Computer Vision and Pattern Recognition, 2004, CVPR 2004, vol. 2, pp. 53–60. IEEE (2004)
15. Mao, J., Huang, J., Toshev, A., Camburu, O., Yuille, A.L., Murphy, K.: Generation and comprehension of unambiguous object descriptions. In: Proceedings of the IEEE Conference on Computer Vision and Pattern Recognition, pp. 11–20 (2016)
16. Simonyan, K., Zisserman, A.: Very deep convolutional networks for largescale image recognition. arXiv preprint arXiv:1409.1556 (2014)
17. Lin, T.-Y., Maire, M., Belongie, S., Hays, J., Perona, P., Ramanan, D., Dollár, P., Zitnick, C. L.: Microsoft COCO: common objects in context. In: Fleet, D., Pajdla, T., Schiele, B., Tuytelaars, T. (eds.) ECCV 2014. LNCS, vol. 8693, pp. 740–755. Springer, Cham (2014). https://doi.org/10.1007/978-3-319-10602-1_48
18. Jia, Y., Shelhamer, E., Donahue, J., Karayev, S., Long, J., Girshick, R., Guadarrama, S., Darrell, T.: Caffe: convolutional architecture for fast feature embedding. In: Proceedings of the 22nd ACM International Conference on Multimedia, pp. 675–678. ACM (2014)
19. Grubinger, M., Clough, P., Müller, H., Deselaers, T.: The iapr tc-12 benchmark: a new evaluation resource for visual information systems. In: International Workshop Ontoimage, vol. 5, p. 10 (2006)
20. Hochreiter, S., Schmidhuber, J.: Long short-term memory. Neural Comput. **9**(8), 1735–1780 (1997)

Spatio-Temporal Context Networks
for Video Question Answering

Kun Gao and Yahong Han[✉]

School of Computer Science and Technology, Tianjin University, Tianjin, China
{gaokun,yahong}@tju.edu.cn

Abstract. Video Question Answering (Video QA) is one of the important and challenging problems in multimedia and computer vision research. In this paper, we propose a novel framework, called spatio-temporal context networks (STCN). This framework uses long short term memory networks (LSTM) to encode spatial and temporal information of videos, then initializes language model by the encoded visual features. Based on the visual and semantic features, we can get an appropriate answer. In particular, in this STCN framework, we effectively fuse optical flow to capture more discriminative motion information of videos. In order to verify the effectiveness of the proposed framework, we conduct experiments on TACoS dataset. It achieves good performances on both hard level and easy level of TACoS dataset.

Keywords: Spatial and temporal information · Language model
Optical flow

1 Introduction

The recent development of deep learning technologies has achieved successes in many visual and natural language processing (NLP) tasks. Deep convolutional feature has shown strong ability in several visual tasks such as detection [6,10], image classification [9], and object recognition [11]. In addition, recurrent neural networks (RNNs), particularly LSTM [1], are being widely used in NLP field. Recently, more and more researchers make attention to deeply understanding of visual content by jointly modeling visual and language information. Video QA is proposed as a bridge to evaluate the ability of deeply understanding. Thus, the paper proposes STCN framework to solve this task.

Early researches of visual understanding started from image captioning [3,5,14,17] researchers try to understand the present objects in images and utilize language model to rank detected words for output sentences. Afterwards, Vinyals et al. [13] proposed the encoder-decoder framework to generate the caption of images by an end-to-end process. The process of encoder aims to extract deep visual feature, and decoder part uses LSTM model to generate

© Springer International Publishing AG, part of Springer Nature 2018
B. Zeng et al. (Eds.): PCM 2017, LNCS 10736, pp. 108–118, 2018.
https://doi.org/10.1007/978-3-319-77383-4_11

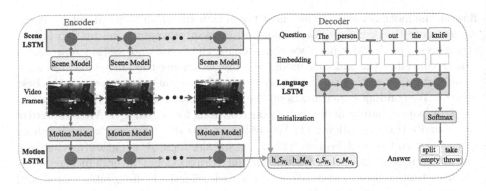

Fig. 1. The proposed spatio-temporal context networks (STCN) framework. This framework includes two components: encoder part and decoder part. For encoder part, we generate the scene and motion representations by two LSTM structures. For decoder part, we concatenate the scene and motion representations to initialize the language model, and use softmax classifier to choose the best answer.

complete sentences. Xu et al. [15] put forward attention model which learns to fix its attention on salient objects while generating the corresponding words in the sequence.

Inspired by the proposed work, the attention model is used to solve image question answering (Image QA) task [2,8,16,19]. The method in [19] can earn the importance of each position according to questions. Compared to the Image QA, Video QA confronts many challenges such as background noises, motion speed, view point changes and so on. How to extract discriminative temporal information is the key to the task of Video QA. The first work on video-based question answering was proposed by Tu et al. [12], which builds a query answering system based on a joint parsing graph from both texts and videos. Then, Zhu et al. [18] presented an encoder-decoder approach to learn temporal structure of videos and answer multiple-choice questions by a ranking loss. This work forces on the temporal domain and trains the model in an unsupervised method with large number of video data. But this temporal model and question pair model use separated training way which weakens the relation between contents and languages. Based on the current research work, there are some problems which need to be addressed on Video QA task. Firstly, how to utilize the scene and motion information effectively. Secondly, how to design an integral model which can be learned by end to end fashion. Lastly, how to benefit from the idea of attention mechanism for Video QA task.

Motivated by above discussions, we present a novel framework named STCN for Video QA. The overall framework of STCN is illustrated in Fig. 1. Our proposed framework is mainly composed of two components: encoder part and decoder part. For encoder part, on the one hand, we generate scene feature by our designed scene model; on the other hand, motion model focuses on how to get temporal information from the consecutive frames. We utilize the optical flow as the motion weight to augment the action variation areas in videos. Next, we generate the scene representation and motion representation by two LSTM structures. For decoder part, we concatenate the scene and motion representations to initialize the language model. Finally, we choose the fully connected layer to aggregate semantic descriptions and use softmax classifier to choose the best answer. We conduct experiments on the public action dataset: TACoS dataset.

This paper mainly makes three contributions for Video QA. We summarize the contributions as follows: (1) We design an integral framework which can be learned by end to end fashion. (2) Based on the idea of attention mechanism, motion weight is inventively acted on the convolutional layer which extracts features from video frames. (3) The network effectively integrates visual and semantic features, and it achieves good performances on TACoS dataset.

2 Proposed Method

In this section, we describe our STCN framework in detail. First, we introduce the processes of generating scene and motion representations by using designed scene and motion models, respectively. Then we concatenate them to initialize the language model. Finally, we detailed discuss how to choose the best answer.

2.1 Generating the Scene Representation Using Scene Model

The scene information in videos provides an overall perspective to comprehend the environment, figures, objects and so on. We can obtain the scene clues from the frames to better understand video content.

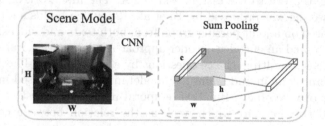

Fig. 2. Scene Model based on the convolutional neural networks (CNNs). We extract the convolutional feature maps of the given video frame with VGGNet [9] at first, and then generate the scene feature vector by sum pooling strategy.

Given a video clip V, we sample N_1 frames and extract feature of each frame by using scene model illustrated in Fig. 2. For the frame f_k ($k = 1, 2, \ldots, N_1$), we extract deep convolutional feature maps F_k, and generate the frame feature vector S_k by sum pooling strategy.

$$F_k = CNN_{vgg}(f_k), \tag{1}$$

$$S_k = SumPooling(F_k). \tag{2}$$

Unlike previous methods [4, 7] which use feature from the fully-connected layer, we get the feature maps F_k from the convolutional layer which retain the spatial structure information of the original frame. In order to explain the process of generating scene representation clearly, we make the following definition: the input frame size is $H \times W$ and the dimension of extracted feature maps F_k is $c \times h \times w$, where $h \times w$ is the spatial scale of each channel on F_k, and c is the number of channels. In addition, we aggregate the extracted feature maps by sum pooling and get the frame feature vector with dimension of c.

Thus, for each frame f_k, we obtain the corresponding vector S_k. Next, we put these video feature vectors into the nodes of LSTM in sequence. Then we get the last hidden state $h\_S_{N_1}$ and memory cell state $c\_S_{N_1}$. Finally, we concatenate $h\_S_{N_1}$ and $c\_S_{N_1}$ to be the final scene representation of the video clip V.

2.2 Generating the Motion Representation Using Motion Model

As mentioned above, through scene model, we obtain precise understanding of spatial information. However, if only consider the scene information, we might lose the important motion information which is crucial for answering questions accurately. In this work, we focus on capturing variation clues from video frames, and enhance the influence of variation regions for the final motion representation.

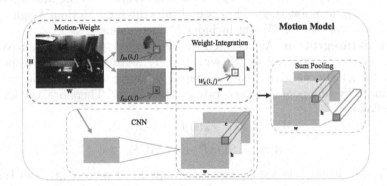

Fig. 3. Motion Model based on the optical flow. We utilize optical flow to reflect the motion variation information, and propose the Motion-Weight method to obtain motion weight. Then we multiply the motion weight with convolutional feature maps in the corresponding location and get the weighted feature maps. At last, we aggregate the weighted feature maps by sum pooling and get the ultimate motion feature vector.

Based on this standpoint, in this subsection, we use optical flow as the motion weight to reflect the motion variation information. Given a video clip V, we sample N_1 frames. For each frame, two optical flow images from the horizontal and vertical components can be extracted. As Fig. 3 depicts, we choose a frame f_k and select its two corresponding optical flow images f_{kx}, f_{ky}. In the optical flow images, high light points manifest the variation areas in the videos. So we utilize this characteristic to propose Motion-Weight method, which can measure the degree of variation among series of consecutive frames. In the following part, we describe the Motion-Weight approach in detail.

Motion-Weight. For a video clip V, we first choose N_1 frames, which are identical to the scene model, to extract the corresponding optical flow images and resize them to the size of $h \times w$. Accordingly, for each frame f_k, we can get the relevant flow images f_{kx}, f_{ky} from horizontal and vertical components. Finally, we can get the Motion-Weight as follows:

$$\eta_{kx}(i,j) = \frac{|f_{kx}(i,j) - N_{kx}|}{N_{kx}}, \tag{3}$$

$$\eta_{ky}(i,j) = \frac{|f_{ky}(i,j) - N_{ky}|}{N_{ky}}, \tag{4}$$

$$W_k(i,j) = \eta_{kx}(i,j) + \eta_{ky}(i,j). \tag{5}$$

Where $f_{kx}(i,j)$ and $f_{ky}(i,j)$ denote the pixel values of the horizontal and vertical optical flow images at point (i,j), respectively. Meanwhile, N_{kx} and N_{ky} denote the mean values of horizontal and vertical flow images, independently. In addition, considering the different directions of motion, we adopt the absolute value to eliminate the differences. $\eta_{kx}(i,j)$ and $\eta_{ky}(i,j)$ denote the intensity values at point (i,j). Finally, we regard the sum $W_k(i,j)$ as the Motion-Weight of the frame f_k at point (i,j). Thus, we obtain the final Motion-Weight W_k of frame f_k, and the Motion-Weight includes $h \times w$ regions.

Weight-Integration. As reflected in Fig. 3, after getting Motion-Weight, we multiply the Motion-Weight W_k with feature maps F_k in the corresponding location to get the weighted feature maps. Then we aggregate the weighted feature maps by sum pooling to generate motion vector. Therefore, the formulas are as follows:

$$WF_k(i,j) = F_k(i,j) \times W_k(i,j), \tag{6}$$

$$WS_k = SumPooling(WF_k). \tag{7}$$

where $F_k(i,j)$ denotes the value of feature maps F_k at point (i,j), and $W_k(i,j)$ represents the weight of the corresponding location. Based on the above formula, we get the weighted feature maps WF_k, and then generate the motion vector WS_k by sum pooling.

After generating motion vectors, we put them to the nodes of LSTM structure one by one. Similarly, we concatenate the last hidden state $h\_M_{N_1}$ and the last memory cell state $c\_M_{N_1}$ together to represent the motion information.

2.3 Generating the Language Representation Using Language Model

After getting the scene representation and the motion representation, we use the new memory cell state $\{c\_S_{N_1}, c\_M_{N_1}\}$ and the new hidden state $\{h\_S_{N_1}, h\_M_{N_1}\}$ to initialize the memory cell state c_L_1 and the hidden state h_L_1 of the language

LSTM. This initialization operation is utilized to joint different visual and semantic features.

The language model we proposed is based on the basic LSTM unit structure. Given a question $Q = \{q_1, q_2, \ldots, q_m\}$, we learn the word tokens as follows:

$$p_i = OH(q_i), \tag{8}$$

$$x_i = W_e p_i. \tag{9}$$

Where $OH(\cdot)$ transforms a word q_i to its one hot representation p_i, a vector that there is only one nonzero value in the position i corresponding to the word vocabulary. The matrix W_e transforms the one hot vector p_i into the d_e dimensional embedding space x_i. Consequently, these embedding vectors $\{x_1, x_2, \ldots, x_m\}$ are fed into the nodes of LSTM structure in sequence.

The number of LSTM nodes is $N_2 (m \leq N_2)$. Meanwhile, we get the hidden state $h\_L_{N_2}$ and the memory cell state $c\_L_{N_2}$ from the last LSTM structure node, separately. Contrary to the conventional approach [18] which makes the last hidden state $h\_L_{N_2}$ to be the final feature, we regard the concatenate vector of $h\_L_{N_2}$ and $c\_L_{N_2}$ as the ultimate representation of the whole question Q.

After getting the whole question representation, we transform the representation to a fixed dimensional space, then execute ReLU and dropout on it. Afterwards, we transform it to the length as same as the number of candidate vocabulary, and train the network using the cross entropy loss.

3 Experiments

In this section, we first describe the TACoS dataset, as illustrated in Fig. 4, which is used for evaluating the performance. Then we introduce the experimental setup. In the following part, we evaluate our proposed STCN from three aspects: the structure of framework, the advantage of motion strategy, and the approach of feature concatenation. At last, comparisons with previous methods which are conducted on TACoS dataset and discussions are presented.

3.1 Dataset

We use the TACoS dataset [18] for Video QA task, which generates the question answering pairs in the cooking scenario. It consists 127 long videos including total 18227 video clips. This dataset generates two difficult levels: hard level and easy level. And they are divided into three splits, separately. For each split, it includes three parts: past part, present part, and future part. In our work, we use the present part to evaluate our proposed STCN. In addition, each present part is divided into training, validation, and testing sets. Besides, the candidate answers contain three distracters and a right answer in easy level and the number of candidate answers is increased to ten in hard level.

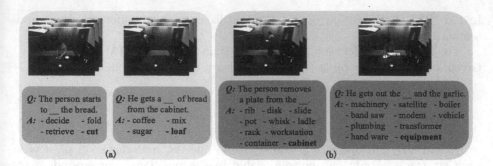

Fig. 4. The TACoS dataset. This dataset generates two difficult levels: easy level (a) and hard level (b). In the easy level, the candidate answers contain three distracters and a right answer; in the hard level, the number of candidate answers is increased to ten. Words colored in red are the correct answers. (Color figure online)

3.2 Experimental Setup

In this subsection, we introduce the experimental setup, and choose the hyperparameters using the validation set. In the encoder part, for each video clip, we set the sampled frames to 26. Accordingly, the nodes of scene and motion LSTM are also set to 26. The dimension of these two LSTM hidden units is set to 256. The frame which is fed into scene model is resized to 240×320, and the optical flow images are resized to 15×20. We set the mean value to be the same configure of 128. For the decoder part, we set the nodes of language LSTM to 26, and the dimension of this LSTM hidden units is set to 512. The number of dropout is set to 0.5. After filtering out low frequency words, we set 650 as the number of answer vocabulary for easy level, and set 2000 for hard level. The model is trained with RMSProp update rule, mini-batch size of 100, and a global learning rate of 3×10^{-4}.

3.3 Evaluation of Framework Structure

As mentioned above, our proposed STCN framework is utilized to joint visual and semantic features based on the encoder-decoder approach. To evaluate the effectiveness of this structure, we design the compared structure, named three stream LSTM networks (TSLN), which only fuses the scene, motion and language features at last. And in this subsection, we compare and analyze the frameworks of STCN and TSLN with the same parameters.

From Table 1, we can see that the performance of proposed STCN has 0.95% and 0.34% improvements than the TSLN framework on hard and easy levels of TACoS. According to the results, we know that the encoder-decoder structure is more efficient than the late fusion structure for Video QA task. Through initialized with encoding features, the language LSTM has a clear understanding of visual information, which helps the language model to make accurate judgments.

Table 1. Comparison of STCN and TSLN frameworks on TACoS dataset. The TSLN stands for the compared three stream LSTM networks.

Framework	Hard				Easy			
	$split_1$	$split_2$	$split_3$	Mean	$split_1$	$split_2$	$split_3$	Mean
STCN	85.52%	86.40%	83.97%	85.30%	92.50%	93.00%	90.97%	92.16%
TSLN	84.56%	85.44%	83.05%	84.35%	92.03%	92.56%	90.87%	91.82%

3.4 Evaluation of Motion Strategy

Motion information is the key difference between Video QA and Image QA. So we evaluate the performance of motion strategy in this subsection. In order to verify conveniently, we remove motion part from STCN and build the compared framework, named spatial context networks (SCN). In the SCN framework, we only take scene representation as the initialization of language LSTM structure. The dimension of language LSTM hidden units is set the same as scene LSTM.

Table 2. Comparison of STCN and SCN frameworks on TACoS dataset. The SCN stands for the compared spatial context networks.

Method	Hard				Easy			
	$split_1$	$split_2$	$split_3$	Mean	$split_1$	$split_2$	$split_3$	Mean
STCN	85.52%	86.40%	83.97%	85.30%	92.50%	93.00%	90.97%	92.16%
SCN	85.37%	85.63%	83.77%	84.92%	92.22%	92.52%	91.02%	91.92%

From Table 2, we can know that the accuracy of our proposed STCN is better than SCN on both hard level and easy level. By comparing the results, we can conclude that motion information plays an important role in Video QA task.

3.5 Evaluation of Feature Concatenation Approach

In the language LSTM structure of proposed STCN framework, unlike the conventional method [18] which makes the last hidden state to be the final feature, we also utilize the memory cell state to enhance semantic information, and regard the concatenation vector of last memory cell state and hidden state as the language representation. To evaluate the effectiveness of this viewpoint, we design the compared STCN_h framework. In the language LSTM structure of STCN_h, we only take the last hidden state as the ultimate language representation.

From Table 3, we can see that the accuracy of STCN framework is higher than STCN_h on two difficult levels of TACoS dataset. By comparing and analyzing, we know that the concatenation of last hidden state and memory cell state can enhance semantic information.

Table 3. Comparison of STCN and STCN_h frameworks on TACoS dataset. In the language LSTM of STCN_h, we only take the last hidden state as the final feature.

Method	Hard				Easy			
	$split_1$	$split_2$	$split_3$	Mean	$split_1$	$split_2$	$split_3$	Mean
STCN	85.52%	86.40%	83.97%	85.30%	92.50%	93.00%	90.97%	92.16%
STCN_h	85.37%	85.37%	83.47%	84.74%	92.33%	92.89%	90.98%	92.07%

3.6 Comparison with Previous Methods Conducted on TACoS

In this subsection, we compare our results with several recently published methods conducted on TACoS dataset to tackle Video QA task, which include the GRUmodel method [18], the ConvNets method [18], and the CCA method [18].

Table 4. Comparison with previous methods conducted on TACoS dataset.

Method	Hard				Easy			
	$split_1$	$split_2$	$split_3$	Mean	$split_1$	$split_2$	$split_3$	Mean
STCN	85.52%	86.40%	83.97%	85.30%	92.50%	93.00%	90.97%	92.16%
GRUmodel [18]	66.90%	66.20%	68.20%	67.10%	79.10%	81.90%	78.10%	79.70%
ConvNets [18]	-	-	-	65.50%	-	-	-	76.30%
CCA [18]	-	-	-	-	67.10%	64.90%	63.20%	65.10%

As shown in Table 4, compared with the GRUmodel method, our proposed STCN has a 18.20% advantage on hard level and 12.46% on easy level. Besides, it outperforms the ConvNets method 19.8% on hard level and 15.86% on easy level. In addition, it can boost the performance of CCA by 27.06% on easy level of TACoS dataset.

4 Conclusions

In this paper, we propose a novel STCN framework to tackle Video QA task. This framework is designed based on the encoder-decoder architecture, which can learn the visual and semantic information by end to end fashion. We design the scene model and motion model to encode video visual features, and the visual information assists language model to decode video sematic information effectively. Thus, our proposed STCN achieves good performances on both hard level and easy level of TACoS dataset.

Acknowledgment. This work was supported by the NSFC (under Grant U1509206, 61472276).

References

1. Hochreiter, S., Schmidhuber, J.: Long short-term memory. Neural Comput. **9**(8), 1735–1780 (1997)
2. Ilievski, I., Yan, S., Feng, J.: A focused dynamic attention model for visual question answering. arXiv preprint arXiv:1604.01485 (2016)
3. Karpathy, A., Joulin, A., Li, F.F.F.: Deep fragment embeddings for bidirectional image sentence mapping. In: Advances in Neural Information Processing Systems, pp. 1889–1897 (2014)
4. Ma, L., Lu, Z., Li, H.: Learning to answer questions from image using convolutional neural network. arXiv preprint arXiv:1506.00333 (2015)
5. Mao, J., Xu, W., Yang, Y., Wang, J., Huang, Z., Yuille, A.: Deep captioning with multimodal recurrent neural networks (M-RNN). arXiv preprint arXiv:1412.6632 (2014)
6. Ouyang, W., Wang, X.: Joint deep learning for pedestrian detection. In: Proceedings of the IEEE International Conference on Computer Vision, pp. 2056–2063 (2013)
7. Ren, M., Kiros, R., Zemel, R.: Exploring models and data for image question answering. In: Advances in Neural Information Processing Systems, pp. 2953–2961 (2015)
8. Shih, K.J., Singh, S., Hoiem, D.: Where to look: focus regions for visual question answering. In: Proceedings of the IEEE Conference on Computer Vision and Pattern Recognition, pp. 4613–4621 (2016)
9. Simonyan, K., Zisserman, A.: Very deep convolutional networks for large-scale image recognition. arXiv preprint arXiv:1409.1556 (2014)
10. Szarvas, M., Yoshizawa, A., Yamamoto, M., Ogata, J.: Pedestrian detection with convolutional neural networks. In: Intelligent Vehicles Symposium (2005)
11. Szegedy, C., Liu, W., Jia, Y., Sermanet, P., Reed, S., Anguelov, D., Rabinovich, A.: Going deeper with convolutions. In: Proceedings of the IEEE Conference on Computer Vision and Pattern Recognition, pp. 1–9 (2015)
12. Tu, K., Meng, M., Lee, M.W., Choe, T.E., Zhu, S.C.: Joint video and text parsing for understanding events and answering queries. IEEE MultiMedia **21**, 42–70 (2014)
13. Vinyals, O., Toshev, A., Bengio, S., Erhan, D.: Show and tell: a neural image caption generator. In: Proceedings of the IEEE Conference on Computer Vision and Pattern Recognition, pp. 3156–3264 (2015)
14. Wu, Q., Shen, C., Liu, L., Dick, A., van den Hengel, A.: What value do explicit high level concepts have in vision to language problems? In: Proceedings of the IEEE Conference on Computer Vision and Pattern Recognition, pp. 203–212 (2016)
15. Xu, K., Ba, J., Kiros, R., Cho, K., Courville, A., Salakhudinov, R., Bengio, Y.: Show, attend and tell: neural image caption generation with visual attention. In: International Conference on Machine Learning, pp. 2048–2057 (2015)
16. Yang, Z., He, X., Gao, J., Deng, L., Smola, A.: Stacked attention networks for image question answering. In: Proceedings of the IEEE Conference on Computer Vision and Pattern Recognition, pp. 21–29 (2016)
17. Yao, L., Torabi, A., Cho, K., Ballas, N., Pal, C., Larochelle, H., Courville, A.: Describing videos by exploiting temporal structure. In: Proceedings of the IEEE International Conference on Computer Vision, pp. 4507–4515 (2015)

18. Zhu, L., Xu, Z., Yang, Y., Hauptmann, A.G.: Uncovering temporal context for video question and answering. arXiv preprint arXiv:1511.04670 (2015)
19. Zhu, Y., Groth, O., Bernstein, M., Fei-Fei, L.: Visual7w: grounded question answering in images. In: Proceedings of the IEEE Conference on Computer Vision and Pattern Recognition, pp. 4995–5004 (2016)

Object Discovery and Cosegmentation Based on Dense Correspondences

Yasi Wang, Hongxun Yao[⊠], Wei Yu, and Xiaoshuai Sun

School of Computer Science and Technology, Harbin Institute of Technology,
Harbin, China
{wangyasi,h.yao,w.yu,xiaoshuaisun}@hit.edu.cn

Abstract. We propose to do object discovery and cosegmentation in noisy datasets with utilization of CNN features. We use an object discovery framework which supposes that common object patterns are sparse concerning transformations across images. The key issue is then how to take advantage of the interrelations among images. Since an image normally matches better with similar images containing the same object than noise images, we exploit the image matching situations of a dataset to capture the interrelations information in it. Comparing with local feature matching, we aim to estimate the dense correspondences between regions with common semantics using mid-level visual information, which captures the visual variability within the whole dataset. Besides, due to the powerful feature learning ability of deep models, we adopt VGG features to do unsupervised clustering and find representative candidates as a prior knowledge. Experiments on noisy datasets show the effectiveness of our method.

Keywords: Object discovery · Cosegmentation
Dense correspondences · Image matching

1 Introduction

1.1 Object Detection and Segmentation

Image is one of the main media which humans use to transmit information. There exist many fundamental and common problems in computer vision field, e.g., image classification, object detection, scene understanding and so on. When we consider images that contain objects, the problems turn into the issues that are more relevant to objects, e.g., object detection, recognition, localization, segmentation and so on. When the computer is being shown an image with objects, these above-mentioned issues try to interpret the knowledge which we human beings see and perceive (the process of vision perception and cognition). That is, *which* pixels of the image belong to the object, *what* is the object, *where* is it roughly or exactly and even *how* does it move.

Object detection is a basic issue in computer vision research. The main target of object detection is to determine whether a certain object (for example a face

© Springer International Publishing AG, part of Springer Nature 2018
B. Zeng et al. (Eds.): PCM 2017, LNCS 10736, pp. 119–128, 2018.
https://doi.org/10.1007/978-3-319-77383-4_12

or a car) exists in the image, and then evaluate the location and scale of the object accurately. A large number of reliable achievements have been made based on decades of researches [1–3], in which sliding window approach is the most widely studied method because of its straight-forward structure and relatively high detection precision. Currently, deep learning approaches based on convolutional neural networks have achieved the state-of-the-art performance [4,5].

Object Segmentation is a subtask of image segmentation. Image segmentation is the process of partitioning an image into multiple nonoverlapping segments, according to image intensity, color, texture, shape and other features, in order that these features present a similarity in the same segment, while present an obvious discrepancy between different segments [7–9]. The goal of segmentation is to simplify the representation of an image into a new one that is more meaningful and easier to analyze [6]. Similarly, object segmentation partitions an image into two segments, the *object* part and the *non-object* part. There are also attempts to use deep neural networks to do segmentation [10,11]. In some work, researchers tried to do detection and segmentation simultaneously, e.g. [12].

1.2   Object Discovery and Cosegmentation

In the aforementioned content, we considered the situation of one image containing one major object. When we extend this situation to another one in which there are multiple images containing the same object, the previous issues also turn into new topics, object discovery and cosegmentation, i.e. object detection and segmentation under the circumstance of an image set.

Object Discovery learns to discover the objects presented in the images in an unsupervised manner by analyzing unlabeled data and searching for reoccurring patterns [18]. From the definition, we can have the prior knowledge that there exist "something similar" in the given set of images. Object discovery can be seen as detecting the common object from the perspective of multiple images, rather than within only one image. It is widely recognized that more labeled training data help produce better performance, however, the expensive manual annotation process hampers this progress. Therefore, unsupervised and weakly supervised methods are investigated. As the task of object discovery is in an unsupervised setting, if we do it well, we are able to acquire a lot of labeled data in an unsupervised manner. This studied topic has two trends of evolution. The first trend is the different forms of marking the object when we discover the common object, from bounding box [19] to segmentation [20,21], which identifies the object with a more accurate and detailed tendency. The second trend is the datasets used in the problem, from small and neat datasets (e.g. MSRC and iCoseg) to large, diverse and noisy datasets (e.g. Internet images).

Cosegmentation was first proposed in 2006 [13]. It is still in active research and cosegmentation generally outperform single image segmentation from the performance reported [15–17]. The explicit definition of cosegmentation was proposed in [14] as the task of jointly segmenting out "something similar" in a given set of images. The key problem of cosegmentation is how to take advantage of the interrelations among images, which contribute to segmenting out the common object. The topic studied has also evolved from the original cosegmentation of a pair of images to concurrent cosegmentation of multiple images. However, these algorithms still have certain limitations, for example, we have to know the number of objects or the object must appear in all images. There still has large research space with regard to segmenting out the common object from a large number of images accurately and automatically.

In this paper, we consider the problem of unsupervised object discovery and cosegmentation simultaneously in noisy Internet images, as done in [20,21], which is discovering the common object and marking the object regions by cosegmentation.

2   Method

We do unsupervised joint object discovery and cosegmentation with utilization of CNN features. For a given dataset of a particular object, in which there are not only images of the object with big variances, but also noise images, the goal is to discover the common object without supervision, which is unsupervised

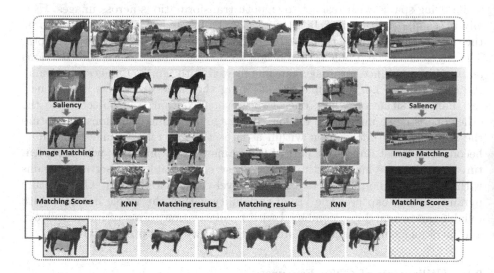

Fig. 1. The framework of unsupervised object discovery and cosegmentation. The first row is the original dataset, including eight images, most of which contain the object *horse*. The last row contains the segmentation results. As shown in the middle part, for an image that contains the object (left part with blue background), its nearest neighbors within the dataset probably also contain the object and have similar appearance. Pairs of images both contain the same object can match well and obtain a high matching score. While for an image that does not contain the object (right part with orange background), its nearest neighbors within the dataset will contain both object images and noise images, neither of which match well, and thus obtain a low matching score. (Color figure online)

Fig. 2. Some examples of two groups of k-means clustering results for the object *airplane*. The first row includes more representative images obtained after clustering, while the second row includes less representative images and noise images.

object discovery, and segment out the object in images in which there exists the object simultaneously (the noise images will be segmented out nothing), which is **cosegmentation**, as shown in Fig. 1.

2.1 Framework

We use an object discovery and cosegmentation framework based on [20]. The key insight is that common object patterns should be salient within each image, while being sparse with respect to smooth transformations across images. Usually it is supposed that more salient part of the image has more tendency to be the object, and also that the visual variability among similar images is smooth. The key issue of the problem then is how to take advantage of the interrelations among images. Since an image can match well with similar images containing the same object, i.e., two images containing the same object can match better than the situation where one of the images contains the object while the other one is noise image. We exploit the image matching situations to capture the interrelations information within a dataset. Thus reliable image matching becomes the most important part of the framework. Comparing with local feature matching, we aim to estimate the dense correspondences between regions with common semantic objects using mid-level visual information - CNN feature pyramid, which captures the visual variability within the whole dataset. With reliable image matching, combined with regularization terms of image saliency and intra-image consistency, we are able to deal with the problem better.

2.2 Utilization of CNN Features

Positive Examples Clustering. We utilize the VGG features for unsupervised clustering and find representative object image candidates as a prior knowledge. Due to the powerful feature learning ability of deep models, we use the VGG model to extract features of images and take the output of the first fully-connected layer as new features. Then we do unsupervised k-means clustering and divide the dataset into two groups. Generally, one of the groups contains more representative images of the particular object and the other group contains some less representative images of the object and outlier candidates, all of which can be served as a prior knowledge. Figure 2 shows some examples of the two groups for the *Airplane* dataset, from which we can see the difference clearly. In the first row, there contains very representative airplane images, including airplanes in the air or at the airport, while the images in the second row are noise images or images in which the airplane object is hard to identify.

Dense Correspondences Estimation. We utilize the DNN flow proposed in [22], which is a category-level image matching algorithm based on CNN feature pyramid, to estimate the dense correspondences across images. Given two images, CNN feature pyramid are used to achieve coarse to fine matching, where top level coarsely matches two images in object level, middle level matches two images in part level, and low level finely matches two images in pixel level. Examples of the matching results are shown in the middlemost part of Fig. 1. For a given image, we match it to its K nearest neighbors to get a matching score. High matching scores indicate a higher possibility of images containing the object, while low matching scores indicate a higher possibility of noise images. In the examples shown in the middle part of Fig. 1, for the horse image in the left part with blue background, the four nearest neighbors in the dataset are also horse images which have similar appearance to it. Under the instruction of effective image matching based on CNN feature pyramid, pairs of horse images match well and obtain a relatively high matching score. While for the field image in the right part with orange background, it can not match well with its neighbors (which are also horse images since the dataset is small for illustration), thus obtain a relatively low matching score.

2.3   Regularization Terms and Optimization

We add two regularization terms to the problem. The first regularization term is image saliency. Since one of the assumptions is that common object patterns should be salient within each image, an off-the-shelf saliency measure in [23] is added. The saliency value of a pixel is defined based on its color contrast to other pixels, i.e., the more different a pixel is from other pixels, the more salient it is. This term encourages more salient pixels to be labeled as foreground. The second regularization term is intra-image consistency, which encourages the spatially consistency of the masks, and the neighboring pixels to have the same label. We use a similar optimization strategy as done in [20]. The optimization is done alternatively between the dense correspondences and the final binary segmentation masks. We use coordinate descent method and optimize one image at each step. Note that we use only one iteration in the process.

3   Experiment

3.1   Datasets

In the experimental part, we use datasets of Internet images proposed in [20] to do object discovery and cosegmentation, which are larger and more diverse compared with traditional cosegmentation datasets. An crucial difference is that the datasets of Internet images contain a certain proportion of noise images.

The datasets are concerning three kinds of objects: *car*, *horse*, and *airplane*. We do **not** use the whole datasets of three common objects, because we only find part of groundtruth results on the website of the datasets[1], including 1,306/4,347 groundtruth images for *Car* dataset, 879/6,381 groundtruth images for *Horse* dataset and 561/4,542 groundtruth images for *Airplane* dataset. The latter number represents the number of images in the dataset, while the former number represents the number of groundtruth images we have for the dataset. Thus we use the subsets of 100 images for three objects as used in [20,21]: *Car100*, *Horse100*, and *Airplane100*, to have comparison results with other methods.

3.2   Evaluation Criteria

We use three evaluation criteria in total, two of which are P and J. These two evaluation criteria are commonly used in the problems of segmentation and object discovery. P is precision, which represents the ratio of correctly labeled pixels, including both foreground and background, and J is Jaccard similarity, which represents the intersection over union of the result and ground truth segmentations for the foreground objects. The two original evaluation criteria P and J measure different metrics of the algorithm and supplement each other, high value of one of the criteria and low value of the other one would not represent a good result. From the quantitative results of previous methods shown in Table 1, Baseline1 is obviously a bad result by achieving good results on the evaluation criterion P but the value of zero on the evaluation criterion J.

Thus, we add another evaluation indicator I to take consideration of a tradeoff between the two original evaluation criteria P and J, which is defined in the following equation. In the definition, P_{opt} and J_{opt} represent current optimal values we have obtained for P and J, so both P/P_{opt} and J/J_{opt} are no greater than 1. The value of I would be between 0 and 1, and the higher the better. We take into account how easily/hard it is to improve the values of the criteria to a certain extent in this definition, rather than simply adding up the values and averaging it.

$$I = P/2 * P_{opt} + J/2 * J_{opt} \tag{1}$$

3.3   Qualitative Results

Qualitative results are shown in Fig. 3 for *Car100*, *Horse100*, and *Airplane100* datasets respectively. For the qualitative results shown in Fig. 3, the first three rows are for *Car100* dataset, the middle three rows are for *Horse100* dataset and the last three rows are for *Airplane100* dataset. The last column shows several wrong examples. The wrong examples include noise images (e.g., the wheel) and images in which the objects are hard to identify (e.g., the horse with a person riding or the crashed airplane).

---

[1] http://people.csail.mit.edu/mrub/ObjectDiscovery/.

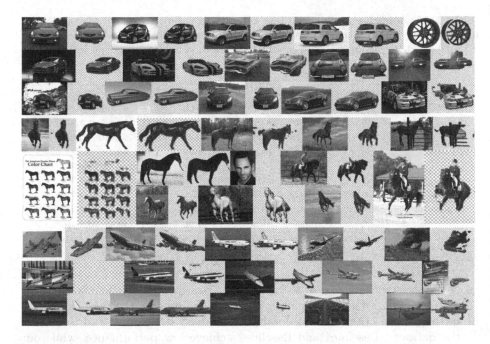

Fig. 3. Qualitative results for three datasets. The first three rows, the middle three rows and the last three rows are results for *Car100*, *Horse100*, and *Airplane100* datasets respectively. The last column contains some wrong examples.

3.4 Quantitative Results

Quantitative results are shown in Table 1 for *Car100*, *Horse100*, and *Airplane100* datasets respectively. We have comparison results with five methods and two baselines as proposed in [20], on three evaluation criteria P, J and I. The first baseline is that all pixels are classified as background (Baseline 1), and the second baseline is that all pixels are classified as foreground (Baseline 2).

As shown in Table 1, there are two findings.

(1) Our method almost achieved the best performance on all the criteria[2] for *Car100*, *Horse100* and *Airplane100* datasets, as shown in the last column of Table 1 (the best performance are shown in bold, and the second best performance are shown in italics), which demonstrates the effectiveness of our method. The performance enhancements of our method are mainly reflected on J and I, meanwhile, we obtain comparable results with the best performance on P.

(2) For *Horse100* and *Airplane100* datasets, Baseline1 achieves good results in terms of criterion P, even higher than several methods available. But at the same time, the values on criterion J are just zero. If we only look at

---

[2] We don't achieve the best performance on P. Our performance on P is quite comparable with the best performance though, especially for *Horse100* dataset.

Table 1. Quantitative results for three datasets. [21] outperformed [20] on P, but underperformed it with a not small gap (18.26% and 15.48% respectively) on J for *Horse100* and *Airplane100* datasets, while our method achieves best performance on J and I, and also comparable performance on P among all datasets.

Dataset	Criteria	Baseline1	Baseline2	[15]	[17]	[16]	[20]	[21]	Ours
Car100	P	68.91	31.09	58.70	59.20	68.85	85.38	**87.65**	*86.48*
	J	0	34.93	37.15	35.15	0.04	64.42	*64.86*	**73.85**
	I	0.3931	0.4139	0.5864	0.5757	0.4199	0.9232	*0.9392*	**0.9934**
Horse100	P	81.54	18.46	63.84	64.22	75.12	82.81	**86.16**	*86.15* (see footnote 2)
	J	0	19.85	30.16	29.53	6.43	*51.65*	33.39	**53.19**
	I	0.4671	0.2923	0.6492	0.6455	0.4908	*0.9599*	0.8074	**0.9935**
Airplane100	P	87.48	12.52	49.25	47.48	80.20	88.04	**90.25**	*89.98*
	J	0	15.26	15.36	11.72	7.90	*55.81*	40.33	**56.19**
	I	0.4774	0.2041	0.4055	0.3634	0.5080	*0.9770*	0.8514	**0.9910**

criterion P without regard to criterion J, Baseline1 could be considered as a good result, which is absolutely wrong. This indicate the reasonability to introduce the criterion I to obtain the tradeoff between P and J. For all the datasets, Baseline1 and Baseline2 achieve low performance, while our method achieves the best performance on criterion I.

4   Conclusion

In this paper, we take advantage of the powerful representation ability of CNN features to do unsupervised object discovery and cosegmentation. First, we use VGG features to do k-means clustering and find for positive examples as a prior knowledge. Then we use mid-level visual information - CNN feature pyramid to estimate the dense correspondences between regions with common semantics within the whole dataset to achieve reliable image matching. Last, we combine with two regularization terms to do overall optimization and obtain the final segmentation results. Experiments on complicated Internet images show the effectiveness and superior performance of our method.

References

1. Viola, P., Jones, M.: Rapid object detection using a boosted cascade of simple features. In: IEEE Computer Society Conference on Computer Vision and Pattern Recognition, vol. 1, pp. 511–518. IEEE Press, Kauai (2001)
2. Papageorgiou, C.P., Oren, M., Poggio, T.: A general framework for object detection. In: International Conference on Computer Vision, vol. 108, pp. 555–562. IEEE Press, Bombay (1998)
3. Felzenszwalb, P.F., Girshick, R.B., Mcallester, D., Ramanan, D.: Object detection with discriminatively trained part-based models. IEEE Trans. Pattern Anal. Mach. Intell. **32**, 1627–1645 (2014)

4. Szegedy, C., Toshev, A., Erhan, D.: Deep neural networks for object detection. In: Advances in Neural Information Processing Systems, vol. 26, pp. 2553–2561 (2013)
5. Girshick, R., Donahue, J., Darrell, T., Malik, J.: Rich feature hierarchies for accurate object detection and semantic segmentation. In: Computer, Science, pp. 580–587 (2014)
6. Barghout, L., Lee, L.: Perceptual information processing system. Adv. Comput. 28, 1–116 (2003)
7. Shi, J., Malik, J.: Normalized cuts and image segmentation. IEEE Trans. Pattern Anal. Mach. Intell. 22, 888–905 (2000)
8. Felzenszwalb, P.F., Huttenlocher, D.P.: Efficient graph-based image segmentation. Int. J. Comput. Vis. 59, 167–181 (2004)
9. Rother, C., Kolmogorov, V., Blake, A.: GrabCut: interactive foreground extraction using iterated graph cuts. In: ACM SIGGRAPH, vol. 23, pp. 309–314. Los Angeles (2004)
10. Long, J., Shelhamer, E., Darrell, T.: Fully convolutional networks for semantic segmentation. IEEE Trans. Pattern Anal. Mach. Intell. 39, 640 (2015)
11. Chen, L.C., Papandreou, G., Kokkinos, I., Murphy, K., Yuille, A.L.: Semantic image segmentation with deep convolutional nets and fully connected CRFs. In: Computer, Science, pp. 357–361 (2014)
12. Hariharan, B., Arbeláez, P., Girshick, R., Malik, J.: Simultaneous detection and segmentation. In: Fleet, D., Pajdla, T., Schiele, B., Tuytelaars, T. (eds.) ECCV 2014. LNCS, vol. 8695, pp. 297–312. Springer, Cham (2014). https://doi.org/10.1007/978-3-319-10584-0_20
13. Rother, C., Minka, T., Blake, A., Kolmogorov, V.: Cosegmentation of image pairs by histogram matching - incorporating a global constraint into MRFs. In: IEEE Conference on Computer Vision and Pattern Recognition, vol. 1, pp. 993–1000. IEEE Press, New York (2006)
14. Hochbaum, D.S., Singh, V.: An efficient algorithm for co-segmentation. In: IEEE International Conference on Computer Vision, vol. 30, pp. 269–276. IEEE Press, Kyoto (2009)
15. Joulin, A., Bach, F., Ponce, J.: Discriminative clustering for image cosegmentation. In: IEEE Conference on Computer Vision and Pattern Recognition, vol. 238, pp. 1943–1950. IEEE Press, San Francisco (2010)
16. Kim, G., Xing, E.P., Li, F.F., Kanade, T.: Distributed cosegmentation via submodular optimization on anisotropic diffusion. In: IEEE International Conference on Computer Vision, vol. 23, pp. 169–176. IEEE Press, Barcelona (2011)
17. Joulin, A., Bach, F., Ponce, J.: Multi-class cosegmentation. In: IEEE Conference on Computer Vision and Pattern Recognition, vol. 157, pp. 542–549. IEEE Press, Providence (2012)
18. Tuytelaars, T., Lampert, C.H., Blaschko, M.B., Buntine, W.: Unsupervised object discovery: a comparison. Int. J. Comput. Vis. 88, 284–302 (2010)
19. Zhu, J.Y., Wu, J., Wei, Y., Chang, E.: Unsupervised object class discovery via saliency-guided multiple class learning. In: IEEE Conference on Computer Vision and Pattern Recognition, vol. 37, pp. 3218–3225. IEEE Press, Providence (2012)
20. Rubinstein, M., Joulin, A., Kopf, J., Liu, C.: Unsupervised joint object discovery and segmentation in internet images. In: IEEE Conference on Computer Vision and Pattern Recognition, vol. 9, pp. 1939–1946. IEEE Press, Portland (2013)
21. Chen, X., Shrivastava, A., Gupta, A.: Enriching visual knowledge bases via object discovery and segmentation. In: IEEE Conference on Computer Vision and Pattern Recognition, vol. 40, pp. 2035–2042. IEEE Press, Columbus (2014)

22. Yu, W., Yang, K., Bai, Y., Yao, H., Rui, Y.: DNN flow: DNN feature pyramid based image matching. In: British Machine Vision Conference, vol. 109, pp. 1–10. Nottingham (2014)
23. Cheng, M.M., Zhang, G.X., Mitra, N.J., Huang, X., Hu, S.M.: Global contrast based salient region detection. In: IEEE Transactions on Pattern Analysis and Machine Intelligence, vol. 37, pp. 569–582. IEEE Press (2011)

Semantic Segmentation Using Fully Convolutional Networks and Random Walk with Prediction Prior

Xiaoyu Lei$^{(\boxtimes)}$, Yao Lu$^{(\boxtimes)}$, Tingxi Liu$^{(\boxtimes)}$, and Xiaoxue Shi$^{(\boxtimes)}$

Beijing Laboratory of Intelligent Information Technology,
School of Computer Science, Beijing Institute of Technology,
Beijing 100081, China
{leixiaoyu,vis_yl,liutx,shixiaoxue}@bit.edu.cn

Abstract. Fully Convolutional Networks (FCNs) for semantic segmentation always lead to coarse predictions, especially in border regions. Improved models of FCNs with conditional random fields (CRFs), however, cause significant increase in model complexity and scattered distribution of pixels in border regions. To address these issues, we propose a novel approach combining random walk with FCNs to capture global features and refine border regions of segmentation results. We design a double-erosion mechanism on the prediction results of FCNs to initialize random walk, and apply prediction scores as a global prior of random walk model by adding an extra item into the weight matrix of the graph constructed from an image. Experimental results show that the proposed method acts better than Dense CRF in pixel accuracy and mean IoU, and obtains smoother results. In addition, our method significantly reduces the time cost of refinement process.

Keywords: Semantic segmentation · Fully Convolutional Networks
Random walk

1 Introduction

Fully convolutional networks (FCNs) [13] are proposed for pixelwise prediction tasks like semantic segmentation by transforming fully connected layers in classification models like VGG16 [16] into convolution layers. This insight enables convolutional networks to make dense predictions.

Inspired by FCNs, Deeplab [1,2] proposes "atrous convolution" to enlarge the resolution of feature map, and uses atrous spatial pyramid pooling (ASPP) to segment objects at multiple scales. Unfortunately, despite using many sophisticated mechanisms like atrous convolution, the innate properties of convolutional and pooling layers in convolutional neural networks still lead to coarse results with regard to pixelwise prediction, especially in border regions between semantic objects and background.

Prior works like [8,9] have applied probabilistic graphical models to make structure prediction. [1,2] use DenseCRF as a post-processing step after convolution neural network, which fails to accurately capture semantic relationships

© Springer International Publishing AG, part of Springer Nature 2018
B. Zeng et al. (Eds.): PCM 2017, LNCS 10736, pp. 129–138, 2018.
https://doi.org/10.1007/978-3-319-77383-4_13

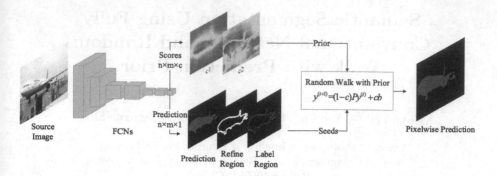

Fig. 1. Architecture of our approach. The prediction scores of FCNs which has dimensions $m \times n \times c$ is used as prior of random walk, and the prediction results ($m \times n \times 1$) will be split into three parts: border regions, label regions and fixed regions. The details of partition criterion will be introduced in Sect. 4.

and leads to spatially scattered distribution of pixels in border regions. While [12,19] attempt to integrate CRFs into convolutional network and train them in end-to-end style, which cause vastly increase in model complexity and time cost due to a large number of parameters or recurrent layers.

Random walk (RW) [14] is used in many tasks like segmentation [3–5,7], web page ranking [15], classification [17] etc. RW is firstly used for interactive image segmentation in [4,5]. Based on it, many improved methods like RWR [7], PARW [18] are introduced to obtain better performance for challenging images with weak boundaries and complex textures. X. Dong et al. [3] summarize these methods that satisfy the sub-Markov property [10] in a unified framework.

In this paper, we introduce a novel approach combining FCNs and random walk with prior for semantic segmentation. We modify random walk model by adding a prior probability map, which is computed from the prediction scores in FCNs, into the random walks formulation, making the process segment out the details that most RW-based algorithms omit. This random walk module is used to refine the segmentation results of FCNs. Thus, our proposed method leads to preferable performance in terms of both spatially smoothness and accuracy. The main contributions of our work are summarized as follows:

(1) We design a double-erosion mechanism on the prediction results of FCNs to define border regions need to be refined and perform initialization of random walk;
(2) We propose a random walk model with prediction prior, which use per-class prediction scores from FCNs as global prior, instead of generating prior from manual labeled seeds (like in [3]);
(3) Unlike prior methods that use CRFs, we implement an innovative approach which use Random Walk to refine the segmentation results of FCNs.

Our experiments show that our method acts better than original FCNs and DenseCRF [8,9] in pixel accuracy and IoU, while spends less time than Dense-CRF. The procedure of our proposed approach is depicted in Fig. 1.

2   Random Walk with Prior

2.1   Sub-Markov Random Walk

Let $G = (V, E)$ denote an undirected graph with a set of nodes V and a set of edges E. Each node v_i in V uniquely identifies an image pixel x_i, and each edge e_{ij} in $E \subseteq V \times V$ connects two nodes v_i and v_j in 8-connected neighborhood system. The weight $w_{ij} \in \mathbf{W}$ is assigned to the edge e_{ij} to measure the similarity between two nodes. $\mathbf{W}$ is defined as follows:

$$w_{ij} = exp(-\frac{\|I_i - I_j\|^2}{\sigma}) + \epsilon, \tag{1}$$

where I_i and I_j indicate the intensities at two nodes v_i and v_j in Lab color space. σ is a controlling parameter which is set as $1/60$ in this paper, and ϵ is a small constant as 10^{-6}. Let $\mathbf{D}$ indicate a $n \times n$ diagonal matrix, which stores the degree values for each node: $d_{ii} = \sum_{j=1}^{n} w_{ij}$ for all j except $i = j$. n is the number of nodes. Then generally, we can express random walk transition matrix as $\mathbf{P} = \mathbf{D}^{-1}\mathbf{W}$.

According to [7], a random walker leaves a graph G from a node v_i with probability c_i and walks to the other adjacent nodes in G with probability $1 - c_i$. Let $r_{im}^{l_k}$ be the staying probability that this random walker stays at the m-th labeled nodes $v_m^{l_k}$ with label l_k, then the vector notation $\mathbf{r}_m^{l_k} = [r_{im}^{l_k}]_{n \times 1}$ is formulated as follows:

$$\mathbf{r}_m^{l_k} = (\mathbf{I} - (\mathbf{I} - \mathbf{D}_c)\mathbf{P})^{-1}\mathbf{D}_c\mathbf{b}_m^{l_k}, \tag{2}$$

where $\mathbf{b}_m^{l_k}$ is an indicating vector indicates whether $v_i = v_m^{l_k}$, $\mathbf{D}_c$ is a diagonal matrix whose diagonal element is c_i.

Actually, since we should consider all seeded nodes with a same label, an average staying probability $r_i^{l_k}$ on a set of seeded nodes with label l_k is used as the likelihood of assigning this node to label l_k. A vector formulation of this average steady-state probability $\mathbf{r}^{l_k}$ can be given as follows:

$$\mathbf{r}^{l_k} = \frac{1}{Z_k M_k} \sum_{m=1}^{M_k} \mathbf{r}_m^{l_k} = \frac{1}{Z_k M_k}(\mathbf{I} - (\mathbf{I} - \mathbf{D}_c)\mathbf{P})^{-1}\mathbf{D}_c\mathbf{b}^{l_k}, \tag{3}$$

where $\mathbf{b}^{l_k}$ is an indicating vector indicates whether v_i has label $l_k(k \in [1, K]$, K is the number of labels), M_k is the number of seeds with label l_k, Z_k is a normalized constant. The final labeling result $\mathbf{R}$ (i.e., the segmentation result) for each node $v_i \in V$ is obtained as follows:

$$\mathbf{R}_i = \arg\max_{l_k} r_i^{l_k}. \tag{4}$$

2.2   SubRW with Prediction Prior

Our segmentation model is based on a generative process where a random walker moves along the nodes of a graph with some specific seeds, which are obtained from the output of FCNs in this work. Thus, our algorithm is sensitive to the segmentation result of FCNs. In other word, if FCNs lose some details of foreground region, the probabilities of a random walker starts from these seeds to the detail parts will be small. Intuitively, the elongated details in an image "disappear" during random walk process. Most RW-based algorithms omit these kind of tiny parts as well. To address this issue, we modify the sub-Markov random walks mentioned above by adding a prediction prior information into weight $\mathbf{W}$.

Assume a label l_k has an intensity distribution H_k for each node, where u_i^k denotes the probability density belonging to H_k at node v_i. This distribution is obtained from prediction scores of the FCNs here. Given these prior distributions, we can reconsider the weight matrix $\mathbf{W}$ as follows:

$$\mathbf{W} = \mathbf{W}_o + \lambda \mathbf{W}_u, \tag{5}$$

where matrix $\mathbf{W}_u$ implies the added prior information computed from the prediction scores of FCNs. λ is a regularization parameter, which measures the importance of the prior distribution. $\mathbf{W}_o$ is the original weight defined in Eq. 1.

Partition the nodes into two sets: seed nodes and unseeded nodes. We may assume without loss of generality that the nodes in $\mathbf{W}_o$ and $\mathbf{W}_u$ are ordered such that seed nodes are first and unseeded nodes are second: $\mathbf{W}_u = [\mathbf{W}_u^* \ \mathbf{0}]$. We may further assume that these seed nodes in $\mathbf{W}_u^*$ are ordered by label l_k, i.e. $\mathbf{W}_u^* = [\mathbf{W}_1, \mathbf{W}_2, \ldots, \mathbf{W}_K]$. Then the piror probability density u_i^k is set as the element of each $\mathbf{W}_k$. In order to match the original wight, the added wight matrix is stretched out to M_k times: $\mathbf{W}_k = \frac{1}{M_k}[\mathbf{u}^k, \mathbf{u}^k, \ldots]_{n \times M_k}$, where $\mathbf{u}^k$ is $[u_i^k]_{n \times 1}$. So, the weight matrix $\mathbf{W}$ in Eq. 5 with label piror is given as follows:

$$w_{ij} = w_o^{ij} + \lambda \frac{1}{M_j} u_i^j b_j, \tag{6}$$

where $b_j = 1$ if v_j is seeded and vice versa. Then the random walk transition matrix $\mathbf{P} = \mathbf{D}^{-1}\mathbf{W}$ can be obtained as follows:

$$
\begin{aligned}
p_{ij} &= \frac{w_{ij}}{\sum_{j=1}^n w_{ij}} = \frac{w_o^{ij} + \lambda \frac{1}{M_j} u_i^j b_j}{d_o^{ii} + \lambda \sum_{k=1}^K u_i^k} \\
&= \frac{w_o^{ij}}{d_o^{ii} + \lambda \sum_{k=1}^K u_i^k} + \frac{1}{M_k} \frac{\lambda u_i^k}{d_o^{ii} + \lambda \sum_{k=1}^K u_i^k},
\end{aligned}
\tag{7}
$$

where d_o^{ii} is element of the original diagonal degree matrix.

Given the transition probability $\mathbf{P}$ formulated by Eq. 7 on a graph with prior, the staying probability $r_{im}^{l_k}$ that random walker starts at v_i stays at the m-th labeled nodes $v_m^{l_k}$ with label l_k can be formulated just as mentioned previously in Eqs. 2 and 3. According to the decision rule of each pixel x_i for image segmentation in Eq. 4, the final segmentation result with a prediction prior is obtained.

3   Combination of FCNs and Random Walk

RW-based algorithms mostly concentrate on interactive segmentation, which means users need to offer manual inputs (for example, user-specified scribbles) to initialize the model and propagate label information across the whole image. In this work, we propose a novel double-erosion mechanism to utilize the prediction outputs of FCNs and perform the initialization of random walk.

Double-erosion mechanism is depicted in Fig. 2. Briefly, we perform two steps of erosion at all of semantic classes (including background) in prediction map, and divide the map into three parts: border, label and fixed regions. We will explain the details in the following subsections.

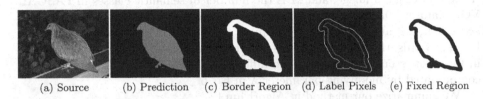

(a) Source   (b) Prediction   (c) Border Region   (d) Label Pixels   (e) Fixed Region

Fig. 2. Partition of FCNs prediction results. After the first erosion on each of the classes (background and bird in this example), the removed pixels are defined as border regions that need to be refined. Similarly, the pixels removed in the second erosion are used as label pixels, and the rest regions are fixed during random walk process.

3.1 Border Region

As mentioned above, we attempt to refine border regions between each semantic objects and background. [11] defines the pixels in these areas as "extremely hard pixels", not only because of coarse prediction, but also about 30% annotation error.

The first erosion step determines the regions need to be refined. Here we define e_s^1 as erosion stride, which means the size of structure element used in first erosion. For example, if we use a disk structure element to perform erosion, then e_s^1 equals the radius of disk element. We define the regions that are removed after first erosion as border regions. Obviously, the area of border regions increase along with e_s^1.

3.2 Initialization

RW-based methods requires label pixels from user-specified scribbles or inter-action for initialization. Generally, the random walk methods achieve best per-formance when these manual remarks distribute near the boundary of different objects.

In order to obtain proper points as label pixels, we apply the second erosion step at size of e_s^2 ($e_s^1 < e_s^2$), and define the subtraction between first and second erosion steps as label pixels. Denote $e_m = e_s^2 - e_s^1$ as the margin of two erosion steps, which controls the number of label pixels and has a remarkable effect on the time cost of random walk process.

In Sect. 4, we will illustrate the influence of these parameters on the segmentation results.

3.3   Prior of Random Walk

As we mentioned above, the user-specified label only works at the seeded nodes. What we want to do is to construct the prior distribution of all unseeded nodes. This distribution can be learned via many approach such as Gaussian Mixture Model (GMM) in [3].

The FCNs outputs contains the prediction scores of each pixel. As shown in Fig. 1, the outputs of layer fc8 has dimensions $300 \times 500 \times 21$, where 300×500 is the size of original image, and 21 is the number of semantic classes in PASCAL VOC dataset. Obviously, there is a positive correlation between the prediction $score = [i, j, c]$ and the possibility of pixel p_{ij} to be labeled as semantic class c. In other words, the prediction scores and the prior of random walk are consistent in terms of essence and form, while different in scale. This difference could be compensated by modifying parameter λ in Eq. 5.

We summarize our method in Algorithm 1.

Algorithm 1. Overall algorithm of the proposed approach.

Require: Original image $I_{m \times n \times 3}$ with k classes, $m \times n$ indicates the size of image.
Ensure: Prediction result $R_{m \times n}$ in pixelwise.
1: Obtain the FCNs prediction scores $S_{m \times n \times k}$, prediction map $M = \arg \max S$;
2: Adapt scores $S_{m \times n \times k}$ as prior u as shown in Sect. 2.1;
3: Split M into 3 parts: border regions, fixed regions and label pixels $L = \{l_1, l_2, ..., l_k\}$ using double-erosion;
4: Compute weight matrix W by Eq. 5 and transition probabilities P by Eq. 7;
5: Compute reaching probabilities $r_{m \times n \times k}$ by Eq. 3;
6: Obtain segmentation results $R_{m \times n} = \arg \max r_{m \times n \times k}$.

---

4   Experiment

We evaluate our approach in PASCAL VOC 2012 Segmentation Dataset, which contains 4369 samples for training and validation, and 21 semantic classes. Several state-of-the-art models including Deeplabv2-VGG16 and Deeplabv2-Resnet101 are used as baselines. The comparison is based on two metrics of common semantic segmentation evaluation, pixel accuracy and intersection over union (IoU).

Let n_{ii} denote the number of pixels predicted correctly, and n_{ij} is the number of pixels of class i predicted to belong to class j. n_c is the number of classes, $t_i = \sum_i n_{ij}$ is the total number of pixels of class i. Then we have:

(1) pixel accuracy: $Acc = \sum_i n_{ii} / \sum_i p_i$
(2) mean accuracy: $mAcc = Acc / n_c$
(3) mean IoU: $IoU = \sum_i n_{ii} / (t_i + \sum_j n_{ji} - n_{ii}) / n_c$

In addition to numerical comparisons, Fig. 3 shows part of prediction results comparing with base models and CRFs. We could infer from the results that

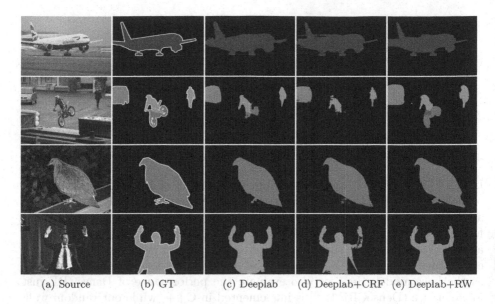

(a) Source   (b) GT   (c) Deeplab   (d) Deeplab+CRF (e) Deeplab+RW

Fig. 3. Comparison between our approach and base model with DenseCRF. Here we use Deeplab-ResNet101 as the base model.

our approach outperforms the base models with CRFs, reflected in more precise outlines and smoother border pixels distribution.

We use caffe [6] to build the base models and implement the random walk algorithm in Matlab. All the methods are tested on Intel Core i7-4790k CPU and Nvidia GTX Titan X GPU.

4.1   Comparison with Base Model and CRFs

Table 1 shows the performance of our approach comparing with base models and post-processing CRFs measured in pixel accuracy. Our approach yields 0.9%–1.3% promotion above the baselines according to mean IoU, and outperforms CRFs by 0.8%–1.8% in terms of mean pixel accuracy.

Table 1. Comparison according to pixel accuracy and IoU

Method	Pixel accuracy	Mean accuracy	Mean IoU
Deeplabv2-VGG16	92.605%	80.963%	68.957%
Deeplabv2-VGG16 + CRF	**93.482%**	81.376%	**71.567%**
Deeplabv2-VGG16 + RW	93.303%	**82.107%**	71.269 %
Deeplabv2-Resnet101	94.626%	84.160%	76.460%
Deeplabv2-Resnet101 + CRF	94.975%	84.233%	77.561%
Deeplabv2-Resnet101 + RW	**95.091%**	**86.041%**	**77.708%**

Table 2. Performance comparison among CRFs, RW-GMM and our method

Method	Pixel accuracy	Mean IoU	Time cost
DenseCRF	84.233%	77.561%	2.805 s
RW with GMM prior	85.733%	77.054%	2.071 s
RW with FCNs prior	**86.041%**	**77.708%**	**1.541 s**

4.2 Time Performance

Unlike GMM methods in [3], we utilize the outputs of FCNs as prior instead of leaning from labeled nodes distribution. This insight not only improves the accuracy, but also significantly reduces the time cost. In Table 2, we give the performances of random walk with FCNs prior and GMM prior in terms of time cost and pixel accuracy. The time cost is represented by averaging processing time of every single image in PASCAL VOC test set and tested on Deeplab-Resnet101 as the base model. Here we also evaluate the performance of DenseCRF just for reference (DenseCRF [1,2] is implemented in C++, while our random walk methods are programmed in Matlab). As shown in Table 2, the time cost of our method is reduced by 46.2% and 25.6% compared with CRFs and random walk with GMM prior respectively.

4.3 Effects of Different Parameters

As introduced in Sect. 3, we use double-erosion to split the prediction results into three parts. It is observed that the size of erosion elements e_s^1, e_s^2 and the margin between two steps of erosion $e_m = e_s^2 - e_s^1$ has a certain degree influence on the results. We can draw a conclusion from Fig. 4 intuitively that when e_s^1 locates in 5–8, our approach could achieve better performance. If $e_s^1 \leq 4$, some pixels near the border region, which might be wrong predicted, would be selected as label nodes. The other extreme is when $e_s^1 \geq 10$, label pixels will lose informations of border and contours, which probably leads to decrease in segment accuracy.

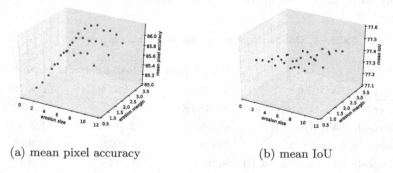

    (a) mean pixel accuracy   (b) mean IoU

Fig. 4. Influences of e_s^1, e_m on mean pixel accuracy and mean IoU, respectively.

Besides, we also explore the effects of iteration. The experimental results show that after several iterations, the mean pixel accuracy will increase significantly, but the background pixel accuracy, overall pixel accuracy and mean IoU decline along with the iteration steps. One possible explanation for this phenomenon might be that, semantic objects tend to 'dilate' and the probabilities of border pixels to be predicted as semantic objects will increase during the iteration.

5 Conclusion

In this work, we propose a novel approach combining random walk model with prior into FCNs to refine border regions of segmentation results. We design a double-erosion mechanism to perform initialization using the prediction results of FCNs, and apply prediction scores as a global prior of random walk model. Comparing with base models and CRFs, our approach yields an improvement according to mean IoU and pixel accuracy. As shown in Fig. 3, our approach outperforms the base models with CRFs in the details of border region, specific performances: (1) more precise outlines; (2) smoother border pixels distribution. Meanwhile, our method significantly reduces the time cost of segmentation.

Acknowledgments. This work was supported by the National Natural Science Foundation of China (No. 61273273).

References

1. Chen, L.C., Papandreou, G., Kokkinos, I., Murphy, K., Yuille, A.L.: Semantic image segmentation with deep convolutional nets and fully connected CRFs. arXiv preprint arXiv:1412.7062 (2014)
2. Chen, L.C., Papandreou, G., Kokkinos, I., Murphy, K., Yuille, A.L.: DeepLab: semantic image segmentation with deep convolutional nets, atrous convolution, and fully connected CRFs. arXiv preprint arXiv:1606.00915 (2016)
3. Dong, X., Shen, J., Shao, L., Van Gool, L.: Sub-Markov random walk for image segmentation. IEEE Trans. Image Process. **25**(2), 516–527 (2016)
4. Grady, L.: Random walks for image segmentation. IEEE Trans. Pattern Anal. Mach. Intell. **28**(11), 1768–1783 (2006)
5. Grady, L., Funka-Lea, G.: Multi-label image segmentation for medical applications based on graph-theoretic electrical potentials. In: Sonka, M., Kakadiaris, I.A., Kybic, J. (eds.) CVAMIA/MMBIA -2004. LNCS, vol. 3117, pp. 230–245. Springer, Heidelberg (2004). https://doi.org/10.1007/978-3-540-27816-0_20
6. Jia, Y., Shelhamer, E., Donahue, J., Karayev, S., Long, J., Girshick, R., Guadarrama, S., Darrell, T.: Caffe: convolutional architecture for fast feature embedding. In: Proceedings of the 22nd ACM International Conference on Multimedia, pp. 675–678. ACM (2014)
7. Kim, T.H., Lee, K.M., Lee, S.U.: Generative image segmentation using random walks with restart. In: Forsyth, D., Torr, P., Zisserman, A. (eds.) ECCV 2008. LNCS, vol. 5304, pp. 264–275. Springer, Heidelberg (2008). https://doi.org/10.1007/978-3-540-88690-7_20

8. Koltun, V.: Efficient inference in fully connected CRFs with Gaussian edge potentials. Adv. Neural Inf. Process. Syst 2(3), 4 (2011)
9. Krähenbühl, P., Koltun, V.: Parameter learning and convergent inference for dense random fields. In: ICML, pp. III-513–III-521 (2013)
10. Lawler, G.F., Limic, V.: Random Walk: A Modern Introduction, vol. 123. Cambridge University Press, Cambridge (2010)
11. Li, X., Liu, Z., Luo, P., Loy, C.C., Tang, X.: Not all pixels are equal: difficulty-aware semantic segmentation via deep layer cascade. arXiv preprint arXiv:1704.01344 (2017)
12. Lin, G., Shen, C., van den Hengel, A., Reid, I.: Efficient piecewise training of deep structured models for semantic segmentation. In: Proceedings of the IEEE Conference on Computer Vision and Pattern Recognition, pp. 3194–3203 (2016)
13. Long, J., Shelhamer, E., Darrell, T.: Fully convolutional networks for semantic segmentation. In: Proceedings of the IEEE Conference on Computer Vision and Pattern Recognition, pp. 3431–3440 (2015)
14. Lovász, L.: Random walks on graphs. Combinatorics, Paul erdos is eighty 2, 1–46 (1993)
15. Page, L., Brin, S., Motwani, R., Winograd, T.: The pagerank citation ranking: bringing order to the web. Technical report, Stanford InfoLab (1999)
16. Simonyan, K., Zisserman, A.: Very deep convolutional networks for large-scale image recognition. arXiv preprint arXiv:1409.1556 (2014)
17. Szummer, M., Jaakkola, T.: Partially labeled classification with Markov random walks. In: NIPS, vol. 14 (2001)
18. Wu, X.M., Li, Z., So, A.M., Wright, J., Chang, S.F.: Learning with partially absorbing random walks. In: Advances in Neural Information Processing Systems, pp. 3077–3085 (2012)
19. Zheng, S., Jayasumana, S., Romera-Paredes, B., Vineet, V., Su, Z., Du, D., Huang, C., Torr, P.H.: Conditional random fields as recurrent neural networks. In: Proceedings of the IEEE International Conference on Computer Vision, pp. 1529–1537 (2015)

Multi-modality Fusion Network for Action Recognition

Kai Huang, Zheng Qin$^{(\boxtimes)}$, Kaiping Xu, Shuxiong Ye,
and Guolong Wang

School of Software, Tsinghua University, Beijing, China
{huang-k15,xkp13,ysx15,
wanggl16}@mails.tsinghua.edu.cn,
qingzh@tsinghua.edu.cn

Abstract. Deep neural networks have outperformed many traditional methods for action recognition on video datasets, such as UCF101 and HMDB51. This paper aims to explore the performance of fusion of different convolutional networks with different dimensions. The main contribution of this work is *multi-modality fusion network* (MMFN), a novel framework for action recognition, which combines 2D ConvNets and 3D ConvNets. The accuracy of MMFN outperforms the state-of-the-art deep-learning-based methods on the datasets of UCF101 (94.6%) and HMDB51 (69.7%).

Keywords: Action recognition · 2D ConvNets · 3D ConvNets
Fusion

1 Introduction

Human action recognition mainly focuses on recognizing specific events performed by humans from a sequence of video frames. It can be applied on many scenarios including video surveillance, customer attributes, human-computer interaction and elderly protection devices. The performance of action recognition depends on temporal and spatial features extracted from video. In real-world scenarios, it becomes a challenging problem due to view point variations, background clutter, cameras dithering, etc.

Recently, Convolutional Neural Networks (ConvNets) have shown their power of visual representations [1]. ConvNets have quickly taken over majority of image classification tasks, ranging from objects, scenes to complex events [3–5]. Then, ConvNets were also extended to action recognition in video in recent years [6, 7]. However, current ConvNets have no significant advantage over early methods using hand-crafted video features.

As shown in [1], 2D ConvNets have strong analysis ability on spatial features. However, it is hard to extract temporal information with 2D kernel from single frame or several frames of input video, which is a crucial issue for action recognition. The 3D convolution is achieved by convolving a 3D kernel on the video volume formed by stacking consecutive frames. 3D ConvNets prevent from missing spatio-temporal information by keeping feature map in the form of cube during feature extraction procedure.

© Springer International Publishing AG, part of Springer Nature 2018
B. Zeng et al. (Eds.): PCM 2017, LNCS 10736, pp. 139–149, 2018.
https://doi.org/10.1007/978-3-319-77383-4_14

Though 3D ConvNets can extract more extra features than 2D ConvNets, there is no good pre-trained model for 3D ConvNets like the ImageNet [2] pre-trained model for 2D ConvNets. Therefore, the performance of 3D ConvNets is not good enough in action recognition task. Two-stream network [8] combining the feature of single frame and multiple optical flow frames is significantly better than single modality recognition, which proves that fusion of networks will achieve good performance. Inspired by this breakthrough, we propose an effective network fused by 2D ConvNets and 3D ConvNets, called *multi-modality fusion network* (MMFN). This framework is a combination of different modalities, including 3D spatio-temporal, 2D spatial and 2D temporal modalities. Our contributions in this paper are:

- Fusion of 2D ConvNets and 3D ConvNets significantly improves the performance of action recognition.
- We find out the best average method for vectors of video clips in C3D framework.
- Our performance outperforms the current state-of-the-art deep-learning-based methods on UCF101 and HMDB51.

2 Related Works

Action recognition aims to find the actions in a short video, which is a hot topic in computer vision community. It has been studied for many years [6–11]. According to the features extracted from videos, previous related works can be divided into three categories: (1) Traditional-features-based methods, (2) 2D-ConvNets-based methods, (3) 3D-ConvNets-based methods.

Traditional-features-based methods. These methods consist of two steps: (1) extract traditional features, (2) classify features with classifiers. The first step is obviously more significant. To improve recognition performance, several descriptors were introduced. Robotics [12] proposed SIFT descriptor, which is distinctive, invariant to rotation and robust to large distortion. Dalal and Triggs [13] have shown that using HOG descriptor gives good results in person detection. HOF introduced by Laptev *et al.* [14] enhances the performance on a variety of datasets. Dalal *et al.* [15] proposed the motion boundary histograms (MBH) descriptor for human detection, which is robust to camera motion. Laptev [16] presented spatio-temporal interest points (SIPs) to extract features from video. Later, some other spatio-temporal features like Cuboids [17] and HOG3D [18] have shown great abilities in action recognition. A series of descriptors based on trajectory, like dense trajectories [19] and improved dense trajectories [20], can eliminate camera motion and improve the performance significantly.

2D-ConvNets-based methods. Simonyan and Zisserman [8] proposed a two-stream ConvNets consist of 2D spatial ConvNets and 2D temporal ConvNets finetuned with the ImageNet pre-trained model. Yue-Hei Ng *et al.* [21] combined the 2D ConvNets with LSTM and exploited the Sports-1M dataset pre-trained model for 2D ConvNets. Sun *et al.* [22] introduced a 2D ConvNets called $F_{ST}CN$, which is a cascaded deep architecture learning the effective spatio-temporal features. Wu *et al.* [23] introduced a novel 2D ConvNets explored inter-feature and inter-class relationships that improved video classification performance. Wang *et al.* [10] proposed a temporal segment networks (TSN) combining the idea of two-stream and sparse temporal sampling strategy surpassed the performance of the state of the art.

3D-ConvNets-based methods. Ji *et al.* [11] proposed a 3D ConvNets, fed with gray features, optical flow features and gradient features extracted from contiguous frames, for human action recognition. Zhu *et al.* [24] introduced a deep framework together with stochastic out operation. Convolutional 3D (C3D) method proposed by Tran *et al.* [9] learned 3D ConvNets with all kernel size of 3 × 3 × 3 on clips of video can yield good performance. Varol *et al.* [7] presented and evaluated the long-term temporal convolutions (LTC), which improved the performance significantly.

3 Multi-modality Fusion Network

In this section, we describe our method for action recognition with fusion network in detail, namely multi-modality fusion network. This architecture has three main parts, namely C3D framework, TSN framework and fusion scheme. We first introduce the basic structure and concept of C3D framework and describe the approach to extract spatio-temporal modality score from this framework. Then, we give detailed descriptions of TSN framework and explain how to extract RGB, TVL1 and warped TVL1 temporal modality score from this framework. Finally, we demonstrate how to conduct fusion for these two frameworks. The structure of the multi-modality fusion network is illustrated in Fig. 1. The video frames are fed to C3D and TSN and then compute four modality scores respectively. The final score is the fusion of these four modality scores.

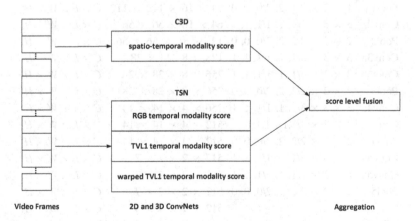

Fig. 1. Multi-modality fusion network

3.1 C3D Framework

We used C3D framework proposed by Tran *et al.* [9] to extract spatio-temporal features from videos. To distinguish them from other features extracted by other networks, we name them spatio-temporal modality features.

Figure 2 illustrates the difference between 2D convolution and 3D convolution. 2D convolution applied in an image and slid on height and width dimensions results in an image. Due to the 2D image, we can hardly extract temporal information from it. 3D convolution can avoid losing temporal information. It is applied in a volume and slid on height, width and length dimensions, which still generates a volume. Similarly, the pooling operation is a 3D operation as well, so that the output can be always a volume during the convolution procedure.

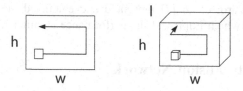

Fig. 2. Difference between 2D convolution and 3D convolution

The hyperparameters of C3D is summarized in Table 1, where C denotes channels, L denotes length, W and H denotes width and height, F denotes the dimension of the feature vector and N denotes the number of classes.

Table 1. C3D hyperparameters

Layer	Size/Stride/Pad	Input size	Dimension order
Conv1	$3 \times 3 \times 3/1, 1, 1/1, 1, 1$	$3 \times 16 \times 112 \times 112$	$C \times L \times W \times H$
Pool1	$1 \times 2 \times 2/1, 2, 2/0, 0, 0$	$64 \times 16 \times 112 \times 112$	$C \times L \times W \times H$
Conv2	$3 \times 3 \times 3/1, 1, 1/1, 1, 1$	$64 \times 16 \times 56 \times 56$	$C \times L \times W \times H$
Pool2	$2 \times 2 \times 2/2, 2, 2/0, 0, 0$	$128 \times 16 \times 56 \times 56$	$C \times L \times W \times H$
Conv3a	$3 \times 3 \times 3/1, 1, 1/1, 1, 1$	$128 \times 8 \times 28 \times 28$	$C \times L \times W \times H$
Conv3b	$3 \times 3 \times 3/1, 1, 1/1, 1, 1$	$256 \times 8 \times 28 \times 28$	$C \times L \times W \times H$
Pool3	$2 \times 2 \times 2/2, 2, 2/0, 0, 0$	$256 \times 8 \times 28 \times 28$	$C \times L \times W \times H$
Conv4a	$3 \times 3 \times 3/1, 1, 1/1, 1, 1$	$256 \times 4 \times 14 \times 14$	$C \times L \times W \times H$
Conv4b	$3 \times 3 \times 3/1,1,1/1/1,1$	$512 \times 4 \times 14 \times 14$	$C \times L \times W \times H$
Pool4	$2 \times 2 \times 2/2, 2, 2/0, 0, 0$	$512 \times 4 \times 14 \times 14$	$C \times L \times W \times H$
Conv5a	$3 \times 3 \times 3/1, 1, 1/1, 1, 1$	$512 \times 2 \times 7 \times 7$	$C \times L \times W \times H$
Conv5b	$3 \times 3 \times 3/1, 1, 1/1, 1, 1$	$512 \times 2 \times 7 \times 7$	$C \times L \times W \times H$
Pool5	$2 \times 2 \times 2/2, 2, 2/0, 0, 0$	$512 \times 2 \times 7 \times 7$	$C \times L \times W \times H$
fc6	–	$512 \times 1 \times 4 \times 4$	$C \times L \times W \times H$
fc7	–	4096	F
fc8	–	4096	F
softmax	–	N	N

As shown in Table 1, the network contains 5 convolution layers, 5 pooling layers, 3 full connected layers and a softmax layer. In order to adapt the C3D framework, we need to preprocess the input videos. First, we extract frames from videos and resized all frames into 128 × 171. Then, we do random crops on frames with a size of 112 × 112. Finally, we split each video into non-overlapped 16-frame clips and drop the last clip whose length is less than 16. After preprocessing, the input dimensions are 3 × 16 × 112 × 112.

The training process is just the same as [9]. First, we train a pre-trained model on Sports-1M dataset. Then, we preprocess our dataset as described above. Finally, we finetune our model with the pre-trained model.

After training, the model can be used as a feature extractor. We can extract the output of softmax layer for the test set, which is called spatio-temporal modality score.

3.2 TSN Framework

Due to the great performance, we select TSN framework [9] as the 2D ConvNets in our network. TSN consist of three spatial networks and three temporal networks. The spatial network takes RGB images as input, while the temporal network takes stacked optical flow fields extracted by TVL1 [25] or warped [20] TVL1 as input. We named these three features as RGB spatial modality features, TVL1 temporal modality features and warped TVL1 temporal modality, respectively.

As shown in Fig. 3, we can see three type images of the three modalities. The two images in column 1 are two consecutive RGB frames of a video. The two gray images in column 2 are the x and y directions of optical flow fields extracted by TVL1 algorithm. The two images in column 3 are the x and y directions of optical flow fields extracted by warped TVL1 algorithm, which eliminates the camera motion.

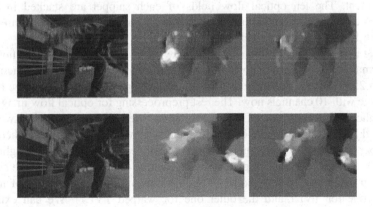

Fig. 3. Example of three types of modality: RGB images, TVL1 images (x, y directions) and warped TVL1 images (x, y directions)

The architecture of spatial network is illustrated in Fig. 4(a), which is similar to [9]. The input video is divided into three segments and a single frame is randomly selected from each segment. Then each single frame is input as a RGB image and fed to BN Inception network [26]. Finally, the scores of three single frames are fused by average function.

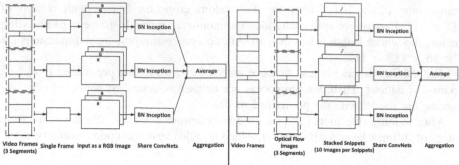

(a) The architecture of spatial network | (b) The architecture of temporal network

Fig. 4. The fundamental components of TSN

Before training, we do some preprocessing for videos. Frames extracted from videos are resized to 256 × 340 and randomly cropped to 256 × 256, 224 × 224, 192 × 192 or 168 × 168. Before feeding to BN Inception, all cropped regions are resized to 224 × 224. Then, we finetune our network with pre-trained BN Inception model on the ImageNet.

The architecture of temporal network is illustrated in Fig. 4(b), which is similar to [9]. First, we extract optical flow field for arbitrary two consecutive frames. Then the optical flow fields are divided into three segments. A short snippet with ten optical flow fields (five for x directions and the other five for y directions) is randomly selected from each segment. The ten optical flow fields of each snippet are stacked in channel dimension and then fed to BN Inception network. Finally, the scores of three single frames are fused by average function.

Owing to the uncertain range of optical flow displacement, optical flow fields need to be normalized by linear transformation. After normalization, all displacements range from 0 to 255, which is the same as gray image. An optical flow field can be regarded as an image with 10 channels now. The rest preprocessing for optical flow images is the same as the preprocessing of RGB images above. We still finetune our network with pre-trained BN Inception model on the ImageNet. However, the difference here is that the number of channels is not equal to three, so we need to average the weights of the three RGB channels and then copy this average to the ten optical flow image channels.

After training, we have a model of spatial network and two models of temporal network (one for TVL1 and the other one for warped TVL1). We can extract the outputs of softmax layer for the test set by using these three models, which are called RGB spatial modality score, TVL1 temporal modality score and warped TVL1 temporal modality score, respectively.

3.3 Fusion Scheme

We have got four modality scores for test set according to the work above. After score fusion, we can get the final score of a video. Fusion scheme will be provided for these scores in this section.

C3D modality score is extracted from a clip of a video, but the others are extracted from a whole video. In order to fuse the four modality scores, we need to compute C3D modality score for the whole video. The score can be formulated as

$$C3D'^{(v)} = \frac{1}{n}\sum_{i=0}^{n} s(v_i),$$ (1)

where v is the video id, n is the number of clips of video v, i is the clip id of video v, $s(v_i)$ is the score vector of all classes of clip i of video v and $C3D'(v)$ denotes the average score vector of all clips of video v.

There is another method, which can be formulated as Eq. (2).

$$C3D''^{(v)} = \frac{1}{\sum_{i=0}^{n} I(h(v_i) = majority(v))}\sum_{i=0}^{n} s(v_i) \cdot I(h(v_i) = majority(v)),$$ (2)

$$majority(v) = \mathrm{argmax}_y \sum_{i=0}^{n} I(h(v_i) = y),$$ (3)

$$h(v_i) = \mathrm{argmax}_j \left(s(v_i)_j \right),$$ (4)

where $h(v_i)$ is the predicted label of clip i of video v, I is an indicator function, $majority(v)$ is the major labels predicted by all clips of v, $C3D''(v)$ denotes the average score vector of clips whose predicted labels are equal to $majority(v)$.

The fusion scheme depends on a score fusion function, which is a weighted average function. It is formulated as Eq. (5).

$$f(v) = w_1 \cdot C3D(v) + w_2 \cdot RGB(v) + w_3 \cdot TVL1(v) + w_3 \cdot wTVL1(v),$$ (5)

where w_1–w_4 are the weights of four modality scores. $C3D(v)$ can be represented as $C3D'(v)$ or $C3D''(v)$. $RGB(v)$, $TVL1(v)$ and $wTVL1(v)$ denote the score vectors computed by RGB, TVL1 and warped TVL1 modality features, respectively. $f(v)$ is the final score vector of the video v. The values of w_1–w_4 are determined by the validation sets.

4   Experiment

In this section, we first introduce the datasets evaluated in this paper. Then, we explore the average methods for vectors of video clips in C3D framework. Finally, we compare the performance of our method with the state of the art.

4.1   Dataset

We empirically evaluate our experiment on the most popular two datasets, UCF101 [27] and HMDB51 [28]. The UCF101 dataset contains 13, 320 videos from 101 human actions. Videos in each class are divided into 25 groups. Each group approximately consists of 5 episodes. The episodes in the same group have similar the scenes and persons. The size of all videos is 320×240. We adopt three training/testing splits provided by the THUMOS13 challenge [29]. The HMDB51 dataset contains 6, 766 videos from 51 actions. Each action consists of over 101 videos. We adopt the three training/testing splits provided by dataset organizers.

4.2 Comparison of Average of All and Average of Majority

In C3D framework, each video is divided into many clips, so we have to determine the final label for the whole video according to the labels predicted by all clips. We propose two methods to make decision, which are shown in Eqs. (1) and (2). The experimental results are demonstrated in Table 2.

Table 2. Exploration of different average methods

Method	Dataset					
	UCF101			HMDB51		
	split1	split2	split3	split1	split2	split3
Average of all	82.6%	82.7%	81.9%	51.3%	47.8%	50.7%
Average of majority	82.0%	82.5%	81.3%	50.8%	45.4%	49.0%

Average of all has clearly advantage over average of majority in all dataset splits. This phenomenon is impressive especially on HMDB51.

4.3 Comparison with the State of the Art

After experimenting with different networks, we build up the best fusion scheme for multi-modality fusion network. Specifically, we fuse four modality scores and test it on UCF101 and HMDB51. We report the results averaged over all 3 splits and compare our results with other state-of-the-art methods in Table 3.

Table 3. Performance comparison on UCF101 and HMDB51

Method	UCF101	HMDB51
DT+MVSV [30]	83.5%	55.9%
iDT+FV [20]	85.9%	57.2%
iDT+HSV [31]	87.9%	61.1%
MoFAP [32]	88.3%	61.7%
Two-stream [8]	88.0%	59.4%
$F_{ST}CN$ (SCI fusion) [22]	88.1%	59.1%
LTC [7]	91.7%	64.8%
KVMF [24]	93.1%	63.3%
C3D (3 nets) [9]	85.2%	–
TSN (3 modalities) [10]	94.2%	69.4%
MMFN (ours)	**94.6%**	**69.7%**

Compared with traditional methods such as dense trajectories [30] and improved trajectories [20], and methods based on deep learning like Two-stream [8], C3D [9] and TSN [10], our method outperforms the best of them by 0.4% on UCF101 and 0.3% on HMDB51. Experiments present observable improvement on two challenging datasets, which proves that fusion of multiple modalities is effective.

5 Conclusion

In this paper, we present a multi-modality fusion network for action recognition, a novel framework that takes advantage of different types of spatial and temporal features. Experiments show that average of all achieves higher performance than average of majority in C3D framework. Besides that, this work takes the state of the art of deep-learning-based methods for action recognition to a new level.

References

1. Krizhevsky, A., Sutskever, I., Hinton, G.E.: Imagenet classification with deep convolutional neural networks. In: Advances in Neural Information Processing Systems, pp. 1097–1105 (2012)
2. Deng, J., Dong, W., Socher, R., Li, L.J., Li, K., Fei-Fei, L.: Imagenet: a large-scale hierarchical image database. In: IEEE Conference on Computer Vision and Pattern Recognition (CVPR 2009), pp. 248–255. IEEE (2009)
3. Yang, H., Zhou, J.T., Zhang, Y., Gao, B.B., Wu, J., Cai, J.: Exploit bounding box annotations for multi-label object recognition. In: Proceedings of the IEEE Conference on Computer Vision and Pattern Recognition, pp. 280–288 (2016)
4. Herranz, L., Jiang, S., Li, X.: Scene recognition with CNNs: objects, scales and dataset bias. In: Proceedings of the IEEE Conference on Computer Vision and Pattern Recognition, pp. 571–579 (2016)
5. Xiong, Y., Zhu, K., Lin, D., Tang, X.: Recognize complex events from static images by fusing deep channels. In: Proceedings of the IEEE Conference on Computer Vision and Pattern Recognition, pp. 1600–1609 (2015)
6. Karpathy, A., Toderici, G., Shetty, S., Leung, T., Sukthankar, R., FeiFei, L.: Large-scale video classification with convolutional neural networks. In: Proceedings of the IEEE Conference on Computer Vision and Pattern Recognition, pp. 1725–1732 (2014)
7. Varol, G., Laptev, I., Schmid, C.: Long-term temporal convolutions for action recognition. arXiv preprint arXiv:1604.04494 (2016)
8. Simonyan, K., Zisserman, A.: Two-stream convolutional networks for action recognition in videos. In: Advances in Neural Information Processing Systems, pp. 568–576 (2014)
9. Tran, D., Bourdev, L., Fergus, R., Torresani, L., Paluri, M.: Learning spatiotemporal features with 3D convolutional networks. In: Proceedings of the IEEE International Conference on Computer Vision, pp. 4489–4497 (2015)
10. Wang, L., Xiong, Y., Wang, Z., Qiao, Yu., Lin, D., Tang, X., Van Gool, L.: Temporal segment networks: towards good practices for deep action recognition. In: Leibe, B., Matas, J., Sebe, N., Welling, M. (eds.) ECCV 2016. LNCS, vol. 9912, pp. 20–36. Springer, Cham (2016). https://doi.org/10.1007/978-3-319-46484-8_2

11. Ji, S., Xu, W., Yang, M., Yu, K.: 3D convolutional neural networks for human action recognition. IEEE Trans. Pattern Anal. Mach. Intell. **35**(1), 221–231 (2013)
12. Lowe, D.G.: Distinctive image features from scale-invariant keypoints. Int. J. Comput. Vis. **60**(2), 91–110 (2004)
13. Dalal, N., Triggs, B.: Histograms of oriented gradients for human detection. In: IEEE Computer Society Conference on Computer Vision and Pattern Recognition (CVPR 2005), vol. 1, pp. 886–893. IEEE (2005)
14. Laptev, I., Marszalek, M., Schmid, C., Rozenfeld, B.: Learning realistic human actions from movies. In: IEEE Conference on Computer Vision and Pattern Recognition (CVPR 2008), pp. 1–8. IEEE (2008)
15. Dalal, N., Triggs, B., Schmid, C.: Human detection using oriented histograms of flow and appearance. In: Leonardis, A., Bischof, H., Pinz, A. (eds.) ECCV 2006. LNCS, vol. 3952, pp. 428–441. Springer, Heidelberg (2006). https://doi.org/10.1007/11744047_33
16. Laptev, I.: On space-time interest points. Int. J. Comput. Vis. **64**(2–3), 107–123 (2005)
17. Dollár, P., Rabaud, V., Cottrell, G., Belongie, S.: Behavior recognition via sparse spatio-temporal features. In: 2nd Joint IEEE International Workshop on Visual Surveillance and Performance Evaluation of Tracking and Surveillance, pp. 65–72. IEEE (2005)
18. Klaser, A., Marszalek, M., Schmid, C.: A spatio-temporal descriptor based on 3D-gradients. In: 19th British Machine Vision Conference (BMVC 2008), p. 275-1. British Machine Vision Association (2008)
19. Wang, H., Kläser, A., Schmid, C., Liu, C.L.: Action recognition by dense trajectories. In: IEEE Conference on Computer Vision and Pattern Recognition (CVPR), pp. 3169–3176. IEEE (2011)
20. Wang, H., Schmid, C.: Action recognition with improved trajectories. In: Proceedings of the IEEE International Conference on Computer Vision, pp. 3551–3558 (2013)
21. Yue-Hei Ng, J., Hausknecht, M., Vijayanarasimhan, S., Vinyals, O., Monga, R., Toderici, G.: Beyond short snippets: deep networks for video classification. In: Proceedings of the IEEE Conference on Computer Vision and Pattern Recognition, pp. 4694–4702 (2015)
22. Sun, L., Jia, K., Yeung, D.Y., Shi, B.E.: Human action recognition using factorized spatio-temporal convolutional networks. In: Proceedings of the IEEE International Conference on Computer Vision, pp. 4597–4605 (2015)
23. Wu, Z., Jiang, Y.G., Wang, J., Pu, J., Xue, X.: Exploring inter-feature and inter-class relationships with deep neural networks for video classification. In: Proceedings of the 22nd ACM International Conference on Multimedia, pp. 167–176. ACM (2014)
24. Zhu, W., Hu, J., Sun, G., Cao, X., Qiao, Y.: A key volume mining deep framework for action recognition. In: Proceedings of the IEEE Conference on Computer Vision and Pattern Recognition, pp. 1991–1999 (2016)
25. Zach, C., Pock, T., Bischof, H.: A duality based approach for realtime TV-L1 optical flow. Pattern Recognition, pp. 214–223 (2007)
26. Ioffe, S., Szegedy, C.: Batch normalization: accelerating deep network training by reducing internal covariate shift. In: Proceedings of the 32nd International Conference on Machine Learning, pp. 448–456 (2015)
27. Soomro, K., Zamir, A.R., Shah, M.: UCF101: a dataset of 101 human actions classes from videos in the wild. arXiv preprint arXiv:1212.0402 (2012)
28. Kuehne, H., Jhuang, H., Garrote, E., Poggio, T., Serre, T.: HMDB: a large video database for human motion recognition. In: IEEE International Conference on Computer Vision (ICCV), pp. 2556–2563. IEEE (2011)
29. Jiang, Y., Liu, J., Zamir, A.R., Toderici, G., Laptev, I., Shah, M., Sukthankar, R.: Thumos challenge: action recognition with a large number of classes (2014)

30. Cai, Z., Wang, L., Peng, X., Qiao, Y.: Multi-view super vector for action recognition. In: Proceedings of the IEEE Conference on Computer Vision and Pattern Recognition, pp. 596–603 (2014)
31. Gan, C., Yang, Y., Zhu, L., Zhao, D., Zhuang, Y.: Recognizing an action using its name: a knowledge-based approach. Int. J. Comput. Vis. **120**(1), 61–77 (2016)
32. Wang, L., Qiao, Y., Tang, X.: MoFAP: a multi-level representation for action recognition. Int. J. Comput. Vis. **119**(3), 254–271 (2016)

Fusing Appearance Features and Correlation Features for Face Video Retrieval

Chenchen Jing, Zhen Dong, Mingtao Pei[✉], and Yunde Jia

Beijing Laboratory of Intelligent Information Technology, School of Computer Science, Beijing Institute of Technology, Beijing 100081, People's Republic of China
{jingchenchen1996,dongzhen,peimt,jiayunde}@bit.edu.cn

Abstract. Face video retrieval has drawn considerable research attention recently. Most prior research mainly focused on either appearance features or correlation features, which could degrade retrieval performance. In this paper, we fuse appearance features and correlation features to exploit rich information of face videos for face video retrieval via a deep convolutional neural network. The network extracts appearance feature and correlation feature from a frame and the covariance matrix of a face video, respectively, and fuses them to obtain a comprehensive video representation. The fused feature is projected to a low-dimensional Hamming space via hash functions for the retrieval task. The network integrates feature extractions, feature fusion, and hash learning into a unified optimization framework to guarantee optimal compatibility of appearance features and correlation features. Experiments on two challenging TV-Series datasets demonstrate the effectiveness of the proposed method.

Keywords: Face video retrieval · Deep CNN · Appearance features
Correlation features

1 Introduction

Recent years have witnessed a tremendous explosion of multimedia data, especially videos. Millions of videos are uploaded every day to the Internet via social networking websites, mobile applications, etc. Face video retrieval aims to retrieve videos of a particular person from a video database given one face video of him/her, and has increasingly attracted more attention. It has a wide range of applications such as locating and recognizing suspects from surveillance videos, intelligent fast forward of movies, and collecting all videos of favorite character from the TV-Series.

Face video representation is critical in face video retrieval. Existing face video representation methods can be roughly divided into two categories: appearance based methods and correlation based methods. Appearance based methods focus on characterizing human faces via appearance features such as such as color and texture [3,6,11,18]. They regard a face video as a set of images and fuse the

© Springer International Publishing AG, part of Springer Nature 2018
B. Zeng et al. (Eds.): PCM 2017, LNCS 10736, pp. 150–160, 2018.
https://doi.org/10.1007/978-3-319-77383-4_15

well-learned representations of each frame to get the final video representation. In general, a face video comprises multiple consecutive frames, and each frame depicts appearance features of the face, which could vary greatly from frame to frame. Hence, ignoring correlation features and simply treating videos as image sets is inadvisable. Correlation based methods treat a video as a whole and utilize the second-order statistics information such as the covariance matrix (Cov) feature of a video to capture the video data variations in a statistical manner [14–16]. Albeit covariance matrix has been proved natural and efficient for video representation, it only represents linear correlations of frames and does not capture the appearance feature of each frame. In this paper, we fuse appearance features and correlation features to obtain comprehensive video representations for face video retrieval.

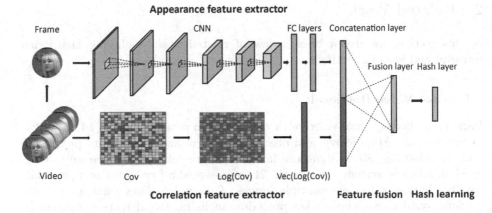

Fig. 1. The architecture of the proposed network.

Figure 1 shows the architecture of the proposed network. Given a frame of a face video as the appearance feature and the covariance matrix as the correlation feature, the network generates a comprehensive face video representation. The network contains four components: appearance feature extractor module, correlation feature extractor module, feature fusion module, and hash learning module. The appearance feature extractor module is utilized to learn discriminative appearance features to alleviate the problem of large intra-class variations of videos in face video retrieval. The correlation feature extractor module projects nonsingular covariance matrices to a Euclidean space and then vectorizes them, since these matrices lie on a Riemannian manifold [14]. The following feature fusion module fuses appearance features and correlation features to obtain comprehensive video representations via a concatenation layer and a fusion layer. The hash learning module is exploited to project high-dimensional fused features to a low-dimensional Hamming space, considering that the fused features are designed for the retrieval task, which have an eagerly demand of time and space saving. Implemented via neural network and trained jointly, all these modules actually form an end-to-end architecture.

The appearance feature extractor module and the correlation feature extractor module appropriately process the input frame and covariance matrix, respectively, aiming to provide effective appearance features and correlation features for the feature fusion module. The feature fusion module fuses these features perfectly to utilize rich information of face videos. The hash learning module generates compact representations to make the fusion more compact for retrieval. The four components are integrated into a unified optimization framework to ensure that appearance features and correlation features are compatibly fused for the final retrieval task. We conduct experiments on two challenging TV-Series datasets (*the Big Bang Theory* and *the Prison Break*) [16]. The excellent experimental results demonstrate the superiority of fusing appearance features and correlation features for face video retrieval.

2 Related Work

In this section, we give a brief review of related works including face video retrieval and hashing methods.

2.1 Face Video Retrieval

Various methods for face video retrieval have been proposed [1,2,6,14,16,19,21] in recent years. Arandjelovic and Zisserman [1,2] utilized an identity preserving and variation insensitive signature image to represent a face video and developed an retrieval system. Sivic et al. [21] represented a face video as a probability distribution to harness multiple frames of the video. They built a complete retrieval system covered every key procedure including face detection, face tracking, etc. The high-dimensional features used in above methods are not applicable to retrieval task by the current view. Li et al. [14] proposed compact video code (CVC) for face video retrieval. They computed covariance matrix from frames' DCT features to utilize the second-order statistics information. Furthermore, they proposed hierarchical hybrid statistic based video binary code [16]. This method first utilizes different parameterized fisher vectors as frame representation and then executes CVC in the Reproducing Kernel Hilbert Space. Dong et al. [6] proposed an end-to-end deep network to learn discriminative and compact frame representations and fuse them to get final video representation, which is the first attempt to employ a neural network to face video retrieval. Aiming to capture local relationships between frames, Qiao et al. [19] designed a multi-branch CNN, which learns video-level features by temporal feature pooling. Above methods mainly focuses on either appearance features or correlation features. Different from these works, our network fuses both the appearance features and correlation features to obtain comprehensive video representations for face video retrieval.

2.2   Hashing Methods

Hashing methods are efficacious solutions to nearest neighbor search problem and have been widely studied recently. Locality sensitive hashing (LSH) [7] is a representative data-independent hashing methods. Since random projections functions instead of hash functions learned from data are adopted, LSH still needs long hash codes to achieve satisfactory performance. Therefore, learning based data-dependent hashing methods have become increasingly popular because of the benefit that taking full advantage of data structure or supervision information of training data. The data-dependent methods can be further divided into unsupervised, semi-supervised and supervised methods. Unsupervised methods learn hash functions only exploiting feature information of training data without supervision information, including spectral hashing [23], iterative quantization hashing (ITQ) [8], gaussian mixture model embedding [9]. Due to supervision information utilized in semi-supervised and supervised methods, performance of these methods superior to unsupervised methods in general. Maximizing variance and independence of hash bits over both labeled and unlabeled data, semi-supervised hashing [22] is a typical semi-supervised method. Both utilizing supervision information, discriminative binary coding [20] use point wise labels, and supervised hashing with kernels [17], robust multiple instance hashing [4] use pair wise labels. In addition, ranking label such as triplet label which aims to preserve rank order among samples are widely used. Ranking based methods include column generation hashing [13], part-based deep hashing [26]. In this work, triplet label supervision is exploited in the final binary space for the improvement of the retrieval performance.

3   Method

3.1   Appearance Feature Extractor Module

The appearance feature extractor module of our architecture is based on the well-known AlexNet [12]. The AlexNet has five types of layers: convolutional layer, max-pooling layer, local contrast normalization layer, fully connected layer and the non-linear ReLU activation layer. The last but one fully connected layer, "FC7" layer is followed by a fully connected layer with 1,000 output neurons and a softmax layer to compute the probability distribution over the categories. Previous studies presented better performances of the 4096-dim features of the "FC7" layer than a large amount of the hand-crafted features [12]. The original AlexNet, which is trained on the ImageNet [5], is not specifically designed for face recognition. Hence, we fine-tune the Alexnet on CASIA-WebFace [25] to transfer the network from natural image domain to face image domain. The layers before "FC7" layer of the fine-tuned AlexNet is utilized as better initializations to learn our appearance feature extractor module.

3.2   Correlation Feature Extractor Module

The correlation feature extractor module projects covariance matrices to a Euclidean space and vectorizes them. With the fine-tuned AlexNet, CNN feature of each frame is extracted through forward propagation. Let $F = [f_1, f_2, ..., f_n] \in \mathbb{R}^{d \times n}$ be the CNN features of a video where d represent the dimension of CNN feature and n is the number of frames, f_i denotes the ith frame with d-dim CNN feature. The covariance matrix of this video is defined as

$$C = \frac{1}{n-1} \sum_{i=1}^{n} (f_i - \overline{f})(f_i - \overline{f})^T, \tag{1}$$

where $\overline{f}$ denotes the mean of all the frame features of this video. Since nonsingular covariance matrices lie on a Riemannian manifold [14], Log-Euclidean Distance is resorted to bridge the gap between Riemannian manifold and Euclidean space. Projecting points on the Riemannian manifold to a Euclidean space via logarithm map, then the distance of two points C_1, C_2 is given by

$$d_{LED} = \|log(C_1) - log(C_2)\|_F, \tag{2}$$

where log is the matrix logarithm operator, and $\|\cdot\|_F$ denotes the matrix Frobenius norm. Since the off-diagonal entries of the matrix $log(C)$ is counted twice during norm computation, we vectorize the covariance matrix in the form of

$$vec(log(C)) = [v_{1,1}, \sqrt{2}v_{1,2}, ..., v_{2,2}, \sqrt{2}v_{2,3}, ..., v_{d,d}], \tag{3}$$

to generate a $d(d+1)/2$-dim feature vector, where $v_{i,j}$ is the ith row, j^{th} column element of $log(C)$.

3.3 Feature Fusion Module

In order to fuse the outputs of the two feature extractor modules, namely the CNN feature and the Cov feature, into an unitary feature, the feature fusion module is introduced in the proposed network. The feature fusion module contains a concatenation layer and a fusion layer. Given two vectors of d_1-dim and d_2-dim, respectively, a concatenation layer concatenates them together to get a $d_1 + d_2$-dim vector. Let $f \in \mathbb{R}^{d_1}$ be the CNN feature, and $c \in \mathbb{R}^{d_2}$ denotes the Cov feature. The output of the catenation layer is

$$x = [f, c] \in \mathbb{R}^{(d_1 + d_2)}. \tag{4}$$

As a simple concatenation of two features, x is an intermediate result provided for the fusion layer. The following fusion layer is a fully connected layer whose output is computed by

$$y = W^T x + b, \tag{5}$$

where W and b are weight and bias of this layer. Followed by the hash learning module, the feature fusion module guarantees the two features are combined directly for the retrieval task, i.e., the features are fused for hashing, and the performance of hash codes is able to guide the fusion of two features. Moreover, the feature fusion module ensures CNN features are constrained by Cov features through back propagation, i.e., parameters of the appearance feature extractor module are influenced by vectorized Cov features [24]. Hence, by introducing the feature fusion module, the whole network are designed to fuse CNN features and Cov features optimally for the final retrieval task.

3.4   Hash Learning Module

The output of the fusion layer are comprehensive but high-dimensional video representations which are not fit for the retrieval task. Hence the hash learning module is utilized to map fused features to a low-dimensional Hamming space. Specially, we enforce triplet ranking loss to hash functions to preserve the data similarity.

Suppose that the deep CNN have mapped face videos to a binary space: $\{+1, -1\}^s$, where s is the length of hash code. The triplet ranking loss reflects the relative similarities in the form as "video $\mathbf{q}$ is more similar to $\widetilde{\mathbf{q}}$ than $\widehat{\mathbf{q}}$". Let $(\mathbf{q}, \widetilde{\mathbf{q}})$ be positive pair whose samples are from the same person, and $(\mathbf{q}, \widehat{\mathbf{q}})$ be the negative pair whose samples are from different individuals, the loss of one triplet is thus formulated as

$$l(\mathbf{q}, \widetilde{\mathbf{q}}, \widehat{\mathbf{q}}) = \max\Big(d(\mathbf{q}, \widetilde{\mathbf{q}}) - d(\mathbf{q}, \widehat{\mathbf{q}}) + \delta, 0\Big), \tag{6}$$

where $d(\boldsymbol{\theta}_1, \boldsymbol{\theta}_1) = (s - \boldsymbol{\theta}_1^T \boldsymbol{\theta}_2)/2$ is the Hamming distance in the binary space, and $\delta \geq 0$ denotes the margin of the distance differences between positive and negative pairs. Define the training video set as $\mathbf{Q} = [\mathbf{Q}_1, \mathbf{Q}_2, ..., \mathbf{Q}_C]$ of C classes, the objective of the our deep CNN is

$$\min_{\mathbf{W}^*, \mathbf{W}} \sum_{i=1}^{C} \sum_{\substack{\mathbf{q}, \widetilde{\mathbf{q}} \in \mathbf{Q}_i \\ \mathbf{q} \neq \widetilde{\mathbf{q}}}} \sum_{j \neq i, \widehat{\mathbf{q}} \in \mathbf{Q}_j} l(\mathbf{q}, \widetilde{\mathbf{q}}, \widehat{\mathbf{q}}), \tag{7}$$

where $\mathbf{W}$ is the parameters of the last layer (hash functions), and $\mathbf{W}^*$ represents the parameters of the front layers.

To solve Eq. (7), the gradients of Eq. (6) is needed. Since the hash function contains the sign function $sgn(\cdot)$ which is non-smooth and non-differentiable, we use $\tanh(\cdot)$ instead of the sign function during the fine-tuning procedure. Therefore, the gradients of Eq. (6) w.r.t. hash codes are given by

$$\frac{\partial l}{\partial \mathbf{q}} = \frac{1}{2}(\widehat{\mathbf{q}} - \widetilde{\mathbf{q}}) \times I, \frac{\partial l}{\partial \widetilde{\mathbf{q}}} = -\frac{1}{2}\mathbf{q} \times I, \frac{\partial l}{\partial \widehat{\mathbf{q}}} = \frac{1}{2}\mathbf{q} \times I, \tag{8}$$

where I is a binary function which returns 1 when $d(\mathbf{q}, \widetilde{\mathbf{q}}) - d(\mathbf{q}, \widehat{\mathbf{q}}) + \delta > 0$ and 0 for other occasions. Obtaining these gradients, the optimization procedure can be conducted via the back-propagation algorithm.

4   Experiments

4.1   Dataset and Experimental Settings

We conduct experiments on the ICT-TV dataset [16] to evaluate the proposed method. The ICT-TV dataset contains two large scale video sets from two American shows: the Big Bang Theory (BBT) and Prison Break (PB). The two TV-Series are quite different in filming styles. The BBT is a sitcom with 5 main

Table 1. Comparison mAPs of our methods.

Methods	The Big Bang Theory						Prison Break					
	8 bits	16 bits	32 bits	64 bits	128 bits	256 bits	8 bits	16 bits	32 bits	64 bits	128 bits	256 bits
Ours (EC-RS)	0.9407	0.9376	0.9362	0.9437	0.9373	0.9413	0.4370	0.4716	0.5122	0.5300	0.5382	0.5672
Ours (EC-AP)	0.9430	0.9525	0.9445	0.9628	0.9563	0.9625	0.4873	0.5320	0.5869	0.5988	0.6184	0.6438
Ours (WC-RS)	0.9604	0.9687	0.9705	0.9702	0.9742	0.9746	0.6997	0.7195	0.7493	0.7554	0.7694	0.7844
Ours (WC-AP)	**0.9665**	**0.9849**	**0.9909**	**0.9917**	**0.9853**	**0.9924**	**0.7667**	**0.7956**	**0.8056**	**0.8188**	**0.8377**	**0.8461**

Table 2. Comparison mAPs with comparison methods.

Methods	The Big Bang Theory						Prison Break					
	8 bits	16 bits	32 bits	64 bits	128 bits	256 bits	8 bits	16 bits	32 bits	64 bits	128 bits	256 bits
LSH [7]	0.4302	0.5301	0.6874	0.7486	0.8541	0.8761	0.1308	0.1299	0.1906	0.2672	0.3487	0.4264
RR [8]	0.8252	0.8738	0.8381	0.8558	0.8910	0.9131	0.2801	0.3806	0.4209	0.4637	0.4916	0.5115
ITQ [8]	0.8419	0.9019	0.8889	0.9130	0.9252	0.9345	0.3571	0.4450	0.5074	0.5337	0.5370	0.5332
SH [23]	0.6403	0.5425	0.5633	0.5332	0.4915	0.4447	0.2615	0.3135	0.3346	0.3293	0.2944	0.2675
SSH [22]	0.8113	0.8173	0.6791	0.6008	0.5571	0.5250	0.3435	0.4380	0.3293	0.2794	0.2651	0.2598
KSH [17]	0.8338	0.9116	0.9388	0.9441	0.9430	0.9435	0.5028	0.6155	0.6313	0.7041	0.7227	0.7456
SITQ [8]	0.8515	0.9439	0.9516	0.9500	0.9508	0.9483	0.4848	0.6072	0.6715	0.7008	0.6903	0.6742
DBHR [6]	0.9497	0.9696	0.9805	0.9803	0.9742	0.9814	0.7496	0.7775	0.7576	0.7857	0.8262	0.8293
HHS-VBC [16]	0.5099	0.5934	0.6718	0.6821	0.7170	0.7401	0.1388	0.1445	0.1560	0.1629	0.1784	0.1982
SPC-CVC [15]	0.5202	0.6471	0.7325	0.7543	0.7740	0.7899	0.1401	0.1525	0.1674	0.1903	0.2099	0.2287
Ours (WC-AP)	**0.9665**	**0.9849**	**0.9909**	**0.9917**	**0.9853**	**0.9924**	**0.7667**	**0.7956**	**0.8056**	**0.8188**	**0.8377**	**0.8461**

characters, in which most scenes are taken indoors. Each episode lasts about 20 min. Differently, many shots of the PB are taken outside during the episodes of about 42 min long. This results in a large range of different illumination conditions. All the face videos are collected from the whole first season of both TV series, *i.e.*, 17 episodes of BBT, and 22 episodes of PB, and the number of face videos of the two sets are 4,667 and 9,435, respectively.

We compare our method with seven state-of-the-art hashing methods: LSH [7], SH [23], ITQ [8], SITQ [8], RR [8], SSH [22], KSH [17], and three face video retrieval methods: DBHR [6], HHS-VBC [16], and SPC-CVC [15]. For each TV-Series dataset, we randomly select 10 face videos per actor or actress for training hash functions, and use the rest face videos for testing. Same to [16], the query set consists of 10 face videos of each main character. To evaluate the quality of our method, we use four evaluation criterions: the mean Average Precision (mAP), the Precision Recall curve (PR curve), Precision curve w.r.t. different number of top returned samples (PN curve), and Recall curve w.r.t. different number of top returned samples (RN curve). For fair comparisons, all the methods use the same training and testing sets.

The network is trained using Caffe deep learning tool [10]. Stochastic gradient descent is utilized to optimize the network, with momentum of 0.9 and weight decay of 0.0005. The learning rate of the optimization is initialized as 0.001 and decreased according to the polynomial policy with power value of 0.6. The mini-batch size of the training samples is 64, and the triplets are randomly generated based on the labels. The total number of the iterations is 50, 000. In our experiments, we execute PCA to get 100-dim CNN features of faces and the dimension of the final Cov features is 5050.

4.2 Results and Discussions

In testing, we generate representations of test face videos in two ways: random selection and average pooling:

- **Random Selection (RS):** We randomly select a frame of a face video and compute the covariance matrix as the inputs of the network. A binary video representation is obtained through forward propagation.
- **Average Pooling (AP):** As for a face video with m frames, all m frames of this video are first inputted into the network with the covariance matrix to obtain m video representations. Then these representations are fused by average pooling to obtain a more robust binary video representation for retrieval.

Moreover, in order to verify the effectiveness of the correlation features, we exclude correlation the feature extractor module and the feature fusion module of the proposed network, *i.e.*, remain the appearance feature extractor module and the hash learning module only, and get a single branch network.

We test the single branch network and the whole proposed network with different representation generation methods. The mAPs are shown on Table 1,

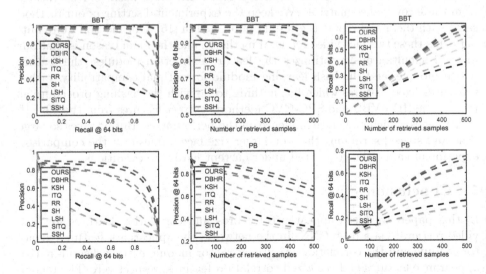

Fig. 2. Comparisons of PR, PN, and RN curves of the face video retrieval experiment on two TV-series datasets.

where "EC" means "Exclude Correlation features", "WC" means "With Correlation features". It can be seen that video representations generated by average pooling are more robust because of large variations in each video of two datasets. The performance differences between "Ours (EC-RS)" and "Ours (WC-RS)", "Ours (EC-AP)" and "Ours (WC-AP)" demonstrate the effect of correlation features. Our single branch network which only contains the appearance feature extractor module and the hash learning module can achieve comparable results with other methods.

Table 2 lists the mAPs of our method and the comparison methods, and Fig. 2 depicts the comparisons of curves. For the seven hashing methods, mean vector of learned frame representations is computed as the final video hash representation. For fair comparisons, these hashing methods use the 4096-dim input features generated by the AlexNet fine-tuned on the WebFace dataset. As shown in Table 2 and Fig. 2, the proposed method significantly outperforms other comparison methods. The advantages of the proposed method mainly lie in two aspects: the utilization of correlation features and the unified optimization procedure which makes the feature extractor modules, the feature fusion module, and the hash learning module optimally compatible for the retrieval task.

The face video retrieval method DBHR [6] builds an end-to-end deep network to learn discriminative and compact frame representations and fuse them to get final video representations. The low-rank discriminative binary hashing which is proposed to pre-learn hash functions, is utilized to achieve state-of-the-art performances. The comparison results of our method and DBHR are shown on Table 2 and Fig. 2, which certify that fusing appearance features and correlation features is efficient for face video retrieval. HHS-VBC and SPC-CVC use multiple size-variant covariance matrices calculated from fisher vectors and raw intensities as video features, respectively, and learn video hash representations from these covariance matrices. We keep the experimental setting of our method same with them and report the results published in [15]. Our method quite outperforms these two face video retrieval methods, and the main reason is that our method simultaneously optimizes the feature extraction modules, the feature fusion module, and the hash learning module for optimal compatibility, rather than uses fixed features which has nothing to do with the hashing procedure as input. The HHS-VBC and SPC-CVC methods extract features from the 20×16 gray images, which may have influence on the performance. But, it takes so large time and space for running them on larger size face frames that the comparison experiment cannot be conducted under current hardware conditions.

5   Conclusion

In this paper, we fused appearance features and correlation features for face video retrieval via a deep CNN. In the network, the appearance feature extractor module and the correlation feature extractor module extract discriminative appearance features and vecorized correlation features, respectively. The following feature fusion module fuses these features together to exploit rich information of face videos. The hash learning module projects the fused feature to a low-dimensional Hamming space. The network integrates these modules into a unified optimization framework to ensure that appearance features and correlation features are optimally fused for the retrieval task. Our method achieved excellent performances on two challenging TV-Series datasets.

Acknowledgments. This work was supported in part by the Natural Science Foundation of China (NSFC) under Grant No. 61472038 and No. 61375044.

References

1. Arandjelovic, O., Zisserman, A.: Automatic face recognition for film character retrieval in feature-length films. In: IEEE Computer Society Conference on Computer Vision and Pattern Recognition (CVPR 2005), vol. 1, pp. 860–867. IEEE (2005)
2. Arandjelović, O., Zisserman, A.: On film character retrieval in feature-length films. In: Interactive Video, pp. 89–105 (2006)
3. Cevikalp, H., Triggs, B.: Face recognition based on image sets. In: IEEE Conference on Computer Vision and Pattern Recognition (CVPR), pp. 2567–2573. IEEE (2010)
4. Conjeti, S., Paschali, M., Katouzian, A., Navab, N.: Learning robust hash codes for multiple instance image retrieval. arXiv preprint arXiv:1703.05724 (2017)
5. Deng, J., Dong, W., Socher, R., Li, L.J., Li, K., Fei-Fei, L.: Imagenet: a large-scale hierarchical image database. In: IEEE Conference on Computer Vision and Pattern Recognition (CVPR 2009), pp. 248–255. IEEE (2009)
6. Dong, Z., Jia, S., Wu, T., Pei, M.: Face video retrieval via deep learning of binary hash representations. In: AAAI, pp. 3471–3477 (2016)
7. Gionis, A., Indyk, P., Motwani, R., et al.: Similarity search in high dimensions via hashing. In: VLDB, vol. 99, pp. 518–529 (1999)
8. Gong, Y., Lazebnik, S.: Iterative quantization: a procrustean approach to learning binary codes. In: CVPR, pp. 817–824. IEEE (2011)
9. Hoang, T., Do, T.T., Tan, D.K.L., Cheung, N.M.: Enhance feature discrimination for unsupervised hashing. arXiv preprint arXiv:1704.01754 (2017)
10. Jia, Y., Shelhamer, E., Donahue, J., Karayev, S., Long, J., Girshick, R., Guadarrama, S., Darrell, T.: Caffe: convolutional architecture for fast feature embedding. In: Proceedings of the 22nd ACM International Conference on Multimedia, pp. 675–678. ACM (2014)
11. Kim, T.K., Kittler, J., Cipolla, R.: Discriminative learning and recognition of image set classes using canonical correlations. IEEE Trans. Pattern Anal. Mach. Intell. **29**(6), 1005–1018 (2007)
12. Krizhevsky, A., Sutskever, I., Hinton, G.E.: Imagenet classification with deep convolutional neural networks. In: Advances in Neural Information Processing Systems, vol. 25, pp. 1097–1105. Curran Associates, Inc. (2012)
13. Li, X., Lin, G., Shen, C., Van Den Hengel, A., Dick, A.R.: Learning hash functions using column generation. In: ICML, vol. 1, pp. 142–150 (2013)
14. Li, Y., Wang, R., Cui, Z., Shan, S., Chen, X.: Compact video code and its application to robust face retrieval in TV-Series. In: BMVC (2014)
15. Li, Y., Wang, R., Cui, Z., Shan, S., Chen, X.: Spatial pyramid covariance-based compact video code for robust face retrieval in TV-Series. IEEE Trans. Image Process. **25**(12), 5905–5919 (2016)

16. Li, Y., Wang, R., Shan, S., Chen, X.: Hierarchical hybrid statistic based video binary code and its application to face retrieval in TV-Series. In: FG, pp. 1–8. IEEE (2015)
17. Liu, W., Wang, J., Ji, R., Jiang, Y.G., Chang, S.F.: Supervised hashing with kernels. In: CVPR, pp. 2074–2081. IEEE (2012)
18. Parkhi, O.M., Simonyan, K., Vedaldi, A., Zisserman, A.: A compact and discriminative face track descriptor. In: Proceedings of the IEEE Conference on Computer Vision and Pattern Recognition, pp. 1693–1700 (2014)
19. Qiao, S., Wang, R., Shan, S., Chen, X.: Deep video code for efficient face video retrieval (2016)
20. Rastegari, M., Farhadi, A., Forsyth, D.: Attribute discovery via predictable discriminative binary codes. In: Fitzgibbon, A., Lazebnik, S., Perona, P., Sato, Y., Schmid, C. (eds.) ECCV 2012. LNCS, vol. 7577, pp. 876–889. Springer, Heidelberg (2012). https://doi.org/10.1007/978-3-642-33783-3_63
21. Sivic, J., Everingham, M., Zisserman, A.: Person spotting: video shot retrieval for face sets. In: Leow, W.-K., Lew, M.S., Chua, T.-S., Ma, W.-Y., Chaisorn, L., Bakker, E.M. (eds.) CIVR 2005. LNCS, vol. 3568, pp. 226–236. Springer, Heidelberg (2005). https://doi.org/10.1007/11526346_26
22. Wang, J., Kumar, S., Chang, S.F.: Semi-supervised hashing for scalable image retrieval. In: CVPR, pp. 3424–3431. IEEE (2010)
23. Weiss, Y., Torralba, A., Fergus, R.: Spectral hashing. In: Advances in Neural Information Processing Systems, pp. 1753–1760 (2009)
24. Wu, S., Chen, Y.C., Li, X., Wu, A.C., You, J.J., Zheng, W.S.: An enhanced deep feature representation for person re-identification. In: IEEE Winter Conference on Applications of Computer Vision (WACV), pp. 1–8. IEEE (2016)
25. Yi, D., Lei, Z., Liao, S., Li, S.Z.: Learning face representation from scratch. arXiv preprint arXiv:1411.7923 (2014)
26. Zhu, F., Kong, X., Zheng, L., Fu, H., Tian, Q.: Part-based deep hashing for large-scale person re-identification. IEEE Trans. Image Process. 26(10), 4806–4817 (2017)

A Robust Image Reflection Separation Method Based on Sift-Edge Flow

Shaomin Du, Xiaohui Liang$^{(\boxtimes)}$, and Xiaochuan Wang

State Key Laboratory of Virtual Reality Technology and Systems,
Beihang University, Beijing, China
{dushaominbuaa,liang_xiaohui,wangxc}@buaa.edu.cn

Abstract. Motion computation is an important part for image reflection separation methods using image sequence. As the motion of background and reflection is separated on image edges, in this paper we present a robust image reflection separation method based on sift-edge flow. Edge motion is firstly computed using sift-edge flow. Based on it, the sparse motion field of image edges is clustered into two parts and refined by RANSAC, which are then used to interpolate the dense motion fields of the background and reflection. The initial image decomposition is conducted by warping the input images to reference image using the dense motion fields of background and reflection respectively. Finally, with the initial solution provided, the background and reflection images can be separated using alternating optimization. Experiment results showed that our method can achieve a robust performance compared with the state of art.

Keywords: Reflection separation · Reflection removal
Layer decomposition · Sift-edge flow

1 Introduction

Image reflection separation, also called reflection removal, is of great importance not only for the purpose of original separation, which can produce desired background images that most people and photographers want to obtain, but also for the specific use such as vehicle automatic driving [10], image based rendering [11] and optical flow estimation [16].

The problem of image reflection separation can be written in the form of $I = I_B + I_R$, where I_B and I_R refer to background image and reflection image respectively. Existing methods to solve this problem can be classified into three main categories by the number of input images: single image [3,5,9], image pairs captured from the same view point but with different imaging condition such as polarized filter [2] or flash [1], and image sequence [4,12,15]. As the problem is highly ill-posed, methods using single image usually introduce different priors, which limit their usage when the priors are not well-fitted. Methods using polarizer or flash are not practical for ordinary people as they require specific

© Springer International Publishing AG, part of Springer Nature 2018
B. Zeng et al. (Eds.): PCM 2017, LNCS 10736, pp. 161–171, 2018.
https://doi.org/10.1007/978-3-319-77383-4_16

techniques. Utilizing the motion between images, methods using image sequence can handle more general cases compared with former two categories, but the accurate motion computation for images containing reflection is difficult.

We use image sequence as input. For methods using image sequence, the main problem is how to compute motion correctly between input images containing reflection. Traditional optical flow methods fail to handle this case because the motions of background and reflection layers are superimposed in the same pixel. To solve this problem, we proposed a method, called sift-edge flow, using feather matching and gradient ownership prior.

Our contributions are as follows: (1) we propose a robust method to compute motion of images containing reflection, called sift-edge flow. (2) we propose a robust method to conduct initial motion field separation and initial image decomposition. The paper is organized as follow. Section 2 summarizes the related work. Section 3 is overall of our method and the experiment is in Sect. 4. The conclusion is presented in Sect. 5.

2 Related Work

Existing methods for image reflection separation can be classified into three main categories by the number of images used: (1) single image, (2) image pairs and (3) image sequence.

For the first category, different approaches tend to introduce specific prior to increase the number of constraints in order to solve the ill-posed problem. On the base of natural image gradient sparsity prior, Levin et al. [3] proposed to add user interaction to mark the background and reflection edges separately, and the background image and reflection image can be reconstructed using IRLS optimization. But the human labeling is a tedious job. Li et al. [5] assumed photographers were more interested in the background image, as a result, the background would be focused and reflection blurrier. Shih et al. [9] proposed to remove reflection using the cue that reflection could be double, for example, the reflection on both sides of window. The last two methods can produce nice results when the priors are well-suited, but the priors are not always suited for not all the reflections are blurrier or double.

The second category uses image pairs. [2] proposed to conduct reflection separation using image pairs with different polarizer angles, as the combination coefficients of the background and reflection vary with the direction of the polarized filters. [1] used a pair of flash and no-flash images as input, and conducted reflection separation using projection of gradients between flash image and no-flash image. But all of these methods need specific technique, which are not practical for ordinary people.

The third category uses image sequence, which is also referred as motion based reflection separation. These methods can be further classified into two categories by the usage of motion cues. The first category uses motion to label background and reflection edges. Both Li et al. [4] and Sun et al. [12] used sift flow [6] to align input images. They assumed that the background motion would be dominant and background would be roughly static after image alignment and the edges could be marked by the computation of edge probability or motion score. Then the problem was reduced to single image reflection separation problem solved by Levin et al. [3]. The second category uses motion to warp images, combining reflection separation and optical flow computation together, which shows a better result compared to previous works. They update the layer images and motion fields simultaneously, as done by Xue et al. [15] and Yang et al. [16]. But their methods heavily rely on initial solution of the motion computation, and their initialization methods are not robust for some cases.

3 Our Method

3.1 Method Overview

We exploit the fact that the background and reflection usually have different motions across input image sequence, as they have different visual depth to the camera, so we use it to separate the reflection. Our pipeline is shown in Fig. 1, which is similar to the pipeline in [15]. For ease of illustration, we first give the form of our objective function

$$\min_{I_B, I_R, \{V_B^t\}, \{V_R^t\}} \sum_t \|I^t - W(V_B^t)I_B - W(V_R^t)I_R\|_1 + E_{prior}(I_B, I_R) + \sum_t E_{prior}(V_B^t, V_R^t) \quad (1)$$

The function uses image sequence and their dense motion fields as input, and outputs background and reflection images of the reference image, which is one image chosen from input sequence. In Eq. 1, the first term is data term, which encodes the warp error of background and reflection components to input images,

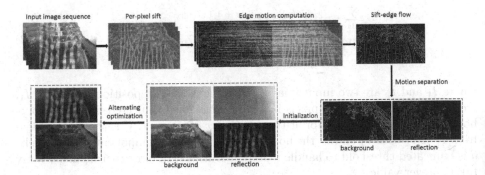

Fig. 1. Method overview. We first compute per-pixel sift descriptor for input images, and compute the motion vectors using sift-edge flow on image edges extracted from input images using Canny, then divide the resulting sparse motion field into two parts, which we use to interpolate the dense motion fields of the background and reflection images. Based on them, initial image decomposition is conducted. The final result is obtained by using alternating optimization with the initial layer images and dense motion fields provided.

the second term is prior terms on layer images and the third term is prior terms on motion fields. t is index for input images, V_R^t and V_B^t are dense motion fields of the reflection and background components from image t to reference image. $W(\cdot)$ is function that constructs warping matrix using motion field. I_R and I_B are reflection and background images of reference image. $W(V_B^t)I_B$ is warped background image using background motion field, similar for $W(V_R^t)I_R$. The objective function can be minimized by updating the layer images and motion fields alternately. We will give a concrete objective function expression and optimization procedure in later sections.

3.2   Sift-Edge Flow

It is necessary to provide a good initialization for motion fields and layer images to conduct the optimization above. For images containing reflection, traditional optical flow method often fails for the complex intensity change, which is caused due to two motions for one pixel in the region of reflection. Li [4] uses sift flow as the motion of input images, as the sift feature is more robust and less affected by the reflection compared to pixel intensity. However, it fails in the case where the feature of background and reflection is confusing, As a result, it is hard to determine whether the calculated motion belongs to background or reflection.

Our method is based on the prior that an observed image gradient (or an image edge) belongs to either the background or reflection layer, but the probability that it belongs to both two layers is very small, which is also called gradient ownership prior. As a result, the motion of background and reflection is separated on the image edge and motions on one edge should be similar. To handle the complex intensity change caused by reflection, we use sift descriptor as image similarity indictor. The energy function of sift-edge flow is defined as

$$\min_V \sum_{x \in Edge(I_1)} \| s(I_1(x)) - s(I_2(x + V(x))) \|_1$$
$$+ \sum_{\substack{x,x' \in Edge(I_1) \\ x,x' \in \Omega}} \min(\alpha|V_1(I_1(x)) - V_1(I_1(x'))|, d) + \min(\alpha|V_2(I_1(x)) - V_2(I_1(x'))|, d) \tag{2}$$

where I_1 and I_2 are two input images, x and x' are pixel positions in image I_1, $Edge(I_1)$ is the set of edge pixels in I_1 and Ω is four-connected pixel neighborhood. $s(I(x))$ is sift descriptor at the position x of image I, V is the motion field from I_1 to I_2 with V_1 and V_2 the horizontal and vertical components respectively. d is truncated threshold to handle matching outliers. In our experiments, V only takes integer value.

The first term in Eq. 2 is data term that describes how well the image patch is matched along the flow vector through feature matching. The second term is regulation term, which enforces motions on neighboring edge pixels to be similar. The energy function can be modeled by Markov Random Field. We solve it using loopy belief propagation and use the resulting edge motion vectors to construct sparse motion fields of background and reflection layers.

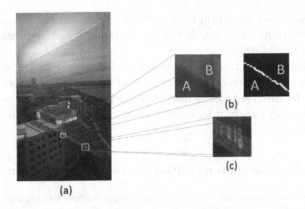

Fig. 2. Illustration for the comparison of using four-connected neighboring pixels and neighboring edge pixels. (a) image containing reflections. (b) zoomed-in region for the boundary of reflection and background and corresponding edge map. (c) zoomed-in region where the interplay of reflection and background is more complex for motion computation

Notice that the sparse motion field is only calculated on image edges, in other words, the Markov random field is only defined using image edge structure, which is different from sift flow and other optical flow algorithms that calculated on four-connected image grid structure, and we will demonstrate that we can get separated motions of background and reflection in this way. As shown in Fig. 2b, an image edge belonging to reflection is highlighted, and in region A the background is dominant, but contrarily reflection is dominant in region B. In traditional optical flow algorithm using four-connected pixel neighborhood, when computing motion near the boundary of region A and B, the motions are regularized to be as similar as possible because they are in the same four-connected pixel neighborhood. But there are both background pixels and reflection pixels in this neighborhood and their motions are different in fact. Trying to regularize them to have similar motion will lead to error in motion computation, which may be worse for regions where the interplay of background and reflection is complex, for example, Fig. 2c. But if we only calculate the motion on edges, problem is solved as neighboring edge pixels belong to the same image layer, which can suppress the interplay of background and reflection. In addition, the probability of that the background and reflection edges intersect or connect in four-connected pixel neighborhood is small, which also contributes to getting separated background and reflection motions at edges.

The reason that sift flow preforms better for images containing reflection than traditional optical flow, as used by Li [4] and Sun [12], is that sift descriptor can handle the interference from other layers to some degree, but as it is based on four-connected neighborhood, the interplay of background and reflection may lead to false motion computation result and reduce robustness. Xue et al. [15] also calculates motion on image edges and proposes edge flow, but as edge flow only uses normalized cross correlation to measure the similarity of image patches, the result is noisy and contains a number of mismatches, which reduces the accuracy of the motion computation.

As the technique for feature detection and description has achieved great development in recent years [8,14], we can also generalize our method to a more general model, feature based edge flow. The only work needed to do is to replace the sift in our energy function by other features. We choose sift in our work just for its robustness.

3.3   Motion Separation and Initial Layer Decomposition

After obtaining the sparse motion field on image edges, we separate it into two parts, one for background and the other for reflection. We first conduct a coarse clustering for the motion vectors, as a result, the sparse set of motion vectors is separated into two parts. We use k-means for the coarse clustering. Even using sift descriptor for edge motion computation, there may be some mismatches, so we eliminate error motion vectors using RANSAC. For each set of motion vectors, we use it to fit a perspective transformation, and assign pixels whose motion vectors best fit the transformation to the corresponding background or reflection layer respectively. In normal conditions, the motion for reflection part may be more complex than background, so we use different values for reprojection error when fitting transformations and the value for reflection part is a little larger than that for background. In our experiment, the value for background is 0.5 pixel and 1.5 pixels for reflection.

After getting sparse motion fields for each layer, we use them to construct dense motion fields by interpolation. Define the dense motion fields of two layers as W_B^t and W_R^t, which refer to background and reflection dense motion fields from image t to reference image respectively, and we can get initial image decomposition through image warping. When warping the input image sequence to reference image using W_B^t, we will get a resulting image sequence with background nearly static, and the reflection will be nearly static when warped using W_R^t. We can get the initial image decomposition using these two sequences.

To get the initial background image, we first warp all input images to the reference image using background motion field W_B^t, then get the minimum value for each pixel across the aligned resulting images and use it as the initial solution for the background image, as the contributions from the reflection layer can only add the intensity at a given pixel in the observed image [13].

To get the initial reflection image, we first warp the initial background image to image I^t using W_B^t, and get the difference image D^t by subtracting the initial background image from original input image I^t. Then we warp the difference image D^t to the reference image using reflection motion field W_R^t. For the resulting image sequence, the reflection component is nearly static, and we compute the median for each pixel as the initial solution for reflection image, which is less affected by noise.

3.4   Optimization

The objective function we use is Eq. 3, where $\| \cdot \|_1$ means L-1 norm, I_t, I_B and I_R are $n \times 1$ vectors which represent the input images, background image and reflection image respectively, n is the number of pixel. For ease of computation, we normalize the value of pixel intensity to range $[0, 1]$. ∇ is gradient operator. V_B^t and V_R^t are sets of motion vectors for background and reflection respectively, both in the form of $n \times 2$ matrix. $W(V_B^t)$ is $n \times n$ matrix such that $W(V_B^t)I_B$ is warped background image according to the background motion field V_B^t, and it is same for $W(V_R^t)$.

$$\min_{I_B, I_R, \{V_B^t\}, \{V_R^t\}} \sum_t \|I^t - W(V_B^t)I_B - W(V_R^t)I_R\|_1 + \lambda_1 (\|\nabla I_B\|_1 + \|\nabla I_R\|_1)$$

$$+\lambda_2 \sum_x (\nabla I_B(x))^2 (\nabla I_R(x))^2 + \lambda_3 \sum_t (\|\nabla V_B^t\|_1 + \|\nabla V_R^t\|_1) \qquad (3)$$

$$0 \le I_B, I_R \le 1$$

The first term in objective function is data term, which encodes the reconstruction error between the warped background image, warped reflection image and input image sequence. The second term enforces gradient sparsity prior [3] on I_B and I_R as they are both natural images. The third term enforces the gradient ownership prior by penalizing the product of the gradients of background and reflection at the same pixel position. The fourth term enforces smoothness of the motion field. The parameters λ_1, λ_2 and λ_3 we use are same as Xue [15].

We solve the objective function using alternating gradient descent method. We first fix $\{W_B^t\}$ and $\{W_R^t\}$ and solve for I_B and I_R, then fix I_B and I_R and solve for $\{W_B^t\}$ and $\{W_R^t\}$. For each alternating step, we solve the minimization using iterative reweighted least squares (IRLS) [7]. To accelerate the computation, as done by many optical methods, we use multi-scale processing and we only compute sift-edge flow at the coarsest level.

4   Experiments

In this section, we show the experiment results of our method. First, we compare the initial motion separation result with [15], which also uses edge motions to construct motion fields of two layers. As shown in Fig. 3, there are less misclassifications for the background and reflection edge motions in our method, which is due to the accurate motion computation of sift-edge flow. And the following optimization will benefit.

For the final reflection separation, we compare with methods in [4, 15], which also use image sequence as input. Both these two methods outperform related methods proposed these years, and could represent the start of art. For method in [4], we use the source code from author's webpage. Since the source code of [15] is not available, we implemented it and optimized the result as better as we can. The comparison results are shown from Figs. 4, 5 and 6 (better view on

Fig. 3. Experiment result for edge motion separation. For each column from left to right: input image, edge map of input image, motion separation result of [15] and ours, the classified background and reflection edge motions are colored in red and blue respectively (Color figure online)

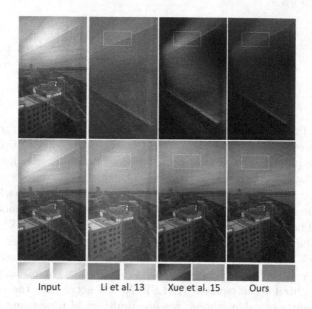

Input   Li et al. 13   Xue et al. 15   Ours

Fig. 4. For each column from left to right: image input, result of [4,15] and ours. For each row from top to bottom: separated reflection, background and zoomed-in local region

screen). The image sequence we use is from [4,15]. We implement our method using Matlab and run it on Intel Xeon CPU with 32 GB memory. It takes about 25 min to processing images with resolution 648 × 1152, which is a little longer compared with [4] and almost the same with [15].

Obviously, our method shows a better result than Li's method [4] for a clear separation of reflection and background with less residual. Also, our method gives better results in the details compared to Xue's method [15], which owes to the accurate edge motion computation (sift-edge flow) and robust motion separation method used in our method. For dusk sequence (Fig. 4), our result has less reflection residual in the resulting background image but there is some reflected window trace in Xue's result, such as the region square marked. For marked region in night sequence (Fig. 5), our method gives a better result in the

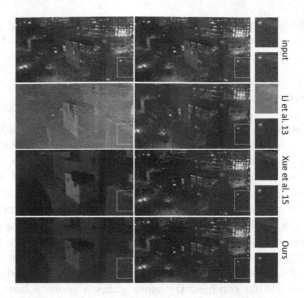

Fig. 5. For each row from top to bottom: image input, result of [4,15] and ours. For each column from left to right: separated reflection, background and zoomed-in local region

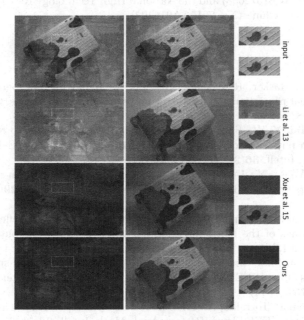

Fig. 6. Image reflection separation results of box image sequence. The meaning of each row and each column are same as Fig. 5

details of the cabinet. And for box sequence (Fig. 6), our method gives a better separation of the reflected window and background box (see marked region for detail).

5 Conclusion

We have presented a robust image reflection separation method based on sift-edge flow. First, we propose sift-edge flow to compute the sparse motion field of image edges based on gradient ownership prior. Second, the sparse motion field is separated into two parts using clustering and refined by RANSAC with different threshold for background and reflection components. Then dense motion fields of two layers are interpolated and the initial layer images are obtained by warping input image sequence to the reference image using the dense motion fields of background and reflection respectively. The separated images are reconstructed using alternating optimization with the initial solution provided. Experiment results show that our method can give clear separated background and reflection images with less visible residual, therefore gains a more robust performance compared with the state of the art.

Acknowledgement. This paper is supported by the National Natural Science Foundation of China (No. 61572058) and the National High Technology Research and Development Program of China (No. 2015AA016402).

References

1. Agrawal, A., Raskar, R., Nayar, S.K., Li, Y.: Removing photography artifacts using gradient projection and flash-exposure sampling. ACM Trans. Graph. (TOG) **24**(3), 828–835 (2005)
2. Kong, N., Tai, Y.-W., Shin, J.S.: A physically-based approach to reflection separation: from physical modeling to constrained optimization. IEEE Trans. Pattern Anal. Mach. Intell. **36**(2), 209–221 (2014)
3. Levin, A., Weiss, Y.: User assisted separation of reflections from a single image using a sparsity prior. IEEE Trans. Pattern Anal. Mach. Intell. **29**(9), 1647–1654 (2007)
4. Li, Y., Brown, M.S.: Exploiting reflection change for automatic reflection removal. In: Proceedings of the IEEE International Conference on Computer Vision, pp. 2432–2439 (2013)
5. Li, Y., Brown, M.S.: Single image layer separation using relative smoothness. In: Proceedings of the IEEE Conference on Computer Vision and Pattern Recognition, pp. 2752–2759 (2014)
6. Liu, C., Yuen, J., Torralba, A.: SIFT flow: dense correspondence across scenes and its applications. IEEE Trans. Pattern Anal. Mach. Intell. **33**(5), 978–994 (2011)
7. Meer, P.: Robust techniques for computer vision. In: Emerging Topics in Computer Vision, pp. 107–190 (2004)
8. Rublee, E., Rabaud, V., Konolige, K., Bradski, G.: ORB: an efficient alternative to SIFT or SURF. In: 2011 IEEE International Conference on Computer Vision (ICCV), pp. 2564–2571. IEEE (2011)

9. Shih, Y., Krishnan, D., Durand, F., Freeman, W.T.: Reflection removal using ghosting cues. In: Proceedings of the IEEE Conference on Computer Vision and Pattern Recognition, pp. 3193–3201 (2015)
10. Simon, C., Park, I.K.: Reflection removal for in-vehicle black box videos. In: Proceedings of the IEEE Conference on Computer Vision and Pattern Recognition, pp. 4231–4239 (2015)
11. Sinha, S.N., Kopf, J., Goesele, M., Scharstein, D., Szeliski, R.: Image-based rendering for scenes with reflections. ACM Trans. Graph. **31**(4), 100:1–100:10 (2012)
12. Sun, C., Liu, S., Yang, T., Zeng, B., Wang, Z., Liu, G.: Automatic reflection removal using gradient intensity and motion cues. In: Proceedings of the 2016 ACM on Multimedia Conference, pp. 466–470. ACM (2016)
13. Szeliski, R., Avidan, S., Anandan, P.: Layer extraction from multiple images containing reflections and transparency. In: IEEE Conference on Computer Vision and Pattern Recognition, Proceedings, vol. 1, pp. 246–253. IEEE (2000)
14. Weinzaepfel, P., Revaud, J., Harchaoui, Z., Schmid, C.: DeepFlow: large displacement optical flow with deep matching. In: Proceedings of the IEEE International Conference on Computer Vision, pp. 1385–1392 (2013)
15. Xue, T., Rubinstein, M., Liu, C., Freeman, W.T.: A computational approach for obstruction-free photography. ACM Trans. Graph. (TOG) **34**(4), 79:1–79:11 (2015)
16. Yang, J., Li, H., Dai, Y., Tan, R.T.: Robust optical flow estimation of double-layer images under transparency or reflection. In: Proceedings of the IEEE Conference on Computer Vision and Pattern Recognition, pp. 1410–1419 (2016)

A Fine-Grained Filtered Viewpoint Informed Keypoint Prediction from 2D Images

Qingnan Li[1,2], Ruimin Hu[1,2,3(✉)], Yixin Chen[1,2,3,4], Jingwen Yan[1,2], and Jing Xiao[1,2,4]

[1] School of Computer Science,
National Engineering Research Center for Multimedia Software,
Wuhan University, Wuhan 430072, China
{qingqing,hrm,blairchen,yanjingwen,jing}@whu.edu.cn
[2] Hubei Key Laboratory of Multimedia and Network Communication Engineering,
Wuhan University, Wuhan 430072, China
[3] Collaborative Innovation Center of Geospatial Technology,
Wuhan 430079, China
[4] Research Institute of Wuhan University, Shenzhen, China

Abstract. Viewpoint informed keypoint prediction from 2D images is an essential task in computer vision, which captures the fine details of rigid objects, however, the cases of ambiguous viewpoint predicted by the convolutional neural network, especially for two peaks of high confidence viewpoint proposals, may specify a set of erroneous keypoints. To address the above issue, we present multiscale convolutional neural networks and propose a filter to ensure high confidence viewpoint informed, which provides a global perspective for keypoint prediction. Leveraging the global precedence, we combine multiscale local appearance based keypoint likelihood with filtered viewpoint conditioned likelihood to induce a considerable performance gain. Experimentally, we show that our framework outperforms state-of-the-art methods on PASCAL 3D benchmark.

Keywords: Filter · Viewpoint conditioned · Keypoint prediction

1 Introduction

Keypoint prediction has been widely studied over the last decade. There are two ways of predicting keypoints. Tree structured methods model the spatial relationships between different parts [4,7], usually for human keypoint localization. The other methods focus on local appearance using convolutional neural networks, which have demonstrated outstanding performance in keypoint prediction [1,5], usually for rigid objects. In this paper, we aim to predict keypoints from 12 categories of rigid objects.

Inspired by the global precedence and local appearance [5], our overall approach deals with viewpoint prediction as well as keypoint prediction. The former models the global spatial relationships between different parts of objects, and the latter localizes the keypoints directly based on the local appearance. Coupled with global appearance, we can develop a finer understanding of objects, which is crucial to the discrimination performance of keypoint prediction. The previous works [5] on the above idea have improved the performance by summing viewpoint conditioned keypoint likelihood and appearance based keypoint likelihood together in their framework. However, the existing works [2] prove that the viewpoint predictions have common confusions, which may play an even negative role for keypoint prediction, as illustrated in Fig. 1.

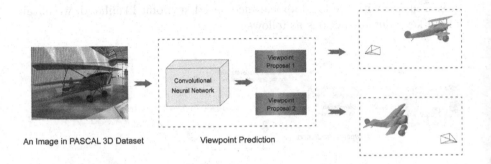

An Image in PASCAL 3D Dataset   Viewpoint Prediction

Fig. 1. An error mode of viewpoint prediction.

The image in Fig. 1 is labeled with the ground truth bounding box in PASCAL 3D dataset. The previous works [2] use Convolutional Neural Network (CNN) to estimate the viewpoint proposals, and adopt the most likely viewpoint proposal, whereas the second viewpoint proposal is probably closest to the ground truth. So we argue that the CNN has been trapped in the ambiguous viewpoints due to the similar peaks of high confidence in the two candidate viewpoint proposals.

To address the above problem, we introduce a filter to ensure high confidence viewpoint informed in our overall framework, as illustrated in Fig. 2, which has the following components -

Viewpoint Predition: We characterize the problem of viewpoint prediction for rigid objects as predicting the euler angles: azimuth(θ), elevation(ϕ) and in-plane rotation(ψ). A CNN model has been proposed to implicitly capture the features of rigid objects and build the spatial relationships among different local features for viewpoint classification.

Keypoint Prediction: We formulate the problem of keypoint prediction for rigid objects as predicting the response maps corresponding to different categories of keypoints. A multiscale CNN model has been proposed to model the relationships between the keypoint localization and the response map based on keypoint likelihood distribution.

Viewpoint Filtered: The two peaks of high confidence viewpoint proposals predicted by CNN may play a negative role in our overall approach for keypoint prediction. Leveraging the filter, we propose a fine-grained viewpoint filter formulation, which passes the viewpoint proposal with a unique peak of high confidence and attenuates the two ambiguous viewpoint proposals with similar confidence at the meanwhile.

Viewpoint Filterd Keypoint Likelihood: For a certain image, the exact locations of keypoints are specified geometrically when given the accurate viewpoint. For images of the same category, however, the proper locations of keypoints are identified as a probability distribution when given the similar viewpoints. Coupled with the local appearance based keypoint likelihood, we obtain our final keypoint predictions as follows -

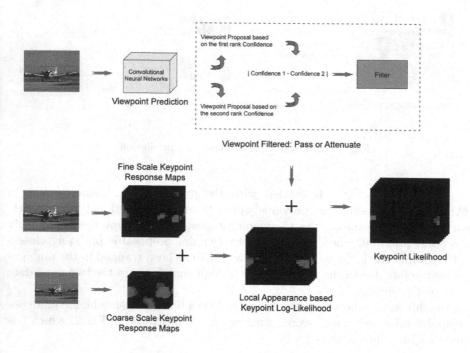

Fig. 2. Overview of our approach.

We obtain viewpoint proposals from a CNN model, and use the filter structure to determine whether the proposals are ambiguous. Given accurate viewpoint predictions based on the unique high confidence, we define a nonparametric mixture of gaussians to model the distribution of keypoints based on the similar viewpoints. Our final keypoint likelihood is the sum of viewpoint conditioned keypoint likelihood and local appearance based keypoint likelihood. And meanwhile, if the given viewpoint predictions are ambiguous, the filter attenuates them and therefore the final keypoint likelihood equals the local appearance based keypoint likelihood only.

We present our filtered viewpoint informed keypoint prediction in Sect. 3, and evaluate our performance on the standard PASCAL 3D validation set [9] in Sect. 4. Furthermore, we will analyze the relationship between PCK and threshold τ in Sect. 5, and suggest insights for future works.

2   Relative Works

Convolutional Neural Network (CNN) has the great power in extracting the intrinsic features and modeling the spatial relationships between local features, which has demonstrated its outstanding performance in many image understanding tasks. In this work, we train CNNs for global perspective based viewpoint prediction as well as local appearance based keypoint prediction.

Viewpoint Prediction: Deformable Part Model (DPM) [10] can be extended to estimate the viewpoint based on their mixtures of multiscale deformable part models, which explicitly captures the deformations between certain pairs of parts. DPM has achieved the powerful performance, however, recently, CNN has outperformed the DPM methods by implicitly modeling the local appearance and relationships between parts. Inspired by the growing availability of 3D models, an image synthesis pipeline with a specifically tailored CNN is proposed to predict viewpoint [2], which generates the training data to avoid over-fitting. Furthermore, subcategory-aware convolutional neural network [13] is proposed for object detection and pose estimation, which introduce the subcategory information to guide the training process. Their results achieve state-of-the-art performance on both detection and pose estimation. Meanwhile, a framework based on deep learning and geometry [12] is proposed for 3D object detection and pose estimation from a given image. Their method combines the estimates that predicted by their CNN model with geometric constraints provided by a 2D object bounding box to produce a 3D bounding box, which outperforms monocular state-of-the-art approaches on the challenging KITTI benchmark for vehicle detection and orientation. Therefore, we leverage the CNN architectures to predict viewpoint, which is one of the core pillars in our framework.

Keypoint Prediction: We focus on the keypoint prediction of objects with known bounding box. The classic model [3] is proposed to capture contextual co-occurrence relations between parts, and recently features extracted from images are proved to be effective for understanding local appearance [1]. CNN based approaches [14,15] have demonstrate their outstanding performance on keypoint prediction for human. For rigid objects, deep MANTA [11] presents a robust convolutional network for vehicle detection, part localization, visibility characterization and 3D dimension estimation from a given image, which wins the first place on the KITTI vision benchmark for vehicle object detection and orientation estimation evaluation. We build our framework on the previous approach [5], which estimates the viewpoint and the keypoint simultaneously. By leveraging the viewpoint estimates, the local appearance based keypoint likelihood is combined with the filtered viewpoint informed keypoint likelihood to obtain the final keypoint likelihood as our final results, which have achieved outstanding performance on 12 categories of rigid objects on PASCAL 3D validation set [9].

3   Filtered Viewpoint Informed Keypoint Prediction

3.1   Viewpoint Network

We classify the viewpoint into $3 * N_c * N_a$ disjoint bins, where the number ahead stands for azimuth(θ), elevation(ϕ) and in-plane rotation(ψ). N_c indicates the number of classes that will be detected, and N_a is specified as a particular number of bins. Therefore, the output layer of our CNN architecture has $3 * N_c * N_a$ neurons. To exploit the low level features between different classes effectively, the convolutional layers and fully connection layers ahead are shared by all classes, as illustrated in Fig. 3. Models proposed in [2,5] are probably the closest to our viewpoint CNN architecture.

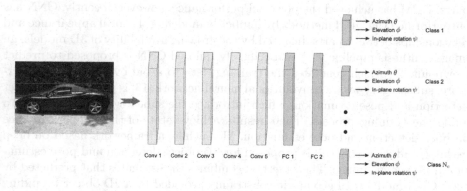

Fig. 3. CNN architecture for viewpoint prediction.

We adopt a logistic loss to process the back-propagation for each class, and train our viewpoint network on PASCAL 3D train dataset as well as ImageNet dataset. The PASCAL VOC 2012 validation set [9] is used for our performance evaluation.

3.2   Keypoint Network

We classify the keypoint into $N_c * (\sum_{c=1}^{N_c} N_{ck}) * N_r$ disjoint bins, where N_c stands for the number of classes, and N_{ck} is the number of keypoints for each class from class 1 to class N_c. We note that N_{ck} varies according to the different classes. For instance, the category of aeroplane is arranged as the first class with $N_{1k} = 16$, which has 16 part names corresponding to 16 response maps, whereas the second class of bicycle has 11 keypoints corresponding to 11 response maps, with $N_{2k} = 11$.

N_r is specified as 144 corresponding to $12 * 12$ response map for a keypoint local-ization in convolutional neural network. The image in the input layer is resized to a fixed size of $384 * 384$. Therefore, a keypoint localization predicted by our CNN model in the response map corresponds to an area of $32 * 32$ in the input image, as illustrated in Fig. 4. Contrary to the details described in the Sect. 3.1, we imple-ment euclidean loss to process the back-propagation for each class, and train the keypoint network using the annotations provided by [8].

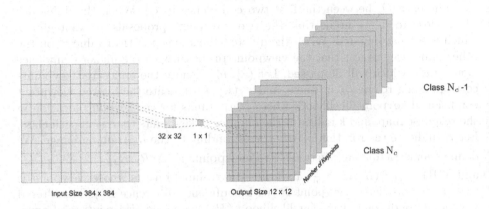

Fig. 4. The correspondence between the input and the output.

The above CNN captures the local appearance, which implicitly models the relationship between different parts at a fine level. However, fine details may result in a fine response map but would probably be trapped in a failure case. Therefore, we adopt a coarse fully convolutional neural network to obtain a coarse response map in a robust way, which has a smaller input size $192 * 192$ and a smaller output size $6 * 6 * N_{ck}$ for each class. We upsample the coarse keypoint response maps, and combine them with the fine keypoint response maps to obtain spatial likelihood response maps, as illustrated in Fig. 2 in the Sect. 1.

3.3 Filtered Viewpoint

We observe that keypoint localization follows a statistic distribution in similar perspectives, as illustrated in Fig. 5. The cars in the first row are rendered from similar viewpoints, and the keypoints in the second row are the ground truth, which are shifted and scaled from the images in the first row. We find that the locations of keypoints from all of the images follow a statistic distribution, which helps us re-locate the keypoint predicted by CNN in Sect. 3.1.

The final keypoint likelihood is the sum of appearance based keypoint like-lihood and viewpoint conditioned keypoint likelihood, as illustrated in Fig. 1. However, the performance of keypoint prediction would be worsen if the view-point is inaccurate or even far apart from the ground truth. In this work, we propose a confidence based filter to solve the above problem. Let C_i denote the

Keypoint Locations

Fig. 5. Keypoint Locations.

confidence corresponding to viewpoint proposals of the i_{th} image. We achieve the difference D_i between the first two confidence in C_i. When the difference D_i is close to 0, we argue that the two viewpoint proposals are ambiguous, which will be attenuated. When the difference exceeds a critical value τ, on the other hand, we suggest that the viewpoint proposal with the higher confidence is accurate, which will be passed. Let (x_k^i, y_k^i) denote the annotated keypoints corresponding to the i_{th} instance, and $P_f(i, j, k)$ indicate the filtered viewpoint conditioned keypoint likelihood, where (i, j) stands for the keypoint location in the response map, and k indicates the number of keypoints (parts) in each class. Let R_i indicate the rotation matrix corresponding to the i_{th} training image. We define geometric distance between two viewpoints as $\Delta(R_1, R_2) = \frac{\|log(R_1^T R_2)\|}{\sqrt{2}}$, and $N(R) = \{i | \Delta(R, R_i) < \frac{\pi}{6}\}$ indicates the training images whose viewpoint is close to the predicted viewpoint R (with confidence difference D_r). The filtered viewpoint conditioned keypoint likelihood (P_f) is defined as a mixture of gaussians. The final keypoint likelihood is the sum of (P_f) and the local appearance based likelihood (L) as follows -

$$P_f(\cdot, \cdot, k) = \frac{(1)^n}{|N(R)|} \sum_{i \in N(R)} \mathcal{N}((x_k^i, y_k^i), \sigma I), \quad n = \begin{cases} 1, & D_r > \tau \\ 0, & otherwise \end{cases} \quad (1)$$

$$(x_k, y_k) = \arg\max_{y,x} \ log(P_f(x, y, k)) + L(x, y, k) \quad (2)$$

An improvement has been achieved based on the modified viewpoint conditioned likelihood formula [5], where n = 1 indicates that the viewpoint conditioned keypoint likelihood P_f is used for keypoint prediction, whereas n = 0 means that the predicted viewpoint is probably ambiguous, and therefore P_f is abandoned. We sort the viewpoint predictions according to ascending order in the confidence difference D, and define a certain proportion of all viewpoint predictions as the ambiguous viewpoints. The adaptive threshold τ is specified by the above certain proportion.

4   Experiments

We evaluate our performance in the settings with known bounding box in PASCAL 3D validation set [9], and follow the PCK evaluation metric proposed in [3]. We abandon 10% of viewpoint predictions (probably ambiguous) using adaptive confidence filter thresholds τ_i for the i_{th} class. The τ_i is specified around

0.3 according to the proportion above for most classes. The performance of our framework and comparison to [1,5] are shown in Table 1. Our result 'conv6 + conv12 + filtered-pLikelihood' outperforms the previous predictions presented in [5], which are shown as 'conv6', 'conv12', 'conv6 + conv12' and 'conv6 + conv12 +pLikelihood'. Generally, we suggest that the viewpoint filter plays a positive role in keypoint prediction (Fig. 6).

PCK: The keypoint prediction is identified as the correct keypoint if it lies within $\alpha * \max(h, w)$ of the annotated image, which has a dimension of (h, w). We predict the keypoint corresponding to each part of rigid objects.

Fig. 6. Filtered viewpoint informed keypoint likelihood. We take 'Nosetip' of aeroplanes, 'CranksetCenter' of bicycles for examples.

Table 1. Keypoint Localization.

PCK[$\alpha = 0.1$]	Aero	Bike	Boat	Bottle	Bus	Car	Chaire	Table	Mbike	Sofa	Train	TV	Mean
Long et al. [1]	53.7	60.9	33.8	72.9	70.4	55.7	18.5	22.9	52.9	38.3	53.3	49.2	48.5
conv6 [5]	51.4	62.4	37.8	65.1	60.1	59.9	34.8	31.8	53.6	44.0	52.3	41.1	49.5
conv12 [5]	54.9	66.8	32.6	60.2	80.5	59.3	35.1	37.8	58.0	41.6	59.3	53.8	53.3
conv6+conv12 [5]	61.9	74.6	43.6	72.8	84.3	70.0	45.0	44.8	66.7	51.2	66.8	56.8	61.5
conv6+conv12+ pLikelihood [5]	66.0	77.8	52.1	83.8	**88.7**	81.3	65.0	47.3	68.3	58.8	**72.0**	65.1	68.8
conv6+conv12+ f_pLikelihood	**71.6**	**78.9**	**59.0**	**87.4**	88.0	**86.1**	**66.4**	**55.1**	**72.7**	**59.2**	71.3	**69.2**	**72.1**

5   Analysis

In this section, we analyze the relationship between PCK and τ in our framework, which suggest insights for the future work. The viewpoint filter plays a positive role in avoiding the ambiguous viewpoint proposals but also a negative role in attenuating the accurate viewpoint proposals. We take four categories of rigid objects for examples, as illustrated in Fig. 7.

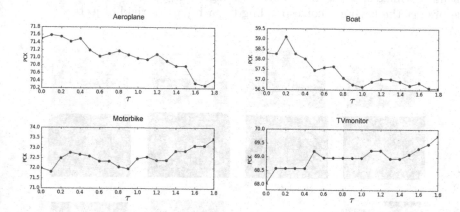

Fig. 7. The PCK evaluation for aeroplane, boat, motorbike and TV monitor.

When the τ increases, the PCK varies, which means that the ambiguous viewpoint predictions are attenuated as well as the probably accurate viewpoint predictions. Particularly, for the classes of aeroplane and boat, the PCK decreases as the τ increases, which indicates that a broader range of ambiguous viewpoints determined by τ do not induce a considerable performance gain. For classes of TV monitor and motorbike, on the other hand, the PCK increases generally as the τ increases, which denotes that many of viewpoints predicted by CNN in Sect. 3.1 are probably inaccurate.

In addition, for TV monitor, the PCK keeps constant sometimes as the τ increases, which is different from the previous experimental results. Through the analysis of this case, we find that the most of viewpoint proposals are probably accurate with the unique high confidence.

6   Conclusion

We propose a method that leverages the CNN architectures to predict keypoint with filtered viewpoint informed keypoint likelihood, and demonstrate an improvement over previous state-of-the-art results [1,5] on the PASCAL 3D dataset. We evaluate our performance following the PCK evaluation metric and hope that our algorithm will contribute towards progress on the task of keypoint prediction.

Acknowledgments. This work was partly supported by the National High Technology Research and Development Program of China (863 Program) No. 2015AA016306, National Nature Science Foundation of China (No. 61231015), EU FP7 QUICK project under Grant Agreement No. PIRSES-GA-2013-612652*, National Nature Science Foundation of China (61502348), Hubei Province Technological Innovation Major Project (No. 2016AAA015), science and technology program of Shenzhen (JCYJ20150422150029092).

References

1. Long, J., Zhang, N., Darrell, T.: Do convnets learn correspondence? In: Advances in Neural Information Processing Systems, vol. 2, pp. 1601–1609 (2014)
2. Su, H., Qi, C.R., Li, Y., Guibas, L.J.: Render for CNN: viewpoint estimation in images using CNNs trained with rendered 3D model views. In: IEEE International Conference on Computer Vision, pp. 2686–2694 (2014)
3. Yang, Y., Ramanan, D.: Articulated pose estimation using flexible mixtures of parts. In: Computer Vision & Pattern Recognition, vol. 32, no. 14, pp. 1385–1392 (2011)
4. Gkioxari, G., Hariharan, B., Girshick, R., Malik, J.: Using k-poselets for detecting people and localizing their keypoints. In: Computer Vision & Pattern Recognition, pp. 3582–3589 (2014)
5. Tulsiani, S., Malik, J.: Viewpoints and keypoints. In: Computer Vision & Pattern Recognition, pp. 1510–1519 (2015)
6. Zhang, N., Shelhamer, E., Gao, Y., Darrell, T.: Fine-grained pose prediction, normalization, and recognition. Comput. Sci. **69**(2), 207–221 (2016)
7. Gkioxari, G., Arbelaez, P., Bourdev, L., Malik, J.: Articulated pose estimation using discriminative armlet classifiers. In: IEEE International Conference on Computer Vision, vol. 9, no. 4, pp. 3342–3349 (2013)
8. Bourdev, L., Maji, S., Brox, T., Malik, J.: Detecting people using mutually consistent poselet activations. In: European Conference on Computer Vision, pp. 168–181 (2010)
9. Everingham, M., Van Gool, L., Williams, C.K.I., Winn, J., Zisserman, A.: The PASCAL Visual Object Classes Challenge 2012 (VOC2012) Results (2012)
10. Felzenszwalb, P.F., Girshick, R.B., Mcallester, D., Ramanan, D.: Object detection with discriminatively trained part-based models. IEEE Trans. Pattern Anal. Mach. Intell. **32**(9), 1627–1645 (2010)
11. Chabot, F., Chaouch, M., Rabarisoa, J., Teulire, C., Chateau, T.: Deep MANTA: a coarse-to-fine many-task network for joint 2D and 3D vehicle analysis from monocular image. In: Computer Vision & Pattern Recognition (2017)
12. Mousavian, A., Anguelov, D., Flynn, J., Kosecka, J.: 3D bounding box estimation using deep learning and geometry. In: Computer Vision & Pattern Recognition (2017)
13. Xiang, Y., Choi, W., Lin, Y., Savarese, S.: Subcategory-aware convolutional neural networks for object proposals and detection. In: IEEE Winter Conference on Applications of Computer Vision (2017)
14. Toshev, A., Szegedy, C.: DeepPose: human pose estimation via deep neural networks. In: Computer Vision & Pattern Recognition, pp. 1653–1660 (2014)
15. Tompson, J., Jain, A., Lecun, Y., Bregler, C.: Joint training of a convolutional network and a graphical model for human pose estimation. In: Eprint Arxiv, pp. 1799–1807 (2014)

More Efficient, Adaptive and Stable, A Virtual Fitting System Using Kinect

Chang-Tai Xiong, Shun-Lei Tang, and Ruo-Yu Yang$^{(\boxtimes)}$

National Key Laboratory for Novel Software Technology, Nanjing University,
Nanjing 210023, China
xiongcht@outlook.com, tshunlei@outlook.com, yangry@nju.edu.cn

Abstract. Under the trend of online shopping, requirements for virtual
fitting continue to increase. However, there still lacks a mature system
that can display realistic garment effects in real-time. In this paper we use
Microsoft Kinect to gather user data, and based on the real-time human
body modeling technique designed by us, the human body model that
adapts to different gestures and body sizes are generated. With suitable
clothing models (4–6k vertices on average) for the target human body,
we use Position Based Dynamics (PBD) constraints to model cloth physical properties and utilize GPU based parallelism method to accelerate
constraint resolving and collision detection. As a result, our system can
provide realistic effects for the virtual fitting while meeting the real-time
and robustness requirements.

Keywords: Virtual fitting · Human body modeling
Cloth simulation · Position Based Dynamic (PBD)

1 Introduction

With the extensive use of depth-captured camera, and the great development
of 3D reconstruction as well as cloth simulation algorithm, more and more
researchers put focus on virtual fitting. Practical virtual fitting systems should
meet a wide range of requirements. For example, it should not be restricted to
any specific scenarios, and it should be efficient and robust enough to produce
dynamic effects for many kinds of clothing in various poses of different people.

In view of the above objectives, there is no mature system yet. However,
some related works [1,2] making admirable progress in virtual fitting system.
In this paper, referring to those great works and focusing on the stability and
efficiency, we propose a virtual fitting system that can provide rich experiences
of dynamic cloth fitting.

Our system uses the silhouette and depth data obtained from Kinect to measure the human body. Then it constructs a 3D human body model close to
the target human in Kinect in real-time based on the joint positions and the
bone orientations provided by Kinect. After that, the cloth simulation module

treats the human body model as a collision geometry and uses cloth simulation method to generate realistic effects. Specifically, our system simulates cloth based on the PBD approach, and our implementation utilizing GPU parallelism highly accelerates the performance. With all these features, our system not only generates realistic cloth effects for different poses and body sizes, but also meets the efficiency and robustness requirements of the virtual fitting system.

The rest of this paper is organized as follows. Section 2 gives a brief introduction to related works of virtual fitting systems. Section 3 introduces the real-time human body modeling module of our system. Section 4 introduces the principle and implementation of the cloth simulation module of our system. Section 5 is about the architecture, introducing key parts of our implementation, as well as the performance and effects of our system. Finally, conclusion and future works are presented in Sect. 6.

2   Related Work

Human Body Modeling. [3] builds a personalized parametric model based on a known kinematic structure. [2] takes a skinned human model as a template and estimates body shape as well as constructs the mannequin model based on the twist-based deformation representation and energy based optimization, however, it requires the preprocessing for depth data filtering, and a global transformation plus a rough initial pose of the human body should be given. [4] achieve high-quality modeling from 3D scans using conformal regularization and angle-preserving deformation, but it's not suitable for real-time human modeling. [5] fitting models from templates with multiple RGB-D images and then retrieve results from the human model database. As for human body measurement, styku (http://www.styku.com) can achieve relatively precise measurements efficiently, so we use the similar method for measurements in our system.

Cloth Simulation. [6] proposes the PBD approach, where deformation energy of clothing mesh is treated as constraints, and each step of simulation is to resolve all particles' projections from predicted positions to relative constraint manifolds. [7] points out that PBD is a special case of time integration method where the stiffness of material is positive infinite. PBD is unconditionally convergence, and it can be implemented efficiency with GPU acceleration. [8] models every objects as collections of particles, applies constraints on particles directly. [9] proposes a random graph coloring method to make partitions of constraints, achieving great improvement on parallelized Gauss-Seidel constraint solver on GPU. [10] rewrites the mass of each vertex to a matrix, and restricts vertex's displacement on certain direction by eliminating the correspond component in the mass matrix. [11] computes collision penalty force or impulse according to local geometry. This method should resolve collision carefully to avoid introducing extra energy, which may lead to instability. [6] models collision as a kind of constraint directly, solves these collision constraints the same way as other normal constraints, making collision handling procedure stable and efficient.

Virtual Fitting System. [1] uses image-based method to implement the virtual fitting system, which can provide virtual fitting effects with dynamic actions. The system generates the user's skeletal poses and uses them to retrieve frames from pre-recorded fitting video database in order to synthesize virtual fitting effect, which relies heavily on the quality of those videos in the database. UniqloTry (http://www.uniqlo.com/try/) provides pre-defined human body and clothing model for users, and a fitting effect is generated within a few minutes based on offline computations, which can only provide static fitting experiences. [2] estimates body shape and constructs human body models in real-time and applies mass-spring model to do cloth simulation with PBD constraints to resolve cloth-human collision handling, which can provide users with virtual fitting effects given some basic poses.

3　Real-Time 3D Human Body Modeling

Collision geometry aligned with the human body is required for cloth simulation. In order to adapt to different genders and body shapes, a divide-and-conquer method is utilized in this paper. Taking accounts of robustness and diverse range of movement in different parts of the human body, pre-segmented components of a mannequin model that are relatively rigid are deformed and transformed according to the data that come from Kinect. Then relatively flexible parts that connect adjacent components are generated by interpolation. Finally all the models are stitched, and Laplacian-based mesh smoothing is applied to make the result smoother. Our method doesn't need preprocessing for depth data filtering and is robust in some relatively complicated scenes. Moreover, it meets the diversity and real-time requirements for virtual fitting systems.

3.1　Body Measurement and Model Component Generation

Measurements of human body rely on both joint positions and the body silhouette provided by Kinect. At the beginning of the measurement, T-pose is required. From the joint points on the depth image, straight lines are stretched perpendicular to longitudinal direction of bones, and their intersections with the body silhouette are mapped back to 3D space. The Euclidean distance between every two intersections is used as a reference for model deformation.

Since triangular mesh is not suitable for stitching, our model components are obtained by sampling along its medial axis. All the sampling points constitute a hierarchical model component, which is consistent with the definition of generalized cylinder [12]. A generalized-cylinder-based presentation is easy to stitch and suitable for constructing models along the skeleton. However, the topological structure of buttocks is quite different from cylinder, so we divide it into two parts along its axis of symmetry and sample them respectively, and finally these two parts are stitched together. The above process is shown in Fig. 1(a).

Further, we deform those components in order to match with the target human in Kinect. The tangent direction of each interpolation point at the medial axis of the model is used as the normal direction of corresponding cross section, and then vertices on the cross section are scaled planarly depend on measurements; In addition, the cross sections are stretched on the axial direction of the model by ratio determined by the length of the corresponding bone in Kinect.

Next, we assemble all the model components to match with the target human body using the joint locations and bone orientations obtained from Kinect. Since joints in Kinect may jitter in some situations, so we apply joint smoothing to filter the positions of joints and average quaternion-based joint orientations [13] within a fixed time window, where the average weights are determined by credibility of joints provided by Kinect. The final result is shown in Fig. 1(b).

3.2 Connection Model Generation and Optimization

In this paper, we define the connection model, which connects adjacent model components, as the model generated along the skeleton that connects the given top and bottom cross sections, and if an intermediate cross section exists, it should also pass through that section. The construction process is divided into two parts: to compute the shape of each cross section by linear interpolation between the corresponding vertices and to determine the orientation of each cross section by spherical linear interpolation. When the intermediate cross section is given, the procedure is further divided into two parts: one is from the top cross section to the middle cross section, and the other is from the middle cross section to the bottom cross section, and finally those two parts are combined. Above process is shown in Fig. 1(c) and a concrete example is shown in Fig. 1(d).

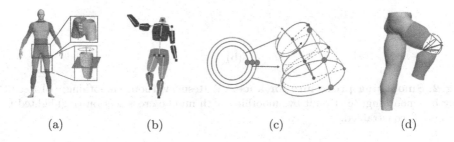

(a)   (b)   (c)   (d)

Fig. 1. (a) Colored parts except green ones are model components, and green parts are connection models. (b) Model components are deformed and transformed into the right positions. (c) Connection models are generated by interpolation along the skeleton. (d) The procedure of generating connection model between thigh and shank. (Color figure online)

In particular, the cross sections at the top of the trunk and bottom of the neck are quite different in shape. Therefore, the method mentioned before is not appropriate enough here. We therefore use the spline surface interpolation scheme proposed in [8] to deal with this problem, which can construct interpolated surfaces with local support. However, when using this scheme, all interpolation points on the model need to be traversed when generating the interpolated surface. Note that the computations of $\phi(u-i,a)$ and $\phi(v-j,a)$ in the formula in Sect. 5.1 in [14] are not related in the inner loop. To improve efficiency, we reduce computation complexity by memoization technique.

As another special case, the model component for buttocks should match with the one for thigh when the pose of body is changing. In this paper, we deform the buttocks model by using SR-ARAP deformation [15], which can achieve a volumetric deformation effect compared with [16]. Specifically, vertices at the top and midline of buttocks are constrained to be fixed, and those on the bottom cross sections of buttocks are constrained to corresponding vertices on the top cross sections of the left and right thigh models respectively. As a result, buttocks model is guaranteed to be consistent with adjacent trunk models.

In order to deal with non-smooth defects in the models and junctions between them, we adopt the method in [17] that solve a constrained bi-Laplacian linear system. More concretely, some vertices on adjacent model components near junctions are constrained to be fixed, and those at the connection model are set as unconstrained vertices. However, the result seems to be over-smoothed and distort since the models are required to lie along the skeleton. So in addition, we constrain the vertices at the middle cross section of knee to be fixed, and get a more reasonable result. Figure 2 illustrates an example for the knee.

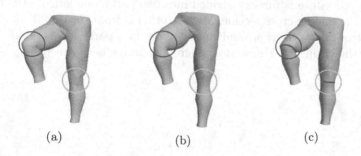

(a)   (b)   (c)

Fig. 2. Smoothing procedure for knee. (a) Result without smoothing; (b) Result only by smoothing; (c) Result by smoothing with middle cross section (highlighted in the figure) constrained.

4 Real-Time Cloth Simulation

Cloth simulation module is in charge of generating vivid effects with the human body model as the collision geometry, and should guarantee that: (1) user can get the cloth effects at real-time; (2) the cloth may penetrate the human body model in some circumstances, but should not cause the system to fail. Efficiencies and stability are the primary focuses in this module.

Considering all these factors, the system model the cloth based on PBD [6] approach: using the PBD constraints to handle physical properties of the cloth as well as the cloth-body collision and self-collision problem. The PBD approach treats energy as constraint functions of positions, and defines conditions that the constraint functions should satisfy. These conditions describe valid manifolds of positions, and the solutions are the projections from predicted positions to these position manifolds. To find the displacement from the existing position to the position that satisfies the condition, that is, a projection from the current position to a reasonable position area.

To take advantage of parallel processing technology to speed up the cloth simulation procedure, our system applies the unified particle method [8]. The method treats each object as a collection of particles, where all kinds of collisions are directly degraded into collision constraints between particles, and all types of constraints are treated as constraints among several particles. So in this system, human body and cloth are both collection of particles; physical properties of the cloth, including in-plane and bending elasticities, are measured by constraints between cloth particles; self-collisions and cloth-body collisions are both particle collision problems, rather than complex spatial geometric problems. Selected results are illustrated in Fig. 3.

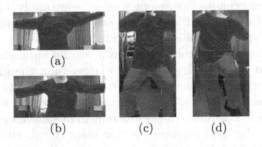

Fig. 3. Stable and robust simulation effects. (a) Detailed wrinkles without penetrations during fast movement; (b) Large buckles without self-collision in the chest; (c) Robust cloth effect when user squatting; (d) Robust cloth effect with left leg lifted.

4.1   Acceleration of Constraint Resolving

The constraints of the cloth simulation method have two main properties suitable for parallelism: (1) locality, each constraint usually involves only a few particles, and these particles tend to have locality at position; (2) independence, even if some constraints are dependent as sharing one common particle, those constraints are usually only associated with few other constraints.

There are two approaches [8] that can solve constraints in parallelism: (1) Jacobi style particle-centric approach. Each thread corresponds to a particle, solves all related constraints, and finally gets this particle's projection. Each thread is exclusive to the particle it solves, and all threads can run in one pass. However, this approach has a relatively slower convergence rate; (2) Gauss-Seidel style constraint-centric approach. Each thread corresponds to a constraint, solves this constraint and updates all related particles. It has significantly faster convergence rate than Jacobi style method, but the non-exclusive reading and writing operations in threads cause data race condition when solving in parallelism.

In this paper, to utilize the advantages of both approaches, we use Gauss-Seidel approach to solve all the permanent constraints, i.e. constraints modeling cloth physical properties. Only the independent constraints are solved in parallelism in one pass to prevent data race. If all constraints are treated as nodes and all particles are treated as edges in a graph, the constraints sharing one particle are adjacent nodes connected by an edge. So the problem of finding independent constraints which can be solved in parallelism is reduced to a graph coloring problem, which can be solved in parallelism using the parallel random graph coloring algorithm [9]. We use Jacobi approach to solve the temporary constraints, i.e. constraints generated by collision. Jacobi method does not have problems of data race, so all the temporary constraints can be solved in one pass.

4.2   Collision Detection

The body model may change fast among frames, so we apply a parallel approach similar to [18] and Chap. 32 of [19], which constructs time-independent spatial data per frame to speed up collision detection.

Our method first divides the space into a regular subdivision grid of cube cells, ensuring that the cell edge's length is larger than the maximum particle radius. Each particle is registered to the cube cell where its spherical center locates, and can easily get their collision candidate particles nearby. There are several advantages of this method: (1) different from spatial octree or boundary volume hierarchy, the data structure is non-hierarchical, suitable for parallel processing; (2) it is trivial to retrieve the corresponding grid cell with a given particle; (3) each particle can span at most eight cube cells, it is easy to get storage locality and reduce the false positive of the candidate collision particles.

5   System

Based on the works in Sects. 3 and 4, we construct an integral virtual fitting system using Kinect. The process and main modules are shown in Fig. 4.

5.1   Implementation of Human Body Modeling

First, we split a referenced mannequin model into components shown in Fig. 1(a) corresponding to those parts in Fig. 1(b) respectively, each of them is stored as offline file for subsequent processing. Second, in order to improve the robustness of measurements, we collect the measurement results in a certain period of time and only retain those in the range of 0.75 to 1.25 times of the mean value up till now. By symmetry, measurement errors can be also reduced by averaging. Measurements of the side parts are obtained by empirical scaling based on the results of the front parts. In addition, the scale values for each cross sections are

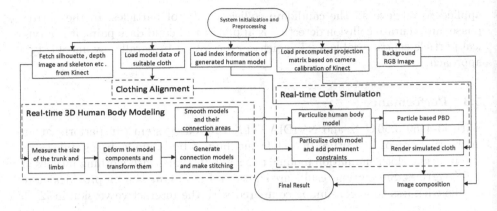

Fig. 4. Architecture for our system. In the Image composition module, we use the method similar to [2] to compose the simulated cloth with the background image to achieve a realistic effect. To automatically align clothing model with body model, we use the method in [20] of our own.

generated by spline interpolation given the scale values for the top, middle and bottom cross sections. We also accelerate the procedure for generating model components that are independent of each other by using multithreading technology. Furthermore, different initial parameters are given according to different genders, and the breast part for female users is generated based on an empirical mathematical model. Finally, all the model components are pieced together to form a complete 3D human body model. In particular, in order to avoid redundant data transmission, we transmit the index information from human body modeling module to cloth simulation module at initialization time, so we only need to transmit the position information during cloth simulation.

5.2   Implementation of Cloth Simulation

Our system applies triangulation and remeshing to convert the given clothing mesh to a relatively regular triangular mesh. The mesh vertices are treated as particles, whose radius is limited to less than half length of the shortest edge in the mesh. For each pair of adjacent vertices in the mesh, our system assigns a distance constraint to them for in-plane elasticity; for each pair of adjacent faces, our system assigns a distance constraint to the two vertices not on the shared edge for bending elasticity.

In some situations, we need to control the simulated cloth through its anchored vertices, which are kinematic and cannot be affected by other particles. For example, the points at the waistband should not be affected by other particles of the trousers. In this system, mass of each of these anchor points is all set to positive infinity, i.e. these anchor points cannot be affected by forces.

The collision detection procedure consists of a board phase and a following narrow phase. During the board phase, spatial hashing technique [18, 19] is applied to retrieve all the candidate collision pairs of particles. In the narrow phase, an accurate collision detection is applied to all candidate pairs, it is a typical particle-centric problem [8], which can be solved in parallel by Jacobi-style approach.

5.3   Performance

With i3-4150 3.50 GHz and NVIDIA GTX 745, our system can perform at an interactive rate of 10-13FPS. In each frame, human body modeling module takes about 35 ms, cloth simulation module takes about 55 ms, with clothing meshes of 4–6K vertices. Simulation results are shown in Fig. 5. Our system provides more details with less time consuming compared with the interactive version in [2].

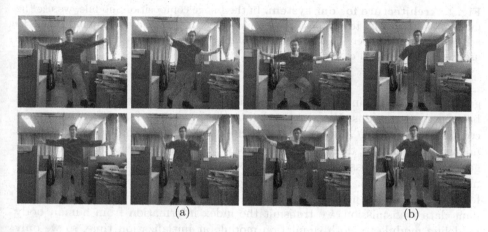

(a)   (b)

Fig. 5. Virtual fitting results. (a) Simulation results of silk like material with several poses and different kinds of clothings; (b) Simulation results of denim like material.

6   Conclusion and Future Work

In this paper, we present a new design of virtual fitting system using Kinect. With our efforts, the system is able to achieve realistic effects while being efficient, stable and adaptive. However, our system has some limitations. Kinect assumes that people are facing it. Therefore, our virtual fitting system is not good at the situation when people stand sideways to the Kinect. Besides, we also need to bring in more accurate methods to get the virtual fitting effect of different materials, while keeping PBD's robustness and efficiency.

Acknowledgements. This work was supported in part by the National Natural Science Foundation of China under Grant Nos. 61672273.

References

1. Zhou, Z., Shu, B., Zhuo, S., Deng, X., Tan, P., Lin, S.: Image-based clothes animation for virtual fitting. In: SIGGRAPH Asia 2012 Technical Briefs, p. 33. ACM (2012)
2. Ye, M., Wang, H., Deng, N., Yang, X., Yang, R.: Real-time human pose and shape estimation for virtual try-on using a single commodity depth camera. IEEE Trans. Visual Comput. Graphics 20(4), 550–559 (2014)
3. Zhang, Q., Fu, B., Ye, M., Yang, R.: Quality dynamic human body modeling using a single low-cost depth camera. In: Proceedings of the IEEE Conference on Computer Vision and Pattern Recognition, pp. 676–683 (2014)
4. Yoshiyasu, Y., Ma, W.-C., Yoshida, E., Kanehiro, F.: As-conformal-as-possible surface registration. In: Computer Graphics Forum, vol. 33, pp. 257–267. Wiley Online Library (2014)
5. Chen, G., Li, J., Zeng, J., Wang, B., Guodong, L.: Optimizing human model reconstruction from RGB-D images based on skin detection. Virtual Reality 20(3), 159–172 (2016)
6. Müller, M., Heidelberger, B., Hennix, M., Ratcliff, J.: Position based dynamics. J. Vis. Commun. Image Represent. 18(2), 109–118 (2007)
7. Bender, J., Müller, M., Macklin, M.: Position-based simulation methods in computer graphics. In: Eurographics (Tutorials) (2015)
8. Macklin, M., Müller, M., Chentanez, N., Kim, T.-Y.: Unified particle physics for real-time applications. ACM Trans. Graph. (TOG) 33(4), 153 (2014)
9. Fratarcangeli, M., Tibaldo, V., Pellacini, F.: Vivace: a practical gauss-seidel method for stable soft body dynamics. ACM Trans. Graph. (TOG) 35(6), 214 (2016)
10. Baraff, D., Witkin, A.: Large steps in cloth simulation. In: Proceedings of the 25th Annual Conference on Computer Graphics and Interactive Techniques, pp. 43–54. ACM (1998)
11. Bridson, R., Fedkiw, R., Anderson, J.: Robust treatment of collisions, contact and friction for cloth animation. ACM Trans. Graph. (ToG) 21(3), 594–603 (2002)
12. Gingold, Y., Igarashi, T., Zorin, D.: Structured annotations for 2D-to-3D modeling. In: ACM Transactions on Graphics (TOG), vol. 28, p. 148. ACM (2009)
13. Landis Markley, F., Cheng, Y., Crassidis, J.L., Oshman, Y.: Averaging quaternions. J. Guid. Control Dyn. 30(4), 1193–1197 (2007)
14. Zhang, R.-J., Ma, W.: An efficient scheme for curve and surface construction based on a set of interpolatory basis functions. ACM Trans. Graph. (TOG) 30(2), 10 (2011)
15. Levi, Z., Gotsman, C.: Smooth rotation enhanced as-rigid-as-possible mesh animation. IEEE Trans. Visual Comput. Graphics 21(2), 264–277 (2015)
16. Sorkine, O., Alexa, M.: As-rigid-as-possible surface modeling. In: Symposium on Geometry Processing, vol. 4 (2007)
17. Botsch, M., Sorkine, O.: On linear variational surface deformation methods. IEEE Trans. Visual Comput. Graphics 14(1), 213–230 (2008)
18. Teschner, M., Heidelberger, B., Müller, M., Pomerantes, D., Gross, M.H.: Optimized spatial hashing for collision detection of deformable objects. In: VMV, vol. 3, pp. 47–54 (2003)
19. Nguyen, H.: GPU Gems 3. Addison-Wesley Professional, New Jersey (2007)
20. Huang, L., Yang, R.: Automatic alignment for virtual fitting using 3D garment stretching and human body relocation. Visual Comput. 32(6–8), 705–715 (2016)

Exploiting Sub-region Deep Features for Specific Action Recognition in Combat Sports Video

Yongqiang Kong, Zhaoqiang Wei, Zhengang Wei[✉],
Shengke Wang, and Feng Gao

College of Information Science and Engineering, Ocean University of China,
No. 238, Songling Road, Qingdao, China
kongyongqiang1992@gmail.com, zqwei1989@gmail.com,
{wzgwzq,neverme,gaofeng}@ouc.edu.cn

Abstract. Current research works for human action recognition in videos mainly focused on the case in different types of videos, that is coarse recognition. However, for recognizing specific actions of one object of interest, these methods may fail to recognize, especially if the video contains multiple moving objects with different actions. In this paper, we proposed a novel method for specific player action recognition in combat sports video. Object tracking with body segmentation are used to generate sub-frame sequences. Action recognition is achieved by training a new three-stream Convolutional Neural Networks (CNNs) model, where the network inputs are horizontal components of optical flow, single sub-frame and vertical components of optical flow, respectively. And the network fusion is applied at both convolutional and softmax layers. Extensive experiments on real broadcast combat sports videos are provided to show the advantages and effectiveness of the proposed method.

Keywords: Object tracking · Three-stream CNNs · Specific action recognition
Combat sports video

1 Introduction

Human action recognition in videos has become an active area of computer vision, which is a very challenging task due to noisy and small training data, and other challenges of variations in motion and viewpoint. Recent advances in this task are driven by the success of two-stream CNNs [1]. Conventional video action recognition with CNNs often dominated by training still frames which ignored motion information. The two-stream architecture incorporates spatial and temporal networks which trained on not only still images but also stacked dense optical flow between consecutive video frames. This architecture takes advantage of motion information and gives a superb performance although training data is very limited. Based on this two-stream method, several approaches for video action recognition has been reported. [2] proposed factorized spatio-temporal CNNs that factorize 3-dimensional (3D) convolutional into 2D and 1D, where 2D convolutional is learning in spatial layers while 1D in temporal layers. In [3], the authors learn 3D CNNs by setting all convolutional kernels with

B. Zeng et al. (Eds.): PCM 2017, LNCS 10736, pp. 192–201, 2018.
https://doi.org/10.1007/978-3-319-77383-4_19

small size $3 \times 3 \times 3$ over spatial and temporal. One recent attempt for taking full advantage of spatial and temporal information is proposed in [4], the authors find that spatial and temporal networks can be fused at convolutional layers in several ways. Their fusion strategy can reduce parameters in the networks without loss of performance. The above-mentioned methods perform well for recognizing actions in different types of videos, where the experimental datasets include UCF-101 [5] and HMDB-51 [6]. However, they may not be able to work in the case of specific action recognition which focuses on one object of interest.

State-of-the-art action recognition in sports videos also aimed at recognizing actions from different types of videos [7–9], the experimental datasets are UCF-Sports [10] and Sports-1 M [9]. For the case of one type of video, many attempts have been made for various sports fields such as soccer [11, 12], tennis [13], and basketball [14], where the tasks mainly include event detection, video summarization, video annotation, object tracking etc. However, specific player action recognition has hitherto remained unstudied. In this paper, compared with aforementioned works, we propose a novel approach for specific player action recognition in various combat sports videos based on computer vision and deep learning. Up to the best of our knowledge, our work is the first attempt to recognize specific actions in one type of video. Combat sports videos are used as case study due to the following motivations:

- Combat sports video has hitherto remained unstudied in multimedia field.
- Broadcast combat sports videos contain significant camera motion, which brings strong noise to video analysis.
- Multiple moving objects (mainly refer to two similar players and a random-walk referee) and complex object actions make the specific action recognition a quite challenging task.

The main contributions of this paper include:

- An effective object tracking and body segmentation method is presented, which performs well on broadcast combat sports videos with moving background.
- A novel temporal-spatio-temporal CNNs architecture is proposed, which operate on horizontal components of multi-frame optical flow, still frames and vertical components of multi-frame optical flow, respectively.
- We investigate the sub-region data as network inputs to train the three-stream CNNs model, which is essential for specific action recognition.

2   Proposed Method

Our method starts with player tracking and body segmentation, to extract region-of-interest from each frame of a video sequence in a specific resolution (detailed in Sect. 2.1). Sub action image sequence could be seen as de-noised consecutive frames. Subsequently, dense optical flows between these sub-frames are computed using OpenCV toolbox, where the horizontal and vertical components of flow are extracted separately. Finally, the temporal-spatio-temporal CNNs are trained on the single sub-frame, stacked horizontal and vertical components of dense optical flow, to

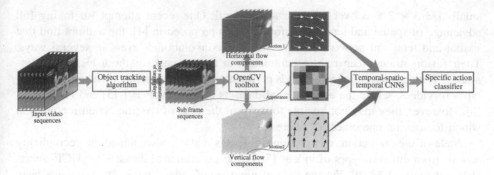

Fig. 1. Schematic overview of the proposed method.

obtain a specific action classifier (detailed in Sect. 2.2). Figure 1 gives an overview of the proposed method.

2.1 Object Tracking and Body Segmentation

We define three fixed bounding boxes B_t, B_{tl} and B_{tr} with the same height, where B_t captures the location information of the target player at time t. In consideration of the movement of a player in one direction is the same as in the opposite direction, box B_{tl} and B_{tr} are added respectively on both sides of B_t in each frame. It is worth noting that both B_{tl} and B_{tr} are half the width of B_t. Three boxes together side by side at the same level, which can build up a large bounding box for body segmentation. Inspired by the work [15], our tracking model is obtained using structured learning [16]. Given a video sequence $V=\{\mathbf{v}_1, \mathbf{v}_2, \ldots, \mathbf{v}_n\}$, the goal is to learn a prediction function f that predicts the locations of the target player:

$$f_{\mathbf{w}}(V) = \arg\max \sum_{t=1}^{n} \mathbf{w}_t^T \phi(\mathbf{v}_t, B_t) \qquad (1)$$

where $\phi(\mathbf{v}_t, B_t)$ is the feature map which corresponds to locations in the bounding box at time t, and the parameter vector $\mathbf{w}$ denotes the weights on the features. In our model, HOG features [17] are extracted from all frames to describe the object patches. And the features in each frame are concatenated into a vector, i.e., $\phi(\mathbf{v}_t, B_t)$. According to [16], we need to minimize the SVM loos l to obtain the optimal $\mathbf{w}$:

$$l_{\mathbf{w}}(\mathbf{v}_t, B_t) = \max_{\bar{B}_t} \left(\mathbf{w}_t^T [\phi(\mathbf{v}_t, \bar{B}_t) - \phi(\mathbf{v}_t, B_t)] + [1 - (B_t \cap \bar{B}_t)] \right) \qquad (2)$$

where we assume that $\bar{B}_t$ represents presentation and B_t represents groundtruth.

Once the player is detected, our aim is to update the model to adjust to both appearance and background changes. During the model updating process (i.e., parameter $\mathbf{w}$ update), the bounding box regions in previous frames are used as positive samples while the surrounding background regions are used as negative samples. In our case, the passive-aggressive algorithm [18] is employed to perform the parameter updates in real time, which is defined as follows:

$$\mathbf{w}_{t+1} \leftarrow \mathbf{w}_t - \frac{l_{\mathbf{w}}(\mathbf{v}_t, B_t)}{\|\nabla_{\mathbf{w}} l_{\mathbf{w}}(\mathbf{v}_t, B_t)\| + \frac{1}{2C}} \nabla_{\mathbf{w}} l_{\mathbf{w}}(\mathbf{v}_t, B_t) \tag{3}$$

where $C \in (0, +\infty)$ is a hyperparameter which governs "aggressiveness". The weights $\mathbf{w}$ are initialized by training SVM that classifies positive samples from 20 negative examples (randomly selected). Like [15], the target object is manually annotated in the first frame of a video sequence.

2.2   Three-Stream CNNs

Our CNNs model is inspired by the two-stream CNNs [1], which incorporates spatial and temporal networks with late fusion. The temporal network is built on dense optical flow between L consecutive frames, where the horizontal and vertical components of flow are stacked to form the input (2L-channel). Unlike [1], we stack the horizontal and vertical components of flow (in a scale between $(t-L/2)$ and $(t+L/2)$) separately, and train them using two temporal networks to take full advantage of the motion information. Each of the three streams is implemented using very deep CNNs (VGG-16) [19]. Note that the flows are linearly rescaled to a range of [0, 255] and saved as JPEG images before training.

Network fusion. At the last convolutional layer (RELU5_3 in VGG-16), we fuse three streams into two spatio-temporal streams. The fusion in our three-stream model is inspired by [4], the authors evaluated several fusion strategies and demonstrated that fusion applied at convolutional layers can significantly reduce the number of parameters of CNNs model without loss of performance. Therefore, we also apply convolutional layers fusion to combine spatio-temporal features, where 3D convolutional and 3D pooling [3] are used to achieve this goal. Given the inputs $\mathbf{x} \in \mathbb{R}^{H \times W \times D}$ of convolutional fusion layers, we first stack two feature maps across time $t=1, 2, ..., T$, to general new input maps $\mathbf{x}_{spatio} \in \mathbb{R}^{H \times W \times T \times D}$ and $\mathbf{x}_{tempral} \in \mathbb{R}^{H \times W \times T \times D}$, with height H, width W and number of channels D. Next, we concatenate them across channels to obtain a new map $\mathbf{y}_{concat} \in \mathbb{R}^{H \times W \times T \times 2D}$, where the concatenation is defined as follows:

$$\mathbf{y}_{concat}^{2d-1} = \mathbf{x}_{spatio}^d; \ \mathbf{y}_{concat}^{2d} = \mathbf{x}_{tempral}^d, d = 1, 2, ..., D \tag{4}$$

Subsequently, we convolve $\mathbf{y}_{concat}$ using 3D convolutional kernels $\mathbf{f} \in \mathbb{R}^{H' \times W' \times T' \times 2D \times D'}$, with number of kernels D', to general a fusion feature map $\mathbf{y}_{fusion}$:

$$\mathbf{y}_{fusion} = \mathbf{y}_{concat} * \mathbf{f} + b \tag{5}$$

where $b \in \mathbb{R}^{2D}$ represents biases. 3D convolutional combines weights of two streams in a local spatio-temporal neighborhood, and followed by 3D pooling. We employ max-pooling using a cube with size $H'' \times W'' \times T''$. 3D pooling first stacks convolutional maps across time, and then pools them from local spatio-temporal neighborhoods to shrink the dimension of maps. At the softmax layer, the class scores are obtained by averaging the predictions of two spatio-temporal streams. The layer configuration and fusion strategy of our three-stream architecture is shown in Fig. 2. The three networks are applied to the input video at time $t, t+\tau, \ldots, t+T\tau$ (τ represents frame stride), to capture long-term information. The inputs of network are resized beforehand, where we fix the image size as 256×256. We set the 3D fusion kernel $\mathbf{f}$ of size $3 \times 3 \times 3 \times 1024 \times 512$ with stride $1 \times 1 \times 1$, because the number of concatenated channels of ReLU5_3 is 1024, and the number of input channels of FC-4096 is 512. And the size of 3D pooling kernel is $2 \times 2 \times 2$ with stride $2 \times 2 \times 2$.

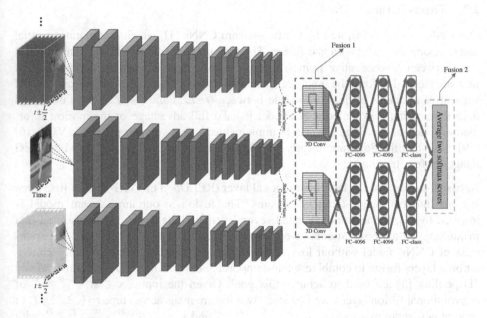

Fig. 2. Illustration of our temporal-spatio-temporal architecture which is based on VGG-16. Rectified Linear Units (ReLUs) are used in all hidden layers, and dropout ratio of 0.9 is applied in the first two fully-connected (FC) layers. And $L=10$ in our case.

Model initialization. We adopt the ImageNet [20] pre-trained model to initialize the spatial and two temporal networks. It is worth noting that the temporal input channel number is different from the spatial input. Therefore, we average the pre-trained kernels of the first layer across the channel, and copy the results 10 times to initialize two temporal streams.

Training. Stochastic gradient descent (momentum=0.9) is used in our case. We fine-tune both spatial and temporal networks with a mini-batch size of 96, learning rate of 0.001 (decreased by a factor of 10 once the test accuracy saturates). At each training iteration, we sample the starting frame of each of the 96 sequences randomly, to apply the networks at $T=5$ frames. And the frame stride $\tau \in [1, 10]$ is also sampled randomly.

It is worth noting that training deep CNNs is very prone to overfitting. To avoid this from happening, data augmentation strategies (crop and horizontal flip) are employed to increase the number of training samples. Instead of random cropping [1, 4], we crop 4 corners and 1 center of the input images (256 × 256), where the size of cropped regions is fixed to 224 × 224. After that, all of these sub-images undergo horizontal flipping to double the training samples. From each selected frame, we generate 10 inputs (4 corners + 1 center, and horizontal reflections) for the three-stream model. We perform training on 4 GPUs (NVIDIA GTX 1080 card) with cuDNN version 5.1, which is implemented using Caffe toolbox [21]. Following [22], the GPUs are synchronized before the first FC layer, while the propagations of the FC layers are performed on one GPU.

Testing. Given a sequence, we sample $T=5$ frames with the corresponding horizontal and vertical components of flows (including their corners and reflections). The final prediction score is obtained by averaging across these sampled frames and their cropped regions. With the multi-GPU implementation, the average speed is approximately 0.17 s for obtaining recognition results of a test sequence using our three-stream CNNs classifier, which is fast enough for real-time recognition.

3 Experiments

3.1 Datasets

We collect two specific action recognition datasets of broadcast combat sports video, Taekwondo (*Dataset-T*) and Boxing (*Dataset-B*), to evaluate the proposed method. *Dataset-T* contains 1.5 K videos of 10 actions while *Dataset-B* includes 0.9 K videos of 6 actions, where each class contains 150 samples. Note that each video captures one action of the target player.

Dataset Preprocessing. All videos in these two datasets are standardized with frame rate of 25 fps. The target player in each video is annotated manually and tracked by our tracking technique in real time. During tracking, each frame undergoes body segmentation by the large bounding box to generate sub-frame sequence (see Sect. 2.1). Figure 3 shows some example sub-frames of actions in two datasets.

Dataset splitting for training/testing. For each dataset, we sample 2/3 sub-frame sequences as training set while the remaining ones are used for testing, where each class has the same number of training/test samples. Tests are performed 3 times where each time the training sequences are sampled. And the test results are obtained by averaging the predictions across 3 times.

3.2 Results on Single Dataset

In this section, we perform confusion matrix analysis to evaluate the performance of each class. The confusion matrices of the classification accuracy, obtained from two datasets by the three-stream CNNs classifier, are presented in Fig. 4(a) and (b), respectively. On average, we obtain higher classification accuracy on *Dataset-T*

Front kick   Back kick   Push kick   Side kick   Roundhouse kick   Downward kick   Spin kick   Tornado kick

Clinch   Fall   Jab   Cross   Hook   Upper-cut   Clinch   Fall

Fig. 3. Example sub-frames from two combat sports datasets.

compared to *Dataset-B*, although with the same number of training samples in each class. As can be observed, misclassification is generally appeared in the actions with similar movements. For example, in some view angles, *Side kick* and *roundhouse kick* are often hard to distinguish from each other even with the human eye. Interestingly, we achieve perfect classification accuracy for *Clinch* class on *Dataset-T*. However, in *Dataset-B*, the *Clinch* class is confused with *Cross* and *Upper-cut* classes, while three classes (*Cross*, *Hook* and *Upper-cut*) are also confused with *Clinch* class. We surmise that this is because two players in boxing video are too close to each other in these cases, which is easy to be misrecognized.

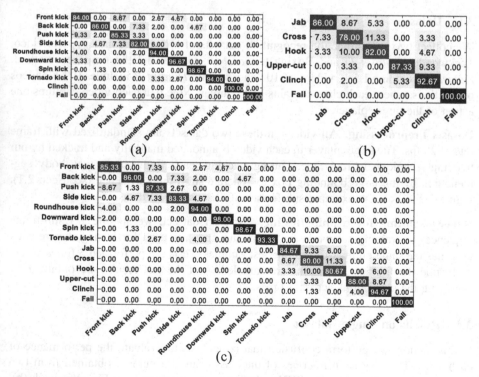

(a)

	Front kick	Back kick	Push kick	Side kick	Roundhouse kick	Downward kick	Spin kick	Tornado kick	Clinch	Fall
Front kick	84.00	0.00	8.67	0.00	2.67	4.67	0.00	0.00	0.00	0.00
Back kick	0.00	86.00	0.00	7.33	2.00	0.00	4.67	0.00	0.00	0.00
Push kick	9.33	2.00	85.33	3.33	0.00	0.00	0.00	0.00	0.00	0.00
Side kick	0.00	4.67	7.33	82.00	6.00	0.00	0.00	0.00	0.00	0.00
Roundhouse kick	4.00	0.00	0.00	2.00	94.00	0.00	0.00	0.00	0.00	0.00
Downward kick	3.33	0.00	0.00	0.00	0.00	96.67	0.00	0.00	0.00	0.00
Spin kick	0.00	1.33	0.00	0.00	0.00	0.00	98.67	0.00	0.00	0.00
Tornado kick	0.00	0.00	0.00	0.00	3.33	2.67	0.00	94.00	0.00	0.00
Clinch	0.00	0.00	0.00	0.00	0.00	0.00	0.00	0.00	100.00	0.00
Fall	0.00	0.00	0.00	0.00	0.00	0.00	0.00	0.00	0.00	100.00

(b)

	Jab	Cross	Hook	Upper-cut	Clinch	Fall
Jab	86.00	8.67	5.33	0.00	0.00	0.00
Cross	7.33	78.00	11.33	0.00	3.33	0.00
Hook	3.33	10.00	82.00	0.00	4.67	0.00
Upper-cut	0.00	3.33	0.00	87.33	9.33	0.00
Clinch	0.00	2.00	0.00	5.33	92.67	0.00
Fall	0.00	0.00	0.00	0.00	0.00	100.00

(c)

	Front kick	Back kick	Push kick	Side kick	Roundhouse kick	Downward kick	Spin kick	Tornado kick	Jab	Cross	Hook	Upper-cut	Clinch	Fall
Front kick	85.33	0.00	7.33	0.00	2.67	4.67	0.00	0.00	0.00	0.00	0.00	0.00	0.00	0.00
Back kick	0.00	86.00	0.00	7.33	2.00	0.00	4.67	0.00	0.00	0.00	0.00	0.00	0.00	0.00
Push kick	8.67	1.33	87.33	2.67	0.00	0.00	0.00	0.00	0.00	0.00	0.00	0.00	0.00	0.00
Side kick	0.00	4.67	7.33	83.33	4.67	0.00	0.00	0.00	0.00	0.00	0.00	0.00	0.00	0.00
Roundhouse kick	4.00	0.00	0.00	2.00	94.00	0.00	0.00	0.00	0.00	0.00	0.00	0.00	0.00	0.00
Downward kick	2.00	0.00	0.00	0.00	0.00	98.00	0.00	0.00	0.00	0.00	0.00	0.00	0.00	0.00
Spin kick	0.00	1.33	0.00	0.00	0.00	0.00	98.67	0.00	0.00	0.00	0.00	0.00	0.00	0.00
Tornado kick	0.00	0.00	2.67	0.00	4.00	0.00	0.00	93.33	0.00	0.00	0.00	0.00	0.00	0.00
Jab	0.00	0.00	0.00	0.00	0.00	0.00	0.00	0.00	84.67	9.33	6.00	0.00	0.00	0.00
Cross	0.00	0.00	0.00	0.00	0.00	0.00	0.00	0.00	6.67	80.00	11.33	0.00	2.00	0.00
Hook	0.00	0.00	0.00	0.00	0.00	0.00	0.00	0.00	3.33	10.00	80.67	0.00	6.00	0.00
Upper-cut	0.00	0.00	0.00	0.00	0.00	0.00	0.00	0.00	0.00	3.33	0.00	88.00	8.67	0.00
Clinch	0.00	0.00	0.00	0.00	0.00	0.00	0.00	0.00	0.00	1.33	0.00	4.00	94.67	0.00
Fall	0.00	0.00	0.00	0.00	0.00	0.00	0.00	0.00	0.00	0.00	0.00	0.00	0.00	100.00

Fig. 4. Confusion matrices of classification accuracy on two datasets. (a) *Dataset-T*. (b) *Dataset-B*. (c) Mixed dataset.

3.3 Results on Mixed Dataset

To verify the effectiveness of proposed method, we build a mixed dataset on *Dataset-T* and *Dataset-B*, which includes 2.4 K videos of 14 classes. *Clinch* and *Fall* classes contains 300 samples respectively, while each of the remaining classes contains 150 samples. The confusion matrix of the accuracy for the mixed dataset is shown in Fig. 4(c). It can be observed that our method is still able to achieve very good performance. Moreover, some classes obtain improved performance compared to single-dataset results (e.g., *Front kick*, *Push kick*, *Cross*). However, there are also some classes with a decrease in performance (e.g., *Tornado kick*, *Jab*, *Hook*).

3.4 Comparison with the State-of-the-Art

Finally, we compare the proposed method with recent deep CNNs based state-of-the-art methods [1–4, 21] on *Dataset-T* and *Dataset-B*, where the performance is measured by the mean classification accuracy (averaging recognition accuracy across classes). For fair comparison, the training/test samples are preprocessed sub-region sequences (each frame contains one player of interest). The resulting performance is reported in Table 1. It can be observed that our approach outperforms all the state-of-the-art methods on both single and mixed datasets. A prominent conclusion drawn from the comparison between [1] and [4, 21] is that deeper networks achieves better performance. And our three-stream architecture shows that the horizontal and vertical components of flows trained on two temporal networks leads to improved performance, as compared to stacking the flow components across channels [1, 4, 21] trained on one temporal network.

Table 1. Performance comparison with state-of-the-art.

Method	Dataset-T	Dataset-B	Mixed
Two-stream CNNs (VGG-M) [1]	83.2%	81.9%	80.6%
Factorized CNNs [2]	82.5%	77.3%	80.3%
3D CNNs [3]	80.9%	79.1%	77.2%
Two-stream CNNs (VGG-16) [21]	87.8%	83.8%	87.1%
Two-stream fusion CNNs (VGG-16) [4]	90.6%	85.0%	87.5%
Ours (operate on full-region data)	31.6%	33.8%	35.5%
Ours	92.1%	87.7%	89.6%

We also evaluated the performance of training full-region data (i.e., original video frames and optical flow without preprocessing). For this case, we obtained very poor accuracy: less than 40% on both single and mixed datasets, as shown in Table 1. Specific action recognition aims to recognize action details of one object, rather than general video classification. Original frames of combat sports video include "lethal" noises such as complex moving background and the similar moving objects of non-interest. Therefore, tracking the target object to generate sub-frames (de-noised data) is essential for specific action recognition.

3.5   Discussion

The limitations of our method include:

- The performance of specific action recognition strongly depends on sub-region features learning based on tracking and body segmentation. However, the target object must be annotated manually in the first frame.
- Our method is only conducted on two types of combat sports videos.
- Our three-stream CNNs model has higher computational requirements compared to state-of-the-art, where multi-GPU training is essential.

For future study, we aim to build a pre-trained object detector that initializes the object of interest automatically in the first frame according to different requirements. And we also plan to perform extensive tests on other combat sports videos, such as wrestling, karate and mixed martial arts. Moreover, collecting more training videos for each class is another intriguing direction for our future research.

4   Conclusion

This paper presented a novel method for specific player action recognition in combat sports video, which lies object tracking and body segmentation. We stack horizontal and vertical components of dense optical flow separately as input to two independent temporal networks. And a temporal-spatio-temporal CNNs model is trained on sub-region data to obtain a specific action classifier. Our method gives a superb performance on two challenging combat sports video datasets. Comparisons show that our method outperforms the deep CNNs based state-of-the-art methods in terms of mean classification accuracy. And our evaluation suggests the importance of sub-region features learning.

Acknowledgments. This work was supported by the National Natural Science Foundation of China (Grant nos. 41606198 and 61301241) and in part by the China Postdoctoral Science Foundation under Grant No. 2015M582140.

References

1. Simonyan, K., Zisserman, A.: Two-stream convolutional networks for action recognition in videos. In: Advances in Neural Information Processing Systems, pp. 568–576 (2014)
2. Sun, L., Jia, K., Yeung, D.Y., Shi, B.E.: Human action recognition using factorized spatio-temporal convolutional networks. In: IEEE International Conference on Computer Vision (ICCV), pp. 4597–4605. IEEE (2015)
3. Du, T., Bourdev, L., Fergus, R., Torresani, L., Paluri, M.: Learning spatiotemporal features with 3D convolutional networks. In: IEEE International Conference on Computer Vision (ICCV), pp. 4489–4497. IEEE (2015)
4. Feichtenhofer, C., Pinz, A., Zisserman, A.: Convolutional two-stream network fusion for video action recognition. In: IEEE Conference on Computer Vision and Pattern Recognition (CVPR), pp. 1933–1941. IEEE (2016)

5. Soomro, K., Zamir, A.R., Shah, M.: UCF101: a dataset of 101 human actions classes from videos in the wild. arXiv preprint arXiv:1212.0402 (2012)
6. Kuehne, H., Jhuang, H., Garrote, E., Poggio, T., Serre, T.: HMDB: a large video database for human motion recognition. In: IEEE International Conference on Computer Vision (ICCV), pp. 2556–2563. IEEE (2011)
7. Zhen, X., Shao, L., Tao, D., Li, X.: Embedding motion and structure features for action recognition. IEEE Trans. Circuits Syst. Video Technol. **23**(7), 1182–1190 (2013)
8. Everts, I., Van Gemert, J.C., Gevers, T.: Evaluation of color stips for human action recognition. In: 2013 IEEE Conference on Computer Vision and Pattern Recognition (CVPR), pp. 2850–2857. IEEE (2013)
9. Karpathy, A., Toderici, G., Shetty, S., Leung, T., Sukthankar, R., Li, F.F.: Large-scale video classification with convolutional neural networks. In: IEEE Conference on Computer Vision and Pattern Recognition (CVPR), pp. 1725–1732. IEEE (2014)
10. Rodriguez, M.D., Ahmed, J., Shah, M.: Action MACH a spatio-temporal maximum average correlation height filter for action recognition. In: IEEE Conference on Computer Vision and Pattern Recognition (CVPR), pp. 1–8. IEEE (2008)
11. Mendi, E., Clemente, H.B., Bayrak, C.: Sports video summarization based on motion analysis. Comput. Electr. Eng. **39**(3), 790–796 (2013)
12. Dao, M.S., Babaguchi, N.: A new spatio-temporal method for event detection and personalized retrieval of sports video. Multimed. Tools Appl. **50**(1), 227–248 (2010)
13. Almajai, I., et al.: Anomaly detection and knowledge transfer in automatic sports video annotation. In: Weinshall, D., Anemüller, J., van Gool, L. (eds.) Detection and Identification of Rare Audiovisual Cues. SCI, vol. 384, pp. 109–117. Springer, Heidelberg (2012). https://doi.org/10.1007/978-3-642-24034-8_9
14. Liu, J., Carr, P., Collins, R.T., Liu, Y.: Tracking sports players with context-conditioned motion models. In: IEEE Conference on Computer Vision and Pattern Recognition (CVPR), pp. 1830–1837. IEEE (2013)
15. Dehghan, A., Tian, Y., Torr, P.H., Shah, M.: Target identity-aware network flow for online multiple target tracking. In: IEEE Conference on Computer Vision and Pattern Recognition (CVPR), pp. 1146–1154. IEEE (2015)
16. Tsochantaridis, I., Joachims, T., Hofmann, T., Altun, Y.: Large margin methods for structured and interdependent output variables. J. Mach. Learn. Res. **6**(2), 1453–1484 (2005)
17. Dalal, N., Triggs, B.: Histograms of oriented gradients for human detection. In: IEEE Computer Society Conference on Computer Vision and Pattern Recognition (CVPR), pp. 886–893. IEEE (2005)
18. Crammer, K., Dekel, O., Keshet, J., Shalev-Shwartz, S., Singer, Y.: Online passive-aggressive algorithms. J. Mach. Learn. Res. **7**(3), 551–585 (2006)
19. Simonyan, K., Zisserman, A.: Very deep convolutional networks for large-scale image recognition. arXiv preprint arXiv:1409.1556 (2014)
20. Deng, J., Dong, W., Socher, R., Li, L.J., Li, K., Fei-Fei, L.: Imagenet: a large-scale hierarchical image database. In: IEEE Conference on Computer Vision and Pattern Recognition (CVPR), pp. 248–255. IEEE (2009)
21. Jia, Y., Shelhamer, E., Donahue, J., Karayev, S., Long, J., Girshick, R., Guadarrama, S., Darrell, T.: Caffe: convolutional architecture for fast feature embedding. In: Proceedings of ACM International Conference on Multimedia, pp. 675–678. ACM (2014)
22. Wang, L., Xiong, Y., Wang, Z., Qiao, Y.: Towards good practices for very deep two-stream convnets. arXiv preprint arXiv:1507.02159 (2015)

Face Anti-spoofing Based on Motion

Ran Wang[1], Jing Xiao[1,3,4(✉)], Ruimin Hu[1,2,3], and Xu Wang[1]

[1] School of Computer Science, National Engineering Research Center
for Multimedia Software, Wuhan University, Wuhan 430072, China
{wangran1994, jing}@whu.edu.cn,
hurm1964@gmail.com, wangxu9191@gmail.com
[2] Hubei Key Laboratory of Multimedia and Network Communication
Engineering, Wuhan University, Wuhan 430072, China
[3] Collaborative Innovation Center of Geospatial Technology,
Wuhan 430079, China
[4] Research Institute of Wuhan University in Shenzhen, Shenzhen, China

Abstract. People can have access to biometric system easily by face spoofing attack. Recent researches have proposed many anti-spoofing strategies based on eye blinking, facial expression changes, mouth movements or skin texture. As for the face which has slight trembling, there are few specific methods about it. To solve this problem, we have proposed a method which could discriminate human real face and face print by using parameters of slight face motion and equal-proportion property in projection. In order to validate our method, we also established a new video database containing 720 moving faces. After getting the facial landmarks, aligning image of each frame and calculating the variance as feature value, final data would be sent to the support vector machine (SVM) to verify the reality of faces. From the experiment results, the proposed method shows its high accuracy in different lighting conditions and different face amplitude for anti-spoofing and will have good prospect in engineer.

Keywords: Anti-spoofing · Face · Motion · Projection · Classification

1 Introduction

Biometric system which relies on biometric identifier taken from the inherited traits of user, has developed rapidly in applications recently [1, 2]. With the widespread use of biometric system, many kinds of attack which try to get pass access has arisen.

Unfortunately, it is proved that biometric system can't prevent the face spoofing attack because the biometric system is based on the biometric identities, it doesn't consider the liveness of identity [3]. The most common kind of face spoofing attack is print attack, this attack performed using a face print in front of the collecting device of biometric system to disguise the real identity of imposter [4]. Beside this, face spoofing attack also includes video attack and mask attack [5].

Liveness detection is the typical countermeasure of face spoofing attack. It means that facial physiological changing such as eye blinking, facial expression changes and mouth movements can all be used as the characteristics for the face anti-spoofing methods [6]. In recent research, lots of related papers proposed their methods in many kinds of aspects, but most of the methods were based on the same situation: the detected faces should be in front of the camera without any trembling. In order to adjust to this situation, before the experiments, researchers always chose the appropriate faces which collected from public databases such as NUAA (Fig. 1) [1] and PRINTAT-TACK [7] or the database developed on their own. In these databases, a client is required to stay still, just blink or roll eyes, smile or open mouth. These experiments could usually give us satisfactory results.

But these proposed methods have the same limitation. On the one hand, consider this situation, if a client doesn't follow the instruction which let him be still or an attacker put a face print in front of the camera with trembling because of the cold weather, it is difficult to collect the accurate facial information, and these methods seem to make the final discrimination hardly because most papers don't consider this situation. If the algorithm of the method discriminate the human as attacker, it will be too arbitrary. In fact, this situation is usual in the normal life; On the other hand, slight trembling of face print can really cause attack because the motion of a print image such as translation and rotation will disguise itself as a three dimensional (3D) face.

In order to solve this problem, in this paper, we proposed a new face anti-spoofing method by using parameters of face slight trembling motion and the differences projection characteristics between plane image and 3D subject. We considered the faces collection process as a projection: for a face print, projection has the property named equal-proportion. It means print face will have special characteristic in projection. When we move or rotate the print face in front of a camera, it corresponds to project the image multiple times. This will make obviously different feature parameters which can be easily classified by the SVM [8].

The development of a new method to solve the problem is not possible without an appropriate database. As we mentioned above, almost all the databases contains abundant print attack images or videos, but few of them have the subjects with face trembling. It will limit our experiment if we choose the public database. To solve this limitation, we developed a new database, which consisted of client dataset and imposter dataset. Each video clip has the face sequences we need. To improve the persuasiveness and accuracy of our database, besides the consideration of different lighting conditions, we invited 60 people in different ages and not only collected the videos with trembling of face, we also collected still face videos like normal print attack database such as PRINTATTACK.

The rest of the paper is organized as follows. Section 2 discusses related works on countermeasures of face spoofing attack. Section 3 gives the details of our proposed method. Our developed database, which consists of client and imposter datasets are introduced in Sect. 4, the experiment of our proposed method in different conditions and the results of them are also given in this section, the results are thoroughly analyzed and also compared with each other. A conclusion is drawn in Sect. 5.

Fig. 1. Example of images captured from real faces (upper row) and from face prints (lower row) in NUAA database

2 Related Work

Face anti-spoofing is a popular research direction in recent years after the biometric system proposed. A lot of related works have been carried out to find effective methods in order to resist face spoofing attack.

As we mentioned above, liveness detection is the typical countermeasure of face spoofing attack [6]. The most basic features of liveness are eye blinking and mouth movements. This is because these facial expressions are very difficult to be imitated [9]. According to this features, for instance, as for eye blinking detection, Pan et al. [10] proposed a face anti-spoofing method based on eye blinking, they collected and detected eye blinking of human in a few seconds and found the differences between real human face and face print [6]. Of course, these physiological signs could be used together, Roberto et al. [11] made the fusion of multiple clues, and analyzed both video and static information to obtain excellent effect of discrimination.

There are still other method based on different theory in face anti-spoofing, Andre et al. [7] thought a public database and a baseline could be really useful to resist face spoofing attack. Jukka et al. [6] used micro-texture analysis method by local binary patterns (LBP) [12] to solve the attack problem. Local ternary pattern (LTP) [13] method in texture analyze of face anti-spoofing also gained wide range of applications. Optical-flow theory was also presented to capture subtle movement and velocity, because the captured optical-flow was obviously different between real human face and face print [6, 14]. For instance, Bao et al. used optical-flow for motion estimation and detected attacks which produced with planar media, the experiments showed a 6% false-alarm against about 14% false-acceptance [15].

It appears that most of the existing methods for spoofing detection not consider the motion differences between the real human face and face print. In fact, the liveness information detection can not only find in the almost still face with little eye blinking motion, when face has some motion, the differences are more obvious. Therefore, we proposed a new kind of discrimination method by using parameters of face slight motion in this paper.

3 Proposed Method

This section provides details of our proposed method. The general overview of our method is summarized in Fig. 2.

Fig. 2. General overview of our proposed method

As we all know, one of the property of projection is its equal-proportion. It means that for a plane figure, whether the projection direction, if point M is the midpoint of a line segment AB in origin graph, the projection point of the M named M' is also the midpoint of the projection line segment $A'B'$ (Fig. 3).

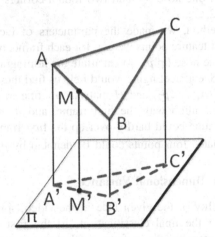

Fig. 3. Equal-proportion of projection, after the projection, it still has the equation $AM : MB = A'M' : M'B'$

In our proposed method, we tried to find obvious evidence to discriminate real faces and face prints by using the characteristic of projection we mentioned above. When we put a face print in front of a camera, it corresponded to the projection from the print. Prints trembling could be seemed as motion. Moved or rotated the prints could be equivalent as changing the direction of the projection. We could also seem it as a still print but it would be projected on a moved or rotated projection surface. Because of the equal-proportion of projection, all points on the print would have the same motion mode.

As for real face, points on the face didn't have the same deep information because the points were not at the same surface. It would cause the disparity of motion mode among all the points. We described the motion mode by homography matrix.

Attention the flowchart in Fig. 2, for the given video, we first got the feature points of the face. The face alignment algorithm in SeetaFaceEngine[1] would help us get some facial landmarks in each frame; then we used three of them to do radiation transformation and calculated homography matrix between the first frame and the others; after that, the left points we had should be aligned with the same points in the first frame by using the homography matrix. The deviation value of the left points should be calculated if they didn't overlap, and we would get the variance from the whole video frame sequences; at last, by using the high dimensional variance, we could get the discriminate result from SVM classification.

3.1   Feature Points Processing

Feature points as the initial value are necessary for the final discrimination of the face. For the proposed method, we chose the SeetaFaceEngine to obtain the feature points in each frame. We could get n facial landmarks by the SeetaFace Alignment modular, such as two eye centers, one nose tip, and two mouth corners. Denoted their coordinates by $p_i(x, y), i = 1, 2, \ldots, n$.

In our proposed method, we made the parameters of face slight motion more intuitive. Consider seven feature points we got, for each frame, used three of them (two eye centers p_1, p_2 and one nose tip p_3) to calculate the homography matrix (H matrix) with the first frame, the SeetaFaceEngine would help us find these points in each frame. Then let the left points ($p_4, \ldots, p_7$) and H matrix do affine transformation. This step would make every frame align with the first frame, and it was easy to know that $p_4, \ldots, p_7$ of the latter frame could hardly overlap the first frame because of the face transformation. The updated four points could be denoted by $p_4', \ldots, p_7'$.

3.2   Calculate of High Dimensional Variance

In order to judge reliability of the given face in the video, some defined parameters should be calculated for the final classification. At the first stage, we used facial information to connect every follow-up frame with the first one.

As we mentioned at first, real human faces and face prints showed different properties when faces had any slight transformation. For each frame of the video, a real human face could be seen as a still picture while a face print could be seen as a picture-in-picture. This would make the left four points have obviously deviation in the whole video frames. The deviation could be described by the variance of the video frame sequences. To simplify the process of variance calculation, we selected 100 serial frames of the whole video frame sequences randomly. For the extracted 100 frames, $p_m^n(x)$ present the x direction value of the No. m feature point in the No. n frame.

---

[1] https://github.com/seetaface/SeetaFaceEngine.

Denote the variance by $\sigma_{ij}, i = 4, 5, 6, 7; j = x, y$. Clearly, we will have eight σ data to send to the SVM finally. For example, σ_{4x} can be defined as:

$$\sigma_{4x} = D(p_4^n(x))|n = 1, 2, \ldots, 100 \tag{1}$$

Where D means the variance.

4   Experiments and Analysis

In this section, we will introduce the experiment details of our proposed method and discuss about the results in order to do some analysis. We begin with the introduction of our developed database. Then we will show the experiment results by some intuitive charts. The results will be given by some comparisons among different conditions of experiment.

4.1   Database

We developed a database which contained the human faces and face prints video clips in three lighting conditions: strong light, moderate light and weak light. According to

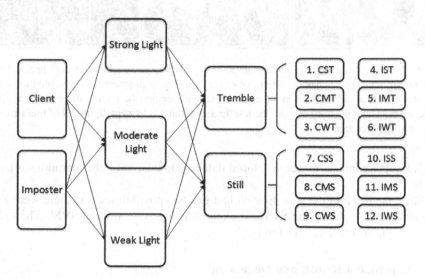

Fig. 4. Overview of our developed database which is classified by twelve labels. The naming convention for labels is using acronyms of the each experiment condition, each label has 60 face video clips

the amplitude of the face motion, video clips in each condition were divided into two kinds of group. The general overview of the database is given in Fig. 4.

For the real faces (client) dataset, we invited 60 people to participate in the video recording. People were consisted of different ages and different gender. The amount of each group were basically equal. In each video, the clients needed to turn their faces left and right to stimulate trembling, the amplitude was controlled in $\pm 15°$. The whole video would be last for about 10 s. We chose the Canon camera to make video and controlled the resolution in 270×480 and the filming distance in 50 cm.

For the face prints (imposter) dataset, in order to ensure the effectiveness and reliability of the whole database, we chose all clients in real face dataset, and took their photograph samples using a white curtain as the background. Then put them in front of the camera, did the same motion like the real faces dataset. The face area should take at least 2/3 of the whole area of the photograph. Also kept the video resolution in 270×480 and the filming distance in 50 cm.

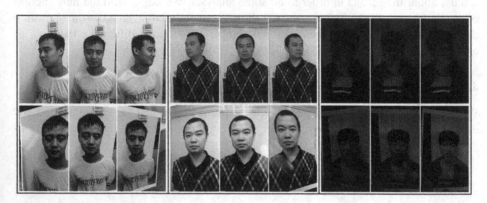

Fig. 5. Example of images captured from real faces (upper row) and from face prints (lower row) in our developed database. The three clients are stay in different lighting conditions, first one (the first three columns) is in strong light, second person (the middle three columns) is in moderate light, and the third person (the last three columns) is in weak light. All of them are still or have slight face trembling.

The capture images of our developed database in different light conditions is given in Fig. 5.

Since the result of the classification had just two possibilities, and there were eight feature vectors (eight σ), the SVM we chose was high dimensional SVM. The kernel type was linear to avoid over fitting.

4.2 Experiment Results and Discussion

From the labels in the Fig. 4, we emphatically considered the effect of our proposed method in different lighting conditions and in different amplitude of the face motion. For the whole database, including the client dataset and imposter dataset, we selected 30 videos from each label as training data (360 videos as training data in all) and the rest of the videos were seemed as test data. Then selected 7 facial landmarks by SeetaFace Alignment modular ($n = 7$).

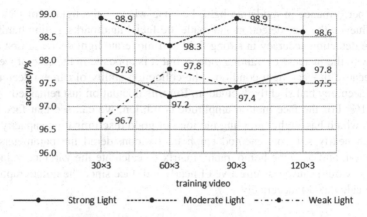

Fig. 6. Comparison of accuracy among different lighting condition. Strong light condition labels (*S*): CST, IST, CSS, ISS. Moderate light condition labels (*M*): CMT, IMT, CMS, IMS. Weak light condition labels (*W*): CWT, IWT, CWS, IWS. 30 × 3 means selecting 30 videos randomly from every light condition label

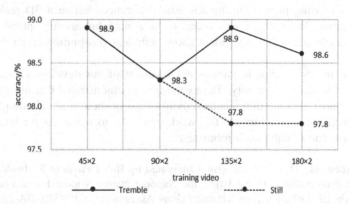

Fig. 7. Comparison of accuracy between different motion amplitude. Face trembling labels (**T): CST, CMT, CWT, IST, IMT, IWT. Moderate light condition labels (**S): CSS, CMS, CWS, ISS, IMS, IWS. 45 × 2 means selecting 45 videos randomly from every face motion amplitude condition label

The comparison of accuracy among different lighting conditions is given by the line chart in Fig. 6 and this criteria between different motion amplitude is also given in Fig. 7.

Since the current anti-spoofing methods always use images rather than videos to test the authenticity of faces, we didn't compare the accuracy of our proposed method with other anti-spoofing methods, our method need the face video clips to calculate the homography matrix.

From the line charts of different experiment conditions, we can get the accuracy percentage of our proposed method. In general, the method results can all get above 96% of accuracy in any conditions. For the light condition, the method shows an excellent performance in moderate light, because whether the light strong or weak, it would influence the face detection and made the facial landmarks getting hardly. From Fig. 6, the detection accuracy in strong light and moderate light decrease first and then increase with the increase of training videos, but it is opposite in the case of weak light. This is because in weak light condition, the collection ability of camera decreased, the detection accuracy had slightly fluctuation. But this fluctuation just remained within the range of 1%. For the face motion amplitude condition, we can see that face in video sequences which has slight trembling motion got good discrimination capacity than the face which nearly still: our method emphatically considered the parameters of face slight motion, and used the homography matrix to calculate the variance value of 100 frames, this would cause less effective of nearly still face since the homography matrix would be calculated inaccurately.

5 Conclusion

In this paper, we found that current face anti-spoofing methods had limitations in face motion situation. So we proposed a face anti-spoofing recognition method that worked on print attack using projection characteristic differences between 3D real face and plane face print. The method was based on a simple but useful optical principle. By SVM classification, the experiment shows efficient recognition result in different conditions.

Furthermore, video clips in various environment of our developed database simulate different situations in reality. The experiments demonstrated that our method can be used in almost extreme illuminating environment or motion amplitude of the face. Another direction to carry forward this work would be to make our method adjust to more situation and to enhance it robustness.

Acknowledgements. This work was partly supported by Hubei Province Technological Innovation Major Project (No. 2016AAA015), the National Nature Science Foundation of China (61502348), the EU FP7 QUICK project under Grant Agreement No. PIRSES-GA-2013-612652, and the science and technology program of Shenzhen (JCYJ20150422150029092).

References

1. Tan, X., Li, Y., Liu, J., Jiang, L.: Face liveness detection from a single image with sparse low rank bilinear discriminative model. In: Daniilidis, K., Maragos, P., Paragios, N. (eds.) ECCV 2010. LNCS, vol. 6316, pp. 504–517. Springer, Heidelberg (2010). https://doi.org/10.1007/978-3-642-15567-3_37
2. Jain, A.K., Flynn, P., Ross, A.A.: Handbook of Biometrics. Springer, USA (2008)
3. Chingovska, I., Anjos, A., Marcel, S.: On the effectiveness of local binary patterns in face anti-spoofing. In: Biometrics Special Interest Group, pp. 1–7. IEEE (2012)
4. Galbally, J., Marcel, S.: Face anti-spoofing based on general image quality assessment. In: International Conference on Pattern Recognition, pp. 1173–1178. IEEE (2014)

5. Erdogmus, N., Marcel, S.: Spoofing in 2D face recognition with 3D masks and anti-spoofing with Kinect. In: IEEE Sixth International Conference on Biometrics: Theory, Applications and Systems, pp. 1–6. IEEE (2013)
6. Maatta, J., Hadid, A., Pietikainen, M.: Face spoofing detection from single images using micro-texture analysis. In: International Joint Conference on Biometrics, pp. 1–7. IEEE Computer Society (2011)
7. Anjos, A., Marcel, S.: Counter-measures to photo attacks in face recognition: a public database and a baseline. In: International Joint Conference on Biometrics, pp. 1–7. IEEE Computer Society (2011)
8. Duda, R.O., Hart, P.E., Stork, D.G.: Pattern Classification, pp. 119–131. Wiley, New York (2001)
9. Pan, G., Sun, L., Wu, Z., et al.: Monocular camera-based face liveness detection by combining eyeblink and scene context. Telecommun. Syst. 47(3–4), 215–225 (2011)
10. Pan, G., Wu, Z., Sun, L.: Liveness detection for face recognition. In: Recent Advances in Face Recognition. InTech (2008)
11. Tronci, R., Muntoni, D., Fadda, G., et al.: Fusion of multiple clues for photo-attack detection in face recognition systems. In: International Joint Conference on Biometrics, pp. 1–6. IEEE Computer Society (2011)
12. Ojala, T., Pietikäinen, M., Mäenpää, T.: Multiresolution gray-scale and rotation invariant texture classification with local binary patterns. In: European Conference on Computer Vision, pp. 404–420. Springer-Verlag (2000)
13. Parveen, S., Ahmed, S., Mumtazah, S., et al.: Texture analysis using local ternary pattern for face anti-spoofing. Sci. Int. 28(2), 968–970 (2016)
14. Kollreider, K., Fronthaler, H., Bigun, J.: Non-intrusive liveness detection by face images. Image Vis. Comput. 27(3), 233–244 (2009)
15. Bao, W., Li, H., Li, N., et al.: A liveness detection method for face recognition based on optical flow field. In: International Conference on Image Analysis and Signal Processing, pp. 233–236. IEEE (2009)

A Novel Action Recognition Scheme Based on Spatial-Temporal Pyramid Model

Hengying Zhao and Xinguang Xiang[✉]

School of Computer Science and Engineering,
Nanjing University of Science and Technology,
Nanjing 210094, People's Republic of China
HengyingZhao@163.com, xgxiang@mail.njust.edu.cn

Abstract. Recognizing actions is one of the most important challenges in computer vision. In this paper, we propose a novel action recognition scheme based on spatial-temporal pyramid model. Firstly, we extract the basic visual feature descriptors for each video. Secondly, we construct visual dictionary on the whole visual features set. Thirdly, we construct a novel spatial-temporal pyramid model by dividing the visual features set of each video into multi-scale blocks in 2-dimensional space domain and 1-dimensional time domain separately. Then we calculate the distribution histogram representation for each block of different scales by using the bag-of-features model and our new visual dictionary. At last, we normalize the final descriptors for videos and then recognize the actions using SVM. Experimental results show that our scheme achieves more accurate for action recognition compared with several state-of-the-art methods.

Keywords: Action recognition · Spatial-temporal · Multi-scale
Visual dictionary

1 Introduction

Human action recognition and analysis [1] have shown their importance in a large amount of applications from video surveillance, automatic video indexing to human computer interaction [2]. Many recent researches focusing on classical image features have been generalized to videos, e.g., 3D-SIFT [3], extended SURF [4], HOG3D [5], Local Trinary Patterns [6], and dense trajectories [7–9], among these local space-time features, dense trajectories have been shown the best performance for action recognition on many video datasets. So, many descriptors like oriented gradients, optical flow and motion boundary are computed along the trajectories of feature points to capture the appearance, shape and motion information of videos, which have achieved improving results in recognizing actions.

© Springer International Publishing AG, part of Springer Nature 2018
B. Zeng et al. (Eds.): PCM 2017, LNCS 10736, pp. 212–221, 2018.
https://doi.org/10.1007/978-3-319-77383-4_21

Many recent researches show that these effective local features mentioned above can achieve improving results for action recognition when combined with a bag-of-features model. For example, [10] uses Harris 3D method to detect the feature points in the video, and the bag-of-features model is used to describe the videos, [11] uses the 2D Gauss filter on every frame of the video and 1D Gabor filter on the temporal dimension of the video to detect the spatial and temporal feature points of the video, which is also combined with the bag-of-features model getting good results.

However, when we construct the visual dictionary and the bag-of-features model to generate the final distribution histogram representations for videos, we may miss a large amount of global spatial and temporal structure information of videos. So some researches propose various methods to improve the bag of word model, e.g., [12] uses K-means to build visual dictionary, and then constructs a higher level descriptor according to the adjacent words of the feature points, then the new descriptor clusters, which improves the accuracy of action recognition. [13] proposes a new model named spatial pyramid model based on the bag-of-features model, which improves the performance of the bag-of-features model especially for image representation. [9,14] both extend the spatial pyramid model for images to the spatial-temporal pyramid model for videos, [14] learns a discriminative codebook and computes the cuboids' sparse representations by sparse coding, then classifies actions in videos using the STPM based on the max pooling achieving perfect results.

As we all know, the structural information in 1D time domain and 2D space domain of videos have very different characteristics. Therefore, in our paper, the main contribution of this work is to propose an efficient and simple model which takes into account the global spatial and temporal structure information of videos by handling the 2D space domain and 1D time domain separately, rather than in a joint 3D space domain as the traditional spatial-temporal pyramid model did. We can get a higher accuracy to recognize the actions in videos when we use our new spatial-temporal pyramid model based on bag-of-features model to represent the videos compared with the original bag-of-features model for action recognition.

The other contribution of this paper is that we construct two new visual dictionary of HOG and HOF for the video dataset KTH [15], for the HOF dictionary, we randomly select a subset of 100000 from all the visual features set of HOF based on the dense trajectories [8], for the HOG dictionary, we randomly select a subset of 60000 from all the visual features set of HOG based on the dense trajectories. When making these dictionaries, we randomly sample from the feature vectors set of each video separately rather than randomly sample from the big feature vectors set of the whole dataset, so our visual dictionaries contain the information of every video, which lays a good foundation for the next clustering in bag-of-features model and improves the performance of action recognition.

This paper is organized as follows. In Sect. 2, we introduce the method of our novel action recognition scheme based on our new spatial-temporal pyramid model, we mainly describe the procedures of constructing visual dictionary, our spatio-temporal pyramid model and the approach of normalization for the final descriptors of videos. Section 3 presents the experimental results on the KTH dataset by our proposed scheme based on our spatial-temporal pyramid model, and then compares the performance of action recognition with the results of some state-of-the-art methods respectively. Finally, we conclude this paper in Sect. 4.

2 Our Proposed Scheme for Action Recognition

In this section, we will describe the main steps in our action recognition scheme based on our new spatial-temporal pyramid model. The flowchart of our proposed scheme can be seen in Fig. 1. Firstly, we briefly introduce the extraction of original visual features in Sect. 2.1. Then the visual dictionary is constructed in Sect. 2.2. Nextly, in spatial-temporal pyramid model part, we detailedly describe the division method for videos in our model and the procedure of generating the final histogram by our new spatial-temporal pyramid model based on the bag-of-features model. In Sect. 2.4, we normalize the final descriptors for videos. At last, with the weighted descriptors, human actions in videos are classified by support vector machine.

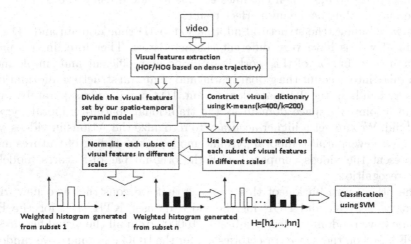

Fig. 1. Flowchart of our proposed action recognition scheme.

2.1 Visual Features Extraction

Dense trajectories methods [7,8] were shown to be an efficient video representation for action recognition and also achieved perfect results on a variety of video datasets. So, in our action recognition scheme, we use the approach of dense trajectories proposed in [8] to get the histogram of optical and the histogram of oriented gradients descriptors as the original visual features for each video.

2.2   Construct Visual Dictionary

In our experiment, we construct our new visual dictionaries for the original visual feature vectors (HOF and HOG based on the dense trajectories [8]) on the KTH dataset. Firstly, we sample from the visual feature vectors set of each video one by one on the KTH dataset randomly and averagely, to make up a features set containing 100000 visual feature vectors which can almost represent the motion and appearance information of all the videos on the KTH dataset, then cluster the subset using k-means to get the central points of the clusters. To limit the complexity, we fix the parameter k of k-means to be 400 and 200, after several iterations, when the sum of squared error is less than a fixed value, we get the final clusters and then regard the central points of the final clusters as the visual words of our new visual dictionary, so we get four visual dictionaries of HOF (k = 200), HOF (k = 400), HOG (k = 200) and HOG (k = 400), which just need moderate calculation and are enough for containing the motion and appearance information of the whole video dataset.

2.3   Novel Spatial-Temporal Pyramid Model

We construct a novel spatial-temporal pyramid model to add the spatial-temporal structure information of videos to the bag-of-features model. As an extension of spatial pyramid for images, we build our model by separately handling the 2D space domain and 1D time domain in videos to capture the spatial structure information and the temporal structure information of videos. We use three different temporal scales and two different spatial scales in our model. For the first level of our model, we use the full video clip without any division to be the level 1 of our model, using t1 to represent the entire duration time of each video for the second level in the 1D time domain, we averagely divide the video clip into two parts in the temporal domain, and then use t2 to represent the duration time of each block in level 2 of our model, for the last level in the time domain, we averagely divide the video clip into four parts in the temporal domain, we use t3 to represent the duration time of each block in level 3 of our model, for the second level in the 2D space domain, we averagely divide the video clip into four parts. The full illustration of our spatial-temporal pyramid model can be seen in Fig. 2, it illustrates our four levels of our model, for each cell of the level, a separate bag-of-features histogram is computed. In the 1D time domain, the histogram representation for each level is concatenated according to the Eq. (1), and in the 2D space domain, the histogram representation for each level is concatenated according to the Eq. (2):

$$H_s = (h_{(s,1)}, h_{(s,2)}, \ldots, h_{(s,n)}), n = 2^{s-1} . \tag{1}$$

$$H_s = (h_{(s,1)}, h_{(s,2)}, \ldots, h_{(s,n)}), n = s . \tag{2}$$

Where H_s is the histogram representing the level s, $h_{(s,n)}$ is the separate histogram for the block n in level s, we shall divide the level s into n blocks in 1D time domain or 2D space domain. The video is, finally, represented by the concatenation of all the histograms of all of the levels and its corresponding weights by the Eqs. (3) and (4):

$$H = (W_1 H_1, \ldots, W_s H_s) .$$ (3)

$$W_s = \begin{cases} \dfrac{1}{2^{(S-s)}}, s = 1, 2, 3 \\ 1 - \displaystyle\sum_{p=1}^{S-1} W_p, s = 4 \end{cases} .$$ (4)

where H represents the final feature vector for the video, H_s is the histogram for the level s, and W_s is the weight for the feature vector of level s, S refers to the whole number of levels in our model.

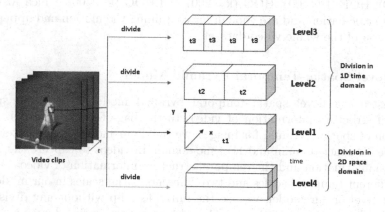

Fig. 2. Illustration of video division in 1D time domain and 2D space domain separately in our novel spatial-temporal pyramid model.

2.4   Normalization

In our works, we use the HOF and the HOG based on the dense trajectories [8] as the basic visual feature descriptors for our scheme. Considering that the number of dense sample points may varies for different videos, leading to the total number of original visual feature vectors of each video is different for the bag-of-features model, which may greatly reduce the comparability between the descriptors generated from the bag-of-features model for different videos. So we normalize the total number of visual feature descriptors generated from the dense trajectories approach [8] for each video according to the Eq. (5) when we construct our spatial-temporal pyramid model based on the bag-of-features model.

$$F = H * \left(\frac{4000}{D_j}\right) .$$ (5)

Where F refers to the final distribution histogram for videos after normalization, H is the histogram to be normalized, D_j represents the whole number

Table 1. Algorithm 1.

Input : a visual feature vector set $f = \{f_d\}$ of video j and our novel visual dictionary Dic of KTH dataset.

Output: a final descriptor for the video j.

1: count the number of f_d in visual feature vector set f.

2: divide the visual feature vector set $f = \{f_d\}$ into some smaller blocks in 1D time dimention and 2D space dimention separately by our spatial-temporal pyramid model.

3:**in 1D time domain:**

4: **for** level $s = 1 \cdots 3$, **do**

5:    **for** block $n = 1 \cdots 2^{s-1}$, **do**

6:        compute the distribution histogram on our visual dictionary Dic using bag of features model for block n.

7:    **end for**

8:    compute the final representation Hs for level s concatenated by Eq (1) .

9: **end for**

10:**in 2D space domain:**

11: **for** level $s = 1, 4$, **do**

12:    **for** block $n = 1 \cdots s$, **do**

13:        compute the distribution histogram on our visual dictionary Dic using bag of features model for block n.

14:    **end for**

15:    compute the histogram representation Hs for level s concatenated by Eq (2).

16: **end for**

17: compute the final representation H for video j concatenated by Eqs (3) and (4).

18: normalize the histogram representation H for video j to achieve the final descriptor F for the video j by Eq (5).

---

of the HOF or HOG feature vectors of the video j. This process can normalize the total number of the dense sample points to 4000 for each video, which has shown to empirically give good results for a wide range of datasets. The details of the procedure from constructing a new visual dictionary to normalization can be seen in Table 1.

2.5 Classifier for Action Recognition

In our experiment, we use the SVM classifier for action classification. Naturally, SVM is a binary classification model, in our example, we realize the multi-classification with the one-against-rest approach and select class with the highest score, our a large number of experiments show that our optimal parameters the kernel function option t is 1, namely polynomial kernel, giving the best accuracy for action recognition.

3 Experiment

In this section, we firstly describe the dataset used for action recognition. After that, the results of our novel scheme for action recognition will be shown and compared with several state-of-the-art action recognition methods. We also will do a set of experiments to prove that our novel spatial-temporal pyramid model, as the most important part in our scheme, has perfectly improved the performance of action recognition for our proposed scheme.

3.1 Dataset

The KTH dataset includes six human action classes: jogging, walking, clapping, boxing, running, and waving, see Fig. 3. Every action is performed several times by 25 persons. The videos were recorded in four different scenarios: indoors, outdoors, outdoors with scale variation and outdoors with different clothes. The background of most videos are homogeneous and static. In total, this dataset consists of 600 video samples, we randomly divide the whole samples into test set (4 subjects: 22, 23, 24, 25) for each human action class, 96 videos in all, and training set (the remain 21 subjects), 503 videos in all.

Fig. 3. Six actions in KTH dataset [15].

3.2 Results and Discussion

In Table 2, we firstly compare the accuracy of our proposed scheme based on spatial-temporal pyramid model for action recognition with Wang Heng's works [8] when we both use the same basic local visual features HOF. Results show that our proposed scheme based on spatial-temporal pyramid model has achieved an improving accuracy for action recognition compared with the Wang's works [8], in our proposed scheme, we use the same method of extracting visual features as wang's work, but we have added a new visual dictionary and a novel spatial-temporal pyramid model, which can capture more global spatial-temporal structure information, to get a better final descriptor for videos, so we can see that our approach outperforms Wang's works [8] for action recognition.

Nextly, in Table 2, we compare our scheme with not only Wang Heng's works [8] but also Somasundaram's works [16] when we all use the same basic local visual features HOG, and Somasundaram's works [16] used the global spatio-temporal features derived from sparse representations to get the global spatio-temporal structure information of videos, results show that our approach has achieved a better performance for recognizing action in videos.

Finally, in Table 2, we compare our proposed scheme with Zhang's works [17], which has also used a spatial-temporal pyramid model, but their pyramid model is constructed in a joint 3D spatial-temporal domain. As we known, the features in 1D time domain and 2D space domain in videos have very different characteristics, so in our works, we build the spatial-temporal pyramid model in 1D time domain and 2D space domain separately, which can better describe the spatial-temporal structure information of videos. Results in Table 2 show that our proposed scheme based on our novel spatial-temporal pyramid model outperforms the pyramid model of Zhang's works [17].

Table 2. Action recognition average accuracies of our proposed scheme based on spatial-temporal model and some state-of-the-art methods based on HOF or HOG on the KTH actions dataset.

Method/descriptor	Accuracy
HOF+BOF (Wang [8])	93.2%
HOF+BOF (k = 400) (our scheme based on spatial-temporal pyramid model)	**95.8%**
HOG+BOF (Wang [8])	86.5%
HOG+Somasundaram [16]	85.3%
HOG+BOF (k = 400) (our scheme based on spatial-temporal pyramid model)	**87.5%**
Spatial-Temporal Pyramid Sparse Coding (Zhang [17])	92.6%
HOF+BOF (k = 400) (our scheme based on spatial-temporal pyramid model)	**95.8%**

To prove the importance of our novel spatial-temporal pyramid model in our proposed scheme, we have done eight sets of experiments, the results are shown in Table 3. In our scheme, for the two kinds of basic visual features HOF or HOG, and the parameter of bag-of-features model k is 200 or 400, we all did a comparative experiment for the two cases, one is that recognizing actions by our proposed scheme based on spatial-temporal pyramid model, the other is that recognizing actions by our proposed scheme but deleting the steps of our novel spatial-temporal pyramid model. The comparative results in Table 3 show that our spatial-temporal pyramid model can really improve the accuracy of action recognition for our proposed scheme by separately capturing the global spatial structure information and temporal structure information of videos.

Table 3. Action recognition average accuracies of our novel action recognition scheme without spatial-temporal pyramid model and our scheme with spatial-temporal pyramid model on the KTH actions dataset.

Method/descriptor	Accuracy
HOF+BOF (k = 200) (our scheme without spatial-temporal pyramid model)	88.8%
HOF+BOF (k = 200) (our scheme with spatial-temporal pyramid model)	**93.0%**
HOF+BOF (k = 400) (our scheme without spatial-temporal pyramid model)	92.3%
HOF+BOF (k = 400) (our scheme with spatial-temporal pyramid model)	**95.8%**
HOG+BOF (k = 200) (our scheme without spatial-temporal pyramid model)	80.5%
HOG+BOF (k = 200) (our scheme with spatial-temporal pyramid model)	**84.7%**
HOG+BOF (k = 400) (our scheme without spatial-temporal pyramid model)	83.3%
HOG+BOF (k = 400) (our scheme with spatial-temporal pyramid model)	**87.5%**

4　Conclusion

This paper has introduced an action recognition scheme based on a novel spatial-temporal pyramid model which improves the bag-of-features model by separately taking into account the global spatial information and global temporal information of different scales for every videos. Our model has covered the shortage of missing a large amount of spatial and temporal structural information of videos for bag-of-features model, and we have achieved an improvement of performance for action recognition on the KTH dataset. Our action recognition scheme with new visual dictionary and our novel pyramid model also simplify the calculation and improve the speed naturally for action recognition. Such a scheme generating the descriptors for videos has shown to be efficient not only for action recognition, but also in other areas, such as video retrieval and action localization.

Acknowledgments. This work was supported in part by the Natural Science Foundation of China under Grant 61301106, 61327013 and U1611461.

References

1. Shao, L., Zhen, X., Tao, D., Li, X.: Spatio-temporal laplacian pyramid coding for action recognition. Cybern. IEEE Trans. **44**(6), 817 (2014)
2. Marfil, R., Dias, J., Escolano, F.: Recognition and action for scene understanding. Neurocomputing **161**(1), 1–2 (2015)
3. Scovanner, P., Ali, S., Shah, M.: A 3-dimensional sift descriptor and its application to action recognition. In: International Conference on Multimedia 2007, Augsburg, Germany, pp. 357–360, September 2007
4. Willems, G., Tuytelaars, T., Van Gool, L.: An efficient dense and scale-invariant spatio-temporal interest point detector. In: Forsyth, D., Torr, P., Zisserman, A. (eds.) ECCV 2008. LNCS, vol. 5303, pp. 650–663. Springer, Heidelberg (2008). https://doi.org/10.1007/978-3-540-88688-4_48

5. Klser, A., Marszalek, M., Schmid, C.: A spatio-temporal descriptor based on 3D-gradients. In: British Machine Vision Conference 2008, Leeds, September 2008
6. Yeffet, L., Wolf, L.: Local trinary patterns for human action recognition. In: IEEE International Conference on Computer Vision, pp. 492–497 (2009)
7. Kataoka, H., Hashimoto, K., Iwata, K., Satoh, Y., Navab, N., Ilic, S., Aoki, Y.: Extended co-occurrence hog with dense trajectories for fine-grained activity recognition. In: Asian Conference on Computer Vision, pp. 336–349 (2015)
8. Wang, H., Klaser, A., Schmid, C., Liu, C.L.: Action recognition by dense trajectories. In: IEEE Conference on Computer Vision and Pattern Recognition, pp. 3169–3176 (2011)
9. Wang, H., Klser, A., Schmid, C., Liu, C.L.: Dense trajectories and motion boundary descriptors for action recognition. Int. J. Comput. Vis. 103(1), 60–79 (2013)
10. Laptev, I., Lindeberg, T.: On space-time interest points. Int. J. Comput. Vis. 64(2), 107–123 (2005)
11. Dollar, P., Rabaud, V., Cottrell, G., Belongie, S.: Behavior recognition via sparse spatio-temporal features. In: IEEE International Workshop on Visual Surveillance and PERFORMANCE Evaluation of Tracking and Surveillance, pp. 65–72 (2005)
12. Kovashka, A., Grauman, K.: Learning a hierarchy of discriminative space-time neighborhood features for human action recognition, pp. 2046–2053 (2010)
13. Lazebnik, S., Schmid, C., Ponce, J.: Beyond bags of features: spatial pyramid matching for recognizing natural scene categories. In: 2006 IEEE Computer Society Conference on Computer Vision and Pattern Recognition, pp. 2169–2178 (2006)
14. Liu, C.H., Yang, Y., Liu, Y.H.: Spatio-temporal pyramid matching using sparse coding for action recognition. J. Chin. Comput. Syst. 33(1), 169–172 (2012)
15. Sch, C., Laptev, I., Caputo, B.: Recognizing human actions: a local SVM approach. In: International Conference on Pattern Recognition, pp. 32–36 (2004)
16. Somasundaram, G., Cherian, A., Morellas, V., Papanikolopoulos, N.: Action recognition using global spatio-temporal features derived from sparse representations. Comput. Vis. Image Underst. 123(7), 1–13 (2014)
17. Zhang, X., Zhang, H., Cao, X.: Action recognition based on spatial-temporal pyramid sparse coding. In: International Conference on Pattern Recognition, pp. 1455–1458 (2012)

Co-saliency Detection via Sparse Reconstruction and Co-salient Object Discovery

Bo Li, Zhengxing Sun$^{(\boxtimes)}$, Jiagao Hu, and Junfeng Xu

State Key Laboratory for Novel Software Technology,
Nanjing University, Nanjing, China
szx@nju.edu.cn

Abstract. Co-saliency detection aims at discovering common and salient objects in a group of related images, which is useful to variety of visual tasks. We propose a novel co-saliency detection framework via sparse reconstruction and co-salient object discovery. By taking advantage of the common background in-formation, we first reconstruct images with the common background bases and computer sparse reconstruction error. Second, we discover the common salient objects using high-level and low-level features. Then the reconstruction errors are refined using co-salient object information to get the superpixel-level co-saliency. Third, pixel-level saliency is computed by an integration of multi-scale superpixel-level co-saliency maps, with the help of intra-saliency propagation and Gaussian refinement. The quantitative and subjective experimental results on two benchmark datasets show that our method outperforms both the state-of-art saliency detection methods and co-saliency detection methods.

Keywords: Co-saliency detection · Sparse reconstruction · Object discovery
Saliency model

1 Introduction

Motivated by simulating human visual attention mechanism to predict human fixations [1], saliency detection has been a booming research topics in the computer vision community in the past decade. A number of visual applications, including object segmentation, image retrieval and content based image editing, have benefits from image saliency detection. Traditional saliency detection models however mainly focus on detecting salient objects in a single image. Recently, the ubiquitous usage of Internet results in an explosion of multimedia data, which drives researchers to extend their studies from detecting individual image saliency to exploring common saliency in image group. The goal of co-saliency detection is discovering common and salient objects in a group of related images [2, 3]. Co-saliency model generates a set of co-saliency maps from a sequence of images, which highlight common foreground objects and suppress irrelevant background regions, can be naturally used in many

© Springer International Publishing AG, part of Springer Nature 2018
B. Zeng et al. (Eds.): PCM 2017, LNCS 10736, pp. 222–232, 2018.
https://doi.org/10.1007/978-3-319-77383-4_22

computer vision tasks such as image co-segmentation [4], image matching [5], and image collage [6]. Thus, co-salient object detection has become an interesting research issue in recent years.

Co-saliency detection usually exhibits the following two properties: (1) co-salient regions should be salient regions in the individual image. (2) all those co-salient regions from different images should have high similarity with respect to certain feature representation. Guided by the properties, most of existing models [7–9] formulate co-saliency by exploring single-image saliency detection, i.e. the intra-image saliency, and correspondence of the saliency regions, i.e. the inter-image saliency, to discover the salient object within each image and describe how frequently the object occurs across the images. In current works, saliency in each image is either generated by a single image saliency detection model [10] or redesigned as a combination of saliency maps generated by several different saliency models. However, a single saliency detection may fail to highlight saliency region in some cases, while it is rather complex and time-consuming to run multiple saliency models [11]. Based on the fact that in co-saliency detection datasets as well as the real-world data, common objects usually occur in common backgrounds [12], we propose to take advantage of the common background information within an image group by employing sparse reconstruction to solve aforementioned problems. By fully using the common background information, not only background parts are better suppressed, but also the salient object which originally fails to be detected is successfully recovered.

As a generic object detection method, objectness [13] has shown its effectiveness to complement saliency detection in a single image [14–16]. Object prior is usually expressed as bounding box or window proposed by object detection method to reflect which image regions are more likely to be objects rather than backgrounds. Naturally, it can be used to help discovering the common object in co-saliency detection [12]. In previous works, the salient score of each pixel or region generated from objectness is calculated by the number of bounding boxes that cover it. However, there are always some non-salient parts with in the bounding boxes, directly assigning pixels a salient score according to the number of bounding boxes that cover it will make some non-salient regions with high saliency. And the overlap of the bounding boxes proposed by object detection would just make the salient result even unsatisfied. Unlike previous works, we propose a different strategy of using objectness in our inter-saliency discovery process, which is more effective for characterizing objects while suppressing non-salient region and better preserving edges of co-salient object.

The main contributions of this paper are as follows:

1. A novel inter-background suppression method is proposed by using the common background information, which not only better suppresses background in each image, but also highlights the salient object which originally fails to be detected.

2. A new inter-saliency discovery process is presented. Combining high-level and low-level feature, we effectively discover common salient objects. With a different strategy of using objectness discovered, we highlight co-salient objects while suppress uncommon-salient regions and preserve edges of co-salient objects.

3. With the help of an intra-saliency propagation method and Gaussian refinement, more favorable saliency results are achieved.

2 The Proposed Method

The framework of proposed co-saliency detection method is illustrated in Fig. 1. Given an image set, we first segment each image into superpixels. We select background bases for all images using boundary connectivity [17]. Next, we reconstruct each image by using background bases of its own and background bases from other images in the image set, respectively. The sparse reconstruction error of each image is generated by gathering tow reconstruction results above. Afterwards, with the help of object pro-posal method [18], we generate salient object candidates for each image based on its reconstruction error. We then discover the common salient objects by applying k-means clustering on all salient object candidates. The sparse reconstruction error is refined by the common objectness we discovered to obtain the superpixel-level sal-iency. Finally, the final co-saliency results are generated by integrating multi-scale superpixel-level saliency, with the help of intra-saliency propagation and Gaussian refinement. Details of the proposed method are given below.

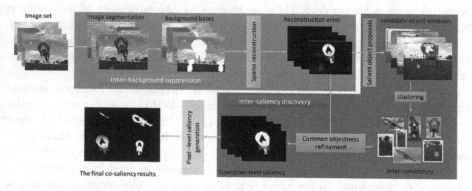

Fig. 1. The framework of the proposed co-saliency detection method.

2.1 Inter-background Suppression via Sparse Reconstruction

In our method, we intuitively consider image saliency detection as an estimation of sparse reconstruction error of whole image with background bases. And there are two important observations: 1. There is a large difference between the reconstruction errors of foreground and background regions using the same bases. 2. Background regions of an image can be well reconstructed by the background bases from other images in the image set which are similar to this image. With the help of the common background information, we better suppress the common background regions over images, and highlight salient objects in each image.

Given the input image set $\mathcal{I} = \{I^i\}_{i=1}^{N}$, we firstly generate superpixels using the simple linear iterative clustering(SLIC) algorithm [19] to segment each input image I^i into multiple uniform and compact regions. We then use the mean color features and coordinates of pixels to describe each segment $\mathbf{x} = \{L, a, b, R, G, B, x, y\}$. So each image

I^i can be represented as $\mathbf{X}^i = \left[\mathbf{x}_1^i, \mathbf{x}_2^i, \cdots \mathbf{x}_{n^i}^i\right] \in \mathbb{R}^{D \times n^i}$, where n^i is the number of segments in each image and D is the feature dimension.

In natural images, foreground regions usually have a less connectivity with image borders than background regions have. The connectivity between a region and image borders is helpful for region-based saliency detection. We calculate *boundary connectivity* [17] for every segments in each image. For every image I^i we set a threshold by employing *OTSU* algorithm [20] as a criterion to distinguish foreground segments and background segments according to their *boundary connectivity*. Therefore, for each image I^i we obtain a background base set as $\mathbf{B}^i = \left[\mathbf{b}_1^i, \mathbf{b}_2^i, \cdots \mathbf{b}_{m^i}^i\right]$, where m^i is the number of background bases. In order to capture the common background information, we using Gist and Color histogram as the global feature to represent each image and then cluster them into two groups based on the Euclidean distance. For each image I^i, the images which are in the same cluster with it are its visual similar neighbors. We can obtain another background base set $\mathbf{U}^i$, which consists of all background bases from visual similar neighbors of image I^i.

For each image I^i, we first use the background base set $\mathbf{B}^i$ as the bases for sparse reconstruction, and encode the image segment $\mathbf{x}_p^i$ by:

$$\beta_p^i = \underset{\beta_p^i}{\operatorname{argmin}} \ \left\|\mathbf{x}_p^i - \mathbf{B}^i \beta_p^i\right\|_2^2 + \lambda \left\|\beta_p^i\right\|_1 \tag{1}$$

and the reconstruction error is:

$$\varepsilon_p^i = \left\|\mathbf{x}_p^i - \mathbf{B}^i \beta_p^i\right\|_2^2 \tag{2}$$

To better suppress the common background, we then reconstruct image I^i with another background base set $\mathbf{U}^i$. Since the common background regions may not always appear in same positions in each image, we remove coordinates feature from segment $\mathbf{x}_p^i$ in sparse reconstruction. And then we can get another reconstruction error η_p^i for segment $\mathbf{x}_p^i$. We combine the two reconstruction error ε_p^i and η_p^i to get final reconstruction error κ_p^i for segment $\mathbf{x}_p^i$ by averaging them.

2.2 Inter-saliency Discovery

In order to capture the co-saliency information, we proposal an inter-saliency discovery process with common salient object selection and objectness refinement on the reconstruction error to get the superpixel-level co-saliency maps.

In order to select the common salient objects over the image set, we need to find all salient object candidates for every image. Previous models [12, 15] usually use an object proposal method to get the object prior. However, the object proposal method may not be able to propose all objects correctly because of its scalability. To overcome this shortage, in our method, we first employ an object proposal method faster-rcnn [18] to propose several object windows with high object probably for each image.

And then, for each image I^i, the proposed object windows would cover some salient segments x^i_c in its reconstruction error map. So the other salient segments which are not covered are also salient regions who are not proposed correctly by the proposal method. We generate bounding boxes for these salient regions. Thus, for each image I^i, we propose all its salient object candidates as $\mathbf{W}^i = [\mathbf{w}^i_1, \ \mathbf{w}^i_2, \cdots \mathbf{w}^i_{h^i}]$, where h^i is the number of salient object candidates.

Since co-saliency is the common saliency in all images, the common salient objects should have high similarity with respect to certain feature representation, and must be repeated emerge in the candidate set and acquire the advantage of the quantity. Based on this, given all salient object candidates $\mathcal{F} = \{\mathbf{W}^i\}^N_{i=1}$ of image set $\mathcal{I}$, to better capture their consistency, we first extract their high-level features using vgg-net [21] and low-level features (the average color feature of all segments covered by the object window) to represent the salient object candidates. However, neither low-level feature nor high-level feature can handle all the cases in co-saliency detection alone, we use them in different situations. According to the recognition results from vgg-net, if most of the salient object candidates belong to one class which means the high-level cannot well distinguish them, we use low-level feature to represent them, otherwise we use high-level feature. We then employ k-means to cluster all salient object candidates into K clusters $\mathbf{C} = \{C_k\}^K_{k=1}$. And we calculate a histogram $\mathbf{t} = \{t_k\}^K_{k=1}$ for each cluster to describe the occurrence rate of all the clusters $\mathbf{C}$ in the N input images:

$$t_k = \frac{1}{N} \sum_{i=1}^N f(C_k, I^i), \qquad k = 1 \cdots K \qquad (3)$$

where $f()$ indicates whether the cluster C_k appears in image I^i. If C_k appears in image I^i, $f = 1$, otherwise $f = 0$. When t_k is great than or equal to the threshold α_1 (we set $\alpha_1 = 0.8$ in our work), cluster C_k will be selected as common salient object cluster. At last, for each image I^i we generate a label set $\mathbf{D}^i = [d^i_1, \ d^i_2, \cdots d^i_{h^i}]$ corresponding to its salient object candidates $\mathbf{W}^i$ to represent whether an object candidate is the common salient object. If $\mathbf{w}^i_j$ is the common salient object $d^i_j = 1$, otherwise $d^i_j = -1$. The process of common salient object candidates discovery is illustrated in Fig. 2.

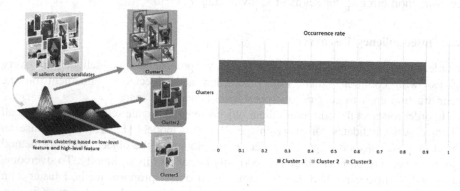

Fig. 2. Illustration of the common salient object candidates discovery.

After we find all common salient objects for image set $\mathcal{I}$, we use them as object prior to refine the reconstruction error and generate superpixel-level co-saliency map for each image. Traditionally, the salient score of each pixel or region generated from objectness is calculated by the number of bounding boxes that cover it. However, not all regions which are covered by bounding boxes are salient region. Unlike the previous works, for each bounding box $\mathbf{w}_j^i$ we reconstruct all segments covered by it using the segments that surround the box as bases. So the salient segments and the un-salient segments are well distinguished. Finally, each bounding box $\mathbf{w}_j^i$ will refine the reconstruction error of all segments it covers by:

$$\kappa_t^i = \kappa_t^i + d_j^i \times v_t^i \tag{4}$$

where t is the label of segment covered by bounding box $\mathbf{w}_j^i$. Thus, we highlight the co-salient objects while suppress the uncommon salient region and get the superpixel-level co-saliency map for each image.

2.3   Pixel-Level Saliency

Intra-saliency propagation. We propose a graph-based intra-saliency propagation method to smooth the superpixel-level saliency. We construct an undirected graph with superpixels as nodes. The weight between two nodes is only defined as their color similarity. As neighboring nodes are very likely to share similar appearance and saliency, we use k-regular constraint on the graph to capture the local grouping cues. That is, each node is only connected to both the nodes neighboring it and the nodes sharing common boundaries with its neighboring nodes. So the segments are divided into several groups. The propagated saliency of segment $\mathbf{x}_p^i$ belonging to group q ($q = 1, 2, \ldots, Q$), is modified by considering its appearance-based context consisting of the other segments in group q as follows:

$$\tilde{\kappa}_p^i = \tau \sum_{j=1}^{N_c} \varpi_{pqj} \tilde{\kappa}_{q_j}^i + (1 - \tau)\kappa_p^i, \tag{5}$$

$$\varpi_{pqj} = \frac{\exp\left(-\frac{\left\|\mathbf{x}_p^i - \mathbf{x}_{q_j}^i\right\|^2}{2\sigma_\mathbf{x}^2}\right)(1 - \delta(q_j - p))}{\sum_{j=1}^{N_c} \exp\left(-\frac{\left\|\mathbf{x}_p^i - \mathbf{x}_{q_j}^i\right\|^2}{2\sigma_\mathbf{x}^2}\right)}, \tag{6}$$

where $q_j (j = 1, 2 \cdots N_c)$ denote the N_c segment labels in group q and τ is a weight parameter. The weight of each segment context ϖ is defined by its normalized similarity with segment $\mathbf{x}_p^i$ in Eq. 6, where $\sigma_\mathbf{x}^2$ is the sum of the variance in each feature dimension of $\mathbf{X}$ and $\delta(\cdot)$ is the indicator function. The proposed graph-based intra-saliency propagation mechanism smooths the superpixel-level saliency in a group, thereby uniformly highlighting the co-salient objects.

Multi-scale saliency integration. For a full-resolution saliency map, we follow Li [10] assigning saliency to each pixel by integrating results from multi-scale superpixel-level saliency. To handle the scale problem, we compute sparse reconstruction errors and refine them at multi-scale. We generate pixel-level saliency by integrating multi-scale superpixel-level saliency

$$E(z) = \frac{\sum_{s=1}^{N_s} \omega_{zn^{(s)}} \tilde{\kappa}_{n^{(s)}}}{\sum_{s=1}^{N_s} \omega_{zn^{(s)}}}, \ \omega_{zn^{(s)}} = \frac{1}{\|f_z - \mathbf{x}_{n^{(s)}}\|_2} \tag{7}$$

where N_s is the number of scale, and $\tilde{\kappa}_{n^{(s)}}$ is the superpixel-level saliency in scale s. f_z is the feature vector of pixel z and $n^{(s)}$ denotes the label of the segment containing pixel z at scale $s.\omega_{zn^{(s)}}$ regards the similarity of pixel z with its corresponding superpixel as the weight to average the reconstruction errors in multi-scale.

Object-based Gaussian refinement. In traditional saliency detection methods, center prior has been wildly used and usually formulated as a Gaussian model

$$G(z) = \exp\left[-\left(\frac{(x_z - \mu_x)^2}{2\sigma_x^2} + \frac{(y_z - \mu_y)^2}{2\sigma_y^2}\right)\right] \tag{8}$$

where $\mu_x = x_c$ and $\mu_y = y_c$ denote the coordinates of the image center and x_z and y_z are the coordinates of pixel z. However, salient objects do not always appear at the image center, the center-biased Gaussian model may include background pixels or miss the foreground regions. We introduce an object-based Gaussian refinement process by applying several Gaussian models on each image. For each common salient object window $\mathbf{w}_j^i$ of image I^i, we can generate a Gaussian model G_j with $\mu_x = x_j$, $\mu_y = y_j$ and $\sigma_x = 0.5 \times H_j$, $\sigma_y = 0.5 \times W_j$, where x_j and y_j denote the center coordinates of $\mathbf{w}_j^i$ while H_j and W_j respectively denote the width and height of $\mathbf{w}_j^i$. The final co-saliency of pixel z is computed by

$$S(z) = E(z) * \sum_{j=1}^{N_o} G_j(z) \tag{9}$$

where N_o is the number of common salient objects in each image and j denotes the label of common salient object.

3 Experiment

We evaluated the proposed algorithm on two benchmark datasets: the iCoseg dataset [22] and the MSRC dataset [23]. The former one is the largest publicly available dataset so far used for co-saliency detection and co-segmentation. It consists of 38 image groups of totally 643 images along with manually labeled pixel-wise ground truth data. The latter one consists of 8 image groups (240 images) with manually labeled pixel-wise ground truth data. Compared with the iCoseg dataset, different colors and shapes are allowed for the co-salient objects appearing in image groups of the MSRC dataset, making it more challenging for co-saliency detection.

To evaluate the performance of the proposed method, we adopted four widely used criteria, i.e. the precision recall (PR) curve, the average precision (AP) score, the F-measure and mean F-score(mF). PR curves and AP scores are generated by thresholding pixels in a co-saliency map into binary co-salient object masks with a series of fixed integers from 0 to 255. The resulting true positive rate versus the precision rate at each threshold value forms the PR curve. The average precision and recall values over the images are obtained following the benchmark introduced in [24], as the F-measure defined by $F - measure = \frac{(1 + \beta^2) \times Precision \times Recall}{\beta^2 \times Precision + Recall}$, where $\beta^2 = 0.3$ as suggested in [24].

For quantitative evaluation, we compared the proposed approach with 5 state-of-the-art methods, i.e., CBCS [7], SACS [9], CSDW [12], LR [25] and DSR [10], where the first three methods are the state-of-the-art co-saliency detection methods and the last two methods are the state-of-the-art saliency detection methods. We also evaluate the effectiveness of each part in the proposed framework, including without using objectness refinement (OURS-NOR), without using intra-saliency propagation (OURS-NSP) and without using Gaussian refinement (OURS-NGR). The experimental results are shown in Fig. 3(a), Tables 1 and 2. As can be seen, the proposed framework (OURS) outperforms both the state-of-the-art saliency detection methods and co-saliency detection methods in PR curves and F-measure curves in two datasets. And our method overcomes all the other saliency approaches on AP scores and mF scores.

We also show some experimental results in Fig. 3(b) for subjective evaluation, which contains examples of four image groups, i.e., the *pyramid* group and the *women soccer* group from iCoseg dataset and the *cattle* group and *face* group from MSRC dataset. As can be seen, compared with the state-of-the-art methods CBCS [7], SACS [9] and CSDW [12], the co-saliency results of our method are more correct and robust. By taking advantage of the common background information, we better suppress background in each image and highlight the salient object which originally fails to be detected (i.e., the pyramid at the left side in third column images in the *pyramid* group). The inter-saliency discovery using both high-level features and low-level features helps we highlight the common salient objects and suppress the uncommon salient regions. With objectness refinement, intra-saliency propagation and Gaussian refinement uniformly smooth the co-saliency results and preserve edges of co-salient objects.

The proposed algorithm is run on a workstation with 3.3 GHz CPU, 64G RAM and additionally with a GeForce GTX Titan GPU for high-level feature acceleration. The remaining codes were implemented in Matlab without any optimization and GPU acceleration. Table 3 lists the average execution time in processing an image by using different approaches.

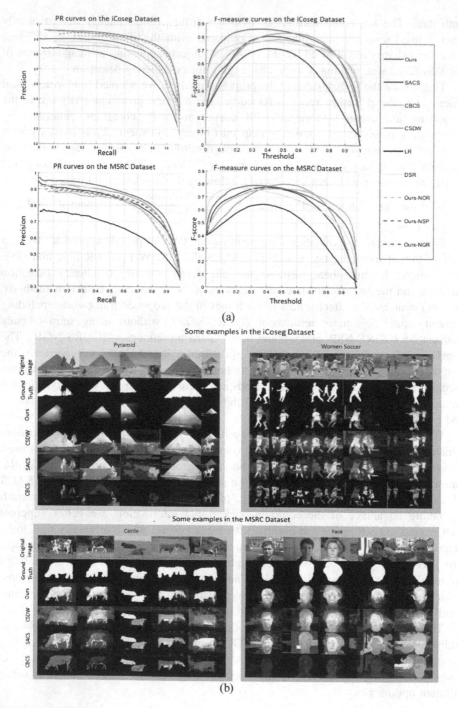

Fig. 3. Quantitative and subjective evaluation of the proposed approach in the iCoseg and MSRC datasets.

Table 1. AP and mF scores on the iCoseg dataset

Methods	LR [25]	DSR [10]	CBCS [7]	SACS [9]	CSDW [12]	OURS-NOR	OURS-NSP	OURS-NGR	OURS
AP	0.727	0.771	0.805	0.865	0.873	0.811	0.859	0.885	**0.902**
mF	0.516	0.701	0.688	0.644	0.676	0.707	0.738	0.741	**0.745**

Table 2. AP and mF scores on the MSRC dataset

Methods	LR [25]	DSR [10]	CBCS [7]	SACS [9]	CSDW [12]	OURS-NOR	OURS-NSP	OURS-NGR	OURS
AP	0.557	0.811	0.713	0.799	0.835	0.802	0.806	0.817	**0.863**
mF	0.465	0.651	0.679	0.623	0.630	0.643	0.649	0.655	**0.683**

Table 3. Average running time per image

Methods	LR [25]	DSR [10]	CBCS [7]	SACS [9]	CSDW [12]	OURS
Time(s)	19.88	0.771	1.61	7.36	6.52	5.33

4 Conclusion

In this paper, we propose a novel co-saliency detection framework via sparse reconstruction and co-salient object discovery. By taking advantage of the common background information, we use sparse reconstruction to better suppress background and highlight the salient object in each image. By inter-saliency discovery, our method is able to capture the common salient objects and suppress the uncommon salient regions. With the help of an intra-saliency propagation method and Gaussian refinement, more favorable saliency results are achieved. For the future work, we plan to extend our method to video processing tasks.

Acknowledgements. This work was supported by National High Technology Research and Development Program of China (No. 2007AA01Z334), National Natural Science Foundation of China (Nos. 61321491 and 61272219), Innovation Fund of State Key Laboratory for Novel Software Technology (Nos. ZZKT2013A12 and ZZKT2016A11), and Program for New Century Excellent Talents in University of China (NCET-04-04605).

References

1. Itti, L., Koch, C., Niebur, E.: A model of saliency-based visual attention for rapid scene analysis. IEEE Trans. Patt. Anal. Mach. Intell. **20**(11), 1254–1259 (1998)
2. Jacobs, D., Goldman, D., Shechtman, E.: Cosaliency: where people look when comparing images. In: Proceedings of ACM UIST, pp. 219–228, October 2010
3. Cheng, M.M., Mitra, N.J., Huang, X., Hu, S.M.: SalientShape: group saliency in image collections. Vis. Comput. **30**, 443–453 (2013). https://doi.org/10.1007/s00371-013-0867-4

4. Chang, K., Liu, T., Lai, S.: From co-saliency to co-segmentation: an efficient and fully unsupervised energy minimization model. In: Proceedings of IEEE CVPR, pp. 2129–2136, June 2011
5. Xue, J., Wang, L.: Automatic salient object extraction with contextual cue and its applications to recognition and alpha matting. Pattern Recognit. **46**(11), 2874–2889 (2013)
6. Zhang, L., Huang, H.: Hierarchical narrative collage for digital photo album. Comput. Graph. Forum **31**(7), 2173–2181 (2012)
7. Fu, H., Cao, X., Tu, Z.: Cluster-based co-saliency detection. IEEE Trans. Image Process. (TIP) **22**(10), 3766–3778 (2013)
8. Li, H., Ngan, K.: A co-saliency model of image pairs. IEEE Trans. Image Process. **20**(12), 3365–3375 (2011)
9. Cao, X., Tao, Z., Zhang, B., Fu, H., Feng, W.: Self-adaptively weighted co-saliency detection via rank constraint. IEEE TIP **23**, 4175–4186 (2014)
10. Lu, H., Li, X., Zhang, L., Ruan, X., Yang, M.H.: Dense and sparse reconstruction error based saliency descriptor. IEEE Trans. Image Process. **25**(4), 1592–1603 (2016)
11. Li, Y., Fu, K., Liu, Z., Yang, J.: Efficient saliency-model-guided visual co-saliency detection. IEEE Signal Process. Lett. **22**(5), 588–592 (2015)
12. Zhang, D., Han, J., Li, C., et al.: Detection of co-salient objects by looking deep and wide. Int. J. Comput. Vis. **120**(2), 215–232 (2016)
13. Alexe, B., Deselaers, T.: What is an object? In: Proceedings of IEEE CVPR, pp. 73–80, June 2010
14. Chang, K., Liu, T., Chen, H., Lai, S.: Fusing generic objectness and visual saliency for salient object detection. In: Proceedings of IEEE ICCV, pp. 914–921, November 2011
15. Jiang, P., Ling, H., Yu, J., Peng, J.: Salient region detection by UFO: uniqueness, focusness and objectness. In: Proceedings of IEEE ICCV, pp. 1976–1983, December 2013
16. Jia, Y., Han, M.: Category-independent object-level saliency detection. In: Proceedings of IEEE ICCV, pp. 1761–1768, December 2013
17. Zhu, W., et al.: Saliency optimization from robust background detection. In: Proceedings of IEEE CVPR (2014)
18. Ren, S., et al.: Faster R-CNN: towards real-time object detection with region proposal networks. In: Advances in Neural Information Processing Systems (2015)
19. Achanta, R., Shaji, A., Smith, K., Lucchi, A., Fua, P., Susstrunk, S.: SLIC superpixels. Technical report 149300. EPFL (2010)
20. Otsu, N.: A threshold selection method from gray-level histograms. IEEE Trans. Syst. Man Cybern. **9**(1), 62–66 (1979)
21. Simonyan, K., Zisserman, A.: Very deep convolutional networks for large-scale image recognition. In: International Conference on Learning Representations (2015)
22. Batra, D., Kowdle, A., Parikh, D., Jie, L., Chen, T.: iCoseg: interactive co-segmentation with intelligent scribble guidance. In: CVPR (2010)
23. Winn, J., Criminisi, A., Minka, T.: Object categorization by learned universal visual dictionary. In: ICCV (2005)
24. Achanta, R., Hemami, S., Estrada, F., Susstrunk, S.: Frequency-tuned salient region detection. In: CVPR (2009)
25. Shen, X., Wu, Y.: A unified approach to salient object detection via low rank matrix recovery. In: CVPR (2012)

Robust Local Effective Matching Model
for Multi-target Tracking

Hao Sheng[1($\boxtimes$)], Li Hao[1], Jiahui Chen[1], Yang Zhang[1], and Wei Ke[2]

[1] State Key Laboratory of Software Development Environment,
School of Computer Science and Engineering, Beihang University, Beijing, China
{shenghao,haoli,chenjh,yang.zhang}@buaa.edu.cn
[2] Macao Polytechnic Institute, Macao, China
wke@ipm.edu.mo

Abstract. Occlusion is one of the main challenges in multi-target tracking, which causes fragments in tracking. In order to handle with fragments, various motion models were proposed. However, motion model has limited effect on dealing with long-term fragments, because the predictability of target motion declines with increase in fragment length. Thus we propose a robust local effective matching model for partial detections to reduce fragment length first. The proposed model is integrated into a network flow based hierarchical framework to solve long-term fragments step-by-step. Initial tracklets are generated for later analysis in the first level. The robust local effective matching model is used in the second level to reduce fragment length. A motion model is utilized in the third level to solve fragments between tracklets. The benchmark results on 2D MOT 2015 dataset were compared with several state-of-the-art trackers and our method got competitive results with those trackers.

Keywords: Multi-target tracking · Network flow
Long-term fragment · Partial detection
Local effective matching model

1 Introduction

Multi-target tracking [12] is the basis of action recognition, behavior analysis. It is used in numerous applications such as visual surveillance and medical image processing. In recent years, great progress is made in multi-target tracking. However, it is still a challenging task due to false detections and occlusions.

Occlusion is the reason of fragments. Various motion models were proposed to solve fragments in tracking. However, motion model has limited effect on dealing with long-term fragments, because the predictability of target motion declines with increase in fragment length. We add links between tracklets and partial detections to reduce fragment length at first. Partial detections are detections smaller than the actual sizes of targets. In previous approaches, partial detections are either ignored or used without refinement. Thus we proposed a robust

© Springer International Publishing AG, part of Springer Nature 2018
B. Zeng et al. (Eds.): PCM 2017, LNCS 10736, pp. 233–243, 2018.
https://doi.org/10.1007/978-3-319-77383-4_23

local effective matching model that consists of an affinity measure and a refine method for partial detections. The proposed model is integrated into a hierarchical framework for tracking. Initial tracklets are generated in the first level of the framework. The robust local effective matching model is used in the second level to reduce fragment length. Finally, fragments are solved by a motion model in the third level. Multi-target tracking is formulated as a minimum-cost flow problem and is solved by linear programming in the proposed framework.

2   Related Work

According to the way of data processing, multi-target tracking is categorized into online tracking and offline tracking. Online tracking [7,15,18] estimates current object state based on past frames. Online tracking is very fast. But it has the drawback that the solution may be trapped in local optimal value. Offline tracking utilizes a batch way to process data. All frames are used to get global optimal solution. Offline tracking [3,9] is slower but more robust to errors than online tracking. The following discussion is about offline tracking methods.

With the remarkable advance in image-based object detection [5,16], the task is converted to a data association optimization problem. Tracking-by-detection paradigm is proposed by Breitenstein et al. [2]. First, detection responses, which mean potential positions of interested targets, are generated by an object detector. Then, detections that belong to the same target are assigned with the same ID label. Multiple hypothesis tracking [9] builds a tree of potential track hypothesis for each target. The most likely combination of tracks is selected. However, it is time-consuming and memory intensive. Zhang et al. [19] proposed a network flow based optimization method for multiple target tracking. The minimum-cost flow to the network corresponded to the solution of tracking problem.

Object motion model is important for multi-target tracking because it predicted the potential positions of targets. The motion model assumes objects moved with constant velocity. Milan et al. used a constant motion model in [14]. McLaughlin et al. [13] incorporated a motion model into a minimum-cost network flow tracker. Their method computed the distances of estimated positions and actual positions between two tracklets, and achieved good performance on public surveillance sequences of Oxford town center [1] and PETS S2.L1 [8].

Local optical flow based affinity measure had been previously explored by Choi [3]. Their aggregated optical flow descriptor encoded how interest points in a detection box moved with respect to another detection box. Their work was focused on using interest points trajectories to measure detection similarity. We used tracking state of interest points to refine partial detections and add links between refined partial detections and tracklets.

3   Robust Local Effective Matching Model

The robust local effective matching model has two components, an affinity measure and a method to refine the partial detections. Partial detection covers only a local part of the target. So the affinity measure between partial detections and tracklets should be able to associate the local part with full target. The proposed model uses the PTP (percent of tracked points) score as affinity measure and refined partial detections using tracking state of interest points.

3.1 PTP Score

If detection O_i and detection O_j belong to the same target, interest points in O_i could also be tracked in O_j. Let $\mathcal{P}^{ij} = \{p_k^{ij} : k = 1, 2, ...m\}$ be the interest point set selected from O_i and tracked in O_j. m is the number of selected points. Each interest point is $p_k^{ij} = \left(x_k^i, x_k^j, y_k^i, y_k^j, f_k^{ij} \right)$, where x_k^i and y_k^i are coordinates of p_k^{ij} in O_i, x_k^j and y_k^j are coordinates of p_k^{ij} in O_j, f_k^{ij} is a binary indicator that shows whether the point is tracked.

$$f_k^{ij} = \begin{cases} 1 & \text{if } p_k^{ij} \text{ is tracked} \\ 0 & \text{otherwise} \end{cases} \tag{1}$$

The PTP score between detection O_i and detection O_j takes the max value calculated in two directions, from O_i to O_j and from O_j to O_i. The definition of PTP score is as follows:

$$\mathcal{S}_{O_i, O_j} = \max\{ \frac{\sum_{p_k^{ij} \in \mathcal{P}_{ij}} f_k^{ij}}{\sum_{p_k^{ij} \in \mathcal{P}_{ij}} 1}, \frac{\sum_{p_k^{ji} \in \mathcal{P}_{ji}} f_k^{ji}}{\sum_{p_k^{ji} \in \mathcal{P}_{ji}} 1} \} \tag{2}$$

In this paper, interest points are selected and tracked using KLT [11]. Local optical flow is the optical flow inside detection bounding boxes.

3.2 Refinement Algorithm for Partial Detection

Partial detection is FP in evaluation, because the overlap between partial detection and ground truth is too small. So partial detections need to be refined.

If $\mathcal{S}_{O_i, O_j} \geq \mathcal{S}_{min}$, $\{O_i, O_j\}$ is known as a matched pair. $\mathcal{S}_{O_i, O_j}$ is the PTP score of O_i and O_j as described in Sect. 3.1. $\mathcal{S}_{min}$ is a minimum threshold. For a matched pair $\{O_i, O_j\}$, O_i is a partial detection if $h_i < \alpha * h_j$. h_i is the height of O_i, h_j is the height of O_j and α is a factor that controls acceptable height difference. Here are two assumptions. One is that the detection size of same target will not change much in neighboring frames. The other is at least one detection of the matched pair has an appropriate size. The first assumption is satisfied with adequate frame rate. The second assumption is satisfied by setting constraints.

As is shown in Algorithm 1. x_i and y_i are the coordinates of upper left corner of O_i, t_i is the frame of O_i, w_i is the width of O_i and h_i is the height of O_i. The notations used in O_j have similar meanings. Other notations are described in Sect. 3.1. Suppose O_i is a partial detection in matched pair $\{O_i, O_j\}$, we need to get a proper size and position to refine it. Since the detections of same target

---

Algorithm 1. Refinement Algorithm for Partial Detection

Input: $O_i = \{t_i, x_i, y_i, w_i, h_i\}, O_j = \{t_j, x_j, y_j, w_j, h_j\}, \mathcal{P}^{ij} = \{p_k^{ij} : k = 1, 2, ...m\}$,
       O_i is a partial detection.

Output: O_i'

1: **for all** $p_k^{ij} = (x_k^i, x_k^j, y_k^i, y_k^j, f_k^{ij}) \in \mathcal{P}_{ij}$ **do**

2:    **if** f_k^{ij} is 1 **then**

3:        $\Delta x_k \leftarrow x_k^j - x_k^i, \Delta y_k \leftarrow y_k^j - y_k^i$

4:    **else**

5:        $\Delta x_k \leftarrow 0, \Delta y_k \leftarrow 0$

6:    **end if**

7: **end for**

8: $\Delta x \leftarrow \dfrac{\sum_{k=1,2,...,m} \Delta x_k}{\sum_{k=1,2,...,m} f_k^{ij}}, \Delta y \leftarrow \dfrac{\sum_{k=1,2,...,m} \Delta y_k}{\sum_{k=1,2,...,m} f_k^{ij}}$

9: **return** $O_i' = \{t_i, x_j - \Delta x, y_j - \Delta y, w_j, h_j\}$

---

will not change much in neighboring frames, we use the size of O_j as the refined size. The refined position is calculated using the average displacement of interest points and position of O_j.

4 Hierarchical Tracking

Our tracking method works in a hierarchical way. The first level analyzes detection-detection relationship and generates tracklets for later analysis. The robust local effective matching model is used in second level to reduce fragment length. In third level, a motion model is utilized to solve fragments between tracklets.

4.1 Tracklets Generation

Since tracklets generated in this stage are the basis for later analysis, we chose a conservative strategy to get them.

Given a detection set $\mathcal{O} = \{O_1, O_2, ...O_n\}$, the pairwise cost between detection O_i and detection O_j is defined as:

$$C(O_i, O_j) = \begin{cases} \mathcal{C}(V_{i,j}, V_{max}^{i,j}) + 1 - cos(f_i, f_j) & (O_i, O_j) \in \mathcal{A} \\ +\infty & \text{otherwise} \end{cases} \quad (3)$$

where $V_{i,j}$ is the velocity between detection O_i and detection O_j, $V_{max}^{i,j}$ is the max velocity between O_i and O_j, $V_{max}^{i,j} = h_a * \beta$, h_a is the average height of O_i and O_j and β is a factor. f_i is a 256-dimensional feature vector of detection O_i trained by deep learning and f_j is the feature vector of O_j, $cos(f_i, f_j)$ is the cosine distance of f_i and f_j, function $\mathcal{C}$ is defined as:

$$\mathcal{C}(\gamma, \lambda) = 1 - e^{\sqrt{\frac{\gamma}{\lambda}}} \quad (4)$$

$\mathcal{A} = \{(O_m, O_n) : m, n \text{ satisfy that } \Delta T_{m,n} \leq T_{max}, V_{m,n} \leq V_{max}^{m,n}, Overlap(m, n) \geq Overlap_{min}\}$. $\Delta T_{m,n}$ is the absolute time difference between detection O_m and detection O_n, T_{max} is the maximum threshold for time gap between detections. $Overlap(m, n)$ is the bounding box overlap between detection O_m and detection O_n, $Overlap_{min}$ is the minimum threshold for overlap.

We get conservative tracklets for later processing by setting strict threshold in this stage. This reduces the search space in the meanwhile.

4.2 Tracklet-Detection Analysis

In order to reduce fragment length of tracklets, we use the robust local effective matching model to explore evidence of targets in unused detections.

Given tracklets set $\mathcal{T} = \{T_1, T_2, \ldots, T_m\}$ and detections set $\mathcal{O}$, we get an unused detection set U. The pairwise cost between tracklet $T_i = \{O_{i1}, O_{i2}, \ldots, O_{il_i}\}$ (l_i is the length of T_i) and an unused detection O_j is defined as follows:

$$C(T_i, O_j) = \begin{cases} 1 - S_{O_{i1}, O_j} & 0 < t(O_{i1}) - t(O_j) < T_{max}, S_{O_{i1}, O_j} \geq S_{min} \\ 1 - S_{O_{il_i}, O_j} & 0 < t(O_j) - t(O_{il_{T_i}}) < T_{max}, S_{O_{il_i}, O_j} \geq S_{min} \\ +\infty & \text{otherwise} \end{cases} \quad (5)$$

where O_{i1} is the first detection of T_i, O_{il_i} is the last detection of T_i, $t(O_{i1})$ is the frame of O_{i1}, $t(O_{il_i})$ is the frame of O_{il_i}, S_{O_{i1}, O_j} is the PTP score of O_{i1} and O_j, $S_{O_{il_i}, O_j}$ is the PTP score of O_{il_i} and O_j, S_{min} is the minimum threshold.

If first condition in Eq. 5 is met and $h_j < \alpha * h_{i1}$ or second condition in Eq. 5 is met and $h_j < \alpha * h_{il_i}$, then O_j is a partial detection and is refined using the algorithm in Sect. 3.2. h_j is the height of O_j, h_{i1} is the height of O_{i1}, h_{il_i} is the height of O_{il_i} and α is a factor that controls acceptable height difference. The cost is one minus PTP score of O_j and its nearest-frame detection in T_i when the PTP score exceeds a minimum threshold and T_i and O_j are not overlapped in time. Otherwise the cost is infinity.

4.3 Tracklet-Tracklet Analysis

After the detection-detection analysis and tracklet-detection analysis, no more detection information could be explored to solve fragment. Thus a motion model is used to analyze relationship between tracklets.

For a tracklet $T_k = \{O_{k1}, O_{k2}, \ldots, O_{kl_k}\}$, l_k is the length of T_k, we use detections in the first 1 s to backwardly estimate its velocity and use detections in the last 1s to forwardly estimate its velocity. Linear regression is performed over x, y coordinates of detections with time as the predictor variable. The forwardly predicted position of T_k in Δt frames later is written as $T_k^f(t(O_{kl_k}) + \Delta t)$, $t(O_{kl_k})$ is the frame of O_{kl_k}. The backwardly predicted position of T_k in Δt frames earlier is written as $T_k^b(t(O_{k1}) - \Delta t)$, $t(O_{k1})$ is the frame of O_1.

The pairwise cost between tracklets T_i and T_j (T_i happens before T_j) is defined as:

$$C(T_i, T_j) = \begin{cases} 1 - e^{\sqrt{\frac{E_{i,j}}{E_{max}}}} & \Delta T_{il_i,j1} \leq T_{max}, E_{i,j} \leq E_{max} \\ +\infty & \text{otherwise} \end{cases} \tag{6}$$

where $E_{i,j}$ is the energy to link T_i and T_j, $\Delta T_{il_i,j1}$ is the absolute time difference between O_{il_i} and O_{j1}, O_{il_i} is the last detection of T_i, O_{j1} is the first detection of T_i, T_{max} is the maximum threshold for time difference, E_{max} is the maximum energy threshold. $E_{i,j}$ is defined as:

$$E_{i,j} = \frac{1}{F} \sum_{t'=1}^{F} |T_i^f(t(O_{j1}) + t') - T_j(t(O_{j1}) + t')| +$$

$$\frac{1}{F} \sum_{t'=1}^{F} |T_j^b(t(O_{il_k}) - t') - T_j(t(O_{il_k}) - t')| \tag{7}$$

where F is the window length used to calculate energy, F equals to the value of FPS (frames per second) in our experiments. The cost function is designed to encourage tracklet pairs with small residual between predicted position and actual position of tracklets.

4.4   Minimum-Cost Network Flow Optimization

The MOT problem is formulated as a minimum-cost network flow problem. The objective function for the problem is:

$$\mathcal{T}^* = \underset{\mathcal{T}}{\operatorname{argmin}} \sum_{T_k \in \mathcal{T}} -\log P(T_k) + \sum_i -\log P(O_i|\mathcal{T})$$

$$= \underset{\mathcal{T}}{\operatorname{argmin}} \sum_i C_{en,i} f_{en,i} + \sum_{i,j} C_{i,j} f_{i,j} + \sum_i C_{ex,i} f_{ex,i} + \sum_i C_i f_i \tag{8}$$

$$s.t. \ f_{en,i} + \sum_j f_{j,i} = f_i = f_{ex,i} + \sum_j f_{i,j}, \forall i$$

where $\mathcal{T}$ is the hypothesis set, T_k is a tracklet hypothesis, O_i is a detection. $C_{en,i}$ is the cost of entry edge between source node and O_i, $C_{ex,i}$ is the cost of exit edge between sink node and O_i, C_i is the cost of detection edge of O_i, $C_{i,j}$ is the cost of transition edge between detection O_i and detection O_j, $f_{en,i}$, $f_{ex,i}$, f_i, $f_{i,j}$ are binary indicators show whether those edges are selected.

The transition edge cost between detection nodes is defined as above three subsections. The cost of detection edge is negative normalized confidence of the detection. The entry/exit edge cost takes a constant zero. Number of targets is obtained using a Fibonacci search in the possible value interval.

In order to avoid the accumulation of errors, we use tracklet-detection analysis and tracklet-tracklet analysis to add some new edges between detections to the network, instead of building new network of tracklets.

5 Experiments

The MOT challenge benchmark provides a standardized evaluation of multiple target tracking methods. So we conducted our experiments on 2D MOT2015 [10] datasets. The selected datasets have a total of 22 sequences. We used public detections for excluding the influence of detection quality. Raw detections were pre-processed using a non-maximum suppression method.

5.1 Implementation Details

The feature vectors used in the first level were trained by deep learning. In our first level to generate tracklets, parameters were set as follows: $\beta = 3$, $T_{max} = 2$ frames, $Overlap_{min} = 0.5$. In our second level, $T_{max} = 4$ frames, $S_{min} = 0.8$, $\alpha = 0.8$. In our third level, $E_{max} = 300$, $T_{max} = 4s$. In the calculation of PTP score, we observed that if total number of selected points are too small, wrong pairs will be produced. So we set a minimum value min_{ns} of total number of selected points. In our experiments, $min_{ns} = 12$. Matlab built-in solver linprog finished the linear programming.

5.2 Evaluation Metrics

MOTA is multiple object tracking accuracy. MOTP is multiple object tracking precision. Each track in ground truth is classified to MT ($\geq 80\%$), PT or ML ($\leq 20\%$) according to total percent of successfully tracked parts. FP (false positives or false alarms), FN (false negatives), IDs (ID switches) and FM (fragments) are different errors made in tracking progress.

5.3 Framework Verification

Stage I is the result of first level. Stage II is the result with first level and second level. Stage III is the result with all three levels. A histogram of fragment length is shown in Fig. 1. As the figure shows, number of long-term fragments (Length $\geq 1s$) decreases while number of short fragments (Length $< 1s$) increases in stage II. This is because the robust local effective matching model reduces fragment length at first. In stage III, there is a sharp decline in number of short fragments, because the fragments are solved using the motion model. Decline in number of long-term fragments is much smaller than decline in number of short fragments, which proves that the longer the fragment is, the worse the motion model works.

Tracking result on ETH-Bahnhof is shown in Fig. 2. Odd frames are omitted in the figure. The fragment of target exists in frames from 71 to 79 in top row. In bottom row, partial detections (red boxes) in frames 71 to 73 and frames 78 to 89 are refined (green boxes). The fragment length reduced by 4 frames. Then the fragment is solved by a motion model.

The total result on training set is listed in Table 1. ↑ is a positive indicator meaning the higher the value, the better, while ↓ means the lower the value, the

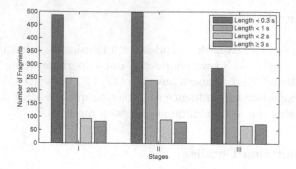

Fig. 1. Fragment statistics on 2D MOT2015 training set.

Table 1. Main evaluation metrics on training set.

Stage	Rcll↑	Prec↑	ML↓	FP↓	FN↓	IDs↓	FM↓	MOTA↑	MOTP↑
I	37.7	81.5	278	3407	24863	786	693	27.2	73.9
II	39.4	80.8	266	3735	24163	741	681	28.2	74.0
III	45.8	76.8	246	5513	21632	469	461	30.8	73.8

better. FN reduces in stage II, because partial detections are refined and used to reduce the length of fragments. FN reduces in stage III because fragments between tracklets are solved using the motion model. FP increases in stage II and stage III, because some wrong links were added to the network. Increase of MOTA shows that both the robust local effective matching model and the motion model improves the tracker performance.

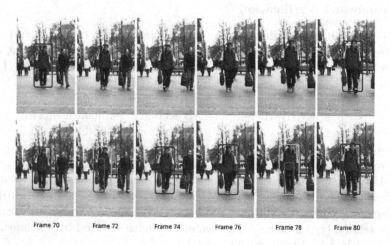

Fig. 2. Tracking results of stage I (top) and stage III (bottom) on ETH-Bahnhof. (Color figure online)

Table 2. Comparison on 2D MOT 2015 Benchmark. All trackers use public detections only. FAF: the average number of false alarms per frame. Hz: tracker speed in frames per second. (accessed on 5/4/2017)

Tracker	MOTA	MOTP	FAF	MT	ML	FP	FN	IDs	FM	Hz
SegTrack	22.5	71.7	1.4	5.8%	63.9%	7890	39020	697	**737**	0.2
JDPA_m	23.8	68.2	1.1	5.0%	58.1%	6373	40084	365	869	32.6
LINF1	24.5	71.3	1.0	5.5%	64.6%	5864	40207	**298**	744	7.5
ELP	25.0	71.2	1.3	**7.5%**	**43.8%**	7345	37344	1396	1804	5.7
LP_SSVM	25.2	71.7	1.4	5.8%	53.0%	8369	**36932**	646	849	**41.3**
LFNF(Ours)	**26.1**	**72.5**	**0.8**	5.0%	51.9%	**4487**	39872	1075	1165	4.0

5.4 Benchmark Results

In order to compare with state-of-the-art trackers, we ran the proposed tracker on 2D MOT 2015 test set. The parameters are trained on training set and listed in Sect. 5.1. The benchmark results are listed in Table 2.

The table shows the comparison of SegTrack [18], JDPA_m [6], LINF1 [4], ELP [13], LP_SSVM [17] and our method LFNF. LFNF outperforms other state-of-the-art trackers in both terms of MOTA and MOTP. It is noteworthy that our method achieves the lowest false alarms per frame too. Our approach is most close related to ELP [13], because both work used network flow optimization and motion model. Our approach achieves fewer fragments than ELP, which proves that our approach handles fragments more effectively.

6 Conclusion

In order to cope with long-term fragments, we proposed a robust local effective matching model for partial detections to reduce fragment length first. The proposed model is integrated into a hierarchical framework to solve fragments. The first level generates initial tracklets for later analysis. The second level utilizes the robust local effective matching model to reduce fragment length and refine partial detections. The third level solves fragments between tracklets by using a motion model. Experiments were conducted on 2D MOT 2015. Results on training set showed that our method improves tracking performance, especially in terms of Rcll, FN, FM and MOTA. Benchmark results on test set showed that our method get competitive results with other state-of-the-art trackers.

Acknowledgment. This study is partially supported by the National Natural Science Foundation of China (No. 61472019), the National Science Technology Pillar Program (No. 2015BAF14B01), the Macao Science and Technology Development Fund (No. 138/2016/A3), the Programme of Introducing Talents of Discipline to Universities, the Open Fund of the State Key Laboratory of Software Development Environment under grant SKLSDE-2017ZX-09 and HAWKEYE Group.

References

1. Benfold, B., Reid, I.: Stable multi-target tracking in real-time surveillance video. In: IEEE Conference on Computer Vision and Pattern Recognition (CVPR), pp. 3457–3464. IEEE (2011)
2. Breitenstein, M.D., Reichlin, F., Leibe, B., Koller-Meier, E., Van Gool, L.: Robust tracking-by-detection using a detector confidence particle filter. In: IEEE 12th International Conference on Computer Vision, pp. 1515–1522. IEEE (2009)
3. Choi, W.: Near-online multi-target tracking with aggregated local flow descriptor. In: Proceedings of the IEEE International Conference on Computer Vision, pp. 3029–3037 (2015)
4. Fagot-Bouquet, L., Audigier, R., Dhome, Y., Lerasle, F.: Improving multi-frame data association with sparse representations for robust near-online multi-object tracking. In: Leibe, B., Matas, J., Sebe, N., Welling, M. (eds.) ECCV 2016. LNCS, vol. 9912, pp. 774–790. Springer, Cham (2016). https://doi.org/10.1007/978-3-319-46484-8_47
5. Felzenszwalb, P.F., Girshick, R.B., McAllester, D., Ramanan, D.: Object detection with discriminatively trained part-based models. IEEE Trans. Pattern Anal. Mach. Intell. **32**(9), 1627–1645 (2010)
6. Rezatofighi, S.H., Milan, A., Zhang, Z., Shi, Q., Dick, A., Reid, I.: Joint probabilistic data association revisited. In: Proceedings of the IEEE International Conference on Computer Vision, pp. 3047–3055 (2015)
7. Hong Yoon, J., Lee, C.R., Yang, M.H., Yoon, K.J.: Online multi-object tracking via structural constraint event aggregation. In: Proceedings of the IEEE Conference on Computer Vision and Pattern Recognition, pp. 1392–1400 (2016)
8. Izadinia, H., Saleemi, I., Li, W., Shah, M.: $(MP)^2T$: multiple people multiple parts tracker. In: Fitzgibbon, A., Lazebnik, S., Perona, P., Sato, Y., Schmid, C. (eds.) ECCV 2012. LNCS, vol. 7577, pp. 100–114. Springer, Heidelberg (2012). https://doi.org/10.1007/978-3-642-33783-3_8
9. Kim, C., Li, F., Ciptadi, A., Rehg, J.M.: Multiple hypothesis tracking revisited. In: Proceedings of the IEEE International Conference on Computer Vision, pp. 4696–4704 (2015)
10. Leal-Taixé, L., Milan, A., Reid, I., Roth, S., Schindler, K.: Motchallenge 2015: towards a benchmark for multi-target tracking. arXiv preprint arXiv:1504.01942 (2015)
11. Lucas, B.D., Kanade, T., et al.: An iterative image registration technique with an application to stereo vision (1981)
12. Luo, W., Xing, J., Zhang, X., Zhao, X., Kim, T.K.: Multiple object tracking: a literature review. arXiv preprint arXiv:1409.7618 (2014)
13. McLaughlin, N., Del Rincon, J.M., Miller, P.: Enhancing linear programming with motion modeling for multi-target tracking. In: IEEE Winter Conference on Applications of Computer Vision, pp. 71–77. IEEE (2015)
14. Milan, A., Roth, S., Schindler, K.: Continuous energy minimization for multitarget tracking. IEEE Trans. Pattern Anal. Mach. Intell. **36**(1), 58–72 (2014)
15. Possegger, H., Mauthner, T., Roth, P.M., Bischof, H.: Occlusion geodesics for online multi-object tracking. In: Proceedings of the IEEE Conference on Computer Vision and Pattern Recognition, pp. 1306–1313 (2014)
16. Ren, S., He, K., Girshick, R., Sun, J.: Faster R-CNN: towards real-time object detection with region proposal networks. IEEE Trans. Pattern Anal. Mach. Intell. 1 (2015)

17. Wang, S., Fowlkes, C.C.: Learning optimal parameters for multi-target tracking with contextual interactions. Int. J. Comput. Vis. 1–18 (2016)
18. Wen, L., Du, D., Lei, Z., Li, S.Z., Yang, M.H.: JOTS: joint online tracking and segmentation. In: Proceedings of the IEEE Conference on Computer Vision and Pattern Recognition, pp. 2226–2234 (2015)
19. Zhang, L., Li, Y., Nevatia, R.: Global data association for multi-object tracking using network flows. In: IEEE Conference on Computer Vision and Pattern Recognition (CVPR 2008), pp. 1–8. IEEE (2008)

Group Burstiness Weighting for Image Retrieval

Mao Wang[1(✉)], Qiang Liu[1], Yuewei Ming[1], and Jianping Yin[2]

[1] College of Computer, National University of Defense Technology,
Changsha 410073, Hunan, China
{wangmao,qiangliu06,ywming}@nudt.edu.cn
[2] State Key Laboratory of High Performance Computing,
National University of Defense Technology, Changsha 410073, Hunan, China
jpyin@nudt.edu.cn

Abstract. In Bag-of-Word based image retrieval, burst phenomenon is a common issue and should be carefully addressed for improving retrieval accuracy. Current state-of-the-art solutions, e.g., the intra- and inter-image burstiness weighting methods, ignore burstiness problem in query image. In this paper, a group burstiness weighting approach is proposed to address this issue by introducing penalties to burst features of query image. Specifically, burst features are detected at query side such that different groups consisting of burst features can be determined. Then, penalties are imposed on the detected burst features when computing images similarity. It is worthwhile to highlight that the proposed approach is compatible with current burstiness processing methods and effective to improve their performance for image retrieval. Experimental results over several public datasets demonstrate that the proposed approach can well fit for existing burstiness processing methods and significantly improve the performance of image retrieval in terms of accuracy, especially for retrieving landmark images.

Keywords: Image retrieval · Visual bursts · Group burstiness

1 Introduction

Last decade has witnessed the success of Bag-of-Word (BoW) model [18] in image retrieval that extracts local features from an image and represents them as an orderless set of visual words quantized by a pre-trained codebook. However, the visual burstiness phenomenon [6] significantly challenges the application of the BoW model, especially for retrieving landmark [11]. The phenomenon means some visual elements, e.g., bricks, windows and texture in building images, frequently appear, making the assumption of visual elements eject independently no longer satisfied. The burst features representing these similar visual elements will match others many times due to the non-exclusive matching in BoW, resulting in an over-estimated similarity score for irrelevant images and spoiling the initial

© Springer International Publishing AG, part of Springer Nature 2018
B. Zeng et al. (Eds.): PCM 2017, LNCS 10736, pp. 244–253, 2018.
https://doi.org/10.1007/978-3-319-77383-4_24

results. But the initial results are important for some post-processing steps, such as spatial verification [3,13,16,25], query expansion [4,5] and rank fusion [23,24] as they are usually only performed on top-ranked results because of the expensive computation overhead. Hence, it is vital to address the burstiness problem in image retrieval.

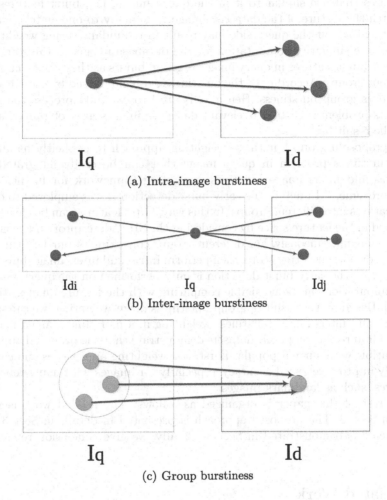

(a) Intra-image burstiness

(b) Inter-image burstiness

(c) Group burstiness

Fig. 1. Illustration of different types of burstiness pattern. I_q and I_d represent query and database image, respectively. Dots mean local features, and arrows mean matches between query and database features.

Many approaches have been proposed for tackling burstiness problem to improve the accuracy of initial results. The most popular approaches are the intra- and inter- image burstiness weighting, which are widely deployed in image retrieval [16] and place recognition [1,15]. As illustrated in Fig. 1(a) and (b), the one-to-many matches among a database image (intra-image burstiness) or cross database images (inter-image burstness), i.e., matches caused by burst features, are penalized to discount their voting scores. However, these strategies ignore the burst features in query image which may also match other features in a database image several times and lead to an over-estimated similarity score. As illustrated in Fig. 1(c), if a feature in a query image matches one in a database image, others features that are similar to it in the query image, i.e., burst features, will also match the feature of the database image. The many-to-one matches caused by burst features at the query side may result in redundant voting weights and dominate the similarity computation for the database image. In this paper, we denote the burst features in query image as group bursts as they can be clustered to different groups. Accordingly, the burstiness problem caused by these features is named as group burstiness. Hence, it is vital to carefully process the group burstiness problem such that irrelevant database images are not ranked at the top of the result list.

We propose a group burstiness weighting approach to explicitly handle the group burstiness problem in query image that can be easily integrated into the intra- and inter- image burstiness weighting framework for further accuracy improvement. In detail, the early burst detection [17] is employed to divide query features into different groups. In this way, burst features can be clearly distinguished in the feature space by considering the SIFT descriptor and geometric information simultaneously. For different groups consisting of burst features, we directly reduce their voting score, then perform intra- and inter- image burstiness weighting. As the early burst detection is only performed on the query side, the extra computation can be negligible comparing with the feature quantization in retrieval. Based on the result of group burstiness down-weighting, we can utilize the intra- and inter- image burstiness weighting in a more fine-grained manner. Experimental results on public datasets demonstrate that the proposed approach is compatible with current popular burstiness weighting approaches and can significantly improve retrieval accuracy, especially for images with many repetitive structures, such as landmark images.

The rest of this paper is organized as follows: The related work is introduced in Sect. 2. The proposed approach is presented in details in Sect. 3. The experiments is demonstrated in Sect. 4. Finally, we give conclusion remarks in Sect. 5.

2   Related Work

As the content of an image is highly redundant, the local features extracted from an image may contain much correlated and less discriminative information [2]. The burst occurrence of some local features can participate in many redundant matches and result in assigning a high similarity score to irrelevant images.

To tackle the burstiness problem, many approaches are proposed to discount the contribution of burst features. The intra- and inter- images weighting are standard steps in BoW model to weaken burst matches based on the visual word information. Depart from this strategy, local features sharing same visual word are aggregated to form a compact representation for matching in [19]. In [15], the authors have observed burstiness problem can also appear after spatial verification, especially for place recognition, and a geometric burstiness processing approach is proposed to improve retrieval recall. In [21], contrast to previous works, burst features are detected and used as discriminative information to replace original BoW-based representation for place recognition. The above approaches are performed on the discrete visual word space, which utilize the quantized visual word information of local features for convenient burstiness processing.

Another kind of burstiness processing approach is performed directly on the continuous feature space. The power-law normalization is employed in the Vector of Locally Aggregated Descriptors (VLAD) [8] framework, which aggregates local features into a uniform representation. The early burst detection [17] is proposed to explicitly detect self-similar visual elements of an image based on the similarity in feature space and geometric information, and then pools local features to feed into the VLAD and Aggregated Selective Match Kernel (ASMK) [19] retrieval framework. Implicitly processing burstiness in the feature space, such as power-law normalization in VLAD, fails to directly process burst features as the normalization is performed on aggregated local features. Explicitly detection of burst feature can find accurate burst groups, but the detection of all images is time consuming and not scalable for large scale retrieval.

3 The Proposed Approach

In this work, we concentrate on the burstiness problem in query side. Based on the work of early burst detection [17], we detect burst groups of query image in the feature space, and then directly down-weight the voting score of features among burst groups before intra- and inter- image burstiness weighting. The proposed approach can be easily integrated into current retrieval framework and compatible with state-of-the-art burstiness weighing approaches. The overall framework of the proposed approach is illustrated in Fig. 2.

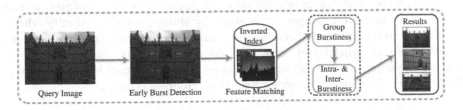

Fig. 2. The framework of the proposed group burstiness weighting.

3.1 Burst Group Detection

For a matching pair of local features (f_i, f_j) between a query image $\mathbf{I}_q$ and a database image $\mathbf{I}_d$, we can represent f_i by $[\mathbf{d}_i, s_i, \theta_i]$, where $\mathbf{d}_i$ is the 128 dimensions SIFT descriptor of local feature, s_i and θ_i are geometric parameters denoting the characteristic scale (log scale) and dominant orientation, respectively. Based on the SIFT and geometric information, we can detect burst groups in a query image. Similar to the work in [17], local features are modeled as vertices in a graph, and three kernel functions are merged to model the weight (similarity) of edges between vertices (local features). Then, connected component analysis is performed on the graph to find connected components as burst groups, which contains local features (vertices) with high similarity (edge weight).

Specificity, similarity kernel of two SIFT descriptors is given by

$$k_\Delta(f_i, f_j) = |\phi(d_i)\phi(d_j)| \tag{1}$$

where $\phi()$ is the normalized triangular embedding [9] of SIFT descriptor, and the absolute cosine distance can be applied as a good metric to distinguish related and unrelated features in [9]. This is different from the original version in [17], where a probabilistic prediction model is learned from matched and un-matched patches.

Furthermore, the following two kernel functions in [17] are respectively used to model the similarity measure of scale and orientation

$$k_s(f_i, f_j) = \exp\{-\frac{(s_i - s_j)^2}{\sigma_s^2}\} \tag{2}$$

$$k_\theta(f_i, f_j) = \frac{\exp(\kappa(\theta_i - \theta_j)) - \exp(-\kappa)}{2\sinh\kappa} \tag{3}$$

Similar to work in [21] and [17,20], the parameter σ_s and κ are set to 10 and 6, respectively.

The final kernel function is given by

$$k(f_i, f_j) = k_\Delta(f_i, f_j)k_s(f_i, f_j)k_\theta(f_i, f_j) \tag{4}$$

With the affinity matrix representing pairwise similarity of local features, we can perform the connected component analysis by thresholding the affinity with a threshold τ to find connected components, which contain similar visual patterns both in SIFT descriptor and geometric property, i.e., burst features. For each connected component, we regard it as a burst group. The problem we tackled is the burstiness in each group, so we refer it to group burstiness.

3.2 Burst Group Down-Weighting

For local features in different burst groups, they have different discriminative ability. The more local features in a burst groups, the less distinctive of these local features as they represent similar visual elements. These features tend to match local features of other images frequently and redundantly. For burst groups with only one feature, however, it can be regarded as a unique feature without burstiness. So, the importance of local features in different burst groups should be considered due to their different distinctiveness.

For each matched feature pair, the voting weight is the product of the inverse document frequency (IDF) value of their visual word. In this work, we focus on the current state-of-the art Hamming Embedding (HE) framework, which has shown good performance in retrieving object and landmark images [7,22]. The voting score [6] of the matched pair (f_i, f_j) is given by

$$score(f_i, f_j) = \exp\{-\frac{h^2(b_i, b_j)}{\sigma^2}\}idf^2(q(f_i))\tag{5}$$

where b_i and b_j are binary signatures of the two SIFT features after hamming embedding, $h()$ is the hamming distance between signatures and σ is the bandwidth parameter. $q(f_i)$ is the quantized visual word of feature f_i, and $idf()$ is the IDF value of the corresponding visual word.

With the result of burst group detection, we propose to down-weight the voting score by

$$score\_group(f_i, f_j) = w(f_i) \times score(f_i, f_j)\tag{6}$$

where $w(f_i)$ is a weighting parameter used to handle group burstiness problem. For a query local feature among a large burst group, its distinctness is less than the one among a small burst group, so its voting weight should be discounted. In order to improve flexibility, the down-weighting is only performed on burst groups that contain local features more than a threshold, avoiding down-weighting groups with only a few local features that may not be a burst occurrence. Inspired by the work of [15], a simple down-weighting approach can be adopted by considering the size of burst groups or its square root. The final weighing function is given by

$$w(f_i) = \begin{cases} \frac{1}{\sqrt{|g(f_i)|}} & \text{if } |g(f_i)| > t \\ 1 & \text{otherwise} \end{cases}\tag{7}$$

where $|g(f_i)|$ represents the number of local features in current burst group of query feature f_i. We select the square root version based on our experiments. The parameter t is a threshold that controls burst groups to be processed, which is also selected by experiments.

4   Experiments

4.1   Experimental Setup

Dataset. Three public datasets are used in our experiments: the Oxford5k building [13], the Paris6k building [14] and the Holidays1k [7] dataset. In order to test the scalability of our approach, we combine an extra distractor dataset

Flickr100k [13] with Oxford5k and Paris6k to form the Oxford105k and Paris106k dataset, respectively. For the Holidays1k dataset, we use 100k images from Flickr1M dataset [7] as distractor to form the Holidays101k dataset. For the Oxford5k, Paris6k and Flickr100k datasets, we extract local features with gravity assumption as in [12]. For the Holidays1k and Holidays101k datasets, we use the data provided in [7].

Hamming Embedding. We use the current state-of-the-art HE image retrieval framework to conduct our experiments. Similar to previous works, we set the same parameter as in [6], i.e., each SIFT descriptor is assigned to a 64 bits binary code, the bandwidth parameter σ is set to 16 and the hamming distance threshold is set to 22 for multiple assignment (MA). For the MA strategy, each descriptor is assigned to 5 nearest neighborhood visual words. The codebook of the Oxford5k is trained on the Paris6k, and vice versa. The codebook for the Holidays is trained on an independent Flickr60k dataset [7]. All the codebooks are with a size of 20k. The mean average precision (mAP) is used to evaluate the retrieval result of the proposed approach.

4.2 Parameter Analysis

In the proposed approach, there exist two parameters needed to be selected, the threshold τ in detecting burst groups of query image and the threshold t to judge whether a burst group should be processed. To analysis and select the two parameters, experiments on the Holidays1k and Oxford5k datasets are conducted respectively as their query images have different burstiness properties. The Holidays1k consists of scenery and object images, while the Oxford5k consists of landmark images. We also test the two weighting functions linear weighting and square root weighting based on the size of burst group.

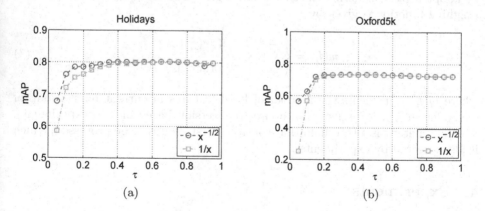

Fig. 3. Parameter analysis on the Holidays1k and Oxford5k dataset.

From the retrieval result illustrated in Fig. 3, we can see that the square root weighting is better than the linear weighting, and the accuracy is stable in a wide range of τ. Hence, we select the square root function in the down-weighting schema. Based on the experimental results, the τ is fixed to 0.5 for the Oxford and Paris datasets, and 0.7 for the Holidays dataset in the following experiments. For the threshold t, we set it to 4 based on our experiments.

4.3   Results and Analysis

Table 1 shows retrieval results of HE framework, HE with intra- and inter- image burstiness weighting (i2-Burstiness) and HE with our group burstiness weighting (g-Burstiness). We can see that the proposed approach, compared with the standard intra- and inter- image burstiness, can achieve a significant performance improvement in terms of mAP, especially for the Oxford105k and Paris106k dataset. The result implies that the burstiness phenomenon is also notable in large-scale datasets. As the Holidays1k dataset consists of many scenery and object images, the burst phenomenon is not obvious as the Oxford5k and Paris6k building datasets. For the two building datasets, there exist many repetitive structures that lead to the occurrence of burst features. So, the group burstiness weighting can achieve a better improvement on these datasets.

Table 1. The mAP% of HE framework with different burstiness weighting.

Dataset	HE	i2-Burstiness [6]	g-Burstiness
Holidays1k	78.7	79.8	**80.2**
Holidays101k	63.8	71.3	**71.4**
Oxford5k	71.2	72.3	**73.3**
Oxford105k	64.8	69.0	**71.3**
Paris6k	68.1	69.9	**71.3**
Paris106k	58.2	62.4	**65.2**

The group burstiness weighting targets at discounting the voting score of burst features in query image, which is ignored in previous burstiness weighting. These burst features in query image can participate in many invalid matches and result in an over-estimated similarity for irrelevant images. By tackling the group burstiness problem, the redundant voting score deriving from burst features can be reduced. Since the group burstiness weighting is performed only on the query side, the proposed approach can be easily embedded into the current image retrieval framework and is compatible with the intra- and inter- image burstiness weighing for further improvement. In practice, we have found some regions are more importance than others for retrieval. The future work will consider the saliency of different regions [10] to further weight burst features for improvement.

5 Conclusions

In this paper, an approach of group burstiness weighting has been proposed to tackle the burstiness problem in query image. Based on the previous work of early burst detection, we can discover burst groups in query image. Then, combing with the popular intra- and inter- image burstiness weighting, the proposed approach directly reduce the voting score of local features among burst groups. Experiments show that this approach can be embedded into current retrieval framework and burstiness processing methods and achieve an accuracy improvement, especially for retrieving large scale building images.

Acknowledgments. The authors would like to thank the financial support of National Natural Science Foundation of China (Project No. 61672528, 61403405, 61232016, 61170287).

References

1. Arandjelović, R., Zisserman, A.: DisLocation: scalable descriptor distinctiveness for location recognition. In: Cremers, D., Reid, I., Saito, H., Yang, M.-H. (eds.) ACCV 2014. LNCS, vol. 9006, pp. 188–204. Springer, Cham (2015). https://doi.org/10.1007/978-3-319-16817-3_13
2. Chen, T., Yap, K.H., Zhang, D.: Discriminative soft bag-of-visual phrase for mobile landmark recognition. IEEE Trans. Multimed. **16**(3), 612–622 (2014)
3. Chu, L., Jiang, S., Wang, S., Zhang, Y., Huang, Q.: Robust spatial consistency graph model for partial duplicate image retrieval. IEEE Trans. Multimed. **15**(8), 1982–1996 (2013)
4. Chum, O., Mikulk, A., Perdoch, M., Matas, J.: Total recall II: query expansion revisited. In: CVPR 2011, pp. 889–896 (2011)
5. Chum, O., Philbin, J., Sivic, J., Isard, M., Zisserman, A.: Total recall: automatic query expansion with a generative feature model for object retrieval. In: IEEE 11th International Conference on Computer Vision, pp. 1–8, October 2007
6. Jegou, H., Douze, M., Schmid, C.: On the burstiness of visual elements. In: IEEE Conference on Computer Vision and Pattern Recognition, pp. 1169–1176, June 2009
7. Jegou, H., Douze, M., Schmid, C.: Hamming embedding and weak geometric consistency for large scale image search. In: Forsyth, D., Torr, P., Zisserman, A. (eds.) ECCV 2008. LNCS, vol. 5302, pp. 304–317. Springer, Heidelberg (2008). https://doi.org/10.1007/978-3-540-88682-2_24
8. Jgou, H., Perronnin, F., Douze, M., Snchez, J., Prez, P., Schmid, C.: Aggregating local image descriptors into compact codes. IEEE Trans. Pattern Anal. Mach. Intell. **34**(9), 1704–1716 (2012)
9. Jgou, H., Zisserman, A.: Triangulation embedding and democratic aggregation for image search. In: IEEE Conference on Computer Vision and Pattern Recognition, pp. 3310–3317, June 2014
10. Li, L., Jiang, S., Zha, Z.J., Wu, Z., Huang, Q.: Partial-duplicate image retrieval via saliency-guided visual matching. IEEE MultiMed. **20**(3), 13–23 (2013)
11. Min, W., Bao, B.K., Xu, C.: Multimodal spatio-temporal theme modeling for landmark analysis. IEEE MultiMed. **21**(3), 20–29 (2014)

12. Perd'och, M., Chum, O., Matas, J.: Efficient representation of local geometry for large scale object retrieval. In: IEEE Conference on Computer Vision and Pattern Recognition, pp. 9–16, June 2009
13. Philbin, J., Chum, O., Isard, M., Sivic, J., Zisserman, A.: Object retrieval with large vocabularies and fast spatial matching. In: IEEE Conference on Computer Vision and Pattern Recognition, pp. 1–8, June 2007
14. Philbin, J., Chum, O., Isard, M., Sivic, J., Zisserman, A.: Lost in quantization: improving particular object retrieval in large scale image databases. In: IEEE Conference on Computer Vision and Pattern Recognition, pp. 1–8, June 2008
15. Sattler, T., Havlena, M., Schindler, K., Pollefeys, M.: Large-scale location recognition and the geometric burstiness problem. In: IEEE Conference on Computer Vision and Pattern Recognition (CVPR), pp. 1582–1590, June 2016
16. Schönberger, J.L., Price, T., Sattler, T., Frahm, J.M., Pollefeys, M.: A vote-and-verify strategy for fast spatial verification in image retrieval. In: Asian Conference on Computer Vision (ACCV) (2016)
17. Shi, M., Avrithis, Y., Jgou, H.: Early burst detection for memory-efficient image retrieval. In: IEEE Conference on Computer Vision and Pattern Recognition (CVPR), pp. 605–613, June 2015
18. Sivic, J., Zisserman, A.: Video Google: efficient visual search of videos. In: Ponce, J., Hebert, M., Schmid, C., Zisserman, A. (eds.) Toward Category-Level Object Recognition. LNCS, vol. 4170, pp. 127–144. Springer, Heidelberg (2006). https://doi.org/10.1007/11957959_7
19. Tolias, G., Avrithis, Y., Jégou, H.: Image search with selective match kernels: aggregation across single and multiple images. Int. J. Comput. Vis. **116**(3), 247–261 (2016). https://doi.org/10.1007/s11263-015-0810-4
20. Tolias, G., Furon, T., Jégou, H.: Orientation covariant aggregation of local descriptors with embeddings. In: Fleet, D., Pajdla, T., Schiele, B., Tuytelaars, T. (eds.) ECCV 2014. LNCS, vol. 8694, pp. 382–397. Springer, Cham (2014). https://doi.org/10.1007/978-3-319-10599-4_25
21. Torii, A., Sivic, J., Okutomi, M., Pajdla, T.: Visual place recognition with repetitive structures. IEEE Trans. Pattern Anal. Mach. Intell. **37**(11), 2346–2359 (2015)
22. Wang, S., Jiang, S.: INSTRE: a new benchmark for instance-level object retrieval and recognition. ACM Trans. Multimed. Comput. Commun. Appl. **11**(3), 1–21 (2015). http://doi.acm.org/10.1145/2700292
23. Zhang, S., Yang, M., Cour, T., Yu, K., Metaxas, D.N.: Query specific rank fusion for image retrieval. IEEE Trans. Pattern Anal. Mach. Intell. **37**(4), 803–815 (2015)
24. Zheng, L., Wang, S., Tian, L., He, F., Liu, Z., Tian, Q.: Query-adaptive late fusion for image search and person re-identification. In: IEEE Conference on Computer Vision and Pattern Recognition (CVPR), pp. 1741–1750, June 2015
25. Zhou, Z., Wang, Y., Wu, Q.M.J., Yang, C.N., Sun, X.: Effective and efficient global context verification for image copy detection. IEEE Trans. Inf. Forensics Secur. **12**(1), 48–63 (2017)

Stereo Saliency Analysis
Based on Disparity Influence
and Spatial Dissimilarity

Lijuan Duan[1,2,4], Fangfang Liang[1,3,4], Wei Ma[1,3,4](✉), and Shuo Qiu[1,3,4]

[1] Faculty of Information Technology, Beijing University of Technology, Beijing, China
mawei@bjut.edu.cn
[2] Beijing Key Laboratory on Integration and Analysis of Large-Scale Stream Data,
College of Computer Science and Technology, Beijing University of Technology,
Beijing 100124, China
[3] Beijing Key Laboratory of Trusted Computing, Beijing 100124, China
[4] National Engineering Laboratory for Critical Technologies of Information Security
Classified Protection, Beijing 100124, China

Abstract. This paper presents a simple approach for detecting salient
regions in stereo images. The approach computes saliency by considering three factors: disparity influence, central bias and spatial dissimilarity. Firstly, an image is split into equal-sized patches to be down-
sampled. Next, disparity influence is estimated based on the disparity
map. Besides, central bias value is assigned to every patch and spatial
dissimilarity is measured between patches in reduced dimensional space.
Thereafter, the product of all factors extracted from the image is computed. Finally, through a process of normalization, the saliency map is
obtained. In the experiments four state-of-the-art methods are used for
comparison with PSU stereo saliency benchmark dataset (SSB). The
experimental results show that our method has better performance than
the others for stereo salient region detection.

Keywords: Stereo · Saliency · Disparity influence · Central bias
Spatial dissimilarity

1 Introduction

Saliency receives much attention because it attempts to simulate human visual
attention mechanisms. Saliency analysis is of interest in neuroscience [5],
robotics, computer vision [16], and is particularly promising for augmenting in
object recognition [14], image relocation [2], object tracking [11], image segmentation [27] and human fixation shift analysis [30,31]. Most research on this topic
has focused on two-dimensional images. However, stereoscopic TV and video are
becoming quite common and 3D salient region detection is increasingly drawing much attention to improve 3D quality. Analyzing features from stereoscopic
images is one branch developing saliency.

© Springer International Publishing AG, part of Springer Nature 2018
B. Zeng et al. (Eds.): PCM 2017, LNCS 10736, pp. 254–263, 2018.
https://doi.org/10.1007/978-3-319-77383-4_25

A lot of work has been done on 2D saliency. These can be classified into data-driven bottom-up models [3,22,23], and knowledge-driven top-down models [16,21], or into local based [8,9,16,18] and global based [1,4,7,10,13] approaches. A typical method was proposed in [21], which constructed different visual saliency models for various scenes. Li [20] explored a multi-task learning algorithm to avoid over-matching problems. Given weak labeling data, Li et al. [20] modeled visual saliency as a sort-learning problem and solved it using a cost-sensitive learning framework. Huang et al. [14] merged the methods in [20,21] to extract saliency and then enveloped the maps and skeleton maps to denoise the result. Li also combined different raw maps produced by the methods in [1,9,12,13,16,28], called "experts group", to generate saliency maps. Also Huang et al. [15] proposed a multiple level saliency map detection algorithm and produced high quality fine scale saliency maps for image retargeting.

Recently, many 3D saliency computation methods have been proposed. Lang et al. [19] provided a theoretical basis for deepness feature extraction methods. By conducting viewpoint tracking experiments on a large number of 2D images and 3D images, they derived four observations. These four observations strongly suggested that the existence of depth features can greatly affect the saliency on images. A Gaussian model was used to fit empirical depth probability density function. The final saliency map was a combination of the saliency map computed by 2D cues and the one obtained by depth information. In addition, Desingh et al. [6] extended the work in [19]. They extended the testing procedure, including a test for a high depth blurred background. They applied the method in [4] and a point-cloud segmentation technique to extract depth features. By combining depth features and 2D cues, they obtained 3D saliency maps. In [26], Niu et al. proposed two methods for stereoscopic analysis: a global disparity contrast-based stereo saliency (CSS) model, and a knowledge-assisted stereo saliency (KSS) model. They combined the two methods to extract stereoscopic saliency. Here we focus on computing stereo saliency accurately considering disparity as an additional cue. Figure 1 shows left and right images (a), (b) and estimated disparity map (c). We integrate a disparity influence factor, central bias factor and a spatial dissimilarity factor to predict stereoscopic saliency.

Our method explores the advantage of disparity information extracted from a pair of left-right stereoscopic images for saliency predicting. At first, disparity

(a)   (b)   (c)

Fig. 1. A stereo pair of images. (a) Left image; (b) Right image; (c) Disparity map.

influence is computed by a probability-weighted vector distance between patches. Computed by vector distances, the influence of background factors is reduced because the disparity influence tends to be negative. Moreover, our method incorporates central bias and spatial dissimilarity to complement the insufficient part of the 3D saliency computation. Besides, central weight are widely adopted on the ground that Judd et al. [17] and Tatler et al. [29] showed that central bias is important in human saliency. Hence, the saliency likelihood of a patch should reduce with increasing distance from the center of the image. On the other hand, inspired by the algorithm [7], we use a PCA-like method to reduce the image representation feature. In the reduced space, we calculate a patch-based eigenvector difference as a measure of dissimilarity. To evaluate the performance of our algorithm, we apply a stereoscopic image dataset built upon [26] for image saliency analysis.

2   The Proposed Method

To calculate stereo saliency, three factors are considered: the disparity influence, the central bias and spatial dissimilarity in a reduced dimensional space. As shown in Fig. 2, at first, sift flow [24] is utilized to estimate disparity. Following that, we divide the image into equal-size patches, and calculate the three saliency factors (dissimilarity, disparity influence, central-bias) for each patch. Then, the saliency value of each patch is taken to be the product of these three factors. Finally, the saliency map is then normalized and smoothed by a Gaussian filter ($\sigma = 13$).

2.1   Calculation of Disparity Influence

An original image and a disparity map of size $(M * N)$, are divided into patches, whose sizes are both $k * k$. Therefore, the total amount of patches is symbolized as $T = ((M * N))/((k * k))$. For one patch $p_i, (i = 1, 2, 3, \ldots T)$, how to acquire final saliency map according to formulas is interpreted in the following sections. The disparity influence of each patch on disparity map is computed according to Eq. (1):

$$s_d(p_i) = \Sigma_{p_i \neq p_j}^T (D_r(p_i, p_j)), \tag{1}$$

where $D_r(\cdot)$ is the distance between two different patches p_i and p_j, defined as:

$$D_r(p_i, p_j) = \Sigma_{k=1}^n \Sigma_{l=1}^n (f(c_{k,i}) f(c_{l,j}) D(p_i, p_j)), \tag{2}$$

in which $f(\cdot)$ is the probability density on disparity map, $c_{k,i}$ and $c_{l,j}$ denote disparity values of the kth, l^{th} pixel in patch p_i and p_j respectively, and n represents the number of pixels in a patch. Hence, $D_r(\cdot)$ represents a probability-weighted vector distance. If a patch possesses a higher frequency of disparity value and a greater probability-weighted vector distance, it will be more salient. The definition of vector distance between two patches is defined as:

$$D(p_i, p_j) = \Sigma_{m=1}^n (x_{i,m} - x_{j,m}), \tag{3}$$

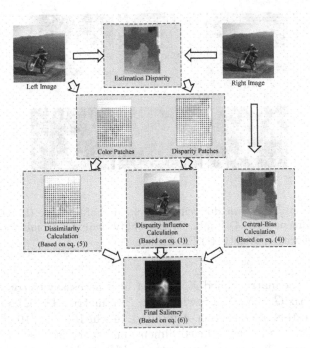

Fig. 2. Main framework of our method.

where $x_{i,m}$ and $x_{j,m}$ are the mth pixel disparity values of patch p_i and p_j, and n is the number of pixels in a patch. If we estimate the distance by the absolute differences, background values will be positive. Thereby, for those values that belong to background are negative in accordance with the disparity influence. Figure 3(c) gives a disparity influence map corresponding to disparity map in Fig. 3(b).

2.2 Central Bias

The tendency of the eyes frequently cast their gaze of image center on a display is a well-known phenomenon [16]. Therefore, we consider the central bias factor is important. In Eq. (4): p_i is a patch, $w(p_i)$ indicates the central−bias weight of p_i, DTC is the Euclidean distance from patch (p_i) to the center of the image, and D_{max} is the largest possible distance between a pixel and the image center.

$$w(p_i) = 1 - \frac{DTC(p_i)}{D_{max}}. \tag{4}$$

2.3 The Dissimilarity of Spatiality

Similar to PCA to reduce the overall patch data dimension, each patch on left image is represented by a column vector of pixel values to yield a sample matrix, named $X = [f_1, f_2 \ldots f_i \ldots f_T]$. Then, mean value is subtracted from

(a)   (b)   (c)

(d)   (e)   (f)

Fig. 3. Results obtained with different factors. (a) Left image; (b) Disparity map; (c) Disparity influence; (d) Dissimilarity Spatiality map; (e) Combination of central bias and dissimilarity spatiality; (f) Final saliency.

each column of the matrix called X. Further, it is necessary to construct the co-occurrence matrix $G = X^T X / T^2$, which is a $T*T$ matrix. The d largest eigenvalues and eigenvectors of G are then computed, in which $d = T/10$. The representation of the patches in the reduced dimensional space is $U = [U_1, U_2 \ldots U_d]^T$, where U_i represents the largest eigenvector and U is a $d*T$ matrix. Then the spatial dissimilarity between patches is accurately calculated in the reduced dimensional space, as followed:

$$dissimilarity(p_l, p_k) = \Sigma_{s=1}^d |x_{s,l} - x_{s,k}|, \tag{5}$$

where $x_{s,l}$ is an element of the eigenvector X_s having k elements. Figure 3(e) shows a saliency map by combination of dissimilarity of spatiality as Fig. 3(d) and center bias prior.

2.4 Stereo Saliency Map

To obtain a saliency value for each patch, the process of multiplying the three saliency factors including disparity influence, the central bias and the spatial dissimilarity, is obtained by Eq. (6). The final stereo saliency map is acquired by normalizing the salient image. As shown in Fig. 3(f), a final saliency is obtained.

$$Sal(p_i) = w(p_i) S_d(p_i) \Sigma_{p_i \neq p_k}^T (dissimilarity(p_i, p_k)). \tag{6}$$

2.5 Experiments

We evaluate the performance of our method on a dataset of 700 stereo images. The dataset is from [26]. The source gallery has about 1000 pairs of left-right stereo images. Their rule for evaluating the available images is as following. For each image, three subjects identify the salient objects. If the three users' results are consistent, the image is available to use. We believe that using only three

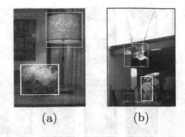

(a)   (b)

Fig. 4. Some images have two or more salient areas, ex. (a) and (b). The main salient area is not obvious so that users cannot identify the most salient object consistently.

people is questionable. Fewer samples increase randomness, so it is likely that random errors exist in their human saliency results. As shown in Fig. 4, we retain those images in which only a single salient object is found. Because multi-salient-objects may exist, the experimental dataset consisting of 700 images are those with a single salient object from the dataset in order to make the recognition of salient targets less ambiguous.

In this section, we evaluate the performance of our method on the dataset. We compare our method with four state-of-the-art saliency detection algorithms, including RC from [4], SS from [26], SWC from [7], and Margolin from [25] respectively. We get three experimental results from open codes except for the SS [26]. We implement the algorithm [26] upon patches because their code is not publicly available. Figure 5 shows some instances of visual saliency maps, where our method achieves much more uniform saliency values. The evaluation methods include precision-recall curve and F-measure. A precision-recall curve is obtained as follows. We binarize the scores from a saliency map using an increasing threshold. The binary map is compared with ground truth to compute the precision rate and recall rate for each threshold, resulting in the precision-recall curves shown in Figs. 6 and 7. Figure 6 illustrates the effects of disparity influence, dissimilarity spatiality and their uniting. It can be seen from Fig. 7 that the performance of our method on the dataset is better than SS, SWC, Margolin and RC. Since it takes both precision and recall into account, the F-statistic is a common evaluation standard in information retrieval, which is defined as:

$$F_\beta = \frac{(\beta^2 + 1)PR}{\beta^2 P + R},\tag{7}$$

where P and R are respectively precision and recall rate. We sample points on the $P - R$ curve to generate a F_β vector. Then we average the values of the F_β in order to yield the final value where we take $\beta^2 = 0.3$ [4]. In Table 1, we provide the analysis of single factor in terms of F-measure while comparison of our method and other models is shown in Table 2. It can be seen from the Table 2 that our method delivers the highest F value, meaning that the performance of our method is better than the other compared methods. In order to decrease

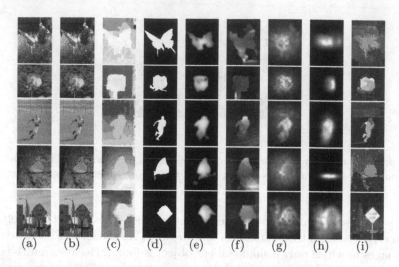

Fig. 5. Stereo saliency maps from our method and others. (a) Left image; (b) Right image; (c) Disparity; (d) Ground Truth; (e) Ours; (f) SS [26]; (g) SWC [7]; (h) Margolin [25]; (i) RC [4].

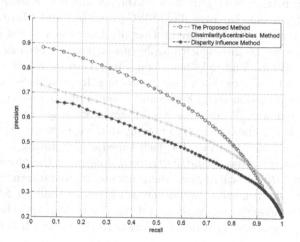

Fig. 6. Individual factor analysis.

the computation time, we down-sample each image while preserving the aspect ratio of the original images. The algorithm is implemented in Matlab. When calculating the saliency map (160 ∗ 120) on an Intel Core i7-3770 with a 3.40 GHz CPU and 16G of memory platform, the overall algorithm costs 37 s. We believe that the computation speed will be much faster if the code is refactored to C++.

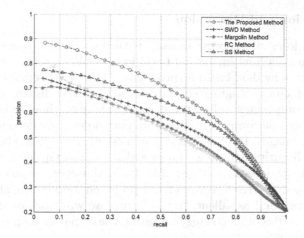

Fig. 7. PR curves of our method and other saliency models.

Table 1. F-statistic of single factor

Factor	F-statistic
Disparity influence	0.41
Dissimilarity and central	0.44
The proposed method	0.53

Table 2. F-statistic of compared methods

Method	F-statistic
Margolin [25]	0.39
SWC [7]	0.40
RC [4]	0.40
SS [26]	0.44
The Proposed Method	0.53

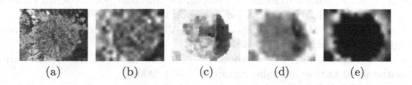

    (a)   (b)   (c)   (d)   (e)

Fig. 8. Example of erroneous detection. (a) Input; (b) Dissimilarity spatiality; (c) Disparity map; (d) Disparity influence; (e) Salient object.

2.6   Conclusion and Discussion

This paper explores stereoscopic saliency with disparity clues obtained from a pair of stereo images (Left image and Right image). When estimating disparity's influence degree, a method based on probability density is proposed. In addition, the other two factors including central bias and spatial dissimilarity are both integrated to complement saliency detection. The experiment shows that our proposed approach performs well and our saliency objects are detected accurately in stereoscopic images. In some scene, our method will fail as shown in Fig. 8. We apply the disparity influence map provided the assumption that the salient subject has higher intensity in disparity map. However, in some case where background is nearer than foreground, our proposed method might detect these objects on background as salient. In the future, we will work on distinguishing such cases and setting up a strategy adjusting the disparity map to prohibit the effect of background.

Acknowledgments. This research is partially sponsored by National Natural Science Foundation of China [61370113, 61672070, 91546111, 61572004]; and Beijing Municipal Natural Science Foundation [4152005, 4152006, 4162058]; the Science and Technology Program of Tianjin [15YFXQGX0050]; the Science and technology planning project of Qinghai Province [2016-ZJ-Y04]; the Beijing Municipal Education Commission Science and Technology Program [KZ201610005009, KM201610005022, KM201510005015].

References

1. Achanta, R., Hemami, S.S., Estrada, F.V., Susstrunk, S.: Frequency-tuned salient region detection, pp. 1597–1604 (2009)
2. Achanta, R., Susstrunk, S.: Saliency detection for content-aware image resizing, pp. 1005–1008 (2009)
3. Bruce, N.D.B., Tsotsos, J.K.: Saliency based on information maximization, pp. 155–162 (2005)
4. Cheng, M., Mitra, N.J., Huang, X., Torr, P.H.S., Hu, S.: Global contrast based salient region detection. IEEE Trans. Pattern Anal. Mach. Intell. **37**(3), 569–582 (2015)
5. Koch, C.: Biophysics of Computation: Information Processing in Single Neurons. Oxford University Press, New York (1999)
6. Desingh, K., Madhava Krishna, K., Rajan, D., Jawahar, C.V.: Depth really matters: improving visual salient region detection with depth (2013)
7. Duan, L., Wu, C., Miao, J., Qing, L., Fu, Y.: Visual saliency detection by spatially weighted dissimilarity, pp. 473–480 (2011)
8. Gao, D., Mahadevan, V., Vasconcelos, N.: The discriminant center-surround hypothesis for bottom-up saliency, pp. 497–504 (2007)
9. Goferman, S., Zelnikmanor, L., Tal, A.: Context-aware saliency detection, pp. 2376–2383 (2010)
10. Gopalakrishnan, V., Hu, Y., Rajan, D.: Salient region detection by modeling distributions of color and orientation. IEEE Trans. Multimed. **11**(5), 892–905 (2009)

11. Guo, W., Xu, C., Ma, S., Xu, M.: Visual attention based motion object detection and trajectory tracking. In: Qiu, G., Lam, K.M., Kiya, H., Xue, X.-Y., Kuo, C.-C.J., Lew, M.S. (eds.) PCM 2010. LNCS, vol. 6298, pp. 462–470. Springer, Heidelberg (2010). https://doi.org/10.1007/978-3-642-15696-0_43
12. Harel, J., Koch, C., Perona, P.: Graph-based visual saliency, pp. 545–552 (2006)
13. Hou, X., Zhang, L.: Saliency detection: a spectral residual approach, pp. 1–8 (2007)
14. Huang, T., Tian, Y., Li, J., Yu, H.: Salient region detection and segmentation for general object recognition and image understanding. Sci. China Ser. F Inf. Sci. 54(12), 2461–2470 (2011)
15. Huang, Z., He, F., Cai, X., Zou, Z., Liu, J., Liang, M., Chen, X.: Efficient random saliency map detection. Sci. China Ser. F Inf. Sci. 54(6), 1207–1217 (2011)
16. Itti, L., Koch, C., Niebur, E.: A model of saliency-based visual attention for rapid scene analysis. IEEE Trans. Pattern Anal. Mach. Intell. 20(11), 1254–1259 (1998)
17. Judd, T., Ehinger, K.A., Durand, F., Torralba, A.: Learning to predict where humans look, pp. 2106–2113 (2009)
18. Kanatani, K.: Geometric information criterion for model selection. Int. J. Comput. Vis. 26(3), 171–189 (1998)
19. Lang, C., Nguyen, T.V., Katti, H., Yadati, K., Kankanhalli, M., Yan, S.: Depth matters: influence of depth cues on visual saliency. In: Fitzgibbon, A., Lazebnik, S., Perona, P., Sato, Y., Schmid, C. (eds.) ECCV 2012. LNCS, pp. 101–115. Springer, Heidelberg (2012). https://doi.org/10.1007/978-3-642-33709-3_8
20. Li, J., Tian, Y., Huang, T., Gao, W.: Cost-sensitive rank learning from positive and unlabeled data for visual saliency estimation. IEEE Signal Process. Lett. 17(6), 591–594 (2010)
21. Li, J., Tian, Y., Huang, T., Gao, W.: Probabilistic multi-task learning for visual saliency estimation in video. Int. J. Comput. Vis. 90(2), 150–165 (2010)
22. Li, Z.: A saliency map in primary visual cortex. Trends Cognit. Sci. 6(1), 9–16 (2002)
23. Li, Z., Fang, T., Huo, H.: A saliency model based on wavelet transform and visual attention. Sci. China Ser. F Inf. Sci. 53(4), 738–751 (2010)
24. Liu, C., Yuen, J., Torralba, A.: Sift flow: dense correspondence across scenes and its applications. IEEE Trans. Pattern Anal. Mach. Intell. 33(5), 978–994 (2011)
25. Margolin, R., Zelnikmanor, L., Tal, A.: Saliency for image manipulation. Vis. Comput. 29(5), 381–392 (2013)
26. Niu, Y., Geng, Y., Li, X., Liu, F.: Leveraging stereopsis for saliency analysis, pp. 454–461 (2012)
27. Rahtu, E., Kannala, J., Salo, M., Heikkilä, J.: Segmenting salient objects from images and videos. In: Daniilidis, K., Maragos, P., Paragios, N. (eds.) ECCV 2010. LNCS, vol. 6315, pp. 366–379. Springer, Heidelberg (2010). https://doi.org/10.1007/978-3-642-15555-0_27
28. Seo, H.J., Milanfar, P.: Static and space-time visual saliency detection by self-resemblance. J. Vis. 9(12), 15 (2009)
29. Tatler, B.W.: The central fixation bias in scene viewing: selecting an optimal viewing position independently of motor biases and image feature distributions. J. Vis. 7(14), 4 (2007)
30. Tatler, B.W., Baddeley, R., Gilchrist, I.D.: Visual correlates of fixation selection: effects of scale and time. Vis. Res. 45(5), 643–659 (2005)
31. Treisman, A., Gelade, G.A.: A feature-integration theory of attention. Cognit. Psychol. 12(1), 97–136 (1980)

Object Classification of Remote Sensing Images Based on Rotation-Invariant Discrete Hashing

Hui Xu, Yazhou Liu, and Quansen Sun[(✉)]

School of Computer Science and Engineering,
Nanjing University of Science and Technology, Nanjing, China
xhjn4637@126.com, {yazhouliu,sunquansen}@njust.edu.cn

Abstract. Object classification is one of the most fundamental but challenging problems faced for large-scale remote sensing image analysis. Recently, learning based hashing techniques have attracted broad research interests because of their significant efficiency for high-dimensional data in both storage and speed. Despite the progress made in nature scene images, it is problematic to directly apply existing hashing methods to object classification in very high resolution (VHR) remote sensing images because they didn't consider the problem of object rotation variations. To address this problem, this paper proposes a novel method called Rotation-invariant Discrete Hashing (RIDISH), which jointly learns a discrete binary generation and rotation-invariant optimization model in the hashing learning framework. Experimental evaluations on a publicly available VHR remote sensing dataset demonstrate the effectiveness of proposed method.

Keywords: Discrete hashing · Rotation-invariant optimization
Object classification · Remote sensing

1 Introduction

Due to the rapid advances of remote sensing satellites, the resolution of remote sensing images become higher and we can get more and more objects' details from them. Thus, the object-based image processing is an important research area, especially for the urban scientific configuration, objection detection and sensitive military target location [1]. However, with the higher resolution of remote sensing images, the sample selection, model training and testing speed for each class is a great challenge because we need large-scale data to describe the detail information in VHR remote sensing images. In fact, many applications of VHR images can be regarded as a classification problem such as object detection and target location [2,3]. As an essential step in VHR image processing, our paper aims to learn a novel object classification method which can be further used for applications of VHR images effectively both in accuracy and speed.

© Springer International Publishing AG, part of Springer Nature 2018
B. Zeng et al. (Eds.): PCM 2017, LNCS 10736, pp. 264–274, 2018.
https://doi.org/10.1007/978-3-319-77383-4_26

Recently, hashing has become a popular method applied to large-scale vision problems due to its high time-efficient search capability and high data storage capability [4]. Hashing methods initially embed high-dimensional image features into a low-dimensional Hamming space, where the image features are represented by binary hash codes [5]. Recent research attentions have been shifted to learning data-dependent binary codes by incorporating various machine learning techniques, which can be divided into unsupervised hashing and supervised hashing methods. Unsupervised hashing methods, such as spectral hashing (SH) [6], isotropic hashing (IsoHash) [7], scalable graph hashing (SGH) [8] and unsupervised bilinear local hashing (UBLH) [9], only use the feature information of the data points for learning without using any semantic information. On the contrary, supervised hashing methods try to leverage semantic information for hashing function learning. Representative supervised hashing methods include supervised hashing with kernels (KSH) [10], latent factor hashing (LFH) [11], FastH [12], supervised discrete hashing (SDH) [13] and column sampling hashing (COSDISH) [14].

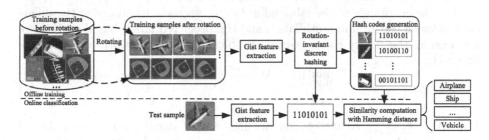

Fig. 1. Framework of the proposed approach.

While various hashing methods have been proposed, most of them only demonstrate their effectiveness on nature scene images. It is problematic to directly apply existing hashing methods to object classification in VHR remote sensing images because they didn't consider the problem of object rotation variations [15]. This paper proposes a rotation-invariant discrete hashing (RIDISH) learning framework to learn compact binary codes efficiently that addresses abovementioned problem. Inspired by SDH [13], to produce compact yet discriminative binary codes, we directly incorporate the quantization optimization into the objective and efficiently solve the discrete optimization problem in the Hamming space to optimize bits of binary codes iteratively through coordinate descending. In particular, to achieve rotation-invariance, we impose a rotation-invariant constraint on the objective function which enforces the training samples before and after rotating to share the similar binary codes. Figure 1 illustrates the framework of the proposed approach.

Our main contributions are summarized as follows: (1) We introduce the hashing method for object classification in large-scale VHR image processing to provide significant efficiency in both storage and speed. (2) We propose a novel hashing approach called RIDISH which jointly learns a discrete binary generation and rotation-invariant optimization model in the hashing learning framework to effectively handle the problem of object rotation variations in remote sensing images. (3) Empirical results demonstrate the effectiveness of our approach both in accuracy and in speed. On one hand, our method outperforms the state-of-the-art hashing methods by a large margin when the length of binary code is very short. On the other hand, it can efficiently improve the speed of classification on the premise of a high accuracy compared with typical classifiers.

2   Rotation-Invariant Discrete Hashing

2.1   Objective Function

Suppose there are n samples $X = \{x_i\}_{i=1}^n \in \mathbb{R}^{d \times n}$, where x_i is a data point of d dimension. The objective is to learn a binary code matrix $B = \{b_i\}_{i=1}^n \in \{-1, 1\}^{q \times n}$ to well preserve their semantic similarities, where the ith column b_i denotes the q-bit binary code for training point x_i.

To take advantage of the label information, we want to minimize the difference between the ground truth labels and the predicted labels based on B. Here we consider the binary codes learning problem in the framework of multi-class linear classification:

$$\min_{B,W} ||Y - W^T B||^2 + \lambda_1 ||W||^2$$
$$\text{s.t. } B \in \{-1, 1\}^{q \times n} \tag{1}$$

Here $W = \{w_k\}_{k=1}^c \in \mathbb{R}^{q \times c}$ is the classifier weight matrix, c is the number of categories and λ_1 is the regularization parameter; $Y = \{y_i\}_{i=1}^n \in \mathbb{R}^{c \times n}$ is the ground truth label matrix, where $y_{ki} = 1$ if x_i belongs to class k and 0 otherwise. It is noticed that formulation (1) directly solves the discrete optimization without any relaxations by imposing discrete constrains on the objective.

The above objective enables to exploit the semantic affinities of manual labels and then we want to preserve the similarity relationships between data samples simultaneously by binary embedding. We define a hash function $H(X)$ and rewrite problem (1) as

$$\min_{B,W,H} ||Y - W^T B||^2 + \lambda_1 ||W||^2 + \lambda_2 ||B - H(X)||^2$$
$$\text{s.t. } B \in \{-1, 1\}^{q \times n} \tag{2}$$

Here $H(X)$ is the projection function which embeds original features into q bits. The last term in (2) measures the fitting error between the data structures of the binary codes and the data samples, and λ_2 is the penalty parameter. While various hashing methods have been proposed in recent years, most of them aim to seek a single projection matrix, which is essentially linear and cannot preserve the nonlinear structure of data samples. Here we want to emphasize that the learned binary codes should well preserve the similarities between original data points. To obtain the desirable binary codes, a good form of hash function is important.

To this end, in this paper, we consider a nonlinear form for embedding, which is widely used as the kernel hash function in, $e.g.$, BRE [16] and KSH [10].

$$H(X) = P^T K(X) \tag{3}$$

Where $K(X) \in \mathbb{R}^{m \times n}$ is a matrix obtained by the RBF kernel mapping. Each column $K(x) = [\exp(-||x-x_{(1)}||^2/\sigma), \cdots, \exp(-||x-x_{(m)}||^2/\sigma)]^T$, where $\{x_{(j)}\}_{j=1}^m$ are m samples randomly selected from the training samples and σ is the kernel width. When we utilize all the n training samples, we can obtain the matrix $K(X) \in \mathbb{R}^{m \times n}$ with mapped data. The matrix $P \in \mathbb{R}^{m \times q}$ projects the mapped data $K(X)$ onto the low dimensional space. As we can see from (3), with the hash function $H(X)$, the last term in (2) explicitly minimizes the reconstruction error between the original distances and the Hamming distances by binary embedding in a nonlinear way.

2.2 Rotation-Invariant Constraint

Despite the great success made in nature scene images, it is problematic to directly apply existing hashing methods to object classification in VHR remote sensing images because they didn't consider the problem of object rotation variations. Similar to the solution to learn rotation-invariant HOG feature [15], in this paper, we expect the learned hash codes to be rotation-invariant [17]. In particular, we impose a rotation-invariant constraint on the objective function. The details are as following.

We define R rotation angles $\alpha = \{ \alpha_1, \alpha_2, \cdots, \alpha_R\}$ and their rotation transformations $T_\alpha = \{ T_{\alpha_1}, T_{\alpha_2}, \cdots, T_{\alpha_R}\}$, where each transformation T_{α_r} denotes the rotation of a sample with the angle of α_r. Applying rotation transformations T_α to all training samples $X = \{x_i\}_{i=1}^n$ can yield a new set of rotated training samples $T_\alpha X = \{T_\alpha x_i\}_{i=1}^n$, where $T_\alpha x_i = \{T_{\alpha_r} x_i | r = 1, 2, \cdots, R\}$. The total training samples before and after rotation $X = \{X, T_\alpha X\}$ will be used together to train our RIDISH model. In our implementation, we set $R = 35$ and $\alpha = \{10°, 20°, ..., 350°\}$.

Here is an assumption that if the training samples before and after rotating share the similar hash codes, our hashing method is sought to be approximately rotation-invariant. Based on this idea, the rotation-invariant constraint term is defined as

$$C(B, T_\alpha B) = \lambda_3 \sum_{i=1}^n ||b_i - \overline{T_\alpha b_i}||^2 = \lambda_3 ||B - \overline{T_\alpha B}||^2 \tag{4}$$

Where $\overline{T_\alpha b_i} = \frac{1}{R}(T_{\alpha_1} b_i + T_{\alpha_2} b_i + \cdots + T_{\alpha_R} b_i)$ denotes the mean values of binary codes generated by all the rotated versions of the training sample x_i. As can be seen from (4), this term enforces the hash codes of each training sample to be close to the mean values of hash codes obtained by its rotated versions.

Then we impose the regularization constraint term on the objective function and rewrite problem (2) as

$$\min_{B,W,H} ||Y - W^T B||^2 + \lambda_1 ||W||^2 + \lambda_2 ||B - H(X)||^2 + \lambda_3 ||B - \overline{T_\alpha B}||^2$$

$$\text{s.t. } B \in \{-1,1\}^{q \times n}.$$

$$(5)$$

Above problem is the final objective function we want to optimize. The last term in (5) enforces the training samples before and after rotating, namely, X and $T_\alpha X$ to share the similar hash codes. That is to say, the generated hash codes corresponding to X and $T_\alpha X$, namely, B and $T_\alpha B$ should be extremely same.

2.3   Alternative Optimization

To solve the optimization problem described in (5), we decompose the problem into three sub-problems that are optimized in an alternative procedure. More specially, we optimize P with W and B fixed. Similarly, W is optimized with P and B fixed; B is optimized with P and W fixed. This three-step alternating optimization procedure will be repeated iteratively for several times till the procedure converges.

Optimize P with W and B fixed: By fixing all variables but P, the projection matrix P can be easily computed by regression: $P = (K(X)K(X)^T)^{-1}K(X)B^T$.

Optimize W with P and B fixed: By fixing B, it is easy to solve W by the regularized least squares problem, which has a closed-form solution: $W = (BB^T + \lambda_1 I)^{-1}BY^T$.

Optimize B with P and W fixed: With all variables but B fixed, this sub-problem is formulated as:

$$\min_{B} ||Y - W^T B||^2 + \lambda_2 ||B - H(X)||^2 + \lambda_3 ||B - \overline{T_\alpha B}||^2$$

$$\text{s.t. } B \in \{-1,1\}^{q \times n}.$$

$$(6)$$

With simple mathematical derivation, one can arrive at the equivalent formulation as

$$\min_{B} tr(B^T W W^T B) - 2tr(B^T U)$$

$$\text{s.t. } B \in \{-1,1\}^{q \times n}.$$

$$(7)$$

Where $U = WY + \lambda_2 H(X) + \lambda_3 \overline{T_\alpha B}$ and $tr(\cdot)$ is the trace norm. It is more challenging to solve for B due to the discrete constraints. However, we can achieve one row of B by fixing all other rows, it means we generate the hash codes bit by bit. Then the binary code matrix B can be updated row by row in the cyclic coordinate descending (CCD) scheme [18]. Let b_i be the ith row of B, $i = 1, ..., q$ and $\tilde{B}$ be the matrix of B excluding b_i. Similarly, u_i and $\tilde{U}$, and w_i and $\tilde{W}$ could be defined. Then each row of B can be pursued by CCD method

$$b_i = \text{sgn}(u_i - (\tilde{B}^T \tilde{W} w_i^T)^T)$$

$$(8)$$

According to (8), the optimal solution of (6) can be obtained and we can finally solve the whole objective.

3   Experiments

3.1   Dataset Description and Implementation Details

We evaluate the performance of the proposed RIDISH method on a publicly available dataset: NWPU VHR-10 dataset [19]. This is a challenging 10-class dataset which can be used for multi-class object classification. These ten object classes are airplane, ship, storage tank, baseball diamond, tennis court, basketball court, ground track field, harbor, bridge and vehicle. This dataset contains a total of 800 VHR optical remote sensing images, where 715 color images were acquired from Google Earth with the spatial resolution ranging from 0.5 to 2 m, and 85 pan sharpened color infrared images were acquired from Vaihingen data with a spatial resolution of 0.08 m.

In these VHR remote sensing images, there are 757 airplanes, 302 ships, 655 storage tanks, 390 baseball diamonds, 524 tennis courts, 159 basketball courts, 163 ground track fields, 224 harbors, 124 bridges and 477 vehicles manually annotated with bounding boxes. Figure 2 shows some of these targets in NWPU VHR-10 dataset. We extract these targets and randomly divide them in two groups: 1000 for test and the rest for training. To augment training data, we set $R = 35$ and $\alpha = \{10°, 20°, ..., 350°\}$ to obtain 36× training samples. The total training samples before and after rotating will be used jointly to train the RIDISH model. Each sample is represented by a 512-dimensional GIST vector. In order to improve the accuracy of experiment, we randomly generate the experiment data ten times with the above method, every time can yield a new set of training samples and test samples used for independently experiment. The average values are took as the final result. All the experiments are implemented via MATLAB on a standard PC with Intel Core i7-6820HQ CPU 2.70 GHz, 16 GB RAM.

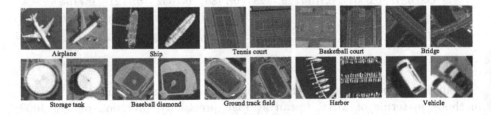

Fig. 2. Example of two targets for each category in NWPU VHR-10 dataset.

3.2   Comparison with State-of-the-Art Hashing Methods

The results of our RIDISH approach are compared with six state-of-the-art hashing methods which cover both unsupervised method and supervised method, including SH [6], SGH [8], KSH [10], LFH [11], COSDISH [14] and SDH [13].

Table 1. Results of MAP on NWPU VHR-10. Results with 8 bits, 12 bits, 16 bits, 24 bits, 32 bits, 48 bits and 64 bits are reported. The highest values are shown in bold numbers.

Method	8	12	16	24	32	48	64
SH	0.1977	0.1958	0.1971	0.2031	0.2249	0.2100	0.2111
SGH	0.2617	0.2550	0.2625	0.2563	0.2598	0.2673	0.2740
KSH	0.6616	0.6925	0.7059	0.7308	0.7386	0.7421	0.7536
LFH	0.4861	0.5635	0.6490	0.6796	0.7456	0.7484	0.7548
COSDISH	0.7015	0.7400	0.7731	0.7852	0.8044	0.8107	0.8144
SDH	0.6935	0.8349	0.9102	0.9241	0.9269	0.9304	0.9340
RIDISH	**0.8669**	**0.9053**	**0.9175**	**0.9266**	**0.9288**	**0.9317**	**0.9344**

Table 2. Results of precision of top 1000 returned samples on NWPU VHR-10. Results with 8 bits, 12 bits, 16 bits, 24 bits, 32 bits, 48 bits and 64 bits are reported. The highest values are shown in bold numbers.

Method	8	12	16	24	32	48	64
SH	0.2600	0.2671	0.2822	0.3000	0.3388	0.3359	0.3238
SGH	0.3887	0.4131	0.4550	0.4828	0.5211	0.5531	0.5688
KSH	0.7099	0.7403	0.7547	0.7741	0.7864	0.7890	0.7970
LFH	0.4256	0.5018	0.5969	0.6226	0.7041	0.7050	0.7114
COSDISH	0.6551	0.7014	0.7328	0.7485	0.7652	0.7721	0.7754
SDH	0.7108	0.8540	0.9212	0.9310	0.9327	0.9350	**0.9370**
RIDISH	**0.8855**	**0.9169**	**0.9258**	**0.9315**	**0.9333**	**0.9354**	0.9366

Tables 1, 2 and 3 respectively shows the performance of different hashing methods in terms of MAP (mean average precision), precision of top 1000 returned samples and precision of Hamming distance with radius 2 with respect to different length of binary code. We can see that our RIDISH method outperforms all other methods by a large margin for any evaluation metric when the length of binary code is very short and keeps optimal performance with code length becoming longer.

Table 3. Results of precision of Hamming distance with radius 2 on NWPU VHR-10. Results with 8 bits, 12 bits, 16 bits, 24 bits, 32 bits, 48 bits and 64 bits are reported. The highest values are shown in bold numbers.

Method	8	12	16	24	32	48	64
SH	0.2150	0.2817	0.3792	0.5457	0.4040	0.0440	0.0055
SGH	0.2782	0.3826	0.5071	0.6806	0.4185	0.0744	0.0170
KSH	0.5653	0.6948	0.7375	0.7752	0.7937	0.7480	0.6803
LFH	0.3734	0.4254	0.3979	0.2429	0.1446	0.0718	0.0422
COSDISH	0.5702	0.6385	0.5433	0.4599	0.4025	0.3432	0.3208
SDH	0.4041	0.6668	0.9078	0.9260	0.9263	0.9101	0.8922
RIDISH	**0.5947**	**0.8709**	**0.9159**	**0.9269**	**0.9278**	**0.9176**	**0.8956**

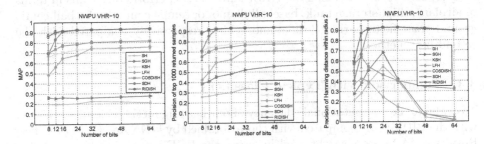

Fig. 3. Results of the compared methods in MAP, two kinds of precision scores and their standard deviation experimented in 10 times with code length from 8 to 64.

Table 4. Performance comparisons of different hashing methods in terms of AP values. Results with 8 bits are reported. The bold numbers denote the highest values in each row.

	SH	SGH	KSH	LFH	COSDISH	SDH	RIDISH
Airplane	0.2549	0.2988	0.8766	0.7601	0.8651	0.7947	**0.9564**
Ship	0.1377	0.1253	0.5287	0.1879	0.5213	0.6769	**0.8593**
Storage tank	0.3179	0.5673	0.9380	0.8150	0.9140	0.7994	**0.9843**
Baseball diamond	0.1735	0.1872	0.5392	0.2685	0.6510	0.7871	**0.8516**
Tennis court	0.2083	0.2784	0.7650	0.5680	0.9125	0.6886	**0.9514**
Basketball court	0.0511	0.0702	0.1533	0.0728	0.1392	0.3178	**0.4336**
Ground track field	0.0546	0.0912	0.2303	0.0863	0.2318	0.3100	**0.6114**
Harbor	0.0923	0.0840	0.1806	0.1272	0.2656	0.4619	**0.7244**
Bridge	0.0508	0.0432	0.1339	0.0511	0.2015	0.3806	**0.4582**
Vehicle	0.1936	0.1698	0.6108	0.3131	0.7373	0.7739	**0.9032**
MAP	0.1977	0.2617	0.6616	0.4861	0.7015	0.6935	**0.8669**

In order to illustrate the advantages of proposed method more intuitively, Fig. 3 shows the results of compared methods in terms of MAP, precision scores and their standard deviation experimented in 10 times, with code length from 8 to 64. Apart from the similar superior performance shown in Tables 1, 2 and 3, we can see that the standard deviation of our RIDISH method is extremely small even when the code length is 8-bit, it demonstrates the stability and robustness of proposed method.

Table 4 shows the quantitative comparison results of different hashing methods, measured by AP (average precision) values of each object category. MAP values are also computed. It should be noted that, since the number of test samples from each object category is different, the results of MAP are calculated by test samples from all of ten categories, rather than the mean values of the above computed AP values. As can be seen from them, when the code length is 8-bit, our RIDISH method obtained 16.17%, 18.24%, 18.43%, 6.55%, 26.28%, 11.58%, 30.14%, 26.25%, 7.76% and 12.93% performance gains in terms of airplane, ship, storage tank, baseball diamond, tennis court, basketball court, ground track field, harbor, bridge and vehicle respectively compared with the second-best method.

3.3   Comparison with Typical Classifiers

To evaluate the computational efficiency of our hashing method, results achieved with the RIDISH are compared with those obtained by k-NN and SVM classifier. Results of SVM are also obtained by using the RBF kernel (the same used in RIDISH). Table 5 provides the results in terms of the average and standard deviation of classification accuracy and average test time required for 1000 samples obtained in 10 trials. We can see that the presented hashing method significantly reduces the computational time with a higher classification accuracy compared with k-NN and SVM.

Table 5. Average (Ave) and standard deviation (Std) of classification accuracy and the average test time (in seconds) required for 1000 test samples' classification by the k-NN, the SVM, and the presented RIDISH.

Method	Feature	Ave	Std	Test time
k-NN	512-GIST	0.7822	0.0143	373.78
SVM	512-GIST	0.8732	0.0069	31.037
RIDISH	8 bits	0.9092	0.0135	2.9066
RIDISH	32 bits	0.9426	0.0052	2.9711
RIDISH	64 bits	0.9461	0.0050	3.0010

Apart from the superiority in terms of time complexity, the storage complexity of binary codes generated by RIDISH is significantly reduced.

For example, in NWPU VHR-10 dataset, for the samples used in the experiments, the storage complexity is 98.6 KB, when the code length is 8-bit. However, without hashing, storing the original image features (those that are required to be stored as double floating-point numbers, i.e., 8 bytes) requires a memory of 394.3 MB, when the feature length is 512. If the feature length increases, the amount of required memory significantly rises. These results clearly illustrate how the hash codes significantly improve the speed of classification and reduce the amount of memory required for storing the images.

4 Conclusions

In this paper, we introduced hashing methods for object classification in VHR remote sensing images to provide significant efficiency in both storage and speed. However, most of existing hashing methods only demonstrated their effectiveness on nature scene images. It is problematic to directly apply them to object classification in VHR remote sensing images because they didn't consider the problem of object rotation variations. To address this problem, this paper proposed a novel hashing method called RIDISH, which jointly learned a discrete binary generation and rotation-invariant optimization model in the hashing learning framework. Experimental evaluations on a publicly available VHR remote sensing dataset demonstrated the effectiveness of RIDISH.

Acknowledgments. This work was supported in part by the National Nature Science Foundation of China under Grant no. 61673220 and 61672286.

References

1. Boya, Z., Hao, S., Liang, C., He, C., Fukun, B.: Object classification of remote sensing images based on BOV. In: IET International Radar Conference 2015, pp. 1–5 (2015)
2. Han, J., Zhang, D., Cheng, G., Guo, L., Ren, J.: Object detection in optical remote sensing images based on weakly supervised learning and high-level feature learning. IEEE Trans. Geosci. Remote Sens. **53**(6), 3325–3337 (2015)
3. Zhang, Y., Zhang, L., Du, B., Wang, S.: A nonlinear sparse representation-based binary hypothesis model for hyperspectral target detection. IEEE J. Sel. Topics Appl. Earth Obs. Remote Sens. **8**(6), 2513–2522 (2015)
4. Demir, B., Bruzzone, L.: Hashing-based scalable remote sensing image search and retrieval in large archives. IEEE Trans. Geosci. Remote Sens. **54**(2), 1–13 (2015)
5. Zhu, X., Zhang, L., Huang, Z.: A sparse embedding and least variance encoding approach to hashing. IEEE Trans. Image Process. **23**(9), 3737–3750 (2014)
6. Weiss, Y., Torralba, A., Fergus, R.: Spectral hashing. In: Advances in Neural Information Processing Systems, pp. 1753–1760 (2009)
7. Kong, W., Li, W.-J.: Isotropic hashing. In: Advances in Neural Information Processing Systems, pp. 1646–1654 (2012)
8. Jiang, Q.-Y., Li, W.-J.: Scalable graph hashing with feature transformation. In: Proceedings of IJCAI (2015)

9. Liu, L., Yu, M., Shao, L.: Unsupervised local feature hashing for image similarity search. IEEE Trans. Cybern. (2015)
10. Liu, W., Wang, J., Ji, R., Jiang, Y.-G., Chang, S.-F.: Supervised hashing with kernels. In: Computer Vision and Pattern Recognition, pp. 2074–2081 (2012)
11. Zhang, P., Zhang, W., Li, W.-J., Guo, M.: Supervised hashing with latent factor models. In: Proceedings of the 37th International ACM SIGIR Conference on Research and Development in Information Retrieval, pp. 173–182 (2014)
12. Lin, G., Shen, C., Shi, Q., van den Hengel, A., Suter, D.: Fast supervised hashing with decision trees for high-dimensional data. In: Proceedings of the IEEE Conference on Computer Vision and Pattern Recognition, pp. 1963–1970 (2014)
13. Shen, F., Shen, C., Liu, W., Shen, H.T.: Supervised discrete hashing. In: Proceedings of the IEEE Conference on Computer Vision and Pattern Recognition, pp. 37–45 (2015)
14. Kang, W.-C., Li, W.-J., Zhou, Z.-H.: Column sampling based discrete supervised hashing. In: Thirtieth AAAI Conference on Artificial Intelligence (2016)
15. Cheng, G., Zhou, P., Yao, X., Yao, C., Zhang, Y., Han, J.: Object detection in VHR optical remote sensing images via learning rotation-invariant hog feature. In: International Workshop on Earth Observation and Remote Sensing Applications, pp. 433–436 (2016)
16. Kulis, B., Darrell, T.: Learning to hash with binary reconstructive embeddings. In: Advances in Neural Information Processing Systems, pp. 1042–1050 (2009)
17. Lin, K., Lu, J., Chen, C.-S., Zhou, J.: Learning compact binary descriptors with unsupervised deep neural networks. In: IEEE Conference on Computer Vision and Pattern Recognition (CVPR), pp. 1183–1192 (2016)
18. Neyshabur, B., Srebro, N., Salakhutdinov, R., Makarychev, Y., Yadollahpour, P.: The power of asymmetry in binary hashing. In: Advances in Neural Information Processing Systems, pp. 2823–2831 (2013)
19. Cheng, G., Han, J.: A survey on object detection in optical remote sensing images. ISPRS J. Photogramm. Remote Sens. **117**, 11–28 (2016)

Robust Principal Component Analysis via Symmetric Alternating Direction for Moving Object Detection

Zhenzhou Shao[1,2], Gaoyu Wu[1,3], Ying Qu[4(✉)], Zhiping Shi[1,2],
Yong Guan[1,2], and Jindong Tan[3,4]

[1] College of Information Engineering, Capital Normal University, Beijing, China
[2] Beijing Advanced Innovation Center for Imaging Technology, Beijing, China
[3] Beijing Key Laboratory of Light Industrial Robot and Safety Verification,
Beijing, China
[4] Engineering College, The University of Tennessee, Knoxville, USA
yqu3@vols.utk.edu

Abstract. Robust Principal Component Analysis (RPCA) has been proved to be effective for the moving object detection with background variation. Alternating Direction Method (ADM) based RPCA takes full advantages of the separable structure of the objective function to achieve better results than traditional RPCA methods. But it suffers from the heavy computing burden and low efficiency. In this paper, a Symmetric Alternating Direction Method (SADM) is proposed to solve above problems. SADM optimizes the iterative strategy of ADM by updating the multiplier of the linear constraint twice every iteration which speeds up the convergence, thus reduces the execution times of Singular Value Decomposition (SVD). Besides, the new equilibrium parameter and interrupt mechanism are introduced to guarantee the object detection accuracy and avoid the unnecessary iterations. Compared with ADM, the experimental results show that not only the detection accuracy of proposed method is improved by 46.8%, but also the time consumption is reduced by 97.5%.

1 Introduction

Moving object detection is one of the most fundamental problems in computer vision. It is widely applied in various applications, such as video surveillance [1],

This work was supported by the Project of Beijing Municipal Commission of Education (KM201710028017), the National Natural Science Foundation of China (61572331, 61472468, 61373034), the National Key Technology Research and Development Program (2015BAF13B01), the International Cooperation Program on Science and Technology (2011DFG13000), the Project of Beijing Municipal Science & Technology Commission (Z141100002014001), the Project of Construction of Innovative Teams and Teacher Career Development for Universities and Colleges Under Beijing Municipality (IDHT20150507), and Training young backbone talents personal projects (2014000020124G135).

© Springer International Publishing AG, part of Springer Nature 2018
B. Zeng et al. (Eds.): PCM 2017, LNCS 10736, pp. 275–285, 2018.
https://doi.org/10.1007/978-3-319-77383-4_27

video content analysis [2], traffic surveillance [3], automatic drive [4], etc. The classical methods for moving object detection include frame difference, background subtraction and optimal flow. However, the former two methods have low robustness, and the optimal flow method usually fails due to the illumination changes and dynamic backgrounds [5]. Moreover, with the increment of image resolution, more efficient algorithms are required to process the increasing data volume with high accuracy.

As a parsimony model, Robust Principal Component Analysis (RPCA) is recently becoming increasingly important to solve the moving object detection problem [6,7]. The core idea of this method is transforming sequential multiple frames into a matrix $\mathbf{C}$, which can be decomposed into a sparse matrix x and a low-rank matrix y. Each column of x and y corresponds to the foreground and background of each image, respectively. Candes $et\ al.$ proposed a convex optimization to solve the RPCA problem [8]. It converts the decomposition to following convex optimization problem:

$$\underset{x,y}{\mathrm{argmin}} \|x\|_* + \delta\|y\|_{l_1}, \ subj\ C = x + y, \tag{1}$$

where $\|\cdot\|_{l_1}$ is l_1 norm, $\|\cdot\|_*$ is nuclear norm, $\delta > 0$ is an arbitrary regularize parameter, $\mathbf{C}$ is the input data matrix, x is a sparse matrix and y is a low-rank matrix. The optimization in Eq. (1) can be solved by iterative thresholding technique [9] or accelerated proximal gradient (APG) algorithm [10]. But these methods converge very slowly. Lin $et\ al.$ proposed both exact ALM (EALM) and inexact ALM (IALM) based on augmented Largrange multipliers (ALM) to alleviate the slow convergence [11]. But both methods do not take into account separable structure in both the objective function and the constraint in Eq. (1) [12]. Yuan $et\ al.$ proposed an Alternating Direction Method (ADM) to solve this problem [13]. However, this algorithm invokes more than once Singular Value Decomposition (SVD) in each iteration, which makes the algorithm time-consuming.

In this paper, we propose a Symmetrical Alternating Direction Method (SADM) for RPCA to detect the moving object. The contributions of the proposed method are two-fold: (1) An optimization method is proposed based on symmetrical theory to optimize the iterative strategy by updating the multiplier of linear constraint twice every iteration. This improvement automatically reduces the iterations of SVD to make the convergence faster. (2) Inspired by NADM method [14], both new equilibrium parameter and interrupt mechanism are proposed to solve the problem more efficiency. The new equilibrium parameter guarantees a better convergence, while the new interrupt mechanism avoids unnecessary iterations thus reduces the time consumption of proposed algorithm.

The rest of the paper is organized as follows. Section 2 describes the proposed algorithm with new iterative strategy, equilibrium parameter and interrupt mechanism elaborated. Section 3 evaluates the algorithm using image sequences with variational background. Conclusion is drawn in Sect. 4.

2   SADM-RPCA: Symmetrical Alternating Direction Method Based RPCA

In this section, a Symmetrical Alternating Direction Method Based RPCA (SADM-RPCA) is presented in details, including the iterative strategy based on symmetrical theory, equilibrium parameter and interrupt mechanism.

2.1   Iterative Strategy Optimization Based on Symmetrical Theory

To resolve a single image into a sparse matrix x (moving object) and a low-rank matrix y (background), an efficient iterative strategy is required to speed up the optimization of RPCA problem. As we know, the primal ADM suffers from heavy computing burden and long time consumption. This paper proposes a SADM with an iterative strategy based on symmetrical theory.

Let $f(x) = \|x\|_*$ and $g(y) = \delta\|y\|_{l_1}$, Eq. (1) can be rewritten as $\underset{x,y}{\operatorname{argmin}} f(x) + g(y)$, $subj\ C = x + y$. The corresponding augmented Lagrangian function is

$$
\begin{aligned}
L_\beta(x, y, Z) =& f(x) + g(y) - \langle Z, x + y - C\rangle \\
& + \frac{\beta}{2}\|x + y - C\|^2,
\end{aligned}
\tag{2}
$$

where $x \in X$ is sparse matrix and $y \in Y$ is low-rank matrix, $Z \in \mathbb{R}^r$ is the multiplier of the linear constraint, $\langle\cdot\rangle$ denotes the standard trace inner product, $\|\cdot\|$ is the induced Frobenius norm, $\beta > 0$ is the penalty parameter for the violation of the linear constraint. The definitional domain of Eq. (2) is $U = X \times Y \times \mathbb{R}^r$.

The primal solution of (2) based on ADM is

$$
\begin{cases}
x^{k+1} = \underset{x}{\operatorname{argmin}}\ L(x^k, y^k, Z^k), \\
y^{k+1} = \underset{y}{\operatorname{argmin}}\ L(x^{k+1}, y^k, Z^k), \\
Z^{k+1} = Z^k - \beta(x^{k+1} + y^{k+1} - C),
\end{cases}
\tag{3}
$$

x^k, y^k and Z^k represent the value of kth iteration. This solution takes advantages of the separable structure, but it employs the time-consuming SVD several times when solving y. The explicit solution of y is

$$
y^{k+1} = U^{k+1}diag(\max \sigma_i^{k+1}, 0)(V^{k+1})^T,
\tag{4}
$$

$U^{k+1} \in \mathbb{R}^{m\times r}$ and $V_{k+1} \in \mathbb{R}^{n\times r}$ can be obtained by

$$
C - x^{k+1} + \frac{1}{\beta}Z^k = U^{k+1}\sum^{k+1}(V^{k+1})^T.
\tag{5}
$$

We can find that ADM uses SVD more than twice every iteration. As the SVD is a time-consuming process, the efficient way to reduce the time consumption of ADM is to decrease the times of iteration.

In Eq. (3), the linear constraint multiplier Z is updated just once after the augmented Lagrangian is minimized with respect to y. According to the symmetrical theory [15], updating Z after x and y respectively is equivalent to Douglas-Rachford and Peaceman-Rachford methods with the optimal condition $C = x + y$. Therefore, we optimize Z twice in each iteration with respect x and y in this paper. The first optimization of Z after x is denoted by $Z^{k+\frac{1}{2}}$,

$$Z^{k+\frac{1}{2}} = Z^k - \beta(x^{k+1} + y^k - C), \tag{6}$$

where β is the step for Z update. The second one after y is

$$Z^{k+1} = Z^{k+\frac{1}{2}} - \beta(x^{k+1} + y^{k+1} - C). \tag{7}$$

The linear constraint multiplier is the key parameter for the convergence. This improvement makes the linear constraint update to the convergence faster, so that the times of SVD implementation are reduced accordingly.

2.2 Equilibrium Parameter and Interrupt Mechanism

In this section, the equilibrium parameter is introduced to further improve the convergence and accuracy of SADM-RPCA. In [14], NADM is proposed for the variational inequality problem. We have proved that NADM can be applied to the convex optimization problem. The proof procedure can be found in the supplemental material. The equilibrium parameter is defined by $\gamma = 2e^{-\delta} \in (0, 2)$. According to the proof in [15], the equilibrium parameter can improve the convergence of formula with the symmetric structure. δ is the regularization parameter to update the multiplier of linear constraint Z, as shown in Eq. (8). It can adjust the weights of moving object x and background y to optimize the distribution of x and y every iteration.

$$\begin{cases} Z^{k+\frac{1}{2}} = Z^k - \gamma\beta(x^{k+1} + y^k - C) \\ Z^{k+1} = Z^{k+\frac{1}{2}} - \gamma\beta(x^{k+1} + y^{k+1} - C). \end{cases} \tag{8}$$

Besides, an error parameter is introduced as the extra interrupt mechanism, as shown in Eq. (9).

$$e_y(y^k, \beta) = y^k - P_y[g(y^k) - Z^k] \tag{9}$$

where $P_y[\cdot]$ is a projection from $\mathbb{R}^n$ to y. This parameter indicates the change of background y after every iteration. Due to the slight change of y at the beginning especially, it sometimes results in a misjudgement of interrupt mechanism. Thus, the error parameter is refined in this paper by involving x with y in Z^k. It can also avoid unnecessary iteration to improve the computational efficiency. In summary, the implementation of SADM-RPCA is described in Algorithm 1.

Algorithm 1. Symmetrical Alternating Direction Methed Based RPCA

Input: Single image, initialization of sparse matrix x, low-rank matrix y and linear constraint multiplier Z, $\gamma \in (0,2)$, $\beta \in (0,1)$, threshold $\epsilon > 0$, number of iterations T.

1: **for** $k = 0$ to T **do**
2:     Update x^{k+1}, y^{k+1}, Z^{k+1} using the following rules:

$$\begin{cases} x_{k+1} = \underset{x}{\operatorname{argmin}}\ L(x^k, y^k, Z^k), \\ Z^{k+\frac{1}{2}} = Z^k - \gamma\beta(x^{k+1} + y^k - C), \\ y_{k+1} = \underset{y}{\operatorname{argmin}}\ L(x^{k+1}, y^k, Z^{k+\frac{1}{2}}), \\ Z^{k+1} = Z^{k+\frac{1}{2}} - \gamma\beta(x^{k+1} + y^{k+1} - C). \end{cases} \tag{10}$$

3:     Calculate the error e using Eq. (9),
4:     **if** $e \le \epsilon$ **then**
5:       The interrupt mechanism is triggered. Terminate execution of the loop.
6:     **end if**
7: **end for**

Output: Sparse matrix x (moving object).

3   Experimental Results and Discussion

To evaluate the effectiveness and accuracy of proposed method, we perform the moving object detection on image sequences by applying proposed SADM-RPCA and seven state-of-the-art methods, including EALM [11], IALM [11], FPCP [16], MoG [17], R2PCP [18], LSADM [15] and ADM [13]. Three dynamic image sequences with nonuniform backgrounds are chosen from Wallflower dataset [19], including Camouflage (C), Moved Object (MO) and Waving Trees (WT). Besides, the effect of equilibrium parameter is also verified with respect to the accuracy and effectiveness using the above dataset.

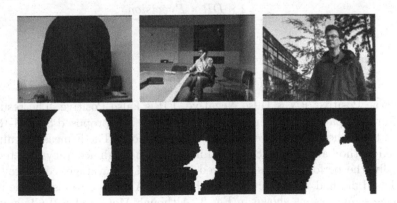

Fig. 1. Samples and corresponding ground truth in the Wallflower dataset. From left column to the right: Camouflage, Moved Object and Waving Trees.

Totally 100 images with the resolution of 160 × 120 in each sequence are randomly chosen with their corresponding ground-truth foreground. The sample data and ground truth of moving object are shown in Fig. 1. Each input matrix $[P_1, P_2, \cdots, P_{100}]$ for moving object detection is built with vector P_i reshaped from the corresponding ith image in the chosen sequence. Both F-measure and computational cost are calculated to evaluate the detection performance. All algorithms are written in Matlab, and run on CPU Intel(R) Core(TM) i7-4790 3.60 GHz with 8 GB memory.

3.1 Performance of Moving Object Detection

The detection results using different image sequences are illustrated in Fig. 2. From visualization, results from MoG-RPCA, R2PCP and the proposed SADM-RPCA are more robust to different dynamic backgrounds.

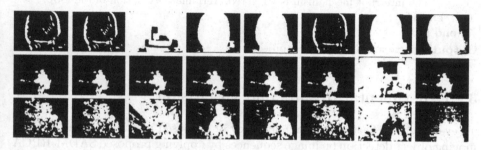

Fig. 2. Experimental results on the Wallflower dataset. From left column to the right: EALM, IALM, FPCP, MoG, R2PCP, LSADM, ADM and proposed method SADM-RPCA. From top to bottom: Camouflage, Moved Object and Waving Trees.

For the quantitative comparison, F-measure is adopted to estimate the accuracy of moving object detection [20], as depicted in Eq. 10.

$$F = \frac{2 \times DR \times Precision}{DR + Precision} \tag{10}$$

where

$$\begin{cases} DR = \frac{TP}{TP+FN} \\ Precision = \frac{TP}{TP+FP}. \end{cases} \tag{11}$$

TP is True Positive, FN is False Negative, FP is False Positive. The results of F-measure comparison are summarized in Table 1. The proposed SADM-RPCA achieves the highest F-measure among all the methods. The F-measure values of proposed method are all over 81, which indicates the high accuracy of detection. Especially, the performance is improved by **46.8%** on average, compared with ADM based method. In particularly, SADM-RPCA is more robust to the different image sequences, as shown in Fig. 3. Although MoG and R2PCP have the comparable performance on the Camouflage dataset, the accuracy is reduced on the datasets of Moved Object and Waving Trees.

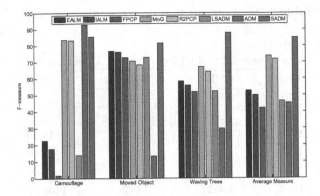

Fig. 3. Comparison of F-measure results.

3.2 Effectiveness Test

For efficiency comparison, the average running time to process 100 images of each sequence is calculated and summarized in Table 2. Compared with ADM based method, the average time of proposed method is reduced by **97.5%**. It indicates that the proposed iterative strategy, equilibrium parameter and interrupt mechanism are able to improve the convergence speed greatly.

Besides, the iterations of each method using different image sequences are compared to verify the convergence of proposed method. As shown in Table 3, the average iterations of SADM is 222, while ADM does not converge after 5000 cycles. IALM and FPCP take less iterations, but the accuracy is much lower than the proposed method, as shown in Fig. 3.

According to Tables 1, 2 and 3, SDAM outperforms over the state-of-the-art methods. There is a trade off between detection accuracy and efficiency using the proposed method. Although the running time of IALM, FPCP, MoG, R2PCP and LSADM is shorter than SADM-RPCA, the accuracy is lower.

Table 1. F-measure results.

Method	Dataset			
	Camouflage	Moved Object	Waving Trees	Average Measure
EALM	22.68	76.65	58.36	52.56
IALM	17.70	76.01	55.89	49.87
FPCP	1.73	72.71	51.89	42.11
MoG	83.56	70.58	67.13	73.76
R2PCP	83.20	68.25	64.16	71.87
LSADM	13.85	72.85	53.32	46.34
ADM	**92.67**	13.21	29.73	45.20
SADM	85.30	**81.57**	**87.85**	**84.91**

Table 2. Total running time on 100 continuous images.

Method	Dataset			
	Camouflage	Moved Object	Waving Trees	Average Time (s)
EALM	90.69	62.33	85.13	79.39
IALM	5.40	5.58	5.46	5.48
FPCP	1.75	1.25	1.16	1.39
MoG	16.56	18.95	22.37	19.30
R2PCP	11.73	11.14	17.93	13.60
LSADM	11.84	12.56	11.88	12.09
ADM	**1575**	1566	1547	1562.67
SADM	43.01	35.74	35.74	38.76

Table 3. Iterations using different methods.

Method	Dataset			
	Camouflage	Moved Object	Waving Trees	Average Iterations
EALM	464	401	497	454
IALM	217	210	197	208
FPCP	**163**	**168**	**168**	**166**
MoG	251	234	218	234
R2PCP	238	215	211	221
LSADM	248	267	289	268
ADM	>5000	>5000	>5000	>5000
SADM	**225**	**213**	**227**	**222**

Thus, the proposed algorithm is able to achieve the moving object detection with the better accuracy within the reasonable time.

3.3 Effect of Equilibrium Parameter

To verify the effect of introduced equilibrium parameter in SADM, SADM without equilibrium parameter is implemented using above image sequences. The detection results are illustrated in Fig. 4. The result without equilibrium parameter is yielded incompletely, and some artifacts are involved. It means the equilibrium parameter has a influence on the decomposition of low-rank and sparse matrix.

Table 4 shows the F-measure results with respect to the equilibrium parameter. The average measure is 66.68, which is lower than SADM by 21.5%. Especially for the Move Object dataset, the accuracy is only 47.17, while SADM performs much better with the F-measure of 81.57.

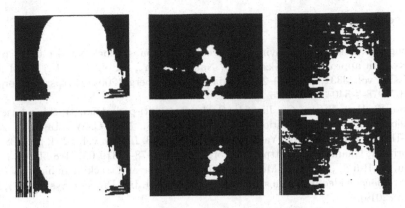

Fig. 4. Performance comparison with and without equilibrium parameter using different dataset. Dataset from left column to the right: Camouflage, Moved Object and Waving Trees.

Table 4. F-measure results with respect to the equilibrium parameter.

Method	Dataset			
	Camouflage	Moved Object	Waving Trees	Average Measure
SADM w/t equilibrium parameter	71.27	47.17	81.61	66.68
SADM	**85.30**	**81.57**	**87.85**	**84.91**

4 Conclusion

In this paper, a novel RPCA via symmetrical alternating direction method (SADM-RPCA) is proposed to solve the moving object detection problem. The symmetrical theory is adopted to optimize the iterative strategy by updating the multiplier of linear constraint twice every iteration, which reduces the iterations of time-consuming SVD decomposition. A new equilibrium parameter is proposed to guarantees a better convergence, and a new interrupt mechanism is proposed to avoid unnecessary iterations, thus reduces the time consumption of the proposed algorithm. Experimental results demonstrate that the computing time is reduced significantly compared to the traditional ADM method and the detection accuracy is increased to a large extend.

References

1. Zeng, W., Huang, Q.: Moving object segmentation: a block-based moving region detection approach. In: Aizawa, K., Nakamura, Y., Satoh, S. (eds.) PCM 2004. LNCS, vol. 3331, pp. 280–287. Springer, Heidelberg (2004). https://doi.org/10. 1007/978-3-540-30541-5_35
2. Gao, S., Han, Z., Li, C., Jiao, J.: Real-time multi-pedestrian tracking based on vision and depth information fusion. In: Huet, B., Ngo, C.-W., Tang, J., Zhou, Z.-H., Hauptmann, A.G., Yan, S. (eds.) PCM 2013. LNCS, vol. 8294, pp. 708–719. Springer, Cham (2013). https://doi.org/10.1007/978-3-319-03731-8_66
3. Mu, K., Hui, F., Zhao, X.: Multiple vehicle detection and tracking in highway traffic surveillance video based on sift feature matching. J. Inf. Process. Syst. 12(2), 183–195 (2016)
4. Zhang, X., Gao, H., Mu, G., Li, G., Liu, Y., Li, D.: A study on key technologies of unmanned driving. CAAI Trans. Intell. Technol. 1(1), 4–13 (2016)
5. Bouwmans, T., Sobral, A., Javed, S., Jung, S.K., Zahzah, E.-H.: Decomposition into low-rank plus additive matrices for background/foreground separation: a review for a comparative evaluation with a large-scale dataset. Comput. Sci. Rev. 23, 1–71 (2017)
6. Bouwmans, T., Zahzah, E.H.: Robust PCA via principal component pursuit: a review for a comparative evaluation in video surveillance. Comput. Vis. Image Underst. 122, 22–34 (2014)
7. Yuan, W., Liang, X., Chen, H., Na, L., Zou, T.: A NSGA-II with alternating direction method of multipliers mutation for solving multiobjective robust principal component analysis problem. J. Comput. Theor. Nanosci. 13(6), 3722–3733 (2016)
8. Candès, E.J., Li, X., Ma, Y., Wright, J.: Robust principal component analysis? J. ACM (JACM) 58(3), 11 (2011)
9. Wright, J., Ganesh, A., Rao, S., Peng, Y., Ma, Y.: Robust principal component analysis: exact recovery of corrupted low-rank matrices via convex optimization. In: Advances in Neural Information Processing Systems, pp. 2080–2088 (2009)
10. Lin, Z., Ganesh, A., Wright, J., Wu, L., Chen, M., Ma, Y.: Fast convex optimization algorithms for exact recovery of a corrupted low-rank matrix. In: Computational Advances in Multi-Sensor Adaptive Processing (CAMSAP), vol. 61, no. 6 (2009)
11. Lin, Z., Liu, R., Su, Z.: Linearized alternating direction method with adaptive penalty for low-rank representation. In: Advances in Neural Information Processing Systems, pp. 612–620 (2011)
12. Guyon, C., Bouwmans, T., Zahzah, E.-H.: Moving object detection by robust PCA solved via a linearized symmetric alternating direction method. In: Bebis, G., et al. (eds.) ISVC 2012. LNCS, vol. 7431, pp. 427–436. Springer, Heidelberg (2012). https://doi.org/10.1007/978-3-642-33179-4_41
13. Yuan, X., Yang, J.: Sparse and low-rank matrix decomposition via alternating direction methods, p. 12 (2009). Preprint
14. He, H., Zhang, M., Han, D., Chen, Y.: A new alternating direction method for solving separable variational inequality problems. Scientia Sinica Mathematica 42(2), 133–149 (2012)
15. Glowinski, R., Tallec, P.L.: Augmented Lagrangian and operator-splitting methods in nonlinear mechanics. In: SIAM (1989)
16. Rodriguez, P., Wohlberg, B.: Fast principal component pursuit via alternating minimization. In: 2013 20th IEEE International Conference on Image Processing (ICIP), pp. 69–73. IEEE (2013)

17. Zhao, Q., Meng, D., Xu, Z., Zuo, W., Zhang, L.: Robust principal component analysis with complex noise. In: ICML, pp. 55–63 (2014)
18. Hintermüller, M., Tao, W.: Robust principal component pursuit via inexact alternating minimization on matrix manifolds. J. Math. Imaging Vis. 51(3), 361–377 (2015)
19. Toyama, K., Krumm, J., Brumitt, B., Meyers, B.: Wallflower: principles and practice of background maintenance. In: Proceedings of the Seventh IEEE International Conference on Computer Vision, vol. 1, pp. 255–261 (1999)
20. Maddalena, L., Petrosino, A.: A fuzzy spatial coherence-based approach to background/foreground separation for moving object detection. Neural Comput. Appl. 19(2), 179–186 (2010)

Driver Head Analysis Based on Deeply Supervised Transfer Metric Learning with Virtual Data

Keke Liu[1], Yazhou Liu[1(✉)], Quansen Sun[1], Sugiri Pranata[2], and Shengmei Shen[2]

[1] School of Computer Science and Engineering,
Nanjing University of Science and Technology, Nanjing, China
{kekeliu,yazhouliu,sunquansen}@njust.edu.cn
[2] Panasonic R&D Center Singapore, Singapore, Singapore
{sugiri.pranata,shengmei.shen}@sg.panasonic.com

Abstract. Driver head analysis is of paramount interest for the advanced driver assistance systems (ADAS). Recently proposed methods almost rely on training with labeled samples, especially deep learning. However, the labeling process is a subjective and tiresome manual task. Even trickier, our application scene is driver assistance systems, where the training dataset is more difficult to capture. In this paper, we present a rendering pipeline to synthesize virtual-world driver head pose and facial landmark dataset with annotation by computer 3D animation software, in which we consider driver's gender, dress, hairstyle, hats and glasses. This large amounts of virtual-world labeled dataset and a small amount of real-world labeled dataset are trained together firstly by deeply supervised transfer metric learning method. We treat it as a cross-domain task, the labeled virtual data is a source domain and the unlabeled real-world data is a target domain. By exploiting the feature self-learning characteristic of deep networks, we find the common feature subspace between them, and transfer discriminative knowledge from the labeled source domain to the labeled target domain. Finally we employ a small number of real-world dataset to fine-tune the model iteratively. Our experiments show high accuracy on real-world driver head images.

Keywords: Head pose estimation · Facial landmark localization
Virtual-world dataset · Deeply supervised transfer metric learning

1 Introduction

Driver head analysis belongs to the advanced driver assistance systems (ADAS), aiming to provide warnings in dangerous situations to ensure traffic safety, including head pose estimation and facial landmark detection. In the field of computer vision, a head pose is typically interpreted as an egocentric orientation of a person's head, which is represented by three angles: pitch, roll and yaw. And facial landmark is expressed by at least 5 points: eyes, nose tip and mouth corners. The task of head analysis is challenging because of the large head appearance variation (gender and expression) and environmental factors (occlusion and illumination).

© Springer International Publishing AG, part of Springer Nature 2018
B. Zeng et al. (Eds.): PCM 2017, LNCS 10736, pp. 286–295, 2018.
https://doi.org/10.1007/978-3-319-77383-4_28

There are many methods for head pose estimation and facial landmark localization. The approaches of pose estimation are summarized in [1]. Papazov et al. [2] introduced a triangular surface patch (TSP) descriptor to match facial point clouds to a gallery of synthetic faces and to infer their pose. Lee et al. [3] employed a filter bank to map head image patches to a large feature space by compressive sensing. As for the facial landmark localization, Active Shape Model (ASM) [4] and Active Appearance Model (AAM) [5] are popular face alignment methods at present. Li et al. [6] proposed Sparse Representation Shape Models (SRSM) in place of PDM. Yong et al. [7] classified and verified the facial emotion using a fuzzy k-NN classifier. Cao et al. [8] utilized the framework and put forward an efficient and accurate shape explicit regression model. However, these methods often face a problem that the visual features extracted are not discriminative or not reliable enough to predict facial landmark, because of not directly extracting texture context information over the whole face region, since they contain rich information.

Recent years, deep learning method shows good performance in many computer vision tasks [9–11]. Sun et al. [12] proposed a cascaded regression approach for facial landmark localization (5 points) with three-level convolutional networks. Wu et al. [13] proposed a face shape prior model based on Restricted Boltzmann Machines. However, getting a large amount of labeled data for the model training is difficult because the labeling process is a human intensive and subjective task. Moreover, our application scene is driver assistance systems.

Since the development of computer image technology, many researchers employ synthesized data for training. Javier et al. [14] learned a pedestrian classifier using only samples from virtual world and compared real-world based pedestrian detectors. Shotton et al. [15, 16] used a large, realistic, and highly varied synthetic set of training images to learn models. Vazquez et al. [17] designed a domain adaptation framework to train a domain adapted classifier which will operate in the target domain.

In this paper, we present a rendering pipeline to construct a virtual-world driving scene model and generate a large amount of virtual-world driver head pose and facial landmark dataset with annotation. In this dataset, we consider driver's gender, dress, hairstyle, hats and glasses, including 280000 labeled driver head images. Different from most deep learning methods, which aiming to learn feature representations via deep model rather than similarity measure. We employ deeply supervised transfer metric learning method by considering the distribution difference between source domain and target domain in a unified framework. The experiments show our method is excellent and has high accuracy on real-world driver head images. Another contribution of this paper is that our virtual-world driving scene model can also be used to generate driver whole body images for other tasks, such as driver pose estimation.

2   Virtual-World Driver Dataset

In this section, we use a computer 3D animation software named 3DS Max to construct a virtual-world driving scene model and extract large amounts of virtual-world driver head images with annotation for the next training, including head pose and facial landmark (Fig. 1).

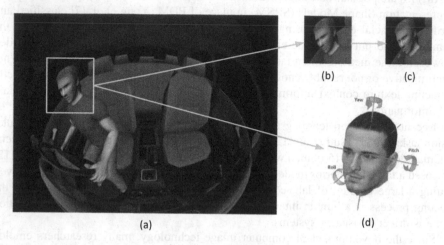

(b)   (c)

(a)   (d)

Fig. 1. Process of synthesizing virtual-world driver dataset. (a) Virtual-world driving scene. (b) Virtual-world driver head image. (c) Facial landmark annotation. (d) Head pose can be described by the egocentric rotation angles of pitch, roll, and yaw.

2.1   Modeling Module

Firstly, we use the modeling module to construct some high quality bone binding character models and car models, and then combine them together to simulate a driving scene (Fig. 1a). For the trained model to work well, the samples must contain good coverage of the environmental factors we hope to recognize at test time. Thus, we add illuminator and reflection effect. Totally, we build 280 models, in which half is male and the rest is female with different dress, hairstyle, wearing different hats and glasses. In order to label the facial landmark, we add spheres to eyes, nose tip, and mouth corners respectively, moving as the head movement. Therefore, the coordinates of these five spheres can represent the facial landmark.

2.2   Animation Module

The head pose can be defined as $\Theta = (\theta_x, \theta_y, \theta_z)$, where θ_x, θ_y and θ_z represent three egocentric rotation angles of pitch, roll and yaw [1] respectively (Fig. 1d). The driver's head is capable of an enormous range of poses which are difficult to simulate. We cannot thus record all possible poses. We use the animation module to construct a random movement of each driver's head in human head motion constraints by 1000 frames. We use the Maxscript to output the Euler angles of head rotation as head pose annotation, and the coordinates of spheres as facial landmark annotation, according to which, we can program to draw the head pose and facial landmark of each head images (Fig. 1c).

2.3 Render Module

A major advantage of using virtual training images is that the ground truth labels can be generated almost for free, allowing one to scale up supervised learning dataset to very large scales. The complete rendering pipeline allows us to rapidly synthesize hundreds of thousands of labeled driver head images.

Before rendering, we place a camera in the rearview mirror towards the interior with fisheye. We utilize V-ray renderer to render the driving scene model automatically, and extract driver head images (Fig. 1b) to synthesize virtual driver head pose and facial landmark dataset, which totally including 280000 driver head images. Additionally, the models can also be used to synthesize driver pose dataset for other tasks, such as pose estimation.

3 Deeply Supervised Transfer Metric Learning Based on Virtual Dataset

It's easy to synthesize hundreds of thousands of virtual data with annotation by computer 3D animation software, but the data characteristic is different from the real-world images captured by cameras. Inspired by [18], we employ a deeply supervised transfer metric learning method to find the common feature subspace between source domain and target domain and transfer discriminative knowledge from the labeled source domain to the unlabeled target domain (Fig. 2). Next we introduce the notation used in this work and the deep supervised transfer metric learning framework.

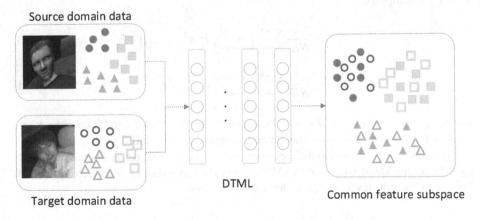

Source domain data

DTML

Common feature subspace

Target domain data

Fig. 2. The basic idea of the deep transfer metric learning.

We consider the virtual-world dataset as the source domain of deep transfer metric learning, including large amounts of labeled virtual driver head images, denoted as $X_s = \{(x_{si}, y_{si})|i = 1, 2, \ldots, N_s\}$, where N_s is the number of training samples, $x_{si} \in R^d$ is a d-dimensional feature vector, $y_{si} \in \{1, 2, \ldots, C_s\}$ is the label of x_{si}, and C_s is the number of classes. The target domain is real-world dataset, consisting of large amounts of unlabeled real-world driver head images and small number of labeled real-world head images. Similarly, we denote the labeled images of target domain as $X_t = \{(x_{ti}, y_{ti})|i = 1, 2, \ldots, N_t\}$, where N_t is the number of training example.

Our networks consist of input layer, several hidden layers and output layer. The number of input feature node in the input layer is the same as the dimension of the output layer, and the output layer is a classifier, usually logistic regression being selected. Each layer of deep networks can be seen as nonlinear mapping process. Let x be the input feature, assume there are M layers, then the output at the mth layer is computed as:

$$f^{(m)}(x) = h^{(m)} = s\left(W^{(m)}h^{(m-1)} + b^{(m)}\right) \tag{1}$$

where $W^{(m)} \in R^{p^{(m)} \times p^{(m-1)}}$ is the weight matrix between the mth layer and $m + 1$th layer, $b^{(m)} \in R^{p^{(m)}}$ is the bias of the parameters, $p^{(m)}$ is the number of node in the mth layer, s is a nonlinear activation function. For the first layer, we assume $h^{(0)} = x$, $P^{(0)} = d$.

In the feature space of hidden layer, the distance metric between each pair of samples x_i and x_j can be measured by computing their squared Euclidean distance:

$$d^{(m)}(x_i, x_j) = \left\|f^{(m)}(x_i) - f^{(m)}(x_j)\right\|_2^2 \tag{2}$$

where $f^{(m)}(x_i)$ and $f^{(m)}(x_j)$ are the output of x_i and x_j in the m th layer respectively. Then Let $S_c^{(m)}$ and $S_b^{(m)}$ be the intra-class compactness and the inter-class separability, which are computed as:

$$S_c^{(m)} = \frac{1}{NK_1} \sum_{i=1}^{N} \sum_{j=1}^{N} P_{ij} d_{f^{(m)}}^2 (x_i, x_j) \tag{3}$$

$$S_b^{(m)} = \frac{1}{NK_2} \sum_{i=1}^{N} \sum_{j=1}^{N} P_{ij} d_{f^{(m)}}^2 (x_i, x_j) \tag{4}$$

where $P_{ij} = 1$ if x_j is one of k_1-intraclass nearest neighbors of x_i, and 0 otherwise; and $Q_{ij} = 1$ if x_j is one of k_2-interclass nearest neighbors of x_i, and 0 otherwise.

To reduce the distribution difference of source domain and target domain, we apply the Maximum Mean Discrepancy (MMD) criterion to measure their distribution difference at the mth layer, which is defined as follows:

$$D_{ts}^{(m)}(\chi_t, \chi_s) = \left\|\frac{1}{N_t} \sum_{i=1}^{N_t} f^{(m)}(x_{ti}) - \frac{1}{N_s} \sum_{i=1}^{N_s} f^{(m)}(x_{si})\right\|_2^2 \tag{5}$$

Then the deep transfer metric learning is formulated as the following optimization problem:

$$\min_{f^{(M)}} J = S_c^{(M)} - \alpha S_b^{(M)} + \beta D_{ts}^{(m)}(\chi_t, \chi_s) + \gamma \sum_{m=1}^{M} (\|W^{(m)}\|_F^2 + \|b^{(m)}\|_2^2) \quad (6)$$

where α is a free parameter which balances the importance between intra-class compactness and interclass separability; $\|Z\|_F$ denotes the Frobenius norm of the matrix Z; $\gamma(\gamma > 0)$ and β are regularization parameters.

To better exploit discriminative information from the output of both the top layer and the hidden layers, we change the formulation (6) to the follow:

$$\min_{f^{(M)}} J = J^{(M)} + \sum_{m=1}^{M-1} \omega^{(m)} h\left(J^{(m)} - \tau^{(m)}\right) \quad (7)$$

where

$$J^{(m)} = S_c^{(m)} - \alpha S_b^{(m)} + \beta D_{ts}^{(m)}(\chi_t, \chi_s) + \gamma(\|W^{(m)}\|_F^2 + \|b^{(m)}\|_2^2) \quad (8)$$

Here $J^{(M)}$ is the loss of the top layer and $J^{(m)}$ is the loss of the m th hidden layer. The hinge loss function $h(x) = \max(x, 0)$ is used to measure the loss; $\tau^{(m)}$ is a positive threshold.

Finally, we employ the gradient descent method to solve the optimization problem in (7).

4   Evaluation

4.1   Experiment and Result

Following the method of Sect. 2, we obtain a virtual driver dataset including 280000 different virtual driver head images with annotation. The annotation contains head pose and facial landmark. In addition, we before have already captured 80000 real-world driver images taken by camera and labeled them manually. In total, our dataset contains a large number of virtual-world driver dataset and a small number of real-world driver dataset.

Figure 3 shows the framework of our driver head analysis process. Firstly, considering 14000 virtual faces and 4000 real-world labeled faces as testing dataset, the rest 266000 virtual faces and 76000 real-world labeled faces as training dataset, we train an initial model by deeply supervised transfer metric learning. Then, we apply the 80000 real-world labeled faces to fine-tune the initial model iteratively until convergence. Finally we use the model to estimate the real-world head pose and locate the facial landmark.

The experimental result is shown in Fig. 4. The left figure is the ROC curves of each head direction (Yaw, Pitch and Roll), and the right is each facial landmark (eyes, nose tip and mouth corners). The horizontal axis is threshold, representing the distance between test result and ground truth, while the vertical axis means the detection rate correspondingly.

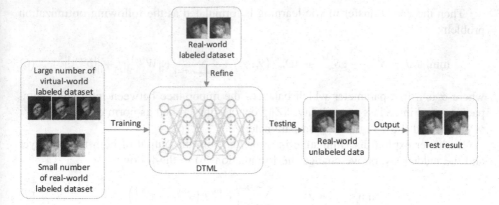

Fig. 3. The framework of our method.

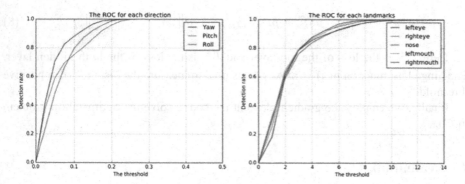

Fig. 4. The ROC curves of our method testing on real-world driver dataset.

4.2 Comparison

To prove the effectiveness of our dataset, we also training only on a small number of real-world driver dataset and evaluate the test result (Fig. 5). The ROC curves of these two training datasets show that our dataset (a large number of virtual-world driver dataset + a small number of real-world driver dataset) greatly improve the accuracy by 6.46% on head pose estimation and 33.24% on facial landmark localization. Figure 6a, b show the test result in real-world driver head images. The red lines and circles are ground truth, representing head direction and facial landmark respectively. The green lines and circles are test result. Figure 6a is the result of training on our dataset, and Fig. 6b is the result of training only on a small number of real-world dataset. We can obviously conclude the former one is better the latter. The main reason is that the number of real-world dataset is too small to extract enough features by the networks. Our large amounts of virtual-world dataset can fill the gap and solve the problem very well.

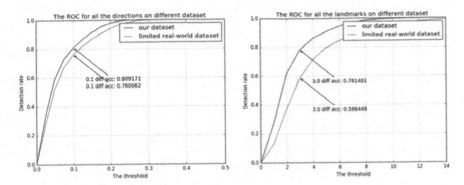

Fig. 5. The ROC curves of different training dataset. (a) Head pose estimation (b) Facial landmark localization.

To prove the effectiveness of our method on facial landmark localization, we also evaluate CFAN [19] and ERT [20] on our real-world driver dataset. The CFAN method cascades multiple deep models (stacked self-coding networks) and regresses facial landmark. And the ERT method employs an ensemble of regression trees to regress the location of facial landmark from a sparse subset of intensity values extracted from an input image. Figure 6c, d are their test results on real-world driver head images, respectively. And Fig. 7 shows the ROC curves of these two methods and our method on our real-world driver dataset. We can observe that our method outperform the other two methods.

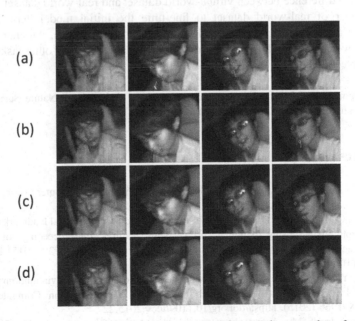

Fig. 6. Test results on real-world driver images. (a) Training on a large number of virtual-world driver dataset and a small number of real-world driver dataset. (b) Training only on a small number of real-world driver dataset. (c) CFAN method. (d) ERT method. (Color figure online)

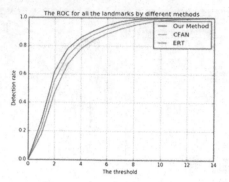

Fig. 7. Comparison of facial landmark localization between CFAN, ERT and our method.

5 Conclusion

In this paper, we propose a method that constructing a virtual-world driving scene model and synthesizing labeled virtual-world driver head dataset by computer 3D animation software. Our virtual-world dataset includes 280000 driver head images, which considers the gender, dress, hairstyle, hats and glasses. We combine this virtual-world dataset and a small number of real-world driver dataset as our training dataset, and employ a deeply supervised transfer metric learning method for real-world driver head analysis including head pose estimation and facial landmark localization. To reduce the difference between virtual-world dataset and real-world dataset, we apply small number of real-world dataset to fine-tune the initial model iteratively. Our evaluation shows high accuracy on real-world driver head images. Another contribution is that we can utilize the virtual-world driving scene model for other tasks, such as driver pose estimation.

Acknowledgments. This work was supported in part by the National Nature Science Foundation of China under Grant no 61672286 and 61673220.

References

1. Murphy-Chutorian, E., Trivedi, M.M.: Head pose estimation in computer vision: A survey. IEEE Trans. Pattern Anal. Mach. Intell. **31**(4), 607–626 (2009)
2. Papazov, C., Marks, T.K., Jones, M.: Real-time 3D head pose and facial landmark estimation from depth images using triangular surface patch features. In: Proceedings of the IEEE Conference on Computer Vision and Pattern Recognition, pp. 4722–4730 (2015). https://doi.org/10.1109/cvpr.2015.7299104
3. Lee, D., Yang, M.H., Oh, S.: Fast and accurate head pose estimation via random projection forests. In: Proceedings of the IEEE International Conference on Computer Vision, pp. 1958–1966 (2015). https://doi.org/10.1109/iccv.2015.227
4. Blake, A., Isard, M.: Active shape models. In: Active Contours, pp. 25–37. Springer, London (1998). https://doi.org/10.1007/978-1-4471-1555-7_2

5. Cootes, T.F., Edwards, G.J., Taylor, C.J.: Active appearance models. IEEE Trans. Pattern Anal. Mach. Intell. **23**(6), 681–685 (2001)
6. Li, Y., Feng, J., Meng, L., Wu, J.: Sparse representation shape models. J. Math. Imaging Vis. **48**(1), 83–91 (2014). https://doi.org/10.1007/s10851-012-0394-3
7. Lee, Y.H., Han, W., Kim, Y., Kim, B.: Facial feature extraction using an active appearance model on the iPhone. In: 2014 Eighth International Conference on IEEE Innovative Mobile and Internet Services in Ubiquitous Computing (IMIS), pp. 196–201 (2014). https://doi.org/10.1109/imis.2014.24
8. Cao, X., Wei, Y., Wen, F., Sun, J.: Face alignment by explicit shape regression. Int. J. Comput. Vis. **107**(2), 177–190 (2014). https://doi.org/10.1007/s11263-013-0667-3
9. Dong, Z., Wu, Y., Pei, M., Jia, Y.: Vehicle type classification using a semisupervised convolutional neural network. IEEE Trans. Intell. Transp. Syst. **16**(4), 2247–2256 (2015)
10. Ouyang, W., Wang, X., Zeng, X., Qiu, S., Luo, P., Tian, Y., Tang, X.: Deepid-net: deformable deep convolutional neural networks for object detection. In: Proceedings of the IEEE Conference on Computer Vision and Pattern Recognition, pp. 2403–2412 (2015). https://doi.org/10.1109/cvpr.2015.7298854
11. Dong, Z., Jia, S., Wu, T., Pei, M.: Face video retrieval via deep learning of binary hash representations. In: AAAI, pp. 3471–3477 (2016)
12. Sun, Y., Wang, X., Tang, X.: Deep convolutional network cascade for facial point detection. In: Proceedings of the IEEE Conference on Computer Vision and Pattern Recognition, pp. 3476–3483 (2013). https://doi.org/10.1109/cvpr.2013.446
13. Wu, Y., Wang, Z., Ji, Q.: Facial feature tracking under varying facial expressions and face poses based on restricted boltzmann machines. In: Proceedings of the IEEE Conference on Computer Vision and Pattern Recognition, pp. 3452–3459 (2013). https://doi.org/10.1109/cvpr.2013.443
14. Marin, J., Vazquez, D., Geronimo, D., Lopez, A.M.: Learning appearance in virtual scenarios for pedestrian detection. In: Computer Vision and Pattern Recognition (2010). https://doi.org/10.1109/cvpr.2010.5540218
15. Shotton, J., Sharp, T., Kipman, A.A., Fitzgibbon, A., Finocchio, M.J., Blake, A., Moore, R.: Real-time human pose recognition in parts from single depth images. Commun. ACM **56**(1), 116–124 (2013). https://doi.org/10.1109/cvpr.2011.5995316
16. Shotton, J., Girshick, R., Fitzgibbon, A., Sharp, T., Cook, M., Finocchio, M.J., Blake, A.: Efficient human pose estimation from single depth images. IEEE Trans. Pattern Anal. Mach. Intell. **35**(12), 2821–2840 (2013). https://doi.org/10.1109/iccv.2013.429
17. Vazquez, D., Lopez, A.M., Marin, J., Ponsa, D., Geronimo, D.: Virtual and real world adaptation for pedestrian detection. IEEE Trans. Pattern Anal. Mach. Intell. **36**(4), 797–809 (2014). https://doi.org/10.1109/tpami.2013.163
18. Hu, J., Lu, J., Tan, Y.P.: Deep transfer metric learning. In: Proceedings of the IEEE Conference on Computer Vision and Pattern Recognition, pp. 325–333 (2015). https://doi.org/10.1109/cvpr.2015.7298629
19. Zhang, J., Shan, S., Kan, M., Chen, X.: Coarse-to-Fine Auto-Encoder Networks (CFAN) for real-time face alignment. In: Fleet, D., Pajdla, T., Schiele, B., Tuytelaars, T. (eds.) ECCV 2014. LNCS, vol. 8690, pp. 1–16. Springer, Cham (2014). https://doi.org/10.1007/978-3-319-10605-2_1
20. Kazemi, V., Sullivan, J.: One millisecond face alignment with an ensemble of regression trees. In: Proceedings of the IEEE Conference on Computer Vision and Pattern Recognition, pp. 1867–1874 (2014). https://doi.org/10.1109/cvpr.2014.241

Joint Dictionary Learning via Split Bregman Iteration for Large-Scale Image Classification

Yanyun Qu$^{(\boxtimes)}$, Hanqian Li, and Yan Zhang

Computer Science Department, Xiamen University, Xiamen, China
yyqu@xmu.edu.cn, saberleo2016@gmail.com,
zy@gznu.edu.cn

Abstract. This paper aims at the hierarchical learning for large-scale image classification. Due to flexibility and capability, sparse representation is widely used in object recognition. The hierarchy is introduced to joint dictionary learning for large scale image classification. Because the joint dictionary learning model is non-quadratic, Split Bregman Iteration is used to solve the shared dictionary and the class-specified dictionary. Moreover, the deep feature generated by Inception-v3 is used for image representation. When a query image is input, two label prediction schemes are investigated: SVM and residual. The proposed approach is implemented on three benchmark datasets: ILSVRC2010, Oxford Flower image set and Caltech 256 and the experimental results demonstrate that our approach is better than the original joint dictionary learning method and achieves excellent accuracy compared with other handcrafted features.

Keywords: Large-scale image classification · Deep features
Joint dictionary learning · Split Bregman Iteration · Hierarchical classification

1 Introduction

Great progresses have been witnessed in image classification in recent years. Not only theoretical research moves forward, but also many achievements have been applied in practical applications such as face recognition, pedestrian identification, and vehicle license plate recognition and so on. Now, due to the widely accessible Internet, the available image data has increased dramatically. Both the number of image classes and the number of images increase greatly. Hence, the large-scale image classification has attracted significant research efforts, especially when the number of classes scales up. One of the key challenges in the large-scale image classification is to achieve efficiency in term of both computation and memory without compromising classification accuracy.

Considerable work has discussed how to exploit the hierarchy to guide the model learning in order to improve the efficiency and accuracy of large scale image classification. These methods usually construct a tree which organized the set of image classes. Among these methods, joint dictionary learning (JDL) [1] is the typical hierarchical dictionary learning method for large-scale image classification. JDL learns the shared dictionaries and the class-specified dictionaries for a two-level tree structure of image classes. For each non-leaf node, JDL explicitly constructs shared visual atoms by using the dictionaries of its member classes. Thus, the shared dictionary is used for image representation of a non-leaf node and the class-specified dictionary is used for image representation of a leaf node. Joint dictionary learning was transformed to an optimal sparse representation problem. The two-stage shrinkage method (TwIST) [14] was used to solve the non-quadratic problem. However, TwIST is not better for the non-quadratic problem in term of the convergence. It has been proved that Split Bregman Iteration (SBI) is superior to TwIST on the non-quadratic optimal problem. In this paper, the SBI is used to solve the optimal problem, which keeps the optimal convergence faster. Moreover, inspired by the success of deep learning, we will use the deep feature extracted from Inception-v3 [9] instead of the hand-crafted feature. Furthermore, we design two schemes of the class label prediction: SVM and residual. The former uses the SVM classifier, and the latter uses residual for classification. We name the proposed method JDL-SBI.

2 Related Work

Current dictionary learning methods can be classified into two types: unsupervised and supervised dictionary learning. Unsupervised dictionary learning is widely used in image restoration and object recognition. Yang et al. [15, 16] used unsupervised dictionary for image super-resolution. Peng et al. [17] used unsupervised dictionary for face recognition. And Zheng et al. [18] implemented unsupervised dictionary learning on person re-identification. The disadvantage of unsupervised dictionary learning is the fact that it lacks sufficient discriminant capability. In order to improve the discrimination of the dictionary, the supervised dictionary learning attracts more and more attentions. Zhang et al. [4] proposed the Fisher discriminative dictionary learning method which improves the performance of object recognition. They also discussed the collaboration dictionary learning and discussed how the dictionary learning scheme influences the performance of multi-class classification. Gu et al. [19] proposed the projective dictionary pairwise learning method (DPL). In this method, a synthesis dictionary and an analysis dictionary are learned jointly, thus it achieves the goal of signal representation and discrimination. DPL method can not only greatly reduce the time complexity but also lead to very competitive accuracies in a variety of visual classification tasks. However, the mentioned methods suffer high computation complexity in both training and testing for large-scale image classification, which makes them less attractive.

In order to avoid the disadvantage of the supervised dictionary learning, the hierarchy is introduced to large-scale image classification. Zhou et al. [1] proposed the joint dictionary learning methods which extend the Fisher discriminative dictionary learning from the flat learning way to the hierarchical learning way. Shen et al. [13] designed a multi-level dictionary learning method which incorporates the discrimination for classification task into dictionary learning and improve the accuracy of image classification. Our method aims at improving JDL by using SBI in terms of convergence and investigating the effect of the deep feature on hierarchical learning model.

3 The Framework of JDL-SBI

The flowchart of our model is shown in Fig. 1. It has four components: deep feature extraction, visual tree construction, sparse representation based on joint dictionary learning and visual tree based multi-class prediction. Firstly, deep feature is extracted by using Inception-v3. Secondly, visual tree is constructed based on spectral clustering [2, 3] in which an affinity matrix records each pairwise inter-class similarity. The image classes with similar visual appearance are grouped and assigned a non-leaf node of a visual tree, and each element class of the group is assigned a child node. After that, joint dictionary learning is made and the shared dictionary is learned for a non-leaf node, and the class-specified dictionary is learned for a leaf node. Finally, the sparse representation is made for the non-leaf node and the leaf node by using their corresponding dictionary respectively. The two-level classifiers are made for each non-leaf node and each leaf node. During testing, deep feature is firstly extracted for a query image based on Inception-v3. Secondly, it is represented by the shared dictionary and classified into a non-leaf node whose SVM confidence value is the maximum or whose residual is the minimum among the prediction values of non-leaf nodes. At last, it is further represented by the leaf dictionary and evaluated by the leaf classifiers. It will be classified into a class whose SVM confidence value is the maximum or whose residual is the minimum among the leaf-node prediction values.

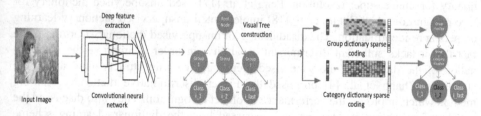

Fig. 1. The flowchart of our integration JDL-SBI hierarchical model. There are four components: deep feature extraction, visual tree construction, joint dictionary learning based hierarchical sparse representation and multi-class prediction. The final result is determined by the non-leaf classifier and the leaf classifier according to the visual tree.

3.1 Joint Dictionary Learning

Assume that there are M visual related categories. Let $X_i \in \mathbb{R}^{d \times N_i}, (i = 1, \ldots, M)$, denote a collection of training samples for ith class, and $D_i \in \mathbb{R}^{d \times v_i}$ is its visual dictionary, where d is the dimension of a training sample, N_i is the number of training samples for the ith group, and v_i is the number of visual atoms in dictionary D_i. For the classes belonging to a non-leaf node, its dictionary is partitioned into two parts: (1) the shared atoms, denoted as $D_0^{(i)} \in R^{d \times v_i^0}$, which are used to describe the common visual properties for the image classes contained in the same group; (2) the class-specified atoms contain $v_i - v_i^0$ visual words, denoted as $\widehat{D}^i \in R^{d \times (v_i - v_i^0)}$, which describes the distinctive visual properties of the ith category. For the purpose of simplicity, the joint dictionary learning problem can be formulated as an optimal problem neglecting the group index,

$$\min_{\{D_0, \hat{D}_i, A_i\}_{i=1}^M} \sum_{i=1}^M \left\{ \left\| X_i - \begin{bmatrix} D_0, \hat{D}_i \end{bmatrix} A_i \right\|_F^2 + \lambda \|A_i\|_1 \right\} + \eta(tr(S_w) - tr(S_B)) \quad (1)$$

where $A_i = [\alpha_{i1}, \ldots, \alpha_{iN_i}] \in \mathbb{R}^{v_i \times N_i}$ is the sparse coefficient matrix of X_i over the ith visual dictionary D_i, and λ is a scalar parameter which relates to the sparsity of the coefficient matrices to promote the discrimination of the dictionaries. And $\eta \geq 0$ is a parameter which controls the trade-off between reconstruction and discrimination, and $tr(.)$ is the matrix trace operator.

The discrimination promotion term is introduced according to Fisher linear discrimination analysis [5]. Discriminative coefficients can be obtained by minimizing the within-class scatter and maximizing the inter-class scatter at the same time. And the within-class scatter matrix and the inter-class scatter matrix are formulated as (2) and (3):

$$S_w = \sum_{j=1}^M \sum_{a_i \in A_j} (a_i - \mu_j)(a_i - \mu_j)^T \quad (2)$$

$$S_B = \sum_{j=1}^M N_j \left(\mu_j^0 - \mu^0 \right) \left(\mu_j^0 - \mu^0 \right)^T \quad (3)$$

where μ_j is the mean column vector of matrix A_j, a_i is a column vector in A_j, and T denotes the matrix transposition. Considering the structure of the dictionaries for a group of visually correlated classes, the sparse coefficient matrix A_j for the jth class is concatenated by two sub-matrices A_j^0 and $\hat{A}_j$ in the form of $[A_j^0; \hat{A}_j]$, where A_j^0 is the sparse representation matrix over the common dictionary D_0, and $\hat{A}_j$ is the sparse representation matrix over the class-specific visual dictionary $\hat{D}_j$, μ_j and μ^0 are the mean of the jth image class and μ^0 is the mean of all the image classes contained in a group, which is detailed as JDL [1].

3.2 Split Bregman Iteration for JDL

The optimal problem Eq. (1) is non-quadratic, so it is solved by two sub-procedures: (1) computing the sparse coefficients by fixing the dictionaries, and (2) updating the dictionaries by fixing the sparse coefficients. In procedure (1), we update A_i by fixing A_j, $j \neq i$, and the objective function is given as:

$$F(A_i) = \left\| X_i - \begin{bmatrix} D_0, \hat{D}_i \end{bmatrix} A_i \right\|_F^2 + \lambda \|A_i\|_1 + \|A_i - M_i\|_F^2 - \sum_{i=1}^M \left\| M_j^0 - M_{(j)}^0 \right\|_F^2 \quad (4)$$

where M_i consists of N_i copies of the mean vector u_i as its columns. And the matrices M_j^0 and $M_{(j)}^0$ are produced by stacking N_j copies of u_j^0 and u^0 as their column vectors, respectively. TwIST [14] was used to solve Eq. (4) in the original JD method. However, TwIST is not better for non-quadratic problem.

Algorithm 1 Split Bregman Iteration (SBI)
1. Set k=0, initiate $\lambda > 0$, $u^{(0)} = 0, d^{(0)} = 0, b^{(0)} = 0$,
2. Repeat
3. $u^{k+1} = \arg\min_{u} H(u) + \dfrac{\lambda}{2}\left\| d^k - J(u) - b^k \right\|_2^2$;
4. $d^{k+1} = \arg\min_{d} \mid d \mid + \dfrac{\lambda}{2}\left\| d - J(u^{k+1}) - b^k \right\|^2$;
5. $b^{k+1} = b^k + (J(u^{k+1}) - d^{k+1})$;
6. $k \leftarrow k+1$;
7. Until stopping rule is satisfied

SBI [20] is a typical method for a class of l_1 norm related minimization problems. And it has been proved that SBI can converge fast when it is used in the l_1 optimization problem. For a general optimal problem:

$$\min |d| + H(u) \quad s.t. \quad d = J(u) \tag{5}$$

SBI works as Algorithm 1. Let's go back to Eq. (4) and point out how to utilize SBI to solve it. According to SBI, Line 3 in Algorithm 1 becomes

$$A_i^{k+1} = argmin \| X_i - DA_i \|_F^2 + \eta \psi_i(X_i) + \frac{\lambda}{2} \left\| d^{(k)} - A_i - b^{(k)} \right\|_F^2 \tag{6}$$

where $\psi_i(X_i) = \| A_i - M_i \|_F^2 - \sum_{i=1}^{M} \left\| M_j^0 - M_{(j)}^0 \right\|_F^2$. And the solution of Eq. (6) can be solve through Lyapunov equation. To solve the optimal problem in Line 4 in Algorithm 1 which is coupled with the l_1 portion of the minimization problem, shrinkage operators are used to compute the optimal value of d. Thus, the solution of Eq. (4) corresponding to Line 4 is as follow:

$$d_j^{k+1} = shrink\left(A_i + b_j^k, \frac{1}{\lambda}\right) \tag{7}$$

where $shrink(x, \gamma) = \frac{x}{|x|} \cdot \max(|x| - \gamma, 0)$.

The JDL-SBI algorithm is summarized in Algorithm 2.

Algorithm 2 JDL-SBI algorithm
1. repeat {Jointly updating $\{\widehat{D}_i\}_{i=1}^C$, D_0 and A_i.}
2. For each class i in the group with C classes, update A_i by optimizing (4) using Split Bregman Iteration.
3. For each class i in the group with C classes, update $\widehat{D}_i$ by solving the Lagrange dual forms in [1].
4. Update D_0 by solving the Lagrange dual forms in [1].
5. Until convergence.

4 The Classification Scheme

We design a hierarchical classification scheme for a query image, which makes label prediction from coarse to fine. In the hierarchical classification scheme, we take two strategies to classify a query image: (1) the SVM classifier is used for a label prediction and (2) residual are used for a label prediction. For the convenience of explanation, we define the root node as the zero level, the non-leaf nodes as the first level, and the leaf nodes as the second level. In the zero level, we construct a new dictionary by concatenating all the shared dictionaries for the non-leaf nodes, as shown in Fig. 2, the new dictionary is denoted by $D^0 = \left[D_0^1, D_0^2, \ldots, D_0^T\right]$. In order to train a classifier for a non-leaf node, we firstly represent a training image based on the dictionary D^0. After we obtain all the feature vector for the training samples, we train a classifier for each non-leaf node and train a leaf classifier for each leaf node, which is detailed in JDL [1].

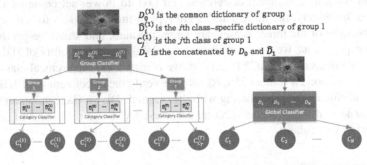

Hierarchical classification scheme   Flat classification scheme

Fig. 2. Illustration of the two-layer hierarchical classification scheme and flat classification scheme.

For the residual classification scheme, we use a global classifier for label prediction. In this scheme, a sparse code is got by solving the optimal problem,

$$\dot{\alpha} = argmin_\alpha \left\{ \|x - D\alpha\|_2^2 + \gamma \|\alpha\|_1 \right\} \tag{8}$$

where γ is a constant. Denote $D = [D_1, D_2, \ldots, D_n]$, and its corresponding sparse code by $\alpha = [\alpha_1, \alpha_2, \ldots, \alpha_n]$, where α_i is the coefficient vector associated with sub-dictionary D_i. The residual for classification is defined as:

$$e_i = \|y - D_i \dot{\alpha}_i\|_2^2 + \omega \cdot \|\dot{\alpha} - m_i\|_2^2 \tag{9}$$

where the first term is the reconstruction error, and the second term is the distance between the sparse coefficient α and the learned mean vector of the ith class m_i, and ω is the preseted weight. During the application of the global classifier, in the zero level of the visual tree, the dictionary in Eq. (8) should be the new constructed dictionary, that is $D^0 = [D_0^1, D_0^2, \ldots, D_0^T]$, and the corresponding sparse coding coefficients is denoted by $\alpha^{(0)} = \left[\alpha_1^{(0)}, \alpha_2^{(0)}, \ldots, \alpha_T^{(0)}\right]$, where $\alpha_i^{(0)}$ is the sparse coding coefficient corresponding to the dictionary D_0^i. In the first level, the dictionary in Eq. (8) should be changed to the concatenation of class-specified dictionaries belong to the ith non-leaf node, that is $[\widehat{D}_1^{(i)}, \widehat{D}_2^{(i)}, \ldots, \widehat{D}_{C_i}^{(i)}]$. In both levels of classification, the query image is classified into a node whose residual is the minimum.

5 Experimental Results

In this section, we evaluate our approach on three datasets: ILSVRC2010 [8], Caltech-256 [6] and Oxford flower set [7]. ILSVRC2010 contains 1000 categories, and Caltech256 contains 256 object categories, and Oxford flower set contains 17 flower fine classes. Intuitively, the three datasets are typical image datasets for our approach, because the sizes of the three datasets are large, medium, and small, respectively.

In our experiments, we firstly validate the scalability and flexibility of JDL-SBI on the large-scale dataset ILSVRC2010. Then, we compare the hierarchical classification and flat classification on Caltech256. At last, we verify the effectiveness of JDL-SBI in accuracy and efficiency by comparing with the original JDL on Caltech256 and discuss the effectiveness of the two classification schemes: SVM and residual on Caltech256 and Oxford flower dataset.

5.1 Experiment Setup

- **Feature extraction:** The deep features are extracted for all training images by using Inception-v3 [9, 10]. And an image can be represented by a vector of 2048 dimensions.
- **Visual tree construction:** We first calculate the similarity matrix between each pair of image categories according to the method of Sect. 3.1. And then, the spectral

clustering method is used to construct a two-layer visual tree. For the ILSVRC2010 dataset, there are 32 non-leaf nodes, For the Caltech-256 dataset, there are 16 non-leaf nodes. We don't construct visual tree for the Oxford flower image set because of the dataset is too small, we only use flat classification for the label prediction.

- **Classifiers:** We use two classification schemes: SVM classifier and residual classifier. The LIBLINEAR software [21] is employed to train the basic linear SVM classifiers. For each basic SVM classifier, we use the same penalty parameter and the same kernel parameter.

5.2   Evaluation on ILSVRC2010

The ILSVRC2010 dataset contains 1.4M images of 1,000 categories. The standard training/validation/testing split is used (1.2M, 50K and 150K images respectively). First, we compare JDL-SBI and JDL [1] in terms of classification accuracy, the result has been showed in Table 1. In the first row of Table 1, there are two numbers, the first number is the number of shared atoms and the second number is the number of the original class atoms. It demonstrates that JDL-SBI is superior to JDL for each setting of dictionary size and the performance gain is from 1% to 3% with the increase of the number of atoms of shared dictionary and the number of the class-specified dictionary. And when each shared dictionary has 5 atoms in the dictionary of each class with 16 atoms, JDL-SBI achieves the highest classification accuracy.

Table 1. JDL-SBI and JDL are compared on ILSVRC2010

Dictionary size	3/8	3/16	5/16
JDL + Inception-v3	59.4%	59.8%	61.3%
JDL-SBI + Inception-v3	59.7%	60.4%	63.4%

Further, we compare JDL-SBI with several state-of-the-art methods on this dataset: JDL with SIFT feature (JDL + SIFT), JDL with CNN feature (JDL + CNN), sparse coding with HOG and LBP [11] (HOG + LBP + CODING), Fisher vector [12]. Table 2 gives the comparison results. It demonstrates that JDL-SBI with Inception-v3 feature achieves the significant improvement compared to other hand-crafted features and Inception-v3 feature is more discriminative than the CNN feature.

Table 2. Comparision with the state-of-the-art methods on the ILSVRC2010.

Method	Accuracy
JDL + SIFT [1]	38.9%
JDL + Inception-v3	61.3%
HOG + LBP + CODING [11]	52.9%
Fisher Vector [12]	45.7%
JDL-SBI + Inception-v3 (our method)	**63.4%**

5.3   Evaluation on Caltech-256

Caltech-256 contains 30607 images with 256 categories. We manually split training/ testing set to be 3:1. In this experiment, we discuss the two components of the hierarchical learning: the hierarchical structure and the label prediction scheme. We consider the combination of the two components, and we get four different configurations: (1) hierarchical structure + SVM classifier, (2) hierarchical structure + residual classifier, (3) flat structure + SVM classifier, (4) flat structure + residual classifier. Table 3 shows the comparison of the four schemes in terms of classification accuracy. We can see that the flat structure is a little better than the hierarchical structure, but the model of the flat structure is much more time consuming than the hierarchical structure, and the training time is much more. For the label prediction scheme, the SVM scheme is better than the residual scheme.

Table 3. Classification accuracy on three dataset for four different configurations. The dictionary size used in this experiment are set to 5/16 in which each category dictionary has 16 words and there are five shared words and 11 class-specified atoms.

Configuration	Caltech-256	Oxford flower	ILSVRC2010
The number of groups	16	1	32
Flat + SVM	68.87%	82.31%	–
Flat + Residual	67.33%	81.32%	–
Hierarchical + SVM	69.47%	–	63.4%
Hierarchical + Residual	68.32%	–	–

5.4   Evaluation on Oxford Flower Image Set

The Oxford flower benchmark contains 1,360 flower images of 17 classes, and each category has 80 images. Three predefined training, testing and validation splits provided by the authors are used in our experiments. Since the 17 flower classes have strong visual correlation, we use the proposed JDL-SBI algorithm to learn discriminative dictionaries by treating them as a single group. On this dataset, we compare effects of the different classifiers on the results with flat structure, and the result can be seen in Table 3. From the table, we can conclude that the residual classifier on the small data set is better than the SVM classifier.

6   Conclusions

In this paper, we design a novel fast algorithm JDL-SBI for JDL model in which SBI are used to solve the non-quadratic problem and apply it to large-scale image classification. Besides, both SVM classifier and residual classifier are investigated for large-scale classification. Experiments show that SBI can improve the effectiveness of the joint dictionary learning algorithm. And it also proves that the combination of deep features and joint dictionary learning algorithms can improve significantly the classification accuracy.

Acknowledgements. This work was supported by the National Natural Science Foundation of China under Grant 61373077.

References

1. Zhou, N., Fan, J.: Jointly learning visually correlated dictionaries for large-scale visual recognition applications. IEEE Trans. Pattern Anal. Mach. Intell. **36**(4), 715–730 (2014)
2. Ng, A.Y., Jordan, M.I., Weiss, Y.: On spectral clustering: analysis and an algorithm. In: Advances in Neural Information Processing Systems, vol. 14, no. 2 (2001)
3. Zelnik-Manor, L., Perona, P.: Self-tuning spectral clustering. In: Advances in Neural Information Processing Systems, vol. 17, pp. 1601–1608 (2004)
4. Yang, M., Zhang, L., Feng, X., Zhang, D.: Sparse representation based Fisher discrimination dictionary learning for image classification. Int. J. Comput. Vis. **109**(3), 209–232 (2014)
5. Duda, R.O., Hart, P.E., Stork, D.G.: Pattern Classification. Wiley, New York (2012)
6. Griffin, G., Holub, A., Perona, P.: Caltech-256 object category dataset (2007)
7. http://www.robots.ox.ac.uk/ ~ vgg/data/flowers/
8. Russakovsky, O., Fei-Fei, L.: Attribute learning in large-scale datasets. In: Kutulakos, K.N. (ed.) ECCV 2010. LNCS, vol. 6553, pp. 1–14. Springer, Heidelberg (2012). https://doi.org/10.1007/978-3-642-35749-7_1
9. Szegedy, C., Vanhoucke, V., Ioffe, S., Shlens, J.: Rethinking the inception architecture for computer vision. In: Proceedings of the IEEE Conference on Computer Vision and Pattern Recognition (2016)
10. http://caffe.berkeleyvision.org/
11. Lin, Y., Lv, F., Zhu, S., Yang, M., Cour, T., Yu, K., Cao, L., Huang, T.: Large-scale image classification: fast feature extraction and SVM training. In: IEEE Conference on Computer Vision and Pattern Recognition (CVPR). IEEE (2011)
12. Akata, Z., Perronnin, F., Harchaoui, Z., Schmid, C.: Towards good practice in large-scale learning for image classification. In: Proceedings of the IEEE Conference on Computer Vision and Pattern Recognition, pp. 3482–3489, June 2012
13. Shen, L., Wang, S., Sun, G., Jiang, S., Huang, Q.: Multi-level discriminative dictionary learning with application to large scale image classification. IEEE Trans. Image Process. **24** (10), 3109–3123 (2015)
14. Bioucas-Dias, J.M., Figueiredo, M.A.T.: A new twist: two-step iterative shrinkage/thresholding algorithms for image restoration. IEEE Trans. Image Process. **16**(12), 2992–3004 (2007)
15. Yang, J., Wang, Z., Lin, Z., Cohen, S., Huang, T.: Coupled dictionary training for image super-resolution. IEEE Trans. Image Process. **21**(8), 3467–3478 (2012)
16. Yang, J., Wright, J., Huang, T.S., Ma, Y.: Image super-resolution via sparse representation. IEEE Trans. Image Process. **19**(11), 2861–2873 (2010)
17. Peng, C., Gao, X., Wang, N., Li, J.: Sparse graphical representation based discriminant analysis for heterogeneous face recognition. arXiv preprint arXiv:1607.00137 (2016)
18. Zheng, W., Gong, S., Xiang, T.: Towards open-world person re-identification by one-shot group-based verification. IEEE Trans. Pattern Anal. Mach. Intell. **38**(3), 591–606 (2016)
19. Gu, S., Zhang, L., Zuo, W., Feng, X.: Projective dictionary pair learning for pattern classification. In: Advances in Neural Information Processing Systems (2014)
20. Tom, G., Osher, S.: The split Bregman method for L1-regularized problems. SIAM J. Imaging Sci. **2**(2), 323–343 (2009)
21. http://www.csie.ntu.edu.tw/ ~ cjlin/liblinear/

Multi-operator Image Retargeting with Preserving Aspect Ratio of Important Contents

Qian Zhang[1], Zhenhua Tang[1,2(✉)], Hongbo Jiang[3], and Kan Chang[1,2]

[1] School of Computer and Electronic Information, Guangxi University, Nanning, China
tangedward@126.com
[2] Guangxi Key Laboratory of Multimedia Communications and Network Technology,
Guangxi University, Nanning, China
[3] School of Electronic Information and Communications, Huazhong University of Science
and Technology, Wuhan, China

Abstract. Content-aware image retargeting can preserve the quality of visually important objects during image resizing. However, some previous approaches fail to provide desired results as the sizes of the important objects in original images are larger than the target resolution of resized images. In this paper, we propose a novel multi-operator image retargeting scheme, which combines seam carving (SC) methods with uniform scaling techniques. To guarantee the quality of visually important objects, we stretch original images in both vertical and horizontal directions and then perform similarity transformation by using the indirect SC and uniform scaling methods. Besides, the direct SC method with gradient vector flow (GVF) is also employed to shrink the image finally. Experiments demonstrated that the proposed scheme could produce more desirable resized images than the existing methods.

Keywords: Image retargeting · Multi-operator · Saliency detection
Seam carving · Gradient vector flow

1 Introduction

In recent years, content-aware image retargeting has gained extensively research attentions. The goal of content-aware image retargeting is to change the resolution or aspect ratio of images adaptively while guaranteeing the quality of visually important objects in images. This technique is helpful to solve the compatibility issue of various display devices.

The existing image resizing methods can be roughly classified into five types: uniform scaling, cropping, warping [1], seam carving (SC) [2] and its improved

This work was supported in part by the National Natural Science Foundation of China (Nos. 61461006, 61401108) and the Guangxi Natural Science Foundation Project (No. 2016GXNSFAA380216).

© Springer International Publishing AG, part of Springer Nature 2018
B. Zeng et al. (Eds.): PCM 2017, LNCS 10736, pp. 306–315, 2018.
https://doi.org/10.1007/978-3-319-77383-4_30

algorithms [3–5], and multi-operator approaches [6, 7]. Due to the simplicity, uniform scaling and cropping are commonly used to solve the problem of image resizing. The uniform scaling approach is to resize the whole image equably according to the target resolution, while the visually unimportant contents in images are discarded by usage of the cropping method. Later, an algorithm named as warping [1] that divides input images into several stripes and then squeezes these stripes with different weights was developed. Recently, the SC technique [2] was proposed to perform retargeting by deleting or adding that consist of pixels according to their energy values. After that, improved algorithms for SC [3, 4, 8, 9] were presented, which mainly focus on creating new energy functions or rules to determine the seams. More recently, multi-operator methods [6, 7] that combine multiple approaches, e.g. SC and cropping, have been developed.

However, these methods fail to provide desired results for all the cases, especially for the case that the sizes of the visually important objects in original images are larger than the target resolution of resized images. We illustrate an example of reducing the width of an original image to the half, shown in Fig. 1. It can be seen that some parts of important objects are cut, e.g. in Fig. 1(b), (e), and (h). Furthermore, distortions or deformation are introduced even though visually important objects are preserved demonstrated in Fig. 1(c), (d), (f), and (g). This implies that these content-aware resizing approaches cannot guarantee the quality of the important object as the size of it is larger than the target resolution of a retargeted image. In contrast, our scheme can obtain a better result than the above-mentioned methods, illustrated in Fig. 1(i).

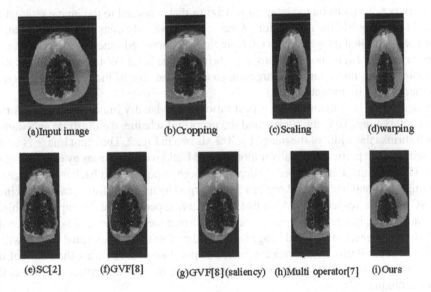

(a)Input image   (b)Cropping   (c)Scaling   (d)warping

(e)SC[2]   (f)GVF[8]   (g)GVF[8](saliency)   (h)Multi operator[7]   (i)Ours

Fig. 1. Comparison of different resizing methods.

In this paper, we propose a novel multi-operator image retargeting scheme, which aims at maintaining the aspect ratio of visually important objects during retargeting. To preserve the quality of visually important objects in original images, we firstly conduct saliency detection to distinguish the visually important and unimportant portions from an original image. Then the image is stretched by using uniform scaling and indirect SC methods. And the similarity transform for the enlarged image is performed while maintaining the aspect ratio of important contents. Finally, the improved SC method based on gradient vector flow (GVF) is applied to shrink the image slightly according to the target image size.

Our main contributions are as follows. First, to guarantee the quality of the visual important contents, we present the scheme that wholly preserve the proportion of visually important objects instead of only changing the width or height of the image. To that end, we stretch the background and important portions by using the indirect SC uniform scaling approaches, respectively. Second, we utilize the improved SC method based on GVF to avoid the case that the deleted seams cross the visually important objects during image retargeting. Third, we determine the number of added or cut seams according to the sizes of visually important regions and target resized image instead of using the bi-directional warping (BDW) technique like [6, 7] which may occupy much computational time.

The remainder of the paper is as follows. Section 2 introduces the proposed multi-operator image retargeting scheme. Section 3 demonstrates the experimental results compared with other state-of-the-art methods, and Sect. 4 concludes this paper.

2   Proposed Scheme

In this paper, we focus on the image downsizing that is crucial to the image retargeting [10, 11]. To simplify the description of the scheme, we only consider the case that the width of an original image is reduced. Note that the proposed scheme can be applied to other cases with slight modifications, e.g. shrinking the height of images. Additionally, we mainly concentrate on the retargeting case that the size of the retargeted image is less than that of important objects.

Our scheme is to maintain the aspect ratio of the visually important objects during image retargeting. To better understand the proposed scheme, we illustrate an example which shrinks the width of the image by 30% shown in Fig. 2. The input image is firstly divided into two parts: the visually important and background portions by using saliency map. Then the image is stretched vertically for both important and background regions. The important and background regions are enlarged by using uniform scaling and indirect SC methods, respectively. After that, to preserve aspect ratio of the important object, the width of the image is enlarged accordingly. Since the ultimate goal is to reduce the width of the image, the enlarged image is rescaled uniformly to the original height, which is termed as similarity transformation in this paper. Finally, we shrink the width of the scaled image to the target size by employing the improved SC algorithm which uses the GVF technique [12].

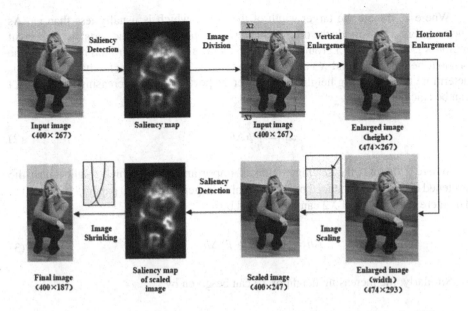

Fig. 2. The general procedure framework to shrink the width of an image by 30%.

2.1 Saliency Map Generation

To distinguish the important and background regions, we deal with saliency detection by using the method presented in [13], which is able to detect important objects and the corresponding scenes. This saliency detection approach applied in our scheme is to protect the image integrity during retargeting.

2.2 Enlargement

As shown in Fig. 1, when the widths of the important region in original images are larger than the target resolution of resized image, cropping the image directly would introduce distortion for the reason that the aspect ratio of important region in original images is changed. Hence, to preserve the aspect ratio of the important region, we should enlarge the height and width of the input image properly correctly at first.

2.2.1 Vertical Enlargement

Let h and w be the height and width of the input image, respectively. The height and width of the important area are represented as h_1 and w_1, respectively. Let Δh denote the vertical increment of the image, and it can be computed by

$$\Delta h = h \times \left(\frac{w_1}{w_f} - 1 \right). \tag{1}$$

Where w_f denote the target width of the image, which is usually less than w_1. As shown in Fig. 2, we divide the original image horizontally into three parts: the important region $X1$, the upper background region $X2$, and the lower background region $X3$. The original height of $X2$ and $X3$ are represented as h_2 and h_3, respectively. Next, Let us determine the increasing height of the different portions. The increasing height of $X1$ can be calculated as:

$$\Delta h_1 = \frac{h_1}{h}\beta\Delta h. \tag{2}$$

Where β denotes the scaling weight of important region which might adjust the stretched distortion introduced by the vertical enlargement. In this paper, β is set as 0.5. The increasing height of $X2$ can be obtained by

$$\Delta h_2 = \frac{h_2}{h_2 + h_3}(1 - \beta)\Delta h. \tag{3}$$

Similarly, the increasing height of $X3$ can be given by

$$\Delta h_3 = \frac{h_3}{h_2 + h_3}(1 - \beta)\Delta h. \tag{4}$$

To guarantee the quality of important objects during enlargement, we adopt different methods to stretch the important and background regions. We stretch the background area by employing indirect SC method, which increases the size of the image by adding the seams with minimum energy. Besides, we use uniform scaling to enlarge the important regions to preserve the quality of this part.

2.2.2   Horizontal Enlargement
To keep the aspect ratio of important objects, we need to perform horizontal enlargement. And the scaling factor of horizontal stretching for the important regions should be in accordance with following the vertical enlargement. We also apply the uniform scaling to conduct horizontal enlargement. Note that the horizontal stretch of the background region is consistent with that of the important region by using the uniform scaling method. The horizontal increasing size of the important region can be expressed by

$$\Delta w_1 = \frac{\Delta h}{h}\beta w. \tag{5}$$

2.3   Similarity Transformation

Since the final purpose is to reduce the width of the images, we need to return the height of the stretched image to the original size. Consequently, we will rescale the enlarged image uniformly to the original height by using the bilinear interpolation method.

Because the aspect ratio of important regions remains unchanged, this step is termed as similarity transformation in this paper.

2.4 Improved SC with GVF

Finally, we employ the improved SC scheme with GVF proposed by [8] to shrink the width of images slightly according to the target size. We show the flow chart of the improved SC scheme with GVF in Fig. 3. The improved SC scheme with GVF is different from the traditional SC algorithm of [2] in two ways. On the one hand, the seams are produced by the direction of the GVF in [8] instead of the energy of pixels. On the other hand, the value of saliency map is viewed as energy for each pixel instead of the gradient. These may be beneficial for protecting the salient regions in our scheme.

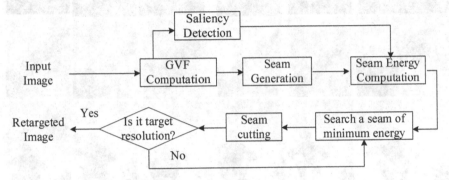

Fig. 3. Image resizing based on improved SC with GVF.

3 Experimental Results

To evaluate the performance of the proposed scheme, we compare it with the following algorithms: SC [2], the improved SC method based on GVF [8] (with and without saliency), multi-operator approach [7]. The testing images are all from the dataset used in [8, 14], which contains 1000 images with various scenes and contents. All the experiments were implemented on a PC with Intel Core2 2.8 GHz CPU and 4 GB of memory. And the experiments were conducted with MATLAB 2012b.

The widths of the images have been reduced to 70% by using different methods, shown in Fig. 4. It can be seen that our scheme can produce resized images with less distortion compared with other approaches, especially for the important objects; while the results with other methods include distortions or deformations, which have been drawn with red rectangular boxes. As demonstrated in Fig. 4(b), some parts of the jumping man, pen and snowman are missed or deformed when using the SC algorithm [2], even missing of the women's face. The reason is that the cutting seams pass through the important objects due to lack of effective protection. Similarly, distortions appear in the results of multi-operator method [7] shown in Fig. 4(c) for the reason that the bi-directional warping (BDW) might fail as the important object occupies large portions of the image. We also show the resized images of the improved SC method with GVF

312   Q. Zhang et al.

in Fig. 4(d) and (e). Since the GVF may enter the important object, the cutting seams will pass through the important objects, which might introduce serious deformation. In contrast, our scheme can obtain better-resized images by remaining the aspect ratio of important objects during retargeting.

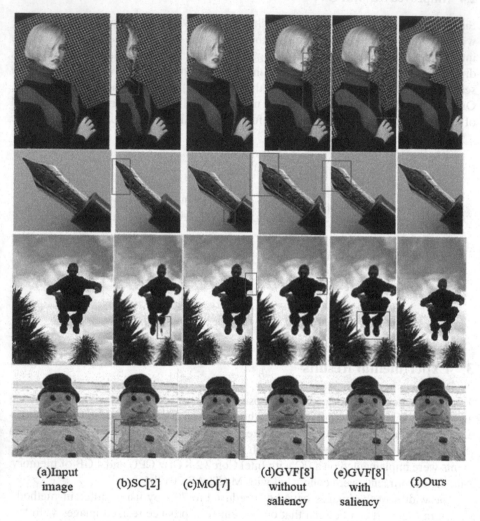

(a)Input image   (b)SC[2]   (c)MO[7]   (d)GVF[8] without saliency   (e)GVF[8] with saliency   (f)Ours

Fig. 4. Results of reducing the width of images by 30%. (Color figure online)

We illustrate the results of reducing the widths of the images by half in Fig. 5. It can be seen that there are a different degree of distortions in important objects by using other methods. In contrast, since our scheme can protect the integrity of the important objects efficiently, the results have a better subjective quality despite a slight stretch in the background area. This also reveals that our scheme is more superior to other methods when the scaling factor of downsizing changes from 70% to 50%.

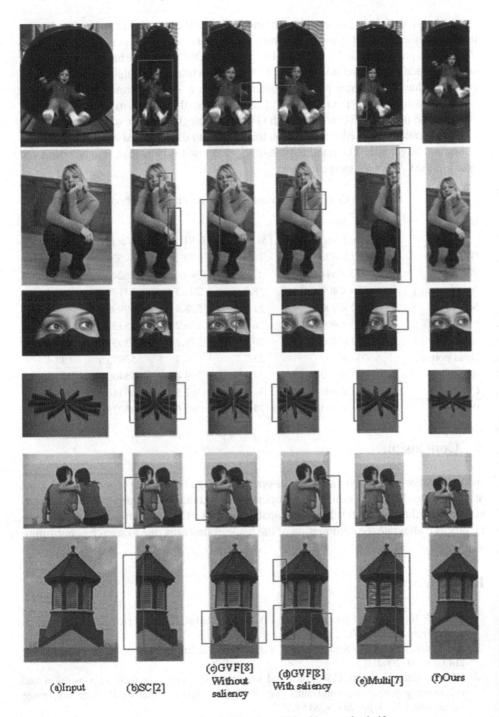

(a)Input   (b)SC[2]   (c)GVF[8] Without saliency   (d)GVF[8] With saliency   (e)Multi[7]   (f)Ours

Fig. 5. Results of reducing the width of images by half.

As shown in Table 1, we compare the computational costs of different methods. The multi-operator method [7] consumes the most time because of repeating computation of the BDW procedure, as the computation of once BDW procedure has high complexity and cost much time because we use the MATLAB; while the SC algorithm [2] cost the least time due to its simple process of seam searching. And the time occupied by our scheme is a little more than the SC [2], but far less than other methods. Note that, although the improved SC scheme with GVF [8] is applied in our scheme, only a few of seams would be deleted for the reason that the width of the scaled image is very close to the final target size. The running time of the proposed scheme can also be optimized by using the C/C++ language further.

Table 1. Comparison of running time for different methods.

Images	Time(s)				
	Image resolution	SC [2]	GVF [8]	Multi [7]	Ours
Busto	267 × 400	16.0	170.7	59523.2	108.0
Pen	400 × 344	27.7	346.6	36243.8	247.3
Jumping man	300 × 400	18.3	205.3	54189.2	102.7
Snowman	400 × 400	31.7	528.4	109998.4	259.7
Little girl	300 × 400	26.4	336.2	165129.1	102.5
Squat women	267 × 400	20.7	278.7	143952.3	152.3
Head portrait	400 × 300	33.2	246.4	53993.1	188.4
Red rods	400 × 300	34.8	359.4	65400.8	204.5
Couple	400 × 300	34.5	367.5	40414.3	206.9
Pagodas	300 × 400	27.2	288.6	95028.3	182.1

4 Conclusion

In this paper, we proposed a novel multi-operator image retargeting scheme, which aims at preserving the aspect ratio of the important objects during retargeting. We demonstrated that the proposed scheme is capable of protecting the important objects efficiently. To alleviate the deformation of the background area due to stretch is our future work.

References

1. Wang, Y.S., Tai, C.L., Sorking, O., Lee, T.Y.: Optimized scale-and-stretch for image resizing. ACM Trans. Graph. **27**(5), 118 (2008)
2. Avidan, S., Shamir, A.: Seam carving for content-aware image resizing. ACM Trans. Graph. **26**(3), 1–10 (2007)
3. Wu, L., Cao, L., Chen, C.W.: Fast and improved seam carving with strip partition and neighboring probability constraints. In: 2013 20th International Conference on Image Processing (ICIP), pp. 2812–2815 (2013)

4. Shafieyan, F., Karimi, N., Mirmahboub, B., Samavi, S., Shirani, S.: Image seam carving using depth assisted saliency map. In: 2014 21st International Conference on Image Processing (ICIP), pp. 1155–1159 (2014)

5. Mishra, A., Scharfenberger, C., Siva, P., Li, F., Wong, A., Clausi, D.: Desire: discontinuous energy seam carving for image retargeting via structural and textural energy functionals. In: 2015 22nd International Conference on Image Processing (ICIP), pp. 3695–3699 (2015)

6. Rubinstein, M., Shamir, A., Avidan, S.: Multi-operator media retargeting. ACM Trans. Graph. **28**(3), 23:1–23:11 (2009)

7. Luo, S., Zhang, J., Zhang, Q., Yuan, X.: Multi-operator image retargeting with automatic integration of direct and indirect seam carving. Image Vis. Comput. **30**, 655–667 (2012)

8. Battiato, S., Farinella, G.M., Puglisi, G., Ravì, D.: Saliency-based selection of gradient vector flow paths for content aware image resizing. IEEE Trans. Image Process. **23**(5), 2081–2095 (2014)

9. Qi, S., Chi, Y.T.J., Peter, A.M., Ho, J.: CASAIR: content and shape-aware image retargeting and its applications. IEEE Trans. Image Process. **25**(5), 2222–2232 (2016)

10. Karaali, A., Jung, C.R.: Image retargeting based on spatially varying defocus blur map. In: 2016 23rd International Conference on Image Processing (ICIP), pp. 2693–2697 (2016)

11. Zhang, L., Wang, M., Nie, L., Hong, L., Rui, Y., Tian, Q.: Retargeting semantically-rich photos. IEEE Trans. Multimedia **17**(9), 1538–1548 (2015)

12. Xu, C., Prince, L.: Snakes, shapes, and gradient vector flow. IEEE Trans. Image Process. **7**(3), 359–369 (1998)

13. Goferman, S., Zelnik-Manor, Z., Tal, L.: Context-aware saliency detection. IEEE Trans. Pattern Anal. Mach. Intell. **34**(10), 1915–1926 (2012)

14. Achanta, R., Hemami, S., Estrada, F., Süsstrunk, S.: Frequency-tuned salient region detection. In: Proceedings of the IEEE International Conference on Computer Vision and Pattern Recognition (CVPR), pp. 1597–1604 (2009)

Human Action Recognition in Videos of Realistic Scenes Based on Multi-scale CNN Feature

Yongsheng Zhou, Nan Pu, Li Qian, Song Wu, and Guoqiang Xiao$^{(\boxtimes)}$

The School of Computer and Information Science in Southwest University,
Chongqing, China
smion@email.swu.edu.cn, gqxiao@swu.edu.cn

Abstract. In this paper, we develop a novel method to design a robust feature representation based on deep convolutional features and Latent Dirichlet Allocation (LDA) model for human action recognition. Compared to traditional CNN features which explore the outputs from the fully connected layers in CNN, we show that a low dimension feature representation generated on the deep convolutional layers is more discriminative. In addition, based on the convolutional feature maps, we use a multi-scale pooling strategy to better handle the objects with different scales and deformations. Moreover, we adopt LDA to explore the semantic relationship in video sequences and generate a topic histogram to represent a video, since LDA puts more emphasis on the content coherence than mere spatial contiguity. Extensive experimental results on two challenging datasets show that the proposed approach outperforms or is competitive with state-of-the-art methods for the application of human action recognition.

Keywords: Human action recognition · Multi-scale pooling
CNN feature representation · Latent Dirichlet Allocation (LDA)

1 Introduction

The task of automatic human action recognition in realistic scenes has gained increasing popularity due to its importance in the applications of video indexing and retrieval, intelligent video surveillance, human-computer interaction, *etc.* However, recognizing human actions in realistic scenes is a challenging task because of the existing camera movement, scale transform, cluttered background, variations in view-point, partial occlusions and shade. General human action recognition is consist of three main procedures: first, visual features extraction; second, encoding the video sequences into a feature representation; third, training a classifier based on the training data with labels and use the final obtained classifier to do the classification and recognition. Hence, a robust and discriminative feature representation of video sequences is crucial to the performance of action recognition. In general, the existing feature representations used for

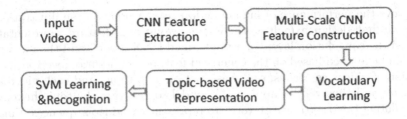

Fig. 1. Flowchart of the proposed method.

human action recognition can be summarized as two categories: hand-crafted features and deep learning features.

Most of the existing human action representations are based on spatio-temporal descriptors [1–8]. These methods mainly contain three procedures: first, the spatio-temporal interest points are detected by Gabor filters [9] or 3D Harris cornet detector [10], then the local descriptors around those interest points are generated, and finally the spatio-temporal descriptors are quantized into video-words. Thus, the local motion information of videos can be represented by the model of bag of video-words.

Recently, deep learning models have achieved breakthrough performance in various computer vision applications, such as image classification, object detection, image segmentation and image search, *etc.*, and in particular, the Convolutional Neural Network (CNN) is the most common deep model in these applications. Due to the high-level and powerful representation learning capability as well as the transfer property of CNN, a pre-trained CNN model can be used to explore the feature representation even there are substantial differences among datasets. Generally, the outputs from the fully connected layers are utilized to generate features. The recent visual representation from activations of deep convolutional layers has also been shown high performance [11,12], and hence, we explore the feature representation on the deep convolutional layers of a pre-trained CNN to recognize the human action.

The latent topic models [13,14] were firstly proposed and used in the field of document analysis and information retrieval. Since the latent topic model has the capability to describe the semantic relationship in the visual feature space, it has been successfully applied to computer vision tasks [1,2,15,16]. For example, Niebles *et al.* [2] proposed to learn the classifier for human action recognition by using latent topic models probabilistic Latent Semantic Analysis (pLSA) [13] and Latent Dirichlet Allocation (LDA) [14]. Liu *et al.* [1] also utilize the LDA model to learn the classifier based on a novel three dimensional Sift local descriptor extracted from the video sequences.

As human actions are consisting of some basic actions (such as: hand waving, leg rise and head movement), inspired by the Latent Dirichlet Allocation model, we can treat each basic action as a topic in LDA model to generate the latent topic histogram, and further to find the sematic relationships among video sequences. Hence, we combine the strength of CNN architecture and LDA model to improve the performance of human action recognition. As the illustration in Fig. 1, we first design a multi-scale deep convolutional feature representation based on the convolution layers of a pre-trained CNN model, and then a vocabulary can be learned based on the generated features. In addition, we specify the collection of videos as corpus, each basic action as a topic, and each video as a document, and thus we can apply LDA model to generate the topic histogram by calculating the occurrence of words to represent the video sequences. Finally, based on topic histogram representations, a liner-SVM [17] is used to train the classifier that can be used for high performance human action recognition.

The rest of this paper is organized as follows: Sect. 2 describes the generation of multi-scale CNN feature as well as the details of the Latent Dirichlet Allocation model. The performance evaluation of human action recognition and the detailed analysis between our method and the compared methods are presented in Sect. 3. The conclusion is given in Sect. 4.

2 Proposed Method

In this section, we describe how to use multi-scale pooling strategy to generate deep convolutional feature and use it to represent each video sequence. For the obtained deep feature representation of each video sequence, we further introduce how to use the LDA to generate topic histogram to represent the video. In Fig. 2, we choose 4 images from UCF-Sport [5] and UCF-11 [6], and overlay some feature maps on the original images for visualization. As can be seen, the activated regions of the sampled feature maps indicate some semantically meaningful regions.

2.1 Scale Pooling Strategy

Generally, the goal of pooling operation is to compute a summary statistics (such as max-pooling, average-pooling and multi-scale pooling) over a local spatial region on the feature map.

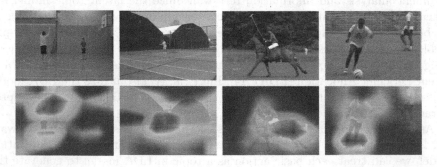

Fig. 2. The visualization of the feature maps extracted from the last convolutional layer of VGG [18].

Given a pre-trained CNN model with L convolutional layers, and an input image I. We feed the image into the pre-trained CNN model, then it will convolve the image with multiple kernels to generate various feature maps. A feature map can be denoted by $\bar{F}_i = \{F_{ij} : i = 1...L; j = 1...C_i\}$, where F_{ij} is equivalent to the jth feature map at ith convolutional layer, and C_i is the number of channels or convolutional kernels. The dimension of F_{ij} is $W_i \times H_i$, where W_i and H_i are the width and height of each channel. Assuming that $f_i(x, y)$ is the response value at the ith convolutional layer with a spatial coordinate (x, y). Thus, the max-pooling on a convolutional layer can be described as follows:

$$\dot{V}_{F_{i,j}} = max(f_i(x, y)); x, y \in F_{i,j} \tag{1}$$

The similar operation is carried on all channels and the final representation can be described as:

$$\dot{V}_i = [\dot{V}_{F_{i,j}} : j = 1...C_i] \tag{2}$$

Average-pooling on a convolutional layer can be constructed as follows:

$$\bar{V}_{F_{i,j}} = \frac{1}{W_i \times H_i} \sum_{y=1}^{W_i} \sum_{x=1}^{H_i} f_i(x, y) \tag{3}$$

The same procedure is performed on all channels, such that the final feature representation is:

$$\bar{V}_i = [\bar{V}_{F_{i,j}} : j = 1...C_i] \tag{4}$$

The max-pooling operation encodes the local maximum response from each feature map and the average-pooling operation encodes all the response in the feature map. Due to the object may appear in different location, shapes and scales, and single scale pooling operation does not consider the spatial and scale

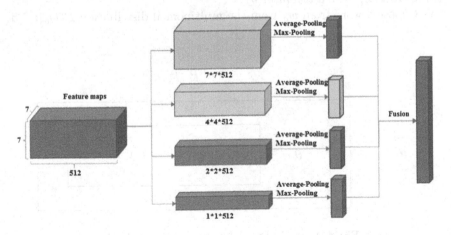

Fig. 3. The illustration of multi-scale pooling scheme.

information of objects in the image, we purpose a multi-scale pooling strategy
to capture object information at multiple scales, which is illustrated as follows:

$$V_i = [V_{F_{i,j,R}} : j = 1...C_i], \; where \; V_{F_{i,j,R}} = P_{x,y \in R}|f_i(x,y)| \tag{5}$$

$$V_i = [V_{F_{i,j}} : j = 1...C_i], \; where \; V_{F_{i,j}} = \sum_{R \in F_{i,j}} V_{i,R} \tag{6}$$

R is a square region of the feature map. $P|\cdot|$ can be max-pooling, average-
pooling or sum pooling on the region R. In our experiment, the width (height)
of R is 1, 2, 4 and 7, which is following the parameter setting in spatial pyramid pooling (SPP) [19]. The extracted features by multi-scale-pooling are then
summed and subsequently normalized to represent each video sequence. The
details of multi-scale-pooling strategy is shown in Fig. 3. In this manner, we can
note that exploring feature representation on deep convolutional feature maps
by using multi-scale-pooling operation has two advantages: first, the generated
feature is robust to the object deformation and scale changes; second, compared
to the high dimensional feature from the fully connected layer in CNN, the deep
convolutional features has higher discrimination with lower dimension.

2.2   Bag of Topics Model

Latent Dirichlet allocation (LDA) is a generative probabilistic model of corpus.
The basic idea of LDA is that documents can be represented as random mixtures
over latent topics, where each topic is characterized by a distribution over words.
   As described in [14], the process that generates each video d_j in the corpus is:

1. Choose $\theta \sim Dirichlet\,(\alpha)$.
2. For each of the N words w_n:
   (a) Choose $Z_n \sim Multinomial(\theta)$.
   (b) Choose a word from w_n from the multinomial distribution $P(w_n|z_n, \beta)$.

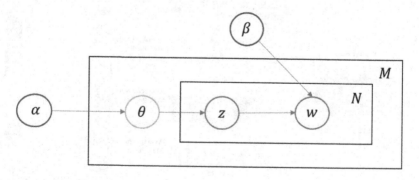

Fig. 4. Graphical model representation of LDA.

First, θ is a multinomial distribution which determines how the categories are mixed in the current video, and each element of θ represents the probability of each topic appears in the current video. α is a parameter of Dirichlet distribution, which is used to generate θ. Second, Z_n is a topic and generated by the multinomial distribution θ. Finally, a matrix β parameterizes the word probabilities on each topic, the constituent of β equals to the probability $p(w_i|z_n)$. Furthermore, N is the number of visual words in each video, and it is independent of all other variables.

The joint distribution of a topic mixture θ, a set of N visual words w, and their corresponding topic z can be represented as:

$$p(\theta, z, w|\alpha, \beta) = p(\theta|\alpha) \prod_{n=1}^{N} p(z_n|\theta)p(w_{n|z_n,\beta}) \tag{7}$$

The illustration of probabilistic graphical model representation of LDA is shown in Fig. 4. As shown in this figure, we can note that the LDA model is represented at three levels:

- Corpus-level: Corpus-level parameters α and β are sampled only once in the generation of a corpus.
- Document-level: For each document, the corpus-level variables θ are sampled once.
- Word-level: The word-level variables z and w are sampled once for each word in each document.

By selecting the topic that generates its corresponding visual word with highest probability, we can label each visual word (deep convolutional representation of each video sequence) with a topic. In this manner, we can generate a topic histogram based on LDA model to represent a video and then perform the human actions classification and recognition.

3   Experiments and Results

In the experiment, we conduct a series of experiments to show the effective and efficient of our proposed framework on the human action recognition. The pre-trained VGG [18] model with 16 layers is used to extract deep convolutional features for each video sequence (note that AlexNet [20], GoogleNet [21] and other CNN architectures [22] can also be used here). In the training phase, the k-means clustering is employed to construct the vocabulary, and we use leave one out cross validation (LOOCV) scheme to train a linear SVM [17]. The experimental environment is a CPU i5-6600k at 3.5 GHz with 8 GB RAM and a 4 GB NVIDIA GTX 960.

322   Y. Zhou et al.

3.1 Datasets

In the present experiment, we use two popular benchmark datasets UCF-Sport [5] and UCF-11 [6] for the evaluation of human action recognition. The two datasets are challenging in terms of large variations in cluttered background, viewpoint transform, camera motion, illumination, etc.

UCF-Sport Dataset contains 10 categories sport actions: diving, golf-swing, kicking, horse-riding, running, skateboarding bench-swing, swing and walking. There are 150 video samples and the frame number per video ranges from 50–130.

UCF-11 Human Action Dataset is a collection of 11 categories, 1600 video samples in total. Human action categories include: basketball shooting (b-shooting), cycling, diving, golf swing (g-swing), horse-riding (h-riding), swinging, tennis swing (t-swing), soccer jugging (s-jugging), trampoline jumping (t-jumping), volleyball spiking (vspiking) and walking (with dogs). Video for each category are divided into 25 relatively independent subsets, where separate groups are taken in different scenes. The number of videos for each group ranges from 4–9.

3.2 Evaluation of the Deep Convolutional Features

In this part, we first conduct experiments to evaluate the strength of the multi-scale pooling strategy. We use CNN features to represent each video frame and generate the topic histogram to represent the video. The performance of traditional CNN feature which using the outputs from the last fully connected layer and the deep convolutional features generated by the operations of max-pooling, average-pooling, multi-scale-max pooling and multi-scale-average pooling on the last convolutional layer in VGG are evaluated on both two datasets. The results in Table 1 highlight the advantages of deep convolutional features as well as the multi-scale pooling strategy: first, the deep convolutional features improve the performance at a lower dimension compared to the features from last fully connected layer; Second, the multi-scale pooling schemes show higher accuracy than single-scale pooling schemes. Moreover, the multi-scale-average pooling achieves the best accuracy on both datasets.

3.3 Comparison with State-of-the-Art

In the following, we compare our method with several published state-of-the-art methods on each dataset. According to the results in Table 1, the multi-scale-average pooling scheme is employed to generate the deep convolutional feature for each video frame. As shown in Tables 2 and 3, we can note that, for human action recognition in realistic scenes, our method achieves the top accuracy, which means that the deep convolutional feature is more discriminative and robust than the widely used spatio-temporal feature. Moreover, Tables 4 and 5

Table 1. Comparison of the approach with multi-scale pooling and single pooling operation. The CNN features extracted from the last fully connected layer (fc7) and the last convolutional layer (conv5). The pooling operations are tested by conv5 features.

Methods	UCF-Sport	UCF-11	Dim
fc7	82.0%	55.84%	4096
max-pooling	83.3%	74.1%	**512**
average-pooling	84.0%	74.3%	**512**
multi-scale-max-pooling	88.6%	74.8%	**512**
multi-scale-average-pooling	**90.0%**	**76.6%**	**512**

Table 2. Comparison of our results to the state-of-the-arts on action recognition dataset UCF-Sport.

UCF-Sport	
Method	Accuracy
Souly and Shah [23]	85.1%
Le et al. [4]	86.5%
Kovashka and Granman [8]	87.2%
Wang et al. [24]	89.1%
Proposed	**90.0%**

Table 3. Comparison of our results to the state-of-the-arts on action recognition dataset UCF-11.

UCF-11	
Method	Accuracy
Hasan et al. [7]	59.7%
Liu et al. [6]	71.2%
Ikizler-Cinbs et al. [25]	75.2%
Proposed	**76.6%**

show the confusion matrix on both datasets using topic histogram generated by the deep convolutional features with multi-scale pooling scheme, which further demonstrate the discrimination of deep convolutional feature as well as the effective of multi-scale pooling strategy.

Table 4. Confusion matrix per action category for UCF-Sport dataset.

	div	golf	kick	lift	h_r	run	skat	s_b	s_s	walk
diving	**100**	0.0	0.0	0.0	0.0	0.0	0.0	0.0	0.0	0.0
golf	0.0	**89.0**	0.0	0.0	11.0	0.0	0.0	0.0	0.0	0.0
kicking	0.0	0.0	**100**	0.0	0.0	0.0	0.0	0.0	0.0	0.0
lifting	0.0	0.0	0.0	**100**	0.0	0.0	0.0	0.0	0.0	0.0
h_riding	0.0	33.3	0.0	0.0	**66.7**	0.0	0.0	0.0	0.0	0.0
running	0.0	7.5	0.0	0.0	7.5	**85.0**	0.0	0.0	0.0	0.0
skating	0.0	0.0	0.0	0.0	0.0	0.0	**92.0**	8.0	0.0	0.0
s_bench	0.0	0.0	0.0	0.0	0.0	0.0	0.0	**100**	0.0	0.0
s_side	0.0	0.0	0.0	0.0	0.0	0.0	0.0	0.0	**92.0**	8.0
walking	0.0	0.0	0.0	4.6	0.0	4.6	13.6	0.0	0.0	**77.2**

Table 5. Confusion matrix per action category for UCF-11 dataset.

	b_sh	cy	div	g_sw	h_rid	s_jug	sw	t_sw	t_ju	v_sp	wa
b_shooting	**83.3**	0.0	0.0	16.7	0.0	0.0	0.0	0.0	0.0	0.0	0.0
cycling	0.0	**75.0**	0.0	0.0	0.0	0.0	0.0	0.0	0.0	0.0	25.0
diving	0.0	0.0	**87.5**	0.0	0.0	0.0	0.0	0.0	0.0	0.0	12.5
g_swinging	14.3	0.0	0.0	**75.4**	0.0	0.0	0.0	0.0	0.0	0.0	10.3
h_riding	0.0	0.0	0.0	10.0	**90.0**	0.0	0.0	0.0	0.0	0.0	0.0
s_juggling	10.0	20.0	0.0	1.0	0.0	**69.0**	0.0	0.0	0.0	0.0	0.0
swinging	1.0	0.0	0.0	0.0	0.0	0.0	**91.0**	7.0	0.0	0.0	1.0
t_swinging	5.2	0.0	0.0	1.8	0.0	0.0	0.0	**93.0**	0.0	0.0	0.0
t_jumping	0.0	0.0	0.0	0.0	7.0	0.0	35.0	0.0	**58.0**	0.0	0.0
v_spiking	0.0	0.0	0.0	25.0	0.0	0.0	0.0	0.0	0.0	**75.0**	0.0
walking	8.0	5.0	12.0	15.0	0.0	0.0	0.0	0.0	0.0	0.0	**60.0**

4   Conclusions

A novel and efficient feature representation for human action recognition in realistic scenes is proposed in this paper. In order to increase the efficient and discrimination of feature extraction on each video frame, we construct a multi-scale deep convolutional features based on a pre-train CNN architecture. Moreover, since LDA model can explore the semantic relationship in video sequences, we propose to use deep convolutional feature to conduct LDA model to further improve the recognition accuracy. The evaluation results show that our method outperforms or is competitive with state-of-the-art methods on two challenging human action datasets.

References

1. Liu, P., Wang, J., She, M., et al.: Human action recognition based on 3D SIFT and LDA model. In: Robotic Intelligence in Informationally Structured Space, pp. 12–17. IEEE (2011)
2. Niebles, J.C., Wang, H., Fei-Fei, L.: Unsupervised learning of human action categories using spatial-temporal words. Int. J. Comput. Vis. **79**(3), 299–318 (2008)
3. Wang, H., et al.: Evaluation of local spatio-temporal features for action recognition. In: British Machine Vision Conference (BMVC 2009), London, 7–10 September 2009. Proceedings DBLP (2009)
4. Le, Q.V., Zou, W.Y., Yeung, S.Y., et al.: Learning hierarchical invariant spatio-temporal features for action recognition with independent subspace analysis. In: Computer Vision and Pattern Recognition, pp. 3361–3368. IEEE Xplore (2011)
5. Rodriguez, M.D, Ahmed, J., Shah, M.: Action MACH a spatio-temporal maximum average correlation height filter for action recognition. In: IEEE Conference on Computer Vision and Pattern Recognition (CVPR 2008), pp. 1–8. IEEE (2008)
6. Liu, J., Luo, J., Shah, M.: Recognizing realistic actions from videos "in the wild". In: IEEE Computer Society Conference on Computer Vision and Pattern Recognition, pp. 1996–2003. DBLP (2009)
7. Hasan, M., Roy-Chowdhury, A.K.: Incremental activity modeling and recognition in streaming videos. In: Computer Vision and Pattern Recognition, pp. 796–803. IEEE (2014)
8. Kovashka, A., Grauman, K.: Learning a hierarchy of discriminative space-time neighborhood features for human action recognition. In: Computer Vision and Pattern Recognition, pp. 2046–2053. IEEE (2010)
9. Laptev, L.: Space-time interest points. In: International Conference on Computer Vision, vol. 1, pp. 432–439. IEEE Xplore (2003)
10. Dollar, P., Rabaud, V., Cottrell, G., et al.: Behavior recognition via sparse spatio-temporal features. In: Joint IEEE International Workshop on Visual Surveillance and Performance Evaluation of Tracking and Surveillance, pp. 65–72. IEEE (2005)
11. Guo, Y., Lao, S., Liu, Y., Bai, L., Liu, S., Lew, M.S.: Convolutional neural networks features: principal pyramidal convolution. In: Ho, Y.-S., Sang, J., Ro, Y.M., Kim, J., Wu, F. (eds.) PCM 2015. LNCS, vol. 9314, pp. 245–253. Springer, Cham (2015). https://doi.org/10.1007/978-3-319-24075-6_24
12. Yosinski, J., Clune, J., Bengio, Y., et al.: How transferable are features in deep neural networks? Eprint Arxiv arXiv:1411.1792, vol. 27, pp. 3320–3328 (2014)
13. Hofmann, T.: Probabilistic latent semantic indexing. In: International ACM SIGIR Conference on Research and Development in Information Retrieval, pp. 50–57. ACM (1999)
14. Blei, D.M., Ng, A.Y., Jordan, M.I.: Latent Dirichlet allocation. J. Mach. Learn. Res. **3**, 993–1022 (2003)
15. Chong, W., Blei, D., Li, F.F.: Simultaneous image classification and annotation. In: IEEE Conference on Computer Vision and Pattern Recognition (CVPR 2009), pp. 1903–1910. IEEE (2009)
16. Cao, L., Li, F.F.: Spatially coherent latent topic model for concurrent segmentation and classification of objects and scenes. In: IEEE International Conference on Computer Vision, pp. 1–8. DBLP (2007)
17. Chang, C.C., Lin, C.J.: LIBSVM: a library for support vector machines. ACM Trans. Intell. Syst. Technol. (TIST) **2**(3), 1–27 (2011)

18. Simonyan, K., Zisserman, A.: Very deep convolutional networks for large-scale image recognition. Computer Science (2014)
19. He, K., et al.: Spatial pyramid pooling in deep convolutional networks for visual recognition. IEEE Trans. Pattern Anal. Mach. Intell. **37**(9), 1904–1916 (2015)
20. Krizhevsky, A., Sutskever, I., Hinton, G.E.: ImageNet classification with deep convolutional neural networks. In: International Conference on Neural Information Processing Systems Curran Associates Inc., pp. 1097–1105 (2012)
21. Szegedy, C., Liu, W., Jia, Y., et al.: Going deeper with convolutions, pp. 1–9 (2014)
22. He, K., et al.: Deep residual learning for image recognition. In: Computer Vision and Pattern Recognition, pp. 770–778. IEEE (2015)
23. Souly, N., Shah, M.: Visual saliency detection using group lasso regularization in videos of natural scenes. Int. J. Comput. Vis. **117**(1), 93–110 (2016)
24. Wang, H., Klaser, A., Schmid, C., et al.: Action recognition by dense trajectories. In: IEEE Conference on Computer Vision and Pattern Recognition, pp. 3169–3176. IEEE Computer Society (2011)
25. Ikizler-Cinbis, N., Sclaroff, S.: Object, scene and actions: combining multiple features for human action recognition. In: Daniilidis, K., Maragos, P., Paragios, N. (eds.) ECCV 2010. LNCS, vol. 6311, pp. 494–507. Springer, Heidelberg (2010). https://doi.org/10.1007/978-3-642-15549-9_36

Automatic Facial Complexion Classification Based on Mixture Model

Minjie Xu[1], Chunrong Guo[2], Yangyang Hu[1], Hong Lu[1], Xue Li[2],
Fufeng Li[2(✉)], and Wenqiang Zhang[1(✉)]

[1] School of Computer Science, Fudan University, Shanghai, China
wqzhang@fuan.edu.cn
[2] Shanghai University of Traditional Chinese Medicine, Shanghai, China
li_fufeng@aliyun.com

Abstract. Classification of facial colors plays a vital role in Traditional Chinese Medicine (TCM), photo beautification, matching cloths and other beauty and cosmetics industry. The face color of a person is considered as a symptom to reflect the physical conditions of organs in the body. Most current methods are difficult to accurately classify the facial colors. In this paper, we propose a facial color classification method based on complexion Gaussion Mixture Model (GMM) and SVM to address this problem. Specifically, we iteratively confirm the complexion pixels belonging to the skin region based on the GMM. In the optimizing process, we extract features based on two-dimensional GMM to describe main color and minor color. Experiments are performed on our dataset with 877 face images. Experimental results demonstrate the accuracy of the proposed classification method compared with the state-of-art facial color classification method.

Keywords: Face skin segmentation · Facial complexion classification
Complexion mixture model · Support Vector Machine

1 Introduction

Facial diagnosis is one of the important methods in the clinical diagnosis of Traditional Chinese Medicine (TCM). TCM divides the facial colors into green, yellow, red, white, black, which also known as the "five colors", and normal. It is an approach to make disease diagnosis through observing the changes of the color and luster of face and understand the physiological functions and pathological changes of the body. The traditional face diagnostic approach is mainly based on observing with nude eyes. The diagnostic results largely depend on personal clinical experience, and different TCM masters may deduce the different conclusion. Hence traditional face diagnosis is not a quantitative and reliable approach which may be affected by many subjective factors. Therefore, it is necessary to robustly and accurately classify facial color of face images for TCM. However, the face images contain more than one main color and the training

© Springer International Publishing AG, part of Springer Nature 2018
B. Zeng et al. (Eds.): PCM 2017, LNCS 10736, pp. 327–336, 2018.
https://doi.org/10.1007/978-3-319-77383-4_32

data lack standardizing, facial color classification is then difficult. On the other hand, facial color classification is widely used in many applications such as photo retouching, matching cloths, cosmetics test and cosmetic surgery [2,3,6,9,11].

In general, the facial complexion distribution among the same face is similar, but some are vary a lot for different face skin parts. Thus it is necessary to propose a facial complexion classification method to adapt to all parts of the facial complexion distribution and blending colors. Many methods on facial complexion classification have been proposed. Specifically, [16,17] propose a cheek complexion classification method. Lab color space is introduced to extract the facial complexion feature. It employs SVM to classify the images into four (white, red, yellow, and healthy) categories. The accuracy is 81% and 82%. However, the cheek region can not indicate disease well because some disease may lead to different colors in other parts of the face. Four categories are not accurate enough to distinguish faces of green and black.

[4,7] propose methods based on RGB color space to address the problem. [4] derives the fixed average RGB values of the pixel spots of typical five-color samples, these then formed a sphere with their own radius. Thus the methods can not adapt to different face images. [7] manually extracted skin blocks with size of 30 * 30 from facial images, and then employs supervised Latent Dirichlet Allocation (sLDA) to classify the images. However, the skin blocks are too small to present the whole face. The process of extracting features with artificial method is not efficient [12].

Another method based on statistical method is proposed in [8]. Five facial parts (two cheeks, forehead, nose, jaw) are segmented, and the color features are extracted on every color channel R, G, B, H, S, V, Y, I, Q. Then Principal Component Analysis (PCA) for dimensionality reduction and SVM for classification. For images with different colors among the extracted five facial parts and other parts such as eyes, it can not obtain satisfactory results. Since every parts of the facial complexion indicates organ conditions, just five parts can not well model the whole condition.

In this paper, we address the challenge of accurate facial color classification by constructing a mixture model and employing a classifier. In recent years, Gaussian Mixture Model (GMM) has been widely used in image segmentation due to its efficacy [5]. It accurately segments the objects in a probabilistic manner. The applications include GrabCut [13], Video SnapCut [1], and Soft Scissors [15], etc. We adopt GMM in facial skin segmentation. We first use the pixels' color of the center ellipse part of the face as training data to build a corresponding complexion GMM for each face image in Lab color space. Then by iteratively reserving the complexion pixels belonging to the skin of the face based on GMM, facial skin can be obtained. We classify the faces via an SVM classifier. Finally, we employ a two-dimensional GMM to improve the classification accuracy.

2   Building the Complexion GMM

First of all, we utilize Haar based classifier to detect a human face from the normalized input image [10,14]. Then we draw an ellipse on the face image center, the height is set 0.5 height of the face and width is set 0.36 width of the face empirically. By discarding the pixels with lowest 20% gray value, the non-skin noise can be removed. Then we can obtain the rough skin region. We use the pixels' color of the ellipse part of the face as the training data to build a GMM for facial skin in Lab color space. Lab color space is selected due to its consistence with human perception. The number of components in GMM is set to 3.

3   Facial Skin Detection

The complexion mixture model has been constructed in the Lab color space. Then for each pixel i in the face image with its color value $x_i = (l_i, a_i, b_i)^T$, its complexion probability generated from the complexion mixture model is computed as

$$p(x_i) = \sum_{k=1}^{3} \pi_k \frac{1}{(2\pi)^{\frac{3}{2}} |\Sigma_k|^{\frac{1}{2}}} exp\{-\frac{1}{2}(x_i - \mu_k)^T \Sigma_k^{-1}(x_i - \mu_k)\} \tag{1}$$

where π_k, μ_k, Σ_k are the weight, mean and the covariance of the k-th Gaussian component in the mixture model.

Algorithm 1. Iteratively detecting the skin.

Require: Set $j = 0$, $N_{skin} = 0$;
Ensure: Threshold T_{skin}.
 1: **repeat**
 2:     **for** each $x_i \in D_{skin}$ **do**
 3:         **if** $p(x_i) \geq it[j]$ **then**
 4:             $N_{skin}{+}{+}$;
 5:         **end if**
 6:     **end for**
 7:

$$R_{skin} = \frac{N_{skin}}{S_e}; \tag{2}$$

 8:     $j{+}{+}$;
 9: **until** $R_{skin} > 0.8$ or $it[j] < 0.01$
10: **return** $T_{skin} = it[j]$;

3.1   Detecting Skin Region

In traditional skin detection methods, normally a fixed threshold is used to determine the pixels belonging to skin region or not. However, the color difference between the skin and other facial sense region vary a lot for different people. We address the problem by an iterative detection method. First, we set an iterative threshold array as $it[j] = 2^{-j}, j = 0...12$. Then we iteratively confirm the threshold T_{skin}, indicating which pixels are skin.

Iteratively detecting the skin. We use the iterative method to detect the skin region in the complexion probability map of the face as below. D_{skin} denotes all pixels in complexion probability map. N_{skin} denotes the number of reserved pixels which is similar to facial complexion in the ellipse template. S_e denotes the size of ellipse template. R_{skin} denotes the skin rate in the ellipse template.

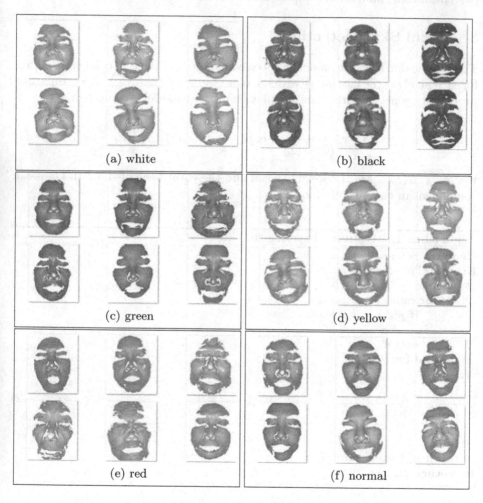

(a) white

(b) black

(c) green

(d) yellow

(e) red

(f) normal

Fig. 1. Face skin images for training. (Color figure online)

3.2   Skin Fine-Tuning Stage

The segmented skin have some noise with lower or higher luminance value after iterative detection of skin. We calculate the cumulative gray-level histogram of skin pixels. Then we remove skin color noise by discarding the lowest 10% and highest 2% pixels. Figure 1 shows some images after detection.

4   Facial Complexion Classification

TCM divides the facial colors into green, yellow, red, white, black, which also known as the "five colors", and normal. Due to large overlap between any two colors, using exiting method can not classify facial colors accurately. One reason is that the training data is not discriminated. Thus, we use the most consistently labelled face image dataset which is judged by five senior doctors to train our classification model. Finally, 33 green, 33 yellow, 31 red, 31 white, 28 black, and 60 normal face images are chosen. The other reason is that, a face containing two colors in some cases. These faces are wrongly classified into one category. To further address the problem, we propose a method with optimization.

Extracting and selecting classification features. Mean of skin color in Lab color space $\bar{l}, \bar{a}, \bar{b}$ are calculated. The result of classifying the six colors by three components in Lab directly is not good. Then the feature selection and optimization is necessary.

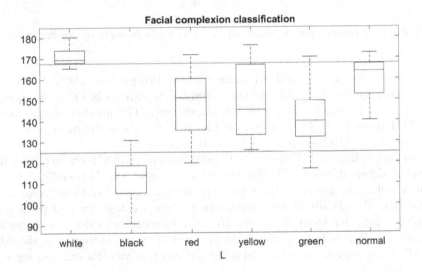

Fig. 2. Facial complexion classification in L component

Optimizing classification features. Normally, black and white categories do not related to hue, so they can separate by L component. As shown in Fig. 2, black, white, and other colors can be separated. We set $\bar{l} < 125$ as black, and $\bar{l} > 168$ as white based on our empirical study.

For other colors, $\bar{a}$ and $\bar{b}$ are selected for classification as is shown in Fig. 3. Then we employ SVM classifier to complete the classification of green, yellow, red, and normal categories. In this experiment, Linear kernel function is used due to its better performance than POLY, RBF, and Sigmoid kernel function.

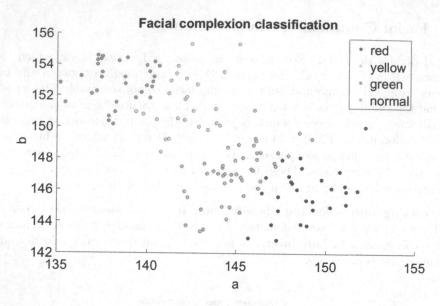

Fig. 3. Facial complexion classification in a and b components (Color figure online)

As shown in Fig. 4(c) and (d), there are both two peaks in the histogram of a and b components. Therefore, we use a and b components in Lab color space to build refined two-dimensional GMMs, respectively. The number of components in GMM is set to 2. The red lines in Fig. 4(c), (d) show the mean values μ_{a1}, μ_{a2}, μ_{b1}, μ_{b2} in the histograms of the a, b components.

For people have mild illness or in the state of sub-health, their faces may have a partial different color with the whole face complexion. Especially, forehead, orbit, cheek, jaw, and nose, these five regions may appear different color as the whole face. We classify these images into the main categories and point out a minor category. For example, in Fig. 4(a), the forehead is redder than other skin region. This face is initially classified into red category. Actually, it should be classified into normal category and point out red category, for existing some red region in the face.

Amendment of the initial classification. We use the value of μ_{a1}, μ_{a2}, μ_{b1}, μ_{b2}, π_1, π_2 to correct the classification and point out the partial color category, where μ, π, are the mean and weight of the GMMs, respectively.

1. Initialization: get the initial category C_0, category C_1 for μ_{a1}, μ_{b1}, category C_2 for μ_{a2}, μ_{b2}, set $\Delta\mu_1 = |\mu_{a1} - \mu_{b1}|$, $\Delta\mu_2 = |\mu_{a2} - \mu_{b2}|$, $\Delta\mu = \Delta\mu_1 + \Delta\mu_2$. If $\pi_1 > \pi_2$, then $C_{max} = C_1$, $C_{min} = C_2$, else $C_{max} = C_2$, $C_{min} = C_1$.
2. Check the faces complexion classification: for the initial classification C_0, if $\Delta\mu \geq 8$ or $\Delta\mu_1 \geq 5$ or $\Delta\mu_2 \geq 5$, it means the pixels appear obvious difference and the category need amendment, go to Step 3, else the initial category has been already right, stop amending.

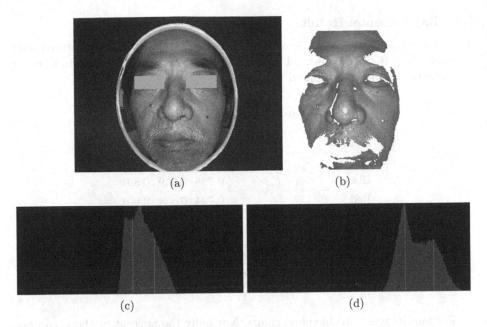

Fig. 4. Face image with red forehead and its a, b components. (a) The detected face image. (b) Skin of the detected face image. (c) Histogram of a component. (d) Histogram of b component. (Color figure online)

3. Compare categories: If $C_0 \neq C_{max}$, correct the category as C_{max}, and point out the minor category C_{min}, stop amending, else go to Step 4.
4. Remain the initial category. If $C_0 \neq C_{min}$, point out the minor category.

After amending, the misclassification caused by partial different colors can be improved. Especially, the faces in the state of sub-health can be picked out to the normal faces have minor category. It will be of great importance in diagnosis. The category overlap can also be improved.

5 Experiment

5.1 Experimental Data and Setting

We use the dataset which contains 877 face images (white 131, black 119, red 131, yellow 136, green 136, normal 224). The images in size of 2816 * 2112 are captured in the Shanghai Shuguang Hospital in a standard environment. We invite 5 doctors to classify these images, and pick out 8 special images contain blending colors as ground truth. We compare the proposed complexion classification method with Li's [7] and Liu's [8] methods. In the evaluation, classification accuracy is used in [7,8]. In this paper, we employ both classification accuracy and blending color recognition accuracy to evaluate the performance of three methods.

5.2 Experimental Results

Table 1 illustrates the comparison of our proposed method with the state-of-art methods [7,8]. It can be observed from Table 1 that our method can obtain better performance than the compared methods.

Table 1. Comparison of classification methods

Method	Li's	Liu's	Ours
White	0.779	0.847	0.740
Black	0.798	0.849	0.891
Red	0.794	0.824	0.901
Yellow	0.801	0.824	0.882
Green	0.831	0.846	0.890
Normal	0.840	0.893	0.902
Classification accuracy	0.811	0.852	**0.872**

For face images with blending colors. Normally the current methods can not well point out the different regions. On the other hand, our proposed method can well address the problem. When we build the two-dimensional GMMs of a, b components of complexion, we reserve the features of main colors and minor colors. In TCM, people whose facial complexion with blending colors may have mild illness or in the state of sub-health. Recognition of minor color is important for diagnosis.

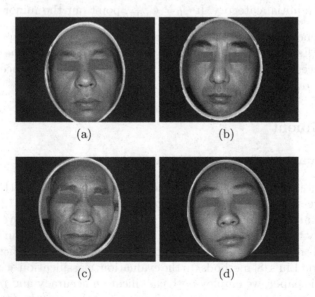

(a)   (b)

(c)   (d)

Fig. 5. Face images correctly categorized after optimization. (Color figure online)

6 Conclusions

In this paper, we propose a complexion Gaussian Mixture Model for robust and accurate face skin segmentation. It is in a probabilistic manner. The accurately segmented face skin is quite useful of skin analysis application. Then we extract six parameters of the two-dimensional GMMs on "a, b" components in Lab space for each picture as features. Finally, we classify the faces via an SVM classifier with Linear kernel function. For face images with partial different colors, the proposed method can well recognize the minor color. This paper also set a quantitative standard for diagnosis in TCM. Experimental results demonstrate that the proposed method can obtain promising performance, and improve the state-or-art classification and recognition accuracy. The facial complexion classification results can be served for TCM and other applications such as photo beautification, matching cloths, etc.

Figure 5 shows images with correct category after optimization in the dataset. These images are wrongly classified into red and yellow categories. They have partial different colors with the whole face. Actually, they should be classified into normal category. Figure 5(a)–(c) have the minor category of red, and Fig. 5(d) has the minor category of yellow.

Acknowledgements. This work was supported in part by National Natural Science Foundation of China (No. 81373555), and Shanghai Committee of Science and Technology (14JC1402200 and 14441904403) for funding. The first two authors contributed equally to this work.

References

1. Bai, X., Wang, J., Simons, D., Sapiro, G.: Video SnapCut: robust video object cutout using localized classifiers. ACM Trans. Graph. (ToG) **28**, 70 (2009)
2. Buchala, S., Davey, N., Gale, T.M., Frank, R.J.: Principal component analysis of gender, ethnicity, age, and identity of face images. In: ICMI, vol. 7 (2005)
3. Feng, X., Fang, J., Qiu, G.: Color photo categorization using compressed histograms and support vector machines. In: International Conference on Image Processing (ICIP), vol. 3, p. III-753. IEEE (2003)
4. Fufeng, L., Dan, D., Xiaoqiang, L., Yiqin, W., Peng, Q., Xiaoyan, Z., Guoping, L.: Facial complexion acquisition and recognition system for clinical diagnosis in traditional Chinese medicine. In: International Joint Conference on Bioinformatics, Systems Biology and Intelligent Computing (IJCBS), pp. 392–396. IEEE (2009)
5. Hu, Y., Lu, H., Cheng, J., Zhang, W., Li, F., Zhang, W.: Robust lip segmentation based on complexion mixture model. In: Chen, E., Gong, Y., Tie, Y. (eds.) PCM 2016. LNCS, vol. 9916, pp. 85–94. Springer, Cham (2016). https://doi.org/10.1007/978-3-319-48890-5_9
6. Kim, B.H., Lee, S.H., Cho, D.U., Oh, S.Y.: A proposal of heart diseases diagnosis method using analysis of face color. In: International Conference on Advanced Language Processing and Web Information Technology (ALPIT), pp. 220–225. IEEE (2008)

7. Li, W., Wang, S., Wu, T., Wu, Y.: Facial complexion recognition based on supervised latent Dirichlet allocation in TCM. In: International Conference on Biomedical Engineering and Informatics (BMEI), vol. 1, pp. 290–293. IEEE (2011)
8. Liu, C., Zhao, C., Li, G., Li, F., Wang, Z.: Computerized color analysis for facial diagnosis in traditional Chinese medicine. In: International Conference on Bioinformatics and Biomedicine (BIBM), pp. 613–614. IEEE (2013)
9. Lyons, M.J., Budynek, J., Akamatsu, S.: Automatic classification of single facial images. IEEE Trans. Pattern Anal. Mach. Intell. 21(12), 1357–1362 (1999)
10. Mita, T., Kaneko, T., Hori, O.: Joint Haar-like features for face detection. In: International Conference on Computer Vision, vol. 2, pp. 1619–1626. IEEE (2005)
11. Niu, J., Zhao, C., Li, G.Z., Zhang, W.: Facial color management for mobile health in the wild. In: International Conference on Bioinformatics and Biomedicine (BIBM), pp. 701–706. IEEE (2015)
12. Phung, S.L., Bouzerdoum, A., Chai, D.: Skin segmentation using color pixel classification: analysis and comparison. IEEE Trans. Pattern Anal. Mach. Intell. 27(1), 148 (2005)
13. Rother, C., Kolmogorov, V., Blake, A.: GrabCut: interactive foreground extraction using iterated graph cuts. ACM Trans. Graph. (ToG) 23, 309–314 (2004)
14. Viola, P., Jones, M.: Robust real-time face detection. Int. J. Comput. Vis. 57(2), 137–154 (2004)
15. Wang, J., Agrawala, M., Cohen, M.F.: Soft scissors: an interactive tool for realtime high quality matting. ACM Trans. Graph. (ToG) 26, 9 (2007)
16. Zhang, J., Wang, C., Zhuo, L., Yang, Y.: Uniform color space based facial complexion recognition for traditional Chinese medicine. In: International Conference on Control Automation Robotics & Vision (ICARCV), pp. 631–636. IEEE (2014)
17. Zhang, J., Zhang, P., Zhuo, L.: Fuzzy support vector machine based on color modeling for facial complexion recognition in traditional Chinese medicine. Chin. J. Electron. 25(3), 474–480 (2016)

Spectral Context Matching for Video Object Segmentation Under Occlusion

Xiaoxue Shi[✉], Yao Lu[✉], Tianfei Zhou[✉], and Xiaoyu Lei[✉]

Beijing Laboratory of Intelligent Information Technology, School of Computer Science, Beijing Institute of Technology, Beijing 100081, China
{shixiaoxue,vis_yl,tfzhou,leixiaoyu}@bit.edu.cn

Abstract. Although numerous algorithms have been proposed for video object segmentation, it is still a challenging problem to segment video object in the case of occlusion. Video object localization is a critical step for an accurate object segmentation. To obtain an initial localization, we propose a new method, Spectral Context Matching (SCM), for a coarse object location. SCM rebuild the affinity Matrix using context information as similarity constraints of features to detect the corresponding areas. Adding with color and optical flow information, the initially estimated object location is selected. For object segmentation, we utilize a spatial-temporal graphical model on the estimated object region to get an accurate segmentation. In addition, we also impose an online update mechanism to detect and handle occlusion adaptively. Experimental results on DAVIS dataset and comparison with the-state-of-the-art method show that our proposed algorithm can efficiently handle heavy occlusion.

Keywords: Video object segmentation · Occlusion
Spectral Context Matching · Online update

1 Introduction

Video object segmentation (VOS) is a problem classifying each pixel of video frames to foreground object or background regions, which has a broad applications in video retrieval, activity recognition, video editing and so on. Numerous approaches have been developed to address the video object segmentation [3,9,12,14], however there remains challenging problems [8] in VOS due to factors such as motion, shape deformation, scale and occlusion. And in this paper, we focus on the segmentation of video object on occlusion.

Optical flow [2] which is used for propagating an object segmentation over time is a general method to estimate initial object location, but it is imprecise when existing large displacement or occlusion. Some of matching method, such as Spectral Matching [10], PatchMatch [1], Locality Sensitive Hashing [6], Coherency Sensitive Hashing [7], finding consistent correspondences between two frames, could remedy the weakness caused by optical flow. Leordeanu [10] propose a spectral

© Springer International Publishing AG, part of Springer Nature 2018
B. Zeng et al. (Eds.): PCM 2017, LNCS 10736, pp. 337–346, 2018.
https://doi.org/10.1007/978-3-319-77383-4_33

technique for correspondence problems using pairwise constraints. Inspired by him, we impose context information as pairwise constraints further improving the matching accuracy. Graph-based model [14,17] define a minimal cut of the graph, which can be formulated in terms of energy minimization, it is worth learning for the refinement of the object segmentation.

In our paper, we propose an improved approach for the initial video object localization by Spectral Context Matching. We utilize context information as similarity constraints of features, which has scale and rotation invariance and robust to occlusion. And then with color and optical flow information, the localization of the object can be further improved. After that, a spatio-temporal graph cut framework is applied to optimize the segmentation. Meanwhile, we utilize an online update strategy to decide whether to modify the appearance and matching model. As shown in Fig. 4, even though in the case of occlusion, our proposed approach could segment the video object sustainably and effectively.

(a)   (b)

Fig. 1. An example of Spectral Context Matching and details of context information. (a) Dividing the images into superpixels, we find the correspondence between the target areas of previous frame and the searching areas of current frame. As shown in (a), i corresponds to i' and j corresponds to j'. (b) pre-frame superpixels i, j respectively correspond current frame superpixels i', j'. Take the centroid of i, i' as center, j, j' as positive direction, build concentric circles and divide it into k sectors simultaneously. The contexts comparison $C_{ij;i'j'}$ is based on features of each sector and small circle. (Color figure online)

2   Video Object Localization and Segmentation

Unlike [9] processing the entire video offline in batch mode, we have the ground-truth in the first frame and aim to propagate the foreground label frame to frame. At the same time, to reduce the computational load and decrease the effect of background noise, the initial step is looking for the coarse object location. And then refine the estimation in a spatial-temporal graphical model for an accurate segmentation.

2.1   Video Object Localization

Localization based on the color and location is accurate in general but sensitive to occlusion while Spectral Context Matching is coarse but robust to occlusion. It will play a complementary effect if combine them reasonably.

Spectral Context Matching. Spectral Matching (SM) [10,15] is a method to find consistent correspondences between two frames. It is an efficient way to locate the approximate targets. Optical flow [2] is used to propagate a coarse mask in videos, however it may result in severe errors when occurs large displacements. We enlarge the searching area when occlusion and SM has little effect on displacement in accuracy and computational load.

Spectral Context Matching is a new method based on SM. In general, the main idea of SM is to find the main clusters C of a assignment graph G whose nodes are the candidate assignment $a = (i, i')$ and whose weights on edges are the compatibility value of the pairwise potential assignment. Formally it aims to maximize the inter cluster score $S = \sum_{a,b \in C} M(a, b)$, where the M is the adjacency Matrix of the G. In [10], it transforms the above problems into a quadratic programming formulation, solved with the principal eigenvector of M to get the best clusters. The construction of affinity matrix M is a critical step for a good result and what we want to improve is the non-diagonal elements construction of M.

Assuming that we have data feature $P = \{p_i | i = 1, 2, ...n_p\}$ and model feature $Q = \{q_j | j = 1, 2, ...n_q\}$, the $a = (i, i')$ and $b = (j, j')$ are two candidate assignments, where $i, j \in P$, $i', j' \in Q$. The original $M(a, b)$, the non-diagonal elements, measures how well the relative pairwise geometry of two model features (i', j') is preserved after putting them in correspondence with the data feature (i, j). Specially, calculate the Euclidean distance p_i and p_j in P, $q_{i'}$ and $q_{j'}$ in Q and then make a difference between them. This method is suitable for equidistant transformation in which the deformation between (i, j) and (i', j') is small.

As you can see in Fig. 1(a), we use the superpixel as a basic unit to match the target superpixel by taking in consideration that the superpixel contains more information and this will reduce computational load. Thus above mentioned feature sets P and Q are calculated on superpixels. The context-based $M(a, b)$ compares the context information noted as $C_{ij;i'j'}$ between pairs of data feature p_i, p_j noted as $F_{i,j}$ and pairs of model feature q'_i, q'_j noted as $F_{i',j'}$. As shown in Fig. 1(b), taking centroid of superpixel i as center, centroid of superpixel j as positive direction, we build concentric circles with radius l, $\frac{l}{2}$ respectively, where l is the size of superpixel. Meanwhile, we divide the larger circular region into K parts by angle from starting axis in clockwise direction.

$$F_{ij}(k) = |p_k - p_i| \qquad (1)$$

where $F_{ij}(k)$ is the difference of features between each sector k, p_k and the smaller circular region i, p_i, green and black slash respectively in Fig. 1(b).

$$C_{ij;i'j'} = \sum_{k=1}^{K} |F_{ij}(k) - F_{i'j'}(k)| \qquad (2)$$

where $C_{ij;i'j'}$ is the comparison of context information between date set superpixels i, j and model set superpixels i', j'. Then we have $M(a, b)$, defined as:

$$M(a, b) = \frac{1}{1 + (C_{ij;i'j'} + C_{ji;j'i'})^2} \qquad (3)$$

Specially, $C_{ij;i'j'}$ is the compatibility between the context information with i relative to j and i' relative to j'. Similarly, $C_{ji;j'i'}$ is the compatibility between the context information with j relative to i and j' relative to i'. We can see that SCM relative to SM has scale invariance as no need to calculate the distance between pairs of features and rotation invariance because we specify a relative positive direction. Now we can get a coarse object location R_t^M in current frame t by SCM and an example of SCM is shown in Fig. 1(a).

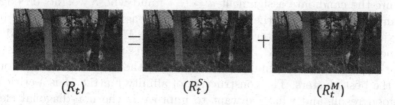

$$(R_t) \qquad\qquad (R_t^S) \qquad\qquad (R_t^M)$$

Fig. 2. R_t^S, the red region of the middle image, is the estimated target based on color and location information. R_t^M, the red region of the last image, calculated by Spectral Context Matching. We found the simple combination of R_t^S and R_t^M achieve good result R_t for localization of the target under occlusion. (Color figure online)

Object Location. Spectral Context Matching localization is coarse and noise. Motivated by [14], we use a scoring function for each pixel further selecting the object location R_t^S in frame t.

$$S_t(x_t^i) = C_t(x_t^i) + L_t(x_t^i) \tag{4}$$

where C_t is the color score on x_t^i and x_t^i is a pixel on local search region R_t^O which expanded from pre-frame mask $\mathcal{M}_{t-1}$. L_t is the location score calculated by Euclidean distance transformation on R_t^O. A threshold is then applied to get the object location R_t^S.

$$R_t = R_t^S \cup R_t^M \tag{5}$$

Although R_t^S is a relative accurate target location, it is sensitive to R_t^O. If R_t^O is not complete due to occlusion or inaccuracy with propagating, R_t^S would be bad which will directly have an influence on the final segmentation. R_t^M is rough but robust to occlusion which can still efficiently match the correspondence. Visual illustration of the effects of the combination of R_t^M and R_t^S is shown in Fig. 2.

2.2 Video Object Segmentation

After the estimated foreground region R_t in frame t for label assignment is roughly computed, next we choose a spatial-temporal graph cut framework to refine each pixel label.

Formally, given the pixel x_i with label $\in \{0, 1\}$, we just consider pixels on the region R_t. Our goal is to find an optimal labelling $\mathcal{L} = \{l_t^i\}_{t,i}$ for all pixels in all frames. Defining an criterion function:

$$\mathcal{L}^* = \arg\min_{\mathcal{L}} E(\mathcal{L}) = \arg\min\{\alpha \sum_{(i,t)\in R_t} \Phi_a(x_t^i) + \beta \sum_{(i,t)\in R_t} \Phi_l(x_t^i, \mathcal{M}_{t-1})$$
$$+ \gamma \sum_{(i,j,t)\in R_t} \Phi_w(x_t^i, x_t^j) + \delta \sum_{(i,j,t)\in R_t} \Phi_b(x_t^i, x_t^j)\} \qquad (6)$$

Where the unary potential Φ_a with weight α is the appearance term, consists of color GMM and an online SVM model with CNN features:

$$\Phi_a = \alpha_{col}\Phi_{col} + \alpha_{cnn}\Phi_{cnn} \qquad (7)$$

The Φ_l is the location term with weight β, measured by Euclidean distance transform of the mask $\mathcal{M}_{t-1}$. And the pairwise potentials Φ_w and Φ_b with weight γ and δ penalize the assignment of different labels between pixels which have similarity in spatial and temporal area respectively.

2.3   Online Update with Occlusion

SCM could efficiently match the objects between frames, and the accuracy of current frame matching results is directly decided by the segmentation of last frame. When occuring occlusion, the results of previous frame must be the partial of the object, which can not efficiently match the object of current frame if the target recurrent suddenly. Inspired by [16], we build a strategy to detect and handle occlusion adaptively.

In order to detect occlusion, we build a sliding windows, in which a successive sequence of H frame is stored. When have segmented a frame, we add a new frame into this sequence and delete the oldest one. And for each frame in this sequence, N_h, the total number of foreground pixels is saved.

$$O_t = \frac{\left| N_{cur} - \frac{\sum_{h=1}^{H} N_h}{H} \right|}{\frac{\sum_{h=1}^{H} N_h}{H}} \qquad (8)$$

where N_{cur} is the current frame foreground pixel number. θ is a threshold determine whether the object has heavy or full occlusion. If O_t is smaller than the θ, we deem that a heavy occlusion is occurred. The appearance model A_{unocc} and mask $\mathcal{M}_{unocc}$ of the latest unobstructed frame is respectively considered as training and matching area for the current frame, which the appearance model is the GMM and CNN model mentioned in Video Object Segmentation section. Otherwise, we use A_{t-1} and $\mathcal{M}_{t-1}$ to train and match the frame t.

3   Experiments

Our proposed algorithm is evaluated on the subset of DAVIS [11] dataset which is accompanied by densely annotated and is well classified by different attributes such as occlusion, deformation, scale-variation, appearance change and so on. According to the annotation of [11], there are 18 videos characterized by occlusion whose objects are partially or fully occluded. These videos with image size 480×854. And to evaluate the proposed algorithm, we first divide the circular region of context information into 6 ($K = 6$) parts. The superpixel length l is decided by the total number of superpixels on the searching area of an image and the searching area is different due to the ratio of occlusion. And we construct the foreground and background color GMMs in the RGB space from the first frame, and set 5 clusters for each GMM. For learning the online SVM model, we extract hierarchical CNN features combining the first 5 convolutional layers from a pre-trained VGG net [14] into 1472 dimensional vectors. We set the parameters in graphical model $\alpha_{col} = 1$, $\alpha_{cnn} = 3$, $\beta = 2$, $\gamma = 3$, and $\delta = 0.2$, the threshold in online update step $\theta = 0.8$.

To outstand the efficiency of our method, we do the experiment in four cases: SCM-only (SCM), Online-Update-only (UP), both SCM and UP (SCM&UP), neither SCM or UP (N-SCM&UP). From Table 1, we can see that SCM with Online Update mechanism efficiently improves the segmentation.

Table 1. The video object segmentation overlap in four cases SCM-only (SCM), Online-Update-only (UP), SCM and UP, neither SCM nor UP.

N-SCM&UP	UP	SCM	SCM&UP
0.66	0.710	0.725	**0.801**

We also compare our approach with various state-of-the-art algorithms including semi-supervised approaches FCP [12], Obj-Flow [14], HSV [5], unsupervised approaches NLC [4], CVOS [13], KEY [9], and so on. We employ the Jaccard index $\mathcal{J}$ defined as the intersection-over-union of the estimated segmentation and the ground-truth mask to measure region similarity. Given an output segmentation M and the corresponding ground-truth mask G, it is defined as:

$$\mathcal{J} = \frac{|M \cup G|}{|M \cap G|} \tag{9}$$

We list 18 video sequences Jaccard index $\mathcal{J}$ in the Table 2 and we can see that although some sequences are not the best, our method achieves the best segmentation performance overall. Furthermore, we introduce overlap plot to evaluate the overall performance of each method. We count the number of successful frames whose overlaps are above a threshold. The overlap plot shows the ratios of successful frames at the thresholds varied from 0 to 1. As shown in Fig. 3(a), we improve the performance by 13% over the second algorithm and far more than other methods. We also evaluate our algorithm on the overall DAVIS dataset. As shown in Fig. 3, it is still outperforms all existing video object segmentation methods. Meanwhile, we pick up example results for segmentation before and

Table 2. Results of region similarity ($\mathcal{J}$) for each video sequence in the dataset. When compared with the state-of-the-art, our scheme outperforms all existing video object segmentation methods. The best performing method of each category is highlighted in bold.

Sequence	[14]	[9]	[12]	[5]	[13]	[4]	Ours
kite-surf	**0.710**	0.586	0.421	0.403	0.343	0.458	0.698
bmx-trees	0.157	0.197	0.242	0.181	0.118	0.212	**0.507**
bmx-bumps	0.320	0.313	0.232	0.272	0.205	**0.473**	0.293
swing	0.560	0.709	0.560	0.114	0.515	**0.851**	0.801
kite-walk	**0.857**	0.201	0.647	0.765	0.436	0.814	0.750
parkour	0.859	0.412	0.316	0.242	0.143	**0.901**	0.818
libby	0.551	0.614	0.300	0.546	0.162	0.627	**0.868**
rhino	**0.894**	0.674	0.790	0.811	0.509	0.681	0.852
bus	0.673	0.787	0.806	0.810	0.648	0.624	**0.725**
lucia	0.898	0.846	0.765	0.775	0.816	0.875	**0.900**
cows	0.911	0.339	0.805	0.778	0.551	0.883	**0.912**
scooter-gray	0.264	0.357	0.470	0.435	0.318	0.585	**0.798**
dance-jump	**0.807**	0.747	0.517	0.680	0.330	0.718	0.771
soccerball	0.097	0.878	0.637	0.081	0.232	0.814	**0.862**
horsejump-high	**0.865**	0.369	0.612	0.764	0.797	0.833	0.806
motorbike	0.477	0.574	0.651	0.688	0.369	0.715	**0.793**
dog-agility	0.863	0.133	0.418	0.464	0.178	0.648	**0.866**
horsejump-low	0.825	0.626	0.567	0.551	0.718	0.653	**0.829**
Mean	0.644	0.520	0.542	0.520	0.410	0.687	**0.769**

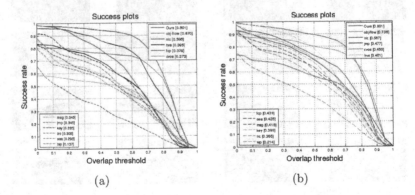

(a)   (b)

Fig. 3. Overlap plots for the DAVIS dataset. The methods are ranked using area under curve of each plot. (a) Results on the subset of DAVIS dataset characterized by occlusion. (b) Results on the overall DAVIS dataset.

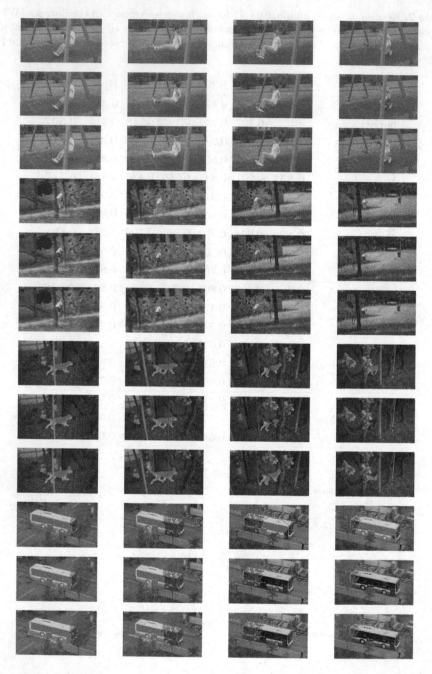

Fig. 4. Visual comparisons of our method (first row of each sequence) with obj-flow [14] (second row of each sequence) and nlc [4] (third row of each sequence) over the video sequences swing, bmx-trees, libby and bus. We choose the frames before, in and after the occlusion and we can see that our method segments the object constantly and effectively.

after occlusion, which is shown in Fig. 4. Noted that the bus is occluded by the trees for a long time, we are still able to find the right location and retarget the object finally.

4   Conclusion

The purpose of our paper is to locate and segment the video object under occlusion. We use a novel method named Spectral Context Matching to correspond the mask of previous frame with that of the next one and further employ color and location information to get a relative good object location. Then graphical model is used to refine the object segmentation. Meanwhile, we also propose a strategy to detect and handle occlusion for adaptively updating the appearance and matching model. The results on published DAVIS occlusion dataset show that our method is more robust and has better performance than the state-of-the-art algorithms.

Acknowledgments. This work was supported by the National Natural Science Foundation of China (No. 01273273)

References

1. Barnes, C.: Patchmatch: a fast randomized matching algorithm with application to image and video. Princeton University (2011)
2. Brox, T., Malik, J.: Large displacement optical flow: descriptor matching in variational motion estimation. IEEE Trans. Pattern Anal. Mach. Intell. **33**(3), 500–513 (2011)
3. Caelles, S., Maninis, K.K., Pont-Tuset, J., Leal-Taixé, L., Cremers, D., Van Gool, L.: One-shot video object segmentation. arXiv preprint arXiv:1611.05198 (2016)
4. Faktor, A., Irani, M.: Video segmentation by non-local consensus voting. In: BMVC, vol. 2, p. 8 (2014)
5. Grundmann, M., Kwatra, V., Han, M., Essa, I.: Efficient hierarchical graph-based video segmentation. In: 2010 IEEE Conference on Computer Vision and Pattern Recognition (CVPR), pp. 2141–2148. IEEE (2010)
6. Indyk, P., Motwani, R.: Approximate nearest neighbors: towards removing the curse of dimensionality. In: Proceedings of the Thirtieth Annual ACM Symposium on Theory of Computing, pp. 604–613. ACM (1998)
7. Korman, S., Avidan, S.: Coherency sensitive hashing. In: 2011 IEEE International Conference on Computer Vision (ICCV), pp. 1607–1614. IEEE (2011)
8. Kudo, S., Koga, H., Yokoyama, T., Watanabe, T.: Robust automatic video object segmentation with graphcut assisted by surf features. In: 2012 19th IEEE International Conference on Image Processing (ICIP), pp. 297–300. IEEE (2012)
9. Lee, Y.J., Kim, J., Grauman, K.: Key-segments for video object segmentation. In: 2011 IEEE International Conference on Computer Vision (ICCV), pp. 1995–2002. IEEE (2011)
10. Leordeanu, M., Hebert, M.: A spectral technique for correspondence problems using pairwise constraints. In: Tenth IEEE International Conference on Computer Vision, ICCV 2005, vol. 2, pp. 1482–1489. IEEE (2005)

11. Perazzi, F., Pont-Tuset, J., McWilliams, B., Van Gool, L., Gross, M., Sorkine-Hornung, A.: A benchmark dataset and evaluation methodology for video object segmentation. In: Proceedings of the IEEE Conference on Computer Vision and Pattern Recognition, pp. 724–732 (2016)
12. Perazzi, F., Wang, O., Gross, M., Sorkine-Hornung, A.: Fully connected object proposals for video segmentation. In: Proceedings of the IEEE International Conference on Computer Vision, pp. 3227–3234 (2015)
13. Taylor, B., Karasev, V., Soatto, S.: Causal video object segmentation from persistence of occlusions. In: Proceedings of the IEEE Conference on Computer Vision and Pattern Recognition, pp. 4268–4276 (2015)
14. Tsai, Y.H., Yang, M.H., Black, M.J.: Video segmentation via object flow. In: Proceedings of the IEEE Conference on Computer Vision and Pattern Recognition, pp. 3899–3908 (2016)
15. Wen, L., Du, D., Lei, Z., Li, S.Z., Yang, M.H.: JOTS: joint online tracking and segmentation. In: Proceedings of the IEEE Conference on Computer Vision and Pattern Recognition, pp. 2226–2234 (2015)
16. Yang, F., Lu, H., Yang, M.H.: Robust superpixel tracking. IEEE Trans. Image Process. 23(4), 1639–1651 (2014)
17. Zhou, T., Lu, Y., Di, H., Zhang, J.: Video object segmentation aggregation. In: 2016 IEEE International Conference on Multimedia and Expo (ICME), pp. 1–6. IEEE (2016)

Hierarchical Tree Representation Based Face Clustering for Video Retrieval

Pengyi Hao, Edwin Manhando, Cong Bai[(✉)], and Yujiao Huang

Zhejiang University of Technology,
Liuhe Road No. 288, Xihu District, Hangzhou, China
congbai@zjut.edu.cn

Abstract. We present a video as a set of people, each person is a sequence of faces clustered by proposed hierarchical tree representation with the purpose of finding all the occurrences of a person in the video without any help of textual information. In the proposed method, faces in a video are detected and tracked to be face-tracks at first, and each face-track is associated with one person. By leveraging temporal constrains, face-tracks that depict the same person in a video are connected. Then we build undirected graphs for a video, and extend discriminative histogram intersection metric learning to generate semantic distances for cutting undirected graphs to be face clusters without predefining the number of clusters. When searching for videos containing the person of query, it is effective to compare faces of query video with sets of people summarized from videos in the dataset. Experimental results show that the proposed face clustering can improve the mean Average Precision of video retrieval and decrease the query time compared to several state-of-the-art approaches.

Keywords: Face clustering · Video retrieval · Undirected graphs
Metric learning

1 Introduction

We are focusing on the following applications, such as all the videos containing the desired criminal suspect could be found from thousands of video sequences captured by CCTV cameras, or if movies in a website containing an actor of interest could be searched for. This kind of applications has given rise to the topic of face based video retrieval. The current state-of-the art mostly use clustering algorithms to classify detected faces [1–4], which may not have much semantic significance. The high level semantic information of videos is carried by entities such as how many person in this video and where people appear in video. With the recent progress in object detection and tracking [5,6] in videos, it is now possible to have a high-level representation of videos in terms of faces. Therefore, an effective way of searching videos is that firstly summarize each video to be a list of person that appear in video, and then search videos by comparing person's

© Springer International Publishing AG, part of Springer Nature 2018
B. Zeng et al. (Eds.): PCM 2017, LNCS 10736, pp. 347–357, 2018.
https://doi.org/10.1007/978-3-319-77383-4_34

representations with those of other videos. From this viewpoint, the problem of face based video retrieval is turned to be the problem of automatically discovering people from videos along with all their occurrences. For solving this problem, Zhang et al. [1] labeled all the detections in a video but requires movie scripts. In [7], researchers labelled training videos having the same characters, then scene segmentation and person discovery were done simultaneously using a generative model with the help of scripts. In [8], researchers defined movie scenes and summaries in terms of characters by using face detections along with movie scripts. An unsupervised version of this task was considered in [9], which performed face clustering by encoding spatio-temporal constraints as clique potentials using a Markov Random Field. In [10] researchers incorporated some spatio-temporal constrints into subspace clustering. But all these methods need to predefine the number of clusters.

In this paper, a novel method is proposed to automatically summarize the faces in a video to be people. In proposed approach, we firstly present 'cannot link/may link' rules to connect face-tracks of the same person in a short time, which forms compact long tracks named as scene-tracks. Then, undirected graphs are constructed to group these tracks that depict the same person but locate in different parts of a video. In this step, discriminative histogram intersection metric learning (DHIML) [11] is used for semantically measuring the similarities between scene-tracks. Training examples are automatically generated from scene-tracks. If two faces came from the same scene-track, they can be a positive pair. If two faces appeared in different scene-tracks that exist in the same time period or have an overlapping, they must not be the same identity, which can form a negative pair. Compared to the common clustering methods, proposed method does not need to predefine the number of clusters, it can hierarchially cluster faces efficiently and is simple to be realized.

The rest of the paper is organized as follows. Section 2 describes the proposed face clustering. Section 3 gives the details of video retrieval. Experiments are reported in Sect. 4, while conclusions and future works are presented in Sect. 5.

2 Hierarchical Tree Representation Based Face Clustering

Suppose I_k is a person appeared in one video, we propose a hierarchical tree structure to find all his (or her) faces appeared in the different parts of this video. Figure 1 shows this process. For person I_k, it has a hierarchical tree, in where the first layer contains detected faces, face-tracks are formed in the second layer based on these faces, and the third layer depicts all the scen-tracks of person I_k. Figure 2 explains how to generate this hierarchical tree, and the details will be given in the following subsections.

2.1 Scene-Tracks Generation

A face detector [12] is first executed on every frame of a video. Then face detections are associated into face-tracks using Kanade-Lucas-Tomasi (KLT)

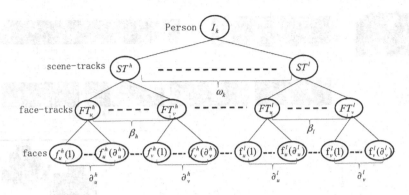

Fig. 1. Person I_k. ω_k is the number of scene-tracks in I_k, β_h is the number of face-tracks in ST^h, and α_u^h is the number of faces in FT_u^h.

tracker [13], such that each face-track corresponds to one person within a shot. LBP descriptors [14] are extracted at five facial components (left and right eyes, tip of nose, left and right corners of mouth) at three different scales, which forms a feature vector of 3840 dimensions. Let FT_i denote the i-th face-track, which is a triad $FT_i = < F_i, \widehat{F}_i, R_i >$. $F_i = \{f_i(1), \cdots, f_i(\alpha_i)\}$ is the set of faces in FT_i, where α_i is the number of faces in FT_i, and $f_i(x)$ is the x-th face in FT_i, $x = 1, \cdots, \alpha_i$. $\widehat{F}_i = \{\widehat{f_i(1)}, \cdots, \widehat{f_i(\alpha_i)}\} \in \Re^{D \times \alpha_i}$ is the feature set, where D denotes the dimension of feature space, and $\widehat{f_i(x)}$ is the feature of $f_i(x)$. $R_i = \{r_a, \cdots, r_b\}$ is a set that records the serial numbers of frames in a video, where $b = a + \alpha_i - 1$.

When tracking faces in a video, fracture is inevitable because of occusion, light changes, camera transfering, etc., resulting in more than one face-track for one person in a short time (e.g. 4 s). This will interfere with quickly browsing and searching for videos. Thus, cannot link/may link rules will be given here for connecting face-tracks of the same person generated in a short time. The connected tracks are call scene-tracks. Given two face-tracks FT_u and FT_v, the cannot link/may link rules are defined based on the following two situations.

- *Intersection and including.* If the elements of R_u are included in R_v, it is called 'intersection' (see Fig. 3(1)-(a)), which means that some faces of FT_u and FT_v come from the same frames. The special case is 'including' (see Fig. 3(1)-(b)). In this situation, FT_u and FT_v must be two different people, so they are labeled as 'cannot link' tracks that means they can not be connected, $\ell_{uv} = -1$.
- *Separation and cut.* If no element of R_u is included in R_v, it is called 'separation' (see Fig. 3(2)-(a)). The special case is 'cut' (see Fig. 3(2)-(b)). In this situation, FT_u and FT_v may either depict two different people or be two tracks of the same person, so they are labeled as 'may link' tracks that means they have the probability to be connected, $\ell_{uv} = 0$.

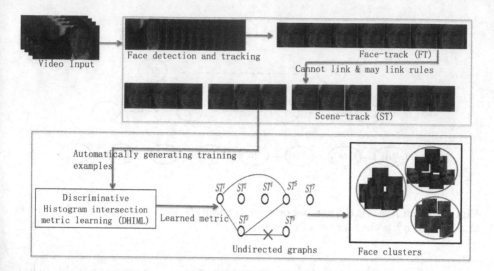

Fig. 2. The flow chart of proposed face clustering

Let X_k denote the set of face-tracks in the k-th scene, ℓ be the matrix to recode the relationship between each two face-tracks in X_k. When FT_u and FT_v have been labeled as 'may link', distances between them need to be calculated. Then ℓ_{uv} will be updated. The algorithm of connecting face-tracks to be scene-tracks in the k-th scene is shown in Algorithm 1, where $d(FT_u, FT_v)$ is the average Euclidean distance over all the face pairs of the two tracks, Y_k is the related set of scene-tracks in k-th scene.

For a video with the length of Max, the algorithm of generating a set of scene-tracks (denoted as Y) is shown in Algorithm 2, where t_1 and t_2 are two time nodes, $t_2 - t_1 = s$. Let $ST^j = < S^j, \widehat{S^j}, \widetilde{R^j} >$ be the j-th scene-track in Y, where S^j is the set of faces united by the faces in ST^j, $\widehat{S^j}$ is the feature set corresponding to S^j, $\widetilde{R^j}$ is the set of frame numbers that are the combination of all the frame numbers in ST^j.

2.2 Discriminative Histogram Intersection Metric Learning from Scene-Tracks

Metric learning aims at finding an appropriate metric from a set of pairs of instances such that the distance between positive pairs should be relatively smaller than that between negative pairs. Unlike most of these methods that learned a Mahalanobis distance [15–17], a discriminative histogram intersection similarity metric [11] that is adapted to the widely used histogram features for faces will be learned in our approach. The training examples are automatically obtained from scene-tracks, which have large variances both in positive pairs and negative pairs.

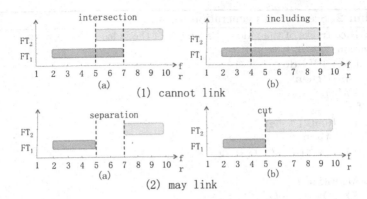

Fig. 3. The two situations between two face-tracks. (1) If two face-tracks are intersected or included, they can not be connected. (2) If two face-tracks are separated or cut, they may be connected.

Let β_j denote the number of face-tracks in ST^j, FT_u^j and FT_v^j denote the u-th and v-th face-tracks in ST^j with the length of α_u^j and α_v^j, respectively. By collecting the face pairs within scene-track, a set of positive training pairs P can be obtained:

$$P = \{(f_u^j(x), f_v^j(y))|u \neq v\}.$$

Similarly, negative training examples can be obtained by collecting the face pairs between two scene-tracks which have the relationship of including or intersection, resulting in the set N:

$$N = \{(f_u^h(x), f_v^l(y))|h \neq l, \widetilde{R^h} \cap \widetilde{R^l} \neq \varnothing\}.$$

Algorithm 1. Scene-tracks generation in the k-th scene

Require: $X_k = \{FT_1, \cdots, FT_n\}$, $n > 1$, $\ell = \{\ell_{11}, \cdots, \ell_{1n}; \cdots; \ell_{n1}, \cdots, \ell_{nn}\}$, Th.
Initialization: $Y_k = \varnothing$.
while there has 0 in ℓ **do**
    1. Calculate a distance set $\chi = \{d(FT_u, FT_v)|u, v = 1, \cdots, n\}$ for all the face-tracks where $\ell_{uv} = 0$.
    2. Update the label of face-track whose corresponding distance is larger than Th to be -1;
    3. Update the label of face-track whose corresponding distance is the smallest in χ and below Th to be 1;
    4. Link the face-tracks whose label $\ell_{uv} = 1$ to be $FT_{u,v}$;
    5. Update X_k and ℓ by deleting FT_u, FT_v and inserting $FT_{u,v}$;
end while
$Y_k \leftarrow X_k$;
return Y_k

Algorithm 2. Scene-tracks generation for a video

Require: Face-tracks of the video, the length of the video Max, a positive value Th.

  Initialization: $t_1 = 0$, $t_2 = s$, $Y = \varnothing$.

  for $k = 1$ to $\lceil \frac{Max}{s} \rceil$ **do**

    if $t_2 > Max$ **then**

      $t_2 \leftarrow Max$;

    end if

    Get X_k, ℓ from t_1 to t_2;

    if $|X_k| \leq 1$ **then**

      $Y \leftarrow Y \cup X_k$; $t_1 \leftarrow t_2$; $t_2 \leftarrow t_2 + s$;

    else

      Do Algorithm 1;

      $Y \leftarrow Y \cup Y_k$; $t_1 \leftarrow t_2$; $t_2 \leftarrow t_2 + s$;

    end if

  end for

  return Y

The distance between scene-tracks ST^h and ST^l is defined as:

$$D(ST^h, ST^l) = \frac{1}{\beta_h \times \beta_l} \frac{1}{\alpha_u^h \times \alpha_v^l} \sum_{u,v} \sum_{x,y} d_{HI}(A\widehat{f_u^h(x)}, A\widehat{f_v^l(y)}), \tag{1}$$

where, $d_{HI}(,)$ is histogram intersection distance, A is a transformation matrix, $A \in \Re^{d \times D}$, $d \leq D$. For learning A, the distance is modeled using the probability:

$$\rho_{u,v}^{h,l}(x,y) = \sigma(c - d_{HI}(A\widehat{f_u^h(x)}, A\widehat{f_v^l(y)})) = \frac{1}{1 + exp(d_{HI}(A\widehat{f_u^h(x)}, A\widehat{f_v^l(y)})) - c)}, \tag{2}$$

where c is a bias term and will be learned together with the metric parameter A. According to [18], in order to suppress noise, the transformation matrix A should be regularized. We use mixed $(2, 1)$-norm to force the sparsity of A. Then our objective function can be written as:

$$\max_{A,c} \Gamma(A, c) = \sum_{h,l} \sum_{u,v} \sum_{x,y} t_{u,v}^{h,l}(x,y) log \rho_{u,v}^{h,l}(x,y)$$

$$+ (1 - t_{u,v}^{h,l}(x,y)) log(1 - \rho_{u,v}^{h,l}(x,y)) + \alpha \sum_{i,j} \kappa(A\widehat{f_u^h(x)} - A\widehat{f_v^l(y)}) + \lambda \parallel A^T A \parallel_{(2,1)}, \tag{3}$$

where $t_{u,v}^{h,l}(x,y)$ denotes the pair label, α and λ are positive trade-off parameters. $\kappa(.)$ is the nuclear norm, as mentioned in [11], correntropy is chosen for $\kappa(.)$, and it can be optimized by half-quadratic optimization technique.

2.3 Undirected Graphs with DHIML

The learned metric is used to verify whether two scene-tracks depict the same person or not. Based on the verification, an undirected graph G is constructed for a video. $G = \langle Y, E \rangle$, Y is the set of scene-tracks, each scene-track is a vertex in G. E is the set of edges among vertexes. If ST^h and ST^l are verified as the same person, there is an edge between them, denoted as (ST^h, ST^l), and ST^h and ST^l constitute a connected component in G. According to the analyses of connected components in G, Y can be separated into clusters without predefining the number of clusters. Let I denote the set of clusters. The algorithm of grouping scene-tracks is given in Algorithm 3. Until here, the faces of a video are clustered based on the processes given above. Figure 1 shows how the faces of each person are clustered intuitively.

Algorithm 3. Clustering scene-tracks of a video

Require: The set of scene-tracks Y, the learned discriminative histogram intersection metric A.

Initialization: $G = <Y, E>$, $E = \varnothing$, $I = \varnothing$.

1. Update E by scene-tracks verification based on DHIML;
2. Compute the number of connected components in G. If no connected component, $I \leftarrow Y$; if the number is larger than 1, do steps 3, 4 and 5;
3. Judge whether exists circles or not in each connected component. If no circle, do steps 4 and 5; else the edges which can not construct a circle are deleted ; Update E;
4. Judge whether a vertex has more than one edge. If no, do step 5; else reserve the edge with the largest similarity and delete other edges ; Update E;
5. Split Y into I based on the connected components in G;
   return I

---

3 Querying from Video Dataset

Suppose that V videos in a dataset are summarized to be a set of people based on the method given in Sect. 2. I_k denote the k-th person in a video dataset. I_k is a two-tuples $<\widehat{I}_k, v_k>$, where $\widehat{I}_k$ is its feature set and v_k is the ID of the video where I_k came from, $k \in [1, \varrho]$, $v_k \in [1, V]$. Since the variance among faces within a scene-track is very small, the mean feature vector is used to describe scene-track, resulting in $\widehat{I}_k \in \Re^{D \times \omega_k}$, where ω_k is the number of scene-tracks in I_k. When given a query, a person I_q will be first extracted, and then the desired videos will be found by measuring the Euclidean distance between I_q and the k-th person in the dataset. Then, a set of matched people can be obtained by using a threshold. The videos containing these people can be got based on the video'IDs stored in the structure of them.

4 Experiments

The whole dataset in [3] is used for evaluation. In the dataset, there are six types of videos: films, TV shows, educational videos, interviews, press conferences and domestic activities. Because the videos in this dataset are too long, it is not easy to judge whether the returned video is correct or not when a person appeared few times in a long video. Thus each long film was segmented to 45 videos, each TV show was segmented to 10 videos, and each educational video was segmented to 10 videos, resulting in total 790 videos with the total length of 29.4 h in the dataset. Then 6287 people were extracted from this dataset using the face clustering given in Sect. 2.

The long film "Along Came Polly" came from the dataset is used to evaluate our proposed scene-tracks generation. The 90 min film gave us 7332 face-tracks, which formed 1781 scene-tracks. The accuracy of scene-tracks generation is calculated by

$$Accuracy = \frac{1}{1781} \sum_{j=1}^{1781} \frac{m_j}{\beta_j},$$

where β_j is the number of face-tracks in the j-th scene-track and m_j is the number of correct face-tracks in the j-th scene-track. According to the manual statistics on the film, 1162 scene-tracks have no error, and 381 scene-tracks have errors. The accuracy of the 1781 scene-tracks was 0.926.

4.1 Scene-Track Clustering

Experiments were done on the film "Along Came Polly". The 1193 scene-tracks belong to 8 main characters were selected from the 1781 scene-tracks generated from this film, and they were manually annotated. The ability of clustering faces by proposed undirected graphs (UG) with DHIML is compared to the following three methods: UG based on LDML [15], the hierarchical clustering (HC) method given in Ref. [3], the agglomerative clustering with signal-linkage (AC) [19], AC combined with DHIML, and AC combined with LDML [15]. We do not fix the number of final sets for each method. The labeling cost and accuracy are shown

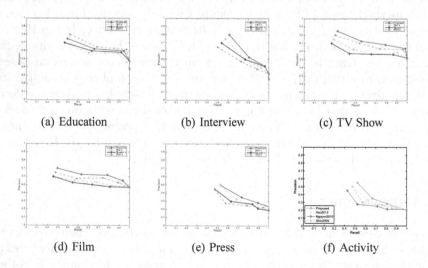

(a) Education   (b) Interview   (c) TV Show

(d) Film   (e) Press   (f) Activity

Fig. 4. Comparison of the proposed method and other three approaches in terms of precision and recall on six different types of videos.

Table 1. Comparison of proposed clustering and others in terms of labeling cost and accuracy.

Method	#Clusters	Cost	Accuracy
HC [3]	17	218	0.663
AC [19]	9	279	0.527
AC+LDML	14	148	0.775
AC+DHIML	13	129	0.805
UG+LDML	10	107	0.837
Proposed	9	84	0.875

in Table 1, where the accuracy is the ratio between the number of correctly grouped scene-tracks and the total number of scene-tracks in the test. Clearly, proposed method performs much better than others, 87.5% of the scene-tracks are correctly organized if we label the scene-tracks in each cluster by the identity of the most frequent person in that cluster.

4.2 Video Retrieval

Precision, recall and mean average precision (mAP) are used to evaluate video retrieval. The precision is the percentage of the videos which contain the same person with the query and the retrieved videos by the searching mechanism. The recall is the percentage between the number of returned videos containing the same person with the query and the number of videos including the desired person in the dataset. The mAP is the mean of average precision scores for a set of queries. In our experiments, the query set has twenty people such as Jennifer Aniston, which covers all of the six types of videos. We manually got the videos containing the same person with each query from the dataset. The statistics about the videos of the query set are the ground truth.

Firstly, the performance of the four methods are evaluated on the six different types of videos respectively. For each type of video, the whole query set is performed. By averaging the precision and recall over the whole query set, Fig. 4 are plotted. It can be seen that all the four methods perform worse on presses and activities than other four types of videos. The reason is that there are so many exposures, flash lamps, and occlusions in the videos of presses and activities. Sivic's method that represents each face track as a histogram over quantized face feature vectors has a clear advantage on educational videos, because the number of faces detected from educational videos is less than that of other types of videos and the intervals between face-tracks are much longer. The proposed method outperforms others in other five types of videos.

Then, the mAP and the retrieval time on the whole dataset are measured. The retrieval time is the time from submitting a query to getting the returned videos. All the processes were performed on an C++ implementation on Windows 7 with a 2.67 GHz CPU and 8 GB memory. Table 2 gives the results. It can be seen that

Table 2. Comparison of the proposed method and other three approaches in terms of mAP and average retrieval time (± standard deviation).

Method	mAP	Retrieval time
Sivic's method [2]	0.498	83.960s ± 0.602s
Nguyen's method [4]	0.464	116.488s ± 0.324s
Hao's method [3]	0.534	9.215s ± 0.014s
Proposed method	0.587	17.114s ± 0.057s

the method of Nguyen et al. gives the lowest mAP. The reason is that the six types of videos in our dataset have large variations than news videos used in their approach. In contrast, the method of Sivic et al. performs slightly better. The proposed method obtains the highest mAP than others in respect that histogram intersection distance metrics are learned from powerful positive and negative pairs and most of the faces are correctly grouped.

5   Conclusions and Future Works

In this paper, we proposed a face clustering method for grouping the faces with large variations but depicting the same person together. Compared to some most famous clustering methods, learning discriminative histogram intersection metrics is more effective for matching face features. The evaluations of video retrieval have demonstrated that the proposed method has the abilities of increasing the mean average precision and decreasing the retrieval time. However, the response time is still unacceptable and the mean average precision is still lower than the real requirement. Therefore, in future, the advance indexing technologies will be employed to shorten the retrieval time as well.

Acknowledgments. This work was supported in part by Zhejiang Provincial Natural Science Foundation of China (LQ15F020008, LY15F020028, LQ15F030005)and National Natural Science Foundation of China (61502424, 61503338)

References

1. Zhang, Y.F., Xu, C.S., Lu, H.Q., Huang, Y.M.: Character identification in feature-length films using global face-name matching. IEEE Trans. Multimedia **11**(7), 1276–1288 (2009)
2. Sivic, J., Everingham, M., Zisserman, A.: Person spotting: video shot retrieval for face sets. In: Leow, W.-K., Lew, M.S., Chua, T.-S., Ma, W.-Y., Chaisorn, L., Bakker, E.M. (eds.) CIVR 2005. LNCS, vol. 3568, pp. 226–236. Springer, Heidelberg (2005). https://doi.org/10.1007/11526346_26
3. Hao, P., Kamata, S.: Efficiently finding individuals from video dataset. IEICE Trans. Inf. Syst. **E95-D**(5), 1280–1287 (2012)
4. Nguyen, T., Ngo, T., Le, D.-D., Satoh, S., Le, B., Duong, D.: An efficient method for face retrieval from large video datasets, pp. 382–389 (2010)

5. Andriluka, M., Roth, S., Schiele, B.: People-tracking-by-detection and people-detection-by-tracking. In: Proceedings of IEEE International Conference on Computer Vision Pattern Recognition (2008)
6. Felzenszwalb, P.F., Girshick, R.B., McAllester, D., Ramanan, D.: Object detection with discriminatively trained part-based models. IEEE Trans. Pattern Anal. Mach. Intell. **32**(9), 1627–1645 (2010)
7. Tapaswi, M., Bauml, M., Stiefelhagen, R.: Knock! Knock! Who is it? Probabilistic person identification in TV-series. In: Proceedings of IEEE Conference on Computer Vision Pattern Recognition (2012)
8. Sang, J., Xu, C.: Character-based movie summarization. In: Proceedings of 18th ACM International Conference on Multimedia, pp. 855–858 (2010)
9. Wu, B., Zhang, Y., Hu, B.-G., Ji, Q.: Constrained clustering and its application to face clustering in videos. In: Proceedings of IEEE International Conference on Computer Vision Pattern Recognition (2013)
10. Xiao, S., Tan, M., Xu, D.: Weighted block-sparse low rank representation for face clustering in videos. In: Fleet, D., Pajdla, T., Schiele, B., Tuytelaars, T. (eds.) ECCV 2014. LNCS, vol. 8694, pp. 123–138. Springer, Cham (2014). https://doi.org/10.1007/978-3-319-10599-4_9
11. Hao, P., Yang, X., Li, X., Kamata, S., Chen, S.: Discriminative histogram intersection metric learning and its applications. J. Comput. Sci. Technol. **32**(3), 507–519 (2017)
12. Viola, P., Jones, M.: Rapid object detection using a boosted cascade of simple features. In: Proceedings of IEEE Conference on Computer Vision Pattern Recognition, pp. 511–518 (2001)
13. Shi, J., Tomasi, C.: Good features to track. In: Proceedings of IEEE Conference on Computer Vision, Pattern Recognition, pp. 593–600 (1994)
14. Ojala, T., Pietikainen, M., Maenpaa, T.: Multiresolution gray-scale and rotation invariant texture classification with local binary patterns. IEEE Trans. Pattern Anal. Mach. Intell. **24**(7), 971–987 (2002)
15. Guillaumin, M., Verbeek, J., Schmid, C.: Is that you? Metric learning approaches for face identification. In: Proceedings of IEEE Conference on Computer Vision, pp. 498–505 (2009)
16. Cherniavsky, N., Laptev, I., Sivic, J., Zisserman, A.: Semi-supervised learning of facial attributes in video. In: Kutulakos, K.N. (ed.) ECCV 2010. LNCS, vol. 6553, pp. 43–56. Springer, Heidelberg (2012). https://doi.org/10.1007/978-3-642-35749-7_4
17. Cinbis, R.G., Verbeek, J., Schmid, C.: Unsupervised metric learning for face identification in TV video. In: Proceedings of IEEE Conference on Computer Vision, pp. 1559–1566 (2011)
18. Huang, K., Ying, Y., Campbell, C.: GSML: a unified framework for sparse metric learning. In: Proceedings of ICDM, pp. 189–198 (2009)
19. Sibson, R.: SLINK: an optimally efficient algorithm for the single-link cluster method. Comput. J. (British Computer Society) **16**(1), 30–34 (1973)

Improved Key Poses Model
for Skeleton-Based Action Recognition

Xiaoqiang Li[1,2](✉), Yi Zhang[1,2], and Junhui Zhang[1,2]

[1] School of Computer Engineer and Science, Shanghai University, Shanghai, China
xqli@shu.edu.cn
[2] Shanghai Institute for Advanced Communication and Data Science,
Shanghai University, Shanghai, China

Abstract. With the development of Kinect sensor, action recognition based on human skeleton becomes a prosperous research field. In this paper, an improved method is proposed to select a few inconsecutive, discriminative and ordinal frames (named Improved Key Poses) to represent a human skeleton action. The main contributions of the proposed method are summarized as follow. First, a novel Key Poses Mining method is presented to keep time order of each frame in action video. Second, we selected a new feature which could reflect the micromotion of specific actions and increase the recognition accuracy. The proposed method is evaluated on three benchmark datasets: MSR Action3D dataset, UTKinect Action dataset and Florence 3D Action dataset. The experiment results show that the proposed approach outperforms than some state-of-the-art methods.

Keywords: Action recognition · Skeleton · Key poses

1 Introduction

Human action recognition has been an active area of research for the past several decades due to its applications in surveillance, video games, robotics, etc. Despite remarkable research efforts and many encouraging advances in recent years [1], accurate recognition of the human actions is still a very challenging task. The difficulty of these tasks arises from several factors, such as intra-class variations, pose changes, incomplete actions, and clutter.

In recent years, with the development of inexpensive RGB-depth sensors such as Microsoft Kinect, a lot of efforts have been made to extract features for action recognition in depth data or skeletons. [7] represents each depth frame as a bag of 3D points along the human silhouette, and utilizes HMM to model the temporal dynamics. Inspired by [11], Seidenari et al. model the movements of the human body using kinematic chains and perform action recognition by Nearest-Neighbor classifier [14]. In [4], skeleton sequences are represented as trajectories in a n-dimensional space, then these trajectories are then interpreted in a Riemannian manifold (shape space). Recognition is finally performed using

© Springer International Publishing AG, part of Springer Nature 2018
B. Zeng et al. (Eds.): PCM 2017, LNCS 10736, pp. 358–367, 2018.
https://doi.org/10.1007/978-3-319-77383-4_35

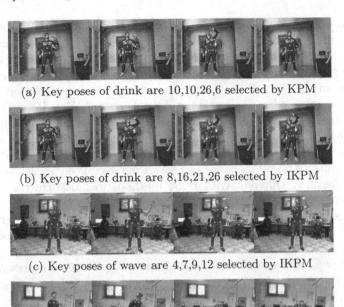

(a) Key poses of drink are 10,10,26,6 selected by KPM

(b) Key poses of drink are 8,16,21,26 selected by IKPM

(c) Key poses of wave are 4,7,9,12 selected by IKPM

(d) Key poses of bow are 2,11,15,18 selected by IKPM

Fig. 1. Comparison between KPM and IKPM

kNN classification on this manifold. [2] extracts a sparse set of active joint coordinates and maps these coordinates to lower dimensional linear manifold before training an SVM classifier. With the development of deep learning, many neural network based approaches are proposed to recognize skeleton action sequences. In order to recognize actions according to the relative motion between limbs and the trunk, [5] uses an end-to-end hierarchical RNN for skeleton based action recognition. [10] uses skeleton sequences to regularize the learning of Long Short Term Memory (LSTM), which is grounded via deep Convolutional Neural Network (DCNN) onto the video for action recognition. Though the deep neural network algorithm show promising result in many research field, it still puzzles us. Many neural network based approaches are proposed to recognize actions by learning spatio-temporal features. Although those features get excellent performance on action recognition, any literatures can not explain what the features represent. There is another issue we could not ignore. Affected by the action speed, behavior habit or action category, usually, the temporal lengths of the action sequences are vary. The problems above motivate us research on the proposed method in this paper.

In earlier work [8], we proposed the Key Poses model (KPM) to define the action sequence. But there are few problems. In the initialization of the model, the length of different sequence is not considered. And the offset o is man-made assigned. It may cause such situation, the Key Pose i appears before Key Pose

$i - 1$ or Key Pose i is equal to Key Pose $i - 1$ though the recognition result is true. Figure 1(a) shows the case. As for the actions such as stand up and sit down, the misorder of Key Poses will influence the recognition results. So we rewrite the algorithm and propose the Improved Key Poses Model (IKPM). In the new model, Key Poses i appears around the base position c_{p_i}. c_{p_i} is not a special integer but a percentage. In other word, Key Pose i is likely to appear around $c_{p_i} \cdot length(X)$-th frame in video X. By introducing the c_{p_i}, the difference of length between different skeleton sequence will be eliminated when training the IKPM. In order to choose Key Poses in turn, we divide each video into n iosmetric subsequence and select one Key Pose in each subsequence by linear classifier. Different with prior method, we initialize the first linear classifier $g_1(x)$ and the training of remaining classifier $g_i(x)$ depends on the help of prior classifier $g_{i-1}(x)$. Earlier feature representations show its deficiency on the actions which occupy little part of the human body such as clapping hands, so in this paper we use another relative position features. With the mentioned work above, we could select more discriminative Key Poses to represent a action and make the recognition process more coinciding with human cognition, as showed in Fig. 1(b). The detail will be discussed in Sect. 2.

In this paper, an improved framework is proposed for action recognition in which key skeleton poses is selected as representation of action in RGB-D video sequences. And the proposed approach has been evaluated on three benchmark datasets: MSR action 3D dataset, UTKinect Action dataset and Florence 3D Action dataset, both are captured with Kinect devices. Experimental results demonstrate that the proposed approach achieve better recognition accuracy than some existing methods. The remainder of this paper is organized as follows. The proposed method is elaborated in Sect. 2. Experimental results are shown and analysed in Sect. 3. Finally, we conclude this paper in Sect. 4.

2 Proposed Method

2.1 Improved Key Poses Model and Action Recognition

Li et al. [9] propose a model that represent a RGB action video by a few key frames, and these key frames are found by the latent support vector machine. In our earlier research [8], this model is applied to the human skeleton action sequence, it shows good performance but is still accompanied with some disadvantage. This is the reason that motivates the research on Improved Key Poses Model.

The same as [8], Improved Key Poses Model is also composed with n Key Poses. For an skeleton sequence X, it is divided to n subsequences. And we hypothesize the Key Pose i could be found around a fixed position $c_{p_i} \cdot length(X)$ in i-th subsequence. How to compute c_{p_i} will be discussed later. For Key Pose i in Key Poses Model, it consist of three parts: (1) The linear classifier $g_i(x)$ distinguishes the Key Pose i form other frames in the i-th subsequence; (2) The relative temporal position c_{p_i} and the relative offset c_{o_i}; (3) The weight of linear classifier w_{g_i} and the weight of temporal position $w_{c_{p_i}}$.

For a given skeleton video sequence contains m frames $X = \{x_1, ..., x_m\}$ and divide it to n fixed length subsequences, the Key Pose i is selected from i-th subsequence. The score of video X will be computed as Eq. (1):

$$f(X) = \sum_{t_i \in T^n} (w_{g_i} \times g_i(x_{t_i}) + w_{c_{p_i}} \times \Delta t_i) \tag{1}$$

$$T^n = \{t_i, i \in [1, n], 1 \leq t_1 < t_i < t_n \leq m\}$$

in which T^n is the Key Poses space, n is the number of Key Poses. t_i is the serial number of Key Pose i in the sequence of X, $(x_{t_i} \in X)$. For example, in Fig. 1(b), $T^n = \{8, 16, 21, 26\}$. And Δt_i is defined as Eq. (2):

$$\Delta t_i = \frac{1}{2\pi c_{o_i}} \exp(\frac{-(c_{t_i} - c_{t_0} - c_{p_i})^2}{2c_{o_i}^2}) \tag{2}$$

in which t_0 is the begin frame of the action, $c_{t_0} = \frac{t_0}{m}$ is the relative position in the video X. The same as c_{t_0}, $c_{t_i} = \frac{t_i}{m}$ represents the real relative position of Key Pose i in video X, and c_{p_i} represents the relative position where the Key Pose i is likely to appear. Δt_i is an Gaussian function and reach the peak when $c_{t_i} - c_{t_0} = c_{p_i}$. t_0 will be computed according to [8].

2.2 Feature Extracting

With the development of the sensor such as Kinect, most of the human action could be characterized by 3D skeleton joints. The raw 3D skeleton joints coordinates contains useful information about the human action sequence and many method have been proposed to extract fine manual features from skeleton data. Pairwise [16] takes the difference of each two joint in a frame as features. The most informative sequences of joint angles (MIJA) establishes a new coordinate system and regards the joint angles as features [13]. Histograms of 3D joints (HOJ3D) computes the 3D spatial histogram as features [17]. Sequence of the most informative joints (SMIJ) selects top 6 joint angle between each two adjoint joints, and extract features with a mapping function [12].

Take the advantage of the methods above, we extract the relative position as the feature. For a given frame $x = \{j_1, ..., j_i, ...j_k\}$, the feature can be compute as follow:

$$\varphi(x) = \{\|j_a - j_b\|_2\} + \{j_a - j_b\} \tag{3}$$

$$(1 \leq a < b \leq k)$$

in which $\|j_a - j_b\|_2$ is the Euclidean Distance between joint a and joint b, $\{j_a - j_b\}$ is the difference between the two joints. Take the informativeness of skeleton itself into consideration, the difference between the two joints ($\{j_a - j_b\}$) is added to the feature. Procrustes Analysis has been done before feature extracting in order to keep the skeleton joint view invariant and eliminate the difference of the subjects. Then we trained a linear classifier for each Key Pose:

$$g(x) = w \cdot \varphi(x) \tag{4}$$

Algorithm 1. Initialize the Improved Key Poses Model

Input:

D_p, D_n, N, n_p;

$pos\_pose, neg\_pose, X_{p1}^1$;

for $i = 1$ **do**

  $pos\_pos = \{\}, neg\_pos = \{\}$

  $tmp\_position = 0$

  $\Phi^{exp} = \Phi(X_{p1}^1)$

  where X_{p1}^1 is the first frame of the first video in D_p

  for $X_j \in D_p$ **do**

    $pos\_pose = \{X_j^i \mid \arg\max_{X_j^i}(Euclidean(\Phi^{exp}, \Phi(X_j^i)))\}$

    $tmp\_position+ = \frac{i}{length(X_j)}$

    where $i \in [1, \frac{1}{N}length(X_j))$

  end for

  for $X_j \in D_n$ **do**

    $neg\_pos = \{X_j^i \mid i = random[1, \frac{1}{N}(length(X_j))]\}$

  end for

  Train $g_1(x)$ with pos_pose and neg_pose

  $c_{p1} = \frac{tmp\_position}{n_p}$

  $c_{o1} = abs(\max(\frac{i}{length(X_j)} - c_{p1}))$

end for

for $i = 2, ..., N$ **do**

  $pos\_pos = \{\}, neg\_pos = \{\}$

  $tmp\_position = 0$

  for $X_j \in D_p$ **do**

    $pos\_pos = \{X_j^i \mid \arg\min_{X_j^i} g_{(i-1)}(X_j^i)\}$

    $tmp\_position+ = \frac{i}{length(X_j)}$

    where $i \in [\frac{i-1}{N}length(X_j), \frac{i}{N}length(X_j))$

  end for

  for $X_j \in D_n$ **do**

    $neg\_pos = \{X_j^i \mid i = random[\frac{i-1}{N}length(X_j), \frac{i}{N}length(X_j)]\}$

  end for

  Train $g_i(x)$ with pos_pose and neg_pose

  $c_{p_i} = \frac{tmp\_position}{n_p}$

  $c_{o_i} = abs(\max(\frac{i}{length(X_j)} - c_{p_i}))$

end for

compute w_{g_i} and $w_{c_{p_i}}$ by training linear SVM

Features described in Eq. (3) reflect the range of the skeleton joint movement. The actions with micro-motion such as clap hands are difficult to recognize because the skeleton joint movement range of these action are not large enough and the skeleton data may contain more noise. To recognize the action with local (arm or leg) micro-motion easily, the feature emphasizes the slight movement of the action. For example, for the Key Poses of action clap, Euclidean Distance between most joints is stable, the Euclidean Distance and difference between left and right wrist is variable. Figure 2 in experiment section showed the effectiveness of improved method.

2.3 Training of the Key Poses Model

Shown in Algorithm 1, the model is first initialized: D_p and D_n are the positive subset and negative subset of D, and the model is initialized with N Key Poses. In order to initialize our model, we first compute $\Phi(X_{p1}^1)$, X represents a video, the subscript represents the serial number of a video, the superscript represent the frame serial number. By computing the Euclidean distance, we select the skeleton poses which are most different from the X_{p1}^1 and put them in pos_pos. In other words, these poses are in the first subsequence in each skeleton sequence and have most obvious motion against the standing pose. The neg_pos is random selected. Then the linear classifier $g_1(x)$ is trained. Next we could train the remainder linear classifier by iteration. To train the i-th linear classifier, pos_pos is found with the help of g_{i-1} in subsequence i in each positive video. In the same scope, neg_pos is random selected. And corresponding c_{p_i} and c_{o_i} will be computed too. Finally, w_{g_i} and $w_{c_{p_i}}$ will be computed by training the linear SVM.

As we can see in Algorithm 1, there are several difference with our earlier work. When the model is initializing, we select pos_pos to training the classifier $g_i(x)(i \neq 1)$ with the help of $g_{i-1}(x)$. For each pose in pos_pos, $g_{i-1}(x)$ get the lowest value at pose in corresponding subsequence. In testing procedure, the quite different classifiers select most discriminative Key Poses to represent the action. In previous work, temporal position and offset is used to select pos_pos, but in Algorithm 1, c_{p_i} and c_{o_i} is computed after the training of linear classifiers.

When the Improved Key Poses Model is initialized, the position of Key Poses could be treated as latent variable according [6]. We minimize the same objective function mentioned in [8] with stochastic gradient descent. In the iteration process, the linear classifiers $g(x)$ is retrained, c_{p_i} and c_{o_i} will be recomputed. When the objective function gets convergence, our model could be used to recognise the action according Eq. (1). Figure 1(b)–(d) shows the results on some actions.

3 Experiment Results

In this section, we evaluate our model on three benchmark datasets: MSR action3D dataset, UTKinect Action dataset and Florence 3D Actions dataset. Following [8], 4 is selected as the Key Poses number. Experiment results demonstrate the effectiveness of proposed method.

3.1 Dataset Introduction

MSR action3D dataset [7] consist of the skeleton data obtained by depth sensor similar to the Microsoft Kinect. The data was captured at a frame rate of 15 frames per second. It contains 20 actions and each action was performed

Table 1. Results on AS1, AS2, AS3

Action subsets	AS_1	AS_2	AS_3	Average
Accuracy	91.53%	90.23%	**97.06%**	92.94%

by 10 subjects in an unconstrained way for two or three times. **UTKinect Action** dataset [17] was captured using a single stationary Kinect and contains 10 actions. Each action is performed twice by 10 subjects in indoor setting. It is recorded with a frame rate of 30 frames per second. **Florence 3D Actions** dataset [14] was collected at the University of Florence during 2012 and captured using a Kinect camera. It includes 9 activities, 10 subjects were asked to perform the above actions for two or three times. This resulted in a total of 215 activity samples. And each frame contains 15 skeleton joints.

3.2　Result on MSR Action3D Dataset

Several studies have already been conducted on the MSR Action3D dataset. According to the protocol by Li et al. [7], we divided the dataset into subsets AS_1, AS_2, AS_3, each consisting of 8 actions, and performed recognition on each subset separately. The subsets AS_1 and AS_2 were intended to group actions with similar movements, while the AS_3 was intended to group complex actions together. And in this experiment, we evaluate our method using a cross-subject test setting: videos of 5 subjects were used to train our model and videos of other 5 subjects were used for test procedure.

Table 1 reports the recognition rates for the proposed approach on three subsets and Table 2 shows the accuracy for various method on MSR Action 3D dataset. Our method gets a very high accuracy up to 97.06% on AS_3 and it proves that our model conquers the complex actions. We can clearly see that the proposed representation almost performs better than the listed method from Table 2. The average accuracy of proposed method is 2% better than our earlier work. It is only lower than Wang et al. [5], but training the Improved Key Poses Model just needs several minutes on the platform with Windows 10 and Intel Core i7-7700K Processor (8M cache, 4.2 GHz). Compared with our method, training a hierarchical recurrent neural network is time-consuming.

3.3　Result on UTKinect Action Dataset

The performance of the proposed method is also assessed based on the UTKinect Action dataset. In this experiment, we also take the cross-subject protocol. Table 3 summarizes the results of our model along with competing approaches on the dataset. We can see that our method achieve the best performance on average accuracy than other approaches. Especially it is 3.3% better than our earlier work. Figure 2 reports the recognition accuracies of each action in UTKinect. For the actions whose skeleton joint movement range of these action are not

Table 2. Comparison our method with others on MSR Action3D dataset

Method	Accuracy
Venulapalli et al. [15]	92.46%
Wang et al. [5]	**94.49%**
Zhou et al. [19]	92%
Salih et al. [18]	90.98%
Li et al. [8]	90.94%
Our method	**92.94%**

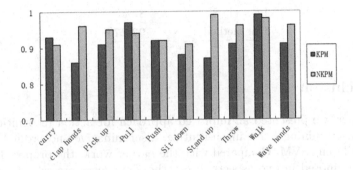

Fig. 2. Results on UTKinect dataset comparison with earlier work [8]

large enough such as clap and wave, the IKPM shows great improvement. For sit down and stand up, IKPM pays attention to the order of Key Poses, So the accuracy gets obviously increased.

Table 3. Comparison our method with others on UTKinect Action dataset

Method	Accuracy
Batabyal et al. [2]	91.45%
Boulahia et al. [3]	94%
Salih et al. [18]	93%
Li et al. [8]	91.5%
Our method	**94.8%**

3.4 Result on Florence 3D Action Dataset

As for Florence 3D Action dataset, we conduct the experiment with the leave-one-actor-out protocol which is suggested by dataset collector. The experimental results are shown in Table 4. By analyzing the experiment result of our method, we can notice that the proposed approach obtains highest accuracy than other methods. It is obvious hat we make a great progress with 5.17% than our previous work. These results clearly demonstrate the superiority of the proposed representation over various existing approaches.

Table 4. Comparison our method with others on Florence 3D Action dataset

Method	Accuracy
Venulapalli et al. [15]	91.88%
Salih et al. [18]	86.13%
Li et al. [8]	87%
Our method	**92.17%**

4   Conclusion

In this paper, we presented an improved approach for action recognition based on skeleton by mining a few inconsecutive, discriminative and ordinal skeleton poses with latent SVM. Compared with the earlier work, the proposed method has been promoted in two aspects. First, the Key Poses are selected in order, they could better represent an action and make the recognition process more coinciding with human cognition. Second, the relative position feature emphasizes the micro-motion of actions. It could get higher accuracy on the action clap and wave. We validated our model on three benchmark datasets: MSR Action3D dataset, UTKinect Action dataset and Florence 3D Actions dataset. Experiment results shows that the proposed approach outperforms than some state-of-the-art methods. Take the cost-effective advantage of our model, we will research on a real-time action monitoring system in the future work.

Acknowledge. This work is partially supported by Shanghai Innovation Action Plan Project under the grant No. 16511101200.

References

1. Aggarwal, J.K., Ryoo, M.S.: Human activity analysis: a review. ACM Comput. Surv. **43**(3), 16 (2011)
2. Batabyal, T., Chattopadhyay, T., Mukherjee, D.P.: Action recognition using joint coordinates of 3d skeleton data. In: 2015 IEEE International Conference on Image Processing (ICIP), pp. 4107–4111. IEEE (2015)
3. Boulahia, S.Y., Anquetil, E., Kulpa, R., Multon, F.: HIF3D: handwriting-inspired features for 3d skeleton-based action recognition. In: 23rd International Conference on Pattern Recognition (ICPR 2016) (2016)
4. Devanne, M., Wannous, H., Berretti, S., Pala, P., Daoudi, M., Del, B.A.: 3-d human action recognition by shape analysis of motion trajectories on Riemannian manifold. IEEE Trans. Cybern. **45**(7), 1340–1352 (2014)

5. Du, Y., Fu, Y., Wang, L.: Representation learning of temporal dynamics for skeleton based action recognition. IEEE Trans. Image Process. **25**(7), 1–1 (2016)
6. Felzenszwalb, P.F., Girshick, R.B., McAllester, D., Ramanan, D.: Object detection with discriminatively trained part-based models. IEEE Trans. Pattern Anal. Mach. Intell. **32**(9), 1627–1645 (2010)
7. Li, W., Zhang, Z., Liu, Z.: Action recognition based on a bag of 3d points. In: Computer Vision and Pattern Recognition Workshops, pp. 9–14 (2010)
8. Li, X., Liao, D., Zhang, Y.: Mining key skeleton poses with latent SVM for action recognition. Appl. Comput. Intell. Soft Comput. (2017)
9. Li, X., Yao, Q.: Action detection based on latent key frame. In: Yang, J., Yang, J., Sun, Z., Shan, S., Zheng, W., Feng, J. (eds.) Biometric Recognition. LNCS, vol. 9428, pp. 659–668. Springer, Cham (2015). https://doi.org/10.1007/978-3-319-25417-3_77
10. Mahasseni, B., Todorovic, S.: Regularizing long short term memory with 3d human-skeleton sequences for action recognition. In: IEEE Conference on Computer Vision and Pattern Recognition, pp. 3054–3062 (2016)
11. Müller, M., Röder, T.: Motion templates for automatic classification and retrieval of motion capture data. In: ACM Siggraph/Eurographics Symposium on Computer Animation, SCA 2006, Vienna, Austria, pp. 137–146, September 2006
12. Ofli, F., Chaudhry, R., Kurillo, G., Vidal, R., Bajcsy, R.: Sequence of the most informative joints (SMIJ): a new representation for human skeletal action recognition. J. Vis. Commun. Image Represent. **25**(1), 24–38 (2014)
13. Pazhoumand-Dar, H., Lam, C.P., Masek, M.: Joint movement similarities for robust 3d action recognition using skeletal data. J. Vis. Commun. Image Represent. **30**, 10–21 (2015)
14. Seidenari, L., Varano, V., Berretti, S., Bimbo, A., Pala, P.: Recognizing actions from depth cameras as weakly aligned multi-part bag-of-poses. In: Proceedings of the IEEE Conference on Computer Vision and Pattern Recognition Workshops, pp. 479–485 (2013)
15. Vemulapalli, R., Arrate, F., Chellappa, R.: Human action recognition by representing 3d skeletons as points in a lie group. In: Proceedings of the IEEE Conference on Computer Vision and Pattern Recognition, pp. 588–595 (2014)
16. Wang, J., Liu, Z., Wu, Y., Yuan, J.: Learning actionlet ensemble for 3d human action recognition. IEEE Trans. Pattern Anal. Mach. Intell. **36**(5), 914–927 (2014)
17. Xia, L., Chen, C.C., Aggarwal, J.: View invariant human action recognition using histograms of 3d joints. In: 2012 IEEE Computer Society Conference on Computer Vision and Pattern Recognition Workshops (CVPRW), pp. 20–27. IEEE (2012)
18. Youssef, C., et al.: Spatiotemporal representation of 3d skeleton joints-based action recognition using modified spherical harmonics. Pattern Recogn. Lett. **83**, 32–41 (2016)
19. Zhou, Y., Ming, A.: Human action recognition with skeleton induced discriminative approximate rigid part model. Pattern Recogn. Lett. **83**, 261–267 (2016)

Pic2Geom: A Fast Rendering Algorithm for Low-Poly Geometric Art

Ruisheng Ng[✉], Lai-Kuan Wong[✉], and John See[✉]

Faculty of Computing and Informatics, Multimedia University,
Persiaran Multimedia, 63100 Cyberjaya, Selangor, Malaysia
1122703066@student.mmu.edu.my, {lkwong,johnsee}@mmu.edu.my

Abstract. Low poly rendering has always been a popular form of art in the art and design community, where the artist draws each polygon (usually triangle) on the image individually. Several state-of-the-art methods were proposed to overcome the laborious process of manual low poly rendering, by rendering the low poly shapes automatically. However, results generated by the aforementioned methods were either not visually pleasing or the algorithms are computationally slow. In this paper, we present Pic2Geom, a fast algorithm that generates low poly geometric art with adequate quality, at low computational cost. The proposed algorithm utilizes edge detection, saliency detection and face detection to generate a set of seed points, which is then used by Delaunay triangulation to generate the low poly abstraction. Comparison with state-of-the-arts approaches demonstrate the efficiency and effectiveness of our algorithm in producing a quality geometric abstraction of a given photograph.

Keywords: Image abstraction · Low poly rendering
Geometric abstraction

1 Introduction

Geometric abstraction is a fork from image abstraction where it aims to discard unnecessary information from the image to create an abstract image, with the difference that it uses geometric shapes to represent its abstraction. Many works have been done on image abstraction, such as pixelated image abstraction by Gerstner et al. [11] and Kuwahara filtering abstraction by Kyprianidis et al. [10], but very few of these works focus on geometric abstraction.

Zhang et al. [2] proposed a real-time low-poly style image and video processing algorithm. To achieve real-time low-poly video processing, the processing speed has to be minimal as a typical video clip contains around 15 to 30 frames per second. Their algorithm achieved an impressive computational speed that hovers around 0.1 to 0.2 s. However, the abstraction produced by their approach lacks perceptual accuracy as photo subjects are not being identified and considered during the abstraction process.

© Springer International Publishing AG, part of Springer Nature 2018
B. Zeng et al. (Eds.): PCM 2017, LNCS 10736, pp. 368–377, 2018.
https://doi.org/10.1007/978-3-319-77383-4_36

Fig. 1. Results of Pic2Geom.

Gai et al. [1] proposed a fully automated low poly rendering method for images. Their approach aims to create high quality low-poly art by constraining edge features and incorporating custom color post-processing to reduce the zigzag artifacts produced during the abstraction process. Besides, to produce a perceptually accurate abstraction, it utilizes salient region detection to identify the photo subjects in an image and use more triangles to represent the photo subjects. The results produced by their algorithm are visually appealing, with accurate abstraction over a wide variety of images. However, this approach lacks computational efficiency. Compared to Zhang et al. [2] approach, the computational time of Gai et al. [1] algorithm is almost 20 times higher.

In this paper, we present an efficient algorithm, Pic2Geom, that aims to produce perceptually accurate geometric abstraction with computational time that is comparable to Zhang et al. [2] algorithm. In a nutshell, our proposed approach first identify the photo subjects. Based on the identified photo subjects, it generates a set of seed points that are then used to produce triangle-based, low poly geometric art. Figure 1 illustrates example results of Pic2Geom. Empirical evaluations conducted illustrate the effectiveness of Pic2Geom in producing high quality abstraction at low computation time.

2   Proposed Method

Figure 2 illustrates the overview of Pic2Geom. Given an input image, Pic2Geom first identify the important area of the image using a combination of saliency, edge and face detection techniques. It then generates a set of seed points, $P=\{P_s, P_e, P_f\}$ to represent the important area, where P_s, P_e and P_f are points generated based on the detected salient regions, edges and faces respectively. These seed points are then used by Delaunay triangulation [7] to generate a set of triangle meshes. To produce the final geometric abstraction of the image, each triangle

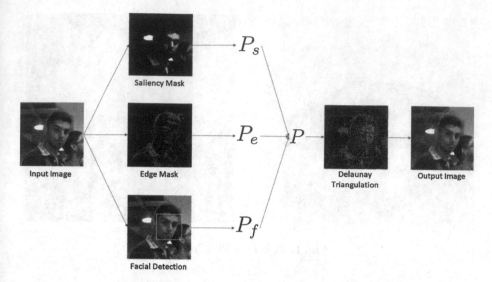

Fig. 2. Overview of Pic2Geom Algorithm. P_s is the salient points. P_e is the edge points. P_f is the facial points. P is the sum of salient points, edge points, and facial points.

mesh will be colored with the average color of the pixels within the mesh as shown in the output image in Fig. 2.

To simplify the user input in performing the abstraction, we utilize a single abstraction parameter, N_t to control the amount of triangles being generated on the image. This N_t parameter is used by the salient detector, edge detector, and facial detector to determine the number of seed points to be generated by each detector. A higher N_t value increases the number of triangles generated, leading to lower level of abstraction of the image and vice versa. In our experiments, we set N_t to 200, as it produces an image that is sufficiently abstract whilst maintaining its detail. Figure 3 illustrates the abstraction results produced using different N_t values.

2.1 Saliency Detection

We adopt Perazzi's saliency model [3] as our salient detector because it has relatively good detection performance and is computationally efficient. From the saliency mask produced by the salient detector, we observed that the salient regions are often very focused and much smaller than the non-salient regions. Thus, based on the assumption that visually salient regions are smaller than the less salient regions, our algorithm segments the saliency mask into four regions; S_a, S_b, S_c, and S_d, with the salient values of each segment in the range of 0 to 63, 64 to 127, 128 to 191, and 192 to 255 respectively. Example of a segmented salient mask is shown in Fig. 4(b). We then allocate N_t seed points to each segmented region. Thus, the number of salient seed points for an image, $|P_s|$ is $4 \times N_t$. This results in higher density triangles being produced in the more salient regions.

Fig. 3. Comparison of results generated using different N_t values. **(top left)** $N_t =$ 100, **(top right)** $N_t = 200$, **(bottom left)** $N_t = 300$, **(bottom right)** $N_t = 400$

Fig. 4. (left) Salient mask. **(right)** Segmented regions based on saliency values in ascending order: black (least salient region), blue, green, red (most salient region). (Color figure online)

2.2 Edge Detection

Prior to performing edge detection, we apply bilateral filter [4] to filter out any excessive noise from the input image. We then apply Canny edge detector [5] to detect the edges. Next, a set of seed points will be generated along the detected edges. To generate points on the edges, we first compute $xGap$ and $yGap$ using the following equations,

$$xGap = \frac{I_w}{N_t} \tag{1}$$

Fig. 5. Use of different N_t values for edge detection. (**left**) N_t=200 (**right**) N_t=350

$$yGap = \frac{I_h}{N_t} \qquad (2)$$

where $xGap$ is the gap between two consecutive edge points on the x-axis; $yGap$ is the gap between two consecutive points on the y-axis; I_w is the width of the image in pixels; and I_h is the height of the image in pixels. We then scan through the image using the computed $xGap$ and $yGap$ values and insert a seed point if the selected pixel lies on an edge. P_e is the set of all the edge points. Figure 5 illustrates the seed points generated using different N_t values.

As the values of $xGap$ and $yGap$ are proportional to the width and height of the image respectively, the number of seed points generated is invariant to the image resolution and our algorithm is scalable for different image resolution. Notably, our algorithm would produce more dense seed points on vertical and horizontal edges compared to diagonal edges but this inconsistency would not affect the visual abstraction result substantially.

2.3 Face Detection

Although the use of both saliency and edge detection are sufficient to create aesthetically pleasing geometric art for many images, it falls short when the algorithm is applied on portrait images. This is due to the nature of portrait images where the face of a person is very sensitive towards abstraction. We adopted Viola's face detection [6] to detect human face. The method used for generating points on the face is similar to that used in edge detection, except that its boundaries are constrained within the detected face region. The x- and y-gaps between the generated seed points on the detected face are computed as:

$$xFaceGap = \frac{2I_w}{N_t} \qquad (3)$$

$$yFaceGap = \frac{2I_h}{N_t} \qquad (4)$$

Notably, the values of $xFaceGap$ and $yFaceGap$ are two times larger than the gap values of $xGap$ and $yGap$. We double the gap values on the face to avoid generating too many points on the face as our experiment shows that using the same gap values as xGap and yGap would result in over realistic abstraction. The set of all the facial points is represented by P_f. If no face is detected by the face detector, no seed points based on face will be generated. Figure 6 illustrates an example of results with and without face detection.

Fig. 6. Comparison of results (**left**) without face detection, and (**right**) with face detection

2.4 Delaunay Triangulation and Colorization

Using the seed points, P, obtained from saliency, edge and face detection as the input, we perform Delaunay triangulation [7] to generate a set of triangular meshes to represent the image. For each triangle generated from Delaunay triangulation, we then color it with the average color of all colors of the pixels contained in the triangle to produce the final low-poly geometric art.

2.5 Performance Optimization

To lower its computational time, we perform several optimization to our algorithm. First, we use a downsampled image as the input to the salient detector. This improves the computational speed by a factor of ten times when an image is downsampled from 1200×800 to 300×200. We then upsample the generated salient mask back to its original resolution for generation of salient points. Notably, the downsampling process is only used for salient mask generation and it does not reduce the resolution of the output abstraction, which is generated based on the input image with the original resolution. We performed numerous comparison between the use of upsampled salient mask and the original salient mask in our algorithm and found that the quality of the resulting low-poly abstraction are comparable.

We also applied parallel processing to the triangulation algorithm by adopting OpenMP [8]. It allows us to fully utilize the CPU processing power by distributing the processing load onto multiple CPUs. This optimization further improved the speed performance by 50%.

3   Experiments and Results

From the results of Pic2Geom illustrated in Figs. 1 and 7, we can observe that our algorithm is able to produce perceptually accurate abstraction, where denser triangles are use to represent the important area of an image. To evaluate the computational efficiency and quality of our approach, we conducted a quantitative evaluation to evaluate the speed of our algorithm and a qualitative user study to evaluate the quality of our geometric abstraction results respectively. A summary of the results of both evaluations are depicted in Table 1.

Table 1. Summary of quantitative and qualitative results

Method	Speed (s)	User preference (%)
Gai et al. [1]	4.791	-
Polyvia [2]	0.247	4.23
DMesh [9]	-	15.77
Pic2Geom	0.476	80.00

Fig. 7. Example results of Pic2Geom.

3.1   Quantitative User Study

To evaluate the computational speed of our algorithm, we compare our proposed algorithm, Pic2Geom against Zhang et al. [2] (Polyvia) and Gai et al. [1] algorithm. The computational time for Polyvia and Gai et al. method are obtained from the user study conducted by Zhang et al. [2] on the Mickey Mouse image illustrated in Fig. 8. We use the same computer specification used in Zhang et al. [2] user study, which is a computer with an Intel Core i7-3770 3.4 GHz and 8 GB RAM, to obtain the computational time for Pic2Geom. The speed comparison depicted in Table 1 shows that the computation time of Pic2Geom is only 2 times slower than Polyvia but 10 times faster than Gai et al. algorithm. From the

| (a) Pic2Geom | (b) Gai et al [1] | (c) Zhang et al [2] |

Fig. 8. Visual comparison with state-of-the-arts low poly rendering methods.

visual comparison of the three methods in Fig. 8, it is obvious that Pic2Geom and Gai et al. approaches can preserve the important features better to produce a more visually appealing abstraction compared to Polyvia. This result shows that our proposed algorithm, Pic2Geom can achieve visual results that are comparable to Gai et al. approach but with significantly less computation time.

3.2 Qualitative User Study

For the qualitative user study, we could not benchmark against Gai et al. [1] method because their source code is not publicly available. Thus, we compare our method against Polyvia [2] and DMesh [9]. DMesh is a commercially available software, in which its algorithm is not disclosed. From the results of DMesh, we believe some salient region detection techniques are applied to generate denser triangles on the important area. Comparatively, DMesh produces perceptually more accurate results than Polyvia. We use a set of 15 images for this user study. For each input image, we generate the results for Pic2Geom, Polyvia and DMesh using the default parameters of the three algorithms. Theoretically, it would be desirable to conduct the evaluation using results with the same number of triangles used for the abstraction for all three approaches. However, in practical, it is difficult to obtain the same number of triangles in the results for each approach because given the same user parameter, the number of triangles generated to represent the image abstraction may differ depending on the content of the input images. From the visual comparison of the three approaches in Fig. 9, we can observe that the triangles used to represent the abstraction differs in terms of the triangle size and distribution but not so much in terms of the numbers. Thus, we opt to use the default parameters for the user study as the

Fig. 9. Comparison of results; **(left)** Pic2Geom, **(middle)** DMesh and **(right)** Polyvia.

default parameters are determined by each researcher experimentally to produce relatively appealing results for their automatic approach.

The user study is conducted online and we recruited a total of 52 respondents. During the user study, the results of the three methods are displayed in a random order and subjects are instructed to select the most appealing abstraction image out of the three results. In total, we collected a total of 780 votes. From the results of the user study depicted in Table 1, Pic2Geom results are highly preferred over the results of Polyvia and DMesh, with over 80% of the 780 votes goes to Pic2Geom. Interestingly, from the analysis of the results for each image illustrated in Fig. 10, Pic2Geom gathered the majority votes for all

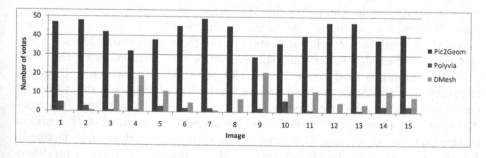

Fig. 10. Results of qualitative study.

the 15 images and outperformed Polyvia and DMesh. This is very likely due to the lack of accuracy in detecting the important areas in the Polyvia and DMesh methods.

The visual comparison of the results in Fig. 9 shows that Pic2Geom can distinguish the photo subject more accurately compared to Polyvia and DMesh, particularly for the images of the deer and the girl. DMesh seems to confuse the textured background with the photo subject and thus produced some very dense triangles in some area of the background. On the other hand, results of Polyvia illustrate a rather uniform distribution of triangles that do not give much focus to the photo subject. These results show that the subjects have a preference for perceptually more accurate abstraction.

4   Conclusion

In this paper, we presented a fast rendering algorithm, Pic2Geom, that automates the low poly rendering to produce good quality geometric abstraction at low computational cost. We were able to achieve perceptually accurate abstraction by using our subject detection techniques that include saliency detection, edge detection, and face detection. We apply several speed optimization to our algorithm to reduce its computational time such as downsampling the input for saliency detection and parallel processing. In our future work, we intend to explore the possibility of incorporating learning-based strategies in pursuit of category-aware geometric abstraction.

References

1. Gai, M., Wang, G.: Artistic low poly rendering for images. Vis. Comput. **32**(4), 491–500 (2016)
2. Zhang, W., Xiao, S., Shi, X.: Low-poly style image and video processing. In: Systems, Signals and Image Processing (IWSSIP) 2015, pp. 97–100. IEEE (2015)
3. Perazzi, F., Krähenbühl, P., Pritch, Y., Hornung, A.: Saliency filters: contrast based filtering for salient region detection. In: Computer Vision and Pattern Recognition (CVPR) 2012, pp. 733–740. IEEE (2012)
4. Tomasi, C., Manduchi, R.: Bilateral filtering for gray and color images. In: 6th IEEE International Conference on Computer Vision, pp. 839–846. IEEE (1998)
5. Canny, J.: A computational approach to edge detection. IEEE Trans. Pattern Anal. Mach. Intell. **8**(6), 679–698 (1986)
6. Viola, P., Jones, M.: Rapid object detection using a boosted cascade of simple features. In: Computer Vision and Pattern Recognition 2001, p, I. IEEE (2001)
7. Delaunay, B.: Sur la sphere vide. Bulletin de l'Acadmie des Sciences de l'URSS, Classe des sciences mathmatiques et naturelles **6**, 793–800 (1934)
8. OpenMP Application Program Interface Version 2.0. http://www.openmp.org/wp-content/uploads/cspec20.pdf
9. DMesh, Triangulation Image Generator. http://dmesh.thedofl.com
10. Kyprianidis, J.E., Kang, H., Döllner, J.: Image and video abstraction by anisotropic Kuwahara filtering. Comput. Graph. Forum **28**(7), 1955–1963 (2009)
11. Gerstner, T., DeCarlo, D., Alexa, M., Finkelstein, A., Gingold, Y., Nealen, A.: Pixelated image abstraction. In: Proceedings of the Symposium on Non-Photorealistic Animation and Rendering, pp. 29–36. Eurographics Association (2012)

Attention Window Aware Encoder-Decoder Model for Spoken Language Understanding

Yiming Wang, Wenge Rong[✉], Jingshuang Liu, Jingfei Han, and Zhang Xiong

School of Computer Science and Engineering, Beihang University, Beijing, China
{wangym,w.rong,jingshuangliu,jfhan,xiongz}@buaa.edu.cn

Abstract. Slot filling task, which aims to predict the semantic slot labels for each specific word in word sequence, is one of the main tasks in Spoken Language Understanding (SLU). In this paper, we propose a variation of encoder-decoder model for sequence labelling. To better use the label dependency feature and prevent overfitting, we use Long Short Term Memory (LSTM) as encoder and Gated Recurrent Unit (GRU) as decoder. We also enhance the model by employing the attention mechanism with attention window as a novel feature, which considers the particularity in slot filling task that each target label corresponds to the specific words and hidden units in the encoder. We test the proposed model using the standard ATIS corpus by adopting different size of attention window. The analysis of trends for the results using different attention window size has shown its application potential of attention window feature.

Keywords: Spoken language understanding
Encoder-decoder model · Attention mechanism · Label dependency
Attention window

1 Introduction

Domain identification, intent classification and slot filling are three typical tasks in Spoken Language Understanding (SLU) [11]. Specifically, the slot filling task focus on predicting the semantic slot labels for each specific word in the word sequence. For example, for the word sequence "I want a ticket from Boston to Seattle", the goal here is to extract the label "departure-city" for the word "Boston", and the label "arrival-city" for the word "Seattle".

A lot of efforts have been devoted for the slot filling task, e.g., conditional random fields (CRFs) [5] and support vector machines (SVMs) [4]. Recently, as the rising of deep learning technologies, some popular models like simple Recurrent Neural Network (simple-RNN) [16] and Long Short Term Memory (LSTM) [15] have been applied to this task. Further extended methods like bidirectional Recurrent Neural Network (bi-RNN) [9] and Convolutional Neural Network (CNN) [13] also have shown satisfied performances solving the problem.

© Springer International Publishing AG, part of Springer Nature 2018
B. Zeng et al. (Eds.): PCM 2017, LNCS 10736, pp. 378–387, 2018.
https://doi.org/10.1007/978-3-319-77383-4_37

Attention mechanism, which has been a huge break through for machine translation task, has the advantage of considering all the information related in the hidden units of encoder, rather than only the last hidden states [1]. In this way, the decoder can "choose" the useful information by themselves to better fulfill the translation task. Moreover, the slot filling task and the machine translation task has common characteristic that they both output a sequence of label. Inspired by this idea, we propose to use the attention based encoder-decoder model for the slot filling task. A convenience of using encoder-decoder model in the slot filling task is that we do not have to consider the different length between the label sequence and the words sequence.

However, attention mechanism comes at cost because it has to go through all the hidden sequence of encoder to find the related information. To overcome this limitation, Luong et al. [8] proposed local attention which only looks at a subset of source words at a time, and achieved great performance in some of machine translation tasks. Moreover, there are two particularities for the slot filling task which fits the extension of local attention: (1) The predicting label corresponds to the specific words in the encoder, and (2) The predicting labels for the word sequence like "New York" or "from Boston to Seattle" largely depends on the phrase around the words itself rather than the whole sentence. Consequently, we extend our model with a feature called attention window, which circles only a few preceding and exceeding hidden units around the specific words and let the decoder focus more on the relevant information.

Furthermore, as label dependency has been proven an useful feature in slot filling [7], we tried to employ this feature in the proposed model as well. In order to prevent overfitting, we propose to use a less complicated but the same competitive decoder called Gated Recurrent Unit (GRU) in the encoder-decoder model. The main contribution of our work is two fold: (1) We extend the encoder-decoder model with LSTM as encoder and GRU as decoder with attention mechanism; (2) We add the attention window as the newly employed feature to the proposed model.

The remainder of the paper is organised as follow. Section 2 will introduce the related work and Sect. 3 will illustrate the proposed methodology. Afterwards Sect. 4 will present the experiment results and discuss the learned lessons. Finally, Sect. 5 will conclude this paper and point out the possible future work.

2   Related Work

The popularity of deep learning ushers the slot filling task into a new era. The RNN [16] and LSTM [15] have proven their ability in overcoming the traditional CRF [5] and SVM [4] models based approaches. Furthermore, the variations like bi-RNN [9], which consider the information from both ends of the sentence, and Deep-LSTM [15] have also achieved great performance.

Encoder-decoder model is firstly used on the machine translation task [12], which encoder the sentence level information in a vector for the decoder to translate. Moreover, the encoder-decoder model has been adopted for many natural language processing tasks. Noticing the similarities of slot filling task and machine translation task, in this paper we propose to use the encoder-decoder model.

Attention mechanism has been widely used on the encoder-decoder model and receive tremendous success in many areas such as machine translation [12] and visual question answering [6]. Local attention, which is less expensive and more efficient than global attention, has been proven to be very competitive [8]. Noticing the particularities of the slot filling task, we adopt the idea of local attention and propose the novel feature called "attention window", which makes the encoder-decoder model more fit for the slot filling task.

Label dependencies have also been used in the slot filling task. The CNN-CRF models the dependencies from the output of CNN [14]. Hybrid RNN is used to combine the Elman-type and Jordan-type RNNs [10]. Liu et al. use the label dependency on RNN and receive better performance [7]. Consider the fact of using label dependency means that more parameters will be added, so in order to prevent overfitting for a more complicated model like encoder-decoder, we propose to use a less complicated decoder GRU in the model.

3   Methodology

The whole model architecture is depicted in Fig. 1, where the top layer is the LSTM encoder and the bottom layer is the GRU decoder. The input $x1$ to $x6$ for both encoder and decoder are the same word sequence to be predicted. For the decoder, another input ($< B >$, $y1$ to $y5$) is the word embedding for the last predicted label, which is the ground truth label for training and the truly predicted label for testing. The attention mechanism is used to consider the hidden states from encoder and the dashed rectangle demonstrate the attention window with size 3. The plot demonstrates an example of how attention mechanism with an attention window is used in this model for different time steps.

3.1   LSTM-GRU Encoder-Decoder with Label Dependency

In this research, we employ the LSTM architecture like [3] for the encoder, which takes the positive word sequence as input. Each word in the sequences is represented by a one-hot-vector V and is transformed to d dimensional matrix through word embedding. In addition, the word context window is used to jointly consider the k preceding and succeeding words around the current input word.

The label dependency is another useful feature for the slot filling task [7]. However, using the label dependency in the complicated model like encoder-decoder might encounter overfitting. Therefore instead of using the same LSTM as encoder, here we use a less complicated decoder GRU to address the overfitting problem, e.g.,

$$r_t = \sigma\left(W_r x_t + U_r h_{t-1} + Y_r y_{t-1}\right) \tag{1}$$

$$z_t = \sigma\left(W_z x_t + U_z h_{t-1} + Y_z y_{t-1}\right) \tag{2}$$

$$\widetilde{h}_t = \tanh\left(W_h x_t + r_t \odot (U_h h_{t-1}) + Y_h y_{t-1}\right) \tag{3}$$

$$h_t = (1 - z_t) \odot h_{t-1} + z_t \odot \widetilde{h}_t \tag{4}$$

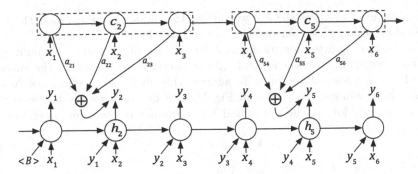

Fig. 1. The plot is the attention window aware encoder-decoder model for spoken language understanding. The plot demonstrates a example of how attention mechanism with attention window is used in the model for the time step 2 and 5, where the size of the attention window equals 3.

where x_t denotes the input at time t, and y_{t-1} denotes the used label dependency for the last time step. r and z are reset gate and update gate respectively, while W, U and Y are transformation matrices.

Furthermore, the used value of y_{t-1} is different in the phase of training and testing because we use the ground truth label for training and truly predicted label for testing. To make the model more robust for handling the predicting mistakes during testing, we adopt the method from [7] to proportionally select the ground truth label and the predicted label for y_{t-1} during training. During testing, the value of y_{t-1} equals to the last predicting label and the left-to-right beam search is used. We initialised GRU's first hidden unit with the mean value of the hidden unit of encoder LSTM for the word sequence. In this way the decoder takes the sentence level information into consideration.

3.2 Attention Mechanism with Attention Window

The architecture of our used attention mechanism is defined as follows:

$$e_{tk} = h_{t-1} \odot c_k \tag{5}$$

$$\alpha_{tk} = \frac{\exp\left(e_{tk}\right)}{\sum\limits_{i=1}^{L} \exp\left(e_{ti}\right)} \tag{6}$$

$$a_t = \sum\limits_{k=1}^{L} \alpha_{tk} c_k \tag{7}$$

where e_{tk} is the cosine similarity between h_{t-1} (the hidden unit of $t-1_{th}$ time step in GRU decoder) and c_k (the memory cell of k_{th} time step in LSTM encoder). The weight a_{tk} is calculated through softmax function because the sum of a_{tk} from 1 to L must equal to 1. L denotes the length of the current word sequence and a_{tk} is the k_{th} weight for the hidden state c_k. a_t is the final acquired attention vector for decoder in time step t.

However, using attention mechanism for the slot filling task has a limitation that the predicting label corresponds to the specific hidden unit in the encoder instead of the whole hidden unit. To address this limitation, we propose to add the attention window (as shown in Fig. 1) as a new feature for the attention mechanism, i.e., for c_k, the upper and lower bounds of the sum operation are different:

$$k \in [t - s, t + s] \tag{8}$$

with $t - s \geq 0$ and $t + s \leq L - 1$, so that

$$\alpha_{tk} = \frac{\exp{(e_{tk})}}{\sum\limits_{i=t-s}^{t+s} \exp{(e_{ti})}} \tag{9}$$

$$a_t = \sum\limits_{k=t-s}^{t+s} \alpha_{tk} c_k \tag{10}$$

where $2s + 1$ is the size of the attention window. For those time steps whose upper and lower bound of the attention window are out of the range of $[0, L]$, consider only the hidden unit within that range.

The attention window makes the decoder only consider a few hidden states around the target word instead of the whole hidden states. In this way, the decoder does not have to consider all the information from the whole hidden state in encoder, especially the hidden unit far from the specific words which may have little information. The attention window makes the decoder more focused and act more efficiency.

The acquired matrix a_t from attention mechanism was used in the softmax layer to jointly predict the label with the hidden unit of decoder, e.g.,

$$s_t = softmax\ (Wh_t + W_a a_t + b) \tag{11}$$

where h_t is the current hidden unit calculated by the decoder, and W and W_a are transformation matrices. For training, the negative log likelihood of the cross entropy cost is minimised with Back Propagation Through Time using Theano.

4   Experimental Study

4.1   Experimental Setup

In this research we test the proposed model on the Airline Travel Information System (ATIS) dataset [2], which has been widely used as a benchmark of the SLU tasks. Figure 2 shows one example of the sentence and the goal label in In-Out-Begin (IOB) representation.

The ATIS corpus contains 4978 sentences as training data and 893 sentences as test data. We randomly select 80% of the training data for training and the

Sentence	show	flights	from	Boston	to	New	York	today
Slots	O	O	O	B-FromCity	O	B-ToCity	I-ToCity	B-Date

Fig. 2. Example of a ATIS sentence and the annotated slots.

other 20% training data for validation. The performance was measured by the F1-score for the test data every time there is an improvement in validation set. For training, we randomly initialised parameters in accordance with the uniform distribution $(-0.2, 0.2)$. Particularly, as [3] suggests, we initialised the bias of the forget gate in the LSTM encoder for one and the other bias for zero. We run the experiment for 100 epochs and use the simple learning rate control as to reduce half of the learning rate when there is no improvement in ten epochs and stop the training as the learning rate is under 10^{-5}.

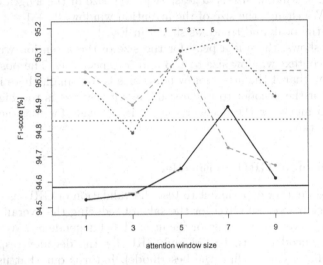

Fig. 3. The plot shows the trend between F1-score and the attention window size. The black, red and green lines represent the trends when the context window size is 1, 3 and 5 respectively. The straight lines denote the baseline when abandoned the feature of attention window. (Color figure online)

4.2 LSTM-GRU Encoder-Decoder with Attention Window

We conducted experiment on the LSTM-GRU encoder-decoder model using attention window, comparing it to the baseline with no attention window to see the improvement. Also, we test different attention window sizes to find the best size which gives us the best test result. For all the experiments, we set the word embedding size to 100 and the number of hidden units to 100 as well. We fix the beam search size to 8. We test different size of context window with the model with no attention window. Then, by adding the attention window, we test different size of attention window with the fixed context window to find the best result, as shown in Table 1.

Table 1. Best F1-score for models with/without context window [%].

Window size	With window	Without window
1	94.89	94.58
3	95.09	95.03
5	95.15	94.84

As the results show, by adding the attention window, there is a improvement compared to the model with no attention window. This indicate that the attention window is a useful and necessary feature for the encoder-decoder model in the slot filling task. Moreover, we also analysis the influence of the attention window size. We can regard the model with no attention window as the model whose attention window size is at least twice the size of the length of the word sequence L. We change the size of the attention window, $2s + 1 \in \{1, 3, 5, 7, 9\}$, and analysis the peak and trend, as shown in Fig. 3.

As Fig. 3 shows, there is a peak for the size of the attention window when we fixed the context window size to 1, 3 and 5 respectively. The possible explanation may be that if the attention window size is too small, there is not much information for the decoder to process; if the window size is too big, the information is too much for the decoder that it is not easy for it to get the truly useful information.

4.3 Validation of GRU as Encoder

We conducted another experiment to test the validation of GRU as decoder. As introduced before, we use GRU for the sake of reducing the overall parameter, so that it can prevent overfitting for the use of label dependency. We use LSTM, GRU for the encoder, with LSTM and GRU for the decoder respectively in the experiments trying to find the best model. It turns out that using LSTM as encoder is slightly better. Specifically, when using the same structure and parameters as the best result (95.15%) does but exchanging the decoder from GRU to LSTM, the result is 94.89%, which in some level validates the using of GRU as decoder.

4.4 Comparison Results and Discussion

We summarise the recently published result in Table 2 on the ATIS slot filling task using only the lexicon feature as ours. It is found that the LSTM-GRU encoder-decoder using attention mechanism with attention window have a really competitive result. By comparing with the published methods, we discuss the advantage of our model and the information from the experiment results.

First, the main difference from our method compared to the previous methods is the use of encoder-decoder model with attention mechanism on the slot filling task. As shown in Table 2, even without the use of attention window, the results of the encoder-decoder model with attention mechanism can still outstrip lots of the baseline, so we add this result to the comparison to show the great potential of attention mechanism. This might show the advantage of using encoder-decoder model and probably due to: (1) The first hidden state of decoder is initialized by the mean value of the hidden state of encoder to get the sentence level information; (2) by feeding the lexicon feature to the encoder and decode twice, the network can memories the information better; (3) by using the attention mechanism, the decoder has ability to choose the useful information from the whole sentence to better predict the label.

Furthermore, the experiment shows that the attention window is indeed a useful feature. We analysis the peak and trend when size of the attention window varies. As Fig. 3 shows, there is a peak for the size of attention window when we fixed the size of context window to 1, 3 and 5 respectively. The possible explanation may be that if the attention window size is too small, there is not much information for the decoder to process, while if the window size is too big, the information is too much for the decoder that it is not easy for it to get the truly useful information. The best size of the attention window is around 5, which is around the normal size of a phrase, indicating that the truly useful for a word in slot filling task is in the phrase around it.

Table 2. Comparison with published results on ATIS slot filling task (with only the lexicon feature) [%].

Method	F1-score
CRF [5]	92.94
RNN [16]	94.11
CNN-CRF [14]	94.35
LSTM [15]	94.85
RNN-SOP [7]	94.89
Deep LSTM [15]	95.08
Our model without attention window	95.03
Our model with attention window	**95.15**

Finally, when using LSTM as encoder, using GRU as decoder receives better results than the LSTM decoder. It might be that in the slot filling task we can regard the encoder as the assistant of the decoder, providing extra information for the decoder to process. In this way, a model which is complicated than the decoder itself may have more extra information, which may result in better consequences.

5 Conclusion and Future Work

In this paper we proposed an encoder-decoder model with LSTM as encoder and GRU as decoder and also adopted the label dependency and the attention mechanism. Furthermore, we added the attention window and analysed the trends and peak when the size of attention window varies. We also analysed the validation of using GRU as decoder. The experiential study on the standard ATIS corpus receive promising results.

In the future, we will test our model on other datasets, e.g., French MEDIA corpus. We may also test the encoder-decoder with different kinds of structure like bi-LSTM, simpe-RNN as encoder or decoder. Furthermore, as attention gives people the ability to interpret and visualise what the model is doing, we may interpret the usefulness of attention window in a visualised way as [1] does.

Acknowledgement. This work was partially supported by the National Natural Science Foundation of China (No. 61332018).

References

1. Bahdanau, D., Cho, K., Bengio, Y.: Neural machine translation by jointly learning to align and translate (2014). CoRR abs/1409.0473
2. Hemphill, C.T., Godfrey, J.J., Doddington, G.R.: The ATIS spoken language systems pilot corpus. In: Proceedings of the DARPA Speech and Natural Language Workshop, pp. 96–101 (1990)
3. Józefowicz, R., Zaremba, W., Sutskever, I.: An empirical exploration of recurrent network architectures. In: Proceedings of 32nd International Conference on Machine Learning, pp. 2342–2350 (2015)
4. Kudo, T., Matsumoto, Y.: Chunking with support vector machines. In: Proceedings of 2nd Meeting of the North American Chapter of the Association for Computational Linguistics on Language Technologies (2001)
5. Lafferty, J.D., McCallum, A., Pereira, F.C.N.: Conditional random fields: Probabilistic models for segmenting and labeling sequence data. In: Proceedings of 18th International Conference on Machine Learning, pp. 282–289 (2001)
6. Lin, Y., Pang, Z., Wang, D., Zhuang, Y.: Task-driven visual saliency and attention-based visual question answering (2017). CoRR abs/1702.06700
7. Liu, B., Lane, I.: Recurrent neural network structured output prediction for spoken language understanding. In: Proceedings of 2015 NIPS Workshop on Machine Learning for Spoken Language Understanding and Interactions (2015)
8. Luong, M.T., Pham, H., Manning, C.D.: Effective approaches to attention-based neural machine translation. In: Proceedings of 2015 Conference on Empirical Methods in Natural Language Processing, pp. 1412–1421 (2015)
9. Mesnil, G., Dauphin, Y., Yao, K., Bengio, Y., Deng, L., Hakkani-Tür, D.Z., He, X., Heck, L.P., Tür, G., Yu, D., Zweig, G.: Using recurrent neural networks for slot filling in spoken language understanding. IEEE/ACM Trans. Audio Speech Lang. Process. **23**(3), 530–539 (2015)
10. Mesnil, G., He, X., Deng, L., Bengio, Y.: Investigation of recurrent-neural-network architectures and learning methods for spoken language understanding. In: Proceedings of 14th Annual Conference of the International Speech Communication Association, pp. 3771–3775 (2013)
11. Shi, Y., Yao, K., Chen, H., Pan, Y., Hwang, M., Peng, B.: Contextual spoken language understanding using recurrent neural networks. In: Proceedings of 2015 IEEE International Conference on Acoustics, Speech and Signal Processing, pp. 5271–5275 (2015)

12. Sutskever, I., Vinyals, O., Le, Q.V.: Sequence to sequence learning with neural networks. In: Proceedings of 2014 Annual Conference on Neural Information Processing Systems, pp. 3104–3112 (2014)
13. Vu, N.T.: Sequential convolutional neural networks for slot filling in spoken language understanding. In: Proceedings of 17th Annual Conference of the International Speech Communication Association, pp. 3250–3254 (2016)
14. Xu, P., Sarikaya, R.: Convolutional neural network based triangular CRF for joint intent detection and slot filling. In: Proceedings of 2013 IEEE Workshop on Automatic Speech Recognition and Understanding, pp. 78–83 (2013)
15. Yao, K., Peng, B., Zhang, Y., Yu, D., Zweig, G., Shi, Y.: Spoken language understanding using long short-term memory neural networks. In: Proceedings of 2014 IEEE Spoken Language Technology Workshop, pp. 189–194 (2014)
16. Yao, K., Zweig, G., Hwang, M., Shi, Y., Yu, D.: Recurrent neural networks for language understanding. In: Proceedings of 14th Annual Conference of the International Speech Communication Association, pp. 2524–2528 (2013)

A New Fast Algorithm for Sample Adaptive Offset

Chentian Sun[✉], Yang Wang, Xiaopeng Fan, and Debin Zhao

Harbin Institute of Technology, Harbin, China
sct@stu.hit.edu.cn

Abstract. Sample Adaptive Offset is a new adopted technology by HEVC in recent years, which improves the visual quality of reconstructed videos significantly. However, there are two problems in current SAO technology. The first is that the statistic phase needs to traverse each pixel to collect relevant information. The other problem is that the complexity of SAO is too high for SAO mode decision stage, which needs to be performed on each CTU. To solve these problems, we proposed a fast SAO algorithm in HEVC encoder. We explore the correlation of SAO type among neighboring CTUs, and then utilize this spatial information to reduce the complexity of SAO. Experimental results demonstrate that our proposed method can achieve about 62%, 80% and 75% SAO encoding time saving on average in AI, RA, and LDB test condition compared with HM16.0 respectively. At the same time, the proposed method just causes negligible compression performance loss.

Keywords: HEVC · SAO · Merge · Statistic

1 Introduction

The High Efficiency Video Coding (HEVC) is under development by the Joint Collaborative Team on Video Coding (JCT-VC). HEVC focus on improving coding efficiency of high definition video. Based on H264/AVC, HEVC has made series improvements, using lots of new technologies, including 64×64 CTU, 35 intra prediction direction [2], quadtree structure, SAO filtering and so on. Its compression efficiency is nearly double compared with popular H.264 standard.

Sample adaptive offset (SAO) filter is applied after deblocking filter to reduce the distortion between reconstructed frames and original ones by adding offsets to each pixel, and could effectively solve the ringing effect in video encoding, improving the quality of it. But at the same time, it also brings some problems such as high coding complexity and large time consumption. To reduce the complexity of SAO encoding, many algorithm have been presented over the past several years.

In [3], Zhang proposed that depth information of the CTU partition could be used to help determine the type of SAO parameters. Meanwhile, a method of predicting the mode of current frame SAO using the correlation between intra-GOP video frames is proposed by Sayed El Gendy [4]. In [5], by limiting the correlation between the SAO patterns within tiles, the goal of improving the parallel ability of SAO mode judgment is achieved. Further, GPU is used to accelerate SAO filtering, which greatly enhance

B. Zeng et al. (Eds.): PCM 2017, LNCS 10736, pp. 388–396, 2018.
https://doi.org/10.1007/978-3-319-77383-4_38

the SAO's running speed [6]. In [7, 8], corresponding VLSI structure of SAO is improved to accelerate the running speed of SAO.

At present, most fast algorithm on SAO is focused on SAO mode decision stage, and few algorithms can further improve the efficiency of data statistics stage. As the data statistics phase accounts for more than 70% of the total SAO time, the key to improving SAO speed is to improve the statistical stage. After lots of testing, we found that among the distribution of SAO, there is a certain correlation in the mode of adjacent CTU. Based on it, we proposed a method which use information of adjacent CTUs to simultaneously reduce the time of data statistic phase and mode decision stage. Experimental result shows that the proposed method can greatly reduce the overall time of SAO.

This paper is organized as follows: in second section details of current SAO algorithm are introduced, the proposed method is given in third section. In fourth section the experimental result is presented. At the end, conclusion is given.

2 Background

Sample adaptive offset (SAO) is a new technique in HEVC. SAO uses offsets which got by statistics in CTU level to adjust each pixel in the image to reduce distortion. According to previous tests, SAO could improve coding performance effectively. In HEVC, SAO has two modes: EO (Edge Offset mode) and BO (Band offset mode).

2.1 Edge Offset

Firstly, SAO needs to choose which gradient mode using for CTB: 0, 45, 90 or 135° (Fig. 1).

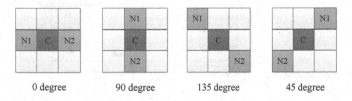

0 degree   90 degree   135 degree   45 degree

Fig. 1. Four EO classes

After chosen the gradient pattern for a CTB, the relationship between current pixel and 2 adjacent pixels in CTB is calculated to determine which edge mode to choose. As shown in Table 1.

In general, the EO pattern is used to refine regions with complex texture. At the same time, the BO pattern is designed for smooth, progressive regions of the texture.

Table 1. EO category classification condition

Edge type	Condition
0	p = n0 and p = n1
1	p < n0 and p < n1
2	p < n0 and p = n1 or p < n1 and p = n0
3	p > n0 and p = n1 or p > n1 and p = n0
4	p > n0 and p > n1

2.2 Band Offset

Band offset (BO) classify all pixels in one CTB region into 32 uniform bands. Some algorithms are selected to compensate 4 consecutive bands. When Luma or Chroma component of a CTB is in the selected band, compensate process would be performed for the sample. It is shown in Fig. 2.

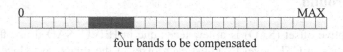

four bands to be compensated

Fig. 2. Compensate for BO offset

2.3 Whole Structure of SAO

Current SAO algorithm is divided into following three parts: a. Statistical stage; b. Mode decision stage; c. SAO filtering stage, which is shown in Fig. 3.

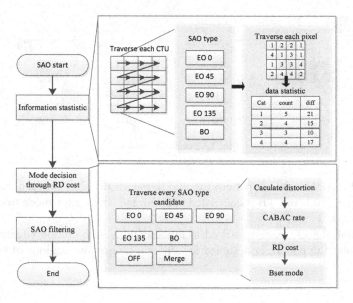

Fig. 3. Whole structure of SAO

In statistical stage, the encoder needs to traverse all the pixels of a frame in turn, and then calculate the relevant information of EO mode and BO mode for each pixel. This phase is the most important phase of SAO algorithm.

In mode decision stage, according to the data obtained by statistical phase, the encoder traverses each CTU in turn, calculates RD cost of EO, BO, OFF, and merge mode, then judges the best SAO mode of each CTU according to RD cost.

In SAO filtering stage, the encoder successively filter each CTU in reconstructed frame.

The proportion of the three steps is shown in Fig. 4.

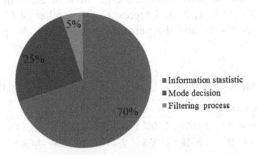

Fig. 4. Proportion of three steps in SAO

It can be seen from the graph that the statistical stage and mode decision stage takes about 95 of SAO time, which means to improve efficiency of SAO, the most important thing is to improve the efficiency of statistical and mode decision stage.

3 Proposed Algorithm

In this paper, we propose an algorithm called SAO adjacent mode fast filtering algorithm (AMF), which is designed base on the correlation in adjacent CTUs to improve the efficient of SAO.

3.1 Motivation

For natural images, adjacent regions have a certain correlation, which also applies to SAO.

Mode distribution of current SAO (takes the HEVC standard test sequence as example) is shown in Table 2.

From the table above it can be seen that for mode distribution of SAO, merge mode accounted for 80–90%, off mode accounted for about 10%, while EO and BO mode only accounted for 5%–10%, from which it can be seen that the merge mode occupies the vast majority in all SAO modes.

Table 2. Distributing of SAO modes in test sequence

Sequence	EO+BO	Off	Merge
Class A	2.10%	9%	88.90%
Class B	4.30%	20.2%	75.50%
Class C	12.30%	25%	62.70%
Class D	10.60%	17%	72.40%
Class E	2.20%	6.1%	91.70%

We further statistical the correlation of merge mode in adjacent CTUs, the result is shown in Table 3. Where 0, 1, 2, 3, 4 represent the number of CTU surrounding the current CTU in merge mode, and the percentage represents the possibility of merge mode for current CTU.

Table 3. Relationship of merge mode in adjacent CTUs

Sequence	0	1	2	3	4
Class A	2.16%	7.30%	8.36%	15.45%	66.73%
Class B	1.59%	5.98%	7.43%	10.18%	74.82%
Class C	2.55%	5.56%	7.04%	20.35%	64.5%
Class D	2.15%	7.17%	10.07%	17.26%	63.35%
Class E	3.43%	8.30%	8.20%	11.56%	68.51%

It can be seen from Table 3 that the left, upper-left, upper and upper-right mode of adjacent CTU are closely associated with the mode of current CTU. When the surrounding four CTUs are all in merge mode or at least three of them are merge mode, current CTU is likely to be merge mode.

3.2 SAO Adjacent Mode Fast Filtering Algorithm

The AMF algorithm could improve SAO both in statistic stage and mode decision stage.

3.2.1 Improvement in Mode Decision Stage

When starting to determine the mode of current CTU, AMF algorithm would first count the current CTU's left, upper-left, upper and upper-right four CTU's mode. If the number of adjacent four CTUs which is in merge mode is larger than or equal to merge_threshold, then it would set the mode of current CTU to be merge mode and enter the merge mode treating process (determine merge-up or merge-left). Otherwise, it enters normal CTU mode judgment process which is the same as in HM 16.0.

In order to ensure that merge mode to be determined as accuracy as possible, the merge_threshold is set to 4, which means only when the four adjacent CTUs are all in merge mode, the current CTU is determined to be merge mode.

Details are as follows:

Step1. Start to deal with a CTU in certain frame

Step2. Collect the mode of adjacent four CTUs

Step3. If the number of adjacent CTU in merge mode is less than merge_threshold, go to step step5, otherwise, go to step 4.

Step4. Execute merge mode decision process, to decide merge-left or merge-right for current CTU, then go to step6.

Step5. Execute EO, BO, OFF and merge mode decision process, to choose the best mode of current CTU

Step6.Mode decision stage for current CTU ended.

3.2.2 Improvement in Statistic Stage

In AMF algorithm, the original statistic phase is removed. CTU information collecting process is integrated into SAO mode decision process. In this way, the encoder does not need to count information of all CTUs in a video frame.

In mode decision stage, when the number of adjacent CTUs in merge mode is less than merge_threshold, the normal SAO mode judgment is entered, only in this case, the information of the pixels in current CTU is needed to be collected. Otherwise, it would directly go into merge mode (up-merge or left-merge) judgment without statistical process for current CTU. Which means only when the information of a CTU is required, would the information collecting process to be perform. The information collecting process is shown in Fig. 5.

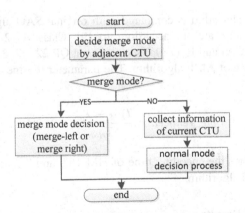

Fig. 5. Improved structure of statistic stage

3.2.3 Overall Framework of AMF Algorithm

Overall framework of AMF algorithm is shown in Fig. 6.

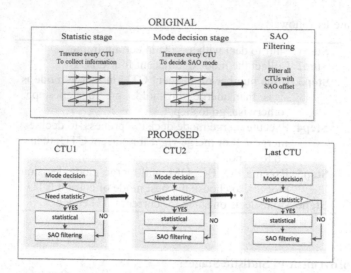

Fig. 6. Framework of original SAO and proposed algorithm

It can be seen that in AMF algorithm, every CTU's mode would be decided firstly and data statistical followed (if necessary). Because AMF algorithm improves the operation efficiency of model decision stage and data statistics stage simultaneously, time consuming of SAO is greatly reduced.

4   Experimental Result

4.1   Test Conditions

The proposed AMF algorithm is compared with original SAO algorithm of HM16.0. Experimental conditions are set according to [9]. Class A_(2 K), B_(1080p), C_(WVGA), D_(QWVGA) and E_(720p) sequences at QP 22, 27, 32 and 37 are used to verify the performance of AMF algorithm. The parameter of time reduced is calculated as follows:

$$time\_reduced = \frac{T_{HM} - T_{pro}}{T_{HM}} \times 100\% \qquad (1)$$

Where T_{HM} denotes the encoding time of HM 16.0 and T_{pro} denotes the encoding time of the proposed algorithm.

4.2   Experimental Results

Experimental results are presented in Table 4.

Because the proposed algorithm can effectively reduce the time consumed in statistical stage and mode decision stage. It can be observed that the proposed algorithm can achieve 61.9% SAO time reducing with almost no loss in AI configuration, and

Table 4. Experimental result

Anchor: HM 16.0		All Intra (AI)		Random Access (RA)		Low Delay (LD)	
		BD rate	Time reduced	BD rate	Time reduced	BD rate	Time reduced
Class A	Traffic	0.00%	54.43%	0.20%	85.55%	0.60%	80.32%
	PeopleOnStreet	0.30%	60.54%	0.60%	74.27%	1.10%	66.25%
Class B	Kimono	0.20%	88.44%	0.10%	80.91%	0.20%	73.46%
	ParkScene	0.10%	52.29%	0.20%	78.61%	0.50%	66.89%
	Cactus	−0.10%	60.60%	0.30%	75.60%	0.30%	65.07%
	BasketballDrive	0.00%	73.72%	0.30%	76.64%	0.50%	68.09%
	BQTerrace	0.00%	56.44%	0.70%	71.34%	0.60%	63.40%
Class C	BasketballDrill	−0.10%	65.12%	0.50%	82.72%	0.40%	70.57%
	BQMall	0.20%	73.51%	0.40%	84.70%	0.40%	71.93%
	PartyScene	0.00%	66.16%	0.20%	83.58%	0.20%	68.41%
	RaceHorses	0.10%	70.25%	0.10%	77.28%	0.50%	68.31%
Class D	BasketballPass	−0.20%	57.04%	0.40%	72.20%	0.50%	64.54%
	BQSquare	0.00%	46.97%	−0.20%	74.96%	0.00%	58.45%
	BlowingBubbles	−0.10%	69.36%	0.00%	54.89%	0.30%	54.89%
	RaceHorses	0.00%	62.42%	0.00%	62.28%	0.10%	67.92%
Class E	FourPeople	−0.10%	38.21%	0.00%	82.08%	0.40%	80.47%
	Johnny	−0.10%	56.61%	−0.10%	84.47%	0.50%	81.32%
	KristenAndSara	−0.10%	54.65%	0.10%	84.69%	0.60%	82.58%
Average	Class A	0.20%	57.49%	0.40%	79.91%	0.90%	73.28%
	Class B	0.00%	63.66%	0.30%	75.25%	0.46%	65.82%
	Class C	−0.10%	69.26%	0.10%	80.07%	0.40%	69.80%
	Class D	−0.10%	58.95%	0.10%	67.58%	0.20%	61.45%
	Class E	−0.10%	49.41%	0.00%	83.61%	0.50%	81.59%

about 80% SAO time reducing in RA and LD configuration with only about 0.4%-0.6% BD rate increasing on average, which is negligible. It means the proposed algorithm is very effective and valuable.

5   Conclusion

In this paper, we analysis the structure of current SAO process. The most time consuming stage of SAO is statistic stage and mode decision stage. So we proposed a fast SAO algorithm which could not only improve the speed of mode determine stage, but also the statistic stage. Result shows that, with proposed method the time of SAO process decreased 61.9% in AI configuration, and almost 80% in LD and RA configuration with little performance loss.

Acknowledgement. This work was supported in part by the National Science Foundation of China (NSFC) under grants 61472101 and 61631017, the National High Technology Research and Development Program of China (863 Program 2015AA015903), and the Major State Basic Research Development Program of China (973 Program 2015CB351804).

References

1. Bross, B., Han, W.-J., Sullivan, G.J., Ohm, J.-R., Wiegand, T.: High Efficiency Video Coding (HEVC) Text Specification Draft
2. Sullivan, G.J., Ohm, J.-R., Han, W.-J., Wiegand, T.: Overview of the high efficiency video coding (HEVC) standard. IEEE Trans. Circuits Syst. Video Technol. **22**(12), 1649–1668 (2012)
3. Zhengyong, Z., Zhiyun, C., Peng, P.: A fast SAO algorithm based on coding unit partition for HEVC. In: 2015 6th IEEE International Conference on Software Engineering and Service Science (ICSESS), pp. 392–395. IEEE (2015)
4. El Gendy, S., Sayed, M.S.: Fast parameter estimation algorithm for sample adaptive offset in HEVC encoder. In: 2015 Visual Communications and Image Processing (VCIP), pp. 1–4. IEEE (2015)
5. Chen, G., Pei, Z., Liu, Z., et al.: Low complexity SAO in HEVC base on class combination, pre-decision and merge separation. In: 2014 19th International Conference on Digital Signal Processing, pp. 259–262. IEEE (2014)
6. De Souza, D.F., Ilic, A., Roma, N., et al.: HEVC in-loop filters GPU parallelization in embedded systems. In: 2015 International Conference on Embedded Computer Systems: Architectures, Modeling, and Simulation (SAMOS), pp. 123–130. IEEE (2015)
7. Kuo, T.Y., Chiu, H., Amirul, F.: Fast sample adaptive offset encoding for HEVC. In: 2016 IEEE International Conference on Consumer Electronics-Taiwan (ICCE-TW), pp. 1–2. IEEE (2016)
8. Zhu, J., Zhou, D., Kimura, S., et al.: Fast SAO estimation algorithm and its VLSI architecture. In: 2014 IEEE International Conference on Image Processing (ICIP), pp. 1278–1282. IEEE (2014)
9. Bossen, F.: Common HM test conditions and software reference configurations. ISO JTC1/SC29/WG11, JCTVCG1200, Geneva, CH, November 2011

Motion-Compensated Deinterlacing Based on Scene Change Detection

Xiaotao Zhu[1], Qian Huang[1,2(✉)], Feng Ye[1], Fan Liu[1], Shufang Xu[1], and Yanfang Wang[1]

[1] College of Computer and Information,
Hohai University, Nanjing 211100, China
huangqian@hhu.edu.cn
[2] Key Laboratory of Symbolic Computation and Knowledge Engineering
of Ministry of Education, Jilin University, Changchun 130012, China

Abstract. This paper proposes to simplify the motion estimation process of motion-compensated deinterlacing based on the results of scene change detection. The design idea consists of four parts: scene change detection, motion estimation, motion state analysis, and motion-compensated interpolation. First of all, scene change detection is performed in the current field and the backward field, followed by intra interpolation or motion-compensated interpolation based on backward, forward or bi-directional motion estimation. Compared with conventional motion estimation schemes, the motion estimation and motion-compensated interpolation processes are simplified for video sequences with frequent scene changes. Experimental results show that the proposed algorithm outperforms traditional ones in terms of objective and subjective qualities. Moreover, the additional complexity is marginal.

Keywords: Scene change detection · Motion estimation
Motion-compensated interpolation · Deinterlacing

1 Introduction

Deinterlacing is a kind of format conversion that converts interlaced signals to progressive signals [1] and can be generally categorized into motion-compensated algorithms and non-motion-compensated algorithms. Non-motion-compensated algorithms [2–4] mainly utilize the spatio-temporal correlations to interpolate missing pixels. This kind of algorithms is used widely due to the simplicity of implementation. However, non-motion-compensated algorithms may produce jagged effects, blurring effects or line-crawling effects.

Motion-compensated algorithms [5–8] are currently the most advanced and most heated techniques for video deinterlacing. With motion estimation and motion analysis, they can eliminate the unsatisfactory effects mentioned above. However, the reliability of motion estimation and motion state analysis rely heavily on the video scenarios. For example, if objects or cameras move, there might be large difference in adjacent pictures, in which case the result of motion estimation is not convincing. Therefore, scene change detection is indispensable for motion-compensated video processing.

In the past decade, several kinds of methods were proposed for scene change detection [9–13]. They can be roughly divided into pixel-based methods, histogram-based methods, edge-based methods, statistics-based methods and methods based on maximum between-class variance. Currently the detection results are satisfactory for cut detection but not so good for gradual change detection. Moreover, satisfactory algorithms are typically based on frame pictures and may not suitable for interlaced videos.

This paper presents a low-complexity motion-compensated deinterlacing method based on scene change detection. The proposed scene change detection is based on field pictures, which reduces computing complexity and improves detection precision compared to frame-based algorithms. The rest of this paper is organized as follows. Section 2 discusses the proposed deinterlacing scheme. Section 3 gives the experimental results. Section 4 draws our conclusion.

2 Proposed Deinterlacing Scheme

Figure 1 sketches the proposed motion-compensated deinterlacing scheme, which consists of four main modules, i.e. Scene Change Detection, Motion Estimation, Motion State Analysis and Motion-Compensated Interpolation. The results of scene change detection can be divided into four categories:

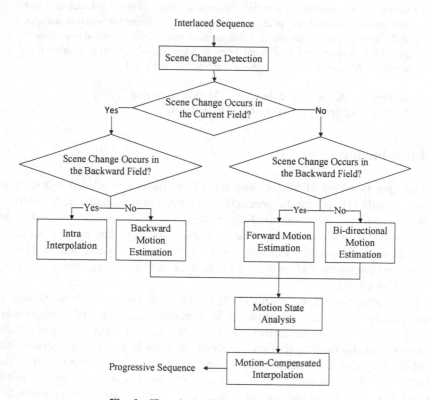

Fig. 1. Flowchart of the proposed scheme

No scene change in the current field. In this case, bi-directional motion estimation is performed, followed by motion state analysis and motion-compensated interpolation.

Scene change occurs in the backward field. In this case, forward motion estimation is performed, followed by motion state analysis and motion-compensated interpolation.

Scene change occurs in the current field. In this case, backward motion estimation is performed, followed by motion state analysis and motion-compensated interpolation.

Scene change occurs in both the backward field and the current filed. In this case, intra interpolation is performed.

2.1 Scene Change Detection

In order to simplify the motion estimation process and improve the accuracy of the optimal motion vector, scene change detection is performed before motion estimation. As shown in Eq. (1), each interlaced motion estimation block in the current field is compared with the corresponding interlaced block in forward or backward field to get the absolute image block difference (AIBD) value.

$$AIBD = \sum_{i=0}^{M-1} \sum_{j=0}^{N-1} |F_n(i,j) - F_{n\pm1}(i\pm1,j)|, \qquad (1)$$

where M and N represent respectively the height and width of an interlaced motion estimation block; $F_n(i,j)$ is a pixel value in the current interlaced motion estimation block; $F_{n\pm1}(i\pm1,j)$ are the values of co-located pixels in the forward and backward fields. Note that i and j are relative vertical and horizontal coordinates, respectively, and that in this paper n refers to the index of the current field. In order to reduce the computational complexity, a 1/4 down-sampling is performed before calculating the AIBD values.

After down-sampling, the number of interlaced motion estimation blocks that have larger values than a predefined experience threshold T are counted. Assume *count_forward* and *count_backward* are forward and backward counted results, respectively. Then the scene change detection process can be described as follows:

(1) If *count_forward* < TC and *count_backward* < TC, there is no scene change in the current field.

(2) If *count_forward* < TC and *count_backward* $\geq$ TC, then scene change occurs in the backward field.

(3) If *count_forward* $\geq$ TC and *count_backward* < TC, then scene change occurs in the current field.

(4) If *count_forward* $\geq$ TC and *count_backward* $\geq$ TC, then scene change occurs in both the current field and the backward field.

Note that TC is calculated as in Eq. (2), where *BlocksInHeight* and *BlocksInWidth* are the number of interlaced image blocks in the vertical and horizontal directions, respectively, and C is an empirical threshold.

$$TC = BlocksInHeight \times BlocksInWidth \times C, \tag{2}$$

2.2 Motion Estimation

The proposed motion estimation is based on the 3D recursive search (3DRS) block matching algorithm [14], the main idea of which is to use the spatio-temporal correlations of motion vectors, and obtain the true motion vector of the current block from spatio-temporal neighboring motion vectors. And the calculation complexity is also very low, hence it is widely used in the process of deinterlacing.

The initial 3DRS references only the forward frame, but it is likely to cause error propagation when selecting the optimal motion vectors due to scene change or camera movement. Therefore, the proposed motion estimation procedure selectively references pixels from the forward interpolated frame and the backward temporarily interpolated frame. Note that the backward frame is temporarily interpolated by the directional interpolation method proposed in [15]. The chosen of optimal motion vector varies according to different scene change detection results:

No scene change in the current field. In this case, the optimal motion vector is chosen from forward and backward motion vector candidates.

Scene change occurs in the backward field. In this case, the optimal motion vector is chosen from forward motion vector candidates.

Scene change occurs in the current field. In this case, the optimal motion vector is chosen from backward motion vector candidates.

Scene change occurs in both the backward field and the current filed. In this case, motion estimation will not be performed hence motion vector selection is unnecessary.

2.3 Motion State Analysis

In this paper, two motion states are identified, i.e. moving and stationary [15]. To improve the precision of motion state analysis, a quad-tree decomposition is performed on interlaced image blocks and the motion vectors are assigned to sub-blocks.

For each sub-block with motion, a 3×3 neighborhood is considered for motion state analysis. If both of the following conditions hold, the current sub-block is considered as motion consistent:

Most neighbors are the same. At least six sub-blocks in the 3×3 neighborhood share the same motion vector as the current sub-block.

SAD/STD Ratio is small. At most three sub-blocks in the 3×3 neighborhood satisfy Eq. (3), where i and j are relative vertical and horizontal coordinates respectively.

$$\frac{SAD}{\sqrt{H \times W \times \sum_{i=0}^{H-1} \sum_{j=0}^{W-1} F_n^2(i,j) - \left(\sum_{i=0}^{H-1} \sum_{j=0}^{W-1} F_n(i,j) \right)^2}} < ST. \tag{3}$$

Note that ST is an empirical value. H and W are the height and width of a motion analysis block, respectively. SAD is the average sum of absolute differences along motion trajectory. Take bi-directional motion estimation for example, SAD is computed as:

$$SAD = \frac{\sum_{i=0}^{H-1} \sum_{j=0}^{W-1} \left(|F_{n-1}(i+mv_y, j+mv_x) - F_n(i,j)| + |F_{n+1}(i-mv_y, j-mv_x) - F_n(i,j)| \right)}{2}. \quad (4)$$

2.4 Motion-Compensated Interpolation

The proposed motion-compensated interpolation relies on scene change detection results.

If no scene change occurs, there's a relatively strong spatio-temporal correlation between adjacent fields. Therefore, both the forward and the backward fields can be utilized for interpolation.

(1) If the current interpolation block is in the boundary region, the missing pixels are interpolated as:

$$F_n(i,j) = median\left(\frac{F_n(i-1, j+offset) + F_n(i+1, j-offset)}{2}, \right.$$
$$\left. \frac{F_n(i-1,j) + F_n(i+1,j)}{2}, \frac{A+B}{2}, A, B \right), \quad (5)$$

where $A = F_{n-1}(i+mv_y, j+mv_x)$ and $B = F_{n+1}(i-mv_y, j-mv_x)$ are the forward and backward reference pixels, respectively; and $offset$ indicates the edge direction in the current field.

(2) Else if the current interpolation block is in a motion consistency region, the missing pixels are interpolated as:

$$F_n(i,j) = median\left(F_n(i-1,j), F_n(i+1,j), \frac{F_n(i-1,j) + F_n(i+1,j)}{2}, A, B \right), \quad (6)$$

(3) Else if the current interpolation block is not in a motion consistency region and the motion state is stationary, then only the current field will be employed for interpolation:

$$F_n(i,j) = median\left(\frac{F_n(i-1, j+offset) + F_n(i+1, j-offset)}{2}, \right.$$
$$\left. F_n(i-1,j), F_n(i+1,j), \frac{F_n(i-1,j) + F_n(i+1,j)}{2} \right), \quad (7)$$

(4) Else if the current interpolation block is not in a motion consistency region and the motion state is moving, then the missing pixels are interpolated as:

$$F_n(i,j) = median\left(F_n(i-1,j), F_n(i+1,j), \frac{F_n(i-1,j) + F_n(i+1,j)}{2}, \frac{A+B}{2}, A, B\right), \quad (8)$$

If scene change occurs in the current field, we simply replace A by B for Eqs. (5), (6) and (8).

If scene change occurs in the backward field, we simply replace B by A for Eqs. (5), (6) and (8).

If scene change occurs in both the current and the backward field, the current field is interpolated by the directional interpolation method proposed in [15].

3 Experimental Results

The interlaced videos used for experiments are down-sampled from progressive videos. And some of the typical scenarios are combined to ensure that scene change does occur in our experiments. In order to demonstrate the robustness of the proposed scheme, different video resolutions are tested in this sub-section, where *BG_16336*, *BG_16337*, *BG_16343* and *BG_37309* are interlaced from the TRECVid 2007 videos, whereas *Comb288i*, *Comb480i*, *Comb576i* and *Comb720i* are generated from different typical sequences, each of which contributes 9 or 10 frames.

Based on extensive experiments, M, N, H, W are set to 8, 16, 4, 8, respectively; whereas T, C and ST are set to $24 \times M \times N$, 0.15 and 2, respectively.

3.1 Objective Performance

Comparison of Scene Change Detection. The higher motion vector accuracy is, the better motion-compensated video processing performance is expected. Therefore, we should improve the recall rate and precision rate of scene change detection, as defined below:

$$\begin{cases} recall\_rate = \frac{detected\ shots}{all\ shots} \times 100\% \\ precision\_rate = \frac{detected\ shots}{all\ annouced\ detection} \times 100\% \end{cases}, \quad (9)$$

where *shots* refer to actual scene changes.

As shown in Table 1, the proposed scene change detection method achieves much higher (almost 100%) precision rates than the global scene change detection method of Lin [10] on interlaced sequences with different scenarios and different resolutions, whereas the recall rates are comparable. In fact, our recall rates are also close to 100%, except when the luminance values are low. Therefore, the proposed scene change detection provides a solid foundation for subsequent motion estimation and motion-compensated interpolation.

Comparison of PSNR (dB). Table 2 illustrates that the proposed deinterlacing scheme is obviously better than traditional deinterlacing methods in terms of PSNR (dB). Moreover, the proposed scheme is stable for different resolution videos.

Table 1. Comparison of recall rate and precision rate

Sequence	Number of frames	Recall of Lin [10]	Recall of proposed	Precision of Lin [10]	Precision of proposed
BG_16336	300	100%	100%	50%	100%
BG_16337	300	100%	100%	42.85%	100%
BG_16343	300	0%	100%	0%	100%
BG_37309	300	100%	100%	50%	100%
Comb288i	300	94.44%	88.89%	47.89%	96.97%
Comb576i	90	100%	100%	45.00%	100%
Comb720i	100	100%	100%	47.62%	100%

Table 2. Comparison of PSNR (dB)

Sequence	Number of frames	Lin [10]	Zhang [16]	Jang [18]	Khan [17]	Mahvash [8]	Proposed
BG_16336	300	31.09	28.81	29.96	31.80	30.79	33.66
BG_16337	300	36.41	32.10	31.25	35.91	37.18	39.64
BG_16343	300	29.84	32.10	25.71	28.63	33.17	34.83
BG_37309	300	34.64	23.56	26.10	27.73	37.75	38.66
Comb288i	300	32.61	27.40	27.67	30.72	30.39	35.70
Comb576i	90	31.71	30.41	30.25	35.04	26.70	35.19
Comb480i	50	34.34	35.85	40.29	44.80	29.09	45.82
Comb720i	100	33.00	31.22	31.62	35.72	27.90	36.05
Average	/	**32.96**	**30.18**	**30.36**	**33.79**	**31.62**	**37.44**

Comparison of Running Efficiency. The running efficiency of some motion-compensated deinterlacing methods is compared in Table 3, where Proposed+intro-duces finer-grained motion estimation based on the proposed scheme, i.e. smaller motion estimation blocks are utilized when motion is not consistent. It can be seen that on average 35.77% more running time is required whereas only 0.37 dB PSNR gain is achieved.

3.2 Subjective Performance

Figure 2 depicts the subjective performance when scene change occurs in the current field. It is obvious that for conventional methods, there exists blur and saw-tooth around edges.

As for the proposed scheme, if there exists scene change in the backward field, the current field will be interpolated using information from the forward interpolated frame and the current field; if there exists scene change in the current field, the current field will be interpolated using information from the backward temporarily interpolated frame and the current field. In this way we successfully avoid introducing interpolation error with median filters, hence the picture quality is enhanced.

Table 3. Comparison of running efficiency

Sequence	Number of frames	PSNR (dB)			Running time (second)		
		[8]	Proposed	Proposed+	[8]	Proposed	Proposed+
BG_16336	300	30.79	33.66	33.75	69.26	31.76	43.62
BG_16337	300	37.18	39.64	40.35	69.79	31.47	42.26
BG_16343	300	33.17	34.83	35.85	68.93	31.87	43.57
BG_37309	300	37.75	38.66	40.28	68.34	32.34	44.92
Comb288i	300	30.39	35.70	35.20	68.82	31.62	43.86
Comb576i	90	26.70	35.19	35.22	270.51	36.83	49.48
Comb480i	50	29.09	45.82	45.71	101.48	18.18	22.35
Comb720i	100	27.90	36.05	36.09	1502.32	91.83	125.31
Average	/	**31.62**	**37.44**	**37.81**	**277.43**	**38.24**	**51.92**

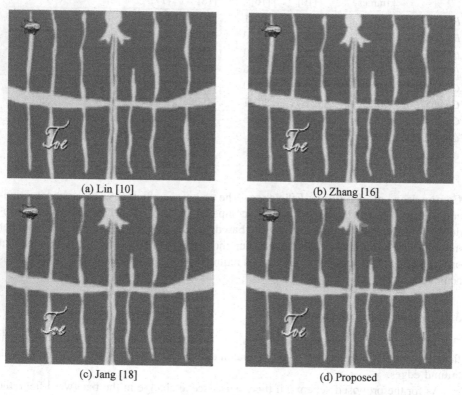

(a) Lin [10]   (b) Zhang [16]

(c) Jang [18]   (d) Proposed

Fig. 2. Subjective evaluation

4 Concluding Remarks

For motion-compensated video processing techniques such as deinterlacing, the selection of motion vectors is affected by scene changes. To improve the accuracy of motion-compensated interpolation, this paper introduces scene change detection before motion estimation and chooses optimal motion vectors accordingly. Experimental results illustrate that the proposed deinterlacing scheme generates clearer de-interlaced pictures with marginal computation burden.

Acknowledgments. This work is partly supported by the National Natural Science Foundation of China under Grant No. 61300122, 61502145 and 61602150, the National Key Technology Research and Development Program of the Ministry of Science and Technology of China under Grant No. 2016YFC0400910 and 2017ZX07104001, and the Fundamental Research Funds of China for the Central Universities under Grant No. 2013B01814.

References

1. De Haan, G., Bellers, E.B.: Deinterlacing–an overview. Proc. IEEE **86**(9), 1839–1857 (1998)
2. Lin, S.F., Chang, Y.L., Chen, L.G.: Motion adaptive de-interlacing by horizontal motion detection and enhanced ELA processing. In: Proceedings of International Symposium on Circuits and Systems, Bangkok, Thailand, pp. II696–II699. IEEE (2003)
3. Kim, W., Jin, S., Jeong, J.: Novel intra deinterlacing algorithm using content adaptive interpolation. IEEE Trans. Consum. Electron. **53**(3), 1036–1043 (2007)
4. Wang, A., Jeong, J.: Deinterlacing using multi direction detection with fixed adaptive tap interpolation filter. In: Proceedings of International Symposium on Broadband Multimedia Systems and Broadcasting, Seoul, Korea, pp. 1–5. IEEE (2012)
5. Gao, X., Gu, J., Li, J.: De-interlacing algorithms based on motion compensation. IEEE Trans. Consum. Electron. **51**(2), 589–599 (2005)
6. Huang, Q., Gao, W., Zhao, D., Sun, H.: An efficient and robust adaptive deinterlacing technique. IEEE Trans. Consum. Electron. **52**(3), 888–895 (2006)
7. Mohammadi, H.M., Langlois, P., Savaria, Y.: A five-field motion compensated deinterlacing method based on vertical motion. IEEE Trans. Consum. Electron. **53**(3), 1117–1124 (2007)
8. Mahvash, H., Savaria, Y., Langlois, J.M.P.: Enhanced motion compensated deinterlacing algorithm. IET Image Proc. **6**(8), 1041–1048 (2012)
9. Radwan, N.I., Salem, N.M., El Adawy, M.I.: Histogram correlation for video scene change detection. In: Wyld, D., Zizka, J., Nagamalai, D. (eds.) Advances in Computer Science, Engineering & Applications, vol. 166, pp. 765–773. Springer, Heidelberg (2012). https://doi.org/10.1007/978-3-642-30157-5_76
10. Lin, C., Liaw, C.: A video de-interlacing with precise interfield information by hybrid scene change detection. In: Proceedings of International Conference on Telecommunications and Signal Processing, Rome, Italy, pp. 848–852. IEEE (2013)
11. Yi, X., Ling, N.: Fast pixel-based video scene change detection. In: Proceedings of International Symposium on Circuits and Systems, Kobe, Japan, pp. 3443–3446. IEEE (2005)

12. Wu, Z., Xu, P.: Shot boundary detection in video retrieval. In: Proceedings of International Conference on Electronics Information and Emergency Communication, Beijing, China, pp. 86–89. IEEE (2013)
13. Reddy, B., Jadhav, A.: Comparison of scene change detection algorithms for videos. In: Proceedings of International Conference on Advanced Computing and Communication Technologies, Rohtak, India, pp. 84–89. IEEE (2015)
14. De Haan, G., Biezen, P.W.A.C., Huijgen, H., et al.: True-motion estimation with 3-D recursive search block matching. IEEE Trans. Cir. Syst. Video Technol. 3(5), 368–379 (1993)
15. Huang, Q., Zhao, D., Ma, S., et al.: Deinterlacing using hierarchical motion analysis. IEEE Trans. Cir. Syst. Video Technol. 20(5), 673–686 (2010)
16. Zhang, H., Rong, M.: Deinterlacing algorithm using gradient-guided interpolation and weighted average of directional estimation. IET Image Proc. 9(6), 450–460 (2014)
17. Khan, S., Lee, D.: Efficient deinterlacing method using simple edge slope tracing. Opt. Eng. 54(10), 103–108 (2015)
18. Jang, S.M., Park, J.H., Hong, S.H.: Deinterlacing method based on edge direction refinement using weighted median filter. In: Proceedings of IEEE International Conference on Signal and Image Processing Applications, Kuala Lumpur, Malaysia, pp. 227–230. IEEE (2009)

Center-Adaptive Weighted Binary
K-means for Image Clustering

Yinhe Lan, Zhenyu Weng, and Yuesheng Zhu[✉]

Communication and Information Security Lab, Institute of Big Data Technologies,
Shenzhen Graduate School, Peking University, Shenzhen, China
{lanyinhe,wzytumbler,zhuys}@pku.edu.cn

Abstract. Traditional clustering methods are inherently difficult to
handle with a large scale of images, since it is expensive to store all
the data and to make pairwise comparison of high-dimensional vectors.
To solve this problem, we propose a novel Binary K-means for accurate
image clustering. After hashing the data into binary codes, the weights
assigned to the binary data are based on the global information and the
weights for the binary centers are adapted iteratively. Then, in each iteration, with the center-adaptive weights the distance between the binary
data and the binary centers is computed by the weighted Hamming distance. As the data and centers are presented in binary, we can build a
hash table to speed up the comparison. We evaluate the proposed method
on three large datasets and the experiments show that, the proposed
method can achieve a good clustering performance with small storage
and efficient computation.

Keywords: Hashing · Image clustering · Center-adaptive weights
Weighted Hamming distance

1 Introduction

In the area of computer vision, image clustering [1,10,11] is widely studied,
since there are many different uses for clustering, such as automatic discovery
of object categories [14,17], reconstructing story lines from photo streams [7]
and detecting spam photos. However, since recently there is a dramatic rise in
the photos on the sharing websites, such as Facebook, Google, and Instagram,
traditional clustering methods are inherently difficult to handle with a large
scale of images. As the images are usually represented as the high-dimensional
feature vectors, for traditional clustering methods, an exhaustive comparison
with all the vectors is prohibitive and storing such a large quantity of high-
dimensional vectors in memory is difficult. In the image retrieval, to handle with
a large number of images, hashing methods [4,5,15,16] are proposed to map the
high-dimensional data into compact binary codes, such that searching for the
binary codes is efficient. Although a lot of hashing methods are developed for
retrieving images, the hashing ideas are rarely applied into the clustering process

© Springer International Publishing AG, part of Springer Nature 2018
B. Zeng et al. (Eds.): PCM 2017, LNCS 10736, pp. 407–417, 2018.
https://doi.org/10.1007/978-3-319-77383-4_40

until recently Gong [3] propose Binary K-means (BK-means). By keeping the data and the centers in form of compact binary codes, BK-means can deal with the high dimensionality and the large scale problems as the binary data can be stored in RAM and the nearest center for each data point can be found fast by building a hashing table [13]. However, a data point may have same Hamming distance to various centers since each bit of binary code is one or zero. Thus, in BK-means, computing Hamming distance between the binary data and the binary centers in the clustering process suffers ambiguity.

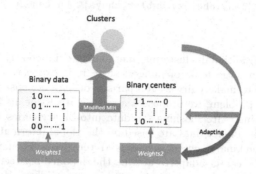

Fig. 1. The illustration of our method

To improve the accuracy of the distance computation between the binary data and the binary centers, in this paper, we propose a accurate clustering method, i.e., Center-adaptive Weighted Binary K-means (CWBK-means), in which the distance between the binary data and the binary centers is calculated by comparing the weights for the binary data with the weights for the binary centers over each bit. In our method, the weights for each bit of the binary data are based on the statistics on the global information. And in each iteration for the clustering process, the weights for each bit of the binary centers are constantly adapted to the centers. Then, the data points are assigned to their nearest center according to the weighted Hamming distance in the clustering process. We build a hash table [13] with some modification on the binary centers such that it can speed up finding the nearest center for each data vector according to the weighted Hamming distance. The framework of the proposed method is shown in Fig. 1.

The main contributions of this paper are as follows: (1) By constantly adapting the binary centers and the weights for them in each iteration of the clustering process, the objective function in our method can converge to a minimum. (2) By assigning the weights to the binary data and the binary centers, respectively, the binary data points are assigned to their nearest center according to the center-adaptive weighted Hamming distance instead of the Hamming distance. It improves the accuracy of clustering images. (3) In our method, the data and the centers are both represented in binary and the storage for the weights can be neglected compared with the binary data. Thus, our method can achieve small storage. (4) We apply the multi-index hashing [13] with some modification to our method, such that our method can perform the clustering process as fast as Binary K-means does.

2   Background and Related Work

In this section, we will give a brief review of the hashing methods. Then, the prior clustering method, BK-means, is introduced.

2.1   Hashing Methods

Assume an image signature set of n points is given, $X = \{x_1, ..., x_n\}$ and $x_i \in \mathbb{R}^D$. To make the computation efficient, in the hashing methods, the image signatures are transformed into compact binary codes, and the Hamming distance between any two codes is used to replace the Euclidean distance to measure the similarity of images. Let h_k be a binary embedding function[1], i.e., $h_k : \mathbb{R}^D \to \{-1, +1\}$. A set $H = \{ h_k, k = 1 \ldots K \}$ of K functions defines a multidimensional embedding function $h : \mathbb{R}^D \to \{-1, +1\}^K$ with $h(x) = [h_1(x), \ldots, h_k(x)]^T$. Usually, each binary embedding function consists of two stages [8]. In the first stage, the high-dimensional data is embedded into a real value. Then, in the second stage, the real value is quantized into a bit value. The function can be decomposed as follows:

$$h_k(x) = q_k[g_k(x)] \qquad (1)$$

where $g_k : \mathbb{R}^D \to \mathbb{R}$ is the real-valued embedding function, and $q_k : \mathbb{R} \to \{-1, +1\}$ is the quantization function. We define $g : \mathbb{R}^D \to \mathbb{R}^K$ with $g(x) = [g_1(x), \ldots, g_k(x)]^T$. The data points x_i are preprocessed to be binary codes by ITQ [2], which is as follows

$$b_i = h(x_i) \qquad (2)$$

Then, we have binary data $B = \{b_1, ..., b_n\}$.

2.2   BK-means

K-means is one of the common clustering algorithms, since it is easily interpretable and simply computable. Assume n data points x_i need to be grouped into $m(\leqslant n)$ clusters, $S = \{S_1, S_2, ..., S_m\}$, and $u_i \in \mathbb{R}^D$ is the center of S_i. However, storing such large quantity of high-dimensional vectors in memory is difficult, especially when the scales of the data and the centers are both huge.

To solve the above problem, BK-means [3] adopts the idea from the hashing methods to constrain both the data and the centers binary. Dealing with the

---

[1] For binary codes, we can represent them as 0/1 or −1/1 interchangeably since we use Hamming distance.

binary codes can enjoy small storage and efficient computation. The data points x_i are preprocessed to be binary codes, which is as follows

$$b_i = h(x_i) \tag{3}$$

Then, we have binary data $B = \{b_1, ..., b_n\}$. Assume we cluster the data points to a set of m centers $C = \{c_1, ..., c_m\}$. The distortion error is defined as the sum of the squared distances between each binary data and its corresponding binary center, and the objective function of BK-means is to minimize the distortion error, which is as follows

$$\min \sum_{i=1}^{m} \sum_{b \in S_i} \|b - c_i\|^2 \tag{4}$$

$$s.t. \quad c_i \in \{1, -1\}^K$$

The problem is solved by an EM style alternative optimization algorithm. Compared with K-means, BK-means can handle a large amount of data and achieve fast clustering with some sacrifice of clustering accuracy.

3   Center-Adaptive Weighted Binary K-means

In this section, we present our clustering method, Center-adaptive Weighted Binary K-means (CWBK-means). It is built on the BK-means. By representing the binary data and binary centers with different expectation values, it improves the accuracy of the distance computation between the binary data and the centers, and achieves a better clustering performance.

3.1   The Objective Function

Assume n binary data points b_i need to be grouped into $m(\leqslant n)$ clusters $S = \{S_1, S_2, ..., S_m\}$, thus, we have m binary centers $C = \{c_1, ..., c_m\}$. In BK-means, the difference in each dimension between the binary data and the binary centers is zero or one, which causes ambiguity to assign the binary data to their nearest center. In our method, the binary data and the binary centers are represented with one expectation value as a weight in each bit, respectively. Then, we assign the binary data to their nearest center according to their weighted Hamming distance rather than their Hamming distance, which can alleviate the ambiguity. Our method is shown in Fig. 1.

We have the following objective function:

$$\min \sum_{i=1}^{m} \sum_{b \in S_i} \sum_{k=1}^{K} \left\| \alpha_k^{b_k} - \beta_k^{c_{ik}} \right\|^2 \tag{5}$$

$$s.t. \quad c_i \in \{1, -1\}^K$$

where α_k is the expectation value for the kth bit of the binary code, and β_k is the expectation value for the kth bit of the binary center. The problem can be solved by an EM style alternative optimization algorithm, i.e., alternating between the assignment step and the update step.

Initially, we can calculate the expectation value of each bit of the binary data according to [4]. According to each dimension k of embedded data, we partition X into two subsets: X_k^1 contains the data point x_i such that $h_k(x_i) = 1$, and X_k^{-1} contains the data point x_i such that $h_k(x_i) = -1$. Then the expectation value of each bit of the binary data is calculated as

$$\alpha_k^1 = \frac{1}{|X_k^1|} \sum_{x \in X_k^1} g_k(x) \tag{6}$$

$$\alpha_k^{-1} = \frac{1}{|X_k^{-1}|} \sum_{x \in X_k^{-1}} g_k(x) \tag{7}$$

The centers c are randomly selected from $B = \{b_1, ..., b_n\}$ and $b_i \in \{-1, 1\}^K$ initially. And the expectation value of each bit of the binary center β_k has the same value as α_k initially.

In the assignment step, each data point b_i is assigned to its nearest center, which is

$$idx_i = \arg \min_j \sum_{k=1}^{K} ||\alpha_k^{b_{ik}} - \beta_k^{c_{jk}}||^2 \tag{8}$$

In the update step, the mean value for each cluster S_j is denoted as η_j, which is calculated as

$$\eta_{jk} = \frac{1}{|S_j|} \sum_{b \in S_j} \alpha_k^{b_k} \tag{9}$$

where k denotes the kth dimension for the binary data and its expectation value. The binary center c_j of the cluster S_j is calculated as

$$c_{jk} = sign(\eta_{jk}) = \begin{cases} +1 & if \quad \eta_{jk} \geqslant 0 \\ -1 & if \quad \eta_{jk} < 0 \end{cases} \tag{10}$$

where k denotes the kth dimension for the binary center. According to each dimension k of the mean values of the clusters η_{jk}, the cluster set S can be partitioned into two subsets: S_k^1 contains the cluster s_j such that $\eta_{jk} \geqslant 0$, and S_k^{-1} contains the cluster s_j such that $\eta_{jk} < 0$. Then, the expectation value for each bit of the binary center β_k is calculated

$$\beta_k^1 = \frac{1}{|S_k^1|} \sum_{\eta_{jk} \in S_k^1} \eta_{jk} \tag{11}$$

$$\beta_k^{-1} = \frac{1}{|S_k^{-1}|} \sum_{\eta_{jk} \in S_k^{-1}} \eta_{jk} \tag{12}$$

Overall, our method alternates between the assignment step and the update step. In the assignment step, binary data are assigned to their nearest center according to the weighted Hamming distance. And in the update step, the binary centers are updated according to the grouped binary data, and the weights for the binary centers are adapted to them.

Compared with the storage for the binary data and binary centers, the overhead for storing the expectation values for binary data and binary centers can be neglected in our method.

3.2 Modified Multi-index Hashing

In the assignment step, each binary data point is assigned to its nearest binary center. In BK-means, it adopts multi-index hashing (MIH) [13], which can efficiently find the nearest center of each data without comparing with all the centers. In our method, since the data and the centers are both represented in binary, we can use MIH with a little modification according to [13]. Like BK-means, a hash table is also set up in our method. Then, the binary centers are also divided into L disjoint binary sub-strings, each sub-string used as the hash keys for the hash table. For each binary data vector, to find its nearest neighbor, one can progressively increase the Hamming search radius per substring, until the nearest neighbor candidates are found. And then the nearest center is found by computing the weighted Hamming distance between the binary data vector and the binary center candidates according to the weights on the data vector and the center.

By adopting MIH with the weighted Hamming distance, our method is shown in Algorithm 1.

4 Experiments

We perform experiments on the GIST1M dataset [6], MNIST dataset [9] and GTSRB dataset [12]. The first one is an unlabeled dataset while the other two datasets with labels. GIST1M dataset contains 1,000,000 960-D GIST features. MNIST dataset contains 70,000 hand-written digit samples which are classified as 10 classes. Each sample is $28 * 28$ pixels which are used as a feature to describe the image in our experiments. German Traffic Sign Recognition Benchmark (GTSRB) is a large multi-category classification benchmark. The dataset was used in a competition at IJCNN 2011. The dataset contains 39,209 images in 43 classes. Each image is represented by the 1568-D HOG feature.

In the experiments, we compare our method with K-means and BK-means. Since K-means is a typical clustering method, we take the result of K-means as a reference. K-means clusters the original features, while BK-means and CWBK-means uses the binary codes which are quantized by ITQ [2] from the original features. Since three methods are all local-convergent, their results are unstable. The reported results are averaged on 10 repetitions to alleviate the randomness.

Algorithm 1. Center-adaptive Weighted Binary K-means

Input:
    the binary code $B = \{b_1, ..., b_n\}$; the expectation values of the binary data α; the number of the clusters m;
Output:
    clusters of the data;
1: Initialize centers as $C = \{c_1, ..., c_m\}$ where c_i are randomly selected from data B;
2: Make the centers C represented with the expectation-values β
3: **Each iteration has:**
4: (1) the assignment step:
5: Build a multi-index table A on center C;
6: **for** $i = 1$ to n **do**
7:    idx=A.Lookup1NN(b_i);
8: **end for**
9: (2) the update step:
10: **for** $j = 1$ to m **do**
11:    Compute the mean η_j for points in each cluster;
12:    Update all c_j by η_j;
13:    Make the centers C represented with an expection-value in each bit according to Eqn. (9)(10);
14: **end for**

4.1 Comparison with Unlabeled Data

The 960-D GIST descriptors are hashed into 32-bit binary codes. When they are grouped into 1000 clusters and 10000 clusters, respectively, from Fig. 2, we can see that the objective function of our method can converge to a minimum. We use the distortion error to evaluate the clustering performance on the GIST1M dataset. The distortion error is defined as the sum of the squared differences between the original features and the centers of their corresponding clusters. The smaller distortion error, the better clustering performance. The assignment of the original features to the clusters in each iteration is achieved by clustering the 32-bit binary data through CWBK-means and BK-means, respectively. CWBK-means and BK-means start with the same random centers. The results are shown in Fig. 3. From the figure, we can find that our method can reach a smaller minimum distortion error than that of the BK-means, in no matter the case of 1000 clusters or the case of 10000 clusters. Especially for the case of 10000 clusters, our method can reach a minimum faster than BK-means, since BK-means needs almost 25 iterations while our method just needs 12 iterations.

    The time complexity of different methods is shown in Table 1. From the table, we can see that the time complexity of the typical clustering method K-means is $O(nm)$, which depends on the number of data n and the number of centers m, while BK-means and CWBK-means only has linear time complexity with the number of data points n, under the assumption that finding the nearest center by hash table lookup has constant time in MIH. The running time for different clustering methods with 32 bits in the cases of 100 clusters, 1000 clusters and 10000 clusters on GIST1M dataset is reported in Table 2. From the table,

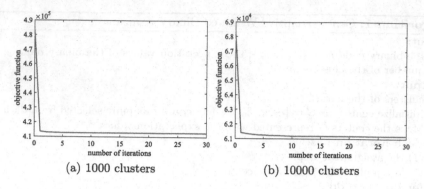

(a) 1000 clusters   (b) 10000 clusters

Fig. 2. Objective function convergence of our method.

Table 1. Time complexity comparison

K-means	BK-means	CWBK-means
$O(nm)$	$O(n)$	$O(n)$

we can see that with the number of clusters increasing, the time for K-means is increasing fast, while the time for BK-means and CWBK-means increases slowly. It is shown that CWBK-means is almost as fast as BK-means. We can see that our method can achieve a lower distortion error than BK-means while the time cost for them is almost the same.

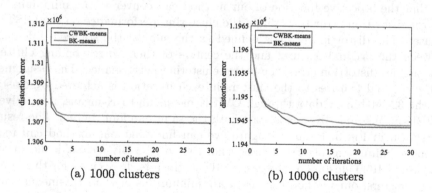

(a) 1000 clusters   (b) 10000 clusters

Fig. 3. Comparison of distortion error on 960-D GIST descriptors.

4.2   Comparison with Labeled Data

Purity and Entropy are usually adopted as the measures to evaluate the performance of the clustering methods with the labeled data. The purity is shown in Fig. 4 by performing clustering to group the images into clusters of which

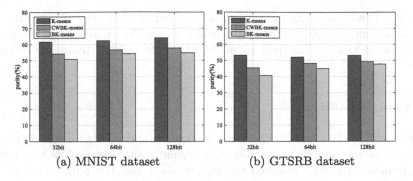

(a) MNIST dataset   (b) GTSRB dataset

Fig. 4. Comparison of clustering purity on two datasets.

the number is equal to the number ground truth classes with 32 bits, 64 bits and 128 bits on two datasets. From the figure, we can see that K-means always achieves the best performance. It is because K-means clusters the original features, BK-means and CWBK-means uses the binary codes to handle large number of images. No matter 32, 64 or 128-bit, our method always has the higher purity than BK-means. The less bits, the larger advantage of CWBK-means. When the length of the binary code is becoming smaller, more information is lost during the process of hashing the data into binary codes and the ambiguity is more common in assigning the data to their nearest centers. Since our method uses weights for the bits to preserve more information, the ambiguity can be alleviated. So our method can achieve a better performance in clustering the data than BK-means, especially for the lower bits.

The entropy is reported in Table 3 by performing clustering to group the images into different numbers of clusters with 32, 64 and 128 bits on GTSRB

Table 2. Timing (seconds) for clustering on GIST1M dataset (one iteration)

Method/clusters	100	1000	10000
K-means	920.946	8997.724	86921.443
BK-means	20.264	21.901	65.593
CWBK-means	20.908	22.424	65.845

Table 3. The entropy on GTSRB dataset

Cluster	10			100		
Bit length	32	64	128	32	64	128
K-means	0.399			0.288		
BK-means	0.468	0.449	0.433	0.368	0.338	0.314
CWBK-means	0.454	0.429	0.409	0.353	0.326	0.303

datasets. The smaller the entropy value, the better clustering result. From the tables, the entropy of CWBK-means is always smaller than that of BK-means, which means that our method is consistently better than BK-means in all the cases.

5   Conclusions

By hashing the data into binary codes, a large number of high-dimensional data can be clustered with small storage and efficient computation. Since computing the Hamming distance between the binary data and the binary centers may cause ambiguity, in our method, we use weights to present the binary data and the binary centers respectively, and calculate the weighted Hamming distance between them to alleviate the ambiguity. The weights for the binary data are based on the global information while the weights for the binary centers are adapted in each iteration. As our method still has the data and centers in binary at hand, combined with modified MIH, our method can enjoy the benefits of BK-means and achieve a better clustering performance.

Acknowledgments. This work is supported by the Shenzhen Municipal Development and Reform Commission (Disciplinary Development Program for Data Science and Intelligent Computing), and the Shenzhen Engineering Laboratory of Broadband Wireless Network Security.

References

1. Bilen, H., Pedersoli, M., Tuytelaars, T.: Weakly supervised object detection with convex clustering. In: Proceedings of the IEEE Conference on Computer Vision and Pattern Recognition, pp. 1081–1089 (2015)
2. Gong, Y., Lazebnik, S.: Iterative quantization: a procrustean approach to learning binary codes. In: Proceedings of the IEEE Conference on Computer Vision and Pattern Recognition, pp. 817–824 (2011)
3. Gong, Y., Pawlowski, M., Yang, F., Brandy, L., Bourdev, L., Fergus, R.: Web scale photo hash clustering on a single machine. In: Proceedings of the IEEE Conference on Computer Vision and Pattern Recognition, pp. 19–27 (2015)
4. Gordo, A., Perronnin, F., Gong, Y., Lazebnik, S.: Asymmetric distances for binary embeddings. IEEE Trans. Pattern Anal. Mach. Intell. **36**(1), 33–47 (2014)
5. Heo, J.P., Lee, Y., He, J., Chang, S.F., Yoon, S.E.: Spherical hashing. In: Proceedings of the IEEE Conference on Computer Vision and Pattern Recognition, pp. 2957–2964 (2012)
6. Jegou, H., Douze, M., Schmid, C.: Product quantization for nearest neighbor search. IEEE Trans. Pattern Anal. Mach. Intell. **33**(1), 117–128 (2011)
7. Kim, G., Sigal, L., Xing, E.P.: Joint summarization of large-scale collections of web images and videos for storyline reconstruction. In: Proceedings of the IEEE Conference on Computer Vision and Pattern Recognition, pp. 4225–4232 (2014)
8. Kong, W., Li, W.J., Guo, M.: Manhattan hashing for large-scale image retrieval. In: Proceedings of the 35th International ACM SIGIR Conference on Research and Development in Information Retrieval, pp. 45–54 (2012)

9. Lcun, Y., Bottou, L., Bengio, Y., Haffner, P.: Gradient-based learning applied to document recognition. Proc. IEEE **86**(11), 2278–2324 (1998)
10. Lee, Y.J., Grauman, K.: Shape discovery from unlabeled image collections. In: Proceedings of the IEEE Conference on Computer Vision and Pattern Recognition, pp. 2254–2261 (2009)
11. Mahmood, A., Mian, A., Owens, R.: Semi-supervised spectral clustering for image set classification. In: Proceedings of the IEEE Conference on Computer Vision and Pattern Recognition, pp. 121–128 (2014)
12. Namor, A.F.D.D., Shehab, M., Khalife, R., Abbas, I.: The German traffic sign recognition benchmark: a multi-class classification competition. In: The 2011 International Joint Conference on Neural Networks (IJCNN), pp. 1453–1460 (2011)
13. Norouzi, M., Punjani, A., Fleet, D.J.: Fast exact search in hamming space with multi-index hashing. IEEE Trans. Pattern Anal. Mach. Intell. **36**(6), 1107–1119 (2013)
14. Sivic, J., Russell, B.C., Zisserman, A., Freeman, W.T., Efros, A.A.: Unsupervised discovery of visual object class hierarchies. In: Proceedings of the IEEE Conference on Computer Vision and Pattern Recognition, pp. 1–8 (2008)
15. Torralba, A., Fergus, R., Weiss, Y.: Small codes and large image databases for recognition. In: Proceedings of the IEEE Conference on Computer Vision and Pattern Recognition, pp. 1–8 (2008)
16. Wang, J., Liu, W., Kumar, S., Chang, S.: Learning to hash for indexing big data - a survey. Proc. IEEE **104**(1), 34–57 (2015)
17. Weber, M., Welling, M., Perona, P.: Towards automatic discovery of object categories. In: Proceedings of the IEEE Conference on Computer Vision and Pattern Recognition, pp. 101–108 (2010)

Aligned Local Descriptors
and Hierarchical Global Features
for Person Re-Identification

Yihao Zhang, Wenmin Wang[(✉)], and Jinzhuo Wang

School of Electronic and Computer Engineering, Shenzhen Graduate School,
Peking University, Shenzhen, China
`ethanyhzhang@pku.edu.cn, wangwm@ece.pku.edu.cn, cr7or9@163.com`

Abstract. Person re-identification aims at identifying the same person
from different non-overlapping camera views, in which one of the fundamental issues is to have a robust feature under various conditions. In
order to deal with the misaligned problem, most works incline to fuse the
feature of less associated patches together. Such strategy might result in
the loss of their relative location information and hinder the better performance. Therefore, in this paper we introduce aligned local descriptors
to preserve the information of patches' relative location and design hierarchical global features to improve the robustness of image representation for person re-identification. We attempt to apply affine transformation to our framework and find it effective for resolving the viewpoint and
pose changes. Experiments are implemented on three challenging datasets
VIPeR, QMUL GRID and CUHK Campus. We obtain competitive or
superior performance compared to state-of-the-art methods.

Keywords: Person re-identification · Image representation
Aligned local descriptors · Affine transformation
Hierarchical global features

1 Introduction

Person re-identification is one of the important research topics in computer
vision. It aims to establish the correspondence between images of the same person
from different scenes. Due to the low resolution of static images, some classical
biometric cues (e.g. face, gait) are not available. Additionally, the illumination,
viewpoint, pose *etc.*, might vary a lot from disjoint non-overlapping cameras.
These challenges would make the task difficult to handle, especially when different persons are dressed in the same style.

In order to address these problems, researchers are mainly working on two
aspects, one is feature design and the other is metric learning [1–5]. Recently,
the methods of deep learning are gradually applied to person re-identification.
However, due to the small training sample size problem, it seems to be one of the
few vision tasks that deep learning has not been able to shine. Although it has

© Springer International Publishing AG, part of Springer Nature 2018
B. Zeng et al. (Eds.): PCM 2017, LNCS 10736, pp. 418–427, 2018.
https://doi.org/10.1007/978-3-319-77383-4_41

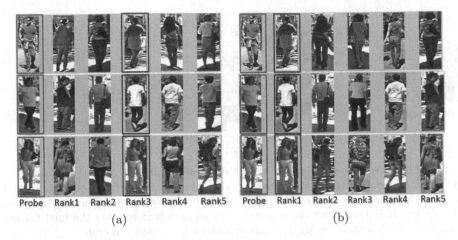

Probe   Rank1   Rank2   Rank3   Rank4   Rank5   Probe   Rank1   Rank2   Rank3   Rank4   Rank5

(a)   (b)

Fig. 1. Some matching results of using LOMO feature and ours on VIPeR dataset. The column bounded in green is the probe images and the others are the top-5 re-identified results with the correct one bounded in red. (a) The matching results using LOMO feature. (b) The matching results using our feature. (Color figure online)

made noteworthy progress, there still leaves much space for improvement with traditional methods. This paper focuses on the extraction of robust image representation.

For the past few years, many effective hand-crafted features are proposed. Symmetry-driven accumulation of local features (SDALF) is one of the classical features proposed by Farnzena et al. [6]. It utilized the symmetry and asymmetry properties of human body to extract three complementary kinds of features. Ma et al. [7] described each image point with a low dimensional descriptor and then turned the local features into Fisher vector to produce global representation. Similarly, Matsukawa et al. [8] described a region area in an image via hierarchical Gaussian distribution. In [4], local maximal occurrence (LOMO) representation was proposed against viewpoint variations. However, while dealing with misaligned problems by integrating local features into a unified space, most methods lost the information of relative location among patches. This might weaken their capacity of discrimination. Therefore, we consider to preserve such information and deal with the viewpoint variations via affine transformation.

Our proposed feature is most similar to that introduced by Liao et al. [4], where a particular patch is represented by color and texture histograms after the preprocessing of Retinex algorithm. Differently, instead of preserving only the maximal occurrence, we try to preserve as many patch features as possible. Besides, we integrate with hierarchical global features to enhance the robustness of image representation. The contributions of this paper are summarized as follows.

- First, we propose a novel framework to extract aligned local descriptors to preserve the information of relative location among patches and introduce affine transformation to deal with viewpoint variations.

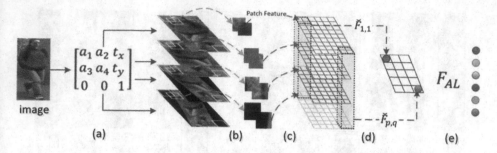

Fig. 2. The extraction process of aligned local descriptors. (a) Affine transformation including horizontal flipping and shearing. (b) Patch feature extraction of color and texture histograms. (c) The corresponding feature maps generated from (b) are piled up. (d) Patch features with the adjacency are summarized to form the final feature map. (e) All the features in (d) are concatenated into a feature vector.

- Second, the novel global features of three hierarchical patch groups are designed to avoid the negative impact of background and improve the robustness of image representation.
- Third, we implement experiments on several benchmark datasets and validate the effectiveness of our method.

2   Image Representation

Through the analysis of LOMO feature used in [4], we find that there are two problems hindering the performance. As shown in Fig. 1(a), the correct matches are confused by those people in dissimilar appearance, and the irrelevant background might also exert a negative influence due to the fuzziness. We try to eliminate the problems from two aspects. One is to preserve the information of relative location among patches, which can help increase the capacity of discriminating the difference. Therefore we propose a framework to extract the local features named aligned local descriptors. The other is to design a novel hierarchical global features based on the extracted salience map, which is also complementary to the insufficiency of local features.

2.1   Aligned Local Descriptors

The design of our aligned local descriptors is mainly for preserving the information of relative location among less associated patches and dealing with the problem of viewpoint changes. The framework is illustrated in Fig. 2. Unlike the other works [7–10] that resolve the misaligned problem by using clustering or Gaussian fitting, *etc.*, we find it another way to introduce affine transformation into our method. Specifically, given an image $\mathbf{I}$, we first calculate its flipping version $\mathbf{I_h}$ horizontally. Then we adopt transformation of horizontal shearing on the copies of these two images, formulated as

$$
\begin{bmatrix} x' \\ y' \\ 1 \end{bmatrix} = \begin{bmatrix} 1 & 0 & 0 \\ \lambda & 1 & 0 \\ 0 & 0 & 1 \end{bmatrix} \begin{bmatrix} x \\ y \\ 1 \end{bmatrix}, \tag{1}
$$

where λ determines the shearing degree, generating $\mathbf{I}'$ and $\mathbf{I_h'}$.

After affine transformation, four images are produced $(\mathbf{I}, \mathbf{I_h}, \mathbf{I}', \mathbf{I_h'})$. We use sliding windows to describe local details of them. The subwindow is of size 8×8 with stride of 4 pixels, dividing each image into $M \times N$ local patches. Within each subwindow, we extract two scales of SILTP histograms ($SILTP_{4,3}^{0.3}$ and $SILTP_{4,5}^{0.3}$), $8 \times 8 \times 8$-bin joint HSV and nRGB histograms and 32-bin joint Lab histograms.

Then we regard these images as four feature maps, with $4 \times M \times N$ points. Each point has a value $F_{m,n}^i (m \leq M, n \leq N, i \in 1, 2, 3, 4)$ that represents the feature vector of the corresponding patch. Next, we pile up the feature maps, and carry out a non-overlapping sum pooling operation on them. The size of the pooling operator is $2 \times 2 \times 4$, where adjacent features are added together as follows

$$
\widetilde{F_{p,q}} = \sum_{i=1}^{4} (F_{m,n}^i + F_{m+1,n}^i + F_{m,n+1}^i + F_{m+1,n+1}^i)
$$
$$
m = 2 \times (p-1) + 1 \tag{2}
$$
$$
n = 2 \times (q-1) + 1, p \leq \lfloor \frac{M}{2} \rfloor, q \leq \lfloor \frac{N}{2} \rfloor).
$$

These generated features are finally concatenated into a feature vector to represent an image, denoted as F_{AL}. Note that we only integrate the features of adjacent patches by sum pooling. Information of relative location among the less associated patches is preserved to the utmost. In addition, the transformation of horizontal flipping can help reduce the misaligned problem because there exists symmetry property between images of the same person under different camera views (e.g. the person captured by one camera faced to left but right in the other views). However, some people under different camera views might only show slight variations in pose. In this case, horizontal shearing can be beneficial to improve the alignment.

2.2   Hierarchical Global Features

We design hierarchical global features to avoid the negative impact of background and enhance the robustness of image representation. The process of our method is depicted in Fig. 3. At the beginning, we extract the foreground of the person by saliency detection via cellular automata proposed by Qin et al. [11], which assumes the marginal pixels belong to the background. Therefore, pixels that belong to the person body would be considered as background if they are close to the edge.

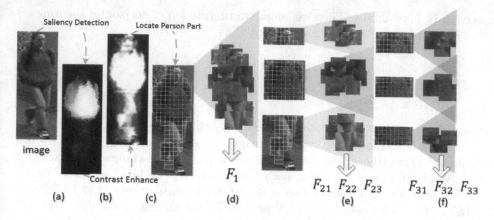

Fig. 3. The extraction process of hierarchical global features. (a) Foreground extraction by saliency detection via Cellular Automata. (b) Contrast enhancement of saliency map within the same row. (c) Localization of the patches belonging to the person after turning (b) into binary image. (d)(e)(f) The first, second and third hierarchical global features.

This may lead to the significative area with low weight in the produced saliency map. Thus, before turning the saliency map into a binary image, we implement a trick by enhancing the contrast ratio in the same row as follows

$$p'_{r,i} = \lfloor \frac{p_{r,i}}{\max(p_{r,j=1,2...n}) - \min(p_{r,j=1,2...n})} \times 255 \rfloor, \tag{3}$$

where $p_{r,i}$ is the ith point value in the rth row of the saliency map.

Subsequently, we transform the saliency map into a binary image with adaptive threshold selected by OTSU algorithm [12]. We use sliding windows to detect the informative patches, the size of which is 10×10 with stride of 5 pixels. Within a subwindow, the value (1 or 0) of all the points inside are added together, denoted as S_{mn}. We define the weight W_{mn} of each patch as follows

$$W_{mn} = S_{mn}/N, \tag{4}$$

where N represents the number of points inside a window. W_{mn} is ranged from 0 to 1 indicating the probability of the corresponding patch belonging to the person. Only those with weight larger than 50% are preserved, denoted as P_{mn}. Each patch is represented in the same way as the local patches mentioned in the last section.

So far, we have obtained the patches (P_{mn}) belonging to the person. Our first hierarchical global features, denoted as F_1 is calculated by average pooling on all P_{mn}. Then we divide P_{mn} into three groups based on the statistics analysis. Each represents the head (P_{mn} with $m \leq 15$), upper body (P_{mn} with $15 \leq m \leq 60$) and lower body (P_{mn} with $m \geq 60$) of a person, denoted as H_{mn}, U_{mn}, L_{mn}. The second hierarchical global features F_{21}, F_{22}, F_{23} are calculated by average pooling on each group. Since the upper body can be more distinguishable, we further divide U_{mn} into three sub groups (U_{mn} with $m \leq 30$, $30 \leq m \leq 45$ and $m \geq 45$) and operate average pooling on each of them as the third hierarchical global features F_{31}, F_{32}, F_{33}. All of these features are then concatenated to be the final vector $F_{HG} = \{F_1, F_{21}, F_{22}, F_{23}, F_{31}, F_{32}, F_{33}\}$.

3   Experiments

We evaluate the proposed method on three public datasets VIPeR, QMUL GRID and CUHK Campus. The results are shown in terms of recognition rate by the Cumulative Matching Characteristic (CMC) curve.

3.1   Implementation Details

In the experiments, we scale all the images in different datasets as 128×48. The aligned local descriptors are extracted from multiscale, namely the original, half and quarter size of the image. In addition, the hierarchical global features are extracted only from the original scale. We randomly select half number of the images for training and the remaining for testing.

We use XQDA algorithm [4] to measure the similarity between the gallery and the probe images. Given a pair of images x and z from different views, the distance function is defined as

$$d(x, z) = d_W(x_{F_{AL}}, z_{F_{AL}}) \tag{5}$$
$$+ \beta \times d_W(x_{F_{HG}}, z_{F_{HG}}), \tag{6}$$

where $d_W(f_1, f_2)$ is the XQDA distance function between the feature vector f_1 and f_2. β indicates the weight of global features. Average performance is calculated by repeating the procedure for 10 times.

Table 1. Comparison with other features on VIPeR

Method	r = 1	r = 5	r = 10	r = 20	Reference
Ours	**46.2**	**74.2**	**85.3**	**94.4**	Proposed
LOMO [4]	40.0	68.0	80.5	91.1	CVPR 2015
Deep Ranking [13]	38.4	69.2	81.3	90.4	TIP 2016
MKML [14]	37.0	69.9	80.7	90.1	ICIP 2016
SCNCD [15]	37.8	68.5	81.2	90.4	ECCV 2014
kBiCov [16]	31.1	58.3	70.7	82.5	IVC 2014
LDFV [7]	26.5	56.4	70.9	84.6	ECCVW 2012

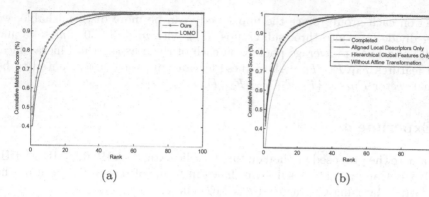

(a)   (b)

Fig. 4. CMC curve results on VIPeR. (a) Comparison of our proposed method with LOMO feature (b) The performance of each part of our proposed method.

3.2   Experiment on VIPeR

VIPeR dataset is one of the most challenging datasets for person re-identification. It consists of 632 pairs of pedestrians, each with 2 images captured by different cameras in an outdoor environment.

In this experiment, we set the parameters of horizontal shearing and the weight of global features as follows: $\lambda = 0.2$ and $\beta = 1.3$. The result of CMC curve is depicted in Fig. 4(a). Apparently, we achieve better performance than the baseline work using LOMO feature. Considering the matching results shown in Fig. 1(b), we can infer that some of the problems we mentioned previously are effectively solved to a certain extent. Our method is more likely to match the correct person from dissimilar ones in gallery. Furthermore, compared with some other state-of-the-art methods listed in Table 1, we also achieve competitive performance, with 46.2% of rank-1 accuracy, which is 6.2% better than the second best.

3.3   Experiment on QMUL GRID

The QMUL underGround Re-IDentification (GRID) dataset contains 250 pedestrian image pairs. It is another challenging person re-identification benchmark, with 775 additional images that do not belong to the 250 persons but used for testing as gallery.

In this experiment, we set parameters λ and β as 0.2 and 1.3. The CMC curve is depicted in Fig. 5(a), which shows that our method outperforms the baseline. We also achieve the best performance compared with other state-of-the-art results as seen in Table 2. The accuracy of the proposed method is 1.4%, 2.4%, 2.5% and 1.1% better than the second best of rank 1, rank 5, rank 10 and rank 20 respectively. It proves our image representation is robust to the variations of pose, colors and lighting changes with poor image quality.

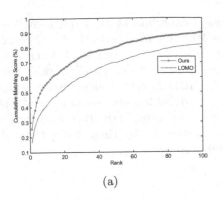 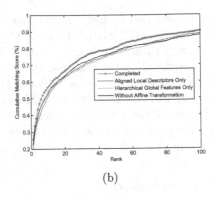

(a)   (b)

Fig. 5. CMC curve results on QMUL GRID. (a) Comparison of our proposed method with LOMO feature (b) The performance of each part of our proposed method.

Table 2. Comparison with state-of-the-art results on GRID

Method	r = 1	r = 5	r = 10	r = 20	Reference
Ours	**25.6**	**47.0**	**56.6**	**66.3**	Proposed
LOMO [4]	16.6	33.8	41.8	52.4	CVPR 2015
SCSP [17]	24.2	44.6	54.1	65.2	CVPR 2016
DR-KISS [18]	20.6	39.3	51.4	62.6	TIP 2016
SSDAL [19]	22.4	39.2	48.0	58.4	ECCV 2016
NLML [20]	24.5	35.9	43.5	55.3	arXiv 2015

3.4   Experiment on CUHK Campus

The CUHK Campus dataset contains 971 persons captured by two camera views in a campus environment. The images are of relatively higher resolution. In this experiment, we set both parameters of β and λ to be 0, and the accuracy of rank 1 reaches 64.9%, which is 1.7% slightly better than LOMO feature. However, when the parameters are set the same as that in VIPeR and QMUL GRID, the accuracy drops a little, with 61.4% of rank 1. By analyzing the dataset, we find the pose variations of all the person from different views are almost the same, with body turning 90°, which slight shearing would not help. And the background is relatively monotonous, which can help re-identify the correct match. Therefore, the method with only flipping operation can perform better.

3.5   Ablation Studies

The approach we propose in this paper boosts the performance of person re-identification, which benefits from the combination of aligned local descriptors and hierarchical global features. We would like to see how each of them exerts an influence on the final result. The ablation experiments are implemented on VIPeR and QMUL GRID datasets. Figures 4(b) and 5(b) shows the CMC curves of those with and without a certain part. With only aligned local descriptors or hierarchical global features, the accuracy drops 2.4% or 15.5% in rank 1 on VIPeR dataset and 5.4% or 3.0% on QMUL GRID dataset. It demonstrates that both aligned local descriptors and hierarchical global features are functional, but may play different roles on different datasets. Moreover, with affine transformation, the performance on both datasets can perform better than that without it, which implies it does help resolve the misaligned problem.

4   Conclusion

In this paper, we propose a novel framework to exploit the information of relative location among patches to boost the performance of person re-identification. Affine transformation is applied for the first time in our method to deal with the viewpoint and pose variations. Moreover, we design hierarchical global features to reduce the impact of background and improve the robustness of image representation. The experiments implemented on VIPeR, QMUL GRID and CUHK Campus show the effectiveness of the proposed method.

Acknowledgments. This work was supported by Science and Technology Planning Project of Guangdong Province, China (2014B090910001), Shenzhen Peacock plan (20130408-183003656).

References

1. Zheng, W.S., Gong, S., Xiang, T.: Person re-identification by probabilistic relative distance comparison. In: Computer Vision and Pattern Recognition (CVPR), pp. 649–656 (2011)
2. Kostinger, M., Hirzer, M., Wohlhart, P., Roth, P.M.: Large scale metric learning from equivalence constraints. In: Computer Vision and Pattern Recognition (CVPR), pp. 2288–2295 (2012)
3. Li, Z., Chang, S., Liang, F., Huang, T.S., Cao, L., Smith, J.R.: Learning locally-adaptive decision functions for person verification. In: Computer Vision and Pattern Recognition (CVPR), pp. 3610–3617 (2013)
4. Liao, S., Hu, Y., Zhu, X., Li, S.Z.: Person re-identification by local maximal occurrence representation and metric learning. In: Computer Vision and Pattern Recognition (CVPR), pp. 2197–2206 (2015)
5. Liao, S., Li, S.Z.: Efficient PSD constrained asymmetric metric learning for person re-identification. In: IEEE International Conference on Computer Vision, pp. 3685–3693 (2015)
6. Farenzena, M., Bazzani, L., Perina, A., Murino, V., Cristani, M.: Person re-identification by symmetry-driven accumulation of local features. In: Computer Vision and Pattern Recognition (CVPR), pp. 2360–2367 (2010)
7. Ma, B., Su, Y., Jurie, F.: Local descriptors encoded by fisher vectors for person re-identification. In: European Conference on Computer Vision (ECCV), pp. 413–422 (2012)

8. Matsukawa, T., Okabe, T., Suzuki, E., Sato, Y.: Hierarchical gaussian descriptor for person re-identification. In: Computer Vision and Pattern Recognition (CVPR), pp. 1363–1372 (2016)
9. Nanda, A., Sa, P.K.: Person re-identification using clustering ensemble prototypes. In: Asian Conference on Computer Vision (ACCV), pp. 96–108 (2014)
10. Zhao, R., Ouyang, W., Wang, X.: Learning mid-level filters for person re-identification. In: Computer Vision and Pattern Recognition (CVPR), pp. 144–151 (2014)
11. Qin, Y., Lu, H., Xu, Y., Wang, H.: Saliency detection via cellular automata. In: Computer Vision and Pattern Recognition (CVPR), pp. 110–119 (2015)
12. Otsu, N.: Threshold selection method from gray-level histograms. IEEE Trans. Syst. Man Cybern. 9(1), 62–66 (1979)
13. Chen, S.Z., Guo, C.C., Lai, J.H.: Deep ranking for person re-identification via joint representation learning. IEEE Trans. Image Process. 25(5), 2353 (2016). A Publication of the IEEE Signal Processing Society
14. Syed, M.A., Jiao, J.: Multi-kernel metric learning for person re-identification. In: IEEE International Conference on Image Processing, pp. 784–788 (2016)
15. Yang, Y.: Salient color names for person re-identification. In: European Conference on Computer Vision (ECCV), pp. 536–551 (2014)
16. Ma, B., Su, Y., Jurie, F.: Covariance descriptor based on bio-inspired features for person re-identification and face verification. Image Vis. Comput. 32(6–7), 379–390 (2014)
17. Chen, D., Yuan, Z., Chen, B., Zheng, N.: Similarity learning with spatial constraints for person re-identification. In: Computer Vision and Pattern Recognition (CVPR), pp. 1268–1277 (2016)
18. Tao, D., Guo, Y., Song, M., Li, Y.: Person re-identification by dual-regularized kiss metric learning. IEEE Trans. Image Process. 25(6), 2726–2738 (2016)
19. Su, C., Zhang, S., Xing, J., Gao, W., Tian, Q.: Deep attributes driven multi-camera person re-identification. In: Leibe, B., Matas, J., Sebe, N., Welling, M. (eds.) ECCV 2016. LNCS, vol. 9906, pp. 475–491. Springer, Cham (2016). https://doi.org/10.1007/978-3-319-46475-6_30
20. Huang, S., Lu, J., Zhou, J., Jain, A.K.: Nonlinear local metric learning for person re-identification (2015). arXiv preprint arXiv:1511.05169v1

A Novel Background Subtraction Method Based on ViBe

Jian Liao[1], Hanzi Wang[1(✉)], Yan Yan[1], and Jin Zheng[2]

[1] Fujian Key Laboratory of Sensing and Computing for Smart City,
School of Information Science and Engineering, Xiamen University,
Xiamen 361005, China
hanzi_wang@163.com

[2] Beijing Key Laboratory of Digital Media, School of Computer Science
and Engineering, Beihang University, Beijing 100191, China

Abstract. In recent years, a large number of background subtraction methods have been proposed. Among these methods, the visual background subtraction method (ViBe) receives much attention due to its high efficiency and good performance. However, it can not work well in complex environments. Therefore, in this paper, we propose a novel background subtraction method based on ViBe, including a new foreground object detection strategy, a bilateral aperture detection strategy, and two effective strategies for foreground noise detection and ghost region detection. The proposed method can effectively alleviate the problems caused by foreground aperture, dynamic backgrounds and ghosts in background subtraction. Experiments on the benchmark dataset show that, the proposed method not only obtains better results compared with a couple of ViBe-based variants, but also achieves competitive results against several state-of-the-art methods.

Keywords: Background subtraction · Bilateral aperture detection
Foreground noise · Ghost region · ViBe

1 Introduction

Background subtraction aims to detect meaningful foreground objects and remove background regions, which can be incorporated into a variety of computer vision applications, such as intelligent video surveillance [1], human-machine interaction [2] and video tracking [3]. However, there are still many unsolved problems due to the complicated situations in the real-world applications.

According to [4], there are 13 kinds of challenging problems existing in the task of background subtraction. Especially in outdoor environments, the situations become more complicated, where one has to handle with several problems at the same time, including foreground aperture, dynamic backgrounds, ghosts, and so on. Therefore, it is of great importance to develop robust background subtraction methods.

A popular background subtraction method called ViBe has originally been proposed by Barnich and Van Droogenbroeck [5,6]. ViBe firstly constructs a

© Springer International Publishing AG, part of Springer Nature 2018
B. Zeng et al. (Eds.): PCM 2017, LNCS 10736, pp. 428–437, 2018.
https://doi.org/10.1007/978-3-319-77383-4_42

background model which contains 20 background samples for each pixel. Then for a pixel at the current frame, if there exists more than one background samples close to this pixel in the background model, the pixel will be classified as a background pixel. Finally, the background model at each pixel location will be updated. Recently, some ViBe-based variants have also been developed. The representative methods include LOBSTER [7] and PBAS [9]. Especially for the PBAS method, it integrates the gradient information into the background model and can automatically choose the thresholds for good performance. However, it can not deal with ghosts very well.

In the proposed method, we not only develop a new strategy for foreground object detection with better performance, but also propose some novel post-processing strategies to deal with foreground aperture, foreground noise and ghosts, respectively. The main contributions of this paper are summarized as follows: Firstly, we propose a novel foreground object detection strategy, which can obtain better detection results than ViBe [6] and its variants [7,9]. Secondly, we propose a bilateral aperture detection strategy to deal with foreground aperture. Thirdly, based on edge detection, we propose two novel effective strategies for foreground noise detection and ghost region detection.

2 The Proposed Method

In this section, we present an overview of the proposed method in Sect. 2.1, and then we detail the implementations of the main components of the proposed method from Sects. 2.2 to 2.4.

2.1 Overview

The overall framework of the proposed method mainly consists of three steps, and each step is briefly introduced as below.

Step I: Foreground object detection. In this step, the initial detection will be performed according to the pixel value of each pixel at the beginning. Secondly, the foreground redetection will be performed according to the pixel gradient magnitude. Finally, the proposed bilateral aperture detection strategy will be adopted to deal with the foreground aperture.

Step II: Foreground noise removal. In this step, the foreground noise detection will be performed, and the edges of each foreground blob are firstly obtained by edge detection. After that the edges of each foreground blob are determined whether they belong to the foreground object. Finally, each foreground blob is judged whether it belongs to the foreground noise.

Step III: Ghost region removal. The ghost region is mainly caused by the moving objects in the first several video frames or the abrupt scene changing in the video sequence. Therefore, two strategies will be adopted in this step, which are respectively based on the statistics of the ghost pixels and the temporal-spatial discontinuity, to remove the ghost region.

2.2 Foreground Object Detection

As depicted in Fig. 1, the proposed strategy of foreground object detection consists of three stages, and each stage will be given in detail as follows. Specifically, we firstly adopt the same way as PBAS [9] to construct the background model $B(x_i)$, which consists of N background samples at the pixel location x_i: $B(x_i) = \{B_1(x_i), \ldots, B_k(x_i), \ldots, B_N(x_i)\}$. For each pixel location x_i in the input frame, the corresponding features $I(x_i) = \{I^v(x_i), I^g(x_i)\}$ consist of the pixel value $I^v(x_i)$ and the gradient magnitude $I^g(x_i)$. Accordingly, the background sample $B_k(x_i) = \{B_k^v(x_i), B_k^g(x_i)\}$ also consists of two corresponding elements, where $B_k^v(x_i)$ corresponds to the background sample of the pixel value at the pixel location x_i and $B_k^g(x_i)$ corresponds to the background sample of the pixel gradient magnitude at the pixel location x_i.

Similar to ViBe [6], in the initial detection stage, we firstly perform foreground detection according to the pixel value of each pixel. Thus, for each x_i, we use the Euclidean metric to measure the distance between the pixel value $I^v(x_i)$ and the corresponding value of $B_k^v(x_i)$ as follows.

$$Edist(I^v(x_i), B_k^v(x_i)) = ||I^v(x_i) - B_k^v(x_i)||_2 \qquad (1)$$

If the background model $B(x_i)$ at x_i has more than two background samples are close to the pixel value $I^v(x_i)$ according to the distance $Edist(I^v(x_i), B_k^v(x_i))$, it will be considered as a background pixel, otherwise it is a foreground pixel.

After the first stage, we further use the pixel gradient magnitude to perform foreground redetection. Since we have already obtained the initial foreground/background detection results, we only focus on the background pixels existing in the foreground blobs, which are considered as wrongly detected pixels. Thus, for each wrongly detected pixel x_i^*, we calculate the distance between

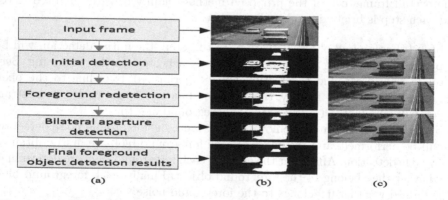

Fig. 1. The intermediate results obtained by the foreground object detection step of the proposed method. (a) The flow-chart of foreground object detection. (b) The intermediate results obtained by each step. (c) The detected foreground.

the features of the pixel $I(x_i^*) = \{I^v(x_i^*), I^g(x_i^*)\}$ and the features of each background sample $B_k(x_i^*) = \{B_k^v(x_i^*), B_k^g(x_i^*)\}$ in the background model at x_i^* as [9],

$$dist(I(x_i^*), B_k(x_i^*)) = \frac{\alpha}{\overline{I^g}} \cdot |I^g(x_i^*) - B_k^g(x_i^*)| + |I^v(x_i^*) - B_k^v(x_i^*)| \qquad (2)$$

where α is a constant value (we set the value of α to the same value as [9]), and $\overline{I^g}$ is the average gradient magnitude. If the background model $B(x_i^*)$ at x_i^* has no more than two background samples close to it according to the distance $dist(I(x_i^*), B_k(x_i^*))$, the pixel will be considered as a foreground pixel.

As shown in Fig. 1, the above two stages can not eliminate the false negatives completely, which will lead to the problem of foreground aperture for some foreground blobs. Therefore, we propose a new strategy called bilateral aperture detection, which can effectively deal with the foreground aperture problem. More specifically, the proposed strategy mainly includes four steps: (1) A rectangular box is generated to cover each foreground blob; (2) For each column pixels in the rectangular box, the background pixels which exist in the middle of foreground pixels are considered as the suspicious aperture pixels in the vertical direction of the rectangular box, marked as V_{SAP}, but they will contain the true negatives; (3) For each row pixels in the rectangular box, the background pixels which exist in the middle of foreground pixels are considered as the suspicious aperture pixels in the horizontal direction of the rectangular box, marked as H_{SAP}, but they will also contain the true negatives; (4) The intersection between V_{SAP} and H_{SAP} will be used to remove the true negatives and obtain the real aperture pixels.

2.3 Foreground Noise Detection

A great number of foreground noises will be detected due to the dynamic background with the swinging trees or in a snowing day. An example is given in Fig. 2(a). The initial detection results contain many foreground noise blobs due to the swinging trees. In other words, the proposed method should have the ability to properly deal with those foreground noise blobs under different situations. Note that the edges of the foreground noise blob are not as salient as those of the foreground object. Therefore, we propose an edge detection based foreground noise detection strategy, which can well handle with the above mentioned problems. More specifically, the edge detection will be firstly performed on the foreground mask and the current frame, respectively (as shown in Fig. 2(b)). Then we can perform the intersection operation on the edge detection results. Secondly, according to the intersection results obtained from the first step, the overlapped edges can be obtained (as shown in Fig. 2(c)). Thirdly, we keep the salient edges (marked as red in Fig. 2(d)) which belong to the foreground object and eliminate the other edges. We also notice that, according to the size of each edge, a bounding box can be generated to cover each edge (marked as green in Fig. 2(c)). And the nearby foreground pixels of each edge can be obtained

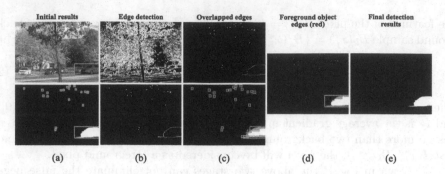

| Initial results | Edge detection | Overlapped edges | Foreground object edges (red) | Final detection results |

(a)   (b)   (c)   (d)   (e)

Fig. 2. The process of foreground noise detection. (a) The initial detection results, where the foreground blob is covered by a green bounding box. (b) Edge detection results of the foreground mask and the current frame in (a). (c) The overlapped edges obtained by performing the intersection operation on the edge detection results (shown in the first row). And each overlapped edge is marked as red and surrounded by the green bounding box (shown in the second row, where the nearby foreground pixels of each edge are marked as the sky-blue points). (d) The foreground blobs with the salient edges (marked as red) and surrounded by the green bounding box are the foreground objects, while the other foreground blobs are treated as the foreground noises. (e) The final detection results obtained by eliminating the foreground noises. (Color figure online)

(marked as the sky-blue points in Fig. 2(c)). These foreground pixels can be used to determine whether each edge belongs to the foreground object as follows,

$$FOE_{e_i}(N_{FP}, N_{EP}) = \begin{cases} 1 & P_{e_i} > T_p \\ 0 & otherwise \end{cases} \tag{3}$$

where $FOE_{e_i}(N_{FP}, N_{EP})$ means that for each edge e_i, N_{FP} is the number of the nearby foreground pixels of each edge marked as the sky-blue points in Fig. 2(c) and N_{EP} is the number of the edge pixels (marked as red in Fig. 2(c)). Moreover, as depicted in Fig. 2(d), the salient edges which belong to the foreground object are long curves in general, and thus the value of N_{FP} of these edges will be higher than the other edges. Therefore, if the ratio value $P_{e_i} = N_{FP}/(N_{EP} + N_{FP})$ is larger than the threshold T_p, the edge e_i will be considered as a foreground object edge (marked as 1). Otherwise it is not considered as a foreground object edge (marked as 0). Therefore, for foreground noise detection, if all the edges of one foreground blob do not belong to the foreground object, the foreground blob will be classified as the foreground noise and thus it will be eliminated.

2.4   Ghost Region Detection

For the step of ghost region detection, two strategies will be adopted, which are based on the statistic of the ghost pixels, and the temporal-spatial discontinuity, respectively.

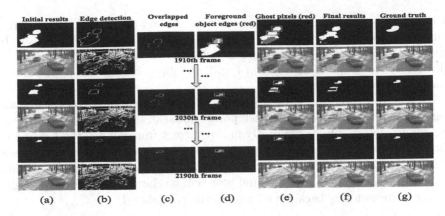

Fig. 3. The process of ghost region detection. (a) The initial detection results. (b) The edge detection results of the images in (a). (c) The overlapped edges obtained by performing the intersection operation on the images in (b). (d) The foreground object edges are marked as red and surrounded by the green bounding box, where the nearby pixels of each edge are marked as the sky-blue points. (e) The foreground object area is surrounded by the purple bounding box, and the ghost pixels are marked as red. (f) The final detection results obtained by eliminating the ghost pixels. (g) The ground truth. (Color figure online)

On one hand, in Sect. 2.3, we describe a strategy to determine whether the edges of each foreground blob belong to the foreground object. If a part area of one foreground blob is surrounded by the edges which belong to the foreground object, it will be considered as the foreground object area (see the purple bounding box in Fig. 3(e)), and marked as A_1. The rest part of the foreground blob is defined as the area without the foreground object (which is not surrounded by the purple bounding box in Fig. 3(e)), and marked as A_2. On the other hand, we compute $N_{times}(x_i^T)$ for each pixel x_i, which counts the number of times of each pixel falling in the area of A_2 at the T-th frame. If the pixel x_i is a foreground pixel and it falls in the area of A_2 at the T-th frame, then the value of $N_{times}(x_i^T)$ will be increased by one; Otherwise the value of $N_{times}(x_i^T)$ will be decreased by two, but the value of $N_{times}(x_i^T)$ should be no less than zero. The reason for adopting such a way is because that according to the value of $N_{times}(x_i^T)$, we not only need to classify the pixels which fall in the area of A_2 as the ghost pixels, but also need to prevent the pixels falling in the area of A_1 from classifying as the ghost pixels. If the pixel is a background pixel, the value of $N_{times}(x_i^T)$ will be directly set to zero. The above process is shown as,

$$N_{times}(x_i^{T+T_0}) = \begin{cases} N_{times}(x_i^T) + 1 & x_i^T \in A_1 \\ N_{times}(x_i^T) - 2 & x_i^T \in A_2 \\ 0 & \text{otherwise} \end{cases} \tag{4}$$

where T is the index number of each frame. $N_{times}(x_i^{T+T_0})$ means that the process of counting will be performed every T_0 frames, where T_0 is set to be

10 in the experiments. If the count value of a pixel $N_{times}(x_i^{T+T_0})$ is larger than a threshold T_{times}, it will be considered as a ghost pixel, which needs to be removed. Accordingly, its background model will be updated and $N_{times}(x_i^{T+T_0})$ will be reset to zero. As depicted in Fig. 3, the ghost region will be iteratively eliminated.

For a ghost region caused by abrupt scene changing, we can detect such ghost regions based on the property of temporal-spatial discontinuity. Specifically, a foreground blob is obtained abruptly in the current frame. Then the foreground blob can be continuously detected in the same place for a long time. In the meanwhile, the number of foreground pixels of the foreground blob has no obvious change. In such a case, the foreground blob will be classified as the ghost region and the corresponding background model will be updated.

3   Experiments and Analysis

In this section, we will present the experimental results and the comparative analysis to demonstrate the superior performance of the proposed method.

3.1   Datasets

The evaluation dataset adopted in our experiments is the CDnet 2014 dataset [10]. The CDnet 2014 dataset is a commonly used public database for background subtraction evaluation[1] in recent years. It contains eleven video categories as follows: Baseline (BL), Intermittent Object Motion (IOM), Dynamic Background (DB), Shadow (SD), Camera Jitter (CJ), Thermal (TM), Bad Weather (BW), Low Frame Rate (LFR), Night Videos (NV), Turbulence (TB) and PTZ. And each video category has four to six videos.

In our experiments, the F-Measure (FM) evaluation metric of the CDnet 2014 dataset [10] is used for performance comparison because it can well reflect the performance of the background subtraction methods. More specifically, F-Measure (FM) can be obtained by: $FM = (2 * Recall * Precision)/(Recall + Precision)$, which reflects the balance between Recall and Precision of each method.

3.2   Parameter Settings

The proposed background subtraction method mainly relies on two parameters, including the threshold T_p in Sect. 2.3 and the threshold T_{times} in Sect. 2.4. We keep the other parameters the same as ViBe [6]. According to the experiments, for foreground noise detection, we only need to detect the edges which have the low ratio value P_e. Hence, the value of T_p is experimentally set to be 0.20. But for ghost region detection, we need to remove the edges of ghosts. Therefore, the value of T_p should be larger, and we experimentally set it to be 0.55, which can obtain good performance. Furthermore, according to the experiment observations, the best choice of the threshold T_{times} is 5.00.

---

[1] www.changedetection.net (CDnet).

3.3 Experimental Results and Analysis

The FM-based comparison on the CDnet 2014 dataset is shown in Table 1. Notice that in Table 1, except for the PTZ video category which is captured by a moving camera (note that our background subtraction method is proposed for the fixed-camera scene), we use all the other ten video categories in the CDnet 2014 dataset for evaluation. In the meanwhile, in order to illustrate the superior performance of the proposed method, we compare the proposed method with six competing methods, where the codes of all these methods are provided by the respective authors. Specifically, the competing methods include ViBe [6] and its variants (i.e. PBAS [9] and LOBSTER [7]). A codebook-based method Multicue-BGS [11] and two state-of-the-art methods, i.e., IMBS-MT [12], SubSENSE [8] are also used for comparing with the proposed method. The parameters of each competing method are set to be the same as the original papers.

As we can see in Table 1, based on the category-wise performance competition, the proposed method obtains the best performance in the categories of IOM, DB, TM, BW and LFR. In the categories of BL, SD, although the proposed method only obtains the third-best experimental results, the experiment results of ours are much better than most of the competing method and close to the best results. In the categories of NV and TB, the proposed method also obtains the third-best experimental results. However, compared with the best results, the experimental results of ours are not very well. This is because the videos in this two video categories exist strong illumination changes and the proposed method can not handle it very well. We can also noticed that, for most of the video categories, the performance of the proposed method is superior to ViBe [6] and its variants (i.e. PBAS [9] and LOBSTER [7]), this is due to the effective strategies used in the proposed method. Compared with the state-of-the-art

Table 1. The average F-Measure metric comparison obtained by the competing methods on the CDnet 2014 dataset, where the best, the second best and the third best results are marked with '*', '**' and '***' in the upper right corner of the numbers, respectively.

Method	ViBe [6]	PBAS [9]	Multicue BGS [11]	IMBS-MT [12]	LOBSTER [7]	SubSENSE [8]	Ours
BL	0.8132	0.7292	0.7672	0.8588	0.9237**	0.9497*	0.9012***
IOM	0.3132	0.3450	0.4757	0.5455	0.5611***	0.6034**	0.6091*
DB	0.6161***	0.5813	0.1932	0.5997	0.5780	0.8212**	0.8222*
SD	0.7582	0.7489	0.7743	0.7263	0.8678**	0.8996*	0.8576***
CJ	0.5753	0.6157	0.5696	0.7642**	0.7402***	0.8085*	0.6931
TM	0.5256	0.5632	0.6853***	0.5942	0.5686	0.6881**	0.7709*
BW	0.6076	0.7863	0.7122	0.6588	0.7863***	0.8550**	0.8585*
LFR	0.3671	0.5287	0.6006	0.6543	0.6570***	0.6690**	0.7214*
NV	0.3712	0.3587	0.5432*	0.3915	0.4269	0.4874**	0.4644***
TB	0.8019**	0.6843	0.6114	0.5350	0.6588	0.8681*	0.7582***
Average	0.5750	0.5941	0.5932	0.6328	0.6615***	0.7650*	0.7300**

Table 2. The average processing time (seconds per frame) of all the competing method for each video category, where the fastest, the second fastest and the third fastest results are marked with '*', '**' and '***' in the upper right corner of the numbers, respectively.

Method	ViBe [6]	PBAS [9]	Multicue BGS [11]	IMBS-MT [12]	LOBSTER [7]	SubSENSE [8]	Ours
BL	0.0020*	0.0213	0.0139**	0.0238	0.0313	0.0556	0.0167***
IOM	0.0017*	0.0172	0.0149***	0.0196	0.0244	0.0476	0.0133**
DB	0.0020*	0.0189***	0.0233	0.0270	0.0357	0.0667	0.0137**
SD	0.0015*	0.0204	0.0156**	0.0233	0.0286	0.0526	0.0161***
CJ	0.0022*	0.0244**	0.0313	0.0278	0.0333	0.0667	0.0256***
TM	0.0011*	0.0164	0.0125***	0.0161	0.0200	0.0417	0.0123**
BW	0.0038*	0.0588	0.0182**	0.0588	0.0769	0.1667	0.0435***
LFR	0.0027*	0.0345	0.0222**	0.0417	0.0556	0.1000	0.0278***
NV	0.0027*	0.0400	0.0185**	0.0476	0.0667	0.1250	0.0370***
TB	0.0039*	0.0556	0.0233***	0.0667	0.0833	0.1667	0.0196**
Average	0.0024*	0.0305	0.0194**	0.0352	0.0459	0.0889	0.0226***

methods, the performance of the proposed method is also very competitive, and we can see that the overall average F-Measure obtained by the proposed method is the second-best, which is superior to IMBS-MT [12]. However, the proposed method can not well handle with the categories of CJ, where the video is captured by the camera jitter. The main reason is that the gradient value of each pixel significantly changes under such a situation and it affects the performance of the proposed method.

In Table 2, we measure the average processing time of all the competing methods in each video category on an Intel Core i7-4790 HD 4600 CPU @ 3.6 GHz, 8 GB RAM. We can see that the proposed method achieves the best average processing time among all the competing methods except for ViBe [6] (which obtains the highest efficiency) and Multicue BGS [11]. Although the final average processing time of the proposed method is slower than ViBe and Multicue BGS, the overall foreground detection accuracies are superior to ViBe and Multicue BGS because it uses the proposed foreground object detection strategy and bilateral aperture detection strategy, and two effective strategies for foreground noise detection and ghost region detection.

4   Conclusion

In this paper, we propose a new ViBe-based background subtraction method, which includes a new foreground detection strategy, and a bilateral aperture detection strategy that helps to reduce the false negatives for foreground detection. Moreover, two effective strategies for foreground noise detection and ghost region detection are proposed to effectively alleviate the problems of dynamic backgrounds and ghosts. Experimental results on the CDnet 2014 dataset show that the proposed method is not only superior to a couple of ViBe-based methods, but also is competitive and outperforms several state-of-the-art background subtraction methods for some video categories. In the meanwhile, the proposed method achieves high efficiency performance on the CDnet 2014 dataset.

Acknowledgements. This work was supported by the National Natural Science Foundation of China under Grants U1605252, 61472334, 61571379 and 61370124 by the Natural Science Foundation of Fujian Province of China under Grant 2017J01127.

References

1. Maddalena, L., Petrosino, A.: A self-organizing approach to background subtraction for visual surveillance applications. IEEE Trans. Image Process. **17**(7), 1168–1177 (2008)
2. Biswas, K.K., Basu, S.K.: Gesture recognition using microsoft kinect®. In: IEEE International Conference on Automation, Robotics and Applications, pp. 100–103 (2011)
3. Yang, T., Pan, Q., Li, J., Li, S.Z.: Real-time multiple objects tracking with occlusion handling in dynamic scenes. In: IEEE Conference on Computer Vision and Pattern Recognition, pp. 970–975 (2005)
4. Bouwmans, T.: Traditional and recent approaches in background modeling for foreground detection: an overview. Comput. Sci. Rev. **11**, 31–66 (2014)
5. Barnich, O., Van Droogenbroeck, M.: ViBe: a powerful random technique to estimate the background in video sequences. In: IEEE International Conference on Acoustics, Speech and Signal Processing, pp. 945–948 (2009)
6. Barnich, O., Van Droogenbroeck, M.: ViBe: a universal background subtraction algorithm for video sequences. IEEE Trans. Image Process. **20**(6), 1709–1724 (2011)
7. St-Charles, P.L., Bilodeau, G.A.: Improving background subtraction using local binary similarity patterns. In: IEEE Winter Conference on Applications of Computer Vision, pp. 509–515 (2014)
8. St-Charles, P.L., Bilodeau, G.A., Bergevin, R.: SubSENSE: a universal change detection method with local adaptive sensitivity. IEEE Trans. Image Process. **24**(1), 359–373 (2015)
9. Martin, H., Tiefenbacher, P., Rigoll, G.: Background segmentation with feedback: the pixel-based adaptive segmenter. In: IEEE Conference on Computer Vision and Pattern Recognition Workshops, pp. 38–43 (2012)
10. Wang, Y., Jodoin, P.M., Porikli, F., Konrad, J., Ishwar, P.: CDnet 2014: an expanded change detection benchmark dataset. In: IEEE Conference on Computer Vision and Pattern Recognition Workshops, pp. 387–394 (2014)
11. Noh, S.J., Jeon, M.: A new framework for background subtraction using multiple cues. In: Lee, K.M., Matsushita, Y., Rehg, J.M., Hu, Z. (eds.) ACCV 2012. LNCS, vol. 7726, pp. 493–506. Springer, Heidelberg (2013). https://doi.org/10.1007/978-3-642-37431-9_38
12. Bloisi, D.D., Pennisi, A., Iocchi, L.: Parallel multi-modal background modeling. Pattern Recogn. Lett. **96**, 45–54 (2017)

Layout-Driven Top-Down Saliency Detection for Webpage

Xixi Li, Di Liu, Kao Zhang, and Zhenzhong Chen[✉]

School of Remote Sensing and Information Engineering, Wuhan University,
Wuhan 430079, Hubei, People's Republic of China
zzchen@whu.edu.cn

Abstract. Webpage is a significant part of internet content and a pervasive medium for information communication. Studying the distribution properties of eye fixation for webpage can help improve the quality of webpage design. In this paper, we investigate the web-viewing behavior caused by webpage layout and propose a novel webpage saliency method based on this top-down knowledge. We derive a layout saliency map by probability model as top-down knowledge according to different layout styles and incorporate it with the bottom-up saliency map computed by conventional models. Experimental results demonstrate that with the proposed layout-driven top-down saliency, webpage saliency detection can be improved for almost all the conventional saliency models.

Keywords: Webpage saliency · Top-down knowledge
Webpage layout · Web-viewing behavior

1 Introduction

Webpage has become an increasingly important information platform with the wide spread of internet in recent years. The fast growing trend of browsing webpage has greatly reshaped the living style, working pattern and marketing campaign of human. Since webpage is a significant fraction of internet content and a pervasive medium for information communication, many researchers put efforts in optimizing web performance [1–3], and those studies which investigate how human deploy and direct their attention when viewing webpages freely have both academic and commercial values [4–6].

Studies on webpage have been a common issue over decades e.g. webpage scanpath, webpage structure classification for recommendation and advertisement blocking [7], web browsing behavior, human computer interaction, relevant dataset, website designing, etc. Most of these researches aim to direct users' attention via scanpath on websites, constructing a model that enables web design interaction. Some groups segment different webpages serving various purposes to better understand the content and function. Webpage designers could optimize the page typography (as shown in Fig. 1) and layout rationally benefiting from these researches since our eye movements are informative about the interacts with stimuli and provide us with clues about what we most likely pay attention to, how long

© Springer International Publishing AG, part of Springer Nature 2018
B. Zeng et al. (Eds.): PCM 2017, LNCS 10736, pp. 438–446, 2018.
https://doi.org/10.1007/978-3-319-77383-4_43

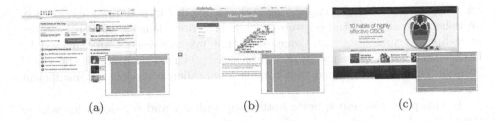

(a)   (b)   (c)

Fig. 1. Illustrations of webpage layout

we spend on the elements in graphic designs, and how we redirect attention between elements [8]. Therefore, they can arrange different page elements legitimately and put the most important part on conspicuous position to enhance user experience. These studies dedicate to both the usability and utility of websites, considering either webpage's distinct characteristics or human viewing behavior. Therefore, we aim at designing a saliency detection method to automatically predict the webpage saliency, i.e., viewers' attention on the webpage, based on the state-of-the-art work on web design [9], eye movements [10], etc.

Saliency detection and eye fixation prediction, which aim to mimic human visual system, are both hot topics in computer vision and bring a wide range of applications such as visual tracking, image retrieval and object recognition. Human visual attention is mainly drawn by two factors: bottom-up factor (that is memory-free, biased and stimulus-driven) and top-down factor (that is memory-dependent, knowledge-driven and with many selective criteria) [11]. Bottom-up methods can predict fixations in images effectively, indicating the importance of low-level features (which resemble the receptive fields of neurons in V1, where neurons represent a bottom-up saliency map). While top-down saliency aims to locate all intended objects in the scene and existing methods typically learn the 'knowledge' from category-specific training data to guide top-down saliency detection [12]. Mounting computational and physiological evidences show that both low-level and high-level features affect the visual attention. These high-level features including faces and text will be recognized in higher areas such as V4 and IT and are related to gaze deployment [13].

Viewing in webpages is different from that in natural images. There are many other kinds of stimuli on webpage, such as text, logos, animations and faces [14], which all belong to high-level features and strongly attract our attention [15]. Most of the conventional saliency models pay more attention to features like color, contrast and orientation. In [15], Shen *et al.* published the first eye tracking dataset on webpages and proposed a computational model for webpage saliency by integrating multi-scale feature maps, face map and positional bias in an MKL framework and later intensive work is involved in DNN. However, empirical studies have shown that human's web-viewing behavior follows some certain principles such as the F-bias to scan top-left region at the beginning of browsing [16,17] and the banner blindness to avoid banner-like advertisement naturally [18,19]. These distinct characteristics may result from certain design guidelines on webpage layout and people's general reading habit and prior experience. Josephson *et al.* [20] studied web-viewing behavior focusing on the category of webpage visual design and suggested that eye movements are affected by both visual design of webpages and habitually preferred path across the visual stimuli. Thus, it is suggested that conventional saliency models are insufficient for webpages.

In this paper, we incorporate bottom-up saliency and top-down knowledge together and construct a novel saliency model for webpages using eye tracking dataset based on webpages' inherent distinctions. The main contributions in this paper are listed as follows:

1. Taking discrimination between websites and natural images into consideration, from the perspective of webpage layout, we regard the layout as non-negligible prior knowledge in visual attention on webpages and we derive a top-down layout saliency map from this.
2. A novel layout-driven model is constructed to integrate bottom-up saliency map derived from conventional saliency models with top-down knowledge together that outperforms other methods.

The remaining of the paper is organized as follows. In Sect. 2, the proposed method is described in detail. Section 3 presents the experimental validation of the derived mathematical models. The final section concludes the paper.

2 The Proposed Method

2.1 Layout Saliency Map

A successful website should attract attention, and enhance readership and readability. The visual layout of a page is typically organized to help users understand how to use a site. Generally, the layout tends to be hierarchically templated obeying a standardized HTML grammar in which case learning becomes easier. There have been many algorithms for layout style classification and we take ideas in [7,21] for reference.

Similar to methods in [21], we can learn the graphic design of webpage and using optimization to generate layouts in various styles. Then we analyze their geometric structure and classify them into several representative types by clustering algorithms. This layout is often hierarchical and reflected in a recursive table layout that can be detected in the parse tree of the HTML document.

The layout styles involved in the dataset can be roughly classified consulting numerous webpage design resources online as shown in Fig. 2. Since webpage saliency is surely related to webpage layout and empty space and different layout styles lead to different browsing patterns, it is essential to manage to get the 'location prior' corresponding to layout as a layout saliency map (LSM).

In the area of saliency map generation, Bayesian analysis is widely used in various ways [22,23]. Thus, we construct a probabilistic model and define the location saliency of each pixel as the probability of the point being gazed at.

$$S_l = p(O = 1 | L = l_z, C = C_i) \tag{1}$$

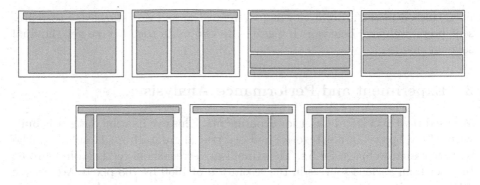

Fig. 2. 7 types of layout style

where O is a binary random variable denoting whether or not a point is gazed at; l_z is the location of point z, C_i represents the ith category of layout styles which the test image belongs to, S_l is location saliency of point z. Then we build our model in concept of probability distribution by learning from eye movement data of webpage saliency (FiWI dataset) obtained by free-viewing browsing.

2.2 Join Bottom-Up and Top-Down Saliency for Webpage

As aforementioned, we take the specific characteristics of webpages into account and combine the learned location prior with bottom-up saliency to improve the accuracy of fixation prediction. The bottom-up saliency S_b is obtained by the existing classical algorithms (we covered 13 methods in later experiment part).

Generally computational models that predict eye fixations on images are built on the hypothesis that the saliency of a region depends on its distance from the neighbor in terms of low-level image statistics, such as luminance, color, edge and density. We regards these stimuli-driven factors as bottom-up saliency.

The next task is to join the bottom-up and top-down saliency maps together. The former studies realize this step in diverse ways such as add operation, multiplication or summation with adaptive weights. Here, we intend to do a hybrid operation as

$$S_{w_i} = \overline{S_b \times S_{l_i}} + S_{l_i} \tag{2}$$

where i represents different layout styles and $\overline{S_b \times S_{l_i}}$ denotes a normalization step after multiplication. First we take the S_l as a probability distribution because what we find conspicuous in natural images is inconsistent with what we observe in webpage. For example: we always overlook the white space. Thus bottom up saliency may introduce some noise. Moreover, it's a remarkable fact that we inevitably lose some non-negligible information after multiplication due to that what we miss in bottom-up model remain to be zero whatever it multiplies. For instance, we usually concern about the title and center area but these may not be prominent in bottom-up models. As the Center-bias habit that has been verified in the natural viewing, we regard S_l as prior knowledge to represent users' webpage behavior. Integrate the two parts together we get the final saliency map S_w.

3   Experiment and Performance Analysis

We used the FiWI [15] dataset for experiments. This eye fixation dataset is built with 149 webpages in 3 categories and eye tracking data from 11 subjects who free-view each webpage for 5 s. The stimuli are screenshots rendered in Chrome browser from various sources in the resolution of 1360 by 768 pixels. We choose GBVS algorithm as an example to elaborate our experiment. As discussed in Sect. 2.1, we separate the dataset into seven categories roughly according to layout styles and we simplify them in Fig. 2. The size of each box is an approximately expression other than a fixed value since the styles are diverse online. Then we divide the data randomly into training images and testing images so that we can learn the location prior from the training data and test the saliency model with testing data. Next we acquire bottom-up saliency from GBVS. Finally we fuse the layout saliency map and bottom-up saliency together to get the final webpage saliency. For performance analysis, we use 4 widely used saliency evaluation metrics including sAUC, AUC_Judd, CC and NSS like most relevant work for saliency to judge whether there is improvement. As shown in Table 1, compared with original GBVS, all evaluation values of our method improves a lot showing a promising performance and illustrating that location is an important factor of web visual attention. Figure 3 gives the diverse maps for comparison. Nevertheless, the accuracy seemingly is not perfect enough for the expectation. We explain that two factors bring about this phenomenon. One is our less rigorous classification and another is the too small amount of data that incompletely generalize webpage layout patterns. But at any rate we have to admit the existence of difference between layouts and they indeed affect the saliency distribution.

Additionally, we evaluate our proposed method with a series of existing saliency detection algorithms AIM [25], CA [26], COV [27], FES [28], GBVS [24], GR [29], MC [30], PCA [31], RBD [32], SeR [33], SIM [34], SUN [22], SWD [35] aiming at a quantitative contrast. All related codes are available on the website[1].

We evaluate the performance sAUC, AUC_Judd, CC and NSS like most relevant work for saliency. The codes and descriptions are all available in [36].

Table 1. The performance of GBVS and our improved method

Methods	AUC_Judd	sAUC	CC	NSS
GBVS	0.6935	0.6595	0.2112	0.6480
Ours	0.7927	0.7759	0.3639	1.1512

---

[1] https://github.com/MingMingCheng/SalBenchmark.

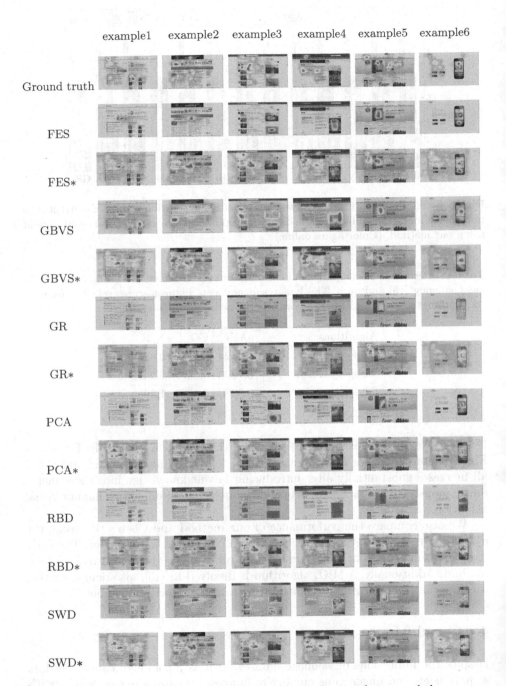

Fig. 3. Diverse maps for comparison. We list 6 examples in columns and the * represents our approach integrating layout information with bottom-up saliency.

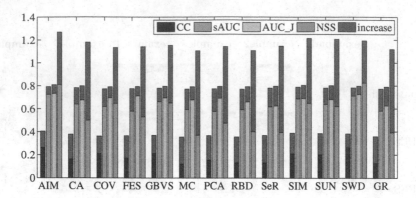

Fig. 4. Evaluations of 13 methods, we plot 4 sorts of evaluation results of conventional bottom-up methods, and the red block on the top of each bar denotes the improvement using our method. (Color figure online)

Table 2. Performance comparison of conventional image saliency models, Shen's webpage saliency [15] and ours. The Image saliency lists highest scores selected from 13 conventional models, and the last row lists the score of our method.

Algorithms	sAUC	CC	NSS
Image saliency	0.6524	0.2667	0.8247
Webpage saliency [15]	0.7206	0.3977	1.2475
Ours	0.8089	0.4073	1.3285

Besides, we draw a histogram to visualize the results as shown in Fig. 4. As Fig. 4 demonstrates, for 13 conventional models, AUC_Judd, CC, NSS and sAUC all increases substantially after introducing layout knowledge into these methods demonstrating a fact that webpage layout actually influences human visual attention.

We also compare the performance of our method and Chen's [15] using the evaluation results in terms of sAUC, CC and NSS listed in the paper. The comparison results shown in Table 2 indicates a relatively better performance of our method. Additionally, a MKL algorithm is involved in [15], also demonstrating the superiority of our proposed method with lower algorithm complexity.

4   Conclusions

Despite the limitations of webpage dataset such as incomplete categories data acquirement, and ungenerous number of images, we cannot ensure whether it's perfectly fit our experiment. But taking users' viewing behavior into consideration we construct a novel layout-driven computational model of saliency prediction and factually verify our idea that webpage layout really has an impact on web visual attention. Moreover, we plan to classify the layout style more scientifically, update the dataset and explore new bottom-up saliency model for website to improve the webpage saliency in the future.

Acknowledgement. This work was supported by National Natural Science Foundation of China (No. 61471273).

References

1. Butkiewicz, M., Wang, D., Wu, Z., et al.: Klotski: reprioritizing web content to improve user experience on mobile devices. In: 12th USENIX Symposium on Network Systems Design and Implementation, pp. 439–453 (2015)
2. Netravali, R., Goyal, A., Mickens, J., et al.: Polaris: faster page loads using fine-grained dependency tracking. In: 13th USENIX Symposium on Network Systems Design and Implementation, pp. 123–136 (2016)
3. Wang, X.S., Balasubramanian, A., Krishnamurthy, A., et al.: Demystifying page load performance with WProf. In: 10th USENIX Symposium on Network Systems Design and Implementation, pp. 473–485 (2013)
4. Bixby, J.: Case study: the impact of HTML delay on mobile business metrics (2011). http://bit.ly/2cbN22l
5. Bixby, J.: 4 awesome slides showing how page speed correlates to business metrics at Walmart.com (2012). http://bit.ly/2cbN22l
6. Eaton, K.: How one second could cost Amazon $1.6 billion in sales. In: Fast Company (2012)
7. Shih, L.K., Karger, D.R.: Using URLs and table layout for web classification tasks. In: 13th International Conference on World Wide Web, pp. 193–202. ACM Press, New York (2004)
8. Bylinskii, Z., Borkin, M.A., Kim, N.W., Pfister, H., Oliva, A.: Eye fixation metrics for large scale evaluation and comparison of information visualizations. In: Burch, M., Chuang, L., Fisher, B., Schmidt, A., Weiskopf, D. (eds.) ETVIS 2015. MV, pp. 235–255. Springer, Cham (2017). https://doi.org/10.1007/978-3-319-47024-5_14
9. Pang, X., Cao, Y., Lau, R.W., Chan, A.B.: Directing user attention via visual flow on web designs. ACM Trans. Graph. **35**, 1–11 (2016)
10. Eraslan, S., Yesilada, Y., Harper, S.: Eye tracking scanpath analysis on web pages: how many users? In: 9th Biennial ACM Symposium on Eye Tracking Research & Applications, pp. 103–110. ACM Press, New York (2016)
11. Itti, L., Koch, C.: A saliency-based search mechanism for overt and covert shifts of visual attention. Vis. Res. **40**, 1489–1506 (2000)
12. He, S., Lau, R.W., Yang, Q.: Exemplar-driven top-down saliency detection via deep association. In: The IEEE Conference on Computer Vision and Pattern Recognition, pp. 5723–5732. IEEE Press, New York (2016)
13. Kootstra, G., de Boer, B., Schomaker, L.R.: Predicting eye fixations on complex visual stimuli using local symmetry. Cogn. Comput. **3**, 223–240 (2011)
14. Still, J.D., Masciocchi, C.M.: A saliency model predicts fixations in web interfaces. In: 5th International Workshop on Model Driven Development of Advanced User Interfaces, pp. 25–28. MDDAUI, Georgia (2010)
15. Shen, C., Zhao, Q.: Webpage saliency. In: Fleet, D., Pajdla, T., Schiele, B., Tuytelaars, T. (eds.) ECCV 2014. LNCS, vol. 8695, pp. 33–46. Springer, Cham (2014). https://doi.org/10.1007/978-3-319-10584-0_3

16. Nielsen, J.: F-shaped pattern for reading web content (2006). http://www.nngroup. com/articles/f-shaped-pattern-reading-web-content
17. Buscher, G., Cutrell, E., Morris, M.R.: What do you see when you're surfing?: using eye tracking to predict salient regions of web pages. In: Proceedings of the SIGCHI Conference on Human Factors in Computing Systems, pp. 21–30. ACM Press, New York (2009)
18. Cho, C.H., University of Texas at Austin: Why do people avoid advertising on the internet? J. Advert. **33**, 89–97 (2004)
19. Hervet, G., Gurard, K., Tremblay, S., Chtourou, M.S.: Is banner blindness genuine? Eye tracking internet text advertising. Appl. Cogn. Psychol. **25**, 708–716 (2011)
20. Josephson, S., Holmes, M.E.: Visual attention to repeated internet images: testing the scanpath theory on the world wide web. In: Proceedings of the 2002 Symposium on Eye Tracking Research & Applications, pp. 43–49. ACM Press, New York (2002)
21. O'Donovan, P., Agarwala, A., Hertzmann, A.: Learning layouts for single-pagegraphic designs. IEEE Trans. Visual Comput. Graph. **20**, 1200–1213 (2014)
22. Zhang, L., Tong, M.H., Marks, T.K., Shan, H., Cottrell, G.W.: SUN: a Bayesian framework for saliency using natural statistics. J. Vis. **8**, 32 (2008)
23. Chen, Z., Yuan, J., Tan, Y.P.: Hybrid saliency detection for images. IEEE Signal Process. Lett. **20**, 95–98 (2013)
24. Harel, J., Koch, C., Perona, P.: Graph-based visual saliency. In: NIPS (2006)
25. Bruce, N., Tsotsos, J.: Attention based on information maximization. J. Vis. **7**, 950 (2007)
26. Goferman, S., Zelnik-Manor, L., Tal, A.: Context-aware saliency detection. IEEE Trans. Pattern Anal. Mach. Intell. **34**, 1915–1926 (2012)
27. Erdem, E., Erdem, A.: Visual saliency estimation by nonlinearly integrating features using region covariances. J. Vis. **13**, 11 (2013)
28. Rezazadegan Tavakoli, H., Rahtu, E., Heikkilä, J.: Fast and efficient saliency detection using sparse sampling and kernel density estimation. In: Heyden, A., Kahl, F. (eds.) SCIA 2011. LNCS, vol. 6688, pp. 666–675. Springer, Heidelberg (2011). https://doi.org/10.1007/978-3-642-21227-7_62
29. Yang, C., Zhang, L., Lu, H.: Graph-regularized saliency detection with convex-hull-based center prior. IEEE Signal Process. Lett. **20**, 637–640 (2013)
30. Jiang, B., Zhang, L., Lu, H., Yang, C., Yang, M.H.: Saliency detection via absorbing Markov chain. In: The IEEE International Conference on Computer Vision, pp. 1665–1672. IEEE Press, New York (2013)
31. Margolin, R., Tal, A., Zelnik-Manor, L.: What makes a patch distinct? In: The IEEE Conference on Computer Vision and Pattern Recognition, pp. 1139–1146. IEEE Press, New York (2013)
32. Zhu, W., Liang, S., Wei, Y., Sun, J.: Saliency optimization from robust background detection. In: The IEEE Conference on Computer Vision and Pattern Recognition, pp. 2814–2821. IEEE Press, New York (2004)
33. Seo, H.J., Milanfar, P.: Static and space-time visual saliency detection by self-resemblance. J. Vis. **9**, 15 (2009)
34. Murray, N., Vanrell, M., Otazu, X., Parraga, C.A.: Saliency estimation using a non-parametric low-level vision model. In: The IEEE Conference on Computer Vision and Pattern Recognition, pp. 433–440. IEEE Press, New York (2011)
35. Duan, L., Wu, C., Miao, J., Qing, L., Fu, Y.: Visual saliency detection by spatially weighted dissimilarity. In: The IEEE Conference on Computer Vision and Pattern Recognition, pp. 473–480. IEEE Press, New York (2011)
36. Bylinskii, Z., Judd, T., Borji, A., Itti, L., Durand, F., Oliva, A., Torralba, A.: MIT saliency benchmark (2015). http://saliency.mit.edu

Saliency Detection by Superpixel-Based Sparse Representation

Guangyao Chen and Zhenzhong Chen[(⊠)]

State Key Laboratory of Software Engineering, School of Computer,
Wuhan University, Wuhan 430079, Hubei, People's Republic of China
{chenguangyao,zzchen}@whu.edu.cn

Abstract. In this paper, we propose a novel model for predicting visual saliency by superpixel-based sparse representation. A superpixel-based sparse representation utilizes the Simultaneous Orthogonal Matching Pursuit algorithm to extract the sparse features from color maps and activation maps of complex cells. The saliency is calculated according to the sparse features from different dictionaries. To guarantee the robustness of the proposed method, the proposed method is performed on a multi-scale basis thus the final saliency result is obtained by using the saliency maps from different scales. Experimental results on multiple datasets show that the proposed model outperforms several advanced methods for saliency prediction.

Keywords: Saliency prediction · Superpixel · Sparse representation

1 Introduction

The Human Vision System (HVS) can quickly prioritize external visual stimuli and pick out interesting parts from a scene. Simulating such human capability with computer has been a topic of interest for researchers in the field of computer vision over the past few decades. Saliency detection aims at highlighting visually salient regions or objects in an image, and results of it can be used to facilitate other computer vision tasks such as image segmentation [5], object detection [14], person re-identification [25], etc. Due to the importance of saliency detection, a large number of models have been proposed to capture different saliency cues. Saliency detection models can be categorized as bottom-up and top-down approaches. Bottom-up methods are data-driven, fast and pre-attentive, while top-down methods are goal-driven, slow and entail supervised learning with class labels. In this paper, we focus on the bottom-up method for images saliency detection.

Current studies reveal that the sparse representation of image statistics exists in the primate visual system [16]. These studies in neuroscience suggest that sparse coding strategy is an efficient way for modelling natural scene as sparse representation, which simulates the V1 population responses to natural stimuli. Extracting the independent sparse features from images has been demonstrated

© Springer International Publishing AG, part of Springer Nature 2018
B. Zeng et al. (Eds.): PCM 2017, LNCS 10736, pp. 447–456, 2018.
https://doi.org/10.1007/978-3-319-77383-4_44

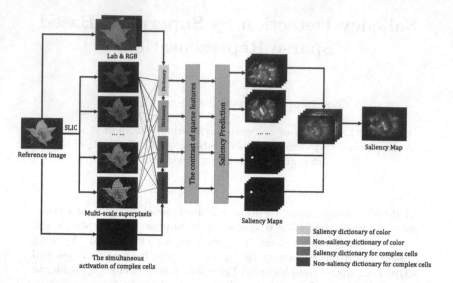

Fig. 1. Framework overview of the proposed model. The model utilises the Simultaneous Orthogonal Matching Pursuit algorithm to extract the sparse features from color maps and complex cells' activation map. Then, the saliency map is formed by the contrast of sparse features under different scales and different dictionaries. (Color figure online)

to be highly effective for many computer vision tasks, leading to better performance for saliency detection.

Saliency models based on sparse representation [6] have been proposed to extract the saliency map of the input image by computing the center-surround differences between image patches mainly. However, these models ignore the fact that image patches can span multiple distinct image regions. Image patches are local regions with fixed size and shape. They may not effectively exploit spatial information of the image thus leading to lower accuracy in saliency detection. Compared with image patches, superpixels are obtained from an over-segmented image, and they aggregate visually homogeneous pixels while respecting natural boundaries. Therefore, superpixels are superior to patches in saliency detection and superpixel-based sparse representation are more likely to simulate the V1 population responses to natural stimuli. Zhang et al. [24] and Li et al. [12] have considered superpixels and sparse representation. They all utilize data-specific features of superpixels to build a dictionary. But, superpixel is a small spatial region whose shape and size can be adaptively changed for different spatial structures. These methods may lose detailed features of superpixels using data-specific features.

To overcome the above shortcomings, we propose a novel sparse representation based on superpixels. The simultaneous orthogonal matching pursuit algorithm [19] is utilized to extract the sparse features of pixels in a superpixel by the joint sparse regularization. We also apply this method to construct a multi-layer sparse coding network [8] based on the theory argued in [9]. The framework overview of the proposed model is shown in Fig. 1. The proposed model firstly extracts sparse features of multi-scale superpixels, which have been proved to be an important cue to improve the saliency region detection in [18], from the color map and complex cells responses. Then, the model measures saliency by calculating the contrast of sparse features over the entire image, combining saliency maps from multi-scale superpixels. To evaluate the performance of the proposed model, we apply it on several datasets for eye fixation prediction. The experimental results show the better performance of the proposed saliency detection model over other existing ones.

The rest of this paper is organized as follows. In Sect. 2, the adopted perceptual domain knowledge for the proposed model are briefly reviewed. Section 3 introduces the proposed framework for saliency detection. Experimental results on two benchmark datasets are presented in Sect. 4. The final section concludes this paper and suggests future research directions.

2 Preliminaries

2.1 Sparse Representation

Sparse representation model is a linear model, where the original input signal can be represented as a linear combination of basis vectors. Here, the response is sparse to stimulate the basis vectors of the input image and shows the same characteristics of the human visual system. Formally, sparse representation model depicts signals by the linear combination of a few items from a pre-specified dictionary. The performance of the sparse representation relies heavily on the quality of the dictionary D. Recently, many dictionary learning algorithms have been proposed to achieve compact representation. One widely used dictionary learning algorithm is the K-SVD [2].

Given an over-complete dictionary $D = [d_1, d_2, ..., d_n] \in R^m$, where normally $m \leq n$, n represents the size of dictionary, and an input signal $I \in R^m$, m is the dimension of the signal. Then the sparse coding coefficients α for x is obtained by solving:

$$\min_{\alpha} \|\alpha\|_0 \quad s.t. \quad \|I - D\alpha\|_2^2 \leq \epsilon \tag{1}$$

The above model aims to seek the most compact representation for the input signal x based on the given dictionary D. However, the optimization for (1) is NP-hard combinatorial optimization problem which can be solved with Orthogonal Matching Pursuit (OMP) algorithm [15].

Unlike traditional saliency models based on sparse representation utilize sparse features to represent local regions of fixed size and shape, the proposed model can effectively capture the correlations of each superpixel by utilizing the joint sparse representation. This model is further described in the following sections.

2.2   Multi-layer Sparse Coding Model

The spatial classical receptive fields (CRFs) of neurons in the primary visual cortex (V1) of primates are selective for location, orientation, and frequency [9]. Hubel and Wiesel in [9] argued that most neurons can be grouped into two categories: simple cells and complex cells. They have different responses to the outside signal stimulation. Simple cells have strong and linear responses to the specific characteristics, such as location, orientation, and frequency, while complex cells are not sensitive to the outside stimuli because of their larger receptive field area. Their responses have nonlinear characteristics. Inspired by this, Hoyer proposed a multi-layer sparse coding model [8] to describe the response properties of high-level neurons further.

To model the V1 complex cells responses, the multi-layer sparse coding [8] takes squares and sums up the linear filtering results of the two quadrature Gabor filters. The output of a model complex cell can be described as follows:

$$C_{\{x_c,y_c,\theta\}} = (\sum_{x,y} G_{\{e,x_c,y_c,\theta\}} I(x,y))^2 + (\sum_{x,y} G_{\{o,x_c,y_c,\theta\}} I(x,y))^2 \qquad (2)$$

when fed with the image $I(x,y)$. Here $G_{\{e,x_c,y_c,\theta\}}$ and $G_{\{o,x_c,y_c,\theta\}}$ are even- and odd-symmetric (respectively) Gabor filters, centered on (x_c, y_c) and of orientation θ. In our model, we utilize this method to construct complex cells' activation maps of images.

3   Saliency Detection by Superpixel-Based Sparse Representation

As is shown in Sect. 2.2, simple cells and complex cells are sensitive to the specific characteristics, such as location, orientation, and frequency, but they are not sensitive to the color. However, color is an important factor influencing people to pick out interesting parts from a scene. Apart from response maps of complex cells, we also choose both RGB and Lab color spaces as color descriptors.

As the overview of the proposed saliency detection model shown in Fig. 1, the SLIC algorithm [1] is used, and the image is converted into the RGB and Lab color space to segment the original image into multi-scale superpixels. Non-saliency regions can be represented by a sparsely coded dictionary [13]. To maximize the difference between sparse coefficients of superpixels in saliency regions and non-saliency regions, we define four over-complete dictionaries trained by the K-SVD algorithm [2] on FIGRIM Fixation Dataset [4]. Half of this dictionary belongs to saliency dictionaries which are regarded as the potential saliency regions. The other half belongs to the non-saliency dictionary. Two saliency dictionaries correspond to color features and complex cells responses (respectively), and non-saliency dictionaries have the same classification. Then, the sparse features of each superpixel are captured based on the color and complex cells responses as follows:

3.1   Superpixel-Based Sparse Representation

Superpixel is a perceptually meaningful atomic region by grouping pixels and can be used to replace the rigid structure of the pixel grid. However, superpixels' shape and size can be adaptively changed for different spatial structures. Each superpixel is composed of some pixels $[p_{i,1}, p_{i,2}, ...]$, and pixels within each superpixel are assumed to have very similar characteristics. Based on this theory, superpixel-based sparse representation is similar to simultaneous sparse approximation problem.

A simultaneous sparse approximation problem can be described as:

Given several input signals, approximate all these signals at once using different linear combinations of the same elementary signals, while balancing the error in approximating the data against the total number of elementary signals that are used [19].

As described above, a superpixel can be treated as a collection of multiple signals, where the signal is equivalent to a pixel in an image. To solve the simultaneous sparse approximation problem, the Simultaneous Orthogonal Matching Pursuit algorithm is proposed in [19]. Given a set of signals $X = [X^1, \ldots, X^n]$ in $R^{m \times N}$, where the X^i are in $R^{m \times n_i}$, and an over-complete dictionary D in $R^{m \times p}$, the Simultaneous Orthogonal Matching Pursuit algorithm solves a matrix of coefficients $A = [A^1, \ldots, A^n]$ in $R^{p \times N}$ which is an approximate solution of the following NP-hard problem

$$\forall i \quad \min_{A^i \in R^{p \times n_i}} \|X^i - DA^i\|_F^2 \ s.t. \ \|A^i\|_{0,\infty} \leq L. \tag{3}$$

For superpixels-based sparse representation, it can be described as follows:

Each pixel is seen as a signal, then pixels within each superpixel can be arranged into a matrix S_i and are assumed to have very similar characteristics. Pixels within each superpixel S_i shall be simultaneously decomposed by linear combinations of a few common atoms from the dictionary, which can be seen as the joint sparse regularization. Let a matrix A_i be the sparse coefficients of the S_i. The joint sparse matrix A_i is an approximate solution of the following optimization problem:

$$\forall i \quad \min_{A^i \in R^{p \times n_i}} \|S_i - DA_i\|_2 \ s.t. \ \|A_i\|_0 \leq K. \tag{4}$$

where A_i is the sparse coefficients of the superpixel S_i and D is the over-complete dictionary utilizing the method mentioned above. Here, the superpixel-based sparse representation is described a simultaneous sparse approximation problem and the Simultaneous Orthogonal Matching Pursuit algorithm is used to solve the problem above efficiently. The solving process is shown in as Algorithm 1. The output of the Simultaneous Orthogonal Matching Pursuit algorithm, A set Λ_t containing T indices, determines the sparse coefficients A_i of the superpixel S_i.

Pixels within each superpixel are assumed to have very similar characteristics, so their sparse coefficients are also similar. In our model, we use the means of the joint sparse coefficients A_i as the sparse coefficient α_i of the superpixel S_i.

Algorithm 1. Simultaneous Orthogonal Matching Pursuit

Input: – A $m * N$ signal matrix S,
             – The stopping criterion and the reconstruction error ϵ,
             – An over-complete dictionary D.
Output: A set Λ_t containing T indices, where T is the number of iterations completed.
1: Initialize the residual matrix $R_0 = S$, the index set $\Lambda_0 = \emptyset$, and the iteration
   counter $t = 1$.
2: Find an index λ_t that solves the easy optimization problem

$$\max_{\omega \in \Omega} \sum_{n=1}^{N} |\langle R_{t-1}e_n, d_\omega \rangle|.$$

   e_k denotes the kth canonical basis vector in R_{t-1} and d_ω is ωth column of the
   over-completed dictionary D, where the parameter ω ranges over an index set Ω.
3: Set $\Lambda_t = \Lambda_{t-1} \cup \{\lambda_t\}$.
4: Determine the orthogonal projector P_t onto the span of the atoms indexed in Λ_t.
5: Calculate the new approximation and residual:

$$R_t = S - P_t S.$$

6: Increment t, and return to Step 2 unless the stopping criterion is met.

In this way, each superpixel S_i is turned to be a linear combination of basis vectors with a sparse coefficients α_i. And this is used to be the feature vector in saliency detection.

3.2   Saliency Calculation Based on Sparse Features

The analysis noted that a superpixel with much difference compared with the others has a higher probability of attracting human's attention. Spatial relationship plays an important role. The closer the distance, the stronger effect between superpixels. Therefore, the Gaussian function can be a good choice to describe this:

$$G_\delta(\|a - b\|) = e^{-\frac{\|a-b\|^2}{\delta^2}} \tag{5}$$

Human eye-tracking studies have shown that gaze fixations are biased toward the center of natural scene stimuli [20]. Center bias has been much discussed in the saliency literature. Here, center bias appears more directly as a factor that influences the relative weights assigned to the score of saliency defined by local superpixels. This effectively means that superpixels closer to the center have more influence in determining saliency value.

Obtain the saliency of each superpixel by calculating the sum of sparse features difference between the superpixel itself and other superpixels. This process can be described as follows:

$$Sal_i^{SP} = \sum_{j=1}^{n} D_{i,j} G_\delta(\|P_i - P_j\|) G_{\delta_c}(\|P_i - P_c\|) \tag{6}$$

where, $D_{i,j}$ is the superpixel difference between superpixels i and j, c is the spatial center of the image, G_{δ_c} is a Gaussian function which controls the amount of center bias based on δ_c, G_δ is a Gaussian function which controls the influence of the distance between the superpixel itself and other superpixels based on δ, Sal_i^{SP} is the saliency value of superpixel i. Here we use the distance between superpixels as the weight of the superpixels difference to calculate the saliency map. We compute $D_{i,j}$ based on sparse features α as follows:

$$D_{i,j} = \frac{\alpha(i) \cdot \alpha(j)}{\|\alpha(i)\| \cdot \|\alpha(j)\|} \tag{7}$$

Every sparse feature is based on the same basis, so the sparse features can be taken as sparse vectors based on same basis vector. Cosine similarity is easy to interpret and simple to compute for sparse vectors. It always performs better for the contrast of sparse vectors. Therefore, we utilize cosine similarity to improve the accuracy of saliency maps.

Combining the saliency map with four sparse responses by four different dictionaries and several scales as computed above. We calculate the average saliency under different scales as saliency value of one pixel:

$$Sal_i^P = \frac{1}{m} \sum_{s=1}^{m} \sum_{d=1}^{4} Sal_{i,r,d}^{SP} \tag{8}$$

where, $Sal_{i,r}^{SP}$ is the saliency value of the superpixel where pixel i is located at scale s by dictionary d, m is the number of superpixels scales.

Implementation Details. Each input image is first converted into the RGB and Lab color space and segmented into superpixels by four scales. Then, get complex cells' activation map of the input image by multi-layer sparse coding network [8]. The Gaussian envelope had an aspect ratio of 1.5, and the spatial frequency of the sinusoid was chosen to give 2–3 main inhibitory regions. Four activation values of four complex cells with four orientations is extracted from every texel. These values construct complex cells' activation map of the input image. We define four over-complete dictionaries trained by the K-SVD algorithm [2] on FIGRIM fixation dataset [4]. FIGRIM fixation dataset consists of 2787 natural scenes from 21 different indoor and outdoor scene categories. After superpixel-based sparse representation for color maps and activation map, the model combines the saliency map with four sparse responses by four different dictionaries and several scales. Before making the summation, each saliency map is normalized.

4   Experimental Results

In this section, the performance of the model we proposed is evaluated in MIT1003 dataset [11] and Toronto dataset [3]. The MIT1003 dataset [11] consists of 1003 natural indoor and outdoor scenes. The eye tracking data in MIT1003

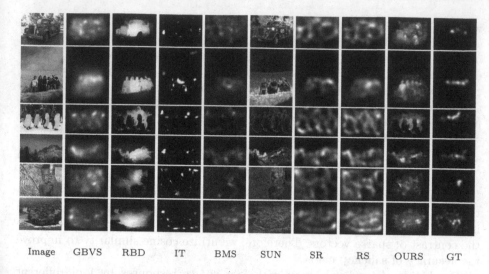

Image   GBVS   RBD   IT   BMS   SUN   SR   RS   OURS   GT

Fig. 2. Comparison between our model with the state-of-art fixation prediction models.

Table 1. Comparison results of Similarity, CC, AUC-Judd and AUC-Borji on the MIT1003 dataset. *Scores in bold means the best performance.*

Metrice	Toronto DataSet				MIT1003 DataSet			
	Similarity	CC	AUC-Judd	AUC-Borji	Similarity	CC	AUC-Judd	AUC-Borji
GBVS [17]	0.466	0.527	0.819	0.807	0.343	0.380	0.806	0.796
RBD [26]	0.465	0.480	0.798	0.750	0.376	0.382	0.801	0.774
IT [10]	0.415	0.383	0.764	0.752	0.294	0.252	0.721	0.713
BMS [22]	0.401	0.356	0.720	0.675	0.326	0.291	0.744	0.701
SUN [23]	0.349	0.216	0.671	0.652	0.264	0.188	0.667	0.653
SR [7]	0.288	0.157	0.661	0.531	0.236	0.129	0.645	0.534
RS [21]	0.478	0.510	0.815	0.797	0.354	0.386	0.799	0.785
Proposed	**0.527**	**0.596**	**0.836**	**0.816**	**0.402**	**0.443**	**0.826**	**0.808**

dataset is collected using a head-mounted eye tracking device for 15 different viewers. The Toronto dataset [3] consists of 120 color images of outdoor and indoor scenes. A large portion of images in Toronto dataset do not contain particular regions of interest. The proposed saliency model is compared with several eye fixation prediction methods GBVS [17], RBD [26], IT [10], BMS [22], SUN [23], SR [7] and RS [21].

For an exhaustive performance evaluation, almost all of the commonly used evaluation metrics, including AUC(Area Under the Receiver Operation Characteristics Curve), CC(Correlation Coefficient) and similarity, are adopted in this paper. Among these evaluation metrics, AUC, containing two accepted version: the Borja's version and Judd's version, is the most widely used metric and is a comparison between saliency map and all eye fixation points. While CC and similarity are the comparisons between saliency map and eye fixation density map.

As shown in Table 1, the proposed saliency model achieves the best performance on CC, Similarity, AUC_Borja and AUC_Judd evaluation metrics on the Toronto dataset. On the MIT1003 dataset, the proposed saliency model also outperforms all of the evaluation metrics. Analyze the results shown in Table 1 and our model extracts from the better sparse features of superpixels, and cosine similarity can better measure the difference between sparse features. The multiscale superpixel is also proved to be an important cue to improve the saliency region detection. Samples of fixation prediction results in this two experimental datasets are shown in Fig. 2.

5 Conclusions

In this paper, we propose a novel saliency detection model based on superpixel-based sparse representation. The novel method of superpixel-based sparse representation utilizes the Simultaneous Orthogonal Matching Pursuit algorithm to extract the sparse features from color maps and complex cells' activation map. Then, the saliency map is formed by the contrast of sparse features under different scales and different dictionaries. Experimental results show that our approach is effective when compared to the several advanced methods.

Acknowledgments. This work was supported by National Natural Science Foundation of China (No. 61471273).

References

1. Achanta, R., Shaji, A., Smith, K., Lucchi, A., Fua, P., Süsstrunk, S.: Slic superpixels compared to state-of-the-art superpixel methods. IEEE Trans. Pattern Anal. Mach. Intell. **34**(11), 2274–2282 (2012)
2. Aharon, M., Elad, M., Bruckstein, A.: rmk-svd: an algorithm for designing overcomplete dictionaries for sparse representation. IEEE Trans. Signal Process. **54**(11), 4311–4322 (2006)
3. Bruce, N.D.B., Tsotsos, J.K.: Saliency based on information maximization. Adv. Neural Inf. Process. Syst. **18**(3), 298–308 (2005)
4. Bylinskii, Z., Isola, P., Bainbridge, C., Torralba, A., Oliva, A.: Intrinsic and extrinsic effects on image memorability. Vision. Res. **116**, 165–178 (2015)
5. Donoser, M., Urschler, M., Hirzer, M., Bischof, H.: Saliency driven total variation segmentation. In: IEEE International Conference on Computer Vision, pp. 817–824 (2009)
6. Fang, Y., Lin, W., Fang, Z., Chen, Z., Lin, C.W., Deng, C.: Visual acuity inspired saliency detection by using sparse features. Inf. Sci. **309**, 1–10 (2015)
7. Hou, X., Zhang, L.: Saliency detection: a spectral residual approach. In: IEEE Computer Society Conference on Computer Vision and Pattern Recognition, pp. 1–8 (2007)
8. Hoyer, P.O., Hyvärinen, A.: A multi-layer sparse coding network learns contour coding from natural images. Vision. Res. **42**(12), 1593–1605 (2002)

9. Hubel, D.H., Wiesel, T.N.: Receptive fields and functional architecture of monkey striate cortex. J. Physiol. **195**(1), 215–243 (1968)
10. Itti, L., Koch, C., Niebur, E.: A model of saliency-based visual attention for rapid scene analysis. IEEE Trans. Pattern Anal. Mach. Intell. **20**(11), 1254–1259 (1998)
11. Judd, T., Ehinger, K., Durand, F., Torralba, A.: Learning to predict where humans look. In: IEEE International Conference on Computer Vision (2009)
12. Li, N., Sun, B., Yu, J.: A weighted sparse coding framework for saliency detection. In: IEEE Conference on Computer Vision and Pattern Recognition, pp. 5216–5223 (2015)
13. Li, X., Lu, H., Zhang, L., Ruan, X., Yang, M.H.: Saliency detection via dense and sparse reconstruction. In: Proceedings of the IEEE International Conference on Computer Vision, pp. 2976–2983 (2013)
14. Luo, P., Tian, Y., Wang, X., Tang, X.: Switchable deep network for pedestrian detection. In: IEEE Conference on Computer Vision and Pattern Recognition, pp. 899–906 (2014)
15. Mallat, S.G., Zhang, Z.: Matching pursuits with time-frequency dictionaries. IEEE Trans. Signal Process. **41**(12), 3397–3415 (1993)
16. Olshausen, B.A., Field, D.J.: Emergence of simple-cell receptive field properties by learning a sparse code for natural images. Nature **381**(6583), 607 (1996)
17. Schlkopf, B., Platt, J., Hofmann, T.: Graph-based visual saliency. Adv. Neural Inf. Process. Syst. **19**, 545–552 (2006)
18. Tong, N., Lu, H., Zhang, L., Xiang, R.: Saliency detection with multi-scale super-pixels. IEEE Signal Process. Lett. **21**(9), 1035–1039 (2014)
19. Tropp, J.A., Gilbert, A.C., Strauss, M.J.: Algorithms for simultaneous sparse approximation. Part I: greedy pursuit. Sig. Process. **86**(3), 572–588 (2006)
20. Tseng, P.H., Carmi, R., Cameron, I.G., Munoz, D.P., Itti, L.: Quantifying center bias of observers in free viewing of dynamic natural scenes. J. Vis. **9**(7), 4 (2009)
21. Yan, J., Liu, J., Li, Y., Niu, Z., Liu, Y.: Visual saliency detection via rank-sparsity decomposition. In: IEEE International Conference on Image Processing, pp. 1089–1092. IEEE (2010)
22. Zhang, J., Sclaroff, S.: Saliency detection: a boolean map approach. In: IEEE International Conference on Computer Vision, pp. 153–160 (2013)
23. Zhang, L., Tong, M.H., Marks, T.K., Shan, H., Cottrell, G.W.: SUN: a Bayesian framework for saliency using natural statistics. J. Vis. **8**(7), 32.1–32.20 (2008)
24. Zhang, L., Zhao, S., Liu, W., Lu, H.: Saliency detection via sparse reconstruction and joint label inference in multiple features. Neurocomputing **155**, 1–11 (2015)
25. Zhao, R., Ouyang, W., Wang, X.: Unsupervised salience learning for person re-identification. In: IEEE Conference on Computer Vision and Pattern Recognition, pp. 3586–3593 (2013)
26. Zhu, W., Liang, S., Wei, Y., Sun, J.: Saliency optimization from robust background detection. In: IEEE Conference on Computer Vision and Pattern Recognition, pp. 2814–2821 (2014)

Reading Two Digital Video Clocks
for Broadcast Basketball Videos

Xinguo Yu[1], Xiaopan Lyu[1(✉)], Lei Xiang[1], and Hon Wai Leong[2]

[1] National Engineering Research Center for E-Learning,
Central China Normal University, Wuhan, China
xgyu@mail.ccnu.edu.cn, xiaopanlv@mails.ccnu.edu.cn
[2] Department of Computer Science, National University of Singapore,
Singapore, Singapore

Abstract. This paper presents an algorithm for reading two digital video clocks of broadcast basketball videos by using context-aware pixel periodicity method and deep learning technique. Reading two digital video clocks is a very challenge problem as a difficulty special case of reading video text. The first challenge task is the clock digit localization. The existing pixel periodicity is a very good method for localizing second-digit place if a single clock is in video, but it is not applicable to localizing two second-digit places. This paper proposes a context-aware pixel periodicity method to identify the second-pixels of each clock based on the domain knowledge of digital video clocks. The second challenge task is clock-digit recognition. For this task, the CNN-based procedures are proposed to recognize clock digits. The experimental results show that the proposed algorithm can achieve 100% of accuracy in both localization and recognition for two clocks at very low computational cost by using very short input clips.

Keywords: Clock digit localization · Clock digit recognition
Deep learning · Digit-sequence · Context-aware pixel periodicity

1 Introduction

Reading digital video clocks has been an active problem for decades [3,7,9,10]. It is an application-oriented research problem because clock time is the critical information of multiple applications in video analysis, video surveillance, panorama video production, and video indexing and retrieval [3,7,9,10]. Reading clocks, especially reading two digital video clocks of a video, is a very challenge problem as a difficult special case of reading text from overlaid video object [1–3,7,9,10].

The clock time plays a critical role in video semantics analysis. The time on clocks often indicates the game time or event time in sports and video surveillance [7,9]. A lot of videos have superimposed digital video clocks or/and timestamps for various reasons—such as to show game-related time or to show the time of the recording. For example, reversely-running game clocks in basketball videos indicate the remaining game time at a frame and reversely-running

© Springer International Publishing AG, part of Springer Nature 2018
B. Zeng et al. (Eds.): PCM 2017, LNCS 10736, pp. 457–466, 2018.
https://doi.org/10.1007/978-3-319-77383-4_45

shot clocks indicate the longest remaining time of the current ball possession. Examples of two digital video clocks in broadcast basketball videos are shown in Fig. 1.

Fig. 1. The sample clock boards with two digital video clocks.

The problem of reading two digital video clocks can be divided into two sub-problems: clock-digit localization and clock-digit recognition. The first sub-problem is a special case of the character localization problem. However, text localization, which is a main step of character localization, is a difficult problem too and the existing algorithms cannot have a satisfactory performance in term of the industrial criteria [4,5,8,11], especially for localizing digits due to that it is hard to differentiate some digits [3,7,9,10]. Thus, researchers change to design custom algorithms for localizing clock digits [3,9,10].

Some methods mainly take an image processing approach to localize clocks [3]. However they are tedious and not robust. For clock-digit localization Yu et al. [10] proposed a pixel periodicity method. This method has a very good performance for localizing the second-digit place if only a single digital clock is in video, but it is not applicable to localization of two second-digit places because two clocks probably have asynchrony periodicities in digit transit.

The second sub-problem of reading digital video clocks is clock-digit recognition, a special case of OCR (Optical Character Recognition) problem. The existing deep learning algorithm can not achieve perfect performance [6]. Again researchers developed the custom algorithms for recognizing clock digits. The digit-sequence method by Yu et al. [10] can robustly recognize second-digits when a video has a single clock. However, this method requires that the transit frames are known in advance and require that the input clip is at least 11 s long.

This paper develops an algorithm that can read two digital video clocks of broadcast basketball video. For second place localization, a context-aware pixel periodicity method is proposed to improve the pixel periodicity method presented in [10]. For clock-digit recognition, this paper proposes the custom algorithms based on domain knowledge and deep learning technique to recognize digit-sequence and repeated digits.

The rest of the paper is organized as follows. Section 2 presents the technical details of the proposed algorithm for reading two digital video clocks. Experimental results are presented in Sect. 3. Section 4 concludes the paper.

2   Reading Two Digital Video Clocks

This section first formulizes the problem of reading two digital video clocks of a broadcast basketball video. Then it presents the proposed algorithm and its technical details.

2.1   Problem Statement

A broadcast basketball video may have two clocks. The number of digits on a digital video clock can vary from 2 to 6, but the core task is to read the four clock-digits representing second, ten second, minute, and ten minute, denoted as s-digit, ts-digit, m-digit, and tm-digit, respectively. And x-digit is defined to represent ts-digit, m-digit, and tm-digit in the rest of this paper when we treat the ts-digit, m-digit, and tm-digit as the same way. Thus the problem of reading digital video clocks is stated as follows.

Problem of Reading Two Digital Video Clocks: Let $B_i^k = (r_i^k, c_i^k, w_i^k, h_i^k)$ for $i = 1$ to 4 and $k = 1$ to 2 be the bounding boxes of s-digit, ts-digit, m-digit, and tm-digit of k_{th} working digital video clock, respectively. The problem of reading two digital video clocks is for $i = 1$ to 4 and $k = 1, 2$ to do two jobs: (a) localize $B_i^k = (r_i^k, c_i^k, w_i^k, h_i^k)$; and (b) recognize digits in $B_i^k = (r_i^k, c_i^k, w_i^k, h_i^k)$.

2.2   Algorithm

An algorithm for reading two digital video clocks is depicted in Algorithm 1. The proposed algorithm for reading two digital video clocks possesses two main phases: clock-digit localization, and clock-digit recognition.

Algorithm 1. Reading two digital video clocks

    Input: A video with two working digital video clocks
    Output: Bounding boxes of digits and recognized clock digits and its
              frame number for each clock
1 *Step 1: Clock-digit localization*
2 *1.1: S-digit localization*
3 *1.2: X-digit localization*
4 *Step 2: Clock-digit recognition*
5 *2.1: S-digit recognition*
6 *2.2: X-digit recognition*

2.3   Clock-Digit Localization

Finding the bounding boxes of clock-second (s-digit) places leverages on the proposed context-aware pixel periodicity method (CPP), which uses not only the periodicity of s-digit pixels but also the context information of the s-digit pixels. This new method captures the facts that some pixels in s-digit region will significantly change their gray values when s-digit transits its digit, some other pixels in s-digit region or on s-digit bounding boxes have relatively constant gray values, and these pixels from the same s-digit are neighbor. The pixel periodicity captures that the observation that some pixels in s-digit region of a working video clock change their grey values every second. Figure 2 gives the illustration of this pixel periodicity on the s-digit place. The notations and concepts are defined first, and then the formulae for computing the s-digit bounding box are presented.

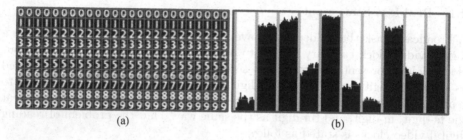

| (a)   (b)

Fig. 2. The second-pixel periodicity illustration of a sample pixel in s-digit region in 10 s. (a) The red dots are the positions of a monitored pixel in s-digit region through 10 s. (b) The graph of the grey value of the monitored pixel in 10 s. Each short horizontal line indicates the average of the corresponding second of the gray values of the monitored pixel. (Color figure online)

Let F_i be the considered frame. Then F_{i-R}, F_{i-R+1}, ..., F_{i-1} and F_i, F_{i+1}, ..., F_{i+R-1} are the R frames in the preceding second and the succeeding second, respectively. Let $c(k, p)$ be the grey value of pixel p in frame F_k. Then we have following definitions.

Definition 1: (Constant Pixel) Let F_k for $k = 1$ to be L frames including at least 3 s consecutive frames. Pixel p is called as a constant pixel if it meets the following condition.

(i) $|c(k, p) - C_1| < \beta_1$ for $k = i$ to L, where $C_1 = \frac{1}{L} \sum_{k=1}^{L} c(k, p)$; where β_1 is a threshold.

Definition 2: Pixel p is called a periodicity pixel at frame i if it simultaneously meets the following three conditions. And β_2 and β_3 are two thresholds.

(i) $|c(k,p) - C_2| < \beta_2$ for $k = i - R + 1$ to $i - 1$, where $C_2 = \dfrac{1}{R} \sum_{k=i-R}^{i-1} c(k,p)$;

(ii) $|c(k,p) - C_3| < \beta_2$ for $k = i$ to $i + R - 1$, where $C_3 = \dfrac{1}{R} \sum_{k=i}^{i+R-1} c(k,p)$;

(iii) $|C_2 - C_3| > \beta_3$.

Definition 3: (Periodicity Pixel) Pixel p is called a (O,k) periodicity pixel if it meets the following conditions.

(i) It is a second periodicity pixel at $i_1, i_2, ..., i_k$ frames;
(ii) $abs((i_u - i_v) \bmod R) < 2$ for $1 \leqslant v < u \leqslant k$.

Definition 4: (S-Digit Pixel Candidate) Pixel p is called an s-digit pixel candidate if it is (O,k) periodicity pixel for $k \geqslant 2$ and it is less than β_4 pixels away from a constant pixel or another s-digit pixel candidate.

Definition 5: (S-Digit Region) A cluster of s-digit pixel candidate is considered as an s-digit place if its cardinality is larger than β_5.

Once an s-digit place is found the bounding box of this s-digit place can be obtained through a local analysis. After s-digits are localized we can learn colors from the instances of s-digits. Then we use a Hough-like procedure to obtain the exact locations of the x-digits. Thus, we finish the task of localizing clock-digits.

2.4 Clock-Digit Recognition

This paper first present a procedure, called as dCNN, which directly uses CNN to recognize s-digits [6]. Procedure dCNN is prepared by directly using CNN to recognize s-digit and find s-digit transit frames but it cannot achieve 100% of accuracy. In fact, frames from $t + k * R + 1$ to $t + (k + 1) * R$ have the same s-digit if frame t is s-digit transit frame because the s-digit transits every R frames. Thus, the s-digit in the frames $t + k * R + 1$ to $t + (k + 1) * R$ is number k if the s-digit in the frames from t to $t + R$ is "0". In other words, the s-digits in the frames from t to $t + v * R$ form a digit periodic increasing sequence according to the clock knowledge, supposed that the input clip is v second long ($v < 10$). Based on these facts, then this paper proposes a 3-digit sequence CNN recognition procedure for finding both s-digit transit frames and recognizing s-digits, denoted as Procedure I. We use the open-source CNN [6].

---

dCNN. The direct CNN procedure for recognizing s-digit

Input: A j second long clip with two running clocks and the bounding
        boxes of all s-digits
Output: The frame number of the first s-digit transit frame and the
        recognized s-digit on the first transit frame for each clock

1 **for** *each s-digit bounding box* **do**
2   Extract the $j * R$ s-digit instances for all the frames of the given clip
     according to the given s-digit bounding box;
3   Use CNN recognize each s-digit instance and get a $j * R$ recognized
     digit sequence;
4   Scan the sequence of recognized s-digits to identify the first change of
     s-digits, then this change frame is the first s-digit transit frame and
     its s-digit is the wanted s-digit;
5 **end**

Procedure I. The 3-digit sequence CNN recognition procedure

Input: A 4 second long clip with single or two clocks and the bounding box of
        each s-digit
Output: The first frame number that all the s-digits are correctly recognized
        and the recognized s-digits on each frame for each clock

1 Let $s = 0$, $e = R$, and $m = [(s + e)/2]$;
2 **while** $e \mathrel{!=} s$ **do**
3   Sequence $1 = F_s, F_{s+R}, F_{s+2R}$, Sequence $2 = F_m, F_{m+R}, F_{m+2R}$, Sequence
     $3 = F_e, F_{e+R}, F_{e+2R}$;
4   Use the trained CNN to recognize these three 3-digit sequences;
5   **if** *all the recognized results of Sequence 1 to 3 are the same or different* **then**
6   return the clock is not a proper running clock;
7   **end**
8   **if** *the recognized results of Sequence 1 and 2 are the same* **then**
9          $s = m$, $m = [(s + e)/2]$;
10   **end**
11   **if** *the recognized results of Sequence 2 and 3 are the same* **then**
12          $e = m$, $m = [(s + e)/2]$;
13   **end**
14   **if** $s = e$ **then**
15   return frame s is the s-digit transit frame and the number on frame s,
         terminate the procedure;
16   **end**
17 **end**

Procedure II. The repeated-digit CNN recognition procedure

Input: A 4 second long clip with two running clocks, the first s-digit
transit frame, and the bounding box of all x-digits

Output: The recognized x-digits on each frame for each clock

1 An odd number v is the parameter of this procedure, indicating how
   many instances are recognized at the same time;

2 Denote the first s-digit transit frame as s, then each x-digit place has the
   same digit in frame s to frame $s + 75$;

3 Extract 75 instances from each x-digit place;

4 **for** *each x-digit place* **do**

5 | Evenly select v instance with respect frame number;

6 | Recognize v instances and consider the most frequently-occurred
   | number as the number of the corresponding x-digit;

7 | Terminate the procedure;

8 **end**

Once s-digit transit frames are known by Procedure I, all the transit frames
for all x-digits are known. Thus, we can take at least 50 frames with the same
digit for any x-digit from a 4 s long clip (Notice that our video is 25 frames per
second). Hence an odd number of frames from these 50 frames can be selected
to recognize an x-digit in Procedure II.

Procedure I and II together can recognize all digits of all clocks. In other
word, clock-digit recognition task is finished.

3   Experimental Results

The algorithm for reading two digital video clocks is implemented in C++. To
evaluate the proposed algorithm a dataset is built. This dataset comprises of 300
broadcast soccer videos and 300 broadcast basketball videos, where each clip is
15 s long. Each of 300 broadcast soccer videos has a single clock; each of 300
broadcast basketball videos has two clocks. All clocks in the clips are working
clocks. These clips vary in digit color, digit background color, size, and font.

3.1   Performance of Clock Digits Localization

Paper [10] presented a pixel periodicity method (shorted as PPM) to localize
the second digit of digital video clock. This paper proposes a context-aware
pixel periodicity method (shorted as CPP) that is enhanced from PPM. This
low-cost method can successfully localize not only single s-digit region but also
multiple s-digit regions with a short length of input clip. The experiments are
conducted to compare the accuracies of PPM and CPP for localizing single and
two s-digits. And the results are given in Table 1.

In Table 1, "Single Clock" means 300 clips that each clip carries a single
digital video clock and "Two Clocks" means 300 clips that each clip carries two

Table 1. Comparison on accuracies PPM and CPP for localizing s-digit on 300 clips with single digit clock and 300 clips with two digit clocks.

Length in second of clip			4	5	6	7	8	9	10	11
Accuracy in %	Single clock	PPM	0	0	3	72	81	82	91	100
		CPP	86.4	100	100	100	100	100	100	100
	Two clocks	PPM	X	X	X	X	X	X	X	X
		CPP	80.3	100	100	100	100	100	100	100

digital video clocks and they are tested in batch; "X" means that the method is not applicable for the corresponding cases. Table 1 shows that CPP can localize two s-digits only requiring 5 s length of clips as input.

3.2   Performance on Clock Digit Recognition

The experiments are conducted to compare the performances of s-digit recognition of three different methods, which are dSequence (digit-sequence procedure presented in [10]), dCNN and Procedure I.

Table 2. Accuracy comparison of recognizing s-digit by using dSequence, dCNN, and Procedure I on 300 clips with two clocks.

Clip length	2	3	4	5	6	7	8	9	10
dSequence	X	X	X	X	X	X	X	X	X
dCNN	92.5	92.5	92.5	92.5	92.5	92.5	92.5	92.5	92.5
Procedure I	99.8	100	100	100	100	100	100	100	100

In Table 2, "X" has the same meaning as in Table 1. Table 2 presents accuracy of recognizing s-digit by using dSequence, dCNN and Procedure I proposed in this paper. We can have three conclusions from Table 2. The first one is that dSequence can not be used to recognize s-digits of two digital clocks. The second one is that dCNN can not get 100% of accuracy. Third one is that Procedure I can recognize two s-digits and it can achieve a 100% of accuracy when the input video is longer than 3 s.

Table 3. Accuracy change of recognizing x-digits by using Procedure II against the number of repeated frames on 300 clips with two clocks.

v (algorithm parameter)	1	3	5	7	9	11
Two clocks	99.4	99.9	100	100	100	100

In Table 3, "v (procedure parameter)" is the parameter of Procedure II, indicating how many instances are used in recognition process; "Two Clocks" have the same meaning as in Table 1. Table 3 shows that the proposed Procedure II can achieve a 100% of accuracy if v is equal or larger than 5, i.e. $v \geqslant 5$ for not only single digital clock but also two digital clocks.

3.3   Evaluation on Computational Time Costs

The experiments are conducted to evaluate the computational time costs of each task of the proposed algorithm. In the experiment, 300 clips with two clocks are split into three 100-clip groups. In Table 4, μ and σ are the means and the variances of the computation times of finishing a task for a batch of 100 clips. From the table, we have two conclusions. The first one is that each step of our algorithm is very fast and the whole algorithm finishes within 3.6 s. From Table 2 and Table 4 we have the following conclusion. The proposed algorithm is very fast and can achieve a 100% of accuracy for recognizing s-digits for two digital clocks when the length of the input clips reaches 3 s.

Table 4. Computational time costs of each task of the proposed algorithm on 300 clips with two clocks of broadcast.

Task	s-digit localization		Other digits localization		s-digit recognition		Other digits recognition		Total time	
Method	CSP				Procedure I		Procedure II			
#total	μ	σ	μ	σ	μ	σ	μ	σ	μ	σ
1st-100	0.237	0.024	0.004	0.001	1.419	0.085	1.556	0.076	3.216	0.666
2nd-100	0.242	0.026	0.003	0.001	1.422	0.087	1.563	0.077	3.227	0.722
3rd-100	0.227	0.029	0.003	0.001	1.655	0.078	1.677	0.069	3.562	0.858

4   Conclusions, and Future Work

This paper has presented an algorithm that can read not only single digital clock but also two digital video clocks at a low computational time cost requiring a short length of input clip.

This paper has made multiple contributions. The first contribution is that it designed the first algorithm that can read two digital video clocks. The second contribution is that it proposed the context-aware periodicity method that can identify the pixels belong to the two s-digit places, overcoming the demerit that the existing periodicity method only can localize the s-digit place of single digital video clock. Another important contribution is that it proposed a 3-digit-sequence CNN procedure, which has an excellent performance. The proposed algorithm is easy to be implemented because it converts the digit localization procedure into computing several functions. These functions properly implemented the context-aware pixel periodicity method, which captures the facts that some second-pixels change their grey value secondly, some other second-pixels keep constancy for several seconds, and they are neighbors. Experimental results show that our new algorithm achieves an excellent performance in reading two digital video clocks.

In the near future we want to apply our algorithms to event detection, video indexing, and video retrieval of broadcast basketball video. We will also want to design a deep neural network to do the multiple s-digit localization. Then we further design a deep neural network to read multiple digital video clocks, i.e. it does both localization and recognition.

Acknowledgments. This work is supported by the National Science and Technology Support Program of China (No. 2015BAH33F01)

References

1. Ghanei, S., Faez, K.: Robust localization of texts in real-world images. Int. J. Pattern Recognit. Artif. Intell. **29**(07), 1555012 (2015)
2. Ghanei, S., Faez, K.: A robust approach for scene text localization using rule-based confidence map and grouping. Int. J. Pattern Recognit. Artif. Intell. **31**, 1753002 (2016)
3. Li, Y., Xu, C., Wan, K.W., Yan, X., Yu, X.: Reliable video clock time recognition. In: Proceedings of the 18th International Conference on Pattern Recognition, vol. 04, pp. 128–131. IEEE Computer Society (2006)
4. Neumann, L., Matas, J.: Real-time scene text localization and recognition. In: 2012 IEEE Conference on Computer Vision and Pattern Recognition (CVPR), pp. 3538–3545. IEEE (2012)
5. Pan, Y.F., Hou, X., Liu, C.L.: A hybrid approach to detect and localize texts in natural scene images. IEEE Trans. Image Process. **20**(3), 800–813 (2011)
6. Sermanet, P., Kavukcuoglu, K., LeCun, Y.: Eblearn: open-source energy-based learning in C++. In: 2009 21st IEEE International Conference on Tools with Artificial Intelligence, pp. 693–697. IEEE (2009)
7. Xu, C., Wang, J., Wan, K., Li, Y., Duan, L.: Live sports event detection based on broadcast video and web-casting text. In: ACM International Conference on Multimedia, Santa Barbara, CA, USA, October, pp. 221–230 (2006)
8. Yi, C., Tian, Y.: Localizing text in scene images by boundary clustering, stroke segmentation, and string fragment classification. IEEE Trans. Image Process. **21**(9), 4256–4268 (2012)
9. Yu, X., Cheng, J., Wu, S., Song, W.: A framework of timestamp replantation for panorama video surveillance. Multimed. Tools Appl. **75**(17), 10357–10381 (2016)
10. Yu, X., Ding, W., Zeng, Z., Leong, H.W.: Reading digital video clocks. Int. J. Pattern Recognit. Artif. Intell. **29**(04), 1555006 (2015)
11. Zhu, S., Zanibbi, R.: A text detection system for natural scenes with convolutional feature learning and cascaded classification. In: Proceedings of the IEEE Conference on Computer Vision and Pattern Recognition, pp. 625–632 (2016)

Don't Be Confused: Region Mapping Based Visual Place Recognition

Dapeng Du, Na Liu, Xiangyang Xu, and Gangshan Wu[✉]

State Key Laboratory for Novel Software Technology, Collaborative Innovation
Center of Novel Software Technology and Industrialization, Nanjing University,
Nanjing 210023, China
dudp.nju@gmail.com, liunana1993@gmail.com, xiangyang.xu@smail.nju.edu.cn,
gswu@nju.edu.cn

Abstract. Visual place recognition is usually formulated as a general image retrieval problem which suffers from numerous demanding and realistic environment challenges. In this paper, we exploit the particularity of place images which can be surprisingly helpful on place recognition. Specifically, we find that images of identified places can be effectively matched by remarkable regions like building facades under limited geometry and illumination changes. Based on that observation, a novel region mapping based method is proposed to comprehensively tackle the influences caused by geometric and illumination variance as well as irrelevant interference. Given a query image, we extract remarkable regions with color constancy feature performed at processing illumination variant conditions. We leverage a two-fold transformation estimation based verification strategy dealing with geometry transformation caused by viewpoint changes for matching. The experimental results demonstrate that the proposed method is powerful for visual place recognition.

1 Introduction

Visual place recognition, which is dedicated to finding images depicting the same place via a query image of a particular street or a building [1], is of fundamental importance to many applications, such as image-based localization [2], landmark recognition [3], and loop closure detection of SLAM (simultaneous localization and mapping) in robotics [4].

Visual place recognition is often tackled with image retrieval techniques, which suffers from numerous demanding and realistic environment challenges. For example, in case (a) of Fig. 1, two images depicting totally different places improperly exhibit a good similarity due to matching of interference features. In case (b), two images of the same place appear quite different because of viewpoint and illumination changes.

In this paper, we present a novel region mapping based method to address these challenges. After an in-depth study to this problem, we find that searching remarkable regions (e.g., building facades) instead of entire images is surprisingly effective in place recognition. Further, the retrieval of remarkable regions

© Springer International Publishing AG, part of Springer Nature 2018
B. Zeng et al. (Eds.): PCM 2017, LNCS 10736, pp. 467–476, 2018.
https://doi.org/10.1007/978-3-319-77383-4_46

Fig. 1. Examples of challenges in visual place recognition. (a) two images depicting different places get mismatched caused by irrelevant interference match (yellow keypoints). (b) two images depicting the same place from quite different viewpoints with illumination changes. (Color figure online)

can be simplified as a region matching problem considering geometry and illumination changes. Towards this goal, we first employ YOLO [5] to train a building detector extracting remarkable regions from a query image. The region extraction effectively makes the recognition less influenced by common non-distinctive interference, like vehicles, billboards, trash cans and so on when measuring the similarity of places. Then we alleviate the illumination changes by illumination invariant imaging processing using color constancy feature. A two-fold transformation estimation based verification homography is performed to map query regions to reference images in database, which dedicates to dealing with viewpoint changes via geometric transformation constraint. At last, reference images in database are ranked based on quantity of matching inliers which depicts the overall similarity against query image.

To evaluate the performance of the proposed method, we evaluate our method on a public dataset. Besides, to make comprehensive comparison, we build a new challenging dataset which covers more demanding and realistic changing environments such like significant illumination variance, large viewpoint change, realistic photographing noise, and conditions with irrelevant interference. This dataset has made a very significant makeup for the existing datasets which are usually comprehensiveness scarcity on those challenges. The experimental results on both datasets show that our method outperforms competitive visual place recognition methods.

The major contributions of this paper are briefly summarized as follows.

- We propose a novel method for place recognition which exploits the particularity of place images based on remarkable regions.
- We simplify the problem as a region matching process considering viewpoint and illumination variance, which performs effectively in place recognition.
- We introduce a new dataset exhibiting challenging viewpoint and appearance variation as well as rich irrelevant interference in daily life.

2 Related Work

The aim of image retrieval is at finding as many relevant database images for a given query image as possible which also provides a meaningful context for other applications. Instead of retrieving all the relevant images, imaged-based place recognition tends to retrieve these relevant images which should be exactly the same place of the query and just one matched result is sufficient in measurement metrics. In [8], a BOF image retrieval system uses the analogy of visual words that tends to represent local features in a global feature representation manner. Many visual place recognition methods build on efficient image retrieval techniques and results rely heavily on the clustering precision of visual words [1,10].

CNN features have been proved powerful for numerous computer vision tasks, such as object classification and detection [12]. In [13], Sünderhauf et al. extracted image descriptors from the stacked output of a single CNN layer and evaluated different layers finding that the lower convolutional layers to be the relatively robust against image appearance change while higher layers to viewpoint changes. In [7], object proposal technique is leveraged to obtain patches for representing landmarks from query image and images in database and pretrained CNN features are used to calculate region similarities. However, the "landmarks" patches they get are generated from specific objectness technique, many of which inevitably contain kinds of trivial and interference objects which would affect the measurement performance. Instead, we propose to target more representative regions and simplify the problem as region matching procedure with specific features processed in stead of relying on blackbox feature representation.

3 Approach

In this section we describe how we tackle this problem. We give an overview of our framework in Fig. 2. Given an input image as query, we utilize a specific detector for extracting remarkable regions. For those extracted regions, we handle them with color constancy for the robustness of illumination invariance. Then, a twofold transformation estimation based verification strategy is performed when mapping query regions to the reference images in database. At last, we measure the overall similarity between image pairs through region matching results.

3.1 Representative Region Extraction

Good region extraction is very important to this problem because it eliminates the interference from background and represents the peculiarity of the place image. We leverage a powerful object detection method [5] to train a building detector. Training data is mainly from Flickr[1] in which we could obtain all kinds of building facade cases. We get remarkable regions in the form of detected

---

[1] https://www.flickr.com/.

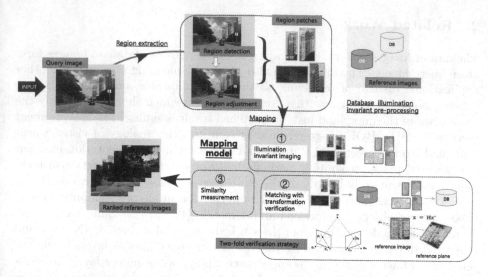

Fig. 2. The framework of our method (Color figure online)

bounding boxes by this trained detector. According to our further observation, surroundings or peripherals of buildings play important roles in helping recognize a place. However, these bounding boxes generated for building regions often fail to envelop the whole detected objects, so we do not directly use these ones as query regions. The adjustment of bounding boxes is adapted from [6] in which we make it so that we could keep more tolerance for extension than tightness in our method (See Fig. 2, bounding box adjustment from initial ones (yellow) to adjusted ones (red)). In other words, high recall of pixels around the initial regions is more welcomed here and we also find this pixel straddling based strategy could help alleviate the error accumulation for later procedure. Remarkable regions extracted for the place are obtained then, see Fig. 2.

3.2   Illumination Invariant Imaging

Illumination changes make many powerful feature descriptors fail to correctly match the same place, as shown in Fig. 1. It is necessary to eliminate the most of its influences for better discrimination between places. As color constancy demonstrates comprehensive relationship of an object's material property, illuminant intensity and lighting spectrum, we utilize it as a pre-processing [11] before region matching procedure. In this way, it suffers less from illumination variance and thus provides a robust condition for the region similarity measurement. Following [11], we use a one-dimensional color space $\mathcal{I}$ consisting of three sensor responses R_1, R_2, R_3 corresponding to peak sensitivities at ordered wavelengths $\lambda_1 < \lambda_2 < \lambda_3$:

$$\mathcal{I} = \log(R_2) - \alpha \log(R_1) - (1 - \alpha) \log(R_3) \tag{1}$$

Fig. 3. Using illumination invariant color space to eliminate illumination changes at different times of day. RGB images are converted to an illumination invariant color space.

The intensity of pixel x in $\mathcal{I}$ could be uniquely identified if the parameter α satisfies the following constraint:

$$\frac{1}{\lambda_x} = \frac{\alpha}{\lambda_1} + \frac{(1-\lambda)}{\lambda_3} \tag{2}$$

The values of λ_i depend on the camera. In [11], several groups of reference values are given. Considering data distribution we use an approximate reference value here. In practice, approximation almost does not hurt matching performance. An example of producing illumination invariant color space is illustrated in Fig. 3. Despite large changes in sun angle, shadow pattern and illumination spectrum between images captured at different times of day, both illumination invariant images exhibit minimal variation. We conduct this processing on all images in database with raw images preserved. Similar processing goes on extracted regions as well.

3.3   Region Mapping

Viewpoint changes often lead to dramatic geometric variance. In this problem we simplified it as a plane to plane mapping procedure because buildings are generally man-made flat objects which could be approximately regarded as planar surfaces. Theoretically, no solution is available in cases that homography is not strictly applicable. However, in real applications, there is no perfect homography relation, even for planar scenes. Hence, the problem is actually derived to a minimization problem and an approximate solution is returned. Even for those buildings with curved surfaces, we find it sufficient to utilize a plane approximation since the structural variance of the surface can be ignored due to the view distance.

Specifically, we adopt a two-fold spacial estimation strategy considering the trade-off. Firstly we estimate affine epipolar geometry (i.e. the geometric relation using fundamental matrix) and the matches are listed ordered by their number of inliers. Unlike the planar homography which provides a point to point mapping, outliers might be considered as inliers since the constraint of fundamental matrix is that the correspondence must lie on the epipolar line, which is not a very strong restriction. To filter out false positives while trying to keep as many true positives as possible, a simple but effective heuristic is used in our experiment: a loose planar homography is fitted by RANSAC [15] to the inliers of the fundamental matrix and if less than 60% of these inliers are consistent with the homography then the image match is rejected. We use Hessian Affine detector [18] and SIFT descriptor [16] to extract local invariant features. For each region we make two mappings. One is from raw regions to raw reference images while the other is in the similar vein but pre-processed with color constancy before matching. Results from these two mappings will get fused in similarity measurement step.

3.4 Similarity Measurement

We measure the similarity between query and referenced place images by region mapping performance. We rank the reference images in database ordered by the fused number of matching inliers. Let f_i be the function to calculate the number of inliers for the ith region extracted from query image to match the jth reference image in database. The overall similarity between this pair images is calculated by the total number of inliers N_j, as shown in Eq. 3

$$N_j = \sum_i f_i \tag{3}$$

Note that f_i calculates two kinds of inliers for each region as described in Sect. 3.3, i.e., from raw region to raw reference image and region-image after color constancy processing. Average weighted strategy is performed when we fuse these two kinds of inliers for robustness. In our experiment, the coefficient is set to 0.5.

4 Experiments and Analysis

In this section, we describe the experiments and analyze the results. We adopt the common evaluation metric [1,3,10], i.e., the query place is regarded as correctly recognized if at least one relevant image (within distance = 25 m) is contained in the top N retrieved images. This has been a common place recognition evaluation metric. The percentage of correctly recognized queries is then plotted for different values of N, the so-called recall@N.

4.1 Datasets

We conduct our experiments on the public Gardens Point dataset[2] which has been widely used to evaluate place recognition methods [7]. One subset of it was recorded keeping on the left side of the walkways, while another from the right side. The dataset thus presents viewpoint changes.

---

[2] http://tinyurl.com/gardenspointdataset.

Besides, considering that existing place recognition datasets only cover simple cases like near-duplicate contents and lack of challenges such as large viewpoint change, illumination variance and diverse interference, we introduce a new dataset called "MGC Places dataset". The collection source is mainly from Mapillary[3], Google Street Views and Photos captured by ourselves and this dataset covers more Challenging cases. We collect 806 pictures of about 80 places manually. We also intentionally add a few interference and noisy images to our dataset. The ground truth is derived from the GPS information of images' meta data.

4.2 Compared Methods and Experimental Settings

We compare our method with these methods as follows:

Baseline. We set the baseline according to that in [1].

Hamming Embedding with Burstiness. The 64-bit SIFT Hamming Embedding (HE) [9] is proved to outperform the state-of-the-art methods when applied with burstiness normalization in the place recognition problem [19].

Coupled Multi-index. Coupled Multi-Index (c-MI) [20] builds an effective multi-index on Hamming Embedding coupled with Color Names descriptor and is open sourced. A color codebook of 200 size is trained on independent data.

ConvNet Landmarks. In [7] (Conv-landmark), Zitnick et al. extract object proposals (50 or 100) both from query images and reference images as region landmarks using [21], pre-trained AlexNet is used to extract conv3 feature to calculate similarity with cosine Euclidean distance.

Ours-ConvNet. As ConvNet-Landmarks also works with regions, we provide a variant of our method for comprehensive analysis. We extract conv3 feature for our remarkable regions with the same similarity measurement as [7] does.

4.3 Experimental Results

On the "MGC Places dataset", our method outperforms image retrieval based methods by a significant gap, as shown in Fig. 4. Specifically, we improve the recall percentage by about 15% at the best match over c-MI and HE, and 35% over baseline. This can be explained by that the comparison methods lack of effective illumination, viewpoint variance handling. The interference objects such as vehicles also affect their performance. It is interesting that though c-MI employs color cue for better performance the promotion is quite limited compared to HE. We think this is because local features and color cue only reduce the influences of false positive matches, and the discrimination of different appearances of the same place has limited improvement. As for ConvNet-Landmark, we conduct an extensive experiment using extracted regions from our method with pre-trained CNN features to evaluate like [7]. The extensive experiment's result shows that our method has better region extraction strategy which displays more

---

[3] http://www.mapillary.com.

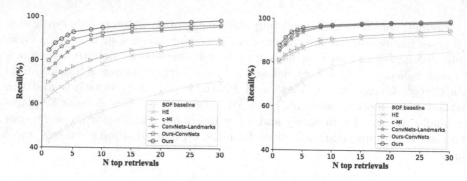

Fig. 4. Results on MGC Place dataset (left), and Garden Point dataset (right)

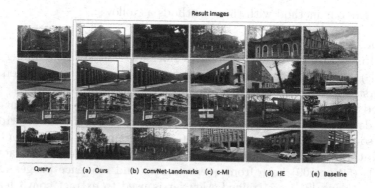

Fig. 5. Challenging examples from MGC dataset with Top 1 results displayed. Positive results are labeled with green frames while negative ones with red. Regions detected in queries are labeled with yellow frames. (Color figure online)

representative and alleviates interference for recognizing a place. With specific feature processed, our method achieves a surprising performance for this task.

Comparison on Garden Point dataset presents similar results, as shown in Fig. 4. The difference is that all of the comparison methods perform better than that on "MGC Places dataset". This is easy to explain since the images of the Garden Point dataset are captured sequentially, which exhibits near-duplicate scenarios in daytime. Besides, there are only 2–3 m of camera movement, thus there are minor viewpoint changes. We note that there are some interesting failure cases for our method. These cases are kind of indoor scenarios as the walker who recorded the dataset went through an open type house during some sequences. It can be inferred that our method would work better when working on the shortlist from large image retrieval results in this condition.

Figure 5 shows some challenging examples of place recognition showing the Top 1 results returned by our method, the ConvNet-Landmarks, the c-MI, the HE and baseline, in columns (a), (b), (c), (d) and (e) respectively. Rows from top to bottom exhibit different conditions including large viewpoint change, illumination variance, and non-distinctive interference (the last two rows, trash can and car as interference respectively). In the first example, the query has quite large viewpoint change with relevant images, thus other methods fail to handle this condition effectively. The next example shows a distinct illumination condition with intense shadow. Since features in other methods fail to do well in describing illumination invariance while we leverage color constancy, only our method and ConvNet-Landmarks get the right result. In last two examples, most methods get fake "good" matching confused by interference object in scenes, however, we overcome this challenge by matching proper regions.

5   Conclusion and Future Work

In this paper, we have presented a novel region mapping based method for image-based place recognition. By utilizing color constancy and two-fold estimation verification strategy on remarkable regions, we produce an impressive result in severe challenging conditions. Consider the shortage in existing datasets, we also introduce a new challenging dataset exhibiting extreme viewpoint and illumination variance as well as rich irrelevant interference and their combinations.

CNN based features have shown great power in this task without bells and whistles, especially the power for illumination change discrimination. We also prove that geometry transformation verification demonstrates significant in coping with viewpoint change in this problem. In the future, we will try to explore the CNN based spatial constraints in geometry transformation for better performance.

Acknowledgments. This work is supported by the National Science Foundation of China under Grant No. 61321491, and Collaborative Innovation Center of Novel Software Technology and Industrialization.

References

1. Torii, A., Sivic, J., Pajdla, T., Okutomi, M.: Visual place recognition with repetitive structures. In: CVPR (2013)
2. Schindler, G., Brown, M., Szeliski, R.: City-scale location recognition. In: 2007 IEEE Conference on Computer Vision and Pattern Recognition. IEEE (2007)
3. Chen, D.M., Baatz, G., Köser, K., Tsai, S.S., Vedantham, R., Pylvänäinen, T., Roimela, K., Chen, X., Bach, J., Pollefeys, M., et al.: City-scale landmark identification on mobile devices. In: CVPR. IEEE (2011)
4. Cummins, M., Newma, P.: FAB-map: probabilistic localization and mapping in the space of appearance. Int. J. Robot. Res. **27**, 647–665 (2008)
5. Redmon, J., Divvala, S., Girshick, R., Farhadi, A: You only look once: unified, real-time object detection. In: CVPR. IEEE (2016)
6. Chen, X., Ma, H., Wang, X., Zhao, Z.: Improving object proposals with multi-thresholding straddling expansion. In: CVPR. IEEE (2015)
7. Sunderhauf, N., Shirazi, S., Jacobson, A., Dayoub, F., Pepperell, E., Upcroft, B. and Milford, M.: Place recognition with convnet landmarks: viewpoint-robust, condition-robust, training-free. In: Proceedings of Robotics: Science and Systems XII (2015)

8. Sivic, J., Zisserman, A.: Video Google: a text retrieval approach to object matching in videos. In: ICCV. IEEE (2003)
9. Jegou, H., Douze, M., Schmid, C.: Hamming embedding and weak geometric consistency for large scale image search. In: Forsyth, D., Torr, P., Zisserman, A. (eds.) ECCV 2008. LNCS, vol. 5302, pp. 304–317. Springer, Heidelberg (2008). https://doi.org/10.1007/978-3-540-88682-2_24
10. Sattler, T., Weyand, T., Leibe, B., Kobbelt, L.: Image retrieval for image-based localization revisited. In: BMVC (2012)
11. Maddern, W., Stewart, A., McManus, C., Upcroft, B., Churchill, W., Newman, P.: Illumination invariant imaging: applications in robust vision-based localisation, mapping and classification for autonomous vehicles. In: ICRA (2014)
12. Razavian, A.S., Azizpour, H., Sullivan, J., Carlsson, S.: CNN features off-the-shelf: an astounding baseline for recognition. In: CVPR Workshops (2014)
13. Sünderhauf, N., Shirazi, S., Dayoub, F., Upcroft, B., Milford, M.: On the performance of convnet features for place recognition. In: IROS (2015)
14. Hartley, R., Zisserman, A.: Multiple View Geometry in Computer Vision. Cambridge University Press, Cambridge (2003)
15. Fischler, M.A., Bolles, R.C.: Random sample consensus: a paradigm for model fitting with applications to image analysis and automated cartography. Commun. ACM 24, 381–395 (1981)
16. Lowe, D.G.: Distinctive image features from scale-invariant keypoints. IJCV 60, 91–110 (2004)
17. Arandjelović, R., Zisserman, A.: Three things everyone should know to improve object retrieval. In: CVPR. IEEE (2012)
18. Mikolajczyk, K., Schmid, C.: Scale & affine invariant interest point detectors. IJCV 60, 63–86 (2004)
19. Arandjelović, R., Zisserman, A.: DisLocation: scalable descriptor distinctiveness for location recognition. In: Cremers, D., Reid, I., Saito, H., Yang, M.-H. (eds.) ACCV 2014. LNCS, vol. 9006, pp. 188–204. Springer, Cham (2015). https://doi.org/10.1007/978-3-319-16817-3_13
20. Zheng, L., Wang, S., Liu, Z., Tian, Q.: Packing and padding: coupled multi-index for accurate image retrieval. In: CVPR (2014)
21. Zitnick, C.L., Dollár, P.: Edge boxes: locating object proposals from edges. In: Fleet, D., Pajdla, T., Schiele, B., Tuytelaars, T. (eds.) ECCV 2014. LNCS, vol. 8693, pp. 391–405. Springer, Cham (2014). https://doi.org/10.1007/978-3-319-10602-1_26

An Effective Head Detection Framework via Convolutional Neural Networks

Canmiao Fu, Yule Yuan, Qiang Zeng, Siying He, and Yong Zhao[✉]

School of Electronic and Computer Engineering,
Shenzhen Graduate School of Peking University, Shenzhen, China
{fcm, zengqiang, hesiying}@pku.edu.cn,
lemmas@foxmail.com, yongzhao@pkusz.edu.cn

Abstract. In this paper, we propose a conceptually simple, advanced and effective head detection framework based on convolutional network. To robustly detect the smaller size of the head in crowded scenes, we propose a new feature extraction strategy which uses a top-down structure and uses lateral connection to combine hierarchical features. Moreover, multi-scale RPN and weight sensitive layer are also explored without increase in the computation costs, as that can reinforce feature representation which is important for identifying small objects. Furthermore, in order to adapt to the needs of the actual application scenarios, we design a model whose size is reduced from 520 M to only 12 M and modify the classification network, which perfect realization of the low calculation and light-weight. We validated our approach on the Brainwash dataset where we show an admirable result compare to the state-of-the-art head detection.

Keywords: Head detection · Multi scale RPN · Weight sensitive layer

1 Introduction

Object detection has made great progress over the past several years because of the use of convolutional neural networks. In fact, whereas speed and accuracy are difficult to be good at the same time. Although, such as Regions with CNN (RCNN) [4], Spatial Pyramid Pooling Net (SPPNet) [5], Fast RCNN [3], Faster RCNN [2], R-FCN [16] etc. have made a great success on MS COCO, PASCAL VOC [17], and ILSV-RC [18] detection tasks, they are heavy computational cost and it's lead to an challenging on speeding up. On the other hand, some framework like You only look once (YOLO) [8], Single Shot MultiBox Detector (SSD) [9], which have an advantage over speed, but pool performance when detecting small objects that is fatal in practical applications. [1] proposed a new and commendable framework, which can use a LSTM layer for sequence generation to detect head in crowed scenes that is Faster RCNN [2] or SSD [9] difficult to do. But it runs about 15 fps on a GPU, it can't reach real-time. As mentioned above, AlexNet [19], ZF-net [20], VGG [21], GoogLeNet [11] and ResNet [22], which have achieved good results on Image-net [18], are being wildly used in object detection as feature extraction net-work. And in this paper, VGG16 [21] is used as a feature extraction network. Nevertheless these networks are all memory intensive, it's impossible to deploy them on embedded system with limited hardware resources. We need lightweight networks which are more feasible to deploy on embedded system. Our goal in this paper is to propose a high accuracy head detection framework and explore the possibility of embedded implementation.

Fig. 1. Our predictions. In the left figure, we use green arrows to identify samples that are difficult to recognize, which including strong light changes and partial occlusion. In the right figure, we use red arrow to identify the sample which we don't recognize. (Color figure online)

Based on the above facts, in order to achieve higher accuracy, we learned that deep convolutional neural networks are capable of learning hierarchical feature layer by layer, and the discriminative feature maps have different spatial resolutions and semantic information. On the one hand, the bottom layers reserve high spatial resolution feature maps which have low-level features that are very useful for precise localization but harmful for object recognition. On the other hand, the top layers are low-resolution but strong semantic features which we can use to gain a precise recognition. Following this observation, we redesign the feature extraction part. Our goal is to be well localization and well recognized, so we combine high-resolution layers with more semantic information layers, more details are described in Sect. 3.

Many precious studies have shown that semantic segmentation and object detection are closely linked. Naturally, we can use semantic information for feature representation. And inspired by [6] which proposes a class activation mapping to localize the discriminative image regions. And [13] used weakly segmentation-aware, which only used bounding box annotation for detection, based on this, we propose a weigh sensitive layer (WSL) to gain well feature representation, as illustrated in Fig. 2. Furthermore, objects have different scales in different scenes. To achieve higher recall and be suitable to multi-scale, we improve the original RPN used in Faster RCNN [2] and redesign a multi-scale RPN (MS-RPN). The motivation for this comes from ResNet [22] and GoogLeNet [11], which used residual connection and Inception architecture which contain multiple scales of sliding windows. And the MS-RPN is illustrated in Fig. 3.

Moreover, the hardware conditions in the actual application scenario limit the size of the model and the high speed requirements. For the sake of reducing the network parameters as fewer as possible and deploying on embedded system, we take Squee-zeNet [7] as the feature extraction network and the whole head detection network is less than 12 M because of it. What's more, we have noticed that we can use fully convolution subnetwork as the last classification network after Roi-pooling rather than fully connect layer by experience, and we can further reduce parameters and computational cost with little accuracy reducing by this way.

To summarize, our contribution mainly includes the following points: (1) We redesign feature extraction subnetwork so that can combine coarse and fine feature. (2) We extend the model and propose a weigh sensitive layer by using semantic information without too much computation addition. (3) We present a multi-scale RPN. (4) What's more, we achieve a lightweight, real-time and high precision head detection that makes embedded implementations possible.

2   Related Work

Object detection contains two parts: feature extraction and object classification. In feature extraction, there are originally artificial design of SIFT [32], HOG [33] and other characteristics. When AlexNet [19] had been published in 2012, VGG [21], GoogLeNet [11], ResNet [22], SqueezeNet [7] etc. have been published one after another, which achieve good results on ImageNet [18], as well as training to get a fine feature expression. Thanks to these groundbreaking research, we can easily fine-tuning the model and transfer to other tasks and object detection is a representative work. There are two main types of object detection framework. One is based on regional proposal, like RCNN [4]. RCNN [4] applied selective search [34] to extra proposals and then combines them with convolutional network, which make an amazing improvement in object detection. After that, regions with convolutional network methods began to become popular. But the original R-CNN [4] approach has a lot to be optimized such as: time consuming during proposals extraction process; repeating feature calculation; unable end-to-end training and so on. SPPNet [5] proposed the use of spatial pyramid pooling makes to enable multi-scale detection, and reused convolutional features to accelerate R-CNN [4]. On the basis of SPPNet [5], Fast R-CNN [3] proposed multi-task optimization loss which first proposed in the MultiBox [15], making end-to-end training methods can be achieved. The above framework need to pre-extract the proposals, Faster R-CNN [2], which our work related to, presented a region proposal network to extract proposals. And [2] creatively proposed a novel anchor pyramid to solve multi-scale & ratio detection. Further more, [2] achieved a multi-scale feature sharing and improve the efficiency of detection. There another set of architecture which skip the proposal select step, like Overfeat [23], YOLO [8], YOLOv2 [24], SSD [9], DSSD [25] etc. Additional, [1] which related to Overfeat [23] and is also the source of the dataset for this paper used LSTM, an newfangled method, to predict variable length outputs.

In the term of extracting features, there are plenty of ways to adopt the integration of multi-layer features, the field of object detection are involved. The general idea is that deep convolutional network has different resolution layers at different depths with hierarchal feature, which have different effects on localization and classification. We can fuse the multiple, hierarchal feature map to improve the accuracy of detection. Related studies include SSD [9], Multi-Scale CNN [26], MultiPath Network [27] which predict object at different layer and HyperNet [10], Inside-outside net (ION) [14] etc. which combine the multiple features first and do detection later.

3 Head Detection Framework

This section presents our head detection framework. Similar to the current regional-based approach, we also use convolutional networks as feature extraction part and then follow the region proposal + RoI classification models. Our goal is to design a better feature extraction method to further enhance the feature representation to achieve head detection with the highest accuracy.

We discuss the details of each component and the motivation for choosing this method as follows. At first, we propose our own feature selection methods and weight sensitive layer in Subsect. 3.1. Then we explain how to design a multi-scale RPN in Subsect. 3.2. Finally, Subsect. 3.3 presents how to design a model that can be deployed on an embedded system. Need to emphasize that the feature extraction network are used VGG16 [21] if we do not make any special instructions, and this paper in the realization of light-weight models to adapt the embedded transplant is used SqueezeNet [7], which will be described in detail later.

3.1 Hierarchical Feature and Weight Sensitive Layer

Convolution neural networks have a strong ability to express features. And different depths, different resolutions of the feature maps on the object recognition and localization have a different role. Intuitively, the integration of hierarchical feature can improve the accuracy of object detection. And we extract hierarchical feature maps from the convolutional networks, which also effectively avoid the repeated calculation. We are based on the structure of VGG16 [21], the main use of feature map is the conv3, conv4 and conv5, as illustrated in Fig. 1. Our approach is different from PVANET [12], HyperNet [10], ION [14], which directly obtain the output of each layer and then sampled to a uniform scale, respectively, used the strategies are (1) take the layer whose scale is $2\times$ of the last layer as the benchmark and the other layers were down sampling and up sampling; (2) with the last layer as the base and the other layers are $2\times$ and $4\times$ down samples, respectively; (3) first, the feature map through the Roi-pooling to uniform size and then connected together via L2 normalize. Our approach is change the channel and enhance the feature via lateral connection firstly. Each lateral connection ensures that the spatial size of the feature map is the same as the original. And then, in order to finally get the same size of the feature map, we have taken a different sampling strategy for each layer. For the conv3 feature map, we employ a max pooling layer which the kernel is 3×3 and stride is 2. Conv4 feature map in the forward propagation process is the same size, so do not need to do any processing. And conv5 with $2\times$ up-sample. After taking out the layers feature, then combined together.

Based on the hierarchical feature obtained above, we can use it directly for object detection. However, as mentioned above, the high-level feature maps will have better semantic features. We design the WSL on conv5's up-sample map, inspired by [6] which proposed a class activation map to indicate the discriminative image regions. And [13] used the fully convolutional network framework to weakly supervise the training of the segmentation network and then extracted the semantic information, using only the bounding box annotations for detection without any other segmentation

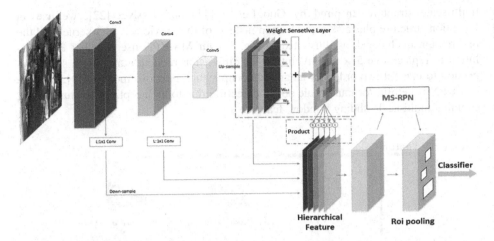

Fig. 2. Our head detection framework. An input image into a fully convolutional network (feature extraction network) and then different sampling operations are performed on Conv3, Conv4, Conv5 respectively to obtain hierarchical features. WSL is obtained on the basis of the Up-sample layer, then multiplied by Hierarchical Feature to get feature map and finally passed to the classifier through MS-RPN and ROI pooling.

label information. In this paper, we seek to get semantic information as simple as possible. We directly use the method of detection to pre-training network, after training, we extract the up-sample feature map, because the convolution network will have a good semantic features without any specific segmentation training. Our implementation details are as follows, first for the given up-sample feature map of 512 channels, let $I^k(x, y)$ represent the kth map of up-sample layer, (x, y) represent the spatial location. Then each map multiplied by a weighting factor w_k which can be seen as a convolution kernel, and then output to get a WSL which is expressed in Formula (1) and the C in Formula (1) represents the size of channels, which is 512 in this paper. Also, we need to ensure that WSL and hierarchical feature maps are the same channels. The strong interaction between WSL and the location of the object makes the WSL have a large amount of transcendental information that automatically indicates the location of the object.

$$WSL = \sum_{k=1}^{C} w_k I^k(x, y) \tag{1}$$

3.2   Multi-Scale RPN

RPN was firstly proposed by Faster RCNN [2]. The original RPN is a fully convolutional network and it slides a 3×3 kernel with stride 2 over conv5 to get a 512-channel feature map. After the mapping is done by the ReLU [31] non-linear processing and then the feature were obtained by two 1×1 kernel processing to get the object classification score and bounding box regression score. Different from the above is that we are not directly using 3×3 sliding windows, but the design of a multi-scale structure. Inspired by GoogLeNet [11] and ResNet [22], we use an Inception structure plus a skip-connection instead of the previous 3 × 3 kernel and the rest remain unchanged, as illustrated in Fig. 3. Our MS-RPN use two 3 × 3 convolution to replace one 5 × 5 convolution for dimension reduction and use a skip connection to make it two orders of magnitude deeper than previous models [30]. And the MS-RPN is helpful for multi scale object detection due to its inception structure which contains multi-scale sliding window feature.

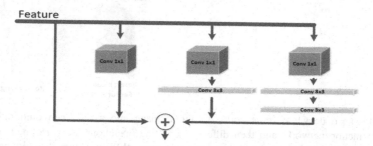

Fig. 3. The framework of MS-RPN. We use two conv 3 × 3 to replace one conv 5 × 5 and this architecture contains multi-scale sliding window feature which is helpful for feature representation.

3.3   Adaption to Embedded Design

In some object detection tasks, ZFnet [20], VGG [21], GoogLeNet [11], ResNet [22], because of their excellent performance, are often used to as feature extraction networks. But there is a drawback is that these networks occupy the storage space is particularly large, which is not suitable for embedded platform to achieve. So we do the first modification is the use of the lightweight network SqueezeNet [7], which is the first time the use of this network to do the object detection. And our goal is to reduce the amount of parameters and increase the speed. Of course, the accuracy will be reduced, which can be senn from the analysis of the experimental results in Sect. 4. SqueezeNet [7] is not aim to get the best convolutional network recognition accuracy, but want to simplify the network complexity, while achieving the public network (AlexNet [19]) recognition accuracy. So SqueezeNet [7] is designed to reduce the number of CNN model's parameters. SqueezeNet's [7] main advantage is to achieve AlexNet-level accuracy on ImageNet [18], but 50× the reduction of parameters, if the use of model compression techniques can reach 510× the parameters of the reduction. In this paper, we use a 50× fewer parameters model.

Moreover, the common detection pipeline uses fully connect layer to fully connect layer then connect the (N + 1) output scores and the 4 N bounding box regression outputs. In order to ensure the accuracy and speed, based on the pipeline, we use a fully convolutional layer, which contains 1 × 1 kernel and 1024 outputs, instead of the traditional FC-FC mode. Experiments show that's a good choice. And thanks to the observation by [12], the feature input to RPN does not need to be the same deep as the inputs to the classifiers. So, we feed the first 384 channel into MS-RPN which helps to reduce the computation costs, too.

4 Experiments

In this section we evaluated the head detection variants on the Brainwash dataset and for all our experiments, we use [1] as a common baseline. Our framework is implemented on Caffe [28] and modifies the Faster RCNN [2]. We initialize the feature extraction network and two FC layer with pre-trained network on ImageNet [18]. So as to test the time of our model, we use a machine with Inter i7-4790k@4GHz processor, 32 GB RAM and an NVIDIA GeForce GTX Titan X GPU card. And all the pictures are of a unified size of 630*840.

4.1 Dataset and Evaluation Metrics

We evaluate our framework on the Brainwash [1] benchmark. The Brainwash dataset contains 11917 images. [1] allocate 1000 images for testing and validation and the remaining for training. In this paper we made minor changes that the original testing dataset contains some image (~ 9 images) without head so we use some of the validation dataset instead of these images.

Like [1], we also use the standard PASCAL VOC [29] evaluation metrics. When its intersection-over-union (IoU) is greater than 0.5, it is judged as correct.

In order to demonstrate that our approach is valid, we mainly compare the results of the [1], and in the course of the experiment we first trained one of the most simple model, which is the original Faster RCNN [2] framework, and then on the basis of this to implement other methods. In this part, all of our experiments use the base network are VGG16 [21] and SqueezeNet [7] and we will clearly state in the follow-up analysis. Our VGG16-based network of experimental results are shown in Table 1 and the recall-precision curves are shown in Fig. 4.

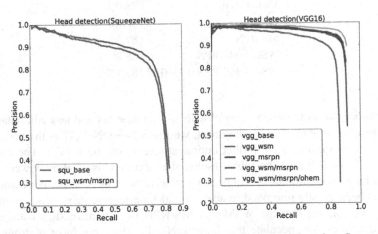

Fig. 4. Performance evaluation. The left is the results of our methods based on SqueezeNet [7], the right is the results of our methods based on VGG16 [21].

In Table 1, the first five results come from the common baseline [1], VGG-based is the easiest framework which simply using the VGG16 [21] network, WSL and MS-RPN respectively refer to weight sensitive layer and multi-scale RPN on the basis of VGG-based, WSL + MS-RPN is a fusion of two methods. And both WSL and MS-RPN have redesigned feature extraction networks whose details are mentioned above. From Table 1 we can see that we designed the WSL and MS-RPN on the basis of the common base framework have a significant improvement in accuracy which proves that our design is very effective, and the two together will make the whole detection framework more robust. In order to further improve the accuracy, we used the OHEM [35] and the results show that OHEM [35] is very effective. As shown in Fig. 1, the left figure shows the successful test results, we use the green arrows identify hard samples which vary greatly and serious occlusions. This intuitively shows that our framework is very effective. And in the right figure, we use red arrow to identify the failed sample which is badly covered and is what we need to keep trying to improve. Also, as shown in Fig. 5, the top row is the results of [1] recognition failure and the bottom row is our results. This figure shows that our framework can well recognize heads that are not recognized by [1]. Our framework is tested on our experimental platform with a speed of ~ 110 ms/image.

Table 1. VGG16 [21] performance evaluation.

Methods	AP
Overfeat – AlexNet [1]	62.0%
Overfeat – GoogLNet [1]	67.0%
L_{fix} [1]	60.0%
L_{firstk} [1]	63.0%
L_{hung} [1]	78.0%
VGG-based	78.0%
WSL	87.6%
MS-RPN	87.3%
WSL + MS-RPN	88.8%
WSL + MS-RPN + OHEM	**89.7%**

In addition, so as to obtain a model with less parameters and less computation and be able to adapt to embedded deployment, we use SqueezeNet [7] as the basic feature extraction network and make further optimizations on the basis of it. The results are shown in Table 2. From the table results, the accuracy is slightly lower than the common framework, but the model parameters have been large-scale reduction and the speed has been greatly improved to achieve real-time requirements. As a result of the analysis, we can see that the WSM and MS-RPN do not have significant effect as described above. We speculate that SqueezeNet [7] does not have a strong feature representation like VGG16 [21].

Fig. 5. Example detection results between [1] (top row) and our approach (bottom row). The top row are failure cases of [1]. The results from the figure show that our method can correctly identify heads that are not recognized by [1]. (Color figure online)

Table 2. SqueezeNet [7] performance evaluation.

Methods	AP	Size	Speed(Titan X)
SqueezeNet-based	72.4%	11.14 M	∼38 ms/image
WSL + MS-RPN	74.2%	11.52 M	∼41 ms/image

5   Conclusion

This paper proposes an efficient head detection framework and validate its performance on a large-scale head dataset which showed our proposed framework obtained the highest accuracy. The main contribution includes: The lateral connection is used to realize the fusion of multi-layer features and the weight sensitive layer which is extracted on the basis of hierarchical feature maps improves the accuracy. In addition, we design a novel MS-RPN, which can also be a good feature enhancement. The combination of WSL and MS-RPN makes the model more robust. Experimental results demonstrated that the highest accuracy of 89.7% was achieved after the fusion of OHEM [35]. Moreover, we further explore the possibility of embedded implementation by taking SqueezeNet [7] as the feature extraction network. We also employ a 1024-channel fully convolutional layer replacing the previous 2-FC layer which makes the model parameters and computation consumption are greatly reduced. Finally, our model is downsized from 520 M to only 11.14 M with the accuracy of 72.4% and the speed of 38 ms/image, so the model size and real-time requirements are guaranteed.

References

1. Stewart, R., Andriluka, M., Ng, A.Y.: End-to-end people detection in crowded scenes. In: Proceedings of the IEEE Conference on Computer Vision and Pattern Recognition (2016)
2. Ren, S., et al.: Faster R-CNN: towards real-time object detection with region proposal networks. In: Advances in Neural Information Processing Systems (2015)
3. Girshick, R.: Fast R-CNN. In: Proceedings of the IEEE International Conference on Computer Vision (2015)
4. Girshick, R., et al.: Rich feature hierarchies for accurate object detection and semantic segmentation. In: Proceedings of the IEEE Conference on Computer Vision and Pattern Recognition (2014)
5. He, K., Zhang, X., Ren, S., Sun, J.: Spatial pyramid pooling in deep convolutional networks for visual recognition. In: Fleet, D., Pajdla, T., Schiele, B., Tuytelaars, T. (eds.) ECCV 2014. LNCS, vol. 8691, pp. 346–361. Springer, Cham (2014). https://doi.org/10.1007/978-3-319-10578-9_23
6. Zhou, B., et al.: Learning deep features for discriminative localization. In: Proceedings of the IEEE Conference on Computer Vision and Pattern Recognition (2016)
7. Iandola, F.N., et al.: SqueezeNet: AlexNet-level accuracy with 50x fewer parameters and <0.5 MB model size. arXiv preprint arXiv:1602.07360 (2016)
8. Redmon, J., et al.: You only look once: unified, real-time object detection. In: Proceedings of the IEEE Conference on Computer Vision and Pattern Recognition (2016)
9. Liu, W., Anguelov, D., Erhan, D., Szegedy, C., Reed, S., Fu, C.-Y., Berg, Alexander C.: SSD: single shot multibox detector. In: Leibe, B., Matas, J., Sebe, N., Welling, M. (eds.) ECCV 2016. LNCS, vol. 9905, pp. 21–37. Springer, Cham (2016). https://doi.org/10.1007/978-3-319-46448-0_2
10. Kong, T., et al.: HyperNet: towards accurate region proposal generation and joint object detection. In: Proceedings of the IEEE Conference on Computer Vision and Pattern Recognition (2016)
11. Szegedy, C., et al.: Going deeper with convolutions. In: Proceedings of the IEEE Conference on Computer Vision and Pattern Recognition (2015)
12. Kim, K.-H., et al.: PVANET: Deep but Lightweight Neural Networks for Real-time Object Detection. arXiv preprint arXiv:1608.08021 (2016)
13. Gidaris, S., Komodakis, N.: Object detection via a multi-region and semantic segmentation-aware CNN model. In: Proceedings of the IEEE International Conference on Computer Vision (2015)
14. Bell, S., et al.: Inside-outside net: detecting objects in context with skip pooling and recurrent neural networks. In: Proceedings of the IEEE Conference on Computer Vision and Pattern Recognition (2016)
15. Erhan, D., et al.: Scalable object detection using deep neural networks. In: Proceedings of the IEEE Conference on Computer Vision and Pattern Recognition (2014)
16. Dai, J., et al.: R-FCN: object detection via region-based fully convolutional networks. In: Neural Information Processing Systems, pp. 379–387 (2016)
17. Everingham, M., Van Gool, L., Williams, C.K., Winn, J., Zisserman, A.: The PASCAL visual object classes (VOC) challenge. IJCV 88, 303–338 (2010)
18. Deng, J., Berg, A., Satheesh, S., Su, H., Khosla, A., Fei-Fei, L.: ImageNet Large Scale Visual Recognition Competition (ILSVRC2012) (2012). http://www.image-net.org/challenges/LSVRC/2012/
19. Krizhevsky, A., Sutskever, I., Hinton, G.E.: Imagenet classification with deep convolutional neural networks. In: Advances in Neural Information Processing Systems (2012)

20. Zeiler, Matthew D., Fergus, R.: Visualizing and understanding convolutional networks. In: Fleet, D., Pajdla, T., Schiele, B., Tuytelaars, T. (eds.) ECCV 2014. LNCS, vol. 8689, pp. 818–833. Springer, Cham (2014). https://doi.org/10.1007/978-3-319-10590-1_53

21. Simonyan, K., Zisserman, A.: Very deep convolutional networks for large-scale image recognition. arXiv preprint arXiv:1409.1556 (2014)

22. He, K., et al.: Deep residual learning for image recognition. In: Proceedings of the IEEE Conference on Computer Vision and Pattern Recognition (2016)

23. Sermanet, P., et al.: Overfeat: Integrated recognition, localization and detection using convolutional networks. arXiv preprint arXiv:1312.6229 (2013)

24. Redmon, J., Farhadi, A.: YOLO9000: Better, Faster, Stronger. arXiv preprint arXiv:1612.08242 (2016)

25. Fu, C.-Y., et al.: DSSD: Deconvolutional Single Shot Detector. arXiv preprint arXiv:1701.06659 (2017)

26. Cai, Z., Fan, Q., Feris, Rogerio S., Vasconcelos, N.: A unified multi-scale deep convolutional neural network for fast object detection. In: Leibe, B., Matas, J., Sebe, N., Welling, M. (eds.) ECCV 2016. LNCS, vol. 9908, pp. 354–370. Springer, Cham (2016). https://doi.org/10.1007/978-3-319-46493-0_22

27. Zagoruyko, S., et al.: A multipath network for object detection. arXiv preprint arXiv:1604.02135 (2016)

28. Jia, Y., et al.: Caffe: convolutional architecture for fast feature embedding. In: Proceedings of the 22nd ACM International Conference on Multimedia, ACM (2014)

29. Everingham, M., et al.: The pascal visual object classes challenge: a retrospective. Int. J. Comput. Vis. 111(1), 98–136 (2015)

30. Veit, A., Wilber, M.J., Belongie, S.: Residual networks behave like ensembles of relatively shallow networks. In: Advances in Neural Information Processing Systems (2016)

31. Glorot, X., Bordes, A., Bengio, Y.: Deep sparse rectifier neural networks. In: Aistats, vol. 15, no. 106 (2011)

32. Lowe, D.G.: Distinctive image features from scale-invariant keypoints. Int. J. Comput. Vis. 60(2), 91–110 (2004)

33. Dalal, N., Triggs, B.: Histograms of oriented gradients for human detection. In: IEEE Computer Society Conference on Computer Vision and Pattern Recognition, 2005, CVPR 2005, vol. 1. IEEE (2005)

34. Uijlings, J.R., et al.: Selective search for object recognition. Int. J. Comput. Vis. 104(2), 154–171 (2013)

35. Shrivastava, A., Gupta, A., Girshick, R.: Training region-based object detectors with online hard example mining. In: Proceedings of the IEEE Conference on Computer Vision and Pattern Recognition (2016)

Identifying Gambling and Porn Websites
with Image Recognition

Longxi Li[1,2], Gaopeng Gou[1,2], Gang Xiong[1,2], Zigang Cao[1,2(✉)], and Zhen Li[1,2]

[1] Institute of Information Engineering, Chinese Academy of Sciences, Beijing, China
caozigang@iie.ac.cn

[2] School of Cyber Security, University of Chinese Academy of Sciences,
Minzhuang Road 89 A, Haidian District,
Beijing 100093, People's Republic of China

Abstract. Gambling and porn websites are more and more harmful to the health and growth of the youth with the rapid development of the Internet, however, the text contents and URLs based website classification methods could not get satisfying on gambling and porn websites detection because domain names of them change fast. Meanwhile, the visual based website classification has gotten perfect results in phishing website detection which encourages us. Therefore, we introduce the visual feature to identify gambling websites and porn websites in this paper. Firstly, we develop a website screenshot tool which could save the full contents of a website to be a image, Secondly, the effective feature is chosen by BoW model to recognize the screenshots of gambling websites and porn websites, and the appropriate parameters are chosen to promote the efficiency of classification. Finally, experimental results on our collected gambling websites and porn website datasets demonstrate that our proposed method is able to recognize the gambling and porn websites and gets satisfying results.

Keywords: Bag of words model · Local feature · Websites identify

1 Introduction

With the rapid expanding of the Internet, more and more people obtain information from websites. However, there are malicious contents in some websites such as phishing websites, gambling websites, porn websites and so on. Seriously, the gambling and porn websites are bad for the healthy growth of the teenagers, how to filter these web contents is badly in need for the parents of teenagers. Therefore, the website classification become the research hot spot recently and what could be used to find a malicious website, analyze the topic of a specific web links, recognize the content structure of the web, improve the quality of web search engines, filter some web contents and so on.

The website classification methods could be divided to be text contents based ones, URLs based ones and visual feature based ones. The text contents based

© Springer International Publishing AG, part of Springer Nature 2018
B. Zeng et al. (Eds.): PCM 2017, LNCS 10736, pp. 488–497, 2018.
https://doi.org/10.1007/978-3-319-77383-4_48

ones are most common. The text contents are major components in the web pages such as HTML/XML tags, hyperlinks, HTML contents, JavaScript codes *etc.* Bhalla extracts features from an HTML document, then these features are assigned with different weights based on the collection of a domain-specific keyword list, and finally, kernel SVM is used as the classification tool [1]. Zheng focuses on large-scale web page classification problems and propose an algorithm which utilize anchor graph hashing to reduce the original feature dimensions and integrate the K-Nearest Neighbour (KNN) for classifying [2]. Sarode utilizes the rough set based quick reduct algorithm to reduce the dimension of the features of web pages, and the Naive Bayesian method is used for classification [3]. The text content based methods suffer from the curse of dimensionality because the websites become more and more complex and massive. Thus, the researchers focus on URLs based ones.

Sirageldin provides a framework for detecting a malicious web page by using artificial neural network based on the URL dictionary and page contents features [4]. Rajalakshmi extracts n-gram based features from URLs alone, and the classification step is done by Support Vector Machines and Maximum Entropy Classifiers [5]. Maurer calculates the URL similarity between original and fraudulent websites by sophisticated spelling mistakes to detect phishing attacks [6]. Although URLs based methods could get satisfying results, the patterns of URLs need to be adjusted simultaneously because the URLs of malicious websites change fast and irregularly.

Comparing with the intensive research on text contents and URLs based methods, little work has been done on the use of the visual content of a web page. Most of the visual based methods focus on phishing website detection. Zhou proposes an anti-phishing method based on the combination of local and global visual features [7]. Rao uses the Speeded-Up Robust Features (SURF) detector to extract discriminative key point features from both suspicious and targeted websites, and the features are used for computing similarity degree between the legitimate and suspicious pages [8]. Afroz introduces PhishZoo which uses profiles of trusted websites to detect phishing. The method can classify zeroday phishing attacks [9]. Bozkir employs Histogram of Oriented Gradients (HOG) descriptor in order to capture cues of page layout without the need of time consuming intermediate stage of segmentation [10]. These phishing website detection algorithms based on visual content mentioned above get perfect results.

Inspired by the work of visual content based website classification on phishing, and gambling and porn websites are harmful to health and growth of the youth, so a visual based gambling and porn website classification method is proposed in this paper. Figure 1 gives the flowchart of our proposed method. The method could be divided to be three parts. Firstly, we try to collect the domains of gambling websites and porn websites from the network traffic. Then we visit the collected domains of the websites, convert the page of each website to be a screenshot image and build a website screenshot database. Secondly, the visual features are extracted from each screenshot based on the bag of words (BoW) model [12]. Finally, the support vector machine (SVM) classifier is utilized to distinguish gambling websites and porn websites from normal websites [13].

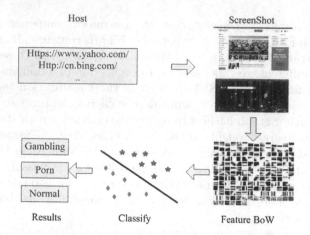

Fig. 1. The flowchart of website classification based on visual feature

The contribution of this paper is:

1. We introduce the visual content based website classification to identify the gambling and porn websites;
2. We develop a website screenshot tool which could get better results than others, and we also construct a gambling website database and a porn website database;
3. We find that SURF descriptor in the BoW model could efficiently recognize the screenshots of gambling websites and porn websites;
4. We find that the appropriate parameters of the BoW model which can be used to recognize the screenshots of gambling websites and porn website and speed up the processing time.

The remainder of this paper is organized as follows: in Sect. 2, we introduce the visual feature based website classification method; in Sect. 3, the experimental results are mentioned to verify the proposed method; and in Sect. 4, we summarize this paper and give the conclusion.

2 Our Approach

2.1 Image Acquisition

After the domains of gambling websites and porn websites are obtained, we should convert the domains to their corresponding full page screenshots. We have tested several full-web page screenshot tools like Webshot and SnapshotterPro. Unfortunately, these softwares cannot overcome the influence caused by lazy load, and many screenshots have blank in themselves because images in the web page are not loaded. In addition, the load time of these tools is fixed, which results in the fact that some tools perform screenshot actions before the web page is loaded completely. In a word, although Webshot take screenshots fast, the quality of images is not satisfying.

In order to get more actual full page screenshots, we develop a tool in Java. Firstly, the tool opens Chrome to load the web page and then scroll to the bottom to make all images in the web page loaded. Secondly, the tool applies JavaScript to detect whether the web page are loaded completely. Finally, the tool invokes a Chrome extension Nimbus Screenshot to take full page screenshots. These procedures are automatically performed until corresponding screenshots of all domains are generated. The screenshots are named by domain names so we can distinguish them. Figure 2 gives the screenshots generated by Webshot and the tool we developed. It could be found that our tool gets better screenshots.

a. Webshot   b. Our tool   c. Webshot   d. Our tool

Fig. 2. The screenshots generated by Webshot and the tool we developed.

2.2 Image Representation Based on the BoW Model

Figure 3 shows the steps of the website screenshot represented by BoW model: (1) keypoints extracting; (2) keypoints description; (3) visual codebook generation; and (4) histogram computing. Figure 4 gives the details of the four steps mentioned above.

The keypoints extracting methods aim to find the maximal and minimal points from a transformed function applied in scale space to a series of smoothed and resampled images. Low contrast candidate points and edge response points along an edge are discarded. The extracted keypoints are the interesting part of an image and more stable for matching and recognition. The efficient keypoints extracting algorithms are FAST [14], SURF [15], SIFT [16] and STAR [17].

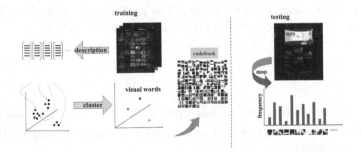

Fig. 3. The pipeline of image representation based on the BoW model.

Keypoints description methods want to generate descriptors, which are vectors of each keypoint that could be highly distinctive and partially invariant to the remaining variations such as illumination, 3D viewpoint, etc. The efficient keypoints description methods are SURF [15], SIFT [16], ORB [18], and BRIEF [19].

Visual codebook generation method plays a dominant role in BoW model. In this paper, we use popular vector quantization algorithm k-means to do clustering. The goal of this algorithm is to find K centers such that after assigning each data vector to the nearest center, the sum of Euclidean distance from the centers is minimized. These centers are called visual words in BoW model. We write these centers into an xml file and then the codebook is formed.

In histogram computing step, each local feature extracted from one image could be mapped to a certain visual word in the codebook based on Euclidean distance. Therefore, the image can be represented by a histogram over the visual words. So the histogram could reflect the distribution of local features which are extracted from the image through the visual codebook. In the below section, the histogram is used to train classifiers.

2.3   Learning and Recognition Based on the BoW Model

Our objective classifier is built to distinguish gambling website images and porn website images from normal ones, and in this paper we choose the support vector machine (SVM) algorithm.

The SVM classifier is used to find a hyper plane which could separate two class data from maximal margin. The maximal margin is defined as the distance from the closest training point to the separating hyper plane. For the given image sample X, and it's corresponding label Y which takes values ± 1, the classification function $f(x)$ could be defined as:

$$f(x) = sign(w^T x + b) \tag{1}$$

where w and b are the parameters of the hyper plane. However, the training and testing samples are not always linearly separable. In order to solve the non-linear problem, the kernel method is introduced to SVM.

The feature vectors extracted from the screenshot are nonlinear ones. So in this paper we introduce the RBF kernel. The RBF kernel on two samples x and x', represented as feature vectors in some input space, is defined as

$$K(x, x') = exp(-\frac{\left\| x - x' \right\|^2}{2\sigma^2}) \tag{2}$$

$\left\| x - x' \right\|^2$ may be recognized as the squared Euclidean distance between the two feature vectors. σ is a free parameter. An equivalent, but simpler, definition involves a parameter:

$$K(x, x') = exp(-\gamma \left\| x - x' \right\|^2) \tag{3}$$

In the kernel formulation, the decision function can be expressed as

$$f(x) = sign(\sum_i y_i \alpha_i K(x, x_i) + b) \tag{4}$$

where x_i is the training feature vectors from data space X, y_i is the label of x_i.

3   Experimental Analysis

3.1   Image Database

The gambling website screenshot database contains 670 gambling website screenshots and 757 normal ones. In this paper, 209 gambling website screenshots and 223 normal ones are used as the training samples, and rest ones and normal ones are used as the testing samples.

The porn website screenshot database contains 757 porn website screenshots and 758 normal ones. In this paper, 250 porn website screenshots and 250 normal ones are used as the training samples, and rest ones and normal ones are used as the testing samples.

3.2   Feature Choose

In this paper, we choose FAST [14], SURF [15], and STAR [17] to extract keypoints from the images, because these keypoint extracting methods are state of the art. The keypoint describing methods we have chosen are SURF [15], ORB [18], and BRIEF [19], because these descriptors are state of the art. SIFT is not a realtime keypoint extracting and description method, so we give up SIFT.

From Tables 1 and 2, we find the SURF feature (keypoint extracting and description) could get excellent precision rate and recall rate on gambling database and porn database. Therefore, we choose the SURF feature as the feature extracting method in this paper.

Table 1. The performance of the different keypoint extracting and keypoint description on gambling website database

Keypoints extract	Min keypoints num	Max kepoints num	Decsriptor	Decsriptor size	Proportion	Cluster num	Precision rate	Recall rate
FAST	128	42694	SURF	64	0.1	1000	0.862	0.935
SURF	169	21283	SURF	64	0.1	1000	0.933	0.935
STAR	7	5304	SURF	64	1	1000	0.885	0.937
FAST	68	42605	ORB	32	0.1	1000	0.849	0.941
SURF	150	21215	ORB	32	0.1	1000	0.87	0.944
STAR	7	5304	ORB	32	1	1000	0.859	0.937
FAST	70	42627	BRIEF	32	0.1	1000	0.882	0.922
SURF	152	21226	BRIEF	32	0.1	1000	0.871	0.922
STAR	7	5304	BRIEF	32	1	1000	0.872	0.935

Table 2. The performance of the different keypoint extracting and keypoint description on porn website database

Keypoints extract	Min keypoints num	Max kepoints num	Decsriptor	Decsriptor size	Proportion	Cluster num	Precision rate	Recall rate
FAST	128	42694	SURF	64	0.1	1000	0.963	0.919
SURF	169	21283	SURF	64	0.1	1000	0.969	0.97
STAR	7	5304	SURF	64	1	1000	0.943	0.956
FAST	68	42605	ORB	32	0.1	1000	0.921	0.947
SURF	150	21215	ORB	32	0.1	1000	0.894	0.917
STAR	7	5304	ORB	32	1	1000	0.917	0.911
FAST	70	42627	BRIEF	32	0.1	1000	0.917	0.978
SURF	152	21226	BRIEF	32	0.1	1000	0.933	0.927
STAR	7	5304	BRIEF	32	1	1000	0.939	0.917

3.3 Comparison of Different Proportion About SURF Feature descriptors

In bag-of-words model, the extracted local features are used to build a codebook. In order to reduce the time and space consumption, a small proportion of feature descriptors of each image is used to build the codebook.

We test the descriptor proportion ranging from 0.1 to 0.3 in the gambling dataset. And the result is as follows.

In order to analyze how the descriptor proportion could influence the detecting result, we keep other parameters and training and testing samples to be constant.

Table 3. Comparison of different proportion about SURF feature descriptors on gambling website database

	Descriptor proportion	Cluster number	Precision rate	Recall rate
Scheme 1	0.1	4000	94.1%	92.6%
Scheme 2	0.15	4000	94.1%	93.5%
Scheme 3	0.2	4000	94.2%	92.4%
Scheme 4	0.3	4000	94.3%	93.7%

From the Table 3, we could find that the precision rate and recall rate are satisfying even if only 10% of local features are used to build the codebook. Both precision rate and recall rate exceed 92%. It can also be found that bigger proportion has little benefit on the precision rate and the recall rate. In the porn dataset, we get similar results. Therefore, we choose the proportion of feature descriptors to be 10%, and time consumption can be remarkably reduced.

3.4   Comparison of Different Cluster Numbers

Cluster Number k for Gambling Website Classification

Cluster number k is the size of the codebook and the dimension of histogram feature vector of each image which is the key parameter in the experiment. So we did the following experiment in gambling dataset to choose appropriate k and the result is as follows:

From Table 4, it could be found when the cluster number increases, precision rate increases and recall rate increases and then decreases. Recall rate has reached the peak when cluster number is 2000. With the continuous increase of the cluster number, precision rate still goes up and recall rate goes down.

Table 4. Comparison of different cluster numbers on gambling website.

	Descriptor proportion	Cluster number	Precision rate	Recall rate
Scheme 1	0.1	500	92.5%	93.3%
Scheme 2	0.1	1000	93.3%	93.5%
Scheme 3	0.1	2000	93.6%	95.0%
Scheme 4	0.1	3000	93.7%	93.3%
Scheme 5	0.1	4000	94.1%	92.6%
Scheme 6	0.1	5000	94.3%	92.6%
Scheme 7	0.1	6000	95.5%	92.4%

On the other hand, if the cluster number increases by one thousand, clustering time cost doubles. Therefore, considering time consumption and efficiency, we choose the appropriate cluster number to be 2000.

Cluster Number k for Porn Website Classification

Like the experiment mentioned above, we use the same method to test porn website detecting system and compare the influence of using different cluster numbers. And here is the result:

From Table 5, we can see that the precision rate is kept in a rather high level especially when cluster number is bigger than 1250, and on the other side, the recall rate decreases significantly. Both the precision rate and the recall exceed 96% when k is 1000. Similar to the gambling websites testing, the efficiency will decrease if the cluster number increases. Hence, we set k to be one thousand and the precision rate, the recall rate and the efficiency are all very satisfying.

Table 5. Comparison of different cluster numbers on gambling website.

	Descriptor proportion	Cluster number	Precision rate	Recall rate
Scheme 1	0.1	500	96.5%	96.8%
Scheme 2	0.1	1000	96.9%	97.0%
Scheme 3	0.1	1250	98.2%	95.1%
Scheme 4	0.1	1500	98.2%	95.7%
Scheme 5	0.1	2000	98.1%	92.7%
Scheme 6	0.1	3000	98.3%	92.3%
Scheme 7	0.1	4000	98.5%	92.5%

4 Conclusion

In this paper, we use the visual features and bag of words model to recognize the gambling websites and porn websites from the encrypted network traffic, the experimental results demonstrate the proposed method is helpful. In the future work, we will test the algorithm on larger dataset, the experiment will be taken under the large-scale encrypted network traffic and on millions of websites to find gambling websites and porn websites. The method also could be used to find other malicious websites such as violence websites, terrorist websites.

Acknowledgements. This work is supported by The National Natural Science Foundation of China (No. 61602472, No. U1636217), The National Key Research and Development Program of China (NO. 2016YFB0801200).

References

1. Bhalla, V.K., Kumar, N.: An efficient scheme for automatic web pages categorization using the support vector machine. New Rev. Hypermedia Multimed. **22**, 223–242 (2016)
2. Zheng, Y., Sun, C., Zhu, C.: LWCS: a large-scale web page classification system based on anchor graph hashing. In: IEEE International Conference on Software Engineering and Service Science, pp. 90–94 (2015)
3. Sarode, S., Gadge, J.: Hybrid dimensionality reduction approach for web page classification. In: International Conference on Communication, Information and Computing Technology (2015)
4. Sirageldin, A., Baharudin, B.B., Jung, L.T.: Malicious web page detection: a machine learning approach. In: Jeong, H.Y., Obaidat, M.S., Yen, N.Y., Park, J.J.J.H. (eds.) Advances in Computer Science and its Applications. LNEE, vol. 279, pp. 217–224. Springer, Heidelberg (2014). https://doi.org/10.1007/978-3-642-41674-3_32
5. Rajalakshmi, R., Aravindan, C.: Web page classification using n-gram based URL features. In: International Conference on Advanced Computing, pp. 15–21 (2013)

6. Maurer, M.-E., Höfer, L.: Sophisticated phishers make more spelling mistakes: using URL similarity against phishing. In: Xiang, Y., Lopez, J., Kuo, C.-C.J., Zhou, W. (eds.) CSS 2012. LNCS, vol. 7672, pp. 414–426. Springer, Heidelberg (2012). https://doi.org/10.1007/978-3-642-35362-8_31

7. Zhou, Y., Zhang, Y., Xiao, J., Wang, Y., Lin, W.: Visual similarity based anti-phishing with the combination of local and global features. In: International Conference on Trust, Security and Privacy in Computing and Communications, pp. 189–196 (2014)

8. Rao, R.S., Ali, S.T.: A computer vision technique to detect phishing attacks. In: Fifth International Conference on Communication Systems and Network Technologies (2015)

9. Afroz, S., Greenstadt, R.: PhishZoo: detecting phishing websites by looking at them. In: Fifth IEEE International Conference on Semantic Computing, pp. 368–375 (2011)

10. Bozkir, A.S., Sezer, E.A.: Use of HOG descriptors in phishing detection (2016)

11. Cao, Z., Xiong, G., Zhao, Y., Li, Z., Guo, L.: A survey on encrypted traffic classification. In: Batten, L., Li, G., Niu, W., Warren, M. (eds.) ATIS 2014. CCIS, vol. 490, pp. 73–81. Springer, Heidelberg (2014). https://doi.org/10.1007/978-3-662-45670-5_8

12. Dong, K., Guo, L., Fu, Q.: An adult image detection algorithm based on bag-of-visual-words and text information. In: International Conference on Natural Computation, pp. 556–560 (2014)

13. Chang, C.C., Lin, C.J.: LIBSVM: a library for support vector machines, pp. 389–396 (2001). http://www.csie.ntu.edu.tw/~cjlin/libsvm

14. Yao, N., Bai, T.C., Chen, J.: Improved fast corner detection based on Harris algorithm for Chinese characters, pp. 767–770 (2013)

15. Bay, H., Tuytelaars, T., Gool, L.V.: SURF: speeded up robust features. Comput. Vis. Image Underst. 110(3), 404–417 (2006)

16. Lowe, D.G.: Distinctive image features from scale-invariant keypoints. Int. J. Comput. Vis. 60(60), 91–110 (2004)

17. Agrawal, M., Konolige, K., Blas, M.R.: CenSurE: Center surround extremas for realtime feature detection and matching. In: European Conference on Computer Vision, pp. 102–115. IEEE (2008)

18. Rublee, E., Rabaud, V., Konolige, K., Bradski, G.: ORB: an efficient alternative to SIFT or SURF. vol. 58, pp. 2564–2571 (2011)

19. Calonder, M., Lepetit, V., Strecha, C., Fua, P.: Brief: binary robust independent elementary features. In: European Conference on Computer Vision, pp. 778–792. IEEE (2010)

Image-Set Based Collaborative Representation for Face Recognition in Videos

Gaopeng Gou[1,2], Junzheng Shi[1,2], Gang Xiong[1,2], Peipei Fu[1,2], Zhen Li[1,2], and Zhenzhen Li[1,2(✉)]

[1] Institute of Information Engineering, Chinese Academy of Sciences, Beijing, China
lizhenzhen@iie.ac.cn
[2] School of Cyber Security, University of Chinese Academy of Sciences, Minzhuang Road 89 A, Haidian District 100093, Beijing, People's Republic of China

Abstract. Video-based face recognition has become one of the hottest topics in the domain of face recognition because it has a wide range of applications in multi-media processing conference, human-computer interaction, judicature identification, video surveillance, and entrance controlling, etc. Methods of video based face recognition could be divided to be two main aspects: the models used to represent the individual image sets; and the similarity metric used to compare the models. Based on image-set based object classification methods, we present an image-set based on collaborative representation based classification (SCRC) method for face recognition in videos. Firstly, the query face video is divided to be many sub sets. Secondly, every sub set is represented by the collaborative representation based classification. Finally, we combine the recognition results of sub sets to be a final classification. Experiments test on three public video face datasets, the experimental results demonstrate that the proposed SCRC method can be able to outperform a number of existing state-of-the-art ones.

Keywords: Collaborative representation · Feature extract
Video face recognition · Pattern recognition

1 Introduction

Face recognition has been an important topic in the field of automatic biometrics recognition for a long time [1,2]. However, accurate video face recognition remains as a challenging task in complicated environments since noise conditions, occlusion, the subject's location and illumination can vary significantly from frame to frame [3–5].

Compared with the traditional face recognition in still images, video-based face recognition has great advantages because videos contain much more abundant information than single images do. Therefore, more robust and stable recognition could be achieved by fusing information of multi-frames. Moreover, the temporal information also could be exploited from videos to improve the accuracy of face recognition. The multi frames and temporal information would help us to avoid the effect of occlusion, illumination variation and other negative factors, and better estimate the target. Meanwhile, video is different from still image, it is possible to analyze not only facial appearance but also head and facial motion, therefore, human faces in video can be considered as a hybrid biometric identifier [6].

Because of the reasons mentioned above, researchers have developed great interest in video-based face recognition and got important progress in recent days, It is worth mentioning that in video based face recognition both the enrolment and recognition sets are facial videos. However, face recognition in typical applications such as surveillance and access control remains challenging due to the following reasons: poor video quality, low quality facial images, illumination changes, pose variations and so on. Hence, a robust face recognition method is required in a practical environment.

Image-set based object classification has recently obtained significant attention from the research community [7–10]. In image-set based object classification, the gallery consists of one or more sets for each class and each image-set contains multiple images of the same class complementing a wide range of rigid and non-rigid variations as well as illumination changes. In the case of video based face recognition, pose variations are relatively rigid while expression variations are non-rigid. The query set also contains an arbitrary number of images of the same subject and is assigned with the label of the nearest gallery set by maximizing some similarity measure. The problem of image set classification may naturally arise in a wide range of biometric applications including video-based face recognition, surveillance and classification base on long term observations [11].

Inspired by the success of image-set based object classification, this paper tries to recognition face from videos by image-set base algorithm. Although the image-set based face recognition provides an opportunity of better recognition, it poses many challenges as well. The main challenge is how to efficiently model an image-set in a compact representation without losing discriminative information. Existing algorithms which have relatively more accuracy exhibit more computational complexity [9], while simple and efficient algorithms such as nearest neighborhood based classifiers exhibit would reduce the accuracy and robustness. In contrast to the existing algorithms, the image-set based collaborative representation method introduced in this paper is both compact and computationally efficient. This method is tested in a wide range of experiments on three standard datasets, the experimental results demonstrated the image-set based collaborative representation exhibited more accuracy than existing algorithms, with significant execution time speedup.

Based on the image-set based object classification methods, we present an image-set based collaborative representation method for face recognition in videos. We use collaborative representation method to get the outputs of different sizes of sub image sets, and obtain the final result by optimally combining these outputs. Experimental results on databases demonstrate that our image-set based collaborative representation method can be able to achieve a more robust recognition rate than the other leading methods.

The remainder of this paper is organized as follows: in Sect. 2, we introduce the related work on video base face recognition, in Sect. 3, the proposed SCSC method is introduced in details, the experimental results are mentioned to verify the proposed method in Sect. 4, and in Sect. 5 we summarize this paper and give the conclusion.

2 Related Work

Existing classification methods using image sets in different ways in which they model the sets and compute distances between them. Fitzgibbon and Zisserman [12] use image sets to recognize the principal characters in movies. They model faces detected in contiguous frames as affine subspaces in feature space, and then use Joint Manifold Distance (JMD) to measure distances between these, they apply a JMD-based clustering algorithm to discover the principal cast of the movie in the end. Another approach [11] is to fit a parametric distribution function to each image set, and then use Kullback-Leibler divergence to measure the similarity between the distributions.

However, as noted in [13], these image-set based methods must solve a difficult parameter estimation problem, for they are not very robust when the test sets have only weak statistical relationships to the training ones, and large set size may be needed to approximate the distribution functions accurately. Hu et al. [9] proposed that each of the two points should be approximated by a sparse combination from the samples of the respective sets. They argued that the sparse approximated nearest points (SANP) will lie close to some facet of the affine hull and hence, implicitly incorporate structural information of the sets as well.

There are also many methods that seek to build nonlinear approximations of the manifold of face appearances, the typical method is embedding a local linearity feature within a globally nonlinear model. This idea has been used widely in both descriptor dimensionality reduction and single-image face recognition [14,15].

Recently, [13,16] used approaches of mainfold for image set based face recognition. Fan and Yeung [16] use hierarchical clustering to discover local structures, approximate each local structure with a linear (not affine) subspace, quantify similarities between subspaces using canonical angles, and finally measure similarities between face image sets by combining these local similarities using majority voting. Wang et al. [13] proposed Manifold-Manifold Distance (MMD) which clustered each image set into multiple linear local models and represented each model by a linear subspace. The similarity between two sets was defined as the canonical correlation between the nearest local models. In addition, the nearest point distance was also combined with the structural similarity to calculate the final similarity between two sets. Wang et al. [17] presents a novel discriminative learning method, called Manifold Discriminant Analysis (MDA), to solve the problem of image set classification. By modeling each image set as a manifold, they formulate the problem as classification-oriented multi-manifolds learning. Aiming at maximizing the margin of manifold, MDA seeks to learn an embedding space, where the manifolds with different class labels are better separated, and the local data compactness within each manifold is enhanced.

Meanwhile, the deep learning becomes the research hot spot in recently, There are some work on video based face recognition by deep learning. Tang et al. [18] using deep learning method which could achieves 99.47% face verification accuracy on Labeled Faces in the Wild (LFW), higher than human performance. The deep learning based method gets excellent performance in pattern recognition. However, the deep learning method is not suitable for video based face recognition because of the nearly real-time processing speed requirement.

3   Image-Set Based on Collaborative Representation Based Classification (SCSC)

3.1   Collaborative Representation

Zhang et al. [19] proposed to use the regularized least square model for collaborative representation based classification (CRC) of face images. In this paper, we introduce the CRC method first and promote it to be SCSC in Sect. 3.2.

Given a set of training samples, denoted by $X_k \in \Re^{m \times n_k}$ the dataset of the k-th class, and each column of X_k is a sample of class k. Suppose that we have c classes of subjects, and let $X = [X_1, X_2, ..., X_c]$. Given a query sample y, the collaborative representation of it is

$$\hat{a} = \arg \min_{\rho} \{ ||y - Xa||^2 + \lambda ||a||_2^2 \} \tag{1}$$

The solution of CRC is

$$\hat{a} = (X^T X + \lambda \cdot I)^{-1} X^T y \tag{2}$$

The classification of CRC is performed by checking which class yields the minimal regularized reconstruction error. The recognition output of the query sample y is

$$Indentity(y) = \arg \min k\{r_k\} \tag{3}$$

where

$$r_k = \frac{||y - X_k \hat{a}_k||}{||\hat{a}_k||_2}, \hat{a} = [\hat{a}_1; \hat{a}_2; ...; \hat{a}_c] \tag{4}$$

3.2   Image-Set Based on CRC (SCSC)

But the CRC method has limitation, when the linear system determined by dictionary X is under-determined, the linear representation of the query sample over X can be very accurate while regularization on $\hat{a}$ is necessary for a unique and stable solution [20]. Once the available samples per subject are very limited,

CRC may fail because the linear representation of the query sample y may not be accurate. Therefore, the CRC method could not get satisfying results because the distribution of face samples in video is not linear.

In order to alleviate the problem of CRC and extend the CRC to video based face recognition, we proposed an image-set based CRC method name SCRC. Therefore, In this paper, we compare our proposed SCRC with other some state-of-the-art algorithms except CRC, because CRC would fail when the available samples is not enough. Figure 1 gives the pipeline of SCRC.

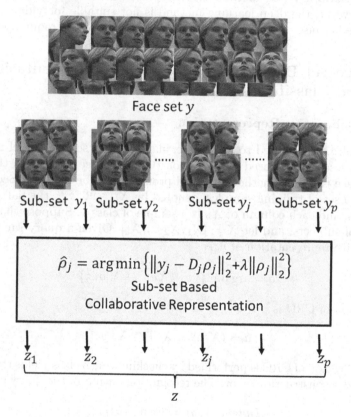

Face set y

Sub-set y_1 Sub-set y_2 Sub-set y_j Sub-set y_p

$$\hat{\rho}_j = \arg\min\left\{\|y_j - D_j\rho_j\|_2^2 + \lambda\|\rho_j\|_2^2\right\}$$

Sub-set Based
Collaborative Representation

z_1 z_2 z_j z_p

z

Fig. 1. Image-set based CRC (SCRC)

As shown in Fig. 1, the SCRC could be divided to be three parts. We will introduce the three steps of SCRC in details in the below.

Firstly, the query image set y is divided into many sub sets $\{y_1, y_2, ..., y_q\}$.

Secondly, the sub set y_j is represented over the local dictionary D_j , which is extracted from the training samples X at the corresponding set y_j, since the linear system determined by local dictionary D_j tends to be under-determined.

Finally, plurality or linear weighted combination method can be applied to the many set based recognition outputs for a final classification. For each face image, the local features such as LBP and Gabor features can be used in image-set based CRC.

Considering that the focus of this paper is to validate the effectiveness of the proposed SCRC strategy instead of local features, for simplicity and clarity the raw gray value features in each patch are used. For patch y_j, its representation over D_j is obtained by Eq. 5.

$$\hat{\rho}_j = \arg\min\{\|y_j - D_j\rho_j\|_2^2 + \lambda\|\rho_j\|_2^2\} \tag{5}$$

D_j is a local dictionary, denoted by D_{jk} the sub-dictionary of the k−th class, and each column of D_{jk} is a patch of class k. Then $D_j = [D_{j1}, D_{j2}, ..., D_{jc}]$. The recognition output z_j of patch y_j is

$$Identity(y_j) = \arg\min_k(r_{jk}) \tag{6}$$

where

$$r_{jk} = \frac{\|y_j - D_{jk} \cdot \hat{\rho}_{jk}\|_2}{\|\hat{\rho}_{jk}\|_2} \tag{7}$$

and $\hat{\rho}_j = [\hat{\rho}_{j1}, \hat{\rho}_{j2}, ..., \hat{\rho}_{jc}]$.

The classification outputs of all patches can then be combined together. Majority voting [15], linear weighted combination [12], kernel plurality [14] and probabilistic model [13] could be employed to combine them. As shown in [15,17], the weighted combination may lead to little improvement compared to the simple majority voting. Therefore, we use the majority voting for the final decision making to fusion the recognition result of sub sets $\{y_1, y_2, ..., y_q\}$.

4   Experimental Analysis

In order to evaluate the proposed algorithm, we have performed our proposed methods on three standard video face databases. The algorithm of Viola and Jones [21] is used to acquire the face region from the video frame. Then, Camshift [22] is employed for face tracking and the face region is clipped from each frame. Finally, we resize the detected face image patch to 32×32 pixels. The proposed algorithm is compared with some state-of-the-art algorithms for recognition rate performance and execution time complexity. We evaluate the computational cost of our method and some state-of-the-art algorithms on an Intel Core (TM) i5 2.53 GHz processor and Matlab platform for all the experiments.

4.1   Dataset Details

In this paper, YouTube celebrity database [23], Honda/UCSD Video database [24] and CMU MoBo dataset were used to test the performance of our method and some state-of-the-art ones.

The YouTube celebrity database [23] includes video clips of 47 celebrities, mostly actors/actresses and politicians, from YouTube. Most of the videos in the database are recorded at high compression rates, which leads to noisy and low resolution image frames. Some sample frames in the YouTube datasets are shown in Fig. 2. [23] manually segmented the clips into homogeneous sequences where the celebrity of interest does appear. There are about 1910 video clips in the database, each subject has about a range of 30 to 100 clips, and the frames' sizes range from (180 × 40) to (240 × 20). This database is challenging for face trackers and recognizers as the videos exhibit large variations in face pose, illumination, occlusion, expression, and other factors.

The Honda/UCSD Video database [24] includes 20 individuals moving their heads with different combinations of 2-D and 3-D rotation, expressions and speed. Some face samples in the Honda/UCSD database are shown in Fig. 2. This database comprises a training video for each of the 20 individuals and another set of 39 test videos. The resolution of each video sequence is 640 × 480. we can see that the face region scale changes in size and the shifting of head is large, even we can only see the top of the head or the chin in some frames.

The CMU MoBo dataset contains 96 video sequences of 25 individuals walking on a treadmill in the CMU 3D room. The subjects perform four different walk patterns: slow walk, fast walk, inclined walk and walking with a ball. All subjects are captured using by six high resolution color cameras distributed evenly around the treadmill. Some face sample frames in the CMU MoBo dataset are shown in Fig. 2.

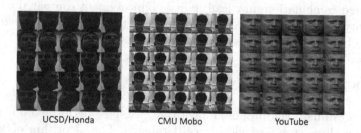

UCSD/Honda   CMU Mobo   YouTube

Fig. 2. Face samples in UCSD/Honda datasets, CMU Mobo datasets and YouTube datasets

4.2   Recognition Based on SCRC

The first experiment is conducted in order to evaluate the performance of our proposed SCRC method. Figure 3 shows the recognition accuracy based on SCRC using different numbers of training samples on CMU Mobo, Honda/UCSD database and YouTube database. From the experimental results, we can see that when the size of sub set is 9 (include 9 face images), increasing the training samples will raise the recognition rate.

Figure 4 shows the recognition accuracy based on SCRC using different sizes of subsets. As we can see during the growing of the size of a subset, the recognition rates are getting higher and higher. This is because that the larger the

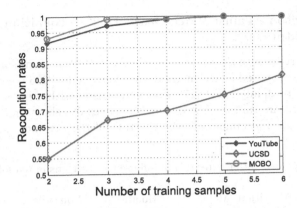

Fig. 3. Recognition accuracy based on SCRC using different numbers of training samples

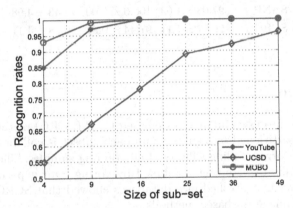

Fig. 4. Recognition accuracy based on SCRC using different sizes of subset

size of the subset contains much more identity information. We also analyze the reasons why we do not obtain a high recognition rate in the UCSD/Honda database. That is because we randomly select some face images in the set to build a subset, and the faces in UCSD/Honda database have more significant pose variation than the those in other two databases. A face in one subset may be entirely different from faces in several other subsets, which reduces our recognition rate. Nevertheless, we build a subset of size 49 (a subset includes 49 face images, because we could detection enough face samples from video), and use two subsets as training samples, and 8 other subsets as test samples. We obtain a 96% recognition rate on the UCSD/Honda database.

If we expand the subset as some state-of-the-art methods: for each subject in the dataset, frames of one object's face in the training video are used for training, and the remaining face frames in video sequences for testing, we can also get 99% to 100% recognition rate on the UCSD/Honda database.

4.3   Comparison Against Video-Based Face Recognition Approaches in Literatures

To allow comparison with the previous methods, we followed the same protocol as used by [9]. The proposed SCRC method was compared with 3 recent algorithms: SANP [9], MMD [13] and MDA [17]. The comparison with other state-of-the-art methods is shown in Table 1. The experimental results show that our proposed methods outperform a number of existing state-of-the-art ones.

Table 1. Average recognition rates (%) of different algorithms in ten fold experiments

Algorithm	Mobo	Honda	YouTube
MMD	89.72 ± 3.48	94.87 ± 1.16	85.72 ± 8.29
MDA	95.97 ± 1.90	88.89 ± 0.91	80.50 ± 6.81
SANP	97.08 ± 1.03	100.0 ± 0.00	72.43 ± 4.98
SCRC	96.07 ± 1.11	97.44 ± 0.87	90.68 ± 4.11

5   Conclusion

In this paper we proposed an image-set based CRC (SCRC) method. The query image set was partitioned into sub set and each subset is collaboratively represented over the corresponding subsets of all training samples. The classification outputs of all subsets were then combined by voting. Our experimental results on controlled and uncontrolled face databases showed that SCRC outperforms state-of-the-art image set based methods.

Acknowledgements. This work is supported by The National Natural Science Foundation of China (No. 61602472, No.U1636217), The National Key Research and Development Program of China (NO. 2016YFB0801200).

References

1. Chellappa, R., Wilson, C., Sirohey, S.: Human and machine recognition of faces: a survey. Proc. IEEE **83**(5), 705–741 (1995)
2. Zhao, W., Chellappa, R., Phillips, P., Rosenfeld, A.: Face recognition: a literature survey. ACM Comput. Surv. **35**(4), 399–458 (2003)
3. Arandjelović, O., Cipolla, R.: Achieving robust face recognition from video by combining a weak photometric model and a learnt generic face invariant. Pattern Recognit. **46**, 9–23 (2013)
4. Nasrollahi, K., Moeslund, T.: Complete face logs for video sequences using face quality measures. IET Signal Process. **3**(4), 289–300 (2009)
5. Lin, J., Ming, J., Crookes, D.: Robust face recognition with partial occlusion, illumination variation and limited training data by optimal feature selection. IET Comput. Vis. **5**(1), 23–32 (2011)

6. Matta, F., Dugelay, J.: Person recognition using facial video information: a state of the art. J. Vis. Lang. Comput. **20**(3), 180–187 (2009)
7. Arandjelovic, O., Shakhnarovich, G., Fisher, J., Cipolla, R., Darrell, T.: Face recognition with image sets using manifold density divergence. In: Proceedings of CVPR, vol. 1, pp. 581–588. IEEE (2005)
8. Cevikalp, H., Triggs, B.: Face recognition based on image sets. In: Proceedings of CVPR, pp. 2567–2573. IEEE (2010)
9. Hu, Y., Mian, A.S., Owens, R.: Face recognition using sparse approximated nearest points between image sets. IEEE Trans. Pattern Anal. Mach. Intell. **34**(10), 1992–2004 (2012)
10. Kim, T.-K., Kittler, J., Cipolla, R.: Discriminative learning and recognition of image set classes using canonical correlations. IEEE Trans. Pattern Anal. Mach. Intell. **29**(6), 1005–1018 (2007)
11. Shakhnarovich, G., Fisher, J.W., Darrell, T.: Face recognition from long-term observations. In: Heyden, A., Sparr, G., Nielsen, M., Johansen, P. (eds.) ECCV 2002. LNCS, vol. 2352, pp. 851–865. Springer, Heidelberg (2002). https://doi.org/10.1007/3-540-47977-5_56
12. Fitzgibbon, A.W., Zisserman, A.: Joint manifold distance: a new approach to appearance based clustering. In: Proceedings of CVPR, vol. 1, pp. I-26. IEEE (2003)
13. Wang, R., Shan, S., Chen, X., Gao, W.: Manifold-manifold distance with application to face recognition based on image set. In: Proceedings of CVPR, pp. 1–8. IEEE (2008)
14. Roweis, S.T., Saul, L.K.: Nonlinear dimensionality reduction by locally linear embedding. Science **290**(5500), 2323–2326 (2000)
15. Hinton, G.E., Dayan, P., Revow, M.: Modeling the manifolds of images of handwritten digits. IEEE Trans. Neural Netw. **8**(1), 65–74 (1997)
16. Fan, W., Yeung, D.-Y.: Locally linear models on face appearance manifolds with application to dual-subspace based classification. In: Proceedings of CVPR, vol. 2, pp. 1384–1390. IEEE (2006)
17. Wang, R., Chen, X.: Manifold discriminant analysis. In: IEEE Conference on Computer Vision and Pattern Recognition CVPR 2009, pp. 429–436. IEEE (2009)
18. Sun, X.T.Y., Wang, X.: Deeply learned face representations are sparse, selective, and robust. In: Proceedings of CVPR, pp. 2892–2900. IEEE (2015)
19. Zhang, D., Yang, M., Feng, X.: Sparse representation or collaborative representation: which helps face recognition? In: Proceedings of ICCV, pp. 471–478. IEEE (2011)
20. Wright, J., Ganesh, A., Yang, A., Zhou, Z., Ma, Y.: Sparsity and robustness in face recognition. arXiv preprint arXiv:1111.1014 (2011)
21. Viola, P., Jones, M.: Rapid object detection using a boosted cascade of simple features. In: Proceedings of CVPR, p. 511. IEEE, USA (2001)
22. Carnegie, R.C.: Mean-shift blob tracking through scale space. In: CVPR, vol. 2, pp. 234–240 (2003)
23. Kim, M., Kumar, S., Pavlovic, V., Rowley, H.: Face tracking and recognition with visual constraints in real-world videos. In: Proceedings of CVPR, pp. 1–8 (2008)
24. Lee, K., Ho, J., Yang, M., Kriegman, D.: Video-based face recognition using probabilistic appearance manifolds. In: Proceedings of CVPR, vol. 1, pp. I-313. IEEE (2003)

Vectorized Data Combination and Binary Search Oriented Reweight for CPU-GPU Based Real-Time 3D Ball Tracking

Ziwei Deng$^{(\boxtimes)}$, Yilin Hou, Xina Cheng, and Takeshi Ikenaga

Graduate School of Information, Production and Systems, Waseda University,
Kitakyushu, Japan
vivideng@toki.waseda.jp

Abstract. 3D ball tracking is of great significance to sports analysis, which can be utilized to applications such as TV contents and tactic analysis. Some applications require real-time implementation, but a highly accurate tracking algorithm is usually time-consuming. This paper proposes a CPU-GPU platform based particle filter for multi-view ball tracking, including 2 proposals: vectorized mask data combination and binary search oriented reweight. The vectorized masks data combination unites HSV mask and inter-frame subtraction mask into one to reduce memory access time. The binary search oriented reweight helps getting and saving reweighted data with low complexity which could directly be used for binary search. The proposed methods are evaluated by both tracking accuracy and execution time. Experiment is based on GPU, the AMD R9 Fury, and compared to the serial implementation on CPU. The tracking accuracy keeps the same, while the execution time is reduced by a factor of 13.

Keywords: GPU acceleration · Heterogeneous computing · OpenCL
Particle filter · 3D ball tracking · Sports analysis

1 Introduction

In sports analysis field, 3D ball tracking plays a crucial role which can obtain the ball's position, velocity and trajectory for applications such as TV contents and tactic analysis. However, to meet with the high tracking accuracy, the algorithms usually carry a heavy computation complexity, increasing the difficulty in real-time implementation. Therefore, our research aims at implementing a 3D ball tracking algorithm to obtain both high accuracy and real time.

Due to the development of computer vision and heterogeneous computing, real-time tracking has shown its importance and value for various utilization. Some 3D tracking works only achieves real-time under some certain situation or time costing would floats violently [1]. And another prevailed tracking algorithm KLT tracks target by feature detection [2]. However, when it comes to 3D ball

© Springer International Publishing AG, part of Springer Nature 2018
B. Zeng et al. (Eds.): PCM 2017, LNCS 10736, pp. 508–516, 2018.
https://doi.org/10.1007/978-3-319-77383-4_50

tracking, the complex circumstances and uncertainties during competition would cause numerous noises. What's more, the target ball is lack in feature point. Thus, we choose to implement multi-view 3D ball tracking by particle filter [3] to access real time, which mostly satisfies our demand.

The chosen algorithm [3] of 3D ball tracking by particle filter achieves a highly accurate tracking result, with 99.14% success rate based on sets of volleyball sequences. The frame work of [3] is shown in Fig. 1. On CPU, the calculation of each particles are processing sequentially, while the observation process which includes color likelihood and foreground likelihood calculation would iterate several times for processing every camera views. Thus, it's difficult to reach real-time tracking only based on a normal CPU.

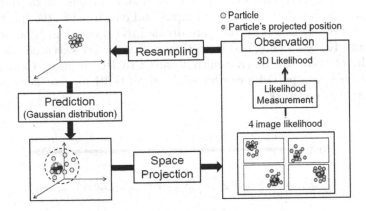

Fig. 1. Framework of the target 3D ball tracking algorithm

However, the heterogeneous computing makes it possible to become real time. More people are focusing on heterogeneous platforms developing recently since the prevailing of dependent processors. By assigning sections of one system in befitting devices, the system would present the optimum performance to users. Thus, heterogeneous platforms are now disseminating in computer science fields especially in computer vision. For 3D ball tracking algorithm, using a CPU-GPU platform is an affordable and reasonable choice.

The conventional work [4] also implemented a particle filter based 3D ball tracking on a CPU-GPU platform, but their solution in resampling could be affected by particle count severely since the compute complexity $O(\sqrt{N})$ is still high. And the optimization of image processing such as convert color(RGB to HSV) and inter-frame subtraction are not considered. Two proposals are presented in our work to solve these problems.

The main contribution of our work is a GPU-accelerated particle filter for multi-view 3D ball tracking. The multiple command queues are arranged to fully parallel the different tasks in the program that have no data dependency. The vectorized masks data combination is applied in observation model, fully utilized resources and reduces time cost in memory access. The binary search oriented reweight decreases the computation complexity upon data dependency, which will be no longer affected significantly by particle count.

This paper is arranged as follows. Sections 2 and 3 cover the detail of the implementation of 3D ball tracking algorithm. The experiment and the conclusion are in Sects. 4 and 5.

2   3D Ball Tracking Framework

The framework of the chosen tracking algorithm [3] is shown in Fig. 1, which consists of prediction, projection, observation and resampling parts. This work is based on 4 views' synchronous videos, so that there're 4 images in the observation space. Apart from initialization, video input and output, the other parts can be implemented on GPU. Five kernels are divided: K1.prediction, K2.observation, K3.reweight, K4.resampling and K5.cvtmask. Kernels are executed inside GPU and results of them can be transmitted back to CPU in array. Generally, the parallelism between particles can be achieved on GPU in most kernels, except for K5 kernel in our work.

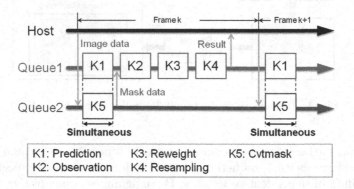

Fig. 2. Framework of CPU-GPU implementation

In the K1.prediction kernel, there're mainly 2 aspects: random number generator and space projection. The particles' 3D position $(P_{x_k}, P_{y_k}, P_{z_k})$ is predicted with Gaussian system noise, so that 3 Gaussian random numbers are needed for each particle to specify 3 dimensions. What's more, a uniformErandom number is required for each particle in resampling part, so that one more random number is generated here and transmitted to the resampling kernel by using Pipes [5]. After that, the 3D positions are projected to 2D space for likelihood evaluation based on images of 4 views.

Likelihood is calculated for each particles in the K2.observation kernel, while it is based on the image masks generated in K5.cvtmask kernel. In the K2, the global size (thread count) is enlarged to 4 times of particle count in order to parallel the likelihood calculation of 4 views. The color likelihood and moving likelihood are calculated based on the data of the masks. In order to reduce time cost in memory access in these 2 kernels, vector data type is utilized, which will be described in detail in Sect. 3.

In the K3.reweight kernel, the weight of each particle is normalized based on its likelihood, and the cumulative distribution function (CDF) is calculated for particle selection of resampling part. The calculation of CDF is data dependent between each thread, so that the binary search oriented reweight is proposed to improve performance.

The K4.resampling kernel is to select particles based on binary search and estimate the 3D position and velocity results based on the selected particles' position and their weight. After finishing this kernel, the 3D position and velocity results are transmitted to CPU for video output.

The framework of our implementation within multiple command queues are arranged as Fig. 2 shows. While there is data dependency between K2 and K5, and K1-K4 can only be processed sequentially, 2 command queues are declared to access task parallelism to some extent. The first command queue involves K1, K2, K3 and K4 and the other one includes K5 only. In CPU-GPU implementation, these two command queues can operate simultaneously.

3   Proposals

3.1   Vectorized Mask Data Combination

A vector of type *vecn* has n components of type *vec*; that is, a vector is a fixed-length collection of scalar data elements. The vector data can be directly mapped to the hardware vector registers, which allows some space to improve performance in the part with plenty of memory access, such as the K5.cvtmask and K2.observation kernel.

As [6] describes, there're 2 similar approaches of vector data usage: *inter-vdt* and *intra-vdt*. In our case, we utilize the *intra-vdt*, which is to vectorize the work performed by one work item (thread).

Firstly, in the K5.cvtmask kernel, the input 1080p images of 4 views are transmitted from CPU to GPU memory. Because of the type of input images is RGB which has 3 channels, we choose to use *vload3()* [5] function to read vectors from the memory. In this way, the coalesced memory access [7] can be achieved, which is the most important performance consideration in programming to reduce the time cost of memory access.

What's more, when storing the mask results, vector data can be utilized to combine both HSV mask and inter-frame subtraction mask together. Knowing that any 3-component vector data has the same alignment and size as the 4-component vector data, the usage of *uchar3* to store HSV mask has 1 component space wasted. Therefore, we combine the inter-frame subtraction mask together with the HSV mask to store in a *uchar4* mask data buffer, which can fully utilize the allocated memory. After the K5, the K2.observation kernel will load the mask data buffer for color likelihood and moving likelihood calculation, which is based on the same region of interest for each particle. Thus, the combined mask data can reduce the data loading time in the K2.

Compared with using scalar buffer, the vector buffer suggests a faster memory access. The detail results will be shown in Sect. 4.

3.2 Binary Search Oriented Reweight

Reweight and resampling kernels include all data dependency in the chosen algorithm. At the core of most standard schemes is a cumulative sum of weights. Binary search oriented reweight decreases time consumption by avoid cumulative distribution function(CDF) calculation.

After observation, each particle gets it's likelihood in current frame. Their weight is normalized as below:

$$W_k^{(i)} = \frac{L(\mathbb{X}_k^{(i)})}{\sum_{i=0}^{N}(L(\mathbb{X}_k^{(i)}))} \tag{1}$$

In general work, summations of particles' weight according to formula composed a CDF from 0 to 1:

$$C_k^{(l)} = \frac{\sum_{i=0}^{l}(W_k^{(i)})}{\sum_{i=0}^{N}(W_k^{(i)})} \tag{2}$$

It should be informed that $W_k^{(i)}$ stands for the weight of particle i while $L(\mathbb{X}_k^{(i)})$ is the likelihood of it. $C_k^{(l)}$ is the cumulated weight with the total number of particles N. This function could be used for selection by comparing with random number. Some work proposed methods to decrease the complexity of building this function [4], while time consumption still floats violently while particle count changes. As Fig. 3 shows, the proposed reweight method seems to be similar with reduction, which takes a group of data and reduce it to a single element. What's different is that we not only obtain the total summation value, but also the value that can be used for binary search in the next kernel. The final saved value of each thread is highlighted as Fig. 3 shows. By storing data like this, the calculation for $C_k^{(l)}$ can be replaced, so that the data dependency is reduced. With the summation saving in the last thread, normalized weight $W_k^{(i)}$ of each thread could be easily received.

In the beginning of resampling, one random number is needed for one particle's selection. With the saved value of different summed level, binary search becomes operable. In this example, the first step of selection starts from thread 7, then the compared index goes to thread 3 or thread 11 according to the first step's result. With the generated random number comparing to values from higher level to lower, selected index of one particle can be achieved readily.

The number of steps of binary searching oriented reweight is $O(\log N)$, and process for each particle is equivalent. Thus, processing time won't alter intensively while particle number changes. The concrete effectiveness of this work will be introduced in Sect. 4.

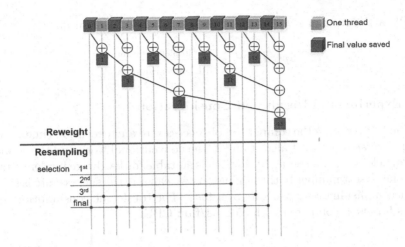

Fig. 3. An example of proposed binary search oriented reweight with 16 threads

4   Experiment

Heterogeneous platform was used to implement the acceleration of the whole algorithm. The experiment was based on GPU, the AMD R9 Fury, and compared to the conventional work [4] and the serial implementation based on the Intel i7-6700K, 4 GHz, CPU. The program was written by OpenCL C language.

4.1   Dataset and Evaluation Method

Videos used for the experiment is of an official volleyball match (2014 Inter High School Games of MenEs Volleyball held in Tokyo Metropolitan Gymnasium in Aug. 2014). For each sequence, synchronous videos taken from 4 cameras located at corners of the court were applied. Resolution of the videos is 1920×1080 and the frame rate is 60fps. Camera's shutter speed is 1000 per second to ensure that there is less blur in videos.

Tracking accuracy evaluation method is same as Cheng's [3]. A definition of HIT was given, which presents a period between two consecutive ball hitting. When the ball is tracked continuously in one HIT, it's considered as success HIT. Success rate is calculated as below:

$$Success\ rate = \frac{\sum Success\ HIT}{\sum HIT} \times 100\% \tag{3}$$

For acceleration evaluation method, the time consumption T is considered as the main measurement. Speedup can be calculated based on the equation below. The time consumption of data transmission between CPU and GPU, and GPU kernel execution time are included, while initialization, reading image from files on CPU and outputting videos parts are not in our consideration.

$$Speedup = \frac{T_{\text{CPU implementation}}}{T_{\text{GPU implementation}}} \qquad (4)$$

4.2 Experimental Result and Consideration

In Table 1, it presents the comparison of success rate and execution time between the CPU version of target algorithm [3], the conventional work and the proposed one. Particle count was set as 1024 which is suitable for hardware implementation and is the closest number to the original. As we can see, the success rate is similar, both accomplishing a success rate over 99%. The total time consumption of our work is 5.7 ms/f, compared with 75.1 ms/f on CPU.

Table 1. Evaluation of execution time.

1024 particles	CPU version	Conventional work	Proposed version
Success HIT	688	689	689
Success rate	99.14%	99.23%	99.23%
Execution time	75.1 ms/f	11.7 ms/f	5.7 ms/f

However, when the algorithm is applied to different ball tracking, such as ping-pong and tennis, larger particle count may be needed for obtaining high accuracy. Thus, we also analyzed the speedup changing with the particle count, from 1024 to 16384.

In the Figs. 4 and 5, the proposed methods were evaluated separately, combined with comparisons with conventional work [4] and other trial version. The Fig. 4 shows that the performance improvement by vectorized mask data combination is relatively high compared with the scalar version. The Fig. 5 presents that our work obtain a large performance promotion by applying binary search

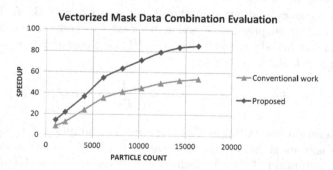

Fig. 4. Evaluation of P1.Vectorized Mask Data Combination, considering the time of K2.observation and K5.cvtmask.

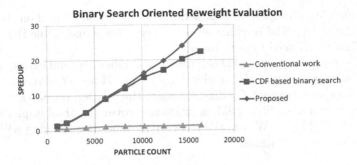

Fig. 5. Evaluation of P2.Binary Search Oriented Reweight, considering the time of K3.reweight and K4.resampling.

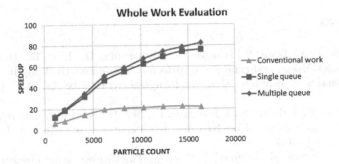

Fig. 6. Evaluation of whole work

in resampling compared with conventional work, while the binary search oriented reweight also has small improvement compared with calculating CDF by $work\_group\_inclusive\_add()$ function [5].

The Fig. 6 shows the speedup of our whole work with different particle count. With the increasing of the particle count, the speedup is more considerable and the time cost doesn't increase too much. For example, for 16384 particles, the time cost is $10.7\,\text{ms/f}$, which can also be real-time based on 60fps videos. Therefore, our work has space for development for different tracking algorithm based on particle filter.

5   Conclusion

This work presents an implementation of a multi-view 3D ball tracking algorithm by particle filter on a CPU-GPU platform. The framework is built in multiple command queues, obtaining a task parallelism between some kernels. The vectorized masks data combination unites HSV mask and inter-frame subtraction mask into one to reduce memory access time. The binary search oriented reweight helps getting and saving reweighted data with low complexity which could directly be used for binary search. The experiment is based on GPU, the

AMD R9 Fury, and compared to the serial implementation based on the Intel i7-6700K, 4GHz, CPU. The tracking accuracy keeps the same, while the execution time is 5.7 ms/f, reduced by a factor of 13.

For various applications in 3D ball tracking, further demand exists, which will increase the complexity of the tracking algorithm. However, our work remains some space for development for different algorithms based on particle filter.

The further efforts will be paid on tracking recovery method implementation, which is proposed in [3]. Within the recovery method, the tracking will be more robust for complex situations.

Acknowledgments. This work was supported by KAKENHI (16K 13006) and Waseda University Grant for Special Research Projects (2017K-263).

References

1. Newcombe, R.A., Izadi, S., Hilliges, O., Molyneaux, D., Kim, D., Davison, A.J., et al.: KinectFusion: real-time dense surface mapping and tracking. In: 10th IEEE International Symposium on Mixed and Augmented Reality (ISMAR), pp. 127–136 (2011)
2. Al-Najdawi, N., Tedmori, S., Edirisinghe, E., Bez, H.: An automated real-time people tracking system based on KLT features detection. Int. Arab J. Inf. Technol. 9(9), 100–107 (2012)
3. Cheng, X., Honda, M., Ikoma, N., Ikenaga, T.: Anti-occlusion observation model and automatic recovery for multi-view ball tracking in sports analysis. In: 41st IEEE International Conference on Acoustics, Speech and Signal Processing, pp. 1501–1505 (2016)
4. Hou, Y., Cheng, X., Ikenaga, T.: Real-time 3D ball tracking with CPU-GPU acceleration using particle filter with multi-command queues and stepped parallelism iteration. In: 2nd International Conference on Multimedia and Image Processing (ICMIP) (2017)
5. The OpenCL Specification, Khronos OpenCL Working Group. http://www.khronos.org/opencl/
6. Fang, J., Varbanescu, A.L., Liao, X., Sips, H.: Evaluating vector data type usage in OpenCL kernels. Concurr. Comput. Pract. Exp. **27**, 4586–4602 (2014)
7. OpenCL Optimization Guide, Advanced Micro Devices, Inc. http://www.developer.amd.com/tools-and-sdks/opencl-zone/amd-accelerated-parallel-processing-app-sdk/opencl-optimization-guide/

Hot Topic Trend Prediction of Topic Based on Markov Chain and Dynamic Backtracking

Feng Xu[1,2(✉)], Jue Liu[3], Ying He[1,2], and Yating Hou[1,2]

[1] College of Computer Science and Technology,
Nanjing University of Aeronautics and Astronautics, Nanjing, China
nuaaos@163.com
[2] Collaborative Innovation Center of Novel Software Technology
and Industrialization, Nanjing, China
[3] Jinshen College, Nanjing Audit University, Nanjing, China

Abstract. Predicting topic trend in social networks can provide good reference value for public opinion guidance and commercial marketing. In this paper, we discuss the hot topic evaluation methods, and then present a method for evaluating the topic popularity of microblog based on multiple factors, which comprehending four factors (the number of micro blog, number of forwarding, number of comments, and number of praise) and using relative ranking method to define the value of micro blog popularity. In order to improve the prediction accuracy of hot topics, we present a prediction algorithm based on Markov chain and dynamic backtracking, which is based our evaluation method. In the algorithm, we use the simulated annealing method to find the optimal parameters and improve the accuracy of the prediction algorithm based on the Markov chain by historical backtracking. Analysis and simulation results demonstrate that the proposed algorithm is more accurate than some conventional methods.

Keywords: Social network · Markov chain · Trend prediction

1 Introduction

With the rapid development of the Internet in recent years, emerging social networks, such as Twitter, Facebook, and Microblog, have been integrated into people's lives. Social networks have become main tools for a person to obtain and release information. From 2009 so far, Sina Weibo has been a huge impact social media in China and Asia, which has more than 500 million registered users and 300,000 authenticated users. Because microblog has become the main network public opinion, information can spread by microblog in a very short time and become a hot topic. Therefore, predicting hot topics of the microblog can provide a reference for the public relations crisis, help organizations to improve their service, and help companies to promote commercial marketing.

However, microblog and traditional media are different in the communication characteristics. Microblogs have 4A (Anytime, Anywhere, Anyone, Anything) characteristics, so they have higher real-time property than traditional media. In general, a news site needs to review and edit the news, which makes it lag compared with

© Springer International Publishing AG, part of Springer Nature 2018
B. Zeng et al. (Eds.): PCM 2017, LNCS 10736, pp. 517–528, 2018.
https://doi.org/10.1007/978-3-319-77383-4_51

microblog. Furthermore, microblogs also have the characteristics of "we media", which can allow the fast flow of information by the "forward" function. This new type of communication is not only different from the linear transmission of traditional media, but also different from the network transmission of the network media. It is more similar to spread of the virus fission. These characteristics bring about more challenges to predict hot topics.

Prediction on social networks has become a hot research field. Based on the target of prediction, the research work can be divided into two directions: user relationship and topic trend. The researches on user relationship prediction mainly involve friend relationship forecast [1, 2], trust degree forecast [3], influence forecast and user behavior prediction [4] etc. Topic prediction research includes topic popularity prediction [5–8] and topic sentiment prediction [9, 10], topic clustering [11, 12], etc. The researches on topic prediction include the hot topic forecast and the emotion prediction.

In addition, microblogs have other characteristics, including the diversified information, text of trivial and short, and no organization and completely issued by the single user, which is different from traditional network public opinion. The user's attention is limited. When a new hot topic occurs, the old topic may be unnoticed. In previous research, the aim of prediction is absolute (such as the number of forwarding, the number of comments, etc.), but it will be very difficult. Absolute number predictions need to predict the results strictly in the actual trend, but the existing technology is hard to do this. Some algorithms can only predict the partial information. Though evaluation methodology has academic value, it is difficult to apply it in practice. In this paper, we present relative evaluation indicator for ranking. This can avoid the impact of other unknown hot spots in the future. Because the influence is the same as all topics, it will not affect the popularity ranking.

The remaining paper is organized as follows. Section 2 describes related work on social network prediction. In Sect. 3, we propose an evaluation method of hot topics and related features of hot spots. In Sect. 4, we present our IABOM algorithm based on a Markov chain and dynamic backtracking. In Sect. 5, we implement a series of experiments. In Sect. 6, we conclude this paper and address our future research work in Sect. 7.

2   Related Work

In recent years, more and more researchers focus on the social network analysis or prediction problems. The major research objects are Twitter, and Facebook [14, 15] etc. In China, they are Sina Weibo and Weixin [16]. Predicted on social media can be user oriented prediction or topic oriented prediction. The user-oriented prediction focuses on user influence and user's preference. The topic-oriented prediction may be topic popularity or topic polarity. The researches about topic's popularity may be divided into the following several aspects. According to feature extractions, they can be social interaction behavior [17], user and location as features [18, 19], or take the influence of user's leadership as features [20], or take the text as features [20, 21]. On the basis of prediction indicators, there are directly predicting the absolute number of related parameters [20] (such as the number of users, forwarding number, or the total number of interactions, etc.) and predicting the degree of the popularity [22]. There are two main approaches based on the assumption whether or not the change of predicted object is linear. One is the traditional forecasting method, which converts the network public opinion data into time series, then modeled by Linear regression (LR), auto regressive (AR) [23], and autoregressive moving average (ARMA) [22] and other models. This method is simple and easy to implement, but the accuracy is based on the assumption that the transformation in social network is linear. However, it is different from the actual characteristics of social networks, so the prediction results are instable. The other is the nonlinear model, using neural network and other theories, such as Gray model [24], Markov chain [25, 26], support vector machine [22, 27], dynamic probability [28–30], etc. In order to improve the accuracy of prediction, the researchers have proposed some combination optimization model based on optimization theory.

At present, the research on the prediction of the microblog topic trend has become a key research field of the social networks. On basis of time series, Tong et al. propose a new method based on adaptive Auto Regression (AR) model, and the parameter estimation algorithm of this model is referred to as Recursive Weighted Least Square (RWLS) [23]. Han et al. propose a novel time series model for predicting the topic social influence. The model is a hybrid model consisting of topical, social and geographic attributes [17]. Gupta et al. encode the rich Twitter using a rich variety of features from microblog data. They explore regression, classification and hybrid approaches, using a large set of popularity, social and event features, to predict event popularity [21]. In term of machine learning algorithm, in addition to the SVM algorithm [22], Zhou et al. analyze the process of topic discussion, and give the formulation of it. Three main factors (individual interest, group behavior, and time lapse) are analyzed and quantized. Based on these factors, they propose a dynamic probability model to predict the user's behavior, i.e. attending the topic discussion or not, and then obtain the number of the attending users [29]. Wang et al. propose an algorithm to predict topics trend. The principle of Grey Model for prediction application is analyzed and Grey Verhulst Model is established [24]. Bao et al. propose a prediction model based on the structure characteristics of topic, such as early user's connection density and the depth of the spread [16]. According to the microblog texts, Fu et al. build a special corpus, and extract the time feature to predict the local trend of special topics [19].

The above researches have a certain effect, but there are some bottleneck problems in the research field. One is the traditional time series prediction method is too dependent specific data. Traditional time series forecasting methods are based on the assumption of linear change. However, the microblog data do not meet the conditions, so the results of the prediction are not ideal. The other is the forecast target. The absolute forecast is too strict to predict. At present, predicting topic trend of the microblog is still an open issue.

The main contributions of the paper are as follows:

(1) In order to improve the traditional popularity evaluation for a single microblog topic, a multi factors evaluation method of topic popularity is proposed.
(2) In order to improve the relative accuracy in the prediction of hot topics, we propose a prediction model based on Markov chain and dynamic backtracking. The model can improve the accuracy of the forecast by using self-learning technology to amend the parameters.

3　Topic Hot Evaluation Method

Popularity is a measure of the attention degree to a topic from users. According to the microblog's parameters, including forwarding number, number of comments, and praise number, we define several concepts about topic popularity as below.

Definition 1 (topic popularity). According to a topic of all the forwarding number, the number of comments, praise number, a topic popularity is defined as below:

$$Popularity = \varepsilon \times \sum_{j}^{j \in S(T)} \alpha \times j_{retweets} + \beta \times j_{comments} + \delta \times j_{attitudes} + \phi \times S(T) \qquad (1)$$

$Popularity$:　A microblog topic's popularity at the time period T,
$S(T)$:　All topics of the microblog collection at the time period T,
j :　A microblog at the time period T,
ε :　Weight coefficient of S(T),
ϕ :　Weight coefficient of each microblog,
$j_{retweets}$:　Forwarding number of microblog j,
$j_{comments}$:　Comment number of microblog j,
$j_{attitudes}$:　Attitude number of microblog j,
α, β, δ :　Weight coefficient of $j_{retweets}$ $j_{comments}$ $j_{attitudes}$.

Definition 2 (average microblog popularity). The average microblog popularity $AVG_{Popularity}$ is the average popularity of all time periods.

Definition 3 (microblog popularity change value). The microblog popularity change value $count_i$ is that the change value of the microblog popularity from the unit time i to unit time $i + 1$. Let $count_i = (Popularity_{i+1} - Popularity_i)$.
　　The $count$ is an absolute value to make a judgment for topics' trend.

Definition 4 (microblog popularity change rate). The microblog popularity change rate s is that the change value of the microblog popularity from the unit time i to unit time $i + 1$. Let $s_i = (Popularity_{i+1} - Popularity_i)/Popularity_i$.
　　The s is a relative value to make a judgment for topics' trend.

4　Prediction Algorithm Based on Markov Chain and Dynamic Backtracking

4.1　Parameter Optimization

In order to ensure the accuracy of the parameters in the prediction algorithm, we use the simulated annealing algorithm to optimization parameters
　　The parameter *up_factor* represents a rising factor, which can adjust the rising speed of the microblog popularity in the prediction process. The parameter *attenuation_factor*

represents an attenuation factor, which can adjust the falling speed of the microblog popularity in the prediction process.

Basic idea of simulated annealing is as follows:

(1) Initialization: Let T be the initial temperature, S be the initial solution state (the starting point of the iterative algorithm), an L be the iteration number for each T;

(2) For $k = 1, 2 \ldots L$; repeat from the third step to the sixth step;

(3) Create new solutions S';

(4) Calculate the incremental $\Delta t' = C(S') - C(S)$, which $C(S)$ is evaluation function;

(5) If $\Delta t' < 0$, then accept the current solution S' as new solution, else accept S' as new solution with probability $\exp(-\Delta t'/T)$;

(6) If the termination condition is satisfied, the current solution is an optimal solution (The termination condition is usually taken as a plenty of continuous new solution have not been accepted).

(7) T is gradually reduced, when $T \to 0$, go to step 2.

This data set includes n time segments following the training set. Set C as the modified data set, $C = \{correction_i | 0 < i < t\}$, and we set initial values of the rising factor and the decay factor: $up\_factor = 1.0$, $attenuation\_factor = 1.0$, and evaluation function is $C(S) = log(Ad) + log(Rd)$. Ad is the absolute difference: $Ad = \sum_{i=1}^{t} correction_i - result_i$. Rd is the relative difference: $Rd = \sum_{i=1}^{t} |\frac{(correction_i - result_i)}{correction_i}|$.

4.2   Specific Prediction Algorithm

Prediction based on Markov chain

According to the current situation of the topic to predict the changes in the future, these time and states are all discrete Markov processes known as Markov chain, denoted as $X_n = X(n), n = 0, 1, 2, \ldots$.

The Markov chain is a sequence of random variables $X_1, X_2, X_3 \ldots$. The X_{n+1}'s conditional probability distribution of the past state is only a function of the X_n:

$$P(X_{n+1} = x | X_0, X_1, X_2, \ldots, X_n) = P(X_{n+1} = x | X_n) \tag{2}$$

Improvement based on dynamic backtracking

(a) *Status improvement*

It is difficult to convert the continuous real popularity into discrete states. Some researchers divide topic popularity into n status through the degree of rising and falling in Markov Chains. But this prediction is more close to the idea of clustering, which can't actually consider the real popularity. In this paper, we choose to abstract the topic's states, and just set only two kinds of states: rising state and falling state. Then we determine the probability of rising and falling according the training set the variation range with recent changes in microblog. By analyzing and comparing the two kinds of situations, we complete prediction of the topic popularity trend.

We set the topic's state set $S = \{state_+, state_-\}$, $state_+$: topic popularity in the next period is a rising period; $state_-$: topic popularity in the next period is a falling period. According to Chapter 3, we get the change probability set $P = (p_{++}, p_{+-}, p_{-+}, p_{--})$. The state transition is shown in Fig. 1.

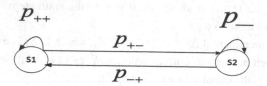

Fig. 1. States transition diagram

(b) *Realization of prediction*

The prediction formula based on Markov chain is shown as follow.

$$predict\_value = front\_value + up + down \tag{3}$$

In the above formula, the *front_value* is the microblog popularity in the previous time unit. The parameter *up* is the rising value. The parameter *down* is the down value. These parameters can be calculated by the following formula.

$$up = up\_factor \times value \times p_+ \times compare_+ \tag{4}$$

$$down = attenuation\_factor \times value \times p_- \times compare_- \tag{5}$$

In the formula 4, p_+ is the probability of the popularity rise, which is obtained by the training set. The *up_factor* is the rising factor, which is obtained by the modified set. The *value* is popularity change value. Based on the classical Markov's theory, if assumes that the popularity of the $n+1$ step is only related to the popularity of the n step, then we can get the following formula.

$$Popularity(t_{n+1}|t_n, t_{n-1}\ldots t_1) = Popularity(t_{n+1}|t_n) \tag{6}$$

But from a practical point of view, there is often more than one step with important impact to the next step when we predict the popularity. The topic popularity of the n+1 step is defined as follow.

$$Popularity(t_{n+1}|t_n, t_{n-1}\ldots t_1) = Popularity(t_{n+1}|t_n, t_{n-1}\ldots t_{n-m+1}) \tag{7}$$

In summary, the final prediction formula is as follows:

$$predict\_value = front\_value + up\_factor \times \frac{\sum_{i=(n-m+1)}^{n} Popularity_i}{m} \times p_+ \times s_+$$

$$\times count_+ + attenuation\_factor \times \frac{\sum_{i=(n-m+1)}^{n} Popularity_i}{m} \times p_- \times s_- \times count_- \qquad (8)$$

5 Experiments

We have collected many popular topics of Sina Weibo, from n April 20, 2014 to May 10, 2014. Then we calculate the popularity of the 6 topics at different times.

In the experiment, we choose T=3 as the prediction time window parameters. In order to evaluate the improved algorithm based on Markov (IABOM), we have compared the existing research work. These work include linear regression model (LR), autoregressive analysis model (AR), and autoregressive integrated sliding average model (ARIM) as traditional prediction methods and support vector machine (SVM) as machine learning prediction model. Through simulation experiments, we get the results of the six topics as shown in Fig. 2.

Through the visual experiment results, we can draw the following conclusions: The algorithm proposed in this paper is close to the actual value, which shows that the algorithm has certain significance in practical application. In comparison with other algorithms, the error of the IABOM algorithm is smaller and the accuracy is better than other algorithms. For the traditional forecasting methods, because they have assumed that the change is linear premise, but the microblog change doesn't accord with this feature. So they have more forecast fluctuations, some predictive value is even negative, which produce a large error.

Figure 3 shows the average relative error of the popularity. In the six topics, IABOM has the lowest error of four, and the error is higher than SVM in other two topics who have a large margin of the "diving" phenomenon. the topic of "civil servants", the popularity fall from 21236.38 to 438.4318 and the topic of "Korean drama" the popularity fall from 43341.75 to 2172.971. There is no way to predict these irregularities from the known characteristics of the topic. So quantity prediction has obvious shortcoming in microblog prediction.

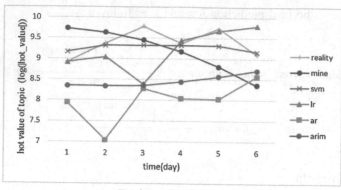

a. Topic1: Housing prices

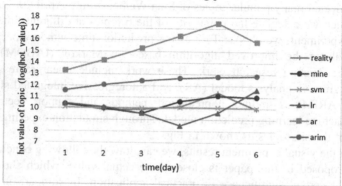

b. Topic2: Civil servants

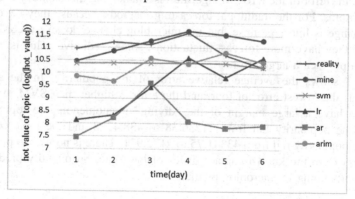

c. Topic3: Korean dramas

Fig. 2. Topic popularity predictive results of the six topics

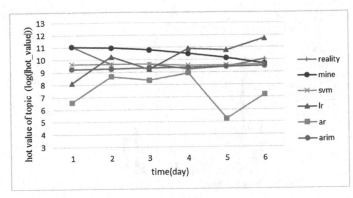

d. Topic4 Hengda

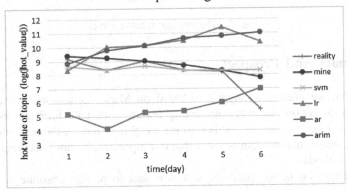

e. Topic5: Rockets

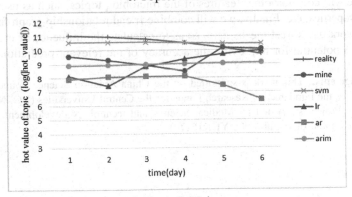

f. Topic6: Meizu

Fig. 2. (*continued*)

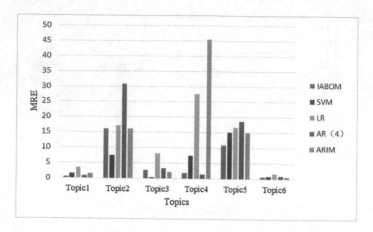

Fig. 3. The average relative error.

6 Summary and Prospect

In this paper, we present an algorithm based on Markov chain and dynamic back-tracking. In the algorithm, when extracting features, we take four factors into consideration, and use a relatively method to set weights to reduce the influence of noise data. The experimentation results show that our algorithm is more accurate than other traditional methods.

But our method is not good for mutation data to predict absolute value. In the future, we will further optimize our work. In order to improve the accuracy of prediction, we will consider other features of the microblog topics, such as user attributes and text properties, etc. Finally, we will combine friend relationship graph features and social network users trust mechanism, so as to calculate the influence of the users and microblog's potential for improving the accuracy of the relevant prediction.

Acknowledgments. This work is supported by the China Aviation Science Foundation (NO. 20101952021), the Fundamental Research Funds for the Central Universities (NO. NZ2013306) and the Key Project supported by Medical Science and technology development foundation, Nanjing Department of Health (NO. YKK15170).

References

1. Hoff, P.D.: Multiplicative latent factor models for description and prediction of social networks. Comput. Math. Organ. Theor. **15**(4), 261–272 (2009)
2. Chen, K.H., Liang, T.J.: Friendship prediction on social network users. In: 2013 International Conference on Social Computing (Social Com), pp. 379–384. IEEE (2013)
3. Borzymek, P., Sydow, M.: Trust and distrust prediction in social network with combined graphical and review-based attributes. In: Jędrzejowicz, P., Nguyen, N.T., Howlet, R.J., Jain, L.C. (eds.) KES-AMSTA 2010. LNCS (LNAI), vol. 6070, pp. 122–131. Springer, Heidelberg (2010). https://doi.org/10.1007/978-3-642-13480-7_14

4. Oentaryo, R.J., Lim, E.P., Lo, D., et al.: Collective churn prediction in social network. In: Proceedings of the 2012 International Conference on Advances in Social Networks Analysis and Mining, ASONAM 2012, pp. 210–214. IEEE Computer Society (2012)

5. Liu, R., Guo, W.: HMM-based state prediction for Internet hot topic. In: 2011 IEEE International Conference on Computer Science and Automation Engineering (CSAE), vol. 1, pp. 157–161. IEEE (2011)

6. Yan, C., Shi, S., Huang, H., et al.: A method for network topic attention forecast based on feature words. In: 2013 International Conference on Asian Language Processing (IALP), pp. 211–214. IEEE (2013)

7. Jiang, P., Zhang, C., Yang, Q., Niu, Z.: Blog opinion retrieval based on topic-opinion mixture model. In: Zaki, Mohammed J., Yu, J.X., Ravindran, B., Pudi, V. (eds.) PAKDD 2010. LNCS (LNAI), vol. 6119, pp. 249–260. Springer, Heidelberg (2010). https://doi.org/10.1007/978-3-642-13672-6_25

8. Zhang, B., Guan, X., Khan, M.J., et al.: A time-varying propagation model of hot topic on BBS sites and blog networks. Inf. Sci. **187**, 15–32 (2012)

9. Wiegand, M., Klakow, D.: Topic-related polarity classification of blog sentences. In: Lopes, L.S., Lau, N., Mariano, P., Rocha, L.M. (eds.) EPIA 2009. LNCS (LNAI), vol. 5816, pp. 658–669. Springer, Heidelberg (2009). https://doi.org/10.1007/978-3-642-04686-5_54

10. Das, D., Bandyopadhyay, S.: Emotions on Bengali blog texts: role of holder and topic. In: 2011 International Conference on Advances in Social Networks Analysis and Mining (ASONAM), pp. 587–592. IEEE (2011)

11. Thi, D.B., Hoang, T.A.N.: Features extraction for link prediction in social networks. In: 2013 13th International Conference on Computational Science and Its Applications (ICCSA), pp. 192–195. IEEE (2013)

12. Hagiwara, K., Takamura, H., Okumura, M.: Constructing blog entry classifiers using blog-level topic labels. In: Cheng, P.-J., Kan, M.-Y., Lam, W., Nakov, P. (eds.) AIRS 2010. LNCS, vol. 6458, pp. 360–369. Springer, Heidelberg (2010). https://doi.org/10.1007/978-3-642-17187-1_35

13. Ruan, Y., Purohit, H., Fuhry, D., et al.: Prediction of topic volume on twitter. In: ACM Web Science, pp. 397–402. ACM (2012)

14. Mathioudakis, M., Koudas, N.: TwitterMonitor: trend detection over the twitter stream. In: Proceedings of the 2010 ACM SIGMOD International Conference on Management of data, pp. 1155–1158. ACM (2010)

15. Pengyi, F., Hui, W., Zhihong, J., et al.: Measurement of microblogging network. J. Comput. Res. Develop. **49**(4), 691–699 (2012)

16. Bao, P., Shen, H.W., Huang, J., et al.: Popularity prediction in microblogging network: a case study on Sina Weibo. In: Proceedings of the 22nd International Conference on World Wide Web Companion, pp. 177–178. International World Wide Web Conferences Steering Committee (2013)

17. Han, Y., Fang, B., Jia, Y.: Predicting the topic influence trends in social media with multiple models. Neurocomputing **144**, 463–470 (2014)

18. Zhao, J., Wu, W., Zhang, X., Qiang, Y., Liu, T., Wu, L.: A short-term prediction model of topic popularity on microblogs. In: Du, D.-Z., Zhang, G. (eds.) COCOON 2013. LNCS, vol. 7936, pp. 759–769. Springer, Heidelberg (2013). https://doi.org/10.1007/978-3-642-38768-5_69

19. Liu, Y., Wang, J., Jiang, Y.: PT-LDA: a latent variable model to predict personality traits of social network users. Neurocomputing **210**, 155–163 (2016)

20. Fu, C., Shaobin, Z., Guangjun, S.: A study on trend prediction in Sina Weibo community. In: 2014 IEEE International Congress on Big Data (Big Data Congress), pp. 364–365. IEEE (2014)

21. Gupta, M., Gao, J., Zhai, C.X., et al.: Predicting future popularity trend of events in microblogging platforms. Proc. Am. Soc. Inf. Sci. Technol. **49**(1), 1–10 (2012)
22. Wang, P., Xu, B.W., Wu, Y.R., et al.: Link prediction in social networks: the state-of-the-art. Sci. China Inf. Sci. **58**(1), 1–38 (2015)
23. Tong, H., Liu, Y., Peng, H., et al.: Internet users' psychosocial attention prediction: web hot topic prediction based on adaptive AR model. In: 2008 International Conference on Computer Science and Information Technology, ICCSIT 2008, pp. 458–462. IEEE (2008)
24. Wang, X., Qi, L., Chen, C., et al.: Grey system theory based prediction for topic trend on Internet. Eng. Appl. Artif. Intell. **29**, 191–200 (2014)
25. Wang, T., Krim, H., Viniotis, Y.: A generalized Markov graph model: application to social network analysis. IEEE J. Selected Topics Sig. Process. **7**(2), 318–332 (2013)
26. Chen, Y., Ying, J.: Modeling community influence in social networks with Markov chains. In: Cloud Computing and Big Data (CloudCom-Asia)
27. Thissen, U., Van Brakel, R., De Weijer, A.P., et al.: Using support vector machines for time series prediction. Chemometr. Intell. Lab. Syst. **69**(1), 35–49 (2003)
28. Li, J., Peng, W., Li, T., et al.: Social network user influence sense-making and dynamics prediction. Exp. Syst. Appl. **41**(11), 5115–5124 (2014)
29. Zhou, Y., Guan, X., Zhang, Z., et al.: Predicting the tendency of topic discussion on the online social networks using a dynamic probability model. In: Proceedings of the Hypertext 2008 Workshop on Collaboration and Collective Intelligence, pp. 7–11. ACM (2008)
30. Ding, H., Wu, J.: Predicting retweet scale using log-normal distribution. In: 2015 IEEE International Conference on Multimedia Big Data, pp. 56–63. IEEE (2015). 2013 IEEE International Conference, pp. 515–520. IEEE

Fast Circular Object Localization and Pose Estimation for Robotic Bin Picking

Linyao Luo[1], Yanfei Luo[2], Hong Lu[1], Haowei Yuan[3], Xuehua Tang[3],
and Wenqiang Zhang[2(✉)]

[1] Shanghai Key Lab of Intelligent Information Processing,
School of Computer Science, Fudan University,
Shanghai, People's Republic of China
[2] Shanghai Engineering Research Center for Video Technology and System,
School of Computer Science, Fudan University,
Shanghai, People's Republic of China
wqzhang@fudan.edu.cn
[3] Shanghai Electric Group CO., LTD. Central Academe, Shanghai, China

Abstract. Detecting and localizing objects in three-dimensional space is essential for robotic manipulation. One practical task is known as "bin-picking", where a robot manipulator picks objects from a bin of parts without any assistance of an operator. For such a task, vision-based object detection and location can be a cost-effective solution. In this paper, we propose a fast and robust approach for picking flanges in a crowd condition. We present a continuous edge detector improved from Canny and a fast ellipse detector based on randomized hough transformation to obtain the outer contours of flange. And then we have implement several picking experiments to verify our proposed approach is fast and robust in practical environment.

Keywords: Bin-picking · Mono vision · Randomized hough transform

1 Introduction

One of the key challenge in highly automated robot-aided manufacturing is the capability to automatically identify and locate parts, thus the robot can grasp and manipulate them in an accurate and reliable way. In general, parts are randomly placed inside a bin or in a conveyor belt, so one needs sophisticated perception systems to identify and precisely locate the searched objects. Usually, this perception task is referred as the "bin-picking" problem, and it has been widely studied in the last decades due to its strong impact in the flexibility and productivity for manufacturing companies.

Vision systems for recognition and localization of objects, based on standard cameras and 2D image analysis, have been widely used in industrial automation for many years. A vision-based recognition system for planar object has been

© Springer International Publishing AG, part of Springer Nature 2018
B. Zeng et al. (Eds.): PCM 2017, LNCS 10736, pp. 529–538, 2018.
https://doi.org/10.1007/978-3-319-77383-4_52

proposed in [1], where a set of invariant features based on geometric primitives of the object boundary are extracted from a single image and matched against a library of invariant features computed from the searched objects models, generating a set of recognition hypothesis. Hypothesis are then merged and verified to reject false recognition hypothesis. In [2], Rahardja and Kosaka presented a stereo vision-based bin-picking system that, starting from a set of model features selected by an operator, search for easy to find "seed" features (usually large holes) to roughly locate the searched objets, and then look for other, usually small, "supporting" features used to disambiguate and refine the localization. In [3], the Generalized Hough Transform (GHT) is used for 3D localization of planar objects, the computational complexity of the GHT is here reduced by uncoupling parameter detection. Shroff et al. [4] presented a vision-based system for specular object detection and pose estimation: authors detect a set of edge features of the specular objects using a multi-flash camera that highlights high curvature regions, a multi-view approach is exploited to compute the pose of the searched object by triangulating the extracted features. An overview of general vision-based object recognition and localization techniques can be found in [5], along with a performance evaluation of many types of visual local descriptors used for 6 DoF pose estimation.

2   Target Location

A large number of industrial parts are almost circular shapes like flanges, thus we will focus on perform an experiment on the flanges. In following sections, we will explain our core algorithms of the mono vision system in several subsection: edge detection, ellipse extraction and pose refinement.

2.1   Edge Detection

Traditional edge detectors like Canny [6], Sobel can extract edge pixels, but meanwhile include much noise. As an object contour is usually continuous, we propose a method of fast continuous edge detection that divides into three steps: compute gradient, find candidate points and extract continuous edges.

The first step is to compute gradient image. The gradient of each pixel is computed as the same algorithm as Canny. However gradient directions are divided into 4 major directions that denote as $C1, C2, C3, C4$, because we do not carry about the accurate gradient direction. The regions of 4 major direction are defined as

$$C1\{(-\frac{\pi}{8}, \frac{\pi}{8}) \cup (\frac{7\pi}{8}, \frac{9\pi}{8})\}, C2\{(\frac{\pi}{8}, \frac{3\pi}{8}) \cup (\frac{9\pi}{8}, \frac{11\pi}{8})\},$$
$$C3\{(\frac{3\pi}{8}, \frac{5\pi}{8}) \cup (\frac{11\pi}{8}, \frac{13\pi}{8})\}, C4\{(\frac{5\pi}{8}, \frac{7\pi}{8}) \cup (\frac{13\pi}{8}, \frac{15\pi}{8})\}$$

Then candidate points need to be found in this step. In order to detect continuous edge, we start with the candidate points. Since candidate points regarded as seeds and extend to a whole edge, we expect that the distribution of these candidate points is dispersed.

As a edge pixel has prominent value in the gradient image, we extract the likely candidates based on its gradient value. However considering the effect of illumination variety, we adopt the local maximum gradient searching to find candidates. A pixel will be brought into candidate point set if it has the local maximum gradient value in $k \times k$ neighborhood. The choice of k depends on the object distribution density that high value k will result in less candidates and sparse distribution, and low value k in more noise. Therefore when we use a high value k to search candidate points, we add a likely local maximum strategy that if the local maximum p_{max} of a $k \times k$ patch is not in the $\frac{k}{2} \times \frac{k}{2}$ neighborhood of the second largest point p_{sec}, the p_{sec} will be involved in candidate set (Fig. 1).

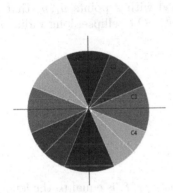

Fig. 1. Regions $\{C_1, C_2, C_3, C_4\}$ represent 4 major gradient directions respectively.

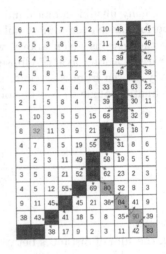

Fig. 2. Process of continuous edge detection.

After candidate points obtained, we start at these points to implement continuous edge extraction. Above all, pixels on a continuous edge are satisfied the following conditions: adjacent in vertical direction of gradient (adopt 8-neighbor judgement) gradient values are quite close; gradient directions are quite close. The detection process is shown in Fig. 2. and result in Fig. 3. Obviously, our proposed continuous edge detection approach includes less noise than Canny detector as shown in Fig. 3.

2.2 Hough-Based Ellipse Extraction

As we know that 5 points determine a ellipse in a plane. That means the time complexity of extracting a ellipse from n points is $O(n^5)$ when implementing randomized hough transform (RHT_5) in [7]. In the crowd industrial environment, the process of RHT_5 is time-consuming in randomly sampling 5 points.

Fig. 3. Edge image. Left: original image. Middle: edge image by our proposed approach. Right: classical Canny edge detection.

A great many invalid samples and accumulations included makes the algorithm poor performance even almost fail in limit time.

For the reasons given above, we propose a improved RHT with 3 points. First, we get a long axis of ellipse L_a determined with 2 points p_1, p_2 that is randomly chosen from edge point set V. The center O of ellipse, long radius r_a and inclination angle θ_a can be computed as

$$O = (\frac{p_1 + p_2}{2}), \tag{1}$$

$$r_a = \frac{\|p_1 - p_2\|_2}{2}, \tag{2}$$

$$\theta_a = \tan^{-1}(\frac{p_1^x - p_2^x}{p_1^y - p_2^y}), \tag{3}$$

Second, the sum of distances between p_3 and focuses f_1, f_2 is equal to the length of long axis, then we have

$$\|p_3 - f_1\|_2 + \|p_3 - f_2\|_2 = 2r_a. \tag{4}$$

We can get the focus coordinates

$$f_1^x = O_x - \cos|\theta|\sqrt{r_a^2 - r_b^2} \tag{5}$$

$$f_1^y = O_y - \sin|\theta|\sqrt{r_a^2 - r_b^2} \tag{6}$$

$$f_2^x = O_x + \cos|\theta|\sqrt{r_a^2 - r_b^2} \tag{7}$$

$$f_2^y = O_y + \sin|\theta|\sqrt{r_a^2 - r_b^2}. \tag{8}$$

The short radius r_b can also be obtained as

$$r_b = \sqrt{\frac{r_a^2\delta^2 - r_a^2\gamma^2}{r_a^2\gamma^2}} \tag{10}$$

where

$$\delta = \|O - p_3\|_2, \quad \gamma = \sin|\theta|(O_y - p_3^y) + \sin|\theta|(O_x - p_3^x). \qquad (11)$$

At last step, after collecting all parameters that a ellipse needed $\{O, r_a, r_b, \theta\}$, we set a accumulator to count how many points $p_i \in V$ fit the ellipse we obtained. It will be accepted as a valid ellipse when the count of points exceed a threshold n_{thresh}. In practical experiment, we get rid of some too long or too short long radius r_a in first step, in order to accelerate the process. The pseudo-code of RHT_3 can be described below.

Algorithm 1. RHT_3 Ellipse

1: Point Set $V\{p_i\}, i = 1, 2, ..., N$
2: **for** p_1, p_2 in V **do**
3:      **if** $Flag[p_1] = 1$ **or** $Flag[p_2] = 1$ **then**
4:          continue
5:      **end if**
6:      **if** $Distance(p_1, p_2) > max_a$ **or** $Distance(p_1, p_2) < min_a$ **then**
7:          continue
8:      **end if**
9:      compute $\{O, a, \theta\}$
10:     init accumulator $Acc := 0$, perimeter $Pe := 0$
11:     **for** p_3 in V **do**
12:         **if** $Flag[p_3] = 1$ **then**
13:             continue
14:         **end if**
15:         $d := Distance(p_3, O)$
16:         **if** $d > a$ **then**
17:             continue
18:         **end if**
19:         compute b
20:         $Acc[b] := Acc[b] + 1$
21:     **end for**
22:     $b\_max\_acc := argmax(Acc)$
23:     **if** $Acc[b\_max\_acc]/Pe[b\_max\_acc] > min\_vote\_rate$ **then**
24:         obtain ellipse $EP\{O, a, b_m ax_a cc, \theta\}$
25:         **for** p_t on EP **do**
26:             $Flag[p_t] := 1$
27:         **end for**
28:     **end if**
29: **end for**

2.3   Pose Refinement

In this section, we show how the pose will be estimated with the ellipse function and how to makes the pose more accurate.

Euler Angle. In this paper, we use euler angle to describe object's 3D pose. The image coordinate system is defined that top-left corner used as origin, right direct as X axis, down as Y axis and inside as Z axis. A object pose is consist of positions $\{Pos_x, Pos_y, Pos_z\}$ and rotations $\{Rot_x, Rot_y, Rot_z\}$. However, we ignore the Z-axis rotation Rot_z in our experiment because it has no effect on picking step, and the Pos_z can only be computed in calibration. Therefore, in the section, we only need to obtain the positions $\{Pos_x, Pos_y\}$ and rotations $\{Rot_x, Rot_y\}$. We define the order of rotation about axis as X, Y, Z. The euler angle [8] can be calculated as below, and we will not show the detail derivation process.

$$\{Pos_x, Pos_y\} = O \tag{12}$$

$$Rot_x = \cos^{-1} \frac{c}{a} \tag{13}$$

$$Rot_y = \cos^{-1} \frac{d}{\sqrt{(d \sin \alpha)^2 + (a \cos \alpha)^2}} \tag{14}$$

In above formula, a, b, O is respectively the long radius, short radius and center of an ellipse, and c, d is the Y-intercept and X-intercept.

Mirror Problem. Obviously, the outer contour of flange is always symmetric, thus we encounter the mirror problem that we are not able to distinguish the correct rotation direct from the mirror direct (as shown in Fig. 4.). In term of this issue, we propose a method to recognize the correct rotation direct, which can also improve the accuracy of fitting the flange for the ellipse. We find noisy points focuses on one side of ellipse in a Canny edge image with a low threshold as shown in Fig. 5., because of the flange thickness effect. We check noise distribution of each $\epsilon \times \epsilon$ patch centered by the point in outer contour, and then regard those points with top 25%–35% density of noise distribution as the outliers.

Fig. 4. Mirror condition. We find no difference between the out contours of left and right image because of symmetrical geometry.

Fig. 5. Noise distribution. Noise points are always converge in one side where the flange is blocked up. Red points are the correct points we obtained.

Actually our method not only imply which rotation direction is accord with the fact, but also make the step of ellipse fitting more accuracy when discarded outliers. The front-view contour and side-view contour are shown in Fig. 6.

Fig. 6. Actual outline. Red edge is the actual flange front outline, and green edge is a side-view contour. (Color figure online)

Fig. 7. Picking process

3   Experiment

3.1   Strategy

For the sake of accurate picking, a flange will be always located twice. For each flange we implement RHT_3 on the first image to obtain a rough position, on which camera will be moved. We stop the camera just above the flange, and then take another image for pose refinement. The strategy is showed in the following steps (Figs. 7 and 8).

1. Take the first image I_0. Implement continuous edge detector (Sect. 2.1) and RHT_3 (Sect. 2.1) to find all ellipse in I_0. The ellipse E_1 with most integrated contour will be picked next, and the center position C_1 is obtained;
2. Move camera to C_1 just above E_1;
3. Take another image I_1, and compute refined pose Pos_1 of E_1 by using the method proposed in Sect. 2.3, and meanwhile find the rough position C_2 of next flange.
4. Pick up the flange on pose Pos_1 by robot manipulator;
5. If the next flange not found, stop picking process. Otherwise, C_2 will be regarded as C_1, and then go to Step 2.

3.2   Experimental Result

In our experiment, we have test the proposed algorithms in these environments: single target and multi-targets randomly placed.

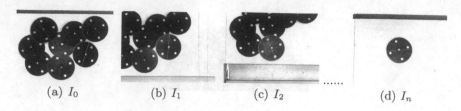

(a) I_0 (b) I_1 (c) I_2 (d) I_n

Fig. 8. Camera view

In single target test, we elevate one side of a flange deliberately with some specific angles, in order to test the accuracy of pose refinement. It is shown in Table 1. that the translation error is almost less than 2 mm and the angle error is less than 3.5°. Specially, we find a small rotation angle will result in a quite big error by pose estimation. This is because $cos^-1\theta$ function is steep decrease around $\theta = 1$, and we have used cos^-1 to calculate Rot_x, Rot_y. However, it does not affect our picking performance, since we can pick it up as well by regarding a small angle as zero.

Table 1. Single target error

Angle	Translation error		Angle error	
	X (mm)	Y (mm)	X (deg)	Y (deg)
4.50	0.51	0.48	3.51	2.88
9.42	1.78	1.34	2.17	2.24
13.29	1.65	1.76	1.05	1.27
17.42	1.82	1.20	1.17	0.74
21.54	1.78	1.76	1.06	0.85
Mean	1.51	1.31	1.79	1.48

In multi-target test, we place several flanges on platform at random, and then record successful times among 50 attempts of picking. In order to test one-time success rate, the robot will bring the flange back automatically to experiment platform after picking up. Of course, the returned position is almost randomized. We do each task 5 times and obtain the average number of successful picking times as shown in Table 2.

In addition, we test the performance of practical bin-picking task that picking all the flanges on platform with the strategy in Sect. 3.2. In this task, success rate of attempts and time consuming of algorithm will be recorded in Table 3. For each task, we also employ the average value of 5 times experiments.

Table 2. Multi-target attempts success rate

Task	Number of flanges	Times of attempts	Success rate (Canny + RHT_5)	Time (Canny + RHT_5)	Success rate (Our approach)	Time (Our approach)
1	5	50	94.0%	1320 ms	97.6%	337 ms
2	10	50	87.8%	8359 ms	93.2%	953 ms
3	15	50	74.6%	26170 ms	88.4%	2754 ms
4	20	50	-	Time out	81.2%	7713 ms

Table 3. Aattempts for Picking All the Flange

Task	Number of flanges	Times of picking
1	5	5.4
2	10	11.2
3	15	18.8
4	20	23.8

4   Conclusion

A mono vision system for picking crowded flanges has been presented in this paper. The core of the system is the location algorithm which is demonstrated ot be robust, fast and accurate. At first we implement a continuous edge detection in order to suppress noise in preprocessing stage, and then put forward a RHT_3 approach to dramatically accelerate the process of ellipse extraction. At last subtly, we make advantage of noise distribution around edge points to solve the mirror problem and to further improve the accuracy of results.

Acknowledgement. This work was supported in part by National Natural Science Foundation of China (No. 81373555), and Shanghai Committee of Science and Technology (14JC1402200 and 14441904403) for funding.

References

1. Rothwell, C.A., Zisserman, A., Forsyth, D.A., Mundy, J.L.: Planar object recognition using projective shape representation. Int. J. Comput. Vis. **16**(1), 57–99 (1995)
2. Rahardja, K., Kosaka, A.: Vision-based bin-picking: recognition and localization of multiple complex objects using simple visual cues. In: IEEE/RSJ International Conference on Intelligent Robots and Systems 1996, IROS, vol. 3, pp. 1448–1457 (1996)
3. Cozar, J.R., Guil, N., Zapata, E.L.: Detection of arbitrary planar shapes with 3D pose. Image Vis. Comput. **19**(14), 1057–1070 (2001)
4. Shroff, N., Taguchi, Y., Tuzel, O., Veeraraghavan, A.: Finding a needle in a specular haystack. In: IEEE International Conference on Robotics and Automation, pp. 5963–5970 (2011)

5. Viksten, F., Forssen, P.E., Johansson, B., Moe, A:. Comparison of local image descriptors for full 6 degree-of-freedom pose estimation. In: IEEE International Conference on Robotics and Automation, pp. 1139–1146 (2009)
6. Canny, J.: A computational approach to edge detection. IEEE Trans. Pattern Anal. Mach. Intell. **8**, 679–698 (1986)
7. Inverso, S.: Ellipse detection using randomized hough transform. Final Project Introduction to Computer Vision (2006)
8. Slabaugh, G.G.: Computing Euler Angles from A Rotation Matrix (1999)

Local Temporal Coherence
for Object-Aware Keypoint Selection
in Video Sequences

Songlin Du$^{(\boxtimes)}$ and Takeshi Ikenaga

Graduate School of Information, Production and Systems,
Waseda University, Kitakyushu 808-0135, Japan
dusonny@fuji.waseda.jp

Abstract. Local feature extraction is an important solution for video analysis. The common framework of local feature extraction consists of a local keypoint detector and a keypoint descriptor. Existing keypoint detectors mainly focus on the spatial relationships among pixels, resulting in a large amount of redundant keypoints on background which are often temporally stationary. This paper proposes an object-aware local keypoint selection approach to keep the active keypoints on object and to reduce the redundant keypoints on background by exploring the temporal coherence among successive frames in video. The proposed approach is made up of three local temporal coherence criteria: (1) local temporal intensity coherence; (2) local temporal motion coherence; (3) local temporal orientation coherence. Experimental results on two publicly available datasets show that the proposed approach reduces more than 60% keypoints, which are redundant, and doubles the precision of keypoints.

Keywords: Video analysis · Local feature extraction
Spatio-temporal keypoint · Object-aware keypoint selection

1 Introduction

With the rapid development of imaging technology and fast increasing of communication bandwidth, video data has played an important role in many industrial applications, such as intelligent traffic control, smart home, robot autonomous navigation, and surveillance system. However, it is hard for human beings to analysis large volume of video data, so automatic video analysis becomes more and more important. An effective solution for automatic video analysis is detecting keypoints in video frames, and then extract distinguishable features from the keypoints with a local descriptor [1]. In recent years, a lot of keypoint detectors have been proposed by detecting corners, blobs, or edges in spatial domain [2]. Since these detectors do not consider the temporal relationship among successive frames in a video, a large number of redundant keypoints would be detected, resulting in heavy computational costs in descriptor generation and high dimensions of features. In most cases, the redundant keypoints are caused by pixels on

© Springer International Publishing AG, part of Springer Nature 2018
B. Zeng et al. (Eds.): PCM 2017, LNCS 10736, pp. 539–549, 2018.
https://doi.org/10.1007/978-3-319-77383-4_53

background which are temporally stationary among successive frames. Although several spatio-temporal keypoint detectors have been proposed, they do not consider the difference between object and background in each frame, so the detected keypoints are still randomly located. To solve this problem, this paper aims at developing an object-aware keypoint selector which eliminates the redundant keypoints on repeated background while precisely keep the keypoints on object in each frame. To achieve this goal, we propose three local temporal coherence criteria, which fully utilize the information of the temporal relationship among successive frames, to select keypoints which are located on object and eliminate the ones on background. The contributions of this paper can be summarized as:

- Three local temporal coherence criteria are proposed for reducing the temporally stationary keypoints in video: (1) local temporal intensity coherence; (2) local temporal motion coherence; (3) local temporal orientation coherence.
- More than 60% keypoints, which are redundant, are reduced, and the precision of keypoints is increased by double.
- Over half of the time consumption spent on keypoint description is reduced.

The remainder of this paper is organized as follows. Section 2 reviews some related works. Section 3 presents the proposed object-aware keypoint selection method. Section 4 shows experimental results and analyses, followed by the conclusion and future works in Sect. 5.

2   Related Works

As mentioned above, a lot of keypoint detectors have been proposed to detect corners, blobs, or edges in spatial domain. The typical detectors include Difference of Gaussian (DoG) [3], Harris corner detector [4], Hessian detector [5], and Smallest Univalue Segment Assimilating Nucleus (SUSAN) detector [6]. However, all these detectors spend heavy computations. To detect keypoints in a simple way, Rosten and Drummond [7–9] proposed the Features from Accelerated Segment Test (FAST) by comparing a center pixel with a circle of sixteen pixels surrounding it to determine whether the center pixel is a corner or not. Besides the above spatial keypoint detectors, several spatio-temporal keypoint detectors have also been proposed in recent years. Zhang et al. [10] proposed a video retrieval and browsing approach by extracting low-level features from video key-frames. Laptev and Lindeberg [11] proposed the space-time interest points (STIP) based on Harris and Förstner interest point operators and analyses of local structures in both space and time. Noguchi and Yanai [12] proposed a spatio-temporal keypoint detector by extracting both of visual feature and motion feature. Baroffio et al. [13] designed a detection mask based spatio-temporal keypoint detector by considering intensity difference and keypoint binning. However, these spatio-temporal detectors do not consider the difference between object and background in each frame, so the detected keypoints are still randomly located. To solve this problem, we propose an object-aware keypoint selection method by designing three local temporal coherence criteria to select keypoints which are located on object and eliminate the ones

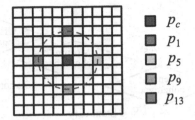

$\blacksquare$ p_c

$\blacksquare$ p_1

$\square$ p_5

$\blacksquare$ p_9

$\blacksquare$ p_{13}

Fig. 1. Graphical illustration of the FAST keypoint detector [7–9].

on background. Since the FAST keypoint detector is utilized to detect the candidates of keypoints in our approach, it is reviewed as follows.

As mentioned above, to detect keypoints in a simple way, the FAST keypoint detector compares a circle of sixteen pixels p_i, $i = 1, 2, \cdots, 16$, with the center pixel p_c. As shown in Fig. 1, the center pixel p_c is defined as a corner if there exists a set of n contiguous pixels on the circle which are all brighter than $f(p_c) + T$ or darker than $f(p_c) - T$, where $f(p_c)$ denotes the gray value of pixel p_c, and T is a threshold. The number of contiguous pixels, i.e. n, is chosen as 12 to balance detection speed and accuracy. To speed up the detection, the FAST keypoint detector firstly examines pixels p_1 and p_9. If the gray values of both pixels p_1 and p_9 are in the range $[f(p_c) - T, f(p_c) + T]$, then p_c is impossible to be a corner. Otherwise, pixels p_5 and p_{13} are examined. Only when at least three pixels among $\{p_1, p_5, p_9, p_{13}\}$ are brighter than $f(p_c) + T$ or darker than $f(p_c) - T$, p_c is possible to be a corner. The full examination can then be applied to the remaining candidates by examining all the 16 pixels.

3   Local Temporal Coherence for Object-Aware Keypoint Selection

Good keypoints are extremely important for the effectiveness, robustness, and efficiency of the whole local feature extraction system. However, as a matter of fact, conventional keypoint detectors detect a large amount of redundant keypoints on background which are temporally stationary among successive frames. The redundant keypoints cause heavy computational costs in descriptor generation and high dimensions of features. To solve this problem, we utilize the FAST detector to detect candidates of keypoints in each video frame, and then propose three local temporal coherence criteria to select keypoints which are located on object and eliminate the ones located on background. The proposed three local temporal coherence criteria include: (1) local temporal intensity coherence C_I; (2) local temporal motion coherence C_m; (3) local temporal orientation coherence C_o. For frame $(n + t)$ in a video sequence, we consider the local temporal coherence between it and the previous frame n, where t is a time interval. As the first step, the candidates of keypoints in frame $(n + t)$ are detected by the FAST keypoint detector, then a corresponding search area in frame n is assigned

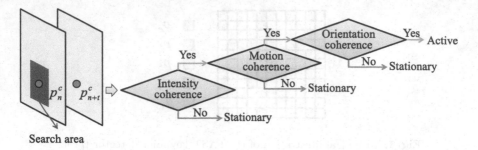

Fig. 2. Graphical illustration of the workflow of the object-aware keypoint selection by the three local temporal coherence criteria. After the selection, the stationary keypoints should be eliminated because they are judged on background, and the active ones should be kept because they are judged on object.

for each candidate of keypoint in frame $(n + t)$. As illustrated in Fig. 2, we then calculate the three local temporal coherence between frame $(n + t)$ and frame n in the corresponding search areas. The keypoints are finally determined by the local temporal coherence criteria one by one.

Local temporal intensity coherence is the first criterion. For a keypoint candidate, if its local temporal intensity coherence is large, it is very possible to be a keypoint on a changing/moving object; otherwise, the local temporal intensity coherence criterion should be tested. Since its local temporal intensity coherence is small, we can calculate its motion vector. If the motion is large, it is also very possible to be a keypoint on a moving object; otherwise, we turn to test the local temporal orientation coherence criterion. Although both of the intensity coherence and motion coherence are small, its orientation coherence is possible to be large. If the orientation coherence is large, it is still possible to be a keypoint on a changing object; otherwise, it should be determined as a stationary keypoint on background which is redundant and should be eliminated. Based on the above analyses, the details of the three local temporal coherence criteria are illustrated in the following three subsections, respectively.

3.1 Local Temporal Intensity Coherence

Intensity is an important kind of information for measuring the temporal relationship between keypoints in successive frames. For each keypoint candidate p_{n+t}^c detected in frame $(n + t)$, we search its corresponding keypoint in frame n with local temporal intensity coherence as follows. As shown in Fig. 3, denoting the histogram of surrounding pixels' intensities of center pixel p_n^c as H_n and the histogram of surrounding pixels' intensities of center pixel p_{n+t}^c as H_{n+t}, the local temporal intensity coherence is defined as the Chi-square distance [14] between H_n and H_{n+t}, i.e.

$$C_I = \frac{1}{2} \sum_{i=1}^{16} \frac{\left(H_n\left(i\right) - H_{n+t}\left(i\right)\right)^2}{H_n\left(i\right) + H_{n+t}\left(i\right)}, \tag{1}$$

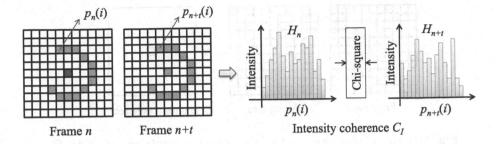

Fig. 3. Graphical illustration of the local temporal intensity coherence C_I.

where $H_n(i)$ denotes the ith surrounding pixel of p_n^c in frame n, and $H_{n+t}(i)$ denotes the ith surrounding pixel of p_{n+t}^c in frame $n+t$. If the local temporal intensity coherence C_I is smaller than a threshold T_I, we turn to calculate the local temporal motion coherence C_m.

3.2 Local Temporal Motion Coherence

As mentioned above, the redundant keypoints caused by the pixels on background, which are temporally stationary, should be removed. Local temporal motion coherence is a good metric to reduce the stationary keypoints in successive frames. If the local temporal intensity coherence C_I between keypoint candidate p_{n+t}^c and keypoint p_n^c is smaller than a threshold T_I, we project p_n^c to the corresponding position in frame $(n+t)$, and then employ the Euclidean distance to measure the motion coherence between p_n^c and p_{n+t}^c. Then the Euclidean distance is defined as local temporal motion coherence. If the local temporal motion coherence C_m is larger than a threshold T_m, that means p_{n+t}^c is not a stationary keypoints, namely, it is possible to be a keypoint on object, and we then turn to calculate the local temporal orientation coherence C_o.

3.3 Local Temporal Orientation Coherence

The FAST keypoint detector attempts to find keypoints with contiguous surrounding pixels which are brighter or darker than the central one. The contiguous surrounding pixels make up a semicircle, we propose to calculate the orientation of each keypoint candidate from the orientation of the corresponding semicircle. As shown in Fig. 4, the orientation of a keypoint in frame $(n+t)$ can be denoted as a vector V_{n+t}, and the orientation of a keypoint candidate in frame n as vector V_n. Then the local temporal orientation coherence can be obtained by

$$C_o = |\angle V_n - \angle V_{n+t}|, \tag{2}$$

where $\angle V_n$ and $\angle V_{n+t}$ denote the orientations of vectors V_n and V_{n+t}, respectively. If the local temporal orientation coherence C_o is smaller than a threshold T_o, the keypoint candidate is determined on object and should be kept.

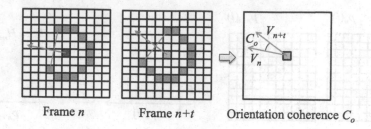

Fig. 4. Graphical illustration of the local temporal orientation coherence C_o.

4   Experimental Results

4.1   Datasets and Settings

Two publicly available datasets PETS2001[1] and LASIESTA[2] [15] are utilized for evaluations. The PETS2001 dataset consists of training sequences and test sequences. All the datasets are taken at two directions of view. The ground-truth images are obtained from the Laboratory for Image and Media Understanding[3]. The LASIESTA dataset provides both of original sequences and ground-truth. In our experiments, the test sequences in PETS2001 dataset #3 from camera #1 (PETS2001_3_2), the dataset #3 from camera #2 (PETS2001_3_2), the I_SI_01 sequence in LASIESTA dataset, and the I_SI_02 sequence in LASIESTA dataset are tested. The sequences from PETS2001 dataset are taken at *outdoor environment*, and the sequences from LASIESTA dataset are taken at *indoor environment*. Since the ground-truth images are of size 320 × 240 pixels, the original frames in the PETS2001 dataset are also resized to the same size before keypoint detection, and only the frames which have corresponding ground-truth images are tested and counted. The experimental environments are C++ language and OpenCV 2.4.10 on a machine of 3.40 GHz CPU and 8 GB RAM.

4.2   Evaluation Metrics

Since background pixels in video are almost the same among successive frames, large amount of local keypoints located on background are redundant, and only the keypoints which are located on objects are active and should be timely updated, the *precision* of keypoints is defined as

$$precision = \frac{\sum_{k=1}^{N} \#ObjKpts\,(k)}{\sum_{k=1}^{N} \#Kpts\,(k)}, \tag{3}$$

where N is the number of frames in the test sequence, "$\#ObjKpts\,(k)$" denotes the number of keypoints which are located on the object in the kth frame, and "$\#Kpts\,(k)$" denotes the total number of keypoints in the kth frame.

---

[1] www.cvg.reading.ac.uk/PETS2001/pets2001-dataset.html.
[2] www.gti.ssr.upm.es/data/lasiesta_database.html.
[3] limu.ait.kyushu-u.ac.jp/dataset/.

The percentage of the number of keypoints reduced by the proposed approach is defined as a metric R_{kr}; the ratio between the improvement of *precision* contributed by the proposed approach and the original *precision* from FAST detector is denoted as another metric R_{ip}. Besides, we use four typical local keypoint descriptors, including SIFT [3], SURF [16], BRIEF [17], and ORB [18], to describe the keypoints before and after using the proposed keypoint selection approach, and the time consumptions are counted. The percentage of time-saving contributed by the proposed approach is then defined as the last metric R_t.

4.3 Parameter Settings

The threshold T in the FAST detector is set as 30; the time interval t is set as 20; the threshold for local temporal motion coherence C_m, i.e. T_m, is set as 5; the threshold for local temporal intensity coherence C_I, i.e. T_I, is set as 160; the threshold for local temporal orientation coherence C_o, i.e. T_o, is set as $2\tan^{-1}(0.5)$, namely, at least 9 out of 12 surrounding pixels on the circle in Fig. 1 are consistent between candidates of keypoints on fame $n+t$ and frame n.

4.4 Results and Analyses

Typical keypoint selection results on PETS2001 dataset and LASIESTA dataset are shown in Figs. 5 and 6, respectively. As can be seen from Figs. 5 and 6, a large amount of keypoints are detected by FAST detector. Compared with FAST detector, the proposed approach selects few keypoints in each frame, which makes it possible to achieve more efficient keypoint description and compacter feature representation in the phase of descriptor generation. It is also important to note that the keypoints on objects in each frame are basically not reduced, which ensures that the information provided by each frame is not lost, because only the stationary keypoints on background are redundant.

Fig. 5. Typical keypoint selection results on the PETS2001_3_1 (top) and PETS2001_3_2 (bottom) sequences. The sequences are taken at *indoor environment*. From left to right in each row: typical frames, keypoints detected by FAST detector, keypoints selected by the proposed approach, ground-truth of objects.

Fig. 6. Typical keypoint selection results on the LASIESTA I_SI_01 (top) and LASI-ESTA I_SI_02 (bottom) sequences. The sequences are taken at *indoor environment.* From left to right in each row: typical frames, keypoints detected by FAST detector, keypoints selected by the proposed approach, ground-truth of objects.

Table 1. Experimental results on the number of keypoints and *precision.* Higher *precision* indicates superior performance.

Sequence	FAST detector			The proposed approach		
	$\sum \#ObjKpts$	$\sum \#Kpts$	Precision	$\sum \#ObjKpts$	$\sum \#Kpts$	Precision
PETS2001_3_1	6359	160054	3.97%	4761	53193	8.95%
PETS2001_3_2	8113	244078	3.32%	4882	76278	6.40%
I_SI_01	4629	63477	7.29%	4368	23647	18.47%
I_SI_02	6956	46941	14.82%	5388	17105	31.50%

The experimental results on the number of keypoints from by FAST detector and the proposed approach, and the corresponding *precision* values, are listed in Table 1. As can be seen from Table 1, the FAST keypoint detector detects a very large amount of keypoints from the test sequences, but most of the detected keypoints are not located on objects in video frames, so both of its $\sum \#ObjKpts$ values and *precision* values are low. The proposed approach reduces the total number of keypoints a lot, but the keypoints located on objects in video frames are basically not reduced. Therefore, the proposed approach achieves higher *precision* values than FAST keypoint detector. The time consumption (seconds) of generating four typical keypoint descriptors on the keypoints are presented in Table 2. One can conclude from Table 2 that the time consumption is reduced a lot by using the proposed keypoint selection approach.

To make the contributions of the proposed approach more clear, Table 3 shows the improvement on precision (R_{ip}), the ratio of keypoint reduction (R_{kr}), and the percentage of time-saving (R_t) contributed by the proposed approach. One can conclude from Table 3 that, for all the test sequences, the proposed

Table 2. Experimental results on time consumption (seconds) of generating four typical keypoint descriptors. Shorter time consumption indicates superior performance.

Sequence	FAST detector				The proposed approach			
	SIFT	SURF	BRIEF	ORB	SIFT	SURF	BRIEF	ORB
PETS2001_3_1	118.52	4.81	9.45	58.97	42.78	1.89	3.28	20.16
PETS2001_3_2	177.24	7.17	14.78	97.50	58.66	2.52	4.70	30.21
I_SI_01	49.55	2.19	3.57	27.69	22.51	1.04	1.52	11.57
I_SI_02	39.59	1.68	3.36	20.90	18.42	0.85	1.35	8.19

Table 3. Ratio of keypoint reduction (R_{kr}), improvement on precision (R_{ip}), and percentage of time-saving (R_t) from four typical descriptors.

Sequence	R_{kr}	R_{ip}	R_t(SIFT)	R_t(SURF)	R_t(BRIEF)	R_t(ORB)
PETS2001_3_1	66.77%	125.44%	63.90%	60.70%	65.29%	65.81%
PETS2001_3_2	68.75%	92.77%	66.90%	64.85%	68.20%	69.02%
I_SI_01	62.75%	153.36%	54.57%	52.51%	57.42%	58.22%
I_SI_02	63.56%	112.55%	53.47%	49.40%	59.82%	60.81%

object-aware keypoint selector reduces more than 60% keypoints, and improves about 100% *precision*, i.e. achieves double *precision*, compared with the result of the FAST detector. Since more than 60% keypoints are reduced, over half of the time consumption spent on keypoint description is reduced, no matter which keypoint descriptor is used.

5   Conclusion and Future Works

A local temporal coherence based object-aware keypoint selection method has been reported in this paper. The proposed approach utilizes the FAST keypoint detector to detect candidates of keypoints in spatial domain, and then propose three local temporal coherence criteria to select the candidates of keypoints which are located on objects in each frame. The three local temporal coherence criteria include local temporal intensity coherence, local temporal motion coherence, and local temporal orientation coherence. Since a large amount of redundant keypoints on background are eliminated by the three local temporal coherence criteria, the proposed approach can significantly reduce the total number of keypoints and improve the precision of the keypoints. Experimental results on two publicly available video datasets show that the proposed object-aware keypoint selection method reduces more than 60% keypoints and doubles the precision. Since more than 60% keypoints are reduced, over half of the time consumption spent on keypoint description is reduced when compared with the FAST keypoint detector.

In the future, the proposed keypoint selection method can be applied to many practical applications, such as pedestrian detection, action recognition, and object tracking, to achieve efficient keypoint description and compact feature representation.

Acknowledgments. This work was supported by KAKENHI (16K13006) and Waseda University Grant for Special Research Projects (2017K-263).

References

1. Fan, B., Wang, Z., Wang, F.: Local Image Descriptor: Modern Approaches. Springer, Heidelberg (2015). https://doi.org/10.1007/978-3-662-49173-7
2. Awad, A.I., Hassaballah, M.: Image Feature Detectors and Descriptors. Springer, Heidelberg (2016). https://doi.org/10.1007/978-3-319-28854-3
3. Lowe, D.G.: Distinctive image features from scale-invariant keypoints. Int. J. Comput. Vis. **60**(2), 91–110 (2004)
4. Harris, C., Stephens, M.: A combined coer and edge detector. In: Alvey Vision Conference, pp. 147–151 (1988)
5. Beaudet, P.: Rotationally invariant image operators. In: International Conference on Pattern Recognition, pp. 579–583 (1978)
6. Smith, S.M., Brady, J.M.: SUSAN: a new approach to low level image processing. Int. J. Comput. Vis. **23**(1), 45–78 (1997)
7. Rosten, E., Drummond, T.: Fusing points and lines for high performance tracking. In: International Conference on Computer Vision, pp. 1508–1515 (2005)
8. Rosten, E., Drummond, T.: Machine learning for high-speed corner detection. In: Leonardis, A., Bischof, H., Pinz, A. (eds.) ECCV 2006. LNCS, vol. 3951, pp. 430–443. Springer, Heidelberg (2006). https://doi.org/10.1007/11744023_34
9. Rosten, E., Porter, R., Drummond, T.: Faster and better: a machine learning approach to corner detection. IEEE Trans. Pattern Anal. Mach. Intell. **32**(1), 105–119 (2010)
10. Zhang, H.J., Wu, J., Zhong, D., Smoliar, S.: An integrated system for content-based video retrieval and browsing. Pattern Recognit. **30**(4), 643–658 (1997)
11. Laptev, I., Lindeberg, T.: Space-time interest points. In: International Conference on Computer Vision, pp. 432–439 (2003)
12. Noguchi, A., Yanai, K.: Extracting spatio-temporal local features considering consecutiveness of motions. In: Zha, H., Taniguchi, R., Maybank, S. (eds.) ACCV 2009. LNCS, vol. 5995, pp. 458–467. Springer, Heidelberg (2010). https://doi.org/10.1007/978-3-642-12304-7_43
13. Baroffio, L., Cesana, M., Redondi, A., Tagliasacchi, M., Tubaro, S.: Fast keypoint detection in video sequences. In: International Conference on Acoustics, Speech and Signal Processing, pp. 1342–1346 (2016)
14. Huong, V.T.L., Park, D.-C., Woo, D.M., Lee, Y.: Centroid neural network with Chi square distance measure for texture classification. In: International Joint Conference on Neural Networks, pp. 1310–1315 (2009)
15. Cuevas, C., Yáñez, E.M., García, N.: Labeled dataset for integral evaluation of moving object detection algorithms: LASIESTA. Comput. Vis. Image Underst. **152**, 103–117 (2016)
16. Bay, H., Tuytelaars, T., Van Gool, L.: SURF: speeded up robust features. In: Leonardis, A., Bischof, H., Pinz, A. (eds.) ECCV 2006. LNCS, vol. 3951, pp. 404–417. Springer, Heidelberg (2006). https://doi.org/10.1007/11744023_32

17. Calonder, M., Lepetit, V., Strecha, C., Fua, P.: BRIEF: binary robust independent elementary features. In: Daniilidis, K., Maragos, P., Paragios, N. (eds.) ECCV 2010. LNCS, vol. 6314, pp. 778–792. Springer, Heidelberg (2010). https://doi.org/ 10.1007/978-3-642-15561-1_56
18. Rublee, E., Rabaud, V., Konolige, K., Bradski, G.: ORB: an efficient alternative to SIFT or SURF. In: International Conference on Computer Vision, pp. 2564–2571 (2011)

A Combined Feature Approach for Speaker Segmentation Using Convolution Neural Network

Jiang Zhong[1,2], Pan Zhang[2(✉)], and Xue Li[1,3]

[1] Key Laboratory of Dependable Service Computing in Cyber Physical Society, Ministry of Education, Chongqing University, Chongqing 400030, China
zhongjiang@cqu.edu.cn, xueli@uq.edu.au
[2] College of Computer Science, Chongqing University, Chongqing 400030, China
zhangpan220@foxmail.com
[3] School of Information Technology and Electrical Engineering, University of Queensland, Brisbane, Australia

Abstract. In this paper, a speaker segmentation algorithm is proposed based on a Combined feature approach using the Convolution Neural Network (CNN), which is used to deal with the speaker segmentation problem of dialogue speech with partial prior knowledge in the CALL_CENTER environment. For the first time, the Mel-Frequency Cepstral Coefficients (MFCC) feature and the SPECTROGRAM feature are combined as the input of CNN to train the speakers' voice feature model and to estimate the change point. In the experiments, a real database about the dialogue voice related to insurance sales and real estate sales industry is used to compare our proposed approach with Bayesian Information Criterion (BIC) approach using different acoustic features sets. The results show that the synthetical performance is improved, and our algorithm has a better segmentation.

Keywords: Combined feature · Speaker segmentation · SPECTROGRAM
MFCC · CNN

1 Introduction

Speaker segmentation aims at detecting the time reversal point of speakers in an audio stream, and focuses on segmenting the audio stream into pieces, each contains only one speaker's voice. Speaker segmentation plays an important role in speech application research as a pre-processing step, such as, multi-speaker recognition, speaker tracking [1], speaker diarization [2, 3] and content-based audio signals analysis [4].

In general, there are two main categories of the speaker segmentation task: one is distance-based segmentation algorithm [5, 6], the other is model-decoding-based segmentation algorithm [7]. The most common segmentation algorithms based on distance include Bayesian Information Criterion (BIC) [8], Kullback-Leibler distance (KL or KL2) [9] and Generalized Likelihood Ratio (GLR) [10], which are used to measure the similarity of speech features in adjacent window to determine whether two

© Springer International Publishing AG, part of Springer Nature 2018
B. Zeng et al. (Eds.): PCM 2017, LNCS 10736, pp. 550–559, 2018.
https://doi.org/10.1007/978-3-319-77383-4_54

adjacent voices are from the same person or not. Among these algorithms, BIC is widely used to deal with speaker segmentation of non-priori knowledge, but because it's particularly sensitive to changes in acoustic characteristics so that too many redundant points are generated in the segmentation process, and it also needs to set the threshold. The model-decoding-based segmentation algorithm, such as Gaussian Mixture Model (GMM) [11], is used to train speaker segmentation model by a priori knowledge about the content of the audio stream. A priori knowledge of a voice refers to the ability to know in advance the identity of the speaker, the sound information, the characteristics and so on. Such voice exists in many areas, for instance, telephone sales industry, communications, news broadcast and customer service calls of the major business services, this kind of voice background environment is called as CALL_CENTER. Therefore, this paper focuses on the model-based speaker segmentation algorithm in CALL_CENTER environment.

CNN is a deep neural network with a special kind of layer the convolution layer. The two characteristics of CNN local perception and parameter sharing can greatly reduce the number of parameters, which can avoid the complex feature extraction and data reconstruction process of traditional identification algorithm, and the models constructed by CNN can be set to different depth and breadth, so CNN has been applied with great success in various disciplines, such as image recognition [12] and speech research [13, 14].

Based on the above analysis, in this paper, for the dialogue speech of CALL_CENTER environment, a speaker segmentation algorithm is proposed based on a Combined feature approach by using CNN, which is used to train the speakers' voice features model and to estimate the speaker change point. The paper uses a voice that contains two speakers, the different voice information between the operator and non-operator can be identified, that is, time reversal point of speakers. Besides, the proposed method does not need to set the threshold value, which greatly reduces the computation complexity and effectively solves the problem of redundant segmentation caused by the changes of acoustic characteristics. Compared with the traditional speaker segmentation algorithm (BIC), some examples are demonstrated to show that the proposed algorithm is more effective in this paper.

This paper is organized as follows. In Sect. 2, the combined feature is proposed. The overall framework of the algorithm is proposed in Sect. 3. In Sect. 4, the experiments for the speaker segmentation are described in detail, and Sect. 5 contains some concluding remarks.

2 Combined Feature

SPECTROGRAM is a kind of graphical display of the squared magnitude of the time-varying spectral characteristics of speech [15]. It focuses on the audio characteristics of the phonetic essence, which is compact and efficient in representation carrying information about energy, pitch, fundamental frequency, formants and timing. SPECTROGRAM combines the characteristics of the spectrum with the time-domain waveform, which can reflect the dynamic spectral characteristics of speech signals, thus, it has very important practical value in speech research, and is called "visual language". Contextual variations in speech are better represented using a SPECTRO-GRAM and hence it is widely used as a tool for speech analysis [16, 17]. Figure 1 shows a 9-s SIGNAL time-domain waveform and SPECTROGRAM.

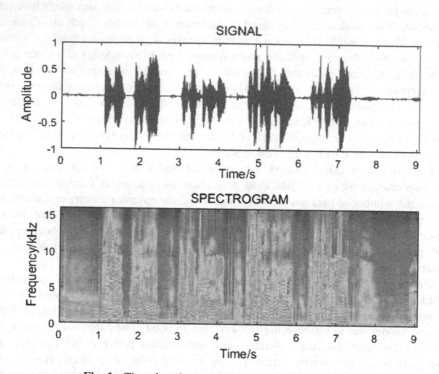

Fig. 1. Time-domain waveform and SPECTROGRAM

The SPECTROGRAM in Fig. 1, the horizontal axis represents the time and the vertical axis represents the frequency. Each coordinate point value represents the energy data of the speech. The SPECTROGRAM consists of the different degrees of color, the different stripe, is also called "voiceprint". It's well known that everyone has different characteristics of the sound, which will produce a different voiceprint, so the voiceprint can be used to distinguish between different people. Therefore, in the following section, this paper introduces the SPECTROGRAM into the problem of speaker segmentation.

On the other hand, Mel-Frequency Cepstral Coefficients (MFCC) [18] is the most common feature extraction technique in speaker identification. The Mel scale was first proposed by Stevens, Volkman and Newman (1937) [19], the Mel frequency can be better to represent the sound from the listener's perspective. Besides, the Mel frequency scale is more consistent with the ear's auditory characteristics and it has strong robustness. Therefore, MFCC has been widely used in signal processing, especially, speech processing [20–23].

According to the introduction of the above two methods, this paper proposes the Combined feature based on SPECTROGRAM and MFCC' characteristics. The process of Combined feature is shown in Fig. 2.

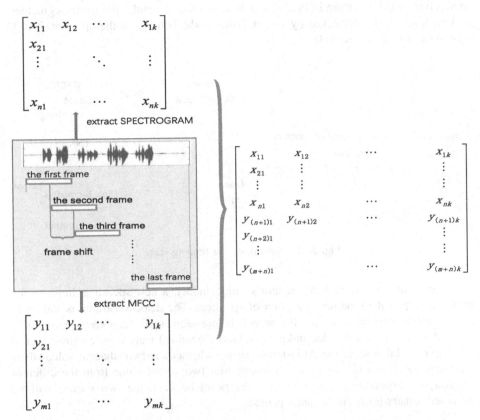

Fig. 2. The process of Combined feature generated from MFCC and SPECTROGRAM

Figure 2 shows that, first, speech signals are divided into many frames, each frame length is 30 ms, and the frame shift is 15 ms, the Hamming window is used to extract the audio frames in the speech process, then sets the number of sampling points equal to the number of windows. Second, MFCC features and SPECTROGRAM features are extracted from each frame, respectively. Finally, the Combined feature is generated after these two features are combined based on the sequence of each frame.

3 The Proposed Algorithm Framework

In this section, first, speech data has a part of speaker prior knowledge in CALL_CENTER environment, that is, the operator's voice information characteristics are known. Then, based on the Combined feature approach, a one-dimensional matrix of original speech is transformed into a two-dimensional features matrix as features input to the CNN to train segmentation model of operator and non-operator. Finally, a speaker segmentation algorithm for the speech data based on Combined feature using CNN is proposed to obtain a label sequence of the speaker. Subsequently, the training model framework is shown in Fig. 3, which shows that the audio file is pre-segmented and each segment is remarked by 1 or 0. If the audio belongs to the operator, it is 1, otherwise it is remarked as 0.

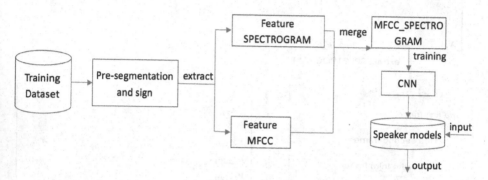

Fig. 3. Framework of the training stage

After obtaining the trained operator's voice model, a new speech is input to the model to detect the time reversal point of speakers. The detection frame is shown in Fig. 4, which demonstrates that the speech is pre-segmented, then each segments is marked in chronological order and the obtained Combined feature as features input to CNN to get a label sequence. At last, comparing whether any two adjacent voice labels are the same, if not the same, which means that two voices come from the different speaker, correspondingly, the time reversal point between the two speech will be achieved, otherwise from the same people.

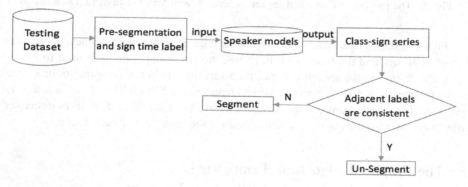

Fig. 4. Framework of speaker segmentation

4 Experiments

4.1 Datasets

In this section, the dataset comes from a telemarketing company, the audios related to two areas of insurance sales and real estate sales industry are single-channel recoding with sampling rate of 16000 Hz from the real environment. In this experiment, first of all, the audio files adopt 30 the different time-length recording files from this dataset, each recording is uniformly segmented into 500 ms pieces. Second, the training set consists of 500 pieces of operator's voice and 500 pieces of non-operator's voice by manually selecting from whole segmented pieces. Last but not least, the complete dialogue voices containing the operator audio and the customer audio which are selected and segmented as the same process of the training set, and 400 pieces are taken as the testing set to detect the time reversal point for different speakers.

4.2 Evaluation Metrics

There are many evaluation parameters of speaker segmentation system. Among these evaluation parameters, precision (PRC) and recall (RCL) [24, 25] is chose in this paper. A false alarm occurs when a speaker change is detected even though it does not exist, this type of error is measured using the precision measure (PRC). Misdetection occurs when the algorithm does not detect an existing speaker change, this type is measured using the recall measure (RCL). They are defined as follows:

$$PRC = \frac{N1}{N2} * 100\% \tag{1}$$

$$RCL = \frac{N1}{N3} * 100\% \tag{2}$$

Where N1: the number of correctly found changes; N2: total number of changes found; N3: total number of correct changes.

The combined F-measure (F) is also used to evaluate the performance and to compare the results with different systems. This measure is defined as:

$$F = \frac{PRC * RCL}{PRC + RCL} * 2 \tag{3}$$

F-measure is the measure of a grammar's accuracy. It considers both the precision and the recall of the grammar to compute the score, according to the formula. When the value of F-measure is higher, indicating that the performance is better.

4.3 Experimental

There are two examples to show the advantages and the effectiveness of the developed methods in our work. Example 1 is presented to show that three parameters obtained by CCN is better than by BIC under the same MFCC feature. Example 2 demonstrates that three evaluation parameters are obtained by CCN based on three different features, namely, MFCC, SPECTROGRAM, Combined feature.

Example 1. In order to preserve the complete audio characteristics information, the frame length is selected as 30 ms, the frame shift is selected as 15 ms, and the number of sampling points is equal to the number of window points. Then, to compare the effectiveness of the CNN approach to BIC approach, we only use MFCC feature in this experiment. The experimental results are shown in Table 1.

Table 1. Segmentation effect of different algorithms under MFCC feature

Algorithm	PRC	RCL	F
BIC	0.865	0.7937	0.8278
CNN	0.9	0.8182	0.8572

Table 1 obviously illustrates that, under the same dataset and the same MFCC feature, the accuracy and recall rate obtained by CNN are better than BIC 3.5% and 2.45%, respectively, and the comprehensive F-measure performance is better than BIC 2.94%. The results reveal that the proposed algorithm based on CNN can get better segmentation results compared with BIC approach, and the RCL indicates that the CNN method reduces the number of redundant points of speaker segmentation.

Example 2. In our work, to prove the segmentation results by the Combined feature results better than other features (MFCC, SPECTROGRAM), we use these three different features as the input of the CNN method to obtain the following results to train the segmentation model 100 times to test the difference of segmentation effect. Figure 5 shows the result find that the comprehensive performance F-measure curves of the detected speakers' time reversal points in three different features. Using the Combined feature, the F-measure is lower than that of MFCC and SPECTROGRAM before the number of training times is 6, but the growth rate of the Combined feature is obvious. When the number of training times is 28, the F-measure is basically stable and obviously higher than MFCC and SPECTROGRAM. Using MFCC features, the F-measure of speaker segmentation is very stable, so the growth rate of precision is very small too. Using the SPECTROGRAM feature, the results are between the other two features'.

The use of Combined features, the comprehensive performance of speaker segmentation is basically stable at 90.2%, up to a maximum of 90.84%. When the model is basically stable, the mean values of the speaker segmentation parameters are shown in Table 2.

It can be seen from Table 2 that when the Combined feature is the input of CNN segmentation algorithm, whose average precision and recall rate are higher than MFCC 3.25% and 5.53%, respectively, and are better than SPECTROGRAM 2% and 3.44%, respectively. The comprehensive performance average F-measure of the Combined feature is better than MFCC 4.48%, is better than SPECTROGRAM 2.77%. It obviously indicates that the proposed algorithm based on Combined feature by using CNN can get better segmentation results compared with MFCC and SPECTROGRAM.

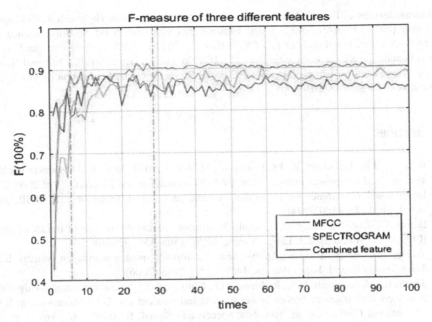

Fig. 5. F-measure curves in three different features

Table 2. Segmentation effect of three different features inputs by the CNN

Features	PRC	RCL	F
MFCC	0.9 (± 0.01)	0.8182 (± 0.0041)	0.8572 (± 0.0058)
SPECTROGRAM	0.9125 (± 0.01)	0.8391 (± 0.0085)	0.8743 (± 0.0092)
Combined feature	0.9325 (± 0.005)	0.8735 (± 0.0089)	0.902 (± 0.0064)

5 Conclusion

In this paper, for the dialogue speech of CALL_CENTER environment, a speaker segmentation algorithm is proposed based on a Combined features approach by using CNN. First, the MFCC and SPECTROGRAM of speech are extracted, and a new Combined feature is generated by fusion operation. Second, the combined feature is input to the CNN for training the speaker segmentation model and finding the time point of the different speakers. Then, The MFCC is used as the acoustic feature to compare two speaker segmentation algorithms of BIC and CNN. At the same time, the MFCC, the SPECTROGRAM and the Combined feature are used as the input for CNN respectively to compare the speaker segmentation effect under the three different features. Finally, the experimental results show that the speaker segmentation algorithm based on the Combined feature by using CNN, presented by this paper, has a better segmentation effect.

Acknowledgement. This work was supported in part by the National High-tech R&D Program of China (NO. 2015AA015308), Social Undertakings and Livelihood Security Science and Technology Innovation Funds of CQ CSTC (No. cstc2017shmsA20013), Frontier and Application Foundation Research Program of CQ CSTC (No. cstc2017jcyjAX0340), National Natural Science Foundation of Chi-na (No. 61402020) and Ph.D. Programs Foundation of Ministry of Education of China (No. 20130001120021).

References

1. Bonastre, J.F., Delacourt, P., Fredouille, C., Merlin, T., Wellekens, C.: A speaker tracking system based on speaker turn detection for NIST evaluation. In: Proceedings of 2000 IEEE International Conference on Acoustics, Speech, and Signal Processing, ICASSP 2000, vol. 2, pp. 1177–1180 (2000)
2. Barras, C., Zhu, X., Meignier, S., et al.: Multistage speaker diarization of broadcast news. IEEE Trans. Audio Speech Lang. Process. **14**(5), 1505–1512 (2006)
3. Tranter, S.E., Reynolds, D.A.: An overview of automatic speaker diarization systems. IEEE Trans. Audio Speech Lang. Process. **14**(5), 1557–1565 (2006)
4. Saeidi, R., Mohammadi, H.S., Rodman, R.D., Kinnunen, T.: A new segmentation algorithm combined with transient frames power for text independent speaker verification. In: IEEE International Conference on Acoustics, Speech and Signal, ICASSP 2007, vol. 4, p. 305 (2007)
5. Chen, S., Gopalakrishnan, P. S.: Speaker, environment and channel change detection and clustering via the Bayesian information criterion. In: Proceedings of DARPA Broadcast News Transcription and Understanding Workshop, vol. 8, pp. 127–132 (1998)
6. Delacourt, P., Wellekens, C.: DISTBIC: A speaker-based segmentation for audio data indexing. Speech Commun. **32**(1), 111–126 (2000)
7. Bakis, R., Chen, S., Gopalakrishnan, P., Gopinath, R., Maes, S., Polymenakos, L., Franz, M.: Transcription of broadcast news shows with the IBM large vocabulary speech recognition system. In: Proceedings of DARPA Speech Recognition Workshop, VA, pp. 67–72 (1997)
8. Cettolo, M., Vescovi, M., Rizzi, R.: Evaluation of BIC-based algorithms for audio segmentation. J. Comput. Speech & Lang. **19**(2), 147–170 (2005)
9. Siegler, M.A., Jain, U., Raj, B., Stern, R.M.: Automatic segmentation, classification and clustering of broadcast news audio. In: Proceedings of DARPA Speech Recognition Workshop, VA, pp. 97–99 (1997)
10. Gish, H., Siu, M.H., Rohlicek, R.: Segregation of speakers for speech recognition and speaker identification. In: 1991 International Conference on Acoustics, Speech, and Signal Processing, ICASSP 1991, pp. 873–876 (1991)
11. Jin, H., Kubala, F., Schwartz, R.: Automatic speaker clustering. In: Proceedings of the DARPA Speech Recognition Workshop, pp. 108–111 (1997)
12. Tompson, J., Stein, M., Lecun, Y., Perlin, K.: Real-time continuous pose recovery of human hands using convolutional networks. ACM Trans. Graph. **33**(5), 169 (2014)
13. Sell, G., Garcia-Romero, D., McCree, A.: Speaker diarization with I-Vectors from DNN senone posteriors. In: Proceedings of Interspeech, pp. 3096–3099 (2015)
14. Abdel-Hamid, O., Mohamed, A.R., Jiang, H., Penn, G.: Applying convolutional neural networks concepts to hybrid NN-HMM model for speech recognition. In: Proceedings of IEEE International Conference on Acoustics, Speech and Signal Processing (ICASSP), pp. 4277–4280 (2012)

15. Quatieri, T.F.: Discrete-time Speech Signal Processing: Principles and Practice. Pearson Education, Delhi, India (2006)
16. Cole, R.A., Rudnicky, A.I., Zue, V.M.: Performance of an expert spectrogram reader. J. Acoust. Soc. Am. **65**(S1), S81–S81 (1979)
17. Zue, V., Lamel, L.: An expert spectrogram reader: A knowledge-based approach to speech recognition. In: IEEE International Conference on Acoustics, Speech, and Signal Processing, ICASSP 1986, vol. 11, pp. 1197–1200 (1986)
18. Davis, S., Mermelstein, P.: Comparison of parametric representations for monosyllabic word recognition in continuously spoken sentences. IEEE Trans. Acoust. Speech Sig. Process. **28** (4), 357–366 (1980)
19. Stevens, S.S., Volkmann, J., Newman, E.B.: A scale for the measurement of the psychological magnitude pitch. J. Acoust. Soc. Am. **8**(3), 185–190 (1937)
20. Deller Jr., J.R., Proakis, J.G., Hansen, J.H.: Discrete Time Processing of Speech Signals, 2nd edn. IEEE Press, New York (2000)
21. Speer, S. R., Warren, P., Schafer, A.: Intonation and sentence processing. In: Proceedings of the 15th International Congress of Phonetic Sciences, pp. 95–105 (2003)
22. Mammone, R.J., Zhang, X., Ramachandran, R.P.: Robust speaker recognition: a feature-based approach. IEEE Sig. Process. Mag. **13**(5), 58–71 (1996)
23. Reynolds, D.A.: Experimental evaluation of features for robust speaker identification. IEEE Trans. Speech Audio Process. **2**(4), 639–643 (1994)
24. Ajmera, J., McCowan, I., Bourlard, H.: Robust speaker change detection. IEEE Sig. Process. Lett. **11**(8), 649–651 (2004)
25. Kadri, H., Davy, M., Rabaoui, A., Lachiri, Z., Ellouze, N.: Robust audio speaker segmentation using one class SVMs. In: 2008 16th European Conference on Signal Processing, pp. 1–5 (2008)

DDSH: Deep Distribution-Separating Hashing for Image Retrieval

Junjie Chen and Anran Wang[✉]

Department of Computer Science, Hong Kong Baptist University,
Kowloon, Hong Kong
{csjjchen,anranwang}@comp.hkbu.edu.hk

Abstract. With the rapid growth of web images, binary hashing method has received increasing attention due to the storage efficiency and the ability for fast retrieval. Recently, deep hashing methods have achieved the state-of-the-art performance by utilizing deep neural networks in hash code learning. Most of these methods are trained with the supervision of triplet labels or pairwise relationships. In this paper, we propose a deep hashing framework called deep distribution-separating hashing (DDSH) method. The main novelty of our learning framework lies in the supervision which enforces to separate the distribution of similar pairs from the distribution of dissimilar pairs. In this way, the gap between similar pairs and dissimilar pairs is enlarged. Experimental results show that our proposed deep hashing method outperforms state-of-the-art approaches on two widely used benchmark datasets: CIFAR-10 and PASCAL VOC 2007.

Keywords: Image retrieval · Hash code learning · Deep hashing

1 Introduction

While the image data with high dimensions are growing explosively on the Internet, approximate nearest neighbor (ANN) search [2] has attracted increasing attention due to its computation efficiency and search quality. Hashing, an effective solution to ANN search, has been widely employed in image retrieval. Specifically, it targets to map a high-dimensional real-value data item into a low-dimensional and binary vector, called hash code.

The existing hashing methods can be generally classified into two categories: data-independent methods [3,9,16] and data-dependent methods [11,13,18,22]. A representative solution of data-independent methods is locality sensitive hashing (LSH) [9], which can generate compact hash codes with random projections in a very efficient way.

For the second category, data-dependant and task-specific hash functions are learned to generate compact binary codes to achieve high search accuracy. Since data-dependent methods learn projections instead of using random ones as in data-independent methods, they generally perform better.

© Springer International Publishing AG, part of Springer Nature 2018
B. Zeng et al. (Eds.): PCM 2017, LNCS 10736, pp. 560–570, 2018.
https://doi.org/10.1007/978-3-319-77383-4_55

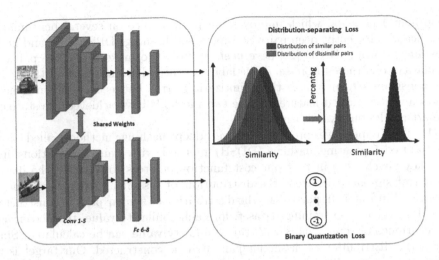

Fig. 1. Overview of our deep distribution-separating hashing (DDSH) framework. The cost function of DDSH contains: (1) the distribution-separating loss; (2) the binary quantization loss.

The data-dependent methods can be further divided into unsupervised methods and supervised methods. Unsupervised methods learn hash functions without utilizing any supervision information. Representative methods include iterative quantization (ITQ) [11,26], spectral hashing [27], graphs hashing [22]. Some deep unsupervised methods based on convolution neural network or binary auto-encoder have also been proposed, including deep neural network hashing DH [8], DeepBit [20] and simultaneous aggregating hash (SAH) [7]. In contrast, supervised methods learn hash functions with the label information from training data. The derived supervision is used to bridge the gap between high-level semantic information and low-level extracted image features. These methods include iterative quantization-canonical correlation analysis (ITQ-CCA) [11], LDAHash [25], two-step hashing (TSH) [19], and supervised hashing with kernel (KSH) [21].

Hand-crafted features have been used in previous hashing methods. These include the use of SIFT [23], GIST [24]. However, in these methods, the construction of hand-crafted feature is independent of the hash code learning procedure, which might lead to suboptimal results. The deep learning revolution shows that deep convolutional neural network (CNN) methods have brought a substantial leap in various computer vision tasks [12,15]. To relief the dependency on hand-crafted features, CNNs have been incorporated in hash code learning methods for image retrieval [17,18,28,29]. For example, convolutional neural network hashing (CNNH) [28] decomposes the hash learning method into two stages. This method learns approximate hash codes in the first stage, and simultaneously learns the feature representation as well as hash functions in the second stage. In network in network hashing (NINH) [17], Lai *et al.* proposed to simultaneously learn hash functions and image representations with a deep neural network, which improves the performance on several benchmarks significantly. Recently, deep pairwise-supervised hashing (DPSH) [18] and Deep Hashing Network (DHN) [29] have been proposed to make use of the pairwise similarity constructed from semantic labels for deep hashing. Both of them add the constraints to minimize the quantization error between the learned hash codes and the learned features. These two methods have achieved the state-of-the-art results on several benchmarks.

In this paper, we propose a novel deep hashing method called deep distribution-separating hashing (DDSH) method with pairwise relationships. The key novelty lies in that our cost function enforces to separate the distribution of similar pairs from the distribution of dissimilar pairs. The idea is illustrated in Fig. 1. In particular, the distribution of similar pairs is constructed as follows: given the training dataset, for each similarity value, the percentage of occurrence of similar pairs with this similarity value can be calculated. Similarly, the distribution of dissimilar pairs can be constructed. Our target is to separate these two distributions by learning effective feature representations and hash codes. By separating these two distributions, the gap between similar pairs and dissimilar pairs will be enlarged. Thus, our method is more likely to make a correct prediction (similar/dissimilar) for an unseen pair in the testing stage.

The proposed DDSH model accepts images of raw pixels and similarity pairwise labels as input, and then processes them through a deep convolution neural network which accepts raw images as input and extracts semantic image features. The optimization is guided with an objective function including a distribution-separating loss term and a binary quantization loss term. The whole model is trained in an end-to-end manner. Experiments on CIFAR-10 [14] and PASCAL VOC 2007 [10] datasets demonstrate that our DDSH method outperforms other deep hashing methods and achieves the state-of-the-art performance for image retrieval.

2   Deep Distribution-Separating Hashing

2.1   Problem Definition

In this paper, we use bold lowercase letters like z to denote vectors. Let $X = \{x_i\}_{i=1}^n$ denote n data points (images), where x_i denotes the raw data of image i. We are also given a set of similarity pairwise labels $S = \{s_{ij}\}$, $s_{ij} \in \{1, -1\}$, which can be constructed from the semantic labels. Specifically, $s_{ij} = 1$ indicates that x_i and x_j is a similar pair, while $s_{ij} = -1$ indicates that x_i and x_j is a dissimilar pair. In our model, we further split the set of similarity pairwise labels into two subsets S^+ and S^-: for all the pairs in S^+, $s_{ij} = 1$, and for all the pairs in S^-, $s_{ij} = -1$.

Given a set of data points $\{x_i\}_{i=1}^n$, the corresponding fixed-length feature representations $\{u_i\}_{i=1}^n$ are produced by the deep convolutional neural network. The binary hash code is computed simply with $b_i = sgn(u_i)$, where $sgn()$ is a sign function which returns 1 if the element is positive and returns -1 otherwise.

In our framework, similarity of pairs are computed with the cosine function:

$$c_{ij} = cos(\mathbf{u}_i, \mathbf{u}_j) \in [-1, 1] \tag{1}$$

We denote $c_{ij}^+ = cos(\mathbf{u}_i, \mathbf{u}_j)$ as the positive similarity when the pairwise label $s_{ij} = 1 \in S^+$, and $c_{ij}^- = cos(\mathbf{u}_i, \mathbf{u}_j)$ as the negative similarity, similarly.

The goal of deep hashing is to learn compact binary K-bit hash code $\mathbf{b_i} \in \{1, -1\}^K$ for each $\mathbf{x_i}$ with the supervised information. The hamming distance between the learned hash codes $\mathbf{b_i}$ and $\mathbf{b_j}$ should be small if $s_{ij} = 1$, and large if $s_{ij} = -1$.

2.2   Feature Learning Structure

Previous hashing models [18,29] have demonstrated that the CNN features can significantly boost the image retrieval performance. In our DDSH model, we adopt a convolutional neural network CCN-F [5] as the component for image feature extraction. The CNN-F model we adopt is pretrained with ImageNet [6]. It consists of five convolutional layers (denoted as $conv1 - 5$) and two fully-connected layers (denoted as $fc6 - 7$). The activation function of all layers is the Rectification Linear Unit (RELU) [15] $a^l(\mathbf{x}) = max(0, \mathbf{x})$. Besides, we add a fully connected layer ($fc8$) to perform linear projection. The representation $\mathbf{u_i}$ produced by $fc8$ has the equal dimensionality with hash code.

2.3   Formulation

We propose a novel objective function with the distribution-separating term and the binary quantization term. With the distribution-separating term, we enforce the deep hashing model from a new perspective of separating the distribution of similar pairs and the distribution of dissimilar pairs. In Fig. 2, we visualize the two distributions. The horizontal axis shows the similarity, and the vertical axis shows the percentage of occurrence for a pair with certain similarity value. Our target is to enlarge the gap between similar and dissimilar pairs.

We formulate the cost function as:

$$L = D + \lambda Q \tag{2}$$

where D is the distribution-separating term, and Q is the binary quantization term. λ is the weight between two terms.

Distribution-Separating Term. Our distribution-separating term D contains two parts: the mean square loss M and the variance loss V:

$$D = M + \eta V \tag{3}$$

η is the weight between mean square loss and variance loss. Mean and variance are two important statistics of a statistical distribution. Inspired by the Linear

Discriminant Analysis (LDA) [4], we consider the deep hashing as a binary classification problem. In the objective function, two elements should be considered: (1) maximize the distance of two distributions; (2) minimize the variance within each distribution.

We denote μ^+ as the mean of the distribution of similar pairs, which can be computed as follows:

$$\mu^+ = \frac{1}{|S^+|} \sum_{(i,j):s_{ij}=1} c_{ij}^+ \tag{4}$$

where c_{ij}^+ can be computed by Eq. 1 and $|S^+|$ is the number of similar pairs. The mean of the distribution of dissimilar pairs μ^- can be computed similarly.

To separate two distributions, our cost function targets to enlarge the distance of two means. Our mean square loss M is formulated as:

$$M = (\mu^+ - 1)^2 + (\mu^- + 1)^2 \tag{5}$$

where μ^+ is pushed to 1 and μ^- is pushed to -1.

To minimize the variance of each distribution, our variance loss V is defined as follows:

$$V = \frac{1}{|S^+| - 1} \sum_{(i,j):s_{ij}=1} (c_{ij}^+ - \mu^+)^2 + \frac{1}{|S^-| - 1} \sum_{(i,j):s_{ij}=-1} (c_{ij}^- - \mu^-)^2 \tag{6}$$

where c_{ij} and μ are computed using Eqs. 1 and 4. By minimizing the variance of each distribution with V, there will be less overlap between two distributions, which gives rise to a better separation.

Quantization Loss. To further boost the performance, we introduce a quantization loss to control the quantization error between hash codes and the feature representations produced by the deep convolutions neural network. The quantization loss is defined as follows:

$$Q = \sum_{i=1}^{n} \|\mathbf{b}_i - \mathbf{u}_i\|_2^2 \tag{7}$$

where $\mathbf{b}_i$ is computed by $\mathbf{b}_i = sgn(\mathbf{u}_i)$ and $\|\cdot\|_2$ denotes the L_2 norm operation. This quadratic quantization loss is incorporated to learn high-quality binary codes.

2.4   Optimization

An alternating optimization algorithm is applied between $\mathbf{b_i}$ and $\mathbf{u_i}$ for model training. We can directly optimize $\mathbf{b_i}$ as follows:

$$\mathbf{b_i} = sgn(\mathbf{u_i}) = sgn(\phi(\mathbf{x}; \theta))$$

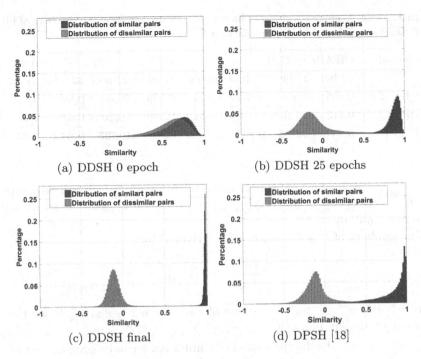

Fig. 2. The positive similarity distribution and negative similarity distribution on identical cifar-10 training set for: (a) initial state computed with initial deep model (b) the similarity distributions computed by the DDSH model after 25 epochs (c) the similarity distributions computed by the DDSH model (d) the similarity distributions computed by the DPSH model for comparison. Blue is for negative similarity distribution and red is for the negative. As seen, DDSH model can dramatically separate two similarity distribution, even without overlap. Best view in color

where $\phi(\mathbf{x}; \theta)$ denotes the CNN model, and θ are the parameters.

Back propagation is performed to update the model parameters θ. To achieve that, one key step is to compute the derivatives of L w.r.t. the kth bit of training sample i (i.e. u_{ik}) as follows:

$$\frac{\partial L}{\partial u_{ik}} = \frac{\partial M}{\partial u_{ik}} + \eta \frac{\partial V}{\partial u_{ik}} + \lambda \frac{\partial Q}{\partial u_{ik}}$$

where we directly get

$$\frac{\partial Q}{\partial u_{ik}} = 2(u_{ik} - b_{ik})$$

The gradient of $cos(\mathbf{u_i}, \mathbf{u_j})$ w.r.t. u_{ik} is denoted as $\delta_{ij,k} = \frac{u_{jk}}{\|\mathbf{u_i}\|_2 \|\mathbf{u_j}\|_2} - \frac{u_{ik}\langle \mathbf{u_i}, \mathbf{u_j} \rangle}{\|\mathbf{u_i}\|_2^3 \|\mathbf{u_j}\|_2}$. For the derivation of $\frac{\partial M}{\partial u_{ik}}$, we have

$$\frac{\partial M}{\partial u_{ik}} = 2(\mu^+ - 1)t_{ik}^+ + 2(\mu^- + 1)t_{ik}^-$$

Table 1. Mean Average Precision of hamming ranking for different numbers of bits on two datasets. The best MAPs are shown in bold.

Method	CIFAR-10 (MAP)				PASCAL VOC 2007 (MAP)			
	12 bits	24 bits	32 bits	48 bits	12 bits	24 bits	32 bits	48 bits
DHN [29]	0.555	0.594	0.603	0.621	0.539	0.563	0.582	0.585
DPSH [18]	0.713	0.727	0.744	0.757	0.589	0.620	0.630	0.638
DDSH	**0.778**	**0.813**	**0.817**	**0.838**	**0.618**	**0.635**	**0.642**	**0.641**

where t_{ik}^+ is the gradient of positive mean μ^+ w.r.t u_{ik}, which can be computed with $t_{ik}^+ = \frac{1}{|S^+|}(\sum_{j:s_{ij}=1} \delta_{ij,k}^+ + \sum_{j:s_{ji}=1} \delta_{ji,k}^+)$. $t_{i,k}^-$ for negative mean μ^- can be computed similarly.

The gradient of V w.r.t. u_{ik} can be derivated by

$$\frac{\partial V}{\partial u_{ik}} = v_{ik}^+ + v_{ik}^-$$

where v_{ik}^+ and v_{ik}^- are the derivations of variance w.r.t. u_{ik}. v_{ik}^+ is for the distribution of similar pairs: $v_{ik}^+ = \frac{2}{|S^+|-1}(\sum_{j:s_{ij}=1} c_{ij}^+ \delta_{ij,k}^+ + \sum_{j:s_{ji}=1} c_{ji}^+ \delta_{ji,k}^+ - |S^+|\mu^+ t_{ik}^+)$. v_{ik}^- for the distribution of dissimilar pairs can be computed similarly.

3   Experiments

To evaluate the effectiveness of our proposed DDSH framework, we perform image retrieval experiments on CIFAR-10 [14] and PASCAL VOC 2007 [10] datasets. The details of the experiments and the results are described in the following subsections.

3.1   Datasets and Setting

We conduct the experiments on two datasets: CIFAR-10 and PASCAL VOC 2007. The CIFAR-10 dataset consists of 60,000 single-label color images in 10 categories. Each class has 6,000 images in size 32 × 32. The PASCAL VOC 2007 dataset consists of 9,963 multi-label color images. There are 20 object classes in this dataset. On average, each image is annotated with 1.5 semantic labels.

For the CIFAR-10 dataset, we follow the experimental setting as [18,29]. We randomly select 100 images per class as test queries, and we select 500 images per class to form the training set. In PASCAL VOC 2007 dataset, we randomly select 1000 images as test query set, and 4000 images as training set. The similarity pairwise labels are constructed using the provided image labels: each pair of images are considered to be similar (dissimilar) if they share at least one (none) common semantic label.

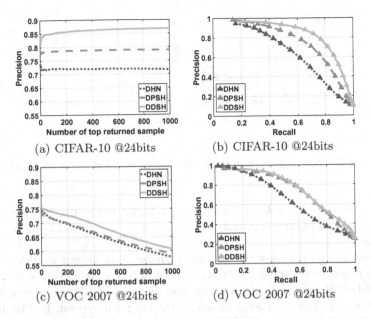

(a) CIFAR-10 @24bits   (b) CIFAR-10 @24bits

(c) VOC 2007 @24bits   (d) VOC 2007 @24bits

Fig. 3. Comparison on CIFAR-10 and PASCAL VOC 2007 datasets: (a) precision curves with respect to top returned samples @24bits on CIFAR-10; (b) precision-recall curves @24bits on CIFAR-10; (c) precision curves with respect to top returned samples @24bits on VOC 2007; (d) precision-recall curves @24bits on VOC 2007.

We compare our DDSH model with the state-of-the-art deep hashing methods: DPSH [18] and DHN [29]. Three evaluation metrics are reported: (1) Mean Average Precision (MAP); (2) Precision curve with respect to different numbers of top returned samples; (3) Precision-Recall curve.

For the experiment of CIFAR-10, the results of DPSH and DHN are directly reported from their original corresponding papers. For PASCAL VOC 2007, the results are obtained by the using the released implementations provided by the authors with parameters tuned by cross validation. We implement our DDSH framework with the open-source TensorFlow framework [1]. The DDSH model is trained with a minibatch based stochastic gradient descent (SGD) learning strategy with the mini-batch size set to be 128. We set $\eta = 1$ for two datasets. We set $\lambda = 10$ for CIFAR-10, $\lambda = 100$ for PASCAL VOC 2007. The parameters are selected by cross validation.

3.2 Results and Discussion

We evaluate all three methods with different lengths of hash code: 12, 24, 32, and 48 bits. The MAP results of DPSH [18], DHN [29], and proposed DDSH are listed in the Table 1. It can be seen that our proposed DDSH method significantly outperforms the two state-of-the-art methods with a large margin. We believe

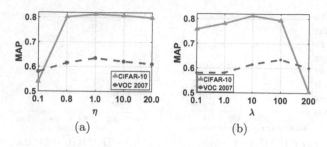

Fig. 4. (a) The effect of choosing different η (b) The effect of choosing different λ

the reason is that our DDSH cost function leads to less overlap between the distributions of similar pairs and dissimilar pairs, which yields more effective hash codes.

Figure 3(a) and (c) show the precision curves with respect to different numbers of top returned samples @24bits on two datasets. It can be seen that the proposed DDSH approach outperforms the two state-of-the-art methods when we only consider top returned samples in the retrieval system. In Fig. 3(b) and (d), Precision-Recall curves @24bits of three methods on two datasets are shown. DDSH achieves the highest precision at all recall levels.

3.3   Parameters Analysis

In this section, we give empirical analysis on the parameter sensitivity. The analysis is conducted with 24-bit hash codes on CIFAR-10 dataset. The parameter η controls the contribution of the variance loss. When η is too small, the performance will degrade as the overlap between two distributions will become larger. If η is too large, the effect of the term M will be small, and the distance of distributions cannot be maximized. It is worth noting that when the mean square loss and variance loss weight equally, (i.e. $\eta = 1$), and the model would achieve the best performance on both datasets. In addition, we show the effect of the parameter λ while fixing η. Figure 4 shows that DDSH can achieve good performance within a wide range of parameter values.

4   Conclusion

In this paper, we proposed the deep distribution-separating hashing (DDSH) method. To the best of our knowledge, DDSH is the first attempt to learn a deep hashing model from a perspective of separating the distribution of similar pairs from the distribution of dissimilar pairs. Extensive experimental results show that DDSH method can learn more effective hash code than other methods. Our proposed DDSH method achieves the state-of-the-art performance on CIFAR-10 and PASCAL VOC 2007 datasets.

References

1. Abadi, M., Agarwal, A., Barham, P., Brevdo, E., Chen, Z., Citro, C., Corrado, G.S., Davis, A., Dean, J., Devin, M., et al.: TensorFlow: large-scale machine learning on heterogeneous distributed systems. arXiv:1603.04467 (2016)
2. Andoni, A., Indyk, P.: Near-optimal hashing algorithms for approximate nearest neighbor in high dimensions. In: FOCS, pp. 459–468 (2006)
3. Andoni, A., Indyk, P., Laarhoven, T., Razenshteyn, I., Schmidt, L.: Practical and optimal LSH for angular distance. In: NIPS, pp. 1225–1233 (2015)
4. Balakrishnama, S., Ganapathiraju, A.: Linear discriminant analysis-a brief tutorial, vol. 18. Institute for Signal and Information Processing (1998)
5. Chatfield, K., Simonyan, K., Vedaldi, A., Zisserman, A.: Return of the devil in the details: delving deep into convolutional nets. arXiv:1405.3531 (2014)
6. Deng, J., Dong, W., Socher, R., Li, L., Li, K., Li, F.-F.: ImageNet: a large-scale hierarchical image database. In: CVPR, pp. 248–255 (2009)
7. Do, T., Tan, D., Pham, N.T., Cheung, N.M.: Simultaneous feature aggregating and hashing for large-scale image search. arXiv:1704.00860 (2017)
8. Erin Liong, V., Lu, J., Wang, G., Moulin, P., Zhou, J.: Deep hashing for compact binary codes learning. In: CVPR (2015)
9. Gionis, A., Indyk, P., Motwani, R., et al.: Similarity search in high dimensions via hashing. In: VLDB 1999, pp. 518–529 (1999)
10. Gong, Y., Jia, Y., Leung, T., Toshev, A., Ioffe, S.: Deep convolutional ranking for multilabel image annotation. arXiv:1312.4894 (2013)
11. Gong, Y., Lazebnik, S., Gordo, A., Perronnin, F.: Iterative quantization: a procrustean approach to learning binary codes for large-scale image retrieval. TPAMI **35**(12), 2916–2929 (2013)
12. He, K., Zhang, X., Ren, S., Sun, J.: Deep residual learning for image recognition. In: CVPR, pp. 770–778 (2016)
13. Kong, W., Li, W.-J.: Isotropic hashing. In: NIPS, pp. 1646–1654 (2012)
14. Krizhevsky, A., Hinton, G.: Learning multiple layers of features from tiny images (2009)
15. Krizhevsky, A., Sutskever, I., Hinton, G.: ImageNet classification with deep convolutional neural networks. In: NIPS, pp. 1097–1105 (2012)
16. Kulis, B., Grauman, K.: Kernelized locality-sensitive hashing. TPAMI **34**(6), 1092–1104 (2012)
17. Lai, H., Pan, Y., Liu, Y., Yan, S.: Simultaneous feature learning and hash coding with deep neural networks. In: CVPR, pp. 3270–3278 (2015)
18. Li, W.-J., Wang, S., Kang, W.C.: Feature learning based deep supervised hashing with pairwise labels. In: IJCAI, pp. 1711–1717 (2015)
19. Lin, G., Shen, C., Suter, D., Van Den Hengel, A.: A general two-step approach to learning-based hashing. In: ICCV, pp. 2552–2559 (2013)
20. Lin, K., Lu, J., Chen, C., Zhou, J.: Learning compact binary descriptors with unsupervised deep neural networks. In: CVPR, pp. 1183–1192 (2016)
21. Liu, W., Wang, J., Ji, R., Jiang, Y., Chang, S.: Supervised hashing with kernels. In: CVPR, pp. 2074–2081 (2012)
22. Liu, W., Wang, J., Kumar, S., Chang, S.: Hashing with graphs. In: ICML (2011)
23. Lowe, D.: Distinctive image features from scale-invariant keypoints. IJCV **60**, 91–110 (2004)
24. Oliva, A., Torralba, A.: Modeling the shape of the scene: a holistic representation of the spatial envelope. IJCV **42**(3), 145–175 (2001)

25. Strecha, C., Bronstein, A., Bronstein, M., Fua, P.: LDAHash: improved matching with smaller descriptors. TPAMI **34**(1), 66–78 (2012)
26. Vinyals, O., Toshev, A., Bengio, S., Erhan, D.: Show and tell: a neural image caption generator. In: CVPR, pp. 3156–3164 (2015)
27. Weiss, Y., Torralba, A., Fergus, R.: Spectral hashing. In: NIPS (2009)
28. Xia, R., Pan, Y., Lai, H., Liu, C., Yan, S.: Supervised hashing for image retrieval via image representation learning. In: AAAI, vol. 1, p. 2 (2014)
29. Zhu, H., Long, M., Wang, J., Cao, Y.: Deep hashing network for efficient similarity retrieval. In: AAAI, pp. 2415–2421 (2016)

An Obstacle Detection Method Based on Binocular Stereovision

Yihan Sun[1], Libo Zhang[2($\boxtimes$)], Jiaxu Leng[1], Tiejian Luo[1], and Yanjun Wu[2]

[1] University of Chinese Academy of Sciences, Beijing 101408, China
[2] Institute of Software, Chinese Academy of Sciences, Beijing 100190, China
zsmj@hotmail.com

Abstract. As the main tasks of Advance Driver Assistance Systems (ADAS), obstacle detection has attracted extensive attention. Traditional obstacle detection methods on the basis of monocular vision will lose its effect when new obstacles appear or the obstacles have severe occlusion and deformation, so this paper proposes an obstacle detection method based on disparity map, which can detect all obstacles on the road accurately. We first determine the disparity of the road in V disparity map through an approach based on weighted least square method. Then we obtain the disparity map contains only the obstacles on the road, and generate corresponding Real U disparity map by projection. Finally, obstacles are detected in Real U disparity map. Experiments show that the proposed method can not only precisely detect the obstacles at greater distances and the obstacles with a large area of occlusion, but also accurately calculate the distance information according to the disparity of the obstacle.

1 Introduction

In recent years, computer vision has made breakthroughs in many fields such as saliency detection [1,2], target tracking [3] and so on. Obstacle detection can improve the safety in driving and reduce traffic accidents as the main tasks of ADAS. Now obstacle detection methods based on vision have attracted wide attention of researchers, for its low cost and the ability to provide a wealth of scene information. In the past few years, different kinds of methods have been proposed. One commonly used method is to segment the image into image fragments, and then employ the similarity measure to classify these fragments. Some methods based on exhaustive search according to object characteristics, or contour information have also been put forward. At present, R-CNN is the most popular method in the field of monocular detection, which extracts feature by CNN, and then utilizes SVM to classify the feature vectors. Deep MANTA train the obstacle model through three layers of network, and then analyze the input image so as to detect the obstacles.

Above methods are based on monocular camera. Although this kind of methods have already made great progress, there are still two problems. (1) These methods implement the process of data acquisition and model training

© Springer International Publishing AG, part of Springer Nature 2018
B. Zeng et al. (Eds.): PCM 2017, LNCS 10736, pp. 571–580, 2018.
https://doi.org/10.1007/978-3-319-77383-4_56

in advance, therefore, once the obstacles in the scene are seriously blocked or the new obstacles appear, the detection algorithm will be invalid. (2) Monocular methods are difficult to calculate the distance of the obstacle accurately, for the reason that its calculation depends on the recognition of objects. In view of the above problems, obstacle detection methods based on binocular vision are beginning to emerge. Labayrade [4] proposed the V-disparity concept aimed at simplifying the process of separating obstacles from road surfaces. Therefore, extraction of 3D road surface and obstacles will be simplified as 2D linear extraction [5]. Hu proposed an U-V-disparity concept based on Labayrade's work, to classify the 3D road scene into relative surface planes and characterize the features of road, roadside, and obstacles [5]. The obstacle detection method based on U-V disparity map can detect obstacles accurately without training the model, and the change of the obstacles'shape does not affect the results.

Inspired by this method, we propose a fast obstacle detection method based on binocular stereovision. The main contributions are as follows: (1) In V-disparity map, a filtering method based on road features is proposed. (2) In V-disparity map, a road extraction method on account of the Hough transformation based on least square method is put forward. (3) For the problem that the obstacles at greater distances are difficult to be detected, we come up with a method to generate Real U disparity map, which can restore two-dimensional information to real spatial information. (4) To solve the problem of the deviation of the disparity, we raise a fast and effective method based on Real U disparity map.

2   Binocular Stereovision Model

Figure 1(a) is the geometric model of binocular stereovision model, which consists of three coordinate systems R_w, R_{cr} and R_{cl}. They represent the world coordinate system established with the ground level, right camera and left camera respectively. θ is the angle between the optical axis of the cameras and the ground level. h represents the height of the cameras above the ground. b is the distance between the cameras (baseline length).

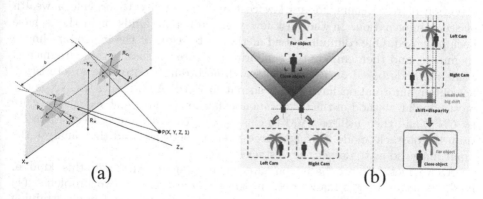

Fig. 1. (a) The model of binocular stereovision. (b) The generation of disparity.

In R_w, if a point is $P(X, Y, Z)$, its corresponding representation in homogeneous coordinate is $P(X, Y, Z, 1)$. Then, we can get the homogeneous coordinate of the imaging positions of point P in cameras and denote it as $p_i(u_i, v_i, 1)$:

$$\lambda \begin{pmatrix} u_i \\ v_i \\ 1 \end{pmatrix} = MT_iR \begin{pmatrix} X \\ Y \\ Z \\ 1 \end{pmatrix} \quad (i = l \text{ or } r) \tag{1}$$

where λ is scale factor, M is parameter matrix inside camera, T is translation matrix, and R is rotation matrix. u_i and v_i is the coordinate of p_i.

$$R = \begin{bmatrix} 1 & 0 & 0 & 0 \\ 0 & \cos\theta & -\sin\theta & 0 \\ 0 & \sin\theta & \cos\theta & 0 \\ 0 & 0 & 0 & 1 \end{bmatrix} \tag{2}$$

$$T_i = \begin{bmatrix} 1 & 0 & 0 & k_i\frac{b}{2} \\ 0 & 1 & 0 & h \\ 0 & 0 & 1 & 0 \\ 0 & 0 & 0 & 1 \end{bmatrix} \tag{3}$$

In Eq. (3), k_i is -1 if i equal to r, otherwise is 1.

The parameter matrix M in Eq. (1) is defined as:

$$M = \begin{bmatrix} f_u & 0 & u_0 & 0 \\ 0 & f_v & v_0 & 0 \\ 0 & 0 & 1 & 0 \end{bmatrix} \tag{4}$$

in which (u_0, v_0) is the central coordinate of the image, f_u and f_v represent the focal length in u and v direction respectively. According to Eqs. (1), (2), (3) and (4), we can generate the imaging positions of P: (u_l, v_l) and (u_r, v_r).

$$\begin{cases} v_{l,r} = \frac{(f_v\cos\theta + v_0\sin\theta)(Y+h) + (v_0\cos\theta - f_v\sin\theta)Z}{Z\cos\theta + (Y+h)\sin\theta} \\ u_{l,r} = u_0 + f_u\frac{X \pm b/2}{Z\cos\theta + (Y+h)\sin\theta} \end{cases} \tag{5}$$

As shown in Fig. 1(b), we can calculate the disparity of P by Eq. (5).

$$\Delta = u_l - u_r = \frac{f_u b}{Z\cos\theta + (Y+h)\sin\theta} \tag{6}$$

Equations (5) and (6) describe the basic relationship between image coordinate (u, v) and disparity Δ, which can be simply represented by the following equations:

$$\begin{cases} u = \Phi_u(X, \Delta) \\ v = \Phi_v(Z, \Delta) \end{cases} \tag{7}$$

Particularly, $Y = 0$ denotes the road surface, and we can generate Eq. (8):

$$v\cos\theta = \frac{h}{b}\Delta - f_v\sin\theta \tag{8}$$

3   The Proposed Method

The first step of obstacle detection is the determination of the road area. Most of the existing monocular based methods require huge amount of computation and are difficult to meet the requirements of real-time. Therefore, we apply the method based on binocular stereovision to determine the road in V-disparity map. We propose a novel method on account of the Hough transformation based on weighted least square method, which can accurately remove the disparity representing the road and outside the road. Besides, the detection of obstacles at greater distances is always a difficulty, for the reason that the disparity points of the those obstacles are few in number and not continuous, thus the missed detection and false detection are much more apt to occur. To solve this problem, we put forward a method to generate Real U disparity map, which can restore two-dimensional information to real spatial information.

Figure 2 demonstrates the flow diagram of our algorithm. The algorithm starts with calculating the V disparity map according to the disparity map obtained by stereo matching, then extracting the road in V disparity map, and removing the disparity representing the road and outside the road. Next, U disparity map is generated via projection, and then mapped to the real space x-z to create Real U disparity map. Finally, the detection is completed in the Real U disparity map. This method is simple and effective, and is characterized by low computation workload and fast speed due to the use of the disparity map based on edge. In addition, it can detect obstacles at greater distances, because of the application of the convertion from disparity map to the real space.

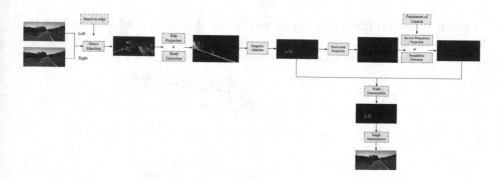

Fig. 2. Algorithm flowchart.

3.1   The Determination of Detection Area

Through the binocular stereovision model, the detection area of the real scenes can be projected to the corresponding disparity map. Taking the center of the center line of the cameras as the origin of coordinates, the detection area of real space is determined by four points: $(X_{left}, 0, Z_{min})$ $(X_{left}, 0, Z_{max})$

$(X_{right}, 0, Z_{min})$ $(X_{right}, 0, Z_{max})$. Do calculation according to the left two boundary points $(X_{left}, 0, Z_{min})$ and $(X_{left}, 0, Z_{max})$, and according to Eq. (9).

$$\begin{cases} \frac{Z}{b/2-x} = \frac{f}{u-w/2} \\ d = \frac{bf}{Z} \end{cases} \tag{9}$$

where w is the width of the image, Z is the real distance, b is the baseline length, x is the true horizontal distance, f is the focal length, u is the column of the image, and d is the disparity. Thus we can obtain a $u - d$ equation what represents the left boundary:

$$d = \frac{b(u - w/2)}{b/2 - x} \tag{10}$$

Similarly, the right boundary equation can be computed. Now the transformation from the real space point (x, z) to (u, d) is achieved. According to the linear equations of left boundary and right boundary, we calculate the boundary disparity of each column in the disparity map. If the disparity of the current column is less than the disparity of road boundary, we set it to be zero to obtain a sub-disparity map containing only the disparity of detection area.

3.2   Road Extraction in V-disparity Map

The V disparity map can be obtained by function $G(D_\Delta) = (D_{v\Delta})$, which counts the number of the same disparity in each row of disparity map. D_Δ is disparity map and $D_{v\Delta}$ is V disparity map, in which the abscissa is disparity, while the ordinate corresponds to the original disparity map. The gray value of each pixel $D_{v\Delta}(v, d)$ is expressed as the number of the pixels with d disparity in the Vth row in original disparity map. To better detect the road, we design a morphological filtering method to filter the V disparity map and enhance the road.

The road in real scenes is usually an arch with lower sides and higher middle, instead of a flat shape. So, it is represented as a long strip with circular shape in V disparity map, and generally the approximately centered line in this strip area is considered as the expression of the road. The drawback of the Hough transformation is that only the straight line through the most points is taken into account. Thus, we put forward an improved road extraction method based on Hough transformation, which uses the least squares method to reduce the impact of noise. Specifically, the pixel points are weighted by the following methods:

$$w(d, v) = \alpha(1 - \frac{v}{h}) + \beta \begin{cases} \frac{n}{(1+\exp(-n))(1-\exp(-d))w} & d > T \\ 1 - \exp(\frac{-n}{wd}) & d \leq T \end{cases} \tag{11}$$

in which $w(d, v)$ denotes the weight of the pixel point (d, v) in the V disparity map. n is the number of current pixels, w and h are the width and height of the original disparity map respectively, α and β are weighting factors, and T is the threshold of disparity. From the equation we can get that the bigger value of the sample point and the smaller the disparity, the less likely it is to be the noise point. The closer the sample point to the bottom, the more likely it is the point represents road, so we give it a greater weight. After the pixels are weighted, we can detect the straight line representing the road. The red line in the graph in the third column of Fig. 2 is the straight line detected by Hough transformation, which is somewhat high and basically extracting the top of the arch. Our method is to detect a straight line by Hough transformation, then use weighted least square method to achieve the process of fitting to generate the second straight line as the road. Specifically, we use Eq. (12) to represent the line detected by Hough transformation:

$$v = kd + b \tag{12}$$

where k and b are parameters of the linear equation:

$$|v' - kd' - b| < \varepsilon \tag{13}$$

$$\min_{k',b'} \sum_{i=1}^{m} (v' - b' - kd') \tag{14}$$

By Eq. (14), we use all the effective pixels (v', d') satisfied Eq. (13), and their corresponding $w(d', v')$, to estimate the straight line representing the road exactly, which is shown as the blue line in the graph in the third column of Fig. 2. This method can not only avoid possible deviations from the road area caused by the drawback of Hough transformation, but also overcome the problem that ordinary least square method is sensitive to noise. By utilizing the detected line of road, we can determine the road's boundaries, and then apply the method in Sect. 3.1 to remove the disparities of the road and outside the road.

3.3   Obstacle Detection Based on Real U-disparity Map

After completing the above steps, we obtain the disparity map contains only the obstacles on the road, and then count the number of the same disparity in each column of disparity map to generate the U disparity map (top view), in which the abscissa corresponds to the original disparity map, while the ordinate represents disparity. The obstacle cannot be detected by detecting the horizontal line segments, because there is usually the errors in the stereo matching. In addition, the disparity points of the obstacles at greater distances are few in number greatly increases the difficulty of detection. To solve above problems, a method based on Real U disparity map is raised, which can revert the two-dimensional information to real spatial information. Here are details about how to transfer U disparity map to Real U disparity map, and how to detect obstacles:

(1) Map the U disparity map u-d to the spatial coordinate u-z, and calculate the distance between the obstacle and the binocular cameras according to $z = BF/d$, and then the pixels in a certain distance interval are counted together. So the obstacle, especially the nearby obstacle, can be compressed into a horizontal line segment, thus can avoid detecting an object as several objects.

(2) Proceed the speckle filtering in u-z graph for removing the hot pixel: Count the number of valid pixels and the sum of the valid pixel values, and then compare them with the corresponding threshold. Let this pixel equal to 0 when the two values are both smaller than the threshold, and equal to 255 otherwise.

(3) To stretch the pixels of the obstacles at greater distances, we map the u-z graph to the x-z graph to produce the Real U disparity map. Assume (x, z) to be one of the pixels in Real U disparity map and compute the corresponding points in the u-z disparity map according to Eq. (15).

$$u = u_0 + (x - B/2)F/(z\kappa) \tag{15}$$

in which B is the baseline length of binocular cameras, F is the focus distance, κ is the physical size of each pixel, and u_0 is the abscissa of the image center. Now we obtain the corresponding points of (x, z) in u-z graph, signed as (u, z). In actual scenes, it is necessary to fill it by interpolation method. A search scope is calculated based on current (x, z) and the given Δx, as shown in Eq. (16).

$$\begin{cases} u_l = u_0 + (x - \Delta x - B/2)F/(z\kappa) \\ u_r = u_0 + (x + \Delta x - B/2)F/(z\kappa) \end{cases} \tag{16}$$

where u_l and u_r denotes the left and right boundary respectively. By doing so, we can remove the hot pixel, and fill the missing disparity of obstacles. To detect horizontal line segments in the Real U disparity map, we move a valid pixel, which is taken as the starting point, to the right, and search the valid values horizontally. At the same time, set the threshold for the length of the line segment. Finally, merge the group of horizontal line segments.

(4) Determine the interval of columns and the scope of disparity of the obstacles according to the detected line segments in Real U disparity map. The pixels that satisfy the scope of disparity are compressed into one column, and the number of the valid disparities in each row is computed. Then search the obstacles from top to bottom. Finally, remove obstacles that are close to the ground according to the height.

4   Result

We evaluate our proposed method on KITTI dataset [6]. The reference images of obstacle detection in KITTI are divided into three categories: Car, Pedestrian and Cyclis, including 7481 images as training data and 7518 as test data. For each category, three levels are set according to the occlusion and truncation of the object: easy, moderate, hard. Our method can detect obstacles without knowing what kind of the obstacle is, therefore it does not require off-line training. The most authoritative method named oracle recall [7] is used to evaluate our method. We first compute the IoU corresponding to each obstacle, where

Table 1. Algorithm performance test.

Method	MHT	RU	Car		Cyclist		Pedestrian	
			Recall	Precision	Recall	Precision	Recall	Precision
ODDM-N2	No	No	0.62	0.78	0.59	0.71	0.51	0.68
ODDM-M	Yes	No	0.72	0.73	0.72	0.68	0.68	0.62
ODDM-R	No	Yes	0.58	0.88	0.55	0.8	0.53	0.79
ODDM-MR	Yes	Yes	0.81	0.95	0.78	0.89	0.75	0.85

IoU represents the degree of overlap between the bounding box and the ground truth. Then we set the threshold as T and receive three kinds of results: positive samples are detected as positive samples (TP), negative samples are detected as positive samples (FP), and the positive samples are detected as negative samples (FN). According to the results, we can calculate recall and precision: $Recall = TP/(TP + FP)$, $Presionl = TP/(TP + FN)$. Finally, we calculate a set of the recall and precision under different threshold T, further generating the R-P graph to compute the Average Precision (AP).

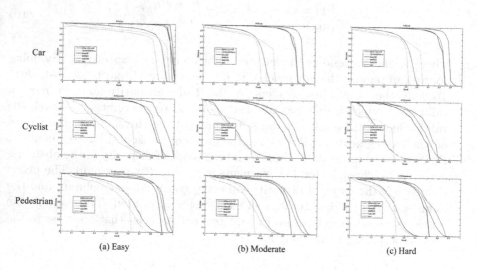

(a) Easy   (b) Moderate   (c) Hard

Fig. 3. Detection results of different method on KITTI dataset.

The result, when threshold T = 70%, is shown in Table 1. ODDM-N2 is the traditional obstacle detection method based on the disparity map, the experimental results show that this method has a large number of false detections and misses partial obstacles. ODDM-M applies the modified extraction method on the basis of ODDM-N2, thus the recall is obviously improved. Based on ODDM-N2, ODDM-R uses Real U disparity map to detect obstacles, which can better detect the obstacles at greater distances and further improve the precision.

Table 2. Average Precision (AP) (in %) on the test set of the KITTI object detection benchmark.

	Cars			Pedestrians			Cyclist		
	Easy	Moderate	Hard	Easy	Moderate	Hard	Easy	Moderate	Hard
SS	75.91	60	50.98	54.06	47.55	40.56	56.26	39.16	38.83
3DOP	91.58	85.8	76.8	61.57	54.79	51.12	73.94	55.59	53
EB	83.91	67.89	58.34	46.8	40.22	33.81	43.97	30.36	28.5
R-CNN	-	-	-	61.61	50.13	44.79	-	-	-
pAUCEnsT	-	-	-	65.26	54.49	48.6	51.62	38.03	33.38
Regionlets	84.75	76.45	59.7	73.14	61.15	55.21	70.41	58.72	51.83
Faster R-CNN	86.71	81.84	71.12	78.86	65.9	61.18	72.26	63.35	55.9
Ours	94.01	93.15	90.28	88.25	85.81	80.42	80.53	77.86	75.24

ODDM-MR is our ultimate method, which has obvious advantages comparing with ODDM-N2. The recall of the Car, Cyclist and Pedestrian detection increased by 19%, 19%, and 24% respectively. The precision of the Car, Cyclist and Pedestrian detection increased by 17%, 18%, and 17% respectively.

To better illustrate the advantages, we compare our method with the currently mainstream obstacle detection methods: Mono3D [8], NMRDO, SubCNN [9], DPM-VOC+VP [10] and LSVM-MDPM-sv [11]. Figure 3 is the R-P graph, which shows the functional relation between the recall and the precision of different methods, and we can find that our method is superior to other detection algorithms in all three categories, even if under the hard level.

We calculate the average precision under different conditions, then compare with other methods. As shown in Table 2, the average precision of our method have absolute advantage in every aspect compared with other methods (SS, 3DOP [12], EB, R-CNN, pAUCEnsT [13], Regionlets [14] and Faster R-CNN [15]). What's more, even under the hard level, our method still maintains good performance. For example, compared with Faster R-CNN, the average precision of our method in Pedestrian detection on different levels (easy, moderate and hard) increased by 7.3%, 11.31% and 19.16% respectively.

5   Conclusion

We propose an obstacle detection method based on binocular stereovision, which does not require off-line training and can detect all obstacles on the road. We first present a method based on weighted least square method in V disparity map to detect the road accurately. Then we propose an approach to project U disparity map to Real U disparity map. Finally, the position of the obstacle is determined by a rapid locating method. The experimental results show that our proposed method is effective and reliable, and can deal with complex scenes very well, especially in case of occlusion and severe deformation of obstacles.

References

1. Zhang, L., Sun, Y., Luo, T., Rahman, M.M.: Note: a manifold ranking based saliency detection method for camera. Rev. Sci. Instrum. **87**(9), 096103 (2016)
2. Zhang, L., Yang, L., Luo, T.: Unified saliency detection model using color and texture features. PLoS ONE **11**(2), e0149328 (2016)
3. Zhang, L., Cai, Y., Ullah, Z., Luo, T.: MLPF algorithm for tracking fast moving target against light interference. In: International Conference on Pattern Recognition, pp. 3939–3944 (2016)
4. Labayrade, R., Aubert, D., Tarel, J.P.: Real time obstacle detection in stereovision on non flat road geometry through "V-disparity" representation. In: Intelligent Vehicle Symposium, vol. 2, pp. 646–651 (2003)
5. Hu, Z., Uchimura, K.: UV-disparity: an efficient algorithm for stereovision based scene analysis. In: Proceedings of the IEEE Intelligent Vehicles Symposium, pp. 48–54. IEEE (2005)
6. Geiger, A., Lenz, P., Urtasun, R.: Are we ready for autonomous driving? the kitti vision benchmark suite. In: 2012 IEEE Conference on Computer Vision and Pattern Recognition (CVPR), pp. 3354–3361. IEEE (2012)
7. Hosang, J., Benenson, R., Dollar, P., Schiele, B.: What makes for effective detection proposals? IEEE Trans. Pattern Anal. Mach. Intell. **38**(4), 814–830 (2016)
8. Chen, X., Kundu, K., Zhang, Z., Ma, H., Fidler, S., Urtasun, R.: Monocular 3D object detection for autonomous driving. In: Computer Vision and Pattern Recognition (2016)
9. Xiang, Y., Choi, W., Lin, Y., Savarese, S.: Subcategory-aware convolutional neural networks for object proposals and detection (2016)
10. Pepik, B., Stark, M., Gehler, P., Schiele, B.: Multi-view and 3D deformable part models. IEEE Trans. Pattern Anal. Mach. Intell. **37**(11), 2232 (2015)
11. Geiger, A., Wojek, C., Urtasun, R.: Joint 3D estimation of objects and scene layout. In: Advances in Neural Information Processing Systems, pp. 1467–1475 (2011)
12. Chen, X., Kundu, K., Zhu, Y., Berneshawi, A.G., Ma, H., Fidler, S., Urtasun, R.: 3D object proposals for accurate object class detection. In: Advances in Neural Information Processing Systems, pp. 424–432 (2015)
13. Paisitkriangkrai, S., Shen, C., van den Hengel, A.: Pedestrian detection with spatially pooled features and structured ensemble learning. IEEE Trans. Pattern Anal. Mach. Intell. **38**(6), 1243–1257 (2016)
14. Long, C., Wang, X., Hua, G., Yang, M., Lin, Y.: Accurate object detection with location relaxation and regionlets re-localization. In: Asian Conference on Computer Vision, pp. 260–275 (2014)
15. Ren, S., He, K., Girshick, R., Sun, J.: Faster R-CNN: towards real-time object detection with region proposal networks. IEEE Trans. Pattern Anal. Mach. Intell. **39**(6), 1137 (2016)

Coding, Compression, Transmission, and Processing

Target Depth Measurement for Machine Monocular Vision

Jiafa Mao, Mingguo Zhang$^{(\boxtimes)}$, Linan Zhu, Cong Bai, and Gang Xiao

College of Computer Science and Technology,
Zhejiang University of Technology, Hangzhou, China
shmilymdt@163.com

Abstract. Most of the existing machine vision positioning technology focused on the technology of double camera geometric positioning, or use a single camera plus non-visual sensor technology for positioning. These two technologies achieve the precise positioning by increasing the amount of data and sacrificing processing speed. In this paper, a new method of target depth measurement for machine monocular vision is proposed. According to the imaging model of the camera, the imaging parameters of the camera (such as focal length, field of view, equivalent focal length, etc.), and the basic principle of analog signal to digital signal, we derived a relationship model between the target depth, field of view, equivalent focal length and the camera resolution. Under the condition of the height of the camera and the height of the target are known, the target depth analysis is carried out. The algorithm shows that our method could effectively locate the target depth.

Keywords: Robot · Machine vision · Depth measurement · Monocular camera

1 Introduction

Machine vision, also known as computer vision or artificial vision, is a simulation of the human eye by computer or machine, which identifies the shape and movement of 3D scenes and objects in the objective world [1–3]. As the demands of robot grow rapidly in industry, military, scientific research and civilian fields [4–7], machine vision has attracted more and more attentions. Machine vision has an important influence on the performance of the robot. The machine vision system is to use the camera to obtain the visual information of the outside world and then control the entire system. The robot could not be separated from the support of the computer vision technology in dealing with the visual problems. The computer vision technology has been applied more and more widely because of its flexibility and adaptability. In computer vision technology, 3D depth information acquisition is one of the most challenging problems in robotic autonomous navigation, 3D scene reconstruction, visual measurement and industrial automation [8].

The robot's ability to operate firstly depends on the connection and cooperation with the external environment, that is, the interaction between the robot and the environment. The interaction between the robot and the environment depends on the three-dimensional positioning ability of the robot to the external target. The three-dimensional positioning

© Springer International Publishing AG, part of Springer Nature 2018
B. Zeng et al. (Eds.): PCM 2017, LNCS 10736, pp. 583–595, 2018.
https://doi.org/10.1007/978-3-319-77383-4_57

capability refers to the three-dimensional spatial positioning capability of the robot using the computer vision technology to restore the target. The image of the objective world captured by the camera have lost the 3-D depth information that is important for the response and operation of the robot. Many researchers have conducted extensive researches on robot positioning. The method of obtaining the depth information of the external target is divided into two categories, one is based on the computer vision target localization method and the other is the non-visual sensor positioning technology [9–11], here we mainly introduce vision - based positioning technology. The vision-based target localization method mainly includes binocular sensing depth method [12, 13], monocular camera calibration method [14–21] and single camera-plane mirror depth acquisition method [22–25]. The accuracy of the binocular perception depth method is affected by the performance of the camera, the light and the length of the baseline (the distance between the two cameras). Because of the complexity of the algorithm, there are many limitations in the application, and the processing data is relatively large, which is not conducive to real-time requirements. The monocular depth perception is widely used in camera calibration technology, which is one of the basic problems of computer vision and is designed to determine the camera's internal and external parameters by using image features and corresponding 3D features. Camera calibration has been extensively studied in computer vision for a long time, and many calibration methods have been proposed. The basic camera calibration method can be divided into the traditional camera calibration and self-calibration. The traditional calibration method has a high calibration accuracy, but requires a specific calibration reference. In the calibration process, due to the constraints of the equipment, it still could not do a very precise record of the corresponding coordinates of a point in the world coordinate system and the image coordinate system. If the coordinates are not accurate enough, the accuracy of the resulting transformation matrix will be constrained, and the accuracy of the coordinate transformation will fluctuate. The self-calibration method does not depend on the calibration reference, but the calibration results are relatively unstable. The monocular camera plus plane mirror method always places the plane mirror on the upper or the side of the tracking target, and is suitable for the tracking target to be fixed in a specific range. Although the problem of occlusion tracking and matching of the target in the specific range is effectively solved, the target activity is not fixed in a particular range, which decrease its practicalities. The non vision sensor uses the sound wave, the infrared, the pressure, the electromagnetic induction and so on to perceive the close degree of the external target and the robot. However, the coordinates of the target 3D space also need to be completed with the visual imaging sensor. This significantly increases the amount of data processed and the memory needed. In view of the limitations, this paper starts from the geometric perspective model of camera imaging, and proposes a new method of depth measurement. This paper studies the geometric model of camera, the target depth information, the relationship between target digital-length and target depth and the influence of the changing of field angle on the digital length of the target, it effectively overcomes the shortcomings of the camera calibration method, and solves the problem of target depth measurement accurately by using single camera measurement.

According to the imaging model of the camera, the imaging parameters of the camera (such as focal length, field of view, equivalent focal length, etc.), and the basic principle of analog signal to digital signal, we derived a relationship model between the target depth, field of view, equivalent focal length and the camera resolution. Under the condition of the height of the camera and the height of the target are known, the target depth analysis is carried out. In this paper, the monocular geometric depth measurement method could effectively avoid the shortcomings of the traditional binocular camera depth perception algorithm, which has high requirements on hardware and high cost. It also solved the problem that the camera calibration method of monocular camera is complicated and easy to be affected by the coordinate point and the problem of need to be calibrated again when the position and parameter changes. At the same time, it solved the problem of narrow scope of application of the single camera plane mirror method. This proposal has the advantages of simple operation, less susceptible to coordinate, lower requirement of hardware, real-time requirements. It could be widely used in industrial automation production line for robot precise positioning of the target, in mobile robot shelter and other fields. The main contributions of this paper are as follows:

(1) The geometric model of the camera and the target depth information is established, this paper deduces the relationship between the target length on the simulated image plane and the distance of the camera to the target. The method is simple and does not need complicated camera calibration procedure.
(2) Digitize the target image on the simulated image plane to solve the mathematical relationship between the target digital length and the target depth, thus solving the practicability of the method. The stability of the mathematical model is better and the data volume is small;
(3) The influence of the changing the field of view on the digitization length of the target is studied, and the mathematical model of the process is deduced. The model effectively solves the relationship between the target depth, the change of the focal length and the digital length of the target in the image.

The rest of this paper is organized as follows: The geometric model of the camera is presented in Sect. 2. The basic concept and relation of camera field of view and focal length is introduced in Sect. 3. Section 4 provides the target depth information calculation reasoning process of monocular vision. Finally the conclusions are presented in Sect. 5.

2   Geometric Model Of The Camera

The imaging model of the camera can be equivalent with the pinhole perspective model, which is a commonly used idealized state model. It approximates the imaging process of the camera, which has the advantages of simple and practical and high accuracy.

Firstly a space coordinate system was set up, as shown in Fig. 1. Assuming the height of the robot (the height of the camera off the ground) is h_1, the robot's target AB (the red part of the map) is h_2, and the target AB is in front of the robot. The CCD (image sensor) in Fig. 1 presents monocular camera in the top of the robot, the target object AB before the camera imaging to its CCD sensor through the pinhole perspective model. Here the problem to be solved is how to calculate the target depth between the target and the robot by these known parameters.

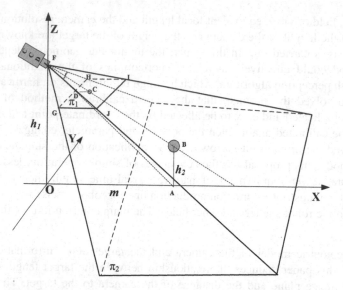

Fig. 1. Schematic diagram of the target object AB in the camera

In order to measure the horizontal distance of the target object AB from the camera, we could firstly set the horizontal distance m, that is, the length of the OA in Fig. 1. The robot is looking at the top of the target object AB, that is, the camera CCD in Fig. 1 focuses on point B. The coordinate system is established with O point at bottom of the robot. The horizontal direction of the machine vision direction is the X axis, that is, the OA side in Fig. 1, the straight line on the ground plane perpendicular to the OX axis is the Y axis. The camera position is remembered as F point, then the OF edge is the Z axis. Assuming that the camera has the focal length FC as f at the time of imaging, and the imagery plane is π_1. The object AB is imaged as a CD by the plane π_1 of the camera. Obviously, points A, B, C, D, O and F are on the plane where XOZ is located. So the following formula could be got.

$$\tan(\angle OFA) = m/h_1 \tag{1}$$

$$\tan(\angle OFB) = m/(h_1 - h_2) \tag{2}$$

Because

$$\angle AFB = \angle OFB - \angle OFA \tag{3}$$

Then

$$\arctan\left(m/(h_1 - h_2)\right) - \arctan\left(m/h_1\right) = \arctan\left(|CD|/f\right) \tag{4}$$

The $|CD|$ in Eq. 4 indicate the distance between C point and D point, f is the focal length of the digital camera. Take the tangent value on both sides of Eq. 4, and the following formula could be got:

$$|CD|m^2 - fh_2m + |CD|h_1^2 - |CD|h_1h_2 = 0 \qquad (5)$$

Equation 6 could be solved shown as follows by Eq. 5

$$|CD| = mh_2f/(m^2 + h_1^2 - h_1h_2) \qquad (6)$$

Based on Eq. 6, the constraint relation between image $|CD|$ of object AB in the image plane π_1 and the target depth m is established. In fact, for machine vision, we get only the height difference of the target object in the image (the pixel difference between point C and point D could be obtained by the image target segmentation technique), the height of the robot itself (could be set in advance), and the height of the target for robot to find (could also set in advance). Therefore, it is necessary to solve the problem of the relationship between the pixel difference of the target height in the image and the actual target height to solve the m in the Eq. 6.

The mapping relationship between the target object AB and the CD is related not only to its imaging principle but also to some parameters of the camera, such as the field of view, the focal length, the camera model, and so on. These parameters are easy to get from the manufacture of digital camera. The basic concepts of field of view and focal length and their relations are introduced in the following passage.

3 The Basic Concept and Relation of Camera Field of View and Focal Length

Because the target through the pinhole imaging model to simulate the projection image plane in the imaging process, the image is affected by the length of camera focal length and size of field of view, it is necessary to establish the relationship between them.

3.1 Basic Concepts of Field of View (FOV) and Focal Length

The so-called field of view refers to the scene could all fall into the imaging size, and the field of view outside the scene will not be taken. In the display system, the field of view is the angle between the edge of the display and the point of view (eye). In optical engineering, the field of view is also referred to as FOV. The FOV is usually used to characterize the scope of the scene. In optical instruments, FOV refers to the angle of the maximum range that can be observed by optical instruments (especially optical instruments such as telescopes).

For optical instruments, FOV is a very important concept, FOV has a significant influence on the measurement accuracy [26]. In the CCD optical system, the calibration of FOV significantly affects the nonlinear geometric distortion between the imaging and the ideal imaging [27]. The size of the FOV determines the range of the optical instrument, the greater the FOV, the greater the visual field, the smaller the optical magnification. FOV is divided into the object field angle and image side angle. General optical equipment users concerned about the object field of view angle. For most optical instruments, the FOV is calculated from the diameter of the image. For the camera, its photosensitive surface is rectangular, the diagonal of the rectangular sensor is used to calculate FOV. Therefore, the angle of view of the lens is related to the target surface of the camera and the focal length of the lens. Figure 2 depicts viewing angle of the visible range diameter. In Fig. 2, $|G'I'|$ is the diameter length of the visible range of the lens, $|FC'|$ is the distance from the camera to the target object, and $\angle G'FI'$ is the viewing angle. Let us set: $|FC'| = s$, $\angle G'FI' = \alpha$, then the following holds:

$$\tan\left(\frac{\alpha}{2}\right) = \frac{|G'C'|}{s} \tag{7}$$

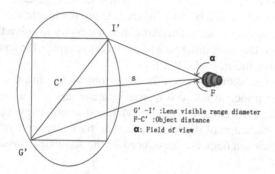

Fig. 2. Field of view determined by the viewing angle

The focal length is the measurement of the aggregation or divergence of the light in the optical system, which refers to the distance from the center of the lens to the focus of the light gathering. It is also the distance from the lens optical center to the imaging plane such as film, CCD or CMOS in the camera. There is a certain mathematical relationship between the FOV and the focal length of the lens and the CCD diagonal.

3.2   Field Angle, Focal Length and CCD Diagonal Relationship

In general, the greater the FOV, the shorter the focal length. For the FOV, it is determined by the CCD and camera focal length. At present, there are many kinds of specifications of the CCD in the camera, such as 1/3" CCD specification, 1/4" CCD specification, etc., and the area of CCD is based on the length of the diagonal length of the rectangle. This is similar to the definition of TV screen size. One inch is 25.4 mm. 1/3" CCD, 1/4" CCD all indicate how many times the CCD diagonal is one inch long. The denominator is small and its numerical value is large, and the corresponding photosensitive element area is also large. For a CCD camera, the size of the CCD is fixed, and the FOV is determined by the focal length. Figure 3 shows the relationship

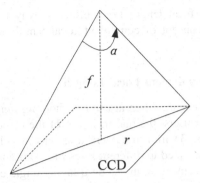

Fig. 3. Geometric relationship between CCD diagonal, FOV, and focal length

between the FOV α, the focal length f and the diagonal line r of the CCD. From this geometric relation, the conversion formula could easily be got between them:

$$\tan\left(\frac{\alpha}{2}\right) = \frac{r}{2f} \tag{8}$$

In the Eq. 8, the diagonal r of the CCD is fixed, and therefore, it can be seen that the focal length is inversely proportional to the tangent value of the field angle. But different camera models, the size of the CCD is not the same, that is, its diagonal r is not the same. Therefore, it is easily come to: the same focal length, with a different CCD, the FOV is also different. For example, if a camera lens focal length is 2.8 mm, if it is paired with a 1/3" CCD, then the camera's field of view is 89.9°. If it with 1/4" CCD, then the camera's FOV was 75.6°, a difference of 14.3° as much. Table 1 lists the same lens focal length with different sizes of CCD FOV difference.

Table 1. The same lens focal length with different sizes of CCD FOV difference

Lens focal length	CCD model		The difference between the two
	1/3" CCD	1/4" CCD	
2.8 mm	89.9°	75.6°	14.3°
3.6 mm	75.7°	62.2°	13.5°
4 mm	69.9°	57.0°	12.9°
6 mm	50.0°	39.8°	10.2°
8 mm	38.5°	30.4°	8.1°
12 mm	26.2°	20.5°	5.7°
16 mm	19.8°	15.4°	4.4°
25 mm	10.6°	8.3°	2.3°
60 mm	5.3°	4.1°	1.2°

It can be seen from Table 1, different types of CCD, the same lens focal length, the FOV is different. In order to compare the size of the FOV with different CCD size cameras, the equivalent focal length is an effective way to normalize the FOV of different cameras. The concept of equivalent focal length will be introduced in the following passage.

3.3   The Concept of Equivalent Focal Length

Only with the lens focal length, different camera shooting range (imaging FOV) could not be compared. But for users, the real meaning of the camera is the shooting range (FOV size). Because the 135 film in camera lens was usually to define the shooting FOV. So people are accustomed to different sizes of photosensitive components on the imaging angle, into 135 camera on the same imaging angle corresponding to the lens focal length. For example, the 50 mm focal length lens on the APS-c (photographic element diagonal length is 2/3 of 135 film) camera the shooting angle is the same as 75 mm focal length of the lens in the 135 film, a difference of about 30°. That is, 50 mm lens conversion into 135 film camera focal length is 75 mm, which is equivalent focal length. Figure 4. shows the relationship between the actual focal length f of the lens and the equivalent focal length f'. Assuming that the equivalent focal length is denoted by f', the actual focal length of the lens is denoted by f, the diagonal length of the 135 film is denoted by r_0, and the actual diagonal length of the CCD is denoted by r, then the equivalent focal length is calculated as follows [28].

$$f' = \frac{r_0}{r} f \qquad (9)$$

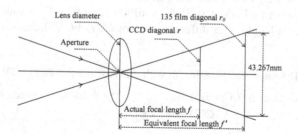

Fig. 4. Equivalent focal length diagram

In order to be consistent with people's habits, this paper takes 135 film camera as a standard for the discussion, in the use of other cameras, converted into the equivalent focal length of 135 film. If the equivalent focal length of the camera is known, the FOV α is:

$$\alpha = 2\arctan\left(\frac{\sqrt{36 * 36 + 24 * 24}}{2f'}\right) = 2\arctan\left(\frac{21.633}{f'}\right) \qquad (10)$$

In Eq. 10, f′ is in mm, and arctan(·) is an arctangent function. In this way, no matter what kind of CCD/CMOS, we could calculate the FOV among different kinds of cameras.

4   The Target Depth Information Calculation of Monocular Vision

The ultimate goal of this paper is to solve the problem of target depth information measurement under single camera. How to achieve the target depth measurement when the height of the camera, the height of the measured object, and some parameter information about the camera are known? The theoretical derivation will be derived below.

4.1   The Relationship Between the Margins of the Imaging Plane and the Focal Length and the Field of View

We assume that the size of the imaging plane π_1 is l * w (l, w are in centimeters), as shown in Fig. 5. Suppose that the four vertices of the plane π_1 are G, H, I, J. The CD in the image plane of the object is extended to the edge of the image plane at E point, then CE is clearly half of the imaging side length l, which is l/2. Since the FC is perpendicular to the analog image plane, that is, perpendicular to the image plane π_1. In a right-angled triangle FCG, it is clear that the length of the GC is half of the diagonal of the rectangular GHIJ, that is:

$$|GC| = \frac{\sqrt{l^2 + w^2}}{2} \tag{11}$$

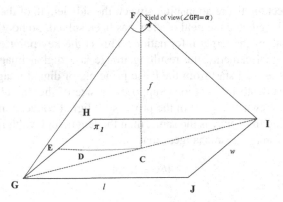

Fig. 5. The relationship between the edge of the image plane π_1 and the focal length and the field of view

So, it is easy to get rid of:

$$|GF| = \sqrt{|FC|^2 + |GC|^2} = \sqrt{f^2 + \left(\frac{\sqrt{l^2 + w^2}}{2}\right)^2} \qquad (12)$$

In the isosceles triangle $\triangle FGI$, $|FG| = |FI|$, GI is the diagonal of the image plane π_1 and the length of GI is $\sqrt{l^2 + w^2}$. In the triangle $\triangle FGI$, using the cosine theorem, we could solve:

$$|GI|^2 = |FG|^2 + |FI|^2 - 2|FG| \times |FI| \times \cos(\alpha) \qquad (13)$$

In the Eq. 13, a is the FOV of the camera. Take the side of image plane l, w and the focal length f into Eq. 13, we could get the following formula:

$$l^2 + w^2 = 2\left(\sqrt{f^2 + \left(\frac{\sqrt{l^2 + w^2}}{2}\right)^2}\right)^2 - 2\left(\sqrt{f^2 + \left(\frac{\sqrt{l^2 + w^2}}{2}\right)^2}\right)^2 \cos\alpha \qquad (14)$$

Finishing Eq. 14, then the relationship model between the side of image plane, the focal length and the field of view could be easily got.

$$l^2 = \frac{4(1 - \cos\alpha)f^2}{1 + \cos\alpha} - w^2 \qquad (15)$$

4.2 Target Depth Information Solution Based on Analog-to-Digital Conversion Technology

In the previous section, the relationship between the side length of the image plane and the camera focal length and the field of view has been solved. So how to use this model to derive the depth of the target information? This is the key point of this paper.

In modern digital cameras, the resulting image is a digital image, not an analog image. We might as well start from the basic principle of digital image transformation to solve the target depth information. Suppose the size of the digital image we got is M*N (pixels), as shown in Fig. 6. In the process of digital conversion, the vertical and horizontal sampling frequency is the same, then the length and width ratio of the analog image and digital image is unchanged, that is:

$$l/w = M/N \qquad (16)$$

Therefore

$$w = Nl/M \qquad (17)$$

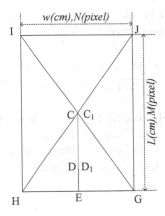

Fig. 6. Analog to digital conversion

Substitute Eq. 17 into Eq. 15 and sort it out:

$$l = \frac{2Mf}{\sqrt{M^2 + N^2}} \sqrt{\frac{1 - \cos \alpha}{1 + \cos \alpha}} \tag{18}$$

In the process of digitizing the simulated image, the simulated image is sampled and quantified according to a certain sampling interval, the ratio of length to width does not change. From the camera imaging principle of the analog-digital conversion relationship, as shown in Fig. 6. Let C_1 and D_1 be the corresponding points of C and D after digitization. The following formula was established.

$$\frac{|C_1 D_1|}{M} = \frac{|CD|}{l} \tag{19}$$

In the Eq. 19, $|C_1 D_1|$ represents the pixel distance between the pixel point C_1 and the pixel point D_1. Take (6) and Eq. 18 into Eq. 19, Eq. 20 could be got as follows:

$$\frac{\dfrac{mh_2 f}{m^2 + h_1^2 - h_1 h_2}}{\dfrac{2Mf}{\sqrt{M^2 + N^2}} \sqrt{\dfrac{1 - \cos \alpha}{1 + \cos \alpha}}} = \frac{|C_1 D_1|}{M} \tag{20}$$

Finishing Eq. 20, then the pixel length of the digitized target $C_1 D_1$ could be got:

$$|C_1 D_1| = \frac{\sin \alpha}{2(1 - \cos \alpha)} \frac{mh_2 \sqrt{M^2 + N^2}}{m^2 + h_1^2 - h_1 h_2} \tag{21}$$

Thus, the constraint relation between the imaging length $|C_1 D_1|$ of the target AB in the final digitized image, and the distance m the target AB from the camera was obtained. The length of $|C_1D_1|$ could be got by image segmentation, the depth m could be calculated by the constraint relationship. The expression of m is as follows:

$$m = \frac{h_2\sqrt{M^2 + N^2}\sin\alpha + \sqrt{h_2^2(M^2 + N^2)(\sin\alpha)^2 - 8|C_1D_1|(1 - \cos\alpha)(h_1^2 - h_1h_2)}}{4|C_1D_1|(1 - \cos\alpha)} \quad (22)$$

In the Eq. 22, α can be obtained by Eq. 10, the depth of the target can be obtained from the digitized image. M and N are determined by the specific camera resolution, h_1, h_2 are known quantities, $|C_1D_1|$ can be obtained by exact segmentation.

So far, the problem of single camera depth analysis is solved.

5   Conclusion

Theoretical derivation results show that the proposed method has simple algorithm and easy operation, and can effectively reduce the cost of production. Because of the simple structure of monocular depth measurement system, it can be widely used in mobile phones and network cameras. It avoids the complexity of stereo matching process, and reduces the computational complexity. The requirement of the hardware is low, which can meet the requirements of the real-time performance of the robot in the industrial production. The disadvantage is that if the camera lens distortion is more serious, the measurement depth error may increase.

Acknowledgements. This work is supported by the Natural Science Foundation of China (No. 61573316, No. 61502424) and the Zhejiang Provincial Natural Science Foundation of China (No. LY15F020032, No. LY15F020028, LQ15E050006).

References

1. Hachmon, G., Mamet, N., Sasson, S., Barkai, T., Hadar, N., Abu-Horowitz, A., Bachelet, I.: A non-Newtonian fluid robot. Artif. Life **22**, 1–22 (2016)
2. Tan, K.: Squirrel cage induction generator system using wavelet petri fuzzy neural network control for wind power applications. IEEE Trans. Power Electron. **31**, 1 (2015)
3. Kong, L.F., Pei-Liang, W.U., Xian-Shan, L.I.: Object depth estimation using translations of hand-eye system with uncalibrated camera. Comput. Integr. Manuf. Syst. **15**(8), 1633–1638 (2009)
4. Hoang, N., Kang, H.: Neural network-based adaptive tracking control of mobile robots in the presence of wheel slip and external disturbance force. Neurocomputing **188**, 12–22 (2016)
5. Mendes, N., Neto, P.: Indirect adaptive fuzzy control for industrial robots: a solution for contact applications. Expert Syst. Appl. **42**, 8929–8935 (2015)
6. Ghommam, J., Mehrjerdi, H., Saad, M.: Robust formation control without velocity measurement of the leader robot. Control Eng. Pract. **21**, 1143–1156 (2013)
7. Charalampous, K., Kostavelis, I., Gasteratos, A.: Thorough robot navigation based on SVM local planning. Robot. Auton. Syst. **70**, 166–180 (2015)
8. Jia, T., Shi, Y., Zhou, Z., Chen, D.: 3D depth information extraction with omni-directional camera. Inf. Process. Lett. **115**, 285–291 (2015)

9. Johnson, S., Nichols, T., Gatt, P., Klausutis, T.: Range precision of direct-detection laser radar systems. In: Laser Radar Technology and Applications IX (2004)
10. Steinvall, O.: Effects of target shape and reflection on laser radar cross sections. Appl. Opt. **39**, 4381 (2000)
11. Yao, J., Yan, H., Zhang, X., Jiang, Y.: Image registration and superposition for improving ranging accuracy of imaging laser radar. Chin. J. Lasers **37**, 1613–1617 (2010)
12. Francisco, A.: Continuous principal distance change for binocular depth perception. Image Vis. Comput. **13**, 101–109 (1995)
13. Yang, J., Xu, R., Ding, Z., Lv, H.: 3D character recognition using binocular camera for medical assist. Neurocomputing. **220**, 17–22 (2017)
14. Xu, Y., Guo, D., Zheng, T., Cheng, A.: Research on camera calibration methods of the machine vision. In: 2011 Second International Conference on Mechanic Automation and Control Engineering (2011)
15. Li, J., Allinson, N.: A comprehensive review of current local features for computer vision. Neurocomputing **71**, 1771–1787 (2008)
16. Song, L., Wu, W., Guo, J., Li, X.: Survey on camera calibration technique. In: 2013 5th International Conference on Intelligent Human-Machine Systems and Cybernetics (2013)
17. Sun, J., Gu, H.: Research of linear camera calibration based on planar pattern. World Acad. Sci. Eng. Technol. **3**, 627–631 (2009)
18. Ricolfe-Viala, C., Sanchez-Salmeron, A.: Optimal conditions for camera calibration using a planar template. In: 2011 18th IEEE International Conference on Image Processing (2011)
19. Yang, X., Huang, Y., Gao, F.: A simple camera calibration method based on sub-pixel corner extraction of the chessboard image. In: 2010 IEEE International Conference on Intelligent Computing and Intelligent Systems (2010)
20. Park, J., Park, S.: Improvement on Zhang's camera calibration. Appl. Mech. Mater. **479–480**, 170–173 (2013)
21. Qi, W., Li, F., Zhenzhong, L.: Review on camera calibration. In: 2010 Chinese Control and Decision Conference (2010)
22. Mao, J., Xiao, G., Sheng, W., Qu, Z., Liu, Y.: Research on realizing the 3D occlusion tracking location method of fish's school target. Neurocomputing **214**, 61–79 (2016)
23. Laurel, B., Laurel, C., Brown, J., Gregory, R.: A new technique to gather 3-D spatial information using a single camera. J. Fish Biol. **66**, 429–441 (2005)
24. Hemelrijk, C., Hildenbrandt, H., Reinders, J., Stamhuis, E.: Emergence of oblong school shape: models and empirical data of fish. Ethology **116**, 1099–1112 (2010)
25. Zhu, L., Weng, W.: Catadioptric stereo-vision system for the real-time monitoring of 3D behavior in aquatic animals. Physiol. Behav. **91**, 106–119 (2007)
26. Zhao, Y.: The study about the effect of the distance and the angle of vision on the precision of temperature measurement using infrared thermal imaging system. Northeastern University (2012)
27. Li, J., Han, H.: Calibrating aberrations and visual angles in the CCD imaging optical system. J. Xi'An Technol. Univ, **2**, 003 (2012)
28. http://mt.sohu.com/20150706/n416241587.shtml

Automatic Background Adjustment for Chinese Paintings Using Pigment Lines

Jie Guo[✉], Chunyou Li, and Jingui Pan

State Key Lab for Novel Software Technology, Nanjing University,
Nanjing, China
guojie@nju.edu.cn

Abstract. Most traditional Chinese paintings are painted on hand-made paper that easily suffers from severe spectral changes caused by prolonged light exposure, resulting in color distortion and low contrast. To recover the original appearance of a Chinese painting, especially its background color, an automatic background adjustment framework is proposed. This framework is based on the insightful observation that the fading model of a painting image is analogue to the common hazy image formation model when the painting image is transformed into the K-M (Kubelka-Munk) space. We demonstrate that this fading model is quite useful in extracting pigment lines from any painting image. These pigment lines represent clusters of distinct color pigments used in a Chinese painting, which is the key to density map estimation and background restoration. Experimental results prove that our approach is able to restore a variety of deteriorated Chinese paintings without any user intervention or training.

Keywords: Image enhancement · Density map
Kubelka-Munk model · Chinese paintings

1 Introduction

Traditional Chinese paintings occupy an important position in China's cultural heritage. Quite different from Western oil paintings, traditional Chinese paintings often leave extensive empty background spaces on the canvas to give human observers more room for imagination. However, the canvas is usually made of Xuan-paper, a kind of hand-made natural fiber paper, that can easily lose its original color and turn yellow with time goes by due to prolonged light exposure (see Fig. 1(a)), resulting in severe color contrast loss between foreground brush strokes and the unpainted background.

As massive numbers of valuable ancient Chinese paintings have been digitized and exhibited on the Internet, there is a pressing need for the computer-assisted techniques that are capable of restoring deteriorated Chinese paintings, especially adjusting the background color. Unfortunately, recovering faded Chinese

B. Zeng et al. (Eds.): PCM 2017, LNCS 10736, pp. 596–605, 2018.
https://doi.org/10.1007/978-3-319-77383-4_58

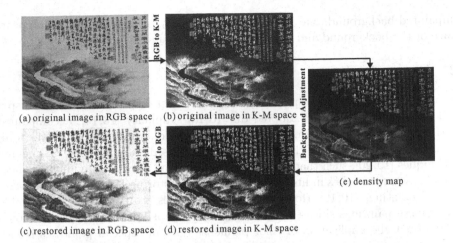

(a) original image in RGB space   (b) original image in K-M space

(c) restored image in RGB space   (d) restored image in K-M space

(e) density map

Fig. 1. Restore a traditional Chinese painting via automatic background adjustment. (Color figure online)

paintings from the yellowish background is not a trivial task since the fading procedures of paper and suspended pigments are complex and vary greatly. The fading percentage may depend on time, density of pigments, and spectrum [8]. As such, there is only a few studies exist on mitigating this problem [13,14,19].

In this paper, we propose a novel color restoration method for traditional Chinese paintings. Our approach is based on the Kubelka-Munk (K-M) model [9], a two-flux radiative transfer model that is widely adopted in both paper-making and coloration industries. When applied to paintings, the K-M model is able to predict the relationship between spectral reflectance of paintings and the optical characterization (i.e., the absorption coefficient K and the scattering coefficient S) of the background paper and constituent pigments. We find that when transforming the original painting image into the K-M space (i.e., from the pixel value to the spectral absorption and scattering ratio K/S), the aged Chinese painting performs like a hazy image. This inspired us to map the color restoration problem to an image dehazing problem in the K-M space.

Unfortunately, such a hazy image in the K-M space easily breaks the assumption of dark channel prior (DCP) [5]. For instance, the black ink in traditional Chinese paintings has a very high value of K/S, and it fades very slowly as time goes by. As a result, the prevalent DCP-based image dehazing method and its variants cannot be utilized in this situation. Instead, we introduce a pigment line model to recover yellow-free painting images in the K-M space. This model is a variant of the haze line model [1] which implies that the number of distinct color pigments used in a traditional Chinese painting is rather limited while the concentration may vary spatially. Each type of pigment spans a pigment line in the K-M space, which can be used to estimate the per-pixel density. With the estimated density and the spectral absorption and scattering ratio K/S of the unpainted background, our approach can efficiently restore the original appearance of the background and enhance contrast for faded Chinese paintings.

2   Related Work

To restore ancient Chinese paintings, color contrast enhancement in some special color spaces is widely adopted due to its simplicity [13,14], accompanied with the risk of metamerism. An alternative solution tries to separate the foreground and background of the painting directly based on multi-spectral imaging techniques [19,20], such that each component can be altered individually. There are also several studies in literature focusing on restoring faded photos or Western oil paintings [10,12]. However, these techniques are not directly applicable to Chinese paintings since their fading percentage is spatially varying. Knowledge about the application of color pigments on some special paintings is also leveraged in painting restoration [18] and fading simulation [15].

Our work is closely related to single image dehazing techniques. Since this problem is ill-posed, most single image dehazing techniques rely on some image priors from natural image statistics to handle ambiguity between haze and object radiance. Early methods [16,17] enhance the visibility of degraded images by maximizing local contrast, assuming that haze-free images have a high contrast while air-light tends to be smooth. Fattal's method [2] is based on the assumption that shading and transmission functions are locally and statistically uncorrelated. Fattal [3] also suggested using color lines [11] of a local patch to generate haze-free images. He et al. [5] observed that a clear outdoor image has at least one color channel with low intensity in a local patch and this dark channel prior could be employed to build a faithful transmission map. Due to its simplicity and effectiveness, DCP-based methods have been widely used in image dehazing. Recently, Berman et al. [1] proposed a non-local prior to estimate transmission, assuming that a haze-free image is well approximated by several hundreds of distinct colors forming tight clusters in the RGB space. Our work is inspired by this haze line model.

3   Our Approach

In this section, we first introduce a physically-based image formation model for Chinese paintings which relates pixel values in the image to the K-M coefficients of paper and constituent pigments. Then, we give a fading model in the K-M space which resembles the haze model in image dehazing problems. After that, we introduce a pigment line model and demonstrate how to de-yellow aged Chinese paintings with pigment lines.

3.1   Image Formation

To digitize a Chinese painting, a scanner or camera will be utilized. In either circumstance, we assume that the incident illumination is diffuse and homogeneous. The only interactions of light with the medium (paper and pigments) are scattering (with coefficient S) and absorption (with coefficient K). According to the K-M theory [4,9], the reflectance R of the medium is given by

$$R = \frac{\sinh bSL}{a \sinh bSL + b \cosh bSL} \qquad (1)$$

with $a = 1 + K/S$ and $b = \sqrt{a^2 - 1}$. L corresponds to the thickness of the medium. In this case, the pixel value $I(\mathbf{x})$ can be approximated by the reflectance $R(\mathbf{x})$, assuming that the incident light's irradiance is normalized to 1.

Traditionally, finished Chinese paintings are mounted on scrolls that probably have similar K-M coefficients with paper. This makes the combined medium so think ($L \to \infty$) that it is effectively opaque and therefore no light will pass through the medium. Under this configuration, we have

$$R_\infty = \lim_{L \to \infty} R = 1 + F - \sqrt{F^2 + 2F} \qquad (2)$$

and

$$F = \frac{K}{S} = \frac{(1 - R_\infty)^2}{2R_\infty}. \qquad (3)$$

F is usually referred as the "K-M function". These two equations can be regarded as the transformation between the traditional RGB color space (R_∞) and the K-M space (F).

3.2 Fading Model

For each pixel position $\mathbf{x}$ of a painting image, its K-M function is actually a mixture of several constituent pigments $F_p(\mathbf{x})$ together with the background paper $F_b(\mathbf{x})$:

$$F_m(\mathbf{x}) = [1 - \rho(\mathbf{x})]F_b(\mathbf{x}) + \rho(\mathbf{x})F_p(\mathbf{x}) \qquad (4)$$

with

$$F_p(\mathbf{x}) = \frac{K_p(\mathbf{x})}{S_p(\mathbf{x})} = \frac{\sum_{i=1}^{N} c_i(\mathbf{x})K_i}{\sum_{i=1}^{N} c_i(\mathbf{x})S_i} \qquad (5)$$

where K_i, S_i are the K-M coefficients of absorption and scattering for N constituent pigments, respectively. $c_i(\mathbf{x})$ is the density of ith pigment at $\mathbf{x}$ while $\rho(\mathbf{x})$ is the overall density of all pigments suspended in the paper. Note that Eq. 4 bears some similarity to the hazy image formation model in the RGB space.

Although both the background paper and constituent pigments could easily fade over time, it is unlikely to restore the original appearance of pigments without sufficient knowledge or user intervention [18]. For this reason, our restoration method focuses on adjusting the background medium F_b, assuming color pigments fade slower than the background paper. This assumption is plausible for many mineral pigments and black ink that are widely used in traditional Chinese paintings. We further assume that the fading percentage is homogenous throughout the paper such that $F_b(\mathbf{x})$ is a constant. Adjusting the background implies replacing F_b in Eq. 4 with another constant F_b' representing the K-M function of the nondeteriorated paper. Then, the new K-M function of the pixel $\mathbf{x}$ becomes

$$F'_m(\mathbf{x}) = [1 - \rho(\mathbf{x})]F'_b + \rho(\mathbf{x})F_p(\mathbf{x}) = F_m(\mathbf{x}) + [1 - \rho(\mathbf{x})](F'_b - F_b). \quad (6)$$

To compute $F'_m(\mathbf{x})$, we have to estimate F_b and build the density map $\rho(\mathbf{x})$.

3.3   Background Color Estimation

The background paper color I_b is analogue to the air-light color in the image dehazing problems. The difference is that I_b is not necessary the pixel with the highest intensity. Most likely, I_b is the dominant color of an image I since most traditional Chinese paintings have a large unpainted background. In our current implementation, we estimate the background color via $I_b = \max\{h(I)\}$ where $h(I)$ returns the histogram of the image I in the RGB space. To reduce the influence of noise, we pre-filter the original image I with a Gaussian kernel. Once we obtain I_b, we transform it into the K-M space based on Eq. 3, i.e., $F_b = (1 - I_b)^2/(2I_b)$.

3.4   Density Map Estimation

Our density map is estimated by the pigment line model in the K-M space, a variation of the haze line model in the RGB space [1]. This model is based on the observation that the number of color pigments used in a traditional Chinese painting is rather limited, while the output color of each image pixel is determined by optical properties of constituent pigments (F_p) and the background paper (F_b), as well as their relative density (ρ).

Extracting pigment lines: Recall that for each image pixel in the K-M space, we have $F_m - F_b = \rho(F_p - F_b)$. This equation indicates that F_b and F_p forms a 1D line in the K-M space for a given pigment (or pigment mixture) F_p, written as

$$F_m - F_b = l_p\mathbf{d}_p \quad (7)$$

in which $\mathbf{d}_p = (F_m - F_b)/l_p$ is the line direction while $l_p = \|F_m - F_b\|$ is the magnitude of F_m. We refer to this line as the pigment line for the pigment F_p. When the background paper is perfectly white, we have $F_b = 0$. In this case, all pigment lines pass through the origin. For instance, Fig. 2 shows a less deteriorated Chinese painting ($F_b \approx 0$) and its corresponding pigment lines. We demonstrate three distinct pigment lines which are marked with different color strokes in the original image. As seen, pixels covered by the same brush stroke are distributed along the same 1D line, and their relative positions encode the density. This suggests that each type of pigment is well represented by the direction of its corresponding pigment line. Therefore, it is possible to extract pigment lines of an image by clustering $\mathbf{d}_p$ on a unit sphere.

   To cluster $\mathbf{d}_p$, we first normalize $F_m - F_b$ for each pixel. Performing normalization on the raw pixel value is poor since the K-M function has a high dynamic

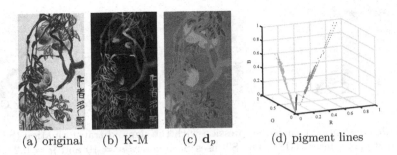

(a) original   (b) K-M   (c) $\mathbf{d}_p$ (d) pigment lines

Fig. 2. Illustration of pigment lines in a less deteriorated Chinese painting. (Color figure online)

range which is several orders of magnitude. To alleviate this problem, we adopt the following log-relative mapping:

$$F_m - F_b \mapsto \log_{10}(|F_m - F_b| + 1). \tag{8}$$

In this case, we have

$$\mathbf{d}_p = \frac{\log_{10}(|F_m - F_b| + 1)}{\| \log_{10}(|F_m - F_b| + 1)\|}. \tag{9}$$

Figure 2(c) shows the result after normalization in the K-M space. Obviously, pixels that belongs to the same pigment line have very similar values of $\mathbf{d}_p$, although their density may vary significantly. It is possible to cluster $\mathbf{d}_p$ on the unit sphere by traditional k-means methods or by a much more efficient binning method proposed in [1].

Building density map: With these pigment lines extracted from a painting image, we are able to estimate the density of each pixel. Specifically, given a pigment line defined by $\mathbf{d}_p$, we first find its maximum magnitude $l_{max} = \max\{l_p\}$ among all pixels along the line. This value l_{max} is assumed to be the magnitude of $F_p - F_b$. Then, the density of any pixel belongs to this pigment line is given by

$$\rho = \frac{F_m - F_b}{F_p - F_b} = \frac{l_p \mathbf{d}_p}{l_{max} \mathbf{d}_p} = \frac{l_p}{l_{max}}. \tag{10}$$

As the initial density ρ is estimated in a per-pixel manner, it is subjected to image noise and inaccuracy of clustering. Therefore, similar to previous work [1,3], we further impose spatial coherency of the input image $F_m(\mathbf{x})$ over the output density map $\rho(\mathbf{x})$ to make it smooth. Mathematically, we seek a refined density map $\hat{\rho}(\mathbf{x})$ that minimize the following cost function:

$$\sum_{\mathbf{x}} \frac{[\hat{\rho}(\mathbf{x}) - \rho(\mathbf{x})]^2}{\sigma^2(\mathbf{x})} + \epsilon \sum_{\mathbf{x}} \sum_{\mathbf{y} \in \mathcal{N}_{\mathbf{x}}} \frac{[\hat{\rho}(\mathbf{x}) - \hat{\rho}(\mathbf{y})]^2}{\|F_m(\mathbf{x}) - F_m(\mathbf{y})\|^2}. \tag{11}$$

This function can be solved by weighted least squares. In this function, ϵ is a regularization parameter controlling the relative importance of each term, and

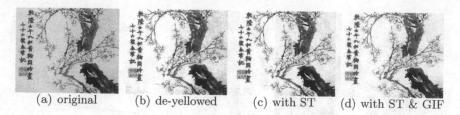

   (a) original   (b) de-yellowed   (c) with ST   (d) with ST & GIF

Fig. 3. Demonstration of noise suppression with the sigmoid transformation (ST) and the guided image filter (GIF). The ST uses parameters $\kappa = 10$ and $\mu = 0.2$. (Color figure online)

$\mathcal{N}_\mathbf{x}$ represents the four nearest neighbors of $\mathbf{x}$ in the image. The data term ensures that $\hat{\rho}(\mathbf{x})$ is similar to $\rho(\mathbf{x})$, and the standard deviation $\sigma(\mathbf{x})$ expresses the uncertainty of the estimated value which is calculated per pigment line. The regularization term penalizes for variation in $\rho(\mathbf{x})$ according to $F_m(\mathbf{x})$.

3.5 Noise Suppression

It is easy to adjust the background of a painting image according to Eq. 6 once its density map is built. To de-yellow the background, we simply set $F'_b = 0$. Thereafter, the output K-M function F'_m is transformed back to the RGB color space using Eq. 2 to obtain the final restored image $I' = 1 + F'_m - \sqrt{(F'_m)^2 + 2F'_m}$.

It should be mentioned that Eq. 2 is sensitive to small perturbation when F is very close to zero. Therefore, noticeable artifacts appear if the deterioration rate of the background paper is not spatially invariant; see Fig. 3(b). To alleviate this problem, we apply a sigmoid transformation (ST) to F before it is transformed back into the RGB color space:

$$F \mapsto \frac{F}{1 + \exp[\kappa(\|F\| - \mu)]}. \tag{12}$$

This transformation tends to diminish small F ($\|F\| < \mu$) while keeping large F ($\|F\| > \mu$) unchanged. Figure 3(c) reveals that the ST counteracts noticeable noise on the background to some extent while respecting sharp features of the foreground, if we choose the parameters κ and μ properly. This is because most foreground stokes still have large values of F after de-yellowing in the K-M space, as opposed to the background paper.

To further average away undesired noise and preserve important features, we can apply a guided image filter [6] to I' as shown in Fig. 3(d). Specifically, we filter the restored image I' under the guidance of the original image I.

4   Results

In this section, we evaluate our approach on a variety of digitized painting images from the Internet. We generate the results on a PC with Intel Core i7-6900K

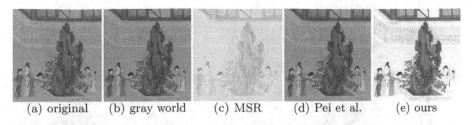

(a) original   (b) gray world   (c) MSR   (d) Pei et al.   (e) ours

Fig. 4. Comparison with several image restoration methods capable of de-yellowing aged paintings or photos. (Color figure online)

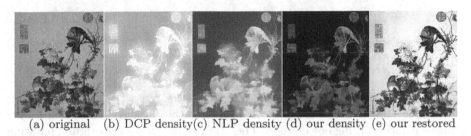

(a) original   (b) DCP density(c) NLP density (d) our density (e) our restored

Fig. 5. Comparison of density maps estimated by different methods.

CPU and 16G RAM. The default values of κ and μ in Eq. 12 are 10 and 0.1, respectively.

Figure 4 compares our approach with several image restoration methods capable of de-yellowing aged paintings or photos. Figures 4(b) and (c) show the restored results of two widely used white-balancing algorithms: the gray world algorithm [10] and the multi-scale retinex (MSR) algorithm [7]. As expected, although both algorithms can remove yellowish tones from an aged painting, they produce rather unnatural results since they enhance the image globally without considering the spatial variance of the fading phenomenon. Pei et al. [13] suggested enhancing the color scheme of an ancient Chinese painting by background adjustment with Von Kries color modification and saturation enhancement. This method is quite efficient, but the result tends to be dark, especially the background. Owing to the estimated density map, our approach can generates a very satisfactory result with recovered light background and less-modified foreground.

In Fig. 5(b)–(d), we compare the density map estimated by our approach in the K-M space with those generated by image dehazing algorithms in the conversional RGB space. Two image dehazing algorithms are adopted for visual comparison: one is the widely used DCP-based algorithm [5] and the other is a state-of-the-art algorithm based on non-local prior (NLP) [1]. As seen, both algorithms over-estimate the density, especially in the regions of the background paper. This is because in the conversional RGB space the observed color of a painting image cannot be expressed as a linear interpolation of two terms via a density map. Instead, such a linear combination only exists in the K-M space as given by Eq. 4.

Fig. 6. More results of automatic background adjustment for Chinese paintings.

Figure 6 shows more examples of adjusting the background of traditional Chinese paintings using our method. The first column shows the original painting images while the other three columns give the resulting images after background adjustment with various types of background.

5   Conclusion and Future Work

We have presented a new technique for automatically adjusting the background of traditional Chinese paintings. A key contribution of our work is the pigment lines that extracted from a painting image in the K-M space. Each pigment line represents one class of color pigment that may have spatially varying density on the image. Built upon these pigment lines, the density map can be estimated through the image, and hence the image can be either de-yellowed or matted on a new background.

Currently, our approach assumes that the fading percentage of the background paper is roughly homogenous such that F_b can be regarded as a constant. This means we can not handle some ancient Chinese paintings that have strong variations of spectral changes on the background. We would like to consider this issue in our future work.

Acknowledgments. This work is supported by NSF China (No. 61502223 and No. 61321491).

References

1. Berman, D., Treibitz, T., Avidan, S.: Non-local image dehazing. In: IEEE Conference on Computer Vision and Pattern Recognition (CVPR) (2016)
2. Fattal, R.: Single image dehazing. In: ACM SIGGRAPH 2008 Papers, SIGGRAPH 2008, pp. 72:1–72:9 (2008)

3. Fattal, R.: Dehazing using color-lines. ACM Trans. Graph. **34**(1), 13:1–13:14 (2014)
4. Guo, J., Pan, J.G.: Real-time simulating and rendering of layered dust. Vis. Comput. **30**(6–8), 797–807 (2014)
5. He, K., Sun, J., Tang, X.: Single image haze removal using dark channel prior. IEEE Trans. Pattern Anal. Mach. Intell. **33**(12), 2341–2353 (2011)
6. He, K., Sun, J., Tang, X.: Guided image filtering. IEEE Trans. Pattern Anal. Mach. Intell. **35**(6), 1397–1409 (2013)
7. Jobson, D.J., Rahman, Z., Woodell, G.A.: A multiscale retinex for bridging the gap between color images and the human observation of scenes. IEEE Trans. Image Process. **6**(7), 965–976 (1997)
8. Kimmel, B.W., Baranoski, G.V.G., Chen, T.F., Yim, D., Miranda, E.: Spectral appearance changes induced by light exposure. ACM Trans. Graph. **32**(1), 10:1–10:13 (2013)
9. Kubelka, P., Munk, F.: Ein beitrag zur optik der farbanstriche. Z. Tech. Phys. (Leipzig) **12**, 593–601 (1931)
10. Nikitenkot, D., Wirthl, M., Trudel, K.: White-balancing algorithms in colour photograph restoration. In: 2007 IEEE International Conference on Systems, Man and Cybernetics, pp. 1037–1042, October 2007
11. Omer, I., Werman, M.: Color lines: image specific color representation. In: Proceedings of the 2004 IEEE Computer Society Conference on Computer Vision and Pattern Recognition, CVPR 2004, vol. 2, pp. 946–953, June 2004
12. Pappas, M., Pitas, I.: Digital color restoration of old paintings. IEEE Trans. Image Process. **9**(2), 291–294 (2000)
13. Pei, S.C., Chiu, Y.M.: Background adjustment and saturation enhancement in ancient chinese paintings. IEEE Trans. Image Process. **15**(10), 3230–3234 (2006)
14. Pei, S.C., Zeng, Y.C., Chang, C.H.: Virtual restoration of ancient chinese paintings using color contrast enhancement and lacuna texture synthesis. IEEE Trans. Image Process. **13**(3), 416–429 (2004)
15. Shi, X., Lu, D., Liu, J.: Color changing and fading simulation for frescoes based on empirical knowledge from artists. In: Zhuang, Y., Yang, S.-Q., Rui, Y., He, Q. (eds.) PCM 2006. LNCS, vol. 4261, pp. 861–869. Springer, Heidelberg (2006). https://doi.org/10.1007/11922162_98
16. Tan, R.T.: Visibility in bad weather from a single image. In: 2008 IEEE Conference on Computer Vision and Pattern Recognition, pp. 1–8, June 2008
17. Tarel, J.P., Hautière, N.: Fast visibility restoration from a single color or gray level image. In: 2009 IEEE 12th International Conference on Computer Vision, pp. 2201–2208, September 2009
18. Wei, B., Liu, Y., Pan, Y.: Using hybrid knowledge engineering and image processing in color virtual restoration of ancient murals. IEEE Trans. Knowl. Data Eng. **15**(5), 1338–1343 (2003)
19. Zhang, J., Zhang, Y., Zhang, S., Yan, L., Chen, J.: Multispectral image matting of ancient Chinese paintings. In: Eurographics (2011)
20. Zhao, Y.: Image segmentation and pigment mapping of cultural heritage based on spectral imaging. Ph.d. dissertation, Rochester Institute of Technology, College of Science, Center for Imaging Science, Rochester, New York, United States, March 2008

Content-Based Image Recovery

Hong-Yu Zhou and Jianxin Wu[✉]

National Key Laboratory for Novel Software Technology, Nanjing University,
Nanjing, China
zhouhy@lamda.nju.edu.cn, wujx2001@nju.edu.cn

Abstract. We propose an interesting challenge: recovering from aspect-ratio distorted images based on their contents. Given a distorted image, we want to construct a model to predict its original aspect ratio. Since this is a general task, we build a database on top of Pascal VOC datasets. On the base of recent deep convolutional neural networks (CNNs), we present a multi-scale architecture and construct a spatial pooling layer to overcome the problem. By utilizing the multi-level and spatial information, our approach surpasses other methods by a large margin. Towards a better understanding of this task, we also perform detailed studies on experimental results.

Keywords: Multi-scale CNN · Spatial information
Image classification · Image aspect ratio recovery

1 Introduction

In recent years, CNNs have achieved great success in various image recognition tasks, e.g., object detection [5], semantic segmentation [6]. Thanks to these great achievements, deep learning is trying to bridge the gap between computers and humans. In image classification, we have surpassed human-level performance on the famous ImageNet challenge [7], and scene classification tasks [8] are no more difficult for deep CNNs [9,10].

However, there are still doubts that high recognition performance means the computer has the same ability to understand image contents as we do. In this paper, we try to propose a new problem which is pretty normal for humans: *predicting the right aspect ratio of a single image*. Given a distorted image, human is able to give its suitable aspect ratio (Fig. 1a). We argue that this ability relies on the recognition of the shapes of typical objects. For example, in Fig. 1a, we can tell that the rightmost image is correct because we know what a person and a dog usually look like, which is a normal ability that all of us should have. Now suppose that we have tens of thousands images with distortion, how can we get back their original versions? Are our computers able to make predictions as accurate as we do? We will talk about this question in the rest of this paper.

In this paper, we try to give a thorough investigation of answers to the question above. Our contributions can be summarized as follows:

© Springer International Publishing AG, part of Springer Nature 2018
B. Zeng et al. (Eds.): PCM 2017, LNCS 10736, pp. 606–615, 2018.
https://doi.org/10.1007/978-3-319-77383-4_59

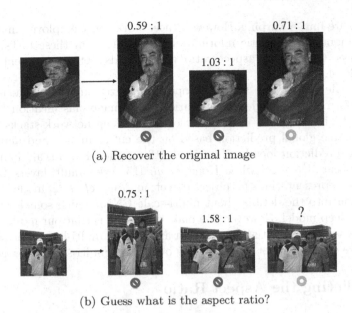

0.59 : 1   0.71 : 1

1.03 : 1

(a) Recover the original image

0.75 : 1

1.58 : 1   ?

(b) Guess what is the aspect ratio?

Fig. 1. Predict the aspect ratio: (a) Considering a distorted image, we can recover the original image by predicting the right aspect ratio (the right picture). (b) Can you guess the original ratio? (answer: 1.33 : 1) Best viewed in color. (Color figure online)

- For the first time, we propose to predict the original aspect ratio given a distorted image which can be regarded as an understanding towards image contents.
- We propose a multi-scale CNN architecture with spatial pooling layers to solve this problem and the proposed approach achieves better results over other traditional methods.
- Towards a better understanding of this problem, we build a new dataset with detailed annotations on top of existing datasets. We also perform ablation studies and statistical analysis on experimental results.

2 Related Work

There have been some works focusing on image transformation based on image contents [11,12,16]. He *et al.* [12] proposed a warping method that creates the perception of rotation and avoids cropping. They designed an optimization-based method that preserves the rotation of horizontal/vertical lines, maintains the completeness of the image content, and reduces the warping distortion. Hoiem *et al.* [11] presented a fully automatic method for creating a 3D model from a single photograph. The main insight is that instead of attempting to recover precise geometry, they statistically modeled geometric classes defined by their orientations in the scene. Li *et al.* [16] used a geodesic-preserving method for content-aware image warping. However, these works only employed image geometry while ignoring semantic information. Different from these tasks, our goal is to recover the correct aspect ratio which needs better representations on semantic level.

Multi-scale CNNs have been developed to utilize multi-level features to get better performance, e.g., depth estimation [14], image classification [2], object detection [13,15]. Eigen et al. [14] employed two deep network stacks: one that makes a coarse global prediction based on the entire image, and another that refines this prediction locally. Kim et al. [13] applied multi-scale hand-crafted features to car detection while Kong et al. [15] used multi-layers to extract CNN-based representations for object detection. Yang et al. [2] made a complete investigation into the details about multi-scale CNNs which somehow helps us design our deep model. However, the main difference is that our model uses *spatial pooling* to utilize spatial information apart from multi-level representations which make our model get better results over other multi-scale approaches.

3   Predicting the Aspect Ratio

We propose to use a multi-scale CNN to directly perform ratio regression. The overview of the model is shown in Fig. 2. Note that we build model based on VGG-16 [4] but similar idea can be easily applied to other popular architectures (e.g., ResNet [17]). We argue that multi-scale and spatial information do help predict the original aspect ratio because they utilize low-level and mid-level representations.

3.1   Architecture

As shown in Fig. 2, we mainly extract features from relu layers right before the pooling layers. The reason why we choose to use the last relu layer of each convolution block is that they can be regarded as the bottleneck of each block and have the ability to describe the whole block. Then we perform an operation called *Spatial Pooling* on these predetermined relu layers. The goal of this operation is to make use of spatial representations. More details about this block are given in Fig. 3. Feature maps for specific scale are split into 2×2 regions and a max pooling layer is added on top of each region. A convolution layer and a relu layer are followed to extract feature vectors with fixed lengths. These feature vectors are then add together to produce the final feature representations.

We take L1 distance as the loss function,

$$\ell(\mathbf{X}, \mathbf{y}) = \sum_{i=1}^{N} |f_\theta(x_i) - y_i| \tag{1}$$

where $f_\theta(\cdot)$ represents the output of the network, x_i and y_i are input image and its label, $\mathbf{X}$ and $\mathbf{y}$ represent images and labels in the dataset, N is the number of training images. In our experiments, *we use the original aspect ratio of each image as its label.*

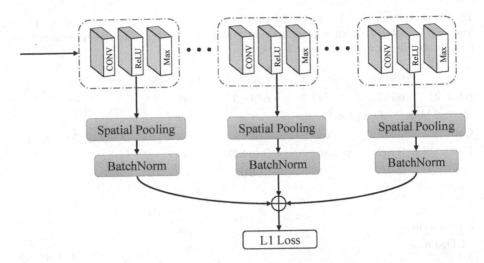

Fig. 2. An overview of our multi-scale model. We create a Spatial Pooling block which is able to utilize spatial information. We perform feature extraction on ReLU layers right before the pooling operations. Note that we use 4 scales in practice while this figure only shows 3 scales.

Spatial Pooling

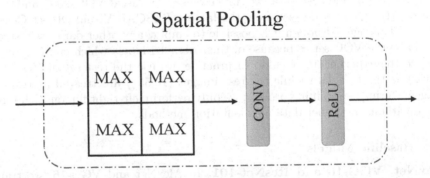

Fig. 3. On each feature map, we split the whole space into 2×2 regions and perform max pooling on each subregion. The pooling layer is then followed by a convolution layer and a relu layer to extract feature vectors. The number of regions can be a free choice and we also perform ablation experiments on different choices (in Table 3).

3.2 Implementation Details

We implement the whole network using MatConvNet [19]. In our experiments, we build a 4-scale model (conv2, conv3, conv4 and conv5). In spatial pooling block, we split the whole image into 2×2 regions. We also use batch normalization on top of the loss function to make the training process easier. The learning rate is 10^{-2} and gradually reduces to 10^{-5} using logspace in 20 epochs. Details of the model architecture can be found in Table 1.

Table 1. Architecture details of the proposed CNN. You can go through the table from top to bottom which follows the implementation order. Note that parameters of batch normalization are the same as those in [18].

scale-1	scale-2	scale-3	scale-4	Filter size
relu2_2	relu3_3	relu4_3	relu5_3	None
Spatial Max Pooling (2 × 2 regions)				None
Conv	Conv	Conv	Conv	$2 \times 2 \times \{128, 256, 512, 512\} \times 512$
BatchNorm	BatchNorm	BatchNorm	BatchNorm	None
ReLU	ReLU	ReLU	ReLU	None
Sum				None
Conv				$1 \times 1 \times 512 \times 1$
BatchNorm				None
L1 Distance				None

4   Experiments

4.1   Dataset

For the training and test data, we directly use the Pascal VOC 2007 and 2012 datasets [1] which are derived from the famous PASCAL Visual Object Classes (VOC) Challenge. Although it is possible to employ any other datasets instead, we choose the VOC series because of their detailed labels which can help us to analyze the experimental results. In practice, we use the test set of VOC2007 (4,952) as the test data while the rest images (16,551) are treated as training images. During the training process, we only perform left-right flip on each input image without any other data augmentation methods.

4.2   Baseline Models

AlexNet, VGG-16 and ResNet-101. In AlexNet and VGG-16, we transform "fc8" from $1 \times 1 \times 4096 \times 1000$ to $1 \times 1 \times 4096 \times 1$ and replace dropout with batch normalization. In ResNet-101, we directly change the number of final layer output from 1000 to 1. We also use batch normalization before the L1 loss to facilitate the training. The learning rate is 10^{-3} and gradually reduces to 10^{-5} using logspace in 20 epochs.

MS-VGGs. These models are all built based on VGG-16. We construct the main bodies of different variants following the same strategy stated in Table 1. It is worth noting that these variants are trained with the same learning rate as told in Sect. 3.2.

4.3   Experimental Results

The regression results of different models are reported in Table 2, and a few interesting points can be observed from it.

Table 2. Experimental results. We mainly perform experiments on AlexNet and VGG-based models. We use *MS-* to represent our multi-scale models. **SP**: spatial pooling (default 2×2); **Scales**: layers involved in multi-scale CNN; **Average Loss**: average L1 distance loss on test set (*the lower the better*).

Method	SP	Scales	Average loss
AlexNet	w/o	w/o	0.27
VGG-16	w/o	w/o	0.18
ResNet-101	w/o	w/o	0.15
MS-VGG	w	Conv5, 4	0.153
MS-VGG	w	Conv5, 4, 3	0.127
MS-VGG	w	Conv5, 4, 3, 2	0.112
MS-VGG	w	Conv5, 4, 3, 2, 1	0.129
MS-VGG	w/o	Conv5, 4, 3, 2	0.126

MS-VGG with 2 scales performs as well as ResNet-101. MS-VGG with conv5, 4 gives 0.153 average loss which is only 0.03 higher than ResNet-101. This phenomenon tells us that multi-scale representations are able to help to recover from distorted images. Note that MS-VGG with 3 scales surpass ResNet-101 by 0.023 which implies that multi layers fusion might have a larger influence on results than simply increasing the depth of network.

More scales do not mean better performance. 3-scale MS-VGG exceed 2-scale model by 0.026 while 4-scale network achieves the best result. However, MS-VGG with full scales (5 scales) not only performs worse than 4-scale model but also loses out to 3-scale network. We can see that more layers might not lead to better results. We argue the reason might be that conv1 are too low to provide valuable representations.

Spatial pooling makes MS-VGG more powerful. MS-VGG with spatial pooling gets 0.014 points lower than that without this operation which suggests that spatial information might contribute to our task. By performing pooling on different regions, we are able to make a fusion of different positions in addition to different feature levels (multi-scale).

Table 3. Comparison between different spatial strategies. **Region size** tells us how to split the feature map.

Base model	Region size	Average loss
MS-VGG	2×2	0.112
MS-VGG	3×3	0.105
MS-VGG	4×4	0.100
MS-VGG	5×5	0.102

We also compare different spatial pooling strategies and report the comparison results in Table 3. MS-VGG with 5×5 shows higher loss than 4×4 model which implies that more regions might not mean better performance.

4.4 Results Analysis

In Fig. 4, we gives an analysis on the results produced by MS-VGG with 4 scales (2×2 regions). Our goal is to find if there exists correlation between the number of instances and high-quality predictions. *By saying high-quality predictions, we mean those images whose L1 loss are lower than 0.03.* In Fig. 4a, we partition the test set (4,952 images) according to the number of instances in each image. *Note that* We can tell that images with few instances take the main part. As shown in Fig. 4b, the percentage of high-quality outputs are almost the same among different types of images with specific number of instances. This might be a little surprising result which suggests that the number of objects has nothing to do with the difficulty of recovering the original images.

Another question is: what is the relationship between the difficulty of recovery and the original image aspect ratio? To answer this question, we also make an investigation and show the results in Table 4, from which we can see that images

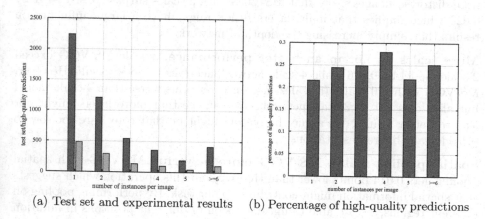

(a) Test set and experimental results   (b) Percentage of high-quality predictions

Fig. 4. (a) We compare the number of instances and high-quality predictions. The blue and yellow histograms represent the number of images in test set and high-quality predictions, respectively. (b) We calculate the ratio between the number of test images and high-quality images. (Color figure online)

Table 4. The percentage of high-quality predictions in different partitions of original image aspect ratios.

0.2–0.6	0.6–1.0	1.0–1.2	1.2–1.4	1.4–1.6	1.6–1.8
0.0435	0.1366	0.1275	0.3346	0.1514	0.0122

Input   Groundtruth   Prediction

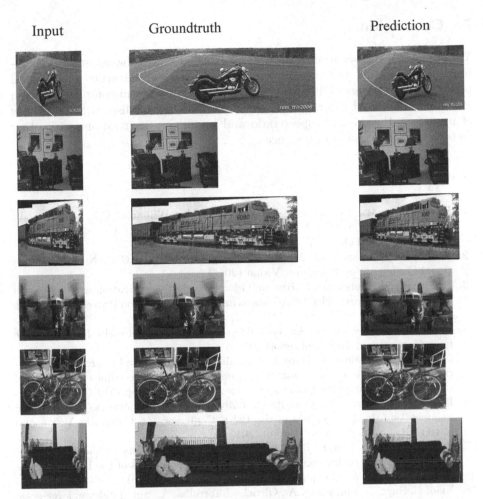

Fig. 5. Some examples of network predictions. The left column is the input image (all resized to 224×224), the middle column is the original image, the right column contains recovered images with predicted aspect ratios. *Note that heights of all images are fixed to the same length.*

whose aspect ratios are between 1.2 and 1.4 are the easiest ones to be recovered. Large aspect ratios (e.g., 1.6–1.8) make it difficult to recover from distorted images.

We also show some predictions of our CNN model in Fig. 5. Although the network still feels hard to recover images with large aspect ratios (row 1, 3, 6 in Fig. 5), most of its outputs are at least acceptable and some of them are undistinguishable (row 2, 4, 5).

5   Conclusion

We propose to recover from aspect-ratio distorted images based on image contents. To solve this problem, we build a multi-scale architecture with spatial pooling that performs well on the recovery task. We perform complete ablation studies on details of the model architecture. Finally, we discuss the difficulty of predicting the original aspect ratio and try mining its relations with other factors, e.g., the number of instances.

References

1. Everingham, M., Eslami, S.M.A., Van Gool, L., Williams, C.K.I., Winn, J., Zisserman, A.: The PASCAL visual object classes challenge: a retrospective. Int. J. Comput. Vis. **111**(1), 98–136 (2015)
2. Yang, S. F., Ramanan, D.: Multi-scale recognition with DAG-CNNs. In: International Conference on Computer Vision (2015)
3. Krizhevsky, A., Sutskever, I., Hinton, G.E.: ImageNet classification with deep convolutional neural networks. In: Advances in Neural Information Processing Systems (2012)
4. Simonyan, K., Zisserman, A.: Very deep convolutional networks for large-scale image recognition. Technical report (2014)
5. Girshick, R., Donahue, J., Darrell, T., Malik, J.: Rich feature hierarchies for accurate object detection and semantic segmentation. In: Proceedings of the IEEE Conference on Computer Vision and Pattern Recognition, pp. 580–587 (2014)
6. Long, J., Shelhamer, E., Darrell, T.: Fully convolutional networks for semantic segmentation. In: Proceedings of the IEEE Conference on Computer Vision and Pattern Recognition, pp. 3431–3440 (2015)
7. He, K., Zhang, X., Ren, S., Sun, J.: Delving deep into rectifiers: surpassing human-level performance on imagenet classification. In: Proceedings of the IEEE International Conference on Computer Vision, pp. 1026–1034 (2015)
8. Xiao, J., Hays, J., Ehinger, K.A., Oliva, A., Torralba, A.: Sun database: large-scale scene recognition from abbey to zoo. In: Proceedings of the IEEE Conference on Computer Vision and Pattern Recognition, pp. 3485–3492 (2010)
9. Xie, G.S., Zhang, X.Y., Yan, S., Liu, C.L.: Hybrid CNN and dictionary-based models for scene recognition and domain adaptation. IEEE Trans. Circuits Syst. Video Technol. **27**, 1263–1274 (2015)
10. Guo, S., Huang, W., Wang, L., Qiao, Y.: Locally supervised deep hybrid model for scene recognition. IEEE Trans. Image Process. **26**(2), 808–820 (2015)
11. Hoiem, D., Efros, A.A., Hebert, M.: Automatic photo pop-up. ACM Trans. Graph. **24**(3), 577–584 (2005)
12. He, K., Chang, H., Sun, J.: Content-aware rotation. In: Proceedings of the IEEE International Conference on Computer Vision, pp. 553–560 (2013)
13. Kim, J., Baek, J., Park, Y., Kim, E.: New vehicle detection method with aspect ratio estimation for hypothesized windows. Sensors **15**(12), 30927–30941 (2015)
14. Eigen, D., Puhrsch, C., Fergus, R.: Depth map prediction from a single image using a multi-scale deep network. In: Advances in Neural Information Processing Systems, pp. 2366–2374 (2014)

15. Kong, T., Yao, A., Chen, Y., Sun, F.: HyperNet: towards accurate region proposal generation and joint object detection. In: Proceedings of the IEEE Conference on Computer Vision and Pattern Recognition, pp. 845–853 (2016)
16. Li, D., He, K., Sun, J., Zhou, K.: A geodesic-preserving method for image warping. In: Proceedings of the IEEE Conference on Computer Vision and Pattern Recognition, pp. 213–221 (2015)
17. He, K., Zhang, X., Ren, S., Sun, J.: Deep residual learning for image recognition. In: Proceedings of the IEEE Conference on Computer Vision and Pattern Recognition, pp. 770–778 (2016)
18. Ioffe, S., Szegedy, C.: Batch normalization: accelerating deep network training by reducing internal covariate shift. Technical report (2015)
19. Vedaldi, A., Lenc, K.: Matconvnet: convolutional neural networks for matlab. In: Proceedings of the 23rd ACM International Conference on Multimedia, pp. 689–692 (2015)

Integrating Visual Word Embeddings into Translation Language Model for Keyword Spotting on Historical Mongolian Document Images

Hongxi Wei[✉], Hui Zhang, and Guanglai Gao

School of Computer Science, Inner Mongolia University, Hohhot, China
cswhx@imu.edu.cn

Abstract. In Bag-of-Visual-Words (BoVW) framework, there is lacking of the semantic relatedness between visual words. Therefore, a visual word embeddings approach has been proposed in this paper, which is similar to the word embedding technique in natural language processing (NLP). First of all, a large number of visual words are extracted and collected from a word image collection under the framework of BoVW. And then, a deep learning procedure is used for mapping visual words into embedding vectors in a semantic space. After that, the visual word embeddings are integrated into a translation language model for attaining the aim of keyword spotting in the scenario of query-by-example. Experimental results prove that the proposed visual word embeddings based translation language model approach for keyword spotting outperforms various state-of-the-art methods, including BoVW, language model (LM), translation language model with mutual information (TLM-MI) and latent Dirichlet allocation (LDA).

Keywords: Visual word embedding · Translation Language Model
Translation probability · Keyword spotting · Historical Mongolian documents

1 Introduction

For a large number of historical document images, how to retrieve them is still a challenging task. There is a traditional approach for accomplishing the task, which utilizes *optical character recognition* (OCR) technology to convert the corresponding historical document images into texts. And then, the retrieval procedure can be performed on the OCR'ed texts. Until now, OCR is still a challenging task for historical documents due to degradation and low image quality.

When OCR is infeasible, *keyword spotting* can be taken as an alternative approach [1]. The aim of keyword spotting is to find all relevant word images from a collection of word images that are similar to a given query keyword image by image matching. Therefore, historical document images need to be segmented into the corresponding word images in advance. Thus, the key issue of keyword spotting is how to represent word images for attaining the aim of real-time image matching. In the traditional keyword spotting, profile-based features are widely used to represent word images [2] and matched using *dynamic time warping* (DTW) algorithm [3, 4]. Although the DTW algorithm works well, it is so time-consuming that cannot be competent for real-time matching at the retrieval stage.

Recently, Bag-of-Visual-Words (BoVW) has been attracted much more attention and shown advantages in the task of keyword spotting [5, 6]. In the BoVW framework, there are two main steps: *encoding* and *pooling*. In order to realize the encoding and pooling, a codebook composed of a number of visual words should be obtained in advance. Given a training collection of word images, the process for creating a codebook is as follows [7]: firstly, *local descriptors* (e.g. SIFT descriptor) are extracted from each word image; secondly, all the local descriptors are collected and divided into different clusters by a clustering algorithm; thirdly, the centroid of each cluster is considered as a *visual word*, and then a codebook can be formulated by obtaining all visual words.

In the BoVW framework, one word image can be converted into a fixed-length histogram of *local descriptors* (i.e. *visual words*). And then, cosine similarity between word images can be calculated on their histograms so that a ranked list of word images can be formed for a given query keyword image. Hence, the BoVW is competent for real-time matching in the case of large-scale word image collections. However, visual words within one word image are independent each other, which results in not only discarding spatial orders of the neighboring visual words but also lacking semantic relatedness between visual words.

In this paper, we propose a *visual word embeddings* approach to capture semantic relations between visual words. To be specific, when a collection of visual words is provided, a similar learning procedure of *word embedding* is utilized as well as in *natural language processing* (NLP). Thus, each visual word can be represented as a vector that is called *visual word embeddings*. The distance (e.g. *Euclidean distance*) or cosine between two embedding vectors is a quantitative indication of the semantic relatedness between the corresponding visual words. Moreover, a *translation language model* is adopted to integrate semantic relations of visual words into keyword spotting on historical Mongolian document images.

The rest of the paper is organized as follows. The related work is given in Sect. 2. The proposed method is described detailedly in Sect. 3. Experimental results are presented in Sect. 4. Section 5 provides the conclusions and future work.

2 Related Work

In the keyword spotting technology, several manners for providing query keyword have been proposed in the literature, which can be divided into *query-by-example* (QBE) and *query-by-string* (QBS) approaches [8]. In the QBS approaches, query keyword is provided by a textual string [9, 10]. But, the QBS approaches need to learn a model to map from textual string to image on a large number of annotated word images. When there is no such annotated word images, the QBE approaches are competent. The QBE approaches [11, 12] require that an example image of the query keyword is provided for being retrieved. In this paper, we address the QBE approach for fulfilling keyword spotting on historical Mongolian document images.

In the recent years, *word embeddings* have shown significant improvements in various NLP tasks, such as word analogy [13], information retrieval [14], and so on. The word embedding technique can assign each word to a low-dimensional vector in a semantic vector space. Word2vec [13] and GloVe [15] are successful examples of word embeddings.

To be specific, Word2vec learns the word embedding vectors using a neural network based language model. Word2vec has two main formulations that are skip-gram and continuous bag-of-words (CBOW). Correspondingly, GloVe learns the word embedding vectors using matrix factorization technique. GloVe incorporates co-occurrence statistics of words that frequently appear together within the document. The training objective of GloVe is to learn word embedding vectors such that their dot product equals the co-occurrence probability of these two words.

In [15], Pennington et al. has been proved that GloVe outperforms Word2vec on word analogy, word similarity and named entity recognition tasks. Therefore, GloVe is used to generate embedding vectors for visual words in this paper. Thus, each visual word will be mapped to a vector of the semantic vector space. And the generated word embeddings are named *visual word embeddings*. By this way, the semantic relatedness between visual words can be measured through calculating *cosine* or *Euclidean distance* on their embedding vectors. As far as we know, this is the first time to learn embedding vectors on visual words.

Recently, Zuccon et al. [16] integrated word embeddings into *translation language model* (TLM). Therein, cosine similarities between embedding vectors were used for estimating translation probabilities as follows.

$$P_t(w|u) = \frac{\cos(u, w)}{\sum_{u' \in V} \cos(u', w)} \tag{1}$$

where $P_t(w|u)$ is the translation probability from word u to word w. $\cos(u, w)$ is the cosine between the embedding vectors of u and w. The denominator is a normalization factor. However, the cosine may be negative in (1), which results in the translation probability may be less than zero. In order to handle the problem, Euclidean distance is alternative in this study. Meanwhile, a *softmax* function is adopted to transform the Euclidean distances into the corresponding translation probabilities (see Sect. 3.3).

3   The Proposed Method

In our study, the handling objects are word images. Hence, each scanned image in the collection of historical Mongolian documents has been segmented into individual word images in advance. The corresponding pre-processing steps have been given in our previous work [17]. Here, the details of our proposed method will be presented in the next sub-sections.

3.1   Local Descriptor and Codebook

In the literature, a variety of local descriptors have been presented. The most well-known is *Scale-Invariant Feature Transform* (SIFT) [18], which has been proved effective due to its invariance to scale and rotation as well for the robustness across considerable range of distortion, noise contamination and change in brightness. Therefore, SIFT descriptors are considered as the local descriptors in our study, which are extracted from each Mongolian word image.

Given a collection of historical Mongolian word images, all SIFT descriptors are extracted and the *k-means* clustering algorithm is used to calculate a certain number of clusters. Each center of the clusters is regarded as a *visual word*. By this way, a codebook can be formed. Figure 1 shows the procedure for constructing a codebook.

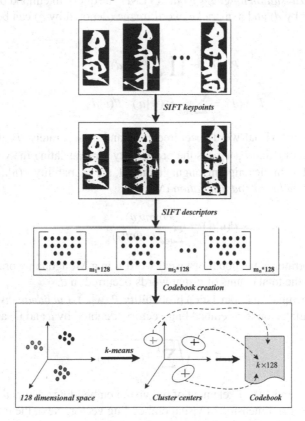

Fig. 1. The flowchart of creating a codebook

3.2   Generating Visual Word Embeddings

After obtaining a codebook, one Mongolian word image can be represented as a sequence of labels of visual words along the writing direction. When a collection of historical Mongolian word images is provided, a training corpus of visual words can be collected by concatenating the corresponding sequences of labels of visual words one after another. And then, a GloVe tool (http://nlp.stanford.edu/projects/glove/) is used to generate embedding vectors of visual words on the training corpus. In this study, the parameters of GloVe are set to as follows. The size of embedding vector and context window are set to 200 and 15, separately. Moreover, the number of iterations is set to 15.

Once visual word embeddings are obtained, the distance (e.g. Euclidean distance) between two embedding vectors will be taken as a quantitative indication of the semantic relatedness between the corresponding visual words.

3.3   Translation Language Model Based on Visual Word Embeddings

In the original *translation language model* (TLM), the query likelihood between a word image (denoted by d) and a query keyword image (denoted by q) can be calculated as follows [19].

$$P(q|d) = \prod_{w \in q} P(w|d) \tag{2}$$

$$P(w|d) = \sum_{u \in d} P_t(w|u) \cdot P(u|d) \tag{3}$$

where u and w are visual words occurred in d and q, separately. $P(u|d)$ is unigram language model of d and $P_t(w|u)$ is the probability for translating the visual word u to the visual word w. In the unigram language model, the probability $P(u|d)$ can be calculated by *maximum likelihood estimation* (MLE).

$$P(u|d) = \frac{count(u)}{\sum_{t \in d} count(t)} \tag{4}$$

where the numerator is the count of visual word u in a Mongolian word image d. The denominator is the total counts of visual words occurred in d.

In order to estimate the translation probability $P_t(w|u)$, *Euclidean distance* between u and w is calculated on their embedding vectors (denoted by $\vec{u}$ and $\vec{w}$) as follows.

$$Sim(\vec{u}, \vec{w}) = \sqrt{\sum_{i=1}^{k} (u_i - w_i)^2} \tag{5}$$

where u_i and w_i denote the ith element of the visual embedding vectors $\vec{u}$ and $\vec{w}$, respectively. k denotes the dimension of visual embedding vector. Next, the translation probability can be estimated by the following softmax function.

$$P_t(w|u) = \frac{\exp(-\alpha \cdot Sim(\vec{u}, \vec{w}))}{\sum_{v \in |V|} \exp(-\alpha \cdot Sim(\vec{u}, \vec{v}))} \tag{6}$$

where α is a free parameter and $|V|$ is the number of vocabularies for visual words. In this study, the value of parameter α is set to **0.8**.

By this means, the semantic relations between visual words are integrated into the TLM. In line with [19], the number of visual words for translation was set to **10** for a given visual word. And the problem of self-translation probability is not concerned in our study.

In (2), q may contain several visual words that do not occur in d. Thus, the probability $P(q|d)$ may be zero. To avoid zero probability, a smoothing scheme should be utilized. In [20], Zhai and Lafferty concluded that the *Jelinek-Mercer* (JM) smoothing method is best for long queries. In the scenario of QBE-based keyword spotting, query keyword images are equivalent to long queries. So, the JM method is chosen to smooth the probability $P(w|d)$. The Eq. (3) can be rewritten into the following formula.

$$P(w|d) = \lambda \cdot [\sum_{u \in d} P_t(w|u) \cdot P(u|d)] + (1 - \lambda) \cdot P(w|C) \qquad (7)$$

where λ $(0 \leq \lambda \leq 1)$ is a smoothing parameter and $P(w|C)$ denotes the probability estimated by the whole collection of visual words. At the retrieval stage, we can substitute (7) into (2). And then, a ranking list of Mongolian word images will be formed for a given query keyword image.

4   Experimental Results

4.1   Dataset

To evaluate performance, a collection of Mongolian historical documents has been collected, which is constitutive of 100 scanned Mongolian Kanjur images with 24,827 words. Each page has been annotated manually to form the ground truth data. Twenty meaningful words are selected and taken as query keywords, which are the same as in [21–23]. In our experiment, evaluation metric is *mean average precision* (MAP).

For creating the codebook, all the SIFT descriptors have been extracted from the 24,827 word images. The total amount of the SIFT descriptors is 2,283,512. After that, the k-means clustering algorithm has been performed on those descriptors. Therein, the number of the clusters varies from 500 to 10,000 and increases 500 each time. In our experiment, the appropriate number of clusters will be determined.

4.2   Baselines

In our experiment, the original BoVW and other state-of-the-art approaches are taken as baselines. The details of these baseline methods are as follows.

BoVW: Each Mongolian word image is converted into a histogram of visual words and *tf-idf* scheme is used for weighing visual words. Cosine similarities can be calculated on the histograms for ranking word images at the retrieval stage.

Language model (LM): Each Mongolian word image can be represented as a probability distribution of visual words. *Query likelihood model* is utilized to rank word images.

For processing easily, only unigram LM is considered. The formula of *Jelinek-Mercer smoothing* for the unigram LM of a Mongolian word image is defined as follows [23].

$$P(t|d) = \lambda \cdot P_{MLE}(t|M_d) + (1 - \lambda) \cdot P_{MLE}(t|M_c) \tag{8}$$

where M_d and M_c are the LMs of a Mongolian word image (denoted by d) and a collection of Mongolian word images (denoted by c), separately. $P_{MLE}(.)$ denotes the prior probability of a visual word t estimated by MLE. λ ($0 \le \lambda \le 1$) is a smoothing parameter.

Translation language model with mutual information (TLM-MI): Karimzadehgan et al. have proposed an approach to estimate translation probability based on mutual information in [19]. Correspondingly, the translation probability $P_t(w|u)$ can be estimated by calculating mutual information between visual words. According to [19], the number of visual words for translation is set to **10** for a given visual word.

Latent Dirichlet Allocation (LDA): Wei et al. [21] proposed a LDA-based representation for Mongolian word images on the same dataset, in which a LDA-based topic model was used to extract semantic relations between visual words. The best MAP of the LDA-based representation can attain **43.78%** when the number of topics and clusters are **100** and **2,000**, severally.

4.3 Performance of BoVW and LM

We have tested the performance of the original BoVW approach. In the BoVW approach, each Mongolian word image was converted into a histogram of visual words and the *tf-idf* scheme was used for weighting visual words. In Fig. 2, the red curve is the performance of the BoVW and its best performance is **13.43%** when the number of clusters increases to **5,500**.

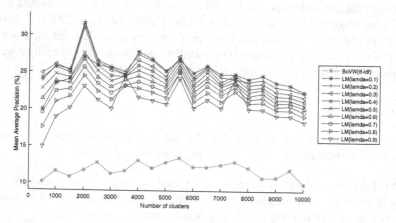

Fig. 2. The performance of BoVW and LM (Color figure online)

For the unigram LM, the *query likelihood model* is applied to rank word images. The performance of the unigram LM is also shown in Fig. 2. The best performance can attain to **31.75%** when the smoothing parameter λ is set to **0.2**. Meanwhile, the appropriate number of clusters is **2000**.

4.4 Performance of the Proposed TLM with Visual Word Embeddings

The performance of the original TLM with mutual information (**TLM-MI**) and the proposed TLM with visual word embeddings (**TLM-VWE**) are shown in Figs. 3 and 4, severally. In Fig. 3, the best performance of TLM-MI is **38.41%** when the number of clusters is **5,500** and the smoothing parameter λ is set to **0.9**.

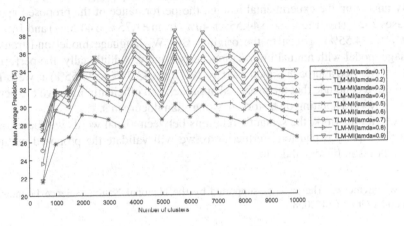

Fig. 3. The performance of TLM-MI

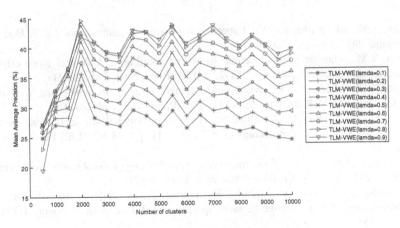

Fig. 4. The performance of the proposed TLM-VWE

In Fig. 4, the best performance of the proposed **TLM-VWE** attains to **44.55%** when the number of clusters is **2,000** and the smoothing parameter λ is set to **0.8**. The performance of the proposed **TLM-VWE** method outperforms **BoVW**, **LM** and **TLM-MI**. Moreover, the proposed **TLM-VWE** is superior to the **LDA** based approach as well. It indicates that the proposed visual word embeddings can obtain much more semantic relatedness between visual words than the **LDA** based approach.

5 Conclusion

In this paper, a visual word embeddings approach is proposed that embedding vectors of visual words are learnt from a collection of visual words by the GloVe. And then, the semantic information between visual words is utilized by a translation language model with the aim of improving the performance of keyword spotting.

By analyzing the experimental results, the performance of the proposed approach increases **232%** (from 13.43% to 44.55%), **40%** (from 31.75% to 44.55%) and **16%** (from 38.41% to 44.55%) against to the original BoVW, language model and translation language model with mutual information, respectively. Additionally, the performance of the LDA based approach is increased by **2%** (from 43.78% to 44.55%) as well. Therefore, we can conclude that the proposed approach can efficiently improve the performance of keyword spotting on historical Mongolian documents.

In our future work, the semantic relations between visual words will be utilized to accomplish query expansion. Furthermore, we will validate the proposed method on other datasets of historical documents.

Acknowledgements. The paper is supported by the National Natural Science Foundation of China under Grant 61463038.

References

1. Rath, T.M., Manmatha, R.: Word spotting for historical manuscripts. Int. J. Doc. Anal. Recognit. **9**(2), 139–152 (2007)
2. Rath, T.M., Manmatha, R.: Features for word spotting in historical manuscripts. In: Proceedings of ICDAR 2003, pp. 218–222. IEEE Press, New York (2003)
3. Rath, T.M., Manmatha, R.: Word image matching using dynamic time warping. In: Proceedings of CVPR 2003, pp. 521–527. IEEE Press, New York (2003)
4. Wei, H., Gao, G., Bao, Y.: A method for removing inflectional suffixes in word spotting of Mongolian Kanjur. In: Proceedings of ICDAR 2011, pp. 88–92. IEEE Press, New York (2011)
5. Shekhar, R., Jawahar, C.V.: Word image retrieval using bag of visual words. In: Proceedings of DAS 2012, pp. 297–301. IEEE Press, New York (2012)
6. Aldavert, D., Rusinol, M., Toledo, R., Llados, J.: A study of bag-of-visual-words representations for handwritten keyword spotting. Int. J. Doc. Anal. Recognit. **18**(3), 223–234 (2015)
7. Lopes-Monroy, A.P., Montes-Y-Gomez, M., Escalante, H.J., Cruz-Roa, A., Gonzalez, F.A.: Improving the BoVW via discriminative visual n-grams and MKL strategies. Neurocomputing **175**, 768–781 (2016)

8. Fornes, A., Frinken, V., Fischer, A., Almazan, J., Jackson, G., Bunke, H.: A keyword spotting approach using blurred shape model-based descriptors. In: Proceedings of HIP 2011, pp. 83–89. ACM Press, New York (2011)
9. Aldavert, D., Rusinol, M., Toledo, R., Llados, J.: Integrating visual and textual cues for query-by-string word spotting. In: Proceedings of ICDAR 2013, pp. 511–515. IEEE Press, New York (2013)
10. Rothacker, L., Fink, G.A.: Segmentation-free query-by-string word spotting with bag-of-features HMMs. In: Proceedings of ICDAR 2015, pp. 661–665. IEEE Press, New York (2015)
11. Wei, H., Gao, G., Su, X.: A multiple instances approach to improving keyword spotting on historical Mongolian document images. In: Proceedings of ICDAR 2015, pp. 121–125. IEEE Press, New York (2015)
12. Wei, H., Gao, G.: A keyword retrieval system for historical Mongolian document images. Int. J. Doc. Anal. Recognit. **17**(1), 33–45 (2014)
13. Mikolov, T., Sutskever, I., Chen, K., Coorado, G.S., Dean, J.: Distributed representations of words and phrases and their compositionality. In: Proceedings of NIPS 2013, pp. 3111–3119. MIT Press, Massachusetts (2013)
14. Zamani, H., Croft, W.B.: Embedding-based query language models. In: Proceedings of the 2016 ACM International Conference on the Theory of Information Retrieval (ICTIR 2016), pp. 147–156. ACM Press, New York (2016)
15. Pennington, J., Socher, R., Manning, C.D.: GloVe: global vectors for word representation. In: Proceedings of EMNLP 2014, pp. 1532–1543. ACL Press, Stroudsburg (2014)
16. Zuccon, G., Koopman, B., Bruza, P., Azzopardi, L.: Integrating and evaluating neural word embeddings in information retrieval. In: Proceedings of the 20th Australasian Document Computing Symposium (ADCS 2015), pp. 12:1–12:8. ACM Press, New York (2015)
17. Wei, H., Gao, G., Bao, Y., Wang, Y.: An efficient binarization method for ancient Mongolian document images. In: Proceedings of the 3rd International Conference on Advanced Computer Theory and Engineering, pp. 43–46. IEEE Press, New York (2010)
18. Lowe, D.G.: Distinctive image features from scale-invariant keypoints. Int. J. Comput. Vis. **60**(2), 91–110 (2004)
19. Karimzadehgan, M., Zhai, C.X.: Estimation of statistical translation models based on mutual information for ad hoc information retrieval. In: Proceedings of SIGIR 2010, pp. 323–330. ACM Press, New York (2010)
20. Zhai, C.X., Lafferty, J.: A study of smoothing methods for language models applied to ad hoc information retrieval. In: Proceedings of SIGIR 2001, pp. 334–342. ACM Press, New York (2001)
21. Wei, H., Gao, G., Su, X.: LDA-based word image representation for keyword spotting on historical Mongolian documents. In: Hirose, A., Ozawa, S., Doya, K., Ikeda, K., Lee, M., Liu, D. (eds.) ICONIP 2016. LNCS, vol. 9950, pp. 432–441. Springer, Cham (2016). https://doi.org/10.1007/978-3-319-46681-1_52
22. Wei, H., Zhang, H., Gao, G.: Representing word image using visual word embeddings and RNN for keyword spotting on historical document images. In: Proceedings of ICME 2017, pp. 1374–1379. IEEE Press, New York (2017)
23. Wei, H., Gao, G.: Visual language model for keyword spotting on historical Mongolian document images. In: Proceedings of CCDC 2017, pp. 1765–1770. IEEE Press, New York (2017)

The Analysis for Binaural Signal's Characteristics of a Real Source and Corresponding Virtual Sound Image

Jinshan Wang[1,2], Xiaochen Wang[1,2,3(✉)], Weiping Tu[1,2],
Jun Chen[1,2], Tingzhao Wu[1,2], and Shanfa Ke[1,2]

[1] School of Computer, National Engineering Research Center for Multimedia Software,
Wuhan University, Wuhan 430072, China
cy_wangjinshan@163.com, clowang@163.com, echotuwp@163.com,
chenj@whu.edu.cn, wutz01@126.com, kimmyfa@163.com
[2] Hubei Key Laboratory of Multimedia and Network Communication Engineering,
Wuhan University, Wuhan 430072, China
[3] Collaborative Innovation Center of Geospatial Technology, Wuhan 430079, China

Abstract. 3D Audio System could rebuild more realistic and immersive sound effects. The existing 3D audio reconstruction methods mainly consider the physical characteristics of sound filed, less take head's effect on sound transmission process into account. However, when human is located in the sound field, there will have an obvious deviation between perceptual sound image and reconstructed image. Some researchers considered head's effects on the reconstruction of sound field, but they only use simple head model to reproduce sound field in some certain loudspeaker configurations. Therefore, if we want to reconstruct an ideal sound filed, we need to analyze head's effects on the reconstruction of sound field in detail. Thus in this paper, we analyzed and compared binaural signal's characteristics under different loudspeaker configurations and gains. The analysis results may be act as a primary reference for further research about sound field reconstruction etc.

Keywords: Sound field reconstruction · Binaural signals · Virtual sound image

1 Introduction

The mainstream 3D audio reconstruction technology mainly include Wave Field Synthesis (WFS) [1], Ambisonics [2–5] and Amplitude panning technology etc. WFS and Ambisonics complete sound field reconstruction based on the physical characteristicsof sound filed. However, when a person is located in the sound field, his (or her)

X. Wang—This work is supported by National Nature Science Foundation of China (No. 61231015, 61671335); National High Technology Research and Development Program of China (863 Program) No. 2015AA016306; Hubei Province Technological Innovation Major Project(No. 2016AAA015).

© Springer International Publishing AG, part of Springer Nature 2018
B. Zeng et al. (Eds.): PCM 2017, LNCS 10736, pp. 626–633, 2018.
https://doi.org/10.1007/978-3-319-77383-4_61

head would bring disturbance to the reconstructed sound field's characteristics thus causing listener's perception for the sound's position deviate the desired reconstructed position.

In some methods such as sine law and tangent law, head's effects are taken into account. These two laws introduce binaural cues to sound image reconstruction. Human's perception to sound's position mainly rely on two important cues: Interaural Level Difference's influence(ILD). and Interaural Time Difference(ITD) [3, 9]. However, sine law and tangent law only utilize ITD to reproduce the virtual sound image generated by loudspeaker pair, not considering the ILD. Since ITD only play main role in low frequency (below 1.5 kHz) sound's location, additionally, these two laws are only suitable for stereo system, thus having limited actual use.

As for the reconstruction for sound image in 3D space, Vector-Based Amplitude Panning (VBAP) [8] and Multiple-Direction Amplitude Panning(MDAP) [6] are usually to be adopted. VBAP achieve the reconstruction of virtual sound image based on the method of vector synthesis. but VBAP has no essential difference compared with sine law and tangent law.

The above mentioned methods mainly consider the physical characteristics of sound filed at listening point or region, less take head's effects on the reconstruction of sound field into account, cannot perfectly reconstruct the sound field in human's head region without perceptual distoration. Therefore, in order to obtain multiple loudspeaker signals to reconstruct 3D audio scene at human's two ears, some researchers have did much work to explore head's disturbance characteristics on sound field according to binaural signals of 3D audio.

In 2013, Breebaart compared interaural intensity differences (IIDs) of a real source and those resulting from a phantom source created by pair-wise amplitude panning. The results show that the translation of panning gain ratios to IIDs depends on the source frequency, the individual's HRTFs, the loudspeaker angle, and the source direction angle [10]. In 2016, Wu pointed out the ILD and Inter-Channel Level Difference (ICLD) cannot be treated as the same, and he made a qualitative and quantitative analysis of the difference between the two parameters [11]. But they did not make a detail analysis for binaural signal's characteristics in different loudspeaker configurations, gain, and azimuth. whether there exist a mapping relationship between the single sound source's binaural signal and the virtual sound image's binaural signal(at the same position with the single sound source) in different loudspeaker configurations? whether we can accurately estimate the position of reconstructed virtual sound image in different loudspeaker configurations? Currently, there are no much attention carried out about these issues.

In this paper, with different loudspeaker configurations, we made a detailed analysis and comparison for binaural signal's characteristics as listener's subjective perception for virtual sound image was approximately consistent with real sound. The analysis results may be act as a primary reference for further research about spatial audio applications such as sound field reconstruction etc.

2   Head's Effect on Physical Characteristics of Sound Field

In a single sound source's sound field reproduced by one loudspeaker, we can use sound pressure and particle velocity to calculate the difference of signal's energy as listener is not located in sound field [11, 15]. But when a listener exist in the sound field, the binaural signal's energy would have a greater difference due to the filtering effect of listener's head, pinna and torso. This difference could be measured by ILD.

2.1   Energy Analysis of Listening Point in Reconstructed Sound Field

Assuming that human's head is a rigid sphere, the sound pressure at point L(left ear) and R (right ear) denoted by P_L and P_R can be calculated by Eq. (1) (Fig. 1).

$$P_L = \frac{g}{r_1} e^{-iKr_1} \quad , \quad P_R = \frac{g}{r_2} e^{-iKr_2} \tag{1}$$

where g is the gain of loudspeaker s, r_1 and r_2 are the distance from S to ears, and the K is the number of wave forms.

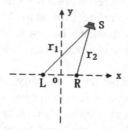

Fig. 1.   Schematic diagram of sound pressure and particle velocity.

The particle velocity at point L and R can be obtained by Eq. (2).

$$\vec{V}_L = \frac{g}{\rho_0 c_0} \frac{e^{-iK|r_1|}}{|r_1|^2} \vec{r}_1 \quad , \quad \vec{V}_R = \frac{g}{\rho_0 c_0} \frac{e^{-iK|r_2|}}{|r_2|^2} \vec{r}_2 \tag{2}$$

where ρ_0 is the air density, c_0 is voice speed. So, we can calculate the energy ratio by Eq. (3).

$$\frac{E_L}{E_R} = \frac{|P_L|^2 + |\vec{V}_L|^2}{|P_R|^2 + |\vec{V}_R|^2} \tag{3}$$

2.2   Energy Analysis of Binaural Signal in Reconstructed Sound Field

Our head's effect on the transmission of sound from sound source to human's ears can be described by Head Related Transfer Function (HRTF). HRTF database can be used to obtain binaural signals we needed. In this paper, the CIPIC HRTF [13] database was adopted to synthesize binaural signals.

The single sound source's binaural signal can be obtained by doing convolution between sound signal and corresponding position's Head Related Impulse Response (HRIR, the HRTF's time domain description) data. We use $S_{sl}(k)$, $S_{sr}(k)$ respectively denote left and right ear signal, they are calculated by Eqs. (4) and (5).

$$S_{sl}(k) = S_s(k) * HRIR_{sl}(index, \theta, \varphi) \tag{4}$$

$$S_{sr}(k) = S_s(k) * HRIR_{sr}(index, \theta, \varphi) \tag{5}$$

Where $S_s(k)$ is the excitation signal (single sound source signal) $HRIR_{sl}(index, \theta, \varphi)$, $HRIR_{sr}(index, \theta, \varphi)$, respectively represented the left and right ear's HRIR data as azimuth is θ, elevation is φ, index is subject's label. Because this paper's experiments focus on horizontal plane, thus φ is always zero.

After obtaining the binaural signal of single sound source, the binaural signal were divide into frames, each frame was transformed to the frequency domain using an FFT of length N ($N = 1024$). The frequency domain signal $S_{bl}(k)$, $S_{br}(k)$ ($k = [0, 1, \ldots \ldots, N/2]$) are divided into nonoverlapping subbands by grouping of FFT bins, the k_b is the start indices of subband b ($b = [1, 2, \ldots \ldots, 25]$). For each subband b, ILD (equivalent to the energy ratio of binaural signal)was computed by Eq. (6) [14].

$$ILD[b] = 10 \log_{10} \frac{\sum_{k=kb}^{kb+1-1} S_{bl}(k) S_{bl}^*(k)}{\sum_{k=kb}^{kb+1-1} S_{br}(k) S_{br}^*(k)} \tag{6}$$

where $*$ denotes complex conjugation.

Based on the above analysis, we can know that head's effect on reconstructed sound field is very conspicuous. we need consider head's effect in the sound field reconstruction, rather than only relying on simple geometric model to implement the sound field reconstruction.

3   Experimental Analysis of Binaural Signal's Characteristics

In order to analyze characteristics of the reconstructed virtual image's binaural signals, we use two loudspeakers to reproduce the virtual sound image in different configuration. In our experiments, we gave six different loudspeaker configurations. Six different loudspeaker configurations on the horizontal plane were as follows: [−20 20], [−25 25], [−30 30], [−35 35], [−40 40], [−45 45], where the first number is the azimuth of left loudspeaker, the second number is the azimuth of right loudspeaker.

For every configuration, we put white noise as an original sound source signal(the sampling rate is 44.1 kHz, the duration is 1 s), selected azimuth every 5° between the left and right loudspeakers and generated binaural signals of single sound source as Eqs. (4) and (5). According to the azimuth of desired reconstructed virtual sound image (single sound source), we could synthesize multiple group binaural signals in different loudspeaker gain by utilizing HRTF database. After obtaining binaural signals of single sound source and loudspeaker pair, we organized listeners to do subjective listening test to select a most suitable virtual sound image that best matched single sound source's position, the experiment results to be averaged for all listeners. Finally, we made a detail comparison and analysis for the ILD of binaural signals. More details are described next.

3.1 Calculation of Loudspeaker Signal's Gain

In our experiments, we used tangent amplitude panning law to calculate the initial gain of loudspeaker signals as shown in Fig. 2.

$$g_l = \frac{\tan \theta - \tan \varphi}{\sqrt{2 \tan^2 \theta + 2 \tan^2 \varphi}} \ , \ \ g_r = \frac{\tan \theta + \tan \varphi}{\sqrt{2 \tan^2 \theta + 2 \tan^2 \varphi}} \tag{7}$$

where g_l and g_r are respectively the gain of left loudspeaker and right loudspeaker, φ is the azimuth of virtual sound, $-\theta$ and θ respectively indicates the left and right loudspeaker's deviation angle. After obtaining the initial gains, guaranteeing the conservation of energy, we regard the initial gains as a center to get multiple group gain by increasing and decreasing gains with a certain small step.

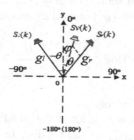

Fig. 2. Tangent amplitue panning law

After getting the gain of loudspeaker signals, we can obtain the weighted loudspeaker signals by Eq. (8).

$$S_l(k) = g_l \cdot S_s(k) \ , \ \ S_r(k) = g_r \cdot S_s(k) \tag{8}$$

where $S_l(k)$ is the adjusted left loudspeaker signal, $S_r(k)$ is the adjusted right loudspeaker signal, $S_s(k)$ is the excitation signal (single sound source signal).

3.2 Generation of Binaural Signals

The binaural signals generated by two loudspeaker signals can be computed by summing binaural signal of each loudspeaker signal.

$$S_u(k) = S_l(k) * HRIR_u(index, \theta, \varphi) \tag{9}$$

$$S_{lr}(k) = S_l(k) * HRIR_{lr}(index, \theta, \varphi) \tag{10}$$

$$S_{rl}(k) = S_r(k) * HRIR_{rl}(index, \theta, \varphi) \tag{11}$$

$$S_{rr}(k) = S_r(k) * HRIR_{rr}(index, \theta, \varphi) \tag{12}$$

Where $S_u(k)$ is the left ear signal generated by left loudspeaker $S_{lr}(k)$ is the right ear signal generated by left loudspeaker, $S_{rl}(k)$ is the left ear signal generated by right loudspeaker, $S_{rr}(k)$ is the right ear signal generated by right loudspeaker.

In our expriments, we used $S_v(k)$ to express the binaural signals of virtual sound generated by loudspeaker pair where $S_{vl}(k)$ represents the left ear signal of virtual sound, $S_{vr}(k)$ represents the right ear signal of virtual sound.

After a 1024-point Fast Fourier Transform(FFT) with 50% overlapped window is applied in $S_u(k)$ and $S_{rl}(k)$, we add their spectrum, then do Inverse Fast Fourier Transform(IFFT) for the sum and dewindow, thus obtaining $S_{vl}(k)$. The calculation method of $S_{vr}(k)$ is similar. They are calculated as follows:

$$S_{vl}(k) = IFFT\left(FFT\left(S_u(k)\right) + FFT\left(S_{rl}(k)\right)\right) \tag{13}$$

$$S_{vr}(k) = IFFT\left(FFT\left(S_{lr}(k)\right) + FFT\left(S_{rr}(k)\right)\right) \tag{14}$$

3.3   Analysis of Binaural Signal's ILD

According to the above expriments, we obtained the following conclusions:

Laws of ILD's norm: it can be observed from Fig. 3. that the norm of the ILD of single sound source is gradually increasing when the azimuth of sound source vary from 0° to 40° in 5° steps. However, the position of first and second through remain approximately unchanged, and with the gradually increase of azimuth of sound source, the norm of ILD at the point of trough increase significantly.

Loudspeaker angle's effect on reconstructed sound image: under[−20 20], [−25 25], [−30 30], [−35 35] configurations, the ILD of binaural signals generated by loudspeakers pair shows a similar law as the ILD of single sound source's binaural signals, but the law of ILD become inconspicuous as the configurations are [−40 40], [−45 45]. And we also find, in our listening tests, that it is difficult to perceive a virtual sound image consistent with a single sound source's location as the angle between two loudspeakers is larger. These phenomena may indicate that loudspeaker pair with smaller angle may be more proper to reconstruct single sound source's sound field.

Laws of ILD's trough point: For a certain azimuth, before the second trough of ILD, the law of binaural signal's ILD approximately remain the same for both single source and loudspeaker pair. From the second row to the fifth row in Fig. 3, we can see that the trough point's position of the ILD of binaural signals generated by loudspeaker pair gradually move to the left with the increase of loudspeaker pair's angle. This may show that the first and second trough point of ILD may play a decisive role in the sound source location, we may use this characteristics to achieve the single sound source's reconstruction in different configurations.

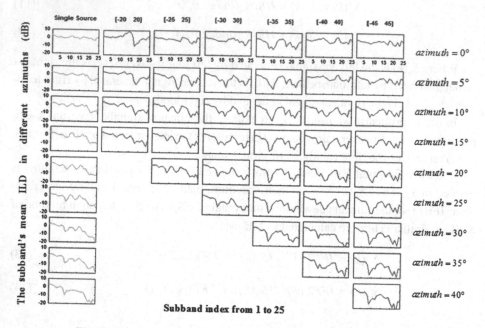

Fig. 3. The mean ILD of binaural signals in different configurations

4 Conclusion

In this paper, with different loudspeaker configurations, we made a detailed comparison and analysis for binaural signal's characteristics as listener's subjective perception for the position of virtual sound image generated by loudspeaker pair was approximately consistent with real sound. Experiments show that loudspeaker pair with smaller angle may be more proper to reconstruct single sound source's sound field. The first and second trough of ILD may play a decisive role in the sound source location. In the future work, we may be able to extract spatial feature parameters to denote the spatial position of synthesized binaural signals, and construct mapping relationships between feature parameters and virtual sound image's position, build location model of virtual sound image generated by multiple loudspeakers, ensure the virtual sound image generated by loudspeakers consistent with human auditory perception, thus achieving the reconstruction of sound field for single sound source without perceptual distortion.

References

1. Berkhout, A.J., de Vries, D., Vogel, P.: Acoustic control by wave field synthesis. J. Acoust. Soc. Am. **93**(5), 2764–2778 (1993)
2. Blauert, J.: Spatial Hearing: The Psychophysics of Human Sound Localization. The MIT Press, Cambridge (1997)
3. Strutt, J.W.: On our perception of sound direction. Philos. Mag. **13**(6), 214–232 (1907)
4. Gerzon, M.A.: Periphony: with-height sound reproduction. J. Audio Eng. Soc. **21**(1), 2–10 (1973)
5. Bernfeld, B.: Attempts for better understanding of the directional stereophonic listening mechanism. In: 44th Audio Engineering Society Convention. Audio Engineering Society (1973)
6. Pulkki, V.: Uniform spreading of amplitude panned virtual sources. In: 1999 IEEE Workshop on Applications of Signal Processing to Audio and Acoustics, pp. 187–190. IEEE (1999)
7. Pulkki, V., Karjalainen, M.: Multichannel audio rendering using amplitude panning [DSP applications]. IEEE Signal Process. Mag. **25**(3), 118–122 (2008)
8. Pulkki, V.: Virtual sound source positioning using vector base amplitude panning. J. Audio Eng. Soc. **45**(6), 456–466 (1997)
9. Pulkki, V., Karjalainen, M.: Localization of amplitude-panned virtual sources I: stereophonic panning. J. Audio Eng. Soc. **49**(9), 739–752 (2001)
10. Breebaart, J.: Comparison of interaural intensity differences evoked by real and phantom sources. J. Audio Eng. Soc. **61**(11), 850–859 (2013)
11. Wu, T., Hu, R., Gao, L., Wang, X., Ke, S.: Analysis and comparison of inter-channel level difference and interaural level difference. In: Tian, Q., Sebe, N., Qi, G.-J., Huet, B., Hong, R., Liu, X. (eds.) MMM 2016. LNCS, vol. 9516, pp. 586–595. Springer, Cham (2016). https://doi.org/10.1007/978-3-319-27671-7_49
12. Gao, L., Hu, R., Yang, Y.: A spatial priority based scalable audio coding. In: 2014 IEEE International Conference on Acoustics, Speech and Signal Processing (ICASSP), pp. 3670–3674. IEEE (2014)
13. Algazi, V.R., Duda, R.O., Thompson, D.M., Avendano, C.: The CIPIC HRTF database. In: Proceedings of 2001 IEEE Workshop on Applications of Signal Processing to Audio and Electroacoustics, pp. 99–102, 21–24 October 2001. Mohonk Mountain House, New Paltz (2001)
14. Breebaart, J., et al.: Parametric coding of stereo audio. EURASIP J. Appl. Signal Process. 1305–1322 (2005)
15. Pierce, A.D.: Acoustics: An Introduction to its Physical Principles and Applications. McGrawHill, New York (1981)

Primary-Ambient Extraction Based on Channel Pair for 5.1 Channel Audio Using Least Square

Dingyan Song[1,2], Ge Gao[1,2(✉)], Yi Chen[3], and Xi Hu[1,2]

[1] National Engineering Research Center for Multimedia Software,
School of Computer Science, Wuhan University, Wuhan 430072, China
songdyan@163.com, gaoge@whu.edu.cn
[2] Hubei Key Laboratory of Multimedia and Network Communication
Engineering, Wuhan University, Wuhan 430072, China
[3] Computer College, Central China Normal University, Wuhan 430072, China

Abstract. According to the growth of reality demand of digital media, the 5.1 surround is widely used and researched. To further improve the listening experience of the 5.1 channel audio, the primary-ambient extraction (PAE) is introduced to facilitate flexible rendering in spatial audio reproduction. The common multichannel PAE approach is principle component analysis (PCA), which suffers from high extraction errors and long computation time. In this letter, we proposed a novel approach based on channel pair for 5.1 channel audio, which considers the five channels as a set of channel pairs. Then a linear estimation framework is applied at any one time to only one pair, which converts the problem of PAE into the estimation of weight matrix, thus the weight of each component can be computed by using the Least Square. The experimental results indicate that the novel approach significantly outperforms the existing approach PCA.

Keywords: Primary-Ambient Extraction (PAE) · Linear estimation
Least Square (LS) · 5.1channel audio · Audio processing

1 Introduction

With the development of digital media such as 3D game and home theater, consumers are demanding a more immersive listening experience to better match 3D visual effects. However the two channels stereo audio has been unable to satisfy these demands, thus, the 5.1 surround is widely used, which is significantly improved over the two channels stereo: front imaging and clarification of dialog was improved by insertion a center to the left and right channels and improved envelopment and rear directional sound was given by adding two surround channels [1]. To further improve the listening experience of the 5.1 channel surround, the perception of the sound scenes is considered as a

---

This work is supported by the National Natural Science Foundation of China (61471271) and the Guangdong Project (2013B090700003).

combination of the foreground sound and background sound [2], which is often referred to as primary and ambient component, respectively [3]. Due to perceptual difference between the primary and ambient component, different rendering schemes should be applied to the primary and ambient component for optimal spatial audio reproduction of sound scene [4]. Channel-based audio is the common audio format that is used in spatial audio reproduction. However, the existing channel-based audio provides only the mixed signal [5]. It indicates that the process of extracting primary and ambient component is demanded. This process is named primary-ambient extraction (PAE).

Moreover, as a spatial audio processing tool, PAE can also play a key role in spatial audio scene coding (SASC) and the audio up-mixing [5, 6]. In SASC, a sound scene is considered as a sum of the primary and ambient component and the localization analysis is carried out separately for the extracted primary and ambient components and the spatial cues is applied in the final synthesis. In up-maxing, such as 5.1 channel systems, a practical method of up-mixing the stereo sound to the 5.1 channel is by separating the primary (localizable) and ambient (non-localizable) component and playing the primary sources on the two front channels to recreate the direct sources as it was intended in the original recording while playing the ambient sources on all channels to give a better listening experience of surround sound.

Several approaches have been proposed to extract the primary and ambient sources from a mixed recording, which most of them are introduced for two channel stereo, and the approach for multichannel is rarely studied. A commonly used PAE approach is using Principal Component Analysis (PCA) mentioned in [5, 7], the method is originally proposed to work for multichannel signals with only dominant amplitude-panned source, which considers the PAE as a problem of finding the maximum eigenvalue of the covariance matrix and its corresponding eigenvector [5]. However, PCA suffers from high extraction errors and long computation time. Thus, we proposed a novel PAE approach based on channel pair for 5.1 channel audio and uses the Least Square to solve the PAE problem on each channel pair. Firstly, to apply the amplitude panning to the 5.1 channel audio, the channel pairs are selected from the five channels in 5.1 channel (except the .1 channel, which is mentioned in the next section), then the process of PAE is applied at any one time to only one pair [8]. And the linear estimation framework is used on each channel pair signals [9], which converts the PAE problem to estimation of the weight matrix. Then, the extracted component of each channel of the audio signals can be computed by using the Least Square. Finally, the objective experiments are applied to compare the novel approach and the existing PCA. The results indicate that the novel method overcomes the disadvantages of PCA: the extraction error of the proposed approach is less than PCA obviously, and better performance of the ambient component can be obtained by using our method, moreover, its computation cost is lower than PCA.

The paper is structured as follows: Section 2 gives the signal model of 5.1 channel audio for PAE, and some assumptions that used in this paper. Section 3 describes the novel method based on the channel pair Least Square. Section 4 shows the evaluation between the proposed method and the previous method PCA. Finally, the conclusion is made for this paper.

2 Signal Model for 5.1 Channel

2.1 Configuration for 5.1 Channel

The current standard for multichannel reproduction recommended by ITU-R BS.775.1 adopted five or seven channels with a channel for low frequency effect content [10]. In this paper, loudspeaker configuration is based on the standard 5.1 surround, show as Fig. 1. For backwards compatibility to stereo in terms of loudspeaker positions, in the front, two loudspeakers are located angles $-30°$ and $30°$. Additionally, there is a center loudspeaker at $0°$, providing a more stable center of the auditory spatial image when listeners are not exactly in the sweet spot. The two rear loudspeaker, located at $-110°$ and $110°$, are intended to provide the important lateral signal components related to spatial impression. There is one additional channel (the .1 in 5.1) intended for low frequency effects (LFE) [11], the LFE channel has only a bandwidth up to 120 Hz and is for effects for which the other loudspeakers cannot provide enough low-frequency sound pressure, which is ignored in the PAE method described in this paper.

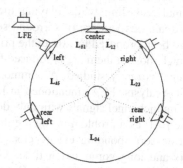

Fig. 1. The standard 5.1 surround loudspeaker configuration

2.2 Channel Pairs Selection

In this paper, the PAE method is based on the channel pair and the amplitude panning is applied to each channel pair. According to the literature [5], it is known that the PAE approaches of stereo can be extended to multichannel, such as the Least Square based method [12], which is estimating the primary and ambient component by minimizing the errors between the estimated component and the original input. However, due to the number of the channel of the 5.1 systems, the amplitude panning and the Least Square method cannot be applied to the PAE of 5.1 channel audio directly. Thus, in this paper, we proposed a novel PAE method, which divides the five channels in 5.1 systems to a set of channel pair, and solved the PAE problem in each channel pair. In the amplitude panning of the 5.1 systems, the LFE loudspeaker is ignored owing to its low frequency signal. Thus, a set of loudspeaker pairs is selected form the loudspeaker configuration, each loudspeaker may belong to two pairs. Shown as Fig. 1, the selected pairs would be L_{12}, L_{23}, L_{34}, L_{45}, L_{51}, then the Vector Based Amplitude Panning (VBAP) can be applied at any one time to only one pair [9]. In the rest of this paper, the process of PAE is based on each channel pair, that is to say, the 5.1 channel PAE is considered as a problem of PAE for a group of channel pair.

2.3 Signal Model Based on Channel Pair

In this letter, the signal model is based on each time-frequency subband, which is converted by short-time Fourier transform (STFT) [5] or some other spatial audio processing approaches. It is generally assumed that within a time frame each subband of the input signal contains only one dominant source, which is considered as the primary component, and PAE is independently carried out on each subband of each frame of the input signal [8]. It considers the signals X as a linear combination of the primary component P and ambient components A in each channel [10]. Therefore, the 5.1 channels signal model can be defined as:

$$x_n[m, l] = p_n[m, l] + a_n[m, l], \quad \forall n \in \{0, 1, 2, 3, 4\}. \tag{1}$$

where the p_n and a_n donates the primary component and ambient component of the n-th channel in the signals, respectively. In general the ambience signals will have comparable levels, that is, $\|a_0\|^2 = \|a_1\|^2 = \cdots = \|a_4\|^2$. The [m,l] are time-frequency index, which can be ignorant.

To insure that the input signal is suitable for the signal model, several assumptions are introduced. Firstly, considering the needs of the simplification of signal model, it assumes that the primary component and ambient component in each channel is correlated and uncorrelated, respectively [5]. And, the primary component is uncorrelated with the ambient component whether in the channel or between channels. Secondly, it considers that the ICLD of the target signal can be ignored. Thirdly, in the loudspeakers configuration shown as Fig. 1, the amplitude panning can be used in each channel pair [9], which means the primary component p_i can be expressed by p_j linearly, i.e., $p_j = \kappa p_i$ (i, j is the selected channel pair), where κ are introduced as the primary panning factors (PPF) [5, 9, 10]. To quantify the differences of power between the primary and ambient components, a factor named primary power ratio (PPR) γ is introduced [10], which is defined as the ratio of total primary power to total signal power in the channel pair, it can be expressed as:

$$\gamma = \frac{E_{p_i} + E_{p_j}}{E_{x_i} + E_{x_j}}, \quad \forall (i, j) \in \{(1, 2), (2, 3), (3, 4), (4, 5), (5, 1)\}. \tag{2}$$

$E_{..}$ denotes the power of the primary component or the source signal in the channel, and the PPR ranges from zero to one. The relationships between the auto- and cross-correlations at zero-lag and the power of these components can be expressed as:

$$r_{ii} = x_i^H x_i = N E_{x_i} = N(E_{p_i} + E_{a_i}). \tag{3}$$

$$r_{ij} = x_i^H x_j = p_i^H p_j = N \kappa E_{p_i}. \tag{4}$$

$$r_{jj} = x_j^H x_j = NE_{X_j} = N\left(\kappa^2 E_{p_i} + E_{a_i}\right). \tag{5}$$

Where H is the Hermitian transpose operator. Thus, according to the Eqs. (2), (3), (4) and (5), the PPF and PPR of the two adjacent channel pair signals are computed as:

$$\kappa = \frac{r_{ii} - r_{jj}}{2r_{ij}} + \sqrt{\left(\frac{r_{ii} - r_{jj}}{2r_{ij}}\right)^2 + 1}. \tag{6}$$

$$\gamma = \frac{2r_{ij} + \left(r_{jj} - r_{ii}\right)\kappa}{\left(r_{jj} + r_{ii}\right)\kappa}. \tag{7}$$

3 PAE Based on Channel Pair for 5.1 Channel Audio Using Least Square

According to the signal model of 5.1 channel audio, the 5.1 channel PAE can be considered as a problem of PAE for a set of channel pairs, which means that the signal is applied at any one time to only one channel pair. In this section, we select one of these pairs to demonstrate the PAE approach based on the Least Square.

In this paper, we address the PAE problem based on a linear estimation framework [10], where the primary and ambient components are estimated as weighted sums of signal in the channel pair. Thus, the extracted primary and ambient components are expressed as:

$$\begin{bmatrix} \hat{p}_i^T \\ \hat{p}_j^T \\ \hat{a}_i^T \\ \hat{a}_j^T \end{bmatrix} = \begin{bmatrix} w_{p_{i,i}} & w_{p_{i,j}} \\ w_{p_{j,i}} & w_{p_{j,j}} \\ w_{a_{i,i}} & w_{a_{i,j}} \\ w_{a_{j,i}} & w_{a_{j,j}} \end{bmatrix} \begin{bmatrix} x_i^T \\ x_j^T \end{bmatrix}. \tag{8}$$

where the $\hat{p}_i$, $\hat{p}_j$ and $\hat{a}_i$, $\hat{a}_j$ are represented as the extracted components of primary and ambient in each channel, respectively. The T is a symbol of transpose, x_i and x_j is the signal of the selected channel pair, $w_{..}$ is the weight of extraction, the "p" and "a" indicate primary and ambient component, respectively, i and j are the selected channel pair $((i,j) \in \{(1,2), (2,3), (3,4), (4,5), (5,6)\})$. Considering the PAE problem under this case, we regard it as a problem of matrix estimation. Following the above formulation (1) and (8), the extracted primary and ambient components can be expressed as:

$$\hat{p}_i = w_{p_{i,i}} x_i + w_{p_{i,j}} x_j. \tag{9}$$

$$\hat{a}_i = x_i - \hat{p}_i. \tag{10}$$

Then, substituting (1) into (9) under the assumption in (3), the formulation can be rewritten as:

$$\hat{p}_i = (w_{P_{i,i}} + \kappa w_{P_{i,j}})p_i + (w_{P_{i,i}} a_i + \kappa w_{P_{i,j}} a_j). \tag{11}$$

Obviously, we can express the formulation of the errors of extracted primary components as follow:

$$\varepsilon_p = \hat{p}_i - p_i = (w_{P_{i,i}} + \kappa w_{P_{i,j}} - 1)p_i + (w_{P_{i,i}} a_i + \kappa w_{P_{i,j}} a_j). \tag{12}$$

Then, the relationship between the error-to-signal ratio (ESR) for primary components and the power of extraction error and true primary components can be expressed as:

$$ESR_p = \frac{E_{\varepsilon_p}}{E_{p_i}}. \tag{13}$$

Finally, the weight of the primary of each channel can be derived by minimizing the mean square error (MSE) using the Least Square [13]. It should be noted that the MSE mentioned here is also can be expressed as the normalized mean square error (NMSE) [14]. And the formulation of MSE is $\mathcal{J} = E\left(\varepsilon_p^H \varepsilon_p\right)$, then combining the formulation (6), (7), (12) and (13) we can get a formulation as follow:

$$\mathcal{J} = E_{p_i}\left\{ \left[1 + (\kappa^2 + 1)\frac{1-\gamma}{2\gamma}\right]w_{P_{i,i}}^2 - 2w_{P_{i,i}} \right. \\ \left. + 2\kappa w_{P_{i,i}} w_{P_{i,j}} + \left[\kappa^2 + (\kappa^2 + 1)\frac{1-\gamma}{2\gamma}\right]w_{P_{i,j}}^2 - 2\kappa w_{P_{i,j}} + 1\right\}. \tag{14}$$

The gradient equation is applied to all least squares problems. Each particular problem requires particular expressions for the model and its partial derivatives [8]. The minimum of the sum of squares is found by setting the gradient to zero. Thus, the weight of primary component $w_{P_{i,i}}$, $w_{P_{i,j}}$, can be derived easily by computing the gradient of J and set it to zero. The results present as follow:

$$w_{P_{i,i}} = \frac{2\gamma}{1+\gamma}\frac{1}{1+\kappa^2}. \tag{15}$$

$$w_{P_{i,j}} = \frac{2\gamma}{1+\gamma}\frac{\kappa}{1+\kappa^2}. \tag{16}$$

Combining the formulations (9), (10), (15) and (16) the extracted components can be obtained. The results of extraction are expressed as:

$$\hat{p}_i = \frac{2\gamma}{1+\gamma}\frac{1}{1+\kappa^2}(x_i + \kappa x_j). \tag{17}$$

$$\hat{p}_j = \frac{2\gamma}{1+\gamma}\frac{\kappa}{1+\kappa^2}\left(x_i + \kappa x_j\right). \tag{18}$$

$$\hat{a}_i = x_i - \frac{2\gamma}{1+\gamma}\frac{1}{1+\kappa^2}\left(x_i + \kappa x_j\right). \tag{19}$$

$$\hat{a}_j = x_j - \frac{2\gamma}{1+\gamma}\frac{\kappa}{1+\kappa^2}\left(x_i + \kappa x_j\right). \tag{20}$$

According to (17), (18), (19) and (20), we can find that the performance of primary and ambient components extraction only rely on PPF and PPR.

4 Experiments and Result

Experiments using synthesized mixed signals were carried out to evaluate the proposed approach. A speech signal was selected as primary component, which is amplitude panned to the adjacent channel with a panning factor 4, 2, 1, whereas a recorded noise was chosen as ambient component, which is decorrelated using all-pass filters with random phase [15]. The input signal is obtained by mixing the primary and ambient components using different values of primary power ratio γ ranging from 0 to 1 with an interval 0.1.

In the existing literatures [5, 16], there are two groups of measures to objectively measure the performance of the extraction approaches, which is commonly used in the researches. The first one considers the accuracy of extracted components, whereas the other one takes the spatial accuracy into count.

Firstly, the extraction performance is quantified by the error-to-signal (ESR, in dB) of extracted component, where the lower ESR indicates a better extraction. The ESR for the primary and ambient component can be computed as [10]:

$$ESR_{y_c} = 10 * \log10\left\{\sum_{c=0}^{4}\frac{\|\hat{y}_c - y_c\|^2}{2\|y_c\|^2}\right\}. \tag{21}$$

Where the y_c is the true component, $\hat{y}_c$ is the extracted component, c is the channel index. The ESR of these approaches with respect to values of γ and κ is illustrated in Fig. 2. Our observations of the ESR performance are as follow:

The ESR of two approaches varies with the value of γ and κ. As the γ increases, the ESR for the primary component of the two methods is decreasing. From the Fig. 2(a)–(c), we can easily find that the extraction performance is better when the lower value of κ is chosen, and the extraction performance of the novel method is more excellent than the PCA, the ESR deduction between the two approaches is up to 15 dB when $\kappa = 2$. Then, from the Fig. 2(d)–(f), it can be found that the ambient extraction of the proposed approach also outperforms PCA, and the lowest ESR can be obtained when $\kappa = 1$.

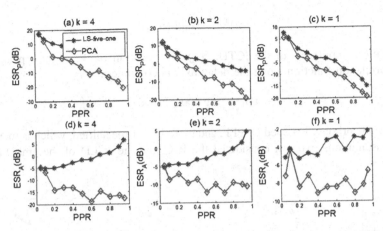

Fig. 2. The ESR of the primary component for the approach we proposed and the existing approach PCA; (d)–(f): the ESR of the ambient component for the approach we proposed and the existing approach PCA. The blue curve represents the ESR of the novel method, the red curve represents the ESR of PCA. (Color figure online)

The second measure is the spatial accuracy of the extracted primary and ambient component. Based on the Jeffress model [17], the inter-channel coherence (ICC) at different lags is computed and the lag number corresponds to the maximum ICC is the estimated inter-channel time difference (ICTD). And the inter-channel level difference (ICLD) can be obtained by taking the ratio of the power between the signals of the channel pair. A better extraction of ambient components is obtained when the ICC and ICLD of the extracted ambient component are closer to one and zero respectively.

The formulations are shown as follow. The ICLD, $\Delta L(n)$, between two signals $x_i(n)$, $x_j(n)$ is given by [12]:

$$\Delta L(n) = 10\lg \frac{E\{x_i^2(n)\}}{E\{x_j^2(n)\}}, (i,j) \in \{(1,2),(2,3),(3,4),(4,5),(5,1)\}. \quad (22)$$

For estimating ICTD and ICC the normalized cross-correlation function is computed.

$$\Phi(n,d) = \frac{E\{x_i(n)x_j(n+d)\}}{\sqrt{E\{x_i^2(n)\}E\{x_j^2(n+d)\}}}. \quad (23)$$

where the n is the frequency index, d is time delay.

The ICC, c(n), is obtained

$$c(n) = \max_d |\Phi(n, d)|. \tag{24}$$

For the computation of the ICTD, $\tau(n)$, the location of the highest peak of the cross-correlation function along the delay axis is computed,

$$\tau(n) = \arg\max_d \Phi(n, d). \tag{25}$$

Since the primary is scaled by PPF, and there is no time shifted, which is mentioned in the assumptions, we just considered the ICC and the ICLD of the ambient com-

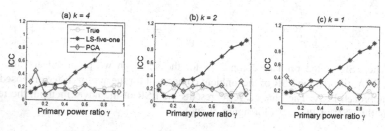

Fig. 3. The ICC of the ambient of the two methods

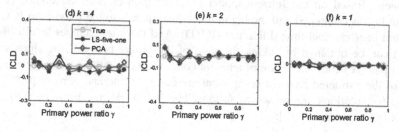

Fig. 4. The ICLD of the ambient of the two methods

ponent of two approaches. Shown as Fig. 3, the ICC of two approaches both increases with the increase of the value of γ, and the ICC of the proposed approach is higher than PCA, which means it can obtain better extracted ambient component by using the proposed approach. However, from the results of ICLD of the ambient shown in Fig. 4, it indicates that the two approaches have similar performance in ICLD.

Finally, we compared the extraction performance as well as the computation time among the two PAE approaches. The simulation was carried out on a PC with Inter

Table 1. The average ESR, ICC, and computation time of PAE approaches

Method	Proposed method	PCA
ESR_P(dB)	−0.5968	−5.8099
ESR_a(dB)	−2.0682	−6.9659
ICC of ambient	0.9480	0.2291
Computation time (ms)	1.6	204.8

(R) Core (TM) i3-2310 M CPU @2.10 GHz, 4 GB RAM, 64-bit windows 10 operating system and 64-bit MATLAB R2014a. The results of computation time averaged across all the γ and κ values are summarized in Table 1. It is obvious that the approach we introduced performs better than PCA on the average, and the novel method is $125\times$ faster than PCA.

5 Conclusion

In this letter, we proposed a novel approach of primary-ambient extraction based on channel pair for 5.1 channel audio, which considers the five channels in 5.1 systems as a set of channel pairs, and the process of PAE is applied at any one time to only one pair. The novel method uses the linear estimation framework to 5.1 channels audio PAE, and converts the PAE to a problem of weighted matrix estimation; then the weight of the primary and ambient component of each channel could be computed by minimizing the MSE using the Least Square. The results of the experiments demonstrate that the proposed approach outperforms PCA: the ESR average deduction of the novel approach is 5 dB and 4.9 dB than PCA for the primary and ambient component respectively. And the diffuse ambient can be obtained by using the novel method. Moreover, its computation time is less than PCA obviously. In the future, we expect that the further study on multichannel PAE, and more approaches for non-ideal case are proposed.

References

1. Lee, K., Son, C., Kim, D.: Immersive virtual sound for beyond 5.1 channel audio. In: Audio Engineering Society Convention 128. Audio Engineering Society (2010)
2. Stefanakis, N., Mouchtaris, A.: Foreground suppression for capturing and reproduction of crowded acoustic environments. In: IEEE International Conference on Acoustics, Speech and Signal Processing (ICASSP). IEEE, pp. 51–55 (2015)
3. Kowalczyk, K., Thiergart, O., Taseska, M., et al.: Parametric spatial sound processing: a flexible and efficient solution to sound scene acquisition, modification, and reproduction. IEEE Signal Process. Mag. 32(2), 31–42 (2015)
4. Menzer, F., Faller, C.: Stereo-to-binaural conversion using interaural coherence matching. In: Audio Engineering Society Convention 128. Audio Engineering Society (2010)
5. He, J.J.: Spatial audio reproduction with primary ambient extraction. Springer, Singapore (2016)
6. Goodwin, M.M., Jot, J.M.: Primary-ambient signal decomposition and vector-based localization for spatial audio coding and enhancement. In: IEEE International Conference on Acoustics, Speech and Signal Processing, ICASSP 2007. IEEE, pp. 1: I-9-I-12 (2007)
7. Ibrahim, K.M., Allam, M.: Primary-Ambient Extraction in Audio Signals Using Adaptive Weighting and Principal Component Analysis (2016)
8. Pulkki, V.: Virtual sound source positioning using vector base amplitude panning. J. Audio Eng. Soc. 45(6), 456–466 (1997)
9. He, J., Tan, E.L., Gan, W.S.: Linear estimation based primary-ambient extraction for stereo audio signals. IEEE/ACM Trans. Audio Speech Lang. Process. 22(2), 505–517 (2014)

10. Recommendation I.: Multichannel stereophonic sound system with and without accompanying picture. International Telecommunication Union, 775–1 (1992)
11. Breebaart, J., Faller, C.: Spatial Audio Processing: MPEG Surround and Other Applications. Wiley, Chicago (2008)
12. Goodwin, M.M.: Geometric signal decompositions for spatial audio enhancement. In: IEEE International Conference on Acoustics, Speech and Signal Processing, ICASSP 2008. IEEE, pp. 409–412 (2008)
13. Faller, C.: Multiple-loudspeaker playback of stereo signals. J. Audio Eng. Soc. **54**(11), 1051–1064 (2006)
14. Browning, T.R.: Applying the design structure matrix to system decomposition and integration problems: a review and new directions[J]. IEEE Trans. Eng. Manage. **48**(3), 292–306 (2001)
15. Kendall, G.S.: The decorrelation of audio signals and its impact on spatial imagery[J]. Comput. Music J. **19**(4), 71–87 (1995)
16. He, J., Gan, W.S., Tan, E.L.: Primary-ambient extraction using ambient spectrum estimation for immersive spatial audio reproduction[J]. IEEE/ACM Trans. Audio Speech Lang. Process. **23**(9), 1431–1444 (2015)
17. Jeffress, L.A.: A place theory of sound localization. Journal of comparative and physiological psychology **41**(1), 35–39 (1948)

Multi-scale Similarity Enhanced Guided Normal Filtering

Wenbo Zhao[1(✉)], Xianming Liu[1], Shiqi Wang[2], and Debin Zhao[1]

[1] School of Computer Science and Technology, Harbin Institute of Technology,
Harbin, China
{wbzhao,dbzhao}@hit.edu.cn, xmliu.hit@gmail.com
[2] Department of Computer Science, University of Hong Kong, Kowloon, Hong Kong
shiqwang@cityu.edu.hk

Abstract. In this paper, we propose a novel mesh denoising scheme in which multi-scale similarity is exploited to improve the performance of non-local normal filtering for feature-preserved mesh restoration. In our scheme, K-ring patches are used to identify multi-scale local structures around faces, and we compare the similarity between patches on multiple levels. The multi-scale similarities are subsequently computed by weighted similarity of patches. Finally, the center faces of similar patches are weighted by similarities in face normal filtering. Experimental results on different models indicate that the proposed method outperforms other local and non-scale-aware similarity based schemes in terms of both objective and subjective evaluations.

Keywords: Mesh denoising · Feature-preserved
Multi-scale similarity · Face normal filtering · K-ring patch

1 Introduction

With the development of computer graphics, the demand of 3D surface mesh models has been increased in many domains, such as CAD, geological model and computer games. However, raw mesh data would be inevitably contaminated by noise due to the limitations of the accuracy of scanning devices and digitization processes. As such, the features in mesh such as sharp edge will be corrupted by noises, which heavily affect the quality of mesh. Hence, mesh denoising has become an important topic in the area of geometry processing.

The main goals of mesh denoising are preserving sharp mesh features and recovering smooth surface from noises simultaneously. To achieve this, some schemes borrowed the idea from the filtering schemes in image denoising. In [3,5], the positions of vertices were directly filtered. Later, the two-step schemes were proposed, in which the face normals are filtered firstly and then the positions of vertices are updated. Zheng et al. [13] adopted the bilateral filter on faces normals, and Zhang et al. [11] exploited the guidance normals in weighting instead of the original normals, which effectively improved the robustness of bilateral filter.

B. Zeng et al. (Eds.): PCM 2017, LNCS 10736, pp. 645–653, 2018.
https://doi.org/10.1007/978-3-319-77383-4_63

These schemes can provide moderate results with low computational resources. However, without the usage of non-local information, unsatisfactory results are still observed in recovering regular features.

To take advantage of non-local information, similarity-based schemes have been proposed for mesh denoising. Digne et al. [2] proposed a point-based scheme, in which a local coordinate system is built for each point. Rosman et al. [6] proposed a patch-based self-similarity point cloud denoising scheme, which extended the well-known BM3D [1] algorithm in 2D image denoising to mesh denoising. In [12], patch is introduced to represent structure around faces, then the normals of faces that in non-local similar structures were used in filtering. However, these schemes may not find similar structures accurately, or make effective use of similarity.

Another focus of research in denoising is the optimization-based scheme. Due to the sparse property of sharp features, He et al. [4] presented a scheme where the L0 minimization is applied on mesh. Similar idea was also applied in [8]. Wang et al. [10] applied L1-analysis compressed sensing optimization to decompose noises and features. However, these schemes are based on the assumption that the noises are independent and identically distributed. When this assumption is not satisfied, the performance of these schemes drops significantly.

The success of non-local normal in filtering [12] provides the effectiveness of combining local and non-local schemes and using similar structures in face normal filtering. However, due to the fact that a fixed small scale patch is sensitive to noise, the method of finding similar structures may not be robust in some situations. On the other hand, increasing large scale patches cannot solve the problem because it may ignore features. To address this problem, we propose a novel mesh denoising scheme with multi-scale similarity. Specifically, the framework of our scheme follows the one in [12]. Patches with different sizes are built for representing multi-scale structure around faces. The similarities of different scales are computed, and the weighted sum of the similarities is used as multi-scale similarity in finding similar patches. Then, both of local and non-local face normals are used in filtering. Local normals will be weighted by both distances and guided normals, while non-local normals will be weighted by the similarity. Finally, the positions of vertexes are updated.

The rest of this paper is organized as follows. In Sect. 2, the proposed method of finding similar patches is described. Section 3 describes the complete process of the proposed scheme. In Sect. 4, we present the objective and subjective experimental results, and Sect. 5 concludes the paper.

2   Multi-scale Similarity

2.1   K-ring Patch

Suppose f_i is a face in a mesh. If f_i and f_j share at least one vertex, f_j and f_i are treated to be adjacent. The generation of a k-ring patch whose center is f_i is achieved by repeatedly adding all the adjacent faces into the patch k times. Since multi-scale similarity needs different sizes of patch, a larger k value is necessary.

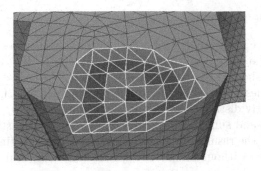

Fig. 1. Illustration of a 3-ring patch. (Color figure online)

In Fig. 1, a 3-ring patch is shown, where the central face is colored with purple, and the 1-ring , 2-ring and 3-ring faces are colored with green, blue and brown, respectively.

2.2 Similarity Between Two Patches

In general, a small scale patch is enough to describe the feature, but it is heavily effected by noise. When the size of patch increases, the robustness to noise gets enhanced. However, feature may also be filtered out in this process. This implies that a fixed scale cannot be adaptive to all cases, and when the scale is not properly chosen, noise and feature cannot be distinguished effectively. Thus, the multi-scale patch representation is utilized to achieve a good trade-off between distinguishing feature and suppressing the noise. To this end, a metric is defined to calculate the similarities between two patches with same number of rings.

Supposing there are two k-ring patches p_1 and p_2, a straightforward idea is that for each face f_i in p_1, we can find a corresponding face f_j in p_2 and calculate the difference between them. The similarity is defined as summing up all the difference, which is calculated with the following procedures.

(1) Moving the centroid of the central face of p_1 coinciding with the centroid of the central face of p_2.
(2) For f_i, finding a face f_j that minimizes:

$$d\left(f_i, f_j\right) = \|c_i, c_j\| \left(1 + \|n_i, n_j\|\right) a_i, \tag{1}$$

where c_i, c_j and n_i, n_j are the centers and normals of f_i and f_j, and a_i is the area of f_i.
(3) The similarity between two patches is calculated by:

$$S\left(p_1, p_2\right) = \frac{\sum\limits_{f_i \in p_1} \min\limits_{f_j \in p_2} d\left(f_i, f_j\right)}{\sum\limits_{f_i \in p_1} a_i \left|p_i\right|}. \tag{2}$$

2.3   Multi-scale Similarity

Assuming there are three faces: f_1, f_2, f_3, where the structures around f_1 and f_2 are similar, and the one around f_3 is not as similar as f_2. If f_2 and f_3 can be distinguished, there should exist some scales in which $S(p_1, p_2) \ll S(p_1, p_3)$. Moreover, in other scales we can have $S(p_1, p_2) \approx S(p_1, p_3)$, which means that they cannot be efficiently distinguished. Thus, if we compute $S(p_1, p_2)$ and $S(p_1, p_3)$ in different scales and sum them up, the scales which can distinguish f_2 and f_3 will heavily affect the results. This indicates that we can distinguish by the sum of similarities, even without the knowledge of the specific scales that lead to the difference.

Let p_{1n} and p_{2n} denote the n-ring patches around f_1 and f_2, respectively, and the multi-scale similarity between the local structure around f_1 and f_2 is formulated as:

$$MS(p_1, p_2) = \sum_{n=2}^{N} W_n S(p_{1n}, p_{2n}), \qquad (3)$$

where N is the max number of ring and W_n is the weighting parameter of different scales.

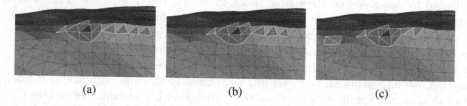

Fig. 2. Illustration of the searching results of the similar structure around an edge. (a) Our method; (b) Only 4-ring patch; (c) Method in [12]. (Color figure online)

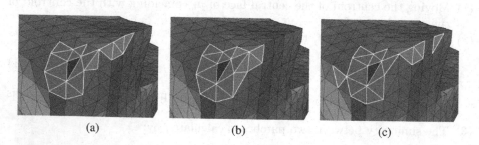

Fig. 3. Illustration of the searching results of the similar structure around a corner. (a) Our method; (b) Only 4-ring patch; (c) Method in [12]. (Color figure online)

As such, the similar structures can be accurately selected. To show the effectiveness of our method, Figs. 2 and 3 show two cases of searching similar structures. Since the local neighbour will be used in filtering directly, similar structures of these faces are not required to be searched. The target face is colored with purple, the geometrical neighbours are green and the center faces of similar structure are blue. The results illustrate that our method outperforms the method in [12] in terms of accuracy. On another hand, large patch may ignore features and then the structures on another side of features are erroneously found.

3   Mesh Denoising

We follow the framework of the scheme in [12] for noise denoising. First we build $2 \sim N$ ring patches for each face, and then find M corresponding similar structures. Subsequently, the guidance normals are computed, and the face normals are filtered as follows,

$$n_i' = e_i \left(\sum_{f_j \in N_i} a_j W_s\left(c_i, c_j\right) W_r\left(g_i, g_j\right) n_j + \sum_{f_k \in G_i} a_k W_m\left(MS\left(p_i, p_k\right)\right) s_p n_k \right), (4)$$

where N_i is the set of geometrical neighbours, S_i is the set of central faces of M similar structures of f_i, and e_i is a normalized factor to ensure n_i' to be a unit vector. s_p is a factor to control the weight of non-locals face normals. W_s, W_r, W_m are the Gaussian kernels [9]:

$$W_s\left(c_i, c_j\right) = \exp\left(-\frac{\|c_i, c_j\|^2}{2\sigma_s^2}\right), \tag{5}$$

$$W_r\left(g_i, g_j\right) = \exp\left(-\frac{\|g_i, g_j\|^2}{2\sigma_r^2}\right), \tag{6}$$

$$W_m\left(MS\left(p_i, p_k\right)\right) = \exp\left(-\frac{MS(p_i, p_k)^2}{2\sigma_m^2}\right), \tag{7}$$

where σ_s, σ_r and σ_m are the weight parameters.

After filtering face normals, the position of vertexes will be updated. An iterative scheme in [7] is employed here. For a vertex v_i whose position is pv_i, its new position is computed by:

$$pv_i' = pv_i + \frac{1}{|fv_i|} \sum_{j \in fv_i} n_j'\left(n_j' \cdot \left(c_j - pv_i\right)\right) \tag{8}$$

where fv_i is a set of faces that one of the vertexes is v_i. The vertex positions updating process will be executed iteratively for N_P times, and the whole process are executed for N_T times.

4   Experimental Results

4.1   Parameter Settings

In this section we provide the settings of the parameters used in this work. In particular, the choices of the parameters N_P and σ_s follow the work in [11]. In all experiments building 2–4-ring patches are enough for finding similar structures. This implies that we can set $N = 4$. As observed in the experiments, $3 \leqslant M \leqslant 5$, $0.2 \leqslant s_p \leqslant 0.5$ can avoid over-smoothing. The parameters σ_m and W_n are decisive factors for similarity, σ_m depends on the size of input mesh, and we choose $W_2 = 1, W_3 = 0.2, W_4 = 0.05$ in all cases. Incorporating similarity in filtering can decrease iteration times, such that N_T is usually smaller than in [11]. The values of parameters mentioned above are shown in Table 1. The parameters used by other schemes can be found in the the supplementary materials in [11,12].

Table 1. Settings of the parameters used in the experiment.

Parameter	Fandisk	Twelve	Shpere	Block	Bunny	Julius
M	5	5	5	5	5	3
N_T	15	60	5	20	4	3
N_P	20	20	20	30	4	4
σ_r	0.25	0.2	0.45	0.3	0.35	0.45
σ_m	0.7	0.6	6	8	0.06	0.06
s_p	0.2	0.2	0.3	0.2	0.2	0.5

4.2   Objective and Subjective Comparisons

We compare our scheme with the state-of-the-art denoising schemes, including the bilateral normal filtering (BNF) [13], the guided normal filtering (GNF) [11], the similarity enhanced normal filtering (SE) [12], and the L0 minimization optimization (L0M) [4]. The following error metrics from [7] which represent the accuracy of face normal and positions of vertices are used to evaluate the performance of denoising:

E_a: The mean angle square error of face normals between the faces in denoised mesh and ground truth.

E_v: L2 vertex-based mesh-to-mesh error, which is calculated by:

$$E_v = \sqrt{\frac{1}{3 \sum_j a_j} \sum_{j \in fv_i} a_j \sum_i dist\left(pv'_i, T\right)^2} \tag{9}$$

where T is the nearest face in the ground truth mesh to the new vertex v'_i, and $dist\left(pv'_i, T\right)$ is the L2 distance between the v'_i and T.

Table 2. Performance comparisons with the state-of-the-art methods.

Model	Noise lv	Metrics	BNF [13]	L0M [4]	GNF [11]	SE [12]	Proposed
Fandisk	0.3	$E_v\,(\times 10^{-3})$	1.504	1.850	1.458	**1.395**	1.442
		E_a	8.094	10.141	7.615	7.439	**6.464**
Block	0.4	$E_v\,(\times 10^{-3})$	5.15	9.273	5.417	5.407	**4.776**
		E_a	11.813	10.722	10.438	11.751	**9.848**
Twelve	0.5	$E_v\,(\times 10^{-3})$	12.41	20.00	5.955	4.852	**4.081**
		E_a	13.465	12.147	11.099	6.304	**6.102**
Shpere	0.3	$E_v\,(\times 10^{-4})$	6.747	7.593	6.742	6.475	**6.376**
		E_a	**14.144**	20.868	20.842	16.280	16.215
Bunny	0.2	$E_v\,(\times 10^{-6})$	7.799	7.897	7.756	7.764	**7.630**
		E_a	7.808	9.359	7.379	7.203	**7.069**
Julius	0.2	$E_v\,(\times 10^{-5})$	**1.571**	1.636	1.589	1.586	1.579
		E_a	9.167	10.664	8.203	**8.012**	8.148

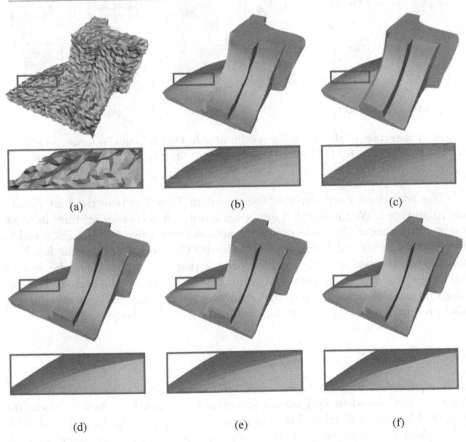

(a)   (b)   (c)

(d)   (e)   (f)

Fig. 4. Illustration of the denoising results of *Fandisk* with Gaussian noise. (a) Noisy mesh; (b) BNF [13]; (c) L0M [4]; (d) GNF [11]; (e) SE [12]; (f) Proposed scheme.

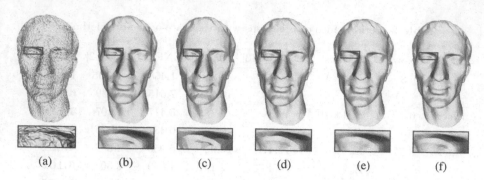

Fig. 5. Illustration of the denoising results of *Julius* with Gaussian noise. (a) Noisy mesh; (b) BNF [13]; (c) L0M [4]; (d) GNF [11]; (e) SE [12]; (f) Proposed scheme.

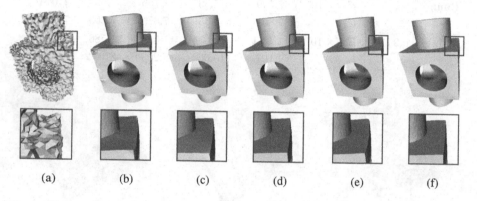

Fig. 6. Illustration of the denoising results of *Block* with Gaussian noise. (a) Noisy mesh; (b) BNF [13]; (c) L0M [4]; (d) GNF [11]; (e) SE [12]; (f) Proposed scheme.

The performance comparisons are shown in Table 2, where the best results are highlighted. We can see that our scheme outperforms other schemes in most cases. Furthermore, the visual quality comparisons are provided. In Figs. 4 and 5, the features in the red boxes are insignificant. We can see our scheme has better feature recovering results, which proves that our multi-scale scheme can effectively improve the accuracy of similarity and improve the performance on insignificant features. In Fig. 6, the feature is a long edge, and our scheme can also produce satisfactory results when dealing with such large-scale features.

5   Conclusion

In this paper, we propose a novel mesh denoising scheme that multi-scale similarity is introduced to find similar structures and non-local face normals are weighted in normal filtering. The multi-scale patches are built around faces, and the similarity between two structures are computed on multiple scales. Finally, the multi-scale similarity is computed by summing up similarities with different weighting factors. The experimental results show that multi-scale similarity can significantly improve the accuracy of similarity, which leads to both visually and numerically better denoising results.

Acknowledgment. This work was supported in part by the National Science Foundation of China (NSFC) under grants 61472101 and 61631017, the National High Technology Research and Development Program of China (863 Program 2015AA015903), and the Major State Basic Research Development Program of China (973 Program 2015CB351804).

References

1. Dabov, K., Foi, A., Katkovnik, V., Egiazarian, K.: Image denoising by sparse 3-D transform-domain collaborative filtering. IEEE Trans. Image Process. **16**(8), 2080–2095 (2007)
2. Digne, J.: Similarity based filtering of point clouds. In: 2012 IEEE Computer Society Conference on Computer Vision and Pattern Recognition Workshops (CVPRW), pp. 73–79. IEEE (2012)
3. Fleishman, S., Drori, I., Cohen-Or, D.: Bilateral mesh denoising. ACM Trans. Graph. **22**, 950–953 (2003)
4. He, L., Schaefer, S.: Mesh denoising via L0 minimization. ACM Trans. Graph. **32**(4), 64 (2013)
5. Jones, T.R., Durand, F., Desbrun, M.: Non-iterative, feature-preserving mesh smoothing. ACM Trans. Graph. **22**, 943–949 (2003)
6. Rosman, G., Dubrovina, A., Kimmel, R.: Patch-collaborative spectral point-cloud denoising. Comput. Graph. Forum **32**, 1–12 (2013)
7. Sun, X., Rosin, P., Martin, R., Langbein, F.: Fast and effective feature-preserving mesh denoising. IEEE Trans. Vis. Comput. Graph. **13**(5), 925–938 (2007)
8. Sun, Y., Schaefer, S., Wang, W.: Denoising point sets via L0 minimization. Comput. Aided Geom. Des. **35**, 2–15 (2015)
9. Tomasi, C., Manduchi, R.: Bilateral filtering for gray and color images. In: 1998 Sixth International Conference on Computer Vision, pp. 839–846. IEEE (1998)
10. Wang, R., Yang, Z., Liu, L., Deng, J., Chen, F.: Decoupling noise and features via weighted L1-analysis compressed sensing. ACM Trans. Graph. **33**(2), 18 (2014)
11. Zhang, W., Deng, B., Zhang, J., Bouaziz, S., Liu, L.: Guided mesh normal filtering. Comput. Graph. Forum. **34**, 23–34 (2015)
12. Zhao, W., Liu, X., Zhou, J., Zhao, D., Gao, W.: Mesh denoising with local guided normal filtering and non-local similarity. In: Yang, X., Zhai, G. (eds.) IFTC 2016. CCIS, vol. 685, pp. 176–184. Springer, Singapore (2017). https://doi.org/10.1007/978-981-10-4211-9_18
13. Zheng, Y., Fu, H., Au, O.K.C., Tai, C.L.: Bilateral normal filtering for mesh denoising. IEEE Trans. Vis. Comput. Graph. **17**(10), 1521–1530 (2011)

Deep Residual Convolution Neural Network for Single-Image Robust Crowd Counting

Mingjie Lu and Bo Yan[⊠]

Shanghai Key Laboratory of Intelligent Information Processing,
School of Computer Science, Fudan University, Shanghai, China
{lumj15,byan}@fudan.edu.cn

Abstract. Crowd counting is still a very challenging task in crowded scenes. The Convolutional Neural Network (CNN) architectures which estimate the density map directly from the input image put up a good performance. While the existing methods mostly use the multi-scale models to widen their networks, we have proposed a very deep network to address the mask. We use the residual block to avoid that too deep network can not converge. Afterwards, we take extensive experiments in three diversity datasets which demonstrate that our method outperforms other state-of-the-art methods. The excellent performance allows our model to be applied not only in counting crowd accurately but also in estimating pedestrian distribution.

Keywords: Residual network · Crowd counting

1 Introduction

With the development of urbanization, more and more people are pouring into the big cities, and the urban roads are becoming more and more crowded. Even large-scale assembly will lead to serious stampede. For the purpose of crowd control and public security, it becomes more and more important to estimate the crowd in the image or video accurately.

The crowd counting method can be roughly summarized into three:

- Detection-based framework: This idea is much natural, with which a detector scans the picture or video and then get the total number of pedestrians. However, this method is mainly applied to the sparse scene. When in the crowded place the performance will be degraded greatly due to the occlusion.
- Regression-based framework: In the process of dealing with crowded scene, the detector is unreliable. The regression based method is a better solution to this problem. Firstly, it extracts various features from a whole image or video frame, such as area of crowd mask, edge count, and texture features

This work was supported by NSFC (Grant No.: 61370158; 61522202).

[1]. Then a regression function is used to map the feature and estimate the number by using a machine learning method.

- CNN framework: This method is similar to regression-based framework. The advantage of CNNs is that they do not have to manually extract features. Lempitsky *et al.* [11] proposed a method using density maps to count cells and pedestrians. The Convolutional Neural Network (CNN) framework can easily convert a image to crowd density map and gain the number by integrating it.

The idea of multi-scale is used commonly in [5,6] to widen network structure. Experiments show that the widened network can indeed improve representation ability because of increasing of parameters. But in theory, deeper network can get a better performance than a wider one. Meanwhile, too deep network will lead to the gradient vanishing, so we use the residual network to avoid this problem. Our approach outperforms the state-of-the-art methods on the ShanghaiTech, UCF_CC_50 and UCSD dataset.

2   Related Work

Chan *et al.* make a series of work [1–4] for crowd counting. [1] utilizes hand-extracted low-level 29-dimensional features to regression the count of crowds. Following work [2] makes some improvements by proposing a new model based on a Bayesian treatment of Poisson Regression instead of Gaussian Process Regression. [3,4] propose a integer programming method for estimating the instantaneous count of pedestrians crossing a line in a video sequence.

Yang *et al.* [13] use the flow velocity field to extract features and use a quadratic regression to get the number of pedestrians cross a line. Wang *et al.* [14] build a spatio-temporal group context model to count people in a group by using the relationships between groups. Idrees *et al.* [8] employ a global consistency constraint of multiple sources information by using Markov Random Field to get the count. Li *et al.* [15] propose a method to people counting based on head-shoulder detection using Faster R-CNN and correlation tracking.

In 2010, Lempitsky *et al.* [11] proposed a method using density maps to count cells and pedestrians. It is very easy and effective to generate the density map for CNN. So the subsequent works of crowd counting via CNN are almost always based on the density map. For example, Zhang *et al.* [9] propose a CNN network framework which has two outputs of crowd count and density map, and train a network using the whole training set firstly. When test images are given, they choose the similar training images to fine-tune the network for various scenes. Zhang *et al.* [6] propose a multi-scale CNN to handle multi-scale crowds by using difference size of convolutional kernels.

3   Our Proposed Method

3.1   Density Map

The method proposed by Lempitsky [11] generates a density map of the crowd and then obtains the count by integration which has more advantages of directly estimating head count. Following Zhang *et al.* [6], we also adopt geometry-adaptive kernels to generate density map. We use the formula below to convert a image to crowd density map:

$$D(x) = \sum_{i=1}^{M} \delta(x - x_i) * G_{\sigma_i}, \; with \; \sigma_i = \beta \bar{d}_i \tag{1}$$

which x_i is the location of a head pixel, $\delta(x - x_i)$ is a delta function, and G_{σ_i} is the adaptive Gaussian kernel. For the ith person, the integration of G_{σ_i} equals 1, so that the integration of $D(x)$ equals the actual person count in the image. The average distance $\bar{d}_i = \frac{1}{m} \sum_{j=1}^{m} d_j^i$ means that the Gaussian kernel concerned about m-nearest neighbors head. In our experiment, $\beta = 0.3, m = 10$.

3.2   Network Architecture

The residual network [10] has achieved great success on ILSVRC, and makes it possible to build a much deeper network. In fact, deeper neural networks are more difficult to converge. Furthermore, deeper "plain" network has higher train error and test error when it is deep enough [10]. Residual network can solve the problems. Based on this idea, we used the residual network to complete the difficult challenge of mapping original image and the density map.

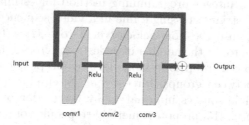

Fig. 1. Residual block

We define a resBlock (Residual Block) similar as [10] in Fig. 1, in which the sum layer sends the sum of two inputs to the next layer. And there are three convolution layers in a resBlock. In Fig. 2, a green block means a resBlock defined in Fig. 1. We use a full-convolution network structure that the input is a batch of original colorful images and the label is a batch of corresponding density maps. The sizes of filters in convolution layers are all $5 \times 5 \times 32 \times 32$ except that the first one is $7 \times 7 \times 3 \times 32$ because the channel of inputs is 3. We use two Max Pooling layers whose size is 2×2. Rectified linear unit (ReLU) is applied as the activation function after each convolution layer. In order to make the network converge better we use three batch normalization layers after the first three convolution layers, which are very effective proved by experiments.

We use filters whose sizes are 1×1 to map the features maps to the density map. In addition, we observe that 99.99% label pixels are in the range [0, 1],

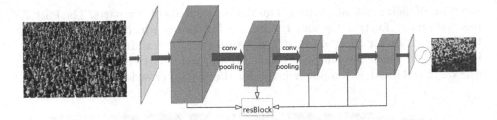

Fig. 2. Our deep residual network framework for crowd counting (Color figure online)

the rest are more than 1 because of the heavy overcrowd which are negligible. For the counting task, we constrain the output in the range of [0, 1] with a sigmoid function. Experiments prove that it is helpful for accelerating network convergence.

Finally, we adopt Mean squared error (MSE) as loss function which is the most commonly used to measure the distance of the output feature map and ground truth. The loss function is defined as follows:

$$L_{MSE} = \frac{1}{M} \sum_{x=1}^{M} (D_x - \hat{D}_x)^2 \qquad (2)$$

L_{MSE} is defined as the loss between predicted density map $\hat{D}_x$ and its corresponding ground truth D_x. Meanwhile, x is the pixels in a image and M is the number of pixels.

4   Experiments

4.1   Evaluation Metric

Following the existing work [6], we evaluate performance on testing set by using mean absolute error (MAE) and the mean squared error (MSE), which are defined as follows:

$$MAE = \frac{1}{N} \sum_{i=1}^{N} |z_i - \hat{z}_i|, \quad MSE = \sqrt{\frac{1}{N} \sum_{i=1}^{N} (z_i - \hat{z}_i)^2} \qquad (3)$$

where N is the number of images in test dataset, z_i and $\hat{z}_i$ are the ground truth and estimate number in the ith image. MAE and MSE indicate the accuracy and robustness of the estimations.

4.2   Shanghaitech Dataset

The Shanghaitech dataset is a challenging large-scale crowd counting dataset [6]. It contains 1198 annotated images which have a total of 330165 people with the locations of their heads annotated. This dataset consists of two parts. The Part_A has 300 images for training and 182 images for testing which are crawled from the Internet. As for the Part_B, it has 400 images for training and 316 images for testing in which the images are taken from the busy streets in Shanghai. In general, the dataset is complex enough for the task of crowd counting.

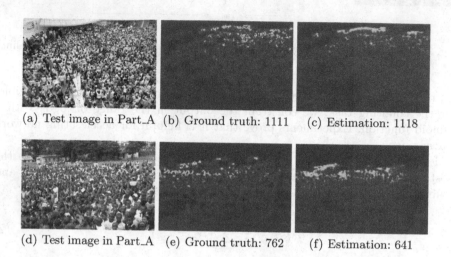

(a) Test image in Part_A   (b) Ground truth: 1111   (c) Estimation: 1118

(d) Test image in Part_A   (e) Ground truth: 762   (f) Estimation: 641

Fig. 3. The ground truth density map and estimated density map of test image in Part_A.

We augment the training set for CNN by cropping 256 × 256 patches with 50% overlap. And the labels are 64 × 64 which are 1/4 size of the input images because of two pooling layers. Finally we gain 6166 patches as training set. In our experiment, momentum is set as 0 and learning rate is 0.0001. Figure 3 shows examples of ground truth density maps and estimated density maps of images in Part_A. We also compare with other methods in Table 1. Our method achieves the best MAE and MSE with existing methods in both Part_A and Part_B.

Table 1. Comparing with other methods on Shanghaitech dataset.

Method	Part_A		Part_B	
	MAE	MSE	MAE	MSE
LBP+RR [6]	303.2	371.09	59.1	81.7
Zhang *et al.* [9]	181.8	277.7	32.0	49.8
MCNN-CCR [6]	245.0	336.1	70.9	95.9
MCNN [6]	110.2	173.2	26.4	41.3
Our method	**93.4**	**144.5**	**20.1**	**32.3**

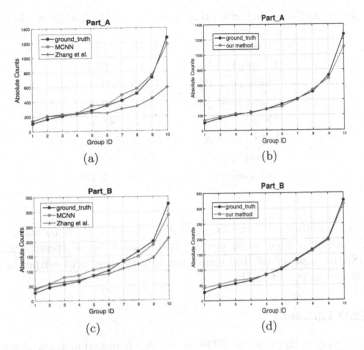

Fig. 4. Comparison with different methods on Shanghaitech testing set. Absolute count in the vertical axis is the average crowd number of images in each group. The left two figures (a) and (c) are gained from MCNN [6]. And the right two figures are our results and ground truth.

In Fig. 4, we compare our result with others in details. Following the setup with [6], we group the testing set of Part_A and Part_B into 10 groups by sorting the crowd count. For Part_A, each group contains 18 test images except the last group which contains 20 images. Similarly for Part_B, each group contains 31 testing images except the last group has 37 images. Since we do not have the specific result data from MCNN, we show the figures from [6] comparing with the generated figure from our result data. We can see our method is more accurate and robust in general obviously.

4.3   UCF_CC_50 Dataset

UCF_CC_50 dataset [8] is another challenge dataset builded by H. Idrees *et al.* The problem is that the dataset only contains 50 images. In addition, the person counts range between 94 and 4543 at an average of 1280 per image. Despite this, our model still has a outstanding performance. We also use 5-fold cross-validation to compare with other methods. And we adopt the same approach for data augmentation as in that in Shanghaitech dataset.

We compare our method with other existing methods in Table 2. We do not get the best result in MSE because the most crowded image which has 4543

Table 2. Comparing with other methods on UCF_CC_50 dataset.

Method	MAE	MSE
Lempitsky et al. [11]	493.4	**487.1**
Idrees et al. [8]	419.5	541.6
Zhang et al. [9]	467.0	498.5
MCNN [6]	377.6	509.1
CNN boosting [7]	364.4	–
CrowdNet [5]	452.5	–
Our method	**355.0**	532.1

persons is so different from others. And it is hard for CNN to learn a pattern without a similar training set in such a small dataset. So one testing image pulls up the MSE because of the big error, but our method still outperforms other methods in the metric of MAE.

4.4 UCSD Dataset

The UCSD dataset [1] contains 2000 frames with notation from a surveillance camera in a UCSD street. Each frame is a 238×158 gray image at 10 fps. The person counts of the frames various from 11 to 46 at an average of 25 which demonstrates the dataset is sparse relative to other two datasets.

Table 3. Comparing with other methods on UCSD dataset.

Method	MAE	MSE
Ridge regression [12]	2.25	7.82
Chan et al. [1]	2.24	7.97
Zhang et al. [9]	1.60	3.31
MCNN [6]	1.07	1.35
CNN boosting [7]	1.10	–
Our method	**1.05**	**1.32**

Unlike some methods in [6,9] that remove the background and only use ROI (region of interest) provided in the dataset as the inputs of the models, we do not use any prior knowledge and directly input the original images. Following the same setup of [6,9], we also set frames 601–1400 as the training set and the rest is regard as testing set. We augment the training set by flipping horizontal images and cropping 120×120 patches with overlap. Similarly, the labels are also flipped horizontal and cropped as 30×30 patches correspondingly. We gain 6400 patches for training finally and the batchsize is set as 32.

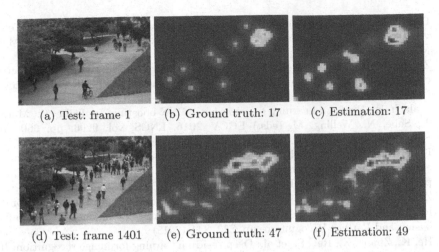

(a) Test: frame 1   (b) Ground truth: 17   (c) Estimation: 17

(d) Test: frame 1401   (e) Ground truth: 47   (f) Estimation: 49

Fig. 5. The ground truth density map and estimated density map of test image in ucsd dataset.

In the process of testing, we take the whole frame as input to pass through the network and get the estimated density map. Experiments prove that our network has the ability to distinguish between the background and the pedestrian as shown in Fig. 5. Table 3 illustrates that our method achieves the state-of-the-art performance in prediction accuracy. It demonstrates that our network structure is suitable for both extremely crowded and relatively sparse scene.

5   Conclusion

In this paper, we have proposed a very deep convolution network to solve the problem of crowd counting in a single image or video frame. Comparing with recent CNN methods, we deepen the network instead of widening it commonly. Our method outperforms the state-of-the-art crowd counting methods on the Frequently-used datasets for evaluation.

References

1. Chan, A.B., Liang, Z.S.J., Vasconcelos, N.: Privacy preserving crowd monitoring: counting people without people models or tracking. In: IEEE Conference on Computer Vision and Pattern Recognition, pp. 1–7 (2008)
2. Chan, A.B., Vasconcelos, N.: Counting people with low-level features and Bayesian regression. IEEE Trans. Image Process. **21**(4), 2160–2177 (2012)
3. Ma, Z., Chan, A.B.: Crossing the line: crowd counting by integer programming with local features. In: Proceedings of the IEEE Conference on Computer Vision and Pattern Recognition, pp. 2539–2546 (2013)
4. Ma, Z., Chan, A.B.: Counting people crossing a line using integer programming and local features. IEEE Trans. Circuits Syst. Video Technol. **26**(10), 1955–1969 (2016)

5. Boominathan, L., Kruthiventi, S.S.S., Venkatesh Babu, R.: Crowdnet: a deep convolutional network for dense crowd counting. In: Proceedings of the 2016 ACM on Multimedia Conference, pp. 640–644. ACM (2016)
6. Zhang, Y., Zhou, D., Chen, S., et al.: Single-image crowd counting via multicolumn convolutional neural network. In: Proceedings of the IEEE Conference on Computer Vision and Pattern Recognition, pp. 589–597 (2016)
7. Walach, E., Wolf, L.: Learning to count with CNN boosting. In: Leibe, B., Matas, J., Sebe, N., Welling, M. (eds.) ECCV 2016. LNCS, vol. 9906, pp. 660–676. Springer, Cham (2016). https://doi.org/10.1007/978-3-319-46475-6_41
8. Idrees, H., Saleemi, I., Seibert, C., Shah, M.: Multi-source multi-scale counting in extremely dense crowd images. In: Proceedings of the IEEE Conference on Computer Vision and Pattern Recognition, pp. 2547–2554 (2013)
9. Zhang, C., Li, H., Wang, X., et al.: Cross-scene crowd counting via deep convolutional neural networks. In: Proceedings of the IEEE Conference on Computer Vision and Pattern Recognition, pp. 833–841 (2015)
10. He, K., Zhang, X., Ren, S., et al.: Deep residual learning for image recognition. In: Proceedings of the IEEE Conference on Computer Vision and Pattern Recognition, pp. 770–778 (2016)
11. Lempitsky, V., Zisserman, A.: Learning to count objects in images. In: Advances in Neural Information Processing Systems, pp. 1324–1332 (2010)
12. Chen, K., Loy, C.C., Gong, S., et al.: Feature mining for localised crowd counting. BMVC 1(2), 3 (2012)
13. Cong, Y., Gong, H., Zhu, S.C., et al.: Flow mosaicking: real-time pedestrian counting without scene-specific learning. In: IEEE Conference on Computer Vision and Pattern Recognition, CVPR 2009, pp. 1093–1100. IEEE (2009)
14. Wang, J., Fu, W., Liu, J., et al.: Spatiotemporal group context for pedestrian counting. IEEE Trans. Circuits Syst. Video Technol. 24, 1620–1630 (2014)
15. Li, Z., Zhang, L., Fang, Y., et al.: Deep people counting with faster R-CNN and correlation tracking. In: Proceedings of the International Conference on Internet Multimedia Computing and Service, pp. 57–60. ACM (2016)

An Efficient Method Using the Parameterized HRTFs for 3D Audio Real-Time Rendering on Mobile Devices

Yucheng Song[1], Weiping Tu[1(✉)], Ruimin Hu[1], Xiaochen Wang[1], Wei Chen[1], and Cheng Yang[2]

[1] National Engineering Research Center for Multimedia Software, School of Computer Science, Wuhan University, Wuhan 430072, China
yuchengsong_youki@foxmail.com, {tuweiping,hrm}@whu.edu.cn, clowang@163.com, erhuchen@163.com
[2] School of Physics and Electronic Science, Guizhou Normal University, Guiyang 550001, China
yangcheng41506@126.com

Abstract. 3D audio real-time rendering is of great importance for virtual reality (VR) application, especially on mobile devices. However, the limited computational power makes it hard to implement fast generation of spatial sound using head-related transfer function (HRTF). To accelerate the procedure of head-related impulse response (HRIR) convolution, we propose an efficient rendering method using the parameterized HRTF. The HRIRs are preprocessed into the parameterized HRTFs with a delayed parameter, so as to realize the fast convolutions in 3D audio synthesis. We found our method could reduce the calculation time of 3D audio rendering significantly. The results were 0.9 times and 0.68 times on average the play duration of the MPEG standard sequences, with Qualcomm Snapdragon 821 and Samsung Exynos 7420. And the subjective test showed that the real-time rendered sounds had the similar audio quality and location perception to the 3D audio rendered with the raw HRIRs.

Keywords: Virtual reality · 3D audio · HRTF · Real-time Mobile device · FFT

1 Introduction

3D audio rendering technology has been widely using in movies, video games, simulation training and many other virtual reality (VR) applications. Real-time 3D audio rendering is necessary for interactive virtual scene. The head-related transfer function (HRTF) technology is considered as the most direct and effective way

Y. Song—This work is supported by National Nature Science Foundation of China (No. 61671335, 61662010), National High Technology Research and Development Program of China (863 Program) No. 2015AA016306.

© Springer International Publishing AG, part of Springer Nature 2018
B. Zeng et al. (Eds.): PCM 2017, LNCS 10736, pp. 663–673, 2018.
https://doi.org/10.1007/978-3-319-77383-4_65

for 3D sound with headphones [1], and rather suitable for mobile devices. However, the high computational complexity resulting from dual-ear convolutions of HRTF-based rendering technology obstructs its being applied on mobile devices.

Low order modeling of HRTFs [2,3] is an efficient way to reduce the computational cost of 3D audio rendering. But the appropriate orders of the models need to be determined by listening tests, which are difficult and time-consuming. Taegyu Lee and Hyun Oh Oh et al., proposed a scalable rendering algorithm by variable order filtering in frequency domain, etc. with binaural room impulse responses (BRIR) [4]. The scalability scheme can compromise between the audio quality and the computational complexity, thus adaptable to a wide range of devices with different computational powers. In other words, the improved efficiency of the method on the devices of poor computational power might be accompanied with the loss of overall audio quality. As area and volumetric sources (such as waterfalls and island) are common in game scenes, Carl Schissler and Aaron Nicholls et al. proposed an efficient HRTF-based approach by projecting the sources into the spherical harmonic (SH) basis [5]. The SH method was demonstrated to be two to three orders of magnitude faster than the general point sampling approach, for the reason that spatial audio of an area-volumetric source can be efficiently computed as a dot product of the SH coefficients of the projection area and the HRTF. However, the SH method is designed for the area and volumetric sources. For the frequent point audio sources, the general method using circular convolution with FFT remains the better solution.

In addition, to construct a Virtual Auditory Display (VAD) available on the poor computation power equipment, such as tablet or smart-phone, Iwaya Yukio and Otani Makoto et al. developed an auditory display system by remote rendering [6]. The remote rendering technology requires the support of network and cost of servers, which might bring extra expenses. Furthermore, Phyo Ko Ko and Kaushik Sunder proposed an Android framework implementation of 3D audio with range control [7]. From an overview of literatures above, how to increase the efficiency of 3D sound synthesis with HRTF still remains the key problem of 3D audio real-time rendering on mobile devices.

In this paper, we propose an efficient convolution method using the parameterized HRTFs, based on FFT. Head-related impulse responses (HRIR) from the database are preprocessed into the parameterized HRTFs with a delayed parameter beforehand. The spectrum of the windowed signal of the sound source is obtained using FFT. Then the frame spectrum is convolved separately with the dual-ear parameterized HRTFs by two operations. The first is dot product between the frame spectrum and the filtering spectrum, and the second is padding the product results with zeros according to the delayed parameter. The speed-up experiment on the Qualcomm Snapdragon 821 and Samsung Exynos 7420 demonstrated that our rendering method could reduce 3D sound synthesis time to 0.9 times and 0.68 times duration of the test sequences, achieving real-time rendering on mobile devices. Besides, the subjective experiment illustrated that the real-time rendered sounds had the similar audio quality and localization perception to the sounds rendered with the raw HRIRs.

2   3D Audio Rendering Using HRTF

When sound propagates from the source to the eardrum of the listener, it interacts with the listeners torso, shoulders, pinnae and head. The information of sound wave propagation can be encapsulated in spatial digital filters, namely, HRTFs [1]. For HRTF databases commonly accessed [8,9], data of filters is provided in the form of HRIR in the time domain, other than HRTF in the spectral domain. Therefore, the basic procedure of 3D audio rendering is the binaural convolutions between the mono signal and the dual-ear HRIRs. In order to make the synthesis practical for 3D audio application, generally, an overlap-add convolution technique based on FFT algorithm is used to accomplish the convolution procedure with intensive computation load [10–12]. And here are the basial steps of the general method of HRTF convolution using FFT:

1. Segmenting the original mono audio into appropriate frames with frame length M;
2. For the i-th audio frame $x_i[n]$, padding the frame $x_i[n]$ and the corresponding transfer function $h[n]$ (left or right HRIR) to the length of L with zeros;
3. Transforming the zero-padding $h[n]$ and $x_i[n]$ into the spectral domain using FFT, as the transfer function $H[k]$ and spectrum $X_i[k]$;
4. Calculating dot product between the $H[k]$ and $X_i[k]$ to obtain the result $Y_i[k]$;
5. Getting the convolution result $y_i[n]$ by inverse fast Fourier transform (IFFT).

To maximum the efficiency of FFT, the value of L is usually the integer power of 2 [11]. And according to the property of convolution, the frame size is set as

$$M = L + 1 - R, \tag{1}$$

where R refers to the length of HRIR.

The calculation time of one real multiplication and one real addition is marked as T_{MUL} and T_{ADD}, respectively. It could be inferred that a complex multiplication includes 4 real multiplications and 2 real additions, as $4T_{\mathrm{MUL}}+2T_{\mathrm{ADD}}$. For L-point FFT, there are $\log_2 L$ stages, one of which contains $L/2$ butterflies [11]. Each butterfly, the basic computational element of the FFT, requires one complex multiplication and two complex additions. Thus, the time consumption of L-point FFT can be computed as

$$T_{\mathrm{FFT}} = L \log_2 L \left(2T_{\mathrm{MUL}} + 3T_{\mathrm{ADD}} \right). \tag{2}$$

From the procedure of the convolution described above, it could also be derived that the time consumption of a single convolution with HRTF could be calculated as

$$T_{\mathrm{SC}} = (6L \log_2 L + 7L) \cdot T_{\mathrm{MUL}} + (9L \log_2 L + 2L) \cdot T_{\mathrm{ADD}}, \tag{3}$$

3 Efficient Convolution Method with the Parameterized HRTFs

3.1 Preprocessing HRIR into HRTF Using Zero Padding

In the general method, HRIR is always transformed into HRTF in the spectral domain during the rendering. Actually, the FFT transformation of filters can be made beforehand. To make use of FFT, the HRIR ought to be padded to the length of the integer power of 2 with zeros [11]. To sum up, in the preliminary works, the HRIRs could be transformed into HRTF, after zero padding with the length of FFT. During the convolution process, only the audio frame need to be transformed by FFT, consequently decreasing the time consumption.

It could be derived that the time consumption of preprocessing optimized spectral convolution could be calculated as

$$T_{\text{POSC}} = (4L \log_2 L + 7L) \cdot T_{\text{MUL}} + (6L \log_2 L + 2L) \cdot T_{\text{ADD}}, \tag{4}$$

For the monaural HRTF convolution with 8192-point FFT, the preprocessing optimized spectral convolution needs 483328 real multiplications, while the general method requires 696320 real multiplications. It could be seen that the number of real multiplications decrease 30.59%.

3.2 Binaural Convolutions Sharing the Frame Spectrum

It could be observed in general method that the convolutions of the left and right channels both include the process of transforming input audio frame $x_i[n]$ into its frequency domain expression, $X_i[n]$. Therefore, the frame spectrum $X_i[n]$ could be shared in the binaural convolutions, and only one FFT is needed. And the structure of binaural convolutions sharing the frame spectrum is illustrated in Fig. 1.

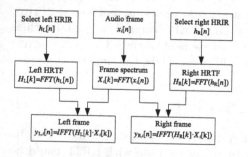
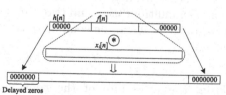

Fig. 1. The structure of binaural convolutions sharing the frame spectrum

Fig. 2. Delayed-zeros optimizing convolution using the delayed parameter D and the filtering section $f[n]$

As for general method, the synthesis of the left and right channel frames needs two convolutions, whose time consumption is

$$T_{\text{BSC}} = 2 \cdot T_{\text{SC}} = (12L \log_2 L + 14L) \cdot T_{\text{MUL}} + (18L \log_2 L + 4L) \cdot T_{\text{ADD}}, \quad (5)$$

If the frame spectrum is shared, the time consumption of binaural convolutions would be reduced to

$$T_{\text{BSS}} = T_{\text{BSC}} - T_{\text{FFT}} = (10L \log_2 L + 14L) \cdot T_{\text{MUL}} + (15L \log_2 L + 4L) \cdot T_{\text{ADD}}, \quad (6)$$

For the binaural convolutions using 8192-point FFT, the binaural convolutions sharing the frame spectrum demands 1179648 real multiplications, while the general method requires 1392640 real multiplications. So, there is 15.29% reduction in the number of real multiplications.

3.3 Delayed-Zeros Optimizing Convolution

From the knowledge of acoustics, it is known that there exists the propagation time before the arrival of the direct sound [4]. Hence, a parameterized HRIR, consisting of a parameter of time delay D and a filtering section $f[n]$, is proposed to model the empirical HRIR. The delayed parameter D records the time delay of the leading edge, or the first arrival of the direct sound. And $f[n]$ refers to the non-zero samples with higher value beyond the threshold in a HRIR.

In this work, the time delay D of a HRIR would be estimated using a relative threshold based on the spectral distortion (SD) estimation. The threshold-based method is regarded as a simple method for estimating the time delay [13]. The SD is a commonly used error criterion for comparing the modeled HRIR to the original empirical ones [14], and is defined as

$$SD^2 = \frac{1}{2\pi} \int_0^{2\pi} \left(20 \log_{10} |H(\omega)| - 20 \log_{10} \left| \hat{H}(\omega) \right| \right) d\omega. \quad (7)$$

where $H(\omega)$ and $\hat{H}(\omega)$ denote the original and reconstructed HRTF, respectively. In the method using a relative threshold, the time delay may vary from 0 to $R - E$ samples, where R refers to the length of HRIR and E denotes the fixed length of filtering section $f[n]$. For the modeled HRIR, the different SDs between the original HRTF, and the HRTFs reconstructed from the HRIRs parameterized with different time delays, would be calculated. The time delay that minimizes the SD would be chosen as the proper delayed parameter D.

As the delay parameter is obtained, the corresponding reconstructed HRIR could be represented as

$$\hat{h}[n] = \begin{cases} f[n-D] & D \leq n < D+E \\ 0 & \text{others} \end{cases}. \quad (8)$$

so, D indicates the number of the delayed zeros in the beginning of the HRIR data. On account of the properties of linear convolution, it could be derived that

$$\begin{cases} y'[n] = \sum_{m=0}^{+\infty} x_i[m] \cdot f[n-m] \\ y[n] = y'[n+D] \end{cases} . \tag{9}$$

To make the best of this in implementation, the delayed zeros could be added in front of the convolution result of $x_i[n]$ and $f[n]$, as illustrated in Fig. 2. While in general method, the frame length is relevant to the length of $h[n]$ (namely, R) as (1), for the convolution using FFT. As the filtering section $f[n]$ is always shorter than R, the frame length could be lengthened to

$$M = L + 1 - E, \tag{10}$$

It means $R - E$ samples more would be obtained in one convolution procedure, compared with the general method.

When R is 1024 [9] and E is set as 200, the delayed-zeros optimizing convolution would calculate 7993 samples in one convolution procedure using 8192-point FFT, while the general convolution method would get 7169 samples. It demonstrates there is 11.49% improvement on the efficiency of the HRIR convolution.

3.4 Complexity Analysis

Here the numbers of the real multiplications are analyzed. As for the implementation of HRTF rendering, windowing and overlap-add techniques are essential [10]. Here it is assumed that the Hanning window of the frame length is used, and the frame over-lapping is half of the window length. It is inferred that the time consumption of the general method would be

$$\begin{cases} M = L + 1 - R \\ L_{\mathrm{ov}} = \left\lfloor \dfrac{M}{2} \right\rfloor \\ L_{\mathrm{re}} = M - L_{\mathrm{ov}} \\ K = \left\lfloor \dfrac{N}{L_{\mathrm{re}}} \right\rfloor \\ T_{\mathrm{BSC}} = 2 \cdot T_{\mathrm{SC}} = (12L \log_2 L + 14L) \cdot T_{\mathrm{MUL}} + (18L \log_2 L + 4L) \cdot T_{\mathrm{ADD}} \\ T = K \cdot T_{\mathrm{BSC}} \end{cases} , \tag{11}$$

where L_{ov} refers to the length of frame overlapping, L_{re} refers the reserved length, K represents the number of frames, N denotes the samples number of the entire mono audio and $\lfloor \rfloor$ notes the round down operation. Accordingly, the time consumption of the proposed method could be computed as

$$\begin{cases} M = L + 1 - E \\ L_{ov} = \left\lfloor \dfrac{M}{2} \right\rfloor \\ L_{re} = M - L_{ov} \\ K = \left\lfloor \dfrac{N}{L_{re}} \right\rfloor \\ T_{FC} = T_{BSC} - 3T_{FFT} = (6L \log_2 L + 14L) \cdot T_{MUL} + (9L \log_2 L + 4L) \cdot T_{ADD} \\ T = K \cdot T_{FC} \end{cases}$$

$$(12)$$

For rendering an audio of 10 s, sampled at 48000 Hz ($N = 10 * 48000 = 480000$), with HRIR of 1024 samples, parameterized with E of 200 samples and 8192-point FFT, the general method requires 185221120 real multiplications, and the proposed method needs only 90439680 real multiplications, which indicates the proposed method could save 51.17% computations of real multiplications in the HRIR convolution procedure.

4   Evaluation

Two typical smart phones are used in the test, namely the Mi 5s Plus cellphone with Qualcomm Snapdragon 821 processor, the Samsung Galaxy Note 5 cellphone with Samsung Exynos 7420, with the detailed configuration is shown in Table 1. The HRIRs are from the PKU&IOA HRTF database [9], which are 1024 samples long. For the parameterized HRIR, filtering section length E is set as 200. And other processing details, including Hanning window, 8192-point FFT and 50% overlapping, are same as the description in Sect. 3.4. For the statistical significance, all the experiment results exhibited below have been averaged.

Table 1. Specs of the test mobile devices

Mobile device	Mi 5s Plus	Samsung Galaxy Note 5
Processor	Qualcomm Snapdragon 821	Samsung Exynos 7420
Number of cores	4*Qualcomm Kryo	4*Cortex A57 + 4*Cortex A53
Clock of processor	2.35 GHz	2.1 GHz (A57) & 1.5 GHz (A53)

Table 2. Results of binaural convolutions time (s) of MPEG audio sequences

Sequences	Duration(s)	Mi 5s Plus			Samsung Note 5		
		General	Proposed	Decrease	General	Proposed	Decrease
es01	10	17.35	8.47	51.18%	12.83	6.57	48.81%
es02	8	13.91	6.78	51.26%	10.34	5.19	49.81%
es03	7	12.16	6.07	50.08%	9.3	4.47	51.94%
sc01	10	17.69	8.42	51.37%	12.96	6.36	50.93%
sc02	12	20.6	10.11	50.92%	16.06	7.8	51.42%
sc03	11	18.7	9.17	50.96%	14.53	7.05	51.52%
si01	8	12.91	6.23	51.78%	10.64	5.53	48.03%
si02	7	12.49	6.15	50.76%	9.4	4.72	49.80%
si03	27	47.97	23.14	51.76%	36.63	18.30	50.04%
sm01	11	18.05	8.76	51.47%	14.45	7.38	48.93%
sm02	10	16.34	8.08	50.55%	12.58	6.10	51.53%
sm03	14	23.36	11.38	51.27%	18.83	9.77	48.11%
Average	-	-	-	51.11%	-	-	50.07%

4.1   Objective Experiment of the Spectral Distortion

When distance is 20 cm, the average SDs between the original HRTFs and the HRTF reconstructed from the parameterized HRIRs, of left channel and right channel, are separately 0.79 dB and 0.72 dB. For all the data (distance of 20–160 cm) from PKU&IOA database [9], the mean SDs of the left and right channel are 0.66 dB and 0.70 dB. These results ensure the effectiveness of the proposed time delay estimation method by a relative threshold.

4.2   Acceleration Experiment of the Time Consumption

The acceleration experiment was carried on the two test devices described in Table 1. The test files are the standard audio sequences (fs = 48000 Hz,16bit) from Moving Picture Experts Group (MPEG). Time consumption of binaural

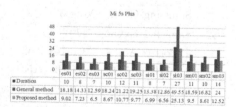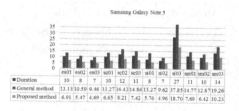

Fig. 3. Total synthesis times (s) of general method and proposed method

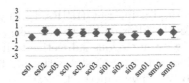

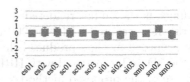

Fig. 4. Audio quality with proposed method compared to general method

Fig. 5. Localization perception with proposed method compared to general method

convolutions (only double convolutions described in Sect. 2) and total synthesis process (including windowing, binaural convolutions, overlap-add operations, etc.) are measured separately.

The results of binaural convolutions time are shown in Table 2. From the analysis in Sect. 3.4, we know that the proposed method could lessen 51.17% computations of real multiplications in the convolution procedure. Since the mean decrease of Mi 5s Plus and Samsung Note 5 are 51.11% and 50.07%, respectively, it has been validated that the proposed method reduces the time consumption of the binaural convolutions procedure indeed.

Here the real-time rendering refers to result that the total synthesis time is shorter than the play duration of the original audio. The plot of total synthesis times is illustrated in Fig. 3. The average ratio (of synthesis time to the duration) over the sequences are 90% and 68%, realizing goal of 3D audio real-time rendering on the Mi 5s Plus and Samsung Note 5. In the Phyo's work, the rendering result showed average 12.556 ms for frame of 26 ms on Samsung S III (fs = 44100 Hz and processor clock of 1.4 GHz). In consideration of differences of the experiment configuration (50% overlap, fs = 48000 Hz and processor clock of 2.1 GHz), the Phyo's result is converted to the counterpart ratio (of synthesis time to the duration) as 70%. As our result (68%) on Samsung Note 5 surpasses 70%, it demonstrates our method outperforms the current result in the efficiency of 3D audio rendering.

4.3 Subjective Experiment of Listening Test

Here a listening test based on comparison mean opinion score (CMOS) [15] was conducted to compare the subjective feeling of rendered 3D audio between the proposed method and the general method (as 3, 2 and 1 means much better, better and slightly better, 0 means about the same, −3, −2 and −1 means much worse, worse and slightly worse). Ten experienced subjects were asked to assess the audio quality and localization perception of the played 3D audio, respectively. The path of audio source is moving along a circle towards head with the radius of 20 cm, and would be stated to the subjects before the listening as a reference of the localization. As for audio quality, the original sequences would be played as references. The scores results are illustrated in Figs. 4 and 5. The CMOS results of the audio quality and localization perception are all nearly close to 0 (about the same). It could be concluded that the 3D audios rendered by the proposed method with the parameterized HRTFs have the similar subjective feelings as the audios rendered by general method using raw HRIRs. In Phyo's work, the measured HRIR is 200 taps long. As the filtering length E is also 200, the proposed method produced the 3D audio with analogous subjective feelings as the 3D audio rendered with HRIR of 1024 samples, which shows the effective feature of the proposed method, compared to the Phyo's method.

5   Conclusion

In this paper, we present three techniques are proposed as preprocessing HRIR into HRTF using zero padding, binaural convolutions sharing the frame spectrum and delayed-zeros optimizing convolution. The acceleration experiment shows the mean decrease of the binaural convolutions time on Mi 5s Plus and Samsung Note 5 are 51.11% and 50.07%, which results in the achievement of real-time rendering of 3D audio on test devices. Besides, the subjective evaluation results illustrate that the 3D audios rendered with proposed method have similar audio quality and localization perception as the general method.

References

1. Sunder, K., He, J., Tan, E.L., Gan, W.S.: Natural sound rendering for headphones: integration of signal processing techniques. IEEE Signal Process. Mag. **32**(2), 100–113 (2015)
2. Torres, J.C., Petraglia, M.R., Tenenbaum, R.A.: Low-order modeling of head-related transfer functions using wavelet transforms. In: Circuits and Systems, ISCAS 2004, p. III-513. IEEE Press (2004)
3. Zhang, J., Xia, R., Xu, C., Li, J., Yan, Y., Sakamoto, S.: Head-related transfer function modeling based on finite-impulse response. In: Intelligent Information Hiding and Multimedia Signal Processing (2013)
4. Lee, T., Oh, H.O., Seo, J., Park, Y.C., Youn, D.H.: Scalable multiband binaural renderer for MPEG-H 3D audio. IEEE J. Sel. Top. Signal Process. **9**(5), 907–920 (2015)
5. Schissler, C., Nicholls, A., Mehra, R.: Efficient HRTF-based spatial audio for area and volumetric sources. IEEE Trans. Vis. Comput. Graph. **22**(4), 1356–1366 (2016)
6. Iwaya, Y., Otani, M., Tsuchiya, T., Li, J.: Virtual auditory display on a smartphone for high-resolution acoustic space by remote rendering. In: Intelligent Information Hiding and Multimedia Signal Processing (IIH-MSP) (2015)
7. Phyo, K.K., Sunder, K., Gan, W.S.: Android framework implementation of 3D audio with range control. In: Audio Engineering Society Convention (2014)
8. Algazi, V.R., Duda, R.O., Thompson, D.M., Avendano, C.: The CIPIC HRTF database. In: 2001 IEEE Workshop on Applications of Signal Processing to Audio and Acoustics, pp. 99–102. IEEE Press (2001)
9. Qu, T., Xiao, Z., Gong, M., Huang, Y., Li, X., Wu, X.: Distance-dependent head-related transfer functions measured with high spatial resolution using a spark gap. IEEE Trans. Audio Speech Lang. Process. **17**(6), 1124–1132 (2009)
10. Storek, D.: Rendering moving sound source for headphone-based virtual acoustic reality aspects of signal processing implementation. In: 2014 International Conference on Applied Electronics (AE), pp. 271–276. IEEE Press (2014)

11. Oppenheim, A.V., Schafer, R.W.: Discrete-Time Signal Processing. Prentice Hall International, Upper Saddle River (2009)
12. Belloch, J.A., Gonzalez, A., Martínez-Zaldívar, F.J., Vidal, A.M.: Real-time massive convolution for audio applications on GPU. J. Supercomput. **58**(3), 449–457 (2011)
13. Katz, B.F., Noisternig, M.: A comparative study of interaural time delay estimation methods. J. Acoust. Soc. Am. **135**, 3530–3540 (2014)
14. Wang, L., Yin, F., Chen, Z.: A hybrid compression method for head-related transfer functions. Appl. Acoust. **70**(9), 1212–1218 (2009)
15. ITU-T Rec. P.800, Methods for Subjective Determination of Transmission Quality, International Telecommunication Union, Geneva (1996)

Efficient Logo Insertion Method for High-Resolution H.265/HEVC Compressed Video

Qi Jing[1], Peng Xu[1], Jun Sun[1,2(✉)], and Zongming Guo[1,2]

[1] Institute of Computer Science and Technology, Peking University, Beijing, China
{jingqi93,xupeng,jsun,guozongming}@pku.edu.cn
[2] Cooperative Medianet Innovation Center, Shanghai, China

Abstract. H.265/HEVC is being widely used in many video applications for its high compression efficiency. Logo insertion of high-resolution H.265/HEVC compressed video has urgent demands. Inserting a logo into video stream quickly with limited quality loss is a challenging task. We propose a logo insertion method composed of region partition algorithm, information reusing scheme and quantization parameter (QP) adjustment algorithm. Region partition algorithm separates each frame into logo region, logo-affected region and logo-unaffected region to stop pixel error propagation. Information reusing scheme reduces computations and saves re-encoding time. QP adjustment algorithm improves re-encoding video quality. Experimental results show that the proposed logo insertion method reduces the total transcoding time by 97.48% with only 3.53% BD-rate increase on average compared with the cascaded pixel-domain transcoding.

Keywords: Logo insertion · H.265/HEVC · Region partition
Information reusing · QP adjustment

1 Introduction

Nowadays, more and more people's communication relies on images and videos instead of text and voice. On many occasions, we insert some amusing logos into a video for having fun. For Internet videos and traditional TV videos, inserting a logo into compressed video is still the most efficient way for copyright protection. Meanwhile, a growing number of high-resolution videos are penetrating into every aspect of our lives. To facilitate encoding and transmission of HD videos, the latest video coding standard H.265/HEVC [8] has been designed. It can achieve equivalent subjective reproduction quality as H.264/AVC [11] when using approximately 50% [5] less bit rate on average. Consequently, it is desirable to find an efficient way for logo insertion of H.265/HEVC video stream. To the best of our knowledge, there are few researches in this area so far.

To insert a logo into a compressed video, one straightforward scheme is the cascaded pixel-domain transcoding (CPDT) method, as shown in Fig. 1. As

© Springer International Publishing AG, part of Springer Nature 2018
B. Zeng et al. (Eds.): PCM 2017, LNCS 10736, pp. 674–682, 2018.
https://doi.org/10.1007/978-3-319-77383-4_66

context-adaptive binary arithmetic coding (CABAC) is the main entropy coding method of H.265/HEVC [9] and context modeling is core algorithm of it, decoding the entire video stream is inevitable. Accordingly, we focus on re-encoding process of logo insertion. There are already some proposed methodologies of logo insertion for MPEG-2 and H.264/AVC. Panusopone *et al.* proposed a closed-loop logo insertion structure [6]. Xiao *et al.* suggested reusing motion vector (MV) for logo insertion in MPEG-2 [12]. Liu *et al.* recommended an interface macroblock-based transcoding scheme for video content editing transcoding [4]. Xu and Nasiopoulos proposed a logo insertion scheme for H.264/AVC using techniques such as partial decoding and re-encoding and syntax level bypassing [13]. Tsuji *et al.* suggested using long-term reference to improve the picture quality for H.264/AVC logo insertion [10]. Common characteristic of these methods mentioned above is that they can copy streams for reusing directly without decoding. However, this does not work in H.265/HEVC because of coding structure changing.

Fig. 1. Flow chart of CPDT logo insertion method

In this paper, an efficient H.265/HEVC logo insertion method is proposed, which is composed of region partition algorithm, information reusing scheme and QP adjustment algorithm. Region partition algorithm separates each frame into logo region, logo-affected region and logo-unaffected region after logo insertion. Logo region will encode in normal coding process. Logo-affected region uses lossless coding to stop pixel error propagation. For logo-unaffected region, information reusing scheme reuses decoding information as much as possible to maximize re-encoding speed. QP adjustment algorithm is used to refine QP of some coding units aimed at improving video quality. Experimental results show that the method achieves 97.48% timesaving with only 3.53% BD-rate increase on average compared with the CPDT method.

This paper is organized as follows. Section 2 presents technical background and challenges of H.265/HEVC logo insertion. In Sect. 3, the proposed logo insertion method is described in details. Experimental results are presented in Sect. 4, and Sect. 5 is the conclusion.

2   Technical Background and Challenges

High Efficiency Video Coding (HEVC) is the latest video coding standard. Many new features are applied in HEVC to improve compression performance. As a result, the new coding standard achieves 50% bit-rate reduction for equal perceptual video quality compared with H.264/AVC [5]. Meanwhile, complexity of H.265/HEVC significantly increases because of these new features.

Different with the previous coding standard H.264/AVC, coding tree unit (CTU) size of H.265/HEVC can be from 64 × 64 to 16 × 16 [8]. Coding unit (CU), prediction unit (PU), and transform unit (TU) are recursively partitioned according to the detail level of video content. Besides, more intra modes [3] and new inter motion prediction technologies arise in H.265/HEVC. The adaptive quadtree splitting structure and new coding features of H.265/HEVC improve encoding efficiency and video quality. However, it is more difficult for logo insertion of H.265/HEVC video stream because of its complicated coding dependencies and increased complexity.

With changes of coding structure and technologies in H.265/HEVC, dependencies and references between CUs become more complex. Video content varies along with logo insertion will propagate to other CUs without control. As CABAC is a context adaptive entropy coding, decoding of video stream is unavoidable. To insert logo quickly with limited quality loss, stopping pixel error propagation and reducing re-encoding computations are the two key issues.

3   The Proposed Logo Insertion Method

Our proposed logo insertion method aims at solving the problems mentioned in Sect. 2. Three core algorithms are applied in our work. Region partition algorithm is for stopping pixel error propagation. Information reusing scheme aims at accelerating re-encoding process. QP adjustment algorithm is for video quality improvement. In following three subsections, detail descriptions of these algorithms will be given.

3.1   Region Partition Algorithm

For controlling of pixel error propagation, each frame of video stream is separated into three regions, namely logo region, logo-affected region, logo-unaffected region. As shown in Fig. 2, logo region includes CUs that have directly connection with insert-ed logo (depicted by color gray in Fig. 2). Logo-affected region is consisted of CUs that have coding dependences with the logo region (depicted by diagonally shaded in Fig. 2). Remaining area is logo-unaffected region.

A CU is counted as logo region no matter entirely covered by the logo or only a few pixels in contact. In this way, it is guaranteed that entire logo are covered by the logo region. Logo region CUs are marked easily according to original splitting information. Because content in this area has changed after logo insertion, it is improper to reuse coding information. Although lossless coding of logo region can acquire better quality, it increases bit rate of video stream as well. Through comparison and analysis, logo region is encoded in normal coding process.

Since logo region CUs have direct relation with inserted logo, they cannot be taken as references. According to decoding information, CUs that taking logo region CU as references are marked as logo-affected region. Meanwhile, CUs in logo-affected region are incapable of encoding in normal coding process, because there are CUs taking them as references as well. To stop pixel error

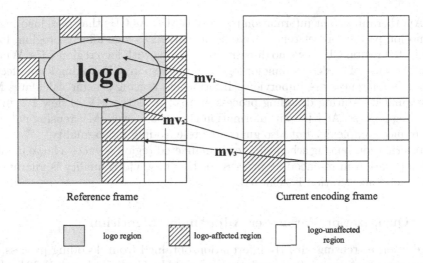

Reference frame   Current encoding frame

logo region   logo-affected region   logo-unaffected region

Fig. 2. Three regions seperated by region partition algorithm

propagation and guarantee reusing information of logo-unaffected region, lossless coding [15] is used for logo-affected region CUs. In lossless mode, the transform, quantization, and other processing that affects the decoded picture are bypassed, and the residual signal is directly fed into the entropy coder. In this way, pixel changes caused by logo insertion are limited within logo region and logo-affected region.

By this region partition algorithm, content changes in pixel domain brought in by logo insertion are terminated.

3.2 Information Reusing Scheme for Logo-Unaffected Region

The most time consuming part of H.265/HEVC is the recursive quadtree splitting structure. Under normal coding circumstance, whether a CU (not in the minimum size) needs to be partitioned depends on the comparison result of rate-distortion cost (RD cost) between the whole CU and sum of four sub-CUs. A large amount of computation is required in this process. Analogously, PU and TU are facing same situation.

To reuse the splitting information of CU, PU, and TU, we record this information during decoding process. For every pixel, its re-encoding partition can be decided by referring its original partition. As a result, there are no recursive splitting process for logo-unaffected region in re-encoding process after logo insertion.

Except for quadtree splitting process, intra mode decision also contains a certain amount of calculation. Encoding an intra CU will calculate all 35 modes and choose the best one in normal coding process. By contrast, only one mode needs to be calcu-lated with reusing original modes information. For some inter CUs, encoding modes can be skip which as a special case of the merge mode. By recording and reusing skip flag information, an inter CU coding mode can be marked as skip directly.

Another important information to reuse is MV. As CUs that take logo region as motion prediction references have been marked as logo-affected region, logo-unaffected region CUs have no directly connections with logo region CUs. What's more, because of lossless coding for logo-affected region, CUs taking logo-affected region as references are impervious. Information reusing scheme calculates MV of original PU during decoding process and set it as the MV of new PU in re-encoding process. As PU split information is reused as well, MV reusing not only can reduce complexity but also guarantee re-encoding video quality.

Information reusing scheme for logo-unaffected region reduces a large number of computation in re-encoding process. In this way, video quality is guaranteed and a good acceleration is achieved.

3.3   Quantization Parameter Adjustment Algorithm

In addition to reusing directly information obtained from decoding process, we endeavor to find more information that is valuable. Compared with H.264/AVC, the quadtree coding structure of H.265/HEVC encodes smoothing regions with large CU size and small ones for the region with more details. After decoding process, we have a better understanding of video texture. Accordingly, computing resources can be distributed better during re-encoding process. Researches of Zhang *et al.* [14] shows that content-based local QP determination approach can achieve better coding efficiency. QP adjustment algorithm is used for some CTUs and experimental results proves that is effective.

To measure complexity (smoothing or detail area) of a CTU, we define a 4×4 block in pixel as a base block. Depth of the ith base block (B_i) in one CTU is only related to the width of CU it belongs to. Use W represents CU width in pixel, W_{max} represents width of CTU, B_i can be calculate by formula (1).

$$B_i = log(W_{max}) - log(W) \tag{1}$$

CU size in smoothing area is larger than that in detail area. Meaning that base blocks have larger depth in area with complex texture. The complexity of one CTU can be measured by the sum of base blocks depth. Define N as numbers of base blocks in one CTU and define $C_{x,y}$ as the complexity of the CTU those frame index is x and CTU index is y. N and $C_{x,y}$ can be calculated by formulas (2) and (3).

$$N = (\frac{W_{max}}{4})^2 \tag{2}$$

$$C_{x,y} = \sum_{i=1}^{N} B_i \tag{3}$$

Figure 3 shows CTU complexity results of one video stream. As we can see in the diagram that $C_{x,y}$ of some CTUs are zero. That is because these CTUs do not split and are in smoothing area. Only a few $C_{x,y}$ are very high meaning that these CTUs are with high complexity. According to experimental results, a

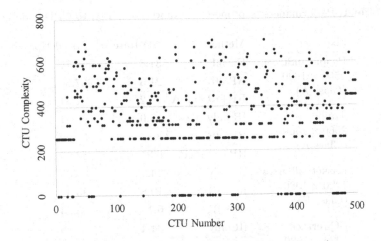

Fig. 3. Complexity of CTUs in video stream

threshold C_{th} of CTU complexity is set to top 3% for one video stream. Finally, adjustments of CTU quantization parameter $(QP_{x,y})$ are made by formula (4).

$$QP_{x,y} = \begin{cases} QP_{x,y} + 1, & (C_{x,y} = 0) \\ QP_{x,y}, & (0 < C_{x,y} < C_{th}) \\ QP_{x,y} - 1, & (C_{x,y} \geq C_{th}) \end{cases} \tag{4}$$

4 Experimental Results

The logo insertion method was implemented based on the H.265/HEVC reference software HM 16.7 [7], and use a default *low delay main* setting [2]. We ran the simulations on the recommended class A and class B 8bit sequences from the common test conditions [2]. The test sequences were fully encoded and with a QP set to 22, 27, 32 and 37. The impact on the coding efficiency was measured by using the BD-Rate [1]. The logo for insertion is a normal static company logo with pixel size 128 × 128 (similar with the channel logo on TV screen).

Taking CPDT method as a reference, we compared the information resuing scheme only (IR only), region partition method with information resuing scheme (RP+IR) and the proposed method (RP+IR+QPA). The IR method marks the entire frame as logo-unaffected region and only reuses decoding information. The RP+IR method abandons QP adjustment algorithm from the proposed method. The computational complexity reduction was measured by the speed-up ratio compared with CPDT method.

As shown in Fig. 4, the class A and class B average RD curve of three different method shows that our region partition algorithm and QP adjustment algorithm are efficient. In addition, experimental results are listed in Table 1. The IR only method achieves highest speed-up ratio but with greater impact on the BD-Rate. The proposed method (RP+IR+QPA) is more recommended as the cost

Table 1. Performances of proposed methods compared to CPDT method

Sequence	Method	BD-Rate[%]	Speed-Up
PeopleOnStreet 2560 × 1600 (Class A)	IR only	31.8	39.77
	RP+IR	21.3	37.60
	RP+IR+QPA	17.2	37.51
Traffic 2560 × 1600 (Class A)	IR only	15.0	62.41
	RP+IR	8.8	57.99
	RP+IR+QPA	6.2	57.85
BasketballDrive 1920 × 1080 (Class B)	IR only	24.4	38.85
	RP+IR	10.8	35.32
	RP+IR+QPA	5.1	35.23
BQTerrace 1920 × 1080 (Class B)	IR only	34.4	48.08
	RP+IR	16.9	44.05
	RP+IR+QPA	9.9	43.95
Cactus 1920 × 1080 (Class B)	IR only	17.5	30.64
	RP+IR	−0.1	27.54
	RP+IR+QPA	−6.9	27.47
Kimono 1920 × 1080 (Class B)	IR only	23.1	37.31
	RP+IR	11.4	34.75
	RP+IR+QPA	6.6	34.66
ParkScene 1920 × 1080 (Class B)	IR only	6.1	45.28
	RP+IR	−7.7	41.70
	RP+IR+QPA	−13.4	41.60
Average	IR only	21.74	43.12
	RP+IR	8.81	39.85
	RP+IR+QPA	3.53	39.75

of a slight reduce of speed achieves significantly BD-Rate decrease. For video streams with less movements, the proposed method outperforms CPDT method as a result of conrolling of pixel error propagation.

Since there are not many other researches in this area, we are not aware of other suitable experimental results for comparison. In addition, comparison between different coding standard is unfair and unconvincing. What's more, taking CPDT method as reference and the comparison results can also prove the validity of the proposed method. In sum, experimental results are satisfactory and show the proposed logo insertion method for high-resolution H.265/HEVC compressed video is effective.

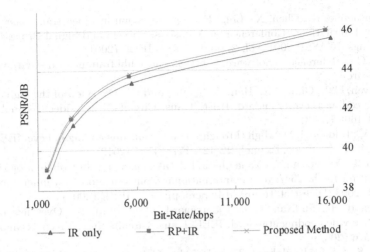

Fig. 4. Average RD curve comparison of different logo insertion methods

5   Conclusion

An efficient logo insertion method for high-resolution H.265/HEVC compressed video is proposed in this paper. It is attractive in many fields as increasing H.265/HEVC applications. Region partition algorithm, information reusing scheme and QP adjustment algorithm are core components of our method. The proposed method overcomes challenges involved by new coding features and maximize speedup ratio while minimize quality loss. Experimental results show that the proposed method outperforms the CPDT method by 97.48% timesaving (39.75x speedup ratio) with only 3.53% BD-rate increase.

Acknowledgments. This work was supported by National Natural Science Foundation of China under contract No.61671025 and National Key Technology R&D Program of China under Grant 2015AA011605.

References

1. Bjontegaard, G.: Calculation of average psnr differences between rd-curves. In: ITU-T Q. 6/SG16 VCEG, 15th Meeting, Austin, Texas, USA, April 2001 (2001)
2. Bossen, F., Common, H.: test conditions and software reference configurations, jct-vc doc. L1100, January 2013
3. Lainema, J., Bossen, F., Han, W.J., Min, J., Ugur, K.: Intra coding of the hevc standard. IEEE Trans. Circuits Syst. Video Technol. **22**(12), 1792–1801 (2012)
4. Liu, Y., Duan, J., Wang, S., Song, S.: Interface mb-based video content editing transcoding. IEEE Trans. Circuits Syst. Video Technol. **25**(2), 261–274 (2015)
5. Ohm, J.R., Sullivan, G.J., Schwarz, H., Tan, T.K., Wiegand, T.: Comparison of the coding efficiency of video coding standards-including high efficiency video coding (hevc). IEEE Trans. Circuits Syst. Video Technol. **22**(12), 1669–1684 (2012)

6. Panusopone, K., Chen, X., Ling, F.: Logo insertion in mpeg transcoder. In: 2001 IEEE International Conference on Acoustics, Speech, and Signal Processing, Proceedings, ICASSP 2001, vol. 2, pp. 981–984. IEEE (2001)
7. HEVC Reference Software. https://hevc.hhi.fraunhofer.de/svn/svn_HEVC Software/
8. Sullivan, G.J., Ohm, J.R., Han, W.J., Wiegand, T.: Overview of the high efficiency video coding (hevc) standard. IEEE Trans. Circuits Syst. Video Technol. 22(12), 1649–1668 (2013)
9. Sze, V., Budagavi, M.: High throughput cabac entropy coding in hevc. IEEE Trans. Circuits Syst. Video Technol. 22(12), 1778–1791 (2012)
10. Tsuji, T., Yoneyama, A., Yanagihara, H., Takishima, Y.: High quality logo insertion algorithm for h. 264/avc. In: International Conference on Consumer Electronics, ICCE 2008, Digest of Technical Papers, pp. 1–2. IEEE (2008)
11. Wiegand, T., Sullivan, G.J., Bjontegaard, G., Luthra, A.: Overview of the h. 264/avc video coding standard. IEEE Trans. Circuits Syst. Video Technol. 13(7), 560–576 (2003)
12. Xiao, S., Lu, L., Kouloheris, J.L., Gonzales, C.A.: Low-cost and efficient logo insertion scheme in mpeg video transcoding. In: Proceedings of the SPIE, vol. 4671, pp. 172–179 (2002)
13. Xu, D., Nasiopoulos, P.: Logo insertion transcoding for h. 264/avc compressed video. In: 2009 16th IEEE International Conference on Image Processing (ICIP), pp. 3693–3696. IEEE (2009)
14. Zhang, F., Bull, D.R.: Hevc enhancement using content-based local qp selection. In: 2016 IEEE International Conference on Image Processing (ICIP), pp. 4215–4219. IEEE (2016)
15. Zhou, M., Gao, W., Jiang, M., Yu, H.: Hevc lossless coding and improvements. IEEE Trans. Circuits Syst. Video Technol. 22(12), 1839–1843 (2012)

Image Decomposition Based Nighttime Image Enhancement

Xuesong Jiang[✉], Hongxun Yao, and Dilin Liu

Computer Science and Technology, Harbin Institute of Technology,
No 92 Xidezhijie Street, Harbin, Heilongjiang Province, China
{xsjiang,h.yao,liudilin}@hit.edu.cn

Abstract. Nighttime image captured at low or non-uniform illumination scene always suffers from the loss of visibility, and contains various noise and objectionable artifact. When we enlarge the amplitude of
the lightness, the noise and artifact in nighttime images will be amplified. Hence, we propose a nighttime image enhancement method based
on image decomposition. We decompose the input image into two components: Structure Layer contains main information of the image, and
Texture Layer contains details, noise and artifact. For the Structure
Layer, we apply an improved-Retinex image enhancement algorithm. To
remain details and suppress noise and artifact in the Texture Layer, we
use Mask Weighted Least Squares method. In the final, we fuse these
two components to get the result. The experimental results demonstrate
that the proposed approach can improve the perceptual quality of nighttime image while suppressing noise and artifact, and avoiding excessive
reinforcement.

Keywords: Nighttime image enhancement
Image decomposition · Noise and artifact suppression
Improved-retinex algorithm

1 Introduction

Due to insufficient illumination at night, images captured at night always suffer
from interference of varieties of noise and loss of visibility, which causes issues
in Photography, forensics, analysis, monitoring, and some other optical imaging systems. The majority of professional or portable cameras widely used in
vision systems cannot capture satisfactory nighttime image. Nighttime image
enhancement techniques which aim to increase the interpretability of the image
by increasing lightness amplitude pixel by pixel, are highly desired in both consumer photography and computer vision applications. This issue has been a hot
and challenging research topic and extensively studied.

A variety of nighttime image enhancement methods were proposed over the
past years. Focus on single low-lighting image enhancement methods, many
impressive algorithms are proposed, such as classical image processing methods (Histogram equalization, Gamma correction, and Tone-mapping) and some

Fig. 1. An example of the proposed nighttime image enhancement (From left to right: input image, noisy result, our result).

variants [1]. Retinex is widely used in contrast enhancement, too. For example, Li et al. [3] and Liu et al. [4] gets impressive results using variants of Retinex. Based on an observation that a pixel-wise inversion of a nighttime image has quite similar appearance with the image acquired at foggy days, Dong et al. [5] introduces single image haze removal algorithm into nighttime image enhancement. Actually, it's a variant of Retinx, too. Following this work, several similar methods [6,7] are proposed to improve the performance of the Dark Channel Prior.

Noise must be taken into consideration in night photography. There are many kinds of noise sources, such as readout, photon shot, dark current, and fixed pattern noise in addition to photon response non-uniformities [2]. Removing noise from nighttime image is difficult. To make matters worse, the noise level would be enlarged when lightness and contrast are amplified, especially in the compressed images. To get more satisfactory results, a noise suppression method is highly demanded. Among the above methods, Zhang [6] smooths results using Bilateral filter and others don't deal with noises. However, the complexity of noise in nighttime images makes the commonly used image smoothing methods poor performance.

Based on the image structure-texture decomposition, we propose a framework which outperforms previous methods. We decompose input image into structure layer and texture layer. Then we deal with two components respectively with the improved-Retinex method and Mask Weighted Least Squares (WLS) smoothing method, and obtain results using composition operation. We show an example in Fig. 1, which can demonstrate the effectiveness of the proposed method. As we can see, the noise and artifact are apparently reduced and visibility improved. We also conduct sufficient experiments with different types of nighttime images. The experimental results demonstrate that the proposed approach can improve the perceptual quality of nighttime image regarding not only enhancing the visibility and contrast, but also effectively suppressing noises and artifacts, and avoiding excessive reinforcement.

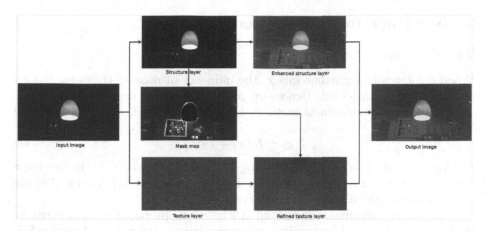

Fig. 2. An overview of the proposed method. Firstly, the input image is decomposed into structure layer and texture layer. Enhance structure layer using improved-Retinex method. A mask map from Structure layer helps to smooth texture layer with Weighted Least Squares (WLS) optimization. The two layers are recombined to get the final result. Here we amplify texture layer and refined texture layer for visualization.

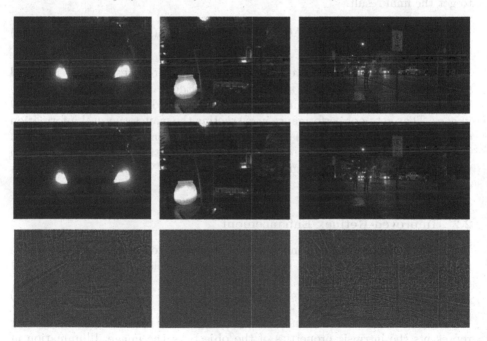

Fig. 3. Results of Structure-texture decomposition. Input images are in the top row. Structure layer (Middle row) consist of objects with larger gradient magnitudes. Texture layer (Bottom row) contains details, noises and artifacts.

2 Nighttime Image Enhancement

2.1 Overview

When dealing with nighttime image, the influence of noise in the enhancement result must be considered. Hence, we present an image decomposition based nighttime image enhancement method. To achieve our goal, we model the input image as

$$I(x) = I_S(x) + I_T(x) \tag{1}$$

Here, x is the pixel index, $I(x)$ is the original input image, $I_S(x)$ is the Structure layer corresponding to the objects with distinct edges, and $I_T(x)$ is the Texture layer containing details, noise and artifact.

Our primary pipeline is illustrated in Fig. 2. The proposed method starts by decomposing the original input image into two layers: structure and texture layers. We enhance Structure layer using an improved-Retinex method and smooth Texture layer by Weighted Least Square (WLS) [13] method. To enhance the details, we deal with texture layer using a mask map extracted from structure layer. Ultimately, we fuse the enhanced structure layer and refined texture layer to get the final result.

$$\min_{I_S} \sum_i (I_S(x) - I(x))^2 + \lambda |\nabla I_S(x)| \tag{2}$$

To obtain the structure layer, we try different approaches, such as Bilateral filter (BF) [6], Guided image filter (GF) [15], Edge-Avoiding Wavelet (EAW) [14], and BM3D [16]. However, image smoothing methods are designed for normal images. They get poor performance in extracting the main structural information of the nighttime images. At last, we choose to minimize the object function designed as Eq. 2 [8], which is based on the total-variation image-reconstruction regularization. Here λ is the regulation parameter, and ∇ represents the gradient operator. In this paper, we set $\lambda = 0.015$.

2.2 Improved-Retinex Enhancement

We use an improved-Retinex enhancement algorithm to improve the lightness of the Structure layer. The input structure layer is modeled as Eq. 3

$$I_S(x) = I_R(x) \cdot I_L(x) \tag{3}$$

Here, $I_R(x)$ represents reflectance and $I_L(x)$ represents illumination. Reflectance represents the intrinsic properties of the objects in the image. Illumination at night is non-uniform. Traditional methods solve this ill-posed problem by Single-Scale Retinex or Multi-Scake Retinex [9].

Instead of using logarithmic operation and Gaussian filter as SSR ans MSR, we estimate $I_L(x)$ using a series of nonlinear operations. We get more reliable illumination map. With edge preserving smoothing method, we can suppress the inherent halo effect cased by Retinex model (Fig. 4).

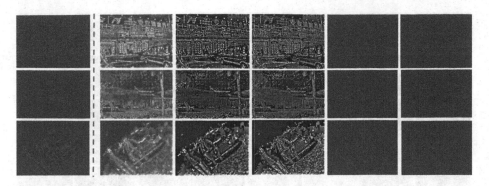

Fig. 4. Denoising results of different smoothing approaches. Input texture images are at left side, on the right side followed by the results with BF, GIF, EAW, BM3D and WLS with mask. To make refined texture visible, we enlarge them using Gamma correction.

Due to multiple light sources and fast attenuation of lightness, illumination in the nighttime images is non-uniform in most cases. Motivated by the Dark Channel Prior, we design an simple algorithm to get an illumination map. First of all, we get max channel of the structure layer:

$$I_M(x) = \max_{c \in (r,g,b)} I_S^c(x) \tag{4}$$

where (r, g, b) means the three channels of the image.

Illumination should be continuous and smooth. Hence, we make the illumination map as smooth as possible. We smooth $I_M(x)$ using median filter first, then remove the details from it.

$$I_L(x) = M(I_M(x)) - D(I_M(x)) \tag{5}$$

Here, $M(\cdot)$ represents median filter and $D(\cdot)$ is the details extracting operation as Eq. 6.

$$D(x) = M(|x - M(x)|) \tag{6}$$

Introducing the illumination map $I_L(x)$ into Eq. 3, we can get enhanced structure layer

$$I_E(x) = \frac{I_S(x)}{I_L(x) + \epsilon} \tag{7}$$

Here ϵ is a small positive value to keep the fraction is meaningful when $I_L(x) = 0$.

2.3 Noise and Artifact Supression

Details, noise and artifact are stirred together as shown in Fig. 3. Image smoothing filters are hard to find a good kernel scale to strike a balance between detail and noise. To improve the ability of noise reducing method means that details

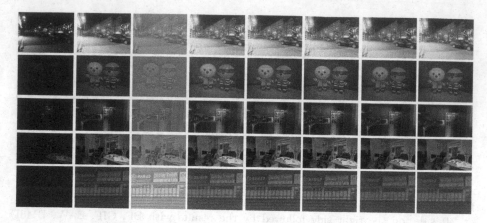

Fig. 5. Comparative results for subjective evaluation. From left to right: Input images, Dong's results [5], MSRCR, Zhang's results [6], Results with GIF [15], Results with EAW [14], Results with BM3D [16], and our results.

will be removed at the same time. Hence, we process the texture layer with not only image smoothing method but also extra mask map.

There is an intuitive observation that the dark regions contain more random noise because of lack of illumination. We calculate a mask map based on this observation. As Eq. 8, We design this operation to weight the importance of the smoothing texture layer.

$$Mask(x) = \min(I_L(x), 1 - I_L(x)) \tag{8}$$

Then, the luminance component is smoothed by Eq. 9.

$$I_F(x) = Mask(x) \cdot WLS(I_T(x)/I_L(x)) \tag{9}$$

Where $I_F(x)$ is the refined texture layer.

To demonstrate the effect of the proposed method, we try several different approaches to reduce the noises, such as BF, GIF, EAW, BM3D and WLS with mask. At last, we add enhanced structure layer and refined texture layer together to get the final result $R(x)$.

$$R(x) = I_E(x) + I_F(x) \tag{10}$$

3   Experiments and Assessment

To evaluate the proposed method, we apply it a total of 310 nighttime images, and make the comparison with different methods for subjective and objective evaluation. We compute several non-reference evaluation metrics (including No-reference Image Quality Evaluator (NIQE) [21], Blind/Referenceless Image Spatial Quality Evaluator (BRISQUE) [22], and IL-NIQE [23]). To demonstrate the

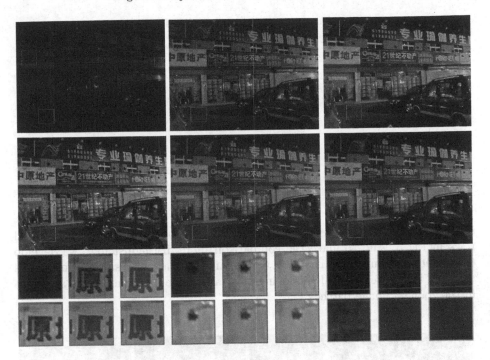

Fig. 6. A comparative experiment of the zoomed results. The above two lines are arranged in the following order: Input image, Dong's result [7], results with BF [6], GIF [15], BM3D [16], and our results. The zoomed image patches are arranged in the same way. (Color figure online)

effect of the proposed method, we apply several different approaches to reduce the noises, such as Multi-scales Retinex with Color Restoration (MSRCR), Dark Channel Prior based nighttime image enhancement method (DCP-NIE) [7], and reducing noises with different methods(Bilateral filter (BF) [6], Guided image filter (GF) [15], Edge-Avoiding Wavelet (EAW) [14], and BM3D [16]). The results are shown in Table 1. According these no-reference image quality evaluators, we can see our approach outperform other image filters and a litter nicer than BM3D. But the proposed method 8 times faster than BM3D.

To get a more intuitive comparison, we display some comparative results for subjective evaluation in Fig. 5. Without noise reduction operation, Dong [5] gets impressive but noisy results, especially in dark areas. MSRCR gets the brightness-enhanced image with inconvenient color distortion. The results under the structure-texture decomposition framework depend on the use of the denoising method. Zhang [6] gets similar objective appraisal as GIF [15] does, but the difference is that BF gets noticeable noise points in the results, and GIF gets fuzzy results with fuzzy noise and artifact. EAW [14] doesn't work well in nighttime image noise removal. BM3D [16] gets impressive results. It reduces the noises and artifacts apparently. Our method can make the enhanced images

Table 1. Quantitative comparison of the average NIQE, BRISQUE and ILNIQE.

Method	NIQE [21]	BRISQUE [22]	ILNIQE [23]
MSRCR	3.9976	33.2330	28.4269
DCP [7]	3.7603	33.8801	32.9433
EAW [14]	3.5196	30.0228	28.3889
Zhang's [6]	5.4412	43.3091	31.8174
GIF [15]	5.3854	49.6131	33.1973
BM3D [16]	5.5098	**51.1790**	32.4671
Our	**5.5106**	50.4614	**34.5517**

smooth enough while preserving useful details, as shown in the second and third rows in Fig. 5. And to make the comparison more distinguishable, we develop the result to see more details in Fig. 6. We can find that our result retains details (red and blue patches) while removing noise and artifact (green patch), as shown in the zoomed image patches.

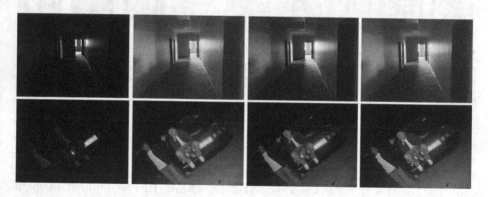

Fig. 7. Comparison experiment of the noise reduction ability. From left to right: Input image, BM3D + Enhancement [7] (denoise before enhancement), Enhancement [7] + BM3D (denoise after enhancement), and our results with BM3D.

In order to demonstrate the role of the structure-texture decomposition, we compare our method with two different denoising ways, including noise reduction before enhancement and after enhancement. Because the visibility is too low, removing noise before enhancement makes the results blurry and noisy. However, noise is amplified after enhancement. It makes eliminating noise difficult, too. In Fig. 7, we can find image decomposition help suppress noise with the same denoising method. This demonstrates the importance of the structure-texture decomposition in nighttime image enhancement.

Because of structure-texture composition, our method is not a real-time method. Through the statistics of all the experiments, we can deal with a color image size of 800×600 in 1.6 s (Intel I5, 8 G RAM, MATLAB code).

4 Conclusion

The main contribution of our work is constructing a framework for enhance nighttime image while suppressing noise and artifact. The main idea is to decompose the input image into structure and texture components. Then we apply a improved-Retinex approach to improving the visibility of the structure layer and reduce noise and artifact in the texture layer with Mask Weighted Least Square. After the above operation, we fuse two components together to gain the final result. Experimental results show that the proposed method has good performance in most conditions. Compared to several similar methods with commonly used image smoothing filtering methods, the proposed approach gets more natural and detail-rich result with fewer noise and artifact.

In the next stage, we will try to use machine learning methods (such as Deep Convolution Neural Network [20]) to make nighttime image look like the image captured during the day time, especially the sky region.

Acknowledgement. This work was supported by the National Natural Science Foundation of China under Project No. 61472103.

References

1. Rao, Y., Chen, L.: A survey of video enhancement techniques. J. Inf. Hiding Multimed. Signal Process. **3**, 71–99 (2002)
2. Reibel, Y., Jung, M., Bouhifd, M., Cunin, B., Draman, C.: CCD or CMOS camera noise characteristics. Europ. Phys. J. Appl. Phys. **21**, 75–80 (2003)
3. Li, B., Wang, S., Geng, Y.: Image enhancement based on retinex and lightness decomposition. In: IEEE International Conference on Image Processing, pp. 3417–3420 (2011)
4. Liu, H., Sun, X., Han, H., Cao, W.: Low-light video image enhancement based on multiscale retinex-like algorithm. In: Chinese Control and Decision Conference, pp. 3712–3715 (2016)
5. Dong, X., Pang, Y.A., Wang, G., Li, W., Gao, Y., Yang, S.: Fast efficient algorithm for enhancement of low lighting video. In: IEEE International Conference on Multimedia and Expo, pp. 1–6 (2011)
6. Zhang, X., Shen, P., Luo, L., Zhang, L., Song, J.: Enhancement and noise reduction of very low light level images. In: IEEE International Conference on Pattern Recognition, pp. 2034–2037 (2012)
7. Jiang, X., Yao, H., Zhang, S., Lu, X., Zeng, W.: Night video enhancement using improved dark channel prior. In: IEEE International Conference on Image Processing, pp. 553–557 (2013)
8. Li, Y., Guo, F., Tan, R.T., Brown, M.S.: A contrast enhancement framework with JPEG artifacts suppression. In: European Conference on Computer Vision, pp. 174–188 (2014)

9. Rahman, Z., Jobson, D.J., Woodell, G.A.: Retinex processing for automatic image enhancement. J. Electron. Imaging **13**, 100–110 (2004)
10. He, K., Sun, J., Tang, X.: Single image haze removal using dark channel prior. In: Conference on Computer Vision and Pattern Recognition, pp. 1–8 (2009)
11. Xiao, C., Gan, J.: Fast image dehazing using guided joint bilateral filter. Vis. Comput. Int. J. Comput. Graph. **28**, 713–721 (2012)
12. Huo, B., Yin, F.: Image dehazing with dark channel prior and novel estimation model. Int. J. Multimed. Ubiquitous Eng. **10**, 13–22 (2015)
13. Min, D., Choi, S., Lu, J., et al.: Fast global image smoothing based on weighted least squares. IEEE Trans. Image Process. Publication of the IEEE Signal Processing Society **23**(12), 5638–53 (2014)
14. Fattal, R.: Edge-avoiding wavelets and their applications. ACM Trans. Graph. **28**, 1–10 (2009)
15. He, K., Sun, J., Tang, X.: Guided image filtering. IEEE Trans. Pattern Anal. Mach. Intell., 1–13 (2013)
16. Dabov, K., Foi, A., Katkovnik, V., Egiazarian, K.: Image denoising by sparse 3-D transform-domain collaborative filtering. IEEE Trans. Image Process. **16**, 2080–2095 (2007)
17. Leonid, I.R., Osher, S., Fatemi, E.: Nonlinear total variation based noise removal algorithms. Phys. D **60**, 259–268 (1992)
18. Wang, Z., Bovik, A.C., Sheikh, H.R., Simoncelli, E.P.: Image quality assessment: from error visibility to structural similarity. IEEE Trans. Image Process. **13**, 111–126 (2014)
19. Sheikh, H.R., Bovik, A.C., de Veciana, G.: An information fidelity criterion for image quality assessment using natural scene statistics. IEEE Trans. Image Process. **14**, 2117–2128 (2005)
20. Cai, B., Xu, X., Jia, K., Qing, C., Tao, D.: DehazeNet: an end-to-end system for single image haze removal. IEEE Trans. Image Process. **25**, 5187–5198 (2016)
21. Mittal, A., Soundararajan, R., Bovik, A.C.: Making a completely blind image quality analyzer. IEEE Signal Process. Lett. **22**, 209–212 (2013)
22. Mittal, A., Moorthy, A.K., Bovik, A.C.: No-reference image quality assessment in the spatial domain. IEEE Trans. Image Process. **21**, 4695–4708 (2012)
23. Zhang, L., Zhang, L., Bovik, A.C.: A feature-enriched completely blind local image quality analyzer. IEEE Trans. Image Process. **24**, 2579–2591 (2015)

PSNR Estimate for JPEG Compression

Ci Wang, Ying Yang$^{(\boxtimes)}$, and Jianhua Shen

Department of Computer Science and Technology, East China Normal University,
Shanghai 200062, China
lpsshg@qq.com, jhshen@cs.ecnu.edu.cn

Abstract. JPEG is wildly used for image compression, which inevitably
introduces some distortions, such as blocking artifacts and blurring. Peak
Signal to Noise Ratio (PSNR) is the most widely used objective criterion to evaluate image distortion, which is a full reference image quality
assessment and requires original image as the reference. However, this
requirement cannot always be guaranteed, so that no reference PSNR
estimate (NRPE) is required in some applications. NRPE is an ill-pose
problem and need some prior knowledge to produce rational results.
DCT coefficients are usually assumed with even or Gaussian distributions, and their parameters are estimated by learning or no learning
based algorithms in PSNR calculation. These works are unsatisfied for
their estimate error is even larger than 3 dB for the heavy compressed
images. Note that the correlations of image pixels will be destroyed and
some artifacts will appear after heavy compression, such as blocking and
blurring. In this paper, the relationship of mean squared difference of
slope (MSDS), pixel correlation, image variance and the left alternating
current (AC) energy is theoretically analyzed, and then PSNR is constructed as the function of MSDS and left AC energy. The left AC energy
cannot be exactly measured in decoded image, hence that it is replaced
by the index of the last nonzero coefficients for simplicity. Benefit from
this arrangement, the proposed algorithm produces more accurate results
over the-state-of-art NRPE algorithms.

Keywords: Mean squared difference of slope · Nonzero coefficients
No reference · PSNR estimate

1 Introduction

JPEG compression is widely used for image delivery and recording, and to monitor its quality is an important issue. Compared with the perceived image quality,
PSNR is an objective metric to truly reflect the signal changes. Therefore, PSNR
is more attractive metric for some applications, for example, to evaluate image
quality of surveillance system or to control the strength of denoising.

Because JPEG and intra-picture of MPEG stream share similar compression
procedure, their PSNR estimates are overviewed as follow. PSNR is to measure
the difference between original and the distorted images, and it requires source

© Springer International Publishing AG, part of Springer Nature 2018
B. Zeng et al. (Eds.): PCM 2017, LNCS 10736, pp. 693–701, 2018.
https://doi.org/10.1007/978-3-319-77383-4_68

signal as reference. For monitoring purposes, the no reference measurement will be more preferred one. Based on the statistical properties of discrete cosine transform (DCT) coefficients, Turaga et al. [1] estimate PSNR for intra-pictures of MPEG-2 video under fixed quantization and get good performance. Knee [2,3] uses DCT coefficients data, the number of coefficient bits, and quantizer-scale to estimate PSNR (named as "PAR"), but it requires to calibrate the parameters through preliminary experiments. Without requirements of the preliminary experiments, Ichigaya et al. [4] give a new method of PSNR estimate for MPEG-2 bit stream under a rate control scheme, which must get the source information from the statistical properties of decoded pictures. Considering the coherence among adjacent blocks, Wang et al. [5] learn this coherence from the image examples and use it for PSNR estimate, rather than the distribution of DCT block itself. Alternatively, Yang et al. [6] use block-based DCT coefficients with shifted block boundary position from the compressed image to estimate the statistical distribution parameter of the DCT coefficients in original image. Although it produces good results, but the influences of the shifting and quantization are not fully studied in [6].

Statistical model of DCT coefficients is the key for PSNR estimate. The individual compressed block cannot offer enough information for modeling, especially for heavily compressed copies. It is well known that there is high correlation among the adjacent pixels and this correlation will be destroyed by compression. The correlation change with the compression is theoretically analyzed in this paper, resulting in that the correlation and variance of original block can be determined by the MSDS and residual energy of the compressed copies. Therefore, PSNR is estimated by MSDS and residual energy. Finally, we utilize the position of last nonzero DCT coefficients to represent residual energy, which makes PSNR estimate more tractable.

In Sect. 2, quantization procedure is formulated and its influences on the factors, such as coherence, variance, MSDS and residual energy, are discussed. Section 2 gives a tractable PSNR estimate. Then, some experiments are implemented to verify the performance of the proposed algorithm in Sect. 4. Finally, some conclusions are given in Sect. 5.

2   Model of JPEG Degradation

2.1   Quantization Noise Description

The compressed image I_d and its low-pass filtered copy I_o have follow relationship

$$I_d = I_o + N_q \tag{1}$$

where N_d is the quantization noise. The correlation of N_q pixels is separable in both horizontal and vertical directions, which can be approximately by a Laplacian distribution with zero mean and a separable covariance

$$r(m, n) = \sigma_f^2 \rho^m \rho^n \tag{2}$$

where m and n are the horizontal and vertical distance between two pixels, σ_f^2 is the variance of the pixel values, and $|\rho| \le 1$ is the correlation coefficient. Follow, we will utilize this statistical property to develop the theoretical model for PSNR estimate.

JPEG utilizes DCT to concentrate the block energy into several coefficients. This procedure is represented by $\hat{I}_o^B = A \cdot I_o^B \cdot A^T$, where A is the basis vector of DCT. I_o^B is the block of I_o, and $\hat{I}_o^B$ is the DCT for I_o^B. The variance of $\hat{N}_q$ will be

$$\hat{\sigma}_F^2(u,v) = \sigma_f^2 \left[ARA^T\right]_{u,u} \left[ARA^T\right]_{v,v} \tag{3}$$

where (u,v) is coefficient index in DCT block, and R is the covariance matrix as

$$R = \begin{bmatrix} 1 & \rho & \rho^2 & & \rho^7 \\ \rho & 1 & \rho & \cdots & \\ \rho^2 & \rho & 1 & & \\ & & & \cdot & \\ & & & & \cdot \cdot \\ \rho^7 & & & & 1 \end{bmatrix}_{8 \times 8} \tag{4}$$

Brandao et al. [9] suggest that DCT coefficients accord with the Laplacian distribution as

$$f(x) = \frac{\lambda(u,v)}{2} \exp(-\lambda(u,v)\,|x|) \tag{5}$$

where $\lambda(u,v)$ is the parameter of the Laplacian function, and x is the value of DCT coefficients. $\lambda(u,v)$ is inversely proportional to the variance of DCT coefficients in (u,v) position as

$$\lambda(u,v) = \frac{\sqrt{2}}{\hat{\sigma}_F^2(u,v)} \tag{6}$$

If image I_o is compressed, $\hat{\sigma}_F^2(u,v)$ is no longer located in the range of $(-\infty, +\infty)$, and will be limited within $(-\Delta/2, +\Delta/2)$, where Δ is quantization step for the (u,v)th coefficients. $\hat{\sigma}_F^2(u,v)$ will be replaced by $\tilde{\sigma}_F^2(u,v)$ as

$$\tilde{\sigma}_F^2(u,v) = \frac{1}{\Delta} \int_{-\Delta/2}^{+\Delta/2} \left(f(x) - \frac{1}{\Delta} \int_{-\Delta/2}^{\Delta/2} f(t)dt\right)^2 dx \tag{7}$$

$\tilde{\sigma}_F^2(u,v)$ is usually less than $\hat{\sigma}_F^2(u,v)$, and $\sum_i \sum_j \tilde{\sigma}_F^2(u,v)$ is also less than $\sum_i \sum_j \hat{\sigma}_F^2(u,v)$ It appears as the lost details, such as blurring. Therefore, $\tilde{\sigma}_F^2(u,v)$ is the function F_1 of ρ, σ_f^2 and Δ as

$$\tilde{\sigma}_F^2(u,v) = F_1(\rho, \sigma_f^2, \Delta) \tag{8}$$

By $\tilde{\sigma}_F^2(u,v)$, we can produce new correlation matrix $\tilde{R}$.

Heavy compression often incurs blocking and ringing. MSDS is widely used to depict the impact of these quantization noises on block boundary, which are

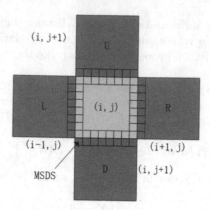

Fig. 1. Demonstration of MSDS calculation

the intensity gradient of the pixels close to the boundary. Let i and j be the block coordinates in horizontal and vertical directions. Suppose that blocks L and R are the left and right blocks of the block (i,j), and U and D are the upper and down blocks of block (i,j), as shown in Fig. 1. MSDS of the block (i,j) is defined as

$$\text{MSDS}_{i,j} = \text{MSDS}_{L,i,j} + \text{MSDS}_{R,i,j} + \text{MSDS}_{U,i,j} + \text{MSDS}_{D,i,j} \qquad (9)$$

MSDS of block (i,j) and its left neighbor is given in (9), and MSDSs in the other directions can be deduced in the same way.

$$\text{MSDS}_{L,i,j} = \sum_{k=0}^{N-1} \left[\frac{1}{2} \left(3I_{i,j}(k,0) - I_{i,j}(k,1) \right) - \frac{1}{2} \left(3I_{i,j-1}(k,N-1) - I_{i,j-1}(k,N-2) \right) \right]^2 \qquad (10)$$

where N is the block size in horizontal or vertical direction. $I_{i,j}(m,n)$ is the pixel value, where (m,n) are the relative coordinate of pixel in block (i,j).

Original images are smoothness ones and without blocking artifacts. Therefore, MSDS usually comes from compression, and its value can also be calculated by the theoretical model of the pixel correlation as

$$\text{MSDS} = F_2(\rho, \sigma_f^2, \Delta) \qquad (11)$$

where F_2 is a quadratic equation. Cooperated with (8), we determine ρ and σ_f^2 from the measurable metrics $\tilde{\sigma}_F^2(u,v)$ and MSDS under the given Δ.

2.2   PSNR Calculation

In the past, quantization noise of JPEG image is often modeled by uniform distribution [10], generalized Gaussian distribution [11], Gaussian mixtures [12], generalized gamma [13], zero-mean Laplace [14] and Cauchy [15,16] PDFs. Among these models, zero-mean Laplace model [7,8] is the most popular one because it balances the accuracy and the simplicity. It is also used in this paper for PSNR estimate.

If the decoded DCT coefficient $X_q(u,v) = x_q$ lies in $[q_l^{u,v}, q_{l+1}^{u,v})$, its probability distribution will be $\gamma \cdot f_{u,v}(x)$ inside the quantization interval and zeros outside this interval, where γ is the normalization constant. The quantization error of the (u,v)-th coefficient is calculated as

$$\sigma_{E_x}^2(u,v) = \gamma \int_{q_l^{u,v}}^{q_{l+1}^{u,v}} (x_q - x)^2 f_{x[u,v]}(x) dx \tag{12}$$

Block PSNR is the sum of all quantization error of its DCT coefficients as

$$PSNR_B = \sum_{u=1}^{8} \sum_{v=1}^{8} \sigma_{E_x}^2(u,v) \tag{13}$$

2.3   Theoretical Model for PSNR Estimate

We have demonstrated that MSDS, and $PSNR_B$ are the functions of ρ and σ_f^2, and their relationship are plotted in Fig. 2. Their ideal relationship is shown in Fig. 2(a), where M represents $\tilde{\sigma}_F^2(u,v)$. PSNR decays with MSDS increasing, which corresponds to the compressed image with more and more obvious block artifacts. PSNR and M have similar relationship. Large M means the compressed block with much residual energy, which is usually with abundant details in its original version. Therefore, PSNRs of these compressed blocks are usually lower than that with small M, if they are compressed with same quantization parameters. Figure 2(a) is just coincident with this general knowledge.

If images are exactly matching with (2), the pair (MSDS,M) will diverge from the curve of Fig. 2(a). We interpolate Fig. 2(a) to produce the fitting surface as Fig. 2(b), which is a more robust model for PSNR estimate.

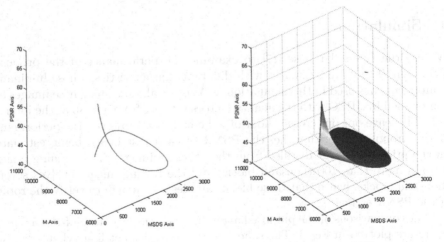

Fig. 2. Theoretical model of PSNR (quality factor = 20)

3   Algorithm Implementation

Because PSNR is the function of MSDS and $\tilde{\sigma}_F^2(u,v)$, we first discuss how to estimate MSDS and $\tilde{\sigma}_F^2(u,v)$, Natural image is usually smoothness, hence that MSDS is resulted from the compression and can be directly calculated on the decoded image by (9) and (10). $\tilde{\sigma}_F^2(u,v)$ rests with ρ, σ_f^2 and quantization parameter (QP). For the given pixel correlation, the amplitude of AC coefficients usually decreases with the frequency increasing. Therefore, we try to use the index of the highest frequency nonzero DCT coefficients (IHFNC) to represent $\tilde{\sigma}_F^2(u,v)$, i.e. modeling $\tilde{\sigma}_F^2(u,v)$ as the function of QP and the positions of nonzero DCT coefficients.

PSNR estimate is decomposed to two steps: training and testing.

Training stage:

1. Images in training set are compressed with different quality scores, such as 5,10,15,20, 25, 30, 35 and 40, to produce JPEG image copies;
2. Decompose JPEG images to some 8×8 blocks, and these blocks are the units for PSNR estimate;
3. Calculate the MSDS, IHFNC, QP and MSE for these blocks to produce their feature set FET_{train}(MSDS, IHFNC, QP, MSE);
4. Use support vector machine to build PSNR estimate model M_{PSNR}, where MSDS, IHFNC, QP are the input variables, and MSE is the output result;

Testing stage:

1. Image to be test is decomposed into blocks as the training stage;
2. Distill the MSDS, IHFNC, QP for each blocks to form the feature set $FET_{test} = (\text{MSDS}, \text{IHFNC}, \text{QP})$;
3. Feed FET_{test} to M_{PSNR}, and estimate its MSE;
4. Average MSEs of all block samples, and calculate PSNR for test image;

4   Simulation

We use the LIVE database [17] to examine the performance of the proposed algorithm. There are 29 images with different characteristics, whose luminance components are used in this simulation as Yang et al. done [6]. These images are compressed by JPEG with the quality factors ranging from 5 to 40 at the interval of 5. The leave one out cross-validation scheme is used to verify the performance of the proposed algorithm, i.e. the PSNR of each test image being estimated on the prior knowledge distilled from the other 28 images. The training images contain more than 100 thousand blocks and the testing image involves several thousand blocks, hence that these block samples are enough to verify the robust of the PSNR estimate.

The comparisons of the proposed algorithm and the last state-of-the-art algorithm are plotted in Fig. 3. The solid line is the equivalent line, where the estimated PSNRs equal to true PSNRs. The scatter plots in Fig. 3(a) are closer to

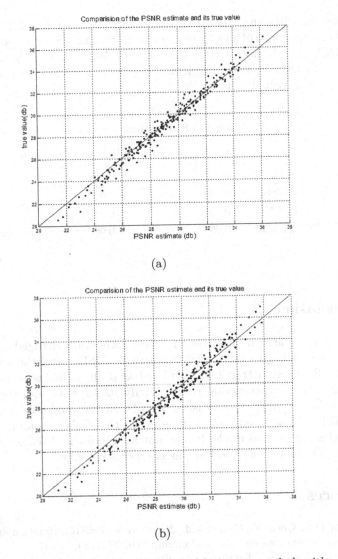

Fig. 3. Scatter plots of PSNR estimate results. (a) the proposed algorithm; (b) Yang algorithm [6].

the equivalent line than that in Fig. 3(b). For better analyses, we evaluate their performances by some numerical metrics often used, such as the mean absolute error (MAE), root mean square error (RMSE), Pearson linear correlation coefficient(PLCC), Spearman rank order correlation coefficient (SROCC). PLCC and SROCC are designed to describe the linear relatedness and monotonous relatedness of two data sets respectively, and their values are located within [0,1]. The PLCC and SROCC of the good estimate should approach 1 at the same time.

Table 1 indicates that the MAE and RMSE are reduced 25.5% and 17.2% respectively than that of the Yang algorithm [6]. Furthermore, both our PLCC and SROCC are 1% higher than that of the Yang [6] algorithm, even though PLCC and SROCC of Yang algorithm have been very close to 1 and to further improve them is very difficult.

Table 1. PSNR estimation results

	Proposed algorithm	Yang algorithm [6]
MAE(dB)	0.41	0.55
RMSE(dB)	0.53	0.64
PLCC	0.99	0.98
SROCC	0.99	0.98

5   Conclusion

In this paper, we first discuss how the pixel correlation changed with the compression, and then give two variables, such as MSDS and the left energy, to reflect PSNR. Then, a tractable learning based algorithm is proposed to estimate PSNR. The experimental results verify its superior and the robustness. Our algorithm produces the satisfied results on the moderate and high compressed JPEG images, but not very suits for the slightly compressed ones for their MSDSs are unmeasurable. It may not be a problem, because most existing PSNR estimators are just good in this compressed range.

References

1. Turaga, D.S., Chen, Y., Caviedes, J.: No reference PSNR estimation for compressed pictures. Signal Process. Image Commun. **19**, 173–184 (2004)
2. Knee, M.: A single-ended picture quality measure for MPEG-2. In: Proceedings of International Broad. Convention (IBC 2000), pp. 95–100, September 2000
3. Knee, M., Diggins, M.J.: World Intellectual Property Bureau, Improvements in Data Compression. International Patent Appl.WO00/22 834 (2000)
4. Ichigaya, A., Kurozumi, M., Hara, N., Nishida, Y., Nakasu, E.: A method of estimating coding PSNR using quantized DCT coefficients. IEEE Trans. Circuits Syst. Video Technol. **16**, 251–259 (2006)
5. Wang, C., Dong, H.Y., Wu, Z.K., Tan, Y.P.: Example-based objective quality estimation for compressed images. IEEE Multimedia **17**(3), 54–61 (2010)
6. Yang, G., Tan, Y.P.: Blind PSNR estimation using shifted blocks for JPEG images. IEEE Int. Symp. Circ. Syst. **19**(5), 1235–1238 (2011)
7. Jayant, N.S., Noll, P.: Digital Coding of Waveforms. Prentice-Hall, Englewood Cliffs (1984)

8. Pao, I.M., Sun, M.T.: Modeling DCT coefficients for fast video encoding. IEEE Trans. Circ. Syst. Video Technol. **9**, 608–616 (1999)

9. Brandao, T., Queluz, M.P.: No-reference image quality assessment based on DCT-domain statistics. Signal Process. **88**(4), 822–833 (2008)

10. Robertson, M.A., Stevenson, R.L.: DCT quantization noise in compressed images. IEEE Trans. Circ. Syst. Video Technol. **15**, 27–38 (2005)

11. Muller, F.: Distribution shape of two-dimensional DCT coefficients of natural images. Electron. Lett. **29**(22), 1935–1936 (1993)

12. Eude, T., Grisel, R., Cherifi, H., Debrie, R.: On the distribution of the DCT coefficients. In: Proceedings of the IEEE International Conference on Acoustics, Speech Signal Processing, vol. 5, pp. 365–368 (1994)

13. Chang, J.-H., Shin, J.W., Kim, N.S., Mitra, S.: Image probability distribution based on generalized gamma function. IEEE Signal Process. Lett. **12**(4), 325–328 (2005)

14. Lam, E., Goodman, J.: A mathematical analysis of the DCT coefficient distributions for images. IEEE Trans. Image Process. **9**(10), 1661–1666 (2000)

15. Eggerton, J., Srinath, M.: Statistical distributions of image DCT coefficients. Comput. Electr. Eng. **12**(3–4), 137–145 (1986)

16. Altunbasak, Y., Kamaci, N.: An analysis of the DCT coefficient distribution with the H.264 video coder. In: Proceedings of the IEEE International Conference Acoustics, Speech and Signal Process., vol. 3, pp. 177–180, May 2004

17. Sheikh, H.R., Wang, Z., Cormack, L., Bovik, A.C.: Live image quality assessment database release 2. http://live.ece.utexas.edu/research/quality

Speech Intelligibility Enhancement in Strong Mechanical Noise Based on Neural Networks

Feng Cheng[1,2,3], Xiaochen Wang[1,2,3(✉)], Li Gang[1,3],
Weiping Tu[1,2], and Jinshan Wang[1,3]

[1] National Engineering Research Center for Multimedia Software, School of Computer,
Wuhan University, Wuhan, China
justry2014@outlook.com, clowang@163.com, ligang10@yeah.net,
echotuwp@163.com, cy_wangjinshan@163.com
[2] Hubei Key Laboratory of Multimedia and Network Communication Engineering,
Wuhan University, Wuhan, China
[3] Research Institute of Wuhan University in Shenzhen, Shenzhen, China

Abstract. Speech intelligibility is a significant factor for successful speech communication. To enhance the intelligibility, many methods have been proposed, mainly by operating the speech signal such as increasing the amplitude or modifying the speech spectrum. However, their effects are limited when the background noise is extremely strong. In this paper, we purpose a preprocessed noise cancellation model to enhance the speech intelligibility by predicting the cancelling signal and superimposing it into the speech signal. We build a deep neural network (DNN) model to make the prediction algorithm have better accuracy. Finally, the effectiveness of the algorithm was verified by objective and subjective tests, the average of signal-to-noise ratio (SNR) improved 4.5 dB, the average of speech intelligibility index (SII) increased 5.4% and the average of comparison mean opinion score (CMOS) rose 1.16 on a variety of test cases.

Keywords: Speech intelligibility enhancement · Noise cancellation
Deep neural network · Signal prediction

1 Introduction

The development of modern communication technology makes cellphone becoming an important way for people to exchange information. We may have a cellphone connected in any environment, such as airport, curbside or noisy factory, so enhance the intelligibility of speech is particularly important when people located in a noisy environment. Most of studies focused on enhancing the far-end speech intelligibility, that is, assuming the speaker located in a noisy environment and trying to restore the clear speech from

X. Wang—This work is supported by National Nature Science Foundation of China (No. 61231015, 61671335); National High Technology Research and Development Program of China (863 Program) No. 2015AA016306; Hubei Province Technological Innovation Major Project (No. 2016AAA015).

the noisy speech. However, when the listener located in a noisy environment, the restored clear speech will still be masked by background noise, thus, the concept of speech intelligibility enhancement (IENH) had been proposed, it is also called near-end speech enhancement (NELE). In 2015, Kleijn published a review in the IEEE Signal Processing Magazine and made a general analysis about this topic [1].

In 1970s, some research has been done on IENH [2, 3], in recent years, numerous methods of this topic were continually being proposed [4–8]. For example, Sauert proposed a method enhancing the speech intelligibility by dynamic tuning the speech signal energy gain, it adopted calculating the signal-to-noise ratio (SNR) as the basis of adjusted parameters [4]. In consideration of acoustic masking characteristics in frequency, Zorila proposed a method non-adaptive to noise, enhancing the intelligibility by modifying the spectrum of the speech, called spectral shaping and dynamic range compression (SSDRC) [5]. Henning proposed a method amplifying the speech by calculating the speech intelligibility index (SII) [6, 9]. Petkov proposed a speech modification method adaptive to noise, called spectral dynamics recovery (SDR) [7]. However, when the environment is extremely noisy, cellphone or other hardware devices are usually limited on the power of loudspeaker, and too large volume may cause serious damage to human hearing, at the same time, too much spectral modification will also make the speech distorted, under these circumstances, we can consider this problem from the perspective of noise cancellation.

In this paper, we propose a preprocessed noise cancellation (PNC) model by superimposed the predicted cancelling signal into the speech signal in advance. We use deep neural networks (DNNs) to predict the cancelling signal. In order to make our algorithm meet the hard real-time requirement, the number of layers of the DNN is not very deep and all the noise signal was taken as additive noise. Actually, most of the noise we encounter can be divided as human noise and mechanical noise, the intensity of human noise is often limited, and the extremely strong noise is usually mechanical noise. Our method is mainly related to the extremal noisy environment, consequently, we use lots of mechanical noise signals as training input data cases. Finally, we confirmed the effectiveness of our algorithm by objective and subjective experiments.

2 Model Design

2.1 Traditional Speech Modification Model

Humans have different perceptual sensitivity to sound in frequency, there are perceptual masking effects between speech and noise. In order to make them have more identification, in many studies, they modified the spectral of speech signal. Methods for speech modification can be divided to non-adaptive and adaptive to noise (Figs. 1 and 2).

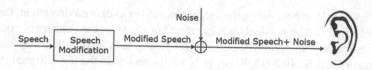

Fig. 1. Non-adaptive speech intelligibility enhancement model.

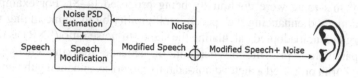

Fig. 2. Adaptive speech intelligibility enhancement model.

SSDRC is a representative algorithm of non-adaptive methods. Considering most noise signals are at low frequency, properly enhancing the frequency of speech signal can improve the perceptive intelligibility, but this method tends to be not effective at noise environments have complex frequency. SDR dynamic tuning the speech spectral to make the modification model has better adaptability, however, too much modification will make the speech distorted when the environment noise is extremely strong. They all focus on speech and left a large space to noise treatment. As a concurrent processing, we proposed the preprocessed noise cancellation (PNC) model to cannel the over-powerful noise signals, such as truck and aero engine's sounds.

2.2 Preprocessed Noise Cancellation Model

When two signals have same amplitude and inverted phase, their waveforms can cancel each other [10]. Based on this principle, we proposed such a method: superimposing the cancelling signal of the noise into the speech signal in advance. However, processing those data will lead to a short time delay, then bring unacceptable errors to the noise cancellation. Considering sound signal has certain autocorrelation in the time domain, accordingly, we can divide the noise signal to short-time frames and predict the next frame by its autocorrelation with the previous frame. With the development of DNN, the predictive signal has a certain degree of accuracy.

$$s'(m) = \left[s(m) + p(m) \right] + n(m) \tag{1}$$

where m is the order number of the frame. $s'(m)$ reflects the m frame of final signal we hearing, $s(m)$ is the m frame of original speech signal, $p(m)$ is the m frame of preprocessed cancellation noise signal, $n(m)$ is the m frame of actual noise signal.

Hence, what we except to achieve is minimizing the difference between the predicted cancelling noise and signal has same amplitude and reversed phase with actual noise, that is minimize

$$e(m) = p(m) - (-n(m)) = p(m) + n(m) \tag{2}$$

where the $e(m)$ is the m frame of final noise signal mixed in the speech signal we hearing. So the final signal we hearing is:

$$s'(m) = s(m) + e(m) \tag{3}$$

the PNC model is shown in Fig. 3.

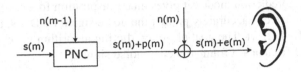

Fig. 3.   The model of PNC we proposed.

In order to let us hear the speech has a higher intelligibility, the goal of our algorithm is to minimize the $e(m)$, as to make $p(m)$ more similar to $-n(m)$. Therefore, we use DNN to predict the $p(m)$ from $n(m-1)$.

2.3   Combination Model

Traditional speech intelligibility methods focus more on adjusting the speech gaining or modifying the speech spectral to enlarge the identification of speech, PNC doesn't concentrate on speech modification but noise cancelling. They can operate independently to enhance the intelligibility in different ways, at the same time, we can combine those two kind of models. Figure 4 shows the combination model:

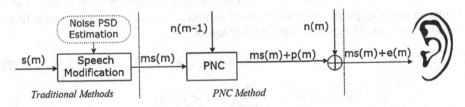

Fig. 4.   The combination model based on speech modification methods and PNC.

where $ms(m)$ means the m frame of modified speech. The final signal we hearing is:

$$s'(m) = ms(m) + e(m) \tag{4}$$

In the following parts of algorithm implementation and experiment modules, we choose the SSDRC represented to the non-adaptive method, SDR represented to the adaptive method to combine with respectively.

3 Algorithm Implementation

In the past several decades, many noise prediction methods have been proposed [10, 11]. Most of them were based on adaptive filter, through the frequency statistics of noise to predict the signal, but due to the non-stationary factor in noise, the tracking sometimes has unsatisfactory results. Recently, as the deep learning has gotten success in many prediction model, it gives much inspiration for speech intelligibility enhancement. If we can accurately predict the noise signal by DNN, the PNC model will have satisfied effect. The goal of our prediction algorithm is get the m frame of predicted signal from $m - 1$ frame of actual noise signal,

$$n(m - 1) \rightarrow p(m) \tag{5}$$

3.1 Neural Networks Structure Design

In order to make the algorithm have better real-time and accuracy, the structure of DNN is not very deep, we use back-propagation (BP) neural networks with 3 hidden layers as structure of DNN, use the mean square error (MSE) as performance function, and use stochastic gradient decent algorithm to minimize the MSE.

$$MSE(m) = \sqrt{\frac{\sum_{i=1}^{j}(p(i) + n(i))^2}{j}} \tag{6}$$

Where m is the frame number, j reflects the number of nodes in output layer. Because the values of signal are normalized and have negative values, moreover, and it is a nonlinear mapping pattern, we use the liner function as the output layer activation function tangent sigmoid function as all of other layers,

$$\alpha = \omega_1 x_1 + \omega_2 x_2 + \cdots + \omega_n x_n + 1 \tag{7}$$

$$y = f(\alpha) = 1 - \frac{2}{1 + e^{-2\alpha}} (-1 < y < 1) \tag{8}$$

Where n is the sum of nodes in previous layer, x_n are outputs value of previous layer, ω_n are values of weight, y is the output value of each node, f is the tangent sigmoid function. When we use one frame as input, it takes its next frame as output, the input and output layer has 160 nodes and hidden layers have 320 nodes. The target MSE performance is 0.005, learning rate is 0.0005, and the total number of epoch is 5000 (Fig. 5).

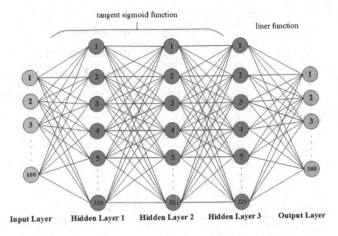

Fig. 5. DNN structure of cancelling signal prediction.

3.2 Neural Networks Training Data

Because the majority of extremely noisy environments we locate in are filled with mechanical noise, so we chose 40 mechanical noise material files from NOISEX-92 database [12] and TS103 224 Background Noise Database [13] as input of DNN, in order to leave some data as test set, we just selected the first 180s of every file from NOISEX-92. As for signal analysis, speech waveform was down-sampled to 8 kHz, and the corresponding frame length was set to 160 samples (20 ms).

3.3 Post Processing

The noise signal has a certain degree of autocorrelation while still very strong randomness, the purpose of the model is to cancelling a part of the noise energy, rather than completely eliminated. As a result, we have added a moving average filter to the predicted noise, which is to smoother the predicted noise so that not introduce more new noise.

$$p'(k) = \frac{1}{N} \sum_{i=0}^{N-1} p(k + i) \tag{9}$$

Where p' is the predicted noise after filter, p is the original predicted noise, k is the number of point, N is the coefficient of the moving average filter. With the increase of N, the signal will be smoother but gentler, so we made the $N = 5$. We chose the first frame of tested results to show the difference between actual noise, predicted noise and filtered predicted noise (Fig. 6).

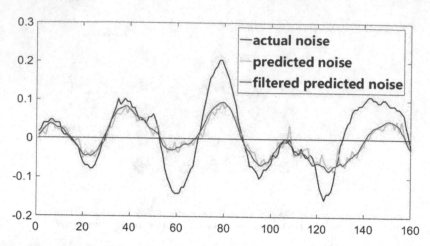

Fig. 6. The waveform comparison of actual noise, predicted noise and filtered predicted noise.

Experimental Results

For test the effect of the algorithm, we conducted objective test and subjective listening test separately. A male and female speech had been chosen from TIMIT database as tested speech signal [14]. We chose the 180 to 210 s of F-16, Leopard and Factory floor noise-1 from NOISEX-92 database as test set as separately present the scenes of noisy airport, roadside and factory.

3.4   Objective Test

SNR Comparison

signal-to-noise ratio (SNR) is an important evaluating indicator of speech intelligibility, there are strong and positive correlations between SNR and intelligibility. We composed the original speech signal and speech processed by SSDRC and SDR methods with three kinds of test noise mentioned above. Compare the SNR of those speech signal with and without PNC.

$$SNR = 10 * \log_{10} \frac{p(s)}{p(s' - s)} \tag{10}$$

Where the $p(s)$ is the total energy of speech signal, and the $p(s' - s)$ is the total energy of deviation between final speech signal we hearing and the original speech signal. The calculation of SNR is computed in dB.

From Figs. 7 and 8, we can see the SNRs have negligible change after the speech processed by SSDRC and SDR, separately descend 0.251 dB and ascend 0.071 dB on average. However, after combining the PNC module, the SNR has been significantly improved, separately ascend 4.499 dB and 4.483 dB on average. It can prove that our algorithm effectively reduces the noise energy from the results.

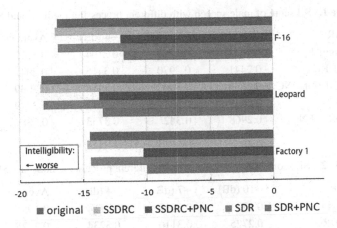

Fig. 7. SNR (dB) of male speech and tested noises.

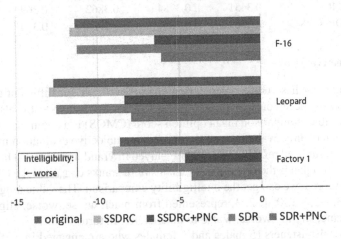

Fig. 8. SNR (dB) of female speech and tested noises.

SII Comparison

Another widely applied measurement method for evaluating speech quality is speech intelligibility index (SII) [9]. we measure the SII of original speech and speech processed by SSDRC and SDR separately with and without PNC. In order to simulate the different level noisy environment, we tested those SII at different SNR. Because our method aims to enhance the intelligibility in strong noise, the SNR of tested situations are at low numerical levels. The results obtained are shown in the following tables.

From Tables 1 and 2, we can see the SII scores have separately improved 60.4% and 87.1% after processed by SSDRC and SDR without PNC on average, at the same time, they have further improved 5.6% and 5.2% combined with PNC. In addition, the further improvement of SII score brought by PNC is more significantly in relatively lower SNR situation, improved 3.4% in −4 dB SNR, 5.4% in −7 dB SNR, 8.0 in −10 dB SNR on average.

Table 1. SII score of male speech with different processing methods and SNRs.

SNR	−10 (dB)	−7 (dB)	−4 (dB)	Average
Original	0.1433	0.1789	0.2104	0.1775
SSDRC	0.2441	0.2970	0.3415	0.2942
SSDRC + PNC	0.2568	0.3062	0.3486	0.3039
SDR	0.2849	0.3311	0.3677	0.3279
SDR + PNC	0.2968	0.342	0.3753	0.3380

Table 2. SII score of female speech with different process methods and SNRs.

SNR	−10 (dB)	−7 (dB)	−4 (dB)	Average
Original	0.1723	0.2017	0.2114	0.1951
SSDRC	0.2725	0.3116	0.3234	0.3025
SSDRC + PNC	0.2865	0.324	0.3303	0.3136
SDR	0.3451	0.3784	0.3862	0.3699
SDR + PNC	0.3569	0.3867	0.3936	0.3791

3.5 Subjective Test

As the human ear has auditory perception characteristic, it's insufficient to judge the intelligibility of speech only by those objective index, Subjective test is also necessary and irreplaceable. comparison mean opinion score (CMOS) is a common method in the field of speech quality evaluation, so we chose it as subjective evaluation methodology [15]. The distorted and reference signals are played in a random order and listeners were not told which signal is the reference. by means of the ranks consulted the CMOS rating the listener scored, we can get the intelligibility comparison. The value range of CMOS rating is −3, −2, −1, 0, 1, 2, 3, represented from much worse, worse, slightly worse, about the same, slightly worse, worse to much better in turn.

We chose 10 listeners (5 males and 5 females who are engaged in audio research, and between the ages of 20 and 30 years old) to score the tested series without knowing

Table 3. CMOS on average: A means the SSDRC method, B means the SDR method, P means the PNC method; S1, 2 are tested speech1, 2; N1, 2, 3 are tested noise1, 2, 3.

Tested Signals	A/O	B/O	A + P/A	B + P/B
S1 N1	1.20	0.60	1.30	1.10
S1 N2	0.40	0.50	0.70	0.90
S1 N3	1.10	0.70	1.20	0.90
S2 N1	1.80	0.80	1.40	1.60
S2 N2	0.90	1.00	1.10	1.20
S2 N3	1.40	0.90	1.50	1.00
Average	1.13	0.75	1.20	1.12

the order, and the tested speech and noise signals we chose were identical with the objective tests.

From the Table 3, we can see that the SSDRC and the SDR separately improve the CMOS 1.13 and 0.75 on average. Besides, the intelligibility further enhances significantly after processed by PNC, separately improve 1.20 and 1.12 on average, it denotes the PNC made the intelligibility of tested speech improved between slightly better and better.

4 Conclusions

In this paper, a speech enhancement models based on the DNN is proposed. Whether from the objective test or subjective test results, we can see the traditional methods and our proposed PNC method cooperate with each other, in terms of modifying the speech spectrum and cancelling the noise to achieve the common effect as enhancing the speech intelligibility, at the same time, they can also operate independently. In the future research, we will focus on taking jointly optimal near-end and far-end, reverberation index and scene discrimination into our model to achieve better results and performance [16, 17].

References

1. Kleijn, W.B., Crespo, J.B., Hendriks, R.C., et al.: Optimizing speech intelligibility in a noisy environment: a unified view. IEEE Signal Process. Mag. **32**(2), 43–54 (2015)
2. Niederjohn, R., Grotelueschen, J.: The enhancement of speech intelligibility in high noise levels by high-pass filtering followed by rapid amplitude compression. IEEE Trans. Acoust. Speech Signal Process. **24**(4), 277–282 (1976)
3. Niederjohn, R., Grotelueschen, J.: Speech intelligibility enhancement in a power generating noise environment. IEEE Trans. Acoust. Speech Signal Process. **26**(4), 378–380 (1978)
4. Sauert, B., Vary, P.: Near end listening enhancement: Speech intelligibility improvement in noisy environments. In: IEEE International Conference on Acoustics, Speech and Signal Processing ICASSP 2006. IEEE, vol. 1, pp. I-I (2006)
5. Zorila, T.C., Kandia, V., Stylianou, Y.: Speech-in-noise intelligibility improvement based on spectral shaping and dynamic range compression. In: Thirteenth Annual Conference of the International Speech Communication Association (2012)
6. Schepker, H.F., Rennies, J., Doclo, S.: Improving speech intelligibility in noise by SII-dependent preprocessing using frequency-dependent amplification and dynamic range compression. In: INTERSPEECH. pp. 3577–3581 (2013)
7. Petkov, P.N., Kleijn, W.B.: Spectral dynamics recovery for enhanced speech intelligibility in noise. IEEE/ACM Trans. Audio, Speech Lang. Process. (TASLP) **23**(2), 327–338 (2015)
8. Goli, P., Karami-mollaei, M.R.: Speech intelligibility improvement in noisy environments based on energy correlation in frequency bands. Digit. Signal Proc. **62**, 238–248 (2017)
9. ANSI A. S3.: 5–1997, Methods for the calculation of the speech intelligibility index. New York: American National Standards Institute, **19**, 90–119 (1997)
10. Widrow, B., Glover, J.R., McCool, J.M., et al.: Adaptive noise cancelling: Principles and applications. Proc. IEEE **63**(12), 1692–1716 (1975)

11. Guarnaccia, C.: Advanced tools for traffic noise modelling and prediction. WSEAS Trans. Syst. **12**(2), 121–130 (2013)
12. Varga, A., Steeneken, H.J.M., Tomlinson, M., et al.: The NOISEX-92 study on the effect of additive noise on automatic speech recognition. Technical Report, DRA Speech Research Unit (1992)
13. ETSI TS 103 224: A sound field reproduction method for terminal testing including a background noise database. European Telecommunications Standards Institute (2014)
14. Zue, V., Seneff, S., Glass, J.: Speech database development at MIT: TIMIT and beyond. Speech Commun. **9**(4), 351–356 (1990)
15. Recommendation I. 800: Methods for subjective determination of transmission quality. International Telecommunication Union (1996)
16. Khademi, S., Hendriks, R.C., Kleijn, W.B.: Jointly optimal near-end and far-end multi-microphone speech intelligibility enhancement based on mutual information. In: IEEE International Conference on Acoustics, Speech and Signal Processing (ICASSP). IEEE, pp. 654–658 (2016)
17. Petkov, P.N., Stylianou, Y.: Adaptive Gain Control for Enhanced Speech Intelligibility Under Reverberation[J]. IEEE Signal Process. Lett. **23**(10), 1434–1438 (2016)

Interactive Temporal Visualization
of Collaboration Networks

Ming Jing[✉], Xueqing Li, and Yupeng Hu

Department of Computer Science and Technology, Shandong University,
Jinan 250001, Shandong, China
{jingming,xqli,huyupeng}@sdu.edu.cn

Abstract. Interactive visual analysis plays an important role to understand complex dataset. Literature data are most often visualized as collaboration networks to show the connection between researchers. However, the static networks barely transfer much information when the dataset including temporal variable. In this paper, we propose an embedded network visualization to display the temporal patterns hiding in the data and to avoid occlusion by intelligent filters. We research different graph style such as temporal display and direction to find the best way to present the temporal feature. Also, we demonstrate the usability of our approach with case studies on real bibliographic databases.

Keywords: Collaboration networks · Temporal visualization
Bibliographic analysis

1 Introduction

A large number of scientific publications have been presented these decades. To analyze and discover the feature hiding in the data is an important task to understand the data quickly and directly. Many online databases, such as DBLP, are available for researchers to survey [1].

The academic social networks are typically based on co-authorship and co-citation relationship among researchers and publications. Some popular variables such as subject, author and citation, are very useful to understand the situation [2, 3]. When the relationship between entities gets intricate, the network would become huge and over-lapping [4]. Technologies such as clustering [5] and threshold filtering, the final view would be simplified to a great extent. Besides, with the help of coloring and shading, network view displays patterns intuitively. However, it becomes more difficult when the dataset contains temporal information. Compared to other unsteady dataset with space and temporal information in scientific computing, academic social network always along with complex lines or curves which is possible to be a mess even for steady data [6].

Given the additional temporal information, bibliographic analysis has to include a new channel to display the features along the time dimension. It is practicable to add a time line separately which often shows up on the bottom of the screen. The time line combines some interested events that can be interacted to observe details. Generally, the more events the data has, the longer the time line is. Sometime, the time line goes

B. Zeng et al. (Eds.): PCM 2017, LNCS 10736, pp. 713–722, 2018.
https://doi.org/10.1007/978-3-319-77383-4_70

cross multiple screens. That is awful to understand the time features. Some other researchers first simplify by clustering and then arrange different color for time dimension [7]. The key of these kinds of methods is the specific algorithm to clustering and coloring. And that display always needs much time to learn the patterns.

In this paper, we address the problem of finding a way to embed the temporal information into networks. We present a novel context preserving visualization technique to integrate temporal displays into networks. Our method utilizes the empty line spaces or the strokes of points (presented as objects of authors or papers) on the network. An algorithm of carving is developed to keep the graph balance when the user interacts with interface. To avoid occlusion, we introduce the method to bundle lines to decrease the number of lines. To the best of our knowledge, it is the first literature study on embedding temporal displays in a collaboration network. We demonstrate our method with case studies on real bibliographic data. The main contributions of our work are summarized as follows.

(1) It is the first attempt that embeds the temporal display onto bibliographic network. Compared to other temporal displays, such as labels, time line, time windows and animation, our method is much clear and simple.
(2) Analyze the key design of embedded temporal visualization including the time line patterns, time orientation and width of time lines.
(3) Application our method on the real IEEE VIS conference series data to demonstrate the result.

The major contents of this paper are summarized as below. First, we summarize the related work on time-oriented information visualization and bibliographic analysis technologies. Then we describe the framework and details of our proposed method in Sects. 3 and 4. And give the case study to show the visualization results in Sect. 5. At last, we draw conclusion based on our discussion and outline of future work.

2   Related Work

2.1   Time-Oriented Data Visualization

Time-oriented data visualization requires dedicated visualization tools. A large variety of time-oriented visualization techniques have been proposed, many of which are useful for domain-specific datasets [8]. For examples, History Flow is used to visualize text edit history and is very effectively at conveying changes over time and revealing typical patterns. Bach et al. [9] proposed a general approach, named time curves, for visualizing patterns of evolution in temporal data by folding the timeline. Other techniques are more generic and can be applied to a wider range of datasets, many of which are derived from space-time cube representation [10], such as small multiples, time-flattened views, animations and 3D space-time cubes.

2.2   The Bibliographic Analysis

Over the last decade, some library datasets have been used to do bibliographic analysis, such as DBLP, IEEE trans [11] or IEEE conferences data. Xu et al. [12] analysis the CNKI series database to study the coauthor cooperation relationship. From these datasets, research topics, co-author, co-citation [13] and collaboration relationships are mined and visualized on the screen. A deep learning model is applied by Wang et al. [2] to represent coauthor network features for relationships identification, which has better performance compared with other state-of-the-art methods. And Daud et al. [14] apply machine learning techniques to predict features in the co-author networks. Billah et al. [15] designed and trained a SVM classifier to identify and predict the emerging researchers. Sándor [16] involved the temporal data into bibliographic coupling to discover cognitive structure of research areas.

While the dataset includes complex information, the network-like visualization always displays the mess result. Some network simplify algorithms are proposed to make the view clearer. Daud et al. [17] apply the Latent Dirichlet Allocation algorithm, one of the topic modeling techniques to capturing the group level structures and temporal trends in the academic social network. Meanwhile, interaction technologies are very useful to explore the interested features among the plenty of objects. Jiang [18] designed a simple effective interface and a hierarchical topic model for mining cross-domain research topic. Varlamis et al. [19] proposed a representation model for visualizing bibliographic databases as graphs and suggest potential synergies between researchers. Besides the basic analysis, the temporal information in the dataset gets more attentions.

3   Proposed Technique

In this paper, we use IEEE VIS conference series data from 1990–2015 to illustrate the usage of our method. The data used in our experiments contain IEEE VIS publication, i.e. InfoVis, SciVis, VAST, or Vis. Each record consists 11 fields: conference type, publication year, paper title, DOI, abstract, author names, references (inside this dataset only), and so on. We treat the papers and authors as nodes respectively, while citation or others as directed edges of a network.

3.1   Motivation

The general goal of our system is to support analysis of temporal patterns in bibliographic networks. We hope to take into account the time-varying information when analyzing patterns of attributes. We observe that few concerned tasks performed commonly in this kind of visualization: (1) What topic is going popular lately? (2) How often the collaboration between authors in the past few years? (3) What's the trend of research topic along time? Based on those tasks, we have few goals for our method as following.

(1)   The design should display the temporal information bundling to each object. Abstract the temporal trend for topics. Embedded these features into the networks

links. Also, we consider some different design candidates to choose appropriate models for the final visual result.

(2) The design should be simple and clear to read. Because the dataset may include complex relationship, information has to be simplified by cutting off or clustering. Setting thresholds for each key parameter can decrease the number of objects to display. Meanwhile, take full advantage of coloring to delight the important patterns.

(3) The design should be easy to interact. According to user's demand, provide an interaction interface to help observing the visual result efficiently. The location of objects can be dragged to a wider space to avoid overlapping and occlusion. Select a specific object to check its details or trends along time.

3.2   System Overview

Figure 1 shows the pipeline of our system that contains three major components. The data component load and pre-process data on demand. The visualization component computes the position and size of each object. According to the task analysis, mentioned in Sect. 3.1, we classify the objects by the topic and field then group them by some specific rules. Concerned their complex relationship, apply lines bundling algorithm and community detection technology to reduce the number of the links. Then, visualization all groups as force-directed network with focused elements. After that, embed the temporal information into the links or objects. In the last component, user can select any

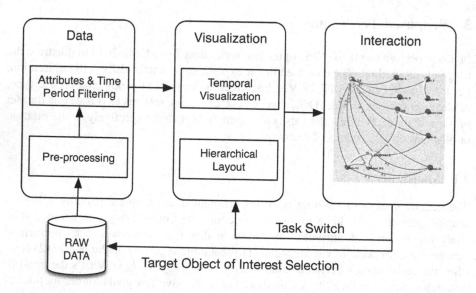

Fig. 1. System overview. The data component deals with pro-processing and filter data according to user's configuration. The Visualization module supports the temporal display technology. The interaction part provides user interactions to help them observing the result more efficiently. (Color figure online)

elements they are interested in and the relative information will display automatically for further analysis.

The force-directed graph layout is one of the most popular graph layout techniques. The layout is preferred in many applications because it can provide appropriate distances between pairs of connected nodes. It assumes that edges of graph have a spring-like forces attempting to keep stable lengths. In addition, the layout can flexibly stabilize the distances of nodes by adjusting the weights of edges [20].

The force-directed layout's drawback, however, is computation time. Many implementations attempt to minimize the sum of the energy of edges by iterative calculation, and the worst case running time is proportional to the square of number of nodes. To solve this problem, many acceleration force-directed techniques have recently been presented [21].

Community detection has many uses in the field of network analysis. Hierarchical clustering is one method to find community structures in network. The technique arranges the network into a hierarchy of groups according to a specified weight function. Hierarchical clustering can either be agglomerative or divisive depending on whether one proceeds through the algorithm by adding links to or removing links from the network, respectively. The fast modularity community structure inference algorithm [22] is a technique based on an agglomerative clustering algorithm, which firstly treat each node as a separate cluster and then progressively merge clusters. Alternatively, divisive clustering algorithms firstly treat the entire graph as a cluster and then recursively split the cluster into smaller clusters. The Girvan–Newman algorithm, which we apply in current implementation, is one of the divisive techniques.

4   Temporal Display Design

4.1   Data Preprocessing

The raw data is a text file in comma separated value format, the data fields of which contains year, paper title, paper doi, abstract, author names, etc. The application retrieves the data of year field and defines the range of time, simultaneously, the co-author network is aggregated from the data of author names fields. Before translating the logical co-author network into geometry space, the Girvan-Newman algorithm, one of the divisive communication detection techniques, is applied to detect the author communication in the network. To enhance the visualization effect, the application turns the geometry space into hierarchical layout by involving the squarified treemaps algorithm to process the network communication information.

4.2   Time Direction

Embedding temporal displays on two dimension networks could disturb the readability if some problems don't be solved reasonably. Time direction of temporal displays on the links is one of them. As the links could be of any slope according to the positions of objects they connect. There are few candidate design choices, such as text labels, color, arrow and so on. Figure 2 shows different design candidates to compare.

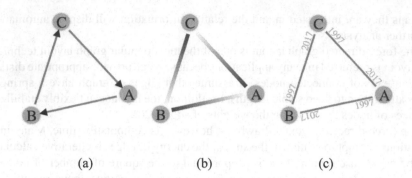

Fig. 2. Different time direction design using arrow (a), color (b), and text labels (c). (Color figure online)

In general, direction obeys on Cartesian coordinate system principle, i.e., the direction of time flow is left to right for horizontal links and bottom to top for vertical links. However, it is not suitable for a mess of lines when the similar nodes are located on the same side and the links would be more likely overlapped. Additional arrows can indicate the time direction on demand without the limitation of nodes' location. But the size of arrows is one of the concerns to match the display. If the arrow were large, it would occupy much space; otherwise, the arrows would be too small to recognize.

Coloring is popular to use in visual analysis because of human's sensitivity to color, such as saturation, opacity, or a sequential color scheme to indicate time direction as shown in Fig. 2(b). But it uses a specific channel which could interfere with the understanding of visualization especially there are other few color channels.

Besides, text label is another choice for time indicator. It can locate on the end of links or along the links. Text label is clearer on time lines than coloring to find the right time point while interacting with interface. However, when the quantity of elements displaying get larger, location of text labels could cause misunderstanding.

We observe that the main problem here is to find a design, which has an easy understanding style like arrow and a simple link; so, we introduce directed curves instead of

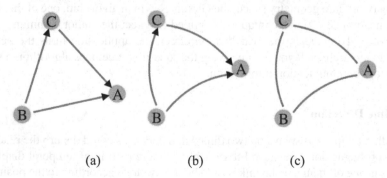

Fig. 3. Time direction designs using (a) arrows, (b) directed curves and (c) undirected curves respectively. (c) is the design we take. (Color figure online)

lines as shown in Fig. 3. Let's take directed line BC as an example. We compute a point p on the right of the line while facing the arrow direction to draw an equilateral triangle. Then set point p as the circle center to draw an arc to cross the B and C. Here the angle theta could be any value between 0 to PI.

For our proposed method, direction between nodes means the contributing direction, which always points from an author to another author more important. Here, we use the amount of the published papers as the author's importance level. For example, the situation in Fig. 3 shows that author A has a high importance level than author B and author C. So, here author A is more like a center of collaboration group. We can find out the most important authors very quickly by the proposed method.

4.3 Temporal Data Visualization

The temporal display is another key design in our proposed method. The ideal design should be clear, simply and intuitive to the temporal features. We have few choices as shown in Fig. 4. Single-side or double-side river (shown in Fig. 4(a) and (b)) is suitable for embedded display which is smooth and harmonious. These kinds of design are popular to visualize temporal data. However, it is inconvenient to interact while some data on a specific time point is asked to show. Figure 4(c) displays bars chart on links.

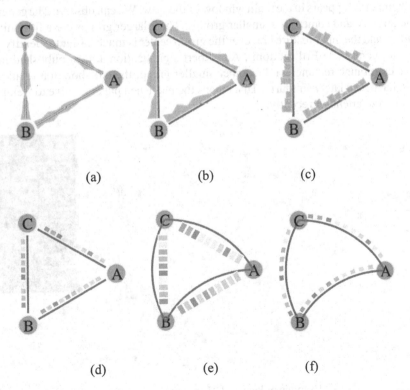

Fig. 4. Different temporal display embedded in links: time river (a), single side river (b), bars (c), color wall ((d), (e) and (f)). (f) is the final design. (Color figure online)

Temporal feature is discrete along the time direction. The height of bars identifies the quantity of feature. Figure 4(d)–(f) display different color walls of our method where Fig. 4(c) is the basic display. If color wall is separated with time direction (shown in Fig. 4(e)), the visual result is hard to match. So we combine the color wall and directed curve to display the temporal feature. Here, each rectangle represents a value on a time spot and the color represents the amount of this value. Color is a popular element to use. We draw the information rectangles as saturation low to high representing the value from small to big.

5   Results

In this section, we demonstrate the usage and effectiveness of our technique by applying to real bibliographic dataset consisting of full papers published during 1990 to 2015, provided by the Digital Library. We filter the title, publication year, abstract, references and authors from file. We implemented the proposed technique with D3 (Data-driven Document), which is a JavaScript library for manipulating documents based on data.

Keyword is a useful filter to select a topic and category. It is the most popular search parameter to find relative literatures. Figure 5 shows a visualization result when a user input keyword "temporal" and set the paper amount threshold as 3. The data containing only "temporal" appears in the main window of the view. We can observe 2 larger groups on the left side and some other smaller groups. The 2 larger groups are a litter difficult to understand the inner feature however the group center is much easier to identify: node Ebert (top) and node Ertl (bottom). And Ebert's publication almost published in past few years (orange rectangles). For other smaller group, the collaboration relationship almost happened lately similarly. That means the published paper relative to "temporal" had got more attention recently.

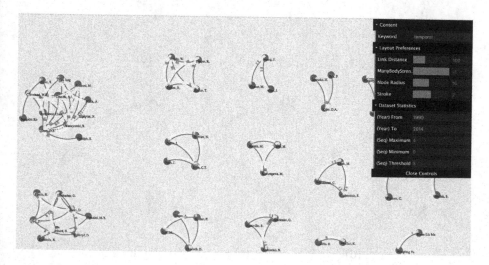

Fig. 5. Example of keyword "Temporal". (Color figure online)

6   Conclusion

We presented a temporal visualization technique of collaboration networks of publication papers. The main goal of this method is to embed the temporal features into the collaboration networks links. We discussed the designs of time direction and temporal display to ensure that the temporal visualization result is meaningful and easy to understand. We applied the technology to a real dataset to demonstrate the efficiency.

As a future work, we would like to research other temporal displays and conduct user evaluation. Also, more complex temporal relationship would be embedded into the networks.

References

1. Horak, Z., Kudelka, M., Snasel, V., Abraham, A., Rezankova, H.: Forcoa. NET: an interactive tool for exploring the significance of authorship networks in DBLP data. In: 2011 International Conference on Computational Aspects of Social Networks (CASoN), pp. 261–266. IEEE (2011)
2. Wang, W., Liu, J., Yu, S., Zhang, C., Xu, Z., Xia, F.: Mining advisor-advisee relationships in scholarly big data: a deep learning approach. In: 2016 IEEE/ACM Joint Conference on Digital Libraries (JCDL), pp. 209–210. IEEE (2016)
3. Chang, Y.-W., Huang, M.-H., Lin, C.-W.: Evolution of research subjects in library and information science based on keyword, bibliographical coupling, and co-citation analyses. Scientometrics 105(3), 2071–2087 (2015)
4. Ishida, R., Takahashi, S., Wu, H.-Y.: Interactively uncluttering node overlaps for network visualization. In: 2015 19th International Conference on Information Visualisation (iV), pp. 200–205. IEEE (2015)
5. Isenberg, P., Heimerl, F., Koch, S., Isenberg, T., Xu, P., Stolper, C., Sedlmair, M., Chen, J., Moller, T., Stasko, J.T.: Vispubdata. org: A Metadata Collection about IEEE visualization (VIS) publications. IEEE Trans. Vis. Comput. Graph. 23, 2199–2206 (2016)
6. Fulda, J., Brehmel, M., Munzner, T.: TimeLineCurator: interactive authoring of visual timelines from unstructured text. IEEE Trans. Vis. Comput. Graph. 22(1), 300–309 (2016)
7. Nakazawa, R., Itoh, R., Saito, T.: A visualization of research papers based on the topics and citation network. In: 2015 19th International Conference on Information Visualisation (iV), pp. 283–289. IEEE (2015)
8. Aigner, W., Miksch, S., Schumann, H., Tominski, C.: Visualization of Time-Oriented Data. Springer, London (2011). https://doi.org/10.1007/978-0-85729-079-3
9. Bach, B., Shi, C., Heulot, N., Madhyastha, T., Grabowski, T., Dragicevic, P.: Time curves: folding time to visualize patterns of temporal evolution in data. IEEE Trans. Vis. Comput. Graph. 22(1), 559–568 (2016)
10. Bach, B., Dragicevic, P., Archambault, D., Hurter, C., Carpendale, S.: A review of temporal data visualizations based on space-time cube operations. In: Proceedings of Eurographics Conference on Visualization (2014)
11. Xu, X., Wang, W., Liu, Y., Zhao, X., Xu, Z., Zhou, H.: A bibliographic analysis and collaboration patterns of ieee transactions on intelligent transportation systems between 2000 and 2015. IEEE Trans. Intell. Transp. Syst. 17(8), 2238–2247 (2016)

12. Xu, X., Jia, W., Tang, M., Feng, Q., Li, Y.: Author cooperation relationship in digital publishing based on social network analysis. In: 2015 12th International Conference on Fuzzy Systems and Knowledge Discovery (FSKD), pp. 1631–1635. IEEE (2015)
13. Zhang, J., Chen, C., Li, J.: Visualizing the intellectual structure with paper-reference matrices. IEEE Trans. Vis. Comput. Graph. **15**(6), 1153–1160 (2009)
14. Daud, A., Ahmad, M., Malik, M.S.I., Che, D.: Using machine learning techniques for rising star prediction in co-author network. Scientometrics **102**(2), 1687–1711 (2015)
15. Billah, S.M., Gauch, S.: Social network analysis for predicting emerging researchers. In: 2015 7th International Joint Conference on Knowledge Discovery, Knowledge Engineering and Knowledge Management (IC3 K), vol. 1, pp. 27–35. IEEE (2015)
16. Soós, S.: Age-sensitive bibliographic coupling reflecting the history of science: the case of the species problem. Scientometrics **98**(1), 23–51 (2014)
17. Daud, A.: Group level temporal academic social network mining using topic models. Tsinghua University (2010)
18. Jiang, X., Zhang, J.: A text visualization method for cross-domain research topic mining. J. Vis. **19**(3), 561–576 (2016)
19. Varlamis, I., Tsatsaronis, G.: Visualizing bibliographic databases as graphs and mining potential research synergies. In: 2011 International Conference on Advances in Social Networks Analysis and Mining (ASONAM), pp. 53–60. IEEE (2011)
20. Hachul, S., Junger, M.: An experimental comparison of fast algorithms for drawing general large graphs. Proc. Graph Draw. **235–240**, 2005 (2005)
21. Noack, A.: Energy models for graph clustering. J. Graph Alg. Appl. **11**(2), 453–480 (2007)
22. Clauset, A., Newman, M.E.J., Moore, C.: Finding community structure in very large networks. Phys. Rev. **E70**, 066111 (2004)

On the Impact of Environmental Sound on Perceived Visual Quality

Wenhan Zhu[1]([✉]), Guangtao Zhai[1], Wei Sun[1], Yi Xu[2], Jing Liu[3],
Yucheng Zhu[1], and Xiaokang Yang[1]

[1] Institute of Image Communication and Network Engineering,
Shanghai Jiao Tong University, Shanghai, China
{zhuwenhan823,zhaiguangtao,sunguwei,zyc420,xkyang}@sjtu.edu.cn
[2] Institute of Cultural and Creative Industry,
Shanghai Jiao Tong University, Shanghai, China
xyphoebe@sjtu.edu.cn
[3] School of Electrical and Information Engineering,
Tianjin University, Tianjin, China
jliu_tju@tju.edu.cn

Abstract. Most of existing visual quality assessment databases are created in controlled conditions where the experimental environments are always kept silent. However, the practical viewing environments often contain diverse environmental sounds. It is our daily experience that different sounds (e.g. chatter, honk and music) can affect our emotions, hence influencing our perceptions of images. So, there is a gap between visual quality under environmental sounds and existing researches of visual quality. Therefore, in this paper, we perform subjective quality evaluations with different types and volumes of environmental sounds. We build a rigorous experimental system to control various conditions of environmental sounds and construct the environmental sound–image database. Afterwards, the influence of environmental sounds on perceived visual quality are analysed from four perspectives: sound categories, sound volumes, distortion levels of images, and image contents.

Keywords: Image quality assessment (IQA) · Environmental sounds
Subjective assessment

1 Introduction

With the rapid development of multimedia techniques and wide applications of digital media devices, contemporary people view digital images via various

This work was supported by the National Science Foundation of China (61422112, 61371146, 61521062, 61527804), National High–tech R&D Program of China (2015AA015905), and Science and Technology Commission of Shanghai Municipality (15DZ0500200).

B. Zeng et al. (Eds.): PCM 2017, LNCS 10736, pp. 723–734, 2018.
https://doi.org/10.1007/978-3-319-77383-4_71

Fig. 1. The diagram of viewing environment accompanied different sounds in practice.

digital devices from virtually anywhere and at any time. Meanwhile, the expectation of humans toward enjoyment of high-quality visual perception is continually ascending. Therefore, image quality assessment (IQA) has drawn great attention from researches [1–4]. In existing subjective IQA experiments [5,6], the experimental environments are always kept silent. However, the ambient sounds, such as music, noise and natural sound, are inevitable in practice, as demonstrated in Fig. 1. In psychology, it is proved that human behaviors and emotion perceptions are affected by audio signals [7,8]. Different sounds may have diverse impact on how viewers perceive images.

In recent years, many researches focus on audio–visual attention [9–11] and quality of services [12–14]. Audio quality assessment (AQA) has been investigated in many literatures. Most AQA methods focus on the coding distortions. By comparing the level-difference between the distorted audio and reference audio, numerous metric were proposed to quantify the degradations based on basilar distance [15], filter bank [16], energy equalization [17] and so on. On the other hand, visual quality assessment (VQA) is also a research emphasis towards the video quality experts group (VQEG) [18]. A number of objective methods for measuring the perceived image and video quality have been proposed over the last two decades. Objective image quality metrics and objective video quality metrics can be classified into three categories, namely full-reference (FR) [19], reduced-reference (RR) [20], and no-reference (NR) [21] based on the availability of the original information [22]. Furthermore, depending on the fact that video usually comes along with audio, some works pay attention on the relationship between video and audio quality to accomplish joint audio–visual quality (AVQ) assessment. Several early studies demonstrated that single audio or video signal have mutual influence on AVQ and the effect of video is larger than audio [23], except audio is more important than video in a teleconference [24]. Some experiments have been evaluated AVQ derived from single audio quality and video quality. Several factors influencing the AVQ such as attention of subjects, audio-visual content itself and usage context are also studied [25]. Moreover, synchronization between audio and video is another important issue in AVQ. A large number of models to assess synchronization have been proposed [26].

Although the relationship between audio and video has been studied in many aspects, most of researches are on the base that the audio is associated with the visual content of the video. These audios and videos have internal relationship. However, the environmental sound which has no correlation with visual content with image or video is not considered. Actually, the environmental sound is inevitable but always neglected in daily life. So we should figure out the influence of different environmental sounds on the viewing comfort.

In general, we should control a single variable to ensure the accuracy of the result in the experiment. Nevertheless, videos always contain audio signals which may have mutual interferences with the environmental sounds. Thus, we study the impact of environmental sounds on image quality to eliminate the potential influence.

In this paper, we establish an environmental sound–image database (ESID), in order to investigate the effects of environmental sounds on perceived visual quality. First, we set up an experimental system to make the research reproducible and eliminate the interference of the sound outside our experiment. Subsequently, we elaborately prepare seven different environmental sounds to constitute three categories of sounds: "Music", "Noise" and "Natural Sound". Three sound volumes (40 dB, 55 dB and 70 dB) are used in our database. So, the number of situations of environmental sounds is fifteen. The image materials generated from 5 reference images and 15 distorted images in three different distortion levels in form of JPEG compression. Thus, this database consists of 300 cases with different situation of environmental sounds. There are 20 participants recruited in our experiment to assess these images. Based on the MOS in our database, we analyse the influence of environmental sounds on perceived image quality from four perspectives: sound categories, sound volumes, distortion levels of images and image contents.

The remainder of this paper is organized as follows. In Sect. 2, we introduce the construction of ESID and describe detailed experimental procedures. Section 3 analyses the influences of different environmental sounds on perceived image quality at four aspects. Finally, conclusions of this paper are presented in Sect. 4.

2 Subjective Quality Assessment

For the convenience of the study about the impacts of different environmental sounds on perceived image quality, we construct the image database with different environmental sounds as background and recruit subjects to evaluate the quality in the form of MOS.

2.1 Database Construction

To make the research precise and reproducible, we set up a experimental system which built in a soundproof lab which surrounded by acoustic insulating material. The whole system consists of a LCD display (BOE LF–55Z7000), a keyboard, eighteen loudspeaker boxes (DYNACORD DC–D8) and a decibel meter

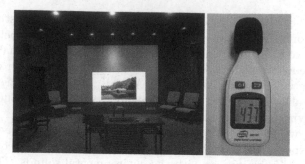

Fig. 2. The experimental system: photos of LCD display, keyboard, loudspeaker boxes and decibel meter.

(BENETECH GM1351). The LCD display is used to show the graphical user interface (GUI) in MATLAB for subjective quality assessment. The keyboard is set to grade or alter the scores of images on the numeric keyboard. The subjects can experience the environmental sounds from eighteen loudspeaker boxes. The decibel meter can accurately measure the decibel of the sound around the subjects. The illustrations of the system is shown in Fig. 2.

In order to study the effect of environmental sounds, we take two significant environmental factors into account.

- Categories of sounds: The categories of environmental sounds may have a significant impact on perceived image quality. We divided the environmental sounds into three genres ("Noise", "Natural Sound" and "Music"). In our study, we select three noises, which are the noise of cutting metal in collision shop, the noise of busy road and the gaussian white noise, called them "Collision Shop", "Busy Road" and "White Noise" for short. The natural sounds represent the sounds existing in the natural, such as sound of the wind, rain, and birds. In this paper, we choose the sound of birds, named it "Birds". Three common types of music (lyric, agile and passionate) are used in our test to increase the diversity of music, where "Variations on the Canon by Pachelbel" ("Canon") for lyric, "Lemon Tree" for agile, "He is a private" ("Private") for passionate. We get rid of lyrics of them to remove the influence of language. Three noises and the sound of birds are available at Adobe Audition Sound Effects [27], and three music was downloaded in high quality (HQ). Several examples of the waveforms and frequency spectra of these sounds are illustrated in Fig. 3.
- Volume of sounds: The volume of sounds is also an important aspect needed to be emphasized. Different volume of sounds will have different degrees of impact on viewing comfort of subjects. Actually, the decibel meter shows that there is a stable ambient sound at about 40 dB in the soundproof lab, which human subjects hard to perceive. According to the Environmental quality standard for noise (GB 3096-2008) [28], the audition of humans may get hurt when staying in a place long time with the noise higher than 80 dB. Thus, we

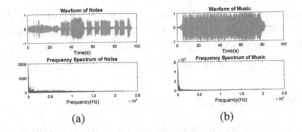

Fig. 3. The examples of waveforms and frequency spectra of sounds with 44100 Hz sampling frequency. (a) The waveform and frequency spectrum of noise: "Collision Shop". (b) The waveform and frequency spectrum of music: "Pirate".

select three degrees of volume: 40 dB (silent), 55 dB and 70 dB to study this influence. Owing to the variation of the volume of the same sound at different moment, we repetitively sample the volume of one sound every two seconds and obtain the equivalent decibel value of it according to below equation:

$$L_{eq} = 10 lg \left(\frac{1}{N} \sum_{i=1}^{N} 10^{0.1 L_i} \right), \tag{1}$$

where L_{eq} represents the equivalent decibel value, and L_i means the ith sampling value of the sound. N is the sampling number.

Image materials of our database includes 15 distorted images and 5 reference images. The original images were captured with professional digital camera (Nikon D610) and the resolutions of them are 1200×800. The distortion type we selected is JPEG compression, which has long been applied to lossy compression of digital images. We compress the reference images with three degree of Quality (25, 15, 5) in the form of JPEG. Figure 4 gives some example images in the database. Using the above mentioned sounds and image materials, we construct

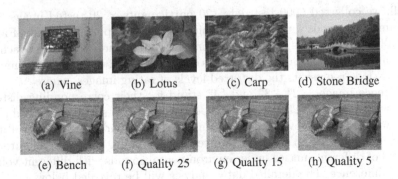

| (a) Vine | (b) Lotus | (c) Carp | (d) Stone Bridge |
| (e) Bench | (f) Quality 25 | (g) Quality 15 | (h) Quality 5 |

Fig. 4. Eight images with resolutions of 1200×800 used in our database. First row and second row are the 5 original images. Third row is the three distorted images of (e) with different degrees of JPEG quality.

the environmental sound–image database (ESID). The total number of designed environmental sounds state is fifteen composed by seven different sounds, two kinds of voiced volume degrees and a silent state. Thus, the proposed database consists of 300 cases under different situations of environmental sounds.

2.2 Subjective Experiment

We perform subjective experiment to gather the subjective opinion scores on our database. In accordance with ITU-R Rec. BT.500-13 [29], twenty inexperienced participants (i.e., 16 males and 4 females) are recruited for our study. Before the experiment, the participants are trained by previewing two group of sample images (reference images with their corresponding distorted images) to prevent viewers from rating optionally. These examples will not appear in the subsequent experiment.

In experiment stage, the viewing distance is fixed at four times the image height. Single–stimulus (SS) method is applied in our experiment. We randomize the presentation order of all testing images to reduce memory effects on grading scores. The playing order of different sounds with different volumes is also stochastic. Subjects are asked to give scores from 1 to 10 (1 for the worst, 10 for the best) to indicate image quality based on visual preference, which has more alternation than five grading scale [30]. The average experimental period is about 18 min and no one experiment lasts more than 30 min, which meets ITU recommendations [29].

After the subjective experiment, we detect the abnormal results based on 3σ principle in the light of Annex 2 of ITU-R Rec. BT.500-13 [29]. If a score is beyond 3σ region of MOS value, it will be regarded as an outlier to be removed. After that the remaining scores are averaged for each image to obtain the final mean opinion scores (MOSs).

3 Experimental Results and Analysis

Overall, we collected 6000 test data (20 participants × 20 tested images × 15 environmental sounds with 3 different volume levels) for purposed study. Figure 5 shows all of MOS values with different images and sound volumes. In each subfigure, diverse symbols in different colors express MOS of different environmental sounds. X-axis represents the distorted levels of rating images, where "1" means the reference images, "2", "3" and "4" stand for their corresponding distorted images with "Quality" 25, 15 and 5 respectively. Y-axis shows MOS of different images with different environmental sounds. We can find that the overall trend of MOS is declining with worse and worse quality of images from this figure. And the MOS of different images under environmental sounds with different volumes all have difference. The detailed data analysis will be revealed below.

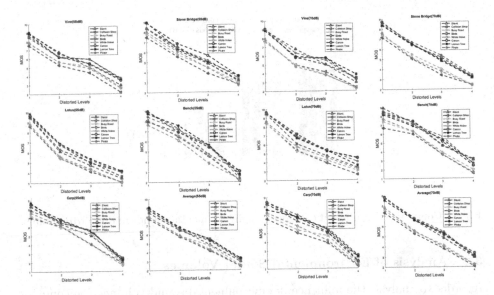

Fig. 5. MOS of images with different environmental sounds in ESID Database. X-axis represents the distorted levels of rating images, where "1" means the reference images, "2", "3" and "4" stand for their corresponding distorted images with "Quality" 25, 15 and 5 respectively. The first two columns are under 55 dB volume and the latter two columns are under 70 dB volume. The bottom subfigures in second column and fourth column are the average scores of five images under 55 dB and 70 dB respectively.

3.1 Analysis of Environmental Sound Categories

To analysis the relationship between MOS and categories of environmental sounds, we average the MOS scores of different sounds in the same categories as divided in the Sect. 2. We choose the situation under 55 dB volume as an example which is expressed in Fig. 6. From the figure and the data table, it is obvious that the environmental sounds have impact on the subjects to perceive the quality of images. "Noise" has bad influence while "Music" promotes the quality. The effect degree of "Noise" is heavier than "Noise". The affection of "Natural Sound" is smallest, the scores of it are roughly the same as the silent environment. Furthermore, relative to the influence of the increasing degree of distortion, the impact of environmental sounds is slight. The similar consequences are acquired under 70 dB.

For more subdivided, "Collision Shop" always obtains the worst scores in whole "Noise" as the purple lines in Fig. 5. We consider that the shrill noise which has many high frequency component shown in Fig. 3(b) has the worst impact on perceiving the quality. In addition, there is no sound in the category of "Music" demonstrating its unique influence. Thus, the impact of different types of music are close.

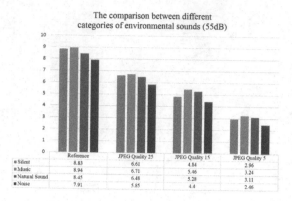

Fig. 6. Comparison of different categories of environmental sounds under 55 dB volume.

3.2   Analysis of Environmental Sound Volumes

In order to analysis the influence of environmental sound volumes, we compare the MOS of all environmental sound categories under different environmental sound volumes as illustrated in Fig. 7. Due to the situation of 45 dB is silent, there is no distinction among different environmental sound categories in this situation. Thus, we mainly compare the disparities between low volume (55 dB) and high volume (70 dB). From Fig. 7, it is distinct that the quality of images with noise decline with the increasing of the sound volume in each distortion level. The MOS of music also has a slight descend when the volume increases, however, the extent of decrease is smaller than noise. It illustrates that the affection of music is positive in a slight volume, while increasing the volume may get bad effect. Actually, when human stay at a environmental with 80 dB sound, they may be agitated [28]. Thus, a slight volume music environment suit human to appreciate images and the high volume music may be regarded as "noise". Moreover, the change of natural sound is small and unfixed. It declines at the situation of JPEG "Quality" 15 and increases at the other three situations. Towards to sound of birds ("Natural Sound"), it consists of transitory stimulations, the influence of volume is small and unstable.

3.3   Analysis of Influence on Different Distortion Levels

We average the difference MOS between situations of environmental sounds and silent situation on different image quality levels. Also, the variance of scores of different environmental sounds on different image quality levels are computed. The data is shown in Table 1. "+" represents the MOS of environmental sound is higher than the silent situation, while "−" expresses the opposite.

From the difference values in above-mentioned table, we can find that music has the minimum impact on reference images (best quality) and affects the poor quality images more. On the contrary, the influence of noise are more overt on good quality images. Towards natural sound, it impedes human to perceive the

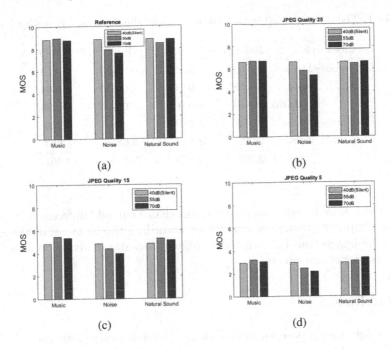

Fig. 7. Comparison of different environmental sound volumes.

high quality images, but it facilitates subjects to grade relatively high score for poor quality images. That is to say, natural sound reduces the difference between high quality images and poor quality images in perception of viewers. In the other hand, from the data of Table 1, the variance of scores are slight larger than common JPEG distortion databases. This means that the environmental sounds may have difference influence degree on different subjects and affect the stability of perception. Also, it is obvious that variances of scores of the best and the worst quality images with environmental sounds are smaller than the middle two quality images. It illustrates that the volatility of subjects to evaluate images will enhance a lot when they view weak distorted images and hear some environmental sounds. This influence will decrease when the quality of image is very good or very poor.

3.4 Discussion

In Sect. 3, we analyse the influences of environmental sounds on perceived image quality from four perspectives. They are the influence of environmental sound categories, the affection of environmental sound volumes, the impact of different image distortion levels and the impress of image contents. All these aspects can be profoundly studied and have abundant application scenarios. For example, there are plenty of online-shopping site in the Internet where the goods are presented to the consumer in the form of images. Currently, these webpages

Table 1. The difference MOS and variance under different image quality levels.

Quality levels		Reference	Quality 25	Quality 15	Quality 5
Difference	Music	+0.017	+0.107	+0.563	+0.195
	Noise	−1.085	−0.968	−0.655	−0.643
	Natural	−0.205	−0.055	+0.365	+0.285
Variance	Music	1.619	2.349	2.668	2.209
	Noise	2.028	2.429	2.687	1.683
	Natural	2.001	2.879	3.156	2.461

are soundless. Based on our research, the merchants can add different background sounds to improve consumers' evaluation according to the types of the goods. Also, the webpages can be designed to offer different sounds to be selected by the preferences of consumers.

4   Conclusion

In this paper, we propose an environmental sound–image database (ESID) in order to study the impacts of environmental sounds on perceived visual quality. Our database contains 300 cases for each subject under 15 different situations of environmental sounds. The environmental sounds consist of three different types: "Music", "Noise" and "Natural Sound". Also, three different volumes: 40 dB (silent), 55 dB and 70 dB are used in our experiment. For each situation of environmental sounds, there are 5 reference images and 15 distorted images with three different distortion levels. Twenty participants are recruited to score the images in form of MOS. Afterwards, we analyse the influence of environmental sounds from five perspectives based on the MOS values in our database. We find that "Music" promotes the perception of images while "Noise" has bad effect. The influence of "Noise" is far stronger than "Music". The visual quality with "Music" and "Noise" decrease with the increasing of the volume of sounds, while "Natural Sound" has the opposite effect. Environmental sounds increase the volatility of perceived quality which is especially obvious for slightly distorted images. Furthermore, the environmental sounds have more influence with less complex image content.

References

1. Zhai, G., Wu, X., Yang, X., Lin, W., Zhang, W.: A psychovisual quality metric in free-energy principle. IEEE Trans. Image Process. **21**(1), 41–52 (2012)
2. Zhai, G., Cai, J., Lin, W., Yang, X., Zhang, W.: Three dimensional scalable video adaptation via user-end perceptual quality assessment. IEEE Trans. Broadcast. **54**(3), 719–727 (2008)

3. Zhai, G.: Recent advances in image quality assessment. In: Deng, C., Ma, L., Lin, W., Ngan, K. (eds.) Visual Signal Quality Assessment, pp. 73–97. Springer, Cham (2015). https://doi.org/10.1007/978-3-319-10368-6_3

4. Gu, K., Zhai, G., Yang, X., Zhang, W.: Using free energy principle for blind image quality assessment. IEEE Trans. Multimed. **17**(1), 50–63 (2015)

5. Sheikh, H.R., Wang, Z., Cormack, L., Bovik, A.C.: Live image quality assessment database release 2. http://live.ece.utexas.edu/research/quality/

6. Xu, Q., Huang, Q., Jiang, T., Yan, B., Lin, W., Yao, Y.: HodgeRank on random graphs for subjective video quality assessment. IEEE Trans. Multimed. **14**(3), 844–857 (2012)

7. Zeng, Z., Pantic, M., Roisman, G.I., Huang, T.S.: A survey of affect recognition methods: audio, visual, and spontaneous expressions. IEEE Trans. Pattern Anal. Mach. Intell. **31**(1), 39–58 (2009)

8. Perrott, D.R., Saberi, K., Brown, K., Strybel, T.Z.: Auditory psychomotor coordination and visual search performance. Attent. Percept. Psychophys. **48**(3), 214–226 (1990)

9. Min, X., Zhai, G., Gu, K., Yang, X.: Fixation prediction through multimodal analysis. ACM Trans. Multimed. Comput. Commun. Appl. **13**(1), 6:1–6:23 (2016)

10. Min, X., Zhai, G., Gao, Z., Hu, C., Yang, X.: Sound influences visual attention discriminately in videos. In: Sixth International Workshop on Quality of Multimedia Experience, pp. 153–158. IEEE (2014)

11. Min, X., Zhai, G., Hu, C., Gu, K.: Fixation prediction through multimodal analysis. In: Visual Communications and Image Processing (VCIP), pp. 1–4. IEEE (2015)

12. You, J., Reiter, U., Hannuksela, M.M., Gabbouj, M., Perkis, A.: Perceptual-based quality assessment for audio-visual services: a survey. Signal Process. Image Commun. **25**(7), 482–501 (2010)

13. Xu, Q., Xiong, J., Huang, Q., Yao, Y.: Online HodgeRank on random graphs for crowdsourceable QoE evaluation. IEEE Trans. Multimed. **16**(2), 373–386 (2014)

14. Xu, Q., Wu, Z., Su, L., Qin, L., Jiang, S., Huang, Q.: Bridging the gap between objective score and subjective preference in video quality assessment. In: IEEE International Conference on Multimedia and Expo, pp. 908–913. IEEE (2010)

15. Colomes, C., Lever, M., Rault, J.B., Dehery, Y.F., Faucon, G.: A perceptual model applied to audio bit-rate reduction. J. Audio Eng. Soc. **43**, 233–240 (1995)

16. Sporer, T.: Objective audio signal evaluation-applied psychoacoustics for modeling the perceived quality of digital audio (1997)

17. Vanam, R., Creusere, C.D.: Scalable perceptual metric for evaluating audio quality. In: Signals, Systems and Computers, pp. 319–323 (2005)

18. Video quality experts group (VQEG). http://www.vqeg.org

19. Wang, Z., Bovik, A.C., Sheikh, H.R., Simoncelli, E.P.: Image quality assessment: from error visibility to structural similarity. IEEE Trans. Image Process. **13**(4), 600–612 (2004)

20. Soundararajan, R., Bovik, A.C.: Video quality assessment by reduced reference spatio-temporal entropic differencing. IEEE Trans. Circuits Syst. Video Technol. **23**(4), 684–694 (2013)

21. Yang, F., Wan, S., Chang, Y., Wu, H.R.: A novel objective no-reference metric for digital video quality assessment. IEEE Signal Process. Lett. **12**(10), 685–688 (2005)

22. Winkler, S.: Video quality and beyond. In: European Conference on Signal Processing, pp. 150–153 (2007)

23. Beerends, J.G., Caluwe, F.E.D.: The influence of video quality on perceived audio quality and vice versa. J. Audio Eng. Soc. **47**(5), 355–362 (1999)

24. Hands, D.S.: A basic multimedia quality model. IEEE Trans. Multimed. **6**(6), 806–816 (2004)
25. Frater, M.R., Arnold, J.F., Vahedian, A.: Impact of audio on subjective assessment of video quality in videoconferencing applications. IEEE Trans. Circuits Syst. Video Technol. **11**(9), 1059–1062 (2001)
26. Blakowski, G., Steinmetz, R.: A media synchronization survey: reference model, specification, and case studies. IEEE J. Sel. Areas Commun. **14**(1), 5–35 (1996)
27. Adobe Audition Sound Effects. http://offers.adobe.com/en/na/audition/offers/audition_dlc/AdobeAditionDLCSFX.html?cq_ck=1407955238126&wcmmode=disabled
28. GB 3096-2008: Environmental quality standard for noise (2008)
29. ITU Recommendation BT.500-13: Methodology for the subjective assessment of the quality of television pictures (2012)
30. Sheikh, H.R., Sabir, M.F., Bovik, A.C.: A statistical evaluation of recent full reference image quality assessment algorithms. IEEE Trans. Image Process. **15**(11), 3440–3451 (2006)

A Novel Texture Exemplars Extraction Approach Based on Patches Homogeneity and Defect Detection

Hui Lai, Lulu Yin, Huisi Wu, and Zhenkun Wen[✉]

College of Computer Science and Software Engineering, Shenzhen University, Shenzhen, China
wenzk@szu.edu.cn

Abstract. Texture exemplar has been widely used in example-based texture synthesis and feature analysis. Unfortunately, manually cropping texture exemplars is a burdensome and boring task. Conventional method over emphasizes the synthesis algorithm analysis and requires frequent user interactions. In this paper, we employ K-means clustering to generate patch distribution maps and calculate K-center similarity as our measurement on patch merge. Patch merging is the key to reduce over-segmentation. Even defective texture exemplars could show high global homogeneity. We detect this kind of exemplars by partitioning patch maps into non-overlapping subblocks. Comparing visual similarity between each block and the global patch map could detect the heterogeneous areas. We also introduce the Poisson disk sampling for achieving uniform exemplar cropping. Visual results show that our approach could accurately extract texture exemplars from arbitrary source images.

Keywords: Homogeneity · Defect detection · Texture exemplars

1 Introduction

With the advent of the era of big data, people can easily obtain various texture images from the Internet. Unconstrained images usually contain kind of heterogeneity textures, from which cropping texture exemplars could be annoying and inefficient. How to pick a desired texture exemplar out of a given natural image becomes a novel issue.

During the last two decades, example-based texture synthesis has attracted much attention [1–4]. Most of the existing example-based texture synthesis methods could be categorized into pixel-based, patch-based and model-based. Efros and Lenung [5], Wei and Levoy [6] synthesized high-quality texture by fetching each pixels from the best matching neighborhood. To reduce computational complexity of copying pixels, Chaos Mosaic [7] proposed patch-based method. They obtained lots of exemplar patches and synthesized texture by mixing transformation. After that, numerous of state-of-the-art methods followed [1, 8–10]. Another model-based method also provides remarkable results in anatomic volume illustration and realistic texture synthesis [11–13]. All methods above only emphasize synthesis algorithm analysis, few researchers have been concerned with extracting desired exemplars from source images.

Recently, Lockerman *et al.* [14] has proposed a texture extraction method using diffusion manifolds to locate textures and extract exemplar tiles. However, this method requires MRF texture synthesis algorithms to generating exemplars, and it needs lots of user interactions. Dai *et al.* [15] although proposed a suggestive way for homogeneity metric, they computed the Euclidean distance between each two regions, which shows absence of practicability with indistinguishable scores.

At the same time, local homogeneity analysis has been widely used in defect detection [16, 17] and image segmentation [18–20]. But it's hard to distinguish sparse texture and defective parts by using the existing homogeneity metric. Few researches can detach sparse texture and defective parts automatically, and apply texture homogeneity to texture exemplar extraction in an efficient manner.

In this paper, we propose a novel approach for automatic texture exemplar extraction based on homogeneity metric and defect detection. We firstly resize the source images into multiple scales and implement the Poisson sampling [21] to guide the cropping randomly and uniformly. And we employ K-means clustering algorithm [22] to generate k centers as our patch categories, and calculate its color distance as our measurement on patch merge. To remove the defective texture exemplar, we compare patch distribution between each sub-block and global patch map. For more accurate matrix distance metric, we applied Chi-Squared distance [23] instead of Euclidean distance. Our method was evaluated with extensive experiments on variety of texture images. Experimental results demonstrated its effectiveness on automatic texture exemplar extraction.

2 Method

The overview of our framework is as shown in Fig. 1. We firstly implement Poisson sampling to crop exemplars from the input image, which has been resized to multi-scales. For each unevaluated exemplar, we extract patch database as 10×10 pixel size and 3 pixel a stride (RGB feature), and the positions of their top-left corners were indexed. Then, we perform K-means clustering to generate k number of patch centers. With the patch index and k number of centers, we can obtain our patch distribution map. As similar patch centers get small RGB distance, we can merge over-segmented patches according to its RGB distance. Texture exemplars with a small area of impurities, which are usually discarded by our artists, could also get high scores. To filter this kind of exemplars, we partition the patch map into 64 non-overlapping subblocks. Comparing RGB similarity between each block and global patch map could detect the heterogeneous areas. Defective blocks get extremely high scores with our histogram cost metric. With our defect detection and homogeneity metric, pleasing and preferable exemplars are ranked in the top of the list.

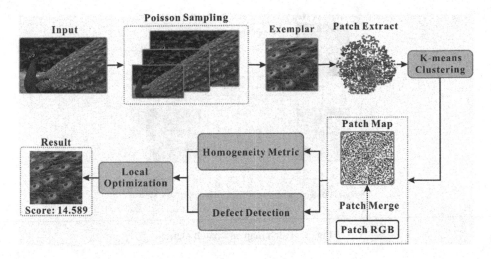

Fig. 1. The overview of our framework.

Given an exemplar x, we assume its extractability score $E(x)$ is composed of deficiency score $D(x)$ and homogeneity score $H(x)$. Defective exemplars, even with small parts of inhomogeneity could cause great distress. High homogeneity exemplars are frequently-used by our artists and researchers. Hence, $H(x)$ plays a positive role in extractability scores. $D(x)$ could be zero or amplified infinitely. That is,

$$E(x) = H(x) \cdot \frac{1}{D(x)+1} \tag{1}$$

We also optimize our extractability score $E(x)$ with random walk strategy, we shift exemplar in eight directions by fine tuning, and pick the texture exemplar with the highest score.

2.1 Patch Map and Patch Merge

Traditional similarity measurement of K-means algorithm is influenced by the number of cluster center K. Similarity texture may be distributed into different regions with larger number of K. Using patch centers' RGB feature distance to merge the over-segmented patches could get close the human visual system on homogeneity (Fig. 2).

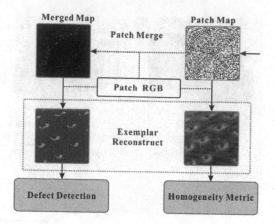

Fig. 2. Patch map and patch merge

After we cluster k number of centers (patch categories), we generate our patch map with the index of patch top-left corners. The merge procedure is composed of the following steps:

Step 1: Calculate the mean RGB value of each patch. If $p_i^c(x,y)$ is the pixel intensity of ith patch center of the position of (x,y) of the cth of the three color components, and the mean intensity of cth channel of ith patch center could be:

$$m_i^c = \sum_{x=1}^{N} \sum_{y=1}^{N} p_i^c(x,y)/(N \times N)(1 \leq i \leq k, 1 \leq c \leq 3, 1 \leq x, y \leq N) \qquad (2)$$

where $N \times N$ is the width and height of each patch.

Step 2: Iteratively compute the RGB distance between each center and the rest. If the RGB Euclidean distance between center i and center j are $d(i,j)$, i.e.,

$$d(i,j) = \sum_{c=1}^{3} \sqrt{\left(m_i^c - m_j^c\right)^2} (1 \leq i \leq k, i+1 \leq j \leq k) \qquad (3)$$

Step 3: Patch merges. Once the RGB distance is smaller than a threshold θ (10 as we implement for defect detection and 4 for homogeneity metric), we rewrite the categories id by the former center. Due to the effect of the threshold θ, we could filter kind of noise and small variation. Exemplar Reconstruction could reduce the distractions on the defect detection.

2.2 Homogeneity Metric

Most of the existing methods extract texture homogeneity based on the co-occurrence matrix. They over-emphasize on the contributiveness of pixel intensity, which is complex in computation. Dai et al. [15] proposed a doable way of homogeneity metric, but they have not considered the influence of K-means clustering. And they evaluate exemplars' homogeneity based on Euclidean distance, which shows lower accuracy than Chi-Squared distance. We propose our homogeneity metric based on the merged patch map.

Two randomly picked regions from the merged map could be uneven, so trial parameters are introduced. On the contrary, we partition the merged map into 3×3 and 4×4 subblocks, and generate the statistical distribution of patch categories in each block. Then, we apply Chi-Squared distance as their similarity metric. That is,

$$H(x) = \frac{\sum_{i=1}^{m-1} i}{\sum_{i=1}^{m-1} \sum_{j=i+1}^{m} C(b_i, b_j) + \varepsilon \cdot \sum_{i=1}^{m-1} i} \tag{4}$$

where m is the number of partitioned regions, $C(b_i, b_j)$ is our matrix cost based on Chi-Squared distance, b_i, b_j is statistical distribution result of block i and block j. We iteratively compute matrix cost between $(m-1)$ number of blocks and the rest, so that's $\sum_{i=1}^{m-1} i$ number of calculations, ε is our tiny factor in case the denominator becomes zero (10^{-2} as we implemented).

2.3 Defect Detection

Texture exemplar with small areas of impurities could rank in the front of the list as higher global homogeneity. And regular texture exemplar may be ignored. Lockerman et al. [14] applied user interaction to pick desired texture, which is a labor intensive task. It's necessary to filter this kind of exemplar automatically.

Exemplars, reconstructed by our merged map and center RGB mean intensity, are less of a distraction on the defect detection. Even for integrated sparse texture, Local regions could take at least half of the RGB feature from global images. It's feasible to use statistical method to filter defective exemplars. In particular, for 256×256 reconstructed exemplar, we partition it into 64 non-overlapping subblocks. Histogram distance of RGB feature is calculated between each block and global exemplar.

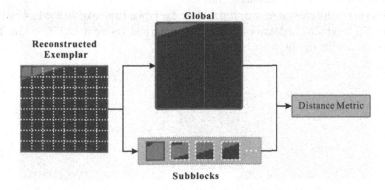

Fig. 3. Defect detection with RGB feature, merge parameters $\theta = 10$.

Once its histogram cost is greater than a threshold (0.6 as we implemented, means they are 60% mismatching), we consider it as a defective block, and multiply by a threshold δ. Otherwise, we set it as zero for innocent homogeneity scores.

$$D(x) = \begin{cases} 0 & (C_j \leq 0.6) \\ \dfrac{1}{n} \sum_{j=1}^{n} (C_j \cdot \delta) & (C_j > 0.6) \end{cases} \tag{5}$$

Formula above is our deficiency metric, where n is the number of subblocks, and $C_j (1 \leq j \leq n)$ is histogram cost between subblocks j and global exemplar, δ is the defect coefficient which we set as a thousand.

2.4   Chi-Squared Distance

Two K-bin histograms similarity matching calls for high accuracy. Euclidean distance between two K-bin histograms can be compact and rough. It's natural to use the Chi-Squared distance [23] to estimate the similarity between observations:

$$C_{ij} = C(p_i, q_j) = \frac{1}{2} \sum_{k=1}^{k} \frac{\left[h_{i(k)} - h_{j(k)}\right]^2}{h_{i(k)} + h_{j(k)}} \tag{6}$$

Chi-Squared distance is a weighted Euclidean distance by taking the inverse of the average proportions as weights, that is $1 / \left[h_{i(k)} + h_{j(k)}\right]$. It's the abundance proportion of the k species in the whole data set.

3   Results

We implement our texture exemplar extraction method using MATLAB R2014a on a Windows 10 operating system. To test the accuracy of our proposed method, we apply our system to thousands of various textures.

For images of different size, we crop texture exemplar in size of 128 × 128 by Poisson sampling. To heighten the detail of texture exemplar, we resize it as 256 × 256. Typical results are as shown in Fig. 4.

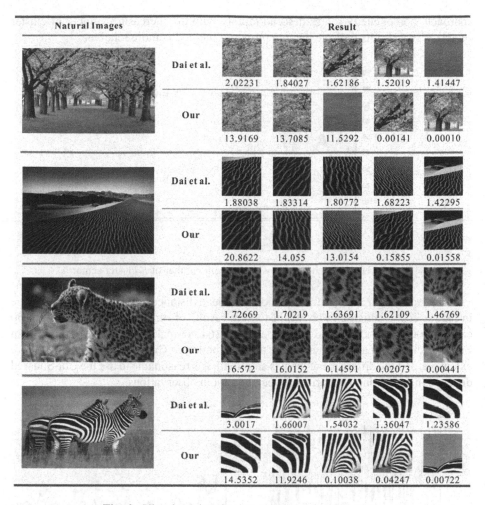

Fig. 4. Visual results of our texture exemplar extraction.

For hundreds of sorted images, we select five typical texture exemplars in the third column. Most of their arrangement rank as what we defined homogeneity. And defective texture can easily be recognized by our algorithm (scores being close to zero). Sparse texture (desert, leopard fur and zebra cutis in Fig. 4.) are arranged in front of the list compared with the defective exemplars. For each same texture exemplar, homogeneity metric by Dai *et al.* [15] is not rigorous and overly centralized, especially for sparse and defective images. With visual results compared with Dai *et al.* [15], our method in homogeneity metric is more efficient and well-organized. According to the higher scores by our homogeneity metric, pleasing texture exemplar is accurately extracted.

We compare the performance of homogeneity scores with different number of K cluster center. As shown in Fig. 5, homogeneity scores of Dai et al. are hovering near 2.5, which is difficult to distinguish between kinds of exemplars. Without our merged approach, homogeneity scores descend rapidly with the increasing number of cluster center. Visual results indicate that our proposed method is more reliable.

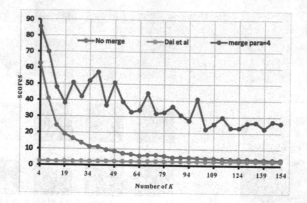

Fig. 5. Homogeneity scores with different number of K cluster center

We also compare the performance of Euclidean distance and Chi-Squared distance in matrix cost evaluation. For two histogram results of our homogeneity metric (150 comparisons we choose) and defect detection (64 comparisons) over exemplar from Fig. 3, visual result as shown in Fig. 6, the distribution of Chi-Squared distance is more extensive, and the difference of them is amplified. It's reasonable to use the Chi-Squared distance in estimating similarity between two k-bin observations.

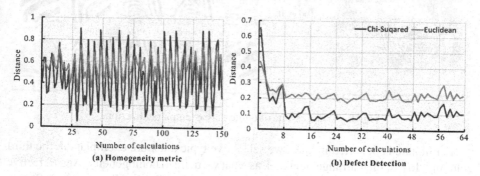

Fig. 6. Comparison of Chi-Squared distance and Euclidean distance as exemplars in Fig. 3

4   Conclusion

In this paper, we propose a novel texture exemplar extraction method based on homogeneity metric and defect detection (RGB feature). Our homogeneity metric with merged patch map, can reduce the influence of K-means algorithm on the over-segmented. We also reconstruct the merged map for defect detection. With our reconstructed exemplar, small variation is filtered. And heterogeneous area is more obvious. The strategy of partitioned subblocks in homogeneity metric can reduce the influence of trails parameter.

And we compare the accuracy of matrix distance evaluation using Chi-Squared distance and Euclidean distance. Due to the weights of Chi-Squared distance, our scores are more discriminative. With our proposed metric, the homogeneity scores range from 0 to 100. We also implement Poisson sampling for uniform and multi-scale cropping. Visual and statistical results prove that this proposed method can automatically extract texture exemplar from arbitrary source images. It's efficient to extend the texture database with satisfying texture exemplars.

Acknowledgments. This work was supported in part by grants from the National Natural Science Foundation of China (Nos. 61303101, 61572328), the Shenzhen Research Foundation for Basic Research, China (Nos. JCYJ20150324140036846, JCYJ20170302153551588, CXZZ201409021 60818443, CXZZ20140902102350474, CXZZ20150813151056544, JCYJ20150630105452814, JCYJ20160331114551175, JCYJ20160608173051207), the Start-up Research Fund of Shenzhen University (Nos. 2013-827-000009), the China-UK Visual Information Processing Laboratory (VIPL) and Maternal and child health monitoring and early warning Engineering Technology Research Center (METRC) of Guangdong Province.

References

1. Ren, Y., Romano, Y., Elad, M.: Example-based image synthesis via randomized patch-matching (2016)
2. Chen, K., Johan, H., Mueller-Wittig, W.: Simple and efficient example-based texture synthesis using tiling and deformation. In: ACM SIGGRAPH Symposium on Interactive 3D Graphics and Games, pp. 145–152. ACM (2013)
3. Liu, G., Gousseau, Y., Xia, G.S.: Texture synthesis through convolutional neural networks and spectrum constraints (2016)
4. Li, Y., Fang, C., Yang, J., Wang, Z., Lu, X., Yang, M.H.: Diversified texture synthesis with feed-forward networks (2017)
5. Efros, A.A., Leung, T.K.: Texture synthesis by non-parametric sampling. In: IEEE International Conference on Computer Vision, vol. 2, pp. 1033. IEEE (1999)
6. Wei, L.Y., Levoy, M.: Fast texture synthesis using tree-structured vector quantization. In: Conference on Computer Graphics & Interactive Techniques, pp. 479–488 (2000)
7. Guo, B., Xu, Y.Q.: Chaos mosaic: fast and memory efficient texture synthesis. Microsoft Research (2000)
8. Efros, A.A., Freeman, W.T.: Image quilting for texture synthesis and transfer. In: Conference on Computer Graphics and Interactive Techniques, pp. 341–346. ACM (2001)
9. Liang, L., Liu, C., Xu, Y.Q., Guo, B., Shum, H.Y.: Real-time texture synthesis by patch-based sampling. ACM Trans. Graph. **20**(3), 127–150 (2001)
10. Lefebvre, S., Hoppe, H.: Parallel controllable texture synthesis. ACM Trans. Graph. **24**(3), 777–786 (2005)
11. Kabul, I., Merck, D., Rosenman, J., Rosenman, J.: Model-based solid texture synthesis for anatomic volume illustration. In: Eurographics Conference on Visual Computing for Biology and Medicine, pp. 133–140. Eurographics Association (2010)
12. Kaynar Kabul, I.: Patient-specific anatomical illustration via model-guided texture synthesis (2012)
13. Zhou, D., 'Farb, G.G.: Model-based estimation of texels and placement grids for fast realistic texture synthesis (2003)

14. Lockerman, Y., Rushmeier, H., Dorsey, J.: Systems and methods for creating texture exemplars. US, US 20130093768 A1 (2013)
15. Dai, D., Riemenschneider, H., Van Gool, L.: The synthesizability of texture examples. In: IEEE Conference on Computer Vision and Pattern Recognition, pp. 3027–3034. IEEE (2014)
16. Rajitha, B., Tiwari, A., Agarwal, S.: A new local homogeneity analysis method based on pixel intensities for image defect detection. In: IEEE International Conference on Recent Trends in Information Systems, pp. 200–206 (2015)
17. Cheng, H.D., Sun, Y.: A hierarchical approach to color image segmentation using homogeneity. IEEE Trans. Image Process. Publ. IEEE Sig. Process. Soc. 9(12), 2071–2082 (2000)
18. Rajitha, B., Tiwari, A., Agarwal, S.: Image segmentation and defect detection techniques using homogeneity. In: International Conference on Futuristic Trends on Computational Analysis and Knowledge Management (2015)
19. Hussain, S., Qi, C., Asif, M.R., Khan, M.S., Zhang, Z., Fareed, M.S., et al.: A novel trignometric energy functional for image segmentation in the presence of intensity inhomogeneity. In: IEEE International Conference on Multimedia and Expo, pp. 1–6. IEEE Computer Society (2016)
20. Kumar, S., Pant, M., Kumar, M., Dutt, A.: Colour image segmentation with histogram and homogeneity histogram difference using evolutionary algorithms. Int. J. Mach. Learn. Cybern. 9, 1–21 (2015)
21. Bridson, R.: Fast Poisson disk sampling in arbitrary dimensions. ACM SIGGRAPH Sketches 49, 22 (2007). ACM
22. Hartigan, J.A., Wong, M.A.: A k-means clustering algorithm. Appl. Stat. 28(1), 100–108 (2013)
23. Yang, W., Xu, L., Chen, X., Zheng, F., Liu, Y.: Chi-squared distance metric learning for histogram data. Math. Prob. Eng. 2015, 1–12 (2015)

Repetitiveness Metric of Exemplar for Texture Synthesis

Lulu Yin, Hui Lai, Huisi Wu, and Zhenkun Wen[✉]

College of Computer Science and Software Engineering, Shenzhen University, Shenzhen, China
wenzk@szu.edu.cn

Abstract. Texture synthesis has become a well-established area. However, researchers are mostly concerned with learning the algorithm of texture synthesis to achieve higher quality and better efficiency. We hereby propose a repetitiveness metric method to pick out an optimal texture exemplar which is used to synthesize texture. Different from conventional methods of texture analysis that emphasize on texture feature analysis for the target textures, our method focuses on repetitiveness metric of texture exemplar. To achieve a more efficient method, we firstly perform a Poisson disk sampling to extract unordered texture exemplars from the input image. Using normalized cross correlation (NCC) based on fast Fourier transformation (FFT) for each exemplar, we can get some matrices. Based on repetitiveness metric, we can assign each exemplar a score. Our method can satisfy visual requirement and accomplish high-quality work in a shorter time due to FFT. Compelling visual results and computational complexity analyses prove the validity of our work.

Keywords: Texture synthesizability · Repetitiveness metric · Texture exemplar
NCC

1 Introduction

Nowadays, texture synthesis has become a hot research topic. There exist abundant methods to achieve a synthesis texture. However, these methods are only concerned with how to synthesize different textures, instead of the pure extent of synthesized textures. We will save lots of work and get ideal synthesis results during the texture synthesis process if we directly select better exemplars to synthesize texture. How to extract a pure and logical texture exemplar from the source image becomes an interesting question. A better exemplar usually can generate better effects of texture synthesis. Given a source image, we can produce arbitrary size of texture exemplars. Generally, acquiring exemplars by manually cropping images is a dreary work if we need to collect masses of exemplars. But we have to crop images manually. So it is imminent to research auto-extraction and repetitiveness metric of texture exemplar.

During the last two decades, example-based texture synthesis usually only emphasized the final synthesis consequence or implemented texture feature analysis on the target textures [1, 2]. One of the most famous methods all over the world was Markov Random Fields (MRF) method [3] which consists of pixel-based texture synthesis and

© Springer International Publishing AG, part of Springer Nature 2018
B. Zeng et al. (Eds.): PCM 2017, LNCS 10736, pp. 745–755, 2018.
https://doi.org/10.1007/978-3-319-77383-4_73

patch-based texture synthesis. In 1999, a pixel-based texture synthesis method was firstly presented by Efros and Lenung [4]. They proposed a texture synthesis model based on the stronger correlations between adjacent pixels of the image. Then in 2000, a patch-based method was proposed by Wei and Levoy [5]. They employed the example as vectors making the patch matching process more efficient. Soon afterwards, to improve the performance of texture synthesis, Ashikhmin [6] further made use of pixel cross correlation in natural texture. On the other hand, Gardner *et al.* [7] presented a patch-based texture synthesis approach for texture synthesis with high randomness. Liang *et al.* [8] also reformed Gardner's method based on patch-based sampling. Another way of dealing with exemplars was to analyze the matching errors between each patch with specific size as a texton [9] to contribute to synthesis. Hertzmann *et al.* [10] directly applied the techniques of texture synthesis to curved surface. Lefebvre [11] proposed a parallel synthesis method based on neighborhood matching patch. To obtain the optimal texture, it constantly made corrections on local texture patch [12].

All above methods only focus on example-based texture synthesis, but little study focuses on the quality of extracted texture exemplars. We cannot emphasize the importance of the quality of texture exemplar for the example-based texture synthesis too much. Although Dai *et al.* [13] proposed a novel texture feature about repetitiveness, their method only quantifies the repetitiveness of the structured single images and doesn't better analyze complex structure texture images. An accepted repetitiveness image, we think, should be a periodic structured texture based on vision. Texture usually can be classified as either repetitive or stochastic. However, many of present world textures are distributed between these two extremes. These textures, as well as repetitive and stochastic textures, form a visual texture spectrum on which the structural repetitiveness continuously varies by randomness in Fig. 1.

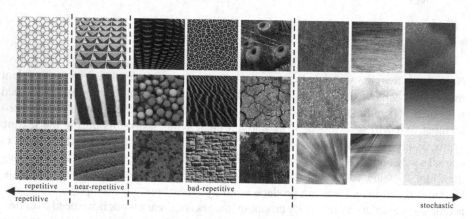

Fig. 1. A texture spectrum on which textures are arranged in good order according to their structural repetitiveness.

In this paper, we propose a novel repetitiveness metric method to pick out an optimal texture exemplar which is used to synthesize texture. Due to so many images that can be easily acquired from the Internet, it is very significant to find an exemplar's repetitiveness metric method. Different from the existing methods, our method focuses on the quality of texture exemplar for the synthesis effects and developing algorithm to extract the ideal texture exemplar. On the other hand, we also perform a Poisson disk sampling algorithm to improve the efficiency of texture exemplar extracting. Based on the Poisson disk sampling algorithm, our method can efficiently extract ideal exemplars randomly and uniformly among masses of images. Finally, we employ NCC matching algorithm based on FFT to improve the precision of repetitiveness texture recognition. We perform our proposed method on masses of images with different scales and different kinds of textures. Compelling visual results and computational complexity analyses prove its validity on repetitiveness metric of texture exemplar.

2 Methodology

To achieve a more robust and more efficient method based on repetitiveness algorithm, we first perform a Poisson disk sampling method to extract masses of unordered texture exemplars among the input image. Using NCC matching algorithm based on FFT for each texture exemplar which is grayed and cut into some identical blocks (16 in the implementation), we can get some NCC matrices in which we throw away the invalid border. Based on repetitiveness metric, we can assign each texture exemplar respectively a repetitiveness score. The higher the score, the better the repetitiveness of the exemplar. The overview of our framework is as shown in Fig. 2.

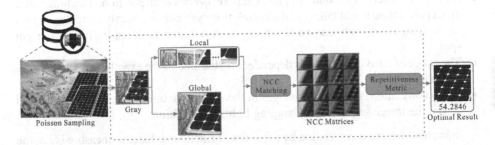

Fig. 2. Overview of our framework

2.1 Sampling Algorithm

Sampling, as defined in the field of analog signal, is a series of samples' values which are generated according to certain interval to obtain continuous time signal. In this section, given an input image, we preprocess it by sampling aimed at getting some texture exemplars. There exist many more sampling technologies such as random sampling, Poisson disk sampling and so on.

Random sampling is a non-uniform sampling. Using this sampling, we obtain some points which can appear too converged or scattered. However, the result of sampling isn't so ideal. It is easy to bring some important information by more sampling or less sampling.

Poisson disk sampling [14] has been widely used in the field of image processing due to adjustability of the spacing of adjacent sampling points. Denoting the distance between p_i and p_j which has to be no less than radius r, we define it as

$$\forall p_i, p_j \in P: \left\| p_i - p_j \right\| \leq 2r \tag{1}$$

Where P is a set of sampling points from the input image, and p_i, p_j are two sampling points which are arbitrary and neighbors.

In our experiment, we choose Poisson disk sampling due to its significant characteristics. Obviously, compared with random sampling, Poisson disk sampling has a huge advantage in adjust ability, and makes sampling points uniform, non-repetitive and random. Based on high-quality sampling points, we can get masses of texture exemplars and pick out an optimal texture exemplar based on repetitiveness algorithm.

2.2 Template Matching by Cross Correlation Algorithm

Cross correlation is a similarity metric of pixel for gray co-occurrence matrix. At first, cross correlation was used for template matching [15] by the squared Euclidean distance measure. Soon it was used for texture synthesizability [13] based on repetitiveness algorithm. However, there are many disadvantages of using cross correlation for template matching [15] as follows:

- If the image energy (the sum of square per pixel) varies with position, matching using cross correlation could fail, *e.g.*, the correlation between an exactly matching region in the image and itself may be less than the correlation between itself and a bright spot.
- The range of cross correlation is dependent on the size of the exactly matching region in the image.
- Cross correlation is variant to changes in the amplitude of images, *e.g.*, those caused across the image sequence by changing lighting conditions.

It is clear that cross correlation by the squared Euclidean distance measure is not the ideal method of template matching for the repetitiveness algorithm. So NCC matching algorithm of [15, 16] was proposed and solved these problems by normalizing the exactly matching region in the image and template image to unit length, yielding a cosine-like correlation coefficient as

$$\Gamma_n(u, v) = \frac{\sum_{i=1}^{N_1} \sum_{j=1}^{N_2} \left(I_{i+u,\, j+v} \cdot T_{ij} \right)}{\sqrt{\sum_{i=1}^{N_1} \sum_{j=1}^{N_2} I_{i+u,\, j+v}^2} \sqrt{\sum_{i=1}^{N_1} \sum_{j=1}^{N_2} T_{ij}^2}} \tag{2}$$

Where $N_1 \times N_2$ is the size of matching template T, $I_{i+u,\, j+v}$ is the gray value of the matching region in the exemplar I at $(i + u, j + v)$, T_{ij} is the gray value of T at (i, j), the denominator denotes the energy of the T and the matching region in the I, and this function denotes NCC coefficient at (u, v). The more the value we want to find by this function is, the more similar two images are.

So far NCC, with strong anti-noise ability and accurate matching, has become a classical matching algorithm. By contrasting cross correlation of template image with input image, we can ensure the matching degree about two images. However, it is boring for low-speed in computing cross correlation. So we change the calculation method to high-speed convolution.

As is known to all, convolution is often used for processing time-domain signal. We formulate convolution of 2-dim discrete signal as

$$f(u, v) = \sum_{m=-\infty}^{+\infty} \sum_{n=-\infty}^{+\infty} f_1(m, n) f_2(u - m, v - n) \tag{3}$$

Where $f_1(m, n)$ denotes the gray value of an image at (m, n), $f_2(u - m, v - n)$ denotes the gray value of another image at $(u - m, v - n)$ which is rotated by $180°$, and this function denotes the value of convolution at (u, v).

We learn that existing template multiplies the image in formula (3), which is similar to convolution in the image processing. But the performance of direct convolution is even slower. Of course, the better the performance is, the more satisfied we are. Therefore, we find that it is effective to speed up the NCC matching algorithm by FFT [15]. We can achieve the value of convolution by FFT transforming the spatial domain to the frequency domain. In our experiment by NCC matching algorithm based on FFT, we magically redefine image cycle, *i.e.*, repetitiveness presented in this paper.

2.3 Repetitiveness Metric

Different from conventional methods, this paper presents a repetitiveness metric which depends on the results of NCC matching algorithm based on FFT and points out these NCC values where a found texture patch matches the gray global image embodying the repetitiveness of this texton, then getting some NCC matrices that are going to participate in the following formula.

Denoting the maximum and minimum values of the tth region P_t by $\max_{P_t CR_n} P_t$ and $\min_{P_t CR_n} P_t$, we formulate the feature score of the input image I as

$$D(\Gamma_n) = \lambda \sqrt{\frac{1}{T} \sum_{t=1}^{T} \left(\max_{P_t C \Gamma_n} P_t - \min_{P_t C \Gamma_n} P_t \right)^2} \tag{4}$$

$$R(I) = \frac{1}{S+1} \left(\max_{1 \leq n \leq N} D(\Gamma_n) + \sum_{k=1}^{S} D(\Gamma_k) \right) \tag{5}$$

Where T is the number of Poisson disk sampled P_t in the Γ_n. But Dai *et al.* set T to be 80 and get 80 randomly sampled regions. It could lose significant datum. We set the size of P_t to be $\lfloor H_I/5 \rfloor \times \lfloor W_I/5 \rfloor$. A size is either so small that it couldn't capture large-scale repetition or so large that it could lose discrimination power. $D(\Gamma_n)$ denotes the difference by normalizing Euclidean distance between $\max_{P_t C \Gamma_n} P_t$ and $\min_{P_t C \Gamma_n} P_t$. To clearly compare the final results, we set parameter λ as 100. The larger the difference, the better the repetitiveness. The principle behind above property is that for repetitive texture patches the matching function should exhibit peaks and valleys. In the next formula, see Fig. 3 for a perfect analysis of repetitiveness metric.

As shown in Fig. 3, we analyze these values by formula (4) in an ascending order. We think the maximum value reveals that the extracted texture patch is the best ideal structural texton we want to find and the minimum value reveals that it is a worse structural texton. In order to better distinguish the differences between final sorted results, we set limitation δ to be 0.2 to capture S values slightly more than the minimum value. Eventually, we work out the average of above-mentioned values as the repetitiveness score. Repetitiveness is similar to the Harmonicity feature of [17], but repetitiveness is more robust because it pools over local regions.

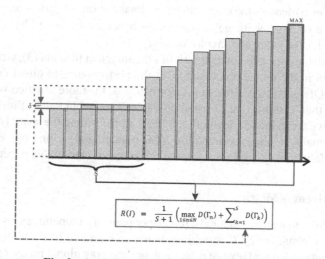

$$R(I) = \frac{1}{S+1}\left(\max_{1 \le n \le N} D(\Gamma_n) + \sum_{k=1}^{S} D(\Gamma_k)\right)$$

Fig. 3. Analysis process of repetitiveness metric

3   Experimental Results and Analyses

We have implemented our method by using MATLAB R2014a on a Windows 10 operating system. To evaluate the effectiveness of our method in dealing with different kinds of texture images and achieving fitter resolutions, we select some 800×500 images that contain repetitiveness textures. In order to get some clearly structural repetitiveness texture exemplars as the ground for comparison, we set the radius of Poisson disk to be 128 and the size of the exemplar to be 256×256. By setting the number of the uniform block to be 4×4, we extract some useful texture patches which are in the gray image and contain some textons. Although we couldn't find a very effective texton by the uniform block, it is enough for the purpose of our experiment. To validate the effectiveness and feasibility of our proposed method, we evaluate our method for both visualization and computational complexity.

3.1 Visual Evaluations

For visual evaluations, we run our presented method to a collected image database and visualize the results of repetitiveness scores, as shown in Figs. 4 and 5. Due to the innovativeness of repetitiveness feature, we only compare ours with Dai *et al.* Our system automatically sorts texture exemplars according to the feature scores.

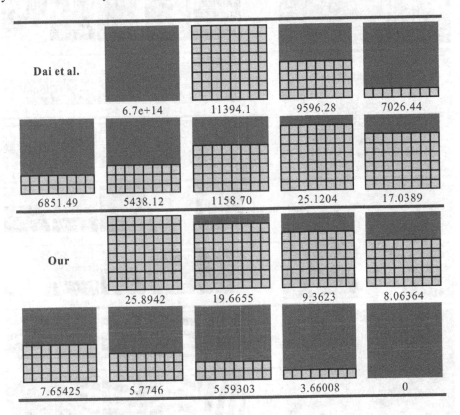

Fig. 4. Repetitiveness scores of experimental images

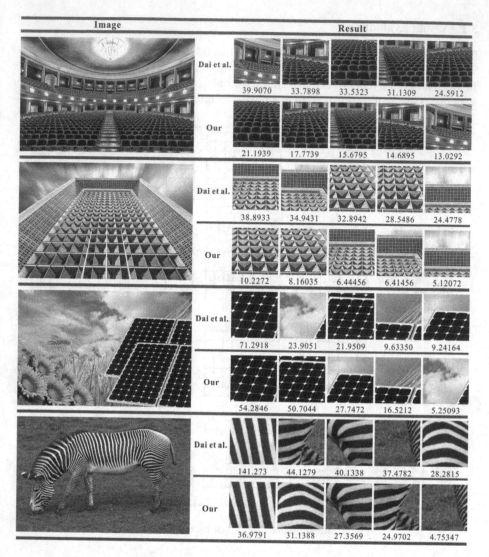

Fig. 5. The visual results of acquiring the repetitiveness-based texture exemplar

Once again, we want to obtain above-mentioned best repetitiveness texture image rather than nonstructural homogeneity texture image. As shown in Fig. 4, we attempt to compare Dai *et al.* and our experimental results with simple images which include more or less repetitive cyan squares as repetitiveness textons in the green background. Satisfactorily, our results are more acceptable than Dai *et al.* From a visual point of view, the results by Dai *et al.* are quite unsorted, but the results by us are in good order and comfortable.

As shown in Fig. 5, using Poisson disk sampling algorithm, we achieve some exemplars from the five input images. In every row, we can observe the sorted results by Dai *et al.* and us. Obviously, our results are more ideal than Dai *et al.* There are larger fluctuations among the repetitiveness scores by Dai *et al*. However, the repetitiveness scores by us range from 0 to 100. For the same method, the higher the score is, the better the repetitiveness of the texture exemplar is. See Fig. 5 where we demonstrate the effect of our method.

3.2 Computational Complexity Analyses

Besides the visual evaluations, we also perform computational complexity analyses for our method to validate the effect of repetitiveness algorithm. In this section, we evaluate the performance of repetitiveness algorithm to find out the difference between these two methods. In our experiments, considering the kinds of texture exemplars, we select 128 textures from images similar to those in Fig. 1. We time the processes of performing repetitiveness algorithm. The following is a quantitative graph.

To evaluate the performance of repetitiveness algorithm, we perform a test about Dai *et al*. and our running time. The results are as shown in Fig. 6. From the computational complexity analyses in Fig. 6, we can clearly see that time gradually increases with the increasing number of exemplar. Obviously, compared with Dai *et al*. for different exemplars, ours performs better and the increasing trend of running time is slower because of FFT in our method. The shorter the running time is, the more satisfying the performance is. Therefore, it takes less time to confirm our expectation.

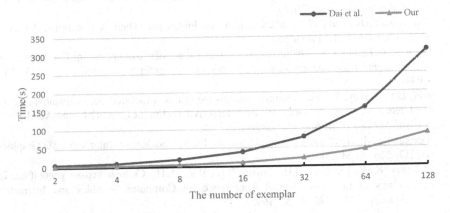

Fig. 6. Comparison of running time

4   Conclusion

In this paper, we present a repetitiveness metric method to pick out an optimal texture exemplar which is used to synthesize texture. Different from conventional methods of extracting texture exemplars which are concerned with texture feature analysis for synthesizing target textures, our method emphasizes the quality of texture exemplars. We automatically get some uniformly distributed texture exemplars in the image with Poisson disk sampling. For each texture exemplar, we can get some values by NCC matching algorithm based on FFT. Using a repetitiveness metric, we can extract some useful information from these values as a standard of recognizing the repetitiveness quality. In a word, we perform an accuracy and efficiency repetitiveness metric method of texture exemplars. Our method can satisfy visual requirement and accomplish high-quality work in a shorter time due to FFT. Compelling visual results and computational complexity analyses prove the validity of our work.

Acknowledgments. This work was supported in part by grants from the National Natural Science Foundation of China (Nos. 61303101, 61572328), the Shenzhen Research Foundation for Basic Research, China (Nos. JCYJ20150324140036846, JCYJ20170302153551588, CXZZ201409021 60818443, CXZZ20140902102350474, CXZZ20150813151056544, JCYJ20150630105452814, JCYJ20160331114551175, JCYJ20160608173051207), the Start-up Research Fund of Shenzhen University (Nos. 2013-827-000009), the China-UK Visual Information Processing Laboratory (VIPL) and Maternal and child health monitoring and early warning Engineering Technology Research Center (METRC) of Guangdong Province.

References

1. Thakur, U., Wien, M., Naser, K.: Dynamic texture synthesis using linear phase shift interpolation. In: Picture Coding Symposium (2017)
2. Liu, G., Gousseau, Y., Xia, G.S.: Texture synthesis through convolutional neural networks and spectrum constraints (2016)
3. Kindermann, R., Snell, J.L.: Markov Random Fields and Their Applications. American Mathematical Society, Providence (1980)
4. Efros, A.A., Leung, T.K.: Texture synthesis by non-parametric sampling. In: The Proceedings of the Seventh IEEE International Conference on Computer Vision, vol. 2, p. 1033. IEEE (1999)
5. Wei, L.Y., Levoy, M.: Fast texture synthesis using tree-structured vector quantization. In: Conference on Computer Graphics and Interactive Techniques, pp. 479–488. ACM Press/ Addison-Wesley Publishing Co (2000)
6. Ashikhmin, M.: Synthesizing natural textures. In: Symposium on Interactive 3D Graphics, pp. 217–226. ACM (2001)
7. Fleischer, K.W., Laidlaw, D.H., Currin, B.L., Barr, A.H.: Cellular texture generation. In: Proceedings of the 22nd Annual Conference on Computer Graphics and Interactive Techniques, pp. 239–248. ACM (1995)
8. Liang, L.: Real-time texture synthesis by patch-based sampling. ACM Trans. Graph. **20**(3), 127–150 (2001)
9. Zhu, S.C., Guo, C.E., Wang, Y., Xu, Z.: What are textons? Int. J. Comput. Vis. **62**(1), 121–143 (2005)
10. Ying, L., Hertzmann, A., Biermann, H., Zorin, D.: Texture and shape synthesis on surfaces. In: Gortler, S.J., Myszkowski, K. (eds.) Rendering Techniques 2001. Eurographics. Springer, Vienna (2001). https://doi.org/10.1007/978-3-7091-6242-2_28
11. Lefebvre, S., Hoppe, H.: Parallel controllable texture synthesis. ACM Trans. Graph. **24**(3), 777–786 (2005)
12. Lazebnik, S., Schmid, C., Ponce, J.: A sparse texture representation using local affine regions. IEEE Trans. Pattern Anal. Mach. Intell. **27**(8), 1265 (2005)

13. Dai, D., Riemenschneider, H., Gool, L.V.: The synthesizability of texture examples. In: IEEE Conference on Computer Vision and Pattern Recognition, pp. 3027–3034. IEEE Computer Society (2014)
14. Bridson, R.: Fast poisson disk sampling in arbitrary dimensions. ACM SIGGRAPH Sketches 2007 **49**, 22 (2007). ACM
15. Lewis, J.P.: Fast normalized cross-correlation. Circ. Syst. Sig. Process. **82**(2), 144–156 (2001)
16. Sun, B.J., Zhou, D.H.: Fast matching method based on NCC. Transducer Microsyst. Technol. **26**(9), 104–106 (2007)
17. Liu, F., Picard, R.W.: Periodicity, directionality, and randomness: wold features for image modeling and retrieval. IEEE Trans. Pattern Anal. Mach. Intell. **18**(7), 722–733 (1996)

Unsupervised Cross-Modal Hashing with Soft Constraint

Yuxuan Zhou[1(✉)], Yaoxian Li[2], Rui Liu[1], Lingyun Hao[3], and Yuanliang Sun[4]

[1] University of Electronic Science and Technology of China, Chengdu 611731, China
yxuanzh@gmail.com
[2] State Key Lab Elect Thin Film and Integrated Device, University of Electronic Science and Technology of China, Chengdu 610054, China
[3] Xidian University, Xi'an 710071, China
[4] Southeast University, Nanjing 211189, China

Abstract. The booming demands for cross-modal retrieval tasks can often bring in its wake the development of retrieval technologies, as people turn to pursuing a more effective way to improve the performance of search results in both accuracy and efficiency, for example by unsupervised cross-modal hashing. It's worth noting that most of the cross-modal hashing methods focus on utilizing merely one approach to generate hash codes. However, each approach has its own intrinsic drawback, which would inevitably diminish the quality of hash codes. In this paper, we propose a state-of-the-art model named *Soft Constraint Hashing* (SCH), using a special soft constraint term defined as an "information tunnel" to achieve the goal that conveys information from one approach to another. In particular, this "tunnel" can eliminate potential data noises to some extent and bridge the gap between two unsupervised discrete hashing allocation approaches to simultaneously reinforce the quality of hash codes. The empirical results on publicly available datasets illustrate that our proposed model outperforms all the existing unsupervised cross-model hashing methods.

Keywords: Unsupervised hashing · Multi-modal data · Soft constraint

1 Introduction

In recent years, the increase of multi-modal data like text and image has contributed to the rapid development of multimedia technologies [1]. As some labels from the single model may be wrong or inaccurate, cross-modal learning schemes are expected to learn more discriminative features and perform better in multi-model retrieval. Consequently, a series of algorithms designed for large-scale cross-modal contents retrieval problems have been put forth [2].

Due to the merits of fewer data storage and better content searching performance, hashing methods have been emerging topic in the cross-modal retrieval tasks [3,4]. In a common scenario, some approaches are transforming data points

© Springer International Publishing AG, part of Springer Nature 2018
B. Zeng et al. (Eds.): PCM 2017, LNCS 10736, pp. 756–765, 2018.
https://doi.org/10.1007/978-3-319-77383-4_74

derived from two modalities into the common space with the guidance of supervised category information, which is called supervised cross-modal hashing [5,6]. Although supervised hashing typically achieves superior performance, it needs a lot of manual works to obtain large-scale labels in current real-world applications. Hence, most of unsupervised hashing methods are applied under a setting that there is no classification information to support the training of hashing.

For unsupervised cross-modal hashing methods, several approaches were proposed in the recent years. As the first approach to use hashing technique to deal with cross-modal retrieval, cross-modal similarity sensitive hashing (CMSSH) [7] maps the different modalities into a common Hamming space. And Collective Matrix Factorization Hashing (CMFH) [8] learns the unified hash codes by collective matrix factorization in the shared latent semantic space from one instance in different modalities. Inter-Media Hashing (IMH) [9] generates nonlinear hash functions to fit the scenario of cross-modality retrieval and takes the differences between multiple modalities into consideration. These proposed ideas tend to utilize matrix projection and factorization methods to get the relaxed solution and calculate hash codes. Therefore, hash codes generated by above ideas are inevitable to lose some information for the semantic gap and quantization loss. To solve these problems, spectral rotation method is proposed, which partly diminishes the deterioration of hash codes. However, neither these unsupervised methods give a discrete solution for hash codes nor do they truly exploit the relationship among instances.

Using image and semantic features to construct similarity matrices is a good approach to solve troubles mentioned above. It is easy to prove that using similarity matrix to allocate hash codes has the same efficiency as spectral rotation in bridging the semantic gap and minimizing the quantization loss. So in the first step of our method, similarity matrices are utilized to generate guide hash codes, which can partly solve the semantic gap problem. However, these guide codes might have overfitted problem under the influence of the incomplete normalization term. To solve the overfitting problem, we mainly use matrix projection method accompanied with soft constraint terms in the second step. The setting of soft constraint term is like a bridge, which can carry the valuable guide hash codes into the second step and fix some "bad bits" in the ultimate hash codes. This method solves hash codes discretely and eliminates quantization loss. In short, our main work is to conduct a unified framework for integrating the advantages of both similarity matrix allocation and matrix projection methods in one model and handle the overfit problem in a discrete way.

In this paper, we propose a novel unsupervised cross-modal hashing approach named *Soft Constraint Hashing* (SCH). The method generates a two-step algorithm. The main contributions of this paper are summarized as below.

- The setting of soft constraint combines the merits of two sorts of hashing algorithms and reduces the noise that exists in hash codes.
- The proposed method solves the hash codes in a discrete way.
- The proposed method deeply exploits the relationship among instances and bridges the semantic gap via similarity matrices.

The remainder of this paper is organized as follows. Firstly, we introduce related works for addressing this problem in Sect. 2. Then we introduce proposed methods in Sect. 3. Experimental results and analysis are reported in Sect. 4, followed by conclusions in Sect. 5.

2   Related Work

The proposed method is relevant to the field in Learning to Hash and Image Information Retrieval. As a result, a large quantity of works are related to our work. In this section, two important models are introduced which are applied in this paper.

2.1   Column Sampling Based Discrete Supervised Hashing

Solving discrete hash codes from similarity matrix is a NP hard problem. The object function for this problem can be formulated as:

$$\min_{B} ||qS - B^T B||_F^2 \tag{1}$$

In this formula, $S \in \{-1,1\}^{n \times n}$ and $B \in \{-1,1\}^{q \times n}$, where n denotes the number of training samples as well as q represents the code length of hash. S is a semantic similarity matrix, where $S_{ij} = 1$ and $S_{i,j} = -1$ mean that point i and point j are semantically similar and dissimilar, respectively. Our goal is to utilize the given similarity matrix S to solve binary hash codes B. When the Eq. (1) reaches its minimum via adjusting B, we get the hash codes. As a kind of hashing allocation procedure, COSDISH [10] shows its great merits for fast optimizing hash codes like Eq. (1) in a discrete way. In fact, it is free to relax S to $(-1, 1)^{n \times n}$ without changing the whole solving process proposed in COSDISH.

2.2   Fast Supervised Discrete Hashing

Inspired by Supervised Discrete Hashing (SDH) [11], a new kind of method called Fast Supervised Discrete Hashing (FSDH) [12] is proposed, with a little adjustment on the original model in SDH. In the SDH model, hash codes need to be updated column by column. Thanks to the little adjustment, all the hash codes can be updated discretely at the same time, which results in an increase in the calculation velocity.

3   Proposed Approach

In order to generate the hash codes, we propose a two-step hash algorithm. In the first step, we utilize the similarity matrices constructed by two modalities to allocate hash codes, which is termed guide hash. Then we apply these guide codes as one side of the "tunnel" to facilitate the optimization of the ultimate hash codes and corresponding projection matrices. These matrices are used for out of sample extension. The framework of soft constraint hashing is illustrated in Fig. 1.

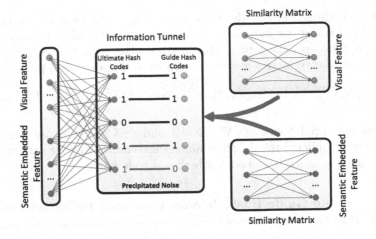

Fig. 1. Our framework about soft constraint hashing

3.1 Preliminary and Notation

Suppose that there is a dataset with n instances. For instance i, we have an image feature vector $x_i^{(1)} \in \mathbb{R}^a$ and a text feature vector $x_i^{(2)} \in \mathbb{R}^b$. We further define $X^{(1)} = [x_1^{(1)} \ x_2^{(1)} \ \cdots \ x_n^{(1)}] \in \mathbb{R}^{a \times n}$ and $X^{(2)} = [x_1^{(2)} \ x_2^{(2)} \ \cdots \ x_n^{(2)}] \in \mathbb{R}^{b \times n}$ to denote two modalities in a dataset. As mentioned, we denote $B_G = [b_{G1}, b_{G2}, \cdots, b_{Gn}] \in \{-1,1\}^{q \times n}$ as the guide hash codes and $B = [b_1, b_2, \cdots, b_n] \in \{-1,1\}^{q \times n}$ as the ultimate hash codes, where q represents the length of hash codes. $P_1 \in \mathbb{R}^{q \times a}$ & $P_2 \in \mathbb{R}^{q \times b}$ are projection matrices, which can convert $X^{(1)}$ and $X^{(2)}$ to the ultimate hash codes B respectively.

In order to better express relationship among instances, we define a kernel function $\phi(x_i, x_j) = 2e^{\frac{\|x_i - x_j\|_2^2}{2\sigma^2}} - 1$, where x_i and x_j are vectors. Furthermore, the similarity matrix is constructed as $\Phi(X^{(m)}, X^{(n)})$, where $\Phi_{i,j}(X^{(m)}, X^{(n)}) = \phi(x_i^{(m)}, x_j^{(n)})$ (e.g. $X^{(1)} \in \mathbb{R}^{a \times n}$, $X^{(2)} \in \mathbb{R}^{b \times n}$ and thus $\Phi(X^{(1)}, X^{(2)}) \in \mathbb{R}^{a \times b}$). Another function used in this paper is the sign function $sign(\cdot)$, which outputs $+1$ for positive numbers or -1 otherwise. Meanwhile, we denote $\|\cdot\|_F$ to represent Frobenius norm in this paper.

3.2 Step One: Guide Hash Allocation

In this section, we conduct our formula for allocating guide hash and the corresponding solving procedure.

Formulation for Guide Hash. In multimedia researching area, a semantic gap is a long-existing problem and troubles researchers a lot. In order to bridge the gap, one simple approach is to set up a rotation matrix so that the gap could be narrowed down [13]. After the rotation process, what changes is the concrete value of every instance, but the distance among these instances is immobile. Inspired by this fact, we find that it is not the concrete value of every instance but the relationship among them that matters. Based on this conclusion, here we use the similarity matrix model to implement the allocation procedure:

$$\min_{B_G} \alpha||q\Phi(X^{(1)},X^{(1)}) - B_G^T B_G||_F^2 + (1-\alpha)||q\Phi(X^{(2)},X^{(2)}) - B_G^T B_G||_F^2 \quad (2)$$

As we sentenced before, $\Phi(X^{(1)},X^{(1)})$ and $\Phi(X^{(2)},X^{(2)})$ are two similarity matrices to indicate relationships among instances. Another variance is B_G, which is given as guide hash codes, where q is code length.

Solution for the Guide Hash. In order to optimize the formulation before, Eq. (2) need to be reformulated as:

$$\min_{B_G} ||\alpha q\Phi(X^{(1)},X^{(1)}) + (1-\alpha)q\Phi(X^{(2)},X^{(2)}) - B_G^T B_G||_F^2 \quad (3)$$

Observing Eqs. (1) and (3), it is easy to conclude that Eq. (3) could be solved discretely by the algorithm proposed in COSDISH [10].

3.3   Step Two: Sparse Hashing with Soft Constraint

In this part, we introduce a soft constraint equation and apply guide hash codes to train final binary codes. In this process, we iteratively update hash codes B and projection matrices P_1 and P_2.

Formulation for Ultimate Hash Codes. The hash codes generated above utilize similarity matrices to bridge the semantic gap successfully. However, hash codes made by this approach put too much weight on the relationship among samples and overlook the possible overfit problem for the missing of any normalization term. To address this problem, we conduct the soft constraint formula, which can optimize guide hash codes efficiently. In Eq. (4), B_G is regarded as reference codes to guide the training of final hash codes B. P_1 and P_2 are projection matrices, which can convert $X^{(1)}$ and $X^{(2)}$ to hash codes.

$$\min_{B,P_1,P_2} ||B_G - B||_F^2 + \beta_1||B - P_1 X^{(1)}||_F^2 + \beta_2||B - P_2 X^{(2)}||_F^2$$
$$+ \eta_1||P_1||_1 + \eta_2||P_2||_1 \quad (4)$$

Update P_1 and P_2. The formula above is non-convex. However, if we fix B, P_2 and update P_1, it is easy to get its exclusive solution. As thus, Eq. (4) can be rewritten as:

$$\min_{P_1} \beta_1||B - P_1 X^{(1)}||_F^2 + \eta_1||P_1||_1 \quad (5)$$

We solve the problem in Eq. (5) by using SLEP [16] package. The same method could be applied to solve P_2 .

Update B. Average methods try to seek a relaxed solution for hash codes, however, it is hard to get discrete ones. Here we apply the solving method FSDH mentioned in Sect. 2 to update B discretely. Compared with the method in SDH, we can obtain hash codes in one step without any iteration. The solution is shown in Eq. (6).

$$B = sign(B_G + \beta_1 P_1 X_1 + \beta_2 P_2 X_2) \tag{6}$$

The the total algorithm combines *Guide Hash Allocation* and *Sparse Hashing with Soft Constraint* can be seen in Algorithm 1 as follow.

Algorithm 1. Algorithm for Hashing with Soft Constraint.

Input: Training image data $X^{(1)}$ and training text data $X^{(2)}$;
Output: Ultimate binary codes B, hash function P_1 and P_2;
  1: Construct image similarity matrix $\Phi(X^{(1)}, X^{(1)})$;
  2: Construct text similarity matrix $\Phi(X^{(2)}, X^{(2)})$;
  3: Update Guide hashing codes B_G by solving the sub-problem in Eq. (3);
  4: Initialize B by evaluating $B = B_G$;
  5: **repeat**
  6:    Update P_1 and P_2;
  7:    Update B according to Eq. (6);
  8: **until** there is no change to P_1, P_2 and B
  9: **return** B, P_1 and P_2;

---

4 Experimental Results

In this section, we introduce baseline methods and compare them with *Soft Constraint Hashing* from the aspects of the cross-modal retrieval accuracy.

4.1 Experimental Settings

We use two cross-modal datasets (MIR-Flickr [17] and LabelMe [18]) to evaluate the performance of our method.

MIR-Flickr is a dataset consisting of images instances accompanied with associated textual tags. For this image database, We remove the instances without labels or textual tags appearing until its image is represented by 150-dimension edge histogram. Derived from PCA on its index tagging vector, its text presents as a 500-dimensional feature vector. For each instance, we take 5% of the dataset as the query set and the rest is the training set and retrieval database. The other dataset is LabelMe, which provides a dataset of digital images. Each image is represented by a 512-dimension GIST [19] feature and each text are represented by an index vector of selected tags. In LabelMe, Image-text pairs are considered to be similar if they share the same scene labels.

As trade-off parameter, α in Eq. (2) is set as 0.35 on both datasets in experiments. In Eq. (4), we set the parameter β_1 and β_2 as 1 and 5, which gives the guide hash codes a proper weight in the optimization process. The two regularization parameters η_1 and η_2 are set as 0.01 and 75, respectively. All of these parameter values are chosen empirically and have proved good enough on all the empirical datasets. Due to the characteristic of COSDISH hash, results might be different in the same parameters. For each pair of parameters, we randomly select one of them as our result. Parameters that used in baselines are all set up as recommendation.

4.2 Baselines

We select several representative methods in unsupervised cross-modal hashing areas as baselines, including Collective Matrix Factorization Hashing (CMFH)[8], Cross-modality Similarity Sensitive Hashing (CMSSH)[7] and Intermedia Hashing (IMH)[9]. For all baseline methods, the source codes are kindly provided by their authors.

4.3 Soft Constraint or Not?

In this subsection we perform a comparison of the proposed models with and without soft constraint term, aiming to see how much the performance in generating hash codes with soft constraint. The comparative results on LabelMe is reported in Table 1, and the results on MIR-Flicker is shown in Table 2.

According to Tables 1 and 2, by adding the soft constraint term in Step 2, the performance of both mAP and precision are obviously improved in general.

Table 1. Hashing with and without soft constraint on LabelMe

Index	Methods	$Image \rightarrow Text$				$Text \rightarrow Image$			
		16 bits	32 bits	64 bits	128 bits	16 bits	32 bits	64 bits	128 bits
mAP	With constraint	0.5656	0.6204	0.6898	0.6901	0.6839	0.7059	0.7597	0.7836
	Without constraint	0.6162	0.578	0.5858	0.5619	0.6693	0.6554	0.6645	0.6306
	Improvement	−8.2%	7.3%	17.8%	22.8%	2.2%	7.7%	14.3%	24.3%
Precision	With constraint	0.5411	0.5849	0.3219	0.2175	0.6447	0.7583	0.7044	0.6774
	Without constraint	0.3103	0.2356	0.2769	0.2105	0.7138	0.6712	0.6945	0.6331
	Improvement	74.4%	148.3%	16.3%	3.3%	−9.7%	13.0%	1.4%	6.5%

Table 2. Hashing with and without soft constraint on MIR-Flickr

Index	Methods	$Image \rightarrow Text$				$Text \rightarrow Image$			
		16 bits	32 bits	64 bits	128 bits	16 bits	32 bits	64 bits	128 bits
mAP	With constraint	0.3022	0.3057	0.31	0.3104	0.3022	0.3064	0.3082	0.3098
	Without constraint	0.3033	0.3031	0.3051	0.3045	0.3019	0.3025	0.3036	0.3022
	Improvement	−0.4%	0.9%	1.6%	1.9%	0.1%	1.3%	1.5%	2.5%
Precision	With constraint	0.5989	0.6239	0.5167	0.3225	0.6063	0.5597	0.3754	0.1841
	Without constraint	0.5894	0.0036	0.003	0	0.6131	0.2106	0.2147	0.0916
	Improvement	1.6%	17230.6%	17123.3%	NaN	−1.1%	165.8%	74.8%	101.0%

As can be seen in Table 2, in particular for precision, results indicate an unsatisfactory performance without constraint. This result indicates that the usage of guide hash codes can actually help generate hash codes with a better quality and subsequently enhances the performance of cross-modal retrieval.

4.4 Overall Comparison with Baselines

As can be seen in Fig. 2, we report the mAP of all methods in LabelMe and MIR-Flickr with different lengths of binary codes, i.e. 16, 32, 64 and 128 bits. It can be observed that SCH substantially outperforms all methods for all cross-modal retrieval tasks. $Text \rightarrow Image$ tasks use text as query to search similar images from text database. And $Image \rightarrow Text$ tasks use images as query to search similar texts from image database. Inheriting merits from COSDISH and the soft constraint, SCH outperforms all the existing methods to the best of our knowledge. In particular, compared to the best shallow baseline CMFH, SCH achieves absolute increases of −2.23%/−1.69%, 0.10%/0.72%, 0.91%/0,62%, 1.17%/1.31% in mAP for $Image \rightarrow Text/Text \rightarrow Image$ on MIR-Flickr, and reaches to an improvement of mAP score in 0.1422/0.1352, 0.2080/0.1502, 0.2731/0.1677, 0.3625/0.4578 on LabelMe. The CMFH performs good in short code-length. However, as code length increases, retrieval performances decay, which might result from the overfit problem. With the increase of multimedia data on social websites, short codes seem inferior due to its low storage capacity. In contrast, relatively long codes can better fulfill requirements of large scale data retrieval tasks. And our proposed method get high-quality results in long code-length. These results verify that SCH is able to get high-quality results for effective cross-modal retrieval.

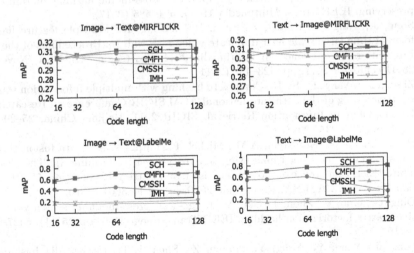

Fig. 2. Results on MIR-Flickr and LabelMe

5   Conclusion

In this paper, we propose a novel model to improve the retrieval efficiency of unsupervised cross-modal hashing methods. With the assistance of a soft constraint term, two different sorts of methods could fuse together to help diminish data noises and the quantization loss. From experiment results, we can find that mAP in proposed method makes a steady growth as the length of code increases, by contrast, that of other methods fluctuate gradually, which probably result from their failures to withstand data noises. When the code length is 128-bit – a reasonable size, our method performs well on both MIR-Flickr dataset and LabelMe dataset. And an inevitable problem for our proposed method is that the result might mutate slightly with same parameters due to the instability of COSDISH. As future work, we suggest improving the stability of COSDISH to get high-quality results.

References

1. Wang, J., Zhou, Y., Duan, K., Wang, J.J.-Y., Bensmail, H.: Supervised cross-modal factor analysis for multiple modal data classification. In: 2015 IEEE International Conference on Systems, Man, and Cybernetics, Kowloon Tong, Hong Kong, 9–12 October 2015, pp. 1882–1888 (2015)
2. Gudivada, V.N., Raghavan, V.V.: Content-based image retrieval systems – guest editors' introduction. IEEE Comput. **28**(9), 18–22 (1995)
3. Liu, L., Lin, Z., Shao, L., Shen, F., Ding, G., Han, J.: Sequential discrete hashing for scalable cross-modality similarity retrieval. IEEE Trans. Image Process. **26**(1), 107–118 (2017)
4. Ding, K., Fan, B., Huo, C., Xiang, S., Pan, C.: Cross-modal hashing via rank-order preserving. IEEE Trans. Multimedia **19**(3), 571–585 (2017)
5. Song, J., Yang, Y., Huang, Z., Shen, H.T., Hong, R.: Multiple feature hashing for real-time large scale near-duplicate video retrieval. In: Proceedings of the 19th International Conference on Multimedia 2011, Scottsdale, AZ, USA, November 28–December 1 2011, pp. 423–432 (2011)
6. Zhang, D., Wang, F., Si, L.: Composite hashing with multiple information sources. In: Proceeding of the 34th International ACM SIGIR Conference on Research and Development in Information Retrieval, SIGIR 2011, Beijing, China, 25–29 July 2011, pp. 225–234 (2011)
7. Bronstein, M.M., Bronstein, A.M., Michel, F., Paragios, N.: Data fusion through cross-modality metric learning using similarity-sensitive hashing. In: The Twenty-Third IEEE Conference on Computer Vision and Pattern Recognition, CVPR 2010, San Francisco, CA, USA, 13–18 June 2010, pp. 3594–3601 (2010)
8. Ding, G., Guo, Y., Zhou, J., Gao, Y.: Large-scale cross-modality search via collective matrix factorization hashing. IEEE Trans. Image Process. **25**(11), 5427–5440 (2016)
9. Song, J., Yang, Y., Yang, Y., Huang, Z., Shen, H.T.: Inter-media hashing for large-scale retrieval from heterogeneous data sources. In: Proceedings of the ACM SIGMOD International Conference on Management of Data, SIGMOD 2013, New York, NY, USA, 22–27 June 2013, pp. 785–796 (2013)

10. Kang, W.-C., Li, W.-J., Zhou, Z.-H.: Column sampling based discrete supervised hashing. In: Proceedings of the Thirtieth AAAI Conference on Artificial Intelligence, 12–17 February 2016, Phoenix, Arizona, USA, pp. 1230–1236 (2016)
11. Shen, F., Shen, C., Liu, W., Shen, H.T.: Supervised discrete hashing. In: IEEE Conference on Computer Vision and Pattern Recognition, CVPR 2015, Boston, MA, USA, 7–12 June 2015, pp. 37–45 (2015)
12. Gui, J., Liu, T., Sun, Z., Tao, D., Tan, T.: Fast supervised discrete hashing. IEEE Trans. Pattern Anal. Mach. Intell. 40(2), 490–496 (2017)
13. Yang, Y., Luo, Y., Chen, W., Shen, F., Shao, J., Shen, H.T.: Zero-shot hashing via transferring supervised knowledge. In: Proceedings of the 2016 ACM Conference on Multimedia Conference, MM 2016, Amsterdam, The Netherlands, 15–19 October 2016, pp. 1286–1295 (2016)
14. Zhu, X., Huang, Z., Shen, H.T., Zhao, X.: Linear cross-modal hashing for efficient multimedia search. In: ACM Multimedia Conference, MM 2013, Barcelona, Spain, 21–25 October 2013, pp. 143–152 (2013)
15. Wu, B., Yang, Q., Zheng, W.-S., Wang, Y., Wang, J.: Quantized correlation hashing for fast cross-modal search. In: Proceedings of the Twenty-Fourth International Joint Conference on Artificial Intelligence, IJCAI 2015, Buenos Aires, Argentina, 25–31 July 2015, pp. 3946–3952 (2015)
16. Liu, J., Ji, S., Ye, J.: SLEP: Sparse learning with efficient projections. Arizona State University (2009)
17. Huiskes, M.J., Lew, M.S.: The MIR flickr retrieval evaluation. In: Proceedings of the 1st ACM SIGMM International Conference on Multimedia Information Retrieval, MIR 2008, Vancouver, British Columbia, Canada, 30–31 October 2008, pp. 39–43 (2008)
18. Russell, B.C., Torralba, A., Murphy, K.P., Freeman, W.T.: LabelMe: a database and web-based tool for image annotation. Int. J. Comput. Vision 77(1–3), 157–173 (2008)
19. Oliva, A., Torralba, A.: Modeling the shape of the scene: a holistic representation of the spatial envelope. Int. J. Comput. Vision 42(3), 145–175 (2001)

Scalable Video Coding Based on the User's View for Real-Time Virtual Reality Applications

Hao Jiang[1(✉)], Gang He[1], Wenxin Yu[2], Zheng Wang[1], and Yunsong Li[1]

[1] School of Telecommunication Engineering, Xidian University,
Xi'an, Shaanxi, China
Jiang8115@outlook.com
[2] Southwest University of Science and Technology, Mianyang, Sichuan, China

Abstract. The transmission of virtual reality (VR) video requires huge bandwidth, which brings great challenges for the system implementation of real-time applications. This paper proposes a scalable panoramic video coding method to adapt the insufficient bandwidth. The feedback of user's movement information from VR device to video encoder is utilized. The regions that user is interested in are first mapped and then coded in high quality while the others in low quality. Experiments show that our optimized system leads to approximately 87% average reduction of bit-rate while there is no significant decrease in quality of region-of-interest in panorama.

Keywords: Virtual Reality (VR) · User vision · Feedback
Panoramic mapping · Scalable High Efficiency Video Coding (SHVC)

1 Introduction

Applications of VR and panoramic videos have attracted considerable attention because of their fully immersive experience. Unfortunately, the current technologies are far from meeting the requirements of a perfect VR show with realistic 3D effects, low delay and high definition. Considering the strong resolving power of the human eye, the maximum angle between adjacent pixels is approximately 1.2 min (1/50°) to achieve good visual effects [1], which means the resolution of an ideal panoramic video could be at least 18 k × 9 k. With such huge data, even the most efficient video coding techniques such as HEVC cannot compress the video into an acceptable size for the transmission system, especially for some real-time applications. The two most common kinds of methods to reduce the bit-rate are optimizing the panoramic mapping algorithms and RoI coding.

Optimizing Mapping Algorithms. The exist video encoders are only capable to encode plane videos [2–4], it is necessary to flatten a scene from a spherical shape into one or several 2D shapes. The equirectangular projection [5] is the most common mapping solution. This projection method can completely record the information of the entire sphere, and the coordinate conversion is simple. However, as we can see in

B. Zeng et al. (Eds.): PCM 2017, LNCS 10736, pp. 766–775, 2018.
https://doi.org/10.1007/978-3-319-77383-4_75

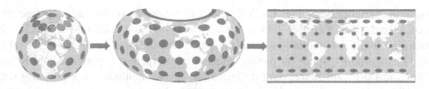

Fig. 1. Equirectangular projection

Fig. 1, there are obvious stretching in the panoramic image obtained by equirectangular projection, which brings redundant data.

Various of other solutions have being proposed like remapping equirectangular projection layout to cube [6] or rhombic dodecahedron [7]. Polyhedral structures can fit the spherical surface better to reduce redundant data and the boundary continuity of adjacent parts after splicing could be used for the prediction coding, but they result in greatly computational complexity and are still not efficient enough for VR applications.

Facebook put forward another effective method. It transforms the video from an equirectangular layout to the pyramid format for each of the 30 viewports and stores them on the server rather than encodes them in real time for each client request [8]. When the client makes a request to the server, the video web site only needs to transmit a view of the video at specific angle. It is claimed that the new solution reduced the stream size by 80% against the original. But the system needs to carry out lots of transform work on servers, plenty of computing resources are required. Since the transforming is based on existing video but not during the encoding process, it is difficult to apply the system in real-time communications.

The RoI Coding. Another kind of approach is to construct a stream of an arbitrary region-of-interest (RoI) from a high-resolution video instead of encoding and transmitting the full video. The VR device is only able to display a portion of the scene, most parts of the panoramic image are not shown on the screen. In principle, the system only need to pass the data of image that the user could see, and lots of bandwidth will be saved. Many solutions of RoI coding have been purposed despite some problems.

Authors in [9] explore two methods for RoI-based streaming, referring to them as tiled streaming and monolithic streaming. The former splits the original video into tiles which are separately encoded, and tiles that overlap with the RoI are sent to the client. This method requires multiple decoders and those pixels who belong to the tiles but not the RoI are superfluous. The second method only transmits the macroblocks falling within the RoI and the macroblocks being depended on either directly or indirectly by other ones falling within the RoI. A pre-processing is required to clarify dependencies. Considering the strong dependency between frames in video coding, the implementation of this scheme is extremely complex and the delay is high.

However, there are mainly three problems being imported by the partial coding. Firstly, it brings the reference problem. When user moves wearing the VR helmet, the contents of the picture may change dramatically, leading to more I frames and increased bit-rate. Yago Snchez purposes to insert Generated Reference Pictures (GRP) for inter prediction, and to use SHVC and Open GOP structures to optimize the reference [10, 11], but the system still only encodes a portion of the picture. Secondly, the system is latency-sensitive. The VR helmet generates a corresponding image on the screen according to the user's motion information. If the user moves quickly at a certain time and the required image is not transmitted in time, the user will see a blank area. The incomplete spherical picture affects the interactive experience of VR badly.

The third problem is mapping deformation. These methods work properly with a precondition that the panoramic videos and the RoI regions are rectangular (only for cylindric panoramic video including horizontal 360 degrees' information). But in VR applications, the videos are spheres containing all the $360° \times 180°$ information. Most of the VR panoramic videos are flattened by equirectangular projection. In this format, a rectangular user view does not correspond to a rectangular region in panoramic video (for more details, see Fig. 5). Since the encoder can only encode rectangular pictures, the panoramic video must be mapped and cropped into rectangular user view by inverse transformation, which brings deformation. So, reconstructed image of the previous frame cannot be used as a reference for the following frame.

Figure 2 shows an example when the user turns to the right. The left marked region is displayed at time t_0 and the right one at time t_1. The mapping deformation breaks the consistency of the same content between frames and affects the inter prediction.

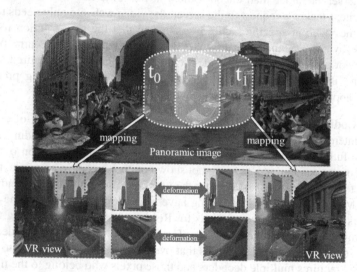

Fig. 2. Content comparison of frames

This paper proposes a user view based scalable video coding [12] system for VR. The messages of user's viewpoint from VR device are transmitted to the encoder (likes RoI methods), and only the part that user could see in VR displayer will be encoded in high quality while the hole panoramic frame is coded as a basic layer to ensure there won't appear blank areas on the screen. In this way, large amounts of video data could be cut down and over 80% transmission bandwidth requirements are reduced comparing with complete encoding.

The proposed scalable coding has several appealing properties. First, its structure is intentionally designed with simplicity, and yet provides excellent performance. Only few modifications are operated on the SHVC encoder, and the SHVC decoder is kept without modification. Second, with the non RoI being coded in the basic layer, there will not appear blank areas on the screens. Even the user moves much too fast or the network is unstable, some details can still be seen, which makes a better VR experience. Third, the basic layer can be utilized as a reference for the RoI in the enhancement layer, which avoids the mismatch problem in the inter prediction. On the other hand, since the coding is based on the entire panorama video and the image will not be transformed, there will not be deformation problem.

2 Proposed Coding Algorithm

2.1 System Flow

Figure 3 (a) illustrates the traditional VR video coding and transmission system. Panoramic videos are usually obtained by multiple cameras working simultaneously. After stitching we can get a 2:1 raw video including all the 360° × 180° environment information. The entire video is first encoded by the conventional encoder and then transmitted to the client. After that, the VR helmet will display the corresponding picture on the screen according to the user's action.

As we can see in Fig. 4, when a user looks in a certain direction, only about one-sixth of the sphere is in the user's vision field under the assumption that the VR video player could offer a 90° rectangle view as most VR applications do. Through equirectangular projection, the rectangle-view should be mapped into corresponding zones marked in green on panorama in Fig. 4(b), which means the other parts are not in sight right now.

In the proposed solution, the encoder need to do the mapping-work according to user's movement information. Shown in Fig. 3 (b), the VR device records user's head-movement information likes the coordinate of visual center and then feed it back. The encoder will map the view into a specific-shape region which will be precisely coded. The whole frame will also be encoded as an unsharp basic layer, because if the system only transmits a part of the picture, when the transmission and codec delay is unstable, there isn't enough time to match the screen and a blank area will appear on the screen, resulting in poor VR experience. On the other hand, the basic layer provides a good reference for predictive coding of higher layers, which plays a very important role in reducing the overall bit stream.

Section 2.2 discusses the equirectangular projection, and the details of the scalable coding will be shown in Sect. 2.3.

2.2 Vision Mapping

The encoder needs to map the correct regions based on the motion information before prediction coding. As shown in Fig. 5, different mapping centers result in different

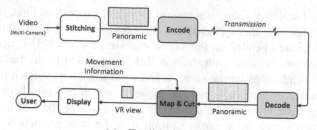

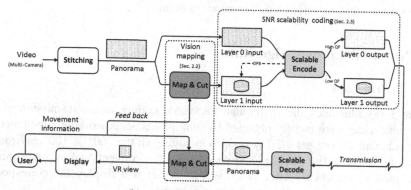

(a)   Traditional process

(b)   Proposed optimized process

Fig. 3. System processing flow

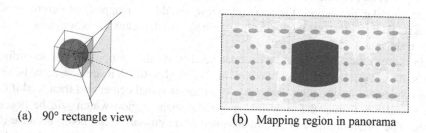

(a)   90° rectangle view   (b)   Mapping region in panorama

Fig. 4. Equirectangular projection (90°)

areas and shapes of regions on panoramic images which means various of situations should be considered.

The coordinate conversion of equirectangular projection is convenient. Take the world map mapping as an example, if we set the coordinate origin to the center of the map and the customer is facing forward at this moment, the relationship between latitude, longitude coordinates and Cartesian coordinates is:

$$
\begin{cases} x = \lambda\rho \\ y = \varphi\rho \end{cases} \quad and \quad \begin{cases} \lambda = x/\rho \\ \varphi = y/\rho \end{cases}
\tag{1}
$$

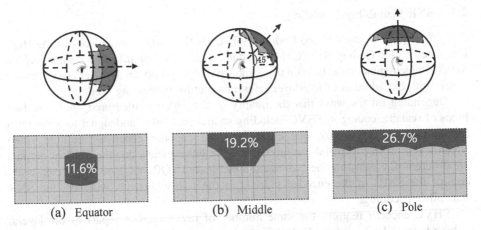

(a) Equator   (b) Middle   (c) Pole

Fig. 5. Panoramic mappings of different angles

λ and φ are the longitude and the latitude of the location to project. x and y are the horizontal and the vertical coordinates of the projected location on the map respectively. ρ is a constant representing the radius.

If there is a point (x', y') on the map which was projected from (λ', φ') satisfying

$$\begin{cases} \lambda' = x'/\rho \\ \varphi' = y'/\rho \end{cases} \tag{2}$$

and meeting the inequality group (3). We will conclude that this point is in the field of vision and it will be displayed on the VR device screen. (The horizontal and vertical visual angles are both set as θ.)

$$\begin{cases} \lambda' \le \theta/2 \\ \tan(\varphi') \le \ \tan(\theta/2) \cdot \cos(\lambda') \end{cases} \quad \theta = 90° \tag{3}$$

When the customer turns to another direction, the origin of the spherical coordinate system and the mapping center are changed. The coordinate should be first rotated and then substituted into the inequality group (3) for judgment.

We can tell a characteristic of the panoramic pictures obtained by equirectangular projection from Fig. 1 that the closer to the two poles, the greater pixels are extended. Shown in Fig. 5, when people are watching the equator of the sphere which corresponds to the center of a panorama, the mapping area gets the minimum value. When observing the top or the bottom gets the maximum value. Measured by experiments, the mapping area is about 11.6% – 26.7% of whole panorama with a 90° user vision shown in Fig. 4(a), corresponding to a plane of a cube. The corresponding areas of vision are marked in green.

2.3   SNR Scalability Encoding

Scalable High Efficiency Video Coding (SHVC) is the scalable extensions of the High Efficiency Video Coding (HEVC) [4] standard. The SHVC architecture design enables SHVC implementations to be built using multiple repurposed single-layer HEVC codec cores, with the addition of interlayer reference picture processing modules.

Depending on the ways that the quality of the video is measured, there are two kinds of scalable coding in SHVC including spatial scalability and signal-to-noise ratio (SNR) scalability. The first one means that the encoder generates multiple video streams with different spatial resolutions and the latter means that the SNR of outputs are different. By adjusting the quantization parameters (QPs) of encoder we can easily control the SNRs of the encoded videos, so the following tests will take the SNR scalability encoding.

SHVC encoder requires the same number of raw sequence inputs as the layers. A base layer (BL) is contained which is the lowest quality representation. One or more enhancement layers (ELs) may be coded by referencing lower layers and provide improved video quality. To simulate and compare the differences between user-view and the other areas of panoramic picture, two layers (one BL and one EL) are used in the following tests. It should be emphasized that the EL coding is delayed by at least one frame than the BL. Considering the high frame rate of VR video, the added delay is only a few milliseconds.

Figure 6 shows the detailed process for scalable coding. Different spot densities represent different video quality levels.

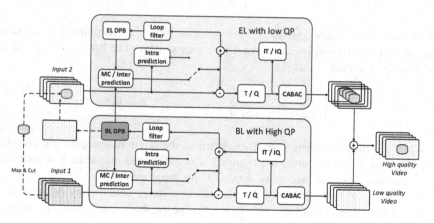

Fig. 6. SNR scalability encoding system

The Input 1 in Fig. 6 is the original raw panoramic video file. In principle, the basic component of Input 2 is the reconstructed sequence in DPB of BL, with a piece of original raw image covering at the regions in user's sight. It should be noted that in order not to modify the SHVC encoder too much in the test, we chose to use the decoded image of BL instead of reconstructed image in DPB to generate Input 2, thence two rounds of coding are required in the following test. The decoding sequences of BL were obtained after the first round, then the specific regions of them were replaced with the original sequences. The regions were selected according to the mapping method mentioned above. In the second round of coding, when the EL encoder compares Input 2 with the reference frames in BL DPB, most areas of the images are the same except the regions had been replaced after round one. Encoder tend to choose the skip mode for these CUs because the residual errors are small enough, bringing extremely few bits. The EL is like a transparent slide covering the BL.

3 Simulation

Three test sequences provided by IEEE 1857 [13] shown in Table 1 were used in the test. All of them have a resolution of 4096 × 2048. To show the difference between non-vision regions and vision regions, the QPs were set as 42 and 22 for BL and EL respectively.

Table 1. Test sequences

Seq. name	Resolution	Frame rate
Fengjing	4096 × 2048	30
Hangpai	4096 × 2048	30
Xinwen	4096 × 2048	30

The SHVC reference software, Scalable HEVC Test Model (SHM), is provided to demonstrate reference implementation of non-normative encoding techniques and normative decoding process. In this paper, SHM-12.0 [14] was used to evaluate the coding performance of the system with two-layer SNR scalability encoding. We processed the videos per Fig. 6 including three kinds of vision mapping centers shown in Fig. 5 called "equator", "middle" and "pole" to simulate different situations. The HEVC anchor was complete with HM-16.0 (HEVC Test Model [15]) and the QP was set as 22, too. Both the SHM and HM tests encode 100 frames of videos with the configuration of "Random access".

Different regions of each frame have different texture features. It is reasonable to compare the qualities of the same position in frames reconstructed by these two encoding algorithms respectively, so the decode outputs of HM-16.0 was also processed into parts of "equator", "middle" and "pole". As we can see in Table 2, the new approach reduces bit stream by 79% – 95% without significant quality loss in RoIs. It is emphasized that a large mapping area does not always imply more coding information because the polar regions were stretched from few points and the images on those parts are simple and repeated, so their performances on stream size and PSNR will be even better than those in the equatorial regions.

Some pieces of different regions are shown in Fig. 7 to compare decoding images obtained by the two methods. The same QP value in vision regions B ensures that scalable encoding achieves the same clarity as the traditional HEVC encoding. It must be admitted that the setting of QPs in different regions will affect compression efficiency, but the gap between vision regions and non-vision regions is visible.

Table 2. Simulation results

Seq.	Angles	RoI area ratio		Bit stream size (KB)			Y-PSNR(dB)[a]		
		Scalable	HEVC	Scalable	HEVC	Reduce	Scalable	HEVC	Loss
Fengjing	Equator	11.64%	100.00%	954	4956	80.75%	42.228	42.082	-0.146
	Middle	19.15%		463		90.66%	46.145	46.242	0.0979
	Pole	26.74%		350		92.94%	48.666	48.857	0.1914
Hangpai	Equator	11.64%	100.00%	573	4878	88.25%	42.072	42.126	0.0538
	Middle	19.15%		247		94.94%	49.901	49.892	-0.009
	Pole	26.74%		245		94.98%	49.584	49.537	-0.047
Xinwen	Equator	11.64%	100.00%	205	986	79.21%	44.785	44.956	0.1705
	Middle	19.15%		166		83.16%	46.495	46.673	0.1786
	Pole	26.74%		174		82.35%	47.139	47.296	0.1577
avg.						87.47%			0.0721

[a] Only for RoIs.

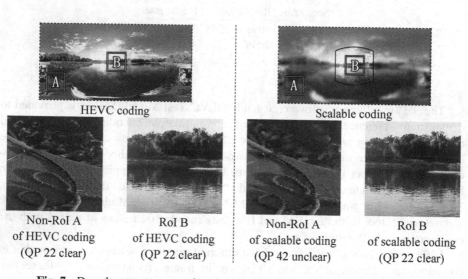

HEVC coding   Scalable coding

Non-RoI A | RoI B | Non-RoI A | RoI B
of HEVC coding | of HEVC coding | of scalable coding | of scalable coding
(QP 22 clear) | (QP 22 clear) | (QP 42 unclear) | (QP 22 clear)

Fig. 7. Decode outputs comparison between HEVC coding and scalable coding

4 Conclusion

We propose a scalable video coding system based on user vision to reduce bit rates of panoramic videos for VR. The scalable encoder in new system requires a feedback of customer's head movement information from VR device when it maps and encodes the video streams in specific view. Specifically, the whole panoramic is encoded in BL, which provides a continuous reference for inter-prediction and avoids the blank screen at the poor network conditions. The RoIs are repeatedly coded in EL. The proposed method is simple in implementation and fully compatible with the scalable HEVC codec standard, thus any SHVC decoder can be utilized to decode the compressed bit streams without modification. Experimental results have demonstrated the effectiveness of the proposed method.

This scalable video coding method is also extensible. If condition permits, the encoder will be capable of outputting multiple angles of enhancement layers to obtain a quality improvement for the whole panorama. In this way, the panoramic videos will be able to be stored and multi-viewers simultaneous viewing will also be possible.

References

1. Russ, J.C.: The Image Processing Handbook (Image Processing Handbook), 5th edn. CRC Press, Inc., Boca Raton (2006)
2. Cote, G., Erol, B., Gallant, M., Kossentini, F.: H. 263+: Video coding at low bit rates. IEEE Trans. Circuits Syst. Video Technol. 8(7), 849–866 (1998)
3. Wiegand, T., Sullivan, G.J., Bjontegaard, G., Luthra, A.: Overview of the H. 264/AVC video coding standard. IEEE Trans. Circuits Syst. Video Technol. 13(7), 560–576 (2003)
4. Sullivan, G.J., Ohm, J., Han, W.J., Wiegand, T.: Overview of the high efficiency video coding (HEVC) standard. IEEE Trans. Circuits Syst. Video Technol. 22(12), 1649–1668 (2012)
5. Snyder, J.P.: Flattening the earth: Two Thousand Years of Map Projections. University of Chicago Press, Chicago (1997)
6. Ng, K.T., Chan, S.C., Shum, H.Y.: Data compression and transmission aspects of panoramic videos. IEEE Trans. Circuits Syst. Video Technol. 15(1), 82–95 (2005)
7. Fu, C.W., Wan, L., Wong, T.T., Leung, C.S.: The rhombic dodecahedron map: An efficient scheme for encoding panoramic video. IEEE Trans. Multimedia 11(4), 634–644 (2009)
8. Next-generation video encoding techniques for 360 video and VR. https://code.facebook.com/posts/1126354007399553/next-generation-video-encoding-techniques-for-360-video-and-vr. accessed Jan 21, 2017
9. Khiem, N.Q.M., Ravindra, G., Carlier, A., Ooi, W.T.: Supporting zoomable video streams with dynamic region-of-interest cropping. In: Proceedings of the first annual ACM SIGMM conference on Multimedia systems, pp. 259–270. ACM, February 2010
10. Sánchez, Y., Skupin, R., Schierl, T.: Compressed domain video processing for tile based panoramic streaming using HEVC. In:IEEE International Conference on Image Processing (ICIP) 2015, pp. 2244–2248. IEEE, September 2015
11. Sánchez, Y., Skupin, R., Schierl, T.: Compressed domain video processing for tile based panoramic streaming using HEVC. In: IEEE International Conference on Image Processing (ICIP), pp. 2244–2248. IEEE, September 2015
12. Boyce, J.M., Ye, Y., Chen, J., Ramasubramonian, A.K.: Overview of SHVC: scalable extensions of the high efficiency video coding standard. IEEE Trans. Circuits Syst. Video Technol. 26(1), 20–34 (2016)
13. 1857.9–01-N0001 Output Document of 201601 IEEE1857.9 1st Beijing
14. SHM-12.0: https://hevc.hhi.fraunhofer.de/svn/svn_SHVCSoftware/tags/SHM-12.0/, accessed Jan 12, 2017
15. HM-16.0: https://hevc.hhi.fraunhofer.de/svn/svn_HEVCSoftware/tags/HM-16.0/, accessed Jan 12, 2017

Towards Visual SLAM with Memory Management for Large-Scale Environments

Fu Li[1,2](✉), Shaowu Yang[1,2], Xiaodong Yi[1,2], and Xuejun Yang[1,2]

[1] State Key Laboratory of High Performance Computing (HPCL),
National University of Defense Technology, Changsha, China
{lifu11,shaowu.yang}@nudt.edu.cn
[2] College of Computer, National University of Defense Technology, Changsha, China

Abstract. Memory consumption of visual SLAM systems grows rapidly with their operation ranges increase. A well-designed organization scheme of map data is important for the scalability of visual SLAM in large-scale environments. In this paper, we present a novel visual SLAM system with an efficient memory management method to manage the map data using a spatial database. Experimental results on two popular public datasets demonstrate the efficiency and accuracy of our system.

Keywords: Visual SLAM · Memory management · Spatial database

1 Introduction

Simultaneous localization and mapping (SLAM) is originally proposed to locate a robot while simultaneously building a consistent map of an unknown environment. It has been a fundamental technology for autonomous navigation of robots in the past decades. Researchers have proposed different SLAM methods using different types of sensors, e.g. cameras or 2D/3D laser scanners. Specifically, visual SLAM systems utilize cameras to obtain sensor-data as input. Recently, with low cost cameras being widely used on robots, cell phones, and tablet devices, visual SLAM has become an attractive research focus in robotics, virtual reality (VR), and augmented reality (AR).

Some milestone visual SLAM systems have been proposed for constrained environments, such as MonoSLAM [1], PTAM [2], and ORB-SLAM2 [3]. These work mainly focuses on the accuracy and the efficiency of solving the SLAM problem using visual features, while keeping all map data in computer memory in cases that the SLAM process requires those data. As a result, how to conduct memory management of the map data, especially in large-scale environments, remains to be an open issue. In many real-world applications, e.g. large-scale or

F. Li – Project 91648204 supported by NSFC, project ZDYYJCYJ20140601 supported by NUDT, and project 201602-01 supported by HPCL.

long-term operations of robots, it is a challenge to solve the memory management issue without affecting the accuracy and the efficiency of visual SLAM systems.

Large-scale environments challenge the scalability of visual SLAM systems. In most modern SLAM systems, the size of map grows unbounded with new places been explored, causing unbounded growth on memory consumption. Moreover, one trend of the SLAM research is to fuse data from multi-modal sensors to improve the accuracy and robustness of the SLAM in complex scenarios. Map data in such SLAM systems will cost much larger size of memory. Therefore, it is important to design SLAM systems with high efficiency on memory consumption. The focus of this paper lies in the memory management method of map data of visual SLAM to reduce memory consumption in large-scale environments.

Recently, research on visual SLAM considering memory consumption can be found in literature. The work in [4,5] proposes to use a long-term memory (LTM) and short-term memory (STM) concept to solve dynamic environmental mapping. The work in [6–9] presents RTAB-Map for long-term large-scale operations of visual SLAM. RTAB-Map keeps the most recent and frequently observed locations in the working memory (WM), and transfers those locations which are less likely to be loop closures from WM to a SQLite database to reduce memory usage. However, the SQLite database in it limits its extension to really large-scale scenarios. The work in [10] presents C²TAM based on a cloud computing framework. C²TAM contains a cloud computing back end which publishes services for map data storage and map fusion of multi-robots, aiming at multi-robot cooperative tracking and mapping. This work focuses on mapping, map storage, map fusion, and real-time performance in the cloud end, while paying little attention on memory consumption in each single robot.

In this paper, we propose a novel visual SLAM system with memory management, to overcome two major challenges in reducing memory consumption of visual SLAM: efficient map data scheduling between the memory and the external storage, and map data persistence method (i.e., the data outlives the process that created it). We redesign the framework of a visual SLAM system to contain a SLAM front end and a database server end. The front end maintains a localization and a mapping process, as well as map data scheduling between the memory and the database. We propose a map data scheduling method to organize map data considering the local spatial character among keyframes. The server end provides data services from a spatial database for global map data storage and accessing. The performance of our system is demonstrated in the experimental results on TUM RGB-D [11] and KITTI [12] datasets.

2   System Overview

The framework of our system is shown in Fig. 1, which includes the front end and the server end. We implement the front end based on ORB-SLAM2 by extending its tracking, local mapping, and loop closing module, and adding one novel memory managing module. The server end publishes data services for map data storage and access.

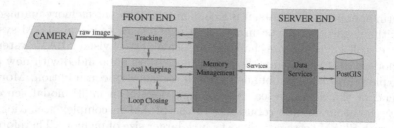

Fig. 1. The overview of our system.

Tracking: The tracking thread processes each raw image frame for pose tracking, and decides which frame should be inserted into the map in the memory as a keyframe. ORB features [17] in raw images are used to match to existing map points to achieve pose tracking. When a new keyframe should be added, it will be transferred to the memory managing module which schedules all map data.

Local Mapping: The local mapping module triangulates new map points from ORB features in keyframes. Moreover, it refines keyframe and map points in the local map, which is a sub-map of the global map affecting current pose tracking and mapping, by using local bundle adjustment (BA).

Loop Closing: The loop closing module detects loop closures among keyframes, and refines the global map using BA whenever a loop closure is found. All keyframes sharing similar ORB features with the new keyframe are used to compute similarity scores to the new keyframe. Several keyframes with the highest scores are selected as loop candidates. The candidates whose similarity transformations are supported by enough inliers will be accepted as loop closures.

Memory Management: The memory management module stores local map data, and schedules map data between the memory and the server end. When a new keyframe is inserted, it transfers related map data between the memory and the database server to update current local map. When a loop closure is detected, all pose data of keyframes and map points will be retrieved from the server to the memory for global map refinement by BA. When BA is finished, all optimized pose data will be updated to the database server to ensure data consistency.

Server: The server module manages map data in a database, and provides several data access services to other modules. It also provides variable interfaces which support complex service development for new application scenarios.

3   Memory Management

As shown in Fig. 2, the memory management module mainly contains three parts, including the data scheduling, data driver, and the memory.

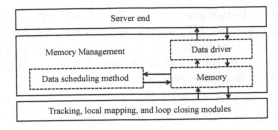

Fig. 2. The structure of memory management module.

3.1   Data Structure Description

The core data structures in our system are keyframes and map points. Each keyframe mainly stores the camera pose, ORB features of the image frame, the identities (IDs) of all map points it observes and IDs of its co-related keyframes in the map. Each map point mainly stores its 3D position, its representative ORB feature, the IDs of keyframes in it is observed.

Another key conception is map which consists of keyframes and map points. The map elements in the map, i.e. keyframes and map points, make up the nodes, and the connections among the map elements make up the edges.

3.2   The Data Scheduling Method

The data scheduling method organizes the global map in the form of grids. It schedules the local map data to the memory and the rest of the global map data to the database. The local map data is selected as a subset of the global map data which affects the current tracking and mapping.

As illustrated in Fig. 3, the 3D global map is mapped into 2D grids by a horizontal decomposition. Then, it is organized in grid cells and managed in the database. Each grid cell has a unique ID, which is encoded as a 32-bit unsigned long integer to support large-scale maps. Multiple keyframes may be mapped to the same grid cell. Map points share the same cell ID as their source keyframe in which they are observed. The map data in a subset of grid cells from the server is selected and scheduled into the memory by the proposed data scheduling method

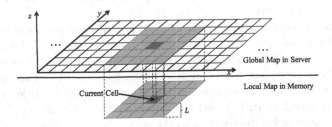

Fig. 3. The data-scheduling method conceptual graph.

with the following selection criteria: (1) the current cell in which the current working keyframe is located; (2) the cells within a distance L to the current cell. These criteria are designed for the reason that the similarities of visual features in two keyframes reduce rapidly as the distance of the two keyframes increases, which will be further verified in Sect. 5.1.

3.3 Data Driver

The data driver provides interfaces to transfer and retrieve data between the server end and the memory module. It packages the data and calls the services provided by the server to remotely transfer and retrieve the required data.

The possible data exchanges between the memory and server end modules can be listed as follows: (1) **Transferring local map data from memory to the server end.** The data driver accepts the map data from the memory, and packages them using the boost serialization library [13]. Then, it calls the server end service to save the data, and removes them from the memory. (2) **Retrieving local map data from the server end to the memory.** The data driver accesses map data from the server database according to the IDs of required keyframes and map points. Then, it deserializes the map data to corresponding data type, and inserts them to the local map. (3) **Retrieving geometric data from server end to the memory.** The data driver calls the service to retrieve geometric data, and deserializes the response data to keyframe poses and map point positions. This is done when geometric data is required by global BA. (4) **Updating geometric data from the memory to the server end.** The data driver packages all optimized pose or position data and calls the service to update the corresponding geometric data in the global map.

3.4 The Memory Module

The memory module stores the local map data and provides interfaces to access the keyframes and map points by their unique IDs.

To support mapping operations, map data in the memory must meet several constraints: (1) Local BA in the local mapping module requires keyframes that share map points with the current keyframe. (2) Loop closure detecting in the loop closing module requires keyframes that share ORB features with the current keyframe. (3) Global BA in the loop closing module requires all keyframe poses and map point positions.

The memory module schedules map data in real-time and runs in a separate thread. It monitors the current grid cell state, and uses the data scheduling interface to get the IDs of cells that need to be taken into or out of the memory. Then, it calls the interface from the data driver to transfer and retrieve relevant map data in cells. The above operations of the memory module can basically satisfy the constraints in (1) and (2). Besides, the memory module provides interfaces for adding keyframes or map points to the map in the memory, getting the connected data by the keyframe ID, getting the source keyframes of map points, and getting or updating geometric data in the global map from the server. The interfaces are designed to specifically meet the constraint in (3).

4 The Server End

The server end module provides services for the front end to access the global map data. It consists of a model layer and a service layer.

The model layer supports the map data persistence and defines the basic data structures of map data in visual SLAM, mainly keyframes and map points. It stores and queries the map data from database tables, and provides basic operations on the data. We use ODB [14] to solve the issue of mapping a C++ object to a record in a database table, instead of using SQL. The ODB is an open source object-relational mapping (ORM) system, which facilitates the persistence of C++ objects to a relational database (RDBMS) without manual effort in processing tables, columns, or SQL. Furthermore, we use PostGIS [15] database to persist SLAM map data in large-scale operations. The PostGIS database is an extension to PostgreSQL to support spatial data analysis and processing.

The service layer implements the service logics on basis of the model layer. The services offered by the service layer are listed as follows: (1) Retrieving keyframes by cell ID; (2) Saving keyframes; (3) Retrieving map points by cell ID; (4) Saving map points; (5) Retrieving all geometric data; (6) Updating all keyframe poses and map point positions.

5 Experimental Results

Our system is implemented in the Robot Operating System (ROS) [16], which provides a run-time environment that facilitates the communication between the front end and the server end. Experiments are conducted to evaluate the performance of our system compared with the original ORB-SLAM2 system. Two popular datasets, TUM RGB-D and KITTI dataset, are processed in the experiments. The KITTI dataset contains stereo sequences recorded from a car in urban environments, and the TUM RGB-D dataset contains indoor sequences from RGB-D cameras. The computer running the experiments features an Ubuntu 14.04 64-bit operating system, an Intel core i7-4790 (8 cores @ 3.6 GHZ) CPU and 8 GB RAM.

5.1 The Data Scheduling Method Verification

The data scheduling method in Sect. 3.2 is designed based on the visual similarities among keyframes. The similarity score is evaluated as the number of shared visual features between two keyframes. Keyframes with a similarity score to the current keyframe larger than $T_{threshold}$ should be kept in memory for local BA, and otherwise be moved to the database. In our system, $T_{threshold}$ is set to 10.

The similarity scores of any two co-related keyframes in our system for the two datasets are shown in Fig. 4. We can find that similarities among keyframes

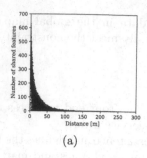 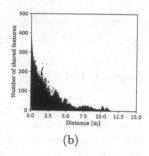

(a)   (b)

Fig. 4. The number of shared visual features w.r.t. the distance of two keyframes.

reduce as the distance of the two keyframes increases. Similarity scores among keyframes with distances larger than approximately 90 m in KITTI sequence02 (in Fig. 4(a)) and larger than approximately 6 m in TUM RGB-D Freiburg2 (in Fig. 4(b)), respectively, decrease to below $T_{threshold}$.

5.2 Memory Consumption

In this section, the dynamic memory consumption between our system and the ORB-SLAM2 system is compared. The dynamic sizes of maps of the two systems in the memory are also compared.

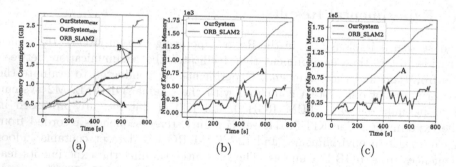

(a)   (b)   (c)

Fig. 5. Memory consumption of our system and ORB-SLAM2 on KITTI sequence02 dataset. (a) The memory consumption, (b) the number of keyframes, and (c) the number of map points.

Figure 5(a) shows the memory consumption of both our system and ORB-SLAM2 on KITTI sequence02 dataset. Our system has much less memory consumption than the ORB-SLAM2 during the exploration. The memory consumption is mainly caused by map data in memory, i.e., keyframes and mappoints. As indicated by Fig. 5(b) and (c), the map size in memory grows nearly linearly over time in ORB-SLAM2, while keeping below a threshold in our system. This is the major cause of the reduction of the memory consumption in our system. Memory consumption $OurSystem_{max}$ is reached when additional data are kept in the memory to fully support loop closing. $OurSystem_{min}$ is reached when only local map data is stored in the memory, without supporting loop closing. The memory consumption in our system theoretically lies between $OurSystem_{max}$ and $OurSystem_{min}$ when different loop closing strategies are implemented.

The memory consumption of our system appears a step (marked as A in Fig. 5(a)) when the size of the map reaches its maximum (marked as A in Fig. 5(b)). Due to the allocation mechanism in C++11, the memory consumption remains unchanged when the size of map reduces (after A in 5(b)). The free memory space is remained in the stack of a process to avoid applying for the system space too frequently. At about 700 s, the memory consumption of both ORB-SLAM2 and our system appear surges. The reason is that the system needs to do the global BA when a loop closure is detected. Global BA expects the system to provide lots of free memory spaces for calculating the intermediate results.

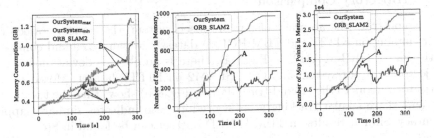

Fig. 6. Memory consumption of our system and ORB-SLAM2 on TUM-RGBD Freiburg2 dataset, with the same notations as in Fig. 5.

We have conducted a similar experiment on TUM-RGBD Freiburg2 with large loop dataset to further prove the advantages of our proposed system in memory consumption. The results are shown in Fig. 6, and we can draw similar conclusions with the case when using KITTI sequence02 dataset.

5.3 Map-Data Scheduling Verification

Figure 7 shows the run-time snapshots of the map in memory at different time-stamps. As can be found in Fig. 7(a) and (b), some keyframes and map points at 50 s (area A in Fig. 7(a)) are transferred to the server end and disappeared at 150 s in Fig. 7(b), when the camera moves forward. As can be found in Fig. 7(d), some keyframes and map points in area C are retrieved from the server end, when the camera moves back. These results show qualitatively that our system can schedule the map data between the front end and the server end reasonably.

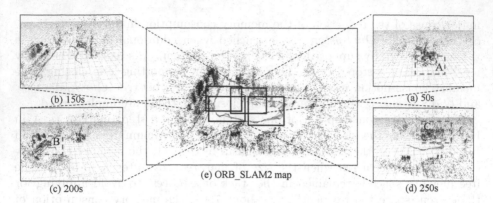

Fig. 7. (a), (b), (c) and (d) Snapshots of the map in the memory of our system at 50 s, 150 s, 200 s, 250 s on the Freiburg2 dataset. (e) The snapshot of the map of ORB-SLAM2 when finishes running on the Freiburg2 dataset.

5.4 Trajectory Comparison

To demonstrate the accuracy of our proposed system, the camera trajectories of it running on KITTI and TUM RGB-D datasets are analyzed and compared with that of ORB-SLAM2. In Fig. 8(a), there is no obvious deviation between trajectories of our system and ORB-SLAM2 on KITTI dataset. Moreover, the trajectory errors to the ground-truth data in Fig. 8(b) shows that the two SLAM systems share similar tracking accuracy, which also indicates similar mapping accuracy. Similar results on TUM RGB-D dataset can be found in 8(c).

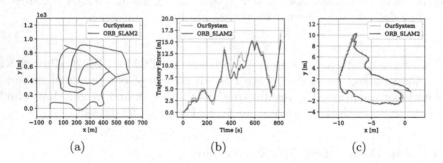

Fig. 8. (a) Trajectories on KITTI sequence02, (b) trajectory error to KITTI sequence02 ground-truth, and (c) trajectories in Freiburg2 dataset of our system and ORB-SLAM2.

6 Conclusions

This paper proposes to reduce the memory consumption of visual SLAM in large-scale environments through an efficient memory management method. The resulting system contains a SLAM front end and a database server end.

The experimental results demonstrate that our system efficiently reduces the memory consumption of visual SLAM, while maintaining its accuracy. The experiments are also shown in a video online[1]. The last contribution of this paper is that we provide the source code of our system to be publicly available[2].

References

1. Andrew, J., Ian, D., Nicholas, D., Olivier, S.: MonoSLAM: Real-time single camera SLAM. IEEE Trans. Pattern Anal. Mach. Intell. **29**(6), 1052–1067 (2007)
2. Georg, K. David, M.: Parallel tracking and mapping for small AR workspaces. In: 6th IEEE and ACM International Symposium on Mixed and Augmented Reality ISMAR 2007, pp. 225–234. IEEE (2007)
3. Raul, M., Juan, D.: ORB-SLAM2: an open-source slam system for monocular, stereo and RGB-D cameras. arXiv preprint arXiv:1610.06475 (2016)
4. Feras, D., Grzegorz, C., Tom, D.: Long-term experiments with an adaptive spherical view representation for navigation in changing environments. Rob. Auton. Syst. **59**(5), 285–295 (2011)
5. Feras, D., Tom, D.: An adaptive appearance-based map for long-term topological localization of mobile robots. In: IEEE/RSJ International Conference on Intelligent Robots and Systems IROS 2008, pp. 3364–3369. IEEE (2008)
6. Mathieu, L., François, M.: Memory management for real-time appearance-based loop closure detection. In: IEEE/RSJ International Conference on Intelligent Robots and Systems (IROS), pp. 1271–1276. IEEE (2011)
7. Mathieu, L., Francois, M.: Appearance-based loop closure detection for online large-scale and long-term operation. IEEE Trans. Rob. **29**(3), 734–745 (2013)
8. Yunlong, W., Bo, Z., Xiaodong, Y., Yuhua, T.: Communication-motion planning for wireless relay-assisted multi-robot system. IEEE Wirel. Commun. Lett. **5**(6), 568–571 (2016)
9. Mathieu, L., François, M.: Online global loop closure detection for large-scale multi-session graph-based slam. In: IEEE/RSJ International Conference on Intelligent Robots and Systems (IROS 2014), pp. 2661–2666. IEEE (2014)
10. Riazuelo, L., Civera, J., Montiel, J.M.M.: C^2tam: a cloud framework for cooperative tracking and mapping. Rob. Auton. Syst. **62**(4), 401–413 (2014)
11. Jürgen, S., Nikolas, E., Felix, E., Wolfram, B., Daniel, C.: A benchmark for the evaluation of RGB-D slam systems. In: IEEE/RSJ International Conference on Intelligent Robots and Systems (IROS), pp. 573–580. IEEE (2012)
12. Andreas, G., Philip, L., Christoph, S., Raquel, U.: Vision meets robotics: The kitti dataset. Int. J. Robot. Res. **32**(11), 1231–1237 (2013)
13. Björn, K.: Beyond the C++ standard library: An Introduction to Boost. Pearson Education, Indianapolis (2005)
14. Bergamaschi, S., Sartori, C., Beneventano, D., Vincini, M.: ODB-Tools: a description logics based tool for schema validation and semantic query optimization in object oriented databases. In: Lenzerini, M. (ed.) AI*IA 1997. LNCS, vol. 1321, pp. 435–438. Springer, Heidelberg (1997). https://doi.org/10.1007/3-540-63576-9_130
15. Paul, R., et al.: PostGIS manual. Refractions Research Inc. (2005)

---

[1] http://v.youku.com/v_show/id_XMjc3MTU5ODU0OA.
[2] https://github.com/lifunudt/M2SLAM.

16. Morgan, Q., Ken, C., Brian, G., Josh, F., Tully, F., Jeremy, L., Rob, W., Andrew, Y.: ROS: an open-source robot operating system. In: ICRA workshop on open source software, vol. 3, p. 5. Kobe (2009)
17. Ethan, R., Vincent, R., Kurt, K., Gary, B.: ORB: An efficient alternative to sift or surf. In: IEEE International Conference on Computer Vision (ICCV), pp. 2564–2571. IEEE (2011)

Entropy Based Sub-band Deletion for Multispectral Image Compression

Worku J. Sori[1]([✉]), Zhao Dongyang[2], Lou Fang[3], Fu Yunsheng[3], Liu Shaohui[1], Feng Jiang[1], and Khan Adil[1]

[1] School of Computer Science and Technology, Harbin Institute of Technology, Harbin, China
worku.jifara@gmail.com
[2] Beijing Institute of Computer Application, Beijing, China
[3] Institute of Computer Application, China Academy of Engineering physics, Mianyang, China

Abstract. This paper proposes effective and efficient multispectral image compression targeting at reducing the extent of storage and transmission time, and at the same time retaining a quality of the reconstructed images. The proposed method is relying on deleting a sub band before compressing the multispectral image. The deleted sub-band is based on the entropy value of each band. Discrete wavelet transform is applied to bands of multispectral image having highest entropy value to delete a sub-band among the four sub-bands and the retained sub-bands are followed by entropy coder for compression. Furthermore, we exploit JPEG2000+principal component analysis (PCA) to more compress the remaining bands. We used multispectral images from NASA website to validate our proposed method. Experimental result on designated dataset reveals that our proposed method improves the reconstructed image quality better than JPEG2000, SPHIT and some other methods in PSNR and SAM metrics.

Keywords: Image compression · Sub-band deletion
Wavelet transform · Entropy

1 Introduction

Multispectral images are extensively employed in a number of applications, like civilian and military activities [1]. The images are obtained from plane or through satellite borne spectrometers and wrap vast areas of the surface of the earth. Multispectral images are composed of six to eleven bands where each band representing the same area of the surface of the earth. Through the inquiry of the spectrum of reflected light existing in these images, it is possible to discriminate what data are existing on the earth and atmosphere [1]. After discrimination, the information can be used in agriculture, military surveillance and the analysis and location of mineral existence. For example, in agriculture, global positioning

© Springer International Publishing AG, part of Springer Nature 2018
B. Zeng et al. (Eds.): PCM 2017, LNCS 10736, pp. 787–797, 2018.
https://doi.org/10.1007/978-3-319-77383-4_77

system (GPS) [2] deliver the location and information for users everywhere in the earth surface by analyzing multispectral data.

As we mentioned earlier, multispectral images are made up of several narrow and neighboring bands of data, wrapping a big spectrum of reflected light. The data produced can be observed as a three dimensional cube as in Fig. 1, where (m,n) is a spatial dimension and the third dimension ρ's are spectral bands. One of the main problem of these images are they need high storage capacity to store [3] and worth much time to transmit [4]. Therefore, its paramount to provide a method which compress them efficiently. In this paper, we propose efficient multispectral image compression method and compare our result with the conventional multispectral image compression methods.

Several work has been done to provide efficient multispectral image compression [5–12]. They can be categorized into lossless compression and lossy compression methods. Lossless algorithms have been studied to preserve all the information. It enables the user to retrieve the original data from the compressed bit stream. Such a compression ratio is limited because of difficulty to meet the requirements of onboard storage and transmission. However, they are extremely significant for achieving the data and distributing to the user. Some of the lossless based multispectral image compression are studied under [5–7,12]. On the other hand, lossy compression techniques have been considered because they provide high compression ratio and it could offer images of different quality at different compression ratios. In this techniques of compression, distortion is introduced in the data so that we cannot retrieve exactly the original data. Some of the lossy based multispectral image are studied under [8–11]. Most of the above aforementioned methods are based on the traditional and widely studied multispectral image compression methods such as JPEG2000, SPHIT, SPECK and CCSDS-IDC.

In this paper, considering these traditional methods, we propose the multispectral image compression by taking the advantage of band arrangement as in [13,14] but based on information entropy of each band where [13,14] are based on correlation coefficient among bands. More specifically, discrete wavelet transform is applied on some selected bands of the data and then three sub-bands are encoded with entropy coder for compression. Also, the non-selected bands are compressed with JPEG2000+PCA. The reconstruction face is obtained by taking the reverse operation. For experimental purpose, we used Landsat 7 ETM+

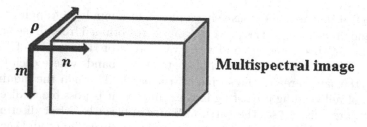

Fig. 1. 3D Cube of multispectral image.

satellite image with seven bands which can be downloaded from NASA website for free. This dataset was launched on April 1999 by NASA.

The rest of the paper is organized as follows. Section 2 briefly review related work. Section 3 introduces the proposed method with detailed explanations of each component. Section 4 gives the evaluation and comparison with state of the art algorithms and finally, Sect. 5 concludes the paper.

2   Related Work

Several multispectral image compression has been proposed by researchers. In [15] the researchers addressed various techniques that were recently used to compress satellite images. Some of these methods are JPEG2000, set partitioning in hierarchical trees (SPIHT), JPEG2000+PCA and CCSDS.

JPEG2000 coding is an extension of the pioneer JPEG coding scheme which uses the discrete wavelet transform (DWT) and is one of the most widely exploited method in multispectral image compression [11]. Several authors adopted DWT and design compression algorithm for multispectral image compression [16]. [17] presented a Daubechies 9/7 filter bank for lossy compression. First, the method applies DWT to each multispectral data. Next coefficient quantization (Q) is applied to individual scales and sub-bands, and then quantized coefficients are coded. In order to increase the coding degree of these methods, first decorralating multispectral image in the spectral domain and then decorralating each band in spatial domain is a common approach. Most of the time, DWT and PCA are employed as spectral decorrelator [10] and 2D-DWT is employed as spatial decorrelator. Also, [18] exploited JPEG2000+DWT as spectral decorrelator and [19] exploited JPEG2000+PCA as spectral decorrelator.

The other most widely used multispectral image compression scheme is the set partitioning in hierarchical trees (SPIHT) [16, 20]. SPIHT is among the successful multispectral image compression techniques benefited from DWT. This method has four basic parts. The first part is initialization. In this stage, the algorithm initializes the list of significant point as empty and then groups a root of similarity trees in the list of insignificant point and list of significant point. The second part is sorting pass in the list of insignificant. At this stage every coefficient in the list of insignificant is checked and then significant coefficient are relocated to the list of significant point and then coded. The third part performs sorting pass in a list of insignificant sets. If an entry in the insignificant list sets is significant, a one is passed, otherwise, if an entry in the list of insignificant is insignificant a zero is passed. Finally, the fourth stage is the refinement pass. In this step every old entry of list significant is checked. If it is significant a one is passed otherwise, if it is insignificant a zero is passed. In the past few years, consultative committee for space data systems (CCSDS) has also provided various methods for data compression. For example, [9] is one of the lossy compression method for hyperspectral and multispectral images. It has two major useful parts as shown in Fig. 2, the first part comprises a data decorrelator (i.e., DWT as data decorrelator) and the second part is the bit plane encoder which encode the decorrelated data. For the detail of this method we refer the reader [9].

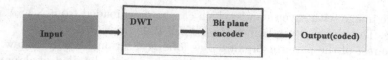

Fig. 2. The CCSDS framework.

3   Proposed Model

Our model has two main parts, the encoder part as shown in Fig. 3 and the decoder part as shown in Fig. 4.

At the encoder side, the proposed method first computes the entropy of each band of an image to identify which bands have higher information. Then, based on the entropy value, the multi spectral image M is categorized into two parts $\{c_q, c_r\}$, where c_q contains three bands $\{x_1, x_2, x_3\}$ with the highest entropy value and c_r contains the rest of the bands. We can formulate each element of c_q and c_r as,

$$x_1 = \arg\max_{x_i}\{E(x_i)\}, i = 1, ..., 7 \tag{1}$$

$$x_2 = \arg\max_{x_i \setminus x_1}\{E(x_i)\}, i = 1, ..., 7 \tag{2}$$

$$x_3 = \arg\max_{x_i \setminus x_1, x_2}\{E(x_i)\}, i = 1, ..., 7 \tag{3}$$

Where E is an information entropy, defined as in Eq. 8. Similarly, we can formulate the rest of the bands as in the above three equations by changing argmax into argmin. To clarify more, we formulate as

$$x_4 = \arg\min_{x_i}\{E(x_i)\}, i = 1, ..., 7 \tag{4}$$

$$x_5 = \arg\min_{x_i \setminus x_4}\{E(x_i)7\}, i = 1, ..., 7 \tag{5}$$

$$x_6 = \arg\min_{x_i \setminus x_4, x_5}\{E(x_i)\}, i = 1, ..., 7 \tag{6}$$

$$x_7 = \arg\min_{x_i \setminus x_4, x_5, x_6}\{E(x_i)\}, i = 1, ..., 7 \tag{7}$$

In c_q, a 2D-DWT is applied and followed by an entropy coder (EC) to delete redundant material within each band. When applying 2D-WT on band x_1 and x_3 the outcome has a wavelet coefficient having redundant information. Due to this, the proposed approach deletes some of these coefficient from bands x_1 and x_3 to reduce the size of the image where the deleted coefficients are reconstructed at the decoder side from band x_2. Then c_r and band x_2 are combined for compression by JPEG2000+PCA as the spectral decorrelation as shown in Fig. 3.

At the decoder side, we assemble two set of bit streams b'_1 and b'_2. With b'_1, the original bands x'_1 and x'_3 can be constructed by entropy decoding, dequantization (DQ) and then followed by inverse 2D-DWT. Before applying the inverse transform, we reconstruct the deleted coefficients from the band x'_2 in b'_2, as shown

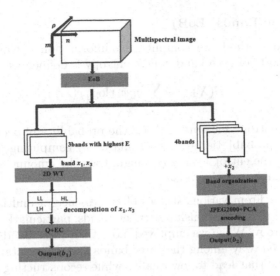

Fig. 3. Proposed multispectral image encoding framework

in Fig. 4. Also, to approximate the rest of bands JPEG2000+PCA decoder is applied. The multispectral image band organization (i.e., organizing based on entropy value) is exploited to reconstruct c'_r and x'_2. Finally, the approximated multispectral image M' is reconstructed by combining the reconstructed section c'_q and c'_r.

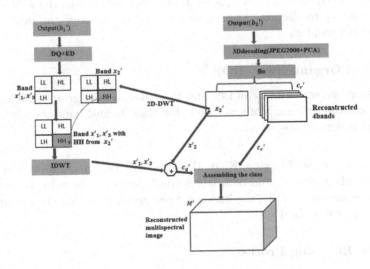

Fig. 4. Proposed multispectral image decoding framework.

3.1 Entropy of Bands (EoB)

In our proposed method, we compute the information entropy (E) measure (**entropy** for short) of each band, where entropy is defined as,

$$E(X) = -\sum_i p(x_i) \log_2 p(x_i) \tag{8}$$

Where E is the entropy measure and p is the probability of occurrence for each pixel value. The probabilities are approximated by computing the histogram of spectral band. If the entropy value E is high, then the amount of information in the data is also high and vice versa.

Band selection: From various studies of the essence of multispectral images, we verify that there is a relationship between bands, particularly the three bands with highest entropy. When we employed more than three bands, the other four entropy value is faraway among the three bands and some detail may be lost in the decoding time that lead to low quality while reconstructing an image.

Deletion of sub-bands: when exploiting 2D-DWT to all bands, we notice that the diagonal changes for three bands are close, and then we employ one of them to code and transmit. In the decoder side we use identical sub-band for the three sub-bands. Due to this reason, we employ the HH sub-band from only one band instead of each three band and the rest of bands are compressed by JPEG2000+PCA. Given the output b_1 at the encoder end, b_1 is coded as,

$$b_1 = co(sb(LL, HL, LH))_{x_1, x_3} \tag{9}$$

where co is a coding and sb is sub-band. Our method deletes the HH sub-band from x_1 and x_3 to decrease the image size and reconstruct the deleted in the decoder from band x_2.

3.2 Band Organization (BO)

At this step, we combine c_q and c_r and then arrange the group of bands based on their entropy values. More concisely, for class c_r and band x_2, the group of bands are ordered using

$$L = o(c_q, x_2) \tag{10}$$

Where o is the order function. First, the order function o, compute the entropy value of bands in class c_r and band x_2. Second, each entropy value is arranged in ascending order and finally, the bands are organized based on the entropy value computed in the second step.

3.3 The Encoding Process

After band organization, to delete parts from two bands that were close in the first three bands, we exploited 2D-DWT. Then, we code L using JPEG2000+PCA. That is

$$b_2 = ec(L) \tag{11}$$

Where ec is an encoding function. First, the encoding function ec decorrelate L with PCA, and then 2D-DWT with four level decomposition is exploited as a spatial decorrelator. BIO [19] reference software is used for implementation and 9/7 filter is used. Hence, we have minimized the size of data that will be coded or transformed and as a result we maximize the bitrate for data in the coding system.

3.4 The Decoding Process

During decoding process, we apply the inverse operation on the encoding process. For b_2 and L in the encoding process, their inverse is computed as

$$L' = ro(d(b'_2)) \tag{12}$$

Where ro is the reorder function and d is the decoding function. First, the decoding function apply the inverse of JPEG2000+PCA. Second, the reorder function ro, reorder these value to obtain the final group data c'_r and x'_2. After this process two basic components; deleted sub-band reconstruction and assembling the class finalize the overall decoder side process.

Deleted Sub-band reconstruction: We reconstruct x'_1 and x'_3 from b'_1 and recover the deleted sub-bands from x'_2 before inverse DWT. (see Fig. 4) That is,

$$L' = d(b'_1) \tag{13}$$

The function d is with HH where LL, HL, LH and HH is obtained by applying 2D-DWT on x'_2 sub-band. Finally, we combine the three bands x'_1, x'_2 and x'_3 into one class c'_q. to more clarify,

$$c'_q = as(x'_1, x'_2, x'_3) \tag{14}$$

Where as is an assemble function which combine the three bands in one class c'_q.

Assembling the class: In class assembling, we combine the class c'_q and c'_r into a data M'. That is

$$M' = as(c'_q, c'_r) \tag{15}$$

Where as is an assembling function which combine the two class as one multispectral data. In the next section we give the experimental results and the evaluation of our proposed scheme.

4 Evaluation and Comparison with State of the Art Algorithms

The proposed method is evaluated on various multispectral images among Landsat images. More specifically, the dataset in our work includes four Landsat7 ETM+ from various locations. We focused on different section of images with 512×512 dimension, where all images are stored as 8 bit per pixel per band (8ppppb).

4.1   Performance Evaluation

To evaluate the reconstructed multispectral image using our model, we compute the widely used metrics PSNR and SAM.

Peak to Signal Noise Ratio (PSNR): Let $M(m, n, \rho)$ be the original multispectral image and $M'(m, n, \rho)$ be the reconstructed images, then $PSNR = 10log_{10}(\frac{P^2}{MSE})$ where $MSE = \frac{1}{m.n.\rho}\sum_{i=1}^{m}\sum_{j=1}^{n}\sum_{k=1}^{\rho}(M(i, j, k) - M'(i, j, k))^2$. Here ρ is the number of multispectral image bands and P is the maximum pixel value of the multispectral image.

Spectral angle mappers (SAM): Given two spectral vectors U and U' where $U = u_1, u_2, ..., u_n$ is the original spectral pixel vectors and $U' = u'_1, u'_2, ..., u'_n$ is its corresponding vector after distortion (i.e. compression-decompression), then the SAM value which represents the absolute value of the spectral angle between a pair of vectors is $SAM(U, U') = cos^{-1}(\frac{<U,U'>}{\|U\|_2.\|U'\|_2})$ where $< U, U' >$ is an inner product of U and U'.

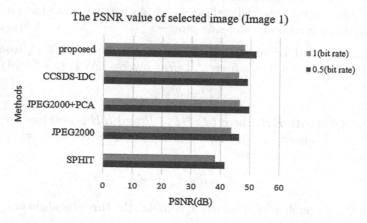

Fig. 5. Graphical illustration of proposed method vs other methods in PSNR value of selected multispectral image.

4.2   Comparison with Other States of the Art Algorithms

The performance of our approach is evaluated and compared with the traditional multispectral image techniques SPIHT, JPEG2000, JPEG2000+PCA and CCSDS-IDC. Our experimental on designated dataset reveals that the proposed approach improves the reconstructed image quality compared with the other compression schemes. Table 1 shows the $PSNR$ values of different methods in comparisons with our method. As shown in this table, our method improves the reconstructed image quality of multispectral image by 2.5 dB–10 dB in $PSNR$ values. Also, Table 2 shows the SAM value of different approaches in comparison with our scheme. As shown in Table 2, our method provides better SAM value where lower SAM value is better. Figure 5 clearly visualize as our method outperforms some other methods.

Table 1. The PSNR result of four compressed images with different methods and our method.

Multispectral image 1: white sand					
Methods→Bitrate↓	SPHIT	JPEG2000	JPEG2000+PCA	CCSDS-IDC	Proposed
0.5	41.40	46.29	49.78	49.20	50.90
1	38.17	43.56	46.43	46.15	47.21
Multispectral image 2: Hawaii					
0.5	44.38	49.56	52.97	52.11	54.48
1	47.29	52.24	56.26	54.43	59.25
Multispectral image 3: New Orleans					
0.5	32.99	39.28	41.30	41.47	44.61
1	36.10	41.77	44.98	44.56	48.50
Multispectral image 4: Los Angeles					
0.5	35.62	41.60	43.58	43.88	46.71
1	38.56	44.38	47.02	46.65	50.20

Table 2. The SAM result of two compressed images with different methods and our method.

Multispectral image 1: white sand					
Methods→ Bitrate↓	SPHIT	JPEG2000	JPEG2000+PCA	CCSDS-IDC	Proposed
0.5	0.017	0.023	0.015	0.017	0.015
1	0.013	0.018	0.010	0.012	0.009
Multispectral image 2: Hawaii					
0.5	0.020	0.028	0.017	0.020	0.017
1	0.015	0.021	0.012	0.015	0.009

5 Conclusion

Effective multispectral image compression model is designed to compress multispectral image. The framework is designed based on deleting sub-bands, band arrangement, entropy value of each band and wavelet transform. First the model organizes the bands based on entropy values, then wavelet transform is applied on some selected multispectral bands to determine the sub-band to be deleted from them. Finally, the rest of the bands are also compressed without deleting sub-bands using JPEG2000 and principal component analysis. From various point of view, we can conclude that the proposed model is effective in comparison with the other methods.

References

1. Kaarna, A., Zemcik, P., Kalviainen, H., Parkkinen, J.: Multispectral image compression. In: International Conference on Pattern Recognition, vol. 2, pp. 1264–1267 (1998)
2. Kaplan, E., Hegarty, C.: Understanding GPS: Principles and Applications. Artech House, Norwood (2005)
3. Mamun, M.A., Jia, X., Ryan, M.: Sequential multispectral images compression for efficient lossless data transmission. In: Second IITA International Conference on Geoscience and Remote Sensing (IITA-GRS), pp. 615–618 (2010)
4. Yeo, C.K., Soon, I.Y., Lau, C.T.: Lossless compression of multispectral satellite images. J. Commun. Netw. 1(4), 226–230 (1999)
5. Arnavut, Z., Narumalani, S.: Lossless compression of multispectral images using permutations. In: Geoscience and Remote Sensing Symposium, IGARSS 1996. Remote Sensing for a Sustainable Future, International, vol. 1, pp. 463–465 (1996)
6. Memon, N.D., Sayood, K., Magliveras, S.S.: Lossless compression of multispectral image data. IEEE Trans. Geosci. Remote Sens. 322, 282–289 (1994)
7. Spring, J.M., Langdon, G.G.: Lossless compression of multispectral images with interband prediction error deltas. In: Conference Record of the Thirtieth Asilomar Conference on Signals, Systems and Computers, vol. 1, pp. 586–590 (1996)
8. Kozhemiakin, R., et al.: Lossy compression of Landsat multispectral images. In: 5th Mediterranean Conference on Embedded Computing (MECO), pp. 104–107 (2016)
9. Consultative Committee for Space Data Systems (CCSDS), Image Data Compression CCSDS, Nov. 2005,: http://public.ccsds.org/publications/archive/122 0b1.pdf
10. Penna, B., Tillo, T., Magli, E., Olmo, G.: Transform coding techniques for lossy hyperspectral data compression. IEEE Trans. Geosci. Remote Sens. 45(5), 1408–1421 (2007)
11. Junxia, W., Ruyi, W., Xiaohui, G.: Multispectral images compression based on JPEG2000. In: 2nd International Conference on Information Engineering and Computer Science (ICIECS), pp. 1–3, Wuhan (2010)
12. Jifara, W., Jiang, F., Zhang, B., et al.: Hyperspectral image compression based on online learning spectral features dictionary. Multimedia Tools Appl. 7623, 25003–25014 (2017)
13. Hagag, A., Hassan, E.S., Amin, M., El-samie, F.E.: Satellite multispectral image compression based on removing sub bands. Optik - Int. J. Light Electron Opt. 131, 1023–1035 (2017)
14. Tate, S.R.: Band ordering in lossless compression of multispectral images. IEEE Tran. Comp. 46(4), 477–483 (1997)
15. Blanes, I., Magli, E., Serra-Sagrista, J.: A tutorial on image compression for optical space imaging systems. IEEE Geosci. Remote Sens. Mag. 2(3), 8–26 (2014)
16. Cuixiang, Z., Minghe, H.: Further Improvement of SPIHT for Multispectral Image Compression. In: International Forum on Information Technology and Applications (IFITA), pp. 337–340, Kunming (2010)
17. Antonini, M., Barlaud, M., et al.: Image coding using wavelet transform. IEEE Trans. Image Process. 1(2), 205–220 (1992)

18. Hagag, A., Amin, M., El-Samie, F.E.: Simultaneous denoising and compression of multispectral images. J. Appl. Remote Sens. **7**(1), 073511 (2013)
19. BOI codec (2014). http://www.deic.uab.cat/francesc/software/boi
20. Minghe, H., Cuixiang, Z.: Application of improved SPIHT for multispectral image compression. In: 5th International Conference on Computer Science and Education (ICCSE), pp. 1058–1061 (2010)

Automatic Texture Exemplar Extraction Based on a Novel Textureness Metric

Huisi Wu[1], Junrong Jiang[1], Ping Li[2], and Zhenkun Wen[1(✉)]

[1] College of Computer Science and Software Engineering,
Shenzhen University, Shenzhen, China
wenzk@szu.edu.cn
[2] Faculty of Information Technology,
Macau University of Science and Technology, Macau, China

Abstract. Traditional texture synthesis methods usually emphasized the final effect of the target textures. However, none of them focus on auto-extraction of the source texture exemplar. In this paper, we present a novel textureness metric based on Gist descriptor to accurately extract texture exemplar from an arbitrary image including texture regions. Our method emphasizes the importance of the exemplar for the example-based texture synthesis and focus on ideal texture exemplar auto-extraction. To improve the efficiency of the texture patch searching, we perform a Poisson disk sampling to crop exemplar randomly and uniformly from images. To improve the accuracy of texture recognition, we also use a SVM for the UIUC database to distinguish the texture regions and non-texture regions. The proposed method is evaluated on a variety of images with different kinds of textures. Convincing visual and statistics results demonstrated its effectiveness.

Keywords: Texture feature · Synthesizability · Textureness
Texture exemplar

1 Introduction

Example-based texture synthesis has been a hot research topic in the last two decades [1–3]. Based on an input example texture, we can efficiently generate arbitrary sizes of textures. Generally, we obtain exemplars manually according to image cropping, which is a tedious task if we need collect a large number of exemplars. A high-quality example usually can produce better texture synthesis effects.

Currently, most of existing methods usually only emphasize on the synthesis effect of the final results or perform texture feature analysis on the target textures [5–7]. One of the most famous methods is Markov Random Fields method, which can be divided into pixel-based texture synthesis and block-based texture synthesis. Efros and Leung [8] firstly proposed a patch-based texture synthesis method. They presented a novel synthesis model based on the correlations between adjacent pixels. Wei and Levoy also proposed patch-based method [9]. They represented the example as vectors and improved the patch matching process to be more efficient. To improve the synthesis efficiency, Ashikhmin [10] further took advantage of pixel relativity in natural texture.

© Springer International Publishing AG, part of Springer Nature 2018
B. Zeng et al. (Eds.): PCM 2017, LNCS 10736, pp. 798–806, 2018.
https://doi.org/10.1007/978-3-319-77383-4_78

On the other hand, Gardner [6] proposed a patch-based texture synthesis method for texture synthesis with high randomness. Liang *et al.* [11] also improved Gardner's method based on patch-based sampling. Another way to process example is to analyze the patching errors of blocks with specify size [12] to help synthesis. Ashikhmin [14] used the techniques of texture synthesis directly on curved surface. More recently, Lefebvre and Hoppe [13] introduced a parallel synthesis algorithm base on neighbourhood patching block. To get the optimal texture, it makes corrections on partial texture constantly [15]. All above methods only focus on synthesis base on example, but little research can focus on texture exemplar extraction. However, the quality of the texture exemplar is very important for the example-based texture synthesis.

In this paper, we present a novel method to extract ideal texture exemplar from image based on textureness metric. Since there have so many images that can be easily obtained from internet, it is very important to develop an automatic texture exemplar extraction method for the example-base texture synthesis. So different from the existing methods, our method emphasizes the quality of the exemplar for the synthesis effects and focus on developing algorithm to extract ideal texture exemplar. To accurately extract texture exemplar from arbitrary image including texture regions, we present a textureness metric based on Gist descriptor [4]. On the other hand, we also perform a Poisson disk sampling to improve the efficiency of the texture patch searching. Based on the Poisson disk sampling, our method can efficiently crop exemplar randomly and uniformly from images. Finally, we employed a SVM for the UIUC database to distinguish the texture regions and non-texture regions to improve the accuracy of texture recognition. Our proposed method is tested on a number of images with different scales and different kinds of textures. Convincing visual and statistics results demonstrated its effectiveness on automatic texture exemplar extraction.

2 Method

The overview of our system is as shown in Fig. 1. Given an input image, we first perform a Poisson disk sampling to crop texture patches uniformly among the source image. To train a LVC model using SVM, we perform Gist feature extractions based on UIUC database [15]. For each cropped texture patch, we extract Gist feature from it to match with trained LVC model. Based on the Gist feature descriptors, we can identify the texture exemplars with a textureness score (0–1), where the better exemplars have higher scores.

2.1 Poisson Disk Sampling

Given an input image, one may suggest to randomly crop texture patches with specify size. However, randomly cropping would require much more time to obtain the optimal exemplar, because there may incur a lot of repeated cropping on the same local region. In our experiment, we employ a Poisson disk sampling to guide the cropping.

We implemented the Poisson disk sampling based algorithm described in [16]. Obviously, compared with random sampling, the generated Poisson disk sampling points have advance features in avoid repeated sampling. Every two Poisson disk

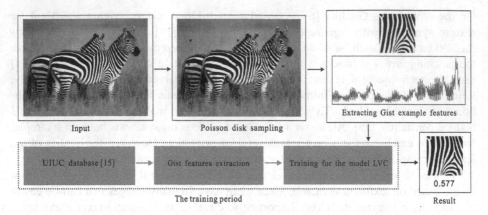

| Input | Poisson disk sampling | Extracting Gist example features |

| UIUC database [15] → Gist features extraction → Training for the model LVC |

The training period   Result

Fig. 1. The overview of our system.

sampling points have remarkable difference in the spatial domain. They have a minimum distance determined by the sampling radius. Thus, Poisson disk samplings preserve both the randomness and uniform distribution among the whole input image. More details about generating sampling points by Poisson disk sampling can be refer to algorithm described in [16]. The generated points of Poisson disk sampling for the input image are as shown in Fig. 1. Based on the Poisson disk sampling points, we can crop a number of texture patches and select an optimal texture exemplar based on textureness metric.

2.2   Gist Feature Extraction

For training the textureness metric to achieve an accurate recognition, we need a distinguish feature to describe the cropped texture patched. In our experiment, we apply the Gist feature extraction on the public UIUC database, which includes about 1000 images with manmade or natural textures. The texture library of UIUC database contains 25 kinds of textures, including bark, lawn, carpet, granite, and etc. On the other hand, UIUC database also has 4485 ordinary scene image to distinguish with the texture images. The ordinary scene images also were divided into 15 classes, such as bedroom, office, forest and street, etc.

Gist feature is a low dimensional representation of the image. It can extract rough information from images to simulate human vision. Gist feature extraction is based on Gabor filters with different directions and dimensions. The final Gist descriptors can be represented with a vector as shown in the Fig. 1. Firstly, we can indicate the input image as $f(x, y)$ with a resolution of $h \times w$. Then, we use n_c channels Gabor filter to convolve the image. By dividing the image into 4×4 cells, we can calculate the mean of data in each cell as an eigenvector. Finally, we can get the whole Gist feature vector by cascading the eigenvectors,

$$G_i(x,y) = \underset{n_c}{cat}(f(x,y) * g_{mm}(x,y)) \qquad (1)$$

where G_i is the Gist feature; n_c equals the product of directions and dimensions of Gabor filter; cat indicates the sign of cascade; $g_{mm}(x,y)$ indicates Gabor filters; And $*$ represents the convolution operator.

2.3 Support Vector Machine

For identifying the optimal exemplar from a number of cropped texture patches, we employ the well-known Support Vector Machine (SVM) to keep a good balance between learning through limited training samples and recognizing samples without faults. Obviously, SVM is a popular machine learning method for the task in computer vision. In this paper, we train texture patches samples by linear SVM and divide the eigen spaces into two parts, C1 and C2. Note that H_1 and H_2 are two parallel dotted lines. We can fit a straight solid line paralleled with H_1 and H_2 to form a separating hyperplane. To distinguish the two classes, no sampling point should be located between the dotted lines (Fig. 2).

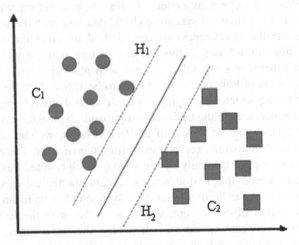

Fig. 2. Sample division basen on SVM.

SVM has two key steps. One is to get support vectors and optimal hyperplane by solving a quadratic programming problem. To obtain optimal hyperplane, H1 and H2 need to separate two kinds of samples to make the vertical distance between them as large as possible. The other step is to map the data in the primal space to those in higher-dimension linear space by kernel function. Let's denote X as the input space. F is the eigen space. For all $x_i \in X$, we have

$$K(x_i, x_j) = \phi(x_i) \cdot \phi(x_j) \tag{2}$$

where $\phi(x)$ is the mapping function from X to F. $K(x_i, x_j)$ the kernel function. $\cdot$ is the inner product of two vectors. Currently four kinds of kernel functions are common used, including linear kernel, RBF kernel, Sigmoid kernel and polynomial kernel. In this paper, we adopt the RBF kernel because we have a large amount of training samples.

$$K(x_i, x_j) = \exp\left(-\frac{|x_i - x_j|^2}{\sigma^2}\right) \tag{3}$$

Compared to other learning machines, SVM classifies finite samples to obtain optimal solution. It can better seize the internal features of data with high accuracy. That is why we choose SVM as the classifier to recognize an optimal texture exemplar.

3 Results

We have implemented our texture exemplar extraction method using MATLAB R2012a on a Windows 7 operating system. To test the both accuracy and speed of our proposed method, we applied our system to UIUC database with thousands of textures.

To demonstrate the effectiveness of our method in automatic texture exemplar extraction, we first applied our method to the images including different kinds of textures. In our experiments, we select images with resolutions of about 800×600, and set the parameters of Poisson disk sampling to be 128×128. Because there have no ground truth for the selected exemplar, we invite several artists to manually select an ideal texture exemplar as a ground truth for comparison. Typical results are as shown in Fig. 3. From the input images shown in the first column, we can observe that it is difficult to crop an ideal texture exemplar even for a human user. The exemplars in the second column are cropped manually by the artists, which cost tedious time to identify the best exemplar. Instead, four best texture exemplars automatically extracted with our method are as shown in the third column. Our system only retains an optimal texture exemplar as the output of our system, which is as shown in the last column. From visual comparisons between the second column and the last column, we can see that our method can accurately extract a texture exemplar, which even outperform the results manually selected by the artists, indicating that our method is effective.

Figures 4 and 5 show more results of our method performed to other images. We can see that our methods generally perform well for both natural textures (Figs. 4(a–c) and 5) and manmade textures Fig. 4(d). In addition, we also test our method in handling exemplars with different resolutions, such as 128×128 and 256×256 in Figs. 4 and 5 respectively. Convincing experimental results also demonstrate that our method can handle the texture exemplar extraction under different resolutions.

Beside visual results, we also perform a statistics on the database. In our experiments, we chose six categories of textures, including grass, fur, sea, bark, flower, and brick. The dataset for testing contains 100 pictures with a resolution of 800×600. We still set the Poisson disk sampling radius to be 128. We collected the scores for all

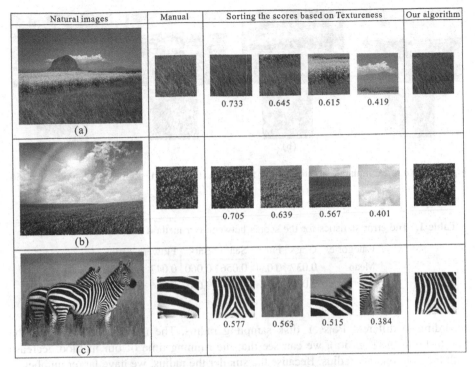

Natural images	Manual	Sorting the scores based on Textureness				Our algorithm
(a)		0.733	0.645	0.615	0.419	
(b)		0.705	0.639	0.567	0.401	
(c)		0.577	0.563	0.515	0.384	

Fig. 3. Visual results of our texture exemplar extration.

Fig. 4. Texture exemplars extracted by our algorithm. Resolution of all exemplars is 128×128.

texture exemplar extractions, and compared the scores between our method and manually cropping by the artists. The statistics results are as shown in the Table 1. From the score statistical results in Table 1, we can see that the scores of our method is close to the manual cropping, pointing out that our extracted exemplars are consistent with the results of the artist in a manually manner.

To evaluate the performance of our method with different parameters, we also performed an experiment to test both the running time and accuracy of our method

(a)   (b)   (c)   (d)

Fig. 5. Texture exemplars extracted by our algorithm. Resolution of all exemplars is 256×256.

Table 1. The error statistics for the scores between our method and the manual cropping.

Categories	Grass	Fur	Sea	Bark	Flowers	Brick
Mean	0.037	0.034	0.056	0.060	0.047	0.052
Std	0.024	0.018	0.039	0.041	0.026	0.030

according to different Poisson disk sampling radius. The result is as shown in the Fig. 6. From the Fig. 6(a), we can see that the running time of our method decrease with the Poisson disk radius. Because the smaller the radius, we have larger number of texture patches for the same input image. There have much more number of texture exemplar candidates to be tested, so it cost more time is confirm to our expectation. However, the situation is different for the accuracy. From the Fig. 6(b), we can see that the accuracy drops with the growing of the Poisson disk sampling radius, which is because texture exemplar usually with higher scores for smaller sampling radius.

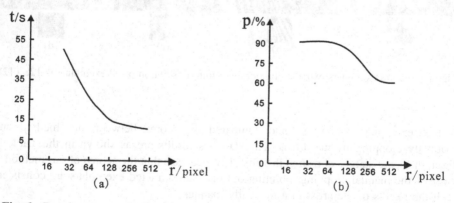

Fig. 6. Running time and accuracy performance *vs.* different Poisson disk sampling radius.

4 Conclusions

In this paper, we presented a novel texture exemplar extraction method based on textureness metric. Unlike traditional methods for example-based texture analysis, which usually more emphasize on the texture feature analysis for the synthesized target textures, our method more focus on auto-extraction of the source texture exemplar. By employing a textureness metric based on Gist descriptor, we can perform an accurate texture exemplar extraction from arbitrary image including texture regions. To improve the accuracy and efficiency of texture recognition, we also employ a SVM and Poisson disk sampling for the UIUC database to distinguish the texture regions and non-texture regions. Our method has been evaluated on a variety of images with different kinds of textures. Convincing visual and statistics results demonstrated its effectiveness on automatic texture exemplar extraction.

Acknowledgments. This work was supported in part by grants from the National Natural Science Foundation of China (Nos. 61303101, 61572328), the Shenzhen Research Foundation for Basic Research, China (Nos. JCYJ20150324140036846, JCYJ20170302153551588, CXZ Z20140902160818443, CXZZ20140902102350474, CXZZ20150813151056544, JCYJ2015063 0105452814, JCYJ20160331114551175, JCYJ20160608173051207), the Start-up Research Fund of Shenzhen University (Nos. 2013-827-000009), the China-UK Visual Information Processing Laboratory (VIPL) and Maternal and child health monitoring and early warning Engineering Technology Research Center (METRC) of Guangdong Province.

References

1. Galerne, B., Gousseau, Y., Morel, J.M.: Random phase textures: theory and synthesis. IEEE Trans. Image Process. **20**(1), 257–267 (2011)
2. Dai, D., Riemenschneider, H., Schmitt, G., et al.: Example-based facade texture synthesis. In: Proceedings of the IEEE International Conference on Computer Vision, pp. 1065–1072 (2013)
3. He, K., Sun, J.: Statistics of patch offsets for image completion. In: Fitzgibbon, A., Lazebnik, S., Perona, P., Sato, Y., Schmid, C. (eds.) ECCV 2012. LNCS, pp. 16–29. Springer, Heidelberg (2012). https://doi.org/10.1007/978-3-642-33709-3_2
4. Dai, D., Riemenschneider, H., Gool, L.V.: The synthesizability of texture examples. In: Proceedings of the 2014 IEEE Conference on Computer Vision and Pattern Recognition, CVPR 2014, pp. 3027–3034 (2014)
5. Peachey, D.R.: Solid texturing of complex surfaces. In: ACM SIGGRAPH Computer Graphics, vol. 19(3), pp. 279–286. ACM (1985)
6. Gardner, G.Y.: Visual simulation of clouds. In: ACM SIGGRAPH Computer Graphics, vol. 19(3), pp. 297–304 (1985)
7. Fleischer, K.W., Laidlaw, D.H., Currin, B.L.: Cellular texture generation. In: Proceedings of the 22nd Annual Conference on Computer Graphics and Interactive Techniques, pp. 239–248 (1995)
8. Efros, A.A., Leung, T.K.: Texture synthesis by non-parametric sampling. In: Proceedings of the Seventh IEEE International Conference on Computer Vision, vol. 2, pp. 1033–1038. IEEE (1999)

9. Wei, L.Y., Levoy, M.: Fast texture synthesis using tree-structured vector quantization. In: Proceedings of the 27th Annual Conference on Computer Graphics and Interactive Techniques, pp. 479–488. ACM Press/Addison-Wesley Publishing Co. (2000)
10. Ashikhmin, M.: Synthesizing natural textures. In: Proceedings of the 2001 Symposium on Interactive 3D Graphics, pp. 217–226 (2001)
11. Liang, L., Liu, C., Xu, Y.Q.: Real-time texture synthesis by patch-based sampling. ACM Trans. Graph. (ToG) 20(3), 127–150 (2001)
12. Julesz, B.: Textons, the elements of texture perception, and their interactions. Nature 290 (5802), 91–97 (1981)
13. Lefebvre, S., Hoppe, H.: Parallel controllable texture synthesis. ACM Trans. Graph. (TOG) 24(3), 777–786 (2005)
14. Ashikhmin, M.: Synthesizing natural textures. In: Proceedings of the ACM Symposium on Interactive 3D Graphics, pp. 217–226 (2001)
15. Lazebnik, S., Schmid, C., Ponce, J.: A sparse texture representation using local affine regions. PAMI 27(8), 1265–1278 (2005)
16. Bridson, R.: Fast Poisson disk sampling in arbitrary dimensions. In: ACM SIGGRAPH Sketches, p. 22 (2007)

In Defense of Fully Connected Layers in Visual Representation Transfer

Chen-Lin Zhang, Jian-Hao Luo, Xiu-Shen Wei, and Jianxin Wu[(⊠)]

National Key Laboratory for Novel Software Technology, Nanjing University,
Nanjing, China
{zhangcl,luojh,weixs,wujx}@lamda.nju.edu.cn

Abstract. Pre-trained convolutional neural network (CNN) models
have been widely applied in many computer vision tasks, especially in
transfer learning tasks. In transfer learning, the target domain may be in
a different feature space or follow a different data distribution, compared
to the source domain. In CNN transfer tasks, we often transfer visual representations from a source domain (e.g., ImageNet) to target domains
with fewer training images or have different image properties. It is natural to explore which CNN model performs better in visual representation
transfer. Through visualization analyses and extensive experiments, we
show that when either image properties or task objective in the target
domain is far away from those in the source domain, having the fully
connected layers in the source domain pre-trained model is essential in
achieving high accuracy after transferring to the target domain.

Keywords: Deep learning · Computer vision · Fully connected layers

1 Introduction

Convolutional neural network (CNN), which is now pervasive in computer
vision [7], is a very successful visual representation learning approach. Research
of CNN in artificial intelligence includes not only the real-world applications, but
also the fundamental developments of CNN itself. However, a systematic study
of classic CNN modules (e.g., the fully connected layer) in various setup (i.e.,
different from the conventional classification usage) is missing in the literature.

The fully connected (FC) layer is one of the most fundamental modules in
CNN. It is widely used in traditional CNN models [7,14]. However, it is known
that FC may cause overfitting, and it requires millions of parameters [14]. In
recent CNN models (such as GoogLeNet [15] and ResNet [5]), a global average
pooling layer replaces the last FC layers, which has much fewer parameters and
improves the classification accuracy on the challenging ImageNet [12] dataset.

This work was supported by the Collaborative Innovation Center of Novel Software
Technology and Industrialization.

© Springer International Publishing AG, part of Springer Nature 2018
B. Zeng et al. (Eds.): PCM 2017, LNCS 10736, pp. 807–817, 2018.
https://doi.org/10.1007/978-3-319-77383-4_79

Thus, more and more deep models prefer discarding FC for better performance and efficiency [5,8,9,18]. The utilities of FC layers in CNN have declined in recent research.

In this paper, however, we are in defense of FC layers in visual representation transfer. In visual representation transfer, the popular way to transfer is fine-tuning, which uses a pre-trained model from the source domain to initialize the deep model in the target domain, and updates its parameters using the target domain data. In general, we have various image data and pre-trained models in source domains like the popular ImageNet [12] data. While, in target domains, there will be fewer image data than ImageNet, or even with different kinds of images.

In our experiments, we treat ImageNet as the source domain, and take diverse kinds of image data as the target domains to perform visual representation transfer, i.e., different numbers of images, object-centric/scene-centric properties and even different granularities (cf. Table 1). We show that when the target domain has a small number of images or the difference between source and target domains is large, FC layers play an important role in achieving high accuracy in target domains by fine-tuning the pre-trained model. To the best of our knowledge, this is the first empirical study that shows the importance of FC layers in transferring CNN visual representations.

2   Related Work

CNN has become the *de facto* standard in many computer vision research. Alex-Net [7] used a model with five convolution layers ($conv_1$, $conv_2$, ..., $conv_5$) with three FC layers (fc_6, fc_7 and fc_8), and achieved rank 1st in the ILSVRC12 classification task. They can both add non-linearity to the models and finish the classification. In spite of these functions, FC layers have serious disadvantages: easily getting overfitted, hard to converge during training, and hampering the generalization ability [8].

Researchers have proposed the global average pooling strategy to replace the FC layers [8]. The global average pooling layer has no parameter, which summarizes the spatial information using an average, and can be seen as a regularizer. GoogLeNet [15] and ResNet [5] are two typical examples without the last FC layers. Both GoogLeNet and ResNet used the global average pooling layer to replace the last fully connected layers, and have achieved best results in the ImageNet competition in 2014 and 2015, respectively.

On the other hand, VGG-Nets [14] also achieved state-of-the-art results. VGG-Nets have similar architecture as that of the Alex-Net. The FC layers are still used in VGG-Nets. An interesting observation is that the VGG-Nets have become a popular feature extraction tool in various computer vision tasks. GoogLeNet and ResNet, however, perform well in tasks with large datasets or tasks which are similar to source domains, but they are not very popular in these transfer learning tasks, and even fail in some tasks [4,10]. In this paper, we show that it is because the FC layers in VGG-16 leads to high accuracy in visual representation transfer.

There is some research on deep transfer learning. It has been shown that pre-trained CNN descriptors are very powerful in many tasks [2,13]. Performing transfer learning based on pre-trained models will benefit the system's accuracy [21]. This procedure is called fine-tuning, and it is also showed that fine-tuning all layers will also improve the final result [20].

In practice, fine-tuning starts from an already learned model like VGG-16, then slightly modifies the network structure. Fine-tuning then initializes the network weights using pre-trained model, and starts training on the target dataset. It has become the most popular transfer learning method in many computer vision tasks in the deep learning scenario. In this paper, we will mainly focus on this type of visual representation transfer learning.

3   In Defense of FC in CNN Transfer Learning

As aforementioned, FC layers are shown as inefficient and inefficacious when training CNN from scratch in only the source domain. In this section, however, we show that the FC layers are essential when transferring the representation in CNN, especially when the source and target domains are far away from each other. To support such a statement, we conduct visual representation transfer experiments on the VGG [14] and ResNet [5] architectures. Based on the two architectures, CNN models with and without FC layers are employed for ablation experiments. Moreover, we prepare several computer vision tasks in different target domains. Finally, by comparing the performance of these CNN models on these target domains, we establish the importance of FC layers in visual representation transfer.

3.1   CNN Models with and Without FC Layers

Experiments are conducted on different CNN models with and without FC based on two architectures. Thus, we have four CNN models from the source domain, i.e., the ImageNet [12] data. Two of them are based on VGG-16 [14], and the other two are based on ResNet [5].

For VGG-16, we name VGG-w.-FC to indicate the pre-trained VGG-16 model with the FC layers. In addition, in order to obtain a VGG model without FC from the source domain, we replace the pool5 layer with a global average pooling layer and remove all subsequent FC layers in original VGG-16. Then, a $1 \times 1 \times 1000$ convolution layer is added to output the predicted results. The modified VGG-16 model is named as VGG-w/o-FC. Then, the ImageNet dataset is used to fine-tune VGG-w/o-FC until converging. The structures of VGG-w.-FC and VGG-w/o-FC are illustrated in Fig. 1a.

A few interesting observations are obtained on these two VGG-based models. First, it can be considered as a transfer learning task in which the target domain is the same as the source domain. For our VGG-w/o-FC, we achieved 10.59% Top-5 error on the ILSVRC 2012 validation set, which is 0.95% lower than that of VGG-w.-FC. The size (i.e., number of parameters) of VGG-w/o-FC is only 11.00%

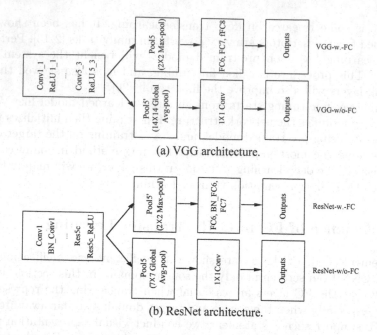

(a) VGG architecture.

(b) ResNet architecture.

Fig. 1. Network structures of different CNN architectures.

of that of VGG-w.-FC (15.22 vs. 138.34 million), but it has higher accuracy than that of VGG-w.-FC. This comparison corroborates the fact that removing FC layers is advantageous when training CNN from scratch with enough training images.

For ResNet models, we use the public ResNet-50 model pre-trained on ImageNet as ResNet-w/o-FC model. Because ResNet-w/o-FC has no FC layer, we add a 2 × 2 local max pooling layer after removing the global average pooling layer and final FC layer. Then, we add a 1024-d FC layer, followed by a batch normalization layer, and finally we add a 1000-d FC layer for classification. We name this model as ResNet-w.-FC. ResNet-w/o-FC got 7.82% Top-5 error on the ImageNet validation set, and ResNet-w.-FC got 8.64% Top-5 error, which also indicates that removing FC layers is advantageous when training CNN from scratch with enough training images.

When both models are transferred to other target domains, we change the number of nodes in the last layer according to the target domain, using the same initialization method to set the new values for the last layer, and fine-tune all parameters in the models using the training data in target domains.

In addition, we also conduct experiments on two more VGG-based models during transferring, i.e., VGG-w.-FC-fix and VGG-w/o-FC-fix. For these models, we fix the representation learning parts. In other words, the CNN representations are used unchangeably.

3.2   Image Data in Different Target Domains

We use four datasets (target domains, see Table 1 for a summary of their properties) and perform three image tasks (classification, content-based retrieval and localization) to study the performance differences with or without the FC layers.

First, four image classification datasets are included (Caltech-101 [3], Indoor-67 [11], RGB-NIR scene [1] and CUB200-2011 [16]). The tasks of these datasets are the same as the baseline models (i.e., classification). However, the images differ from ImageNet in their properties. Second, we transfer the baseline models to perform fine-grained unsupervised image retrieval and object localization, in which the tasks are significantly different in the source and target domains. Examples of these datasets are shown in Fig. 2. Details of these datasets are as follows.

- **Caltech-101.** It has 101 categories of objects [3]. This dataset is the most similar one to ImageNet, because the categories in Caltech-101 are mostly included in the categories in ImageNet.
- **MIT Indoor-67.** It has 67 indoor scene categories [11]. This dataset is less similar to the source ImageNet dataset than Caltech-101. Instead of recognizing objects, the categories are characterized by *scenes*. However, some scene categories are common in both MIT indoor and ImageNet.
- **9-class RGB-NIR scene.** This scene recognition dataset is proposed in [1]. It includes nine scene categories in the RGB-NIR image format. In our study, it is divided into two parts: the RGB image and the NIR image. It has nine classes of outdoor scenes.

  The RGB images in this dataset is getting more distant to ImageNet, because the outdoor scenes in this dataset is different from those in ImageNet. The NIR part of this dataset is taken by different sensors than the ImageNet

(a) ImageNet

(b) Caltech-101   (c) Indoor-67   (d) 9-class RGB   (e) 9-class NIR   (f) CUB

Fig. 2. Example images from the source domain (ImageNet) and target domains, i.e., (b)–(f). We organize these datasets such that the similarity (including *object types*, *image types*, *imaging sensors* and *category granularities*) between the source and target domain decreases from left to right. Note that image classification is performed in the source (ImageNet) and (b)–(f), and fine-grained retrieval and object localization is performed on (f).

(NIR vs. RGB). Due to this difference in imaging sensor, the NIR images are dissimilar to the ImageNet images.

- **CUB200-2011** [16] contains 11788 images of 200 fine-grained bird species. We perform both classification and unsupervised localization/retrieval tasks on CUB200-2011. Fine-grained image classification is performed as similar as the other datasets. For unsupervised fine-grained image retrieval and object localization, we use the SCDA method [17] to show performance of different CNN models.

3.3   Visualization and Observations

Before comparing numerical accuracy rates in various target domains, we take `VGG-w.-FC` and `VGG-w/o-FC` as examples to visualize for giving us some intuitions about their differences. Figure 3 shows their corresponding visualization.

Table 1. Summary of the datasets' properties.

Dataset	♯ images	♯ classes	Style	Granularity	Color space
Caltech-101	9,145	102	Object	Generic	RGB
Indoor-67	6,700	67	Scene	Generic	RGB
9class RGB	477	9	Scene	Generic	RGB
9class NIR	477	9	Scene	Generic	NIR
CUB200-2011	11,788	200	Object	Fine-grained	RGB

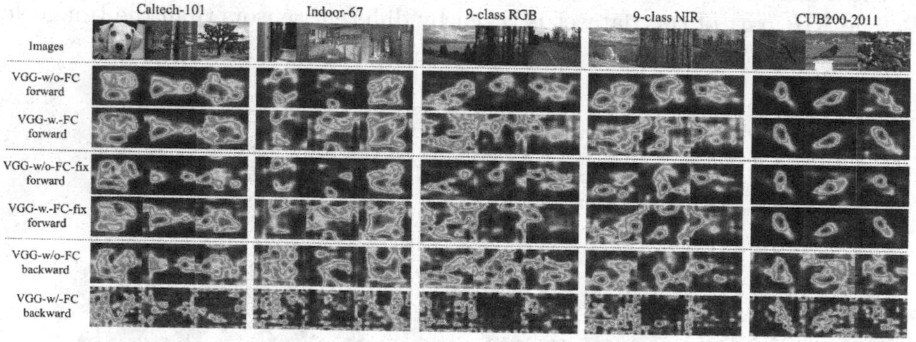

Fig. 3. Visualization of the activations (of $relu_{5\_3}$) for the four baseline models on four classification datasets. The first row shows the input images. The second, third, fourth and fifth rows show the forward feature maps of `VGG-w/o-FC`, `VGG-w.-FC`, `VGG-w/o-FC-fix`, `VGG-w.-FC-fix`, respectively. The sixth and seventh rows show the backward feature maps of `VGG-w/o-FC` and `VGG-w.-FC` models, respectively. Note that we organize the figures such that every two rows between the horizontal bars are directly comparable, i.e., they differ only by the existence or missing of the fully connected layers. Color code is used to visualize the values: the red regions mean larger values and blue regions refer to smaller values. (Color figure online)

Table 2. Comparison of classification accuracy on four datasets. The best result in a column of each sub-table is marked in bold. Note that, the "-fix" version of VGG models indicates their representation learning parts are fixed.

	FC	Caltech-101	indoor-67	RGB scene	NIR scene	CUB
VGG-w.-FC	✓	87.24%	**66.27%**	**80.20%**	**76.40%**	**73.24%**
VGG-w/o-FC	✗	**88.17%**	64.97%	78.80%	75.56%	71.90%
VGG-w.-FC-fix	✓	88.64%	**66.56%**	**81.60%**	**79.12%**	**68.42%**
VGG-w/o-FC-fix	✗	**89.40%**	64.86%	77.76%	76.52%	67.90%
ResNet-w.-FC	✓	90.89%	**74.75%**	**90.20%**	**87.87%**	**81.81%**
ResNet-w/o-FC	✗	**91.03%**	74.44%	89.90%	86.86%	81.50%

We visualize both forward and backward feature maps. For each forward feature map, we show the results after fine-tuning. For the backward feature maps, we visualize the gradient when the two non-fix models start to fine-tune on the visualized input image. For each visualization, we sum the response values of all the channels in the $relu_{5\_3}$ layer for each deep network.

One obvious difference between models with and without FC layers is: while models without FC layers has its activation map (i.e., the red regions) concentrated around the center object, those with the FC layers (e.g., VGG-w.-FC) has activation maps that is more *distributed*, i.e., the activations scatter in many locations in the image.

Hence, we conjecture that when FC layers are missing, the activations is *too concentrated around the object* (i.e., *only features tightly related to the source domain has strong responses*). This close relationship makes such models both efficient and effective in the source domain, but at the same time may make it inappropriate to transfer to a target domain if the source and target are distant from each other. Those models with FC layers show a different property. Although they might be less effective in the source domain, its distributed activations *enable them to capture useful image features in target domains*, even if the target is dissimilar to the source domain.

This difference can be partly explained by the different pooling action after $relu_{5\_3}$ in these two models (cf. Fig. 1). In VGG-w/o-FC, the layer $conv_{5\_3}$ is updated directly using the error signal in the classification. Hence, the visual representation is highly focused for classification of the source domain. In VGG-w.-FC, the error signal will first affect the fc_8 layers, then fc_7 and fc_6, finally it will affect $conv_{5\_3}$. The FC layers fc_6 and fc_7 act like "firewalls" in the transfer process such that the features in $conv_{5\_3}$ are not directly affected by the classification error. Hence it will reflect more general image structures.

As the example in the first column of Fig. 3 shows, VGG-w/o-FC only focuses on the dog's mouth or the ear. Because the target is similar to the source domain in this case, this concentration of attention is a desired property. We observe similar concentration in the examples from fourth column to sixth column. However, when we move on the more distant target domains, the models without FC layers only concentrate around few small regions, which fails to capture useful information in the target domain. VGG-w.-FC, which has the FC layers, on the contrary, activates on many regions that are useful in describing the target domain image. For example, it activates on different types of objects in the fifth column (for indoor images) and different trees in the tenth column. For backward feature maps, we can easily see the same findings: VGG-w/o-FC mainly focuses on parts of dogs, while VGG-w.-FC is more distributed, both for dog parts and background parts.

4 Experiments

We first describe the experimental setting, then the results and analyses follow.

4.1 Experimental Setup

For all the classification tasks, the images are resized to 224×224, and we did not use additional data augmentation techniques. In validation, we use the one image policy. For the source domain models, VGG-w/o-FC is trained by the Caffe toolbox [6] with learning rate 10^{-3}, weight decay 5×10^{-4} and momentum 0.9. For training ResNet-w.-FC, we use the Torch toolkit with the same hyper-parameter values to train ResNet-w.-FC.

Regarding the dataset settings, for most datasets, we follow the traditional protocols or original training/test splitting provided by the datasets.

Specifically, on Caltech-101, We randomly sample 30 images per category for training, and the remaining up to 50 images per category for testing. We repeat five random splits and report the average accuracy. For the 9-class RGB-NIR dataset, we use the RGB images and NIR images for two independent classification tasks. The NIR 1-channel images are replicated into 3-channels as model inputs. For both RGB and NIR tasks, we follow the setup in [19]: 42 images are randomly chosen for training per category, and the rest 11 images for testing. The averaged accuracy is reported on five random splits. For MIT Indoor-67 and CUB200-2011, we follow the training and test splitting included with these datasets.

For fine-tuning models in target domains, we set the base learning rate to 10^{-5}, momentum to 0.9 and weight decay to 5×10^{-4}. The parameters of the last layer are initialized from a zero-mean Gaussian with the standard deviation as 10^{-3}.

For fine-grained image retrieval on CUB200-2011, [17] proposed a simple but effective method to do unsupervised fine-grained image retrieval and object localization, i.e., Selective Convolutional Descriptor Aggregation (SCDA). SCDA only needs a model pre-trained from ImageNet, hence we choose it as our experimental method. SCDA utilizes layers' activations and descriptor aggregation such as average- and max-pooling. For VGG-w.-FC, the activations of $relu_{5\_3}$ and $pool_5$ are used, which are a $14 \times 14 \times 512$ tensor (VGG-w.-FC 14×14 in Tables 3 and 4) and a $7 \times 7 \times 512$ tensor (VGG-w.-FC 7×7 in Tables 3 and 4), respectively. As the

Table 3. Comparison of different outputs' SCDA object localization accuracy on CUB200-2011 with different IoU.

Models	FC	0.35	0.4	0.45	0.5	0.55	0.6	0.65	0.7
VGG-w.-FC 7 × 7	✓	**91.82%**	**87.71%**	**82.86%**	**76.79%**	**68.95%**	**59.89%**	**48.71%**	**36.35%**
VGG-w/o-FC 7 × 7	✗	75.94%	69.40%	62.00%	54.88%	47.29%	40.14%	32.78%	25.72%
VGG-w.-FC 14 × 14	✓	**92.35%**	**88.97%**	**84.28%**	**79.46%**	**73.52%**	**65.86%**	**56.87%**	**46.63%**
VGG-w/o-FC 14 × 14	✗	77.79%	71.07%	64.20%	56.42%	49.72%	43.30%	36.04%	28.98%

Table 4. Comparison of different outputs' SCDA image retrieval accuracy on CUB200-2011.

Models	FC	Avg. pooling		Max pooling		Avg.+Max pooling	
		Top-1	Top-5	Top-1	Top-5	Top-1	Top-5
VGG-w.-FC 7 × 7	✓	**56.42%**	**63.14%**	**58.35%**	**64.18%**	**59.72%**	**65.79%**
VGG-w/o-FC 7 × 7	✗	22.26%	29.33%	24.44%	31.51%	26.20%	33.31%
VGG-w.-FC 14 × 14	✓	**55.33%**	**62.04%**	**58.03%**	**63.93%**	**59.08%**	**65.45%**
VGG-w/o-FC 14 × 14	✗	22.51%	30.06%	24.21%	31.48%	26.61%	33.91%

comparisons with VGG-w/o-FC, we first remove the layers after $relu_{5\_3}$, then add a 2×2 max pooling layer (also call it $pool_5$). Similarly, the outputs of $relu_{5\_3}$ and $pool_5$ are extracted, which also have $14 \times 14 \times 512$ and $7 \times 7 \times 512$ activations, respectively. They are shown as VGG-w/o-FC 14×14 and VGG-w/o-FC 7×7 in Tables 3 and 4. Now we have four methods to compare in total.

In Table 3, we report the object localization accuracy on CUB200-2011 with different Intersection-over-Union (IoU) ratios. In Table 4, the Top-1 and Top-5 mAP as the retrieval performance are reported for these four models. Additionally, since SCDA did not work well on the ResNet-50 based models, the localization accuracy and retrieval results of these models are not reported (about 20% lower than VGG models).

4.2 Results and Analyses

Results of image classification tasks are listed in Table 2. It is obvious that the best result for each dataset appear mostly in w.-FC models except the Caltech-101 dataset. That is, as the target domain is getting more dissimilar to the source domain, having the fully connected layers are becoming more important. However, when the source and target domains are similar, the w/o-FC models are more accurate. In Caltech-101, VGG-w/o-FC outperforms VGG-w.-FC by 0.93%. While in dissimilar datasets like CUB200-2011 and 9-class RGB-NIR, VGG-w.-FC leads VGG-w/o-FC by a 1.34%, 0.84% and 1.40% margin. For ResNet-50 based models, they show the same conclusion as VGG based models: ResNet-w.-FC leads ResNet-w/o-FC by 0.5% to 1% in all four datasets except the Caltech-101 dataset.

The -fix versions of CNN models fix the representation learning parts, whose results are shown in Table 2. In transferring to dissimilar target domains, the models with FC layers consistently outperform those without FC layers; and VGG-w.-FC-fix even has a significant improvement over VGG-w.-FC, the non-fixed version. We guess that for target domains with small data, only fine-tune the FC layers can prevent models from overfitting, and achieve higher accuracy. We conjecture that when the target domain is distant from the source domain, and when the number of training images is very small, applying the visual representation in a pre-trained model (learned with the FC layers) is the optimal option.

For fine-grained image retrieval and object localization tasks, because SCDA is an unsupervised method, the performance is directly decided by the pre-trained model itself. In these two tasks, VGG-w.-FC based models performs significantly better than VGG-w/o-FC based models in all situations. In image retrieval, VGG-w.-FC based models get about 58% Top-1 and 63% Top-5 accuracy, but VGG-w/o-FC based models can only get about 25% Top-1 and 30% Top-5 accuracy, leaving a 30% gap. Similar gaps exist in the object localization tasks. These two tasks are totally different from the ImageNet classification task, which may explain this gap: when the source and target domains differ not only in image properties but also required tasks, having the FC layers are essential too.

Hence, when the source and target domains are similar in both image properties and task objectives, we recommend not using any FC layer in the source domain. However, we defend the importance of FC layers if there is significant dissimilarity in either image property or task objective.

5   Conclusion and Future Work

In this paper, we have studied the usage of fully connected layers in visual representation transfer. By performing visualization analyses and experiments on classification, fine-grained retrieval and object localization on various kinds of datasets in target domains, we conclude that when the target domain is not far away from the source domain, fully connected layers can be replaced by global average pooling for better efficiency and accuracy. However, when a large difference exists in either image property or task objective, fully connected layers are essential in visual representation transfer.

In the future, we will try to improve the performance of CNN models with global average pooling. We want to maintain its small model size and efficiency, and make it suitable for visual representation transfer to distant target domains.

References

1. Brown, M., Süsstrunk, S.: Multi-spectral SIFT for scene category recognition. In: CVPR, pp. 177–184 (2011)
2. Donahue, J., Jia, Y., Vinyals, O., Hoffman, J., Zhang, N., Tzeng, E., Darrell, T.: DeCAF: a deep convolutional activation feature for generic visual recognition. In: ICML, pp. 647–655 (2014)

3. Fei-Fei, L., Fergus, R., Perona, P.: Learning generative visual models from few training examples: an incremental bayesian approach tested on 101 object categories. CVIU **106**, 59–70 (2007)
4. Girshick, R.: Fast R-CNN. In: ICCV, pp. 1440–1448 (2015)
5. He, K., Zhang, X., Ren, S., Sun, J.: Deep residual learning for image recognition. In: CVPR, pp. 770–778 (2016)
6. Jia, Y., Shelhamer, E., Donahue, J., Karayev, S., Long, J., Girshick, R., Guadarrama, S., Darrell, T.: Caffe: convolutional architecture for fast feature embedding. In: ACM MM, pp. 675–678 (2014)
7. Krizhevsky, A., Sutskever, I., Hinton, G.E.: Imagenet classification with deep convolutional neural networks. In: NIPS, pp. 1097–1105 (2012)
8. Lin, M., Chen, Q., Yan, S.: Network in network. In: ICLR (2014)
9. Lin, T.Y., RoyChowdhury, A., Majiu, S.: Bilinear CNN models for fine-grained visual recognition. In: ICCV, pp. 1449–1457 (2015)
10. Long, J., Shelhamer, E., Darrell, T.: Fully convolutional networks for semantic segmentation. In: CVPR, pp. 3431–3440 (2015)
11. Quattoni, A., Torralba, A.: Recognizing indoor scenes. In: CVPR, pp. 413–420 (2009)
12. Russakovsky, O., Deng, J., Su, H., Krause, J., Satheesh, S., Ma, S., Huang, Z., Karpathy, A., Khosla, A., Bernstein, M., Berg, A.C., Fei-Fei, L.: ImageNet large scale visual recognition challenge. IJCV **115**, 211–252 (2015)
13. Sharif Razavian, A., Azizpour, H., Sullivan, J., Carlsson, S.: CNN features off-the-shelf: an astounding baseline for recognition. In: CVPR 14 Workshops (2014)
14. Simonyan, K., Zisserman, A.: Very deep convolutional networks for large-scale image recognition. In: ICLR (2015)
15. Szegedy, C., Liu, W., Jia, Y., Sermanet, P., Reed, S., Anguelov, D., Erhan, D., Vanhoucke, V., Rabinovich, A.: Going deeper with convolutions. In: CVPR, pp. 1–9 (2015)
16. Wah, C., Branson, S., Welinder, P., Perona, P., Belongie, S.: The Caltech-UCSD birds-200-2011 dataset. Technical report. CNS-TR-2011-001, California Institute of Technology (2011)
17. Wei, X.S., Luo, J.H., Wu, J., Zhou, Z.H.: Selective convolutional descriptor aggregation for fine-grained image retrieval. TIP **26**(6), 2868–2881 (2017)
18. Wei, X.S., Xie, C.W., Wu, J.: Mask-CNN: Localizing parts and selecting descriptors for fine-grained image recognition. arXiv preprint arXiv:1605.06878 (2016)
19. Xiao, Y., Wu, J., Yuan, J.: mCENTRIST: a multi-channel feature generation mechanism for scene categorization. TIP **23**, 823–836 (2014)
20. Yosinski, J., Clune, J., Bengio, Y., Lipson, H.: How transferable are features in deep neural networks? In: NIPS, pp. 3320–3328 (2014)
21. Zeiler, M.D., Fergus, R.: Visualizing and understanding convolutional networks. In: Fleet, D., Pajdla, T., Schiele, B., Tuytelaars, T. (eds.) ECCV 2014. LNCS, vol. 8689, pp. 818–833. Springer, Cham (2014). https://doi.org/10.1007/978-3-319-10590-1_53

Block Cluster Based Dictionary Learning for Image De-noising and De-blurring

JianWei Zheng, Ping Yang, Shanshan Fang, and Cong Bai[✉]

School of Computer Science and Technology,
Zhejiang University of Technology, Hangzhou, China
congbai@zjut.edu.cn

Abstract. Image de-noising or de-blurring is an important step in image pre-processing. A great variety of experiments have demonstrated that using image block as a basic operation unit can effectively improve the final results both in efficiency and visual quality. An image block searching algorithm based on the largest variance of inter groups is proposed by referring to HVS. This method could effectively extract the intrinsic information of the image blocks and avoid the change of the Euclidean distance due to the illumination variations. With the better variance value among different image block groups, the correlation of those groups is reduced and a dictionary of wider distribution is obtained such that it can get a better visual effectiveness in the sparse reconstruction. The experimental results show that this method outperforms state-of-the-art algorithms both in visual quality and the PSNR value.

Keywords: De-noising · De-blurring · Block cluster · Dictionary learning
Reconstruction

1 Introduction

Traditional single image de-noising and de-blurring methods all rely on the local smoothness and non-local self-similarity property [1]. These two properties mean that, for a certain size of image block I_b, there should be a collection S satisfying $dis_E(I_b, \forall_1\{S_1, S_2, \ldots, S_i\}) < \varepsilon$, where S_i indicates i-th similar block that matches I_b in the natural image, and $dis_E(,)$ refers to the Euclidean distance. For a random selected column vector I_{I_b} transformed from block I_b, a vector I_{S_j} can be located within the same image, which has high similarity with I_{I_b}. According to [2], this problem could be rewritten as follows:

$$I_b = I_S \cdot \theta + \xi, \tag{1}$$

where $I_S = \{I_{S_1}, I_{S_2}, \ldots, I_{S_n}\}$, θ is the coefficient matrix with elements $\theta = \{\theta_1, \theta_2, \ldots, \theta_n\}$. In the ideal case, ζ can be ignored, and it is clear that only the value of the i-th element is 1 and the remainders are all zero in θ_i. However, in the practical case, θ_i is a sparse vector, and its sparseness is related to the correlation of the interior column vectors in I_S. Furthermore, θ is a full rank sparse matrix. According to [3], the collection I_S can be regarded as a dictionary set, and the solution of coefficient θ is:

$$\hat{\theta} = \arg \min_{\theta} \|I_B - I_S \cdot \theta\|_2^2, s.t. \|\theta\|_0 \leq \varepsilon, \tag{2}$$

where $\hat{\theta}$ is the optimal value of θ, $\|\cdot\|_0$ represents l_0-norm.

In the above process, the similarity is determined by the Euclidean distance. A natural assumption is that a small Euclidean distance leads to a large similarity. Nevertheless, due to the impact of illumination, two selected image blocks with similar structure but with different luminance always get small similarity value, which disobeys the original assumption. Kostadin et al. [4] proposes the BM3D algorithm for image de-noising and achieves appealing experimental results. BM3D also uses Euclidean distance, and it performs a global search for each image block with high computational complexity.

Li et al. [5] deems that the image blocks can be divided into high-resolution and low-resolution blocks. The low-resolution and high-resolution image blocks are used to calculate the similarity and reconstruct image, respectively. However, the block matching operation of low-resolution images is not conducive to improving the matching accuracy due to the lack of structural information in low-resolution domain.

In view of the problems of structural differences caused by Euclidean distance in different illumination, and lack of structural information by using low resolution image, in this paper, a new similar image block selection method is proposed for calculating the variance between different groups. The similarity of two image blocks with small variance is high. And an unsupervised clustering method is introduced in the dictionary learning step to solve the problems of the incompleteness of the local computing method and the high complexity of the global search method.

2 Related Works

Traditional algorithms using image block as the basic operating unit, mostly adopt a sliding window in overlapping segmentation [1]. And similarity measurement method is Euclidean distance. As mentioned above, due to the impact of illumination, two selected image blocks with similar structure but with different luminance always get large Euclidean distance. In order to improve the accuracy of selecting similar blocks, we use the ideas learning from HVS [6].

(a) *Human Visual System (HVS)*

Recent researches on HVS mainly focus on two aspects [7, 8], one is the neuroscience of HVS in order for explaining the principle. Although it has not yet been applied to practical problems, it provides important clues for researchers on understanding them. Another one applies it to computer vision problems according to the characteristics of HVS for ameliorating classical models and enhancing the performance of practical applications. It has been successfully used in optical character recognition and recommendation systems [9]. Based on current research on HVS, we adopt variance instead of Euclidean distance to calculate the similarity of two image blocks.

(b) *Image De-noising and De-blurring Processing*

The degradation process of the image includes a variety of situations and the general model can be written as $y = G \cdot x_{org} + n$ [11], where x_{org} is the original image, y is degraded image, G can be regarded as the operator of the degradation process of the original image, n is the additional noise signal. So the image degradation process can be degraded by the following equation:

$$x_{est} = G^\dagger(y - n), \qquad (3)$$

where x_{est} is represented as the processed image, $G^\dagger$ is pseudo inverse matrix of G. Because G is unknown image degradation process, Eq. (3) cannot obtain a unique solution. To solve this problem, [12] converted into an optimization problem, the degraded image is reconstructed by sparse representation.

(c) *Dictionary Training*

The basic goal of dictionary learning in sparse representation is to include as complete as possible information of the sample and the correlation of information among groups as low as possible to ensure the sparsity of coefficient. The residual between the reconstructed image and the original image can be expressed by $\zeta = \hat{y} - y$. Rubinstein et al. [13] proposes a dictionary learning algorithm, obtains plenty of small image blocks I_b as the training set D, and each image block satisfies:

$$I_b = D \cdot \theta_i + \xi_i, \qquad (4)$$

where ζ_i represents the residual amount, and θ_i is the sparse coefficients. According to [5], the optimization process is to find the optimal dictionary D. The optimization problem can be represented as the probability of maximizing the optimal dictionary set, since each block I_b in the training set is independent distribution and randomly selected, a optimization problem can be expressed as [14]:

$$\max_D P(X|D) = \max_{D,\theta_i}\{\prod_{i=1}^{n} P(I_{b_i}|\theta_i, D)P(\theta_i)\} \qquad (5)$$

where $P(I_{b_i}|\theta_i, D)$ follows Gaussian distribution, $P(\theta_i)$ follows the prior distribution of the coefficients, then the dictionary D and the coefficient θ_i could be solved by the alternate solution method. However, this method is easy to fall into the local optimum, and obviously the convergence is slow.

3   Proposed Method

Traditional single image de-noising and de-blurring algorithms mainly include four steps [15]: (a), similar image blocks searching and matching process; (b), dictionary learning process; (c), transpose domain de-noising process; (d), image reconstruction. This section proposes a dictionary learning method based on block clustering for the first two steps. A dictionary is learned from the set of similar image blocks, and the correlation between groups within the dictionary is reduced by increasing the variance between groups. At the same time, a more accurately similar image blocks searching strategy is established inspired by HVS, weakening the influence of the illumination changes with the same computational complexity.

A comparison of Euclidean distance and variance of same block groups is demonstrated as follows. As shown in Fig. 1, it is clear that the boxes of same color have similar texture structures, but when the brightness changes, their Euclidean distance changes greatly, and their variance changes little. As we can see in the right side of Fig. 1), the size of original image X_{org} is 256×256, and the size of the selected image block b_s is 16×16. Without loss of generality, we pick out three groups to prove the results and each group contains three kinds of columns. The first column is randomly selected, the second column is overlapping block similar to the first one, and the third column is affected by the shadow and has large brightness changes.

Fig. 1. The numerical analysis with image Barbara

Via calculating, the Euclidean distance and the variance of the overlapping block and the initial block were shown at the top of each group. And the results of the third block and the initial block are shown at the lower part. The results show that the rates of change of Euclidean distance are 378%, 112% and 65%, respectively. But variance changes of each group are -14%, 45% and 10% respectively. It can be concluded that using variance as similarity criterion will be more robust. In addition, taking the computational complexity into account, calculating Euclidean distance cost averaged 0.000106 s for each group, and calculating variance cost averaging 0.000169 s per group.

Dividing a natural image X_{org} into $m \times n$ small image squares blocks of the same size $\sqrt{S_{pch}} * \sqrt{S_{pch}}$ without overlapping, rewriting it to vector form x_i, $(x_i \in R^{S_{pch}*1})$ and stacking them together, an untrained dictionary $X = \{x_1, x_2, \ldots, x_p\}$ $(X \in R^{S_{pch}*p})$ is obtained, where $p = m \times n$.

In order to train the dictionary, k clustering centers is defined firstly [16]. For distinguishing from common image blocks, using x_{ki} to represent clustering center vector, then a clustering center matrix $X_k = \{x_{k1}, x_{k2}, \ldots, x_{kk}\}$ could be obtained. Adopting the similarity criterion described in the previous section, a similarity matrix

J could be obtained by calculating the similarity between each vector and the k_i-th cluster center vector, shown as follows:

$$J_{ij} = std(x_{ki} - x_j), \tag{6}$$

where $J \in R^{p*k}$, namely $1 \leq i \leq p, 1 \leq j \leq k$ and $std()$ represents calculating variance. J_{ij} denotes the i-th row and j-th column element in similarity matrix J, and its value denotes the variance between i-th image block and j-th cluster center.

After obtaining the similarity matrix J, we sort the row elements from small to large, pick out corresponding vectors from top q lines in matrix J, and recalculate the cluster centers. The clustering center is $X_k^i = \{x_{k1}^i, x_{k2}^i, \ldots, x_{kk}^i\}$, where i denotes i-th iteration. When the difference between the value of the clustering center obtained by the n-th iteration and the $n + 1$-th iteration is less than a real constant ε, or the algorithm reaches the preset number of iterations, it will jump out of the loop and a trained dictionary is obtained.

Taking image Barbara as example, the original image size is 256×256 pixels, and mage block size is 8×8. The original image is shown in Fig. 2(a). The flow chart of dictionary learning is shown in Fig. 2(b). The first step is to use the unsupervised K-means clustering algorithm [16] to initialize the k vectors as the cluster centers. In the second step, use the similarity criterion mentioned above to find similar vectors, calculate variance and obtain similarity degree matrix J. The third step is to sort each column in matrix J, and pick out the vectors corresponding to the first 30 lines' in J. The fourth step is to calculate the mean of the extracted vectors, update the clustering centers and back to the second step. The break conditions are described above. The trained dictionary D_{Tr} is shown in Fig. 2(c).

After obtaining the dictionary set, the final $\hat{y}$ could be obtained with the optimal value $\hat{\theta}$ by $\hat{y} = D \cdot \hat{\theta}$. Seen from Eq. (2), l_0-norm is used to evaluate the sparsity of the

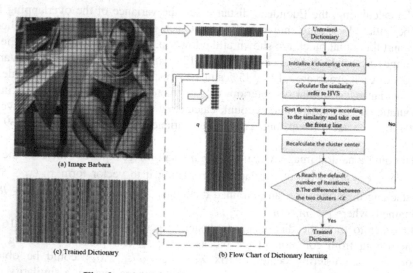

(a) Image Barbara

(c) Trained Dictionary

(b) Flow Chart of Dictionary learning

Fig. 2. Algorithm flow chart and some examples

coefficient $\hat{\theta}$ for enhancing the quality of images after de-noising and de-blurring. In order to solve the non-convex optimization problem, we use the l_1-norm instead of the l_0-norm. According to [10], it can be further transformed into the penalty polynomial form with parameter μ. As mentioned above, we use HVS-based similarity criterion to calculate variance instead of Euclidean distance. The optimal equation for θ can be written as:

$$\hat{\theta} = \arg\min_{\theta}(std(\|\theta \bullet D - y\|_2)^2) + \mu\|\theta\|_1. \tag{7}$$

where $std(\cdot)$ represents calculating variance. It can be seen that Eq. (7) holds the same computational complexity as [17].

4   Experimental Results

In this section, we use the six images of Barbara, House, Boat, Peppers, Lena and Cameraman with 256 gray levels to verify the effectiveness of our algorithm. The size of experimental objects is all 256×256. The most recently proposed algorithm GSR [17], which has proved to outperform most of other state-of-the art methods, is adopted as the competing algorithm. The image quality is evaluated by the ratio of peak signal to noise (PSNR). The blurred and noised images are respectively derived by smooth convolution and Gaussian noise attachment of the original image. The original images, blurred images and noised images are shown in Fig. 3a, b, c respectively. Table 1 lists the degrees of blurring and noising with PSNR.

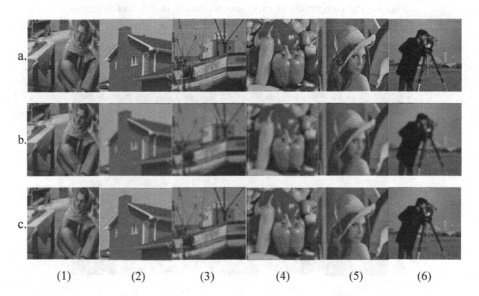

Fig. 3. The original, blurred and noised images of experimental objects

Table 1. PSNR of Blurred and Noised Images

	Barbara	House	Boat	Peppers	Lena	Cameraman
Blurred	22.47	24.08	22.27	21.97	22.89	20.56
Noised	23.81	23.39	25.91	25.12	26.17	23.39

Because adopting cluster method between groups, our algorithm shows higher efficiency in the optimization. Figure 4(a) and (b) show the comparison of de-noising and de-noising effectiveness on PSNR respectively. Taking the image House as example, Fig. 5 shows the results of our algorithm in the image de-blurring and de-noising of different iterations. The upper row is de-blurring results and lower is de-noising results. Column (a) is the initialize image, and column (b) is the result after the first iteration. It can be seen that the algorithm has better effect in contour

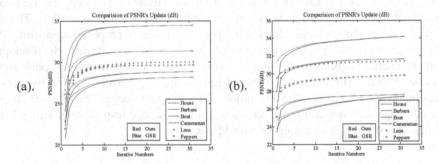

Fig. 4. The comparison of experimental results in different iterations

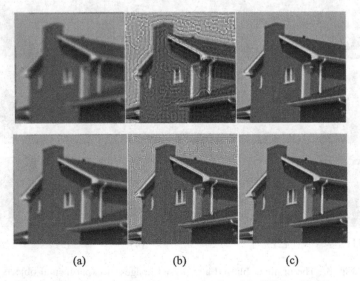

(a)   (b)   (c)

Fig. 5. The display of image House results with different iterations

delineation. Column (c) is the result. It is seen that the image has a good visual quality after the de-blurring and de-noising operation.

Table 2 shows the comparison of experiment results on GSR and ours on PSNR. It could be seen that our algorithm outperforms GSR in all the six images.

Table 2. The comparison of the experimental results on PSNR

Image		House	Barbara	Boats	Peppers	Lena	Cameraman
De-noising	GSR [17]	34.48	28.95	31.34	29.66	30.10	28.28
De-noising	Ours	**34.61**	**29.52**	**31.75**	**30.25**	**30.45**	**28.52**
De-blurring	GSR [17]	34.18	27.39	31.64	27.61	31.43	29.79
De-blurring	Ours	**34.53**	**28.52**	**31.95**	**28.25**	**31.76**	**30.25**

5 Conclusions

In this paper, we present an image de-noising and de-blurring method based on image blocks clustering strategy. Inspired by HVS, we adopt difference selection method, which uses the variance value as the similarity criterion. In order to avoid reducing image blocks' resolution and extracting the edge feature, an image blocks clustering method is proposed to cluster image blocks by structure similarity. After image clustering step, a dictionary with lower correlation of the columns is obtained, which improves the sparseness of the image reconstruction step and ensures the effectiveness of removing low-frequency noise. The experimental results show that our algorithm achieves better de-noising and de-blurring effectiveness but with the same computational complexity compared to state-of-the-art algorithms. The larger variance leads to faster convergence rate and a clearer visual quality. A drawback in this paper is that all the image blocks are transformed into vector form for sub sequential steps. Our future works will focus on the image blocks in the matrix form for better results and efficiency.

Acknowledgments. This work is supported by the National Science Fund of China under Grant Nos. 61602413 and 61502424, and the Natural Science Foundation of Zhejiang Province of China under Grant LY15F030014 and LY15F020028.

References

1. Liu, X., Zhai, D., Zhao, D., et al.: Progressive image denoising through hybrid graph Laplacian regularization: a unified framework. IEEE Trans. Image Process. **23**(4), 1491–1503 (2014)
2. Zhang, J., Zhao, D., Zhao, C., et al.: Compressed sensing recovery via collaborative sparsity. In: Data Compression Conference, pp. 287–296. IEEE (2012)

3. Dong, W., Zhang, L., Shi, G., et al.: Image deblurring and super-resolution by adaptive sparse domain selection and adaptive regularization. IEEE Trans. Image Process. 20(7), 1838–1857 (2011). A Publication of the IEEE Signal Processing Society
4. Dabov, K., Foi, A., Katkovnik, V., et al.: Image denoising by sparse 3-D transform-domain collaborative filtering. IEEE Trans. Image Process. 16(8), 2080–2095 (2007)
5. Shang, L., Liu, S.F., Zhou, Y., et al.: Modified sparse representation based image super-resolution reconstruction method. Neurocomputing 9225, 348–356 (2016)
6. Bhateja, V., Misra, M., Urooj, S.: Human visual system based unsharp masking for enhancement of mammographic images. J. Comput. Sci. 21, 387–393 (2016)
7. Wang, S., Jin, K., Lu, H., et al.: Human visual system-based fundus image quality assessment of portable fundus camera photographs. IEEE Trans. Med. Imaging 35(4), 1046–1055 (2015)
8. Pei, S.C., Chen, L.H.: Image quality assessment using human visual DOG model fused with random forest. IEEE Trans. Image Process. 24(11), 3282 (2015). A Publication of the IEEE Signal Processing Society
9. de Melo, E.V., Nogueira, E.A., Guliato, D.: Content-based filtering enhanced by human visual attention applied to clothing recommendation. In: IEEE International Conference on TOOLS with Artificial Intelligence, pp. 644–651 (2015)
10. Chen, Y., Liu, K.J.R.: Image denoising games. IEEE Trans. Circuits Syst. Video Technol. 23 (10), 1704–1716 (2013)
11. Shao, C., Song, X., Feng, Z.H., et al.: Dynamic dictionary optimization for sparse representation based face classification using local difference images. Inf. Sci. 393, 1–14 (2017)
12. Thuene, P., Enzner, G.: Maximum-likelihood approach with Bayesian refinement for multichannel-wiener postfiltering. IEEE Trans. Signal Process. 65, 3399–3413 (2017)
13. Rubinstein, R., Peleg, T., Elad, M.: Analysis K-SVD: a dictionary-learning algorithm for the analysis sparse model. IEEE Trans. Signal Process. 61(3), 661–677 (2013)
14. Zhou, X., Li, Y., He, B., et al.: GM-PHD-based multi-target visual tracking using entropy distribution and game theory. IEEE Trans. Ind. Inf. 10(2), 1064–1076 (2014)
15. Lai, W.S., Huang, J.B., Hu, Z., et al.: A comparative study for single image blind deblurring. In: IEEE Conference on Computer Vision and Pattern Recognition, pp. 1701–1709. IEEE (2016)
16. Oliveira, G.V., Coutinho, F.P., Campello, R.J.G.B., et al.: Improving k-means through distributed scalable metaheuristics. Neurocomputing 246, 45–57 (2017)
17. Zhang, J., Zhao, D., Gao, W.: Group-based sparse representation for image restoration. IEEE Trans. Image Process. 23(8), 3336 (2014)

Content Adaptive Constraint Based Image Upsampling

Fan Yang[1], Huizhu Jia[1,2]($\boxtimes$), Don Xie[1], Rui Chen[1], and Wen Gao[1]

[1] National Engineering Laboratory for Video Technology,
Peking University, Beijing 100871, China
hzjia@pku.edu.cn
[2] Cooperative Medianet Innovation Center and Beida, Information Research,
Peking University, Binhai, China

Abstract. In this paper, we present a novel image upsampling method within a two-stage framework to reconstruct different image content (large-scale edges and small-scale structures). First, we utilize a total variation (TV) filter for image decomposition which decomposes an image content into structure component and texture component. In the first stage, the structure component is enhanced by a shock filter and an improved non-local means filter, then combines with the texture component to generate initial high-resolution (HR) image. In the second stage, the gradient of initial HR image is regarded as an edge preserving constraint to reconstruct the texture component. Experimental results demonstrate that the new approach can reconstruct faithfully the HR images with sharp edges and texture structures, and annoying artifacts (blurring, jaggies, ringing, etc.) are greatly suppressed. It outperforms the state-of-the-art approaches, based on subjective and objective evaluations.

Keywords: Image upsampling · Content adaptive
Total variation filter · Shock filter · Non-local means filter
Edge preserving constraint

1 Introduction

Image upsampling, reconstructing a sharp HR image from its low resolution (LR) counterpart, has a wide range of applications such as medical imaging, remote sensing, consumer electronics, etc. It is a fundamental and challenging problem in the imaging research area. How to reconstruct sharp edges and texture structures while introducing less visual artifacts, such as such as ringing, aliasing and blurring, is the major difficulty.

Simplest linear interpolators, such as bilinear and bicubic [1] schemes, are very fast but often produce annoying artifacts. To preserve sharp edges, many edge-directed methods have been proposed [2,3], Li [3] proposed to estimate the covariance of the high-resolution image from the low-resolution image, and

© Springer International Publishing AG, part of Springer Nature 2018
B. Zeng et al. (Eds.): PCM 2017, LNCS 10736, pp. 827–837, 2018.
https://doi.org/10.1007/978-3-319-77383-4_81

then use the estimated covariance to adapt the interpolation. Another representative edge-guided interpolators is proposed by Zhang and Wu [4], in which a 2-D piecewise autoregressive model is used to estimate missing pixels in groups. Hung and Siu [5] presented a robust soft-decision interpolation algorithm using Weighted least-squares estimation for both parameter and data estimation steps. However, these methods only consider edges reconstruction, less or without considering textures reconstruction.

The reconstruction based approaches [6] are derived from the LR image generation process, where the LR image is characterized by smoothing and downsampling of the HR image. The total variation (TV) regularization approach [7] is a representative reconstruction based method. It seems most successful in terms of edge preservation and no artifacts. Saito [8] proposed an especially TV approach. This method achieves sharp edge preservation but insufficient super resolution for texture component. Yoshikawa [20] proposed to decompose an input image into a structure component and a texture component, and then enhanced the two components separately. Sakurai [9] proposed to process structure component and texture component through non-linear enhancement filters. To preserve local edges and recover image details well, edge constraints [10, 11] were introduced in the edge-directed reconstruction methods.

Recently, some learning-based methods [12, 21–23] have been proposed. In these methods, the high-frequency information is learned from a reference database. It can obtain good image quality but take very long computational time and depend on the variety of the database. Moreover, It can only be used in fixed upsampling factors.

In this paper, we take advantage of TV-based and edge-directed reconstruction methods, and propose a two-stage sharpness preserving upsampling method, as shown in Fig. 2. In the first stage, LR image is separated into a structure component and a texture component by a TV filter [13–15]. The sharp edges in the recovered structure component are ensured by shock filter [16, 17] and novel non-local means filter. In the second stage, we use a sharpness preserving reconstruction algorithm to recover small-scale textures. Our approach performs significantly better than the state-of-the-art approaches in preserving image sharpness while suppressing artifacts.

The rest of this paper is organized as follows. In Sect. 2, we describe the problem of image decomposition modeling, and discuss how to enhance the structure component through shock filter and improved non-local means filter. Section 3 presents the detail of the texture component reconstruction. Experiment results are given and discussed in Sect. 4 while Sect. 5 concludes the letter.

2   Super-Resolution Based on Total Variation Regularization

The TV-based super-resolution approach proposed in [9] is shown in Fig. 1, while Fig. 2 shows our proposed approach. The difference between these two approaches is that structure component is enhanced by an improved shock filter

[17], in Fig. 1, and by a normal shock filter [16], also incorporate a novel non-local means filter as postprocessing in Fig. 2. We have discovered that the combination of a shock filter and a non-local means filter [18] has very good compatibility. The Texture component magnification is implemented by pulse sharpening filter in Fig. 1, and by reconstruction-based method that uses a gradient constraints to preserve the edge sharpness in Fig. 2.

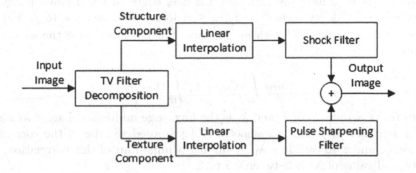

Fig. 1. Super-resolution approach with TV regularization filter and pulse filter

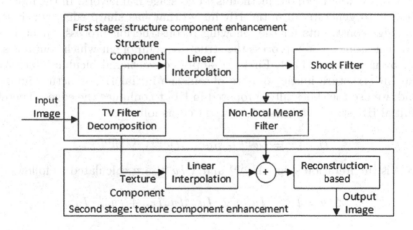

Fig. 2. Proposed approach

2.1   Image Decomposition

Image decomposition is to split an image into two or more component images. An image f can be regarded as the sum of the structural image u (being piecewise smooth and with sharp edge along the contour) and the textural image v (only containing fine-scale details, usually with some oscillatory nature), $f = u + v$.

The TV-based method has been widely used in image structure-texture decomposition models. A general approach for such decomposition [13] is to solve the problem as follows:

$$\min_u \{\|TV(u)\|_A | \|t(u, f)\|_B \leq \alpha\} \tag{1}$$

where $\| \cdot \|_A$ and $\| \cdot \|_B$ are certain norms. The TV regularization term $TV(u) = \int |\nabla u|$ allows u to have discontinuities; hence, edges in the original image are preserved. The fidelity term $\|t(u, f)\|_B \leq \alpha$ forces u to be close to f. Yin [14] proposed to minimize TV with an L^1-norm fidelity term, then the solution is updated as:

$$\min_u \int_\Omega |\nabla u| + \lambda_1 \int_\Omega |f - u| \tag{2}$$

where Ω is the domain of f, and λ_1 is the Lagrange multiplier. Larger λ_1 means that u is closer to f and less smooth. [15] proposed the use of the correlation between u and v to estimate λ_1 by finding a minimum of this correlation, and the typical value of λ_1 is between 0.2 to 2.

2.2   Shock Filter

As previously described, our method is a two-stage framework. In the first stage, our aim is to generate an initial HR image that has sharp edge, which served as the edge constraints for the following reconstruction process. Given this, in the current step, we only process the structure component which contains sharp edges, by using shock filter. First, we apply conventional bicubic interpolation to the LR structure image so as to obtain the initial HR structure image I_u. Second, we use the shock filter proposed in [16] to enhance the edges. Therefore, the initial HR structure image I_u is updated as follows:

$$Iu^{(n+1)} = Iu^{(n)} - sign(\Delta Iu^{(n)})\|\nabla Iu^{(n)}\| t \tag{3}$$

where t is the iteration step. $\Delta Iu^{(n)}$ and $\nabla Iu^{(n)}$ are calculated as follows:

$$\Delta Iu = Iu_{xx} \cdot Iu_x^2 + 2 \cdot Iu_{xx} Iu_x Iu_y + Iu_{yy} \cdot Iu_y^2 \tag{4}$$

$$\nabla Iu = \sqrt{Iu_x^2 + Iu_y^2} \tag{5}$$

where Iu_x and Iu_y are the first-order derivative in horizontal direction and vertical direction.

2.3   Improved Non-local Means Filter

The shock filter is a nonlinear filter that can effectively sharpen edges, however, it is sensitive to noise and also introduces jagged artifact, as shown in Fig. 3(b). To solve these problems, Sakurai [9] proposed to improve the shock filter by replace the $\Delta I u^{(n)}$ [17]. We propose to apply improved non-local means filter to process the shock filter result, where filter error can be modeled as the noise. Experiment results show that we can better preserve edge structures while suppressing visual artifacts, as shown in Fig. 3.

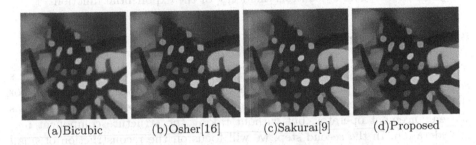

(a)Bicubic   (b)Osher[16]   (c)Sakurai[9]   (d)Proposed

Fig. 3. Structure component enhancement.

Given the initial HR structure image I_u processed by shock filter, for a pixel $I_u(x_0, y_0)$ at location (x_0, y_0), let S be the search window, $I_u(x_0, y_0)$ is computed as a weight average of all the pixels in the search window

$$I_u(x_0, y_0) = \sum_{I_u(x,y) \in S} w(x,y) I_u(x,y) \tag{6}$$

where the weight $w(x,y)$ depends on the similarity between pixel $I_u(x_0, y_0)$ and $I_u(x,y)$. Denote $N(x_0, y_0)$ as the squared neighborhood of $I_u(x_0, y_0)$, $N(x,y)$ as the squared neighborhood of $I_u(x,y)$. The similarity between two pixel $I_u(x_0, y_0)$ and $I_u(x,y)$ is measured by similarity of the gray level intensity and distribution. The distance of gray level intensity between $I_u(x_0, y_0)$ and $I_u(x,y)$ is defined by

$$d(x,y) = \left\| N(x_0, y_0) - N(x,y) \right\|_2^2 \tag{7}$$

where $\| \cdot \|$ is the L_2 norm operator. For the gray level distribution, we use perceptual hashing [19] for block hashing so as to obtain a concise representation of gray level distribution. Denote binary image block $H(x_0, y_0)$ and $H(x,y)$ as the hash value of $N(x_0, y_0)$ and $N(x,y)$. For a block $N(x,y)$, first, the mean of the pixel values is computed. Next, for each pixel in $N(x,y)$, a 1 is assigned to the corresponding coordinate in $H(x,y)$ if the pixel value is greater than the mean; otherwise a 0 is assigned. The distance of gray level distribution between $I_u(x_0, y_0)$ and $I_u(x,y)$ is defined by

$$h(x,y) = \left\| H(x_0, y_0) - H(x,y) \right\|_1^1 \tag{8}$$

Similar to the non-local means denoising [18], we set $w(x,y)$ as the exponential function of distance $d(x,y)$ and $h(x,y)$

$$w(x,y) = \frac{1}{Z(x_0, y_0)} e^{-\frac{d(x,y)}{\sigma_1}} e^{-\frac{h(x,y)}{\sigma_2}} \tag{9}$$

where $Z(x_0, y_0)$ is the normalization constant

$$Z(x_0, y_0) = \sum_{I_u(x,y) \in S} e^{-\frac{d(x,y)}{\sigma_1}} e^{-\frac{h(x,y)}{\sigma_2}} \tag{10}$$

the parameter σ_1 and σ_2 controls the decay of the exponential function.

3   Texture Component Reconstruction

The shock filter and improved non-local means filter can reconstruct sharpness edges. It is the first processing step contained in our two-stage framework. For the texture component, Sakurai [9] proposed to use a pulse-sharpening filter as the enhancement operator, but without taking the structure component into consideration. In the second step, we will focus on the reconstruction of small details on the premise that assures the sharpness of edge structures. First, we apply conventional bicubic interpolation to the LR texture image, so as to obtain the initial HR texture image I_s. Denote the initial HR image I_h^0 as $I_h^0 = I_u + I_s$. Given the LR image I_l, we estimate the HR image by minimizing the following energy function that enforce the constraints in both image domain and gradient domain

$$I_h^* = arg \min_{I_h} \left\| [I_h \otimes G]_{\downarrow(n)} - I_l \right\|_2^2 + \lambda_2 \left\| \sum_{\varphi \in \Psi} \varphi I_h - \varphi I_h^0 \right\|_2^2 \tag{11}$$

where $\otimes$ is the convolution operator. G represents the Gaussian kernel and $\downarrow (n)$ means downsampling image with the factor n. φ and Ψ are gradient extraction operator and corresponding operator set respectively. We use λ_2 to control the relative weights of the data fidelity term and the gradient regularization term. Larger λ_2 places larger importance on the gradient domain constraint, which helps to produce sharp edges with little artifacts.

To solve the objective function, we use the gradient descent method, and in each iteration, the solution is updated as

$$I_h^{t+1} = I_h^t - \tau \Big(([I_h \otimes G]_{\downarrow(n)} - I_l]_{\uparrow(n)}) \otimes G$$
$$+ \lambda_2 (\sum_{\varphi \in \Psi} \varphi^T \varphi I_h^t - \varphi^T \varphi I_h^0) \Big) \tag{12}$$

where t is the iteration number and τ is the iteration step, $\uparrow (n)$ means upsampling image with the factor n. For the gradient extraction operators, we use the operators which are similar to Sobel operators. Let $\Psi = \{\varphi_1, \varphi_2\}$, where

$$\varphi_1 = \begin{bmatrix} -1/4 & 0 & 1/4 \\ -1/2 & 0 & 1/2 \\ -1/4 & 0 & 1/4 \end{bmatrix} \text{ and } \varphi_2 = \begin{bmatrix} -1/4 & -1/2 & 1/4 \\ 0 & 0 & 0 \\ 1/4 & 1/2 & 1/4 \end{bmatrix}.$$

4   Experiment Results

Our method integrates TV-based and edge-directed reconstruction methods, therefore, we compare with three representative algorithms: the bicubic interpolation method [1], the method proposed in [9], the fast image up-sampling via the displacement field method [11]. In all the experimentation we have fixed a search window S of 21×21 pixels and a similarity square neighborhood $N(x, y)$ of 7×7 pixels. The σ_1 is fixed to be the variance of square neighborhood $N(x_0, y_0)$, $\sigma_2 = 0.1$, $\lambda_1 = 0.8$, $t = 0.1$, $\lambda_2 = 0.2$, $\tau = 0.1$. The number of iterations is set to 30. For color images, we apply our method only to the luminance channel and the chromatic channels are interpolated by the bicubic interpolator (Fig. 4).

Fig. 4. The twelve images in our test.

Table 1. PSNR (dB) results. The best in each row is in bold.

Images	Bicubic	Sakurai [9]	Wang [11]	Ours
House	29.64	29.24	31.13	**31.52**
Airplane	29.75	29.28	30.73	**32.04**
Pepper	30.48	30.14	32.15	**32.58**
Baby	33.56	32.79	35.06	**36.56**
Flower	31.40	31.04	32.86	**33.73**
Chip	29.06	28.61	30.94	**32.15**
Parrot	29.03	28.42	29.74	**31.01**
Camera	25.79	25.46	26.56	**27.42**
Hat	30.04	29.98	31.12	**31.76**
Head	33.02	32.66	33.94	**34.56**
Foreman	30.44	30.01	31.94	**32.78**
Lena	31.76	31.20	33.38	**34.67**

For quantitative comparison, in practice, the LR images are obtained by passing the original image through a Gaussian PSF kernel with standard deviation 1 and down-sampling the smoothed image with a factor of 2. The peak

Table 2. SSIM results. The best in each row is in bold.

Images	Bicubic	Sakurai [9]	Wang [11]	Ours
House	0.9462	0.9408	0.9562	**0.9566**
Airplane	0.9286	0.9185	0.9378	**0.9403**
Pepper	0.9737	0.9715	**0.9787**	0.9778
Baby	0.9653	0.9594	0.9707	**0.9755**
Flower	0.9753	0.9727	**0.9821**	0.9819
Chip	0.9418	0.9344	0.9584	**0.9599**
Parrot	0.9468	0.9396	0.9532	**0.9603**
Camera	0.8203	0.8084	0.8365	**0.8565**
Hat	0.9664	0.9651	0.9711	**0.9730**
Head	0.9029	0.8963	0.9111	**0.9159**
Foreman	0.9353	0.9289	0.9469	**0.9516**
Lena	0.9804	0.9778	0.9840	**0.9864**

signal-to-noise ratio (PSNR) and the structural similarity (SSIM) are utilized to measure the quality of the results. Table 1 list the PSNR results of the four algorithms for the test images, and Table 2 list the SSIM results. It can be seen, that our method can improve the PSNR and SSIM higher than the aforementioned methods on most of test images.

Visual comparisons are shown in Figs. 5, 6, 7 and 8. The bicubic interpolator produces very blurred results. Sakurai et al.'s method obtains sharp edges, but there are some visually unpleasant artifacts along the edge, and the texture component is not be well reconstructed. Wang et al.'s method can produce sharp edges and increase the contrast, but there are some visually unpleasant artifacts along the edge, and the detail structures are not very sharp. The proposed method produces the most visually pleasant results, sharp edges and textures with much less artifacts.

(a)Bicubic   (c)Sakurai[9]   (b)Wang[11]   (d)Ours

Fig. 5. Reconstruction results of image Airplane. Please zoom in to see the detail changes.

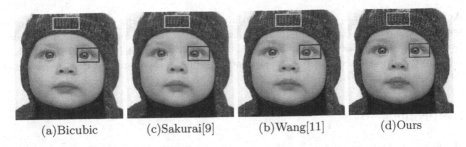

(a)Bicubic   (c)Sakurai[9]   (b)Wang[11]   (d)Ours

Fig. 6. Reconstruction results of image Baby.

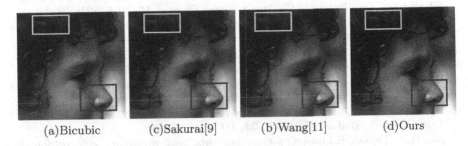

(a)Bicubic   (c)Sakurai[9]   (b)Wang[11]   (d)Ours

Fig. 7. Reconstruction results of image Head.

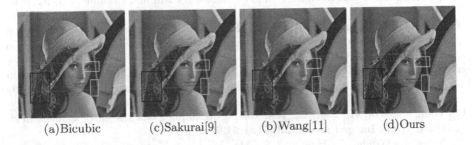

(a)Bicubic   (c)Sakurai[9]   (b)Wang[11]   (d)Ours

Fig. 8. Reconstruction results of image Lena.

5 Conclusion

In this paper, we proposed a novel image upsampling method that combines TV-based and edge-directed reconstruction methods. The input LR image is decomposed into structure component and texture component via TV-based image decomposition model. The shock filter and improved non-local means filter are introduced into structure component reconstruction process. In the texture structures reconstruction, we incorporate a gradient constraint to preserve the edge sharpness obtained in the first stage of our proposed framework. Proper experiments have confirmed that proposed scheme provided a better performance both quantitatively and qualitatively in most cases.

Acknowledgements. This work is partially supported by the National High Technology Research and Development Program of China (863 Program) under contract No. 2015AA015903, the National Science Foundation of China (61421062, 61502013), the Major National Scientific Instrument and Equipment Development Project of China under contract No. 2013YQ030967.

References

1. Keys, R.: Cubic convolution interpolation for digital image processing. IEEE Trans. Acoust. Speech Signal Process. (2003)
2. Zhang, L., Wu, X.: An edge-guided image interpolation algorithm via directional filtering and data fusion. IEEE Trans. Image Process. **15**, 2226–2238 (2006)
3. Li, X., Orchard, M.T.: New edge-directed interpolation. IEEE Trans. Image Process. **10**, 1521–1527 (2001)
4. Zhang, X., Wu, X.: Image interpolation by adaptive 2-D autoregressive modeling and soft-decision estimation. IEEE Trans. Image Process. **17**, 887–896 (2008)
5. Hung, K.W., Siu, W.C.: Robust soft-decision interpolation using weighted least squares. IEEE Trans. Image Process. **21**, 1061–1069 (2012)
6. Baker, S., Kanade, T.: Limits on super-resolution and how to break them. IEEE Trans. Pattern Anal. Mach. Intell. **24**, 1167–1183 (2002)
7. Aly, H.A., Dubois, E.: Image up-sampling using total-variation regularization with a new observation model. IEEE Trans. Image Process. **14**, 1647–1659 (2005)
8. Saito, T., Komatsu, T.: Image-processing approach based on nonlinear image-decomposition. IEICE Trans. Fundam. Electron. Commun. Comput. Sci. **92**, 696–707 (2009)
9. Sakurai, M., Sakuta, Y., Watanabe, M., Goto, T., Hirano, S.: Super-resolution through non-linear enhancement filters. In: IEEE International Conference on Image Processing (2013)
10. Sun, J., Sun, J., Xu, Z., Shum, H.Y.: Gradient profile prior and its applications in image super-resolution and enhancement. IEEE Trans. Image Process. **20**, 1529–1542 (2011)
11. Wang, L., Wu, H., Pan, C.: Fast image upsampling via the displacement field. IEEE Trans. Image Process. **23**, 5123–5135 (2014)
12. Yang, J., Wright, J., Huang, T.S., Ma, Y.: Image Super-Resolution Via Sparse Representation. IEEE Trans. Image Process. **19**, 2861–2873 (2010)
13. Wada, Y., Ogata, A., Kubota, T.: Total variation based image cartoon-texture decomposition. SIAM J. Multiscale Model. Simul. (2005)
14. Yin, W., Goldfarb, D., Osher, S.: A comparison of three total variation based texture extraction models. J. Vis. Commun. Image Represent. **18**, 240–252 (2007)
15. Aujol, J.F., Gilboa, G., Chan, T., Osher, S.: Structure-texture image decomposition-modeling, algorithms, and parameter selection. Int. J. Comput. Vis. **67**, 111–136 (2006)
16. Osher, S., Rudin, L.I.: Feature-oriented image enhancement using shock filters. Soc. Ind. Appl. Math. **27**, 919–940 (1990)
17. Alvarez, L., Mazorra, L.: Signal and image restoration using shock filters and anisotropic diffusion. SIAM J. Numer. Anal. **31**, 590–605 (1994)
18. Buades, A., Coll, B., Morel, J.F.M.: A non-local algorithm for image denoising. In: IEEE Conference on Computer Vision and Pattern Recognition (2005)

19. Mccarthy, E., Balado, F., Slvestre, G.C.M., Hurley, N.J.: A framework for soft hashing and its application to robust image hashing. In: IEEE International Conference on Image Processing (2004)
20. Yoshikawa, A., Suzuki, S., Goto, T., Hirano, S.: Super resolution image reconstruction using total variation regularization and learning-based method. In: IEEE International Conference on Image Processing (2010)
21. Freedman, G., Fattal, R.: Image and video upscaling from local self-examples. ACM Trans. Graph. **30**, 12 (2011)
22. Lu, X., Yuan, H., Yan, P., Yuan, Y.: Geometry constrained sparse coding for single image super-resolution. In: IEEE Conference on Computer Vision and Pattern Recognition (2012)
23. Dong, C., Chen, C.L., He, K., Tang, X.: Image super-resolution using deep convolutional networks. IEEE Trans. Pattern Anal. Mach. Intell. **38**, 295–307 (2016)

Image Quality Assessment for Video Surveillance System

Jianhua Shen, Hongyan Zhang, and Ci Wang(✉)

Department of Computer Science and Technology,
East China Normal University, Shanghai 200062, China
cwang@cs.ecnu.edu.cn

Abstract. With the popularity of surveillance system, traditional method to daily keep watch on its performance by human cannot meet the requirements anymore. Image degradation is a progressive process and its ideal version can be captured at beginning. The objects in the scene may change during its usage, so that the image content to be examined will be significantly different with the referred one. Therefore, the full-reference (FR) image quality assessments (IQAs) are no longer efficient for this application. In this paper, a reduced-reference (RR) IQA is proposed to fit the distribution of MSCN coefficients as the low level feature, and the feature is combined with the content representation. This feature is associated with MOS by SVR to produce the IQA model. We validate the performance of our method with an extensive study involving 1000 surveillance images and experimental results show that the method fits with the subjective evaluation better than the existing FR and NR algorithms.

Keywords: Reduced-reference · Image quality assessment
Mean subtracted contrast normalized · Support vector regression
Video surveillance system

1 Introduction

Various types of distortions, which directly affect image quality, are normally involved in image acquiring, compressing and transmitting. Equipment aging and damage will increase the distortions during its usage, which significantly reduces image information efficiency. For the video surveillance system, some information is important. To guarantee the efficacy of the surveillance system, it is necessary to manage the image quality. Therefore, a practical IQA method for surveillance system is a topic of great interest.

IQA algorithm can be classified into three categories: FR [1, 8, 10], RR [2, 3] and no-reference (NR) [4–6]. FR IQA is a mature and reliable evaluation method at present, while RR and NR IQAs are still in their preliminary stage. All information of reference image should be obtained for FR IQA, and then image quality is analyzed by extracting the effective features and calculating the feature divergence between the referred and distorted images. RR IQAs utilize partial information about the referred one to predict the perceptual quality of the distorted image. As for the third one, NR IQA algorithm works under the situation that is difficult to obtain the reference image. Note that the method only uses the information of the distorted image to evaluate its quality.

© Springer International Publishing AG, part of Springer Nature 2018
B. Zeng et al. (Eds.): PCM 2017, LNCS 10736, pp. 838–846, 2018.
https://doi.org/10.1007/978-3-319-77383-4_82

Nowadays, most communication systems adopt NR IQAs because they are difficult to get the reference images. However, traditional NR assessment method can only effectively evaluate the quality of single distorted images, and we need to know the type of distortions in advance, so its performance on surveillance image of multiple distortions is not so well. In this paper, we focus on video surveillance system, where the images with the best quality are stored after new camera is installed. However, FR method is comparatively invalid for this case, because the objects in surveillance cameras are usually moving things, so that the contents of the referred and distorted images may be different. Based on blind/referenceless image spatial quality evaluator (BRISQUE) [6], a new RR IQA method is formed to evaluate the perceptual quality of surveillance images. In order to ensure the robustness for the proposed applications, we add the referred information in our IQA model and the model is shown to capture key statistical features of surveillance images.

2 Proposed Method

Our proposed model is shown in Fig. 1. Firstly, the referred and distorted images are taken as the training images. The content representation of image as well as the fitting parameters of mean subtracted contrast normalized (MSCN) coefficients are combined to form more robust and efficient spatial features, where Φ_1 is the spatial features of distorted one and $\Delta\Phi$ is the difference of spatial features of the distorted and referred image. Then, our IQA model resorts to the help of the classical support vector regression (SVR) to find the underlying relationship of the visual features and mean opinion score (MOS) scores [7] to produce an IQA training model. Finally, the training model is used to analyze the spatial features of the test images to predict their visual quality. The detailed elaboration is explained in the following sections.

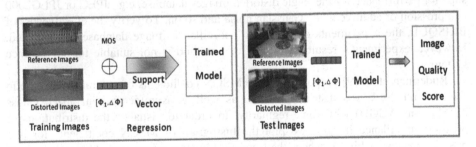

Fig. 1. The framework of our model.

2.1 Problem Formulation

2.1.1 Pristine Image Having Different MSCN Distribution

The Visual Information Fidelity (VIF) [8] assesses the mutual information of referred and distorted version to evaluate the visual quality of the distorted image. The results justify its superiority and efficiency over a number of the classical and the state-of-the-art IQA methods. When VIF algorithm is used to estimate image quality from the video surveillance image database, its results cannot correlate well with human judgments. Figure 2(a) and (b) show examples of the referred and distorted version from video surveillance image database respectively. Figure 2(a) as the referred (distortion-free) one, with the MOS score of 5, is captured from a surveillance camera, and Fig. 2(b) is get from the same surveillance camera later. Obviously, Fig. 2(b) is still a 'clean' image, but its quality score by VIF is only 2.71, which is quite different from its MOS score of 5. This experiment demonstrates that the VIF method cannot effectively handle surveillance images and the reason for the unsatisfactory experimental result is that the referred and distorted surveillance images have different contents.

(a)   (b)

Fig. 2. Sample images from the video surveillance image database. (a) Reference image. (b) A 'clean' image is captured from the same camera as (a).

The BRISQUE model operates directly on the spatial pixel data and achieves superior performance for the single distorted images database, e.g., JPEG or JPEG2000 compression or additive white Gaussian noise and so on. To verify the effectiveness of BRISQUE, the experiments on the video surveillance image database is conducted. However, experimental results show that this method is not suitable for surveillance system.

Ruderman et al. [9] proposed that the MSCN coefficients of natural images are in accord with the Gauss distribution (GD) as well as asymmetric generalized Gauss distribution (AGGD) with some regularity. In order to visualize the distributions of pristine surveillance images, we plot the histogram of MSCN coefficients for two pristine images in Fig. 3, where they have different appearances. Although both of them are pristine images, their MSCN distributions are clearly distinct from the other, hence that we cannot judge image quality only from the MSCN distribution. Because most cameras are fixed, the background and its characteristics are usually unchanged and the referred and distorted images usually share some common visual features, even if the objects have moved. Therefore, the distorted image can help us to identify the scene and deduce its ideal MSCN distribution, which should be involved in the proposed IQA method.

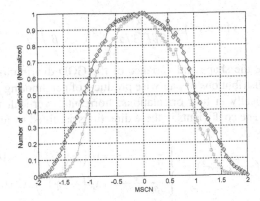

Fig. 3. Histogram of MSCN coefficients for two pristine surveillance images.

2.1.2 Same MSCN Distribution Having Different Image Quality

BRISQUE is a natural scene statistic-based NR IQA model and its visual features are designed on MSCN coefficients [6]. There is a decorrelating effect to use a local non-linear operation to remove local mean displacements from zero log-contrast and normalize the local variance of the log contrast [9]. The normalization can remove the correlation among the adjacent coefficients, and its results $\hat{I}(i,j)$ is expressed as

$$\hat{I}(i,j) = \frac{I(i,j) - \mu(i,j)}{\sigma(i,j) + C} \tag{1}$$

where $I(i,j)$ is the luminance of image in the pixel coordinate (i,j). C is the constant to avoid denominator to be zero. Mean $\mu(i,j)$ and variance $\sigma(i,j)$ are the average luminance and contrast of $I(i,j)$ and its neighbor. If two distorted image patches $I_1(i,j)$ and $I_2(i,j)$ have the same MSCN value, but with different average luminance, i.e. $\mu_1(i,j) \neq \mu_2(i,j)$, we have

$$\frac{I_1(i,j) - \mu_1(i,j)}{\sigma_1(i,j)} = \frac{I_2(i,j) - \mu_2(i,j)}{\sigma_2(i,j)} \tag{2}$$

From (2), we have $\sigma_1(i,j) = \frac{I_1(i,j)-\mu_1(i,j)}{I_2(i,j)-\mu_2(i,j)} \sigma_2(i,j)$ so that $\sigma_1(i,j) \neq \sigma_2(i,j)$ if $\frac{I_1(i,j)-\mu_1(i,j)}{I_2(i,j)-\mu_2(i,j)} \neq 1$, i.e. distorted image patches $I_1(i,j)$ and $I_2(i,j)$ with the same MSCN coefficients but with different $\mu(i,j)$ and $\sigma(i,j)$. Therefore, only the MSCN coefficients of the distorted image cannot reflect the objective quality well.

2.2 Proposed Spatial Features

MSCN coefficient distributions of the distorted images often deviate from GD, so that the generalized Gaussian distribution (GGD) model is utilized to describe the broader spectrum of the distorted image. The GGD expression is

$$f\left(x, \alpha, \sigma^2\right) = \frac{\alpha}{2\beta\Gamma(1/\alpha)} exp\left(-\left(\frac{|x|}{\beta}\right)^\alpha\right) \tag{3}$$

where α and σ^2 are the shape and variance of the GGD distribution.

The empirical distributions of pair wise products of neighboring MSCN coefficients are modeled statistically in four orientations: horizontal, vertical, main diagonal and diagonal direction. The coefficients in these directions are fitted by an AGGD models as

$$f\left(x, v, \sigma_l^2, \sigma_r^2\right) = \begin{cases} \frac{v}{(\beta_l + \beta_r)\Gamma\left(\frac{1}{v}\right)} exp\left(-\left(\frac{-x}{\beta_l}\right)^v\right), x < 0 \\ \frac{v}{(\beta_l + \beta_r)\Gamma\left(\frac{1}{v}\right)} exp\left(-\left(\frac{x}{\beta_l}\right)^v\right), x \geq 0 \end{cases} \tag{4}$$

where v, η, σ_l as well as σ_r are the shape, mean, left variance and right variance of the AGGD distribution.

The reference image and its corresponding distorted image have different feature parameters. We extract 100 pair parameters (α, σ^2) of the referred and distorted images from the video surveillance image database, which are plotted in Fig. 4(a). It is found that the distortion features are undistinguishable in GGD parameter space. As for higher dimensional space, we use the AGGD fitting parameters $\left(v, \sigma_l^2, \sigma_r^2\right)$ of the same image set in horizontal direction as example. Figure 4(b) shows that the AGGD parameters of the referred and distorted objects are still mixed in the proposed feature space. This phenomenon indicates that the reference image and other distorted images may have the same feature parameters.

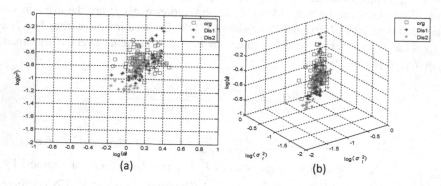

Fig. 4. (a) 2-D scatter plot between α and σ^2 parameters obtained by fitting GGD to the empirical distributions of MSCN coefficients of reference images and distorted images of video surveillance image database. (b) 3-D scatter plot between σ_l^2, σ_r^2 and v parameters obtained by fitting AGGD to horizontal paired products using the same image set as (a). Org: reference images. Dis1: distorted images with the MOS values ranging from 3.5 to 5. Dis2: distorted images with the MOS values ranging from 1 to 2.5.

Because nature image has statistical regularities in spatial domain, we propose a robust and low-level IQA feature for surveillance image, whose characteristics are defined as

$$\Phi = [\Phi_1, \Delta\Phi]$$
$$\Delta\Phi = \Phi_1 - \Phi_2 \tag{5}$$

where Φ_1 is the parameters of GGD and AGGD for the distorted image, and Φ_2 is the same parameters for referred image. Just like BRISQUE, $\Phi_i, i = 1, 2$ is calculated on the parameters of GGD (α, σ^2) [11] and AGGD ($\nu, \sigma_l, \sigma_r, \eta$) [12] on 4 directions, i.e. with 36 parameters in total.

In above section, we demonstrate that Φ_1 cannot reflect the distortion but its divergence from the ideal MSCN distribution affecting image quality. Although the pristine image of Φ_1 is actually unavailable in surveillance system, but its reference image can give us some hints about Φ_1. Given up the first preference, we replace the ideal MSCN distribution with Φ_2 to calculate the divergence $\Delta\Phi$, and the confidence of $\Delta\Phi$ depends on the degree of the scene changed. To describe the reliability of $\Delta\Phi$, Φ_1 is embed into the proposed visual feature to improve its resolution.

Visual quality is the comprehensive feeling about image. Image content must take into consideration for IQA, because different image content can tolerate different degree distortion. In this paper, image content is represented by their MSCN feature, i.e. Φ_1, which is concatenated with $\Delta\Phi$ to constrain the training and testing processes of SVM.

3 Experimental Results

Limited by the cost, surveillance systems often adopt heavy compression and poor-performing components, resulting in its image quality is significantly inferior to the ones in consumer applications. Therefore, surveillance images appear different behavior from the traditional image database, such as LIVE and TID 2003. In this part of experiments, we sample images for the real surveillance system and label their quality by the experts of security industry under the guide of ITU-R BT.500. The test images consist of 500 pair images, which are taken from different cameras corresponding to different scenes. To produce reasonable experimental results, the distorted images are selected with various distortion degrees, i.e. their MOS values ranging from 1 to 5 and uniformly distributed in every score.

To prevent the same images are reused in training and testing, the Cross-validation method [13] is introduced in this paper to ensure the rationality of the experimental results. We randomly select 80% samples from image database and set them as the training set and the remained 20% as set as the test set. We used the libsvm package [14, 15] to build the connection between the proposed visual features and image MOSs in training step, and then use their relationship for testing. Above process is repeated over 1000 times to test the robustness of the proposed algorithm.

We compare the MOS scores and the estimated scores from VIF, BRISQUE and the proposed algorithm, and plot their scatter points and fitting curves in Fig. 5, according to the logarithmic fitting method [16]. As Fig. 5 shown, our method has better linearity and monotonicity than the others do. Besides, the scatter points of the proposed algorithm tightly close to the fitting curve, indicating the homogeneity of the estimated results. Besides subjective illustration, some statistical measurements, such as the Spearman's rank ordered correlation coefficient (SROCC) and Pearson's (linear) correlation coefficient (LCC) are used to measure the coherence between MOSs and the estimated scores [17]. LCC and SROCC values are widely used to evaluate the performances of IQAs, whose values are located within [0, 1]. If LCC and SROCC values approach to 1, the estimate score of the proposed method coincides with MOS score. We compare the results of three IQAs in Table 1, and our LCC and SROCC are above 0.80 and 0.76 respectively. It is better than FR VIF method about 19% and 17%, and better than NR BRISQUE algorithm about 17% and 8% respectively, which proves its efficiency for surveillance applications. As discussed in Sect. 2, VIF performance is poor for the cases that the scenes have changed. BRISQUE is weak for the surveillance images contaminated by several distortions simultaneously, which makes distortions separation and measurement more difficult.

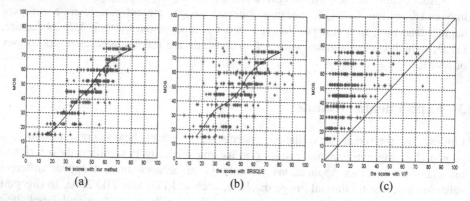

(a)   (b)   (c)

Fig. 5. Scatter plots between true MOS scores and the estimate scores. (a) Our method. (b) BRISQUE. (c) VIF.

Table 1. Comparison with BRISQUE, VIF and our method

	LCC	SROCC
VIF	0.6336	0.5686
BRISQUE	0.7251	0.5880
Our method	0.8018	0.7602

4 Conclusion

In this paper, we first analyze the spatial features of surveillance images and propose a practical RR IQA method for surveillance system. This method combines the advantages of BRISQUE algorithm and solves its shortcomings by calculating the spatial characteristics of the distorted images and adding the feature difference as a reference. We take the experiments on video surveillance image database, and the results illustrate its higher performance over the state-of-the-art VIF and BRISQUE algorithms for CCTV applications.

References

1. Laparra, V., Muñozmarí, J., Malo, J.: Divisive normalization image quality metric revisited. J. Opt. Soc. Amer. **27**(4), 852–864 (2010)
2. Soundararajan, R., Bovik, A.C.: RRED indices: reduced reference entropic differencing for image quality assessment. IEEE Trans. Image Process. **21**(2), 517–526 (2011)
3. Li, Q., Wang, Z.: Reduced-reference image quality assessment using divisive normalization-based image representation. IEEE J. Sel. Top. Sig. Process. **3**(2), 202–211 (2009)
4. Saad, M., Bovik, A.C., Charrier, C.: Blind image quality assessment: a natural scene statistics approach in the DCT domain. IEEE Trans. Image Process. **21**(8), 3339–3352 (2012)
5. Wang, Z., Bovik, A.C.: Modern Image Quality Assessment. Morgan & Claypool Publishers, San Rafael (2006)
6. Mittal, A., Moorthy, A.K., Bovik, A.C.: No reference image quality assessment in the spatial domain. IEEE Trans. Image Process. **21**(12), 4695–4708 (2012)
7. ITU-T Recommendation P.800: Methods for subjective determination of transmission quality, August 1996
8. Sheikh, H.R., Bovik, A.C.: Image information and visual quality. IEEE Trans. Image Process. **15**(2), 430–444 (2006)
9. Ruderman, D.L.: The statistics of natural images. Netw. Comput. Neural Syst. **5**(4), 517–548 (1994)
10. Wang, Z., Bovik, A.C., Sheikh, H.R., Simon-celli, E.P.: Image quality assessment: From error measurement to structural similarity. IEEE Trans. Image Processing **13**, 600–612 (2004)
11. Sharifi, K., Leon-Garcia, A.: Estimation of shape parameter for generalized Gaussian distributions in subband decompositions of video. IEEE Trans. Circ. Syst. Video Technol. **5** (1), 52–56 (1995)
12. Lasmar, N.E., Stitou, Y., Berthoumieu, Y.: Multiscale skewed heavy tailed model for texture analysis. In: Proceedings of the IEEE International Conference on Image Process, pp. 2281–2284, November 2009
13. Geisser, S.: The predictive sample reuse method with applications. J. Am. Stat. Assoc. **70**(350), 320–328 (1975)
14. Chang, C.C., Lin, C.J.: LIBSVM: A Library for Support Vector Machines [Online] (2001). http://www.csie.ntu.edu.tw/~cjlin/libsvm/

15. Schölkopf, B., Smola, A.J., Williamson, R.C., Bartlett, P.L.: New support vector algorithms. Neural Comput. 12(5), 1207–1245 (2000)
16. VQEG, Final report from the video quality experts group on the validation of objective models of video quality assessment, phase II, August 2003. http://www.vqeg.org/
17. Sheikh, H.R., Sabir, M.F., Bovik, A.C.: A statistical evaluation of recent full reference image quality assessment algorithms. IEEE Trans. Image Process. 15(11), 3440–3451 (2006)

Style Transfer Based on Style Primitive Discovery

Hao Wu[1], Zhengxing Sun[1(✉)], Shuang Wang[1,2], Weihang Yuan[1], and Hui-Hsia Chen[3]

[1] State Key Laboratory for Novel Software Technology,
Nanjing University, Nanjing, China
szx@nju.edu.cn
[2] Jiangsu Vocational Institute of Commerce, Nanjing, China
[3] Asia University, Taiwan, China

Abstract. Example-based stylization provides a direct way of making artistic effects for images. However existing methods are not suitable for artistic applications like Chinese embroidery. In this paper, we propose an example-based non-rigid image stylization method tailored for Chinese embroidery art. To this aim, a novel style transfer framework is presented, which works by using different aggregation patterns, i.e. regular primitive and stochastic primitive. We find that these two patterns are surprisingly effective in embroidery description. Specifically, we first extract these two style primitives from an example image according to the directionality and orientation. Then we employ a primitive selection algorithm to filter defected primitives. After that, we employ a sparse representation-based style transfer method, to synthesize the final result. In the experiments, the synthesis results show that our framework is superior to state-of-the-art methods and performs more efficient on large resolution images.

Keywords: Style primitive discovery · Non-rigid primitive discovery
Style transfer · Sparse representation

1 Introduction

Image stylization which aim at transferring a photo into styled image, the existing works can be categorized as stroke-based, filter-based and example-based [1]. Stroke-based [2] image stylization uses carefully designed strokes as primitives to represent the style. Filter-based methods use image processing filter to represent the style. All the two methods need to carefully design primitive model (stroke model and filter model) which is difficult to design properly for some kinds of art [1]. Example-based stylization uses example template (e.g., an oil painting) to extract primitives to represent texture, and the stylized image is synthesized from a real image (e.g., a portrait photo) [3]. This kind of methods provide direct way to extract style primitive which are image patches and transfer the style. However, there are two challenges: how to discover style primitives for different artistic styles, especially for newly style, and how to transfer photo in term of the discovered style primitives into the expected artistic image.

© Springer International Publishing AG, part of Springer Nature 2018
B. Zeng et al. (Eds.): PCM 2017, LNCS 10736, pp. 847–858, 2018.
https://doi.org/10.1007/978-3-319-77383-4_83

To our knowledge, there have been two main approaches to discover style primitive in the example-based image stylization according to texture directionality in the style templates, namely, direction-aware and direction-insensitive method. The direction-aware methods manage to discover primitives with direction information from the art, in which paint by strokes having dominant direction (e.g. stokes of line drawing [4]). For example, Wang et al. [5] rotate template image into 24 directions and use dense sampling at each rotated image to discover primitives which form a primitive repository with discrete direction information. Instead of rotate the template image discretely, Lukáč et al. [6] proposed a discovery method based on primitive which can rotate continuously to sample the texture according to the direction and it's effective to extract the primitive with complex direction field (e.g., oil painting with hair or fur). But when the art is drawn by strokes without direction (e.g., stippling [7]) or with multiple direction strokes (e.g., oil painting), they still try to extract the primitive according to a dominant direction. To discover primitives from these arts, direction-insensitive methods use dense sampling method [8, 9] to extract square patches. Both direction-aware and direction-insensitive approaches are suitable for art painted by one type of strokes but not for art drown by both type of strokes (Fig. 2). Additionally all the works above, only Zhang et al. [8] select the proper primitives from the primitive repository to reduce the complexity of their algorithm, but no effectiveness evaluation is given.

In the style transfer stage, constructing matching relationship between source image and primitives is a critical problem. Most of the existing works model the matching problem as labeling using MRF and use belief propagation to solve the optimization [8, 9]. But because of the complex neighbor relationship between primitives, it is hard to use on the non-rigid primitive. In the non-rigid primitive based method, Lukáč et al. [6] model the matching problem as a global optimization and use EM algorithm to solve. But in their work they only concern the direction instead of texture in the matching, it's not suitable for every art style. Both of the methods only use one type of primitive and need huge number of primitives as candidate labels, the computational complexity is exponential growth to the number of primitives.

As a traditional Chinese craft Embroidery consists of pulling threads through a background material with embroidery needles to stitch patterns. By using different aggregation patterns of threads, namely: regular primitive which is made of strokes with similar direction and stochastic primitive which is made of multiple direction strokes. We use texture directionality to distinguish these two primitives. This art also has two characteristics different from other art. Local directionality means, in some local areas, artists usually use the aggregation patterns with same directionality. Local direction means, some of the aggregation patterns with strong directionality form texture with a dominant direction. Figures 1 and 2 shows such an example. However, even the most popular CNN based image stylization method [13] can't provide convincing results on this kind of art. Our work proposed a style transfer framework for this new art. Compared with existing methods, the contribution of our work can be summarized as follow:

(1) To deal with the local directionality characteristic, we propose two types of style primitive, namely, regular primitive and stochastic primitive according to the directionality. The shape of the primitive is also changeable according to the local directionality.

Fig. 1. Comparison of directionality, (a)(b) is Chinese embroidery image and its corresponding directionality map, (c)(d) is oil painting and its corresponding directionality map

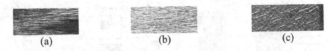

Fig. 2. Comparison of textures from Fig. 1(a). (a) shows sub texture with dominant direction and (b)(c) shows primitive with multiple direction

(2) To extract both type of primitive, we propose a style primitive discovery process based on non-rigid patch which are rotatable and shape variable. We also propose a primitive selection process to select the primitives with better art representativeness. With these primitives we can get a better synthesized result.

(3) To get a better flexibility in representation of both kinds of primitive, we propose a sparse representation based style transfer method with better efficiency.

2 Preliminary

The basic sparse representation problem is to solve the following optimization problem:

$$min_{D,X}\|Y - DX\|_2 s.t. \forall 1 \leq i \leq N, \|x_i\|_0 \leq k \tag{1}$$

Where $Y \in R^{d \times N}$ represent all the image patches sampled from the image, $X \in R^{n \times N}$ is the representation coefficient. Sparse representation aims to find both the dictionary $D \in R^{d \times N}$ and the representation coefficient. k is a given constant controlling the sparsity and the over-completeness of D.

$$min_{D,X}\|Y - DX\|_2 + \lambda\|X\|_1 \tag{2}$$

Equation (2) is the simplified optimization goal of the sparse representation. λ is the regularization parameter to balance the ℓ_2 representation fidelity term and the ℓ_1 sparsity penalty term. This regularized ℓ_1-norm optimization problem can be efficiently solved [10].

3 Overview

Figure 3 illustrate our proposed framework. The framework composed of two processes:

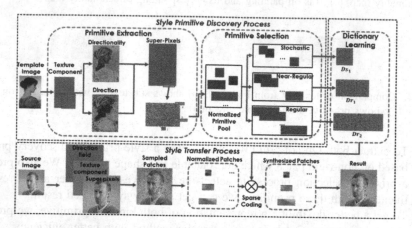

Fig. 3. Overview of our proposed framework.

In the Style Primitive Discovery Process. Firstly, we perform primitive extraction process which is described in component from the template image. On the basis of texture component, we compute directionality and direction maps and super-pixels is extracted via a modified SLIC algorithm. In this example, three types of style primitives, which is described in Sect. 4.1, is extracted from each super-pixel according to the directionality and dominant direction. Then we perform primitive selection to select the primitives with better representativeness which is described in Sect. 4.2.

In the Style Transfer Process. Firstly, we compute direction vector field and directionality of the source image. And a modified SLIC is also used to extract super-pixels. Patches are extracted with the same method used in Sect. 4.2. Then we perform a modified sparse representation algorithm to synthesis the transferred patches using dictionaries trained from different style primitives. Transferred patches is copied to the synthesized image at the same position in the source image according to the direction.

4 Style Primitive Discovery

In this chapter, our goal is to extract primitives with only style. The style of Chinese embroidery is mainly about the texture it contains, so we propose a style-content separation process on template image via: $L_s = L - median(L)$. L is the L channel in

Luv color space, *median*() is median filter. By this method we remove the influence of luminance and acquire a style component with only texture from the template image. We perform our process on the style component L_s of the template image.

4.1 Style Primitive Definition

In this section we extract style primitives from Chinese embroidery. From Figs. 2 and 3, we can find the characteristics of this art described in introduction. Noticing the different types of texture in the image: stochastic and regular texture [11]. We propose two types of style primitives:

Stochastic primitives which contain stochastic texture are sampled as rigid square patches since the directionality intensity of stochastic texture is relatively low. The stochastic primitives which contain no dominant direction are sampled horizontally in the discovery process and will be also placed horizontally in the style transfer process.

Regular primitives which contain regular texture with high directionality are sampled as rotatable non-rigid patches which contain dominant direction. We use rectangle patches which won't cut the long threads, instead of square patches and the long axis is parallel to the dominant direction of texture. Moreover, the regular primitives will be classified into different shapes with different length-width ratio according to their local directionality. The stronger directionality the larger length-width ratio we use.

4.2 Style Primitive Extraction

In the style primitive extraction process, we propose two features: dominant measure and radon transformation to evaluate the directionality and dominant direction. We sample the template image into square patches and calculate two features for each patch and form them into feature maps: directionality and direction map. The size of the patches is slightly larger than the length of largest regular primitive to enable rotation.

Directionality: We compute the directionality map of the template image with dominant measure [11] which evaluate the dominant directionality of local texture. The dominant measure estimation method is based on the PCA algorithm, which at its core uses the singular value decomposition of gradient vector of patch to calculate the local directionality. The primitive has dominant direction when the dominant measure is large, Fig. 2 shows such an example Fig. 1 shows the dominant measure heat map.

Algorithm 1. Representative Style Primitive Selection

Input: A set of image patches $P_i^{input}, i = 1, ..., N$, selection rate r ;
Output: Representative patches: $P_i^R, i = 1, ..., K$;
1: Set $K = N \times r$;
2: Using Eq. (2), compute the representation coefficient X for patches, compute the kurtosis for each coefficient vector and sort in ascending order, get kurArray
3: Using Eq. (3), compute the style quality d_p for each patch and sort in descending order, get quaArray;
4: Set n = 0;//to count how many discriminative patches have been found.
5: **for** i=1; i<=20; i++
    for j=1;j<=i;i++
    if n<K
    Find patches whose kurtosis value is the beginning $i \times 0.05$ in the kurArray
    Find patches whose style quality value is the beginning $j \times 0.05$ in the quaArray
    Find intersection of patches found in last two steps and save to the representative patches $P_i^R, i = 1, ..., K; n = n + p$
    End for
  End for

Dominant direction: We calculate the direction map with radon transform which extract the dominant direction of local texture in patches. Radon transform extracts the edge response along a specific direction We calculate 180 radon transforms along each direction ($\theta \in (0°, 180°)$). In Fig. 4 shows such example.

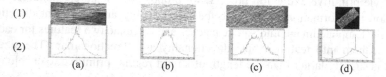

(1)
(2)
    (a)   (b)   (c)   (d)

Fig. 4. 'Radon' transform result for Chinese embroidery. Row (1) shows the patches of different threads pattern, and row (2) is the corresponding radon transform. X axis represents angle degree ($\theta \in (0°, 180°)$), and y axis represents the edge response. We can find that the more directional the patch is the sharper radon transform is. In (a) and (b) we can find the peak of the radon transform represent the dominant direction.

Extraction: Finally, we extract style primitives according to the two features map and a modified SLIC process is used to extract super-pixels Instead of extract super-pixels on color feature, our modified SLIC is based on the former extracted two features. For each super-pixel we extract a style primitive centered at the centroid. When the directionality of the centroid is below a threshold R^*, we extract a stochastic primitive otherwise we extract a regular primitive. When extracting regular primitives, the length-width ratio is set according to the directionality and the length axis of the primitive is set to the direction of the centroid. Figure 5 is the extraction result. In the example, we extract two types of regular primitive with the length-width ratio set to 2 and 3.

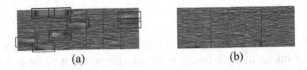

Fig. 5. Primitive selection result, (a) is the dictionary with defected primitives, (b) is the result.

4.3   Representative Style Primitive Selection

The previous chapter construct a style primitive pool in which defected primitives are contained. In the style primitive selection process, we proposed a Representative Style Primitive Selection Algorithm using two effective features which are kurtosis and style quality to evaluate the effectiveness of primitives.

Kurtosis: Since the threads cause strong edge response, the style primitives should consist of as much edge information as possible, so the local texture can be better preserved in the style primitive. As well known the DCT basis is usually used for image compression and has a strong response to the edges in the image. Using DCT as sparse represent dictionary, kurtosis can measure the quantity of edge information in the style primitive. Given a style primitive, instead of training a dictionary from the samples, we use a fixed dictionary with DCT basis. After applying the ℓ_1-ls algorithm [12] to estimate the representation coefficient X in, the kurtosis is evaluated using $\|X\|_1$.

Style quality: Limited by the performance of modern camera, it is difficult to capture texture clearly in some situations. When there are dark color threads or with a bad focus, we can hardly distinguish the threads from each other. We propose a feature called style quality to measure the texture quality of style primitives. Style quality is evaluated by:

$$d_p = \text{avg} \sum\nolimits_{(x,y) \in p} |Median(Y) - Y| \tag{3}$$

where $(x, y) \in p$ means a pixel in style primitive p. The larger d_p is, the higher style quality the style primitive p is. Mathematically, the Representative style primitives are those primitives with low kurtosis (namely, more atoms used for representation) and high style quality (namely, the edges of threads is clearer). In Algorithm 1, we proposed a selection method based on the kurtosis and style quality of the patch, and a parameter (selection rate r) is used to control the process. Since it is difficult to show large number of style primitive in this paper and to tune the parameter easily, we use sparse representation dictionary to show the selection results. Figure 8 shows results of this algorithm and more experimental results will be provided in the experiments chapter to evaluate this algorithm.

5 Style Transfer

In this chapter, we proposed a sparse representation based style transfer method to transfer a source image to style image with the primitives we discovered.

Style primitive representation. We form the style primitive representation as a non-negative problem. To obtain a representation of the style primitives we use sparse coding which is described in the preliminary to build a set of dictionaries for different types of style primitives. In the example template image, we build three dictionaries. The dictionary D_S is built upon the stochastic primitives The dictionaries D_{R1}, D_{R2} is built upon the regular primitives with relatively low directionality and high directionality. In the style-content matching, we use the same style-content separation method described in Sect. 4 to acquire the texture component. Then we compute the direction field and directionality map described in Sect. 4.2. Super pixels are extracted based on the former two maps.

Style-content matching and synthesis. We sample organized image patches according to the types of primitive using the same scheme described in Sect. 4.3. With the source image patches and corresponding style primitive dictionaries we use a modified sparse representation to do the matching. Since the style primitives discovered contain strong style characteristic which bring noises in the sparse coding model, we use two methods to deal with this problem. Firstly, we add Gaussian white noise in the source image patches, then in the sparse coding process, we add median filter in the energy function described in the preliminary:

$$min_{D,X}\|P - Median(DX)\|_2 + \lambda\|X\|_1 \tag{4}$$

In Eq. (4), P is the patches sampled from the source image. Dictionary D is chosen according to the directionality of P. In the final quilting step, we use the corresponding DX to keep the style characteristic and we got a synthesized patch: $p = DX$. Secondly, for simplicity, we use alpha-mapping as quilting [9] process to blend the overlapping areas between patches.

6 Experimentations

We propose several experiments to evaluate our non-rigid style primitive discovery process and style transfer process.

Differences between our newly art with other art style: In this experiment, we compare the difference between embroidery and other art. Figure 6 shows the characteristics of Chinese embroidery. We use 6 embroidery images and 7 images (tem_1 to tem_13) of other arts. Because of these characteristics, we define our two types of primitives according to the directionality and dominant direction.

(1)

(2)

(3)

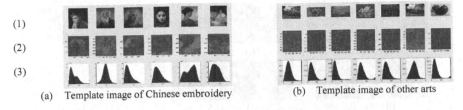

(a)   Template image of Chinese embroidery   (b)   Template image of other arts

Fig. 6. Compare of directionality of Chinese embroidery (a) and other art style (b), in (a) from left to right is tem_1 to tem_13 respectively. Row (1) show the art images, row (2) show the directionality maps computed in Sect. 4.2, and row (3) is directionality histogram. We can find that Chinese embroidery art use same pattern in a local area and other arts doesn't, so we extract two types of primitive according to the directionality. And this art has a high avg. directionality than other art which means it uses more regular primitives than other arts.

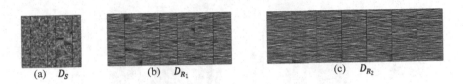

(a) D_S (b) D_{R_1} (c) D_{R_2}

Fig. 7. Dictionary constructed from tem_5, (a) is the stochastic primitive dictionary with weakest directionality. From it we can find the stroke has multiple directions and form stochastic texture, (b) is the regular primitive dictionary with weaker directionality, (c) is the regular primitive dictionaries with strongest directionality in which we can find the stroke similar dominant direction and we normalized them in a horizontal manner. From this figure we show that our directionality feature is effective in distinguishing our primitives and detect the dominant direction accurately.

Effectiveness of primitive extraction: In this experiment, we show the effectiveness of our directionality and direction feature. Figure 7 is the primitive dictionaries of our extract primitives which is extract from the example embroidery image tem_5.

Effectiveness of style primitive selection: In this experiment, we show the effectiveness of our primitive selection algorithm. Figure 8 shows that with a proper parameter setting (select rate r) we can filter most of the defect primitives. And we also use selected primitives to reconstruct the template image to evaluate the effectiveness of primitive selection. We use PSNR [11] which are proposed to evaluate the similarity of two images to evaluate our reconstruct image and original image on the 6 embroidery images. From Fig. 9, we can find that we have a higher PSNR [14] than other method which means our selected primitives is more representative.

Compare with state-of-art methods: In this experiment, we compare the stylization result with our discovered non-rigid primitives and other state-of-art methods especially the CNN based method. Figure 10 shows the results. Our method provides a better synthesized result with a smoother texture than the non-direction aware method [8]. When comparing to the most popular CNN based method, our method also

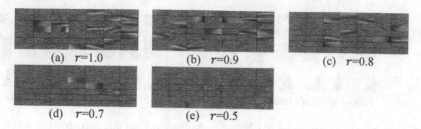

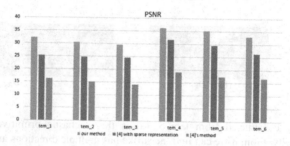

Fig. 8. Primitive selection result, (a)(b)(c)(d) is the select result with different parameter (select rate r in Algorithm 1) in which we can find defected primitives, (e) is the result of proper setting in which, the defect primitives is filtered successfully. Through experiments, we find, 0.5 is a proper setting for every embroidery image in our dataset

Fig. 9. PSNR of our method, Zhang et al. [8]'s method using sparse representation and the original method of Zhang et al. [8]

provides better results. Ignore the color which can be post processed, the texture of embroidery has been hallucinated too much in three results and can't be evaluated as visual pleasing. Moreover, our method requires only a few parameters with clear physical meaning while CNN based method need to tune parameters without clear physical meaning to get better results. And these parameters are very fuzzy and difficult to tune.

Computational complexity: The proposed method has been implemented in Matlab (2015b) without exploiting parallel options or Mex accelerations. The reported tests were performed on a Laptop Windows machine (2.8 Ghz E3-1505 M v5 Intel Xeon CPU, 16 GByte RAM, 64-bits operating system). The run-time for our method stand on 70–130 s for an image of size 3000 × 3000 pixels and 10–15 s for an image of size 512 × 512 pixels. The CNN method need 6 h on 512 × 512 pixels on CPU and 205 s on GPU (single nVidia Titan X) using 1000 iterations. When compared to Gatys' algorithm [13], the proposed method is much faster and simpler.

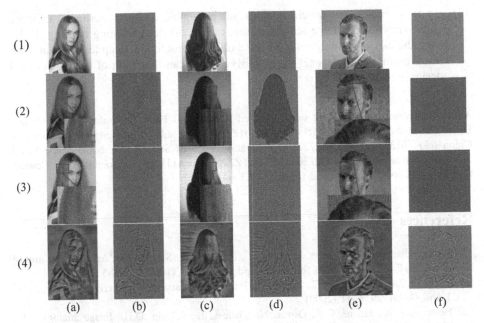

| (a) | (b) | (c) | (d) | (e) | (f) |

Fig. 10. Comparison of our method (row (2)), Zhang's method [8] (row (3)) and the neural style method from Gatys [13] (row (4)) and the source image (row(1)). (b)(d)(f) is the corresponding texture component of (a)(c)(f) When comparing with the non-direction aware method (middle), the detail of hair shows our method is superior in stylizing the image with complex direction field. In the area of face our method performs similar to Zhang's method. When comparing with the CNN based method, our method shows a better preservation of detail texture. CNN based method tend to twist the texture of the style image in the final result. In the background area of (a) (b), emerges strange texture which are not visual pleasing. Zoom 400% to see detail.

7   Conclusion

In this work, we have proposed a non-rigid style transfer framework based on style primitive discovery. Differently from previous approaches, our work is able to extract two types of primitives according to the texture directionality and transfer a real image into Chinese embroidery art style. Two feature is applied to detect the directionality and dominant orientation of local patches and two different types of primitive with different shape are extracted. Moreover, we proposed sparse representation based style transfer method. The experiments show the effectiveness of our method in image stylization and show better results event to the most popular CNN based method. One may question why our method outperform CNN-based method, our answers are as follow:

(1) The CNN based methods is designed as general model and is not optimized for Chinese embroidery which is a very special art form.

(2) The CNN method is usually applied to black box model which is suitable for the application of transferring uncertain style. For Chinese embroidery, its internal mechanism is very explicit and explicit model can get better results.

(3) Being a minor art which belongs to intangible cultural heritage, Chinese embroidery lack of large-scale data sets to support deep learning training. However, the lack of training set has been a difficult problem in deep learning, and the result on the small data set is obviously worse than the result of the handcrafted design model.

Acknowledgements. This work was supported by National High Technology Research and Development Program of China (No. 2007AA01Z334), National Natural Science Foundation of China (Nos. 61321491 and 61272219), Innovation Fund of State Key Laboratory for Novel Software Technology (Nos. ZZKT2013A12 and ZZKT2016A11), and Program for New Century Excellent Talents in University of China (NCET-04-04605).

References

1. Kyprianidis, J.E., Collomosse, J., Wang, T., Isenberg, T.: State of the 'Art': a taxonomy of artistic stylization techniques for images and video. TVCG **19**, 866–885 (2013)
2. Zeng, K., Zhao, M., Xiong, C., Zhu, S.-C.: From image parsing to painterly rendering. ACM Trans. Graph. **29**, 1–11 (2009)
3. Hertzmann, A., Jacobs, C.E., Oliver, N., Curless, B., Salesin, D.H.: Image analogies. In: SIGGRAPH 2001 (2001)
4. Kang, H., Lee, S., Chui, C.K.: Coherent line drawing. In: Proceedings of the NPAR, vol. 1, pp. 43–50 (2007)
5. Wang, B., Wang, W., Yang, H., Sun, J.: Efficient example-based painting and synthesis of 2D directional texture. TVCG **10**, 266–277 (2004)
6. Lukáč, M., Fišer, J., Asente, P., Lu, J., Shechtman, E., Sýkora, D.: Brushables: example-based edge-aware directional texture painting. CGF **34**, 257–267 (2015)
7. Kim, S.Y., Maciejewski, R., Isenberg, T., Andrews, W.M., Chen, W., Sousa, M.C., Ebert, D. S.: Stippling by example. In: NPAR 2009 (2009)
8. Zhang, W., Cao, C., Chen, S., Liu, J., Tang, X.: Style transfer via image component analysis. IEEE TMM **15**, 1594–1601 (2013)
9. Frigo, O., Sabater, N., Delon, J., Hellier, P.: Split and Match: example-based adaptive patch sampling for unsupervised style transfer. In: CVPR 2016 (2016)
10. Efron, B., Hastie, T., Johnstone, I., Tibshirani, R.: Least angle regression. Ann. Stat. **32**, 407–499 (2004)
11. Yang, S., Wang, M., Chen, Y., Sun, Y.: Single-image super-resolution reconstruction via learned geometric dictionaries and clustered sparse coding. TIP **21**, 4016–4028 (2012)
12. Koh, K., Kim, S.-J., Boyd, S.: An interior-point method for large-scale l1-regularized logistic regression. J. Mach. Learn. Res. **8**, 1519–1555 (2007)
13. Gatys, L.A., Ecker, A.S., Bethge, M.: Image style transfer using convolutional neural networks. In: IEEE Conference on Computer Vision and Pattern Recognition, pp. 2414–2423 (2016)
14. Wang, Z., Bovik, A.C., Sheikh, H.R., Simoncelli, E.P.: Image quality assessment: from error visibility to structural similarity. IEEE TIP **13**, 600–612 (2004)

Construction of Sampling Two-Channel Nonseparable Wavelet Filter Bank and Its Fusion Application for Multispectral Image Pansharpening

Bin Liu[1(✉)], Weijie Liu[2], and Longxiang Xu[1]

[1] School of Computer and Information Engineering, Hubei University,
Wuhan 430062, Hubei Province, China
liub@hubu.edu.cn
[2] Computer School, Wuhan University, Wuhan 430072, Hubei Province, China

Abstract. Resulting image of the multispectral fusion method based on separable wavelets has lower spatial resolution and block traces. To solve these problems, a construction method of sampling two-dimensional two-channel nonseparable wavelet filter bank, whose dilation matrix is [1,1;1,−1], is presented and an image fusion method based on this kind of wavelet transform for multispectral pan-sharpening is proposed. Two-channel nonseparable filter banks are constructed and the sampling multi-resolution analysis of the intensity of the MS and panchromatic image are performed. The high-frequency coefficients of the panchromatic image are injected into the multispectral image. The experimental results indicate that the proposed fusion method has good visual effect and the fusion performance is outperforms the classical fusion methods in preserving high spatial resolution and global spectral information. The low spatial resolution multispectral image is pan-sharpened.

Keywords: Image fusion · Two-channel sampling nonseparable wavelet
Filter bank · Multispectral image · Panchromatic image

1 Introduction

The fusion of multispectral (MS) image integrates the images that have higher spectral quality but lower spatial resolution and the panchromatic images with higher spatial resolution. It creates a new image that has better spectral information and higher spatial resolution. It is one of the raging technologies of remote sensing image fusion, and has been widely used [1, 2].

A number of approaches regarding pixel-level fusion have been proposed for merging MS and panchromatic images. The common procedures include intensity hue saturation mergers (IHS mergers) [3], principal component analysis mergers (PCA mergers) [4], and separable discrete wavelet transform based on Mallat algorithm (DWT mergers) [5]. The fusion method of PCA is adequate for all waveband MS images, and it can enhance the spatial resolution of the fused image; however, its spectral resolution is lower and it consumes a great deal of computation. The fusion

© Springer International Publishing AG, part of Springer Nature 2018
B. Zeng et al. (Eds.): PCM 2017, LNCS 10736, pp. 859–868, 2018.
https://doi.org/10.1007/978-3-319-77383-4_84

methods that are adopted most widely in MS image fusion are the IHS transform method and the DWT fusion method [6], but the two methods have their limitations. The IHS transform method can obtain high spatial resolution image, but the fusion result image may seriously lose the spectral information of the original MS image [6]. A fused image with good spectral information can be created by the separable wavelet based on Mallat algorithm [7], but the resulting image has low spatial resolution and block effect because line and column sub-sampling mode is done when the images are decomposed and reconstructed. To solve these problems, Zhang and Hong proposed a fusion method combining IHS transform and DWT [8], and the fused image has good spectral quality and higher spatial resolution. However, the sub-sampling by 2 is used in wavelet multi-resolution analysis, the wavelet transform is not translation invariant and the block effect still exists in the fused image. In addition, researchers also proposed other fusion methods, such as the fusion method combined IHS and additive wavelet decomposition [9, 10], the fusion method based on lifting wavelet transform [11], the fusion method based on IHS and the first generation of curvelet [12], the fusion method based on IHS and the second generation of curvelet [13], and the fusion method based on IHS and the contourlet [14]. Although these methods are found to have good fusion performance, all the mother wavelets used are composed of tensor product wavelets.

Non-separable wavelet transform has good performance in image processing and recognition. The separable wavelet transform is a specialized class of two-dimensional wavelet transform. It approximates image using point information, but the image is a surface, only a two-dimensional wavelet base can be used to approach it perfectly. Non-separable wavelet is a new class of wavelet grew up in the last ten years [15], and is the general class of two-dimensional wavelet. Moreover, when compared to the tensor product wavelet, non-separable wavelet has a lot of excellent features and can produce high spatial resolution resulting image [10]. Our group had researched the construction method of 4-channel, 2-channel, and 3-channel nonseparable wavelet filter banks and applied them to multispectral image fusion [7, 10, 16]. Higher spatial resolution resulting images were obtained. In addition, comparing to the 3-channel or 4-channel nonseparable wavelet transform, two-channel nonseparable wavelet transform has very obvious features for image fusion. First, as it is known, the main information of an object in the image is largely focused on the diamond field of the two-dimensional spectrum. Quincunx sampling of 2-dimensional 2-channel nonseparable wavelet transform can extract this kind of image information effectively. Second, the multispectral image fusion method based on two-channel nonseparable wavelet transform has less computational complexity than that of 4-channel and 3-channel nonseparable wavelet transforms, because there exist only two channels to deal with when the multi-resolution analysis of the images is performed [16].

When compared with the wavelet decomposition of nonsubsampling mode, sampling mode can behave as the natural characteristics of the wavelet transform. In our previous image fusion study based on four-, three-, and two-channel nonseparable wavelet transforms, only nonsubsampled mode is used to decompose and reconstruct images. This mode has obvious limitations. First, nonsubsampling mode can not behave as the sampling characteristic of two-dimensional wavelet transform, and the quincunx sampling mode of the two-channel nonseparable wavelet transform can abstract the image information of the "diamond" field effectively. Second, the size of each layer is almost the same when the original image is decomposed using the non-subsampling mode, and the amount of computation is large. Therefore, it is not suitable for real-time image processing. Thus, to preserve good spectral information and higher spatial resolution as well as cut down the computation amount of fusion procedure, a new fusion method based on sampling two-channel nonseparable wavelets for multi-spectral image pansharpening is presented in this study.

2 Two-Dimensional Two-Channel Nonseparable Wavelet Filter Bank and Its Sampling Mode

2.1 Two-Dimensional Nonseparable Wavelet Transform and Its Sampling Mode of Discrete Lattice

In the two-dimensional transform of discrete wavelets, matrix M represents the sampling mode after wavelet filtering [16], and thus, it is also called as the sampling matrix. For instance, when $M = [1,1;1,-1]$, it shows that quincunx sampling is done to the discrete lattice [15]. The determinant of matrix M has an absolute value of 2. According to the theory of general two-dimensional wavelet transform, there are two filters—a low-pass filter and a high-pass filter. Accordingly, there are one scale function and one wavelet function. In this case, the two-dimensional scale function cannot be decomposed into the tensor product of two one-dimensional scale functions [16], and the wavelet function cannot be decomposed into tensor product of two one-dimensional wavelet functions or a scale function as well as a wavelet function [6].

When the sampling matrix equals to $[1,1;1,-1]$, the sampling process of nonseparable discrete wavelet decomposition is composed of the following two steps:

Step 1: Coordinate transform. According to the coordinate transform formula, $n' = Mn$, the new coordinates are calculated, where $n' = (n'_1, n'_2)^T$, $n = (n_1, n_2)^T$. The coordinate transform processes are presented in Fig. 1(a)–(b).

Step 2: Subsampling for the discrete lattice after Step 1. There exist odd sampling mode and even sampling mode. The sampling processes are presented in Fig. 1(b)–(c).

Interpolation process of the two channel nonseparable wavelet transform is the reverse of the above-mentioned process.

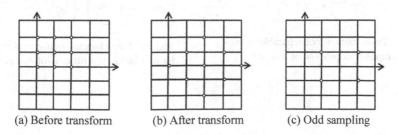

(a) Before transform   (b) After transform   (c) Odd sampling

Fig. 1. Coordinate transform and sampling of two-channel nonseparable wavelet transform

2.2   Image Multi-resolution Decomposition and Reconstruction in the Sampling Mode

Let $H_0 = \{h_0(k)\}_{k \in \mathbb{Z}^2}$ be the low-pass filter and $H_1 = \{h_1(k)\}_{k \in \mathbb{Z}^2}$ be the high-pass filter. According to the method of coordinate transformation and sampling presented in Fig. 1, the multiresolution decomposition and reconstruction processes can be represented as shown in Figs. 2 and 3 respectively, when the sampling matrix is equal to [1,1;1,−1]. The decomposition process consists of two parallel steps:

Step 1:   Coordinate transformation and odd sampling (or even sampling) after low-pass filtering (by H_0). $\downarrow M(E)$ denotes coordinate transformation and even sampling, and $\downarrow M(O)$ denotes coordinate transformation and odd sampling in Fig. 2. The two low-frequency subimages are obtained after Step 1.

Step 2:   Coordinate transformation and odd sampling (or even sampling) after high-pass filtering (by H_1). The two high-frequency subimages are obtained after Step 2.

The reconstruction process is contrary to the decomposition process. $\uparrow M(E)$ and $\uparrow M(O)$ in Fig. 3 denote the reverse process of $\downarrow M(E)$ and $\downarrow M(O)$ respectively, which are the reverse coordinate transformation as well as the even interpolation and reverse coordinate transformation and the odd interpolation, respectively. H_0^* and H_1^* are the low-pass filter and high-pass filter of the reconstruction corresponding to decomposition filters H_0 and H_1 respectively. Only one decomposition level is presented in Fig. 2; however, more levels of decomposition and reconstruction can also be performed similar to that of the one level case shown in Figs. 2 and 3. After multilevel decompositions (e.g. j levels), 2^j low-frequency subimages and 2^j high-frequency subimages are obtained.

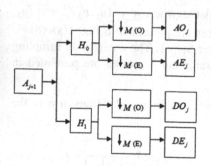

Fig. 2. Two-channel nonseparable wavelet decomposition process of image

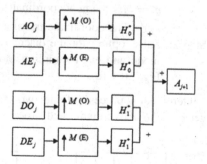

Fig. 3. Two-channel nonseparable wavelet reconstruction process of image

2.3 Construction of Two-Dimensional Two-Channel Nonseparable Wavelet Filter Banks

Let us denote the Fourier transform of low-pass filter H_0 and high-pass filter H_1 as $m_0(\omega)$ and $m_1(\omega)$ respectively, where $\omega = (\omega_1, \omega_2)^T$.

$$m_0(x,y) = \sum_{0 \leq j,k \leq L-1} h_0(j,k)x^j y^k, m_1(x,y) = \sum_{0 \leq j,k \leq L-1} h_1(j,k)x^j y^k \qquad (1)$$

where $x = e^{-i\omega_1}, y = e^{-i\omega_2}$, and $i = \sqrt{-1}$.

According to the literature [17], we can construct two-dimensional two-channel nonseparable filter banks as follows.

Let $s = 2$, constructing $X(x,y) = (1, xy)$, and $D(x,y) = [1,0;0,xy]$, then, the two-dimensional two-channel filter bank with compact support, orthogonality, can be constructed as

$$(m_0(x,y), m_1(x,y)) = \frac{1}{2}(1, xy) \prod_{j=1}^{K} (U_j D(x,y) U_j^T) V \qquad (2)$$

where $x = e^{-i\omega_1}, y = e^{-i\omega_2}$, $U_j(j = 1, 2, \cdots, K)$ and $V/2 = (V_0, V_1)/2$ are the orthogonal matrices, V_1 is a 2×1 vector, and $V_0 = (1, 1)^T$.

To obtain $4 * 4$ filter banks, let $K = 2$, constructing

$$U_j = \begin{pmatrix} \cos(\alpha_j) & -\sin(\alpha_j) \\ \sin(\alpha_j) & \cos(\alpha_j) \end{pmatrix} (j = 1, 2), V = \begin{pmatrix} 1 & 1 \\ 1 & -1 \end{pmatrix} \qquad (3)$$

It can be validated that U_j (for any α_j) and $V/2$ are orthonormal matrices. Consequently, the filter banks which have compactly support and orthonormality can be constructed. The number of filter banks is infinite according to (3) with different values of α_j. We select a filter bank as shown in Eq. (4), which is used to fuse the images, as described in the next section.

$$H_0 = \begin{pmatrix} 0.146946 & 0 & 0 & 0 \\ 0 & .353054 & 0 & 0 \\ 0 & 0 & .646946 & 0 \\ 0 & 0 & 0 & -.146946 \end{pmatrix}, H_1 = \begin{pmatrix} -0.146946 & 0 & 0 & 0 \\ 0 & -.257562 & 0 & 0 \\ 0 & 0 & .551455 & 0 \\ 0 & 0 & 0 & -.146946 \end{pmatrix}$$

$$(4)$$

It can be validated that this is an orthonormal filter bank and H_0, H_1 are nonseparable.

3 Fusion Algorithm

IHS transform changes the color system with Red, Green and Blue channels into the system of intensity, hue and saturation (IHS). An intensity component of the MS image usually presents like a panchromatic image. This characteristic is used in the multispectral image fusion to fuse a high-resolution panchromatic image with a low-resolution color image. The common fusion algorithm is that the intensity of MS image is replaced by the panchromatic image. The high spatial resolution image can be obtained using this fusion algorithm, but the spectral information of the original MS image may be lost badly. There is no block effective in the resulting image using nonseparable wavelet transform. Hence, we combine IHS transform and the two-channel sampling nonseparable wavelet multiresolution analysis in this paper, and fuse the approximate coefficients and detail coefficients after nonseparable wavelet decomposition. Before image fusion, the original multispectral image and the panchromatic image should be registered. When being registered to the high spatial resolution panchromatic image, the low spatial resolution multispectral image needs to be re-sampled [18]. To have a good fusion effect, the panchromatic image usually needs to be matched to the intensity of multispectral image after registration [8]. There are five steps in our fusion algorithm.

Step 1: Register the MS image and panchromatic image.
Step 2: Perform IHS transform with the original MS image [3].
Step 3: Perform histogram matching between the panchromatic image and the intensity component of the original MS image.
Step 4: Fuse the intensity component I of the original MS image and the panchromatic image P' after histogram matching, and generate the fused image F.

Perform multiresolution nonseparable wavelet decomposition of the image I and P' according to the process described in Fig. 2 using the filter bank (4). To obtain a fused image with good spectral information and high spatial resolution, we consider low-frequency of the fused image is the average of the low-frequency subimages of I and P'. For the high-frequency subimages of the fused image, the fusion rule is that the detail components of I are replaced by the corresponding detail components of P' (for all even and odd high-frequency components).

Subsequently, perform the nonseparable wavelet inverse transform, and reconstruct the new intensity image F according to the upsampling mode presented in Fig. 3.

Step 5: Perform IHS inverse transform to F, H, S and generate the fused MS image.

4 Experimental Results and Performance Analysis

4.1 Experimental Results

To validate the feasibility of the proposed method, we performed numerous experiments and obtained identical conclusions. We displayed the analysis of the visual effect and the quantitative indicators for the fusion of the two pair images presented in Figs. 4(a)–(b) (LISS-3 images) and Figs. 5(a)–(b) (ETM+ images) in this paper. The multispectral image is registered and re-sampled to the panchromatic image. The LISS-3 multiband image, which is a fire scene, is composed of the B2 band (Green), B3 band (Red) and B4 band (Near infrared). The spatial resolutions of the MS image and the panchromatic image are 23.5 m and 5.8 m respectively, the size of each image is 512×512. It can be noted that the flame is burning on the upper right corner of the scene. The flame has been extinguished on the lower-left corner of the scene with traces of burning. The flame and combustion traces are expressed through color. For the ETM+ image fusion, we have done the fusion experiment on the Landsat-7 ETM+ multi-band image and panchromatic image of the same area (New York urban). Figures 5(a) and (b) are source images, where, Fig. 5(b) is the ETM+ panchromatic image which spatial resolution is 15 m, and Fig. 5(a) is the composed multi-band image of ETM+ band 1, band 2 and band 3 which spatial resolution is 30 m.

Figures 4(i) and 5(i) show the fused images obtained by the proposed method. To see the fusion effects distinctly, we compare the proposed method with the methods based on IHS [3], DWT [5], IHS-DWT [8], IHS-Contourlet [14], and IHS-Curvelet [13]. To analyze the fusion characteristic deeply, we also compare the proposed method with the fusion method based on IHS and the two-channel nonsubsamped orthogonal nonseparable wavelet ([16], IHS-TCNONW). The fusion rules of the low-frequency coefficients and the high-frequency coefficients of the latter five fusion methods are as the same as that of the proposed fusion method. Figures 4(c)–(i) and 5(c)–(i) present the fused images of the above seven fusion methods, respectively. The experimental results are carried out in the computing environment of MATLAB 7.5.

On comparing the visual effects presented in Figs. 4(i) and 5(i) with those obtained by the other six fusion methods (Figs. 4(c)–(h) and 5(c)–(h)), it can be noted that the fused image of the proposed fusion method can keep good spectral information and higher spatial resolution. Moreover, the flame color of the scene is more natural, and there is no artificial trace in the fused image. On the contrary, the fused image obtained by the IHS fusion method has high spatial resolution, but the spectral information is wried seriously, and the contrast of the fused image is low. The fused images obtained by DWT and IHS-DWT methods have high spectral quality, but there are evident block traces in the place of the mountain ridges. The fused images based on IHS-Contourlet and IHS-Curvelet methods can keep the good spectral quality and high spatial resolution, but when compared with the proposed fusion method, the luminance of the two fused images is darker and the detail information of the original panchromatic image is not kept well. IHS-TCNONW fusion method has high spectral quality, but the spatial resolution is low.

4.2   Objective Performance Analysis

The relative average spectral error (RASE), and relative global dimensional synthesis error (ERGAS) are used to estimate the spectral information of the fused image [12]. The smaller the values of RASE and ERGAS, the better is the spectral quality preservation. The entropy and a type of correlation coefficient (sCC) are used to estimate the high spatial information preserved by the fused image [12]. Higher sCC between the resulting image and panchromatic image reveals that most of the high spatial information of the panchromatic image is injected into the original multispectral image during the fusion procedure.

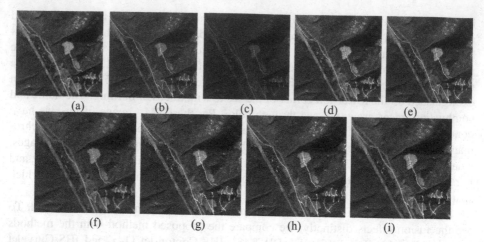

Fig. 4. Fusion of LISS-3 MS image and PAN image. (a) original MS image; (b) original panchromatic image; (c) IHS fused image; (d) DWT fused image; (e) IHS-DWT fused image; (f) IHS-TCNONW fused image; (g) IHS-Contourlet fused image; (h) IHS-Curvelet fused image; (i) fused image of the proposed method.

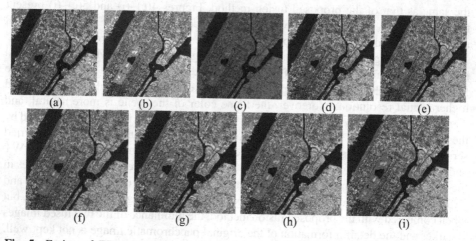

Fig. 5. Fusion of ETM+ images. (a) original MS image; (b) original panchromatic image; (c) IHS fused image; (d) DWT fused image; (e) IHS-DWT fused image; (f) IHS-TCNONW fused image; (g) IHS-Contourlet fused image; (h) IHS-Curvelet fused image; (i) fused image of the proposed method.

Tables 1 and 2 show the objective performance indices of the fused images based on IHS, DWT, IHS-DWT, IHS-TCNONW, IHS-Contourlet, IHS-Curvelet and the proposed fusion method. It can be noted that the values of the proposed method in RASE and ERGAS are smaller than those of the other six methods and the entropy, sCC are greater than those of the other six methods. This indicates that the proposed fusion method outperforms the IHS fusion method, DWT fusion method, IHS-DWT fusion

Table 1. Performance indices of LISS3 image

Method	RASE	ERGAS	sCC	Entropy
IHS (R, G, B)			0.9105	
	49.3643	14.0021	0.9449	6.7218
			0.9713	
DWT (R, G, B)			0.9307	
	5.1329	1.2863	0.972	7.4161
			0.9659	
IHS-DWT (R, G, B)			0.9558	
	1.9363	0.4502	0.9801	7.4366
			0.9758	
IHS-TCNONW (R, G, B)			0.9516	
	9.9535	2.8962	0.9380	7.3198
			0.9656	
IHS-Contourlet (R, G, B)			0.9582	
	1.9325	0.4503	0.9818	7.4358
			0.9781	
IHS-Curvelet (R, G, B)			0.9576	
	2.2503	0.5649	0.9814	7.4262
			0.9776	
The proposed method (R, G, B)			0.9804	
	1.3198	0.4106	0.9861	7.4488
			0.9872	

Table 2. Performance indices of ETM+ image

Method	RASE	ERGAS	sCC	Entropy
IHS (R, G, B)			0.9712	
	34.2768	17.5144	0.8706	7.4618
			0.9619	
DWT (R, G, B)			0.9685	
	2.8806	1.6783	0.9457	7.7901
			0.9643	
IHS-DWT (R, G, B)			0.9847	
	3.4944	2.1474	0.9485	7.8490
			0.9813	
IHS-TCNONW (R, G, B)			0.9573	
	6.4756	2.9126	0.9409	7.8535
			0.9523	
IHS-Contourlet (R, G, B)			0.9858	
	2.8820	1.6202	0.9490	7.8494
			0.9825	
IHS-Curvelet (R, G, B)			0.9872	
	4.537	2.7963	0.9452	7.4262
			0.9842	
The proposed method (R, G, B)			0.9876	
	2.8418	1.6039	0.9634	7.8588
			0.9892	

method, IHS-Contourlet fusion method, IHS-Curvelet fusion method, and IHS-TCNONW fusion method in keeping high spatial resolution and good global spectral information. When we fuse TM image and SPOT image, Quickbird panchromatic and MS images, different band ETM+ images, and the other multispectral and panchromatic images using the proposed method, the same conclusion is obtained.

5 Conclusion

A construction method of 2-D 2-channel sampling nonseparable wavelet filter bank, whose dilation matrix is [1,1;1,−1], has been presented and a fusion method based on this kind of wavelet has been proposed for multispectral image pansharpening. The proposed fusion method, while can preserve good global spectral information, has higher spatial resolution than the fusion methods based on the IHS, DWT, IHS-DWT, IHS-Contourlet, IHS-Curvelet, and IHS-TCNONW. The low resolution multispectral image has been enhanced.

Acknowledgments. This work was supported by the National Natural Science Foundation of China (No. 61471160) and the Key Project of the Natural Science Foundation of Hubei Province (No. 2012FFA053).

References

1. Restaino, R., Vivone, G., Mura, M.D., Chanussot, J.: Fusion of multispectral and panchromatic images based on morphological operators. IEEE Trans. Image Process. **25** (6), 2882–2895 (2016)
2. Zhang, K., Wang, M., Yang, S., Xing, Y., Rong, Q.: Fusion of panchromatic and multispectral images via coupled sparse non-negative matrix factorization. IEEE J. Selected Topics Appl. Earth Observations Remote Sens. **9**(12), 5740–5747 (2016)
3. Tu, T.M., Su, S.C., Shyu, H.C., Huang, P.S.: A new look at IHS-like image fusion methods. Inf. Fusion **2**(3), 177–186 (2001)
4. Chavez, P.S., Sides, S.C., Anderson, J.A.: A comparison of three different methods to merge multiresolution and multispectral data: landsat TM & SPOT panchromatic. Photogram. Eng. Remote Sens. **57**(3), 295–303 (1991)
5. Bai, L., Xu, C., Wang, C.: A review of fusion methods of multi-spectral image. Optik-Int. J. Light Electron Optics **126**(24), 4804–4807 (2015)
6. Liu, B., Liu, W., Peng, J.: Multispectral image fusion method based on intensity-hue-saturation and nonsubsampled three-channel non-separable wavelets. Chinese Optics Lett. **8**(4), 384–387 (2010)
7. Liu, B., Li, K., Liu, W., Liu, F.: Construction method of three-channel nonseparable symmetric wavelets with arbitrary dilation matrices and its applications in multispectral image fusion. IET Image Process. **7**(7), 679–685 (2013)
8. Zhang, Y., Hong, G.: An IHS and wavelet integrated approach to improve pan-sharpening visual quality of natural colour IKONOS and QuickBird images. Inf. Fusion **6**(3), 225–234 (2005)
9. Chen, S.H., Zhang, R.H., Su, H.B., et al.: SAR and multispectral image fusion using generalized IHS transform based on à trous wavelet and EMD decompositions. IEEE Sens. J. **10**(3), 737–745 (2010)
10. Liu, B., Liu, W.: Fusion of multi-spectral image using non-separable additive wavelets for high spatial resolution enhancement. In: Kamel, M., Campilho, A. (eds.) ICIAR 2011. LNCS, vol. 6753, pp. 90–99. Springer, Heidelberg (2011). https://doi.org/10.1007/978-3-642-21593-3_10
11. Zhang, W., Yang, J.Z., Wang, X.H., et al.: The fusion of remote sensing images based on lifting wavelet transformation. Comput. Inf. Sci. **2**(1), 69–75 (2009)
12. Choi, M., Kim, R.Y., Nam, M.R., Kim, H.O.: Fusion of multispectral and panchromatic satellite images using the curvelet transform. IEEE Trans. Geosci. Remote Sens. Lett. **2**(2), 136–140 (2005)
13. Dong, L., Yang, Q., Wu, H., Xiao, H., Xu, M.: High quality multi-spectral and panchromatic image fusion technologies based on curvelet transform. Neurocomputing **159**(2), 268–274 (2015)
14. Mahyari, A.G., Yazdi, M.: Panchromatic and multispectral image fusion based on maximization of both spectral and spatial similarities. IEEE Trans. Geosci. Remote Sens. **49**(6), 1976–1985 (2011)
15. Kovačević, J., Vetterli, M.: Nonseparable multidimensional perfect reconstruction filter bank and wavelet bases for $\mathbb{R}^n$. IEEE Trans. Inf. Theor. **38**(2), 533–555 (1992)
16. Bin, L., Peng, J.: Multi-spectral image fusion method based on two channels non-separable wavelets. Sci. China Ser. F Inf. Sci. **51**(12), 2022–2032 (2008)
17. Chen, Q.H., Micchelli, C.A., Peng, S.L., et al.: Multivariate filter banks having matrix factorizations. SIAM J. Matrix Anal. Appl. **25**(2), 517–531 (2003)
18. Li, Z., Jing, Z., Yang, X., Sun, S.: Color transfer based remote sensing image fusion using non-separable wavelet frame transform. Patt. Recogn. Lett. **26**(13), 2006–2014 (2005)

Data Reconstruction Based on Supervised Deep Auto-Encoder

Ting Rui[1,2], Sai Zhang[1(✉)], Tongwei Ren[2], Jian Tang[1],
and Junhua Zou[1]

[1] PLA University of Science and Technology, Nanjing 210007, China
466908114@qq.com
[2] State Key Laboratory for Novel Software Technology, Nanjing University,
Nanjing 210023, China

Abstract. Digital media information reconstruction has attracted much attention in machine learning, we propose a new method about this problem for supervising learning by using the classical unsupervised auto-encoders (AE), and we also analyze the deep model structure and training strategy. In this paper, we present a supervised deep-based auto-encoder model which has a set of progressive and interrelated learning strategies by multiple groups of supervised single-layer AE. In this structure, the one-to-one training strategy in classical AE model (one output corresponding to one input) is substituted by the multi-to-one training strategy (one output corresponding to many inputs), and it improves the ability to express the feature code. We use the structure and training strategy mentioned above to reconstruct the damaged or obscured images. Experimental results show that the proposed method has good effect and adaptability to the reconstruction of the damaged or occluded samples.

Keywords: Auto-encoder · Supervised learning · Deep structure
Training strategy · Image reconstruction

1 Introduction

In general, many factors can cause the damage or loss of local information in digital media data, such as digital images in the acquisition, transmission, processing, compression and decompression process. In order to ensure the integrity of the information, these damaged parts need to be effectively repaired [1].

Nowadays, deep learning [2] has been a hot spot and an effective way in image processing [3–6]. Auto encoder is one of the classical models of deep learning, and it completes the training through unsupervised learning. Auto encoder not only can finish structure extraction and expression of low dimensional data, but also can extract more abstract feature, improve the classification accuracy, reconstruct data information through concise expression in deep network. However, the expression of the data is only limited to compression of the inherent information. If the training data information damaged, it can lead to the feature extraction incomplete, and produce inevitable impact on the follow-up reconstruction.

© Springer International Publishing AG, part of Springer Nature 2018
B. Zeng et al. (Eds.): PCM 2017, LNCS 10736, pp. 869–879, 2018.
https://doi.org/10.1007/978-3-319-77383-4_85

Based on the observations above, in order to make better use of feature encoding ability of auto encoder, and give play to the training advantages of supervised learning, we propose a new auto encoder model based on the classical auto encoder structure. In this paper, we design a new training strategy and efficiently use sample prior to get more abstract features and more abundant expression to achieve the improvement of the reconstruction ability of the damaged data. In experimental stage, different scale impact noise is mixed into MINIST database to simulate damaged samples, and these mixed samples are used for classification to prove the validity of the method. Grounded on the experimental results, the proposed method can be applied to the reconstruction of partial or missing regions in face regions, and the effectiveness and applicability of our method are verified.

2   Related Work

There have been some research on data reconstruction problem. Bertalmio et al. [7] use the Partial Differential Equation (PDE) model to solve the image restoration problem (the BSCB model). Chan and Shen [8] put forward another image inpainting model based on the variational principle, this model is called the total variation algorithm (TV) model. Criminisi et al. [9] propose a repair method based on sample blocks. This method considers the structure and texture information of the image, uses SSD (Single Shot MultiBox Detector) model to search the optimal matching block. Komodakis et al. [10] propose BP propagation algorithm based on priority, and they describe the image restoration problem as a discrete global optimization problem. Its objective function is the minimization of the energy function of the Markov random field (MRF). With the wide application of MRF in the field of computer vision, Hsin et al. [11] propose a more comprehensive repair algorithm based on BP algorithm, this algorithm increases the edge information to ensure structural image restoration. In recent years, Pathak et al. [12] restore images by image semantic information. Yang et al. [13] infer missing information by content and texture information based on convolutional neural networks. Huanga et al. [14] build a deep face recognition framework based on special Denoising Auto-Encoder (DAE) and image reconstruction.

3   Supervised Auto-Encoder

3.1   Supervised Single Layer Auto-Encoder

Automatic encoder (AE) is one of the classical models in deep learning. In 1986, Rumelhart [15] proposed the concept of automatic encoder and applied it to high-dimensional complex data processing. AE is a deep network that can be stacked over multiple single-layer AE, and the goal of the single layer AE is to minimize the average reconstruction error between the input data X and the reconstructed data Z:

$$J(W, b) = \frac{1}{m} \sum_{i=1}^{m} \left(\frac{1}{2} \|Z_i - X_i\|^2 \right) \tag{1}$$

where M is the number of training samples, Z_i represents the i_{th} reconstruction sample, X_i represents the i_{th} input sample.

AE is closely related to the form of training samples and the expression of features. If the training sample of unsupervised AE is damaged, the feature expression must be incomplete.

In order to make up for the limitation on feature expression and make good use of the advantages of supervised learning, we propose a new supervised learning method for classical unsupervised AE. The new model transforms the objective function of the original unsupervised AE into the minimum mean reconstruction error between the supervised label X_{label} and the reconstructed sample Z. The cost function becomes:

$$J_{supervised}(W, b) = \frac{1}{m} \sum_{i=1}^{m} \left(\frac{1}{2} \| Z^i - X_{label}^i \|^2 \right) \tag{2}$$

Where m is the number of training samples, X_{label}^i represents the i_{th} supervised sample. The model structure is shown in Fig. 1.

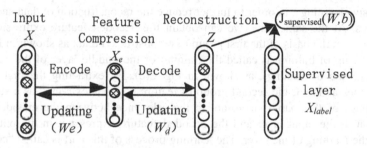

Fig. 1. Framework of supervised single-layer AE

Feature expression of unsupervised AE is single and limited, and the feature extracted by training is only the inherent characteristic of input samples.

In this paper, the classical AE model is supervised, which improves the uniqueness and limitation of the characteristic expression ability of the classical AE model. This paper uses a multi-to-one learning strategy, that is, an input sample has a variety of forms, and the output corresponds to only one training label. This allows the supervised single-layer AE model trained by the new strategy to be able to learn more diverse features than its inherent characteristics. This strategy makes up for the lack of feature expression in the classical AE model, making the feature more robust.

3.2 Deep Auto-Encoder Model Based on Supervised Learning and Training

The deep structure of the classical AE is achieved through an unsupervised greedy algorithm, which is implemented in a stacked form. Each layer of the training process will produce a feature expression, the deeper the number of layers stacked, the more abstract features obtained. For the deep AE model based on supervised learning, multi-layer stacking is also to obtain more abstract, more diversified feature representation (the weight W). Since the supervised label for each layer of the deep AE model based on supervised learning is not the input of the layer, the classical AE stacking method and the training method can not be used. In this paper, we propose a new deep network structure and training method.

In this paper, the training of the new model is divided into three groups, as shown in Fig. 2. Each group of training is based on a supervised learning single-layer AE model, and each training model is independent, but the entire training process is interrelated. The first group of training is the input layer of training (the first layer of training) in the new model, as shown in Fig. 2(a). In the training process, this paper describes the result of the hidden layer as the feature code, the input layer to the hidden layer of the connection weight (W_e) called the encoded feature expression. The connection weight from the hidden layer to the output layer (W_d) is called the decoded feature expression; The second group of training is called the training of the output layer (the third layer of training). Firstly, the first group of reconstructed data is extracted as the input of the second model, and the supervised learning is carried out again with the lossless samples. In this paper, this process of group learning is called "progressive learning", in order to further reduce the reconstruction of data and lossless data errors. At the same time, we can obtain the decoded feature expression in the output layer on the basis of the first group of reconstructed data, as shown in Fig. 2(b); The last group of training is called the training of the middle layer of the new model (the second the of training), as shown in Fig. 2(c). By extracting the first group of feature codes as input, the second group of feature codes is extracted as a supervisor. The purpose of this part is to establish the relevance between the encoded feature expression in the input layer and the decoded feature expression in the output layer through the learning of the layer. The learning process of this part is called "correlation coding". The supervised learning of the two groups of feature codes further improves the ability of deep feature expression and the coding of the features. In the training of each group of supervised single-layer AE models, the sigmoid function f(·) is used as an activation function to map the feature representation, and the learning process is as follows:

$$f_e^i(x) = f(W_e^i * x + b_e^i) \tag{3}$$

$$f_d^i(f_e^i) = f(W_d^i * f_e^i + b_d^i) . \tag{4}$$

Where f_e^i is the coding result of the i_{th} supervised AE model, and b is the decoding result of the i_{th} supervised AE model;

In this paper, the new AE and the classical AE are significant differences in the model structure and training methods. This paper completes the training of the new model structure through "progressive learning" and "relevance coding". The new model adopts the multi-to-one training strategy to achieve the deep abstract characteristic code, and overcomes the singularity of the classical AE to the characteristic expression.

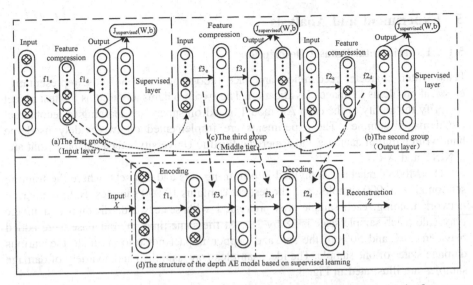

Fig. 2. Training framework of deep AE model based on supervised learning. (a) the first group of supervised training processes; (b) the second group of progressive learning; (c) the third group of relevance codes; (d) the structure of the deep AE model based on supervised.

4   Deep Auto-Encoder Data Reconstruction Based on Supervised Learning

The training of the model is completed by the training method of the model in Sect. 3.2. The feature expression in the model is extracted according to the method in Sect. 3.2, the characteristic weight W. According to the pre-coded and re-decoded network structure, a stacking AE model with two-layer coding and two-layer decoding is constructed. The network structure is shown in Fig. 2(d). Firstly, the deep feature is extracted and encoded from the damaged sample, and then the decoded feature representation is used to decoding to reconstruct the near-destructive sample information described by the feature code. For the trained model, the reconstruction of the damaged samples is done in a feedforward manner. The preprocessing process is as follows:

$$\begin{aligned}
f_e^1(x) &= f(W_e^1 * x + b_e^1) \\
f_e^3(f_e^1) &= f(W_e^3 * f_e^1 + b_e^3) \\
f_d^3(f_e^3) &= f(W_d^3 * f_e^3 + b_d^3) \\
f_d^2(f_d^3) &= f(W_d^2 * f_d^3 + b_d^2)
\end{aligned} \tag{5}$$

5 Experiment and Analysis

5.1 Experimental Dataset Description

Handwritten character recognition and face recognition are the most representative classical problems in image classification. The two problems are used as the test object to verify the ability of the deep AE model based on supervised learning to reconstruct the damaged samples. The experiments are implemented on two widely used the handwritten digital database and American Purdue University's face database, that are, MNIST and AR.

The MNIST database is divided into training sets and test sets, where the training set contains 60,000 samples, and the test set contains 10,000 samples. Before entering network training, each sample was pretreated with scale standardization and image grayscale (each sample scale is 28 by 28). At the same time, the database were added between 20% and 50% of the salt and pepper impact noise to simulate the various damage states of one sample. The ideal samples (raw samples) and a variety of damage samples are illustrated in Fig. 3.

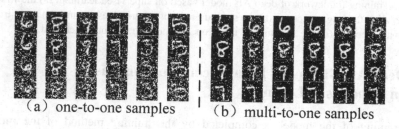

(a) one-to-one samples   (b) multi-to-one samples

Fig. 3. Different levels of damaged samples. (a) A single sample of damage. Four simulated data sets were designed in this experiment, they are 20%, 30%, 40% and 50%; (b) Multi-to-one damaged data sets, each line of a variety of damaged forms corresponding to a lossless sample.

The AR database contains over 4000 face images from 126 people (56 women and 70 men). These images contain frontal view faces with different facial expression, illuminations, and occlusions (sun glasses and scarf). Some face images from AR are illustrated in Fig. 5. In order to reduce the amount of computation, this paper extracts the faces of 50 men in this database, with 1,300 faces. The experiment took these samples from the AR database into four parts. In first part, for each person corresponding to 14 faces, we choose the facial images with neutral expression, frontal pose as a lossless training set, with a total of 700 faces, as shown in Fig. 4(a); The second is to build a corresponding damaged data set by artificial randomly for each nondestructive shade the area of the face, as shown in Fig. 4(b); The third is the test set. It consists of occluded faces (such as wearing sunglasses, wearing scarves) under natural conditions and random secondary destruction of the occluded faces by artificial, each person corresponding to 14 faces, with a total of 700 faces, as shown in Fig. 4(c); The fourth part is that every man in the corresponding face, through the artificial selection of a subjective view in the light, expression and no occlusion of the best face as the training of the label face, as shown in Fig. 4(d). It is used for multi-to-one training strategy.

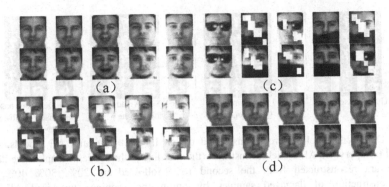

Fig. 4. Some original images from AR database and the damaged ones. (a) Supervised samples (b) Training samples, corresponding to lossless face samples; (c) Test samples, the occluded samples extracted from the AR database and randomly destroyed; (d) Multi-to-one face labels.

5.2 Experimental Methods and Results Analysis

Test Results of MNIST Reconstruction Analysis. The experiment first uses non-destructive samples to pre-train a convolution neural network as a classifier. The damaged samples were reconstructed by different methods and then input into the pre-trained CNN classifier, and then the classification results were compared with the different model. The experimental framework is shown in Fig. 5.

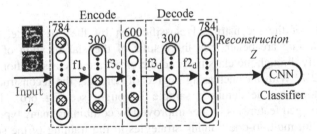

Fig. 5. The MNIST reconstruction framework of supervised deep AE model

In this paper, the unsupervised AE model, the one-to-one supervised single-layer AE model, the multi-to-one supervised single-layer AE model and the multi-to-one supervised deep AE model were trained, and then the damaged MNIST samples are reconstructed using these trained models. The reconstructed results are shown in Fig. 6. The error rate of the classification obtained by CNN is used to compare the advantages and disadvantages of the model. As can be seen from Table 1, the damaged samples reconstructed by unsupervised AE models are more severely damaged and the results are worse. The reconstruction results is shown in Fig. 6(a).

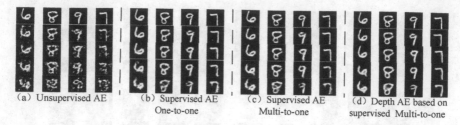

(a) Unsupervised AE   (b) Supervised AE   (c) Supervised AE   (d) Depth AE based on
                          One-to-one   Multi-to-one   supervised Multi-to-one

Fig. 6. Damaged samples were reconstructed under different structural AE models. (a) The classical unsupervised AE model reconstructs (the first line is the lossless samples, the damaged samples are reconstructed from the second row, followed by 20%, 30% 40%, 50%); (b) Reconstruction of damaged samples by one-to-one training supervised AE model; (c) Reconstruction of damaged samples by multi-to-one training supervised AE model; (d) Reconstruction of damaged samples by multi-to-one training deep AE model based on supervised learning;

Table 1. Result of recognition with CNN in a variety of the damaged samples

Model strategy	Noise ratio (%)	20%	30%	40%	50%
CNN direct classification	Error rate (%)	25.76%	48.50%	67.59%	80.13%
Single-layer model Reconstruction classification	Unsupervised	17.73%	34.36%	50.19%	60.46%
	Supervise (one-to-one)	3.11%	5.83%	10.49%	19.56%
	Supervised (multi-to-one)	2.76%	4.55%	8.72%	16.84%
Deep model Reconstruction classification	Supervised (multi-to-one)	2.68%	4.39%	7.53%	14.74%

The results of the reconstructed classification by the AE model based on the supervised learning are better than the results of the classification of the damaged samples directly through the classifier, and the error rate of classification decreased by 22.65%–57.82%. With the increasing degree of damage, the reconstruction of some local information on the damaged sample is rough, see Fig. 6(b). Therefore, the training of damaged features is further improved by combining many types of damaged information with multi-to-one training strategies in the training of the supervised AE model. The test results are shown in Table 1, and the classification error rate of different damaged samples decreased again by 0.08%–2.1%. The reconstructed results are shown in Fig. 6(c). Experiments show that the new training strategies are effective for supervising the training of AE models.

In this experiment, we use the new model to reconstruct the damaged sample more fully under the multi-to-one training strategy. The result is shown in Fig. 6(d). The results show that the proposed method can improve the smoothness of the local edge in the reconstructed image and have the best reconstruction effect, and prove the effectiveness of the deep AE model based on supervised learning.

Test Results of Face Occlusion Area Reconstruction Analysis. In this experiment, the reconstructed face samples were used to quantitatively describe the effect of different reconstruction methods using Pearson correlation [16]. Using the above four AE models, the reconstruction of the face occlusion area is shown in Fig. 7. It can be seen that the reconstructed face of the supervised AE model is superior to that of the unsupervised AE model, as shown in Fig. 7(a). As shown in Fig. 7(b), the results show that the supervised AE model is still superior to the unsupervised AE model, but the one-on-one training strategy cannot satisfy the characteristic expression of the occlusion area. As shown in Fig. 7(c), multi-to-one training strategy is superior to one-to-one training strategy. The effectiveness of the multi-to-one training strategy proposed for the supervised AE model is proved. In this paper, the deep AE model based on supervised learning is used to improve the reconstruction effect of the partial occlusion area of the image by using the multi-to-one training strategy. Compared with the supervised AE model, the image reconstruction is more natural. The experiment proves the effectiveness and applicability of the new model and the new training strategy.

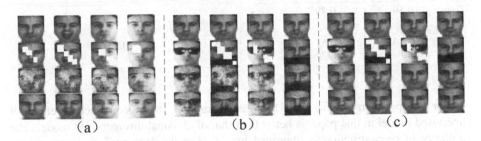

Fig. 7. Face reconstruction results in AE models with different structures. (a) The first row is lossless samples, the second line is the damaged samples, the rest are the reconstruction results by unsupervised AE model and by one-to-one training supervised AE model; (b) The first row is the label face, the second line is the test samples, followed by unsupervised AE model, one-to-one training supervised AE model; (c) The first line is the label face, the second is the test samples, the third is the reconstruction results of multi-to-one training supervised AE, the fourth line is the reconstruction results of multi-to-one training deep AE based on supervised.

In order to quantitatively describe the difference about the reconstructed performance of the above model, this paper uses Pearson correlation to analyze the results of the model reconstruction. The Pearson correlation coefficient is defined as follows:

$$r = \frac{\sum_{i=1}^{n} (X_{label} - \overline{Z})(X_{label}^2 - \overline{Z^2})}{\sqrt{\sum_{i=1}^{n} (X_{label} - \overline{Z})^2} \sqrt{\sum_{i=1}^{n} \left(X_{label}^2 - \overline{Z^2}\right)^2}} \tag{6}$$

Where n represents the number of samples, X_{label} represents the label face, and Z represents the reconstructed face. The experimental framework is shown in Fig. 8.

Calculate the similarity of the 14 pieces of masking face corresponding to a person in the test set, and the average of the 14 similarities as the final result, as shown in Table 2.

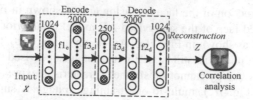

Fig. 8. The face reconstruction framework of supervised deep AE model

Table 2. The results of correlation analysis about face reconstruction

Model	Unsupervised AE	Supervised AE model (one-to-one)	Supervised AE model (multi-to-one)	Supervised deep AE model (multi-to-one)
Training set	0.59	0.79		
Testing set	0.46	0.51	0.93	0.95

For the problem of damaged face reconstruction, the reconstruction effect of supervised model in this paper is better than that of classical unsupervised model. The similarity of reconstruction is improved by 0.2. For the face occlusion area reconstruction test, the similarity of reconstructed face of supervised model is higher than that of unsupervised model. Similarity increased by 0.05. The experimental results demonstrate the applicability of the supervised AE model to the occlusion face reconstruction.

By using the multi-to-one training strategy, the reconstruction effect of the face occlusion area is improved by 0.42. In this paper, the effect of the deep AE model on face reconstruction is compared with that of the supervised single-layer AE model, and the similarity of reconstruction is increased again by 0.02. Compared with the effect of classical unsupervised AE reconstruction, the reconstructed similarity is improved by 0.49. This paper proves the effectiveness and applicability of the new training strategy based on the supervised AE model.

6   Conclusion

Nowadays, a great deal of digital media data will be produced at all times. It is necessary to provide an effective method for massive data. Based on the classic unsupervised AE model, this paper proposes a new method to reconstruct the damaged image by supervised learning based on the analysis and research of the unsupervised AE framework. In this paper, we propose a new training strategy to the supervised AE model, and then design the new deep framework of supervised AE and training method of the deep model. The experimental results were analyzed quantitatively. Experiments show that the proposed method has good contribution and adaptability to the damaged or the occluded samples reconstruction.

Acknowledgments. This work was supported in part by National Natural Science Foundation of China (Grant No. 61473444). This foundation mainly focus on multimedia.

References

1. Zhang, H.Y., Peng, Q.C.: A survey on digital image inpainting. J. Image Graph. **12**(1), 1–10 (2007)
2. Hinton, G.E., Osindero, S., Teh, Y.W.: A fast learning algorithm for deep belief nets. Neural Comput. **18**(7), 1527 (2006)
3. Bengio, Y.: Learning deep architectures for AI. Found. Trends Mach. Learn. **2**(1), 1–81 (2009). (S1935-8237)
4. Zhang, C., Zhang, Z.: Improving multiview face detection with multi-task deep convolutional neural networks. In: IEEE Winter Application and Computer Vision Conference, USA, pp. 1036–1041 (2014)
5. Längkvist, M., Karlsson, L., Loutfi, A.: A review of unsupervised feature learning and deep learning for time-series modeling. Patt. Recogn. Lett. **42**, 11–24 (2014). (S0167-8655)
6. Dahl, G.E., Sainath, T.N., Hinton, G.E.: Improving deep neural networks for LVCSR using rectified linear units and dropout. In: IEEE International Conference on Acoustics, Speech and Signal Processing, Vancouver, Canada, pp. 8609–8613 (2013)
7. Bertalmío, M., Sapiro, G., Caselles, V., et al.: Image inpainting. In: Conference on Computer Graphics and Interactive Techniques, pp. 417–424. DBLP (2000)
8. Chan, T., Shen, J.: Mathematical models for local non-texture inpaintings. SIAM J. Appl. Math. **62**(3), 1019–1043 (2001)
9. Criminisi, A., Perez, P., Toyama, K.: Region filling and object removal by exemplar-based image inpainting. IEEE Trans. Image Process. **13**(9), 1200–1212 (2004)
10. Komodakis, N., Tziritas, G.: Image completion using global optimization. In: Computer Vision and Pattern Recognition, pp. 442–452 (2006)
11. Hsin, H.F., Leou, J.J., Lin, C.S., et al.: Image inpainting using structure-guided priority belief propagation and label transformations, pp. 4492–4495 (2010)
12. Pathak, D., Krahenbuhl, P., Donahue, J., et al.: Context encoders: feature learning by inpainting, pp. 2536–2544 (2016)
13. Yang, C., Lu, X., Lin, Z., et al.: High-resolution image inpainting using multi-scale neural patch synthesis (2016)
14. Huanga, R., Chang, L., Guoqi, L., et al.: Adaptive deep supervised autoencoder based image reconstruction for face recognition (2016)
15. Rumelhart, D.E., Hinton, G.E., Williams, R.J.: Learning representations by back-propagating errors. Nature **323**, 533–536 (1986)
16. Pearson, K.: Mathematical contributions to the theory of evolution (III): regression, heredity, and panmixia. Philos. Trans. Royal Soc. Lond. Ser. A Containing Pap. Math. Phys. Charact. **187**, 253–318 (1895)

A Novel Fragile Watermarking Scheme for 2D Vector Map Authentication

Guoyin Zhang, Qingan Da, Liguo Zhang, Jianguo Sun[✉], Qilong Han,
Liang Kou, and WenShan Wang

Harbin Engineering University, Harbin, China
sunjianguo@hrbeu.edu.cn

Abstract. In this paper, we use a grouping method and feature marking to ensure a good localization accuracy. Then, on the basis of vertex insertion and an embedding strategy that can resist rotation, translation and scaling (RST) attacks, we design a group correlation method. And the RST invariant authentication information are generated with the log-polar transformation (LPT) and encryption technology. We construct two datasets and the invisibility, validity and localization ability are demonstrated through experiments. It can resist the batch features deletion attack accurately and mark out the deleted group.

Keywords: Fragile watermarking · Tamper localization
2D vector map · Batch features deletion

1 Introduction

In recent years, digital vector map has been widely employed in military mapping, GPS navigation, marine development and other fields. However, there are some data security issues in the promotion of digital maps, such as malicious tampering and illegal copying. Then, fragile watermarking technology has become a popular choice to solve these problems [1,2]. It is used to judge the authenticity and integrity of digital works, such as medical image, audio and digital map. According to the embedding position of the watermark, the fragile watermarking algorithm is divided into two categories, one is frequency-based method and the other is spatial-based method.

Some algorithms are embedding the fragile watermark in the frequency domain. In [3], the perceived hash value was embedded in the wavelet sub-band of the carrier data. In [4], a semi-fragile watermarking algorithm based on frequency domain transform embedded the authentication information into high frequency region. These two watermarking strategies can accomplish the purpose of tamper detection, but these algorithms always have high complexity. Li *et al.* used group-based wavelet quantization and proposed another semi-fragile watermarking scheme which can provide good accuracy of tamper localization [5]. But it

© Springer International Publishing AG, part of Springer Nature 2018
B. Zeng et al. (Eds.): PCM 2017, LNCS 10736, pp. 880–889, 2018.
https://doi.org/10.1007/978-3-319-77383-4_86

requires a large image block to ensure a certain degree of robustness. Therefore, the localization accuracy of this watermark strategy will be reduced.

There are lots of spatial-based fragile watermarking strategies in previous studies. In [6], a near-lossless data hiding method for images was proposed, it has the flexibility to control the embedding distortion. However, this method can't guarantee a good tamper localization accuracy. Shi *et al.* proposed a region-adaptive semi-fragile dual watermarking scheme which provided anti-deletion ability [7]. However the capacity of watermark is not very abundant in practical application. In [8], the Douglas algorithm was used to simplify the map before the watermark embedding phase. This method allows users to compress the map, but the contents of the map were damaged to a certain degree. In addition, Neyman *et al.* divided a vector map into groups first on the basis of the number of vertices on the polyline [9]. The fragile watermark was embedded in the coordinates of data points with the least significant bit (LSB) technique. This scheme achieves good localization accuracy, but the addition or deletion attack is easy to affect the grouping result in watermark detection phase and result in failure of test results. To solve this problem, they created additional vertices for each feature to embed watermarks and achieved the purpose of locating geometric attacks on received vector map [10]. Nevertheless, the feature rearrangement or vertex reversing operation may totally disable the localization capability. Wang *et al.* designed a reversible fragile watermarking scheme based on virtual coordinates, which was characterized by high capacity and low complexity [11]. However, this strategy is easily limited in practical applications due to lacking of RST invariance. To this end, they used a watermark embedding strategy proposed by Chou and Tseng [12], and designed a signature technique to enhance the accuracy of positioning [13]. Afterwards, they divide the features into different blocks and embed the watermark based on virtual coordinates and concentric circles technology [14]. Similarly, the method used in [15] is to embed group watermark and object watermark into each object. However, these schemes may not be able to detect the batch features deletion attack and then result in passing a dummy authentication.

In order to solve these problems, we propose a feature group correlation technique to detect the missing group, apply it to the fragile watermarking scheme for 2D vector map. In this scheme, we divide the spatial features into groups and apply the marking method to each feature. Then we use the correlation mark to mark each feature group. After that, we generate a RST invariant watermark and embed it with the method proposed in [12]. In the watermark authentication phase, we can identify the partial data of the missing group by the correlation mark of the feature group. In order to detect the exact location of the tampered content, the system will compare the extracted watermark with the reproduced watermark. Besides, our watermarking scheme inherits the RST invariance.

2 The Proposed Watermarking Method

The content authentication scheme designed in this paper applies to both the line layers and area layers of the digital map. Figure 1 shows the implementation method of digital map authentication system.

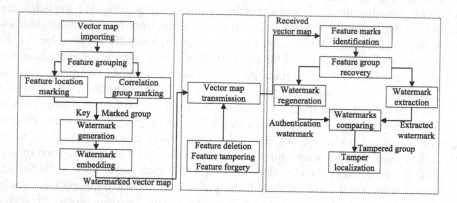

Fig. 1. The implementation model of the proposed fragile watermark algorithm

2.1 Pretreatment for Vector Map

Before the pretreatment process, it is necessary to introduce the theoretical basis [12] of this paper. There are three vertices V_m, V_q and V_s in a plane. In order to hide the watermark $m(0 \leq m < S_m, S_m = 1, 2, 3, ...)$ in V_m, two parameters are set, one is the embedding parameter S_m and the other is K_m used to adjust the maximum distortion. We called the three vertices as watermark-hiding vertex, quantization vertex and standard vertex. First, move the position Q_m so that the Euclidean distance between V_m and V_q is qualified, and the new location V_w^e is obtained.

$$\begin{cases} Q_m = \|V_s V_q\| / K_m \\ V_m^e = V_m - \frac{V_m - V_q}{\|V_m V_q\|} \cdot (\|V_m V_q\| \, mod Q_m), \end{cases} \tag{1}$$

where Q_m is the standard quantization. Second the identification information m is hidden by the offset of the vertex V_m^e and the final position $V_m{}'$ of the watermark vertex is obtained.

$$V_m{}' = V_m^e + \frac{V_m^e - V^q}{\|V_m^e V^q\|} \cdot \frac{Q_m}{S_m} \cdot m. \tag{2}$$

From the method in [12], we can find that the distortion caused by the hidden watermark is less than Q_m. The proposed authentication system has two inputs which are used to set the length of the watermark L and the number of watermark bits a vertex carries c. According to certain attributes, the polylines in the layers are first divided into different groups. And the location of each polyline is identified using the location ID [13]. These marks are hidden into the vertices of the corresponding polylines, which are named as landmarks. Then, in order to achieve the ability to resist the batch feature deletion attack, feature groups should be correlated together. We hide some of the information called the correlation tags in the vertices of the corresponding group which are called as synergy vertices. In this paper, the vertices are divided into two categories, one is used to carry the authentication information (called watermark vertices) and the other is called non-watermark vertices. So we not only need a landmark to hide the location ID, a pair of synergy vertices to carry the correlation tag, but also need a standard vertex and a quantization vertex. These five vertices belong to non-watermark vertices, therefore, only with at least $\lceil L/c \rceil + 5$ vertex's, can a polyline have enough space to hide the authentication information. We call this polyline as an standard polyline.

For a polyline layer L with Z polylines, we first combine the standard poly-lines with the non-standard polylines orderly to obtain a number of polyline groups. The group size is $n(n \geq 1)$. Each group contains at least one standard polyline as the first polyline of each group and we call it as a watermark polyline. The second vertex on the watermark polyline is called parameter1 vertex and the penultimate vertex on it is called parameter2 vertex.

Next, we assign the location ID to each polyline. The total number of groups is $N_g = \lceil Z/n \rceil$. For the $q^{th}(1 \leq q \leq n)$ polyline in the $p^{th}(0 \leq p \leq N_g - 1)$ group, we set its location ID as $m_{p,q} = p \times n + q$.

In order to detect the location of the missing group, we associate the groups with following method. We suppose there are two correlated group $G_p(0 \leq p \leq N_g - 1)$ and $G_q(q = (p+1) \mod N_g)$, whose parameter1 vertices are $v_{1,w}^p(v_{1,w}^{p,x}, v_{1,w}^{p,y})$ and $v_{1,w}^q(v_{1,w}^{q,x}, v_{1,w}^{q,y})$, respectively. The relationship between the two vertices is represented by a vector $\overrightarrow{v_{1,w}^p v_{1,w}^q}$. We denote the distance between them as $l_{p,q}^1$ and convert this data to $d_{p,q}^1 = \log_2 l_{p,q}^q$, express the angle of incli-nation of the vector as $\theta_{p,q}^1$. We embed these information of the offset vector into the synergy vertices. Similarly, the information of offset vector between the parameter2 vertices in G_p and the one in G_q as $d_{p,q}^2$ and $\theta_{p,q}^2$. For a polyline group, we embed parameter1 vertex's tags of the associated group in watermark polyline, embed parameter2 vertex's tags in non-watermark polyline.

2.2   Watermark Embedding

Since at least five vertices are required to mark the polyline, we divide the poly-lines in L into five categories. They are normal polyline (more than 4 vertices), four-points polyline (4 vertices), three-points polyline (3 vertices) and two-points polyline (2 vertices). Figure 2 shows the embedding results of feature's marks, where $m_{i,j}(0 \leq i \leq N_g - 1, 1 \leq j \leq n, m_{i,j} \in [1, Z])$ is the location ID of poly-line which is as an example, v' is used to indicate the order of vertices on the polyline. And we unified d and $\theta(\theta \in [0, 360))$ to represent the correlation tags. Here we focus on the hiding method of correlation tags.

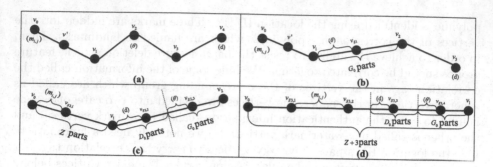

Fig. 2. Method of marking the location for different types of polylines

In order to hide the correlation tags through exist vertices, as shown in Fig. 2(b), according to Eqs. (1) and (2), we embed d into v_3 by regarding the vertices v_1, v_2 and v_3 as the standard vertex, the quantization vertex and watermark-hiding vertex, respectively. The parameter $K_m = len_{max}/\tau$ is defined, where len_{max} is the maximum length of the polylines in the layer L, and τ is the accuracy tolerance of the layer. And we denote the maximum distance of the reference vertex pair in the map as D_0, define a parameter as $S_m = \log_2 D_0$. As shown above, the distortion caused by the hidden information dose not exceed τ, so the hiding method is still able to guarantee the quality of the digital map.

If there is no extra vertices for the embedding of the correlation tags, we need to insert an additional vertex to hide the associated information through the distance between the vertices. Figure 2(b) is still taken as an example. The distance between $v_1(v_1^x, v_1^y)$ and $v_2(v_2^x, v_2^y)$ is first divided into G_0 intervals which is set as 360. We insert vertex $v_{S1}(v_{S1}^x, v_{S1}^y)$ between v_1 and v_2, use the distance between v_1 and the inserted vertex v_{S1} to represent θ. Since the redundant vertex is inserted in a straight line, it is still able to guarantee the quality of the map.

Then, for each marked group G_i^m, assuming that its watermark polyline is Pl^m, according to the watermark generation method in [13], we use all non-watermark vertices of G_i^m to generate authentication information $H_i = \{h_i | h_i \in \{0, 1\}, j \in [0, L-1]\}$ with RST invariance.

Finally, the authentication information H_i is embedded into watermark vertices of the corresponding group. As mentioned earlier, the vertices from v_3 to v_{p+2} ($p = \lceil L/c \rceil$) is used to hide authentication information. According to the input c, H_i is divided into several watermark fragments. These fragments are embedded into watermark vertices in order and the parameter1 vertex and the parameter2 vertex are used as standard vertex and quantization vertex. The parameter S_w is set as 2^c. Finally, each watermark fragment is embedded in the watermark polyline of the group G_i^m. When all the marked groups on the map are processed, the watermarked version L^w is obtained.

2.3   Watermark Authentication

Different types of polylines have different properties. When the number of vertices on a polyline is fewer than 6, the polyline's location ID is deemed invalid and it is detected as tampered directly. When the number of vertices on a polyline is greater than 6, we see it as a possible marked normal polyline. For a polyline Pl^w with only six vertices, we identify its type with the following rules.

First, check if the six vertices of Pl^w are on the same line, if so, see it as a possible marked two-points polyline. Second, check if the first 3 adjacent vertices starting at one end and the first 4 adjacent vertices starting at the other end of Pl^w are collinear, respectively, if so, see it as a possible marked three-points polyline. Third, check if there are two groups of three-vertex collinear. If so, see it as a possible marked four-points polyline, otherwise, see it as a possible marked normal polyline.

Next, the marks and correlation tags of each polyline can be extracted according to the embedding position in Fig. 2. When the location ID of a polyline in the receiving map is known, it is easy to calculate its group number $i(0 \leq i \leq N_g - 1)$ and inner position $j(1 \leq j \leq n)$. Then we can restore the original group according to the position marks, traverse and find the missing group, derive important location information through the correlated group.

For any watermarked polyline group G_i^w, we can obtain parameter1 vertex v_{r1}', parameter2 vertex v_{r2}' and a list of watermark vertices $V_i^{w'} = \{v_j' | j \in [0, \lceil L/c \rceil - 1]\}$ from its watermark polyline. Given the setting of the parameters K_w and $S_w = 2^c$, we can extract the information from each watermark vertex and join them in sequence to get the watermark W_i for the current polyline group. Then, for each G_i^w, we use all non-watermark vertices in G_i^w to regenerate the watermark. Finally, the tampered group will be located accurately by comparing the extracted information with the regenerate one.

3   Experiments and Results

We run experiments on a PC with 2.80 GHz, RAM 4.00 GB, Win7 Ultimate, ArcGIS Version 10.2, ArcGIS Engine 10.2 and Visual C++6.0. We construct two datasets: one contains 40 vector maps and another contains 40 vector maps. These maps are taken from the samples of ArcGIS. The inputs are set as follows: the number of watermark bit a vertex carries $c = 8$, group size $n = 3$ and the watermark length $L = 128$.

3.1   Verification of Invisibility

Six vector maps of the first dataset are used to show the invisibility of our scheme. They are a railway map of Taiwan, southern California map, a river map of China XinJiang, a lake map of south part of China, a railway map of north part of China and a river map of north part of China. The precision tolerance τ of this three maps are 200, 6, 800, 500, 1250 and 1500, respectively.

Three test cases chosen from the first dataset are watermarked by the proposed algorithm, the watermarked versions are shown in Fig. 3. The original railway map of Taiwan is watermarked by our scheme yielding the watermarked map shown in Fig. 3(a). Because the geographic information of this test case is simple, it is easy to reflect that the improved scheme has good invisibility.

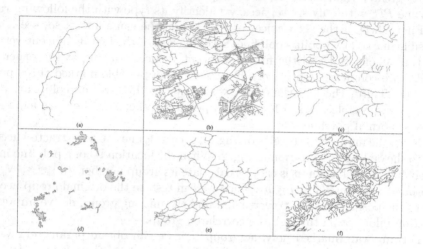

Fig. 3. The watermarked 2D vector maps

3.2   Verification of Validity

For a fragile watermarking scheme, the verification of the validity is more stringent than invisibility and it requires that disturbance caused by the hidden authentication information is within the allowable range of the error. In this paper, we use the maximum distortion $Maxd$ [13] to measure the objective quality of the embedded vector map. Figure 4 shows the results of three contrast algorithms for the validity of each test case. Due to the setting of the embedding parameter K_w, the introduced distortions do not exceed the precision tolerance. Therefore, the validity of the map data can be guaranteed.

3.3   Discussion of Localization Accuracy

In this section, we select a river map in the second dataset to test the localization capability of this algorithm as shown in Fig. 5(a). Figure 5 also shows the watermarked version, tampered version and the results of authentication. Expressly, we deleted 3 polylines from region 'A', deleted 3 polylines from region 'B' and deleted 2 polylines from region 'C'. The red marks is given to identify the location of the tampered group or the missing group. It can be seen that the results of tamper localization is accuracy.

In this section, we use two measures B and E(B) mentioned in [2]. B indicates the number of polylines that are detected after unauthorized tampered.

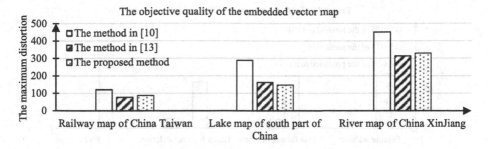

Fig. 4. The objective quality of the embedded vector map

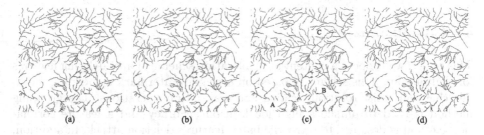

Fig. 5. The changes of a river map at different watermarked stages (Color figure online)

The expectation of β is denoted as $E(\beta)$, which is calculated to compare the localization accuracy of our algorithm with the ones proposed in [10,13].

In [10], Neyman *et al.* divide the polylines into different groups on the basis of the number of vertices on the polyline. But it is hard to evaluate the number of vertices within each polylines. For simplicity, we assume a vector map with 100 polylines is divided into 10 groups, each group has 10 features, the probability of adding/deleting operation of the features in i^{th} group is 1/10. In particular, the probability of the case that a whole group is deleted after removing a small number of features is 0. We assume 10 polylines are missing after the batch features deletion attack. These polylines are in the same group or in two different groups. The probability of these two cases is equal. When we calculate $E(\beta)$ for the method reported in [13], we assume that the probability that the added feature is regarded as a valid feature is 1/2.

Figure 6 shows that the expected values of the three watermarking algorithms under different attacks. The data show that the proposed watermarking algorithm in this paper can accurately locate the tampered place in the authentication phase after the addition or deletion of the feature on the watermark map. Our watermarking algorithm has invariance for the RST editing operations. In particular, this algorithm can detect batch feature deletion operations.

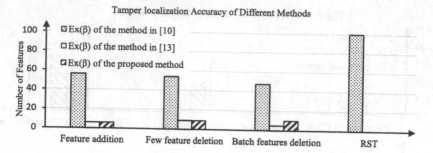

Fig. 6. Tamper localization accuracy of different methods

4 Conclusions

This paper, we propose a content authentication scheme of anti-deleting features for digital map. This scheme is based on a fragile watermark embedding methods that can resist rotation, scaling and translation operations. The grouping method is used to pursue a high localization accuracy and a feature correlation method is designed to resist the batch features deletion attack. In addition, the authentication information generated by the log-polar transformation technique can resist several editing operations such as vertex reversing and feature rearrangement.

Acknowledgments. This work was supported by project of NSFC of China (61202455, 61472096, 61501132).

References

1. Wang, N.N., Zhao, X., Xie, C.: RST invariant reversible watermarking for 2D vector map. Int. J. Multimed. Ubiquit. Eng. **11**(2), 265–276 (2016)
2. Wang, N.N., Men, C.G.: Reversible fragile watermarking for 2-D vector map authentication with localization. Comput. Aided Des. **44**(4), 320–330 (2012)
3. Weng, L., Darazi, R., Preneel, B., Macq, B., Dooms, A.: Robust image content authentication using perceptual hashing and watermarking. In: Lin, W., Xu, D., Ho, A., Wu, J., He, Y., Cai, J., Kankanhalli, M., Sun, M.-T. (eds.) PCM 2012. LNCS, vol. 7674, pp. 315–326. Springer, Heidelberg (2012). https://doi.org/10.1007/978-3-642-34778-8_29
4. Haojun, F.U., Zhu, C., Jian, M.: Multipurpose watermarking algorithm for digital raster map based on wavelet transformation. Acta Geod. Cartogr. Sin. **40**(3), 397–400 (2011)
5. Li, C., Ma, B., Wang, Y., Huang, D., Zhang, Z.: A secure semi-fragile self-recoverable watermarking algorithm using group-based wavelet quantization. In: Lin, W., Xu, D., Ho, A., Wu, J., He, Y., Cai, J., Kankanhalli, M., Sun, M.-T. (eds.) PCM 2012. LNCS, vol. 7674, pp. 327–336. Springer, Heidelberg (2012). https://doi.org/10.1007/978-3-642-34778-8_30

6. Fujiyoshi, M., Kiya, H.: Histogram-based near-lossless data hiding and its application to image compression. In: Ho, Y.-S., Sang, J., Ro, Y.M., Kim, J., Wu, F. (eds.) PCM 2015. LNCS, vol. 9315, pp. 225–235. Springer, Cham (2015). https://doi.org/10.1007/978-3-319-24078-7_22

7. Shi, H., Li, M.C., Guo, C., et al.: A region-adaptive semi-fragile dual watermarking scheme. Multimed. Tools Appl. **75**(1), 465–495 (2016)

8. Ren, N., Wang, Q., Zhu, C.: Selective authentication algorithm based on semi-fragile watermarking for vector geographical data. In: 22nd International Conference on GeoInformatics (2014)

9. Neyman, S.N., Sitohang, B., Cahyono, F.: An improvement technique of fragile watermarking to assurance the data integrity on vector maps. In: IC3INA, vol. 25, pp. 179–184. Springer (2013)

10. Neyman, S.N., Wijaya, Y.H., Sitohang, B.: A new scheme to hide the data integrity marker on vector maps using a feature-based fragile watermarking algorithm. In: International Conference on Data and Software Engineering (ICODSE) (2014)

11. Wang, N.N., Zhang, H., Men, C.G.: A high capacity reversible data hiding method for 2D vector maps based on virtual coordinates. Comput. Aided Des. **47**, 108–117 (2014)

12. Chou, C.M., Tseng, D.C.: Affine-transformation-invariant public fragile watermarking for 3D model authentication. IEEE Comput. Graph. Appl. **29**(2), 72–79 (2009)

13. Wang, N.N., Bian, J., Zhang, H.: RST invariant fragile watermarking for 2D vector map authentication. Int. J. Multimed. Ubiquit. Eng. **10**(4), 155–172 (2015)

14. Wang, N.N., Zhao, X., Zhang, H.: Block-based reversible fragile watermarking for 2D vector map authentication. Int. J. Digit. Crime Forensics **7**(3), 60–80 (2015)

15. Yue, M., Peng, Z., Peng, Y.: A fragile watermarking scheme for modification type characterization in 2D vector maps. In: Asia-Pacific Web Conference (2014)

Hybrid Domain Encryption Method of Hyperspectral Remote Sensing Image

Wenhao Geng[1], Jing Zhang[1(⊠)], Lu Chen[1], Jiafeng Li[1], and Li Zhuo[1,2]

[1] Signal and Information Processing Laboratory, Beijing University of Technology, Beijing, China
{gengwh, chenlu}@emails.bjut.edu.cn,
{zhj, lijiafeng, zhuoli}@bjut.edu.cn
[2] Collaborative Innovation Center of Electric Vehicles in Beijing, Beijing, China

Abstract. With the rapid development of remote sensing technology, hyperspectral remote sensing image as foundation data containing abundant sensitive information has been widely applied in many fields, such as agriculture, resources, ocean, city, and environment, etc. A hybrid domain encryption method is proposed for securely transmitting and storing hyperspectral remote sensing images. Considering the spatial and spectral characteristics, the hyperspectral image is encrypted in hybrid domain (spatial and spectral). Spatial domain encryption is done by using the composite chaos sequences. Then, the spectral sequence is scrambled by the cipher sequence for protecting the spectral feature of the hyperspectral image. Finally, the spectral and spatial information is mixed by a one-to-one mapping. Experimental results on NASA datasets show that our method can effectively protect both spectral and spatial feature of hyperspectral image compared with the other methods.

Keywords: Remote sensing · Hyperspectral image · Encryption
Hybrid domain · Recombination chaos sequences

1 Introduction

In recent years, hyperspectral imaging has been an active area of remote sensing research and development, which can image the same ground object with several tens to hundreds of spectral bands from ultraviolet to the microwave range [1–3]. Because hyperspectral remote sensing image as foundation data containing abundant sensitive information has been widely applied in many fields, such as agriculture, resources, ocean, city, and environment, etc., it is very necessary to ensure to securely transmit and store hyperspectral remote sensing images (hyperspectral image for short).

Image encryption is a technique to prevent the information leakage of the image by using the characteristics of digital images [4]. Researchers have proposed hundreds of encryption algorithms for common image [5–7]. It has been proved that image encryption based on chaos theory can achieve better performance [8, 9], which uses the chaotic characteristic to transform the pixel values. But with the development of image encryption technology, the encryption effect of chaotic system based on a single chaotic sequence shows weaker obviously. Therefore, composite chaos containing two chaos sequences become a new solution to improve the security of image encryption.

Nowadays, remote sensing image encryption has attracted more attention due to the abundant information of surface features, but there is little research about hyperspectral images. Huang et al. [10] proposed an encryption scheme using chaotic system to build up the compressed sensing framework. A two-dimensional generalized Arnold map is adopted to protect the remote sensing image. Yin et al. [11] proposed to use secured TD-ERCS chaotic model to shuffle important EZW coefficients. Muhaya et al. [12] proposed a secure satellite image encryption technique based on chaotic and Advanced Encryption Standard (AES) techniques. These methods can protect the spatial information of the remote sensing images effectively, but ignore the important spectral information of the hyperspectral image. Considering high dimensionality and spectral characteristics of hyperspectral image, traditional encryption methods for common images [13–15] cannot be directly utilized to protect both spectral and spatial information of hyperspectral image.

In this paper, a hybrid domain encryption method of hyperspectral remote sensing image is proposed by combining spatial domain encryption and spectral domain encryption in order to ensure the security of hyperspectral image. Considering the spatial and spectral characteristics, the hyperspectral image is encrypted in hybrid domain (spatial and spectral). Spatial domain encryption is done by using the composite chaos sequences. Then, the spectral sequence is scrambled by the cipher sequence in spectral domain. Finally, the spectral and spatial information is mixed by a one-to-one mapping.

The remainder of this paper is organized as follows: Sect. 2 states the hybrid domain encryption method in detail, which includes spatial domain encryption, spectral domain encryption and hybrid domain encryption. Experimental results are analyzed in Sect. 3 and the conclusions are drawn in Sect. 4.

2 Hybrid Domain Encryption

As we know, hyperspectral image contains both spectral and spatial features. Traditional image encryption method only protects the spatial domain information, which is not security enough for hyperspectral image once the spectral information leakage. Therefore, we propose to encrypt the hyperspectral image in hybrid domain. The overall architecture is shown in Fig. 1. Firstly, we use composite chaos to encrypt the hyperspectral image in spatial domain. Then the spectral bands are scrambled by the cipher sequence. Finally, the spatial and spectral feature is scrambled by domain mixing encryption.

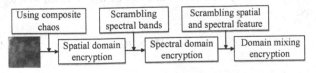

Fig. 1. The process of proposed encryption method.

2.1   Encryption in Spatial Domain

Generally, hyperspectral image encryption in spatial domain is accomplished by changing pixels' values or scrambling the position of pixels. As above mentioned, the security of single chaos sequence is not appropriate enough. Therefore, composite chaos is used in hyperspectral image encryption in spatial domain.

In this paper, the composite chaos is used to obtain the secret key. The composite chaos is composed of chaotic sequence generated by Logistic Map and Chebyshev Map.

Logistic Map: The Logistic Map is described as follows:

$$x_{n+1} = \mu x_n (1 - x_n) \tag{1}$$

where $\mu \in (0, 4]$, $x_i \in (0, 1)$. When $\mu \in (3.5699456..., 4]$, the Logistic Map works in chaos state. The sequence $\{x_i, i = 1, 2, 3,...\}$, generated by the initial value x_0, is non-periodic, non-convergence and sensitive to the initial value.

Chebyshev Map: The Chebyshev Map is described as follows:

$$x_{n+1} = \cos(k \arccos(x_n)) \tag{2}$$

where k is nonlinear strength coefficient of the system. When $k \geq 2$, the Chebyshev Map works in chaos state. The chaos sequence $\{x_i, i = 1, 2, 3,...\}$ is generated by the initial value x_0.

Let $\mathbf{L}(l_1, l_2, l_3,...)$ be the sequence of Logistic Map and $\mathbf{C}(c_1, c_2, c_3,...)$ be the sequence of Chebyshev Map. The composite chaos is generated by:

$$\mathbf{R} = \mathbf{L} \cdot \mathbf{C} \tag{3}$$

where $\mathbf{R}(r_1, r_2, r_3,...)$ is the composite chaos and $r_i = l_i \times c_i$.

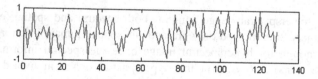

Fig. 2. The composite chaos.

Figure 2 shows the composite chaos generated by two chaos sequences. As can be seen in Fig. 2, the value range of the composite chaos is $[-1, 1]$. To compute with pixel values (all integers), the composite chaos need to be transformed to integers, which can be expressed as:

$$\mathbf{Z} = \lfloor \mathbf{R} \times n \rfloor \tag{4}$$

where $\mathbf{Z}(z_1, z_2, z_3,...)$ is the integers sequence, $\mathbf{R}$ is the composite chaos, n is a integer which is related to the image pixels values and $\lfloor \rfloor$ is rounding down process. Equation (4) can transform the value to integer at the same value range with pixel values. Then we use sequence $\mathbf{Z}(z_1, z_2, z_3,...)$ to encrypt the hyperspectral remote sensing image in spatial domain. Specific procedures are as follows:

Step 1: The parameter μ of Logistic Map, the parameter k of Chebyshev Map and the initial values l_1 and c_1 are determined first.

Step 2: To improve the key sensitivity, we introduce the auxiliary key Ak computed by the input images, which is defined as:

$$Ak = \frac{\mathrm{mod}(\sum I_i, 256)}{256} \qquad (5)$$

where Ak is the auxiliary key and I_i is the pixel values of the input image. Then the new initial values l'_1 and c'_1 is obtained by multiplying l_1 and c_1 by Ak. Due to Ak is computed by pixel values, the initial values will be changed with different input images, which can improve the sensitivity of the initial values.

Step 3: The sequences of Logistic Map and Chebyshev Map are generated by the new initial values l'_1 and c'_1 according to Eqs. 1 and 2. Here we introduce an integer S to change the range of the chaos sequences. Let n be the number of the pixels of the input image. The chaos sequences are generated by iterating $n + S - 1$ times. Then the first S elements are dropped and the rest sequences can generate the final secret sequence $\mathbf{Z}(z_1, z_2, z_3,...)$ according to Eq. 3 to Eq. 5.

Step 4: Due to $\mathbf{Z}(z_1, z_2, z_3,...)$ is a integer sequence, the pixels' values of input image are computed by:

$$x'_i = x_i \wedge z_i \qquad (6)$$

where $\wedge$ is Binary XOR operation, x_i is the pixel values of original image, z_i belongs to $\mathbf{Z}(z_1, z_2, z_3,...)$. Then sequence $\mathbf{Z}'(z_1, z_2, z_3,...z_{M+N})$ is gained from $\mathbf{Z}(z_1, z_2, z_3,...)$ which is used to scramble the position of the pixels, which is defined as:

$$X = \begin{cases} m_i \rightarrow z_i, & i \in [1, M] \\ n_i \downarrow z_i, & i \in [M+1, M+N] \end{cases} \qquad (7)$$

where $\rightarrow$ and $\downarrow$ are the cyclic shift operation of right orientation and down orientation, m_i and n_i are the column vector and row vector of the image, $z_i \in \mathbf{Z}'(z_1, z_2, z_3,... z_{M+N})$.

2.2 Encryption in Spectral Domain

Hyperspectral images are acquired simultaneously in dozens of narrow, adjacent wave-length bands. A continuous spectrum can be extracted from endmembers, which can be used to identify surface materials [1]. Therefore, hyperspectral images contain much sensitive information including minerals, city construction, military base and so on. While traditional encryption methods for remote sensing images ignore to further protect the spectral information which increase the risk of spectral information leakage. A hyperspectral image is made up of hundreds of 2D images which are ranked by the spectrum order. Hence, the spectral information can be protected by changing the spectral bands order. In this section, we propose to scramble the spectral bands order of the hyperspectral image with secret key. The procedures can be summarized as follows:

> **Step 1:** The secret key is obtained by the final secret sequence $\mathbf{Z}(z_1, z_2, z_3,...)$, which is computed in Sect. 2.1.
>
> **Step 2:** Let the hyperspectral image includes n spectral bands. Then n values are selected from $\mathbf{Z}(z_1, z_2, z_3,...)$, which is $\mathbf{Z}''(z_1, z_2, z_3,..., z_n)$.
>
> **Step 3:** As Eq. 8, a matrix $[\mathbf{B}\ \mathbf{Z}'']$ is constructed by sequence $\mathbf{Z}''$ and band order $\mathbf{B}$. Then the matrix is transformed by reranking $\mathbf{Z}'$ in descending order, and we gain a new vector $\mathbf{B}'$ which is the new band order.

$$[\mathbf{BZ}''] \xrightarrow{Rank\mathbf{Z}''} [\mathbf{B}'\mathbf{Z}''']. \tag{8}$$

2.3 Encryption by Domain Mixing

The hyperspectral remote sensing image is a 3D data. Therefore, the analytical approach of cube data may acquire the information of a hyperspectral image. Considering the hyperspectral image contain both spatial and spectral information, and the spatial domain is orthogonal to spectral domain, correlation of two domains is changed to improve the security. Here we introduce to use a Mapping method to shuffle the two domains. The mapping mode is shown in Fig. 3.

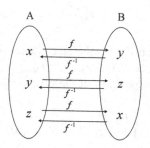

Fig. 3. The mapping mode of domain confusion.

Let a pixel in a hyperspectral image be $X(x, y, z)$. As we can see in Fig. 3, the x value is mapping to y-axis, the y value is mapping to z-axis and the z value is mapping to x-axis, which is defined as:

$$X(x, y, z) \xrightarrow{Mapping} X'(y, z, x) \tag{9}$$

Then the spectral and spatial domains are mixed together and the correlation of two domains is broken. This process can disturb the attacker and prevent the space analysis of the hyperspectral remote sensing image, which leads to further security. To prove the security of our method, the encryption results and analysis will be shown in the next section.

3 Experimental Results and Analysis

In order to evaluate the encryption performance of our method, we conducted experiments with a collection of the high-resolution hyperspectral data sets obtained from German Aerospace Center's (DLR) in Oberpfaffenhofen in Germany and NASA over the World Trade Center (WTC) area in New York. The AVIRIS images contain more than 125 spectral bands between 0.4 and 2.5 μm. The spatial resolution is 20 m, and the spectral resolution is 10 nm. The experimental platform is a PC with 3.30 GHz CPU, 4.00 G memory, Windows 7 operating system. Our dataset contains more than 2000 hyperspectral remote sensing images with different size of images.

In this experiment, we set the initial values of the Logistic Map and Chebyshev Map to 0.32. The parameter μ of Logistic Map is set to 4 and the parameter k of Chebyshev Map is set to 20. And the size of the image is $512 \times 614 \times 224$. Two different single chaotic sequences for image encryption [9] and an encryption method based on AES [12] are compared. In the next section, some well-known security analysis techniques are considered as quality measurement factors such as Histogram analysis, Correlation of adjacent pixels Information entropy, Key space analysis and Key sensitivity analysis.

3.1 Histogram Analysis

To prevent information leakage, it is important to ensure that the encrypted image and original image do not have any statistics similarities. The histogram reflects the distribution of the pixel values which is attacked most. As can be seen in Fig. 4, the histogram of the original image contains continuous rises and declines, while the histogram of encrypted image shows uniform distribution. The results show that our method has stronger ability to resist statistical analysis and attacks.

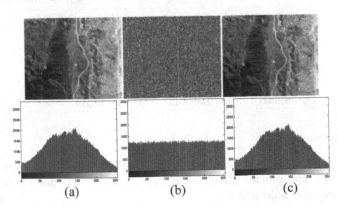

(a)   (b)   (c)

Fig. 4. The encryption results: (a) the original image, (b) the encrypted image, (c) the decrypted image.

3.2 Correlation of Adjacent Pixels

The high correlation between adjacent pixels is one of the major feature of an image. Therefore, the correlation between adjacent pixels of the encrypted image is broken to improve the security. Figure 5 shows the pixel correlation in vertical direction of our method. As can be seen that the points in the figure are uniform distribution after encrypted.

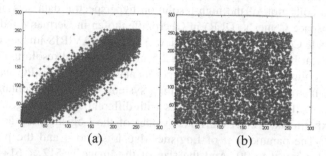

(a)   (b)

Fig. 5. The pixel correlation in vertical direction: (a) the original image, (b) the encrypted image.

Correlation coefficient can reflect the correlation between pixels objectively. First, $E(x)$ is the means of series x_i. Correlation coefficient r is described as:

$$r_{x,y} = \frac{\sum_{i-1}^{N} (x_i - E(x))(y_i - E(y))}{\sqrt{\sum_{i-1}^{N} (x_i - E(x))^2} \sqrt{\sum_{i-1}^{N} (y_i - E(y))^2}} \tag{10}$$

The correlation coefficients of the encrypted image in vertical and horizontal direction is shown in Table 1. The results show that the correlation of encrypted image is very low, and our method and AES-256 are much better.

Table 1. The correlation coefficients of different encryption methods.

Encryption method	Vertical direction	Horizontal direction
Original image	0.973810	0.977445
Logistic Map [9]	0.025141	0.017214
Chebyshev Map [9]	0.032118	0.022741
AES-256 [12]	0.010221	0.013217
Our method	0.010012	0.012014

3.3 Information Entropy

Information entropy was first proposed by Shannon [16, 17]. The entropy and related information measures provide useful descriptions of the random process behavior. The information entropy is defined as:

$$H(m) = \sum_{i=0}^{2N-1} P(m_i)\log_2 \frac{1}{P(m_i)} \tag{11}$$

The calculated information entropy value is given in Fig. 6. The value obtained from the computed experiment results is very near to the theoretical ideal value of 8. And our method and AES-256 has a great impact and improve the security level.

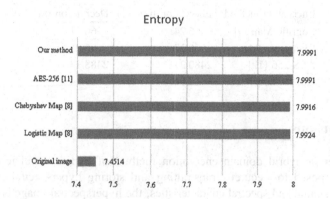

Fig. 6. The information entropy of different encryption methods

3.4 Key Space Analysis

To secure hyperspectral image from brute-force and similar attacks, the key space should be large enough. In our method, the key consists of initial values of Logistic and Chebyshev Map, parameter μ and k. Due to the value range of μ, k and initial values, the key space is more than 10^{28}. Therefore, the key space is large enough to reduce the risk of a brute-force attack.

3.5 Key Sensitivity Analysis

The encryption algorithm should be sensitive to the secret key. The change of a single bit in the secret key should produce completely different output results. In our method, the key sensitivity is related to the initial values and parameters sensitivity for the chaotic sequences. As can be seen in Fig. 7, the initial values and k changing a little will produce a completely different chaotic sequences. This can be explained by the fact that Chebyshev Map is sensitive to the initial value.

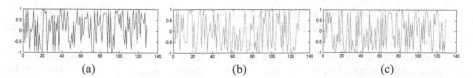

(a)   (b)   (c)

Fig. 7. The chaos sequences: (a) $x_1 = 0.4113$, $k = 20$, (b) $x_1 = 0.4113001$, (c) $k = 20.000001$.

3.6 Performance Analysis

Besides the security analysis by evaluating statistical analysis and measurements, the time consumption is also an important issue. From Fig. 7, Tables 1 and 2, the security of our method and AES-256 is stronger, but the time consumption of AES-256 is much higher than other methods. Therefore, our method has a better performance.

Table 2. Time consumption results for different encryption methods.

Encryption method	Encryption time (s)	Decryption time (s)
Logistic Map [9]	66.24	66.21
Chebyshev Map [9]	66.17	66.05
AES-256 [12]	2480.21	2488.13
Our method	67.96	67.74

4 Conclusions

In this paper, a hybrid domain encryption method of hyperspectral remote sensing image is proposed for securely transmitting and storing hyperspectral images. Considering the spatial and spectral characteristics, the hyperspectral image is encrypted in hybrid domain (spatial and spectral). Spatial domain encryption is done by using the composite chaos sequences. Then, the spectral sequence is scrambled by the cipher sequence for protecting the spectral feature of the hyperspectral image. Finally, the spectral and spatial information is mixed by a one-to-one mapping. Three methods are compared in our experiments, our method was successfully implemented and showed a better encryption performance for hyperspectral image. In the future work, we will further reduce the correlation between adjacent pixels and enlarge the key space by improving the construction to enhance the security of our proposed method.

Acknowledgments. The work in this paper is supported by the National Natural Science Foundation of China (No. 61370189, No. 61531006, No. 61372149, and No. 61471013), the Beijing Natural Science Foundation (No. 4163071), the Science and Technology Development Program of Beijing Education Committee (No. KM201510005004), the Importation and Development of High-Caliber Talents Project of Beijing Municipal Institutions (No. CIT&TCD20150311), Funding Project for Academic Human Resources Development in Institutions of Higher Learning Under the Jurisdiction of Beijing Municipality.

References

1. Smith, R.B.: Introduction to Hyperspectral Imaging, pp. 1–24. Microimages (2006)
2. Zhang, E., Zhang, X., Yang, S.: Improving hyperspectral image classification using spectral information divergence. IEEE Geosci. Remote Sens. Lett. **11**(1), 249–253 (2014)
3. Veganzones, M., Tochon, G., Dalla-Mura, M., Plaza, A., Chanussot, J.: Hyperspectral image segmentation using a new spectral unmixing-based binary partition tree representation. IEEE Trans. Image Process. **23**(8), 3574–3589 (2014)

4. Chen, G., Mao, Y., Chui, C.K.: A symmetric image encryption scheme based on 3D chaotic cat maps. Chaos, Solitons & Fractals **2**(3), 749–776 (2004)
5. Cao, W., Zhou, Y., Chen, C.P., Xia, L.: Medical image encryption using edge maps. Sign. Process. **132**, 96–109 (2017)
6. Zhang, S., Gao, T.: An image encryption scheme based on DNA coding and permutation of hyper-image. Multimed. Tools Appl. **75**(24), 17157–17170 (2016)
7. Ayoup, A.M., Hussein, A.H., Attia, M.A.: Efficient selective image encryption. Multimed. Tools Appl. **75**(24), 17171–17186 (2016)
8. Yi, X., Tan, C.H., Siew, C.K.: A new block cipher based on chaotic tent maps. IEEE Trans. Circ. Syst. I Fundam. Theory Appl. **49**(12), 1826–1829 (2002)
9. Usama, M., Khan, M.K., Alghathbar, K., Lee, C.: Chaos-based secure satellite imagery cryptosystem. Comput. Math Appl. **60**(2), 326–337 (2010)
10. Huang, X., Ye, G., Chai, H., Xie, O.: Compression and encryption for remote sensing image using chaotic system. Secur. Commun. Netw. **8**(18), 3659–3666 (2015)
11. Yin, L., Zhao, J., Duan, Y.: Encryption scheme for remote sensing images based on EZW and chaos. In: The 9th International Conference for Young Computer Scientists, Hunan, China, pp. 1601–1605 (2008)
12. Muhaya, F.T.B.: Chaotic and AES cryptosystem for satellite imagery. Telecommun. Syst. **52**(2), 573–581 (2013)
13. Liu, Z., Xu, L., Liu, T., Chen, H., Li, P., Lin, C., Liu, S.: Color image encryption by using Arnold transform and color-blend operation in discrete cosine transform domains. Opt. Commun. **284**(1), 123–128 (2011)
14. Zhou, N., Wang, Y., Gong, L., He, H., Wu, J.: Novel single-channel color image encryption algorithm based on chaos and fractional Fourier transform. Opt. Commun. **284**(12), 2789–2796 (2011)
15. Tan, R.C., Lei, T., Zhao, Q.M., Gong, L.H., Zhou, Z.H.: Quantum color image encryption algorithm based on a hyper-chaotic system and quantum Fourier transform. Int. J. Theor. Phys. **55**(12), 5368–5384 (2016)
16. Shannon, C.E.: A mathematical theory of communication. Bell Syst. Tech. J. **27**(3), 379–423, 623–656 (1948)
17. Shannon, C.E.: Coding theorems for a discrete source with a fidelity criterion. IRE Nat. Convention Rec. **7**, 142–163 (1959)

Anomaly Detection with Passive Aggressive Online Gaussian Model Estimation

Zheran Hong, Bin Liu[(✉)], and Nenghai Yu

Key Laboratory of Electromagnetic Space Information,
Chinese Academy of Science, School of Information Science and Technology,
University of Science and Technology of China, Hefei, China
flowice@ustc.edu.cn

Abstract. Anomaly detection is an important topic for surveillance video analysis and public security management. One of the major challenges comes from the fact that there is no abnormal data for training in most cases. Gaussian modelling has proven to be one of the most successful approaches to solve this one-class classification problem. Existing algorithms load features of all the training data and learn the Gaussian model in an offline way, which consumes a lot of memory and training time. Besides, they cannot handle the normal streaming data with varying patterns over time in real scenarios. In this paper, we propose an anomaly detection algorithm with passive aggressive online Gaussian model estimation. The algorithm is able to reduce the memory occupation and training time significantly without loss of model discriminability. The online learning strategy can also well adapt to the varying patterns. According to the experiments, the proposed algorithm can cut off over 99% memory occupation and 80% training time consumption.

Keywords: Anomaly detection · Passive aggressive online learning

1 Introduction

Nowadays, the almost omnipresent surveillance cameras play a critical role in public security management, which put forward an urgent demand on intelligent computer algorithms to help analyze the huge and increasing number of surveillance videos, alleviating the heavy reliance on manual inspection. Anomaly detection is one of the most important task in surveillance video analysis, which means to detect the abnormal events or behaviors in videos.

However, anomaly detection is a complex and difficult problem due to the following challenges: (1) Different from other computer vision problems like segmentation or tracking, the definition of anomalies or anomalous behaviors is not clear. Many suspicious behaviors like theft or stealing a ride look very similar with normal behaviors like walking or running. A certain kind of action or object may be regarded as normal in some scenes while as anomalous in some other scenarios.

© Springer International Publishing AG, part of Springer Nature 2018
B. Zeng et al. (Eds.): PCM 2017, LNCS 10736, pp. 900–910, 2018.
https://doi.org/10.1007/978-3-319-77383-4_88

(2) Current computer vision tasks benefit a lot from discriminative models with large amount of well annotated training data. However, this is not the case in anomaly detection. Due to the unclear definition of anomaly, it's hard to enumerate all kinds of anomaly and collect sufficient data for each of them. Anomaly detection is more like a one-class classification problem, where we can easily obtain large amount of normal data. (3) Since surveillance videos are living videos in real scenarios, anomaly detection algorithms should be smart enough to adapt to the changing environments (like day and night, season changes, etc.) and unusual but normal events. For example, gathering on a public square is abnormal in most cases but normal during important festivals. The living videos demands an online learning system that can quickly learn the normal patters with little human interaction.

Though many works have been proposed for anomaly detection with good performance on accuracy and real-time capability, they often adopt an offline setting for the model training stage. They train models from all the training features, consuming a lot of memory and training time. Besides, how to determine the appropriate time of pattern changes and select the adequate number of training data is a challenging problem. Motivated by these problems, we propose an online learning algorithm to handle the anomaly detection problem in real applications, which has advantages of low memory consumption, fast model training, and better discriminability.

Specifically, we choose the deep fully convolutional features rather than the hand-crafted features to represent the video content and motion. Convolutional Neural Networks (CNNs) have become one of the most popular and best performing methods for many tasks in computer vision. Recent researches on convolutional neural networks for video anomaly detection indicate that deep convolutional features also work well in representing object appearance and motion [18]. For anomaly discrimination, we adopt the Gaussian model to approximate the normal patterns. Gaussian model has been widely explored and has shown good anomaly detection performance in [17,18,21]. To speed up the training process and adapt to the varying patterns, we propose an online passive aggressive algorithm to learn the Gaussian model efficiently and effectively. Our overall framework is depicted in Fig. 1.

The main contributions of this paper include:

1. We propose an online passive aggressive algorithm for the estimation of Gaussian, which can reduce the memory occupation and training time consumption significantly.
2. We adopt the deep convolutional features and extensively validate the effectiveness of different layers from different network architectures.

The remainder of the paper is organized as follows: Sect. 2 introduces the related work on anomaly detection. Section 3 illustrates the anomaly detection framework and the Gaussian discriminative model. Section 4 introduces the proposed online passive aggressive learning algorithm for Gaussian model estimation. Empirical evaluation is presented in Sect. 5 and conclusions are drawn in Sect. 6.

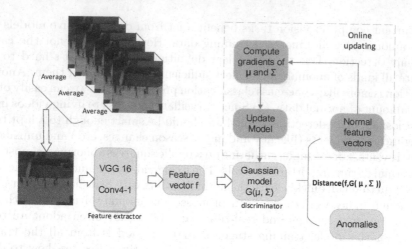

Fig. 1. The proposed anomaly detection framework.

2 Related Works

The commonly accepted definition of anomaly lies mainly in two kinds, motion irregularities and abnormal appearances. In our approach we fuses motion information into appearance, similar to [18], so as to combine both of the definitions.

Most anomaly detection algorithms can be summarized into one architecture: a feature extractor that depicts the input frame abstractively or frames and a discriminator that makes decisions to tell which features are abnormal.

To refine the feature extractor, works in [13,15] aim to find a better form of representation to motion and appearance within video frames. However, their methods base mainly on hand-crafted features like optical flow which lacks computational efficiency and works poorly when compared with deep features. Also when the scene is large and crowded, which is not rare to see in surveillance videos, hand-crafted features that is designed to depict trajectories or motions, such as [22], are often unable to perform accurately. Recently, deep features extracted from layers of convolution and pooling are proposed for anomaly detection. Researchers train a spacial-temporal CNN whose last layer is a binary value that labels normal and anomaly [24]. Long Short-Term Memory Network (LSTM) uses features from convolutional layers which efficiently keeps the important influences that happened long time before [14]. However, training a deep architecture like LSTM or CNN is difficult due to the lack of labeled training data. Moreover, the trained LSTM or CNN model shows their reliance on the certain scenes which are used for training. Some works start to use unsupervised learning approaches such as sparse reconstruction or autoencoder as feature extractor [5,20] which is trained only on normal video frames. In this way, they transfer anomaly detection into an one-class learning task and attain good performance and generalization ability.

As for the discriminator, Cheng et al. choose to cluster features by many steps in order to attain a high level representation for appearance and motion and gains great performance in detection accuracy [4]. However this method runs slowly making it too difficult to apply in real tasks. Unsupervised method like sparse coding [5] uses features from normal frames to reconstruct the input frame when detecting anomalies, which creates a reconstructing error that shows the similarity between normal training features and the testing ones. The input frame or feature vectors are labeled as anomaly when this error is greater than a certain threshold.

Real-time processing is another stiff problem to solve in real applications. Authors of [12,17,18] train generative models to extract features and try to accelerate the testing procedure through simplifying model structure or algorithm complexity. They achieve up to 370 fps of frame rate when detecting anomalies. During experiments we find that even if their testing speed is dramatically high, their training step still costs hours and even days of time to accomplish. Motivated by [9,16], we notice that online learning is a better alternative to train the discriminator, which is proved to be helpful in reaching the real time goal in our work. Further more, different from [9,16], our method uses deep features from generative models as [18,24] do in their works rather than clustering handcrafted features.

3   Deep Feature Extractor and Discriminative Model

Our overall framework consists of two stages: feature extraction and model learning as shown in Fig. 1. In feature extraction, we fuse six successive frames into one RGB image, from which we extract deep features for model learning with the pre-trained networks. In model learning, we use the proposed online learning algorithm to save memory occupation and time consumption.

In the image fusion step, we average two continuous gray frames into one image and then fuse three averaged image as three color channels together to make the movement between images transforms into shape and appearance. Frames should be converted into gay scale for RGB inputs before fusion. Then we feed the conjuncted RGB image into the feature extractor.

Using deep features from layers of convolution or pooling shows outstanding effect when exploited to video tracking or segmentation tasks. Features from CNNs are of great sensitivity toward appearances of the objects inside the image or video frame. This characteristic makes CNN an effective method to work in anomaly detection tasks where unusual shapes or patterns are important categories of anomaly. Features of the off-the-shelf CNNs which are pre-trained in many other large datasets like ImageNet are proved to be sufficient for detecting anomalies in [18]. We choose to use this kind of mechanism for our basic goal of time saving. Since we mainly use the outputs from the convolutional layers of CNNs, the feature extractor network can be regarded as a Fully Convolutional Network (FCN).

Features extracted from a certain layer of a feature extractor (FCN) is denoted as:

$$f_x^t(i,j,l) = [f_x^t(i,j,1), f_x^t(i,j,2), ..., f_x^t(i,j,m_x)]_{w_x,h_x} \tag{1}$$

which refers to the output f at time t from a certain layer x are l (l = 1, 2, ..., m_x. m_x denotes the number of kernels belong to the layer x) feature maps of size $w_x \times h_x$. Equation (1) can be rewritten in this form:

$$f_x^t(i,j,l) = [f_x^t(1,1,m_x), f_x^t(1,2,m_x), ..., f_x^t(w_x,h_x,m_x)] \tag{2}$$

which means that there are $w_x \times h_x$ feature vectors of length m_x of a certain output layer x at time t.

To detect anomalies, we need to train a discriminator to classify the features from deep networks. We choose to apply a gaussian model to fit the feature distribution and Mahalanobis distance to measure the similarity between an input vector and the trained distribution. We use the single gaussian model for the computational efficiency and convenience of our further online update mechanism.

So given the features f_x^t our discriminative model can be written as:

$$G(f_x^t(i,j,l)) = \begin{cases} normal & \text{if distance}(f_x^t(i,j,l), G) \leq \alpha \\ abnormal & \text{if distance}(f_x^t(i,j,l), G) > \alpha \end{cases} \tag{3}$$

The Mahalanobis distance is a frequently used distance to measure whether a input vector belongs to a gaussian distribution or not, which performs better than Euclidean metrics and is given by:

$$mahalanobis(\mathbf{x}, G(\boldsymbol{\mu}, \Sigma)) = \sqrt{(\mathbf{x} - \boldsymbol{\mu})^T \Sigma^{-1} (\mathbf{x} - \boldsymbol{\mu})} \tag{4}$$

Where $\boldsymbol{\mu}$ and Σ stand for the mean and covariance of the multivariant gaussian distribution respectively. Our feature vector is m_x dimensional, so we fit an m_x dimensional multivariate gaussian distribution on normal features.

4   Online Passive Aggressive Learning

Training a gaussian model to fit the distribution of normal patterns consumes a lot of time and memory when the feature set is very large. As in [17,18] the gaussian discriminator is trained on about 2000 normal training frames and the extractor creates more than a million feature vectors for calculating mean and covariance. This fact makes the training procedure impossible to complete when we have a lot more frames to update the model or when the feature space becomes larger i.e. larger w_x and h_x.

In this case, we propose an batch-wise online learning method to update the parameters of gaussian model. Simply setting the Mahalanobis distance as loss function to compute gradient for $\boldsymbol{\mu}$ and Σ is bound to cause huge gradient and fails the training process, which is explicitly discussed in [8]. As illustrated in [6], the training process should follow the passive aggressive rule to make proper step after each iteration of updating and to avoid over updating. Moreover, motivated by [7], we choose to minimize the KL divergence between the learned distribution of different updating step and the Mahalanobis distance at the same time, where the KL divergence guarantees the passive rule and the Mahalanobis distance ensures the aggressive rule. After this modification the result converges into values that greatly fit our training feature space.

Our primary goal is to design a objective function from which we can learn mean and covariance, and make the updated distribution fits the distribution of training data as well as possible. We assume that the normal features appear in a frames follows a normal distribution. In this case, we write the objective function as the minus log-likelihood of x under a multi-variant gaussian density function, as inspired by [8]:

$$\underset{\mu,\Sigma}{\arg\min}\, l(\mu,\Sigma) = \underset{\mu,\Sigma}{\arg\min} -\ln \frac{1}{\sqrt{det(2\pi\Sigma)}} exp\{-\frac{1}{2}(x-\mu)^T\Sigma^{-1}(x-\mu)\} \tag{5}$$

Or in a batch-wise representation (omitting the 2π coefficient):

$$\underset{\mu,\Sigma}{\arg\min}\, l(\mu,\Sigma) = \underset{\mu,\Sigma}{\arg\min} \frac{1}{2N}\sum_{i=1}^{N}(x_i-\mu)^T\Sigma^{-1}(x_i-\mu) + \frac{1}{2}\ln\det(\Sigma) \tag{6}$$

$$x_i,\mu \in \mathbb{R}^{m_x},\ \Sigma \in \mathbb{R}^{m_x \times m_x}$$

where x_i is the input training vector that is m_x dimensional and N is the batch size which is set to be $w_x \times h_x$ experimentally. In (6), the first term equals to (4) without the sqrt, while the last term can be regarded as a constraint or penalty term. Then we get the gradient to update our μ and Σ from computing the partial derivative:

$$\frac{dl}{d\mu} = -\frac{1}{N}\sum_{i=1}^{N}\Sigma^{-1}(x_i-\mu) \tag{7}$$

$$\frac{dl}{d\Sigma} = -\frac{1}{2N}\sum_{i=1}^{N}\Sigma^{-1}(x_i-\mu)(x_i-\mu)^T\Sigma^{-1} + \frac{1}{2}\Sigma^{-1} \tag{8}$$

As stated before, simply minimizing the distance within the normal class only satisfies the aggressive rule and could not make the process converge. Motivated by [7], we add the KL divergence into the objective function. D_{KL} represents the divergence between the distribution before and after a step of updating which makes the updated distribution look more alike the one before updating. So we modify the objective function as follows:

$$\underset{\mu,\Sigma}{\arg\min}\, L(\mu,\Sigma) = \underset{\mu,\Sigma}{\arg\min}\ D_{KL}(\mathbf{N}(\mu_{t-1},\Sigma_{t-1})\|\mathbf{N}(\mu,\Sigma))$$

$$+ \frac{\lambda}{2}\frac{1}{N}\sum_{i=1}^{N}(x_i-\mu)^T\Sigma^{-1}(x_i-\mu) + \lambda\ln(\det\Sigma) \tag{9}$$

We further expand the D_{KL} and represent the formula in a explicit way:

$$
L(\mu, \Sigma) = \frac{1}{2} \ln(\frac{\det \Sigma}{\det \Sigma_{t-1}}) + \frac{1}{2} Tr(\Sigma^{-1}\Sigma) + \frac{1}{2}(\mu - \mu_{t-1})^T \Sigma^{-1}(\mu - \mu_{t-1})
$$
$$
- \frac{d}{2} + \frac{\lambda}{2} \frac{1}{N} \sum_{i=1}^{N} (x_i - \mu)^T \Sigma^{-1}(x_i - \mu) + \lambda \ln(\det \Sigma) \tag{10}
$$

Where the subscript $t-1$ means the value is calculated one iteration before and the value of $t-1$ represents the total times of iterations. N is the batch size. We adopt the block-coordinate optimization algorithm [3] to solve the above objective function. In the first step, we update μ while keeping Σ fixed, i.e. $\Sigma = \Sigma_{t-1}$, and write the objective function as:

$$
\arg \min_{\mu} L_1(\mu, \Sigma_{t-1}) = \arg \min_{\mu} D_{KL}(\mathbf{N}(\mu_{t-1}, \Sigma_{t-1}) \| \mathbf{N}(\mu, \Sigma_{t-1}))
$$
$$
+ \frac{\lambda}{2} \frac{1}{N} \sum_{i=1}^{N} (x_i - \mu)^T \Sigma_{t-1}^{-1}(x_i - \mu) \tag{11}
$$

In which the λ equals to $\frac{1}{t-1}$. This coefficient forces the influence of Mahalanobis distance decrease after iterations. Then we set the partial derivative of (11) with respect to μ to zero as:

$$
\frac{dL_1(\mu, \Sigma_{t-1})}{d\mu} = \Sigma_{t-1}^{-1}(\mu - \mu_{t-1}) + \lambda \frac{1}{N} \sum_{i=1}^{N} \Sigma_{t-1}^{-1}(\mu - x_i) = 0 \tag{12}
$$

For Σ_{t-1}^{-1} is a fixed number in this step, we get the update of μ as:

$$
\mu_t = \frac{1}{1+\lambda}\mu_{t-1} + \frac{\lambda}{1+\lambda} \frac{1}{N} \sum_{i=1}^{N} x_i \tag{13}
$$

The updated mean is denoted as μ_t. In the second step, we update the covariance σ when making μ fixed to μ_{t-1}. And similarly we have:

$$
\arg \min_{\Sigma} L_2(\mu_{t-1}, \Sigma) = \arg \min_{\Sigma} D_{KL}(\mathbf{N}(\mu_{t-1}, \Sigma_{t-1}) \| \mathbf{N}(\mu_{t-1}, \Sigma))
$$
$$
+ \frac{\lambda}{2} \frac{1}{N} \sum_{i=1}^{N} (x_i - \mu_{t-1})^T \Sigma^{-1}(x_i - \mu_{t-1}) + \lambda \ln(\det \Sigma) \tag{14}
$$

Where the last term is the penalty term that regularizes the update in a constrained extent. Finally we set the partial derivative of (13) to equal to zero and get the update of Σ as:

$$
\Sigma_t = \frac{1}{1+\lambda}\Sigma_{t-1} + \frac{\lambda}{(1+\lambda)} \frac{1}{N} \sum_{i=1}^{N} (x_i - \mu_{t-1})(x_i - \mu_{t-1})^T \tag{15}
$$

Where the updated covariance is denoted as Σ_t. With (13) and (15) we can calculate the mean and covariance of the gaussian model in a online way.

Table 1. The time consuming and memory occupation comparison between online updating with batches and model computing with the entire input feature set loaded.

Quantity ($N \times 1024$)	Training with entire loaded data		Online training	
	Memory	Total time	Memory	Total time
500 × 1024	12.9 GB	320.01 s	60 MB	72.35 s
1000 × 1024	25.7 GB	655.91 s	60 MB	144.76 s
1500 × 1024	37.2 GB	979.99 s	60 MB	219.31 s
2000 × 1024	51.1 GB	1396.74 s	60 MB	291.34 s
2500 × 1024	Run out	—	60 MB	363.12 s

5   Experiments and Results

The widely used anomaly detection dataset include: UCSD[1], UMN[2] and Subway [2], in which UCSD is most commonly referred. Compared with other datasets like UMN or Subway, UCSD has higher crowd density and anomaly frequency. The anomaly in UCSD includes more categories like wheelchair, skateboard, cars and bicyclists. The dataset includes 2 scenes, ped1 and ped2. We test our algorithm mainly in ped2 dataset which contains 16 video samples, about 2500 frames, for training as well as 12 video samples, 2010 frames and 12 anomalies, for testing. We compare the time consuming and memory occupation capacities and detection performance on a computer with 3.0 GHz i7 CPU and 64 GB RAM.

To illustrate the advantage of processing time and memory saving of our method, we show related results in Table 1. Values in the left column are the quantity of feature vectors for training where N represents the batch number and 1024 equals to $w_x \times h_x$ for VGG16 conv4-1 features in online updating. And we read in the same amount of features (equals to $N \times 1024$) when we calculate the gaussian model parameters directly with all the read feature vectors. With batch size of $w_x \times h_x$, our algorithm only takes up around 60 MB memory by loading the entire feature set batch by batch while computing the parameters directly occupied more than 60 GB memory. In this case our method saves over 99% in memory cost.

When using the online learning mechanism, the training process of the gaussian model can be accomplished in a much more efficient way and more importantly the learned model performs as well as the one that is calculated completely in the entire training feature space. The batch in a learning epoch is set to be equal to $w_x \times h_x$ so that we can process features from one input frame at a time. When compared with the fully calculated model in ROC curves, the learned model fits the curve of calculated model well in both trend and shape and gets nearly same value of AUC. As shown in Fig. 2.

In order to find a better FCN network and a proper output layer, we compared different kinds of architectures that measured by ROC curve on detecting

---

[1] http://www.svcl.ucsd.edu/projects/anomaly/dataset.htm.

[2] http://mha.cs.umn.edu/.

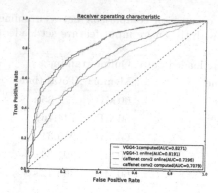

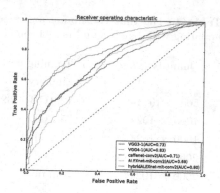

Fig. 2. The comparison between the model get from online updating and the directly computing

Fig. 3. We compared features from VGG16 [19] Alexnet [11] hybridAlexnet [23] and CaffeNet [1]

frame-level anomalies, and give some of the well working frameworks in Fig. 3. As illustrated in the figure, we select the best performing one (VGG16 layer conv4-1) for training the discriminator in the next step. Sabokrou et al. [18] uses the conv2 layer's outputs of CaffeNet as part of their extractor and when we switch to VGG16 conv4-1 we get a 12-percent increase in AUC value. Through experiments we find that features from shallower layers perform poorly for their inadequate depth and that outputs from deeper layers may over-fit to the original task and still perform badly.

We show the anomaly detecting ability in Table 2 and compare the results with some other works at Ped2 data set. We choose to compare deep features with hand-crafted features to show that the reliability of CNN-based feature in anomaly detection tasks. The application of pre-trained CNN features is a newly proposed idea for anomaly detection [18], related works with the similar feature extractor is rare according to our research. Since we have used the similar structure in [18], we mainly compares the detecting speed and accuracy with [18] in the table.

Table 2. The proposed method outperforms algorithms that use hand-crafted features and the similar architecture in [18] in UCSD Ped2 data set.

Method	AUC	EER/%
MDT-Temp [13]	0.765	27.9
Social-Force [15]	0.702	35
MPPCA-MRF [10]	0.71	35.8
Adam et al. [2]	–	42
Extractor, discriminator of [18]	0.71	37
Proposed method	**0.82**	**24.5**

The proposed batch-wise online learning method exhibits its advantage when practically applied in a personal computer that equips insufficient memory or when we need to train our gaussian discriminator in a longer training video with higher resolution and frame rate. And we can set the batch size to fit any feature size and data quantity as we require.

6 Conclusion

In this paper, we propose a passive-aggressive online updating method for gaussian discriminative model estimation, which helps us to reach the goal of online anomaly detection. Our system has high computational efficiency and comparable accuracy while taking up little memory storage. The gaussian model can also be further used in other detection or classification tasks and the proposed approach works as an algorithm accelerator and resource saver. The online updated gaussian distribution can further be concatenated by other different feature extractors which are able to provide more anomaly sensitive and appearance discriminative features, making the system become more adaptive to more complicated scenes or situations.

Acknowledgement. This work is supported by the National Natural Science Foundation of China (Grant No. 61371192), the Key Laboratory Foundation of the Chinese Academy of Sciences (CXJJ-17S044) and the Fundamental Research Funds for the Central Universities (WK2100330002).

References

1. https://github.com/BVLC/caffe/tree/master/models/bvlc_reference_caffenet
2. Adam, A., Rivlin, E., Shimshoni, I., Reinitz, D.: Robust real-time unusual event detection using multiple fixed-location monitors. IEEE Trans. Pattern Anal. Mach. Intell. **30**, 555–560 (2008)
3. Bertsekas, D.P.: Nonlinear Programming. Athena Scientific, Belmont (1999)
4. Cheng, K.W., Chen, Y.T., Fang, W.H.: Video anomaly detection and localization using hierarchical feature representation and Gaussian process regression. In: Proceedings of the IEEE Conference on Computer Vision and Pattern Recognition, pp. 2909–2917 (2015)
5. Cong, Y., Yuan, J., Liu, J.: Sparse reconstruction cost for abnormal event detection. In: 2011 IEEE Conference on Computer Vision and Pattern Recognition (CVPR), pp. 3449–3456. IEEE (2011)
6. Crammer, K., Dekel, O., Keshet, J., Shalev-Shwartz, S., Singer, Y.: Online passive-aggressive algorithms. J. Mach. Learn. Res. **7**, 551–585 (2006)
7. Crammer, K., Kulesza, A., Dredze, M.: Adaptive regularization of weight vectors. In: Advances in Neural Information Processing Systems, pp. 414–422 (2009)
8. Dasgupta, S., Hsu, D.: On-line estimation with the multivariate Gaussian distribution. In: Bshouty, N.H., Gentile, C. (eds.) COLT 2007. LNCS (LNAI), vol. 4539, pp. 278–292. Springer, Heidelberg (2007). https://doi.org/10.1007/978-3-540-72927-3_21

9. Javan Roshtkhari, M., Levine, M.D.: Online dominant and anomalous behavior detection in videos. In: Proceedings of the IEEE Conference on Computer Vision and Pattern Recognition, pp. 2611–2618 (2013)
10. Kim, J., Grauman, K.: Observe locally, infer globally: a space-time MRF for detecting abnormal activities with incremental updates. In: IEEE Conference on Computer Vision and Pattern Recognition, CVPR 2009, pp. 2921–2928. IEEE (2009)
11. Krizhevsky, A., Sutskever, I., Hinton, G.E.: ImageNet classification with deep convolutional neural networks. In: Advances in Neural Information Processing Systems, pp. 1097–1105 (2012)
12. Lu, C., Shi, J., Jia, J.: Abnormal event detection at 150 fps in matlab. In: Proceedings of the IEEE International Conference on Computer Vision, pp. 2720–2727 (2013)
13. Mahadevan, V., Li, W., Bhalodia, V., Vasconcelos, N.: Anomaly detection in crowded scenes. In: 2010 IEEE Conference on Computer Vision and Pattern Recognition (CVPR), pp. 1975–1981. IEEE (2010)
14. Medel, J.R., Savakis, A.: Anomaly detection in video using predictive convolutional long short-term memory networks. arXiv preprint arXiv:1612.00390 (2016)
15. Mehran, R., Oyama, A., Shah, M.: Abnormal crowd behavior detection using social force model. In: IEEE Conference on Computer Vision and Pattern Recognition, CVPR 2009, pp. 935–942. IEEE (2009)
16. Roshtkhari, M.J., Levine, M.D.: An on-line, real-time learning method for detecting anomalies in videos using spatio-temporal compositions. Comput. Vis. Image Underst. 117(10), 1436–1452 (2013)
17. Sabokrou, M., Fathy, M., Hoseini, M., Klette, R.: Real-time anomaly detection and localization in crowded scenes. In: Proceedings of the IEEE Conference on Computer Vision and Pattern Recognition Workshops, pp. 56–62 (2015)
18. Sabokrou, M., Fayyaz, M., Fathy, M., et al.: Fully convolutional neural network for fast anomaly detection in crowded scenes. arXiv preprint arXiv:1609.00866 (2016)
19. Simonyan, K., Zisserman, A.: Very deep convolutional networks for large-scale image recognition. arXiv preprint arXiv:1409.1556 (2014)
20. Tang, X., Zhang, S., Yao, H.: Sparse coding based motion attention for abnormal event detection. In: 2013 20th IEEE International Conference on Image Processing (ICIP), pp. 3602–3606. IEEE (2013)
21. Veracini, T., Matteoli, S., Diani, M., Corsini, G.: Fully unsupervised learning of Gaussian mixtures for anomaly detection in hyperspectral imagery. In: Ninth International Conference on Intelligent Systems Design and Applications, ISDA 2009, pp. 596–601. IEEE (2009)
22. Wang, H., Kläser, A., Schmid, C., Liu, C.L.: Dense trajectories and motion boundary descriptors for action recognition. Int. J. Comput. Vis. 103(1), 60–79 (2013)
23. Zhou, B., Lapedriza, A., Xiao, J., Torralba, A., Oliva, A.: Learning deep features for scene recognition using places database. In: Advances in Neural Information Processing Systems, pp. 487–495 (2014)
24. Zhou, S., Shen, W., Zeng, D., Fang, M., Wei, Y., Zhang, Z.: Spatial-temporal convolutional neural networks for anomaly detection and localization in crowded scenes. Sig. Process. Image Commun. 47, 358–368 (2016)

Multi-scale Convolutional Neural Networks for Non-blind Image Deconvolution

Xuehui Wang[1,2], Feng Dai[1(✉)], Jinli Suo[3], Yongdong Zhang[1],
and Qionghai Dai[3]

[1] Key Lab of Intelligent Information Processing of Chinese Academy of Sciences
(CAS), Institute of Computing Technology, CAS, Beijing 100190, China
{wangxuehui,fdai,zhyd}@ict.ac.cn
[2] Graduate University of Chinese Academy of Sciences, Beijing 100190, China
[3] Department of Automation, Tsinghua University, Beijing 100084, China
{jlsuo,qionghaidai}@mail.tsinghua.edu.cn

Abstract. Image deconvolution appears in many image-related problems. Previous works tried to train neural networks directly on blurry/clean pairs to restore clean images but failed. In this work, we propose a novel neural network, trained end-to-end, pixels-to-pixels, to deblur images from blurry ones. Our key insight is to build multi-scale convolutional neural networks that extract various scale feature maps which is essential for recovering sharp images and removing artifacts. The networks take input image of arbitrary size and produce output within efficient time. We demonstrate that our approach yields better result than the state-of-the-art deconvolution algorithms on a large dataset.

Keywords: Non-blind deconvolution · Multi-scale · CNN

1 Introduction

Many image degradation processes can be modeled as space-invariant convolution, for example, the movement of camera during image capturing [6,11,16] and out-of-focus blur [12]. Mathematically, A blurry image y is given by $y = x * k + n$ where x is the underlying sharp image, k is the PSF and n is usually assumed to be additive, white and Gaussian noise (AWG). The inverse process to restore sharp image, also called image deconvolution, becomes a vital tool in motion deblurring and extended depth of field. It is ill-posed in the presence of lowpass filter and noise.

Most previous methods employ generative models. These models usually make strong assumption, such as sparse image gradient priors which may not hold for all images. In this paper, we build a system not based on physical characteristics, instead by using image statistics to automatically learn the image deconvolution procedure.

© Springer International Publishing AG, part of Springer Nature 2018
B. Zeng et al. (Eds.): PCM 2017, LNCS 10736, pp. 911–919, 2018.
https://doi.org/10.1007/978-3-319-77383-4_89

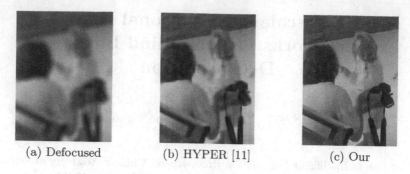

(a) Defocused   (b) HYPER [11]   (c) Our

Fig. 1. Sample results of blur removal for a photograph.

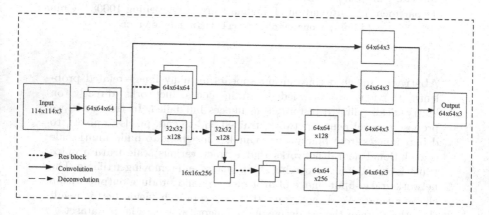

Fig. 2. Our multi-scale convolutional neural networks architecture.

We come up with the multi-scale convolutional neural networks (CNN) to learn the procedure on a large dataset of natural images without the need to know PSF. Unlike [17], we train our network without any pre-processing. Our network is initialized with random weights and trained as a whole, rather than [21] which uses kernel separability to empirically initialize network parameters and trains two submodules separately. Sample results refer to Fig. 1.

In our work, we train neural networks, end-to-end, pixels-to-pixels, and combine multi-scale feature maps to restore sharp images. It presents a general learning procedure for any kind of space-invariant deconvolution. Experiments show that our approach outperforms previous methods in terms of image deconvolution and has a shorter inference time.

2   Related Work

Image deconvolution is studied for decades due to its fundamentality in image processing. Previous methods broadly can be divided into two classes. The first

Clear   Defocused $\mathcal{L}_2$ BM3D[4] HYPER[11] YUV[11] MLP[17]   Our

Fig. 3. Example results of square blur as compared to competitors.

class of methods is based on a generative perspective, whereas the second class of methods applies a deblurring step followed by denoising.

Methods in the first category seek a Bayes estimate of the sharp image x, given a blurry and noisy version y and the PSF k. Formally, one tries to find the x maximizing $p(x|y, k) \propto p(y|x, k)p(x)$. The first term is likelihood and the second term is the marginal distribution of images. Wiener Deconvolution applies Gaussian assumption for both image gradients and noise. It suffers from smoothed edges and ringing artifacts. Recent research on deconvolution shows that sparse image priors are essential to preserve sharp edges and suppress artifacts. The priors present heavy-tailed distribution, for examples, in [11,12], the image gradients follow a hyper-Laplacian distribution and EPLL [22] models priors using a Gaussian Mixture Model (GMM). To capture texture statistics within images, one can model the energy using Conditional Random Field (CRF) framework [15].

The second category of methods take a regularized deblur, followed by a denoising procedure. In the deblur step, regularization are generally a $\mathcal{L}_2$ norm on image gradient. Thus it can be solved in one single step in Fourier domain. The deconvolution can be treated as point-wise division by the blur kernel. This sharps the image but also amplifies noise. The deconvolution transfer to a denoising problem. Deconvolution via denoising requires the denoising algorithm can handle non-flat power spectrum of colored noise which is distinct from additive, white, Gaussian noise. Methods, such as DEB-BM3D [3] and IDD-BM3D [4], are able to remove colored noise and achieve good deconvolution results.

More recently, researchers leverage deep neural network and big data to restore images. Stacked denoising auto-encoder [18] can achieve good results in image denoising and blind image inpainting [19]. Burger *et al.* [1] use plain multi-layer perceptrons to handle different types of noise. Eigen *et al.* [5] ultilize convolutional neural networks to remove raindrop and lens dirt. Schuler *et al.* [17] adopt multi-layer perceptron (MLP) to replace the denoising step in deconvolution by a learning method. Xu *et al.* [21] propose a new convolutional network to bridge the gap between networks and generative models. They train two submodules separately and use kernel separability to guide weight initialization. In this work, we address the image deconvolution problem using a multi-scale convolutional neural network with random initialization, trained end-to-end.

3   Method

Our goal is to train a convolutional neural network $f(\cdot)$ directly on blurry/clean patch pairs that minimizes

$$\frac{1}{N} \sum_{i=1}^{N} \|f(y_i) - x_i\|_2^2, \tag{1}$$

where N is the number of image pairs and y_i is a blurred, noisy image and x_i is the clean version as the ground-truth. Previous work [17] fails to restore clean images with the same goal by using a multi-layer perceptron (MLP). In our method, we come up with multi-scale convolutional neural networks addressing this issue.

3.1   Architecture

Convolutional neural networks are powerful models that yield hierarchical visual features. Our architecture is illustrated in Fig. 2. To extract multi-scale feature maps, we design networks with parallel streams, in a form of increasingly larger size of receptive fields.

Our networks begin with a convolutional layer with large filter size to learn the inherent PSF, which exhibits more interpretability compared to previous works. In [21], they use large-scale one-dimensional kernels to mimic kernel separability. Schuler *et al.* [17] adopt inversion of the blur in Fourier domain, then remove colored noise using MLP, omitting the PSF learning. In Sect. 5, we will demonstrate that our filters with random initialization are learned to possess evident shape of the corresponding PSF.

We then extract multi-scale feature maps based on previous layer output. Coarse scales are achieved by convolving fine scales with stride kernel. As the size of feature maps gets small, we increase the number of feature maps. Each scale contains three residual learning blocks [8] and each block has three convolutional layers. The first convolutional layer uses kernel of size 1×1, and the second produces feature maps with 3×3 kernel and the third layer generates feature maps with 1×1 kernel. We add corresponding padding to maintain the same feature size. Each convolutional layer is followed by a batch normalization [9] which accelerates the learning process. We use the rectified linear unit (ReLU) [14] as activation layer.

Finally, deconvolution layers [13] upsample multi-scale feature maps back into their original resolution. Various features are concatenated as response, then fed into the final output layer to produce prediction result.

3.2   Key Insights

Multi-scale features maps regularize learned filters and remove ringing artifacts in prediction result. In uniform convolution, a blurred image is shifted when the PSF is not in center and can be corrected by convolving with a vector. This causes ambiguities about the location of the PSF when training networks. Inspired by works of blind deconvolution [2,20], which estimate PSF by resizing image to a smaller size and make sure PSF is centered, we combine multi-scale features to eliminate the ambiguity. Meanwhile, different scale features preserve various details. We will show in the Sect. 5, the primary content of the image are retained in fine scales, and the ringing artifacts are detected in coarse scales.

The architecture is fully convolutional. We discard pooling and unpooling in our framework as pooling usually eliminates image details which are essential in low-level image restoration problems. It is worth noting that since our network is fully convolutional, we can achieve pixel-wise prediction and allow arbitrary size of input image. On the contrary, the MLP framework [17] has to do patch-wise inference and averages results in regions where they overlap.

Inspired by residual networks [8], we add skip connections between convolutional blocks. There are two major benefits. First, as networks go deeper, image details can be lost. Skip connections pass feature maps carried with much image details. Second, the skip connections facilitate the gradient back-propagate to bottom layers.

3.3 Training and Testing

Our training dataset contains 8×10^5 patches randomly cropped from 1.5×10^4 natural photos. The networks are implemented and trained using Caffe [10]. We minimize the mean squared error (MSE) formed in Eq. 1. The weights for convolutional layers are initialised using Xavier [7]. We use a large learning rate with step strategy, i.e., learning rate is 0.001, step size is $300,000$, and gamma is 0.1. We adopt Adam for training, as we find empirically it converges faster than SGD. Networks converge after approximately 6×10^5 iteration, corresponding to 20 h of GPU time.

To deblur an image, we only need to feed the image to our trained networks, no matter what size it is. We can remove blur from an image of size 512×512 pixels in a 200 ms on a modern GPU.

4 Results

We explore various network architecture choices, and we compare deconvolution results to the state-of-the-art methods. We choose several typical blur kernels and additive noise to allow for fair comparison. Our approach is tested on a large set of natural images.

4.1 Multi-scale Validation

In this experiment, we validate the importance of multi-scale design in our architecture. We remove the parallel streams in networks (only the third stream in Fig. 2 is left) and maintain other network setting identical. Both networks are

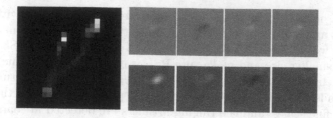

Fig. 4. Motion blur and learned filters from different networks. Left is the true PSF, right top filters are from multi-scale networks, and right bottom ones are from simple networks.

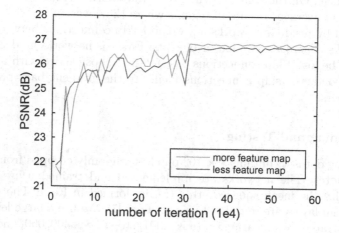

Fig. 5. Networks comparison with different feature maps.

trained on the same dataset. The filters of the first convolutional layer are shown in Fig. 4. We can tell that networks with multi-scale streams learn centered filters, on the contrary, networks without multi-scale feature maps can not ensure the PSF position and raise artifacts in prediction result.

4.2   Number of Feature Maps

Bigger networks usually give better results in computer vision tasks provided enough training data. The number of filters affects the amount of information that passes through the network and also has effect on computational complexity. We compare current networks to one has half size of feature maps. Figure 5 shows the effect of changing number of filters. The reconstruction quality averagely increases about 0.2 dB at the expense of increase of computational complexity.

4.3 Comparison to Other Methods

To compare our approach to previous methods, we perform synthetic experiments on a typical scenario. Square blur with size 19 × 19 and AWG noise with $\sigma = 0.01$. The blur kernel is particularly destructive to image high frequencies and therefor challenging to deconvolution.

We evaluate our method as well as other methods on validate images. Sample examples are shown in Fig. 3. Our method outperforms generative methods on most images by a large margin and our approach exhibits more visual appealing result comparing to [17].

5 Discussion

Our approach achieves decent results in image deconvolution. In this section, we will delve into the networks to provide some insight about how it works.

Fig. 6. Sample filters for square blur in the left-most.

5.1 Input Filters

We start to look at the filters of the first convolutional layer, see Fig. 6. The filters are of size 51 × 51 pixels larger than blur kernel size, which is important to learn full information carried by PSF. Most filters learn the shape of blur in different colors. Since image blur is circular convolution, we see square shapes are concatenated around the center. Although we initialize net weights randomly, the network can automatically learn inherent blur kernel without any handcrafted design. Even if the kernel information spread out, learned filters have the ability to capture all characteristics.

5.2 Output Feature Maps

We now analyze the feature maps in each stream to check what kind of information various scales learn. Figure 7 shows features maps produced by different scale and been up-sampled by deconvolution layer. Obviously, we see that different scale feature maps preserve different components. The primary contents of the image are retained in fine scales, and the ringing artifacts are detected in coarse scales. In some degree, it explains why it works better than networks with only one stream. If there is only one scale, it is difficult for the networks to recover all details and remove undesired artifacts at the same time.

Our networks have millions of parameters and we can not figure out everything inside them. Nonetheless, we are able to make some observation regarding how the networks achieve their results. This is done by looking into the convolutional filters and the feature maps generated by hidden layers.

Fig. 7. Feature maps extracted from fine to coarse scales.

6   Conclusion

In this work, we have proposed the multi-scale convolutional neural networks, trained end-to-end, pixels-to-pixels, to recover sharp images from blurry ones. Our method presents several advantages: We do not rely on any pre-processing, nor do we need the point-spread function to guide training and we do not design any features. The neural networks automatically learn filters to remove image blur and ringing artifacts. Once trained, networks accept image of arbitrary size and produce output within efficient time. We were able to gain insight into how our multi-scale CNN operate: The multi-scale feature maps are critical for eliminating the ambiguity of blur position. Learned filters show strong relevance to the PSF. Different scales attain various features for output, *i.e.*, the primary components of images are retained in fine scales and the ringing components are detected in coarse scales. We demonstrate that our approach achieves high-quality image deconvolution result.

Acknowledgments. This work is supported by National Nature Science Foundation of China (61327013, 61379084, 61402440) and the Key Research Program of the Chinese Academy of Sciences, Grant No. KFZD-SW-407.

References

1. Burger, H.C., Schuler, C.J., Harmeling, S.: Image denoising: can plain neural networks compete with BM3D? In: Proceedings of the IEEE Conference on Computer Vision and Pattern Recognition, pp. 2392–2399. IEEE (2012)
2. Cho, S., Lee, S.: Fast motion deblurring. ACM Trans. Graph. **28**, 145 (2009)
3. Dabov, K., Foi, A., Katkovnik, V., Egiazarian, K.: Image restoration by sparse 3d transform-domain collaborative filtering. In: Electronic Imaging, p. 681207 (2008)
4. Danielyan, A., Katkovnik, V., Egiazarian, K.: BM3D frames and variational image deblurring. IEEE Trans. Image Process. **21**(4), 1715–1728 (2012)
5. Eigen, D., Krishnan, D., Fergus, R.: Restoring an image taken through a window covered with dirt or rain. In: Proceedings of the IEEE International Conference on Computer Vision, pp. 633–640 (2013)
6. Fergus, R., Singh, B., Hertzmann, A., Roweis, S.T., Freeman, W.T.: Removing camera shake from a single photograph. ACM Trans. Graph. **25**, 787–794 (2006)
7. Glorot, X., Bengio, Y.: Understanding the difficulty of training deep feedforward neural networks. In: AISTATS, vol. 9, pp. 249–256 (2010)

8. He, K., Zhang, X., Ren, S., Sun, J.: Deep residual learning for image recognition. In: Proceedings of the IEEE Conference on Computer Vision and Pattern Recognition, pp. 770–778 (2016)
9. Ioffe, S., Szegedy, C.: Batch normalization: accelerating deep network training by reducing internal covariate shift. arXiv preprint arXiv:1502.03167 (2015)
10. Jia, Y., Shelhamer, E., Donahue, J., Karayev, S., Long, J., Girshick, R., Guadarrama, S., Darrell, T.: Caffe: convolutional architecture for fast feature embedding. In: Proceedings of the ACM International Conference on Multimedia, pp. 675–678. ACM (2014)
11. Krishnan, D., Fergus, R.: Fast image deconvolution using hyper-Laplacian priors. In: Advances in Neural Information Processing Systems, pp. 1033–1041 (2009)
12. Levin, A., Fergus, R., Durand, F., Freeman, W.T.: Image and depth from a conventional camera with a coded aperture. ACM Trans. Graph. **26**(3), 70 (2007)
13. Long, J., Shelhamer, E., Darrell, T.: Fully convolutional networks for semantic segmentation. In: Proceedings of the IEEE Conference on Computer Vision and Pattern Recognition, pp. 3431–3440 (2015)
14. Nair, V., Hinton, G.E.: Rectified linear units improve restricted Boltzmann machines. In: Proceedings of the International Conference on Machine Learning, pp. 807–814 (2010)
15. Roth, S., Black, M.J.: Fields of experts: a framework for learning image priors. In: Proceedings of the IEEE Conference on Computer Vision and Pattern Recognition, vol. 2, pp. 860–867. IEEE (2005)
16. Schmidt, U., Rother, C., Nowozin, S., Jancsary, J., Roth, S.: Discriminative non-blind deblurring. In: Proceedings of the IEEE Conference on Computer Vision and Pattern Recognition, pp. 604–611 (2013)
17. Schuler, C.J., Christopher Burger, H., Harmeling, S., Scholkopf, B.: A machine learning approach for non-blind image deconvolution. In: Proceedings of the IEEE Conference on Computer Vision and Pattern Recognition, pp. 1067–1074 (2013)
18. Vincent, P., Larochelle, H., Lajoie, I., Bengio, Y., Manzagol, P.A.: Stacked denoising autoencoders: learning useful representations in a deep network with a local denoising criterion. J. Mach. Learn. Res. **11**, 3371–3408 (2010)
19. Xie, J., Xu, L., Chen, E.: Image denoising and inpainting with deep neural networks. In: Advances in Neural Information Processing Systems, pp. 341–349 (2012)
20. Xu, L., Jia, J.: Two-phase kernel estimation for robust motion deblurring. In: Daniilidis, K., Maragos, P., Paragios, N. (eds.) ECCV 2010. LNCS, vol. 6311, pp. 157–170. Springer, Heidelberg (2010). https://doi.org/10.1007/978-3-642-15549-9_12
21. Xu, L., Ren, J.S., Liu, C., Jia, J.: Deep convolutional neural network for image deconvolution. In: Advances in Neural Information Processing Systems, pp. 1790–1798 (2014)
22. Zoran, D., Weiss, Y.: From learning models of natural image patches to whole image restoration. In: Proceedings of the IEEE International Conference on Computer Vision, pp. 479–486. IEEE (2011)

Feature-Preserving Mesh Denoising Based on Guided Normal Filtering

Renjie Wang[1]([✉]), Wenbo Zhao[1], Shaohui Liu[1], Debin Zhao[1], and Chun Liu[2]

[1] School of Computer Science and Technology, Harbin Institute of Technology,
Harbin 150001, China
{renjiewang,wbzhao,shliu,dbzhao}@hit.edu.cn
[2] College of Computer Science and Information Technology,
Daqing Normal University, Daqing 163712, China
saralc@126.com

Abstract. Mesh denoising is important to improve the quality of the geometry surface acquired by 3D scanning devices. This paper proposes a feature-preserving denoising framework. By classifying the faces into feature and non-feature faces, we use joint bilateral filtering and partial neighborhood filtering to deal with the face normals these two kinds of faces. Experimental results show that our method outperforms the existing methods and achieves higher quality results on the geometry feature.

Keywords: Mesh denoising · Feature face · Joint bilateral filter
Feature preserving · Partial neighbor

1 Introduction

With the wide use of 3D scanning equipment, we can acquire high-resolution 3D models in recent years. 3D mesh model completely describes the 3D structure of the object, and it has been widely used in many domains, such as robotics, virtual reality, protection of cultural relics and so on. However, due to the limitation of the accuracy of the scanning equipment and the influence of surrounding environment, the acquired raw data inevitably contains noise. In order to take advantage of these models for further geometry processing, mesh denoising is essential. A great number of mesh denoising methods are proposed in recent years. We briefly introduce some of these techniques related to our work. The bilateral filter is a nonlinear filter for smoothing images while preserving sharp features such as edges [11]. As its success in image processing, there have been many ways to apply bilateral filtering to geometry processing such as mesh denoising and smoothing. Fleishman et al. [6] and Jones et al. [8] extend the bilateral filter to adjust vertex positions of the mesh using local neighborhoods. Later, instead of directly updating vertex position, two-stage methods which first filter facet normal field and then adjust vertex position have been proposed, such as Lee and Wang [12], Zheng et al. [2], Sun et al. [4,5], the main difference of

B. Zeng et al. (Eds.): PCM 2017, LNCS 10736, pp. 920–927, 2018.
https://doi.org/10.1007/978-3-319-77383-4_90

these methods is that they have used the different weighting functions to filter normals respectively. On the basis of the bilateral filter, Zhang et al. [11] proposed a joint bilateral filter using guidance signal in weighting instead of original signal. Recently, some researches have focused on vertex classification before mesh denoising, such as Fan et al. [3], Bian and Tong [1], Wang et al. [14] and Wei et al. [10,15]. In order to achieve better denoised results, they proposed different vertex classification criteria to classify vertex of the noisy mesh and performed a denoising algorithm [9]. Here, we assume that the underlying surface of a noisy mesh is piecewise smooth and features are always located at the intersection of multiple smooth surface patches [13]. Based on this assumption, we propose a feature-preserving mesh denoising framework, which is more focused on the protection of sharp features than the conventional methods. Firstly, we identify the feature by dividing the vertex into two types, feature vertex and non-feature vertex. We call vertices of sharp edges and corners as feature vertices, and faces as non-feature vertices. It is necessary to note that in this paper we define the face containing the feature vertex as feature face and the remaining face as non-feature face. These feature faces tell us which faces require special consideration during the filtering process. Then, for these two different types face, we use different formula to filter the normals. For the non-feature face, we use the joint bilateral filtering method to filter the normal. For the feature face, we adopt the similarity measure we defined to find the partial neighborhood of the feature face, we hope the geometrical characteristic of these faces we found is as consistent as possible to feature face, then combine the geometric neighborhood and the partial neighborhood to perform the joint bilateral filtering. Finally, we update the vertex position based on the filtered normals. Through the above three steps, the denoising process of the mesh model is completed. The rest of this paper is organized as follows: Sect. 2 briefly explains the guided normal filtering. Section 3 introduces the proposed mesh denoising scheme in details. Experimental results and analyses are presented in Sect. 4. At last, we conclude this paper in Sect. 4.3.

2   Guided Normal Filtering

The joint bilateral filter is a local filter for smoothing images that can preserve sharp features, the main idea is that it uses guidance signal instead of original signal as the weight. Although the joint bilateral filter has been successful on 2D images, it is still a challenge for applying to 3D models. Zhang et al. [11] extended it to mesh denoising, and proposed a method to compute the guidance normal. Given a noisy triangular mesh, the centroid and the normal of each face are denoted as c_i and n_i, the joint bilateral filter has the following form:

$$\bar{n}_i = 1/W_i \sum_{f_j \in N_i} A_j K_s(c_i, c_j) K_r(g_i, g_j) n_j \tag{1}$$

where N_i defines the neighborhood faces of a face f_i, A_i is the area of f_i, g_i is the guidance normal of f_i, and $W_i = \sum_{f_j \in N_i} A_j K_s(c_i, c_j) K_r(g_i, g_j) n_j$ is a normalization factor to sure $\bar{n}_i$ is a unit vector. K_s and K_r are the Gaussian kernels [13]:

$$K_s(c_i, c_j) = exp(-\|c_i - c_j\|^2/(2\sigma_s^2)) \tag{2}$$

$$K_r(g_i, g_j) = exp(-\|g_i - g_j\|^2/(2\sigma_r^2)) \tag{3}$$

where σ_s and σ_r are variance parameters.

3   Feature-Preserving Mesh Denoising

The proposed algorithm includes three parts: feature detection, definition of feature face and the partial neighborhood, denoising. Following, these three parts are given in details.

3.1   Feature Detection

Feature detection in practice is a process of vertex classification, the feature is identified by dividing the vertices of the noisy mesh into feature vertices and nonfeature vertices. Now there are a few vertex classification methods. Normal tensor voting algorithm [9] can accurately classify vertices of the original triangular mesh into face, sharp edge and corner according to the eigenvalues of the normal voting tensor, but it is sensitive to noise. So we directly employ multi-scale tensor voting [7] to classify the vertices of the input noisy mesh. In detail, in the case of noisy, the vertex classification rules depend on the choice of scale. An adaptive neighborhood is used to weigh whether it is a feature vertex or a non-feature vertex. Therefore, adopting a heuristics to get an optimal scale to achieve the normal tensor voting process. Then using a new feature measurement to classify the vertices into feature vertices and non-feature vertices. We define the vertex on the sharp edges and corners as the feature vertex, and the vertex on the face is defined as the non-feature vertex. Here, we give two new definitions, feature face and non-feature face. We define the face containing the feature vertex as feature face and the remaining face as non-feature face. Now, we successfully detect the feature of the input noisy mesh.

3.2   Definition of Feature Face and Partial Neighborhood

Many of the triangular meshes used in computer graphics are piecewise smooth, and it can be also found that a feature is always located at the intersection of multiple smooth surface patch. In each surface patch, the directions of the normals change smoothly. However, the directions of the normals of the two different surface patches are much different. Thus, when we filter the normal of the one of the smooth patch, we hope the influence from the other patches to this patch is as little as possible. Mentioned in the above, the feature face is the face that contains the feature vertex. It can be seen that the positions of these features are located on both sides of the sharp feature edge. Therefore, in order to filter the normal of the feature face more accurately, we try to find some faces that their geometrical features are more consistent with the feature faces. We call these faces we found partial neighborhood, the normals of these faces in the partial neighborhood have similar or smooth changes to the normal of the feature face, That is to say, geometric features between these faces and the feature face change as little as possible. It is worth noting that this method is used only in the feature face where the feature vertex locate, since the non-feature face always locates in a single neighborhood. As mentioned above, in order to find these faces whose geometric feature is similar to the feature face, and more accurately filter feature face normal, we take full advantage of the geometrical information of the triangular mesh, i.e., normal of face, centroid of face, area of face, and the consistency measure of the face's 1-ring neighborhood. We define the similarity measure S to find the partial neighborhood by the four properties. Specially, for a face f_j in the K-ring neighborhood N_i^k of the feature face f_i, we compute the $S(f_j)$, and select several faces with the smallest value as the partial neighborhood of the feature face. The similarity measure is formulated as

$$S(f_j) = \lambda_1 E_1 + \lambda_2 E_2 \tag{4}$$

where $f_j \in N_i^k$, λ_1 and λ_2 is the weighting parameter. And E_1 measures the difference of the normal and distance of the two center between the feature face f_i and f_j, $E_1 = \|\|n_i - n_j\|\| + \|\|c_i - c_j\|\|$. And E2 uses the area and the smoothness of the 1-ring neighborhood to measure the consistency of the two faces $E_2 = abs(H_i - h_j) + abs(A_i - A - j)$.

Finally, we define these faces which have the smallest S as the partial neighborhood of the feature face. Through a large number of experiments, it can be found that if the number of partial neighborhood is five or six, we can get a more accurate partial neighborhood.

3.3 Feature-Preserving Mesh Denoising

Bilateral filtering is performed by filtering the normal of all neighborhood faces on each face, but these neighborhoods may include multiple piecewise smooth region, especially for those faces located at the feature edges. If bilateral filtering is performed directly on these faces, it will cause inaccurate normals, and further result in the blurring of sharp features or the elimination of less pronounced features. We know that these features are always located at the intersection of two or more piecewise smooth planes, so we have to consider these piecewise smooth areas when we filter the feature face. In order to more accurately get the facet normal field, we improve the joint bilateral filtering [11] by adding one more constraint term that consider the partial neighborhood to feature faces. Similar to Zhang et al. [11], our method is an iterative, two-step method. The main process is as follows:

1. Adjust the normal for each face;
2. Update each vertex position according to the adjusted facet normal field.

In Sect. 3.1, we divide these faces in the triangular mesh into feature faces and non-feature faces. In Sect. 3.2, for every feature face, we find the partial neighborhood faces which have the similar geometrical feature to the feature face. Based on the results of the first two steps, for these feature faces and non-feature faces we filter the normals separately. For the feature faces, the normal direction in the neighborhood Ni of the feature face may suddenly appear big change, so we combine the neighborhood Ni and the partial neighborhood Si to implement joint bilateral filtering. For the non-feature faces, the neighborhood of its location is a single neighborhood, where the normal direction changes smoothly and does not suddenly change greatly. Therefore, we use the neighborhood N_i directly to filter the normals. Here, the N_i consists of the f_i and a set of surrounding faces, defined by Zhang et al. [11]. According to the Eq. (1), then the filtered normal N_i' for face f_i can be computed if the face $f_i \notin F$

$$n_i' = \bar{n}_i \tag{5}$$

Otherwise, it will be calculated by weighting neighborhood faces and partial neighborhood:

$$n_i' = \lambda \bar{n}_i + (1 - \lambda)1/W_i \sum_{f_j \in S_i} A_j K_s(c_i, c_j) K_r(g_i, g_j) n_j \tag{6}$$

where F is the set of feature faces, when f_i belongs to the feature faces, S_i represents the partial neighborhood of the feature face f_i. And λ is a positive variable with the range of $\lambda \in [0, 1]$. Here λ is used to control the effect of the neighborhood N_i, if λ is too small, the number of faces included in partial neighborhood is not enough to provide more reference for filtering normal, if λ is too large, it will use the extra information in the neighborhood. After the face normals are filtered, we update the vertex positions to match new normal directions. It is just the iterative scheme proposed by Fleishman et al. [6].

4   Implementation and Results

4.1   Choice of Parameters

Our approach involves a series of parameters, including the parameters mentioned in [1]: the number of iterations kiter for normal filtering, the number of iterations k_{iter} for vertex update, the radius parameter r used for finding a geometrical neighborhood, the spatial and the range kernels variance parameters σ_s and σ_r. As well as the parameters we added in the proposed framework: the similarity measure parameter λ_1 and λ_2 for finding the partial neighborhood of feature faces, the face number n of the partial neighborhood and the weighting parameters λ to filter the normals of feature faces. The parameters used in [11] remain basically the same, for some mesh models, the number of iterations may be more less. For these newly added parameters, through a large number of experiments found, the value of the parameter λ_1 and λ_2 are set to 0.3 and 0.2 respectively, and the number $n \in [5, 6]$, we can get a more accurate result. The weighting parameter $\lambda \in [0.5, 0.6]$ used in the feature face filtering provides a good balance for the neighborhood and the partial neighborhood.

4.2   Results and Comparisons

We have performed our framework on a variety of noisy models, some of them are even non-uniformly sampled. We use these models to verify availability of the method we proposed in dealing with sharp features or irregular surface sampling. In this paper, the noisy models are obtained by adding Gaussian noise to the vertex of the original model along the direction of the vertex normal. We have experimented with a large number of models and selected representative models to show the results. We have compared our method with six representative denoising techniques: Fleishman et al.'s bilateral mesh filter [6], Zhang et al.'s. local bilateral normal filter and its global representation method [2], He and Schaefer's area-based edge filter [7], Wei et al.'s. multistage method [10] and Zhang et al.'s joint bilateral filter [11], all these methods can better preserve features. These models shown in Figs. 1 and 2 have obvious geometric features (sharp edges and corners), and we can see from the magnified details that our method protects the geometric details better.

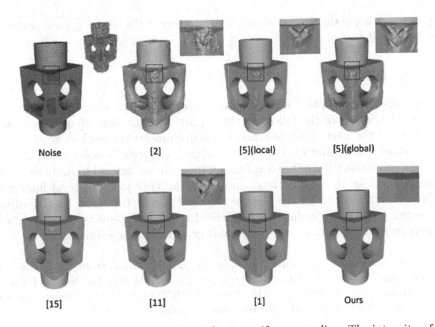

Fig. 1. Denoising of the Block model with non-uniform sampling. The intensity of the Guassian noise applied to this model is 0.4

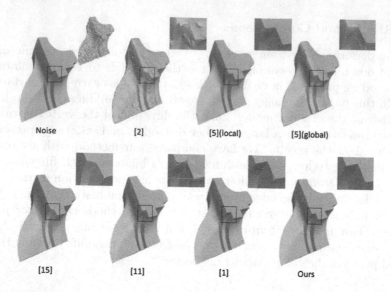

Fig. 2. Denoising of the Fandisk model. The intensity of the Guassian noise applied to this model is 0.3

4.3 Conclusion

In this paper, we presented a feature-preserving mesh denoising framework. The framework consists of the following three parts: feature detection, definition of feature face' the partial neighborhood, feature-preserving mesh denoising algorithm. Based on the theory that the underlying surface of a noisy mesh is piecewise smooth, taking use of the consistency measure we defined to find the partial neighborhood for the feature face, and then applying joint bilateral filter with different neighborhood for the feature face and non-feature face. Lastly, adjusting vertex positions according to the filtered normals. Extensive experiments on various synthetic demonstrate the capability of the proposed method.

Acknowledgments. This work is supported by the Major State Basic Research Development Program of China (973 Program 2015CB351804), the National Science Foundation of China under Grants 61300110 and 61672193, and by the Science Research Foundation of Daqing Normal University under Grant No. 14ZR02.

References

1. Bian, Z., Tong, R.: Feature-preserving mesh denoising based on vertices classification. Comput. Aided Geom. Des. **28**(1), 50–64 (2011)
2. Zheng, Y., Fu, H., Au, O.K.C., Tai, C.L.: Bilateral normal filtering for mesh denoising. IEEE Trans. Vis. Comput. Graph. **17**(10), 1521–1530 (2011)
3. Fan, H., Yu, Y., Peng, Q.: Robust feature-preserving mesh denoising based on consistent subneighborhoods. IEEE Trans. Vis. Comput. Graph. **16**(2), 312–324 (2009)

4. Sun, X., Rosin, P., Martin, R., Langbein, F.: Fast and effective featurepreserving mesh denoising. IEEE Trans. Vis. Comput. Graph. **13**(5), 925–938 (2007)
5. Sun, X., Rosin, P.L., Martin, R.R., Langbein, F.C.: Random walks for feature preserving mesh denoising. Comput. Aided Geom. Des. **25**(7), 437–456 (2008)
6. Fleishman, S., Drori, I., Cohen-Or, D.: Bilateral mesh denoising. ACM Trans. Graph. **22**(3), 950–953 (2003)
7. He, L., Schaefer, S.: Mesh denoising via l0 minimization. ACM Trans. Graph. **32**(4), 1–8 (2013)
8. Jones, T.R., Durand, F., Desbrun, M.: Non-iterative, feature-preserving mesh smoothing. ACM Trans. Graph. **22**(3), 943–949 (2004)
9. Kim, H.S., Choi, H.K., Lee, K.H.: Feature detection of triangular meshes based on tensor voting theory. Comput. Aided Des. **41**(1), 47–58 (2009)
10. Wei, M., Yu, J., Pang, W.M., Wang, J., Qin, J., Liu, L., Heng, P.A.: Bi-normal filtering for mesh denoising. IEEE Trans. Vis. Comput. Graph. **21**(1), 43–55 (2015)
11. Zhang, W., Deng, B., Zhang, J., Bouaziz, S., Liu, L.: Guided mesh normal filtering. Comput. Graph. Forum **34**(7), 23–34 (2015)
12. Lee, K.W., Wang, W.P.: Feature-preserving mesh denoising via bilateral normal filtering. In: International Conference on Computer Aided Design and Computer Graphics, pp. 275–280 (2006)
13. Manduchi R., Tomasi, C: Bilateral filtering for gray and color images. In: IEEE International Conference on Computer Vision (CVPR), pp. 839–846 (1998)
14. Wang, J., Zhang, X.: A cascaded approach for feature-preserving surface mesh denoising. Comput. Aided Geom. Des. **44**(7), 597–610 (2012)
15. Wei, M., Liang, L., Pang, W.M., Wang, J., Li, W., Wu, H.: Tensor voting guided mesh denoising. IEEE Trans. Autom. Sci. Eng. **14**(2), 931–945 (2017)

Visual-Inertial RGB-D SLAM for Mobile Augmented Reality

Williem[1], Andre Ivan[1], Hochang Seok[2], Jongwoo Lim[2], Kuk-Jin Yoon[3], Ikhwan Cho[4], and In Kyu Park[1(✉)]

[1] Department of Information and Communication Engineering,
Inha University, Incheon, Korea
williem.pao@gmail.com, andreivan13@gmail.com, pik@inha.ac.kr
[2] Division of Computer Science, Hanyang University, Seoul, Korea
kaha0707@naver.com, jlim@hanyang.ac.kr
[3] School of Electrical Engineering and Computer Science, GIST, Gwangju, Korea
kjyoon@gist.ac.kr
[4] Media Experience Lab, Corporate R&D Center, SK Telecom, Seoul, Korea
ikhwan.cho@sk.com

Abstract. This paper presents a practical framework for occlusion-aware augmented reality application using visual-inertial RGB-D SLAM. First, an efficient visual SLAM framework with map merging based relocalization is introduced. When the pose estimation fails, a new environment map is generated. Then, a map merging is performed to merge the current and previous environment maps if a loop closure is detected. The framework is then integrated with the inertial information to solve the missing environment map problem. Camera pose is approximated using the angular velocity and translational acceleration value when the pose estimation fails. Experimental results show that the proposed method can perform well in the presence of missing pose. Finally, an occlusion-aware augmented reality application is built over the SLAM framework.

1 Introduction

For the last decades, visual simultaneous localization and mapping (visual SLAM) has become an active research topic in robotics and computer vision. Visual SLAM utilizes a set of images to estimate the camera pose and generate the environment map simultaneously. Recently, visual SLAM plays an important role to provide geometric information for augmented reality (AR) and virtual reality (VR) applications. With the extracted camera pose and environment map, AR application can augment virtual graphic objects to it. Then, viewers can experience the augmented objects aligned in the real world which generates emerging experiences to the viewers. There are various kinds of visual SLAM based on the input type, such as monocular visual SLAM [2,12,13], visual RGB-D SLAM [3,5,6], visual-inertial SLAM [1,9,15,19], etc.

In this paper, we focus on mobile visual-inertial RGB-D SLAM for AR application. Mobile visual SLAM often fails when there are motion blur, occlusion

© Springer International Publishing AG, part of Springer Nature 2018
B. Zeng et al. (Eds.): PCM 2017, LNCS 10736, pp. 928–938, 2018.
https://doi.org/10.1007/978-3-319-77383-4_91

and distortion. Thus, it cannot estimate the relative pose between the previous and current frames. Conventional method [12] performs relocalization until it finds camera pose with enough inliers. Otherwise, we need to build the environment map from the beginning. To solve the failed pose estimation, we develop an efficient feature-based visual SLAM method. Instead of using conventional relocalization method, a map merging based relocalization method is utilized. We generate a new environment map whenever the pose estimation fails, and merge the environment maps when a loop closure is detected across the environment maps. However, it is not suitable for AR application because the current camera pose is reset and previous environment map information is lost. Thus, we integrate the system by employing the inertial information from the mobile device. While the pose estimation fails, the visual-inertial SLAM system exploits the inertial information to approximate the camera pose. Experimental results show that the proposed method can handle the missing pose problem with better visualization. The contribution of this paper is summarized as follows.

- The visual-inertial SLAM framework that is aware of failed pose estimation.
- Map merging based relocalization to correct the accumulated error in the visual-inertial SLAM framework.
- An occlusion-aware augmented reality application over the SLAM framework.

2   Related Works

Henry *et al.* [5] introduced a keyframe based system that utilized a RGB-D camera to generate dense 3D models. Sparse features were extracted to find the correspondence between consecutive frames. Each feature was projected into 3D space and then the camera pose was estimated using RANSAC algorithm. The camera pose was refined using iterative closest point (ICP) algorithm. A global pose optimization was performed to handle the camera drift. They exploited a loop closure detection for a subset of previous keyframes to look for the possible loop closure. The global optimization was done when the loop closure is detected. Fioraio and Stefano [3] introduced SlamDunk that employed a similar system as in [5] with more efficient computation. Instead of performing RANSAC for all possible corresponding keyframes, they utilized feature pool for fast and efficient feature matching. On the other hand, Kerl *et al.* [6] proposed a dense RGB-D SLAM instead of using sparse features. They focused on improving several components to reduce the drift.

Servant *et al.* [15] used inertial sensors to improve the performance of plane based SLAM. They performed the sensor fusion in Extended Kalman Filter (EKF) based framework. Leutenegger *et al.* [9] introduced a non-linear optimization for combining the visual and inertial information. Inertial error terms and landmarks reprojection error terms were utilized in the joint optimization framework. Tiefenbacher *et al.* [19] proposed an off-the-shelf sensor integration for monocular SLAM on mobile devices. They introduced a Unscented Kalman Filter (UKF) based sensor fusion and a UKF motion model. They employed PTAM algorithm [7] as the SLAM approach and used the estimated pose as

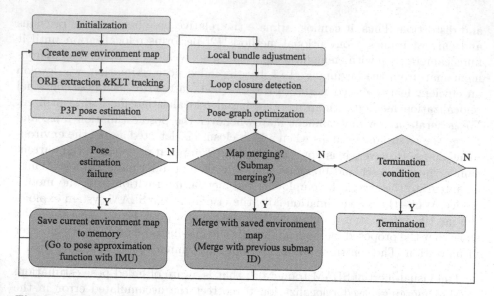

Fig. 1. Overview of the proposed visual (-inertial) SLAM system. It consists of motion estimation, local and global optimization, loop closure detection, and map merging. Pose estimation failure detection and map merging process is highlighted by blue-colored component. The functions used in visual-inertial system are described in the parentheses. (Color figure online)

the measurement input for UKF. Brunetto *et al.* [1] extended SlamDunk framework [3] and integrated it with inertial sensors. There were two filters used for filtering the camera orientation and camera position, separately. First, an orientation EKF was used to integrate the camera rotation and gyroscope information. Then, a position KF was used to integrate the camera position and accelerometer information.

3 Proposed Method

3.1 Visual SLAM

Framework Overview. We propose a feature-based visual SLAM system which operates robustly even when the camera pose estimation fails. First, feature points are extracted and tracked to estimate the camera pose, and the environment map is constructed with the 3D landmarks obtained using the depth information. When the loop closure occurs, the pose-graph is optimized to minimize the accumulated pose errors, thereby improving the accuracy of the entire camera postures and 3D landmark positions. However, if sufficient number of feature points cannot be extracted or tracked due to severe motion blur and occlusion, the estimated camera pose may have large error and it may fail in the worst case. To alleviate this problem, we propose an efficient algorithm to maintain multiple environment maps and merge them if their relative poses are known in loop closure detection. Figure 1 illustrates the overview of the proposed algorithm.

Pose Estimation. In our framework, ORB feature points [12] are used as the feature points for pose estimation. Extracted ORB feature points are tracked using the Kanade-Lucas-Tomasi tracker [16]. As the camera moves, the number of tracked ORB feature points decrease. When the number of tracked feature points is less than the threshold, new ORB feature points are extracted and added for tracking. The depth of feature points are given from the depth images. The relative pose of the camera is calculated by the P3P RANSAC algorithm [8] using the pairs of tracked 2D feature points and 3D landmarks. If the relative translation or rotation of the current camera pose to the most recent keyframe is larger than thresholds, the current frame is registered as a new keyframe, a visual odometer edge links the previous and the new keyframes, and new features are added to the environment map as landmarks. Then local bundle adjustment (LBA) optimizes the poses of recent keyframes and the positions of landmarks.

Loop Closure Detection and Pose-Graph Optimization. Loop closure is tested when a keyframe is registered. First, N candidate keyframes are searched in a vocabulary tree [14]. Then, the feature points of the current keyframe and the candidate keyframes are matched using the P3P RANSAC algorithm. If the total reprojection errors and the inlier ratio satisfy the loop closure criteria, a loop closure edge is added in the environment map [4]. When a loop closure occurs, a pose graph composed of visual odometer edges and loop edges is constructed, and pose graph optimization is performed to minimize the accumulated keyframes pose errors [17].

Pose Estimation Failure Detection. We hypothesize that two cases of pose estimation failure.

1. Pose cannot be estimated - P3P RANSAC failure
2. Pose with very large error is calculated.

To detect the case 2, we use the statistical difference of the number of tracked feature points and the relative pose between previous keyframes. The condition for failure of pose estimation is given as follows.

$$n > \mu_n + 2\sigma_n \quad | \quad T > \mu_T + 2\sigma_T \tag{1}$$

where n and T are the number of features and the relative translation of current keyframe, μ_n, σ_n and μ_T, σ_T are the mean and the standard deviation of the number of features and the relative translation in the previous five keyframes, respectively.

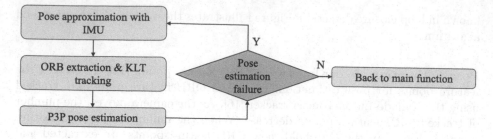

Fig. 2. Overview of the pose approximation function using inertial information.

Map Merging Process. When the pose estimation fails, the pose of the current keyframe cannot be estimated. In our system, the previous environment map is kept in background, and a new environment map is initialized with the current keyframe, into which the subsequent keyframes are added. Since the vocabulary tree contains all keyframes in existing environment maps, the loop closures not only in the current map but also the previous maps are tested using the P3P RANSAC algorithm whenever a new keyframe is added. If the best candidate keyframe is in a previous environment map, it is merged with the current map by adding a loop closure edge between the matching keyframes. In this process the keyframe poses and landmark positions in the previous map need to be adjusted using the estimated relative pose between the keyframes. Note that for a new keyframe at most one loop closure edge can be added regardless of a between-map or within-map loop closure.

3.2   Visual-Inertial SLAM

Framework Overview. The visual SLAM has a limitation that the current camera pose does not have relation with previous camera poses until the map merging process is done. This is a disadvantage when visual SLAM information is used by AR application because the camera pose is reset to initial and become inconsistent. To ameliorate this problem, we utilize inertial information when the pose estimation fails. Note that we do not integrate the visual and inertial information together, but use each of them alternatively. As inertial information is very noisy which can lead to large drift error, we propose a system to correct the camera pose when the visual SLAM can obtain reliable camera pose.

Instead of maintaining multiple environment maps as performed in visual SLAM, we generate only a single environment map with additional group identifier number (submap ID) to manage the keyframes, landmarks, and camera poses. The submap ID separates the keyframes, landmarks, and poses into different groups until they are merged later. Each optimization (local bundle adjustment, loop closure detection, and pose graph optimization) is performed only for keyframes with the same submap ID. Submap merging process, which shares similar concept as map merging, is done when a loop closure occurs across groups

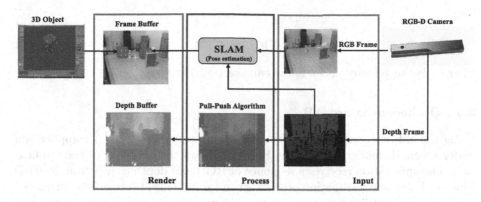

Fig. 3. Overview of the occlusion-aware augmented reality application.

with different submap ID. The overview of the proposed visual-inertial SLAM is shown in Fig. 1 with the updated functions described inside the parentheses.

When the pose estimation fails, the proposed system operates the pose approximation function using inertial sensors as shown in Fig. 2. Instead of utilizing global 3D landmarks, we generate and utilize temporary 3D landmarks in this function to check the pose estimation. We execute the pose approximation function iteratively until the pose estimation does not fail. When it succeeds, the application goes back to the main function and execute other processes.

Inertial Sensors Usage. First, we calibrate the low cost IMU using an IMU-calibration techniques by Tedaldi [18] to estimate the gyroscope and accelerometer biases. Using the angular velocity, we update the camera orientation by the following equation.

$$\theta^k = \theta^{k-1} + \omega^k \Delta t \tag{2}$$

where θ is the camera orientation and ω is the angular velocity. k is the frame index and Δt is the time interval between consecutive frames.

We need to remove the gravity $g = [0, 0, 9.8]$ which is included in the obtained acceleration value a. Thus, we utilize a method in [10] to estimate the orientation of the IMU sensor. Using the obtained orientation, we can measure the linear acceleration a_l as the following equation.

$$a_l^k = \exp(\theta_d)a^k - g \tag{3}$$

where θ_d is the IMU device orientation and $\exp(\theta_d)$ is the function to generate a rotation matrix from an orientation θ_d. Using the linear acceleration, we perform double integration to estimate the position while the pose estimation is failed as follows.

$$v^k = v^{k-1} + a_i^k \Delta t \qquad (4)$$
$$p^k = p^{k-1} + v^k \Delta t \qquad (5)$$

where v is the velocity and p is the camera position.

3.3   Occlusion-Aware AR

Using the obtained camera pose, we develop an occlusion-aware AR application under OpenGL rendering pipeline. Figure 3 shows the overview of the application. The application receives a sequence of RGB and depth frames from RGB-D camera. Then, pose estimation process is run for each input frame. The estimated camera pose is utilized to augment the 3D graphic objects aligned in the real world. To build an occlusion-aware AR application, the depth frame is copied to the depth buffer every time. Pull-push algorithm [11] is utilized to fill the holes in raw depth frame. The 3D objects are loaded in advance and augmented to the environment map when needed. For each frame, the augmented objects are drawn in the world coordinates.

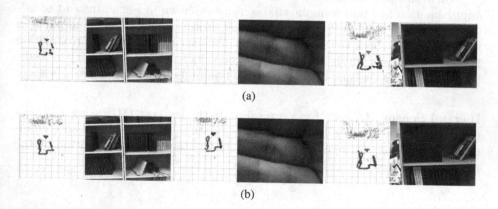

Fig. 4. Sample results of (a) visual SLAM and (b) visual-inertial SLAM. (Left) Frame 323; (Middle) Frame 423; (Right) Frame 523.

4   Experimental Results

The proposed algorithm is implemented on Microsoft Surface 4 Pro with its internal inertial sensors. For the camera, we utilize Intel RealSense R200 and use its SDK to perform the calibration between depth and color cameras. Figure 4(a) shows the qualitative results of the environment maps generated by the visual SLAM algorithm. Frame 323, 423, and 523 are selected to show the performance when the pose is missing. It confirms that the visual SLAM can find the previous environment map and merge it with the current environment map.

Table 1. Maximum and mean angular error.

Start frame	Total frame	Maximum error	Mean error
300	50	2.60°	0.02°
	100	8.08°	0.09°
	200	8.08°	0.07°
600	50	4.70°	0.03°
	100	5.97°	0.07°
	200	6.16°	0.07°

Visual-inertial SLAM refines the performance by keeping the environment map when the pose estimation fails. It is shown in Fig. 4(b) which selects the same frame index. It confirms that the environment map is not missing in frame 423 and can approximate the camera pose because of the inertial information usage. To evaluate the performance of each inertial sensor (gyroscope and accelerometer) in the device, we capture two data which consists of only rotation and only translation, separately. Missing pose is synthetically generated by selecting a portion of frames as the missing frames. Then, we compare the camera poses generated by visual SLAM and visual-inertial SLAM algorithms.

Table 1 shows the maximum and mean angular error between both algorithms. When the pose is missing, visual-inertial algorithm gain at most 8.08° error. This amount of error is acceptable as we do not have any information other than the inertial information. Figure 5(a) and (b) show the plot of angular error in all captured frames. It demonstrates that the camera orientation is corrected after the missing frames. This is due to the proposed submap merging process.

While the gyroscope can provide acceptable measurements for the rotation, the accelerometer has severely noisy measurement. It is difficult to provide accurate camera position by only using the accelerometer. Thus, accelerometer is only used for the rough position approximation and the error is corrected by the proposed submap merging process. In the only translation data, the missing frames start from frame 400. The total missing frames are 50, 100, and 200 and the maximum position error of each scenario is 3.4686, 3.7782, and 11,5271, respectively. It confirms that the accelerometer is acceptable for short period but contains large error for long period. Figure 5(c) and (d) show the plot of position error in all captured frames. It proves that the proposed submap merging process can correct the position error after the missing frames.

Finally, the proposed SLAM framework is tested on the AR application. There are two scenarios to show the usability of the application. The first scenario is by moving the camera with static occlusion and the second scenario is by moving the occlusion (dynamic occlusion) with static camera. Figure 6 shows the sample results of each scenario. It is confirmed that the proposed AR application shows correct occlusion handling by updating the depth buffer and camera pose in each frame.

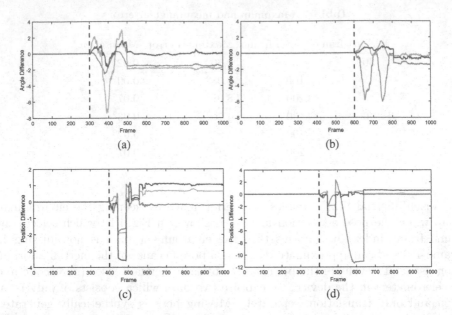

Fig. 5. Plot of angular error with 200 missing frames which start from (a) Frame 300 and (b) Frame 600; Plot of position error which starts from frame 400 with (c) 50 missing frames and (d) 200 missing frames. Red, green, and blue colors denote the difference in x, y, and z directions. The black dash line denotes the starting point of missing frame. (Color figure online)

Fig. 6. Sample results of (a) static occlusion; (b) dynamic occlusion. Dices and globes are the augmented 3D graphic objects.

5 Conclusion

In this paper, we proposed a visual-inertial RGB-D SLAM system that was aware of failed pose estimation problem. A new environment map was generated whenever the camera pose was missing. Then, a map merging process was performed to combine the previous and current environment maps when a loop closure occurred. A visual-inertial SLAM framework was introduced to handle the missing environment map problem. Inertial information was used to approximate the camera pose while the camera pose was missing. Both visual SLAM and inertial information were used alternatively to perform continuous pose estimation. Experimental results confirmed that the proposed framework could solve the failed pose estimation problem. Finally, an occlusion-aware AR application was developed over the proposed SLAM framework.

Acknowledgement. This work was supported by SK Telecom. This work was supported by Institute for Information & communications Technology Promotion (IITP) grant funded by the Korea government (MSIT) (2017-0-00142).

References

1. Brunetto, N., Salti, S., Fioraio, N., Cavallari, T., Stefano, L.D.: Fusion of inertial and visual measurements for RGB-D SLAM on mobile devices. In: Proceedings of IEEE International Conference on Computer Vision Workshops, pp. 148–156 (2015)
2. Davison, A.J., Reid, I.D., Molton, N.D., Stasse, O.: MonoSLAM: real-time single camera SLAM. IEEE Trans. Pattern Anal. Mach. Intell. **29**(6), 1052–1067 (2007)
3. Fioraio, N., Di Stefano, L.: SlamDunk: affordable real-time RGB-D SLAM. In: Agapito, L., Bronstein, M.M., Rother, C. (eds.) ECCV 2014. LNCS, vol. 8925, pp. 401–414. Springer, Cham (2015). https://doi.org/10.1007/978-3-319-16178-5_28
4. Galvez-Lopez, D., Tardos, J.D.: Real-time loop detection with bags of binary words. In: Proceedings of IEEE International Conference on Intelligent Robots and Systems, pp. 51–58 (2011)
5. Henry, P., Krainin, M., Herbst, E., Ren, X., Fox, D.: RGB-D mapping: using kinect-style depth cameras for dense 3D modeling of indoor environments. Int. J. Robot. Res. **31**(5), 647–663 (2012)
6. Kerl, C., Sturm, J., Cremers, D.: Dense visual SLAM for RGB-D cameras. In: Proceedings of IEEE International Conference on Intelligent Robotics and Systems, pp. 2100–2106 (2013)
7. Klein, G., Murray, D.: Improving the agility of keyframe-based SLAM. In: Forsyth, D., Torr, P., Zisserman, A. (eds.) ECCV 2008. LNCS, vol. 5303, pp. 802–815. Springer, Heidelberg (2008). https://doi.org/10.1007/978-3-540-88688-4_59
8. Kneip, L., Scaramuzza, D., Siegwart, R.: A novel parametrization of the perspective-three-point problem for a direct computation of absolute camera position and orientation. In: Proceedings of IEEE Conference on Computer Vision and Pattern Recognition, pp. 2969–2976 (2011)
9. Leutenegger, S., Lynen, S., Bosse, M., Siegwart, R., Furgale, P.: Keyframe-based visualinertial odometry using nonlinear optimization. Int. J. Robot. Res. **34**(3), 314–334 (2015)

10. Mahony, R., Hamel, T., Pflimlin, J.M.: Nonlinear complementary filters on the special orthogonal group. IEEE Trans. Autom. Control **53**(5), 1203–1217 (2008)
11. Marroquim, R., Kraus, M., RCavalcanti, P.: Efficient point-based rendering using image reconstruction. In: Proceedings of Eurographgics Symposium on Point-Based Graphics, pp. 101–108 (2007)
12. Mur-Artal, R., Montiel, J.M.M., Tardós, J.D.: ORB-SLAM: a versatile and accurate monocular SLAM system. IEEE Trans. Robot. **31**(5), 1147–1163 (2015)
13. Newcombe, R.A., Lovegrove, S.J., Davison, A.J.: DTAM: dense tracking and mapping in real-time. In: Proceedings of IEEE Conference on Computer Vision and Pattern Recognition, pp. 2320–2327 (2011)
14. Nister, D., Stewenius, H.: Scalable recognition with a vocabulary tree. In: Proceedings of IEEE Conference on Computer Vision and Pattern Recognition, pp. 2161–2168 (2006)
15. Servant, F., Houlier, P., Marchand, E.: Improving monocular plane-based SLAM with inertial measures. In: Proceedings of International Conference on Intelligent Robots and Systems, pp. 3810–3815 (2010)
16. Shi, J., Tomasi, C.: Good features to track. In: Proceedings of IEEE Conference on Computer Vision and Pattern Recognition, pp. 593–600 (1994)
17. Sünderhauf, N., Protzel, P.: Towards a robust back-end for pose graph SLAM. In: Proceedings of IEEE International Conference on Robotics and Automation, pp. 1254–1261 (2012)
18. Tedaldi, D., Pretto, A., Menegatti, E.: A robust and easy to implement method for IMU calibration without external equipments. In: Proceedings of IEEE International Conference on Robotics and Automation, pp. 3042–3049 (2014)
19. Tiefenbacher, P., Schulze, T., Rigoll, G.: Off-the-shelf sensor integration for mono-SLAM on smart devices. In: Proceedings of IEEE Conference on Computer Vision and Pattern Recognition Workshops, pp. 15–20 (2015)

ODD: An Algorithm of Online Directional Dictionary Learning for Sparse Representation

Dan Xu[1], Xinwei Gao[1,2], Xiaopeng Fan[1(✉)], Debin Zhao[1], and Wen Gao[3]

[1] Department of Computer Science and Technology, Harbin Institute of Technology, Harbin City, Heilongjiang Province, China
{xudan,fxp,dbzhao}@hit.edu.cn
[2] Department of Technology and Architecture, Wechat Business Group, Tencent, Shenzhen City, Guangdong Province, China
vitogao@tencent.com
[3] School of Electronics and Computer Science, Peking University, Beijing City, China
wgao@pku.edu.cn

Abstract. Recently, some sparse representation based image reconstruction methods have demonstrated with a learnt dictionary. In this paper, we propose a block-based image sparse representation approach with an online directional dictionary (ODD). Unlike the conventional dictionary learning approaches for image sparse representation aims at learning some signal patterns from a large set of training image patches, the proposed joint dictionary for each patch is composed by an original offline or online trained sub-dictionary from a training set and an novel adaptive directional sub-dictionary estimated from the reconstructed nearby pixels of the patch itself. A joint dictionary with ODD has two main advantages compared with the conventional dictionaries. First, for each patch to be sparse represented, not only the most general contents, but also the most possible directional textures of the image patch are considered to improve the reconstruction performance. Second, in order to save storage costs, only the original trained sub-dictionary should be stored, the proposed ODD can be obtained consistently. Experimental results show that the reconstruction performance of the proposed approach exceeds other competitive dictionary learning based image sparse representation methods, validating the superiority of our approach.

Keywords: Sparse representation · Dictionary learning
Online directional dictionary · Adaptive prediction · Local similarity

1 Introduction

Recently, there is a growing interest in the research of sparse representation of images. Sparse representation can utilize less cost to store and transmit images by transfer images to a form with the number of zero value far larger than that of

© Springer International Publishing AG, part of Springer Nature 2018
B. Zeng et al. (Eds.): PCM 2017, LNCS 10736, pp. 939–947, 2018.
https://doi.org/10.1007/978-3-319-77383-4_92

nonzero ones. Due to the characteristic of sparsity, an over-complete dictionary can do much benefit to applications like compression, feature extraction, image reconstruction and more. For instance, DCT used in JPEG [1] and DWT used in JPEG2000 [2,3] transform the image pixels to obtain more zero-valued coefficients. However, the above approaches for obtaining the dictionary rely on the predefined bases which are extracted from mathematics models. There is little correspondence between the predefined dictionaries and human vision perception. The predefined dictionaries are limited to the expression of the mathematics models [4] when the image patch contains detailed textures.

By using an over-complete learnt dictionary instead of predefined dictionary, images can be represented as a sparse linear combination of dictionary columns. Usually, each columns of the dictionary represents a pattern called an element which can describe a kind of content modality. To represent the image patch content, a patch commonly consists of one or more texture patterns. It has shown the potential of generating an over-complete dictionary from a training image dataset through machine learning [5]. A learnt dictionary can describe the patch content more specifically and accurately. From this, sparse representation based on learnt dictionary has been widely implemented on computer vision [6] and image progressing [7].

The learnt dictionary is generally generated by offline [7,8] or online training [9–11]. For very large training database, offline training dictionary cant accurately represent the content of image patches and performance so satisfied. Since if there are not same or similar patterns of the current patch to be represented in the offline trained dictionary, image patches may not be represented specifically and accurately. This promotes the development of the online learnt dictionary. For instance, the online learning dictionary [9] and the recursive update dictionary (RLS-DLA) [10] were generated. However, conventional online dictionary learning algorithms are based on training image samples, updating the whole dictionary according to the training patch content. Whats more, conventional dictionary training procedures need more storage and transmitting costs.

Differing from conventional approaches, we propose an online directional dictionary (ODD) learning algorithm and generate a joint dictionary by combining ODD and arbitrary offline or online learnt dictionary to achieve the sparse representation of the testing image. ODD is learnt by testing image content instead of training image dataset. Benefitting from the local similarity of image content, ODD can represent the image more accurately and specifically by estimating the image patch according to the surrounding pixels of it. Furthermore, a joint dictionary can avoid large error by the original sub-dictionary and guarantee the accuracy by ODD.

2   Online Directional Dictionary

2.1   ODD Based Joint Dictionary for Sparse Representation

Sparse representation aims at modeling an image by a linear combination of several elements chosen from the learned dictionary. We consider there is a kth patch x_k extracted by the image X. The residual y_k is obtained by subtracting the patch mean intensity value m_k from the image patch x_k. According to conventional learnt dictionary $D_{original}$, the problem of sparse representation can be formulated as

$$\min \left\| y_k - D_{original} \cdot \alpha_k \right\|_2^2 + \left\| \alpha_k \right\|_0, \tag{1}$$

where α_k is the kth original offline or online coefficients for sparse representation of the image patch. However, $D_{original}$ is a learnt dictionary which is trained by a large set of image patches. As a result of general learning, its likely to occur a situation that there is no accurate pattern to describe the testing image patch. Conventional online learnt dictionary concentrated on training image samples on training dataset with more computation and storage cost. It cant solve this problem effectively.

According to the local similarity of the natural image content, we propose a block-based online directional dictionary (ODD) learning approach to produce a novel online sub-dictionary with respect to the testing image patch content to be sparse represented. Then the problem can be described as

$$\min \left\| y_k - D_{original} \cdot \alpha_k - D_{proposed} \cdot \beta_k \right\|_2^2 + \left\| \alpha_k \right\|_0 + \left\| \beta_k \right\|_0, \tag{2}$$

where $D_{proposed}$ is a dictionary which is learnt by neighbouring image pixels of the testing patch and β_k is the kth coefficients of sparse representation with ODD. To be brief, the function can be simplified as follows

$$\min \left\| y_k - D \cdot \omega_k \right\|_2^2 + \left\| \omega_k \right\|_0, \tag{3}$$

where $\omega_k = (\alpha_k, \beta_k)^T$ and $D = (D_{original}, D_{proposed})$. Since (3) is a NP-hard problem, we use the Orthogonal Matching Pursuit (OMP) [12] algorithm which implies the idea of greedy to obtain the sparse coefficients wk of the patch x_k.

2.2 Details of the Design About ODD

In this sub-section, details of the design about ODD will be elaborated. Inspired by HEVC Intra prediction [13], we design ODD according to the directional block-based prediction as illustrated in Fig. 1. There are 35 prediction modes employed in our approach, including DC mode, planar mode and 33 angular prediction modes. In this paper, mode 0 refers to planar mode, mode 1 to DC mode, and mode 2 to 34 to angular modes. Utilizing the reconstructed values of the surrounding pixels of current patch, prediction values with various directions of current image patch can be obtained.

Like Fig. 2 illustrated, all the prediction modes employ the reference set from above and left of the patch to be sparse represented. And we denote the reference samples by $R_{i,j}$ and the sparse samples by $P_{i,j}$. Planar mode calculates $P_{i,j}$ by bilinear interpolation as

$$\begin{aligned} P_{i,j} = ((n-i) \cdot R_{0,j} + i \cdot R_{n,0} + (n-j) \cdot R_{i,0} + j \cdot R_{0,n}) \\ \gg (\log_2 n + 1) \end{aligned} \tag{4}$$

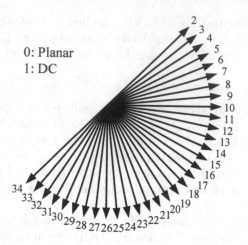

Fig. 1. Prediction mode angular of HEVC.

where $\gg$ denotes a bit shift operation to the right. And for DC mode, all pixels in the current image patch are aligned to the same value which is predicted by (5)

$$DC\_Value = \sum_{i=0}^{n} (R_{0,i} + R_{i,0}) \gg (\log_2 n + 1).\qquad(5)$$

As to angular modes 18 to 34, each sparsed samples $P_{i,j}$ is obtained by projecting its location to the reference row $R_{i,j}$ utilizing the prediction angular and then doing an interpolation scheme for the sample. Interpolation is implemented linearly utilizing the two closest reference samples like (6)

$$P_{i,j} = ((32 - w_j) \cdot R_{u,0} + w_j \cdot R_{u+1,0}) \setminus 32,\qquad(6)$$

where w_j is the weighting value between the reference samples projected to the location $R_{u,0}$ and $R_{u+1,0}$. u denotes the reference sample index. We calculate w_j applying the offset d in Table 1 which is related to the selected angular prediction (7), where mod indicates the module operator. c_j and w_j are only corresponded to j and d. Modes 2 to 17 are derived identically by swapping i and j coordinates in (6) and (7).

$$c_j = \lfloor (j \cdot d) \setminus 32 \rfloor$$
$$w_j = (j \cdot d) \bmod 31\qquad(7)$$
$$u = i + c_j$$

2.3   Image Reconstruction Employing Joint Dictionary with ODD

Then, we introduce the image reconstruction step in which an image can be represented by a sparse and compressible coefficient vector. First, we consider

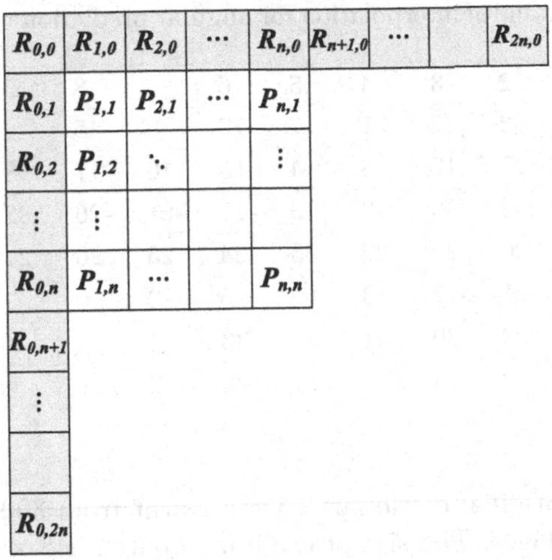

$R_{0,0}$	$R_{1,0}$	$R_{2,0}$	$\cdots$	$R_{n,0}$	$R_{n+1,0}$	$\cdots$		$R_{2n,0}$
$R_{0,1}$	$P_{1,1}$	$P_{2,1}$	$\cdots$	$P_{n,1}$				
$R_{0,2}$	$P_{1,2}$	$\ddots$		$\vdots$				
$\vdots$	$\vdots$							
$R_{0,n}$	$P_{1,n}$	$\cdots$		$P_{n,n}$				
$R_{0,n+1}$								
$\vdots$								
$R_{0,2n}$								

Fig. 2. Reference samples $R_{i,j}$ used in prediction to obtain predicted samples $P_{i,j}$ for a block of size $n \times n$ samples.

that x_k can be represented as the summation of the mean intensity value m_k and the residual y_k like

$$x_k = y_k + m_k. \tag{8}$$

Conventional learnt dictionary based sparse representation approaches describe the residual y_k like following form (9)

$$y_k = D_{original} \cdot \alpha_k + \delta, \tag{9}$$

where $D_{original}$ denotes the original learnt dictionary, denotes the sparse coefficients of the kth image patch employing $D_{original}$, and δ is a minimal value. What differs from our proposed method and conventional learnt dictionary is incorporating adaptive ODD, which is described in Sect. 2.2 into original one to reduce the reconstruction error. Joint dictionary can be modeled by

3 Experimental Results

In this section, we conducted experiments on different testing images to evaluate the PSNR/SSIM performance of the ODD incorporated to various learnt dictionaries and also display the reconstructed image so that it can be evaluated from the perspective of subjectivity.

3.1 Parameters Setting

In our experiments, K-SVD, MOD and RLS-DLA are contained for comparison and their parameter settings were the same as that used in [7,10,14]. The training images were selected from the Berkeley image database and their resolutions are

Table 1. Weighting value of interpolation for angular prediction numbered from 2 to 34

mode	2	3	4	5	6	7	8	9	10
d	32	26	21	17	13	9	5	2	0
mode	11	12	13	14	15	16	17	18	19
d	-2	-5	-9	-13	-17	-21	-26	-32	-26
mode	20	21	22	23	24	25	26	27	28
d	-21	-17	-13	-9	-5	-2	0	2	5
mode	29	30	31	32	33	34			
d	9	13	17	21	26	32			

all 512×512. The original dictionaries were learnt from 30000 random patches from 200 natural images. The size of the image patch is 8×8. And the original Dictionary size for comparison and joint dictionary is 64×291 and 64×256 respectively. And we set the dimension of the proposed ODD is 64×35. The numbers of the elements to represent the patches are from 3 to 6.

3.2   Results and Evaluations of Experiments

In this subsection, we evaluate the reconstructed performance of several standard testing images from USC-SIPI image database in both our approach and other dictionaries.

Tables 2, 3, 4 and 5 shows the PSNR/SSIM performance of the selected images with various numbers of elements to represent image patches. This table demonstrated joint dictionary incorporated ODD to various original dictionaries exceeded original dictionaries themselves with the same size. Meanwhile, as seen from Tables 2, 3, 4 and 5, the reconstructed quality of testing images improved with the increase of element number to represent the image patch.

Figure 3 shows the reconstructed images of MOD and the proposed ODD incorporated into it with 3 elements. The reconstructed image by MOD yields

Table 2. The PSNRS(dB)/SSIMS of reconstructed images by different approaches with 3 elements

Image	K-SVD	K-SVD +ODD	MOD	MOD +ODD	RLS-DLA	RLS-DLA +ODD
Barbara	26.9/0.84	27.0/0.85	26.8/0.84	27.0/0.85	28.0/0.88	28.2/0.88
Boat	35.5/0.94	35.8/0.94	35.5/0.93	35.7/0.94	35.7/0.94	35.8/0.94
Cameraman	33.6/0.95	34.1/0.96	33.5/0.95	34.0/0.96	33.9/0.96	34.4/0.96
Dollar	21.6/0.76	21.8/0.77	21.5/0.76	21.8/0.77	22.0/0.79	22.2/0.80
Lena	33.9/0.92	34.3/0.92	33.9/0.92	34.4/0.92	34.1/0.92	34.4/0.93
Peppers	33.0/0.89	33.3/0.89	33.0/0.89	33.3/0.89	33.2/0.89	33.4/0.89
Woman2	38.8/0.95	39.1/0.96	39.0/0.95	39.2/0.96	39.5/0.96	39.6/0.96

Table 3. The PSNRS(dB)/SSIMS of reconstructed images by different approaches with 4 elements

Image	K-SVD	K-SVD +ODD	MOD	MOD +ODD	RLS-DLA	RLS-DLA +ODD
Barbara	27.6/0.87	27.9/0.88	27.6/0.87	27.8/0.88	29.2/0.91	29.4/0.91
Boat	36.8/0.95	37.1/0.95	36.8/0.95	37.0/0.95	37.3/0.95	37.3/0.95
Cameraman	35.1/0.97	35.6/0.97	35.0/0.96	35.5/0.97	35.8/0.97	36.1/0.97
Dollar	22.2/0.79	22.5/0.80	22.1/0.79	22.4/0.80	22.8/0.83	23.1/0.84
Lena	35.1/0.93	35.4/0.94	35.1/0.93	35.4/0.94	35.4/0.94	35.7/0.94
Peppers	34.0/0.90	34.2/0.90	34.0/0.90	34.2/0.90	34.4/0.91	34.5/0.91
Woman2	40.0/0.96	40.3/0.96	40.1/0.96	40.3/0.96	40.8/0.97	40.8/0.97

Table 4. The PSNRS(dB)/SSIMS of reconstructed images by different approaches with 5 elements

Image	K-SVD	K-SVD +ODD	MOD	MOD +ODD	RLS-DLA	RLS-DLA +ODD
Barbara	28.3/0.89	28.7/0.90	28.2/0.88	28.6/0.90	30.2/0.93	30.5/0.93
Boat	37.9/0.96	38.1/0.96	37.9/0.96	38.1/0.96	38.5/0.96	38.6/0.96
Cameraman	36.5/0.97	36.9/0.97	36.4/0.97	36.8/0.97	37.5/0.98	37.7/0.98
Dollar	22.7/0.82	23.0/0.83	22.6/0.81	23.0/0.83	23.6/0.85	23.8/0.86
Lena	36.0/0.94	36.3/0.95	36.0/0.94	36.3/0.95	36.5/0.95	36.8/0.95
Peppers	34.7/0.91	35.0/0.92	34.7/0.91	34.9/0.91	35.3/0.92	35.4/0.92
Woman2	40.9/0.97	41.2/0.97	41.1/0.97	41.2/0.97	41.8/0.97	41.8/0.97

Table 5. The PSNRS(dB)/SSIMS of reconstructed images by different approaches with 6 elements

Image	K-SVD	K-SVD +ODD	MOD	MOD +QDD	RLS-DLA	RLS-DLA +ODD
Barbara	28.8/0.90	29.3/0.91	28.7/0.90	29.4/0.91	31.2/0.94	31.5/0.94
Boat	38.8/0.96	39.0/0.96	38.8/0.96	38.9/0.96	39.6/0.97	39.6/0.97
Cameraman	37.6/0.98	38.0/0.98	37.5/0.98	38.0/0.98	39.0/0.98	39.1/0.98
Dollar	23.2/0.83	23.5/0.84	23.1/0.83	23.5/0.84	24.3/0.87	24.5/0.88
Lena	36.8/0.95	37.1/0.95	36.8/0.95	37.0/0.95	37.5/0.96	37.7/0.96
Peppers	35.4/0.92	35.6/0.92	35.4/0.92	35.5/0.92	36.0/0.93	36.2/0.93
Woman2	41.7/0.97	41.9/0.97	41.8/0.97	42.0/0.97	42.6/0.98	42.6/0.98

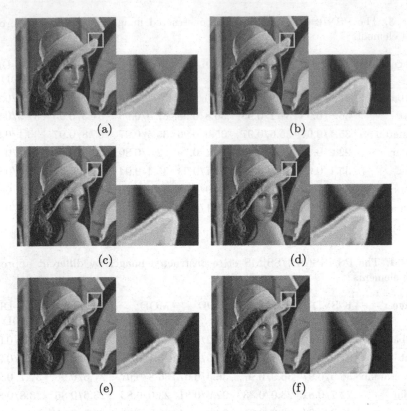

Fig. 3. The reconstructed Lena images (resolution: 512 × 512) with 3 elements. PSNRs and SSIMs of the reconstructed images are (a) K-SVD: 33.9 dB/0.92, (b) K-SVD+ODD: 34.3 dB/0.92, (c) MOD: 33.9 dB/0.92, (d) MOD+ODD: 34.4 dB/0.93, (e) RLS-DLA: 34.1 dB/0.92, (f) RLS-DLA+ODD: 34.4 dB/0.93.

many jagged effects along the edges, but the proposed ODD approach provides better visual quality with more detailed texture, smoother edges, and less blurring/jagged effects. It can be seen that the proposed approach has better quality both objectively and subjectively. Since most natural images normally consist of the objects with different kinds of texture patterns, the proposed ODD can represent the natural images more accurately as a result of make predictions employing the surrounding patch content of the patch to be predicted. On the basis of the avoiding large deviations with original learnt dictionaries, ODD can further improve the reconstructed quality of testing images. What's more, in the applications like image compression and more, it doesn't need so much storage space but guarantees the reconstructed image quality.

4   Conclusions

In this paper, we proposed a online directional dictionary (ODD) approach for image sparse representation. Differing from conventional learnt dictionaries,

ODD can describe the detailed texture of image patch more accurately by employing surrounding patch content of it. Furthermore, without storing ODD, it reduced storage and transmitting costs effectively. Experimental results demonstrate the superiority of the performance of our approach exceeds other competitive algorithm in comparison.

Acknowledgement. This work was supported in part by the National Science Foundation of China (NSFC) under grants 61472101 and 61631017, the National High Technology Research and Development Program of China (863 Program 2015AA015903), and the Major State Basic Research Development Program of China (973 Program 2015CB351804).

References

1. Wallace, G.K.: The JPEG still picture compression standard. Commun. ACM **34**(4), 607–609 (1991)
2. Taubman, D., Marcellin, M.: JPEG 2000: Image Compression Fundamentals, Standards and Practice, 1st edn. Kluwer Academic, Boston (2001)
3. Marcellin, M.W., Gormish, M.J., Bilgin, A., Boliek, M.P.: An overview of JPEG-2000. In: Proceedings of Data Compression Conference, pp. 523–541 (2000)
4. Rubinstein, R., Bruckstein, A., Elad, M.: Dictionaries for sparse representation modeling. Proc. IEEE **98**(6), 1045–1057 (2010)
5. Olshausen, B., Field, D.: Emergence of simple-cell receptive field properties by learning a sparse code for natural images. Nature **381**(13), 607–609 (1996)
6. Wright, J., Ma, M.Y., Mairal, J., Sapiro, G., Huang, T., Shuicheng, Y.: Sparse representation for computer vision and pattern recognition. Proc. IEEE **98**(6), 1031–1044 (2010)
7. Aharon, M., Elad, M., Bruckstein, A.: K-SVD: an algorithm for designing overcomplete dictionaries for sparse representation. IEEE Trans. Sig. Process. **54**(11), 4311–4322 (2006)
8. Lee, H., Battle, A., Raina, R., Ng, A.Y.: Efficient sparse coding algorithms. In: Advances in Neural Information Processing Systems (NIPS), pp. 801–808 (2007)
9. Mairal, J., Bach, F.: Online learning for matrix factorization and sparse coding. J. Mach. Learn. Res. **11**, 19–60 (2010)
10. Skretting, K., Engan, K.: Recursive least squares dictionary learning algorithm. IEEE Trans, Sig. Process. **58**(4), 2121–2130 (2010)
11. Sun, Y., et al.: Dictionary learning for image coding based on multisample sparse representation. Circ. Syst. Video Technol. IEEE Trans. **24**(11), 2004–2010 (2014)
12. Pati, Y., Rezaiifar, R.: Orthogonal matching pursuit: recursive function approximation with applications to wavelet decomposition. In: Conference Record of the Twenty-Seventh Asilomar Conference on Signals, Systems and Computers, vol. 1, pp. 40–44 (1993)
13. Lainema, J., et al.: Intra coding of the HEVC standard. IEEE Trans. Circ. Syst. Video Technol. **22**(12), 1792–1801 (2012)
14. Engan, K., Skretting, K., Husy, J.H.: Family of iterative LS-based dictionary learning algorithms, ILS-DLA, for sparse signal representation. Digit. Sig. Process. **17**(1), 32–49 (2007)

A Low Energy Multi-hop Routing Protocol Based on Programming Tree for Large-Scale WSN

Feng Xu[1,2(✉)], Yating Hou[1,2], Guozhong Qian[1], and Yunyu Yao[1,2]

[1] Nanjing University of Aeronautics and Astronautics, Nanjing, China
nuaaos@163.com
[2] Collaborative Innovation Center of Novel Software Technology
and Industrialization, Nanjing, China

Abstract. In large-scale conditions, due to the number of nodes and the spread of space range are larger, the energy consumption of sensor nodes in the network is more serious, which proposes the higher energy requirements on WSN routing protocols. In this paper, the energy saving scheme of WSN routing protocols is analyzed and classified, and we find that the traditional routing protocols have a lot of room for improvement. In these protocols, cluster head selection usually adopts a random selection method by considering the cluster head rotation, but the cluster head can't keep a reasonable distribution. At the same time, the lack of reasonable planning of the communication path between cluster heads causes a large communication overhead. For this, we put forward a low energy adaptive clustering multi-hop routing protocol based on programming tree (LEACH-PT). The routing protocol takes consideration in the structure within the cluster, the remaining energy of nodes and so on. Based on these factors, the protocol makes the selection of cluster head optimal. Through the method of programming tree, the protocol builds the routing path of the cluster head. Analysis and simulation results show that our protocol provides better balance in energy consumption among nodes and can prolong network lifetime significantly.

Keywords: Large-scale WSN · Low energy · Multi-hop · Programming tree

1 Introduction

Sensor network is widely used at present. The application scenario includes the target imaging, intrusion detection, weather monitoring, security, tactical reconnaissance, distributed computing, and detect environmental conditions, etc. [1].

With microelectronics technology progressing and improving significantly, wireless sensor equipment is made smaller and integrated, and its cost is reduced. It enables deployment in the practical application of more number of sensor nodes to build large-scale wireless sensor networks. Large-scale deployment of the nodes can improve the accuracy of the information, the detection range and so on. So the large-scale wireless sensor network routing protocol research has attracted great attention.

© Springer International Publishing AG, part of Springer Nature 2018
B. Zeng et al. (Eds.): PCM 2017, LNCS 10736, pp. 948–959, 2018.
https://doi.org/10.1007/978-3-319-77383-4_93

In this paper, we analyze the energy saving scheme of WSN routing protocols. According to the ideas, we propose a low energy adaptive clustering multi-hop routing protocol based on programming tree (LEACH-PT). Combining with the characteristics of large-scale network, the protocol optimizes the allocation of nodes and builds a programming tree to reduce communication overhead. This protocol takes comprehensive consideration of these factors: communication routing between clusters, the structure within the cluster, remaining energy of nodes and so on. Through these factors, the protocol adapts to the energy control for large-scale network.

The main contributions of this paper are as follows:

(1) We summarize the common methods of energy saving. In order to reduce the energy consumption of single hop communication, we select cluster head based on energy and the deviation of the cluster center. The method can avoid random positions of the cluster nodes are too biased to the center.
(2) In order to reduce the energy consumption of cluster communication, this paper proposes multi-hop routing protocol based on the programming tree to optimize the routing path of multiple hops.
(3) At last, we compare LEACH, MR-LEACH and LEACH-PT protocol through simulation experiment.

This paper is organized as follows: In the next section, we review related work and research motive. Then in Sect. 3, we put forward a low energy adaptive clustering multi-hop routing protocol based on programming tree. Section 4 provides experimental simulation and analysis. Finally, Sect. 5 summarizes the research results and discusses the further work.

2 Related Work

Many routing protocols are presented for wireless sensor network. Based on the underlying network structure, these routing protocols may generally be categorized as: flat routing protocols, hierarchical routing protocols, and position-based routing protocols [1].

Energy saving problem in wireless sensor network (WSN) has been a key issue. The routing protocol's energy consumption has significant effects on the scalability of the protocol, and it is more prominent in large-scale wireless sensor networks.

There are many ways to improve energy efficiency. Its essence is to reduce the communication between network nodes and computation overhead. These methods to improve energy efficiency are reducing control overhead, mitigating energy consumption, and balancing energy overload [2]. These specific methods are as follows:

(1) Reducing control overhead. The aim of the method is to enhance the energy efficiency by reducing the control overhead. They use innovative designs to simplify the route construction process other methods to substitute the routing process. Thus the control overhead can be reduced. Wu et al. in [3, 4] proposed a routing solution called Off-Network Control Processing (ONCP) that achieves

control scalability in large-scale sensor networks by handing over a certain amount of routing functions to an "off-network" server.

(2) Mitigating energy consumption. The routing protocols exploit various means to achieve this target, such as dynamic event clustering, multi-hop communication, cooperative communication and so on. Ge et al. proposed a novel idea by introducing cooperative communication from a mobile ad hoc network (MANET) to a WSN for energy reduction [5]. They aimed to find the optimal coalition size to minimize the total transmission cost.

(3) Balancing energy overload. Some protocols achieve energy balance through the partition or clusters between nodes, which can prevent excessive death of partial node that may cause reduction of the entire network life cycle. In [6] the authors proposed an energy-efficient distributed clustering protocol, named Geodesic Sensor Clustering (GESC). GESC aims to prolong the network lifetime by distributing energy consumption evenly, considering the localized network structure and the remaining energy of neighboring nodes. In order to utilize the spatial correlation among the sensed data, reference [7] proposed Distributed Clustering Scheme based Spatial Correlation (DCSSC) for grouping sensors based on similarity of data readings. The sensor nodes that have the highest similarity are grouped into the same cluster. They can be scheduled to alternatively report their sensed data for energy saving. Additionally, a dynamic backbone is constructed for efficient data collection.

Traditional LEACH [8] protocol is a typical representative of a hierarchical topology control. But it is a single jump routing protocol. So is not suitable for a large-scale environment. Muhammad et al. [9] proposed a multiple hops low energy adaptive clustering hierarchy routing algorithm (MR-LEACH). The motivation of this work is by increasing the adaptive clustering hierarchy to reduce the energy consumption of sensor nodes. We put forward a FD-LEACH protocol based on fuzzy decision [10], which improves the flexibility and adaptability of the routing protocol to achieve the purpose of energy balance by fuzzy algorithm.

Peng et al. [11] proposed two self-organizing schemes, ECN and ELDCN, for generating clustering-based, degree-constrained and scale-free-inspired for large-scale WSNs. Chidean et al. [12] proposed a general framework for LS-WSN that uses a combination of in-network processing and clustering algorithms to obtain a self-organized and data-coupled network configuration.

In the paper, combining with the characteristics of large-scale wireless sensor networks, we propose a low energy adaptive clustering multi-hop routing protocol based on programming tree (LEACH- PT).

3   Low Energy Adaptive Clustering Multi-hop Routing Protocol Based on Programming Tree

3.1   Energy Saving and Improvement Method

Based on the analysis of the above, we think that hierarchical routing protocols can be further improved in order to improve its energy saving effect. Our LEACH-PT protocol mainly makes improvements in two stages.

Phase of cluster head election: In the whole network electing stage, we choose the same method as LEACH to establish clusters. In the inner cluster electing stage, the candidate cluster heads become head in turn. The candidate cluster heads selecting from nodes based on these factors: center migration degree in cluster, distance from the sink, and surplus energy.

Phase of routing path between clusters: A programming tree is established, in which each cluster heads are mapped as the leaf nodes, and base station is mapped as the destination node. For the points between leaf node and destination node, they are called the relay node. Each relay node is elected through evaluation function. In order to saving energy, establishing programming tree and determining routing path are computed in the base station. The specific definition and algorithm are described below.

3.2   Definitions and Concepts

For the convenience of discussing our algorithm, we make the following definitions:

Definition 1: The Node Hierarchy Level

The sending node is called the source node (SN), and the receiving node is called the destination node (DN). As shown in Fig. 1, the nodes in the area of a square wireless sensor network are the source nodes, and the five-pointed star sign is the destination node. The level of the nodes, which are the first ones received the signal in the network area, is 1. Then these nodes will send the radio message to the neighbor nodes by jumping with the radius of sense. The level of the nodes that have received message stays the same, and the level of the nodes that have not received message increases 1 by the original level. So on, until all the source nodes in the network receive broadcast information. The level of the nodes within the dashed lines in the picture is Level1, and within the dot-dash line is Level2.

Definition 2: The Upper Neighbor Node

In wireless sensor networks, if the nodes are within the radius of sense of node N, they are called N's Neighbor nodes, and if their nodes Level grade are less than or equal to the node Level, it is called N's Upper Neighbor nodes (Upper-Level Neighbor node), shorthand for the UN.

Definition 3: Programming Tree

In order to create an optimal multi-hop routing path, source nodes collect and calculate the information they have to form a tree, whose root node is the destination node and leaf nodes are all the source nodes. We call the tree as the programming tree (PT). There are three kinds of node in programming tree, the leaf node (LN, the source

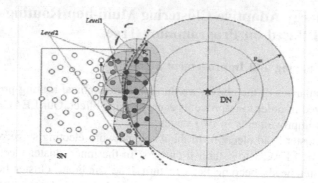

Fig. 1. The node hierarchy level

nodes), the root node (RN, the destination node), and the alternative node (AN, nodes in the middle of the path).

Definition 4: Deviation of Center Gravity

In LEACH-PT protocol, we generate a convex hull from the convex hull algorithm-Graham-Scan algorithm [13]. As shown in Fig. 2, it shows the process of generating the convex.

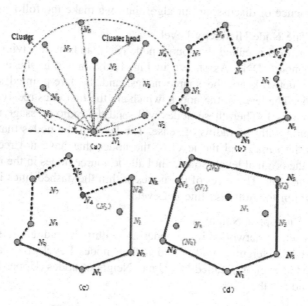

Fig. 2. The establishment of the convex

And then we define the offset with the convex polygons centroid as the node's deviation of center gravity (D_{CG}). Then we assume that the points of the convex hull form a set PS = {P1, P2, ..., Pn}, and connect Pi, Pi + 1 with the origin of coordinates to form n triangles.

3.3 Protocol Description

Each round in this protocol is a cycle. Each cycle can be divided into the following stages: cluster head election stage, cluster set up stage, and cluster routing stage.

3.3.1 Cluster Head Election Stage

At the beginning of the protocol, we use the random selection of cluster head strategy like LEACH protocol. In the initialization, each sensor node N get a random number between 0 and 1, if the random number is lower than the threshold T(N), then the node is elected to be the cluster head. The calculation method of T(N) as follows:

$$T(N) = \begin{cases} \frac{p}{1-p \times [r\bmod(1/p)]}, & N \in G \\ 0 & N \notin G \end{cases} \qquad (3-1)$$

In the formula (3-1), p is the expecting probability of the node to become a cluster head in each round, namely the ratio of the pre-set number of cluster nodes and the total number of all the nodes. In addition, r is the current round number. G is a set of nodes that have not been a cluster head in former 1/p rounds.

A candidate set of cluster heads is set up by the current cluster heads with the receiving message. The message includes the deviation of center gravity of the node Ni DCG(Ni), the distance between the node Ni and the base station D(Ni, BS) and the current energy Ecur(Ni). Based on these three factors, we give a selection factor CHSelsctFun(Ni) as follows:

$$CHSelectFun(N_i) = \frac{E_{cur}}{D_{CG}(N_i) \times D(N_i, BS)} \qquad (3-2)$$

3.3.2 Cluster Set up Stage

The nodes, which are selected as the cluster head nodes, broadcast to the around nodes. The Ordinary nodes according to the received signal strength choose the nearest cluster to join. In the LEACH-PT protocol, cluster nodes consist of ordinary member nodes, candidate cluster head nodes and the cluster head nodes. The communication mode within the cluster chooses a single hop mode "members-the cluster head". This way is suitable for real-time scenarios.

3.3.3 Cluster Routing Stage

The base station finds routing path for each cluster head, according to the mechanism of PT in dynamic programming, in which search the optimal next hop relay node for each cluster head until reaching the base station. The formation of the programming tree branch is a tree, in which the cluster heads are leaf nodes and the base station is the root node.

The process of establishing the programming tree is shown in Figs. 3 and 4. In Fig. 3, the initial state of finding an optimal routing path is described. The green point represents the source node (leaf node, LN), and the red point represents the destination node (root node, RN).

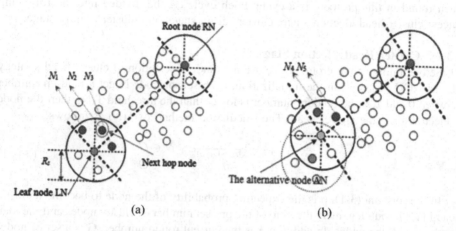

(a) (b)

Fig. 3. The section of AN (Color figure online)

The base station chooses the next hop node for a leaf node based on information about the leaf node's neighbor nodes in its perception radius. The method is drawing a dotted line in LN, which is vertical to the connecting line between LN and RN so we can judge which LN's neighbor nodes belong to its upper neighbor nodes. For example, in Fig. 4, the nodes N1, N2, N3 are LN's upper neighbor nodes. Then, according to the dynamic programming idea, we choose an optimal next hop node in upper neighbor nodes as an alternative node (AN). On the basis of the dynamic programming evaluation function(DFun) and node's dynamic value (DValue) which will be given in following text, LN calculates and selects the next AN according to the below formula (3-3).

$$AN = N_i \text{ where } DFun(LN, N_i) + DValue(N_i) > DFun(LN, N_{j \neq i}) + DValue(N_{j \neq i})$$

$$(3-3)$$

For example, in Fig. 3(a), if N2 is chosen to be the next AN, then N2 will be the new LN and choose the next AN again with the above method. The following nodes will choose their AN according to the dynamic programming principle until they reach the root node. In Fig. 4(a) an optimal routing path of a leaf node is established, and after each leaf node builds the optimal path, the programming tree is established, as shown in Fig. 4(b).

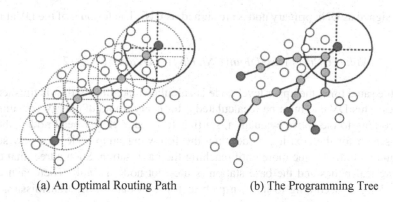

(a) An Optimal Routing Path   (b) The Programming Tree

Fig. 4. An optimal routing path and the programming tree (Color figure online)

Firstly, we can calculate the dynamic programming evaluation function (DFun). The formula is:

$$DFun(LN, UN_i) = (\frac{E_{cur(i)}}{E_o} + \cos\theta_i + \frac{D_{LU(i)}}{C \times R_s})/3, \cos\theta_i = \frac{D_{LU(i)}^2 + D_{RL}^2 - D_{RU(i)}^2}{2 \times D_{LU(i)} \times D_{RL}}$$

$$(3-4)$$

In formula (3-4), Eo and Ecur(i) are the initial energy and current energy of the node UNi respectively. DLU(i) and DRU(i) are the distance of node UNi with the leaf node (LN) and root node (RN). Rs is the radius of sense. DRL is the distance between the leaf node and the root node. θ_i is the angle of line (LN, UNi) and line (LN, RN). When constant C = 1, it means that the UNi is LN's direct upper neighbor node, otherwise, it is non-direct upper neighbor node. LN can choose UNi as the relay node based on DFun.

Secondly, we can calculate the node's state value (DValue). As shown in Fig. 1, according to the level of the node definition to points, each node can be divided into the primary node, the secondary node and so on. The next jump target of the primary nodes is necessarily the base station, namely the root node, without considering the next-hop node selection, then their state value (DValue) is calculated by this formula:

$$DValue(UN_i) = ((S(n+1).yd - ym)/dist(UNi, Bs) + S(i).E/Eo)/2 \qquad (3-5)$$

In the formula (3-5), $S(n+1).yd - ym$ denotes the distance between the base station and the area edge, $dist(UNi, Bs)$ means the distance between node UN_i and the base station, and $S(i).E/Eo$ denotes the radio of the current energy of the node and the initial energy. As shown in the formula, the DValue of primary nodes only considers energy and distance factors.

Then we calculate the DValue of secondary nodes. As the next-hop is the primary node for the secondary nodes, we should consider the choice of the next jump. A secondary node is signed as UNi, primary nodes are signed as UNj. The formula of the DValue is as follows:

$$DValue(UNi) = \max(DFun(UNi, UNj) + DValue(UNj))/2 \qquad (3-6)$$

At the same time, the upper level node is calculated like this, until it is finished with all nodes. This DValue must be recalculated after every round of energy consumption.

According to the above evaluation, starting from each cluster head nodes, the base station search for the next-hop node, then the following jump node as a new starting point, and go to find some more until reaching the base station. Such a tree, that cluster heads are leaf nodes and the base station is the root node, is built. Then each cluster head as long as according to its own path to transmit data in the transmission stable stage.

4   Experiments and Analysis

4.1   Experimental Parameters

We establish a simulation environment using Matlab. In our experiment, we deploy 2500, 5000, and 10000 nodes respectively in the area 500 m*500 m. The sink node is outside the area, and each node has 2J energy at the beginning.

4.2   The Experimental Results and Analysis

The simulation result of the network lifetime is shown in Fig. 5. We compare these three protocols: LEACH, MR-LEACH, LEACH-PT. The result shows that the network lifetime of three protocols in three situations. Compare with LEACH and MR-LEACH, our LEACH-PT protocol can prolong network lifetime significantly.

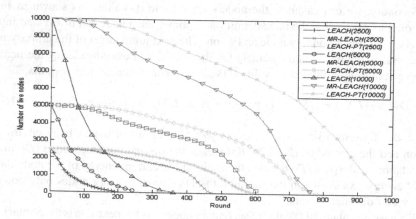

Fig. 5. Network lifetime of LEACH, MR-LEACH, LEACH-PT

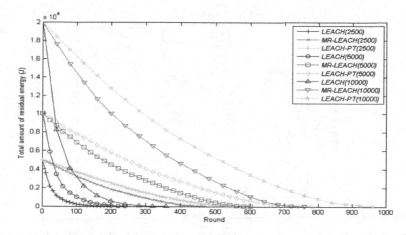

Fig. 6. Network surplus energy of LEACH, MR-LEACH, LEACH-PT

The result of the network surplus energy is shown in Fig. 6, which shows that LEACH-PT can save more energy compared with the other two protocols.

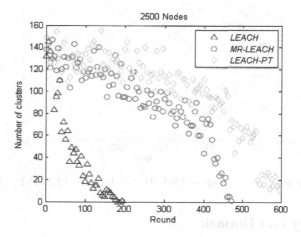

Fig. 7. Number of cluster heads of LEACH, MR-LEACH, LEACH-PT (2500 nodes)

Figures 7, 8 and 9 (2500, 5000, 10000 nodes) describes the number of cluster head in each round of the LEACH, MR-LEACH and LEACH-PT protocol. According to the optimal cluster head number rate, we can calculate the number is 125, 175 and 250 under different number of nodes. The result can reflect that compared with the former two protocols, the number of cluster head in the LEACH-PT protocol is more close to the optimal number of cluster heads, and it can makes the layout of the entire network more balanced (not due to the number of cluster heads is too little, which leads to unbalanced energy consumption).

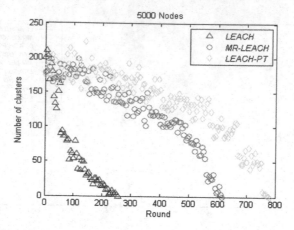

Fig. 8. Number of cluster heads of LEACH, MR-LEACH, LEACH-PT (5000 nodes)

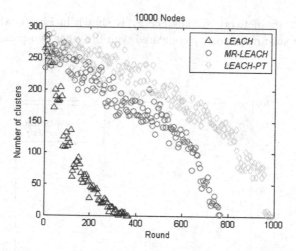

Fig. 9. Number of cluster heads of LEACH, MR-LEACH, LEACH-PT (10000 nodes)

5   Summary and Outlook

At first, the energy saving scheme of WSN routing protocols is analyzed and classified. Then we put forward a general optimization scheme of energy conservation. Taking an example of LEACH, we give a low energy adaptive clustering multi-hop routing protocol based on programming tree (LEACH-PT). At last, we compare LEACH, MR-LEACH and LEACH-PT protocol through experiment. The results show that LEACH-PT protocol has better energy efficiency and prolongs the network lifetime under the condition of large-scale.

In the large-scale network, the cluster heads and key nodes are facing the attack, which can cause the plight of the entire network paralysis. How to defense the attack and designing a routing protocol that has fault tolerance, safety and energy efficiency will be our priority of follow-up work.

Acknowledgments. This work is supported by the China Aviation Science Foundation (NO. 20101952021), the Fundamental Research Funds for the Central Universities (NO. NZ2013306) and the Key Project supported by Medical Science and technology development foundation, Nanjing Department of Health (NO. YKK15170).

References

1. Al-Karaki, J.N., Kamal, A.E.: Routing techniques in wireless sensor networks: A survey. IEEE Wirel. Commun. **11**, 6–28 (2004)
2. Ciancio, A., Ortega, A.: Energy consumption optimization in wireless sensor networks using dynamic programming. In: Proceedings of the 2005 International Conference on Acoustics, Speech and Signal Processing, Philadelphia, USA, pp. 7–10 (2005)
3. Chen, J., Yin, Z., Li, D., Sun, T.: A distributed and effective cluster routing protocol of sensor networks. In: Proceedings of the 1st International Conference on Intelligent Networks and Intelligent Systems, Wuhan, China, pp. 271–275, November 2008
4. Wu, T., Biswas, S.: Off-network control for scalable routing in very large sensor networks. In: Proceedings of the 2007 IEEE International Conference on Communications, Glasgow, UK, pp. 3357–3363, June 2007
5. Ge, W., Zhang, J., Xue, G.: Joint clustering and optimal cooperative routing in wireless sensor networks. In: Proceedings of the 2008 International Conference on Communication, Beijing, China, pp. 2216–2220, May 2008
6. Dimokas, N., Katsaros, D., Manolopoulos, Y.: Energy-efficient distributed clustering in wireless sensor networks. J. Parall. Distrib. Comput. **70**, 371–383 (2010)
7. Le, T.D., Pham, N.D., Choo, H.: Towards a distributed clustering scheme based on spatial correlation in WSNs. In: Proceedings of the 2008 International Wireless Communications and Mobile Computing Conference, Crete Island, Greece, pp. 529–534, August 2008
8. Heinzelman, W., Chandrakasan, A., Balakrishnan, H.: Energy-efficient communication protocol for wireless microsensornetworks. In: Proceedings of the 33rd Annual Hawaii International Conference on System Sciences, pp. 3005–3014. IEEE Computer Society, Maui (2000)
9. Muhammad, O.F., Abdul, B.D., Ghalib, A.S.: MR-LEACH: multi-hop routing with low energy adaptive clustering hierarchy. In: 2010 Fourth International Conference on Sensor Technologies and Applications (ENSORCOMM), pp. 262–268. IEEE Communications Society, New York (2010)
10. Xu, F., Zhu, W., Xu, J., et al.: A low energy adaptive clustering multi-hop routing protocol based on fuzzy decision. J. Intell. Fuzzy Syst. **29**(6), 2547–2554 (2015)
11. Peng, H., Si, S., Awad, M.K., et al.: Toward energy-efficient and robust large-scale WSNs: a scale-free network approach. IEEE J. Sel. Areas Commun. **PP**(99), 1 (2016)
12. Chidean, M.I., Morgado, E., Del Arco, E., et al.: Scalable data-coupled clustering for large scale WSN. IEEE Trans. Wirel. Commun. **14**(9), 4681–4694 (2015)
13. Mark, D.B., Otfried, C., Kreveld, M., et al.: Computational Geometry Algorithms and Applications, 3rd edn., pp. 2–14. Springer, Berlin (2008)

Sparse Stochastic Online AUC Optimization for Imbalanced Streaming Data

Min Yang[1], Xufen Cai[2], Ruimin Hu[1,3], Long Ye[2], and Rong Zhu[1(✉)]

[1] National Engineering Research Center for Multimedia Software, Computer School of Wuhan University, Wuhan, China
{yangmin_16,hrm,zhurong}@whu.edu.cn
[2] Department of Information Engineering, Communication University of China, Beijing, China
xufen.cai@vipl.ict.ac.cn, yelong@cuc.edu.cn
[3] Hubei Provincial Key Laboratory of Multimedia and Network Communication Engineering, Wuhan University, Wuhan, China

Abstract. Area Under the ROC Curve (AUC) is an objective indicator of evaluating classification performance for imbalanced data. In order to deal with large-scale imbalanced streaming data, especially high-dimensional sparse data, this paper proposes a Sparse Stochastic Online AUC Optimization (SSOAO) method. Specifically, we first turn the standard online AUC optimization problem into a stochastic saddle point problem, then optimizing AUC by solving stochastic saddle point problem through AdaGrad optimizer. A sparse regularization term is also added for learning sparse data with high dimension. Comprehensive evaluation has been carried out on the recent benchmark. The experimental results show that the proposed SSOAO has the comparable performance on low-dimensional data, and outperforms other popular AUC optimization methods on high-dimensional sparse imbalanced streaming data. Both time and space complexity for model updating are reduced from $O(d^2)$ to $O(d)$, which equal to the data dimension.

Keywords: Online learning · AUC optimization · Imbalanced data

1 Introduction

With the explosive growth of streaming data in our daily life, streaming data learning attach significance to various aspects of our life, from daily production activities to national security, from corporation management to government macroeconomic decision-making, etc. On some more specific issues, such as face recognition, medical diagnosis, and fault detection, the data we process is often imbalanced. Imbalanced data refers that the number of samples of some categories are significantly less than the number of other categories. The ratio of the

---

M. Yang and X. Cai—Contributed equally to this work.

© Springer International Publishing AG, part of Springer Nature 2018
B. Zeng et al. (Eds.): PCM 2017, LNCS 10736, pp. 960–969, 2018.
https://doi.org/10.1007/978-3-319-77383-4_94

majority and the minority is defined as the imbalanced rate. In some cases, less may be more important, the information contained in a small number of categories is more important. For example, in medical diagnosis, we prefer to detect a few "sick" people among hundreds of healthy people, rather than all people classified as "healthy". Meanwhile, in some extreme cases, the imbalanced rate may even reach more than 10^6. In this case, the classification accuracy is often not as a good evaluation index, because simply all the data are divided into the majority can be achieved very high classification accuracy. For imbalanced problem, measures like AUC and F-measure are better evaluation criteria and this paper mainly focuses on online AUC optimization. Zhao et al. proposed an algorithm for online optimization AUC based on reservoir sampling and the hinge loss [15]. The OAM algorithm needs to store the previous data in the buffer. Gao et al. proposed an OPAUC [8] algorithm based on the squared loss. The advantage of the OPAUC algorithm is that it only needs to traverse the dataset once. However, both OPAUC and OAM have the disadvantage of large computational cost and storage resource consumption for each iteration. They cannot be applied in large scale and high dimensional data. After that, Ying et al. proposed an algorithm for online AUC optimization based on stochastic saddle point problem and square loss [13]. The time complexity is $O(d)$ which is lower than OAM and OPAUC. The SOLAM algorithm, although the efficiency is dominant, when the data is sparse and the dimensions are rather high, the performance still have the space to improve.

In addition, high dimension and sparseness for streaming data are also two vital issues in large-scale machine learning tasks. The general online learning algorithm assumes that all features and results are related, which may result in a nonzero weight corresponding to the feature without information, which in turns degrading the performance. For example, in the spam task, the length of the vocabulary may reach as long as millions. Although the dimensions of feature are rather high, many input values among them are zero and few valid information is provided for the task, which will affect classification performance [14]. The goal of online sparse learning is to solve this problem. By limiting the number of active features, the algorithm learns to get a sparse classifier, that is, most of weights are zero while only a few weights containing information are nonzero. In recent years, many scholars have devoted themselves to studying online sparse learning. FOBOS [5] is based on the sub-gradient descent using Forward-Backward Splitting. Another popular online sparse learning method is Regularized Dual Average (RDA) method [12], which is based on the dual average method [10] using the average of all previous sub-gradients and regularization terms.

In this paper, based on stochastic saddle point problem, we propose an online AUC optimization method named SSOAO by adaptive gradient updates to update the different features in varying degrees for large-scale high-dimensional imbalanced streaming data learning tasks.

2 Related Work

2.1 Online Learning

The traditional batch learning method assumes that all training data has been access at the learning stage and saved in local. Unlike it, online learning updates the model every time for every new arriving samples, and the process continues along with the arrival of the continuous streaming data. In the domain of machine learning, many first-order online learning algorithms have been proposed, including well-known perceptual algorithms [7] and Passive-Aggressive (PA) algorithms [2]. Although the PA algorithm introduces the concept of "maximum margin" in the classification, the PA algorithm cannot update the different features with varying degrees. Consider the task that all features are values by 0 or 1, only the corresponding parameters will be updated when the feature is 1. As a result, the higher frequency the feature appears in, the more the number of updating of the corresponding parameters are. This will result in good estimation for the corresponding parameters for whose feature appears in high frequency, but inaccurate estimation for that in low frequency. In order to solve this problem, in recent years, second-order online learning algorithm [1,4,6,11] have been proposed to achieve better classifiers, these algorithms adopt the confidence information to improve the performance.

2.2 Stochastic Saddle Point (SSP) Problem

The stochastic saddle point problem [13] is the problem represented by formula (2.1)

$$min_{\mu \in \Omega_1} max_{\alpha \in \Omega_2} \{f(\mu, \alpha) := \mathbb{E}[F(\mu, \alpha, \xi)]\} \tag{2.1}$$

Among them, $\Omega_1 \subseteq \mathbb{R}^{d_1}$, $\Omega_2 \subseteq \mathbb{R}^{d_2}$, and Ω_1, Ω_2 is a nonempty convex set; ξ is a random vector, $\xi \in \mathbb{C}$, $\mathbb{C}$ is a nonempty measurable set, and $F : \Omega_1 \times \Omega_2 \times \mathbb{C} \to \mathbb{R}$. Here $\mathbb{E}[F(\mu, \alpha, \xi)] = \int_{\mathbb{C}} F(\mu, \alpha, \xi) dPr(\xi)$, and the function $f(\mu, \alpha)$ is convex on $\mu \in \Omega_1$ and concave on $\alpha \in \Omega_2$. Usually we call μ as the primal variable and α is the dual variable. Saddle point is referred as the optimal solution of stochastic saddle point problem, and first order stochastic algorithms is widely used to solve this problem. The main idea of these algorithms is to replace the real gradient with the unbiased estimation gradient in the process of each iteration, then gradient descent for the primal variable and gradient ascent for the dual variable.

2.3 Area Under the ROC Curve (AUC)

Assume that the ROC curve is connected in order by discrete points whose coordinates are $\{(x_1, y_1), (x_2, y_2), \dots (x_n, y_n)\}$. Then the Area Under the ROC Curve (AUC) can be calculated from formula (2.2):

$$AUC = \frac{1}{2} \sum_{i=1}^{n-1} (x_{i+1} - x_i) * (y_i + y_{i+1}) \tag{2.2}$$

From the perspective of probability, assume the input space $\mathcal{X} \in \mathbb{R}^d$, the output space $y \in \{-1, 1\}$, and the training data $z = \{(x_i, y_i), i = 1, 2...n\}$ is obtained by independently sampling from the unknown distribution ρ defined on $Z = X * Y$. For the decision function $f : \mathcal{X} \to \mathbb{R}$, f consists of any weights of features, AUC value is equal to the probability that the score achieved by positive samples is higher than the negative, under the case that randomly extracting a sample from both positive and negative, respectively. Then the definition of AUC can also be formulated as follows:

$$AUC(f) = Pr\left(f(x) \geq f(x')|y = +1, y' = -1\right) \tag{2.3}$$
$$= \mathbb{E}\left(\mathbb{I}_{[f(x)-f(x')\geq 0]}|y = +1, y' = -1\right)$$

where (x, y) and (x', y') are independently sampled from the distribution ρ.

3 Sparse Stochastic Online AUC Optimization

3.1 Online AUC Optimization

The objective of optimizing AUC is to achieve the optimal decision function f,

$$arg \max_f AUC(f) = arg \min_f Pr(f(x) < f(x')|y = +1, y' = -1)$$
$$= arg \min_f \mathbb{E}\left[\mathbb{I}_{[f(x)-f(x')<0]}|y = +1, y' = -1\right] \tag{3.1}$$

Where $\mathbb{I}$ is the instruction function, take 1 if the condition is true, otherwise take 0. Let $p = Pr(y = 1)$, $\eta(x) = Pr(y = +1|x)$, AUC optimization problem is equivalent to minimizing the expected loss (3.2):

$$R(f) = \mathbb{E}\left[\eta(x)(1 - \eta(x'))l(f, x, x') + \eta(x')(1 - \eta(x))l(x', x, f)\right] \tag{3.2}$$

Among them $l(f, x, x') = \mathbb{I}(f(x) - f(x') < 0), x, x'$ are independently sampled from the same distribution ρ_x. Make Bayesian risk $R^* = \inf_f[R(f)]$, we can get the Bayesian optimal score function set (3.3)

$$\mathcal{B} = \{f : R(f) = R^*\} = \{f : (f(x) - f(x'))(\eta(x) - \eta(x')) > 0$$
$$\text{if } \eta(x) \neq \eta(x')\} \tag{3.3}$$

Since the indicator function $\mathbb{I}(f(x) - f(x') < 0)$ is non-convex and discontinuous, the direct optimization of the indicator function often leads to the problem becoming NP-hard problem. In practice, the indicator function is substituted by its convex surrogate loss $\Phi(f(x) - f(x'))$, where Φ is a convex function. We define the expected risk Φ for

$$R_\Phi(f) = \mathbb{E}_{x,x'\sim\rho_x^2}[\eta(x)(1 - \eta(x'))\Phi(f(x) - f(x'))$$
$$+ \eta(x')(1 - \eta(x))\Phi(f(x') - f(x))] \tag{3.4}$$

And let

$$R_\Phi^* = \inf_f R_\Phi(f) \qquad (3.5)$$

and the surrogate loss Φ is consistent with AUC [9]. So, in this paper, we focus on the linear classification, that is, the function represented by formula (3.6)

$$f(x) = \mathbf{w}^T x \qquad (3.6)$$

the square loss is selected as the surrogate loss of indicator function, and then AUC optimization problem is converted into formula (3.7)

$$arg \min_f \mathbb{E}[(1 - \mathbf{w}^T(x - x'))^2 \,|y = +1, y' = -1]$$

$$= arg \min_f \frac{1}{p*(1-p)} \iint_{\mathcal{Z} \times \mathcal{Z}} (1 - \mathbf{w}^T(x - x'))^2 \, \mathbb{I}_{[y=1]} \mathbb{I}_{[y'=-1]} d\rho(z) d\rho(z') \qquad (3.7)$$

When ρ is the uniform distribution on the training data set z, we have the empirical minimization problem (3.8) for AUC optimization [3,8]

$$arg \min_f \frac{1}{n_+ n_-} \sum_{i=1}^{n} \sum_{j=1}^{n} (1 - \mathbf{w}^T(x_i - x_j))^2 \, \mathbb{I}_{[y_i=1 \wedge y_j=-1]} \qquad (3.8)$$

Where n_+, n_- represents the number of positive samples and the number of negative samples, respectively.

3.2   Sparse Stochastic Online AUC Optimization

In this section, we propose a novel online AUC optimization method named Sparse Stochastic Online AUC Optimization (SSOAO). Now consider the objective,

$$arg \min_f \mathbb{E}[(1 - \mathbf{w}^T(x - x'))^2 \,|y = +1, y' = -1] \qquad (3.9)$$

it can be converted into the problem represented by [13]

$$\mathbb{E}[(1 - \mathbf{w}^T(x - x'))^2 \,|y = +1, y' = -1]$$

$$= 1 + \min_{(a,b) \in \mathbb{R}^2} \max_{\alpha \in \mathbb{R}} \int_{\mathcal{Z}} \frac{F(\mathbf{w}, a, b, \alpha; z) d\rho(z)}{p(1-p)} \qquad (3.10)$$

However, we find that, in the function $F(\mathbf{w}, a, b, \alpha; z)$ in (3.10), the prior probability $p = Pr(y = 1)$ is unknown. In order to solve this problem, we estimate it by formula (3.11) assuming that t data has been received.

$$\hat{p}_t = \sum_{i=1}^{t} \frac{\mathbb{I}_{y_i=1}}{t} \qquad (3.11)$$

Let $v = (\mathbf{w}, a, b)$,

$$f(v, \alpha) = \int_{\mathcal{Z}} F(v, \alpha; z) d\rho(z) \qquad (3.12)$$

Now the optimization problem is transformed into formula (3.13) as a stochastic saddle point problem:

$$\min_{v \in \mathbb{R}^{d+2}} \max_{\alpha \in \mathbb{R}} f(v, \alpha) = \min_{v \in \mathbb{R}^{d+2}} \max_{\alpha \in \mathbb{R}} \int_{\mathcal{Z}} F(v, \alpha; z) d\rho(z) \qquad (3.13)$$

The function $f(v, \alpha)$ is convex on $v = (w, a, b)$ and concave on α. For controlling the model complexity, we introduce the l_2 norm regularization term, and the objective becomes:

$$\min_{v \in \mathbb{R}^{d+2}} \max_{\alpha \in \mathbb{R}} \int_{\mathcal{Z}} \frac{\lambda}{2} ||v||^2 - \frac{\lambda}{2} ||\alpha||^2 + F(v, \alpha; z) d\rho(z) \qquad (3.14)$$

Recall that we mentioned in Sect. 2.1, in the task of online learning, we wish update the different features with varying degrees. In this paper, we realize it by adaptive gradient updates [1,3,6]. Specifically, first suppose $g_t = (\partial_v F_t(v, \alpha; z) - \partial_\alpha F_t(v, \alpha; z))$, $g_{1:t} = [g_1 ... g_t]$ is a matrix including $g_1, ..., g_t$, $G_t = \sum_{\tau=1}^{t} g_\tau g_\tau^T$ and $u_t = (v_t, v_\alpha) x$. Then in each iteration the variable u_{t+1} is updated by

$$u_{t+1} = \prod_{\Omega}^{G_t^{\frac{1}{2}}} (u_t - \eta (G_t)^{-\frac{1}{2}} g_t) \qquad (3.15)$$

where $\prod_{\Omega}^{A}(u) = arg \min_{u' \in \Omega} ||\alpha||_A = arg \min_{u' \in \Omega} <u' - u, A(u' - u)>$. However, the above updates need to compute and store matrix G_t, which makes the algorithm inefficient when the data dimension is large. To solve this problem, we use a diagonal matrix $diag(G_t)$ to approximate G_t. To ensure that the approximation of the diagonal matrix is reversible, we replace the diagonal matrix with $H_t = \delta I + diag(G_t)^{\frac{1}{2}}$, where δ is a small constant used to ensure that the matrix H_t is reversible. At this point in each iteration u_{t+1} is updated by

$$u_{t+1} = \prod_{\Omega}^{H_t} (u_t - \eta H_t^{-1} g_t) \qquad (3.16)$$

Intuitively, we provide the low frequency features with high learning rate, because these features involve more important information. Moreover, in order to improve the efficiency and performance of the algorithm on high dimensional sparse data, the soft l_1 norm regularization $\theta ||u||_1$ is also introduced for the objective. After it, a sparse classifier will be learned, that is, only a small number of parameters of features containing a large amount of information are nonzero while the remaining are all zero. Finally, the objective becomes:

$$\min_{v \in \mathbb{R}^{d+2}} \max_{\alpha \in \mathbb{R}} \int_{\mathcal{Z}} \frac{\lambda}{2} ||v||^2 - \frac{\lambda}{2} ||\alpha||^2 + F(u; z) + \theta ||v||_1 - \theta ||\alpha||_1 d\rho(z) \qquad (3.17)$$

3.3   Optimization and Updates

In order to optimize the objective function (3.17), composite mirror descent algorithm [3, 6] is introduced, which takes a tradeoff between the adaptive gradient item g_t and the regularization term $\varphi(u)$. Let the regularization item $\varphi(u) = \theta||u||_1$, the $i-th$ diagonal element for H_t is $H_{t,ii}$ and $H_{t,ii} = \delta I + ||g_{1:t,i}||_2$. For formula (3.16), suppose $\psi_t(g_t) = <g_t, H_t g_t>$, the dual norm of $||\cdot||_{\psi_t}$ is $||\cdot||^*_{\psi_t}$, and here we have $||g_t||^*_{\psi_t} = ||g_t||_{H_t^{-1}}$. Thus, formula (3.16) can be rewritten by:

$$u_{t+1} = arg\min_{u\in\Omega}\{\eta<g_t,u> + \eta\varphi(u) + B_{\psi_t}(u,u_l)\} \tag{3.18}$$

Where the regularization terms $\varphi_t \equiv 0$, $g_t = (\partial_v F_t(v,\alpha,z) - \partial_\alpha F_t(v,\alpha,z))$ and $B_{\psi_t}(u,u_t)$ are Bregman divergence, which is strong convex and under the differentiable function $\psi_t(g_t) = <g_t, H_t g_t>$. Thus,

$$B_{\psi_t}(u,u_t) = \psi_t(u) - \psi_t(u_t) - <\nabla\psi_t(u_t), u - u_t> \tag{3.19}$$

Now let $\varphi(u) = \theta||u||_1$, we extend formula (3.18) by

$$\min_u \eta<g_t,u> + \eta\varphi(u) + \frac{1}{2}<u - u_t, H_t(u - u_t)> \tag{3.20}$$

For simplicity, we rewrite it as

$$\min_u \eta<\eta g_t - H_t u_t, u> + \frac{1}{2}<u, H_t u> + \frac{1}{2}<u_t, H_t u_t> + \eta\theta||u||_1 \tag{3.21}$$

Suppose $\hat{u}$ is the optimal solution for the problem (3.21), then we have concluded as follows:

1. When $\left|u_{t,i} - \frac{\eta}{H_{t,ii}}g_{t,i} \le \frac{\eta\theta}{H_{t,ii}}\right|$ the optimal solution is $\hat{u}_1 = 0$
2. When $u_{t,i} - \frac{\eta}{H_{t,ii}g_{t,i}}$, then $\hat{u}_i < 0$, at this point the problem (3.21) is differentiable, and let the gradient of (3.21) be zero

$$\eta g_{t,i} - H_{t,ii}u_{t,i} + H_{t,ii}\hat{u}_i - \eta\theta = 0 \tag{3.22}$$

So $\hat{u}_i$ will be updated by

$$\hat{u}_i = u_{t,i} - \frac{\eta}{H_{t,ii}}g_{t,i} + \frac{\eta\theta}{H_{t,ii}} \tag{3.23}$$

3. When $u_{t,i} - \frac{\eta}{H_{t,ii}}g_{t,i} > \frac{\eta\theta}{H_{t,ii}}$, then $\hat{u}_i > 0$, similarly,

$$\eta g_{t,i} - H_{t,ii}u_{t,i} + H_{t,ii}\hat{u}_i + \eta\theta = 0 \tag{3.24}$$

So $\hat{u}_i$ will be updated by

$$\hat{u}_i = u_{t,i} - \frac{\eta}{H_{t,ii}}g_{t,i} - \frac{\eta\theta}{H_{t,ii}} \tag{3.25}$$

Combine these three cases above, update expression for each dimension of coordinate is achieved:

$$u_{t+1,i} = sign(u_{t,i} - \frac{\eta g_{t,i}}{H_{t,ii}})\left[\left|u_{t,i} - \frac{\eta g_{t,i}}{H_{t,ii}}\right| - \frac{\eta\theta}{H_{t,ii}}\right]_+ \tag{3.26}$$

The Pseudo-code for SSOAO is shown in Algorithm 1.

Algorithm 1. SSOAO Pseudo-code

Input: Regularization parameters λ, θ, learning rate η, smooth parameters δ
Variable: $a, b, \alpha \in \mathbb{R}, s \in \mathbb{R}^d, H \in \mathbb{R}^{(d+3)\times(d+3)}, g_{1:t,i} \in \mathbb{R}^t$ for $i \in 1, 2, ..., d+3$
    initiation $w_0 = 0, \alpha_0 = 0, \hat{p}_0 = 0, a_0 = 0, b_0 = 0, g_{1:0} = [], u_0 = 0$

1: **for** $t = 1, ..., T$ **do**
2:     Receive a sample (x_t, y_t)
3:     Update the probility $\hat{p}_t = \sum_{i=1}^{t} \frac{\mathbb{I}_{[y=1]}}{t}$
4:     Calculate $g_t = [\partial_w \hat{F}_t(w_{t-1}, a_{t-1}, b_{t-1}, \alpha_{t-1}, z_t), \partial_a \hat{F}_t(w_{t-1}, a_{t-1,t-1}, \alpha_{t-1}, z_t]),$
        $\partial_b \hat{F}_t(w_{t-1}, a_{t-1}, b_{t-1}, \alpha_{t-1}, z_t]), -\partial_\alpha \hat{F}_t(w_{t-1}, a_{t-1}, b_{t-1}, \alpha_{t-1}, z_t])]$
5:     Update $g_{1:t} = [g_{1:t}g_t], s_{t,i} = \|g_{1:t,i}\|_2$
6:     $H_t = \delta I + diag(s_t)$
7:     $u_{t+1,i} = sign(u_{t,i} - \frac{\eta g_{t,i}}{H_{t,ii}}) \left[\left| u_{t,i} - \frac{\eta g_{t,i}}{H_{t,ii}} \right| - \frac{\eta \theta}{H_{t,ii}} \right]_+$
8:     $w_t = u_t(1:d), a_t = u_t(d+1), b_t = u_t(d+2), \alpha = u_t(d+3)$
9: **end for**

---

4 Experimental Results

4.1 Datasets

For evaluating the performance of our proposed SSOAO method, the experiments were carried out in stochastically selected seven datasets, which can be downloaded from the LIBSVM[1] and UCI[2] web sites. Some of these datasets were originally multi-class data, and we divided it into two classes that were imbalanced. The details of datasets are shown in Table 1.

Table 1. Experimental datasets description

Dataset	Feature number	Data dimension	Imbalance rate $(\frac{n_-}{n_+})$
a9a	32561	123	3.15
usps	7291	256	12.45
mnist	6000	780	10.67
splice	3157	60	5.57
reuters	8293	18933	42.64
farm-ads	4143	54877	1.14
rcv_train	15564	47236	1.10

In our experiments, all feature of samples are standardized, which is $x_t \leftarrow \frac{x_t}{\|x_t\|}$. In this paper, all experiments are completed under the configuration of Intel Xeon E5-2640 v4 2.40 GHz CPU, 64G, and MATLAB 2016b.

---

[1] http://www.csie.ntu.edu.tw/~cjlin/libsvmtools/datasets/.
[2] http://archive.ics.uci.edu/ml.

4.2   Competitors

For comparison, we have chosen three online AUC optimization methods as follows, noting that these algorithms are also based on the square loss function as their surrogate loss function.

- SOLAM [13]: loss function is rewritten into SSP problem then optimized.
- AdaOAM [3]: loss function is optimized by an adaptive gradient descent method.
- OPAUC [8]: loss function is optimized by the stochastic gradient descent method.

4.3   Results and Analysis

We compare the performance of SSOAO algorithm with SOLAM, AdaOAM and OPAUC algorithm in the first four datasets, and compare the performance of SSOAO algorithm and SOLAM algorithm in all seven datasets. In the training phase, we use the five-fold cross validation to determine the parameters for SOLAM $C \in [1 : 9 : 100], R \in 10^{[-1:1:5]}$, and to determine the learning rate $\eta \in 2^{[-8:1:0]}, \lambda \in 2^{[-12:1:2]}$, for AdaOAM and OPAUC. In the first four groups of low-dimensional data, we fix $\theta = 0$, determine $\lambda \in 2^{[-12:1:2]}, \eta \in 2^{[-8:1:0]}$ for SSOAO; in the last three groups of high-dimensional data, we fix $\lambda = 10^{-6}$ and determine $\theta \in 2^{[-8:1:1]}, \eta \in 2^{[-8:1:0]}$ for SSOAO. For all algorithms, five random cross validations are conducted, and the AUC performance is determined by the average of 25 runs.

The experimental results as Table 2 show that, on low dimensional data the SSOAO algorithm is comparable with other algorithms. It should be noted that the time and space complexity of the SSOAO algorithm and the SOLAM algorithm are $O(d)$ for every time the model is updated, while the time and space complexity of the AdaOAM and OPAUC algorithms is $O(d^2)$. The application of AdaOAM and OPAUC will be limited when the data is large scale and on high dimension. On high dimensional data, the AUC performance of SSOAO outperform the SOLAM algorithm, which prove that SSOAO is more efficient for high dimensional data despite in the same complexity.

Table 2. AUC performance comparison

Dataset	SSOAO	SOLAM	AdaOAM	OPAUC
a9a	$.9001 \pm .0037$	$.8997 \pm .0034$	$.8999 \pm .0043$	$.9000 \pm .0028$
usps	$.9793 \pm .0060$	$.9729 \pm .0074$	$.9818 \pm .0052$	$.9820 \pm .0058$
mnist	$.9773 \pm .0069$	$.9484 \pm .0310$	$.9776 \pm .0045$	$.9767 \pm .0046$
splice	$.9684 \pm .0117$	$.9593 \pm .0168$	$.9658 \pm .0140$	$.9681 \pm .0132$
reuters	$.9453 \pm .0240$	$.9302 \pm .0148$	-	-
farm-ads	$.9704 \pm .0048$	$.9667 \pm .0056$	-	-
rcv_train	$.9931 \pm .0012$	$.9918 \pm .0014$	-	-

5 Conclusion

In this paper, the online AUC optimization problem is transformed into SSP problem. Based on the SSP problem, we propose the SSOAO approach for large scale imbalanced data stream. Compared to the previous online AUC optimization algorithms, the time cost and storage space of SSOAO only need $O(d)$ in each iteration. It is also worth mentioning that our proposed algorithm has better AUC performance on high-dimensional sparse data. In future work, we will extend it by exploring the threshold for online classification.

References

1. Bartlett, P.L., Hazan, E., Rakhlin, A.: Adaptive online gradient descent. In: Conference on Neural Information Processing Systems, Vancouver, British Columbia, Canada, pp. 65–72, December 2007
2. Crammer, K., Dekel, O., Keshet, J., Shalevshwartz, S., Singer, Y.: Online passive-aggressive algorithms. J. Mach. Learn. Res. **7**, 551–585 (2006)
3. Ding, Y., Zhao, P., Hoi, S.C.H., Ong, Y.-S.: Adaptive subgradient methods for online AUC maximization. arXiv preprint arXiv:1602.00351 (2016)
4. Dredze, M., Crammer, K., Pereira, F.: Confidence-weighted linear classification. In: Proceedings of the 25th International Conference on Machine Learning, pp. 264–271. ACM (2008)
5. Duchi, J., Singer, Y.: Efficient online and batch learning using forward backward splitting. J. Mach. Learn. Res. **10**, 2899–2934 (2009)
6. Duchi, J.C., Hazan, E., Singer, Y.: Adaptive subgradient methods for online learning and stochastic optimization. J. Mach. Learn. Res. **12**, 2121–2159 (2011)
7. Rosenblatt, F.: The perceptron: a probabilistic model for information storage and organization in the brain. Psychol. Rev. **65**(6), 386–408 (1958)
8. Gao, W., Jin, R., Zhu, S., Zhou, Z.-H.: One-pass AUC optimization. In: Proceedings of the 30th International Conference on Machine Learning, pp. 906–914 (2013)
9. Gao, W., Zhou, Z.-H.: On the consistency of AUC pairwise optimization. In: Twenty-Fourth International Joint Conference on Artificial Intelligence (2015)
10. Nesterov, Y.: Primal-dual subgradient methods for convex problems. Math. Program. **120**(1), 221–259 (2009)
11. Wang, J., Zhao, P., Hoi, S.C.: Exact soft confidence-weighted learning. In: Proceedings of the 29th International Conference on Machine Learning (ICML 2012), pp. 121–128 (2012)
12. Xiao, L.: Dual averaging methods for regularized stochastic learning and online optimization. J. Mach. Learn. Res. **11**, 2543–2596 (2010)
13. Ying, Y., Wen, L., Lyu, S.: Stochastic online AUC maximization. In: Advances in Neural Information Processing Systems, pp. 451–459 (2016)
14. Youn, S., Mcleod, D.: Spam email classification using an adaptive ontology. J. Softw. **2**(3), 43–55 (2007)
15. Zhao, P., Jin, R., Yang, T., Hoi, S.C.: Online AUC maximization. In: Proceedings of the 28th International Conference on Machine Learning (ICML 2011), pp. 233–240 (2011)

Traffic Congestion Level Prediction Based on Video Processing Technology

Wenyu Xu[✉], Guogui Yang, Fu Li, and Yuanhang Yang

College of Computer, National University of Defense Technology, Changsha, China
xuwenyu15@nudt.edu.cn

Abstract. Traffic congestion has become a worldwide problem, seriously restricting the performance of transport network. Prediction of traffic congestion levels composes a significant part of traffic management for improving network performance. With respect to congestion level prediction, although there have been many works, only a few are conducted from the view of overall status of the road network. In this paper, in order to achieve congestion level forecasting, a novel methodology is proposed, which is based on treating network status transformation as a video and processing traffic data from the view of video processing technology. By implementing the model, the experiments based on traffic simulator VISSIM obtain high accuracy (above 0.89), proving the effectiveness of the proposed method.

Keywords: Traffic congestion · Video processing · Machine learning

1 Introduction

With the increasing use of vehicles, traffic congestion has developed as a huge and complicated problem in the urban areas of many countries. To reduce congestion, three ways are usually taken into consideration [7]. One is to improve the infrastructure, e.g., increasing the road capacity, but this requires enormous expenditure. Another way is to promote public transport in large cities, which is not always convenient. The last method is to predict the future states of road network segments, which will support transportation departments and their managers to predictively manage the traffic before congestion appears.

Accurate prediction of future traffic conditions is valuable to traffic management of congested regions and help enhance the performance of urban road network. On the one hand, traffic congestion evaluation and effective predictions of future traffic condition aids commuters to adopt smarter trip strategies, including route and departure time selection. In addition, with the indication of congestion forecasting, traffic departments can take effective traffic management measures, such as traffic dispersion and signal regulation, to avoid grievous jams. Therefore, if the congestion is predicted successfully, it could help to take decisions on noise reduction and energy saving. Also, it could increase the effectiveness and the performance of transport systems, and lead to savings in public infrastructure.

© Springer International Publishing AG, part of Springer Nature 2018
B. Zeng et al. (Eds.): PCM 2017, LNCS 10736, pp. 970–980, 2018.
https://doi.org/10.1007/978-3-319-77383-4_95

Recently, there have been many researches on the prediction of traffic congestion levels. Within these researches, the algorithms of machine learning and data mining tend to be widely utilized. An adaptive data-driven real-time method in [6] was proposed to achieve congestion prediction. Kong et al. [5] utilized floating car trajectory data to predict the urban traffic congestion. Posawang et al. [11] and Thianniwet et al. [13] chose a combined learning framework of neural network and decision tree to classify road traffic congestion into three levels: light, heavy and jam. In the study of [1], a set of seven algorithms of machine learning such as K-nearest neighbors (K-NN), support vector machines (SVM), Bayesian networks (BN) and etc., were selected to prove their effectiveness in the traffic congestion prediction. In particular, the speed, density, distance and etc. were collected as feature data. Although these algorithms have been employed to conduct congestion level prediction and obtained good performance, few work takes the co-movement of different sections of the network into consideration. In other words, it lacks studies focusing on forecasting from the view of the overall status of the whole traffic network.

As machine learning and data mining are data-based methods, massive amount of data for study is in need. The data generally derives from two sources, i.e., real world versus simulation. For the former, Shen et al. [12] and Thianniwet et al. [13] both collected the data through GPS devices while Posawang et al. [11] and Asencio-Cortes et al. [1] captured the data from traffic cameras and detectors. Despite the authenticity of the data, the information collection from the real world is possibly time-consuming and costly owing to the expensive devices, which may further limit the data volume. Recently, many traffic simulators such as TransCAD, SUMO, VISSIM and etc. are employed to evaluate traffic conditions. Compared to empirical data collection, simulators can emulate various traffic conditions and generate sufficient study data, which is time-saving and economical. In [3,8], VISSIM was selected to conduct traffic estimation and verification. VISSIM is a multi-purpose traffic simulation tool to analyze and optimize traffic flows. It offers a wide variety of urban and highway applications, integrating public and private transportation [4]. The tool can effectively and efficiently analyze traffic and transit operations under constraints such as lane configuration, traffic composition, traffic signals, transit stops and etc. Because of the excellent performance on traffic simulation, it is selected as experiment and evaluation tool in this paper.

In this paper, we propose a novel methodology based on the view of video processing technology to predict traffic congestion levels. Specifically, the process of network status transformation is regarded as a video and each link is treated as a pixel of the video frame. The traffic flow simulator is employed to emulate the mobile conditions of traffic flow in a real traffic network. The simulation data are sampled at fixed time interval and prepared based on the video processing technology (e.g. gradients and histograms calculation). To validate the effectiveness, several machine learning algorithms are implemented to forecast congestion levels based on the preprocessed data set.

2   The Proposed Framework

Within this study, we propose an algorithm framework based on video process-ing technology to predict traffic congestion levels. The study data is collected by the traffic simulator VISSIM and prepared for the succeeding framework. From the view of video processing, gradients and histograms of link states are calcu-lated to compose the feature data as descriptor of the whole network condition. Then, machine learning algorithms applied on the data set output the predic-tion results. An overview of the proposed framework with its main constituents is depicted in Fig. 1.

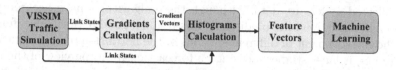

Fig. 1. Overview of the proposed method

2.1   Collection and Preparation of Simulation Data

For the sake of reproducibility, controllability, and generation of a sufficient amount of data, we select the traffic flow simulator VISSIM to model a real traffic network. In the simulation of VISSIM, the network is constructed by connected road links. Then, traffic compositions of a certain period are fed into the network model to emulate traffic conditions and produce traffic data.

VISSIM is equipped with tools for recording and evaluation, making the data sampling easily operable. The status of each link is recorded at a fixed time interval Δt and at each sampling point, three input variables are taken down as the features of link status: vehicle density, vehicle speed and vehicle volume.

The congestion levels that we study are limited to three levels: light, heavy and jam, which is sufficient and appropriate according to the study of [11]. Specifically, the congestion level of a network is determined by the average value of vehicle velocity $\bar{v}$ as follows [11]: if $\bar{v} \geqslant 20\,\text{km/h}$, the congestion level is *light*, if $20\,\text{km/h} > \bar{v} \geqslant 10\,\text{km/h}$, the congestion level is *heavy* and if $10\,\text{km/h} > \bar{v}$, the congestion level is *jam*.

Extraction of Link Status. A video is composed of a series of frames and mainly contains visual modality, thus the visual modality is generally processed based on separate frames in terms of video processing. A frame within a video comprises pixels of different colors and the color of a pixel is represented with a set of values selected from the color space, e.g. RGB (red-green-blue) space. With RGB space, the color of a pixel is composited of three values in three color channels: red, green and blue.

In this paper, we originally treat the traffic network from the view of video processing technology. More specifically, the transformation process of network status is regarded as a video and the instantaneous status at each sampling point is a frame of the video. Moreover, the status of each link in the network composes a "pixel" (referred as "link pixel"). The corresponding RGB channels of a link pixel is: vehicle density, vehicle speed and vehicle volume (referred as DSV).

Calculation of Link Gradient Vectors. As a video is a dynamic process, it is essential to obtain the temporal video information for video study. To fetch the temporal information, the concept of gradient vector is introduced. Generally, the gradient represents the slope of the tangent of the function graph, e.g. the progression between colors as color gradient and rate-of-change of a physical quantity over space as spatial gradient. As for video processing, different oriented gradients in a video image are calculated as gradient vectors, which are utilized to effectively figure the geometrical and optical transformations of the video.

Likewise, as the variation of the network status is treated as a video in this study, the gradient vector of a link pixel denotes the rate-of-change of link status. As mentioned above, three variables, i.e., vehicle density, vehicle speed and vehicle volume, are selected to profile the status of a link at each sampling interval. Let (d_i, s_i, v_i) be the status of link L at the ith sampling point where, d_i, s_i and v_i respectively represents density, speed and volume of L. The gradient vector of L is expressed as $(\nabla d_i, \nabla s_i, \nabla v_i)$ where ∇(the nabla symbol) denotes the vector differential operator. Here, ∇ bounds to the Mean of Difference (MD): $\nabla d_i = [d_{i+1} - d_{i-1}]/2$, $\nabla s_i = [s_{i+1} - s_{i-1}]/2$, $\nabla v_i = [v_{i+1} - v_{i-1}]/2$, and $Gradient(L) = (\nabla d_i, \nabla s_i, \nabla v_i)$.

With the gradient vectors, we could profile the temporal variation of a link.

2.2 Calculation of Histograms

In the study of video processing, the histogram of RGB colors (HRC) and the histogram of oriented gradients (HOG) are frequently used to characterize the features of visual modality.

HLS: Histogram of Link States. HRC mainly counts the amount of different colored pixels in video frames, depicting the proportions and the distribution of different colors. To be specific, for the example of RGB space, the frequency of three colors (i.e. red, green, blue) is counted according to the RGB values of pixels, then converting into HRC.

Accordingly, as DSV are selected as the corresponding RGB channels of link pixels, at each sampling point, we calculate the frequency of different numerical intervals according to the DSV values of link pixels. For The resulting histogram is called the histogram of link states (referred as HLS).

HOG: Histogram of Oriented Gradients. The histogram HOG is used as the feature descriptor in the study of computer vision and pattern recognition. The technique counts occurrences of gradient orientation in localized portions of an image.

In this paper, HOG is utilized to describe the transformation pattern of traffic network condition. We only focus on the time-oriented gradient as mentioned in Sect. 2, thus we count occurrences of temporal gradients of three status variables (DSV) in each sampling interval and obtain the HOG of the network.

2.3 Validation Process: Machine Learning

Based on the calculated histograms and the recorded network status, the data set is constructed and fed into machine learning algorithms to validate their effectiveness.

Preparation of Data Set. At each sampling point, HRC and HOG are merged into a feature vector as descriptor of instantaneous network condition. For unification, the histogram will be normalized beforehand.

Then, information about future occurrence of traffic condition recorded in Sect. 2 will be included in the class. As mentioned before, the class includes three possible levels: light, heavy and jam. In this paper, we use three numbers to represent these three, i.e. 0, 1 and 2, expressed as light $= 0$, heavy $= 1$ and jam $= 2$. Specifically, within the following preset minutes (in this study, those minutes are 10 and 20), if free flow occurs, then value 0 is assigned to the class; If traffic condition is detected heavy, 1 is assigned; if congested, 2 is assigned. These three levels will be the class label and the one expected to be correctly predicted.

As a consequence, the feature vectors with class labels compose the data set which will be fed into the following machine learning.

Validation Process. In this study, considering the spatial and temporal associations of traffic conditions of different sections in the network, two algorithms of machine learning have been selected to evaluate their effectiveness in the prediction of traffic congestion levels, i.e. k-nearest neighbors (K-NN) algorithm, C4.5 decision trees (C4.5) algorithm. As both algorithms are able to address a classification problem, they are regarded as classifiers in this paper. Specifically, the data sets used to validate the performance of traffic congestion prediction have three classes (light, heavy and jam). Since all these are classical algorithms, there is no redundant description to them.

The prediction on the whole network may be not so significant since the network scale is relatively large. Hence, we decide to divide the network into several smaller sub-networks according to the zones covering the related links. Then based on the current condition of the whole network, the prediction will be made on the future status of different sub-networks. Such smaller-scale predictive information can help the managers to locate the congested region more accurately and take pertinent management measures.

3   Experiments and Analysis

In this section, we firstly simulate traffic conditions in a real network. Then, experiments based on the proposed method are devised to estimate the effectiveness of the study.

3.1   Simulation and Data Collection

Basically, the experimental scenario is set on a real network of a region of Changsha City in China and VISSIM is applied to model the mobile conditions of vehicles of the selected area (see Fig. 2).

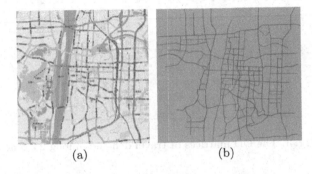

(a)   (b)

Fig. 2. The network model of a region in Changsha City

For modeling real world scenarios, a traffic simulation mainly needs data that describes the infrastructure of transport network as well as data about the real-world travel demand [2]. Firstly, VISSIM constructs the network model based on the map of Changsha City extracted from OpenStreetMap [10]. The network model is divided into 24 zones and contains 145 links of which each link keeps a distinguished ID. Then, we collect travel-demand data of 8:00am–9:00am from the Annual Report of Changsha Traffic in 2015 [9] since the heaviest congestion occurs in this period. Furthermore, the demand data are modeled using Origin-Destination (OD) matrices (see Fig. 3) within which each OD pair indicates the largest vehicle departures from origin zone to destination zone over the period. In order to illustrate different traffic demand, a series of OD matrices are used to represent various demand levels, which are obtained by multiplying the traffic demand with a coefficient (denoted as φ). This coefficient φ varies from 0.1 to 1.0 in the numerical test so as to increase the network OD demand. As for traffic compositions, the desired vehicle speeds are set as: Car: 50(48–58) km/h; Bus: 25(20–30) km/h; HGV (Heavy Goods Vehicle): 25(20–30) km/h. Take the car as example, 50(48–58) km/h means the expected speed of the car ranges from 48 to 58 km/h with 50 as the mean value.

With the network model and OD matrices as input, VISSIM is run to produce study data as output. In order to get stable information, for each OD matrix, we set up 100 simulations with 20 iterations to warm up. For data collection, the sampling interval is set as $\Delta t = 5$ min and the output status of a link at each point is organized as: [ID, Time, Vehicle Density, Vehicle Speed, Traffic Volume].

For example, [1, 300, 6.25, 12.54, 78.34] means link 1 at 300 s accommodates 6.25 vehicles per kilometer, with cars flowing at average speed 12.54 km/h and 78.34 vehicles passing through it per hour.

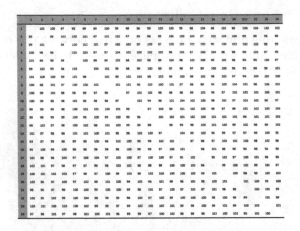

Fig. 3. The OD matrices of travel demand among 24 zones

Based on the simulation data collected in Sect. 2.1, at each sampling point and each link, we compute the gradient vectors of congested links.

3.2 Labels of Traffic Levels

For more indicative predictive information, we make prediction on 8 smaller sub-networks of the network, as roughly shown in Fig. 4. For each sampling interval and each sub-network, the traffic congestion level is determined according to Sect. 2.1 and marked as the corresponding value: 0, 1 and 2 (i.e. light, heavy, jam).

Fig. 4. Partitions of eight sub-networks

3.3   Calculation of Histograms: HLS and HOG

Firstly, we calculate the HLS which contains three dimensions: vehicle density, vehicle speed, vehicle volume. Take density dimension as example and let Max-Den and MinDen be the maximum and minimum density values detected in the experiment. We partition the value range into 12 histogram bins, so the span is (MaxDen-MinDen)/12 for each bin. At each sampling point, each link pixel votes for the bin that covers its density value. Likewise, the speed-dimensional and volume-dimensional histograms are calculated in the similar way. An example of the three-dimensional HLS is displayed in Fig. 5(a).

Then the similar procedure is applied to the calculation of HOG. Specifically, for the three gradient members ($\nabla density, \nabla speed, \nabla volume$), the bin span is one twelfth of the difference between maximum and minimum values. Voting on bins will be employed based on the gradients, resulting in three-dimensional HOG. An example of HOG is displayed in Fig. 5(b).

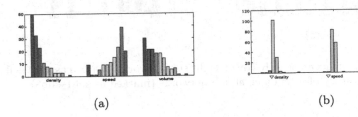

(a)   (b)

Fig. 5. Examples of histograms: (a) HLS and (b) HOG

As HLS and HOG are both three-dimensional histograms and each dimension has 12 bins, either constitutes $12 * 3 = 36$ features. In addition, to contain the information of the co-movement of different sections in network, the congestion levels of 8 sub-networks are included into the feature values. Thus, the combination of two histograms and congestion levels of sub-networks composes an 80-dimensional feature vector ($36 + 36 + 8 = 80$).

3.4   Results and Analysis of Applying Machine Learning

The sampling interval is set with the $\Delta t = 5$ min (i.e., 300 s). We detect the traffic condition at a sampling point and make predictions on the future. Specifically, the future prediction intervals from detection point t are set $2\Delta t$ and $4\Delta t$ (10 min and 20 min) respectively, i.e. the traffic prediction will be made on $(t, t + 2\Delta t)$ and $(t, t + 4\Delta t)$.

In this paper, two algorithms of machine learning (i.e., K-NN and C4.5) are selected to conduct congestion level prediction. Before implementing C4.5, the training set and testing set should be constructed. We use the data collected from the former 100 simulations as training set. In the training set, each element (i.e., a vector) contains 80 features and the class label of traffic condition of the corresponding sub-network and prediction interval. As a consequence, based on different prediction intervals, the machine learning algorithm obtains different training results which will be applied to the subsequent prediction. To obtain testing data set, we run another 100 simulations with random travel demands. The sampling interval is set with the same $\Delta t = 5$ min (i.e., 300 s). Correspondingly, at each sampling point, we record the status of each link, calculate the histograms and mark the congestion level of different sub-network.

As K-NN is a type of lazy-learning and does not need training set to train, we use the same testing set of C4.5 as its testing samples.

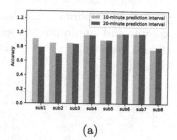

(a)

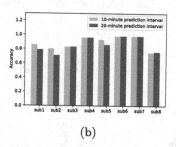

(b)

Fig. 6. (a) Prediction accuracy of K-NN on eight sub-networks (marked as sub1–sub8), (b) Prediction accuracy of C4.5 on eight sub-networks (marked as sub1–sub8)

Table 1. Prediction accuracy of 10-min prediction interval

	sub1	sub2	sub3	sub4	sub5	sub6	sub7	sub8	Total
K-NN	0.91	0.85	0.85	0.96	0.89	0.98	0.98	0.76	0.92
C4.5	0.86	0.80	0.83	0.96	0.93	0.98	0.98	0.75	0.91

Table 2. Prediction accuracy of 20-min prediction interval

	sub1	sub2	sub3	sub4	sub5	sub6	sub7	sub8	Total
K-NN	0.79	0.70	0.84	0.96	0.89	0.98	0.98	0.79	0.90
C4.5	0.79	0.71	0.83	0.96	0.86	0.98	0.98	0.76	0.89

During the testing, the machine learning algorithm takes the input without the class labels and exports a label value as the predictive result for the corresponding sub-network and prediction interval. Finally, the resulting predictions were compared to the actual test classes, producing the prediction accuracy. Overall, as can be seen from the figures and tables of results, both algorithms achieve relatively high prediction accuracy (all above 0.89), which prove the effectiveness of our proposed method. As shown in Fig. 6, for both algorithm, the accuracy sees a decline as prediction intervals increase (from 10 min to 20 min), which is consistent with the actual traffic situation. Specifically, the current traffic condition has stronger influence on future condition in a shorter time, so it becomes less indicative of future as interval grows.

As shown in Tables 1 and 2, for different sub-networks, the proportions of accurate prediction vary which can be attributed to the different structures. Some sub-networks obtain significantly high accuracy such as No. 6 and No. 7 (both above 0.98 even the prediction interval rises to 20 min). After analyzing on the reality, we attribute these outcomes to grievous and continuous congestion of these two section during the simulation time (8:00am–9:00am). Since, the features are relatively distinguishing for the classifiers. As for different prediction intervals, K-NN outperforms C4.5 in their entirely, which can be owing to the better performance of K-NN on depicting the spatial and temporal associations of traffic conditions.

4   Conclusion

In this paper, we take the co-movement of different sections of the network into consideration, proposing a novel methodology based on the view of video processing technology to predict traffic congestion levels. Specifically, the process of network status transformation is regarded as a video and each link is treated as a pixel of the video frame. The simulation data are processed based on the video processing technology (e.g., gradients and histograms calculation). To validate the effectiveness, two algorithms of machine learning (i.e., K-NN and C4.5) are implemented to forecast congestion levels based on the preprocessed data set.

The experimental results show relatively high prediction accuracy (above 0.89), proving that the proposed method makes sense. Moreover, it indicates that the proposed method could be used to provide valuable information for effective and efficient traffic flow management such as real-time prediction.

References

1. Asencio-Corts, G., Florido, E., Troncoso, A., Mart-lvarez, F.: A novel methodology to predict urban traffic congestion with ensemble learning. Soft Comput. **20**(11), 4205–4216 (2016)
2. Bieker, L., Krajzewicz, D., Morra, A.P., Michelacci, C., Cartolano, F.: Traffic simulation for all: a real world traffic scenario from the city of Bologna. In: Behrisch, M., Weber, M. (eds.) Modeling Mobility with Open Data. LNM, pp. 47–60. Springer, Cham (2015). https://doi.org/10.1007/978-3-319-15024-6_4
3. Cho, H., Kim, Y.: Analysis of traffic flow with variable speed limit on highways. KSCE J. Civil Eng. **16**(6), 1048–1056 (2012)
4. Fellendorf, M., Vortisch, P.: Microscopic traffic flow simulator VISSIM. In: Barceló, J. (ed.) Fundamentals of Traffic Simulation. International Series in Operations Research & Management Science, vol. 145, pp. 63–93. Springer, New York (2010). https://doi.org/10.1007/978-1-4419-6142-6_2

5. Kong, X., Xu, Z., Shen, G., Wang, J., Yang, Q., Zhang, B.: Urban traffic congestion estimation and prediction based on floating car trajectory data. Future Gener. Comput. Syst. **61**(C), 97–107 (2016)
6. Li, F., Gong, J., Liang, Y., Zhou, J.: Real-time congestion prediction for urban arterials using adaptive data-driven methods. Multimedia Tools Appl. **75**(24), 1–20 (2016)
7. Jian, C., Gao, Z., Ren, H., Lian, A.: Urban traffic congestion propagation and bottleneck identification. Sci. China Inf. Sci. **51**(7), 948 (2008)
8. Mehar, A., Chandra, S., Velmurugan, S.: Highway capacity through VISSIM calibrated for mixed traffic conditions. KSCE J. Civil Eng. **18**(2), 639–645 (2014)
9. Transport News: Transport of Changsha (2016). tensorflow.org
10. OpenStreetMap: Openstreetmap (2017). openstreetmap.org
11. Posawang, P., Phosaard, S., Polnigongit, W., Pattara-Atikom, W.: Perception-based road traffic congestion classification using neural networks and decision tree. In: Ao, S.I., Gelman, L. (eds.) Electronic Engineering and Computing Technology. Lecture Notes in Electrical Engineering, vol. 60, pp. 237–248. Springer, Dordrecht (2010). https://doi.org/10.1007/978-90-481-8776-8_21
12. Shen, Q., Ban, X., Guo, C., Wang, C.: Kernel based semi-supervised extreme learning machine and the application in traffic congestion evaluation. In: Cao, J., Mao, K., Wu, J., Lendasse, A. (eds.) Proceedings of ELM-2015 Volume 1. Proceedings in Adaptation, Learning and Optimization, vol. 6, pp. 227–236. Springer, Cham (2016). https://doi.org/10.1007/978-3-319-28397-5_18
13. Thianniwet, T., Phosaard, S., Pattara-Atikom, W.: Classification of road traffic congestion levels from vehicle's moving patterns: a comparison between artificial neural network and decision tree algorithm. In: Ao, S.I., Gelman, L. (eds.) Electronic Engineering and Computing Technology. Lecture Notes in Electrical Engineering, vol. 60, pp. 261–271. Springer, Dordrecht (2010). https://doi.org/10.1007/978-90-481-8776-8_23

Coarse-to-Fine Multi-camera Network Topology Estimation

Chang Xing, Sichen Bai, Yi Zhou, Zhong Zhou$^{(\boxtimes)}$, and Wei Wu$^{(\boxtimes)}$

State Key Laboratory of Virtual Reality Technology and Systems,
Beihang University, Beijing 100191, China
{zz,wuwei}@buaa.edu.cn

Abstract. In multiple camera networks, the correlation of multiple cameras can provide us with a richer information than a single camera. In order to make full use of the association information between multiple cameras. We propose a novel approach to estimate a camera topology relationship in a multi-camera surveillance network, which is unsupervised and gradually refined from coarse to fine. First, an improved cross-correlation function is used to get a preliminary result, then a time constraint feature matching model is used to reduce the error caused . by external environment and noise, which can increase the accuracy of our results. Finally, we test the proposed method on several different datasets, and its result indicates that our approach perform well on recovering the topology of the camera and can improve the accuracy on over camera tracking.

Keywords: Multi-camera · Camera topology · Cross-correlation
Feature matching

1 Introduction

As an important part of the security technology system, video surveillance system is always a good studied topic and research hotspot. The need of practical application on this kind of system has being rising rapidly. However, nowadays, most of the traditional surveillance systems rely on human cooperation and brings burden for operators. For example, if a car needs to be found in a city area, the operator has to search every surveillance video in the area by orders. Even he can find the right car, the operator spend too much time to understand the order relationship of occurrence during the different cameras. It is often ineffective and obtain inaccurate result. Therefore, many intelligent surveillance systems have been presented to inference the relationship between multiple videos automatically.

Unlike single camera, a multi-camera surveillance network has a wider field of view. So, it is hard for us to associate cameras at different positions. Over the past few decades, camera topology relationship is presented to determine the relationship between the cameras. Makris et al. [1] proposed a method to

© Springer International Publishing AG, part of Springer Nature 2018
B. Zeng et al. (Eds.): PCM 2017, LNCS 10736, pp. 981–990, 2018.
https://doi.org/10.1007/978-3-319-77383-4_96

estimate the camera topology relationship in a camera network based on the simple occurrence correlation between entering and exiting events. Kinh [2] presented an approach to estimate the topology of a camera network by measuring the degree and nature of statistical dependence between observations in different cameras. Unlike previous work, Kinh explicitly considered the correspondence problem and handles general types of statistical dependence by using mutual information and non-parametric density estimates. Niu [3] proposed a model constructed by the combination of normalized color and overall model size to measure the moving objects appearance similarity across the non-overlapping views, their method combines appearance information and statistics information of the observed trajectories, which can overcome the disadvantages of the approaches that only use one of them. Then, based on Kinhs method, Zehavit [4] proposed a method which divides the camera frame into blocks, and refines the relationship between camera into block level. Chen [5] focuses on decreasing the large variance of transition time of true correspondences, which can compensate for the influence caused by large-scale false correspondences to a certain degree.

The methods mentioned above mainly dependent on the relevance of time, and do not take into account the target speed of movement. Their method generally relies on long term videos to reduce the error. To solve those problem, we propose a novel multi-camera network topology estimation method in this paper. The main contributions of this paper are concluded as follows:

- A coarse-to-fine framework to estimate an accuracy camera topology in the multi-camera surveillance system.
- The proposed approach has good scalability, which can be applied in various field such as over camera tracking which can improve the accuracy and efficiency of existing methods.

2   Our Approach

Our coarse-to-fine multi-camera network topology estimation approach is divided into two main procedures. Firstly, given input entries in videos, we use cross-correlation function model to calculate the transition time and improve it with neighbor accumulate method and peak detection. Then, a time constraint based on feature matching method is used to get a more accuracy transition time distribution. Through the above steps, we can obtain accurate correlation between cameras.

2.1   Improved Cross-Correlation Function Model

As the input of our method, entries in the videos are detected by clustering foreground where objects moving into or leaving from the camera. We consider that objects are directly corresponding to entry. So we uses Faster-RCNN [6], a constructive work of recent years, to detect the (such as human) location of objects in the camera view. Then the entry zones can been easily clustered by the K-means method [7]. Three examples are shown in Fig. 1.

(a) camera 1   (b) camera 5   (c) camera 4

Fig. 1. A example of entries division in cameras (on DukeMTMC [8]).

According to moving direction, the objects are added into corresponding departure sequence and arrival sequence. As for the entry i in camera c_1 and entry j in camera c_2, if there is a strong transition relationship between them, the object leaves from i at time t_1 will move into entry j at time t_2, $t_2 \in [t_1 - \tau_0, t_1 + \tau_0]$, where τ_0 is a parameter that defines the transition time window. We assume that the transition time obeys the Gaussian distribution. The origin cross-correlation function is defined as $R_0^{ij}(\tau) = E[D_i(t) \cdot A_j(t + \tau_0)]$, where $D_i(t)$ is the departure time sequence at entry i, $A_j(t + \tau_0)$ is the arrival time sequence at entry j. τ_0 is the transition time. $R_0^{ij}(\tau)$ will have obvious peak which represent that there is a transition relationship between the two entries.

However, the origin cross-correlation function uses only temporal information, the state of the cross-correlation function is unstable. In order to get a clear and steady peak, an improved cross-correlation function is introduced to calculate the transition time window. We use an n-neighbor accumulated method [5] to improve the stability of the cross-correlation function:

$$
\begin{aligned}
R^{ij}(\tau) &= \sum_{\tau_0 = \tau_n - 5}^{\tau_n + 5} R_0^{ij}(\tau_0) \\
&= \sum_{\tau_0 = \tau_n - 5}^{\tau_n + 5} E[D_i(t) \cdot A_j(t + \tau_0)] \\
&= \sum_{\tau_0 = \tau_n - 5}^{\tau_n + 5} \sum_{t = -\infty}^{+\infty} D_i(t) \cdot A_j(t + \tau_0), \tau_n \geqslant 5
\end{aligned}
\tag{1}
$$

The n is set to 5 empirically, which can solve the problem of excessive accumulation in [5].

Intuitively, at different entries, only those objects which look similar in appearance can be counted to derive the spatio-temporal relation. The $E(,)$ can be transformed to Eq. (2):

$$
E[D_i(t) \cdot A_j(t + \tau_0)] = \sum_{O_i \in D_i(t)} \sum_{O_j \in A_j(t + \tau_0)} similiarity(O_i, O_j)
\tag{2}
$$

$similiarity(,)$ denotes the similarity between two objects (O_i, O_j) in corresponding sequences.

A threshold is empirically set to detect the peak interval of the $R^{ij}(\tau)$ from the mean and variance of the transition time.

$$threshold = avg\left(R^{ij}(\tau)\right) + \omega \cdot std\left(R^{ij}(\tau)\right) \tag{3}$$

The value below the threshold is considered to be the noise. After that, we search for a peak interval in the $R^{ij}(\tau)$, t_k is identified as a candidate if it satisfies the formula $R^{ij}(t_k - 1) \leqslant R^{ij}(t_k) \leqslant R^{ij}(t_k + 1)$, $W^{ij}(t_k)$ represent the interval width of t_k which is extended until $threshold > R^{ij}(t_p)$ or $R^{ij}(t_p) > R^{ij}(t_k)$. In this work, we assume there is only one popular transition time if there is a link between entry i and entry j. If there is more than one candidate t_m and t_n, a threshold α is set to merge them (α is the width of the candidate, empirically set to 0.2W).

$$W^{ij}(t_m) = W^{ij}(t_m) + W^{ij}(t_n), \qquad if \quad t_m - t_n < \alpha \tag{4}$$

Through the repeated iteration, t_k is the final transition time when there is only one interval. And the transition time window W_0^{ij} approximates to its interval width:

$$T^{ij} = t_k, W_0^{ij} = W^{ij}(t_k) \tag{5}$$

Otherwise, there is no direct correlation between two entries. Then, a coarse results is obtained. Figure 2(a) is the cross-correlation function without any process, though the accumulation and the peak detection, the peak is much more clear and smooth and its much easier to be recognized (Fig. 2(b)).

2.2   Time Constraint Feature Matching Model

The improved cross-correlation function helps us to get a preliminary transition relationship between entries, but it still has a possibility of making error: the speed of the object and some noise such as wrong detection are not taken into account that will make the result unreliable and imprecise. For example, there are three sequences: sequence1 is (0, 0, 0, 1, 2, 3, 4, 5, 6.), sequence2 is (1, 2, 3, 4, 5, 6.), sequence3 is (1, 2, 4, 3, 5, 6.). When calculate the correlation relationship between sequence1 and sequence2, the transition time is 3 and the cross-correlation function has a clear peak. Due of the reverse of the number 3 and number 4, the transition time between sequence1 and sequence3 is 0.

To solve these problem, we proposed a time constraint feature matching model. First, domain guided dropout algorithm [9] is used to extract the appearance feature of the object in departure sequence and arrival sequence. For entry i and entry j, which already get the transition time T^{ij} and the width W_0^{ij} preliminary by the improved cross-correlation function approach mentioned before, T^{ij} follows a normal distribution $X(T) \backsim N\left(\mu, \sigma^2\right)$. When an object leaves from entry i at time t, search for the most similar object in the objects sequence moving into entry j during the time transition window $\left[t + T^{ij} - 3*W_0^{ij}, t + T^{ij} + 3*W_0^{ij}\right]$, as shown in Fig. 3(a). Since the coarse

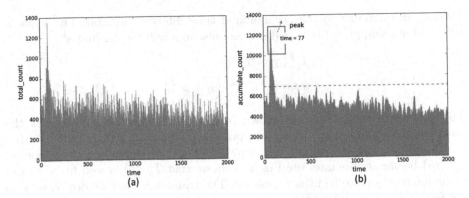

Fig. 2. The coarse result by the proposed method. The dotted line is the threshold. (camera2_zone0, camera1_zone1, on DukeMTMC [8]) (a) cross-correlation function result without accumulate. (b) Peak detection result.

result is already got, it should be a great probability to match the same object in the two sequences. Each matching pair will have a time interval η_0 between them. To calculate the mean and variance for the time interval function $T_0^{ij}(\eta_0)$, the neighbor accumulated method is used:

$$T^{ij}(\eta) = \sum_{\eta_0=\eta_n-5}^{\eta_n+5} T_0^{ij}(\eta_0), \quad \eta_n \geq 5 \tag{6}$$

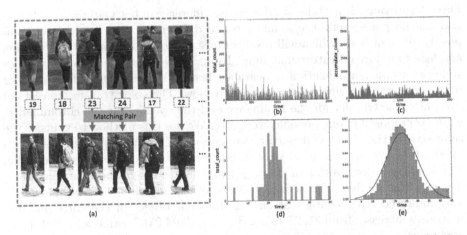

Fig. 3. A example of estimated transition distributions by different method. (a) Feature matching result. (b) Cross-correlation function. (c) Method proposed in Sect. 2.1. (d) Time interval before accumulation. (e) Processed time interval function (on DukeMTMC, camera5_zone0, camera3_zone0).

$T_p^{ij}(\eta)$ corresponding to the accumulated time interval function. The value is still 1 after accumulated is considered as noise and will be eliminated.

$$T_p^{ij}(\eta) = T^{ij}(\eta),$$
$$s.t. \eta \in \left\{ \eta' | T^{ij}\left(\eta'\right) > 1 \right\} \tag{7}$$

The process of our method is shown in Fig. 3. The Fig. 3(b) represents the cross-correlation function without any process. Figure 3(c) is the result by using the improved cross-correlation function. The Fig. 3(d) shows the time interval $T_0^{ij}(\eta_0)$ before accumulate, the Fig. 3(e) shows that $T_p^{ij}(\eta)$ is well fitted to the Gaussian function model after processed. The transition time window is easy to get from this figure. By using the time constraint feature matching method, our results are more accurate than before.

3   Experiments

To evaluate the effect of the proposed method, we test our method on public datasets: DukeMTMC [8] and NLPR_MCT [5] (including two different scenes: NLPR_MCT_1 includes street and indoor scene, NLPR_MCT_2 is campus monitoring video), which are time synchronously and applicable to the proposed approach. We conduct multiple experiments to give a performance test of the proposed method. After using color transfer as a preprocessing, we test our method on camera topology recovery time and over camera tracking across non-overlapping experiments.

Data Preprocessing. Actually, due to the difference in both lighting conditions and camera parameters, the same object in different camera would have completely different hues, which will result in mistakes on cross-correlation function and lead to failure of feature matching. To make them have consistency in color style, we use a normalization appearance feature model to transfer the color from target camera view to source camera view. The color transfer consists of two parts: the transfer for the luminance and the transfer for the chrominance, which is proposed in our previous work [10]. We use this method to transfer the color style of the object in departure sequences and arrival sequences. As shown in Fig. 4, the color style of objects in different cameras turn to be the same. The luminance distribution of the target and source images become consistent. Through this method, the accuracy of the object matching has been remarkably improved (the accuracy of finding the same object in the corresponding sequences increases from 31.4% to 35.0%, on DukeMTMC, camera3_zone1, camera4_zone0).

Camera Topology Recovery. We estimate the performance of the proposed method on recovering the topology structure and calculate the transition time between entries, we use our method to detect the links between the entries in cameras. Table 1 summarizes the results of the inter-camera correspondence for all the cameras and zones in the camera network on DukeMTMC [8]

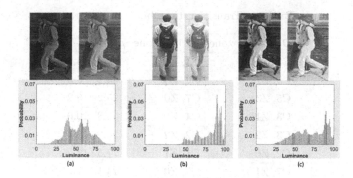

Fig. 4. Color transfer result and luminance cumulative histogram.

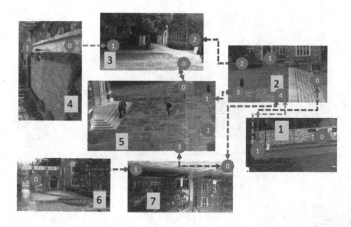

Fig. 5. The camera topology graph by our approach (on DukeMTMC).

(the camera topology is shown in Fig. 5). μ and σ is expectation and variance of the transition time. In order to simplify the calculation, we extract one key frame for every 20 frames (original video@ 59.940059 fps). All the link between cameras are detected and consistent with the ground truth.

We also compare our approach with previous method. As shown in Fig. 6. In Makris's [1] method, the peak is not obvious and difficult to adapt to complex scenes. In Chen's [5] method, a lot of manual parameters is needed and it's difficult to adjust these parameter, furthermore the cross-correlation function is continuously accumulated and excessive accumulation can cause small transition times missing. The previous methods show unclear and noisy distributions for both valid and invalid. As illustrate in Fig. 6(c). The transition time by our approach is much more accuracy and does not need extensive tuning experience.

Table 1. Transition time between cameras

Departure zone	Arrival zone	μ	σ
C5, Z0	C3, Z0	19.9	5.6
C5, Z1	C2, Z3	35.2	6.5
C5, Z3	C7, Z0	25.2	5.2
C3, Z1	C4, Z0	54.8	10.0
C3, Z2	C2, Z2	26.2	5.7
C2, Z0	C1, Z1	77.5	14.2
C7, Z1	C6, Z0	24.1	7.4
C1, Z1	C2, Z4	159.8	13.7
C2, Z4	C7, Z0	97.3	8.1

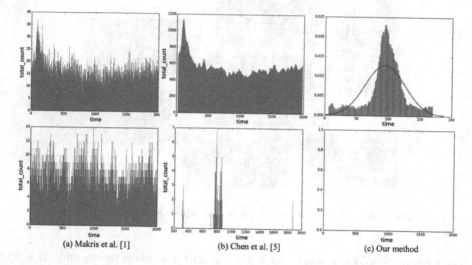

(a) Makris et al. [1]   (b) Chen et al. [5]   (c) Our method

Fig. 6. Performance comparison with other methods. First row: valid link (camera1_zone1, camera2_zone0). Second row: invalid link (camera3_zone1, camera5_zone3)

We also validate our approach on other datasets. The result is illustrated in Table 2. The association number represents the count of all the certain link between entries (over camera). The correct detection represents the number of current link number detected by our approach. We have applied the proposed method for each pair of entries. As the result shows, our method performs generally well on various kind of scene but have some error detection. The reason is that although there is a real path between some entries, it fails to be detected as there are too few object moving between these two entries, and there might have a fork in the blind area between cameras that the crowed is too disperse to have a strong correlation.

Table 2. Result on public datasets.

Dataset \ param	Camera	Entry zone number	Association number	Correct detection
DukeMTMC	7	20	18	18
NLPR_MCT_1	3	9	4	4
NLPR_MCT_2	5	11	10	6

Over Camera Tracking. We notices that building topological relationships on multiple cameras can help us to correlate targets in different cameras. The transition time between cameras can also help us on over camera tracking between cameras with disjoint views. We compare the accuracy between using the transition distributions information and not using. The result is illustrate in Table 3. By using our approach, when the target object departures from a camera, we are no longer need to search all the cameras. The highly reliable transition distributions information can help us to find the neighboring cameras. Clearly, this method narrows the retrieval scope and plays a key role in finding out the object accurately and effectively. Meanwhile, the time of matching the independent object is shortened. The data in the table represents the accuracy of the finding the same object in the next camera when the target object leaving from a camera.

Table 3. Performance comparison with full camera search in over camera tracking

Method/dataset	Duke MTMC	NLPR_MCT_1	NLPR_MCT_2
Full camera	40.9%	24.7%	28.1%
Our method	87.6%	72.6%	84.2%

4 Conclusion

In this paper, a coarse-to-fine multi-camera network topology estimation method is proposed. We learn both the topological and temporal transition characteristics in the multi-camera network. Our approach does not require manual calibration and can automatically learn the transition relationship between the cameras. We test our method on several dataset. The experiments results demonstrate that our method can recovery the camera topology and the transition time between entries in multi-cameras surveillance video accurately than previous methods. And we also demonstrate that, in the over camera tracking application, our method can narrows the retrieval scope and plays a key role in finding out the object accurately and effectively.

Acknowledgments. This work is supported by the Natural Science Foundation of China under Grant No. 61572061, 61472020 and National 863 Program of China under Grant No. 2015AA016403.

References

1. Makris, D., Ellis, T., Black, J.: Bridging the gaps between cameras. In: Proceedings of the 2004 IEEE Computer Society Conference on Computer Vision and Pattern Recognition, CVPR 2004, vol. 2. IEEE (2004)
2. Kinh, T., Dalley, G., Grimson, W.E.L.: Inference of non-overlapping camera network topology by measuring statistical dependence. In: Tenth IEEE International Conference on Computer Vision, ICCV 2005, vol. 2. IEEE (2005)
3. Chaowei, N., Grimson, E.: Recovering non-overlapping network topology using far-field vehicle tracking data. In: 18th International Conference on Pattern Recognition, ICPR 2006, vol. 4. IEEE (2006)
4. Zehavit, M., Shimshoni, I., Keren, D.: Multi-camera topology recovery from coherent motion. In: First ACM/IEEE International Conference on Distributed Smart Cameras, ICDSC 2007. IEEE (2007)
5. Chen, X., Huang, K., Tan, T.: Learning the three factors of a non-overlapping multi-camera network topology. In: Liu, C.-L., Zhang, C., Wang, L. (eds.) CCPR 2012. CCIS, vol. 321, pp. 104–112. Springer, Heidelberg (2012). https://doi.org/10.1007/978-3-642-33506-8_14
6. Shaoqing, R., et al.: Faster R-CNN: towards real-time object detection with region proposal networks. IEEE Trans. Pattern Anal. Mach. Intell. **39**, 1137–1149 (2017)
7. Hartigan, J.A., Wong, W.A.: Algorithm AS 136: a k-means clustering algorithm. J. Roy. Stat. Soc. Ser. C (Appl. Stat.) **28**(1), 100–108 (1979)
8. Ristani, E., Solera, F., Zou, R., Cucchiara, R., Tomasi, C.: Performance measures and a data set for multi-target, multi-camera tracking. In: Hua, G., Jégou, H. (eds.) ECCV 2016. LNCS, vol. 9914, pp. 17–35. Springer, Cham (2016). https://doi.org/10.1007/978-3-319-48881-3_2
9. Xiao, T., et al.: Learning deep feature representations with domain guided dropout for person re-identification. In: Proceedings of the IEEE Conference on Computer Vision and Pattern Recognition (2016)
10. Xing, C., Ye, H., Yu, T., Zhou, Z.: Homogenous color transfer using texture retrieval and matching. In: Chen, E., Gong, Y., Tie, Y. (eds.) PCM 2016. LNCS, vol. 9917, pp. 159–168. Springer, Cham (2016). https://doi.org/10.1007/978-3-319-48896-7_16

An Adaptive Tuning Sparse Fast Fourier Transform

Sheng Shi[1(✉)], Runkai Yang[1], Xinfeng Zhang[2], Haihang You[1], and Dongrui Fan[1]

[1] Institute of Computing Technology, Chinese Academy of Sciences, Beijing, China
{shisheng,yangrunkai,youhaihang,fandr}@ict.ac.cn
[2] Rapid-Rich Object Search Lab, Nanyang Technological University, Singapore, Singapore
xfzhang@ntu.edu.sg

Abstract. The Sparse Fast Fourier Transform (SFFT) is a novel algorithm for discrete Fourier transforms on signals with the sparsity in frequency domain. A reference implementation of the algorithm has been proven to be faster than modern FFT library in cases of sufficient sparsity. However, the SFFT implementation has the drawback that it only works reliably for very specific input parameters, especially signal sparsity k. This drawback hinders the extensive applications of SFFT. In this paper, we present a new Adaptive Tuning Sparse Fast Fourier Transform (ATSFFT). In the case of unknown sparsity k, ATSFFT can probe the sparsity k via adaptive dynamic tuning technology and then complete the Fourier transform of signal. Experimental results show that ATSFFT not only can control the error better than SFFT, but also performs faster than SFFT, which computes more efficiently than the state-of-the-art FFTW.

Keywords: Sparse Fast Fourier Transform · Sparsity
Adaptive tuning · FFTW

1 Introduction

In the era of big data, the cloud technology, referred to the computation or application through the Internet, is explosively developed. The amount of signals increases dramatically, and the corresponding high efficiency signal processing techniques are demanded urgently. The discrete Fourier transform (DFT) is one of the most fundamental and important numerical algorithms which plays central roles in signal processing, communications, and audio/image/video compression [1]. The Fast Fourier Transform (FFT) [2] greatly simplifies the complexity of DFT, and shows importance in a broad range of applications.

It is well known that most signals are sparsity in frequency domain, and this sparsity property has been widely used in various applications including High Efficiency Video Coding (HEVC) [3–6], compressed sensing [7–9] and radio astronomy. Therefore, for sparse signals, the $\Omega(n)$ lower bound for the complexity of DFT is no longer valid. It is necessary to study the new strategy of

© Springer International Publishing AG, part of Springer Nature 2018
B. Zeng et al. (Eds.): PCM 2017, LNCS 10736, pp. 991–999, 2018.
https://doi.org/10.1007/978-3-319-77383-4_97

the Fourier transform based on signal sparsity. In 2012, Hassanieh *et al.* proposed one-dimensional Sparse Fast Fourier Transform (SFFT) [10,11] which is faster than traditional DFT. However, the two dimensional spare Fourier transform cannot simply implement by utilizing two separate one-dimensional Sparse Fourier transform in [10,11]. Since two-dimensional transform for image signals are more widely used in practical applications, in [12], we proposed a method for two-dimensional Sparse Fast Fourier transform.

However, the SFFT implementation has the drawback that it only works reliably for very specific input parameters, especially signal sparsity k. This drawback hinders the extensive applications of SFFT. Therefore, in this paper, we propose a new Adaptive Tuning Sparse Fast Fourier Transform (ATSFFT) to improve the accuracy and robustness of SFFT. By adaptive tuning technology, ATSFFT can probe the sparsity k automatically and achieve the Fourier transform of signals. Experimental results show that ATSFFT not only can control the error better than existing SFFT, but also performs faster than SFFT.

The remainder of this paper is organized as follows. Section 2 briefly introduce the Sparse Fourier Transform (SFFT). Section 3 describes the new Adaptive Tuning Sparse Fast Fourier Transform (ATSFFT). Section 4 reports the simulation results followed by the conclusions in Sect. 5.

2   Sparse Fast Fourier Transform

Several conventions and notations are used in this paper. A space-domain image is represented as a 2D matrix $x \in C^{N \times N}$, the Fourier spectrum of the image is represented as $\hat{x}$. We assume that N is a power of 2, the notation $[N]$ is defined as the set $\{0, 1, ..., N - 1\}$, and $[N] \times [N] = [N]^2$ denotes the $N \times N$ grid $\{(i, j) : i \in [N], j \in [N]\}$. The image support is denoted by supp$(x) \subseteq [N] \times [N]$. All matrix indices are calculated modulo the matrix size, A set of matrix elements can be written as a matrix subscripted with a set of indices, for example $x_{I,J} = \{x_{i,j} | i \in I, j \in J\}$. In addition, we assume that B is a power of 2, and N can be divisible by B.

We define $\omega = e^{-2\pi i/N}$ to be a primitive N-th root of unity. In the following sections, we will use the following definition of the 2D-DFT without the constant scaling factor:

$$\hat{x}_{i,j} = \sum_{u \in [N]} \sum_{v \in [N]} x_{u,v} \omega^{iu+jv}, \quad (i,j) \in \Omega_N$$
$$\Omega_N = \{(i,j) | 0 \le i \le N - 1, 0 \le j \le N - 1\} \tag{1}$$

This makes some proofs easier, but is not relevant in practical implementations.

We briefly describe the structure of SFFT. The presentation of all details is beyond the scope of this paper and can be referred to [11] for more information.

A simplified flow chart of SFFT is shown in Fig. 1 which originally appeared in [12]. The hash function is the core of SFFT. Hash function includes random spectrum permutation, filtering and subsampling in frequency domain.

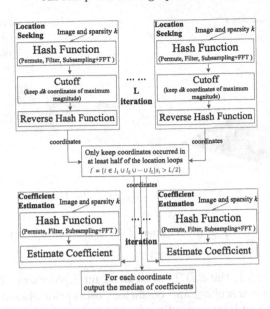

Fig. 1. A simplified flow diagram of SFFT

- SFFT does not have access to the input image's Fourier spectrum, as that would involve performing DFT. The permutation allows to permute the image's Fourier spectrum by modifying the space domain signal x. This can be done by spectrum factor $P_{\sigma_1,\sigma_2,\tau_1,\tau_2}$ where σ_1, σ_2 are the random step sizes and τ_1, τ_2 are the offsets.

$$(P_{\sigma_1,\sigma_2,\tau_1,\tau_2}x)_{i,j} = x_{\sigma_1 i+\tau_1,\sigma_2 j+\tau_2} \tag{2}$$

- In order to achieve a sub-linear computational complexity, SFFT uses the Guassian flat window function to extract a part of the input image for computations. According to the convolution theorem, filtering process can expand the area of non-zero coefficients, in preparation for the subsequent sub-sampling and reverse steps, and further increase the probability of detecting non-zero coefficients.
- SFFT effectively reduces dimension by subsampling input space-domain image and summing up the result. As the signal is sparse in frequency domain, dimension reduction can reduce the complexity of searching position and amplitude of non-zero elements.

The basic idea behind hash function is to hash the $N \times N$ coefficients of the input image into a small number of $B \times B$ bins. B is determined by k, which is set to $\sqrt{Nk}$. From these bins, SFFT only keeps coordinates of top dk points with largest magnitudes. The actual locations of the Fourier coefficients are then approximated.

$$h_{\sigma_1,\sigma_2}(i,j) = round(\sigma_1\sigma_2 ij \frac{B^2}{N^2}), i \in [N], j \in [N] \tag{3}$$

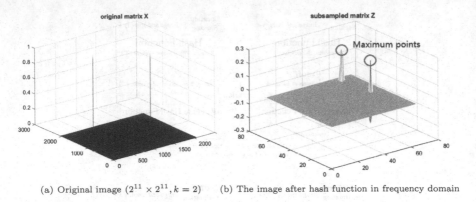

(a) Original image ($2^{11} \times 2^{11}, k = 2$)   (b) The image after hash function in frequency domain

Fig. 2. The relationship of the number of local maximum points and sparisty k

As shown in Fig. 1, the SFFT consists of multiple executions of two kinds of operations: location seeking and coefficient estimation. Location seeking is to generate a list of candidate coordinates which have high probability of being indices of the k nonzero coefficients in frequency domain. While coefficient estimation is used to precisely determine the frequency coefficients.

3   Adaptive Tuning Sparse Fast Fourier Transform

The drawback of SFFT implementation is that it works reliably with prior knowledge of signal sparsity k. This drawback hinders the wide range of applications of SFFT. Although it is well known to all that most signals are sparse, it is almost impossible to foreknow the sparsity k of the signals in advance. Therefore, we propose a new Adaptive Tuning Sparse Fast Fourier Transform (ATSFFT). By adaptive dynamic tuning technology, ATSFFT can predict the sparsity k and achieve the Fourier transform of signal. Experimental results show that ATSFFT not only can control the error better than SFFT, but also performs faster than SFFT.

The hash function hashes the $N \times N$ coefficients of the input image into a small number of $B \times B$ bins. An example of a $2^{11} \times 2^{11}$ image in frequency domain ($k = 2$) is shown in Fig. 2(a). We find that after the hash function, the number of maximum points is the same with the number of original image nonzero coefficients in frequency domain as shown in Fig. 2(b). Therefore, by finding the local maximum points, we can avoid prior knowledge sparsity k.

ATSFFT initially sets a small value to B_0 and k_0. After hashing, we can get k_1 by finding and counting the number of local maximum values in $B \times B$ matrix. Then, B_1 can be updated by analyzing the relationship between k_0 and k_1. For the convenience of description, the change ratio factor r of k is defined as follows,

$$r_i = |1 - \frac{k_i}{k_{i-1}}|. \tag{4}$$

The iterative process is shown as follows

$$B_{i+1} = \begin{cases} \varepsilon_1 B_i, & 0 \leq r_i < \delta_1 \\ B_i, & \delta_1 \leq r_i < \delta_2 \\ (1+\varepsilon_2)B_i, & \delta_2 \leq r_i \end{cases} \tag{5}$$

where $0 < \delta_1 < \delta_2 < 1$ and $0 < \varepsilon_1 < \varepsilon_2 < 1$. When k_i approaches k_{i-1} within a very small range of δ_1, we consider B_i adapts to the full scatter point set where nonzero elements can adequately distributed, so B_{i+1} need to be decreased to find the better size B. When k_i approaches k_{i-1} within a appropriate range between δ_1 and δ_2, we consider B_i adapts to the appropriate scatter point set. If we further reduce the size of B, it will lead to large area overlap. Therefore, B_{i+1} is kept the same with B_i. When k_i fluctuates within a large range of k_{i-1}, we consider B_i is too small to lead large area overlap, so we need to continue to increase B. The visualized representation is shown in Fig. 3. Since B is a power of 2, and N can be divisible by B. ATSFFT sets $\varepsilon_1 = 1/2$, $\varepsilon_2 = 1$, $\delta_1 = 2\%$, $\delta_2 = 5\%$.

$$B_{i+1} = \begin{cases} 1/2B_i, & 0 \leq r_i < 2\% \\ B_i, & 2\% \leq r_i < 5\% \\ 2B_i, & 5\% \leq r_i \end{cases} \tag{6}$$

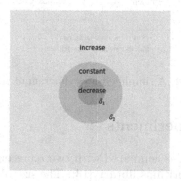

Fig. 3. The relationship between B and r

A simplified flow diagram of ATSFFT is shown in Fig. 4. Compared with SFFT, ATSFFT does not need sparsity k in advance. By running multiple adaptive tuning iterations, it is able to identify candidate coordinates with a high probability of being one of the k nonzero coordinates. Given the set of coordinates I, ATSFFT can use coefficient estimation to precisely determine the frequency coefficients, which basically remove the phase change due to the permutation and the effect of the filtering.

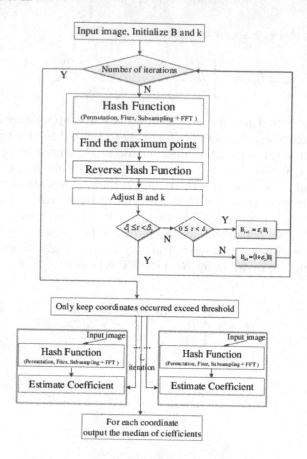

Fig. 4. A simplified flow diagram of ASFFT

4   Numerical Experiments

In this section, ATSFFT is compared with two representative algorithms, SFFT and FFT in FFTW algorithms library [13]. The size of image matrix N is fixed to constant ($N = 2^{10}, 2^{11}, 2^{12}$) and the runtime of the three algorithms with the sparsity k ($k = 50, 100, 200, 500, 1000$) is shown in Table 1. Observing the Table 1, we can get two conclusions: (i) ATSFFT is not only faster than FFTW, but also faster than SFFT which uses the fixed B; (ii) ATSFFT can control the error better than SFFT. That is, the error of ATSFFT is lower than SFFT at the same number of cycles.

More intuitively, the runtime comparison on different sparsity degrees ($N = 2^{11}, 2^{12}$) is shown in Fig. 5. We can see that when the image size is fixed, as the increase of sparsity k, the ATSFFT is faster than SFFT, while the runtime of FFTW is essentially constant, which depends on image size not sparsity k.

The runtime comparison on different sparsity degrees ($N = 2^{10}$) is shown in Fig. 6. We can get the same conclusion that ATSFFT is faster than SFFT.

Table 1. The runtime and error of SFFT, ASFFT and FFTW

k	FFTW	SFFT	ATSFFT	FFTW	SFFT	ATSFFT
N = 1024	Time (s)			MSE		
50	0.093	0.0212	0.0030	3.30E−14	4.45E−05	1.99E−06
100	0.0967	0.0312	0.0046	2.50E−14	4.40E−05	1.86E−09
200	0.0908	0.0602	0.0058	1.87E−14	2.82E−05	2.21E−06
500	0.0900	2.2507	0.0144	1.29E−14	9.85E−04	8.81E−05
1000	0.0902	9.2400	0.0308	9.60E−15	6.15E−03	1.90E−03
N = 2048	Time (s)			MSE		
50	0.4919	0.0489	0.0073	6.55E−14	7.27E−10	5.44E−10
100	0.4817	0.0610	0.0094	4.97E−14	3.49E−09	3.19E−09
200	0.4729	0.0856	0.0077	3.74E−14	1.87E−03	3.46E−05
500	0.4804	0.1194	0.0394	2.56E−14	6.28E−05	7.70E−07
1000	0.4699	0.1447	0.0446	1.91E−14	9.65E−04	7.27E−06
N = 4096	Time (s)			MSE		
50	1.8087	0.1200	0.0099	1.29E−13	1.41E−09	6.15E−10
100	2.0562	0.1396	0.0254	9.85E−14	3.29E−10	5.64E−10
200	2.0477	0.1843	0.0218	7.43E−14	1.66E−09	3.82E−07
500	1.9689	0.2564	0.0306	5.07E−14	1.18E−04	4.68E−06
1000	2.0624	0.3707	0.0386	3.78E−14	1.41E−03	7.05E−06

In addition, SFFT is faster than FFTW when sparsity $k < 200$, while 2D-SFFT presents disadvantage when sparsity $k > 200$. This is because the increase of sparsity k will leads to large area overlap. SFFT must increase the number of iterations to achieve the error standard, which will greatly increase running time. Therefore, SFFT performs better than FFTW when image has sufficient sparsity. By comparing ATSFFT against SFFT, the applicable range of ATSFFT is much wider than SFFT.

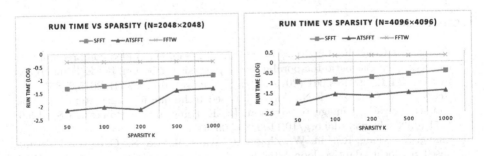

Fig. 5. The runtime comparison on different sparsity degrees ($k = 2048, 4096$)

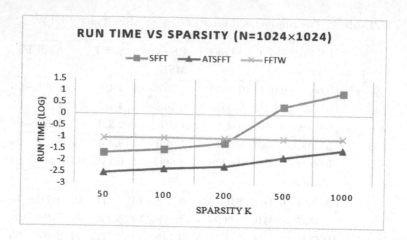

Fig. 6. The runtime comparison on different sparsity degrees ($k = 1024$)

5   Conclusion

SFFT is a novel algorithm for DFT on signals with sparsity in frequency domain. The reference implementation of the algorithm exists and has been proven to be faster than modern FFT library in cases of sufficient sparsity. However, the drawback of SFFT implementation is that it works reliably with foreknown signal sparsity k. It hinders the wide range of applications of SFFT. We present a new Adaptive Tuning Sparse Fast Fourier Transform ASFFT. In the case of unknown sparsity k in advance, ASFFT can identify the sparsity by adaptive dynamic iterative tuning and then complete the Fourier transform of signal. Experimental results show that ATSFFT not only can control the error better than SFFT, but also performs faster than SFFT.

Acknowledgment. This work was supported by the National Key Research and Development Program of China (2016YFE0100300), the 100 Talents Program of the Chinese Academy of Sciences (2920154070) and the Knowledge Innovation Project of the Chinese Academy of Sciences (5120146040).

References

1. Zhang, X., Xiong, R., Lin, W., Ma, S., Liu, J., Gao, W.: Video compression artifact reduction via spatio-temporal multi-hypothesis prediction. IEEE Trans. Image Process. **24**(12), 6048–6061 (2015). https://doi.org/10.1109/TIP.2015.2485780
2. Reddy, B.S., Chatterji, B.N.: An FFT-based technique for translation, rotation, and scale-invariant image registration. IEEE Trans. Image Process. **5**(8), 1266–1271 (1996). https://doi.org/10.1109/83.506761
3. Zhang, X., Xiong, R., Lin, W., Zhang, J., Wang, S., Ma, S., Gao, W.: Low-rank based nonlocal adaptive loop filter for high efficiency video compression. IEEE Trans. Circuits Syst. Video Technol. **27**(10), 2177–2188 (2017). https://doi.org/10.1109/TCSVT.2016.2581618

4. Ma, S., Zhang, X., Zhang, J., Jia, C., Wang, S., Gao, W.: Nonlocal in-loop filter: the way toward next-generation video coding? IEEE MultiMed. **23**(2), 16–26 (2016). https://doi.org/10.1109/MMUL.2016.16

5. Zhang, X., Lin, W., Xiong, R., Liu, X., Ma, S., Gao, W.: Low-rank decomposition-based restoration of compressed images via adaptive noise estimation. IEEE Trans. Image Process. **25**(9), 4158–4171 (2016). https://doi.org/10.1109/TIP.2016.2588326

6. Zhang, X., Lin, W., Wang, S., Ma, S.: Nonlocal adaptive in-loop filter via content-dependent soft-thresholding for HEVC. In: IEEE International Symposium on Multimedia (ISM), Miami, FL, pp. 465–470 (2015). https://doi.org/10.1109/ISM.2015.56

7. Zhang, X., Lin, W., Liu, J., Ma, S.: Compression noise estimation and reduction via patch clustering. In: Asia-Pacific Signal and Information Processing Association Annual Summit and Conference (APSIPA), Hong Kong, pp. 715–718 (2015). https://doi.org/10.1109/APSIPA.2015.7415365

8. Zhang, X., Xiong, R., Fan, X., Ma, S., Gao, W.: Compression artifact reduction by overlapped-block transform coefficient estimation with block similarity. IEEE Trans. Image Process. **22**(12), 4613–4626 (2013). https://doi.org/10.1109/TIP.2013.2274386

9. Shi, S., Xiong, R., Ma, S., Fan, X., Gao, W.: Image compressive sensing using overlapped block projection and reconstruction. In: 2015 IEEE International Symposium on Circuits and Systems (ISCAS), Lisbon, pp. 1670–1673 (2015). https://doi.org/10.1109/ISCAS.2015.7168972

10. Hassanieh, H., Indyk, P., Katabi, D., Price, E.: Simple and practical algorithm for sparse Fourier transform. In: Proceedings of the Twenty-Third Annual ACM-SIAM Symposium on Discrete Algorithms, Japan, pp. 1183–1194 (2012)

11. Hassanieh, H., Indyk, P., Katabi, D., Price, E.: Nearly optimal sparse fourier transform. In: Proceedings of the 44th Symposium on Theory of Computing Conference, New York, pp. 563–578 (2012)

12. Shi, S., Yang, R., You, H.: A new two-dimensional Fourier transform algorithm based on image sparsity. In: 2017 IEEE International Conference on Acoustics, Speech and Signal Processing (ICASSP), New Orleans, LA, pp. 1373–1377 (2017). https://doi.org/10.1109/ICASSP.2017.7952381

13. Frigo, M., Johnson, S.G.: FFTW: an adaptive software architecture for the FFT. In: Proceedings of the 1998 IEEE International Conference on Acoustics, Speech and Signal Processing, Seattle, WA, pp. 1381–1384 (1998)

Author Index

Printed in the United States
By Bookmasters